AVERAGE INFLATION-ADJUSTED RETURNS BY DECADES—COMMON STOCK AND BONDS

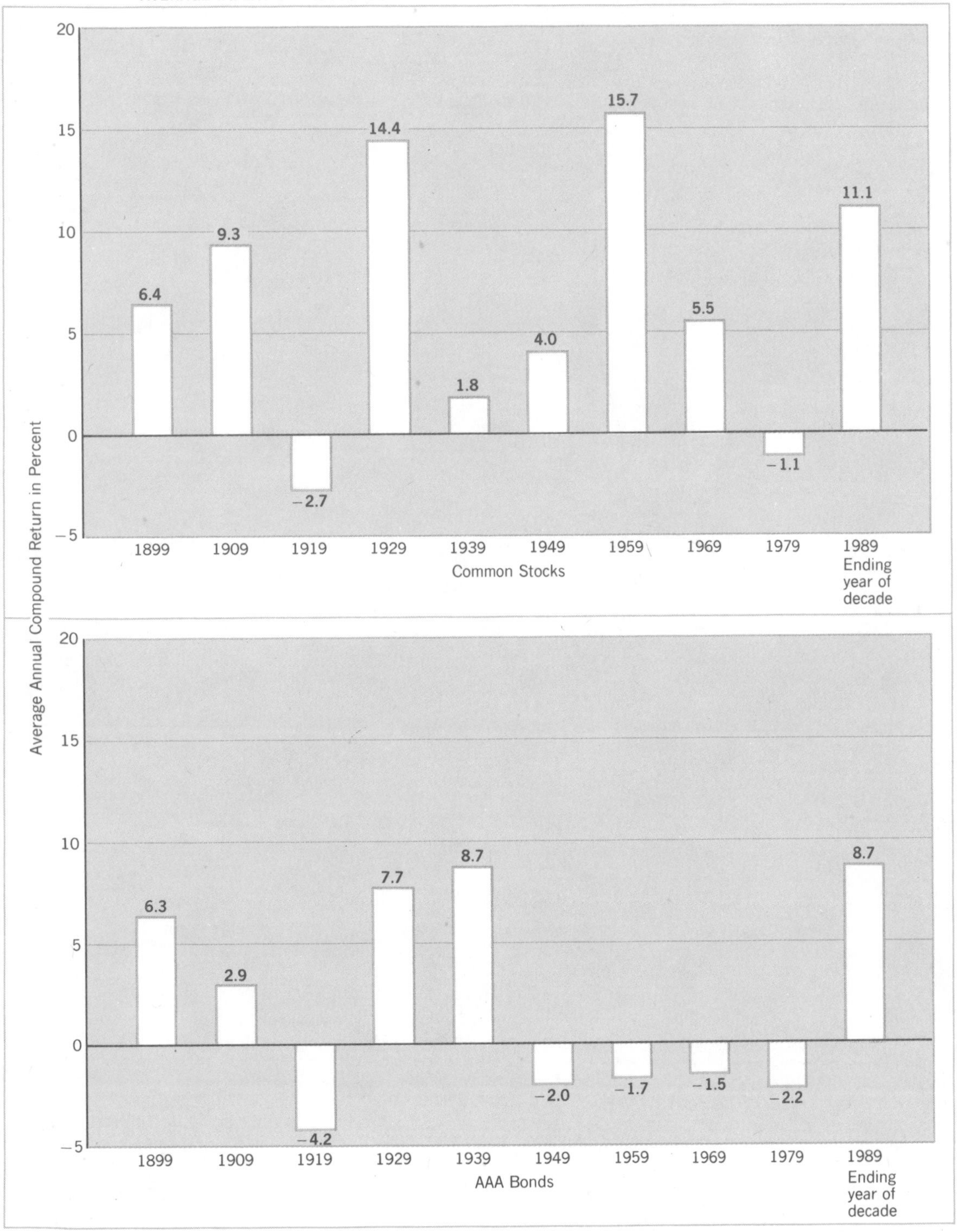

Investments
Analysis and Management
THIRD EDITION

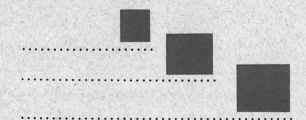

A title in the Wiley Series in Finance

Edwin J. Elton and Martin J. Gruber, Consulting Editors

Investments
Analysis and Management THIRD EDITION

Charles P. Jones
North Carolina State University

JOHN WILEY & SONS, INC.
New York • Chichester • Brisbane • Toronto • Singapore

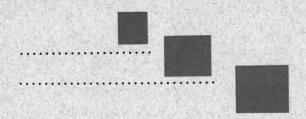

To Kay and Kathryn
and
To Helen

Acquisitions Editor	*John Woods*
Designer	*Sheila Granda*
Cover Illustration	*Roy Wiemann*
Copyediting Supervisor	*Gilda Stahl*
Production Supervisor	*Savoula Amanatidis*
Manufacturing Manager	*Lorraine Fumoso*
Illustration Department	*John Balbalis and Dean Gonzalez*

Library of Congress Cataloging in Publication Data:

Jones, Charles Parker, 1943–
Investments : analysis and management / Charles P. Jones. — 3rd ed.
p. cm.
Includes bibliographical references and index.
ISBN 0-471-52839-0 (cloth)
1. Investments. 2. Investment analysis. I. Title.
HG4521.J663 1991
332.6—dc20 90-48568
CIP

Printed in the United States of America

10 9 8 7 6 5 4 3 2 1

Preface

This book is designed to provide a good understanding of investments while stimulating interest in the subject. This understanding can be very valuable because each of us must make various investment decisions during our lifetime—definitely as individuals, and possibly as managers. My goal is to help students gain an appreciation of what is involved in (1) making investment decisions, (2) recognizing what the investment opportunities are, and (3) recognizing where investment problems arise.

Because the book is designed for the first course in investments, descriptive material must be—and is—thoroughly covered. Equally important, the analytics of investments are presented throughout the book in order to help students reason out investment issues for themselves and thus be better prepared when making real-world investment decisions.

The book is written for the first course in investments, generally taught at the junior–senior level. Standard prerequisites include accounting, economics, and financial management. A course in statistics is useful but not essential. I have sought to minimize formulas and to simplify difficult material, consistent with a presentation of investments that takes into account exactly what is going on in this changing field today. Relevant, state-of-the-art material has been simplified and structured specifically for the benefit of the beginning student.

Organization of the Text

The text is divided into seven parts centered around background, different types of securities, and investment management.

Part One provides a *background* for students before encountering the specifics of security analysis and portfolio management. The goal of this part is to acquaint beginners with an overview of what investing is all about—and not about. It describes the *variety of securities available, the markets in which they are traded, sources of information and its effective utilization, and some insight into the concepts of risk and return.*

Parts Two and Three focus on the basic approach to *security analysis and valuation* by presenting "how-to" tools and techniques. Part Two examines the *analysis and management of bonds,* a logical starting point in learning how to value securities. Part Three builds on these concepts in discussing the *valuation (security analysis) of common stocks.* Appendix 7-B, covering preferred stocks, makes a good transition between Parts Two and Three.

Parts Four and Five proceed to the two strategies typically discussed in the selection of common stocks. Part Four covers *fundamental analysis,* the heart of security analysis. Because of its scope and complexity, Chapters 10, 11, and 12 are required to cover the fundamental approach adequately. The order of these chapters—market, industry, and company—are deliberate, reflecting the recommended order of procedure in doing fundamental analysis.

Part Five discusses the other approach to common stock selection, *technical analysis,* as well as the concept of *efficient markets,* which all investors should understand. Technical analysis, discussed in Chapter 13, remains controversial. Chapter 14 explains the reason for the controversy as well as the efficient market hypothesis. As explained at the outset in Chapter 1, investors should be aware of and carefully consider this hypothesis, although it need not dominate their thinking, nor does it dominate the text. For example, Chapter 14 also discusses market "anomalies," which deserve careful investor consideration.

Parts Three, Four, and Five are devoted to common stocks, a reasonable allocation, given investor interest in common stocks. Part Six discusses the *other major securities available to investors.* Chapter 15 analyzes *options (puts and calls),* a popular investment alternative in recent years. *Stock index options* also are covered. Chapter 16 continues the analysis of equity-derivative securities by focusing on *warrants and convertibles.* Chapter 17 is devoted to *financial futures,* an important new topic in investments. Finally, Chapter 18 analyzes the investor's alternative of indirect investing—*buying shares in an investment company* that, in turn, buys a portfolio of securities.

Part Seven is concerned with *portfolio management and portfolio performance measurement.* Chapter 19 contains a complete discussion of *modern portfolio concepts,* with primary emphasis on the essentials of *Markowitz portfolio theory and the single-index model.* Chapter 20 discusses *capital market theory,* a natural extension of portfolio theory. Chapter 21 discusses extended diversification possibilities, including *foreign securities, real estate, and precious metals.* This chapter contains material necessary for the understanding of today's investing environment. Chapter 22 concludes the text with a discussion of *how to measure portfolio performance.* This is a logical conclusion to both Part Seven and to the entire book, because all investors are keenly interested in how well their investments have performed. Mutual funds are used as examples of how to apply these portfolio performance measures and how to interpret the results.

Special Features

This text offers several important features, some of which are unique.

1. The *sequence of chapters* has been carefully structured and coordinated as a package, reflecting considerable experimentation over the years. While other arrangements are workable, I find this one to be the most satisfactory in a beginning investments course. Starting with background material and progressing through an analysis of various securities to a discussion of portfolio management, the book proceeds from easier to more difficult concepts, and from fewer to more numerous equations. However, should one wish, the chapter order can be rearranged with little or no loss in continuity.
2. I have diligently sought to hold the text to a *length that is manageable* in the standard undergraduate investments course. Although it requires a tight schedule, the entire text can be covered in one semester, including the use of supplementary material. However, instructors may very well choose to omit chapters, depending on preferences and constraints. Doing so will cause no problems in terms of teaching a satisfactory investments course. Still another alternative is assigning some chapters to be read by students with little or no class discussion. Chapter 4 is a good possibility for this, as are Chapters 13 and 16.
3. Each chapter features several items specifically designed for the student's benefit. These include the following:
   - *Key words* appear in boldface, and are carefully defined in the *glossary.* Other important words are italicized.
   - Each chapter contains a *summary of "bulleted" points* for quick and precise reading.
   - Each chapter contains an *extensive set of questions* keyed specifically to the chapter material and designed to review the concepts in each chapter thoroughly.
   - Most chapters have a *separate set of problems* designed to illustrate the quantitative material in the chapters. Some of these problems can be solved in the normal manner, and some are designed to be solved with *The Investment Calculator.* Such problems are marked with a small disk icon.
   - Each text includes *The Investment Calculator software disk,* a self-contained, easy-to-use software package that removes the drudgery

of the more tedious calculations required to work some investment problems. The documentation for this software is included as a text appendix. Those readers who choose not to use this software package will still benefit fully from the text.

- A distinctive feature of this text is the use of *boxed inserts,* which were pioneered in the first edition of this book. These inserts provide timely and interesting material from the popular press, enabling the student to see the real-world side to issues and concepts discussed in the text. These boxed inserts have been very carefully selected from the potentially large number available on the basis of their likely interest to the reader, their relevance in illustrating important concepts, their timeliness, and their overall appeal to students interested in learning about the world of investments.

Changes in the Third Edition

The third edition has been thoroughly updated using the latest information and numbers available. Other changes include the following:

- Several chapters have been reorganized to make them more streamlined and concise.
- A new chapter, International Investing and Extended Diversification, has been added to discuss international investing in detail as well as tangible assets such as real estate and precious metals.
- Some material has been moved to appendixes in order not to slow down some readers who may wish to omit these topics. This includes futures options (Appendix 17-A), which remains a less-well-developed topic that can easily be skipped; the term structure of interest rates (Appendix 7-A), which is an important topic but one that some instructors choose not to emphasize; and simple techniques for determining optimum portfolios (Appendix 19-A), which can be omitted with no loss in continuity.
- Some material that was in an appendix has been incorporated into the chapters, in particular the supernormal growth model used in common stock valuation.
- The text now includes clearly marked-off examples. Although part of the text material itself, these examples are slightly set off in format to make them obvious.
- *Investments Intuition* is another new feature. Separated from the paragraph material, these insights are designed to help the reader think intuitively about what is going on as an aid to developing the reasoning process so vital in investments.
- *Investment Calculations* is a new feature designed to show clearly how

the problem material can be solved with the software that accompanies this text.

- Problems that can be solved using *The Investment Calculator* software appear as the last ones in each problem set and are clearly marked with a small disk icon.
- In the chapters containing the more important problem sets, *Demonstration Problems* have been provided to illustrate the calculations in detail.

A final change to be noted in the new edition is the adoption of the term *total return* for *holding period yield,* and the term *return relative* for *holding period return.* These terms may be more familiar to readers and are consistent with the Ibbotson Associates data, which are used even more extensively in this revision, along with the author's own work in this area.

Supplements

The third edition includes a more complete set of supplements than has been available previously. In addition to the *The Investment Calculator* software, the following elements are also available to assist you and your students in teaching and learning the nature of investments.

- **Study Guide.** This has been prepared by James D'Mello of Western Michigan University. For each chapter it includes a chapter overview, vocabulary exercises, problem sets—to be solved with and without the text software—and multiple-choice practice test questions. All answers to problems and questions are included.
- **Instructor's Manual.** For each chapter, chapter objectives, lecture notes, notes on the use of transparency masters, and additional material that is relevant for the particular chapter are included. Answers to all questions and problems in the text are provided.
- **Transparency Masters.** These will be of selected text art, selected items from other sources, and solutions to selected end-of-chapter problems in the text.
- **Testbank.** The testbank includes numerous multiple-choice and true-false questions for each chapter. Most of these have been extensively tested in class and are carefully checked. Some questions will be included from the study guide for those who would like to include them on tests.

Acknowledgments

A number of individuals have contributed to this project. I particularly thank Jack W. Wilson, North Carolina State University, a highly valued friend and colleague who read the original manuscript and offered many useful comments, provided material for some of the appendixes, and worked out many of the problems (including the extended problems) for the text. He has continued his valuable assistance by supplying data, graphs, suggestions, and insights. Some of the material used in this book and supplements is based on Jack's pathbreaking work in the area of asset returns and has generously been made available by him, for which I am very grateful.

A text does not reach its third edition unless it has met the needs of a large number of instructors who find it to be a useful tool in assisting their teaching. The earlier editions of this text benefitted substantially from the reviews of many instructors whose suggestions for improvements can be found on many pages of this text. I owe a debt a gratitude to these teachers and colleagues, who helped on the first and second editions: Randall Billingsley, Virginia Polytechnic Institute and State University; Pat Hess, Ohio State University; Richard DeMong, University of Virginia; Keith Broman, University of Nebraska; Ron Braswell, Florida State University; Donald Puglisi, University of Delaware; Howard Van Auken, Iowa State University; James Buck, East Carolina University; Malcolm Torgerson, Western Illinois University; Eugene Furtado, Kansas State University; William B. Gillespie, St. Louis University; Edward Sanders, Northeastern University; P. R. Chandy, North Texas State University; D. Monath, University of Louisville; Larry J. Johnson, University of Tulsa; Stan Atkinson, University of Central Florida; Howard W. Bohnen, St. Cloud State University; James M. Tipton, Baylor University; William P. Dukes, Texas Tech University; A. Bhattacharya, University of Cincinnati; and Christopher Ma, University of Toledo.

I wish to thank in particular two users, John Groth of Texas A&M University and Seth Anderson of Auburn University, who supplied me with detailed comments, suggestions, and corrections in the course of using the text. Seth continues to provide me with a close scrutiny of the book and has been very helpful.

In the development of the third edition, I had the benefit of still more input from instructors teaching this course, including Paul Bolstar, Northeastern University; John Lindvall, California Polytechnic State University; Robert McElreath, Clemson University; Roger Palmer, College of St. Thomas; John Williams, California State University, Northridge; Philip Swensen, Utah State University; Clark Holloway, University of South Carolina; James F. Feller, Middle Tennessee State University; Michael McBain, Marquette University; George S. Swales, Jr., Southwest Missouri State University; Lalatendu Misra, University of Texas, San Antonio; Richard E. White, University of North Florida; Donald Monath, University of Louisville; Thomas R. Anderson, Babson College; Randall Billingsley, Virginia Polytechnic Institute and State University; John W. Ellis, Colorado State University; Thomas E. Eyssell, University of Missouri, St. Louis;

James P. D'Mello, Western Michigan University; and Herbert Weinraub, University of Toledo. Their criticisms and suggestions have substantially affected the evolution of this text and made it a better book.

I would also like to thank my former editor at Wiley, Rich Esposito, for his confidence in me. Joe Dougherty was very helpful in planning and preparing the second edition. The current editor, John Woods, has been most supportive of this revision and has made a very significant difference in the final product. John has worked hard to enhance the supplementary material available with the text and to provide the overall support necessary to revise the material substantially and improve the book in numerous ways. The other Wiley professionals with whom I have worked on this project have been excellent, in particular Gilda Stahl, copyediting supervisor, Joe Ford, production manager, Savoula Amanatidis, production supervisor, and Sheila Granda, designer.

Finally, I would like to thank my family, who shared in this burden fully and magnificently. Without their support, a project such as this is difficult at best. I thank in particular my wife, Kay, who helped me tremendously in the preparation of the manuscript and without whose support I would have been unable to finish on schedule. Kay and Kathryn make a difficult job bearable, and worth doing.

Charles P. Jones
North Carolina State University

Brief Contents

Contents

100

PART 1

Background

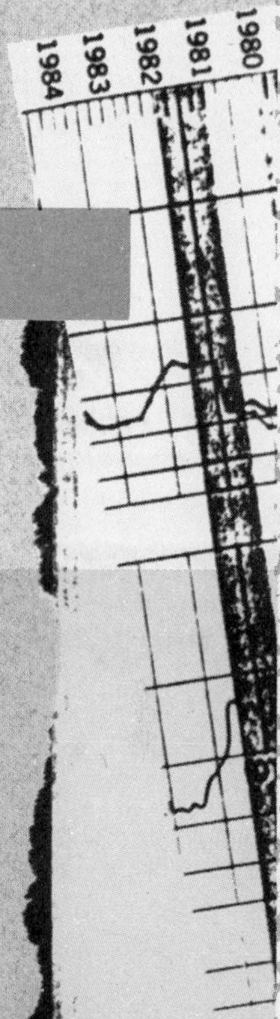

CHAPTER 1

A Background for Understanding Investments

- The stock market opened the 1990s by hitting a new record high. Within three weeks, the market had declined almost 9% (a 250-point drop in the Dow Jones Industrial Average) in value. Why?
- For the six years ending in 1988, only 26% of professionally managed stock portfolios were able to outperform the overall stock market more than 50% percent of the time. Why?
- Is it possible to have earned 40% or more investing in default-free Treasury bonds in only one year?
- Why did the price of Texas Instruments stock fall 32% ($50.75 per share) in only two days (a total drop in market value of $1.2 billion)?
- How can futures contracts, with a reputation for being extremely risky, be used to reduce an investor's risk?
- What is the average annual rate of return on common stocks? What can an investor reasonably expect to earn from stocks in the future?

The objective of this text is to help you understand the investments field as it is currently understood, discussed, and practiced so that you can intelligently answer questions such as the preceding. To accomplish this objective, key concepts are presented to provide an appreciation of the theory and practice of investments.

Both descriptive and quantitative materials on investing are readily available. Some of this material is very enlightening, much of it is debatable because of the many controversies in investments, and some of it is worthless. This text seeks to cover what is particularly useful and relevant for today's investment climate. It offers some ideas about what you can reasonably expect to accomplish by using what you learn, and therefore what you can realistically expect to achieve as an investor in today's investment world. *In fact, learning to avoid the many pitfalls awaiting you as an investor by clearly understanding what you can reasonably expect from investing your money may be the single most important benefit to be derived from this text.* For example, would you entrust your money to someone offering 36% annual return on riskless Treasury securities? Some 600 investors did and lost some $10 million to a former Sunday-school teacher.[1] See Box 1-1 for additional discussion on protecting yourself as an investor.

[1]See Earl C. Gottschalk, Jr., "Churchgoers Are the Prey as Scams Rise," *The Wall Street Journal*, August 7, 1989, p. C1.

BOX 1-1

THE HUSTLER'S BEST FRIEND: YOU

The major dangers that investors face haven't changed. It's still a jungle out there.

The worst menace, as old as markets, is right in your own bosom: greed, the lure of big bucks made easily. The arbs made megamillions in takeovers, but they have hurt individual investors much less than that army of hustlers relying on slick merchandising. Your own greed is the hustler's best friend.

"Come grow with us," the catchy phrase of Robert Brennan's First Jersey Securities, took out thousands of investors while making large fortunes for Brennan and some of his merry band. First Jersy's pitch was probably too blatant for most *Forbes* readers, but there are other, more sophisticated ones to steer clear of.

Among the most important are the claims made by brokers and money and mutual fund managers about their sensational records. A classic example is Fred Alger. His major fund rocketed up in the speculative bubble of 1967–68, only to go down in flames when the go-go market collapsed. Alger says he did not solely manage the fund in the crash, and thus does not debit this disaster to his performance record. That's kind of like playing golf and counting only your good shots.

A multimillion-dollar media blitz claimed that he had beat the S&P's 500 10-to-1 on average annually since 1965. Had you put $10,000 with Alger back in 1965, the advertisements blare, it would be worth $651,228 today. (The fine print states that he had only one account back then and does not indicate whether he has kept it.)

Questionable claims are not the only menace. Some of the Brahmins of the investment business are excellent marketers and not too proud to cash in on the latest speculative fad. So when a salesman tries to talk you into buying, say, the latest new variety of mutual fund, thank him politely and hang up the phone.

As for hot-performing mutual funds, some firms run hatcheries in sizzling investment areas. The process is simple. A number of funds are started in-house in a fast-paced area, with only those chalking up spectacular records eventually being sold to the public. The new fund hits an eager public with an excellent record. Those funds with poorer results quietly sink to the bottom of the pond.

If you haven't already, make a resolution this year to curb your own greed and thus make life a little tougher for those with doubtful merchandise to peddle. Here are a few antigreed rules: Avoid hot stories. Investigate before you buy. Searching a record is time-consuming but worth its weight in gold. (It's amazing that people spend dozens of hours shopping for television sets, cars or dishwashers but invest tens of thousands of dollars on the basis of only a two- or three-minute sales talk.)

If your questions get a reply like "It's moving up, and we're only allotting you stock because we want you as a client," run, do not walk, to the nearest exit. If a performance record has numerous caveats and gives itself wide benefits of the doubt in measurements, again beat a retreat.

The point is, if it looks too easy, it probably is. Avoid it.

Source: Adapted from David Dreman's column. Excerpted by permission of *Forbes* magazine, January 26, 1987.

The Nature of Investments

Some Definitions

The term *investing* can cover a wide range of activities. It often refers to investing money in certificates of deposit, bonds, common stocks, or mutual funds. More knowledgeable investors would include other "paper" assets, such as warrants, puts and calls, futures contracts, and convertible securities, as well as tangible assets, such as gold, real estate, and collectibles. Investing encompasses very conservative positions as well as aggressive speculation.

An **investment** can be defined as the commitment of funds to one or more assets that will be held over some future time period. The field of **investments,** therefore, involves the study of the investment process. Investments is concerned with the management of an investor's **wealth,** which is the sum of current income and the present value of all future income. (Therefore, present value and compound interest concepts have an important role in the investing process.) Although the field of investments encompasses many aspects, as the title of this book suggests, it can be thought of in terms of two functions: analysis and management.

In this text, the term *investments* refers in general to financial assets and in particular to marketable securities. **Financial assets** are paper (or electronic) claims on some issuer, such as the federal government or a corporation; on the other hand, **real assets** are tangible assets such as gold, silver, diamonds, art, and real estate. **Marketable securities** are financial assets that are easily and cheaply tradable in organized markets. Technically, investments includes both financial and real assets, and both marketable and nonmarketable assets. Because of the vast scope of investment opportunities available to investors, our primary emphasis is on marketable securities; however, the basic principles and techniques discussed in this text are applicable to real assets.

Even when we limit our discussion primarily to marketable securities, it is difficult to keep up with the proliferation of new products. Two such assets that did not exist a few years ago are junk bonds (discussed in Chapter 6) and stock index futures (discussed in Chapter 17). The former became a $200 billion dollar market by the end of the 1980s before undergoing a severe crisis, whereas the latter continues to grow at such a rate that their trading often impacts the stock market significantly.

A Perspective on Investing

The investment of funds in various assets is only part of the overall financial decision making and planning that most individuals must do. Before investing, each individual should develop an overall financial plan. Such a plan should include the decision on whether to purchase a house, a major investment for most individuals. Also, decisions must be made about insurance of various types—life, health, disability, and protection of business and property. Finally, the plan should provide for emergency reserve funds.[2]

This text assumes that investors have established their overall financial plan and are now interested in managing and enhancing their wealth by investing in an optimal combination of financial assets. The idea of an "optimal combination" is important, because our wealth, which we hold in the form of various assets, should be evaluated and managed as a unified whole. Wealth should be evaluated and managed within the context of a **portfolio,** which is made up of the asset holdings of an investor.

Why Do We Invest?

We invest to make money! Although everyone would agree with this statement, we need to be more precise (after all, this is a college textbook). We invest to improve our welfare, which for our purposes can be defined as monetary wealth, both current and future.[3] We assume that investors are interested only in the monetary benefits to be obtained from investing, as opposed to such factors as the psychic income to be derived from impressing one's friends with one's financial prowess.

Funds to be invested come from assets already owned, borrowed money, and savings or foregone consumption. By foregoing consumption today and investing the savings, investors expect to enhance their future consumption possibilities by increasing their wealth. Investors also seek to manage their wealth effectively, obtaining the most from it while protecting it from inflation, taxes, and other factors. To accomplish both objectives, people invest.

The Importance of Studying Investments

It is important to remember that all individuals have wealth of some kind—if nothing else, this wealth may consist of the value of their services in the marketplace. Most individuals must make investment decisions sometime in their lives. Some workers, for example, can decide whether their retirement funds are to be invested in stocks or bonds. Others may wish to maximize the return from their "savings account" funds by investing in alternatives to insured savings accounts.

A good example of the investment decisions facing a typical individual, and the critical importance of making good investment decisions, is the

---

[2]Personal financial decisions of this type are discussed in detail in personal finance texts. See, for example, Lawrence Gitman and Michael Joehnk, *Personal Financial Planning, 4th ed.* (New York: The Dryden Press, 1987).

[3]An excellent discussion of the wealth problem for investors can be found in Charles A. D'Ambrosio, *Principles of Modern Investments* (Chicago: SRA, 1976), Chapter 3.

Individual Retirement Account (IRA), still available to income earners despite the landmark Tax Reform Act of 1986. IRA funds can be invested in a wide range of assets, from the very safe to the quite speculative. IRA owners are allowed to have self-directed brokerage accounts, which offer a wide array of investment opportunities. As these funds may be invested for as long as 40 or more years, good investment decisions are critical, as shown by the examples in Table 1-1. Over many years of investing, the differences in results that investors realize, due solely to the investment returns earned, can be staggering.

In the final analysis, we study investments in the hope of earning better returns in relation to the risk we assume when we invest. A careful study of investment analysis and portfolio management principles can provide a sound framework for both managing and increasing wealth. Furthermore, we would like to avoid as many pitfalls as possible, such as those illustrated in Box 1-1—and the many more that await the investor.

Understanding the Investment Process

To view the investment process in an organized manner involves analyzing the basic nature of investment decisions, dividing the activities in the decision process, and examining the major factors in the investors' operating environment that affect their investment decisions.

Common stocks have, on average, produced larger returns over the years than savings accounts or bonds, so why did all investors not invest in common stocks and realize these larger returns? The answer to this question is that to pursue these higher returns investors must assume larger risks. Underlying all investment decisions is the trade-off between return and risk. Therefore, we first consider these two basic parameters that are of critical importance to all investors and the trade-off that exists between them.

Given the foundation for making investment decisions—the trade-off between expected return and risk—we consider the decision process in investments as it is typically practiced today. Although numerous separate

TABLE 1-1 ***Possible Payoffs from Long-Term Investing***

Amount Invested per Year ($)	Number of Years	Final Wealth If Funds Are Invested at 5%	10%	15%
		—Total Number of Dollars ($)—		
2000	20	66,132	114,550	204,880
2000	30	132,878	328,980	869,480
2000	40	241,600	885,180	3,558,000

decisions must be made, for organizational purposes this decision process has traditionally been divided into a two-step process: security analysis and portfolio management. The former involves the valuation of securities, whereas the latter involves the management of an investor's investment selections as a portfolio (unit), with its own unique characteristics.

The Basic Nature of the Investment Decision

Return Why invest? Stated in simplest terms, investors wish to earn a return on their money. Cash has an opportunity cost: By holding cash you forego the opportunity to earn a return on that cash. Furthermore, in an inflationary environment, the purchasing power of cash diminishes, with high rates of inflation (such as that in 1980) bringing a relatively rapid decline in purchasing power.

INVESTMENTS INTUITION

Investors buy, hold, and sell financial assets to earn returns on them. Within the spectrum of financial assets, why do some people buy common stocks instead of safely depositing their money in an insured savings account? The answer is that they are trying to earn returns larger than those available from such safer (and lower-yielding) assets as savings accounts and Treasury bills. They know they will be taking a greater risk of losing some of their money by buying common stocks, but they expect to earn a greater return.

In investments it is critical to distinguish between an **expected return** (the anticipated return for some future period) and a **realized return** (the actual return over some past period). Investors invest for the future—for the returns they expect to earn—but when the investing period is over, they are left with their realized returns. What investors actually earn from their holdings may turn out to be more, or less, than what they expected to earn when they initiated the investment. This point is the essence of the investment process: *Investors must always consider the risk involved in investing*.

Risk Investors would like their returns to be as large as possible; however, this objective is subject to constraints, primarily risk.[4] In 1982 the stock market had a very good year, with total returns in excess of 20% on a broad cross section of common stocks. Nevertheless, several professionally managed funds managed to lose money that year. As this example shows,

[4]Although risk is the most important constraint on investors, other constraints clearly exist. Taxes and transaction costs are often viewed as constraints. Some investors may face legal constraints on the types of securities they can purchase or the amount they can hold.

marketable securities offering variable returns across time are risky! The investment decision must, therefore, always be considered in terms of both risk and return. The two are inseparable.

There are different types, and therefore different definitions, of risk. **Risk** is defined here as the chance that the actual return on an investment will be different from its expected return.[5] Using the term *risk* in this manner, the nominal (current dollar) return on a Treasury bill has no practical risk because there is no reasonable chance that the U.S. government will fail to redeem these obligations as they mature in 13 or 26 weeks. On the other hand, there is some risk, however small, that Exxon or General Electric will be unable to redeem an issue of 30-year bonds when they mature. And there is a very substantial risk of not realizing the expected return on any particular common stock over some future holding period, such as a year, six months, one month, or even one day.

Do investors dislike risk? In economics in general, and investments in particular, the standard assumption is that investors are rational. Rational investors prefer certainty to uncertainty. It is easy to say that investors dislike risk, but we should be more precise and say that investors are risk averse. A **risk-averse investor** is one who will not assume risk simply for its own sake and will not incur any given level of risk unless there is an expectation of adequate compensation for having done so. Note carefully that it is not irrational to assume risk, even very large risk, as long as we *expect* to be compensated for it. In fact, investors cannot reasonably expect to earn larger returns without assuming larger risks.

Investors deal with risk by choosing the amount of risk they are willing to incur. Some investors choose to incur high levels of risk with the expectation of high levels of return. Other investors are unwilling to assume much risk, and they should not expect to earn large returns.

We have said that investors would like to maximize their returns. Can we also say that investors, in general, will choose to minimize their risks? No! The reason is that there are costs to minimizing the risk, specifically a lower expected return. Taken to its logical conclusion, the minimization of risk would result in everyone holding risk-free assets such as savings accounts and Treasury bills. Thus, we need to think in terms of the expected return–risk trade-off that results from the direct relationship between the risk and the expected return of an investment.

The Expected Return–Risk Trade-off Within the realm of financial assets investors can achieve virtually any position on an expected return–risk spectrum such as that depicted in Figure 1-1. The line *RF* to *B* is the as-

---

[5]As we shall see in Chapter 5, expected return is a precise statistical term, not simply the return the investor expects. As indicated in our definition, risk involves chances, or probabilities, which will also be discussed in Chapter 5, along with measures of the dispersion in the expected return.

sumed trade-off between expected return and risk that exists for all investors interested in financial assets. This trade-off always slopes upward, because the vertical axis is *expected* return, and rational investors will not assume more risk unless they *expect* to be compensated for doing so. The expected return should be large enough to compensate for taking the additional risk; however, there is no guarantee that the additional returns will be realized.

RF in Figure 1-1 is the return on a riskless asset such as Treasury bills. This position has zero risk and an expected return equal to the current rate of return available on riskless assets such as Treasury bills. This **risk-free rate of return,** which is available to all investors, will be designated as *RF* throughout the text.

Figure 1-1 shows approximate relative positions for some of the financial assets that will be discussed in Chapter 2. As we move from riskless Treasury securities to more risky corporate bonds, equities, and so forth, we assume more risk in the expectation of earning a larger return. Common stocks are quite risky, in relation to bonds, but they are not as risky as an unhedged purchase of options (puts and calls) or futures contracts (all of these terms will be defined in the next chapter). Obviously, Figure 1-1 depicts broad categories. Within a particular category, such as common stocks, a wide range of expected return and risk opportunities exists at any time.

The important point in Figure 1-1 is the trade-off between expected return and risk that should prevail in a rational environment. Investors

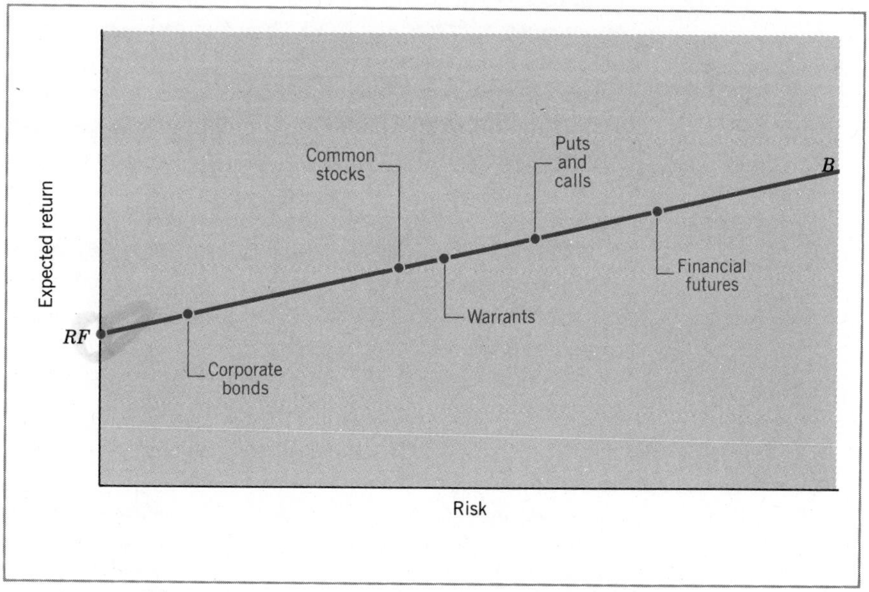

FIGURE 1-1 ***The expected return–risk trade-off available to investors.***

unwilling to assume risk must be satisfied with the risk-free rate of return, *RF.* If they wish to try to earn a larger rate of return, they must be willing to assume a larger risk as represented by moving up the expected return–risk trade-off into the wide range of financial assets available to investors. Although all rational investors like returns and dislike risk, they are satisfied by quite different levels of expected return and risk; or, put differently, investors have different limits on the amount of risk they are willing to assume and, therefore, the amount of return that can realistically be expected. In economic terms, the explanation for these differences in preferences is that rational investors strive to maximize their utility, the perception of which varies among investors.[6]

Always remember that the risk–return trade-off depicted in Figure 1-1 is **ex ante,** meaning "before the fact"; that is, before the investment is actually made, the investor expects higher returns from assets that have a higher risk. This is the only sensible expectation for risk-averse investors, who are assumed to constitute the majority of all investors. **Ex post** (meaning "after the fact" or when it is known what has occurred), for a given period of time, such as a month or a year or even longer, the trade-off may turn out to be flat, or even negative. Such is the nature of risky investments.

Structuring the Decision Process

Investors can choose from a wide range of securities. They invest in an attempt to maximize the expected returns from these opportunities, but they face constraints, the most pervasive of which is risk. Traditionally, investors have analyzed and managed securities using a broad two-step process: security analysis and portfolio management.

Security Analysis The first part of the investment decision process involves the valuation and analysis of individual securities, which is referred to as **security analysis.** Professional security analysts are usually employed by institutional investors. Of course, there are also millions of amateur security analysts in the form of individual investors.

The valuation of securities is a time-consuming and difficult job. First of all, it is necessary to understand the characteristics of the various securities and the factors that affect them. Second, a valuation model is applied to these securities to estimate their price, or value. Value is a function of the expected future returns on a security and the risk attached. Both of these parameters must be estimated and then brought together in a model.

---

[6]Utility theory is a complex subject; however, for our purposes we can equate maximization of utility with maximization of welfare. Because welfare is a function of present and future wealth, and wealth in turn is a function of current and future income discounted (reduced) for the amount of risk involved, in effect investors maximize their welfare by optimizing the expected return–risk trade-off. In the final analysis, expected return and risk constitute the foundation of all investment decisions.

For bonds, the valuation process is relatively easy, because the returns are known and the risk can be approximated from currently available data. This does not mean, however, that all the problems of bond analysis are easily resolved. Interest rates are the primary factor affecting bond prices, but no one can consistently forecast changes in interest rates.

The valuation process is much more difficult for common stocks than for bonds. The investor must deal with the overall economy, the industry, and the individual company. Both the expected return and risk of common stocks must be estimated.

After completing the formal valuation process just outlined, at least one significant question remains to be answered—the issue of market efficiency, which has implications for the valuation and selection of stocks. Sufficient creditable evidence exists to make intelligent investors consider this concept carefully, as will be explained later in the chapter.

Portfolio Management The second major component of the decision process is **portfolio management.** After securities have been evaluated, a portfolio should be selected. Concepts on why and how to build a portfolio are well known. Much of the work in this area is in the form of mathematical and statistical models, which have had a profound effect on the study of investments in this country in the last 30 years.

Having built a portfolio, the astute investor must consider how and when to revise it. This raises a number of important questions. Portfolios must be managed, regardless of whether an investor is active or passive. Questions to be considered include taxes, transaction costs, maintenance of the desired risk level, and so on.

Finally, all investors are interested in how well their portfolio performs. This is the bottom line of the investment process. Measuring portfolio performance is an inexact procedure, even today, and needs to be carefully considered.

External Factors Affecting the Decision Process

The investment decision process as just described can be lengthy and involved, and intelligent investors should be aware of this. Regardless of individual actions, however, certain factors in the investment environment affect all investors. These factors should constantly be kept in mind as investors work through the investment decision process.

The Great Unknown

The first, and paramount, factor that all investors must come to grips with is uncertainty. Investors buy financial assets expecting to earn returns over some future holding period. These returns, with few exceptions, can only be expected—they may never be realized. The simple fact that dominates investing, although many investors never seem to appreciate it fully, is that the realized return on an asset with any risk attached to it may be different from what was expected—sometimes, quite different.

Estimates are imprecise, at best; at worst, they are completely wrong. All that investors can do is make the most informed return and risk estimates they can, act on them, and be prepared for shifting circumstances. They may, and very often do, use past data to make their estimates. Often investors modify these data to incorporate what they believe is most likely to happen. Regardless of how careful and informed investors are, the future is unknown, and mistakes will be made. This will always be true for risky assets.

Some investors try to handle uncertainty by building elaborate quantitative models, and others simply keep it in the back of their mind. All investors, however, are affected by it. What is important to remember is that basing investment decisions solely on the past is going to lead to errors. A 10% average return on all stocks for the last 10 years does not in any way guarantee a 10% return for the next year, or even an average 10% return for the next 10 years.

Someone can always tell you what you should have bought or sold last year. (For example, the author of this text is pleased to tell you that you, or someone on your behalf, should have bought and held Fidelity's Magellan Fund, a mutual fund investing in common stocks with growth as the objective. Magellan had a percentage gain for the 10-year period from mid-1979 to mid-1989 of 1251%, compared to a percentage gain of 150% for the overall market.) No one, however, can guarantee you a successful portfolio for next year. Unanticipated events will affect the stock market. Interest rates, the major factor affecting bonds, cannot be predicted with any significant degree of consistency. No one can forecast consistently what will happen in the financial markets, including the professionals who are paid to make recommendations. Consider the following statement from Mark Hulbert, who monitors investment newsletters that offer investors advice:

> Sometimes I think the market is just plain out to get us. At the end of April 1986, *not one* of the 100-plus investment newsletter services I monitor in my *Hulbert Financial Digest* was predicting what lay ahead: that the market would rise by almost 50%, give it all back in a crash, and then recover to its old high, counting reinvested dividends. All within the space of 36 months. But be reasonable. Who could have predicted this unlikely course of events?[7] [emphasis added]

Although uncertainty is always present, all is not lost. It is often possible to make reasonable and informed judgments about the outcomes of

[7]See Mark Hulbert, "Whiplash?" *Forbes,* June 26, 1989, p. 216. Used with permission.

many investment opportunities; it is not possible, however, to make totally accurate forecasts consistently about risky securities.

Investment decisions are both an art and a science. To succeed in investing, we must think in terms of *what is expected to happen*. We know what has happened, but the past may or may not repeat itself. Although the future is uncertain, it is manageable, and a thorough understanding of the basic principles of investing will allow investors to cope intelligently.

The Investment Environment

Consider the following quote from a "Capital Markets" column of *Forbes*, a popular investment magazine:

> Giants tread Wall Street these days. How is a small investor to compete with them? After all, . . . [they] have access to information the little guy doesn't have.[8]

There are two broad categories of investors: individual investors and **institutional investors.** The latter group—consisting of bank trust departments, pension funds, mutual funds, insurance companies, and so forth—includes the professional money managers, who are often publicized in the popular press. The amount of money managed by these institutions is staggering. For example, in mid-1989 Goldman, Sachs & Company managed some $16 billion in money market and bond funds. Two months after deciding to manage stock portfolios once again (Goldman had abandoned stock management some years earlier), it was offered some $200 million to manage by wealthy individuals before it actually began accepting funds. These amounts pale by comparison to the $105 billion under management by Shearson Lehman Hutton, Inc. Given the figures for individual companies, it is not hard to see why by the beginning of the 1990s, institutional investors in the United States held almost $6 trillion dollars in assets. However, these institutional investors do not constitute a monolithic bloc of investors. Instead, they are made up of thousands of different organizations, most of which have multiple money managers.

Although individuals are the indirect beneficiaries of institutional investors, because they indirectly own or benefit from these institutions' portfolios, on a daily basis they are "competing" with these institutions. Both groups are trying to make intelligent trading decisions about securities. Can individual investors hope to compete fairly with institutions, and how is their decision process affected by these large portfolios?

It is true that the institutional investors are the "professional" investors, with vast resources at their command. Does the average investor have a reasonable chance in the market? Yes—in the sense that he or she can

---

[8] See Ben Weberman, "Pebbles on the Beach," *Forbes*, January 16, 1984, p. 127.

generally expect to earn a fair return for the risk taken. On average, the individual investor will probably do just as well as the big institutional investors, because markets are usually quite efficient and securities fairly priced. And some investors do better. By concentrating on situations they know about, investing regularly and for the long term, and diversifying, a number of investors have enjoyed excellent results over long periods. See Box 1-2 for support of this statement and information about how these results were accomplished.

Continuing the previous quote from *Forbes:*

> Never mind. A lot of individuals do all right. One way they do so is to look for pockets in the market so small that mega-institutions can't be bothered with them—imperfections in the market that smart investors can take advantage of.[9]

These possible imperfections in the market relate to market efficiency, which we will consider next.

The Question of Market Efficiency

One of the most profound ideas affecting the investment decision process and, indeed, all of finance is the idea that the securities markets, particularly the equity markets, are efficient. In an efficient market the prices of securities do not depart for any length of time from the justified economic values calculated for them by investors. Economic values for securities are determined by investor expectations about earnings, risks, and so on, as investors grapple with the uncertain future. If the market price of a security does depart from its estimated economic value, investors act to bring the two values together. Thus, as new information arrives in an efficient marketplace, causing a revision in the estimated economic value of a security, its price adjusts quickly and, on balance, correctly to this information. In other words, securities are efficiently priced on a continuous basis. We will discuss the full implications of this statement in Chapter 14.

INVESTMENTS INTUITION

An efficient market does not have to be perfectly efficient to have a profound impact on investors. All that is required is that the market be *economically efficient*, meaning that after acting upon information to trade securities and subtracting *all* costs (transaction costs and taxes, to name two), the investor would have been as well off with a simple buy-and-hold strategy. If the market is economically efficient, securities could depart somewhat from their economic (justified) values, but it would not pay investors to take advantage of these small discrepancies.

---

[9]Ibid.

BOX 1-2

YES, IT'S TRUE: AMATEUR INVESTORS DO REGULARLY BEAT WALL STREET

They meet once a month in the back office of the local grain company in Jamestown, Ohio, population 2500. Their mission: best Wall Street's stock-picking wizards at their own game.

And they do just that. The Bowersville Investment Club—a group of 11 farmers—has racked up an average total return of 16% a year since 1972.

That's three percentage points better than Standard & Poor's 500-stock index over the same period. In comparison, only a quarter of investment professionals were able to equal or beat the index.

But although the Bowersville club's performance is exemplary, its experience in beating the market and the pros isn't unique. Amateur investors regularly beat Wall Street.

The National Association of Investors Corp., the Royal Oak, Mich., association of the nation's investment clubs, annually monitors the performance of its 6900 clubs for the year ended April 28. Over the latest year, it says, 47% of the clubs surpassed or at least matched the performance of the S&P 500.

How the clubs manage to chalk up such performance should give encouragement to every individual investor who has ever felt beat up by program traders, institutional indexers and cold-calling brokers.

Indeed, as many investment club participants see it, amateur investors frequently have some important advantages over the pros. The trick is to make the most of them. Here are some of their tips:

Invest Close to Home.

Know the Management. Thomas O'Hara, chairman of the National Association of Investors Corp., says top clubs always look hard at management.

Keep It Simple. The all-star clubs generally stay away from technology and other complex stocks.

Invest Regularly. Amateurs have complete control over their flow of money to invest. This allows investors to "dollar-cost average." That is, they purchase the same dollar amount of stock at regular intervals regardless of price. Over time, they tend to end up with more shares bought at low prices than at high prices.

Think Long-Term. Unlike many professional money managers, amateur investors don't have to "attempt to look good every quarter," says Mr. O'Hara. As a result, they don't have to worry about trying to time the market's twists and turns. That leaves them free to follow a long-term buy-and-hold strategy.

Don't Panic.

Diversify. Everybody talks about it; the all-star investment clubs do it.

Source: Adapted from Earl C. Gottschalk, Jr., "Yes, It's True: Amateur Investors Do Regularly Beat Wall Street," *The Wall Street Journal*, January 2, 1990, pp. C1, C19. Reprinted by permission of *The Wall Street Journal*, © 1990 Dow Jones & Company, Inc. All Rights Reserved Worldwide.

Obviously, the possibility that the stock market is efficient has significant implications for investors. In fact, one's knowledge of and belief in this idea, known as the **efficient market hypothesis** (EMH), will directly affect how one views the investment process and makes investment decisions. Those who are strong believers in the EMH may adopt, to varying degrees, a passive investment strategy, because of the likelihood that they will not be able to find underpriced securities. These investors will seek to minimize transaction cost and taxes and the time and resources devoted to analyzing securities, which should, if the EMH is correct, be correctly priced to begin with.

Investors who do not accept the EMH continue to seek out undervalued securities, believing that they can identify such securities and that lags exist in the market's adjustment of these securities' prices to new (better) information. These investors generate more search costs (both in time and money) and more transaction costs, but they believe that the marginal benefit outweighs the marginal costs incurred.

It is important for all investors at the outset of their study of investments at least to be aware of this idea and its potential implications. A tremendous amount of research has been done on the EMH over the last 20 years, and much evidence has accumulated. Very impressive evidence exists that the market is quite efficient. Certainly, the idea cannot be dismissed out of hand. If you think it can be, go back and read the second statement in this chapter—if only such a small percentage of professional money managers is able to outperform the market more than 50% of the time, easy opportunities do not abound. On the other hand, more evidence of market inefficiencies has been accumulating recently. Possibilities for astute investors appear to exist and have been documented. In the final analysis, the issue remains open.

The point to keep in mind at this stage is that investors should learn as fully and carefully as possible about the actual environment that exists in today's investment world. Although startling, the EMH cannot be quickly dismissed. The intelligent course of action is to understand the situation, employ what is useful and disregard or use sparingly the remainder, and make the best decisions possible. Only by understanding the investment process and the issues involved in the efficient markets controversy can one hope to answer the question, "How efficient is the market?"

Organizing the Text

The presentation in the following chapters is organized around the previously discussed decision process involved in investments: security analysis and portfolio management. The investments business has traditionally been divided into these two broad areas, each of which encompasses a wide spectrum of activities.

Four chapters of background material follow this introductory chapter.

The assets available to investors and the markets in which they trade are examined in turn. This is followed by an examination of the sources of information available to investors. Finally, return and risk are examined in some detail, since these two parameters underlie all investment decisions.

Thirteen chapters of the book are devoted to evaluating alternative investment opportunities and explaining the basics of security analysis. We begin with a study of bonds because the valuation process can be learned most quickly by studying bonds. Common stocks are analyzed next. For both of these assets the basics are covered in one chapter, and a separate chapter on valuation techniques follows.

Because of the complexity of common stocks, three additional chapters are needed to describe the basics of fundamental analysis, the most popular method for analyzing stocks. These chapters are purposefully sequenced from market to industry to company analysis. A discussion of technical analysis follows this sequence on fundamental analysis and is in turn logically followed by a discussion of efficient markets.

An in-depth analysis of alternative investment opportunities follows the material on common stocks. Separate chapters cover options, warrants and convertibles, and futures. Finally, indirect investing through investment companies is considered.

The text concludes with four chapters on portfolio management. The basics of portfolio theory and management are examined first, followed by a discussion of extended diversification and capital market theory. The logical capstone to a study of investments, the measurement of portfolio performance, is analyzed last.

Summary

- An investment is the commitment of funds to one or more assets that will be held over some future period. The field of investments involves the study of the investment process.
- The investment opportunities considered in this text consist of a wide array of financial assets (primarily marketable securities), which are financial claims on some issuer, and to a lesser degree real assets, which are tangible assets such as precious metals.
- We invest to improve our welfare, defined here as monetary wealth.
- The basic element of all investment decisions is the trade-off between expected return and risk. Financial assets are arrayed along an upward-sloping expected return–risk trade-off, with the risk-free rate of return as the vertical-axis intercept.
- Expected return and risk are directly related; the greater (smaller) the expected return, the greater (smaller) the risk.
- Investors seek to maximize expected returns subject to constraints, primarily risk.

- Risk is defined as the chance that the actual return on an investment will differ from its expected return.
- Rational investors are risk averse, meaning that they are unwilling to assume risk unless they expect to be adequately compensated.
- For organizational purposes the investment decision process has traditionally been divided into two broad steps: security analysis and portfolio management.
- Security analysis is concerned with the valuation of securities. Valuation, in turn, is a function of expected return and risk.
- Portfolio management encompasses building an optimal portfolio for an investor. Considerations include initial portfolio construction, revision, and the measurement of performance.
- Major factors affecting the decision process include uncertainty in investment decisions, the investments environment, and the efficiency of the market. These factors should be considered carefully by investors as they study investments, evaluate information and claims, and make decisions.

Key Words

Efficient market hypothesis (EMH)
Ex ante
Expected return
Ex post
Financial assets
Institutional investors
Investment
Investments
Marketable securities
Portfolio
Portfolio management
Real assets
Realized return
Risk
Risk-averse investor
Risk-free rate of return
Security analysis
Wealth

QUESTIONS

1-1 Define the term *investments*.

1-2 Describe the broad two-step process involved in making investment decisions.

1-3 Why is the study of investments important to many individuals?

1-4 Distinguish between a financial asset and a real asset.

1-5 Carefully describe the risk–return trade-off faced by all investors.

1-6 In terms of Figure 1-1, when would an investor expect to earn the risk-free rate of return?

1-7 A risk-averse investor will not assume risk. Agree or disagree with this statement.

1-8 Summarize the basic nature of the investment decision in one sentence.

1-9 Distinguish between expected return and realized return.

1-10 Define risk. How many specific types can you think of?

1-11 What other constraints besides risk do investors face?

1-12 Are all rational investors risk averse? Do they all have the same degree of risk aversion?

1-13 What external factors affect the decision process? Which do you think is the most important?

1-14 What are institutional investors? How are individual investors likely to be affected by institutional investors?

1-15 What is meant by the expression *efficient market?*

1-16 Of what significance is an efficient market to investors?

1-17 Why should the required rate of return be different for a corporate bond and a Treasury bond?

Selected References

An excellent discussion of the investment decision and process can be found in

D'Ambrosio, Charles A. *Principles of Modern Investments*. Chicago: SRA, 1976.

A very interesting account of today's investment world is contained in

Ellis, Charles D. *Investment Policy: How to Win the Loser's Game*. Homewood, Ill.: Dow Jones-Irwin, 1985.

CHAPTER 2

Types of Securities

This chapter surveys the major types of securities available to investors. Each will be discussed only briefly, with the purpose of introducing the types of securities available in the money and capital markets. Later chapters will present additional details about these securities, allowing the reader to concentrate specifically on a particular security.

Although our discussion is as current as possible, rapid changes make it necessary for all investors to keep up. New securities have appeared recently, and others undoubtedly will be offered in the coming months and years. The financial markets in the United States are dynamic; new securities are constantly being developed to meet the changing needs and preferences of investors. Investors in the 1990s have a wide variety of investment alternatives they can consider.

According to one estimate, more than 600 new financial products were introduced between 1986 and the end of 1990.[1] Many investors may not realize that until the deregulation of the 1980s, banks and thrifts were unable to offer their own rates on small certificates of deposit. Zero-coupon bonds did not exist until the 1980s; however, by the end of the 1980s zero-coupon bonds provided the largest return of any Treasury security. All of these instruments are reviewed in this chapter. Junk bonds, among the most controversial securities ever, are discussed in detail in Chapter 6.

The emphasis in this chapter (and throughout the text) is on financial assets, which are financial claims on the issuers of the securities. We focus in particular on marketable securities, which are claims that are negotiable, or salable, in various marketplaces, as discussed later in Chapter 3. Although our emphasis is on marketable securities, investors quite often own some nonmarketable financial assets, such as savings accounts or savings bonds. Because these assets are widely known and owned by investors, they warrant a brief discussion and are presented at the beginning of the chapter.

Marketable securities may be classified as either money market or capital market instruments. They can also be classified as either fixed-income or equity securities. Money market instruments are discussed first. Capital market instruments, which are more important to most investors, are separated in our discussion into fixed-income instruments and equity instruments (common stocks), followed by equity-derivative securities and futures contracts.

Finally, *indirect investing* is examined. Rather than invest directly in

[1]See Tom Herman, "Is Financial Product Explosion Perilous for Investors?" *The Wall Street Journal*, December 21, 1989, p. C1.

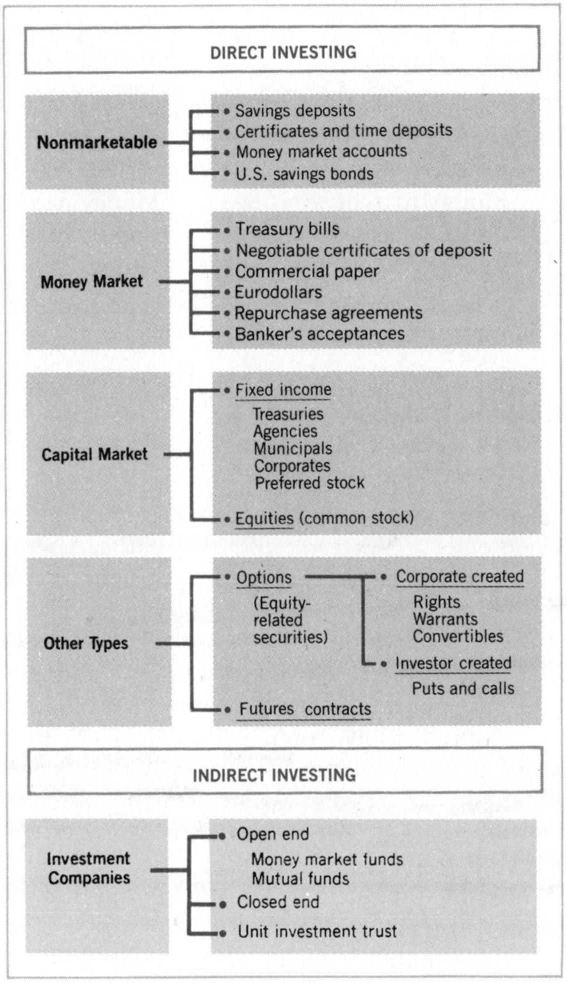

FIGURE 2-1 ***Major types of financial assets.***

securities, investors can invest indirectly in a portfolio of securities by purchasing the shares of an investment company, a financial intermediary that invests in securities of various types on behalf of its shareowners. This is a very important alternative for all investors to consider.

Figure 2-1 charts the types of financial assets to be analyzed in this text. The organization is based on the classifications discussed earlier. Thus, investors have two broad alternatives: direct investing or indirect investing (or a combination of the two). Investing directly, beyond nonmarketable assets, investors can choose money market securities or capital market securities; the latter consist of fixed-income securities and equity securities. Other types of securities include various claims on common stocks (both corporate-created and investor-created) and financial futures contracts. Most, or all, of these assets are also available to investors through indirect investing. In summary:

INVESTORS CAN

Invest Directly in	*Invest Indirectly in*
Money market securities	Money market securities
Capital market securities	Capital market securities
Other types of securities	Other types of securities

Use a Combination of Direct and Indirect Investing

Nonmarketable Financial Assets

Savings Deposits

Savings accounts are undoubtedly the best-known type of investment in the United States. These accounts are held at commercial banks or "thrift" institutions such as savings and loan associations and credit unions.[2]

Savings accounts in insured institutions (and your money should not be in a noninsured institution) offer a high degree of safety on both the principal and the return on that principal. At most commercial banks, accounts are insured by the Federal Deposit Insurance Corporation (FDIC).[3] Liquidity is taken for granted, which, along with their safety, probably accounts for the popularity of savings accounts. **Liquidity** can be defined as the ease with which an asset can be converted to cash; an asset is liquid if it can be sold quickly with, at most, small price changes, assuming no new information in the marketplace.

Historically, the rate of interest paid on these accounts was regulated by various government agencies. For example, in the early 1980s federal regulations permitted banks to pay a maximum of 5.25% in interest on regular savings (compounding at some institutions could increase the effective rate), whereas thrifts could pay a maximum of 5.50%.[4] This low return helped to spawn the rise of competitors for the savings dollar. The money market funds (discussed later in the chapter) that came into existence at this time have enjoyed phenomenal growth.

---

[2]The distinctions between banks and thrifts have decreased since the deregulation of the banking industry in the early 1980s. The trend is toward individual institutions offering a wide range of financial services.

[3]At savings and loan associations and credit unions, accounts are insured by the Federal Savings and Loan Insurance Corporation and the National Credit Union Administration, respectively.

[4]As of January 1, 1984, federal regulations were changed to allow banks to pay a maximum of 5.50% on regular savings.

As of April 1, 1986, the interest rate ceiling on all deposit accounts was removed. Few banks raised their rates at the time, however, apparently believing that "passbook" savers are insensitive to the rates being paid on these accounts (otherwise, the reasoning goes, they would have moved the funds to alternative, higher-yielding investments).

Financial institutions also offer **NOW (negotiable order of withdrawal) accounts,** checking accounts that pay interest at the so-called NOW interest rate. Such accounts typically require a minimum balance to avoid service charges. NOW accounts pay a relatively low rate of interest.

Money Market Deposit Accounts

In 1982 federal regulators allowed financial institutions to offer **money market deposit accounts (MMDAs)** with no interest rate ceilings. This means that these accounts *can* pay rates competitive with money market funds (i.e., rates currently available on money market instruments) and compete directly with such funds for investors' business. In practice, these accounts typically yield from 1 to 3% less than instruments paying competitive money market rates.

A typical bank offers a money market "investment" account, which pays competitive money market rates and is insured up to $100,000 by the FDIC. A minimum deposit may be required by the institution (often $1000) to open this type of acount.[5] As long as the balance remains above this minimum, interest is paid daily during the statement period at the money market rate.[6] If the balance falls below the minimum required, the interest rate drops to the current rate being paid on savings accounts.

Federal regulations restrict the number of transactions allowed each month. Six preauthorized or automatic transfers are allowed each month, up to three of which can be by check. As many withdrawals as desired can be made in person, and there are no limitations on the number of deposits.

Certificates of Deposit

Commercial banks and other institutions offer a variety of savings certificates known as **certificates of deposit (CDs)**. These certificates are available for various maturities, with higher rates offered as maturity increases (larger deposits may also command higher rates, holding maturity constant). The interest rate typically is compounded on a 365-day basis. CDs are insurable up to $100,000.[7]

---

[5]As of January 1, 1986, federal regulations on the minimum denomination required for MMDAs were eliminated.

[6]The minimum balance may be stated as an average daily balance.

[7]CDs are insured by either the Federal Deposit Insurance Corporation or the Federal Savings and Loan Insurance Corporation.

In effect, institutions are free to set their own rates and terms on most CDs. Because of competition for funds, the terms on CDs have been liberalized. Some institutions, for example, periodically raise the rate paid on longer CDs. Although some CD issuers today reduce the stated penalties for early withdrawal, and even waive them, penalties for early withdrawal of funds can be and often are imposed. Investors should investigate carefully the terms offered on CDs by various institutions.[8]

U.S. Government Savings Bonds

One final nonmarketable asset commonly owned by individuals is the nonmarketable debt of the U.S. government in the form of savings bonds. Following this discussion, all references to government securities will be to marketable issues—Treasury bills, notes, and bonds.

Savings bonds are nonmarketable, nontransferable, and nonnegotiable and cannot be used for collateral. They are purchased from the Treasury, most often through payroll deduction plans and banks and savings institutions. Series EE bonds are sold at 50% of face value, which ranges from $50 to $10,000.

Investors receive interest on these bonds in a lump sum at redemption. The rate of interest is calculated twice a year at 85% of the average yield on five-year Treasury securities. A guaranteed minimum rate is offered if the bonds are held for at least five years. Therefore, depending upon how long the bond is held and the prevailing interest rates, investors receive more or less than the face amount at redemption. Federal tax can be deferred until the bond is redeemed, and the interest is exempt from state and local taxes.

Traditionally, savings bonds were considered a poor investment because they had a maximum fixed interest rate that was noncompetitive during periods of high inflation. In 1982 the floating rate and a minimum 7.5% rate were instituted, and savings bonds became competitive. By 1985–1986 they were attractive and popular investment opportunities because of falling interest rates (the current rate paid is based on the average Treasury yield for the preceding six months). Although the Treasury lowered the guaranteed minimum rate to 6% on November 1, 1986, because of the low level of interest rates at that time, the amount of savings bonds outstanding had reached a record level of almost $120 billion by the beginning of 1990.

Money Market and Deposit Yields

Figure 2-2 shows some money market and deposit yields for 1987 through early-1990. The bottom three plots show deposit yields set by financial institutions, whereas the top three show rates determined under competitive money market conditions. This information provides an appreciation

[8]CD rates usually are displayed in the bank or savings and loan, and are updated regularly.

of both the absolute rates paid on these assets and the *relative* relationships that exist. This information is useful as a benchmark by which to judge investment alternatives because these are low-risk investment opportunities available to virtually all investors.

Figure 2-2 shows that NOW accounts and savings accounts pay low, and quite steady, interest rates across time. Money market deposit accounts are above these levels, with the spread widening in 1988 and 1989 and then beginning to narrow somewhat. Small time deposits (primarily certificates of deposit) paid rates very competitive with the money market instruments

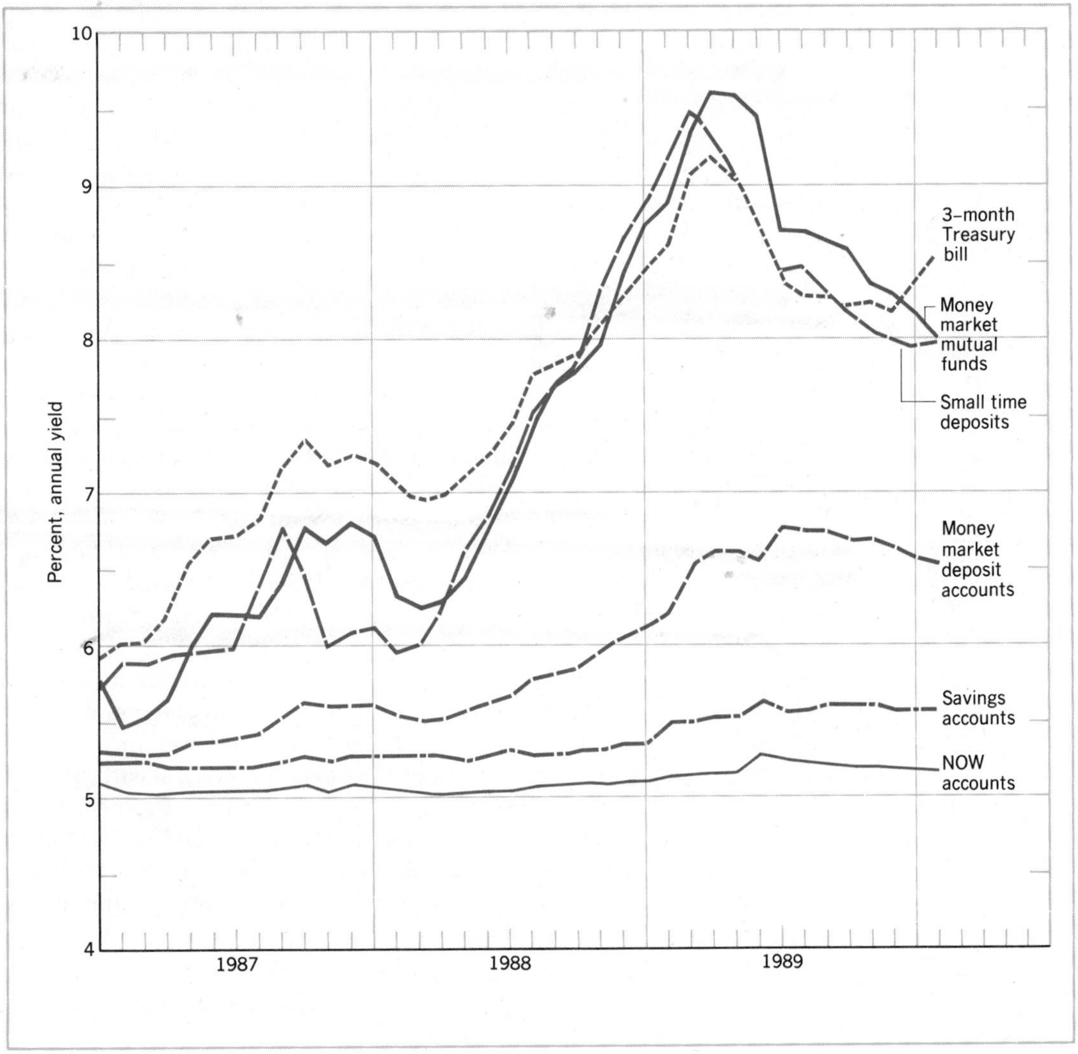

FIGURE 2-2 ***Money market and deposit yields.***
Source: Economic Trends, Federal Reserve Bank of Cleveland, April 1990, p. 5.

discussed in the next section. As the figure indicates, the rate on small time deposits was above the Treasury bill rate during the first half of the period shown, and then declined below it.

Money Market Securities

Money market securities are short-term debt instruments sold by governments, financial institutions, and corporations to investors with temporary excess funds to invest. This market is dominated by financial institutions, particularly banks, and governments. The size of the transactions in the money market typically is large ($100,000 or more). The maturities of money market instruments range from one day to one year and are often less than 90 days.

Some of these instruments are negotiable and actively traded, and some are not. Investors may invest directly in some of these securities, but more often they do so indirectly through money market mutual funds, which are investment companies organized to own and manage a portfolio of securities and which in turn are owned by investors. Thus, many individual investors own shares in money market funds that, in turn, own one or more of these money market certificates.

Another reason a knowledge of these securities is important is the use of the **Treasury bill** (T-bill) as a benchmark asset. Although in some pure sense there is no such thing as a risk-free financial asset, on a practical basis the Treasury bill is risk-free. There is no practical risk of default by the U.S. government. The Treasury bill rate, denoted *RF,* is used throughout the text as a proxy for the risk-free rate of return available to investors (e.g., the *RF* shown and discussed in Figure 1-1).

In summary, money market instruments are characterized as short-term, highly liquid investments, with an extremely low probability of default. The minimum investment is generally large. These debt securities are typically owned by individual investors indirectly in money market mutual funds. Table 2-1 describes the major money market securities.

Figure 2-2, discussed earlier, shows the rate on three-month Treasury bills over a recent period. This rate reflected money market conditions on a current basis. As the figure shows, the general trend was upward, rising from less than 6% at the beginning of 1987 to about 8½% in early 1990. The other money market instruments pay competitive rates of return based on current market conditions. These rates typically are close to each other and higher than the rate on Treasury bills, holding maturity constant. As an example, consider the rates on three-month maturity instruments as of early March, 1990:

Treasury bills	7.72%
CDs	8.12%
Commercial paper	8.15%
Bankers acceptance	8.04%
Eurodollars	8.30%

TABLE 2-1 ***Major Money Market Securities***

1. *Treasury bills.* The premier money market instrument, a fully guaranteed, very liquid IOU from the U.S. Treasury. They are sold on an auction basis every week at a discount from face value in denominations of $10,000 to $1 million; therefore, the discount determines the yield. The greater the discount at time of purchase, the higher the return earned by investors. Typical maturities are 13 and 26 weeks. New bills can be purchased by investors on a competitive or noncompetitive bid basis. Outstanding (i.e., already issued) bills can be purchased and sold in the secondary market, an extremely efficient market where government securities dealers stand ready to buy and sell these securities.
2. *Negotiable certificates of deposit (CD).* Issued in exchange for a deposit of funds by most American banks, the CD is a marketable deposit liability of the issuer, who usually stands ready to sell new CDs on demand. The deposit is maintained in the bank until maturity, at which time the holder receives the deposit plus interest. However, these CDs are negotiable, meaning that they can be sold in the open market before maturity. Dealers make a market in these unmatured CDs. Maturities typically range from 14 days (the minimum maturity permitted) to one year. The minimum deposit is $100,000.
3. *Commercial paper.* A short-term, unsecured promissory note issued by large, well-known, and financially strong corporations (including finance companies). Denominations start at $100,000, with a maturity of 270 days or less. Commercial paper is usually sold at a discount either directly by the issuer or indirectly through a dealer, with rates comparable to CDs. Although a secondary market exists for commercial paper, it is weak and most of it is held to maturity. Commercial paper is rated by a rating service as to quality (relative probability of default by the issuer).
4. *Eurodollars.* Dollar-denominated deposits held in foreign banks or in offices of U.S. banks located abroad. Although this market originally developed in Europe, dollar-denominated deposits can now be made in many countries, such as those of Asia. Eurodollar deposits consist of both time deposits and CDs, with the latter constituting the largest component of the Eurodollar market. Maturities are mostly short-term, often less than six months. The Eurodollar market is primarily a wholesale market, with large deposits and large loans. Major international banks transact among themselves with other participants including multinational corporations and governments. Although relatively safe, Eurodollar yields exceed that of other money market assets because of the lesser regulation for Eurodollar banks.
5. *Repurchase agreement (RPs).* An agreement between a borrower and a lender (typically institutions) to sell and repurchase U.S. government securities. The borrower initiates an RP by contracting to sell securities to a lender and agreeing to repurchase these securities at a prespecified price on a stated date. The effective interest rate is given by the difference between the purchase price and the sale price. The maturity of RPs is generally very short, from three to 14 days, and sometimes overnight. The minimum denomination is typically $100,000.
6. *Banker's acceptance.* A time draft drawn on a bank by a customer, whereby the bank agrees to pay a particular amount at a specified future date. Banker's acceptances are negotiable instruments because the holder can sell them for less than face value (i.e., discount them) in the money market. They are normally used in international trade. Banker's acceptances are traded on a discount basis, with a minimum denomination of $100,000. Maturities typically range from 30 to 180 days, within 90 days being the most common.

Capital Market Investments

The **capital market** encompasses instruments with maturities greater than one year. Risk is generally much higher than that in the money market because of the time to maturity and the financial soundness of some of the issuers. Marketability is poorer in some cases. The capital market includes both debt and equity instruments, with the latter having no maturity date.[9]

Fixed-Income Securities

We begin our review of the principal types of investment opportunities typically considered by individual investors with **fixed-income securities.** All these securities have a *specified payment schedule.* In most cases, such as that with a traditional bond, the amount of each payment and the date of each payment are known in advance. Some of these securities carry a risk that the indicated payment will not materialize according to the specified conditions for reasons other than default.[10] Although some of the newer securities in this area deviate from the traditional-bond format, all have a specified payment schedule.

Fixed-income investment opportunities in the capital markets have traditionally consisted primarily of bonds, which are contracts for the borrowing of money. With a traditional bond, the borrower (who issues the bonds) agrees to repay the principal at a specified maturity date and to pay interest at specified intervals in the interim. All details are specified in the contract, and failure to meet a specified condition can result in default.

There are four major types of bonds in the United States based on the issuer involved. Within each major type there are variations. Finally, preferred stock is classified in this text as a fixed-income security because of the fixed nature of its dividends. Preferred stock is discussed last in this section because it is part debt security and part equity and logically can be placed between the two.

Federal Government Securities The U.S. government, in the course of financing its operations through the Treasury Department, issues numerous notes and bonds with maturities greater than one year.[11] The U.S. government is considered the ultimate creditor; therefore, for practical purposes investors do not consider the possibility of risk of default for these securities. An investor purchases these securities with the expectation of

---

[9]For a detailed discussion of the capital markets, see Herbert E. Dougall and Jack E. Gaumnitz, *Capital Markets and Institutions,* 5th ed. (Englewood Cliffs, N.J.: Prentice-Hall, 1986).

[10]Examples include income bonds and preferred stocks.

[11]Through 1982, Treasury securities were sold in bearer form, meaning they belong to the bearer (whoever possesses them). Most federal, state and local, and corporate bonds issued after January 1, 1983, must be registered in the owner's name (unless the maturity is one year or less).

earning a steady stream of interest payments and with full assurance of receiving the par value of the bonds when they mature.

Treasury Bonds **Treasury bonds** generally have maturities of from 10 to 30 years, although a bond can be issued with any maturity.[12] Like Treasury bills, they are sold at competitive auctions. Unlike bills, they are sold at face value, with investors submitting bids on yields.

Interest payments (coupons) are paid semiannually. Face value denominations are $1000, $5000, $10,000, $100,000, $500,000, and $1 million.

Federal Agency Securities Since the 1920s, the federal government has created various federal agencies designed to help certain sectors of the economy, through either direct loans or guarantee of private loans. These federal credit agencies compete in the marketplace for funds by selling **federal agency securities.**

There are two types of federal credit agencies. Legally, "federal agencies" are part of the federal government. These agencies borrow from the Federal Financing Bank (FFB), which in turn borrows from the Treasury. These securities are fully guaranteed by the federal government.[13] The most important "agency" for investors is the Government National Mortgage Association.

In contrast to federal agencies that are officially a part of the government, "federally sponsored credit agencies" are privately owned institutions that sell their own securities in the marketplace in order to raise funds for their specific purposes. Although these agencies have the right to draw upon Treasury funds up to some approved amount, *their securities are not guaranteed by the government as to principal or interest.* Nevertheless, the rapidly growing agency market is dominated by these federally sponsored credit agencies, which include the Federal National Mortgage Association, the Federal Home Loan Mortgage Corporation, the Federal Home Loan Bank, the Farm Credit System, and the Student Loan Marketing Association.

Perhaps the best known of these agencies in the *Federal National Mortgage Association (FNMA)*, which is designed to help the mortgage markets. The FNMA and its issues—discount notes and bonds—are known by the name *Fannie Mae.* Although government sponsored, FNMA is now a privately owned corporation and its securities are not a direct obligation of the U.S. government. A variety of Fannie Mae issues are available, with maturities ranging from short-term—overnight to one year, in the case of notes—to 25 years for bonds.

---

[12] U.S. securities with maturities greater than one year and less than 10 years technically are referred to as Treasury notes.

[13] Although some of these securities remain available to investors as a result of sales before the creation of the FFB in 1973, it is likely that in the future all federal agency debt will be FFB securities. Federal agencies include the Export–Import Bank, Tennessee Valley Authority, U.S. Postal Service, Federal Housing Administration, and Farmers Home Administration.

Fannie Mae and two other government agencies, the *Government National Mortgage Association* (*Ginnie Mae*) and the *Federal Home Loan Mortgage Corporation* (*Freddie Mac*), issue and guarantee securities backed by conventional mortgages bought from lenders. These securities are part of the rapidly growing market of fixed-income securities known as **mortgage-backed securities,** which are securities representing an investment in an underlying pool of mortgages. All three agencies purchase mortgages from banks and thrift institutions, repackage them in the form of securities, and sell them to investors in the form of mortgage pools.

Investors purchase a piece of the mortgage pool, taking into consideration such factors as maturity and the spread between the yield on the mortgage security and the yield on 10-year Treasuries (considered a benchmark in this market). Investors assume little default risk because most mortgages are guaranteed by one of the three government agencies.

Ginnie Mae issues are well known to investors. This wholly owned government agency issues fully backed securities (i.e., they are full faith and credit obligations of the U.S. government) in support of the mortgage market. The GNMA *pass-through securities* have attracted considerable attention in recent years because the principal and interest payments on the underlying mortgages used to collateralize them are "passed through" to the bondholder *monthly* as the mortgages are repaid.[14]

Pass-throughs present investors with uncertainty because they can receive varying amounts of monthly payments, depending upon how quickly homeowners pay off their mortgages. Although the stated maturity can be as long as 40 years, the average life of these pass-throughs to date has been less than 12 years. These certificates originate in minimum denominations of $25,000 but are available from brokerage firms in the form of investment trust units for about $1000 each.

INVESTMENTS INTUITION

Federal agency securities can be thought of as an alternative to U.S. Treasury securities from the investor's standpoint. The feeling in the marketplace seems to be that the Treasury would not stand by and permit a government-sponsored agency to default; however, these securities have to be viewed as having slightly greater default risk. Longer-term issues may trade less frequently than comparable Treasury bonds. These two factors together cause these securities to carry slightly higher yields than Treasury securities of comparable maturity.

[14]A related mortgage-backed security is "Freddie Mac," issued by the Federal Home Loan Mortgage Corporation. This is a *participation certificate* paying a monthly return. Unlike Ginnie Mae, Freddie Mac is not guaranteed by the U.S. government itself. Fannie Mae also issues pass-throughs called mortgage-backed securities. These also are not guaranteed by the U.S. government; however, payment of interest and principal is guaranteed by Fannie Mae.

Municipal Securities Bonds sold by states, counties, cities, and other political entities (e.g., airport authorities, school districts) other than the federal government and its agencies are called **municipal securities,** or simply *municipals.* There are roughly 50,000 different issuers with almost 2 million different issues outstanding, which have credit ratings ranging from very good to very suspect. Thus, risk varies widely, as does marketability. A well-publicized failure occurred in 1983 with the Washington Public Power Supply System's (nicknamed WHOOPS by Wall Street because of the default) $2.25 billion default on its Nos. 4 and 5 nuclear power plants, the largest municipal bond default in U.S. history. Roughly 80,000 investors received a rude shock when the utility announced that it could not pay the approximately $185 million of annual interest payments on these bonds.[15] As of 1989, these investors were in line to receive some 40 cents on the dollar, although a final resolution had not been achieved. Overall, however, the default experience on municipal bonds has been quite favorable.

Two basic types of municipals are *general obligation bonds,* which are backed by the "full faith and credit" of the issuer, and *revenue bonds,* which are repaid from the revenues generated by the project they were sold to finance (e.g., a toll road or airport improvement).[16] In the former case, the issuer can tax residents to pay for the bond interest and principal. In the latter case, the project must generate enough revenue to service the issue. Most long-term municipals are sold as *serial bonds,* which means that a specified number of the original issues matures each year until the final maturity date. For example, a 10-year serial issue of the municipals might have 10% of the issue maturing each year for the next 10 years.

The distinguishing feature of most municipals is their exemption from federal taxes.[17] Because of this, the stated rate on these bonds will be lower than that on comparable nonexempt bonds. Any capital gains on these bonds are still subject to taxes. The higher an investor's tax bracket, the more attractive municipals become. A taxable equivalent yield can be calculated for any municipal bond return and any marginal tax bracket using the following formula:

$$\text{Taxable equivalent yield} = \frac{\text{tax-exempt municipal yield}}{1 - \text{marginal tax rate}} \qquad (2\text{-}1)$$

---

[15]See Lynn Asinorf, "WPPSS Begins to Cause Pain for Investors," *The Wall Street Journal,* December 28, 1983, p. 15.

[16]Municipalities also issue short-term obligations. Some of these qualify for money market investments because they are short-term and of high quality. Bonds backed by the general revenues of the political entities can be for maturities as short as one year. Notes are also issued, typically with a maturity of less than one year. These notes may be of the tax anticipation or the revenue anticipation form. The former are issued against anticipated tax revenues, whereas the latter are issued against other anticipated revenues (e.g., payments from the federal government).

[17]In some cases, the municipal bondholder can also escape state and/or local taxes. For example, a North Carolina resident purchasing a bond issued by the state of North Carolina would escape all taxes on the interest received.

Thus, an investor in the 28% marginal tax bracket who invests in a 10% municipal bond would have to receive

$$\frac{0.10}{(1 - 0.280)} = 13.89\%$$

from a comparable taxable bond to be as well off.[18]

Corporates Most of the larger corporations, several thousand in all, issue **corporate bonds** to help finance their operations. Many of these firms have more than one issue outstanding. AT&T, for example, has several different issues of bonds listed on the "New York Exchange Bonds" page of *The Wall Street Journal.* Although an investor can find a wide range of maturities, coupons, and special features available from corporates, the typical corporate bond matures in 20 to 40 years, pays semiannual interest, is callable, carries a sinking fund, and is sold originally at a price close to par value, which is almost always $1,000.[19]

There are numerous types of corporate bonds. A *debenture* is an unsecured bond, although the holders usually have first call on the earnings (or assets) of the issuer. Bonds that are "secured" by a legal claim to specific assets of the issuer in case of liquidation are called *mortgage bonds. Income bonds* pay interest only if the corporation earns the required payment amount by a specified date. These bonds are an exception to the rule that bond issuers must pay the interest payments and repay the principal payments when due or risk default and possible bankruptcy. Finally, a *convertible bond* can be converted into a specified number of shares of the common stock of the issuer. All these features are discussed in Chapter 6.

Corporate bonds, unlike Treasury securities, carry the risk of default by the issuer. Two rating agencies, Standard & Poor's and Moody's, provide a relative safety rating for each major bond, and bond buyers usually check these ratings carefully. (These ratings are explained in Chapter 6.)

New Fixed-Income Securities The money and capital markets are constantly adapting to meet new requirements and conditions. The result is new types of securities not previously available.

Zero-coupon bonds represent a radical departure from bonds of the past.[20] As their name implies, these bonds are issued with no coupons, or

---

[18]As a result of tax reform, municipal bonds used to finance nonessential government functions are now taxable—specifically, private-purpose municipal bonds issued after August 7, 1986. Some of these bonds are fully taxable to all investors; others are taxable only to investors subject to the alternative minimum tax.

[19]There are various exceptions to this generalization, of course, including bonds with warrants attached, mortgage-backed bonds, collateral trust bonds (which are backed by financial assets), and zero-coupon bonds.

[20]CDs can also be issued in zero-coupon form, but for convenience we will discuss bonds. Zero-coupon convertible bonds have been issued by several corporations.

interest, to be paid during the life of the bond. The purchaser pays less than par value for zero-coupons and receives par value ($1000) at maturity. The difference in these two amounts generates an effective interest rate, or rate of return. As in the case of Treasury bills, the lower the price paid for the bond, the higher the effective return.

Issuers of zero-coupon bonds include corporations, municipalities, government agencies, and the U.S. Treasury. Treasury zero-coupons are the largest segment of the market. They originated with "derivative" Treasury zeros created by investment banker-dealers who took a regular coupon bond and "stripped" it into the principal and a series of short-maturity zeros representing specific interest payments every six months for the life of the bond. For example, a 20-year Treasury bond becomes 40 separate securities maturing every six months plus a zero-coupon claim on the principal, for a total of 41 claims.[21] "STRIPS," which are specified Treasury issues that can be turned directly into Treasury zero-coupon bonds, now dominate this segment of the market.

The proliferation of new securities with catchy acronyms is rapid, as Box 2-1 illustrates.

In the area of mortgage-backed securities, **collateralized mortgage obligations (CMOs)** have been created to offer investors an alternative mortgage security. CMOs are bonds backed by a trust created to hold Ginnie Mae and other government-guaranteed mortgages. They are issued by brokerage firms. Shorter maturities are typically purchased by institutions whereas individual investors often purchase the longer-term issues known as "companion" CMOs. One advantage of CMOs is their lower minimum investment of $1000, compared to $25,000 for Ginnie Maes. Yields are higher than those for Ginnie Maes, perhaps half a percentage point, presumably because of their lower liquidity. CMOs can be redeemed by random calls by the trust as the principal accumulates in a redemption fund. Like Ginnie Maes, investors in CMOs face the risk of early redemption as a result of mortgage refinancings.

Preferred Stock Although technically an equity security, **preferred stock** is known as a hybrid security, because it resembles both fixed-income and equity instruments. Preferred stock occupies a middle position between bonds and common stock both in terms of priority of payment of income

---

[21] A good illustration of these receipts are the Treasury Investment Growth Receipts (**TIGRs,** or **tigers**) issued by Merrill Lynch, a large stock brokerage firm. For example, in 1982 Merrill Lynch sold an issue of these receipts representing claims on $500 million of principal and over $2 billion of interest on 14% U.S. Treasury bonds maturing in 2011. Maturities on these receipts range from three months to 29 years. Investors buy the receipts at a discount and receive the particular interest or principal payment when it comes due. A custodian bank holds the U.S. government bonds, and Merrill Lynch pays off the receipts with the proceeds from the bonds. The backing of the U.S. government virtually eliminates the risk of default on these receipts.

BOX 2-1

Blame it all on Merrill Lynch & Co. The firm's TIGRs—Treasury investment growth receipts—were successful enough to spawn a slew of imitators. Salomon Brothers Inc. soon followed with CATS, or certificates of accrual on Treasury securities. Now, more than animals are running amok on Wall Street.

How About a Test Drive?

Salomon is selling securities backed by auto loans called CARs, or certificates of automobile receivables. Drexel Burnham Lambert Inc. calls its version of the same thing FASTBACs, or first automotive short-term bonds and certificates.

One type of security can be bought, depending on the firm, as STARS, or short-term auction-rate stock; DARTS, or Dutch-auction-rate transferable securities; MAPS, market-auction preferred stock; AMPS, auction-market preferred stock; and CAMPS, cumulative auction-market preferred stock.

Shearson Lehman Brothers Inc. recently tagged a floating-rate mortgage-backed security with one of the Wall Street's most popular words: FIRSTS, or floating-interest-rate short-term securities.

Merrill Lynch, knowing no boundaries, added COLTS, or continuously offered long-term securities, and OPPOSMS, options to purchase or sell specific mortgage-backed securities. Salomon bolstered its lineup with HOMES, or homeowner-mortgage Eurosecurities, and CARDs, certificates for amortizing revolving debts, backed by credit-card receivables.

ZCCBs and SLOBs

Likewise, by the time a name has been massaged to produce an acronym, it may tell little of the product. For example, Merrill Lynch offers LYONs, or liquid-yield option notes; these are really zero-coupon convertible bonds, but calling them ZCCBs wouldn't sound nearly as good for these companions of TIGRs.

Of course, the uncontrived names of some securities actually form acronyms, but these rarely make useful marketing tools. First Boston, for instance, once underwrote an offering of secured-lease obligation bonds. It used the full name.

Source: Ann Monroe, "LYONs and TIGRs, No BEARs, Oh, My! LYONs and TIGRs, No . . .", *The Wall Street Journal*, February 18, 1987, p. 29. Reprinted by permission of *The Wall Street Journal*, © 1987 Dow Jones & Company, Inc. All Rights Reserved Worldwide.

and in case the corporation is liquidated. Preferred stockholders are paid after the bondholders but before the common stockholders.

As an equity security, preferred stock has an infinite life and pays dividends. Although the corporate issuer is never obligated to redeem it, most preferred stock issued today is callable and therefore may not remain outstanding forever.

Preferred stock resembles fixed-income securities in that the dividend is specified and known in advance and is fixed in amount; in effect, preferred stock can provide a stream of income very similar to that of a bond. The difference is that the stream continues forever, unless the issue is called, or otherwise retired. Because of its stipulated payments, preferred stock is viewed by most investors as a fixed-income security and is therefore considered at this point; however, it is worthwhile to remember that the price fluctuations in preferreds often exceed those in bonds.

Preferred stock dividends often are stated as a percentage of **par value** (i.e., the stated or face value for a security); therefore, a preferred stock's par value is meaningful and important to know. A $100 par value preferred paying a 10% dividend would pay $10 per year, for example, whereas the same rate on a $50 par value preferred would yield only $5 per year. Many preferred stock dividends are stated in annual dollar amounts, such as $10 or $5 in the examples given here.

Preferred stock dividends are not legally binding but must be voted on each period by a corporation's board of directors. If the issuer fails to pay the dividend in any year and if the preferred is cumulative, the unpaid dividend(s) must be paid before any common stock dividends can be paid (if the preferred is noncumulative, dividends in arrears do not have to be paid).[22]

Example. Long Island Lighting Company (LILCO), an electric utility that suffered major problems with its Shoreham nuclear power plant, announced in July, 1989, that it would make up almost $400 million in arrears on all its preferred stock, which had been accruing since 1984 on 19 separate issues. The following month, LILCO announced plans to pay a common dividend, ending a five-year omission. ▪

More than one-third of the preferred stock sold in recent years is convertible into common stock at the owner's option.[23] A large amount of the total outstanding is variable-rate preferred; that is, the dividend rate is tied to current market interest rates. Corporations are the largest buyers of preferreds because of a unique tax advantage—70% of the dividends paid to corporations are not taxable, resulting in an effective tax rate of only 10.2% (assuming the maximum marginal corporate tax rate of 34%).

For years preferred stock has been a relatively minor part of the capital markets, used heavily by utilities that raised large amounts of capital. As the 1980s drew to a close, the preferred market saw significant new activity as banks, both foreign and domestic, became big issuers of preferred stock. As the only country with a developed market for preferred stock, the United States suddenly had a $50 billion market in preferred stocks as

[22]In the event of omitted dividends, preferred stock owners may be allowed to vote for the directors of the corporation.

[23]Convertibility will be discussed in Chapter 16.

banks rushed to take advantage of new international agreements on capital instruments.[24]

New trends in preferred stocks include *auction-rate preferred,* a type of floating-rate preferred in which the dividend is established by auction every 49 days.

Rates on Fixed-Income Securities Once again, to provide a perspective on rates of return available on financial assets, we will consider some recent capital market rates. Figure 2-3 shows average yields on four basic capital market rates over the period of 1985 to April, 1990: FHA mortgage rates, high-quality corporate bonds, long-term Treasury securities, and high-quality municipal bonds. Although this is a nonexhaustive comparison, it does illustrate the primary points that the reader should consider at this point.[25]

Figure 2-3 shows that, as expected, corporate bond rates exceed the Treasury rate, because of the possible risk of default. Mortgage rates are higher than either of these two. The municipal bond rate is below all other rates, but we must remember that this is an after-tax rate. To make it comparable, municipal bond yields should be adjusted to a taxable equivalent yield using equation 2-1. When this is done, the rate will be much closer to those in Figure 2-3, and in some particular cases considerably higher. For example, in mid-1989 the differential between some revenue bonds and 30-year Treasuries for investors in the 33% federal income tax bracket was three percentage points; that is, the taxable equivalent yield on these revenue bonds was roughly 11% versus roughly 8% on Treasuries.

Equity Securities

Unlike fixed-income securities, **equity securities** represent an ownership interest in a corporation. Since preferred stock was discussed earlier in connection with fixed-income securities, this discussion involves only common stock, which is *the* security as far as most investors are concerned.

Common stock represents the ownership of corporations. As a purchaser of 100 shares of common stock, an investor owns $100/n$ percent of the corporation (where n is the number of shares of common stock outstanding). As owners, the holders of common stock are entitled to elect the directors of the corporation and vote on major issues. Each owner is usually allowed to cast votes equal to the number of shares owned for each

---

[24]See Matthew Winkler, "More Issuers Prefer Issues of Preferred," *The Wall Street Journal,* August 17, 1989, p. C1.

[25]The capital market rates shown here do not reflect actual realized returns as calculated, for example, on a year-to-year basis. We will consider this type of calculation in Chapter 5.

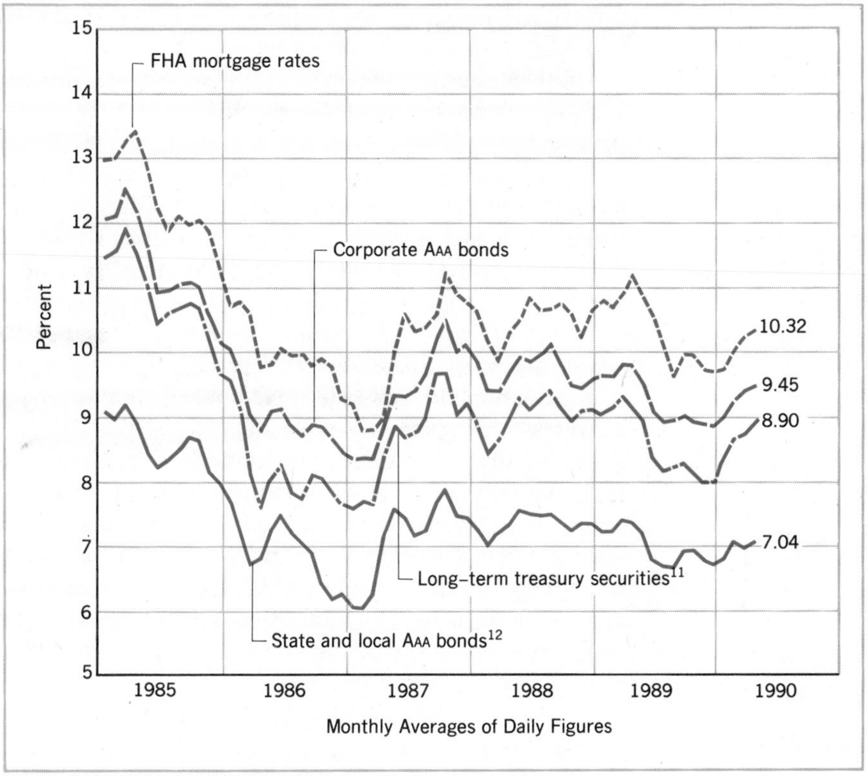

FIGURE 2-3 ***Long-term interest rates, 1985 to April, 1990.***
Source: Monetary Trends, The Federal Reserve Bank of St. Louis, May 1990, p. 12.

director being elected. Such votes occur at the annual meeting of the corporation, which each shareholder is allowed to attend.[26]

If a firm's shares are held by only a few individuals, it is referred to as a "closely held" firm. By being closely held, a company can avoid public disclosures of financial information. Most companies choose to "go public," meaning that common stock is sold to the general public. This is done primarily to enable the company to raise additional capital more easily.

If a corporation meets certain requirements, it can, if it chooses to, be listed on one or more exchanges. Otherwise, it will be traded in the over-the-counter market (to be discussed in Chapter 3). The stock would be referred to as a listed security in the first case and as an unlisted security in

[26]Most shareholders do not attend, often allowing management to vote their proxy. Therefore, although technically more than 50% of the outstanding shares are needed for control of a firm, effective control can often be exercised with considerably less, because not all the shares are voted.

the second case. For large corporations, the regulatory difference between being listed and unlisted is small.

The common stockholder is the residual claimant on both the income and the assets of the corporation, receiving what remains after both the creditors and the preferred stockholders have been paid. In some cases, nothing is left; in others such a claim can be worth a substantial amount of money. Note that the common stockholder has no specific promises to receive any cash from the corporation, since the stock never matures, and dividends do not have to be paid. Dividends are declared by the board of directors, who can raise and lower (or eliminate) them as they see fit. Thus, the dividend could be doubled or eliminated. Common stock dividends, if they are declared, are paid quarterly.

Common stock has no specified return that must be paid, now or ever. Thus, equity securities involve substantial risk. As noted, the dividend is at the company's discretion. Stock prices typically fluctuate sharply, meaning that the value of investors' claims may rise and fall rapidly over relatively short periods of time. This is well demonstrated in Figure 2-4, which shows the market's performance from January, 1987, to late August, 1989. Notice the strong upward trend in 1987, the great market crash of October, 1987, and the long upward climb after that. The market reached new levels in 1989, and most stockholders enjoyed a great year.

Other Types of Securities

Equity-Derivative Securities

Equity-derivative securities are securities with a claim on the common stock of a corporation. The owner of such a security has the right, under

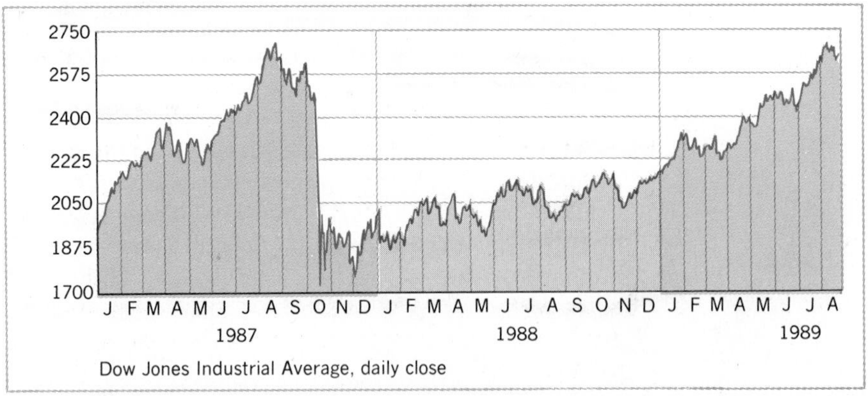

FIGURE 2-4 ***Stock price changes in Dow-Jones Industrial Average, daily close, 1987 to mid-1989.***
Source: The Wall Street Journal, August 25, 1989, p. C1. Reprinted by permission of *The Wall Street Journal,* © 1989 Dow Jones & Company, Inc. All Rights Reserved Worldwide.

specified conditions, to either make delivery on, or take delivery of, a specified amount of common stock. These securities are marketable and trade on secondary markets. Rather than own the stock itself, investors can own a marketable claim on that stock. They need never own the stock to participate in the benefits that accrue if the corporation does well and the price of its stock rises. Equity-derivative securities can be created by corporations or investors (both individuals and institutions).

Corporate-Created Securities Perhaps the most basic claims on equity created by a corporation are *rights,* which permit current stockholders, for a very short-term period (up to 10 weeks), to have the first right to purchase at a specified price new shares of stock being sold by the corporation. Recipients of the rights may exercise them, let them expire, or sell them in the marketplace. They have a market value (price) because they permit the holder to purchase the shares at a discount from current market prices.

Warrants are long-term options to purchase common stock from the corporation, with original maturities typically from five years upward. A holder of warrants can turn the warrants in to the corporation anytime before they expire, together with a stipulated amount of money, and obtain a stipulated number of shares of common stock. (All terms of the warrant are specified by the issuer when the warrants are issued.) Warrants are often attached to the bonds or the preferred stock being sold by a corporation in order to make the issue more attractive. Like rights, warrants are traded in the marketplace. In effect, for investors the purchase of warrants is a substitute for the purchase of the underlying common stock, with both advantages and disadvantages. Advantages include a lower initial investment and an opportunity for a larger percentage return on the investment relative to owning the stock itself. Disadvantages include the limited time period over which they have value and possibly greater downside volatility.

Convertible securities (i.e., convertible bonds and convertible preferred stock) have a built-in conversion feature. The holders of the bonds or preferred have the option to convert whenever they choose. Typically, the bond or preferred stock is turned in to the corporation in exchange for a specified number of common shares, with no cash payment required. Convertibles are two securities simultaneously: a fixed-income security paying a specified interest or dividend payment and a claim on the common stock that will become increasingly valuable as the price of the underlying common stock rises. Thus, the prices of convertibles may fluctuate over a fairly wide range, depending on whether they currently are trading like other fixed-income securities or are trading to reflect the price of the underlying common stock.

Investor-Created Securities In today's investing world the word ***options*** refers to **puts** and **calls.** These are created not by corporations but by investors seeking to trade in claims on a particular common stock. A call (put) option gives the buyer the right to purchase (sell) 100 shares of a particular stock at a specified exercise price within a specified time. Maturities on new puts and calls are available up to several months away. Several exercise prices are created for each underlying common stock, giving investors a choice in both the maturity and the price they will pay or receive.

Buyers of calls are betting that the price of the underlying common stock will rise, making the call option more valuable. Put buyers are betting that the price of the underlying common stock will decline, making the put option more valuable. Both put and call options are written (created) by other investors who are betting the opposite of their respective purchasers. The sellers (writers) receive an option premium for selling each new contract; the buyers pay this option premium. Once the option is created and the writer receives the premium from the buyer, it can be traded repeatedly on an exchange, such as the Chicago Board Options Exchange, the American Stock Exchange, and so on. The premium is simply the market price of the contract as determined by investors.

The price will fluctuate constantly, just as the price of the underlying common stock changes. This makes sense, because the option is affected directly by the price of the stock that gives it value. In addition, the option's value is affected by the time remaining to maturity, current interest rates, the volatility of the stock, and the price at which the option can be exercised.

Puts and calls allow both buyers and sellers (writers) to speculate on the short-term movements of certain common stocks. Buyers obtain an option on the common stock for a small, known premium, which is the maximum that the buyer can lose. If the buyer is correct about the price movements of the common, gains are magnified in relation to having bought (or sold short) the common, because a smaller investment is required; however, the buyer has only a short time in which to be correct. Writers (sellers) earn the premium as income, based upon their beliefs about a stock. They win or lose, depending upon whether their beliefs are correct or incorrect. Options can be used in a variety of strategies, giving investors opportunities to manage their portfolios in ways that would otherwise be unavailable to them.

Futures Contracts

Futures contracts have been available on commodities such as corn and wheat for a long time. Recently, they have become available on several financial instruments. Futures can be purchased on stock market indexes, currencies, Treasury bills, Treasury bonds, bank certificates of deposit, and GNMA's. Futures are marketable, with trading occurring on organized markets, such as the Chicago Board of Trade.

A futures contract is an agreement providing for the future exchange of a particular asset between a buyer and a seller. The seller contracts to deliver the asset at a specified delivery date in exchange for a specified amount of cash from the buyer. Although the cash is not required until the delivery date, a "good faith deposit," called margin, is required to reduce the chance of default by either party. The margin is small compared to the value of the contract.

Most futures contracts are not exercised. Instead, they are "offset" by taking a position opposite to the one initially undertaken. For example, a purchaser of a May Treasury bill futures contract can close out the position by selling an identical May contract before the delivery date, and a seller can close out the same position by purchasing that contract.

Most participants in futures are either *hedgers* or *speculators*. The former seek to reduce price uncertainty over some future period. For example, by purchasing a futures contract, a hedger can lock in a specific price for the asset and be protected from adverse price movements. Sellers, likewise, can protect themselves from downward price movements. Speculators, on the other hand, seek to profit from the uncertainty that will occur in the future. If prices are expected to rise (fall), contracts will be purchased (sold). Correct anticipations can result in very large profits, because only a small margin is required.

One of the newest innovations in financial markets is options on futures. Calls on futures give the buyer the right, but not the obligation, to assume the futures position. One advantage of such options is that the purchaser's potential loss is limited to the purchase price of the option, whereas the potential loss with a futures contract can be large.

The Investor's Alternative—Indirect Investing

The discussion to this point has involved the types of securities that can be bought and traded in various markets. Such instruments as common and preferred stocks, puts and calls, and savings deposits are within reach of almost all investors. Investors can also buy Treasury bills with a $10,000 minimum, or purchase Treasury, municipal, or corporate bonds if they choose (and are willing to accept the lower liquidity of municipals and corporates). Although many investors will never deal in negotiable CDs or banker's acceptances, some investors, including institutions, do buy and sell them.[27]

Investors always have an alternative to direct investing—**indirect investing,** which refers here to the buying and selling of the shares of investment companies, which, in turn, hold portfolios of securities. **Investment companies** are organized for the purpose of investing in securities of various kinds on behalf of their own shareholders. Each has specific objectives,

[27]Repurchase agreements are a specialized item, not designed for individual investors.

such as capital gains, maximum current income from either money market or capital market securities, or tax-free income.

Investors purchasing shares of a particular portfolio managed by an investment company are purchasing an ownership interest in that portfolio of securities and are entitled to a pro rata share of the dividends, interest, and capital gains generated. Shareholders also must pay a pro rata share of the company's expenses and its management fee, which will be deducted from the portfolio's earnings as it flows back to the shareholders. For an open-end investment company holding capital market securities, the price per share of the portfolio of assets is the price per share of the investors' interest.

The contrast between direct and indirect investing is illustrated in Figure 2-5, which shows that indirect investing accomplishes essentially the same thing as direct investing, the real difference being that the investment company stands between the investors and the portfolio of securities. Although technical qualifications will be made at the appropriate time, the point about indirect investing is that investors gain and lose through the activities of the investment company in the same manner that they would gain and lose from holding a portfolio directly. The differences are the costs (any sales charges plus the management fee) and the additional services gained from the investment company, such as record keeping, check-writing privileges, and so on.

Open-End Investment Companies (Mutual Funds)

Investors purchase most investment company shares directly from the company itself and sell their shares back to the company (which is obligated to redeem them). Such investment companies are called **open-end investment companies** and are popularly referred to as **mutual funds.** The companies sell as many shares as investors demand, investing the proceeds in additional securities in accordance with that company's investment objectives. The company stands ready to repurchase shares from investors wishing to sell. When it repurchases such shares this causes a shrinkage in the fund's size.

All sales and purchases of open-end investment companies are made at the *net asset value per share* (a sales charge may also be included), which reflects the actual value of the company's portfolio on the day of the transaction.[28] Thus, if one buys shares of a mutual fund that holds the 30 Dow Jones Industrial stocks and the prices of these 30 stocks rise strongly for several days, the 30 stocks will be worth more and therefore the shares of the fund holding these 30 stocks will be worth more.

One of the two major types of open-end investment companies, the

---

[28]Specifically, the net asset value per share of an investment company is found by totaling the market value of all the securities in its portfolio, subtracting any liabilities that may exist, and dividing by the number of shares of the investment company's stock that is outstanding.

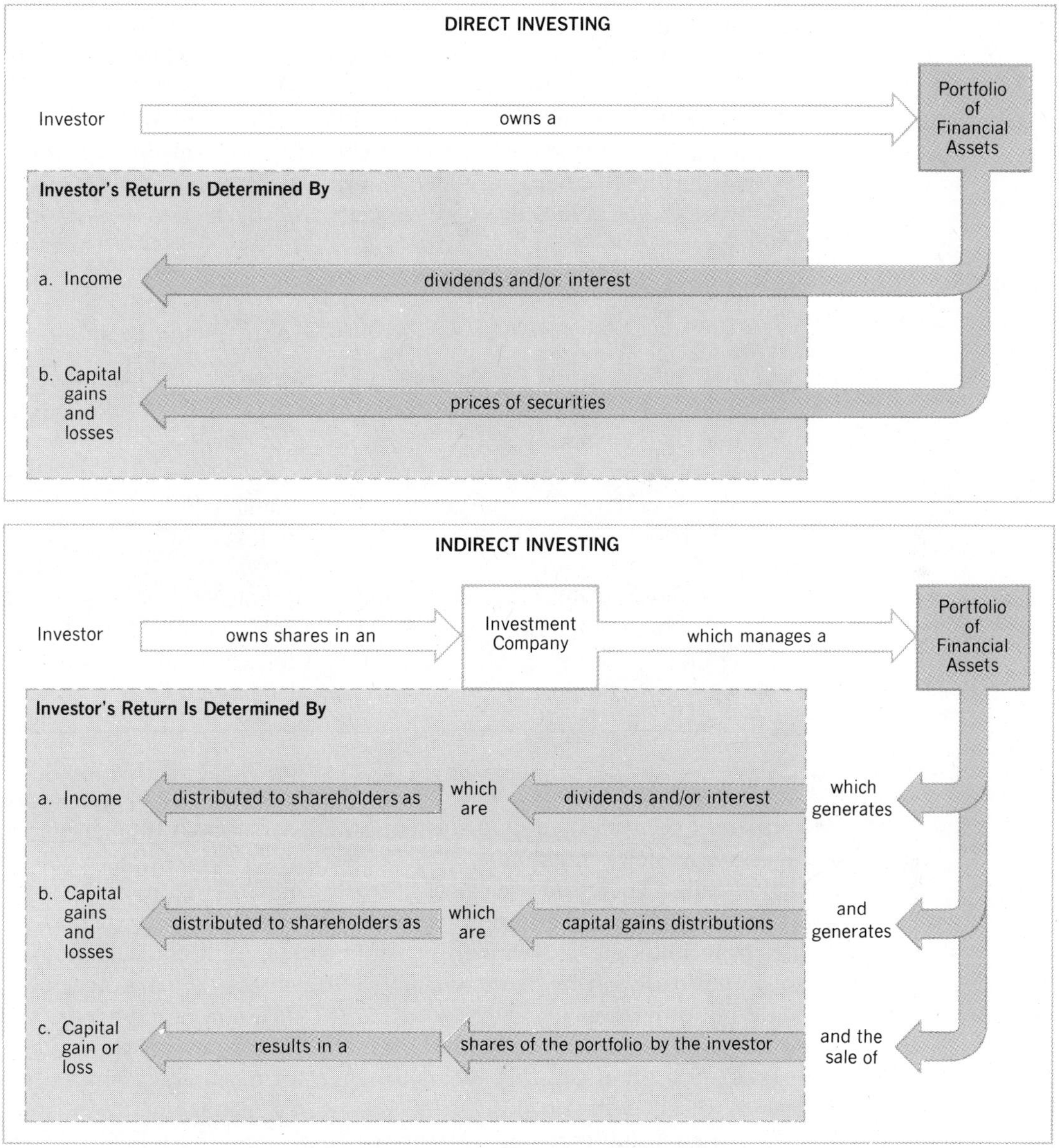

FIGURE 2-5 ***Direct investing vs. indirect investing.***

money market fund, specializes in money market instruments. The more traditional type, the equity and bond fund, invests primarily in capital market instruments.

Money Market Funds In response to new trends that emerged in the 1970s, the investment company industry created **money market funds** to invest in the short-term, highly liquid, low-risk money market instruments discussed earlier in this chapter. The money market funds own portfolios of Treasury bills, negotiable CDs, prime commercial paper, and so forth. Investors can buy into these funds for an initial investment of around $2500 to $3000, with some funds requiring as little as $1000. Interest is earned and declared daily and investors can sell their shares any time they choose. The expenses of the fund are very low. Check-writing privileges are available, usually in amounts of $500 or more. Until the checks clear, investors continue to earn interest on their funds.

INVESTMENTS INTUITION

Money market funds provide investors with an alternative not otherwise available to many. They can participate in the ownership of money market instruments that are liquid and of very low risk and short maturity, earning the competitive rates being paid on these instruments that otherwise might not be available to them. Referring back to Figure 2-2, notice that the "money market mutual funds" rate tracked the three-month Treasury bill rate closely, indicating that their returns closely tracked current money market conditions. The fact that this rate sometimes exceeded the bill rate reflects the portfolio of other money market assets held by these funds, primarily commercial paper, whose rates often exceed the Treasury bill rate.

Stock, Bond, and Income Funds Investment companies also invest in capital market securities, primarily stocks and bonds. Each fund has a stated objective, which it must adhere to, such as income, growth, or maximum capital gains. Therefore, investors know the general nature of the portfolio when they invest. In addition, some funds specialize in particular industries or technologies, providing investors with specific choices. Most funds are very broadly diversified, providing a real service to many investors who could not otherwise achieve adequate diversification. Some funds, known as index funds, attempt to duplicate a market average such as the Standard & Poor's 500. In effect, this allows the investor to purchase shares in "the market" itself, with no input from the fund's management. In contrast, most funds argue that one of their services to investors is providing the expertise of their portfolio managers.

Closed-End Investment Companies

The alternative form of investment company, accounting for a much smaller percentage of total investment company assets, is the **closed-end investment company,** whose shares are traded on exchanges exactly like any other shares of stock. Closed-end companies have a fixed number of shares of their stock outstanding, and investors use their brokers to buy and sell these shares, paying regular brokerage fees. With this exception, closed-end companies operate in a manner similar to open-end companies. However, unlike mutual funds, closed-end companies can (and do) sell for less (at a discount) or more (at a premium) than their net asset values, because the prices of these shares are determined by investors in an open market.

Conclusions on Indirect Investing

In summary, an investment company is a clear alternative for an investor seeking to own stocks and bonds. Rather than purchase and manage a portfolio, investors can, in effect, turn their money over to an investment company and allow it to do all the work and make all the decisions (for a fee, of course). This is an important issue that all investors should think about carefully. There are possible advantages and disadvantages to each alternative. Box 2-2 describes many of the advantages of mutual funds in showing how they have responded to investor needs.

The importance of indirect investing can be recognized immediately by looking at Figure 2-6. These graphs are for mutual funds (open-end investment companies) alone and do not include closed-end companies. The dramatic rise in the number of shareholder accounts and total assets during the 1980s is obvious. By the beginning of 1990 there were almost 3000 mutual funds, with total assets of approximately $1 trillion, a tenfold increase in the decade.

Ownership of Financial Assets

Amounts of Financial Assets Outstanding

Large amounts of U.S. government securities are available to investors. At the end of 1989, over $300 billion of short-term Treasury securities (maturity less than one year) and almost $600 billion of Treasury notes with maturities of two to 10 years were in private holdings, out of a total of $1650 billion.[29]

Small (less than $100,000) and large time deposits constitute a big part of liquid assets, totaling $1142 billion and $554 billion, respectively, at the beginning of 1990. Total savings deposits amounted to $411 billion, and MMDAs came to $485 billion.

Other than Treasury bills, money market instruments are most likely to

[29]The short-term amount excludes depository institutions, Federal Reserve Banks, money market mutual funds, and foreign entities.

BOX 2-2

RESPONDING TO INVESTOR NEEDS

One of the hallmarks of the mutual fund industry is its responsiveness in a rapidly changing economic environment. By keeping attuned to investor needs, the mutual fund industry has been able to adapt and expand its product line and services to suit just about any investor's goals.

As a result, the investor's choice of funds and investment objectives has grown dramatically. In 1975, mutual funds fit neatly into seven main categories. By the end of 1985, the seven fund categories had grown to 15, with many funds further defining their investment objectives according to industry sectors, geographic limitations, or business philosophies. The number of individual funds available almost quadrupled in that period. Continuing innovation in the variety of mutual fund portfolios being offered to the public further increased the investment objective categories in 1987 to 22.

Such a diverse menu has encouraged many investors to sample the products the mutual fund industry has to offer.

Every fund establishes a minimum amount necessary for opening an account, plus minimum increments for adding to it. Some funds have very low minimums or even none at all; still others have minimums of $2,500 and up (some institutional funds may have minimums of $1 million or more). The great majority fall between $250 and $1,000.

Funds try to make investing as easy as possible. Most have payroll deduction plans to take the effort out of making regular contributions, and some funds, upon proper authorization, will regularly deduct a specified amount from the shareholder's bank account.

Mutual funds also offer automatic reinvestment programs in which shareholders can elect to have dividends and capital gains distributions poured back into the fund by automatically buying new shares to expand their holdings.

A similar feature covers automatic withdrawal. Arrangements can be made with the fund to send checks at regular intervals from the fund's earnings or principal to the shareholder or anyone else designated by the shareholder.

Even if a shareholder is not participating in a regular withdrawal plan, the fund makes it easy to withdraw money. By law, the fund must be willing to redeem any or all shares on each business day. All a shareholder needs to do is give proper notification and the fund will send a check. Even easier is a shareholder's ability to write checks drawing from a money market mutual fund account and from some bond funds. While most funds have minimum check amounts of $500, this still proves to be a convenient way of redeeming shares immediately.

If shareholders do not want to withdraw their money but, instead, want to move their assets into a different fund, they can take advantage of a fund's exchange privilege. Many management companies offer more than one fund (known as a "family of funds") to their shareholders. In this way, investors can choose from funds with a variety of investment objectives, each appropriate for different investor needs and economic conditions. An exchange privilege allows the shareholder to contact the fund or a fund representative at any time to exchange shares from one fund within the family to another. Usually funds allow investors to use the exchange privilege several times a year for a low or no fee per exchange.

Some funds may also let investors move their assets within a family of funds via telephone. With the proper notification, and a minimum of $250 or more (the minimum may vary from fund to fund), an investor can execute a telephone exchange in a matter of minutes.

Whenever a shareholder exchanges shares, writes a check from a money market fund, or makes an investment, a statement will be sent to confirm each transaction. Mutual funds have long been noted for their convenient recordkeeping. In addition to confirmation statements, the fund sends account updates on a monthly, quarterly, or annual basis, depending on the fund.

Finally, funds send periodic reports both to the SEC and to shareholders. Complete information is supplied to shareholders at least twice a year, and for most companies, four times a year. These reports list the names and amounts of securities the fund holds, major investment changes since the last report, plus financial statements and related information.

By taking advantage of new technology, the mutual fund industry has made prompt and professional service a priority. Many funds have fax machines that allow shareholders to transmit important documents quickly and easily. Voice-response systems—which let shareholders access information about their funds or even perform simple transactions over the telephone—have expedited service delivery. Shareholders may check their account balances, current yield figures in money market funds, and discover a vareity of other important fund information over the telephone, often 24 hours a day.

The mutual fund industry tries to stay in tune with the needs of its current *and* future shareholders. Healthy competition ensures that the industry will continue to develop new products and services to respond to the needs of mutual fund shareholders better than ever.

Source: The Investment Company Institute, *1990 Mutual Fund Fact Book.* Reprinted by permission of the Investment Company Institute.

be owned by individual investors indirectly through money market funds. Commercial paper totaled some $350 billion at the beginning of 1990.

As for capital market instruments, the total marketable U.S. government debt is second only to that of mortgages, and exceeds by one-third the total of state and local, corporate, and foreign bonds.

Obviously, the aggregate market value of all corporate equities fluctuates widely over time. For example, the market value of all *equity* securities increased some $250 billion in the first two weeks of January, 1987, alone (and it could lose that much just as quickly).

One interesting point about stocks is that their supply is shrinking. Mergers, buyouts of one company by another company, and firms' repurchases of their own stock reduce the supply, whereas the issuance of new stock by companies increases the supply. The former has completely overshadowed the latter in recent years, with the result that an estimated $500 billion of stock was removed from the market in the four-and-one-half-year period from 1985 to mid-1989. Such a shrinkage in the supply of stock is considered a favorable sign by some investors as a support for stock prices.

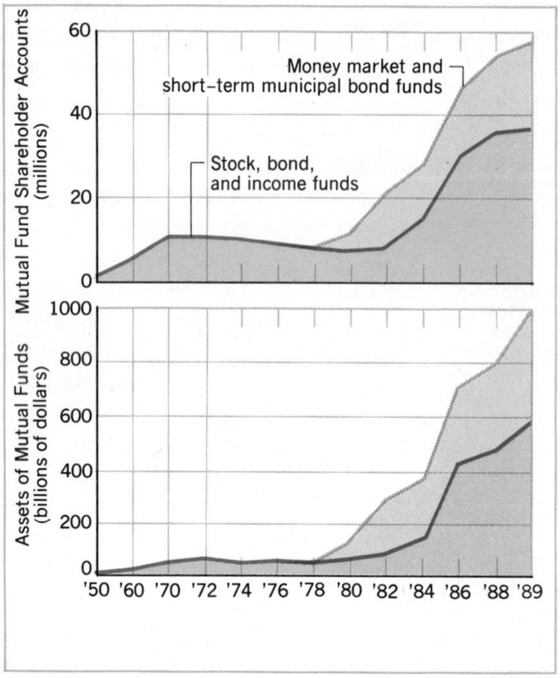

FIGURE 2-6 ***Mutual fund shareholder accounts and assets of mutual funds.*** *Source: 1990 Mutual Fund Fact Book,* Investment Company Institute, p. 23. Reprinted by permission of the Investment Company Institute.

Household Ownership of Financial Assets

More than one-third of households' total financial assets in 1988 were in the form of deposits, including demand deposits, small time and savings deposits, money market mutual fund shares, and large time deposits.[30] Small time and savings deposits constituted a large proportion of total deposits (roughly half), because they are a familiar and popular method of providing liquidity and safety.

Money market fund shares grew rapidly in the early 1980s as investors sought to earn higher money market rates. From a base of less than $4 billion in 1977, households held some $302 billion in such funds by early 1989. However, the creation of money market deposit accounts (MMDAs) in December, 1982, and "Super NOW" accounts in January, 1983, lessened the appeal of money market shares because financial institutions could pay money market rates on these accounts, and the Super NOWs can be used as a checking account. Total MMDAs at commercial banks and thrift institu-

[30]The numbers in this discussion are taken from *Balance Sheets for the U.S. Economy: 1949–1988,* Board of Governors of the Federal Reserve System, Washington, D.C., April 1989.

tions went from nothing in November 1982 to $500 billion by mid-1990, with about 75% of the total held at banks.

As for the marketable securities owned by households, less than 10% of their total financial assets was held in the four major debt securities discussed: U.S. government securities, agency issues, municipals, and corporates. Treasury issues constituted the largest of these four positions, followed by municipals. Corporate and foreign bonds made up less than 1% of total financial assets held by households.

As the 1980s came to a close, approximately 20% of total financial assets of households consisted of individual stocks, down from about 25% at the beginning of the decade. On the other hand, the assets of mutual funds grew tenfold in the 1980s, approaching $1 trillion.

Households own an increasingly large amount of pension fund reserves. Most of this amount is being invested by pension funds, on behalf of households, in equity and fixed-income securities. Many of those affected will have some say in whether their pension fund dollars are invested in fixed-income or equity securities. Furthermore, at the beginning of 1990 individuals held some $275 billion in IRA and Keogh accounts. Thus, study of investments can be useful for many people in terms of retirement planning.

Institutional Ownership of Financial Assets

A resurgence in the number of individuals owning shares of stock occurred between 1975 and 1985, with the number exceeding 47 million by 1985.[31] Survey data indicate that by 1990 one in four adults owned common stocks.[32] Nevertheless, individual investors have been net sellers of stocks (purchases of stocks less sales, including equity mutual funds) for many years. If individuals are selling, who is buying?

By 1980 institutional investors already owned 35% of the market value of all New York Stock Exchange–listed stocks. If omitted institutional investors in common stocks, such as bank-administered personal trust funds, private hedge funds, and nonbank trusts, had been included, the total institutional holdings would probably have amounted to about 50% of the entire market value of all stocks on the NYSE. On balance, institutional investors have been net buyers of stock. Institutional investors include pension funds, insurance companies, investment companies, bank trust departments, and foundations and endowments.

As noted in Chapter 1, by the beginning of the 1990s, U.S. institutional investors had total assets of almost $6 trillion. Their assets grew almost 14%

[31]This includes both corporate shares and stock mutual funds.

[32]Out of the total population, the incidence of ownership was 20%. This type of data can be found in the annual *Fact Book* issued by the New York Stock Exchange.

a year during the 1980s, far outstripping projections. Pension funds are the largest single institutional owner of common stocks. Estimates are that in 1989 the top 100 investment advisors for pension funds had $2 trillion invested. By 1987 pension funds alone owned some 23% of stocks and 15% of bonds. Even after the breakup of American Telephone & Telegraph into several units, its pension fund alone amounted to about $33 billion at the beginning of 1990. At the same time, almost 300 pension funds held more than $1 billion each. The California Public Employee Retirement Sytem, with some $56 billion in assets at the beginning of 1990, was expected to reach $200 billion by the year 2000 and $1 trillion by 2014.[33]

The large percentage of common stocks owned by institutions is a very important factor in U.S. equity markets. These investors purchase and sell thousands of shares per transaction, accounting for over 60% of the daily trades in the New York Exchange. Furthermore, because of legal and practical considerations, they tend to concentrate on a select list of the largest U.S. corporations. Both of these factors can have implications for various stocks. For example, look at the list of most actively traded stocks on the New York Stock Exchange for a given day. Many of the same stocks, which are institutional favorites, tend to show up day after day. This institutional presence also is related to the question of market efficiency, a subject that will be discussed in Chapter 14.

Summary

- Major categories of securities include nonmarketable securities, money market instruments, capital market securities (divided into fixed-income and equity securities), other securities, and indirect investments in the form of investment company shares.
- Nonmarketable investments, widely owned by investors, include savings deposits, nonnegotiable certificates of deposit, money market accounts, and U.S. savings bonds.
- Money market investments, characterized as short-term, highly liquid, very safe investments, include Treasury bills, negotiable certificates of deposit (CDs), commercial paper, Eurodollars, repurchase agreements, and banker's acceptances. The first three are obligations (IOUs) of the federal government, banks, and corporations, respectively.
- Capital market investments have maturities in excess of one year.
- Fixed-income securities, one of the two principal types of capital market securities, have a specified payment schedule. They include four types of bonds: U.S. governments, federal agencies, municipals, and corporates.
- Preferred stock, although technically an equity security, is regarded by

[33]The figures in this discussion are taken from James A. White, "The Decade of Phenomenal Growth for Institutions . . . ," *The Wall Street Journal*, February 26, 1989, pp. C1, C17.

investors as a fixed-income security, because of its stated (and fixed) dividend. Preferred stock has no maturity date but may be retired by call or other means.

- Common stock (equity) represents the ownership of the corporation. The stockholder has a residual claim on both income and assets.
- Other types of securities include several forms of equity-derivative securities and futures contracts.
- Equity-derivative securities derive all or part of their value from the underlying common stock and can be divided into two categories: corporate created and investor created.
- Corporate-created equity-derivative securities include rights, warrants, and convertible bonds and convertible preferred stock.
- Investor-created equity-derivative securities, commonly called options, allow both buyers and sellers (writers) to speculate on and/or hedge the price movements of stocks for which these claims are available. These calls (puts) are multiple-month rights to purchase (sell) a common stock at a specified price.
- Futures contracts provide for the future exchange of a particular asset between a buyer and a seller. A recent innovation is options on futures.
- An alternative to purchasing these financial assets is provided by indirect investing, which involves the purchase of shares of an investment company. These financial intermediaries hold a portfolio of securities on behalf of their shareholders.
- Investment companies are classified as either open end (which includes both money market funds and equity and bond funds) or closed end, depending upon whether their own capitalization (number of shares outstanding) is constantly changing or fixed.
- Large amounts of financial assets are outstanding, particularly U.S. government securities and equity securities.
- Institutional investors own a substantial amount of NYSE stocks and account for a very large percentage of the daily trading in them.

Key Words

Calls
Capital market
Certificates of deposit (CDs)
Closed-end investment companies
Collateralized mortgage obligations (CMOs)
Convertible securities
Corporate bonds
Equity securities
Equity-derivative securities
Federal agency securities
Fixed-income securities
Futures contracts
Investment company
Indirect investing
Liquidity
Money market securities
Money market fund
Money market deposit accounts (MMDAs)
Money market mutual fund
Mortgage-backed securities
Municipal securities
Mutual funds

NOW (negotiable order of withdrawal) account
Open-end investment companies
Options
Par value
Preferred stock
Puts
TIGRs, tigers
Treasury bill
Treasury bond
Warrant
Zero-coupon bond

Questions

2-1 Outline the classification scheme for marketable securities used in the chapter. Explain each of the terms involved.

2-2 What is the difference between a savings deposit and a certificate of deposit?

2-3 How do market accounts at banks and thrifts differ from their other investment opportunities?

2-4 What does it mean for Treasury bills to be sold at discount?

2-5 Distinguish between a negotiable certificate of deposit and the certificates of deposit discussed in the section "Nonmarketable Securities."

2-6 Name the four issuers of bonds discussed in this chapter. Which do you think would be most risky as a general proposition?

2-7 From an issuer's standpoint, what is the distinction between Fannie Mae and Ginnie Mae?

2-8 Name and explain the difference between the two types of municipal securities.

2-9 What does it mean to say that investors in Ginnie Maes and CMOs face the risk of early redemption?

2-10 What are the advantages and disadvantages of zero-coupon bonds?

2-11 Is there any relationship between a "strip" and a zero-coupon bond?

2-12 Why is preferred stock referred to as a hybrid security?

2-13 Why is preferred stock classified in this chapter as a fixed-income security?

2-14 Why is the common stockholder referred to as a "residual claimant"?

2-15 Do all common stocks pay dividends? Who decides?

2-16 What is meant by the term *equity-derivative security?* Distinguish between those that are created by the corporation and those that are created by the investor.

2-17 What are two differences between a warrant and a call?

2-18 How are puts and calls created?

2-19 On which financial instruments can futures contracts be purchased?

2-20 What is meant by indirect investing?

2-21 What is an investment company? Distinguish between an open-end and a closed-end company.

2-22 What is a money market fund? Why would it appeal to investors?

2-23 What is an index fund?

2-24 Do households own more equity securities or more long-term debt securities?

2-25 How do individual investors and institutional investors compare in the ownership of common stocks?

2-26 Distinguish between a serial bond and a term bond.

2-27 How is a Series EE government savings bond like a zero-coupon bond?

2-28 Explain why it may be important to know about the par value on a preferred stock.

Problems

2-1 Assuming an investor is in the 15% tax bracket, what taxable equivalent must be earned on a security to equal a municipal bond yield of 9.5%?

APPENDIX 2-A

Taxes and Investing

The major tax overhaul in 1986 significantly changed the tax laws for investors. Up to that point long-term capital gains received preferential tax treatment. In 1986, 60% of a long-term capital gain was excluded from tax. Since the top tax rate on interest and dividends and short-term capital gains was 50%, the effective maximum tax on long-term capital gains was 20%.

By 1988 the top rates on all three categories were either 28% or 33%, depending on the investor's income. (Technically, a surtax of 5% raises the top rate to 33% for single taxpayers with taxable income between $43,150 and $89,560 and for joint filers with taxable income between $71,900 and $149,250.) Since long-term capital gains no longer receive favorable treatment, the tax rate can reach the maximum of 33%. State taxes, of course, must also be considered and could easily raise the effective marginal tax rate to 40% or more.

Although there is no practical benefit for most investors in distinguishing between short-term and long-term capital gains, since the rate is the same for both, the tax laws retain this distinction. It is quite possible that the distinction between capital gains and ordinary income may be reinstated in the 1990s. The holding period to become a long-term gain or loss was raised to one year from the previous six months for property acquired after 1987 (if acquired before 1987, the cutoff is six months).

Capital losses are deductible in full against capital gains. Up to $3000 per year of *net* capital losses (what remains after netting against capital gains) can be written off against other income.[34] Any unused portion may be carried over to the next year and treated as if it occurred in that year.

[34]If both a net short-term capital gain and a net long-term capital loss occurs, the two must be netted to determine the long-term capital loss; if both a net short-term capital loss and a net long-term capital gain occur, the two must be netted to determine the short-term capital loss.

Any loss carried over retains its original distinction as either short term or long term.

The important effect of the 1986 tax revision is to lower tax rates on investment income such as interest and dividends. Conversely, the maximum rate on long-term capital gains increased some two-thirds, from 20% to 33%.

As for corporations, the marginal tax rate is 34%. While interest income is taxed at ordinary rates, dividends received by one corporation from another are 70% excludable. At a marginal rate of 34%, the effective tax on dividends would be 10.2%. Capital gains are taxed the same as operating income.

CHAPTER 3

Securities Markets

The purpose of this chapter is to outline the structure of the securities markets in the United States and to describe how securities are traded. The emphasis is primarily on stocks, and to a lesser extent bonds, because these are the securities investors most often buy and sell. The mechanics of trading puts and calls and warrants are very similar to those of common stocks. And as noted in the last chapter, most investment company shares are bought from and sold to the investment company itself. The factors involving these other securities are discussed in the chapters dealing specifically with each security.

The structure and operating mechanisms of the security markets in the United States have changed drastically in the last 10 to 15 years. Accordingly, this chapter concludes with a look at some of these changes and what the future may hold.

The discussion will be organized around the two basic types of markets that exist: the primary and secondary. **Primary markets** involve the sale of new securities, whereas **secondary markets** provide a forum for the trading of securities after their initial sale. Before considering these two types of markets, however, we will examine their importance to the economy.

The Importance of Financial Markets

Business firms need tremendous amounts of capital to finance their operations. To grow and expand, they must invest capital in amounts beyond their capacity to save in any reasonable period of time. Similarly, governments must borrow large amounts of money to provide the goods and services demanded of them by the populace. The financial markets permit both business and government to raise the needed funds by selling securities. Simultaneously, investors with excess funds are able to invest and earn a return, enhancing their welfare.[1]

Primary markets are absolutely vital to capitalistic economies if they are to function properly, since they serve to channel funds from savers to borrowers. Furthermore, they provide an important allocative function by channeling the funds to those who can make the best use of them—presumably, the most productive. In fact, the primary function of a capital market is to allocate resources optimally. A securities market with this characteristic is said to be *allocationally efficient*. An *operationally efficient* market, on the other hand, is one with the lowest possible prices for transactions services.

[1]For a discussion of these issues, see J. C. Poindexter and C. P. Jones, *Money, Financial Markets and the Economy* (St. Paul, Minn.: West Publishing Company, 1980), Chapter 10.

Primary markets would not function well without secondary markets. Savers would be reluctant to invest in new securities if they had to hold these securities to maturity or incur large search costs in finding a seller when they were ready to sell. The existence of well-functioning secondary markets, where investors come together to trade existing securities, assures the purchasers of primary securities that they can quickly sell their securities if the need arises. Of course, such sales may involve a loss, because there are no guarantees in the financial markets. A loss, however, may be very much preferred to having no cash at all if the securities cannot be sold readily.

In summary, secondary markets are indispensable in the United States to the proper functioning of the primary markets. The latter, in turn, are indispensable to the proper functioning of the economy.

The Primary Markets

As noted, a primary market is one in which a borrower issues new securities in exchange for cash from an investor (buyer). New sales of Treasury bills, or IBM stock, or North Carolina bonds all take place in the primary markets. The issuers of these securities—the U.S. government, IBM, and the state of North Carolina, respectively—receive cash from the buyers of these new securities, who in turn receive financial claims that previously did not exist. In all three examples some amount of these securities is outstanding before the new sales occur. In other cases the issuer is selling securities for the first time. Regardless, once securities are sold by the original purchasers, they trade in secondary markets. New securities may trade repeatedly in the secondary market, but the original issuers will be unaffected in the sense that they receive no additional cash from these transactions.

The Investment Banker

Since most issuers of securities do not raise long-term capital frequently, they usually lack the expertise needed to do the best job possible; furthermore, suppliers of capital are widely dispersed, and efficiently reaching them all requires organization. In the course of selling new securities, therefore, issuers often rely upon an **investment banking firm.** Along with performing activities such as helping corporations in mergers and acquisitions, *investment banks* specialize in the design and sale of securities in the primary market while operating simultaneously in the secondary markets. For example, Merrill Lynch offers investment banking services while operating a large retail brokerage operation throughout the country.

Investment bankers act as intermediaries between issuers and investors. The issuer sells its securities to investment bankers, who in turn sell the securities to investors. For firms seeking to raise long-term funds, the investment banker provides the following functions, each of which will be discussed: the advisory function, the underwriting function, and the marketing function.

Investment Banking Functions Because of their expertise in selling securities on a continual basis, an important function investment bankers can provide to their clients is advice during the planning stage preceding the issuance of new securities. This advice includes providing information about the type of security to be sold, the features to be offered with the security, the price, and the timing of the sale. Such advisory work occurs in a "negotiated" bid arrangement, whereby the issuer chooses the investment banker at the initiation of the process and the two negotiate and work together thereafter.[2]

The **underwriting** function consists of the investment banker's purchasing the securities (once the details of the issue have been negotiated) and subsequently reselling them to investors.[3] Investment bankers provide a valuable service to the issuers at this stage because the bankers assume the risk of price declines in the securities. The issuer receives its check and can spend the proceeds for the purposes for which the funds are being raised. The investment bankers own the securities until they are resold. The term *underwriting* refers to investment bankers assuming the risk of selling the securities.

Investment bankers bear risk in the underwriting stage. Although many issues are sold out quickly (e.g., the first day they are offered to the public), others may not be sold for days or even weeks. A price decline in the securities during this time could cause the investment bankers a loss. However, most issues are sold successfully, with the price approximating that agreed on during the planning stage before the sale. Investment bankers are compensated by a *spread*, which is the difference between what they pay the issuer for the securities and what they sell them for to the public (i.e., the securities are purchased from the issuer at a discount).

In addition to having expertise in these matters and closely scrutinizing any potential issue of securities, investment bankers can protect themselves by forming a **syndicate,** or group of investment bankers. This allows them to diversify their risk. One investment banker acts as the managing

they are at risk of loss. bet. paid is diff price paid & price sold is underwriting spread.

[2]An alternative arrangement is a competitive bid, whereby the firm decides beforehand the details of the sale, solicits bids from investment bankers, and accepts the best offer. This arrangement is usually required of most public utilities. However, most corporate stock and bond offerings are sold on a negotiated basis rather than a competitive bid basis.
[3]Corporate offerings are classified as either "seasoned" issues or "initial" public offerings. The former refers to new securities sold by companies with existing public markets for their securities; the latter indicates the initial sale of securities by a company.

underwriter, overseeing the underwriting syndicate. This syndicate becomes part of a larger group that sells the securities.

The third function mentioned for investment bankers is marketing. Securities have typically been sold through a selling group consisting of the sales division of the underwriting and selected retail brokerage houses. The selling group operates under a selling group agreement that specifies the operating conditions, such as how the spread will be split among the various parties and how long the group will operate.

Figure 3-1 illustrates a primary offering of securities through investment bankers, a process referred to as a *syndicated offering*. The issuer (seller) of the securities works with the originating investment banker in designing the specific details of the sale. Documents are prepared to satisfy

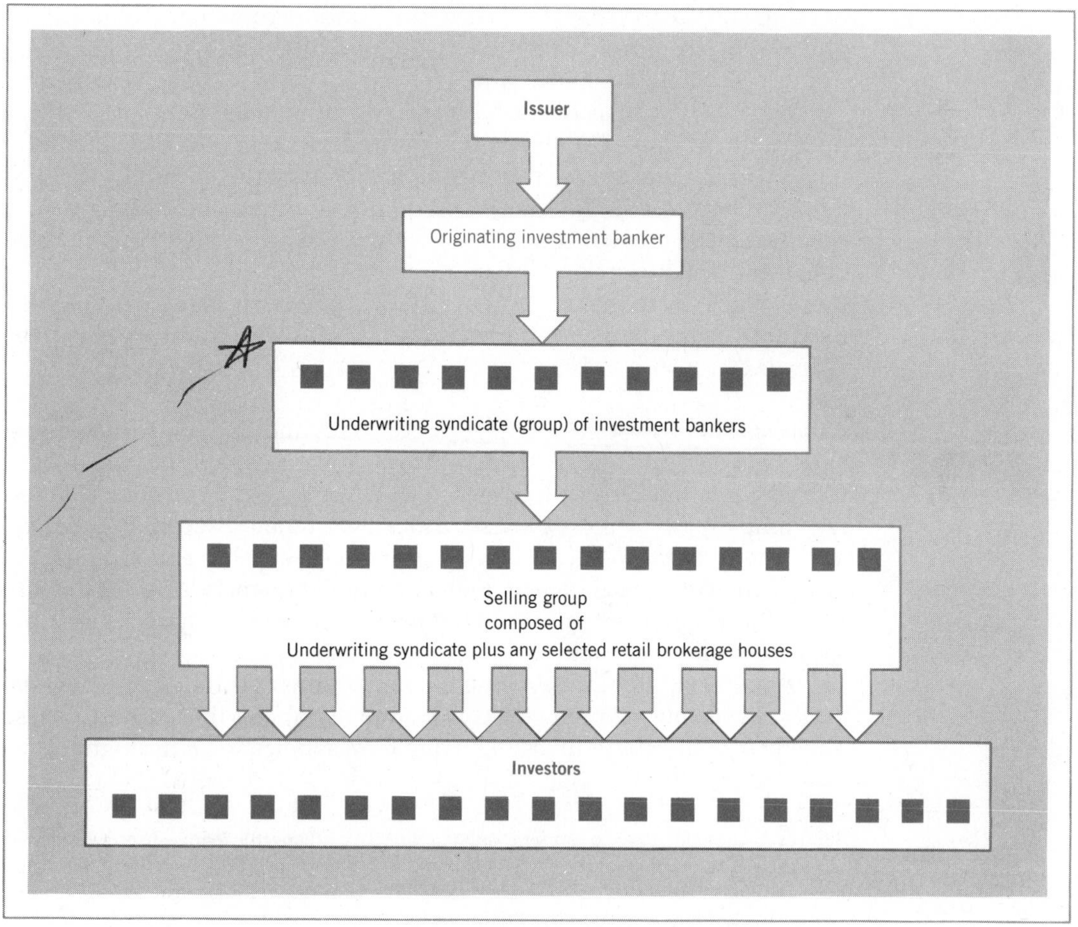

FIGURE 3-1 ***The issuance process for new securities in the primary market.***

federal laws. In particular, the issuer files a registration statement with the **Securities and Exchange Commission (SEC)** containing financial and other information about the company and issues a **prospectus,** which summarizes this information, to offer the securities for sale officially.

The underwriter forms a syndicate of underwriters willing to undertake the sale of these securities. The selling group consists of the syndicate members plus, if necessary, other firms affiliated with the syndicate. The selling group cannot begin its sales efforts until the legal requirements have been met. In particular, new issues must be registered with the SEC at least 20 days before being publicly offered.[4] Upon approval from the SEC, the selling group begins selling the securities to the public. The issue may be fully subscribed (sold out) quickly, or it may require several days (or longer) to sell. During this time the underwriting manager can legally elect to stabilize the market by placing purchase orders for the security at a fixed price. Underwriters feel that such stabilization sometimes is needed to provide for an orderly sale (thereby helping the issuer) and reduce their risk (thereby helping themselves).

Who are the investment bankers, and how much debt and equity is underwritten? Table 3-1 shows the top underwriters of U.S. debt and equity in recent years and the magnitude of their business. By 1989 the industry's profit margins on new issue underwriting and trading had declined over the previous three years some 40% to 45%. New common stock offerings, which provide the largest profits, declined some 45% from the first half of 1988 to the first half of 1989. On the other hand, the volume of fixed-rate debt offerings had reached its highest level in three years, some $72 billion.[5]

New Trends in Investment Banking Securities and Exchange Rule 415 (the **shelf rule**), effective in 1982, permits qualified companies to file a "short form registration" and "place on the shelf" securities to be sold. The issuing company can sell the new securities over time by auctioning pieces of the issue to the lowest-cost bidder, providing flexibility and savings. This rule, along with the general deregulation of the financial services industry, may have a significant impact on investment bankers, shifting their emphasis away from underwriting.

Another significant development in investment banking is the *unsyndicated stock offering,* whereby the corporation distributes the entire stock issue directly to institutional investors rather than syndicating it through the nor-

---

[4]However, the selling group can send out a preliminary prospectus to investors describing the new issue. No offering date or price is shown, and the prospectus is identified clearly as an informational sheet and not a solicitation to sell the securities; for this reason, the preliminary prospectus is often referred to as a "red herring."

[5]These figures are taken from Matthew Winkler, "Merrill Tightens Hold on Top Spot," *The Wall Street Journal,* July 5, 1989, p. C1.

TABLE 3-1 ***Top underwriters of U.S. debt and equity***

Top Underwriters of U.S. Debt and Equity

	First Half 1989		First Half 1988		
Manager	Amount (In Millions)	Market Share (%)	Amount (In Millions)	Rank	Market Share (%)
Merrill Lynch Capital Markets	$25,191.6	17.8	$21,664.0	1	14.9
Goldman, Sachs	16,853.5	11.9	19,674.2	3	13.5
First Boston	16,326.7	11.5	16,436.6	4	11.3
Salomon Brothers	15,216.3	10.7	20,213.7	2	13.9
Shearson Lehman Hutton	12,611.1	8.9	12,465.6	6	8.6
Drexel Burnham Lambert	10,777.6	7.6	10,779.2	7	7.4
Morgan Stanley	9,787.8	6.9	14,578.2	5	10.0
Bear, Stearns	8,038.8	5.7	5,025.4	9	3.4
Prudential Bache Capital Funding	6,227.3	4.4	5,254.6	8	3.6
Kidder, Peabody	4,500.9	3.2	3,091.0	11	2.1
Subtotals	$125,531.6	88.7	$129,182.3		88.7
Industry totals	141,550.1	100.0	$145,719.2		100.0

Source: Matthew Winkler, "Merrill Tightens Hold on Top Spot," *The Wall Street Journal,* July 5, 1989, p. C1. Reprinted by permission of *The Wall Street Journal,* © 1989 Dow Jones & Company, Inc. All Rights Reserved Worldwide.

mal retail distribution network to individual investors. The issuers save the fees paid for a normal syndicated offering, which can be substantial; furthermore, the issuing process may be streamlined because the issuer is dealing with a small number of presumably sophisticated buyers. The underwriters handling these unsyndicated offerings may earn a larger net return, although total fees are lower, because they do not have to share the fees with the underwriting syndicate. In the early 1980s, only 1% to 2% of all common stock issued was unsyndicated, whereas by the mid-1980s as much as one-third was sold in this manner.

Public and Private Placements

There has been a trend in recent years for more corporations to execute **private placements,** whereby new securities issues (typically, debt securities) are sold directly to financial institutions, such as life insurance companies and pension funds, bypassing the open market. The advantages include not having to register the issue with the SEC, thereby saving both time and money. Investment bankers' fees also are saved because they are not typically used in private placements; even if they are used, the underwriting spread is saved.[6] The savings in time can sometimes be important,

[6]Investment bankers in this situation are paid a finder's fee. The bankers have many contacts, which may be helpful, and they provide information to the issuer in evaluating the buyer's offer.

as market conditions can change rapidly between the time an issue is registered and sold.

The disadvantages of private placements include a higher interest cost, because the financial institutions usually charge more than would be offered in a public subscription, and possible restrictive provisions on the activities of the borrower. Also, a lack of marketability exists, because the issue is unregistered; therefore, the buyer may demand additional compensation, in the form of a higher yield, from the lender.

Secondary Markets: Structure

Once new securities have been sold in the primary market, an efficient mechanism must exist for their resale if investors are to view securities as attractive opportunities. Secondary markets provide the means for investors to trade securities among themselves.[7]

Secondary markets exist for the trading of common and preferred stock, warrants, bonds, and puts and calls. The structure of each of these markets is discussed in this section, and the mechanics of trading in secondary markets is discussed in the following section. Figure 3-2 diagrams the structure of the secondary markets.

Common stocks, preferred stocks, and warrants are traded in the equity markets. Some secondary equity markets are **auction markets,** involving an auction (bidding) process in a specific physical location. Investors are represented by **brokers,** intermediaries who represent both buyers and sellers and attempt to obtain the best price possible for either in a transaction. Brokers collect commissions for their efforts and generally have no vested interest in whether a customer places a buy order or a sell order, or, in most cases, in what is bought or sold (holding constant the value of the transaction). However, in the past, some brokers received a larger part of the sales fee for selling in-house mutual funds than for selling other funds (In the past, Merrill Lynch's 11,000 brokers received 8% more for selling the firm's in-house fund. At the beginning of 1990, Merrill Lynch started paying its brokers the same commission regardless of the fund sold).[8]

The other type of secondary equity markets is **negotiated markets,** involving a network of **dealers** who make a market by standing ready to buy and sell securities at specified prices. Unlike brokers, dealers have a vested interest in the transaction because the securities are bought from them and sold to them, and they earn a profit in these trades by the spread, or difference, between the two prices.

---

[7]Again, this does not directly affect the issuer, who sells new securities in the primary market in order to raise funds.

[8]See Michael Siconolfi, "Merrill, in Switch, Puts All Funds It Peddles on a Level Selling Field," *The Wall Street Journal*, January 4, 1990, p. C1.

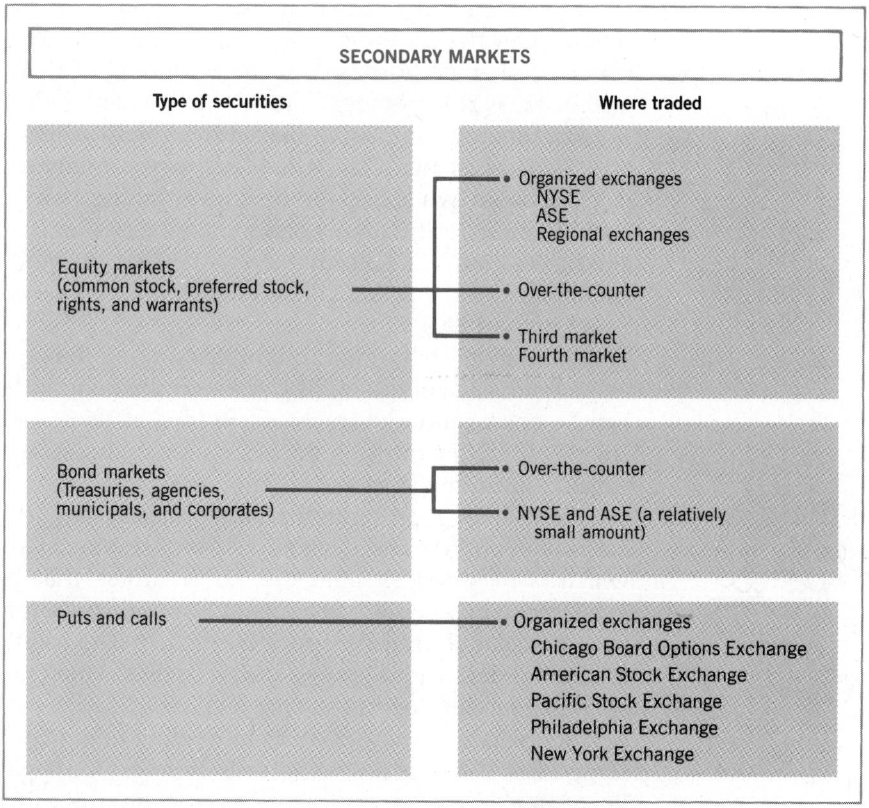

FIGURE 3-2 ***The structure of the secondary markets in the United States.***

The auction markets include the New York Stock Exchange, the American Stock Exchange, and the regional exchanges. Negotiated markets involve the over-the-counter market. We consider each in turn.

New York Stock Exchange Founded in 1792, the **New York Stock Exchange (NYSE)** is the oldest and most prominent secondary market in the United States, if not the world. It is a not-for-profit corporation with 1444 members as of the beginning of 1990, 1366 of whom own a seat.[9] Most of the members are partners or directors of stockbrokerage houses.[10] Members may transfer seats, by sale or lease, subject to the approval of the Exchange. The price of a seat has varied sharply over the years, ranging from less than $100,000 in the mid-1970s to a high during 1987 of $1,150,000 to a level of around $360,000 at the beginning of the 1990s.

[9]The other individuals paid an annual fee to have access to the trading floor. The number of seats has remained constant since 1953.

[10]For example, Merrill Lynch, the largest retail stockbrokerage firm, owns over 20 seats.

Most members of the NYSE act as brokers for customers, buying and selling securities for them. They are called *commission brokers* and are members of brokerage houses.[11] At the beginning of 1990 there were approximately 350 NYSE member firms doing business with the public.

Brokers are the people that individual investors most often think of, and come in contact with, when they invest. Many misperceptions appear to exist about what brokers do, their training and knowledge, life as a broker, and so forth. Box 3-1 offers some interesting insights into the brokerage profession, but note that it was written in 1987, and Wall Street has changed since then. We will end the chapter with a discussion about Wall Street in the 1990s.

Specialists, who own roughly 25% of all the seats on the NYSE, are assigned to each of the trading posts on the floor of the NYSE, where they handle one or more of the stocks traded at that post. In early 1990 there were 49 specialist firms on the NYSE, each possessing a monopoly to make markets in certain stocks.

Specialists, representing a system nearly 200 years old on the NYSE, act as both brokers and dealers. As a broker, they maintain the *limit book,* in which is recorded all limit orders, or orders that have been placed by investors to buy or sell a security at a specific price (or better) and that will not be executed until that price is reached. The commission brokers leave the limit orders with the specialist to be filled when possible; therefore, the specialist receives part of the broker's fee.

Specialists also act as dealers, buying and selling shares of their assigned stock(s) to maintain an orderly market. The stock exchanges function essentially as a continuous market, assuring investors that they can almost always buy and sell a particular security at some price. Assuming that public orders do not arrive at the same time, so that they can be matched, the specialist will buy from commission brokers with orders to sell and sell to those with orders to buy, hoping to profit by a favorable spread between the two sides.

Specialists are charged by the NYSE with maintaining a continuous, orderly market in their assigned stocks. To provide this continuous market, they often must go "against the market," which requires adequate capital. The NYSE requires specialists to be able to assume a position of 5000 shares in their assigned stocks.[12]

How well does the system work? According to NYSE figures, in one

---

[11]Floor brokers, on the other hand, are brokers acting as free-lancers who handle overflows for various commission brokers and share in their commissions. Floor traders trade for their own account, paying no commissions. Such traders are speculating on their own behalf, sometimes buying and selling on the same day ("day-trading"). Their activities have decreased over the years.

[12]Specialists must be approved by the Board of Governors of the NYSE and must have experience, ability as a dealer, and specified minimum capital.

recent year specialists bought and sold 7.9 billion shares.[13] Some 96% of all transactions occurred with no change in price or within the minimum change permissible on the NYSE—one-eighth of a point. The specialists' stabilization rate—defined as the percentage of shares purchased at prices below or sold at prices above the last different price—was 86%.

The New York Stock Exchange has specific listing requirements that companies must meet in order to be listed (i.e., accepted for trading), as shown in Table 3-2. New companies are added each year. For example, a record 128 companies were added to the NYSE in 1989, bringing the total to 1720 companies, accounting for some 2246 stocks (because some companies have listed both common stock and one or more issues of preferred stock).[14] At the end of 1989, the warrants of 16 companies were listed on the "Big Board." Continuing listing requirements must also be met or a firm could be delisted from the exchange. The NYSE can suspend or delist a firm whenever it believes that continued trading would not be advisable.

The NYSE had a 1989 aggregate share volume of almost 42 billion shares, which was almost 50% of the total equities trading in domestic securities markets. By dollar volume the figure was even higher, 67%. Daily trading volume averaged 165 million shares in 1989, compared to less than 40 million shares daily in 1979. In 1989 the record trading volume for one day was over 416 million shares.

A new trend of potential significance that is often discussed in the popular press is **program trading,** defined by the NYSE as the purchase or sale of a basket of 15 stocks or more to accomplish certain trading strategies, such as arbitrage against futures contracts and portfolio accumulation and liquidation strategies. The NYSE published its first report on program trading activities in 1988. For the last half of 1988 and for 1989, program trading volume accounted for approximately 10% of total NYSE volume.[15] Program trading is considered in more detail in other chapters.

American Stock Exchange The American Stock Exchange (Amex) is the only other national organized exchange. Its organization and procedures resemble those of the NYSE, except that it is smaller (approximately 650 seats) and fewer companies are listed there (less than 900 by 1990). The listing requirements for stocks on the Amex are less stringent than those for stocks on the NYSE. Many companies that grow and prosper eventually move their listing to the NYSE. Since 1976 dual listing of stocks on both the NYSE and the AMEX has been permitted.

The Amex accounted for less than 4% of the total 1989 share volume.

---

[13]These figures are taken from *Fact Book 1990,* NYSE, Inc., 1990, p. 22.

[14]The number 128 refers to original new common stocks; because of removals, the net change for 1989 was 32.

[15]See *Fact Book 1989,* NYSE, Inc., 1989, p. 15, and *Fact Book 1990,* p. 21.

BOX 3-1

COLD-CALL COWBOYS

The chance of a lifetime? Nearly 50,000 people became registered to sell stocks, bonds and packaged securities last year alone. In all, there are 404,000 people registered to sell securities of one kind or another. No wonder you get so many calls and letters.

For the stoutest hearts, big money could be there. According to the Securities Industry Association, the average broker earned $80,000 last year. But don't let the average mislead you. It includes superbrokers who gross over $1 million in commissions a year. "A good slug of brokers earn half the average," says SIA General Manager Adrian Banky. "In a bear market a broker oriented toward selling stocks and bonds can see his business drop 30% or 40%." Small wonder only 41% of all brokers remain in the business more than three years.

Still, there is no shortage of applicants, who have two roads to travel. The high road is with a major brokerage firm. But getting hired can seem as hard as getting into medical school. "In 1986 we trained 800 new brokers, but we had 70,000 applicants," says Joel Margolies, head of retail branches at Shearson Lehman Brothers.

Only one new broker in five starts out with one of the major firms, which provide a base salary for up to 16 months, training and name recognition. After that, brokers keep 25% to 50% of their gross commissions.

Merrill Lynch's 17-week training program includes three weeks at its campus-like complex in Princeton, N.J., which features high-tech simulation drills, jacuzzis to cool out in, and fine dining. Merrill says it spends $30,000 to $50,000 per trainee.

The vast majority of potential brokers, however, have to take the low road and get no such coddling. Their training with a small firm usually consists of a few product lectures and the chance to watch an established salesman at work. Then they're given a desk, a phone and a telephone directory. Sometimes the atmosphere is a bit rough.

All new brokers must become registered with the National Association of Securities Dealers, of course. The six-hour, 250-question General Securities exam used to be child's play. Until last June the pass rate for the exam hovered around 65%. The test is now tougher; less than 60% pass.

There is no proven formula for becoming a successful broker. Rich friends and a gift of gab help. A sales background usually is a big plus, too. But advanced degrees can work against you. Says Barrus at Blinder, Robinson, "I hate Harvard M.B.A.s—they think too much. I need doers."

Self-confidence is a must. Says one district manager of a firm: "All I need is a name and number to be successful. I don't care if they are qualified investors. I'll take names off of subway cars."

Rookies and pros alike are constantly on the prowl for new clients, spending upwards of 70 hours a week cold-calling, often using the same directories. Others concentrate on mailings, seminars and teaching night classes to woo customers. Some women brokers find they have an advantage selling to women professionals, but others find they are more successful with male clients.

"The level of rejection is incredible, but there can be no lapse in your mental attitude," says one ex-broker, who admits he couldn't hack it and now does odd jobs for a living. "One day you can be the best guy in the world, the next you can rattle off 150 calls, and no one wants to talk to you."

According to Bill Meyer, a psychologist at Rohrer, Hibler & Replogle, the most successful brokers seem to be driven almost solely by money and profit. They tend not to make other sacrifices and, as a result, have a higher tendency toward divorce. "These people find this pressure to earn very exciting," Meyer says. "They are driven."

Source: Matthew Schifrin, "Cold-call Cowboys," *Forbes,* February 23, 1987, pp. 140–141. Excerpted by permission of *Forbes* magazine, February 23, 1987. ©Forbes, Inc., 1987.

TABLE 3-2 ***Initial Listing Requirements for the New York Stock Exchange***

1. Demonstrated earning power consisting of a minimum level of profitability for the preceding three years.
2. Net tangible assets of $18 million, but greater emphasis on aggregate market value of the common stock.
3. Market value of publicly held shares within a range of $9 to $18 million. The $18 million figure was applicable at the end of 1989.
4. A total of 1,100,000 common shares held by the public.
5. Either 2000 holders of at least 100 shares or 2200 total stockholders together with recent average monthly trading volume of 100,000 shares.

Source: Fact Book 1987, New York Stock Exchange, Inc., 1987, p. 21. With permission.

In dollar volume, it accounted for less than 2%. Typically, the NYSE does more trading in the first hour than the Amex does during the entire day.

Regional Exchanges Several regional exchanges exist, including the Midwest Stock Exchange, the Pacific Stock Exchange, the Boston Stock Exchange, the Philadelphia Stock Exchange, and the Cincinnati Stock Exchange. Although these exchanges are patterned after the NYSE, the listing requirements are considerably more lenient.

Regional exchanges list small companies that may have limited geographic interest. Additionally, they engage in dual listing, listing of securities that are also listed on the NYSE and the Amex. In fact, most of the securities traded on the regional exchanges are also traded on the NYSE or the Amex. This allows local brokerage firms that are not members of a national exchange to purchase a seat on a regional exchange and trade in dual-listed securities.

By offering lower commissions on such stocks, regional exchanges have attracted business that otherwise would go to the larger exchanges. As the 1990s began, institutional investors were aggressively seeking lower trading costs. One way for Wall Street firms to accommodate these demands by their institutional clients is to take some trades to the regional exchanges. In 1989 only 69% of the trades in NYSE-listed stocks were executed on the NYSE, the lowest percentage in the history of the NYSE.[16]

[16]The information in this section is based on Craig Torres, "More Trades Desert Big Board for Regional Exchanges," *The Wall Street Journal,* February 16, 1990, p. C1.

Some large Wall Street firms had decided by early 1990 to take any trade of 5000 shares or less to whatever exchange offered the lowest costs. The NYSE continues to have an advantage in handling big block trades, which is referred to as *liquidity* by traders.

In 1988 total volume on the Midwest Stock Exchange exceeded that for the Amex, one indication of the regional exchanges' ability to compete with the major exchanges.

The Over-the-Counter Market In contrast to auction markets, the **over-the-counter (OTC) market** is a negotiated market. Transactions not handled on an organized exchange are handled in this market; that is, this market essentially handles *unlisted securities,* or securities not listed on a stock exchange. The OTC market has become a major player in the securities markets, and in all likelihood will continue to gain in importance. It already is the second largest U.S. equity market, and the fifth largest in the world, after Tokyo, NYSE, Taiwan, and London, on the basis of dollar volume (as of 1989).

Unlike the NYSE, the OTC market is not a place with a specific location. Rather, it is a way of doing business. It consists of a network of dealers linked together by communications devices, including the latest equipment. These dealers do transactions directly with each other and with customers. In fact, in many respects the OTC market may represent the market of the future, as will be discussed.

The **National Association of Security Dealers (NASD)** is a self-regulating body of brokers and dealers that oversees OTC practices, much as the NYSE does for its members. NASD licenses brokers when they successfully complete a qualifying examination. Violation of the fair practices prescribed by the NASD are grounds for censure, fine, suspension, or expulsion. The NASD disciplines both firms and principals in the firms. The self-regulating function of the NASD serves to protect the public as well as the interest of its members.

Example. In early 1990 the NASD expelled a member firm from membership for failing to file timely statements concerning its financial condition and for failing to maintain adequate records. A principal of the firm was barred from membership with any NASD member. Another firm was expelled, and two principals were fined and suspended for varying periods, for filing an inaccurate statement of financial conditions and conducting business without maintaining required net capital.[17] ▪

The over-the-counter market can best be described by thinking of smaller and smaller parts, as illustrated in Figure 3-3. The entire OTC

[17]See Robert Daniels, "NASD Disciplines 2 Firms, 3 Individuals For Failing to Report Net Capital Deficit," *The Wall Street Journal*, February 2, 1990, p. C19.

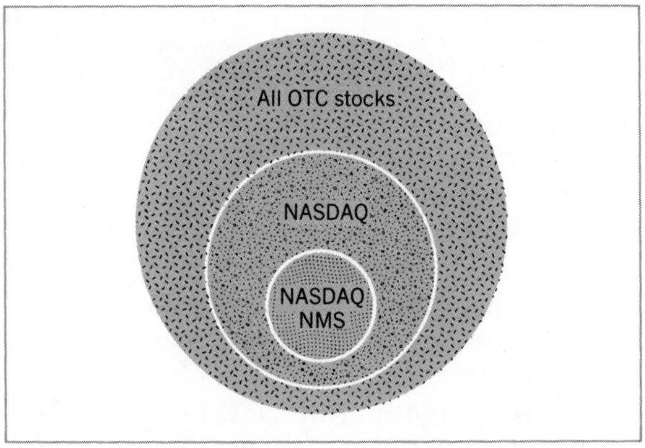

FIGURE 3-3 ***The structure of the over-the-counter market.***

market consists of more than 15,000 stocks. However, some 11,000 of these stocks are quite small and are often inactively traded. These stocks are referred to as "pink-sheet stocks," because the paper on which their quotes are circulated is pink.[18]

In 1971 the NASD initiated a computerized communications network called **NASDAQ** (an acronym for the NASD Automated Quotation System), which offers current (up-to-the-minute) bid–asked prices for thousands of OTC stocks. Interested investors can obtain the current bid and asked prices from all the market makers for a security, assuring them of receiving the best price. Before the advent of NASDAQ, investors had to rely on their brokers placing calls to various dealers to obtain quotes, an inexact process at best. Price spreads on NASDAQ-carried stocks have narrowed even more since 1980 when NASDAQ began releasing the highest bids and lowest askeds rather than representative quotations.

NASDAQ-traded stocks are the key component of the OTC market; that is, although the entire shaded areas in Figure 3-3 represent more than 15,000 OTC stocks, the roughly 4300 stocks in the "NASDAQ circle" in that figure constitute the major trading activity for the OTC market. NASDAQ continues its expansion, with some 34 billion shares traded in 1989, accounting for almost 39% of all equities traded in that year.

A significant development occurred on April 1, 1982, with the start-up of the **NASDAQ National Market System (NASDAQ/NMS),** a component of the NASDAQ market. The NMS is a combination of the competing market makers in OTC stocks and the up-to-the-minute reporting of trades, using data similar to that shown for the NYSE and AMEX (specifically, high, low, and closing quotations, volume, and the net change from one day to the

[18]OTC stocks that meet certain requirements are quoted daily in *The Wall Street Journal*. For those not carried, quotes can be obtained from the National Quotation Bureau, which reports daily prices on several thousand OTC securities.

next). There are an average of 11 market makers per security. By 1989, 2610 firms traded on NASDAQ/NMS, accounting for 72% of all NASDAQ volume.[19] Thus, as shown in Figure 3-3, the NASDAQ/NMS is a component of NASDAQ, accounting for approximately 61% of all NASDAQ companies.

In summary, the common stock issues traded in the OTC market vary widely in size, price, quality, and trading activity. Many are small, struggling, speculative companies, often not far removed from having obtained public financing in a primary offering. Others are comparable to NYSE stocks and could, if they chose, be listed there. In fact, more and more OTC companies are choosing to remain OTC companies rather than move on to the AMEX or NYSE.

An important trend in the OTC market is the emergence of institutional investors as dominant players. Traditionally, the OTC market has been known as the market for mostly small and less-well-known companies, where individual investors trade. Since 1982, the institutions have assumed a larger and larger role. One indication of the presence of institutional investors is that for the two years 1988 and 1989 big-block trades, associated with institutional activity, accounted for 43% of total NASDAQ/NMS volume. Daily volume in 1989 increased relative to 1988 despite the fact that individual investors, fleeing the stock markets following the big crash in October, 1987, had not returned in full force.

The importance of institutional participation, as measured by block volume (large trades), is shown in Figure 3-4 for both the NYSE and NASDAQ/NMS. As the figure shows, the trend is clearly upward for both markets, and reached some 51% for the NYSE by the end of 1989.

Perhaps more important than the increase in trading volume brought about by the institutional investors, they "have brought Nasdaq respectability and liquidity." There apparently is a feeling among some traders at large brokerage houses that the increase in institutional trading adds status to the OTC market, makes the larger stocks traded there more attractive, and helps to keep OTC firms from deciding to move to the NYSE or Amex.[20]

The Third and Fourth Markets All off-exchange transactions in securities listed on the organized exchanges take place in the so-called **third market.** This market was created to serve the needs of large institutional investors who did not want to pay full brokerage costs on large transactions. These large buyers and sellers were brought together by brokers who were not members of organized exchanges, and therefore were not required to charge the high commissions required on the exchanges. With the elimina-

---

[19]This discussion is based on the *NASDAQ 1989 Fact Book,* Washington, D.C.: The National Association of Securities Dealers, Inc., p. 5.

[20]Sonja Steptoe, "OTC Stocks Attract Institutional Investors, Become More Volatile," *The Wall Street Journal,* July 26, 1989, p. A1. The information in this part of the discussion is based on this article.

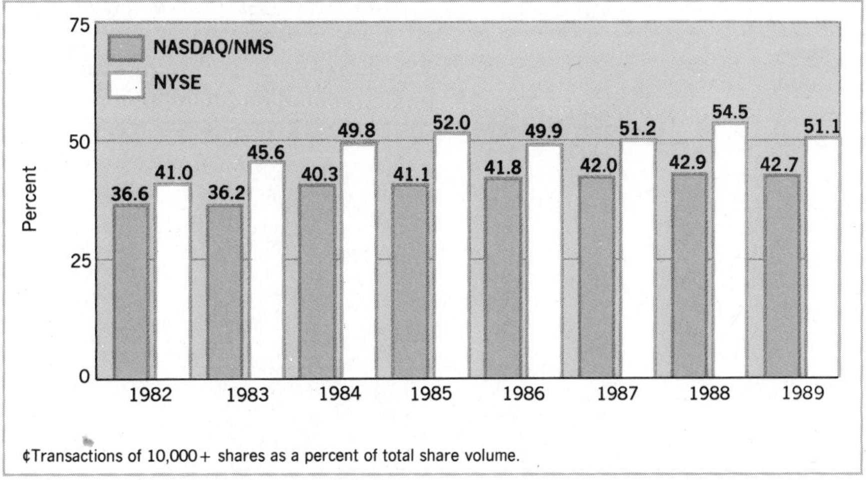

FIGURE 3-4 ***Institutional participation as measured by block volume: NASDAQ/NMS vs. NYSE, 1982–1989.***
Source: 1990 NASDAQ Fact Book, National Association of Securities Dealers, Inc., Washington, D. C., 1990, p. 42. Reprinted by permission.

tion of fixed commissions in 1975, activity in the third market declined significantly. By the beginning of the 1990s, however, the third market had become the third largest trader of NYSE-listed stocks (the NYSE and the Midwest Stock Exchange ranked first and second, respectively).

Today a few third-market brokers provide investors with the flexibility to trade when the NYSE is closed. For example, Jeffries & Co., a leading third-market broker in Los Angeles, specializes in trading big blocks off the floor of major exchanges, particularly when the NYSE is not open. Generally, it makes a market in a stock by matching buyers and sellers (and collecting commissions), but Jeffries often takes positions in stocks to facilitate trading. Another third-market firm, Madoff Investment Securities, paid brokers to execute orders through its system, thereby providing very aggressive competition for both the NYSE and the regional exchanges.

The **fourth market** refers to transactions made directly between large institutions (and wealthy individuals), bypassing brokers and dealers. Essentially, the fourth market is a communications network among investors interested in trading large blocks of stock. Several different privately owned automated systems exist to provide current information on specific securities that the participants are willing to buy or sell. **Instinet** is an electronic trading network that handled some 2.5 billion shares in 1989.

Comparisons of Equity Markets Table 3-3 shows share and dollar volume for all equities trading in domestic markets in 1989. The NYSE continues to dominate in both categories. However, NASDAQ share volume has in-

TABLE 3-3 ***U.S. Equity Markets: 1989 Share and Dollar Volumes***

i	Share Volume (In Millions)	Share Volume Percent	Dollar Volume (In Millions)	Dollar Volume Percent
NASDAQ	33,530	38.6%	$431,381	18.8%
NASDAQ/OTC Trading in Listed Securities	1,794	2.1%	66,378	2.9%
Amex	3,125	3.6%	44,401	1.9%
Regionals (BSE, CSE, MSE, PSE, and Phix)	6,733	7.7%	216,773	9.4%
NYSE	41,699	48.0%	1,542,800	67.0%
Totals	86,881	100.0%	$2,301,733	100.0%

Source: 1990 NASDAQ Fact Book, National Association of Securities Dealers, Inc., Washington, D.C., 1990, p. 8. Reprinted by permission.

creased dramatically since 1979 relative to both the NYSE and the Amex, as shown in Figure 3-5.

Bond Markets

Just as stockholders need good secondary markets to be able to trade stocks and thus preserve their flexibility, bondholders need a viable market in order to sell before maturity. Otherwise, many investors would be reluctant to tie up their funds for up to 30 years. At the very least, they would demand higher initial yields on bonds, which would hinder raising funds by those who wish to invest productively.

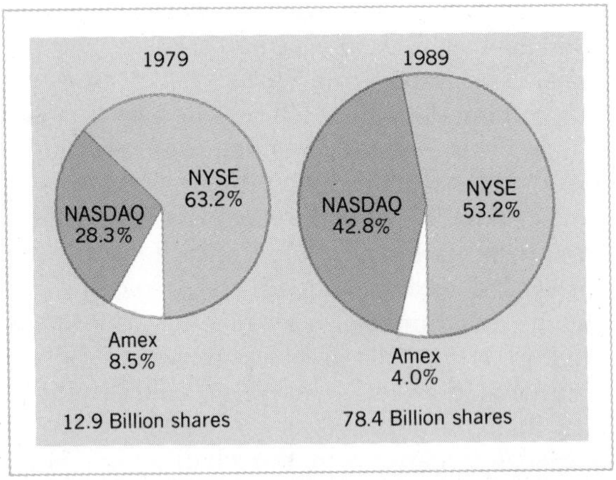

FIGURE 3-5 ***Comparison of share volumes: NASDAQ, NYSE, and Amex.***
Source: 1990 NASDAQ Fact Book, National Association of Securities Dealers, Inc., Washington, D. C., 1990, p. 9. Reprinted by permission.

Investors can purchase either new bonds being issued in the primary market or existing bonds outstanding in the secondary market. Yields for the two must be in equilibrium. If IBM's bonds are trading in the secondary market to yield 12% over a 20-year period, for example, comparable new IBM bonds will be sold with approximately the same yield.

A few thousand bonds are traded on the NYSE and a very few on the Amex, and their prices can be seen daily in *The Wall Street Journal*. However, *the secondary bond market is primarily an OTC market,* with a large network of dealers making markets in the various bonds. The volume of bond trading in the OTC market dwarfs that of all the exchanges combined.

Investors can buy and sell bonds through their brokers, who in turn trade with bond dealers. Certain features of the bond markets should be noted.

Treasury Bonds U.S. Treasury notes and bonds are widely purchased, held, and traded. The Federal Reserve conducts open-market operations with Treasury securities, and institutions such as commerical banks deal in very large quantities. The result is a broad and deep market, with a volume of transactions exceeding that of any other security.

The Treasury bond market consists of selected market makers who trade with the open-market desk of the Federal Reserve Bank of New York. These large dealers include the bond departments of several banks, and this network has widespread branches and dealers. In addition, many large banks act as dealers (make markets) in particular issues. Although larger investors can transact directly with these dealers, most investors use their banks and brokers and pay commissions on the order of $30 to $50 per purchase or sale.

Federal Agency Bonds Federal agency securities trade in good secondary markets, with basically the same dealer market and procedures used as in the case of Treasury securities. Larger issues are more easily traded than smaller issues, and recently issued securities are usually more actively traded than those that have been in existence for some time.

Municipal Bonds Municipal securities often have a relatively thin market, with only moderate activity in the secondary market. This is because most bonds are held to maturity, and therefore are traded infrequently.

Probably fewer than 5% of all securities firms maintain an active municipal bond operation. Some specialize in particular types of issues, but most trade across the spectrum. Of course, an investor's broker can contact and transact with these dealers.

Individual investors can be important in this market. However, when the individual is ready to sell, it may be difficult to find a buyer for just a few bonds unless significant price concessions are made. Investors with less than $50,000 to put into municipals are sometimes advised to buy a unit investment trust, an indirect investing method.[21]

Corporate Bonds Although a substantial number of corporate bonds are listed on the exchanges, with numerous small trades being executed there, exchange trading in corporate bonds is only a very small part of this market. For example, on a typical day some two-thirds of the roughly 3000 issues on the NYSE's bond board do not trade at all, and a typical trade is less than 15 bonds. Liquidity is not always good for these small transactions, with delays occurring in the trade; furthermore, price concessions often have to be made. Investors should be careful in trading small amounts of corporate bonds and be prepared for delays and costs. The price that appears in newspapers for these exchange-traded bonds may vary significantly from the actual price at which the bond trades.

Most corporate bonds are traded off the exchanges by institutions dealing in round lots of at least 250 bonds, and often larger amounts. This institutional market behaves independently of the bond trading on the exchanges, where a computer collects bids to buy and offers to sell from around the country and executes a trade when a match is made. At times, prices between the two markets can differ by several points.[22]

Put and Call Markets

Options trading on organized exchanges began in 1973. There are now five option exchanges, and they have standardized the terms of trade for these securities, thereby increasing their liquidity. The original option buyer or seller (writer) can easily close out a position by making an opposite transaction in one of these markets.

Each of these exchanges has a physical location, with a trading floor and designated areas for the options of each stock listed on the exchange to be traded. Members of each exchange buy and sell directly on the floor, with nonmembers using floor brokers to execute orders. Some exchanges use market makers, who are members of the exchange, to perform a dealer function; other exchanges use specialists. Market makers compete with each other to buy and sell options assigned to them, whereas specialists are charged with maintaining a fair orderly market in their assigned options. Both market makers and specialists are regulated by their respective exchanges as to what they can do in setting bid–asked spreads and in the sequence of prices at which their options trade.

---

[21]These are fixed, diversified portfolios of bonds sold in multiples of $1000 each (with a sales charge of about 4%) that pay interest monthly.

[22]See David Henry, "Patience Rewarded," *Forbes*, May 19, 1986, p. 82.

Regulation of the Securities Markets

Much of the legislation governing the securities markets and industry was enacted during the Great Depression. Many fraudulent and undesirable practices occurred in the 1920s, and the markets as a whole were shattered in the Crash of 1929. Congress subsequently sought to improve the stability and viability of the securities markets, enacting the basis of all securities regulation in the 1930s. Additional acts have been legislated over the last 50 years. Table 3-4 contains a brief description of the major legislation affecting securities markets.

The Securities and Exchange Commission

The **Securities and Exchange Commission (SEC)** was created in 1934 as an independent, quasi-judicial agency of the U.S. government. Its mission is to administer laws in the securities field and to protect investors and the public in securities transactions. The commission consists of five members

TABLE 3-4 ***Major Legislation Regulating the Securities Markets***

1. The Securities Act of 1933 (the "Securities Act") deals primarily with new issues of securities. The intent was to protect potential investors in new securities by requiring issuers to register an issue with full disclosure of information. False information is subject to criminal penalties and lawsuits by purchasers to recover lost funds.
2. The Securities Exchange Act of 1934 (SEA) extended the disclosure requirements to the secondary market and established the SEC to oversee registration and disclosure requirements. Organized exchanges are required to register with the SEC and agree to be governed by existing legislation.
3. The Maloney Act of 1936 extended SEC control to the OTC market. It provides for the self-regulation of OTC dealers through the National Association of Securities Dealers (NASD), which licenses and regulates members of OTC firms. The SEC has authority over the NASD, which must report all its rules to the SEC.
4. The Investment Company Act requires investment companies to register with the SEC and provides a regulatory framework within which they must operate. Investment companies are required to disclose considerable information and to follow procedures designed to protect their shareholders. This industry is heavily regulated.
5. The Investment Advisors Act of 1940 requires individuals or firms who sell advice about investments to register with the SEC. Registration connotes only compliance with the law. Almost anyone can become an investment advisor because the SEC cannot deny anyone the right to sell investment advice unless it can demonstrate dishonesty or fraud.
6. The Securities Investor Protection Act of 1970 established the Securities Investor Protection Corporation (SIPC) to act as an insurance company in protecting investors from brokerage firms that fail. Assessments are made against brokerage firms to provide the funds with backup government support available.
7. The Securities Act Amendments of 1975 was a far-reaching piece of legislation, calling for the SEC to move toward the establishment of a national market. This act abolished fixed brokerage commissions.

appointed by the president for five-year terms. Its staff consists of lawyers, accountants, security analysts, and others divided into divisions and offices (including nine regional offices).

In general, the SEC administers the securities laws previously mentioned (as well as others not mentioned). Thus, under the Securities Act of 1933, the SEC ensures that new securities being offered for public sale are registered with the commission, and under the 1934 act it does the same for securities trading on national exchanges. It is important to note that the registration of securities in no way ensures that investors purchasing them will not lose money. Registration means only that adequate disclosure has been made by the issuer. In fact, the SEC has no power to disapprove securities for lack of merit. The Securities Acts Amendments of 1964 directs the SEC to apply reporting provisions to most OTC stocks.

Under the two acts of 1940, investment companies and investment advisors must register with the SEC and disclose certain information. In effect, the SEC ensures that these two groups will meet the requirements of the laws affecting them. One problem, however, is that the number of registered investment advisers increased fourfold in the 1980s to over 16,000, and the number of investment companies increased to some 3500. The SEC has a staff of some 225 to deal with these two groups.

The SEC is required to investigate complaints or indications of violations in securities transactions. A good example is "insider trading," which has been a primary enforcement emphasis of the SEC. "Insiders" (officers and directors of corporations) are prohibited from misusing (i.e., trading on) corporate information not generally available to the public and are required to file reports with the SEC showing their equity holdings.

Several insider-trading "scandals" have been reported in recent years. Dennis Levine, a key member of the mergers and acquisitions department of Drexel Burnham Lambert, Inc., was charged with insider trading in a major case with many repercussions. A well-known arbitrageur, Ivan Boesky, was fined $100 million by the SEC in a highly publicized insider-trading case. Although questions remain about exactly what constitutes insider trading, even small investors can be charged with possessing "material, nonpublic information," as Box 3-2 illustrates.

Secondary Markets: The Mechanics of Trading

Opening a Brokerage Account

In general, it is quite easy for any responsible person to open a brokerage account. An investor selects a broker or brokerage house by personal contact, referral, reputation, and so forth. Member firms of the NYSE are supposed to learn certain basic facts about potential customers, but only minimal information normally is required; in fact, personal contact be-

BOX 3-2

HOW A ROUND OF GOLF COST $1 MILLION

A real estate developer was puzzled by his golfing buddies. They'd been friends almost all their lives, attending the same high school. They knocked off early nearly every Friday to golf together. But on the afternoon of March 7, 1986, they kept snickering about something they wouldn't share with the developer.

Only in the clubhouse after the round did one of the group who was the hub of this chatter finally tell the developer what he'd already told some of the others: Buy the stock of Revco Drug Stores. It hadn't been announced yet, but the big Ohio-based chain was going to be taken over by its management. "I know the guy doing the deal," the friend confided.

The discloser figured he was doing his friends a favor when he passed along his big secret. When they thought about it at all, they considered the hot tip and their subsequent trading in Revco nothing more than a pleasant and profitable diversion, hardly something they needed to worry about. Nearly two years later, one of the golfers got a phone call from someone who said he was a Securities and Exchange Commission investigator.

"Yeah, right, and I'm Ivan Boesky," he replied.

Not Funny

But in the eyes of the SEC, the businessmen were in a crucial respect indistinguishable from the notorious Wall Street arbitrager and securities felon. Two months ago, both of the individuals, two other friends and their stockbroker were charged by the SEC with insider trading. They have paid about $1 million in penalties and legal fees to settle the case. They have lain awake at night before giving testimony about—and in some cases, against—their oldest friends.

Source: Adapted from Thomas E. Richs, "How 4 Pals Who Mixed Golf and Stock Tips Landed in the Rough," *The Wall Street Journal,* July 21, 1989, p. A1. Reprinted by permission of *The Wall Street Journal,* © 1990 Dow Jones & Company, Inc. All Rights Reserved Worldwide.

tween broker and customer sometimes does not occur, with transactions carried out by telephone or in writing.

The most basic type of account is the **cash account,** whereby the customer pays the brokerage house the full price for any securities purchased. Many customers open a **margin account,** which allows the customer to borrow from the brokerage firm to purchase securities. (Margin is explained in some detail later.) The NYSE requires a minimum margin deposit of $2000 to open this type of account (regardless of the transaction contemplated).

In 1977, Merrill Lynch, the largest retail brokerage firm in the United States, started a new type of account, which it called the cash management account (CMA). This account, which requires a minimum balance to open and the payment of an annual fee, automatically reinvests the account holders' free credit balances in shares of a money market fund chosen by the investor. Account holders are issued bank checks and a VISA card. Checks can be written against the account's assets, both cash and securities. In addition, instant loans based on the marginable securities in the account can be obtained for virtually any purpose, not just securities transactions, at the current broker's call money rate plus 0.75% to 2.25%. Each month the customer receives a comprehensive summary statement. The CMA account was phenomenally successful, and by 1982 virtually all large brokerage firms were offering similar accounts.

The newest tack in brokerage accounts is for brokers to act as middlemen, matching clients with independent money managers.[23] The new phrase is "capturing client assets." Large brokerage houses such as Merrill Lynch and Dean Witter Reynolds offer managed accounts for investors with a minimum of $100,000 to commit. Using the broker as a consultant, the client chooses an outside money manager from a list provided by the broker. Under a "**wrap**" **account,** all costs are wrapped in one fee—the cost of the broker-consultant, the money manager, and transactions costs. For stocks, a typical fee is 3% of the assets managed (and less for larger accounts). Under a "directed commission" approach, the client pays the money manager, who routes orders through the broker-consultant. The brokerage firm uses part of the commissions to compensate the broker for his or her consulting services.

The Securities Investor Protection Corporation (SIPC), a quasi-government agency, insures each customer account of member brokers against brokerage firm failure. Each account is covered for as much as $500,000 (coverage of cash is limited to $100,000).[24] From 1970 to 1990, SIPC paid out in excess of $180 million in helping some 200,000 investors recover over 1 billion from failed brokers with SIPC insurance. (Would you want a broker without such insurance?)

How Orders Work

On the Organized Exchanges *Traditionally,* a typical order from an investor for 100 shares of IBM might be handled as follows. The investor phones his or her broker, or registered representative, and asks how IBM is doing. The broker can punch a few buttons on an electronic console and immediately see the last trade for IBM, as well as other information, such as the high and low for the day and the number of shares traded. Assuming that the investor is willing to pay the last trade price for IBM, or a price close to that,

[23]This discussion is based on James A. White, "Stockbrokers Turning into 'Consultants,' " *The Wall Street Journal,* March 1, 1990, p. C1.

[24]In addition, many brokerage firms carry additional insurance, often for several million dollars, to provide even more protection for customers.

the broker can be instructed to buy, say, 100 shares of IBM "at the market." This order will be transmitted to the broker's New York office, and then to the member partner on the exchange floor (or the broker may work through some other exchange member). The representative on the floor will go to the trading post for IBM, where the specialist handling IBM is located, and ask, "How's IBM?"

The specialist is charged with maintaining a fair and orderly market in IBM. The specialist knows the current quotes for IBM because he or she keeps a record of all limit orders for the stock. Assuming no other member partner has come to the post to sell IBM, the specialist will quote a current bid and asked price for 100 shares. The partner then indicates that there is a purchase order to be filled (at the asking price). A confirmation is relayed back to the investor's broker, who notifies the investor.

The trade will appear on the NYSE consolidated tape, which since June 1975 has printed transactions for all NYSE-listed securities on participating markets; in 1989 this involved six stock exchanges (in addition to the NYSE), the over-the-counter market, and Instinet. Daily papers such as *The Wall Street Journal* report the high and low prices for each stock wherever they occur.[25] Share volume shown on the tape increased to a record 50 billion shares in 1989, with the NYSE accounting for over 84% of consolidated volume.

In actuality, the NYSE has become highly automated.[26] An electronic system matches buy and sell orders entered before the market opens, setting the opening price of a stock. The NYSE has SuperDOT, an electronic order-routing system for NYSE-listed securities. Member firms send orders directly to the post where the securities are traded, and confirmation of trading is returned directly to the member firm over the same system.

As a part of SuperDOT, the Opening Automated Report Service (OARS) automatically and continuously scans member firms' preopening buy and sell orders, presenting the imbalance to the specialist up to the opening of a stock. OARS handles preopening market orders up to 30,099 shares. SuperDOT also includes a postopening market order system designed to accept postopening market orders of up to 2099 shares. Some 99% of market orders in 1989 were executed and reported back to the member firm sending the order within two minutes.

Specialist's volume handling and processing capabilities have been enhanced electronically by the creation of "The Electronic Books," with more than 1900 stocks on such systems by the end of 1989. These work stations are database systems that assist in recording and reporting limit

---

[25]An investor needs to realize that a limit order placed to sell a stock at, say, $101\frac{1}{2}$ may not have been executed, although the quotes from yesterday's trading in today's paper show a price of $101\frac{1}{2}$ as the high. This will happen if the investor's broker placed the order on the NYSE, but the stock's high was reached on the Pacific Stock Exchange, for example.

[26]The same is true for the Amex.

and market orders. This electronic system helps to eliminate paperwork and processing orders.[27]

In the Over-the-Counter Market Traditionally, dealers in the OTC market arrive at the prices of securities by both negotiating with customers specifically and by making competitive bids. Dealers match the forces of supply and demand, with each dealer making a market in certain securities. They do this by standing ready to buy a particular security from a seller or to sell it to a buyer. Dealers quote bid and asked prices for each security; the **bid price** is the highest price offered by the dealer; the **asked price** is the lowest price at which the dealer is willing to sell. The dealer profits from the spread between these two prices.

Stocks traded on NASDAQ average about 10 market makers per security, which can help to keep the spread small. As of 1985, the Small Order Execution System (SOES) included all NASDAQ issues. All SOES trades are automatically executed at the best price available in NASDAQ, as automatically reported to NASDAQ.[28] As explained previously, NASDAQ/NMS stocks are reported differently.

How well does NASDAQ work for the investor? This is not an easy question to answer. It is important to remember that the auction markets use specialists and that the OTC market uses dealers, and the two represent different systems. This issue will be considered in more detail in Chapter 8.

Types of Orders

Three basic types of orders are used by investors: **market orders, limit orders,** and **stop orders.** Each of these orders is explained in Table 3-5. Investors are often advised today to enter limit orders whenever possible in order to avoid the range of prices that may result from a market order.

Investors can enter limit or stop orders as *day orders,* which are effective for only one day, or as *good-until-canceled orders,* which remain in effect for six months unless canceled or renewed.

A standard order is a *round lot,* which is 100 or a multiple of 100 shares; an *odd lot* is any number of shares between 1 and 99. Odd lots have traditionally cost the transactor an extra $\frac{1}{8}$ or $\frac{1}{4}$ of a point. Odd lots are now executed by the NYSE directly by computer. Total odd-lot volume on the NYSE amounted to only 324 million shares in 1989, with sales outnumbering purchases by a substantial amount. Some large brokerage firms now handle their own odd lots, and most investors who transact in odd lots are actually transacting with a dealer.

---

[27]This information is based on *Fact Book 1990,* New York Stock Exchange, Inc., 1990, p. 23.
[28]A 5000-share limit for NASDAQ and a 1000-share limit for NASDAQ/NMS was in effect in 1985.

TABLE 3-5 ***Types of Orders Used by Investors***

1. *Market orders,* the most common type of order, instruct the broker to buy or sell the securities immediately at the best price available. As a representative of the buyer or seller, it is incumbent upon the broker to obtain the best price possible. A market order ensures that the transaction will be carried out, but the exact price at which it will occur is not known until its execution and subsequent confirmation to the customer.
2. *Limit orders* specify a particular price to be met or bettered. They may result in the customer obtaining a better price than with a market order or in no purchase or sale occurring because the market price never reaches the specified limit. The purchase or sale will occur only if the broker obtains that price, or betters it (lower for a purchase, higher for a sale). Limit orders can be tried immediately or left with the broker for a specific time or indefinitely. In turn, the broker leaves the order with the specialist who enters it in the limit book.
   EXAMPLE: Assume the current market price of a stock is $50. An investor might enter a buy limit order at $47; if the stock declines in price to $47, this limit order, which is on the specialist's book, will be executed at $47 or less. Similarly, another investor might enter a sell limit order for this stock at $55; if the price of this stock rises to $55, this investor's shares will be sold.
3. *Stop orders* specify a certain price at which a market order takes effect. For example, a stop order to sell at $50 becomes a market order to sell as soon as the market price reaches (declines to) $50. However, the order may not be filled exactly at $50 because the closest price at which the stock trades may be $49\frac{7}{8}$. The exact price specified in the stop order is therefore not guaranteed and may not be realized.
   EXAMPLE 1: A sell stop order can be used to protect a profit in the case of a price decline. Assume, for example, that a stock bought at $32 currently trades at $50. The investor does not want to limit additional gains, but may wish to protect against a price decline. To lock in most of the profit, a sell stop order could be placed at $47.
   EXAMPLE 2: A buy stop order could be used to protect a profit from a short sale. Assume an investor sold short at $50, and the current market price of the stock is $32. A buy stop order placed at, say, $36 would protect most of the profit from the short sale.

Clearing Procedures

Most securities are sold on a *regular way* basis, meaning the *settlement date* is five *business* days after the trade date.[29] On the settlement date the customer becomes the legal owner of any securities bought, or gives them up if sold, and must settle with the brokerage firm by that time.[30] Most customers allow their brokerage firm to keep their securities in a **street name,** that is, the name of the brokerage firm. The customer receives a monthly statement showing his or her position as to cash, securities held, any funds borrowed from the broker, and so on.

Brokerage houses must settle all transactions with the other party to the transaction, either another brokerage house or the specialist. A clearing

[29] A sale could be made as a "cash" transaction, which requires delivery and settlement the same day.

[30] The purchaser of securities typically will not be able to take physical delivery of the securities on the settlement date because they will not be available by then.

house facilitates this process by taking the records of all transactions made by its members during a day, verifying both sides of the trades, and netting out the securities and money due or to be paid each member. Members of clearing houses include brokerage houses, banks, and others involved with securities. The National Securities Clearing Corporation operates such a central clearing house for trades on the New York and American stock exchanges and in the OTC markets.

Use of stock certificates as part of the settlement is dying out in the United States. The Depository Trust Company (DTC) has helped to eliminate their use by placing these transactions on computers. Members (brokers and dealers) who own certificates (in street name) deposit them in an account and can then deliver securities to each other in the form of a bookkeeping entry. This *book-entry system,* as opposed to the actual physical possession of securities in either registered or "bearer" form, is essential to minimize the tremendous amount of paperwork that would otherwise occur with stock certificates.[31]

Commissions

For most of its long history, the New York Stock Exchange required its members to charge fixed (and minimum) commissions.[32] Although this was a source of bitter contention and gave rise to the third market, as discussed earlier, little changed until 1975, when Congress, as part of the Securities Acts Amendments of 1975, eliminated all fixed commissions. Fees are supposed to be negotiated, with each firm free to act independently.

Investors can attempt to negotiate with their brokers, and different brokers charge different commissions. In practice, the larger retail brokerage houses have set commissions at specified rates for the typical small investor. However, the overall competition in the industry has an effect on the rates that are set. By 1989 the lack of business from investors allowed customers to get 25% off the large firms' posted rates, and investors who generate a couple of commissions could do better. In recognition of the bargaining occurring, Merrill Lynch did not publish a schedule of commission rates. Customers are free to shop around, and smart ones do so.

In contrast, negotiated rates are the norm for institutional customers, who deal in large blocks of stock. The rates charged institutional investors have declined drastically, from an average of 25 cents a shares in 1975 to an average of 6–7 cents a share or less. Institutional investors also receive a

[31]At the beginning of 1986, almost two-thirds of all outstanding corporate bonds and over one-half of all NYSE common stocks and all outstanding municipal bonds had been "immobilized" by deposit in DTC vaults. As of August, 1986, all marketable Treasury securities were issued in book-entry form only.

[32]Technically, this is price fixing and therefore illegal, but the NYSE was exempted from prosecution under the antitrust laws.

TABLE 3-6 ***Representative Brokerage Commission Schedule***

Shares Bought or Sold	Price per Share	Representative Full-Commission Broker	Representative Discount Broker
100	$60	$ 98	$ 49
500	15	181	85
3000	25	879	209

better deal when trading in OTC stocks. The spread, or difference between the bid and the asked price, averages about 23 cents a share for individual investors but only 6 cents to 13 cents a share for institutional investors.

One significant result of the elimination of fixed brokerage commissions is the birth and growth of the **discount brokers.** These brokerage houses concentrate on executing orders and charge only for this service. In contrast, a full-service brokerage house offers a variety of services, particularly advice and research recommendations.

The result of the change in 1975 was to *unbundle* brokerage services so that customers pay only for the services they really want. The discount houses are the ultimate in unbundling, essentially offering only execution services at rates 30% to 70% lower than the full-service houses. By the mid-1980s they had about 20% of the retail market. Table 3-6 illustrates some "representative" brokerage commissions for both a full-service brokerage firm and a typical discount broker (obviously, exact rates vary between firms).[33]

Margin

As previously noted, accounts at brokerage houses can be either cash accounts or margin accounts. With a margin account the customer can pay part of the total amount due and borrow the remainder from the broker, who in turn typically borrows from a bank to finance customers. The bank charges the broker the broker loan rate, and the broker in turn charges the customer this rate plus approximately 1% to 1.5% more.

The Board of Governors of the Federal Reserve System (Fed) has the authority to specify the *initial margin,* which is used as a policy device to influence the economy. Historically, initial margin for stocks has ranged between 40% and 100%, with a current level of 50% for a number of years.[34] Furthermore, all exchanges and brokers require a *maintenance margin* below which the actual margin cannot go. The NYSE requires an investor to

[33]Some discount brokers charge considerably less than the typical discount broker. Known as "deep discount" firms, they may charge 40% less than the average discount brokerage firm.

[34]Exchanges and brokerage houses can require more initial margin than that set by the Fed if they choose.

maintain an equity of 25% of the market value of any securities held (and in practice brokers usually require 30% or more) on long positions; maintenance margins on short positions are higher.

Margin is that part of a transaction's value that a customer must pay to initiate the transaction; that is, it is that part of the total value of the transaction that cannot be borrowed from the broker.

Example. If the initial margin requirement is 50% on a $10,000 transaction (100 shares at $100 per share), the customer must put up $5000, borrowing $5000 from the broker.[35] ▪

If the actual margin exceeds the initial margin, the excess margin could be withdrawn from the account or more stock could be purchased without additional cash. Conversely, if the actual margin declines below the initial margin, problems can arise, depending on the amount of the decline.

Example. Assume that the maintenance margin is 40%, with a 50% initial margin, and that the price of the stock declines from \$100 to \$90 per share. Equation 3-1 is used to calculate actual margin.[36]

$$\text{Actual margin} = \frac{\text{market value of securities} - \text{amount borrowed}}{\text{market value of securities}} \tag{3-1}$$

$$= \frac{\$9000 - \$5000}{\$9000} = 44.44\%$$

The actual margin is now between the initial margin of 50% and the maintenance margin of 40%. This would result in a *restricted account*, meaning that additional margin purchases are prohibited, although no additional equity (cash) has to be put into the account by the customer. ▪

A **margin call** is issued when the actual margin declines below the maintenance margin. If additional cash (or securities) is not advanced, the securities can be sold by the broker. Brokerage houses calculate the actual margin in their customers' accounts daily to determine if a margin call is required. This is known as having the brokerage accounts *marked to market.*

Example. Assume in the previous example that the maintenance margin is 25%. If the price of the stock drops to $80, the actual margin will be 37.5% [($8000 − $5000) / $8000]. Because this is above the maintenance margin, there is no margin call. However, if the price of the stock declines to $66.66, the actual margin will be 25% [($6666 − $5000)/$6666]. Any additional

---

[35]With a 60% requirement, the customer must initially put up $6000.

[36]The difference between the market value of the securities and the amount borrowed is the investor's equity.

decline in price will result in a margin call, given a maintenance margin of 25%. If the price declines to \$60, for example, the amount of the margin call will be

$$\begin{aligned} \$6000 \times 25\% &= \$1500 \text{ the equity required} \\ \$6000 - \$5000 \text{ (the amount borrowed)} &= \underline{\$1000} \text{ current equity} \\ & \quad\;\; \$500 \text{ margin call} \end{aligned}$$

▪

Although the margin requirement for common stocks and convertible bonds is 50%, it is only 30% for "acceptable" municipal and corporate bonds. U.S. government securities require only 8% to 15% margin. Long positions in puts and calls are not marginable; therefore, option buyers must put up 100% cash when taking long positions. Uncovered short positions in puts and calls require margin from the investor. Thus, an investor with \$2000 equity in an option account who writes (sells) uncovered call contracts may have to post additional margin.[37]

INVESTMENTS INTUITION

The appeal of margin trading to investors is that it magnifies any gains on a transaction by the reciprocal of the margin requirement (i.e., 1/margin percentage; for example, with a margin of 40%, the magnification is 1/0.4 = 2.50). Unfortunately, the use of margin also magnifies any losses. Regardless of what happens, the margin trader must pay the interest costs on the margin account. An investor considering a margined stock purchase should remember that the stock price can go up, remain the same, or go down. In two of these three cases, the investor loses. Even if the stock goes up, the breakeven point is now higher by the amount of the interest charges.

Short Sales

The purchase of a security technically results in the investor being "long" the security. The security is bought, and owned, because the investor believes the price is likely to rise. But what if the investor thinks that a security will decline in price? If he or she owns it, it might be wise to sell. If the security is not owned, the investor wishing to profit from the expected decline in price can sell the security short. **Short sales** are a normal part of market transactions.

How can an investor sell short, which is to say sell something not

[37]The margin requirements have to be calculated on an individual basis. These requirements are exchange-imposed minimums, and some brokerage houses may have stricter requirements.

owned? Not owning the security to begin with, it will have to be borrowed from a third party. The broker, on being instructed to sell short, will make these arrangements for this investor by borrowing the security from those held in street-name margin accounts and, in effect, lending it to the short seller.[38]

The short seller's broker sells the borrowed security in the open market, exactly like any other sale, to some investor wishing to own it. The short seller expects the price of the security to decline. Assume that it does. The short seller instructs the broker to repurchase the security at the currently lower price and cancel the short position (by replacing the borrowed security). The investor profits by the difference between the price at which the borrowed stock was sold and the price at which it was repurchased.

Example. Assume an investor named Helen believes that the price of General Motors (GM) will decline over the next few months and wants to profit if her assessment is correct. She calls her broker with instructions to sell 100 shares of GM short (she does not own GM) at its current market price of $50 per share. The broker borrows 100 shares of GM from Kellie, who has a brokerage account with the firm and currently owns GM ("long"). The broker sells the 100 shares at $50 per share, crediting the $5000 proceeds (less commissions, which we will ignore for this example) to Helen's account.[39] Six months later the price of GM has declined, as predicted by Helen, and is now $38 per share. Satisfied with this drop in the price of GM, she instructs the broker to purchase 100 shares of GM and close out the short position. Her profit is $5000 − $3800, or $1200 (again, ignoring commissions). The broker replaces Kellie's missing stock with the just-purchased 100 shares, and the transaction is complete.[40] ▪

Several technicalities are involved in a short sale. These are outlined in Table 3-7.

How popular are short sales? In 1989, 3.0 billion shares (in round lots) were sold short on the NYSE, which was 7.2% of all reported sales. NYSE

---

[38]The securities could be borrowed from another broker. Also, individuals sometimes agree to lend securities to short sellers in exchange for interest-free loans equal to the collateral value of the securities sold short. Collateral value equals the amount of funds borrowed in a margin transaction.

[39]Note that Kellie knows nothing about this transaction, nor is she really affected. Kellie receives a monthly statement from the broker showing ownership of 100 shares of GM. Should Kellie wish to sell the GM stock while Helen is short, the broker will simply borrow 100 shares from Elizabeth, a third investor who deals with this firm and owns GM stock, to cover the sale. It is important to note that all of these transactions are book entries and do not typically involve the actual stock certificates.

[40]Notice that two trades are required to complete a transaction, or "round trip." Investors who purchase securities plan to sell them eventually. Investors who sell short plan to buy back eventually; they have simply reversed the normal buy–sell procedure by selling and then buying.

TABLE 3-7 ***The Details of Short Selling***

1. Dividends declared on any stock sold short must be covered by the short seller. After all, the person from whom the shares were borrowed still owns the stock and expects all dividends paid on it.
2. Short sellers must have a margin account to sell short and must put up margin as if they had gone long. The margin can consist of cash or any restricted securities held long.
3. The net proceeds from a short sale, plus the required margin, are held by the broker; thus, no funds are immediately received by the short seller. The lender must be fully protected. To do this, the account is marked-to-the-market (as mentioned earlier in connection with margin accounts). If the price of the stock declines as expected by the short seller, he or she can draw out the difference between the sale price and the current market price. If the price of the stock rises, however, the short seller will have to put up more funds.
4. There is no time limit on a short sale. Short sellers can remain short indefinitely. The only problem arises when the lender of the securities wants them back. In most cases the broker can borrow elsewhere, but in some situations, such as a thinly capitalized stock, this may not be possible.
5. Short sales are permitted only on rising prices, or an uptick. A short seller can sell short at the last trade price only if that price exceeded the last different price before it. Otherwise, they must wait for an uptick. Although the order to the broker can be placed at any time, it will not be executed until an uptick occurs.

members accounted for almost 70% of short sales on the NYSE, with specialists, who often sell short to meet public buy orders, accounting for about half of this total. Specialists, in their role of maintaining an orderly market, must often sell short to meet an inflow of buy orders. The public accounted for the remainder. Although individual investors have often bypassed short selling in the OTC market, this is changing as short selling has become more accessible to them.

The Changing Securities Markets

For the last 10 to 15 years the securities markets have been changing rapidly, with many more changes expected over the coming years. This is significant for at least two reasons. First, securities markets in the United States underwent relatively few changes for many years. The New York Stock Exchange enjoyed a monopoly position, which it defended vigorously. Second, investors need to understand how the markets are changing, and why. In all likelihood, the procedures and mechanics of trading used in the future will be very different from those of the past.

The Stimulus for Market Changes

At least two reasons account for markets undergoing such rapid changes:

1. The emerging role of the institutional investors in the marketplace.
2. The passage of the Securities Acts Amendments of 1975.

Institutional investors are very different from individual investors, for whom the securities exchanges were primarily designed. They have different requirements and different views, and their emergence as the dominant force in the market has necessitated significant changes in how markets are structured and operated.

The role of institutional investors can be appreciated by considering some statistics. Individual investors have been net sellers of stocks for a number of years, with the institutions absorbing these shares. The institutions owned about 35% of all NYSE-listed stocks by 1980 and accounted for half the value of all shares traded on the NYSE in that year.

Institutional investors often trade in large **blocks,** which are defined as transactions involving at least 10,000 shares. Large-block activity on the NYSE is an indicator of institutional participation. The average size of a trade on the NYSE has grown sharply over the years, doubling between 1981 and 1989. Block trades on the NYSE have increased year after year, and in 1989 an average of 3464 blocks changed hands each day, accounting for more than half of NYSE reported volume.[41] Block volume doubled from 1984 to 1989, and amounted to over 21 billion shares by 1990.

The growth of institutional trading that occurred in the 1960s and 1970s clashed head on with a basic NYSE rule requiring all members to charge a minimum fixed commission. This commission structure was designed with relatively small orders in mind and made no provision for the large institutional orders that were becoming more and more common. Substantial economies of scale exist in executing large orders, because a large element of fixed costs is involved in every trade, regardless of size. Brokerage firms were receiving excess returns on large orders. Knowing this, institutions sought changes in the minimum fixed commissions. The rise of the third market is a good example of changes occurring to accommodate the institutional investors. Negotiated commissions were the end result of the activity by institutions to obtain a change in the commission structure.

The second factor stimulating a change in our markets was the passage of the Securities Acts Amendments in 1975, the most far-reaching securities legislation since the 1930s. The purpose of this act is to promote a fully competitive national system of securities trading. The act called for a **national market system (NMS)** but left its final form undefined. The result was the evolution toward some type of national market, but its final form is not mandated and remains unknown.

---

[41] *New York Stock Exchange Fact Book 1990* (New York: New York Stock Exchange, 1989), p. 17.

The Form for a National Market

Given the congressional mandate for an NMS, and the changes that have occurred to date, what lies ahead? Although no one knows the exact form an NMS will take when fully developed, certain procedures and trends are emerging.

To achieve the goals of the 1975 act, the SEC has suggested four basic parts of an NMS foundation:

1. Negotiated brokerage commissions.
2. A central reporting mechanism for price quotations and transactions.
3. A central order routing system.
4. A national protection of limit orders.

The first of these was accomplished by the SEC in 1975. The second is operational and is a necessary ingredient in reducing market fragmentation, because it provides investors with the best trading data available.

The purpose of a central order routing system is to obtain the best executions possible for investors. This is accomplished by electronically routing orders to whatever market is offering the best price to a buyer or a seller. Such a system promotes competition and should lower spreads, because the dealers with the most attractive prices would automatically receive the orders. This system is progressing slowly, as the SEC experiments to find the most satisfactory procedure. Brokerage houses, in particular Merrill Lynch, now have electronic systems that search out the best market for a customer's order and send the order to that market quickly.

One alternative for a routing system is the **Intermarket Trading System (ITS),** a network of electronic terminals linking together eight markets.[42] The ITS allows brokers—as well as specialists and market makers trading for their own accounts—on any one of the eight markets to interact with their counterparts on any of the other exchanges. These participants would use the nationwide composite quotation system to check for a better price. However, the ITS system does not guarantee that the orders will be routed because NYSE brokers can ignore better quotes on other exchanges. It is the system favored by the NYSE.

Like other recent developments in the marketplace, ITS started slowly but has grown rapidly. Starting with 11 stocks on two exchanges in April 1978, it has expanded to 2082 issues, with volume of 2.3 billion shares, by year-end 1989.[43]

The fourth item, national protection of limit orders, would provide for

[42]The eight are the New York, American, Boston, Cincinnati, Midwest, Pacific, and Philadelphia exchanges and the NASD.

[43]The 2082 eligible stocks at the end of 1989 represented most of the stocks traded on more than one exchange; 1633 were listed on the NYSE and 449 on the Amex.

limit orders from all markets to be brought together, with execution priority depending only on price and time priority. Thus, orders would be filled on whichever exchange a limit price is reached, whereas now a limit order may be executed on the NYSE, although a different price is reached on other exchanges.

This part of a proposed NMS, known as a central limit order book (CLOB), has made the least progress. No nationwide system exists. The NYSE does have a limit order system as part of its superDOT electronic order-routing system. This system electronically files limit orders up to 30,099 shares.

Where do we go from here? Congress continues to press the SEC for an NMS, and the SEC in turn has stepped up the pressure on the industry. More changes will occur, but the final structure of the securities market cannot yet be predicted. An important development that could influence the direction and form of securities markets in the future is the emerging NASDAQ National Market System (NMS) discussed earlier. This system of trading OTC stocks with competitive multiple market makers reporting last-sale data continuously (i.e., real-time trade reporting) has made a significant impact in the relatively short time it has existed. Both individual and institutional investors are attracted by the increased visibility of the securities traded in this manner.

An important issue that remains controversial is the role of the NYSE, the dominant secondary market in the United States. Of special concern to many is the nearly 200-year-old specialist system, which the NYSE continues to defend and justify while others criticize it as a system not attuned to the needs of the modern market. At the beginning of 1990 two unreleased congressional studies were very critical of the way U.S. stocks are traded, with particular emphasis on the specialist system.[44] In effect, the reports expressed doubts that U.S. trading mechanisms were competitive with some in foreign countries, with the result that the NYSE may lose business to foreign exchanges. One person who worked on one of the reports claimed that a significant percentage of the volume in NYSE-listed stocks was being handled in the London market by institutional investors desiring to avoid the specialist system. The NYSE was expected to defend the specialist system vigorously, citing such evidence as the 1987 market crash, when the specialists stayed at their posts to handle orders while many over-the-counter dealers allegedly refused to answer the phone.

The Globalization of Securities Markets

By 1985 U.S. equities exchanges were seeking electronic linkages with foreign markets and barriers to international trading were falling. For

[44]The information in this paragraph is based on Kevin G. Salwen and Craig Torres, "Studies Criticize Big Board's System of Market Makers," *The Wall Street Journal*, January 18, 1990, pp. C1, C9.

example, the "Big Bang" occurred in October, 1986, when the London Stock Exchange eliminated fixed commissions and barriers to competition among brokers, market makers, and underwriters that had existed for many years. The deregulation of the third largest stock *exchange* in the world (after Tokyo and New York) will have important implications for global trading.

By 1988 NASDAQ's communications linkage with its counterpart in London involved quotations and transaction information on about 700 securities. NASD members in the United Kingdom can use NASDAQ as if they were located in this country. Also in 1988 NASDAQ began exchanging quotations on a few securities with Singapore.

As the 1990s began, the move toward around-the-clock trading continued, although slowly. One step in that direction was the start-up of evening sessions for futures trading on the Chicago Board of Trade. Trading in Treasury bond futures was averaging some 15,000 contracts, with the Japanese heavily involved. In early 1990 the NYSE began to study the possibility of an after-hours trading system that would lead to 24-hour trading. The NYSE is being pressured by the SEC to do this, but movement is slow because of resistance from exchange members, such as specialists and brokers. Also in early 1990 the NASD announced plans to expand its planned London trading system to include NYSE and Amex-traded American depository receipts (explained in Chapter 20).[45] It was already planning to start predawn trading in roughly 300 OTC issues in its NASDAQ system sometime in 1990, including about 70 securities listed on the London Stock Exchange. The NASDAQ market would have to open at 4 A.M. Eastern time to accomplish this.

The Changing Nature of Wall Street

To complete our discussion of the changing nature of the securities markets, consider the changes that have been occurring in the daily functioning of the investments business. These changes affect the people who are currently employed in the industry and those thinking about careers in the field.

Areas in demand in the investments field change markedly from time to time. Trading was a major activity in the 1970s, when markets were much more regulated and those not in the business were unable to access basic information such as stock quotes. The stock and bond sales people, the traders, and the securities analysts were in demand and often earned large salaries and bonuses.

By the early 1980s the *sell-side* people, who sell securities to both institu-

[45]This information is based on Richard E. Rustin, "NASD to Offer Big Board Stocks to Catch the Early-Bird Trader," *The Wall Street Journal*, December 7, 1989, p. C1.

tions and individuals, were experiencing a severe decline.[46] Fixed brokerage commissions had been abolished, corporations were allowed to auction their bonds, and individuals began to gain access to once-proprietary information, such as stock quotes, by leasing or purchasing services that make quotes available. Although the traders were still in demand, their situation was starting to change.

The services of top traders became less and less important as technological advances increased. Trading profits seemed more difficult to realize as competition increased, both from foreign securities firms and from domestic banks as deregulation allowed them to conduct activities formerly prohibited. Profit margins continued to decline on most securities handled by the big firms. One large money management firm claimed publicly that it paid an average commission of only 2 cents a share in 1988.

As the 1980s came to a close, the new action on Wall Street was in two areas. Traders and analysts were moving to the *buy side,* a general term covering institutional investors and money managers who manage portfolios and thus buy Wall Street's products. The really hot opportunies in the late 1980s were for specialists in mergers, leveraged buyouts, and junk bonds. In the 1980s, investment banking was where the action, and the rewards, were. This is not expected to be true in the 1990s.

Consider the scope of merger activity in the 1980s. *Fortune*'s annual list of the 50 largest acquisitions, restructurings, public offerings, and stock buybacks for 1988 amounted to about $112 billion, not including the largest leveraged buyout up until that time, the $25 billion RJR Nabisco deal (which was not completed until 1989). *Fortune* estimated that the dealmakers—the investment bankers and related people—took in at least $687 million in advisory fees (not counting commissions on related financings and not counting the RJR deal).[47]

By early 1990, the situation was starting to change drastically. Drexel Burnham Lambert, the epitome of the go-go atmosphere of the 1980s involving corporate takeovers, famous corporate raiders like Pickens and Icahn, and junk bonds (which Drexel made famous, or infamous), filed for bankruptcy in February, 1990. Some 5000 people lost their jobs. On March 1, 1990, Shearson Lehman Hutton announced the layoff of 2000 employees. This brought to more than 40,000 the number of securities industry employees laid off since the market crash of October 1987, with more expected. For example, Merrill Lynch was expected to lay off at least 3000 employees in 1990.

For insights into how Wall Street may change in the 1990s, see Box 3-3.

---

[46]This discussion is based on Matthew Winkler and William Power, "Along Wall Street, Once-Mighty Traders Are Reduced to Pawns," *The Wall Street Journal,* July 20, 1989, p. A1.
[47]See Ronald Henkoff, "Deals of the Year," *Fortune,* January 30, 1989, p. 162.

BOX 3-3

WALL STREET IN THE 1990s

Is the securities firm of the future the securities firm of the past?

That's what some soothsayers predict, looking at the success stories amid Wall Street's recent woes.

What threads these firms together as other securities firms struggle is that they have stuck to their knitting. These firms, to one degree or another, have figured out where their strengths lie and have avoided expanding into areas they know little about. And that, analysts and securities executives say, is likely to define the successful Wall Street investment firm of the 1990s.

That would mark a sharp reversal from the go-go 80s, when many big securities firms bit off far more than they could chew. Merrill Lynch & Co. and Shearson Lehman Hutton Inc. plowed into nearly every hot product, from mortgage-backed securities and high-yield junk bonds to risky real-estate partnerships.

The yen for smaller shops has led to a flurry of investment boutiques. Boutiques will continue to bloom in the 1990s, many executives say.

Whatever the size, focus will work far better than fragmentation. To thrive, securities firms will have to sit back, scrutinize their strengths, and return to basics, say securities executives.

Investment banks are likely to pay more attention to research. But they will focus on research involving junk bonds and merchant banking, not the traditional stock and bond research that many investors increasingly are shunning, executives say. Both merchant banking, where firms invest their own money in deals, and junk bonds have been highly profitable until recently, but have proved treacherous for those firms whose controls have lapsed.

For all Wall Street firms, industry executives say, times will be tough, and cost cutting will continue. Accountability will count. And investment bankers will have to get used to more modest pay, analysts say.

For Wall Street's big, struggling retail firms that cater to individual investors, the saving grace may be asset management, executives say. Despite other financial problems, for instance, Merrill and Shearson have strong money-management units that will generate strong profits. That is because managing investment protfolios for investors is a money machine even when the investors aren't trading much. Analysts look for other firms to step up their money-management activities.

Source: Adapted from Michael Siconolfi, "Will Wall Street Find Its Future in the Past?" *The Wall Street Journal*, February 9, 1990, pp. C1, C12. Reprinted by permission of *The Wall Streeet Journal*,

Summary

- Financial markets include primary markets, where new securities are sold, and secondary markets, where existing securities are traded.
- Primary markets involve investment bankers who specialize in selling

new securities. They offer the issuer several functions, including advisory, underwriting, and marketing services.

- Alternatives to the traditional public placements include private placements and unsyndicated offerings.
- Secondary markets are markets where existing securities trade.
- The equity markets consist of auction markets (exchanges) and negotiated markets (over-the-counter, or OTC, market). Brokers act as intermediaries, representing both buyers and sellers; dealers make markets in securities, buying and selling for their own account.
- On the New York Stock Exchange (NYSE), still the premier secondary market, specialists act to provide a continuous market for NYSE stocks.
- The Amex, on which fewer and generally smaller stocks trade, resembles the NYSE in its operations. Finally, several regional exchanges around the country list small companies of limited interest as well as securities traded on the NYSE and Amex.
- The OTC market is a network of dealers making markets in unlisted securities. The National Association of Security Dealers (NASD) oversees OTC practices.
- NASDAQ, an automated quotation system, provides current bid–asked prices for over 4000 stocks, enhancing OTC trading. A new subcomponent of NASDAQ, the NASDAQ National Market System (NMS), offers multiple market makers and up-to-the-minute price information in a format similar to that on the organized exchanges.
- Although some bonds are traded on the NYSE (and to a lesser extent on the Amex), most bond trading occurs in the OTC market.
- Although Treasury bonds and federal agency bonds enjoy broad markets, the markets for municipal bonds and corporate bonds are often less liquid.
- Puts and calls are traded on five option exchanges under standardized terms of trade. Warrants are traded on the same markets as equities.
- The Securities and Exchange Commission administers the securities laws, investigating complaints or violations.
- With a cash brokerage account, the customer pays in full on the settlement date; with a margin account money can be borrowed from the broker to finance purchases.
- Most orders sent to the exchanges involve a specialist and are now highly automated.
- Market orders are executed at the best price available, whereas limit orders specify a particular price to be met or bettered. Stop orders specify a certain price at which a market order is to take over.
- Brokerage commissions now are negotiable. Full-line brokerage houses charge more than discount brokers but offer recommendations.
- Margin is the equity an investor has in a transaction. The Federal Reserve sets an initial margin, but all exchanges and brokers require a maintenance margin. An insufficient amount of equity in a margined position can result in a margin call.

- An investor sells short if a security's price is expected to decline. The investor borrows the securities sold short from the broker, hoping to replace them through a later purchase at a lower price.
- The securities markets are changing rapidly, stimulated by the demands of the institutional investors and by the mandate of the Securities Acts Amendments of 1975 to create a national market system (NMS). Although the exact form the NMS will take remains unknown, rapid changes in the securities markets will continue.
- Securities markets increasingly are linked globally.
- Wall Street changed significantly in the 1980s and will continue to do so in the 1990s.

Key Words

Asked price
Auction market
Bid price
Blocks
Broker
Cash account
Dealer
Discount broker
Fourth market
Instinet
Intermarket trading system (ITS)
Investment banking firm
Limit orders
Margin
Margin account
Margin call
Market order
NASDAQ
NASDAQ National Market System (NASDAQ/NMS)
National Association of Security Dealers (NASD)
National market system (NMS)
Negotiated market
New York Stock Exchange (NYSE)
Over-the-counter (OTC) market
Primary market
Private placement
Program trading
Prospectus
Secondary market
Securities and Exchange Commission (SEC)
Shelf rule
Short sale
Specialist
Stop order
Street name
Syndicate
Third market
Underwriting
"Wrap" account

Questions

3-1 Discuss the importance of the financial markets to the U.S. economy. Can primary markets exist without secondary markets?

3-2 Discuss the functions of an investment banker.

3-3 Outline the process for a primary offering of securities involving investment bankers.

3-4 Outline the structure of equity markets in the United States. Distinguish between auction markets and negotiated markets.

3-5 In what way is an investment banker similar to a commission broker?

3-6 Explain the role of the specialists, describing the two roles they perform. How do they act to maintain an orderly market?

3-7 Do you think that specialists should be closely monitored and regulated because of their limit books?

3-8 Is there any similarity between an over-the-counter dealer and a specialist on an exchange?

3-9 Explain the difference between NASD and NASDAQ.

3-10 Distinguish between the third market and the fourth market.

3-11 Identify the legislative act that
(a) initiated the regulation of securities markets by the federal government
(b) extended disclosure requirements to secondary issues
(c) established the Securities and Exchange Commission
(d) called for the creation of a national market system (NMS).

3-12 Discuss the advantages and disadvantages of a limit order versus a market order. How does a stop order differ from a limit order?

3-13 What is meant by selling securities on a "regular way" basis?

3-14 What are the advantages and disadvantages of using a street name?

3-15 Explain the margin process, distinguishing between initial margin and maintenance margin. Who sets these margins?

3-16 What conditions result in an account being "restricted"? What prompts a margin call?

3-17 How can an investor sell a security not currently owned?

3-18 What conditions must be met for an investor to sell short?

3-19 What are two primary factors accounting for the rapid changes in U.S. securities markets?

3-20 Name at least four recent changes in securities markets and trading procedures.

3-21 List the four basic parts of a National Market System as suggested by the Securities and Exchange Commission. What is the current status of these four items?

3-22 Why do you think the New York Stock Exchange favors the Intermarket Trading System (ITS)?

3-23 Discuss recent international developments that relate to U.S. financial markets.

3-24 How does the NASDAQ differ from the conventional OTC market? What are its implications for the future?

3-25 Explain the difference, relative to the current market price of a stock, between the following types of orders: sell limit, buy limit, buy stop, and sell stop.

3-26 What is the margin requirement for U.S. government securities?

3-27 What is the basic nature of the changes in Wall Street regarding specialties in demand?

3-28 What is a wrap account? How does it involve a change in the traditional role of the broker?

Problems

3-1 (a) Consider an investor who purchased a stock at \$100 per share. The current market price is \$125. At what price would a limit order be placed to assure a profit of \$30 per share?
(b) What type of stop order would be placed to ensure a profit of at least \$20 per share?

3-2 Assume an investor sells short 200 shares of stock at \$75 per share. At what price must the investor cover the short sale in order to realize a gross profit of \$5000? \$1000?

3-3 Assume that an investor buys 100 shares of stock at \$50 per share and the stock rises to \$60 per share. What is the gross profit, assuming an initial margin requirement of 50%? 40%? 60%?

3-4 Assume an initial margin requirement of 50% and a maintenance margin of 30%. An investor buys 100 shares of stock on margin at \$60 per share. The price of the stock subsequently drops to \$50.
(a) What is the actual margin at \$50?
(b) The price now rises to \$55. Is the account restricted?
(c) If the price declines to \$49, is there a margin call?
(d) Assume that the price declines to \$45. What is the amount of the margin call? At \$35?

Selected References

Factual information concerning major secondary markets can be found in

NASD Fact Book. Annual. Washington, D.C. National Association of Securities Dealers, Inc.

New York Stock Exchange, *Fact Book.* Annual. New York: New York Stock Exchange, Inc.

CHAPTER 4

Sources of Investment Information

Investments is an information-oriented subject. Investors make their investment decisions on the basis of their expectations for the future. The fact that a particular common stock rose or fell 50 (or 150) points last year is of little current value to prospective buyers or sellers. What matters is its prospects for the coming year, and to assess these prospects investors need information about securities.

The problem that most investors face is not obtaining information, but selectively choosing among a bewildering number of sources and an almost endless flow of facts and figures. The United States is an information-oriented society, in which there is a proliferation of printed and computer-accessible data that have no end in sight. How, then, can the investor cope? The answer involves recognizing one's own needs, knowing what is available, and proceeding from there in a reasonable manner.

Before reviewing the sources of investment information, it is worthwhile to evaluate the use of the information.

Users of Investment Information

Chapter 1 discussed some external factors affecting the investment decision process. One of these factors is the environment in which investors find themselves. Two broad categories of investors are playing the investments game, individual and institutional investors. Although both groups have the same basic objectives, they go about their investment process somewhat differently. Each has its own needs and uses for information. In the case of investment information, we can begin to appreciate why this distinction was made in Chapter 1.

Individual Investors

The average investor in securities is a part-timer, with neither the ability nor the time to evaluate a large (and often complex) flow of information. Most individual investors have a job, and a life, apart from investing. Individuals have an opportunity cost in obtaining investment information, such as reading publications, tracking stock prices, and building files (printed or computerized) on securities. This opportunity cost is the time and resources foregone that could have been used in other endeavors.

There is also a question of efficiency. What can most investors expect to collect or learn in the way of basic information (as opposed to "insights") that is not already known by the market as a whole? Unless they are particularly diligent or insightful, chances are that the information has been collected and is available, if only they know where to look.

Where does this leave individual investors who need information to make investment decisions? What information should be sought? The astute investor needs to understand the valuation process and the basics of portfolio management, both of which constitute the remainder of this book. As will be seen in the following chapters, investors should follow certain procedures in analyzing various securities. A knowledge of these procedures will suggest the primary types of information of interest to investors.

After learning about the valuation and management of bonds, for example, investors will quickly appreciate the necessity of knowing about the level of and movements in interest rates, which affect all bonds (and, indeed, all securities); therefore, they should be aware of the general state of the economy, and in particular, government actions in the form of monetary and fiscal policies. Government publications will be helpful here, as will certain analyses of the economy regularly published by banks and brokerage houses.

In the case of equities, a three-step valuation process will be described in Chapter 9. This involves analyzing, first, the overall economy and state of the stock market, then industries, and finally companies. Individual investors need to obtain information that will help them to make intelligent appraisals of each of these three steps, and information is available on all three.

In the final analysis, most individuals who invest can do only so much in the way of obtaining and evaluating information. They need to recognize fully their constraints and limitations. All investors must have information to invest intelligently; the question is what kind and how much.

Institutional Investors

At the other end of the scale are the institutional investors, whose full-time job is to value securities and manage portfolios. These institutions have staffs that specialize by type of job, such as security analyst or portfolio manager; by area, such as common stock analyst versus bond analyst; and by other designations, such as a computer industry analyst or an automobile industry analyst.

Institutional investors have economists, accountants, computer specialists, and others on whom to rely. They have massive computer facilities and information banks. They can purchase information from other specialists or build their own unique databases. In short, institutional investors can do what needs to be done in collecting and managing information.

What does all of this mean? First of all, it is reasonable to assume that institutional investors have access to, and use, a wide variety of information in making their investment decisions. Individual investors should assume that, if information is potentially useful, manageable, and obtainable on a reasonable basis, some institutional investor has it. Second, it means that for most information, it is more efficient to let the institutions and advisory organizations collect and distribute it. Individual investors cannot reasonably expect to duplicate the thorough, ongoing efforts of institutions whose job it is to collect the information and use it and, in the process, make it known.

As discussed in Chapter 1, the disparity between the resources and abilities of the two groups does not mean that individual investors are severely disadvantaged. Individual investors may be able to interpret the same information used by institutional investors in a more insightful manner, thereby deriving additional benefit from it. To do this, however, the investor must know something about the sources of investment information available, to which we now turn.

A Users' Guide to Investment Information

This discussion is organized into two major parts, published information and computerized information. In the next section, the major sources of published information available to individual investors will be discussed *roughly* in order of their general availability and use by investors. The objective in this chapter is to provide a concise view of what is available that is likely to be of use to different investors, depending on their needs and abilities. This information will be expanded on at appropriate places throughout the remainder of the book.

Next, computerized sources of information are considered. Although computer information has traditionally been of little direct use to the typical individual investor, institutions use it extensively and investors can obtain some or all of the results from them. Furthermore, the dramatic rise of the personal computer is radically changing the accessibility of computerized investment information.

Published Sources of Information

The Financial Press

Virtually all investors have access to, and read, the general financial press on a daily or weekly basis because of its widespread availability and timeliness. This information may appear daily and weekly, in the case of newspapers, or weekly or biweekly, in the case of magazines, such as *Business Week* and *Forbes*, respectively.

Newspapers Perhaps the most popular and best-known source of daily financial information is *The Wall Street Journal* (*WSJ*).[1] It provides detailed

[1]An alternative source is *The New York Times*, a daily newspaper known for its large business and financial coverage. Much of this information parallels that contained in the *WSJ*.

coverage of financial and business-related news, on both a national and world level. Daily quotations from the principal bond, option, and stock markets are a well-known feature of the *WSJ*. Of particular interest to many investors is earnings information on various corporations, on both a reported basis, in the form of quarterly and annual earnings reports, and a prospective basis, in the form of news reports concerning expected earnings. The *WSJ* carries several columns that may be of interest to investors, including "Heard on the Street," "Abreast of the Market," "Bond Market," and "Dividend News."

Barron's, like the *WSJ*, is published by Dow Jones; it is a weekly newspaper with more detailed articles on general business topics and particular companies. It carries weekly price and volume quotations for all financial markets as well as a large amount and variety of statistics on assets, markets, economic variables, indicators, and so forth.[2] *Barron's* also includes regular columns on weekly activities in the stock market, the bond market, the options market, commodities, the real estate market, the international situation, and dividend news.

The *M/G Financial Weekly* is a weekly newspaper delivered on Monday. It contains detailed information (e.g., earnings, dividends, prices, and volume) for roughly 3400 securities, separated into industry groups.[3] Each week the performance of these industry groups is shown for the current week and the last 4, 13, 52 weeks. Numerous charts and tables are provided on the market indices, dividend yields, P/E ratios, volume, and so forth. Regular columns include fixed-income securities, the "market week," selected research reports, and other items of current interest.

The Wall Street Transcript is a weekly paper specializing in detailed reports on individual companies. It also features interviews with market professionals.

Magazines A wide variety of financial magazines exist. This discussion outlines some of the better-known general magazines. Specialized magazines include *Pension and Investment Age*, intended for those people involved in managing or overseeing pension fund assets, and the *OTC Review*, obviously focusing on the OTC market. The latter is a source of earnings reports for OTC stocks as well as statistics on OTC trading.

Turning to the general magazines or "popular press," *Forbes* is a biweekly magazine offering articles on various companies and topics of interest to investors, as well as columnists with opinions on particular market segments and activities. *Forbes* publishes an index that measures U.S. economic activity, including graphs of its eight components (industrial production, manufacturers' new orders, housing starts, retail sales etc.). It also

---

[2]Another weekly, *The Commercial and Financial Chronicle*, has daily prices for the leading exchanges and weekly prices for regional exchanges and the OTC market.

[3]The Media General carries every common stock listed on the NYSE and Amex, plus some 700 OTC stocks.

features "The *Forbes* Wall Street Review," showing a graph of the overall market, "Closeup of the Market," which indicates the short-run changes in several market indexes or investment alternatives, and other selected information, such as the best- and worst-performing stocks.

The first issue of *Forbes* in January of each year contains the "Annual Report on American Industry," which shows how the more than 1000 largest U.S. public companies compare in profitability, growth, and stock market performance for five-year periods and the latest 12 months. *Forbes* also evaluates the performance of mutual funds during the year.

Business Week covers the major developments in business during the week. It contains articles about specific companies and industries, and regular features include "Finance," "Industries," "International," "Economic Analysis," and other subjects. The "Business Week Index" page features production indicators, leading indicators, foreign exchange information, prices, monthly economic indicators, monetary indicators, and money market rates.

Fortune is a biweekly magazine with articles on general business trends, written with an emphasis on the perspective of corporate managers. A well-known regular feature of *Fortune* is "Personal Investing."[4]

Money magazine is a monthly publication intended for anyone interested in personal financial matters. It regularly publishes features such as "key economic data," "Money Update," "Wall Street," and so forth. *Money* reports detailed rankings on mutual funds. It also features a variety of articles on the financial situations of specific individuals.

Corporate Reports

An important source of information is the corporation itself. Owners of a company's common stock will receive its annual report; nonshareholders can obtain the annual report from the company or their broker.

Annual reports highlight the most recent fiscal year. Extended discussions of activities, problems, and prospects are often part of the report. In addition, the annual report contains audited financial information. The balance sheet, income statement, and statement of changes in financial position are shown, usually for at least the current and preceding year. A summary of accounting policies may be included, as well as detailed notes to the financial statements. Such information can aid diligent investors in better assessing the current and future condition of the company.

Brokerage Firms

Most investors have access to investment information in the form of oral and written information from their brokers. The typical full-service broker-

[4]Additional publications similar to the three discussed here include *Dun's Review* and *Financial World*. These publications typically carry more detailed articles.

age house has a research department that provides a steady flow of reports for consumption by all investors, whether individuals or institutions. In addition, these firms subscribe to well-known investment information sources that can be used by their customers.

Brokerage houses have their own research staffs of economists and analysts. They make recommendations to buy, hold, or sell securities. Some brokerage houses deal primarily with institutional investors, whereas others, known as "retail" brokerage houses, deal primarily with individuals. Major retail brokerage houses include, among others, Merrill Lynch; Shearson Lehman Hutton; Dean Witter Reynolds; Prudential-Bache; and A. G. Edwards.

Each brokerage house puts out a number of pamphlets for investors. These reports cover the economy, the stock and bond markets, options, and industries, and specific companies. Merrill Lynch, for example, has featured publications such as "Investments for a Changing Economy," "Interest Rates," "Investment Strategy," and "Taxable Bond Indices," among others.

The traditional full-service brokerage firms provide most of this information "free" to their customers; however, the cost of providing this service is presumably built into the commissions paid by their customers. Discount brokers do not provide such information. They are selling execution capability, and the investor makes his or her own decisions. Thus, investors have a choice and should choose brokers according to the types of services needed (and the ability of brokerage houses to deliver cost-effective services).

Brokerage houses are a source of both information and recommendations. The emphasis, however, is on recommendations, because brokers earn commissions based on the amount of trading that investors do. Furthermore, most recommendations are "buy" recommendations, as opposed to "sell" recommendations.

Investment Information Services

A large amont of information is available to investors from companies that specialize in providing investment information and advice. Investors can subscribe to these services, several of which offer a variety of products, or they can read at least some of them free of charge at their library or at the offices of their broker; see Box 4-1 for a discussion of this point. Although some of these services offer both information and investment advice, for *organizational purposes* they will be separated into information services (this section), and advisory (recommendation) services (next section). Remember, however, the same service can provide both information and recommendations.

Investors can access financial information and data from a variety of investment information services. These include such services as Dun & Bradstreet, Inc., the widely known credit-reporting company. But the two

BOX 4-1

FOLLOW THE WINOS' LEAD

Who has more continual access to tidy investment tidbits, stockbrokers or hobos? The hobos, it seems. As a kid I used to hang out in the San Francisco Business Library—just blocks from the brokers. All winter long the hobos and winos flooded in to keep warm, but there was rarely a broker in sight. For top investment results, try following the winos' lead.

From Seattle to Tampa, from Boston to Los Angeles, without doubt, there are better research facilities in any medium-size or larger city library than in most brokerage firms. Of course, you have to be willing to spend time and effort at it, but the information is there to make you an informed investor.

And it's free. Many folks are unfamiliar with the dandy tools they could use if only they would hang out with the winos and bums. I have never met an unhelpful librarian, so ask for aid. But, to get started, here are some of my favorite gizmos.

Standard & Poor's Corporation Records is a must. I couldn't last two days without it. Its seven huge volumes have a ton of basic knowledge on almost every publicly traded stock. When readers write for the address of some obscure stock I have mentioned, I do them a favor by insisting they learn how to look it up themselves in the *S&P's*. It might not have enough data for you to decide to buy a stock, but it often has enough to convince you to avoid one. *Standard & Poor's Stock Guide* gives you recent pricing information, including price/earnings ratios, dividends, yields, etc.

The F&S Index is the best-kept secret since the $64 question. It's like a customized reader's guide to everything in print about a company or industry. In minutes you can track down years of magazine and newspaper articles on a stock—and dig more deeply than most stock buyers and sellers ever take time for. It covers publications ranging from the big financial press to obscure industrial trade journals (available through interlibrary loan if your library doesn't carry them).

By the same publisher (God bless them) as the above is *Predicasts F&S Index of Corporate Change*. It will pilot you through years of organizational gyrations, such as joint ventures, bankruptcies, liquidations, reorganizations, name changes and subsidiary changes. For instance, I like the seemingly fruitless but at times rewarding search for bargains among bankrupt companies. That would be ever so much harder without this source. *The Wall Street Journal Index* covers what the *WSJ* has run by company, industry, topic or whatever. Pick a subject. Quick as a wink, you could check out anything they had printed—either on the subject or specific companies.

The Wall Street Transcript is a great source of what The Street is thinking, feeling and doing. It covers brokerage firm research reports, publishes text from newsletters, has regular interviews with a host of security analysts and money managers. Best of all, it indexes all mentions of stocks from previous issues. If a stock isn't here, it probably isn't in Wall Street's eye (and by contrarian logic might be a good buy). When a stock is mentioned, you can get a quick and dirty assessment of what The Street thinks of it.

Ward's Directory lists—by Zip Code—

almost every corporation, so you can check them out regionally. There was a paragraph on *Ward's* in my Dec. 3, 1984 column, but it is so useful, it's worth a second tout and more than a second of your time.

How would you feel about a stock where the insiders bailed out? The SEC's *Official Summary of Insider Transactions* gives a monthly breakdown on officers and directors who have been buying and selling their own stock. Do you need a quick scan on recent article about a business, person or subject—maybe Texaco, John Templeton or tender offers? *The Business Index* from Information Access Corp. covers articles from over 800 publications.

There's too much at the library to do all of it justice here. Maybe you blow a boodle on newsletters. Try reading them at the library. Did you get 300 shares of American Widget when Uncle Morris died? Do you need its price on the date of his death for estate taxes? Try Standard & Poor's *Daily Stock Price Record.* You need to know about all the publications in a certain field, like chemical processing; you can learn about them from *Cahners.*

Source: Adopted from Kenneth L. Fisher, "Follow the Winos' Lead," *Forbes,* April 22, 1985, p. 168. Reprinted by permission. *Forbes* magazine, April 22, 1985, © Forbes, Inc., 1985.

best-known sources of a wide variety of investment information are Standard & Poor's Corporation (S&P) (a subsidiary of McGraw-Hill) and Moody's Investor Services, Inc. (owned by Dun & Bradstreet), both New York based. These two services issue a systematic, continuous flow of reports on a daily, weekly, and monthly basis. Investors can subscribe to only those parts that are of interest to them, such as the common stock service or the bond service. Both sources are commonly available in larger public and college libraries.

Both services issue basic reference volumes covering corporations in some detail. For example, Moody's *Industrial Manual* devotes several pages, in very small print, to each company covered. Moody's also issues the *OTC Industrial Manual,* the *OTC Unlisted Manual, The Public Utility Manual,* the *Bank & Finance Manual,* the *Transportation Manual,* the *Municipal & Government Manual,* and the *International Manual.* All these manuals are updated in separate binders weekly.[5]

The comparable series of Standard & Poor's is their six-volume *Corporation Records.* These are in alphabetical order and are issued regularly, with daily updates in a seventh volume called *Daily News.* Unlike Moody's, this coverage is not separated by areas such as transportation or public utilities.

Standard & Poor's also issues a two-volume *Industry Surveys,* with very detailed discussions of various industries as organized and reported on by S&P. It also issues *Statistical Services: Current Statistics,* which carries a wide variety of statistics of all types: economic production and consumption, data by industry, price data, and so forth.

Often of special interest to investors seeking information about a par-

[5]The *Transportation Manual* is updated every Friday and the *International Manual* biweekly on Fridays.

EG&G Inc.

NYSE Symbol **EGG** Options on Phila (Mar-Jun-Sep-Dec) In S&P 500

Price	Range	P–E Ratio	Dividend	Yield	S&P Ranking	Beta
Oct. 19'89	1989					
34⅛	35½–28⅜	15	0.68	2.0%	A	0.96

Summary

EG&G provides a variety of specialized scientific products and services to the Government and industrial customers for technical applications. Despite lower results in the instruments and components segments, earnings should increase for the third consecutive year in 1989, aided by stronger demand for services provided to the Government. A further gain is likely in 1990.

Current Outlook

Earnings for 1990 should approximate $2.85 a share, compared with the $2.50 projected for 1989.

The quarterly dividend is likely to be raised modestly late in 1989.

Revenues should grow meaningfully in 1990. EG&G's recent strategic initiative to expand its markets should result in a continuing increase in services provided to the Government, including Department of Energy support work. Somewhat restraining is likely to be a slowdown in instrument demand and weak component demand due to minimal growth in the electronics industry. Margins should benefit from the higher volume, well controlled costs and resolution of difficulties with product qualification and delivery in the commercial segment. An expansion of the company's technological base, including the use of acquisitions, and aggressive efforts to increase Government business should aid long-term results.

TRADING VOLUME
THOUSAND SHARES

1983 | 1984 | 1985 | 1986 | 1987 | 1988 | 1989

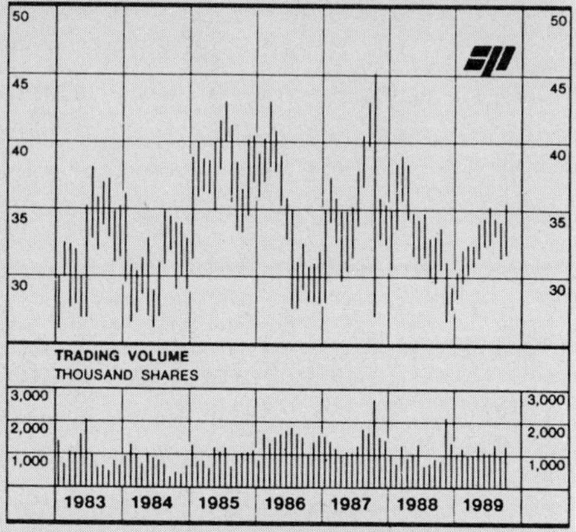

Net Sales (Million $)

13 Weeks:	1989	1988	1987	1986
Mar.	391	332	297	276
Jun.	411	339	304	281
Sep.	---	348	319	287
Dec.	---	386	316	301
	---	1,406	1,236	1,145

Revenues for the six months ended July 2, 1989 increased 19% from those of the comparable year-earlier period. However, due to a 3.4 percentage point decline in the gross profit margin, pretax income was 3.9% lower. After taxes at 31.0%, versus 30.8%, net income declined 4.2%. Earnings per share were $1.16, compared with $1.19.

Common Share Earnings ($)

13 Weeks:	1989	1988	1987	1986
Mar.	0.56	0.56	0.45	0.48
Jun.	0.60	0.63	0.53	0.43
Sep.	E0.62	0.49	0.50	0.33
Dec.	E0.72	0.62	0.52	0.41
	E2.50	2.30	2.00	1.65

Important Developments

Aug. '89— EGG acquired the photoflash lamp product line from GTE's U.S. Lighting Division.

Jul. '89— EGG said its earnings declined in the second quarter due to lower income at the instruments, components and technical services segments.

Next earnings report expected in late October.

Per Share Data ($)

Yr. End Dec. 31	¹1988	1987	1986	1985	1984	¹1983	1982	1981	¹1980	1979
Tangible Bk. Val.	9.78	8.41	7.53	6.50	4.97	7.13	5.93	4.86	3.97	3.89
Earnings	2.30	2.00	1.65	2.07	1.88	1.56	1.38	1.21	0.97	0.79
Dividends	0.60	0.56	0.52	0.48	0.40	0.36	0.32	0.25	0.20	0.15
Payout Ratio	26%	28%	32%	23%	20%	23%	24%	21%	21%	15%
Prices—High	39	45⅛	43	43	36⅛	38⅛	30⅝	22	24⅜	12⅜
Low	26⅝	27	27⅝	31¼	26⅛	26	14½	16⅛	11⅜	6½
P/E Ratio—	17–12	23–14	26–17	21–15	19–14	24–17	22–11	18–13	25–12	16–8

Data as orig. reptd. Adj. for stk. div(s). of 100% Feb. 1982, 100% Feb. 1980. 1. Reflects merger or acquisition. E-Estimated.

Standard NYSE Stock Reports
Vol. 56/No. 207/Sec. 10

October 27, 1989
Copyright © 1989 Standard & Poor's Corp. All Rights Reserved

Standard & Poor's Corp.
25 Broadway, NY, NY 10004

FIGURE 4-1 *A coverage of one NYSE company from Standard & Poor's* **Stock Reports.**
Source: Standard & Poor's *Stock Reports,* New York, Standard & Poor's Corporation, October 27, 1989, p. 789. Reprinted by permission of Standard & Poor's Corporation.

Income Data (Million $)

Year Ended Dec. 31	Revs.	Oper. Inc.	% Oper. Inc. of Revs.	Cap. Exp.	Depr.	Int. Exp.	[1]Net Bef. Taxes	Eff. Tax Rate	Net Inc.	% Net Inc. of Revs.
[2]1988	**1,406**	**123**	**8.7**	**27.9**	**24.6**	**7.5**	**97.4**	**29.5%**	**68.7**	**4.9**
1987	1,236	100	8.1	22.5	21.2	7.4	81.0	31.5%	[3]55.5	4.5
1986	1,145	77	6.7	20.0	16.4	7.4	72.3	37.9%	44.9	3.9
1985	1,155	97	8.4	17.3	15.1	11.5	88.6	37.1%	55.7	4.8
1984	1,072	86	8.0	13.5	13.0	7.0	85.0	37.0%	53.5	5.0
[2]1983	904	69	7.6	11.4	9.9	2.0	77.7	40.0%	46.6	5.2
1982	801	62	7.8	9.6	9.0	2.0	66.5	39.6%	40.2	5.0
1981	704	60	8.5	10.4	7.8	1.5	60.9	44.0%	[3]34.1	4.8
[2]1980	613	52	8.4	11.4	6.3	1.3	48.4	45.6%	26.3	4.3
1979	522	40	7.7	6.8	5.6	1.1	38.0	45.6%	20.6	4.0

Balance Sheet Data (Million $)

Dec. 31	Cash	Curr. Assets	Curr. Liab.	Curr. Ratio	Total Assets	Ret. On Assets	Long Term Debt	Common Equity	Total Inv. Capital	% LT Debt of Cap.	Ret. On Equity
1988	**41.9**	**364**	**173**	**2.1**	**539**	**12.5%**	**14.8**	**332**	**356**	**4.2**	**21.9%**
1987	32.0	308	198	1.6	515	11.5%	21.4	271	308	6.9	21.7%
1986	22.2	264	162	1.6	445	10.2%	20.4	236	275	7.4	20.4%
1985	17.4	268	184	1.5	430	13.5%	15.8	203	237	6.6	31.3%
1984	18.3	245	205	1.2	387	15.6%	15.3	150	178	8.6	31.4%
1983	93.5	257	103	2.5	339	15.2%	11.3	215	231	4.9	23.7%
1982	70.3	213	74	2.9	270	15.9%	12.2	175	193	6.3	25.2%
1981	52.2	188	68	2.8	225	15.9%	10.8	138	155	7.0	27.3%
1980	40.3	167	71	2.3	199	12.8%	12.4	109	125	10.0	24.4%
1979	18.3	135	64	2.1	161	15.5%	11.0	82	95	11.6	31.1%

Data as orig. reptd. **1.** Incl. equity in earns. of nonconsol. subs. after 1980. **2.** Reflects merger or acquisition. **3.** Reflects accounting change.

Business Summary

EG&G is a technologically diversified company. Industry segment contributions in 1988:

	Sales	Profits
Instruments	11%	13%
Components	16%	19%
Technical services	17%	23%
Aerospace	8%	11%
Defense	17%	16%
Department of Energy support	31%	18%

Foreign operations accounted for 7.6% of revenues and 6.9% of pretax income in 1988.

Uses for the company's instruments include physics research, analytical chemistry, life sciences research and geophysical and oceanographic surveys.

EG&G offers standard and custom electronic, optp-electronic, mechanical, electro-mechanical, and frequency-based compnents.

The technical services segment provides testing services to both industry and government, including vehicle and toxicology testing, as well as providing services for NASA.

The aerospace segment designs and manufactures various mechanical components and subassemblies that are used in commercial and military aircraft engines, missiles and propulsion system.

Specialized services (operations, data collection and analysis) and custom hardware to agencies within the Department of Defense.

Components for nuclear weapons and support activites for underground nuclear testing, nuclear power plant safety and other programs are provided to the Department of Energy.

Dividend Data

Dividends have been paid since 1965. A dividend reinvestment plan is available. A "poison pill" stock purchase right was adopted in 1987.

Amt. of Divd. $	Date Decl.	Ex-divd. Date	Stock of Record	Payment Date
0.17	Nov. 22	Jan. 13	Jan. 20	Feb. 10'89
0.17	Mar. 22	Apr. 17	Apr. 21	May 10'89
0.17	May 24	Jul. 17	Jul. 21	Aug. 10'89
0.17	Jul. 26	Oct. 16	Oct. 20	Nov. 10'89

Next dividend meeting: Nov. 21'89.

Capitalization

Long Term Debt: $14,843,000.

Common Stock: 29,980,590 shs. ($1 par). Institutions hold about 57%. Shareholders of record: 17,609.

Office—45 William St., Wellesley, Mass. 02181. **Tel**—(617) 237-5100. **Chrmn & CEO**—J. M. Kucharski. **Pres**—D. M. Kerr. **Treas**—P. A. Broadbent. **Investor Contact**—P. F. Chapski. **Dirs**—D. W. Freed, R. F. Goldhammer, J. B. Gray, K. F. Hansen, D. M. Kerr, J. M. Kucharski, B. J. O'Keefe, W. F. Pounds, S. Rubinovitz, J. F. Thompson, G. R. Tod, J. F. Turley. **Transfer Agent**—First National Bank of Boston. **Incorporated** in Massachusetts in 1947. **Empl**—25,000.

 Paul H. Valentine, CFA

FIGURE 4-1 *(Continued)*

ticular company are the short reports (two pages) on companies put out by each service. Standard and Poor's *Stock Reports* are divided into New York Stock Exchange, American Stock Exchange, and Over the Counter and regional exchanges, each in four volumes. Figure 4-1 shows a S&P *Stock Reports* for a NYSE firm, EG&G, a manufacturer of scientific products. The comparable Moody's service, *Investors Fact Sheets,* is likewise separated by exchanges. These sources are less detailed than those discussed previously but offer the investor both a compact source of current information and a historical balance sheet, income statement, and market data (10 years for Standard & Poor's, seven for Moody's).

Investors can use an even briefer source of information on stocks of interest from Moody's *Handbook of Common Stocks* or Standard & Poor's *Stock Guide.* The former is issued in spring, summer, fall, and winter editions and contains one page of write-up and data for each covered stock. Figure 4-2 shows an excerpt for EG&G, from Moody's *Handbook.* The *Stock Guide,* issued monthly, contains very brief information on several thousand listed and unlisted stocks. These data consist of high and low prices for selected years, sales, and yield information.

Data for small OTC firms are available in Standard & Poor's *OTC Profiles.* Figure 4-3 shows the typical coverage for one firm.

Investors seeking information on the dividends paid on most securities have a wealth of information at their disposal. Standard & Poor's issues a *Quarterly Dividend Record,* with detailed information on the timing and amount of dividends by company. Moody's issues an *Annual Dividend Report* with similar detailed information.

Standard & Poor also publishes a *Bond Outlook,* containing such information as changes in bond ratings, convertibles of interest, new issues, and data about the bond markets themselves. The comparable Moody's publication is the *Bond Survey,* issued weekly. Each issue is a thick, detailed coverage of virtually everything happening currently in the bond market with regard to recent issues, prospective issues, bond averages, and so forth. All types of issues are covered—Treasuries, agencies, corporates, and municipals.

Standard & Poor's also issues the *Bond Guide,* a monthly publication providing concise information for a large number of companies, both domestic and foreign. Figure 4-4 shows a page from the *Bond Guide.*

Investment Advisory Services and Investment Newsletters

A wide variety of investment advisory services and investment newsletters is available to investors. Many offer a combination of analyses and projections along with stock recommendations. Investment advisory services may specialize in particular selection techniques or in particular assets (e.g., options) or areas (e.g., new issues). The larger services may offer several different products for investors. Most investment advisory services and investment newsletters offer trial subscriptions, allowing investors to sample what is available.[6]

Because of the wide variety of services and letters available to investors, we will describe only one in detail. We will then briefly mention others that are well known among many investors.

Value Line *The Value Line Investment Survey* (*VL*) is the largest (by number of subscribers) and probably best-known investment advisory service in the United States. The *VL* covers over 1700 stocks (including NYSE, Amex, and some OTC) organized into 90 plus industries on a regular basis, reviewing each once every three months; specifically, each weekly issue covers several industry groupings, completing the cycle every quarter. In addition to this "Ratings and Reports," every week subscribers also receive a "Summary and Index" and a "Selection and Opinion" section containing an overall review of the market, a highlighted stock, a record of insider transactions, and numerous other data.

The *VL* is both a reference service and a recommendation service. Essential information is presented for each industry grouping as a whole as well as for each individual company. For example, 23 series of financial and operating statistics are provided for each company for the previous 15 years and estimated for the next one or two years. These statistics can be seen in the middle of Figure 4-5, which shows a typical page of coverage for a company, in this case EG&G. Each company report shows both historical data and estimated data.

As for recommendations, the *VL* ranks each company from 1 (top) to 5 (bottom) on the basis of its "probable safety in the future" and its timeliness ("probable price performance in the next 12 months") in relation to the other 1700+ stocks. The top 100 and bottom 100 stocks are in Group 1 and Group 5, respectively, the next 300 top and 300 bottom, respectively, are in Groups 2 and 4; and the middle 900 are in Group 3. Value Line recommends that investors choose stocks out of the top 400 (Groups 1 and 2) that meet their standards for safety and current yield. If any of the selected stocks falls below the investor's standards, a switch is made into those that currently conform. This is convenient for investors because the weekly "Summary and Index" section shows the current performance and safety ratings for each of the 1700 stocks as well as their estimated yields and latest earnings.

Value Line's stock rankings are based on a computer model developed

---

[6]A good source of trial subscriptions is *Barron's*.

EG & G, INC.

LISTED	SYM.	LTPS♦	STPS♦	IND. DIV.	REC. PRICE	RANGE (52-WKS.)	YLD.
NYSE	EGG	72.0	96.2	$0.68*	34	35 - 27	2.0%

UPPER MEDIUM GRADE. EG&G MANUFACTURES LABORATORY AND FIELD-TEST INSTRUMENTS AND ELECTRONIC AND MECHANICAL COMPONENTS FOR A NUMBER OF COMMERCIAL INDUSTRIES.

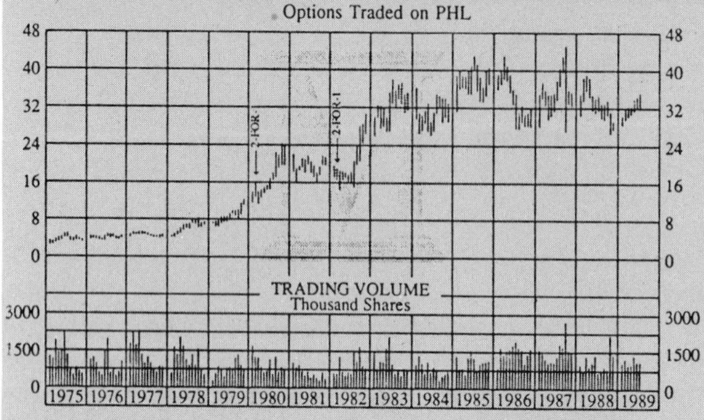

CAPITALIZATION: (12/31/88)

	(000)	(%)
Long-Term Debt	$ 14,843	4.2
Defer. Inc. Tax	8,780	2.5
Com. & Surp.	332,347	93.3
Total	$355,970	100.0

Shs. ($1)-30,011,000

INTERIM EARNINGS:

Qtr.	3/31	6/30	9/30	12/31
1986	0.48	0.43	0.33	0.41
1987	0.45	0.53	0.50	0.52
1988	0.51	0.64	0.51	0.62
1989	0.56	0.60	...	...

INTERIM DIVIDENDS:

Amt.	Dec.	Ex.	Rec.	Pay.
0.15Q	5/25/88	7/18/88	7/22/88	8/10/88
0.15Q	9/28	10/25	10/31	11/10
0.17Q	11/22	1/13/89	1/20/89	2/10/89
0.17Q	3/22/89	4/17	4/21	5/10
0.17Q	5/24	7/17	7/21	8/10
0.17Q	7/26	10/16	10/20	11/10

BACKGROUND:

EG&G, Inc. is a technologically diversified company providing advanced scientific and technical products and services worldwide. EG&G's operations are organized into six business segments. The Instruments segment manufactures scientific equipment for airport and industrial security and the precise measurement of physical, chemical and biological phonomena. The Components segment provides optical, mechanical and electronic divices for commercial markets. Technical Services businesses offer auto and Lubatesting, biomedical research and technical services. Components and subsystems for aviation and aerospace industries are produced by EG&G's Aerospace Group. The Defense and Energy Support Groups provide research and service support systems.

RECENT DEVELOPMENTS:

Due to product delivery and operating cost problems in the components segment, net income for the quarter ended 7/2/89 fell 8% to $17.5 million. EGG's Aerospace segment showed significant improvement toward correcting the test-to-acceptance delays and qualification problems that slowed results for the quarter. Sales were $410.7 million, up 21% despite softness in the Technical Services due to lubricant testing elements in Automotive Research.

PROSPECTS:

Results are expected to improve fueled by the acquisitions of Astrophysics Research Corporation and Dynatrend. Uncertainties exist in orders and bookings for the Instruments segment because of political circumstances in EG&G's Beijing offices in the Peoples Republic of China. Future government results may be tempered due to military budget cuts. An agreement to support Management and Operating Prime Contractor for the Department of Energy's Superconducting Super Collider Laboratory in Texas bode well for long-term growth and has positioned EG&G as a player in the high-energy physics arena. An expansion into Asia will further strengthen EGG's position.

STATISTICS:

YEAR	GROSS REVS. ($mill.)	OPER. PROFIT MARGIN %	RET. ON EQUITY %	NET INCOME ($mill.)	WORK CAP. ($mill.)	SENIOR CAPITAL ($mill.)	SHARES (000)	EARN. PER SH.$	DIV. PER SH.$	DIV. PAY. %	PRICE RANGE	P/E RATIO	AVG YLD. %
79	522.2	6.3	25.2	20.6	71.0	11.0	26,404	0.79	0.15	19	12¼ - 6⅜	11.9	1.6
80	631.1	6.3	24.1	26.3	95.8	12.4	27,510	0.97	0.20	21	24¼ - 11¼	18.4	1.1
81	704.2	7.4	24.8	34.1	120.7	10.8	28,355	1.21	0.25	21	22 - 16⅛	15.8	1.3
82	800.8	6.7	22.9	40.2	139.8	12.2	29,595	1.38	0.32	23	30⅝ - 14½	16.3	1.4
83	904.2	6.5	21.7	46.6	153.6	11.3	30,256	1.56	0.36	23	38⅛ - 26	20.6	1.1
84	1,071.7	7.5	35.7	53.5	40.2	15.3	30,384	1.88	0.40	21	36⅛ - 26⅛	16.6	1.3
85	1,177.1	7.5	27.4	55.7	84.2	15.8	27,427	2.07	0.48	23	43 - 31	17.9	1.3
86	1,145.1	5.3	19.0	44.9	102.3	18.0	27,137	1.65	0.52	32	43 - 27⅝	21.4	1.5
87	1,247.5	6.4	20.4	55.5	109.8	21.4	25,622	2.00	0.56	28	45⅛ - 27	18.0	1.6
88	**1,406.3**	**7.0**	**20.7**	**68.7**	**191.2**	**14.8**	**30,011**	**2.30**	**0.60**	26	39 - 26⅝	**14.3**	1.8

♦Long-Term Price Score — Short-Term Price Score; see page 4a. STATISTICS ARE AS ORIGINALLY REPORTED Adjusted for 100% stock dividend, 2/82 and 2/80.

INCORPORATED:
November 13, 1947 — MA

PRINCIPAL OFFICE:
45 William Street
Wellesley, MA 02181
Tel.: (617) 237-5100

ANNUAL MEETING:
Fourth Tues. in April

NUMBER OF STOCKHOLDERS:
16,300

TRANSFER AGENT(S):
The First National Bank of Boston
Boston, MA

REGISTRAR(S):

INSTITUTIONAL HOLDINGS:
No. of Institutions: 200
Shares Held: 16,954,523

OFFICERS:
Chairman & C.E.O.
J. M. Kucharski
President
D. M. Kerr
Sr. Vice Pres. & C.F.O.
J. R. Dolan
Treasurer
P. A. Broadbent
Investor Relations
P. F. Chapski

FIGURE 4-2 ***A sample page from Moody's*** **Handbook of Common Stocks.**
Source: Taken from Moody's *Handbook of Common Stocks,* Fall 1989 Edition. Reprinted by permission.

Contel Cellular

NASDAQ	Price	P-E Ratio	Dividend	Yield	Ranges		S&P Ranking
	Dec. 29 '89				1989	1988	
†CCXLA	25¼	NM	None	None	27¼-11¾	12-7⅛	NR

Business: Through subsidiaries or partnerships, this company provides cellular telephone service to some 55 metropolitan areas throughout the U.S. It is also seeking authority to provide cellular service in certain rural areas. The company was spun off from Contel Corp. in April 1988, and Contel retains control through all the Class B supervoting stock.

	Share Earnings (Cal. Yr.)	Divs. Paid (Cal. Yr.)	
1988 Sales.: 41.4 mil.			**Chrm:** C. Wohlstetter
1988 Net Inc.: 2.1 mil.	1988 0.02	Nil	**Pres & CEO:** P. G. Kozlowski
Common Shs.: ¹99,913,000	1987 0.01	Nil	**Secy:** W. M. Grant
Long Term Debt: 14.3 mil.	1986 Nil	Nil	**Office:**
	1985 d0.01	Nil	9000 Central Park West
Book Val. Per Sh.: 1.20 Dec. '88	**Interim Earnings: 9 Months**		Atlanta, GA 30328
Latest Div.: None	Sep. '89 0.02 Sep. '88 0.03		**Tel:** (404) 698-6100

Footnotes: †Marginable. **1.** Combined classes. d-Deficit.

Standard & Poor's Corp. Copyright ©1990 Standard & Poor's Corp. All Rights Reserved 25 Broadway, NY, NY 10004

FIGURE 4-3 *A coverage of one OTC firm from Standard & Poor's* **OTC Profiles.**
Source: Standard & Poor's *OTC Profiles*, New York, Standard & Poor's Corporation, January 1990, p. 58. Reprinted by permission of Standard & Poor's Corporation.

and modified over many years. The model includes price history over both a short and long period, earnings changes, and an earnings surprise factor to account for actual earnings significantly above or below those predicted by their analysts. The *VL* discloses the methodology for computing the ranks and regularly reports on how well the ranks have done in practice.

As Figure 4-5 shows, the *VL* coverage also provides such information as the beta (to be discussed in Chapter 5) and the P/E ratio (Chapter 9). Additional information includes the company's financial strength, the price stability of the stock, the price growth persistence, and the earnings predictability. Quarterly sales, earnings, and dividends are shown on both a historical and an estimated basis. Note (in the upper left corner) that both institutional and insider decisions are shown.

As part of its company coverage, Value Line issues an industry report for each of the 90 plus industries it covers. This is typically a two-page report preceding the companies assigned to that industry by Value Line. This discussion analyzes the current and prospective situation for the industry and has a table of composite statistics, including both historical and estimated figures.

Value Line also publishes a separate *Options and Convertibles Service*, which covers all listed options, convertibles, and warrants. Each of the options covered is assigned a performance rank. Finally, Value Line publishes an *OTC Special Situations Service* and a *New Issues Service*.

Corporate Bonds — EAS-ELP 71

Title-Industry Code & Co. Finances (In Italics)	Ind	Fixed Charge Coverage	1986	1987	1988	Year End	Million $ Cash & Equiv.	Curr. Assets	Curr. Liab.	Balance Sheet Date	L. Term Debt (Mil $)		Capital-ization (Mil $)	Total Debt % Capital						
Individual Issue Statistics Exchange	Interest Dates	S&P Debt Rating	Date of Last Rating Change	Prior Rating	Eligible	Bond Form	Redemption Provisions: Regular Price	Regular (Begins) Thru	Sinking Fund Price	Sinking Fund (Begins) Thru	Refund/Other Restriction Price	Refund/Other Restriction (Begins) Thru	Outst'g (Mil $)	Underwriting Firm	Underwriting Year	Price Range 1990 High	Price Range 1990 Low	Mo. End Price Sale(s) or Bid	Curr. Yield	Yield to Mat.
[1]*Eastern Illinois Tel*	*67a*	*Subsid of ALLTEL Corp, see*																		
1st 8.95s 2000	jD15	A+	12/81	A−	X	R	103.33	12-15-90	100	....	....	....	4.20	M3	'70	100⅜	96½	96⅞	9.24	9.41
Eastman Kodak	*40d*		*5.61*	*9.41*	*3.86*	*Dc*	*1183*	*8941*	*6496*	*10-1-89*	*★7386*		*14258*	*51.8*						
• Deb 8⅝s 2016	Jd15	A−	2/88	AA	X	R	105.42	6-14-90	100	(6-15-97)	®103.19	6-14-96	300	M6	'86	90⅛	86⅞	s88	9.80	9.91
Deb 9.95s 2018	jJ	A−			X	R	[2]....	....	....	....	....	....	125	M6	'88	105⅝	100½	100⅞	9.86	9.86
Nts 8¾s '91	mN	A−	2/88	AA	X	R	NC	....	....	....	....	....	300	M3	'87	99⅞	99⅜	99½	8.79	9.05
Nts 9.20s '95	Jj15	A−			X	R	NC	....	....	....	....	....	750	M6	'90	99⅞	97⅞	97⅞	9.40	9.75
Nts[3] 7¼s '97	Ao15	A−	2/88	AA	X	R	NC	....	....	....	....	....	125	M6	'87	88⅜	86	86¼	8.41	9.97
Nts 8.55s '97	Mn	A−	2/88	AA	X	R	NC	....	....	....	....	....	200	F2	'87	97⅝	95	95¼	8.98	9.47
Nts 9⅛s '98	Ms	A−			X	R	100	(3-1-95)	....	....	....	....	1100	M6	'88	97½	94½	94¾	9.63	10.09
Nts 9⅝s '99	mN15	A−	2/88	AA	X	R	100	(11-15-94)	....	....	....	....	275	S1	'87	102⅝	99⅞	100⅛	9.61	9.60
Nts 9½s 2000	Ao15	A−			X	R	100	(4-15-95)	....	....	....	....	400	S1	'88	101¾	98⅝	99	9.60	9.65
Nts 10s 2001	Jd15	A−			X	R	100	(6-15-96)	....	....	....	....	300	F2	'88	104⅛	101¼	101½	9.85	9.78
Nts 9⅜s 2003	Ms15	A−			X	R	NC	....	....	....	....	....	400	G2	'88	96⅞	93	93⅜	10.04	10.30
Nts 9⅞s 2004	mN	A−			X	R	100	(11-1-98)	....	....	....	....	300	F2	'88	100	96⅛	96⅜	10.25	10.36
Nts 9¾s 2004	aO	A−			X	R	NC	....	....	....	....	....	300	F2	'89	100⅜	96⅜	96¾	10.08	10.18
Eaton Corp	*8*		*4.18*	*5.04*	*5.40*	*Dc*	*270.0*	*1377*	*598.0*	*9-30-89*	*853.0*		*2092*	*42.7*						
• SF Deb 8¾s 2001	jJ15	A	1/85	A−	X	R	102.80	7-14-90	100	....	....	....	37.4	M3	'76	No Sale		94¾	9.23	9.51
• SF Deb 7⅞s 2003	jD	A	1/85	A−	X	R	102.835	11-30-90	100	....	....	....	43.8	M3	'73	No Sale		86½	9.10	9.66
• SF Deb 9s 2016	Ms15	A			X	R	107.225	3-14-90	100	(3-15-98)	®104.25	3-14-96	100	M3	'86	92	89⅛	90½	9.94	10.03
Deb[4] 8s '96	[5]fA15	A			X	R	NC	....	....	....	....	....	100	M3	86	95½	93⅜	93⅝	8.54	9.32
• Deb 7s 2011	Ao	A	1/85	A−	X	R	100	....	....	....	....	....	[6]200	M3	'81	No Sale		76¼	9.18	9.65
Deb 8½s 2017	Jj15	A			X	R	106.076	1-14-91	100	(1-15-98)	®103.574	1-14-97	100	S4	'87	91⅛	86⅜	86¾	9.80	9.92
Deb[7] 8⅞s 2019	Jd15	A			X	R	NC	....	....	....	....	....	100	S4	'89	100½	94⅞	95⅜	9.31	9.34
[8]*Eckerd Holdings*	*58e*		*[9]0.41*	*0.03*	*0.97*	*Ja*	*17.10*	*730.0*	*488.0*	*4-29-89*	*955.0*		*991.0*	*110.0*						
♦Disc[10]SubDeb 2006	[11]	B−			Y	R	100	....	100	(5-1-91)	....	....	[6]345	M3	'86	87¼	73	73½	....	Flat
♦Sub Deb 11⅛s 2001	Mn	B−			Y	R	100	(5-1-91)	100	(5-1-97)	....	....	[6]291	M3	'86	90	84	s84¾	13.13	13.83
ECL Indus[12]	*17a*		*0.43*	*0.48*	*d0.04*	*Dc*	*1.26*	*18.60*	*47.10*	*9-30-89*	*4.09*		*16.50*	*201.0*						
• Sub[13](Gtd)[14]Deb[15] 9s '89	§mN15	NR			Z	R			Default 11-15-88 P & I				[6]7.24	Exch.	'69	104	95	94	....	Flat
Ecolab Inc	*64*		*[16]9.16*	*4.33*	*3.28*	*Dc*	*20.40*	*332.0*	*262.0*	*9-30-89*	*259.0*		*753.0*	*41.6*						
SF Deb 10⅜s 2017	jJ15	BBB			X	R	109.338	7-14-90	100	(7-15-98)	®105.188	7-14-97	125	F2	'87	105	100⅝	101	10.27	10.26
Edgcomb Metals Co	*44d*		*0.96*	*1.11*	*1.34*	*Dc*	*4.77*	*173.0*	*113.0*	*9-30-89*	*266.0*		*307.0*	*90.2*						
Sr[17]Sub(Reset[18])Nts 9s '99	fA15	B−			Y	R	106.667	(8-15-94)	100	(8-15-98)	[19]115	8-14-90	139	D9	'89	78	78	78	11.54	....
Edison Elec. Illum,N.Y.	*75*	*See Consol. Edison of N.Y.*																		
• 1st Con 5s 95	jJ	NR			X	C	NC	....	....	....	....	....	1.44		1895	No Sale		79¼	6.31	10.06
El Paso Electric (Texas)	*72a*		*1.46*	*1.29*	*1.62*	*Dc*	*49.30*	*171.0*	*285.0*	*9-30-89*	*587.0*		*1233*	*53.6*						
1st 4⅝s '92	Fa	BB+	7/89	BBB−	Y	CR	100.21	1-31-91	100.15	1-31-91	....	....	10.4	S1	'62	91⅝	91⅛	91⅛	5.08	9.61
1st 6¾s '98	Mn	BB+	7/89	BBB−	Y	R	101.87	4-30-90	100	....	....	....	24.8	E5	'68	84¾	82⅛	82¼	8.21	9.95
1st 7¼s 2001	Ao	BB+	7/89	BBB−	Y	R	103.39	3-31-90	100.78	3-31-90	....	....	15.8	S12	'71	87½	84¼	84½	9.17	10.09
1st 9s 2004	mN	BB+	7/89	BBB−	Y	R	104.11	10-31-90	100	....	....	....	20.0	K1	'74	92½	88⅝	89	10.11	10.48
1st 10½s 2005	mN	BB+	7/89	BBB−	Y	R	105.91	10-31-90	100.78	10-31-90	....	....	15.0	H7	'75	102¾	99⅛	99½	10.55	10.56
1st 8½s 2007	Ao	BB+	7/89	BBB−	Y	R	105.13	3-31-90	100.28	3-31-90	....	....	25.0	M3	'77	89⅝	85⅝	85⅞	9.90	10.26
El Paso Natural Gas[20]	*73a*		*3.18*	*4.34*	*3.96*	*Dc*	*n/a*	*98[illegible]*	*635.0*	*9-30-89*	*648.0*		*2311*	*28.4*						
• SF Deb 12⅞s 2002	jD	A	7/88	A−	X	R	107.71[illegible]		100	....	....	....	125	M3	'83	106⅝	106⅝	103⅝	12.42	12.30
• SF Deb 9⅝s 2011	aO	A	7/88	A−	X	R	[illegible]		100	(10-1-97)	®106.84	9-30-91	100	M6	'86	99	99	97⅞	9.83	9.86

Uniform Footnote Explanations-See Page 1. Other: [1] Now ALLTE' [2] amt based on formula. [3] (HRO)On 4-15-92 at 100. [4] (HRO)On 8-15-96 at 100. [5] Due 8-15-2006.
[6] Incl disc. [7] (HRO)For a Risk Event & on 6-15-04 at 100. [8] Now Jack [10] Int accrues at 13% fr 5-1-91(pd M&n 1). [11] Due 5-1-06.
[12] Was Norlin Ind.sub of Service Resources Corp. [13] 10% of issue due Int of 11-15-85 pd 3-24-86. [15] Trades on $1000 prin amt. [16] Fiscal Jun'86 & prior.
[17] (HRO)On Chge of Ctrl at 101. [18] Int to 8-15-94,15% aft to maturity. El Paso Company(Burlington Resources).

FIGURE 4-4 ***A sample page from Standard & Poor's* Bond Guide,** February 1990. *Source:* Standard & Poor's *Bond Guide,* New York, Standard & Poor's Corporation, February 1990, p. 71. Reprinted by permission of Standard & Poor's Corporation.

Other Advisory Services and Letters There are many other investment advisory services and letters. Another well-known weekly service is Standard & Poor's *The Outlook.* It discusses general market conditions and offers portfolio advice. It also features recommended industries and stocks, with the latter based on a "star" rating system—five stars indicates a buy and one star indicates a sell, with three shadings in between.

Some of the well-known investment newsletters include *The Zweig Forecast, Dow Theory Forecasts, Granville Market Letter, The Professional Tape Reader,* and *The Prudent Speculator. Forbes* magazine now carries Mark Hulbert, who publishes *Hulbert Financial Digest,* which monitors investment letters, as a columnist.

Government Publications

The federal government, through a variety of agencies and departments, provides much information about the economy, industries, and companies.

E G & G, Inc. NYSE-EGG

RECENT PRICE	32	P/E RATIO	12.6 (Trailing: 13.6 / Median: 17.0)	RELATIVE P/E RATIO	0.97	DIV'D YLD	2.4%	VALUE LINE	142

TIMELINESS 3 Average
(Relative Price Performance Next 12 Mos.)

SAFETY 2 Above Average
(Scale: 1 Highest to 5 Lowest)

BETA .95 (1.00 = Market)

	1979	1980	1981	1982	1983	1984	1985	1986	1987	1988	1989
High:	12.3	24.3	22.0	30.6	38.1	36.1	43.0	43.0	45.1	39.0	36.5
Low:	6.4	11.3	16.2	14.5	26.0	26.1	31.3	27.6	27.0	26.6	28.4

1992-94 PROJECTIONS

	Price	Gain	Ann'l Total Return
High	85	(+165%)	29%
Low	60	(+90%)	19%

Insider Decisions

	M	A	M	J	J	A	S	O	N
to Buy	0	0	0	0	0	0	0	0	0
Options	1	0	1	0	0	1	0	0	1
to Sell	0	1	0	1	1	0	0	1	0

Institutional Decisions

	1Q'89	2Q'89	3Q'89
to Buy	37	47	38
to Sell	51	39	39
Hld's(000)	19725	17070	15835

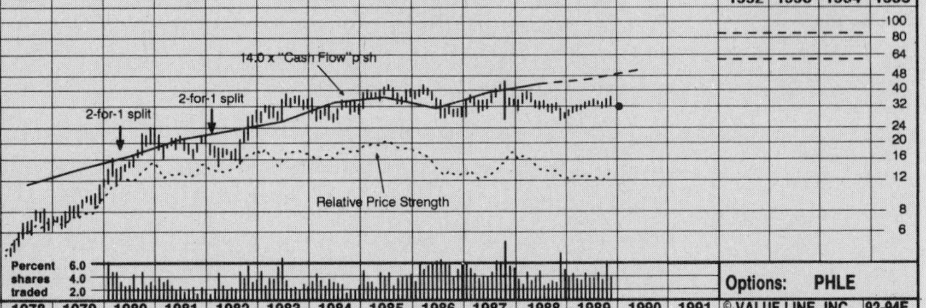

Options: PHLE

1974	1975	1976	1977	1978	1979	1980	1981	1982	1983	1984	1985	1986	1987	1988	1989	1990	1991	© VALUE LINE, INC.	92-94E
7.05	7.31	8.87	11.91	16.89	19.78	22.29	24.83	27.11	29.95	40.00	42.44	41.76	44.58	46.86	**57.75**	**67.85**		Sales per sh	**89.30**
.37	.42	.48	.56	.81	.99	1.19	1.48	1.66	1.87	2.41	2.60	2.24	2.76	3.11	**3.30**	**3.75**		"Cash Flow" per sh	**5.25**
.24	.28	.34	.42	.61	.79	.97	1.21	1.38	1.56	1.81	2.07	1.65	2.00	2.30	**2.35**	**2.75**		Earnings per sh (A)	**4.00**
.03	.03	.04	.09	.12	.15	.20	.25	.32	.36	.40	.48	.52	.56	.60	**.70**	**.78**		Div'ds Decl'd per sh (B) ■	**1.00**
.19	.13	.12	.14	.18	.26	.42	.37	.32	.38	.50	.64	.73	.81	.93	**.85**	**1.00**		Cap'l Spending per sh	**1.25**
1.81	2.02	2.15	2.49	2.44	3.09	3.97	4.86	5.93	7.13	5.59	7.47	8.62	9.79	11.07	**11.20**	**11.95**		Book Value per sh	**19.65**
23.13	24.09	28.29	31.57	26.08	26.40	27.51	28.36	29.54	30.20	26.79	27.22	27.42	27.72	30.01	**29.00**	**28.00**		Common Shs Outst'g (C)	**28.00**
11.8	12.9	12.0	11.1	10.3	11.0	17.3	15.9	14.5	20.6	17.0	18.2	20.6	17.6	14.2	*Bold figures are*			Avg Ann'l P/E Ratio	**18.0**
1.65	1.72	1.54	1.45	1.40	1.59	2.30	1.93	1.60	1.74	1.58	1.48	1.40	1.18	1.17	*Value Line*			Relative P/E Ratio	**1.50**
1.0%	.9%	1.0%	2.0%	1.9%	1.7%	1.2%	1.3%	1.6%	1.1%	1.3%	1.3%	1.5%	1.6%	1.8%	*estimates*			Avg Ann'l Div'd Yield	**1.4%**
						613.1	704.2	800.8	904.2	1071.7	1155.1	1145.1	1235.9	1406.3	**1675**	**1900**		Sales ($mill)	**2500**
						8.4%	8.5%	7.8%	7.6%	8.0%	8.4%	6.7%	8.1%	8.7%	**7.5%**	**7.0%**		Operating Margin	**7.5%**
						6.3	7.8	9.0	9.9	13.0	15.1	16.4	21.2	24.6	**26.0**	**28.0**		Depreciation ($mill)	**35.0**
						26.3	34.1	40.2	46.6	51.5	55.7	44.9	55.5	68.7	**70.0**	**77.0**		Net Profit ($mill)	**112**
						45.6%	44.0%	39.6%	40.0%	39.4%	37.1%	37.9%	31.5%	29.5%	**30.0%**	**30.0%**		Income Tax Rate	**30.0%**
						4.3%	4.8%	5.0%	5.2%	4.8%	4.8%	3.9%	4.5%	4.9%	**4.2%**	**4.1%**		Net Profit Margin	**4.5%**
						95.8	120.7	139.8	153.6	40.2	84.2	102.3	109.8	191.2	**180**	**200**		Working Cap'l ($mill)	**280**
						12.4	10.8	12.2	11.3	15.3	15.8	20.4	21.4	14.8	**8.0**	**8.0**		Long-Term Debt ($mill)	**Nil**
						109.1	137.7	175.2	215.2	149.8	203.4	236.3	271.4	332.4	**325**	**335**		Net Worth ($mill)	**550**
						22.2%	23.5%	22.0%	21.0%	31.6%	26.0%	18.0%	19.4%	20.1%	**21.5%**	**23.0%**		% Earned Total Cap'l	**20.5%**
						24.1%	24.8%	22.9%	21.7%	34.4%	27.4%	19.0%	20.4%	20.7%	**21.5%**	**23.0%**		% Earned Net Worth	**20.5%**
						19.2%	19.7%	17.6%	16.7%	26.6%	21.0%	13.0%	14.7%	15.6%	**15.0%**	**16.5%**		% Retained to Comm Eq	**14.5%**
						20%	21%	23%	23%	23%	23%	32%	28%	25%	**30%**	**28%**		% All Div'ds to Net Prof	**25%**

CAPITAL STRUCTURE as of 10/1/89
Total Debt $72.4 mill. **Due in 5 Yrs** $70.0 mill.
LT Debt $7.8 mill. **LT Interest** $1.0 mill.
(Total interest coverage: 12.0x) (2% of Cap'l)

Pension Liability None in '88 vs. none in '87

Pfd Stock None

Common Stock 28,591,000 shs. (98% of Cap'l)
as of 10/29/89

CURRENT POSITION ($MILL.)	1987	1988	10/1/89
Cash Assets	32.0	42.0	40.8
Receivables	169.6	201.7	211.8
Inventory (LIFO)	84.2	100.9	109.7
Other	22.0	19.8	23.6
Current Assets	307.8	364.4	385.9
Accts Payable	46.7	51.0	54.8
Debt Due	59.2	34.2	64.6
Other	92.1	88.0	87.4
Current Liab.	198.0	173.2	206.8

ANNUAL RATES of change (per sh)	Past 10 Yrs.	Past 5 Yrs.	Est'd '86-'88 to '92-'94
Sales	13.5%	10.0%	12.5%
"Cash Flow"	16.0%	10.0%	11.5%
Earnings	16.0%	7.5%	12.5%
Dividends	21.0%	12.5%	10.0%
Book Value	15.5%	10.5%	12.0%

Cal-endar	QUARTERLY SALES ($ mill.) (A) Mar.31	Jun.30	Sep.30	Dec.31	Full Year
1986	276.4	281.3	286.7	300.7	1145.1
1987	296.6	303.9	319.2	316.2	1235.9
1988	332.6	339.0	348.5	386.2	1406.3
1989	390.9	410.7	426.1	**447.3**	**1675**
1990	**450**	**460**	**470**	**520**	**1900**

Cal-endar	EARNINGS PER SHARE (A) Mar.31	Jun.30	Sep.30	Dec.31	Full Year
1986	.48	.43	.33	.41	1.65
1987	.45	.53	.50	.52	2.00
1988	.56	.63	.49	.62	2.30
1989	.56	.60	.57	**.62**	**2.35**
1990	**.65**	**.70**	**.65**	**.75**	**2.75**

Cal-endar	QUARTERLY DIVIDENDS PAID (B) ■ Mar.31	Jun.30	Sep.30	Dec.31	Full Year
1985	.12	.12	.12	.12	.48
1986	.13	.13	.13	.13	.52
1987	.14	.14	.14	.14	.56
1988	.15	.15	.15	.15	.60
1989	.17	.17	.17	.17	

BUSINESS: EG&G, Inc. provides a variety of scientific and technically oriented products, custom equipment systems, and related or specialized services to government and industrial customers. Markets are comprised of scientific instruments (11% of sales), components (16%), technical services (17%), aerospace (8%), defense (17%), and Department of Energy support (31%). Formed EG&G Venture Partners, 1985. R&D: 1.4% of sales. Labor costs, 30% of sales. Employs 22,500; has 17,600 shareholders. 1988 depreciation rate: 13.2%. Estimated plant age: 5 years. Insiders own 3% of stock. Chairman: John M. Kucharski. President: Donald M. Kerr. Inc.: Massachusetts. Address: 45 William Street, Wellesley, MA 02181. Telephone: 617-237-5100.

The EG&G share price seems to be haunted by the company's past. Profits are considerably higher than they used to be, yet the price has been more or less flat for seven years. This dichotomy probably relates to the occasional setbacks to EG&G's earnings progress which have caused investors to assign a generally declining price-earnings ratio to its stock.
The 1989 bottom line is unlikely to help matters. For the first nine months, earnings were little different from a year earlier. The fourth-quarter result won't change that, we think. Not surprisingly, EG&G stock is ranked 3 (Average) for Timeliness.
There are good reasons to anticipate markedly higher share earnings in 1990 and through 1992-94. • Big new projects include a four-year contract to manage and operate the Department of Energy's Rocky Flats nuclear weapons plant, and to provide logistical and operational support for the United States Antarctic Program over a potential ten-year span. These are not isolated examples; EG&G was awarded many large government jobs this year. • The recent acquisition of the German bioanlytical company, Laboratorium Prof. Dr. Berthold, is the largest commercial product manufacturing acquisition in EG&G's history and enhances its stature as a precision instrument company. With 1989 sales of about $55 million and only 400 employees, we suspect that Berthold is a highly profitable operation, although this information, as well as the purchase price, has not been disclosed. • EG&G's stock repurchases are antidiluitve. About 1.5 million shares were bought in 1989, of which only one-third was used for corporate purposes. Similar action is likely in 1990.
EG&G stock is attractive on more than one count. Although profit growth may continue to be irregular, earnings of $4 a share are likely in 3 to 5 years, with a resulting target price range of $60-to-$85 a share as investors award this equity a higher P/E. Its Safety Grade of 2 (Above Average) is another plus, as is the company's policy of annual dividend increases. (Beginning with the February 9th payment, the quarterly dividend will be boosted to 19¢ a share.)

Lucien Virgile *December 22, 1989*

(A) Based on primary shares outstanding. Excludes nonrecurring gain: '84, 7¢. Next earnings report due early January. (B) Next dividend meeting about February 21. Goes ex-dividend January 19. Dividend payment dates: February 9, May 10, August 10, November 10. ■ Dividend reinvestment plan available. (C) In millions, adjusted for stock splits.

Company's Financial Strength	A+
Stock's Price Stability	80
Price Growth Persistence	35
Earnings Predictability	80

Factual material is obtained from sources believed to be reliable, but the publisher is not responsible for any errors or omissions contained herein.

FIGURE 4-5 *A page from a weekly issue of* **Ratings and Reports, The Value Line Investment Survey.**
Source: Ratings and Reports, The Value Line Investment Survey, Edition 1, Part 3, December 22, 1989, p. 142. Copyright © by 1989 Value Line, Inc. Used by permission.

Although this information is available to investors either free or for a small charge, many do not know of its existence or utilize it very often. Generally, it is more specialized than the previous sources discussed and therefore it has been placed after them.

Government publications are a primary source for data concerning the state of the economy. A summary report of recent and prospective activity is contained in the *Economic Report of the President,* which is sent by the president to the Congress. The report includes over 200 pages covering such issues as monetary policy, inflation, tax policy, the international economy, and review and outlook. In addition, it contains over 100 pages of tables showing historical data for the Gross National Product (GNP), price indices, savings, employment, production and business activity, corporate profits, agriculture, international statistics, and so forth.

The Federal Reserve Bulletin, a monthly publication of the Board of Governors of the Federal Reserve System, is a prime source for monetary data, money and credit data, and figures on GNP, labor force, output, and the international economy. It also contains data pertinent to the Federal Reserve System, including member-bank reserves and reserve requirements, and open-market transactions.

Most of the 12 Federal Reserve Banks also have their own publications, featuring data and analyses of economic activity. The Federal Reserve Bank of St. Louis produces several publications of special interest to economists and other economic observers. For example, *U.S. Financial Data* is a weekly analysis of money market conditions, and *National Economic Trends* is a monthly publication dealing with aggregate business.

Economic Indicators is a monthly publication of the Council of Economic Advisors. It contains data on income, spending, employment, prices, money and credit, and other factors on both a monthly and an annual basis.

Business Conditions Digest (*BCD*), published monthly by the Department of Commerce, contains data on indicators of the economy from the National Bureau of Economic Research (which will be discussed in Chapter 10). Some 90 indicators, and over 300 components, are included. These indicators are important in attempting to discern the economy's movements, which make *BCD* a valuable information source for those interested in forecasting economic activity. *BCD* contains the basic data for many of the charts of economic activity often seen by investors.[7]

A third monthly source of economic data is the Department of Commerce's *Survey of Current Business.* This source provides detailed information on the national income accounts, as well as data on such variables as

[7]The Federal Reserve also publishes a monthly *Chart Book* showing numerous financial and economic series.

industrial production, employment and wages, and interest rates. The *Survey* also reviews recent developments in the economy.

The government provides data on industries, primarily through the Census Bureau. These data include employment figures, number of companies, and sales. Investors who choose to do their own detailed security analysis may find such information of real value. A good source of industry accounting data is *Quarterly Financial Report for Manufacturing Corporations*, published by the Federal Trade Commission and the Securities and Exchange Commission. This report contains aggregate balance sheet and income statement data for all manufacturing corporations. Data are broken down by industry and by size (assets).

Finally, the role of the government in providing investors with information on companies should be noted. Very extensive accounting and financial data are provided to investors in virtually all companies of interest through the requirements of the SEC. Annual reports must be filed within 90 days of the close of the fiscal year with the SEC in 10-K statements, which provide very detailed information. The 10-K statements contain information not available in a company's annual report. Interim reports (8-K) must also be filed if important transactions occur. These reports are available to investors from the SEC and can also be found in many libraries. In many respects, the 10-K report is the most detailed source of company information that can be obtained by an investor.

Academic and Professional Journals

Like government publications, the academic press is available to investors but is not often used. First, investors are often unaware of these journals. Second, in most cases they are too difficult to be read easily. And third, they often contain many articles not of direct interest to the practicing investor.

The more difficult academic journals, of limited use to most investors, include *The Journal of Finance, The Journal of Financial and Quantitative Analysis, The Journal of Financial Economics, The Journal of Business, The Journal of Financial Research*, the *Financial Review,* and the *Journal of Business Research*.

Several journals of both an academic and professional nature are available. Of particular interest to some investors with a good basic understanding of investments is the *Journal of Portfolio Management,* a quarterly intended to make available academic research for the professional portfolio manager. The *Financial Analysts Journal* (formerly published by the Financial Analysts Federation) is a bimonthly with articles intended for financial analysts. Although the average investor may not understand all the articles in these two journals, much of this material is valuable to those with some knowledge of the field.

The Financial Analysts Federation combined in 1989 with the Institute of Chartered Financial Analysts to form the **Association for Investment Management and Research (AIMR).** The AIMR is a nonprofit corporation devoted to the advancement of investment management and security analysis. The AIMR emphasizes research that is practitioner oriented, and conducts a number of seminars and workshops during the year devoted to topics of current interest to people in the investments area.

The Institute of Chartered Financial Analysts is a professional organization composed of members called **Chartered Financial Analysts (CFA).** This professional designation is awarded to people meeting recognized standards of competency and conduct. To earn the CFA designation, a candidate must complete a series of three comprehensive examinations offered once a year in June. The subject areas studied include economics, financial accounting, quantitative techniques, ethical and professional standards, fixed-income securties analysis, equity securities analysis, and portfolio management. The candidate must also accumulate three years work experience in positions related to investments. The CFA designation, first awarded in 1963, is widely respected and continues to gain recognition in the investment community. In 1989 some 8000 total candidates took one of the three exams, with an overall pass rate of 62% (the pass rate at Level I was 54%).

The CFA Digest, a publication of the AIMR, contains abstracts of published articles from academic, government, and professional sources that are felt to be of interest to security analysts and portfolio managers. Each issue may contain 25 to 30 abstracts.

A third professional journal is *Institutional Investor,* intended for money managers. Published monthly, its emphasis is on the current state of the money management industry.

Computerized Investments Information

Although the previous discussion demonstrates the tremendous amount of published financial information available, a large and growing amount of computer-based information is also available. In some cases the latter is similar to the published information, but it is much more convenient for those with access to both it and a computer. Individuals wishing to study securities and to analyze data can accomplish far more with the computer than they could ever hope to accomplish without it.

For several years investors have been able to obtain either databases or computer-based services, or both, from specialized financial service firms. In the case of databases, the buyer typically receives a tape (or tapes) containing substantial financial information on a large number of companies and processes this information on a mainframe computer. Computer-based services, on the other hand, provide the client with the means to access the databases from the client's terminal (again, traditionally, some type of large computer). These databases are almost always quite expensive, often thousands of dollars, as are the computers themselves.

Obviously, most investors do not have mainframe computers or computerized sources of information. However, the rise of the personal computer has changed this situation dramatically and will continue to have a major impact in the future. Investors currently can access or process an incredible array of computerized information from their homes, and the number doing so undoubtedly will grow.

For *organizational purposes,* we will first discuss the traditional sources of computerized information and services that remain important to many users, particularly researchers who wish to analyze and manipulate substantial amounts of data for hundreds, or even thousands, of companies. We will then review the personal computer potential, which is of immediate use to individual investors with access to a personal computer. It should be noted, however, that the division between these two components is not sharp and distinct. For example, Compustat now has available a floppy disk version of its data, and the Media General databank can be accessed by personal computers.

Traditional Computerized Databases and Services

Probably the best-known source of financial information for studies of corporate securities and their issuers is Standard & Poor's Compustat Services, Inc. The **Compustat** database consists of various tapes that can be regularly updated. For example, the Compustat II Annual and Quarterly Format option available to universities consists of several databases covering several thousand active companies.[8] The annual format presents numerous data items for 20 years; the quarterly format presents fewer data items for 40 quarters.[9]

Compustat provides these tapes to many universities and colleges at greatly reduced rates, thereby making them available for scholarly research.[10] Many investments articles have used these data in their analysis.

CRSP The Center for Research in Security Prices (CRSP) at the University of Chicago produces a set of tapes containing both month-end and daily stock prices for every NYSE stock, starting in 1926.[11] These data are in both

[8]One of the 12 databases, the Research file, contains an additional 3600 inactive companies that have filed for bankruptcy, have gone private, were acquired or liquidated, or no longer report.

[9]These databases also contain business segment and aggregate industry data.

[10]For example, in 1986 the Compustat II option had a $10,000 annual fee for universities, and commercial rates totaled more than $60,000.

[11]Tapes for the American Stock Exchange are also available.

raw form (prices and dividends) and returns form. Market indices are also available on a daily and monthly basis.

The CRSP tapes allow researchers to document the price (return) performance of every NYSE stock, either by itself or in relation to a market index, for almost 60 years. Thus, the reaction of a stock, or group of stocks, to a particular event or series of events can be studied.

Media General The publishers of *The Media General Financial Weekly,* referred to earlier, also sell a databank containing major financial information for close to 3000 companies. The tapes include current and historical price and volume information as well as balance sheet and income statement data.

Personal Computer Possibilities

The personal computer is opening up numerous possibilities for investors, providing them the opportunity to examine large amounts of data in an almost endless variety of ways. Until the rise of the personal computer and its mushrooming related-support services, these opportunities were simply beyond the scope of all but a very few individual investors.

Several million personal computers have been sold, and projections call for a vastly expanding market. As more and more individual investors purchase a personal computer, the demand for investment services they can use will increase. The only additional hardware needed by an investor is a modem to connect the personal computer by telephone lines to another computer.

It is impossible to describe all the services and packages now available to investors through the use of personal computers. Existing products change rapidly, and in some cases disappear, as new ones appear daily. What we can do, however, is to organize this area into its principal products and services and describe a few of the better-known offerings. Readers must keep in mind that this is a nonexhaustive list intended only as a general guide.[12]

Our organization is based on the following structure:

1. On-line financial services
2. Disk databases
3. Software packages
   a. For security analysis
      (1) Technical analysis
      (2) Fundamental analysis
   b. For portfolio management

[12]No endorsement of any of the products mentioned here is intended or implied.

On-Line Financial Services A widely known source of information available to all personal computer users is *Compuserve.* It offers current and historical price data, financial statements, and earnings estimates. It features the ability to screen companies, funds, and issues according to over 20 criteria specified by the user as well as the ability to chart and graph technical trends. The user can interface and interact with online brokerage firms 24 hours a day. Obviously, a modem is needed, and charges are involved, depending upon usage.

A major source of investment information for personal computers is the *Dow Jones News/Retrieval,* produced by the publishers of *The Wall Street Journal.* This service provides up-to-the-minute news and information from Dow Jones, which has a vast array of information stored in its computers. This information set includes news from *The Wall Street Journal, Barron's,* and the Dow Jones News Service; Dow Jones Quotes; Media General Financial Services (covering 3200 companies and 170 industries); Disclosure II (detailed data on over 6000 publicly held companies, including data filed with the SEC); an update of weekly economic information; forecasts of corporate earnings for 2400 of the most widely followed companies, weekly forecasts of monetary and economic indicators, and other services. Users must pay a per-minute fee to use the various parts of the service, with different parts having different rates.[13]

The *Dow Jones News/Retrieval* offers a total of over 30 databases. It is considered by many investors to be the premier on-line financial service.

Dow Jones also offers *Professional Investor Report,* which provides real-time price alerts on 5000 stocks. When a stock moves outside its "normal" range, a PC user's screen or printer signals the news. Volume activity is also reported. Follow-up reports can be received moments later.

Several other on-line services are available. For example, Charles Schwab & Co., a discount brokerage firm, offers Schwab's Electronic Brokerage Service. Using its software package, *The Equalizer,* investors can access information from the *Dow Jones News/Retrieval* and from several other organizations such as Standard & Poor's.

Disk Databases Two packages available from well-known investment advisory services are Stock Pak II from Standard & Poor's, and Value/Screen II from Arnold Bernhard & Company (publisher of *The Value Line Investment Survey*).

Stock Pak II consists of separate data disks covering NYSE, Amex, and over-the-counter stocks. Users can design their own screening criteria to use with these data disks and screen the database for all companies meeting the criteria.

Value/Screen II, new in 1989, is an investment software system that

[13]Non-prime-time rates are cheaper than prime-time rates.

helps investors select stocks and keep portfolio records. It contains all of Value Line's decision-making criteria for each of 1600 companies. Subscribers can receive an updated disk quarterly, monthly, or weekly. Users can screen this database using Value Line's criteria such as timeliness and safety, and can load the data into spreadsheets. In addition to constructing lists of stocks to meet specific objectives and obtaining the complete Value Line report on each company, the user can obtain the latest quotes and news on any stocks of interest using Value/Screen's automatic link-up with *Dow-Jones News Retrieval*.

Compustat data, described earlier, is now available in compact disk format. (This format requires a special drive to read.) It includes 20 years of annual data and 10 years of quarterly data for over 7000 active companies, and also includes data for inactive companies.

The *Disclosure* on-line service described earlier is available as a compact disk, which holds 1500 times the data of a floppy disk. The Disclosure Database, updated monthly, provides financial and management information about companies extracted from reports filed with the SEC. It also provides such information as annual reports to stockholders, detailed stock ownership information, management discussion of significant issues, proxy statements, and so forth. Detailed profiles are provided for more than 12,000 companies.

Economica and *Citibase* offer *Econ-DB*, a comprehensive PC database. Over 700 widely used economic time series, such as GNP, exports, consumption, and retail sales, are available on diskette in monthly, quarterly, or one-time-only form.

Software Packages Many software packages are now available for the personal computer, offering both security analysis and portfolio management. We will discuss each of these areas briefly.

In 1986, only a few years after the widespread introduction of personal computers, *PC Magazine* reviewed 25 programs designed for technical analysis, which essentially means that they help prepare a chart of the price and/or volume movements for a particular company.[14] These programs typically come with the ability to access the on-line financial services so that the necessary data can be downloaded. Personal computers are well suited to producing graphs of various types, which form the basis of technical analysis.

The same issue also reviewed seven fundamental analysis software packages, including Stock Pak II and Value/Screen Plus, mentioned earlier. It is clear that much less software has been produced in this area. The reason for this may become apparent after we study fundamental analysis.

Numerous programs for the personal computer are available to man-

[14]See *PC Magazine*, April 15, 1986.

age the portfolio by valuing it, separating items by tax categories, tracking brokerage commissions, and so on. Essentially, these programs build a database (your portfolio information) and allow you to make calculations and generate reports from that database. These programs tend to be divided into two categories, those for professional portfolio managers and those for individual investors. The prices of such programs reflect this, with some ranging into the thousands of dollars.

Summary

- Since the investment process is basically information oriented, a primary problem for investors is finding what is needed and likely to be useful from the vast quantity of information available.
- Users of information can be broadly divided into two groups: individual investors and institutional investors. Individuals must recognize their needs and limitations and act accordingly. Institutional investors, on the other hand, have the resources and the need to collect and process considerable information.
- Information sources can be separated into printed and computerized material.
- Published sources of information can be organized in rough order of general availability and use by investors. They include the financial press (newspapers and magazines), which is widely available as a source of such features as news stories; economy, industry, and company analysis; price and volume information; and columnists.
- Corporate reports are sent automatically by companies to shareholders, and other investors can easily obtain them.
- Brokerage firms provide a steady flow of information and recommendations.
- Investment information services, such as Standard & Poor's and Moody's, publish a variety of reports, manuals, and guides, and probably form the basis of investment information in this country while also recommending securities.
- Numerous investment advisory services exist, which, though they provide information, are usually thought of as "recommendation" services. *The Value Line Investment Survey* is the largest and probably best-known advisory service.
- Other sources of information include government publications and the financial and professional journals.
- Computerized investment information includes the traditional mainframe-oriented databases, a necessity in analyzing securities and researching investment questions and strategies, and computer-based services that allow subscribers to access information through time-sharing techniques.
- Personal computers now offer anyone a way to access information and

services from their home or office. Included in this area are the on-line financial services, floppy disk databases, and various types of software for both security analysis and portfolio management.

Key Sources of Information

- **The Financial Press**
  - **Newspapers**
    - *The Wall Street Journal*
    - *Barron's*
    - *The M/G Financial Weekly*
    - *The Wall Street Transcript*
  - **Magazines**
    - *Forbes*
    - *Business Week*
    - *Fortune*
    - *Money*
- **Annual Reports**
- **Brokerage Firms**
- **Investment Information Services**
  - **Standard & Poor's Corporation**
    - *Bond Guide*
    - *Bond Outlook*
    - *Corporate Records* (*Daily News*)
    - *Stock Guide*
    - *Stock Reports*
    - *Industry Surveys*
    - *Statistical Service: CurrentStatistics*
  - **Moody's**
    - *Bond Survey*
    - *Handbook of Common Stocks*
    - *Investors Fact Sheets*
    - *Manuals* (*Industrial, OTC Industrial, Public Utility Bank & Finance, Municipal & Government, Transportation, and International*)
    - *Stock Survey*
- **Investment Advisory Services**
  - *The Value Line Investment Survey*
  - **Others**
- **Government Publications**
  - *Economic Report of the President*
  - *The Federal Reserve Bulletin*
  - *Federal Reserve Bank of St. Louis*
    - *U.S. Financial Data*
    - *National Economic Trends*
  - *Economic Indicators*
  - *Business Conditions Digest*
  - *Survey of Current Business*
  - *Quarterly Financial Report for Manufacturing Corporations*
- **Academic and Professional Journals**
  - **Academic Journals**
  - **Professional Journals**
    - *Financial Analysts Journal*
    - *Journal of Portfolio Management*
    - *Institutional Investor*
    - *The C.F.A. Digest*
- **Computerized Databases and Services**
  - **Compustat**
  - **CRSP**
  - **Media General**
- **Personal Computers**
  - **On-Line Financial Services**
  - **Disk Databases**
  - **Software Packages**
    - **Security Analysis**
      - **Technical Analysis**
      - **Fundamental Analysis**
    - **Portfolio Management**

Questions

4-1 How should individual investors approach the problem of obtaining investment information?

4-2 What sources of price and volume information for securities are investors most likely to use?

4-3 How does *The Wall Street Journal* and *Barron's* differ in price and volume quotations?

4-4 How can annual reports help investors in trying to analyze the "quality" of a corporation's earnings?

4-5 How do discount brokers and full-service brokers differ in providing investment information?

4-6 Describe how, using Standard & Poor's services, an investor can go from very detailed information about a common stock to a quite brief summary of pertinent information.

4-7 What does a Value Line rating of "4" for timeliness mean?

4-8 Would you expect each stock rated by Value Line to perform in accordance with its rank in every year? What about each of the five groups?

4-9 Outline government publications that would be of help in analyzing the economy.

4-10 What sources of information are available from the government on industries and on companies?

4-11 Which government publication is particularly useful in forecasting economic activity? Why?

4-12 Where could an investor find abstracts of recent articles of interest to security analysts and portfolio managers?

4-13 Explain what Compustat is and its value.

4-14 How could Compustat aid investors in testing possible investment strategies?

4-15 Of what additional value are the CRSP tapes in relation to Compustat?

4-16 What is meant by time-sharing?

4-17 What is the Dow-Jones News/Retrieval?

4-18 Describe the types of software and services available for personal computer users.

Selected References

Abstracts of recent articles related to investments can be found in

The CFA Digest, The Institute of Chartered Financial Analysts; P.O. Box 3668; Charlottesville, Virginia 22903.

The largest investment advisory service for individuals is:

The Value Line Investment Survey and other Value Line services. Arnold Bernhard and Company, Inc.; 5 East 44th Street; New York, New York 10017.

Information on where to find statistics and data of various types can be found in:

Karen J. Chapman, *Investment Statistics Locator* (Phoenix, Arizona: The Oryx Press, 1988).

CHAPTER 5

Return and Risk Concepts

The field of investments traditionally has been divided into security analysis and portfolio management. Chapter 6 and several later chapters discuss security analysis for fixed-income and equity securities. The heart of security analysis is the valuation of financial assets. Value, in turn, is a function of return and risk. These two concepts, therefore, are very important in the study of investments.

Return and risk will be described, measured, and used throughout the text. Particular concepts of return and risk will be used when needed, but it is extremely valuable before beginning an analysis of the various securities to obtain a working knowledge of these concepts. Therefore, in this chapter we shall consider the concepts of return and risk, learn how to measure them, and discuss how to go about estimating them. In the final analysis the investment decision can be described as a trade-off between risk and expected return. The chapter concludes with a detailed examination of the risk–return trade-off that dominates investments.

Return

As noted in Chapter 1, the objective of investors is to maximize expected returns, although subject to constraints, primarily risk. Return is the motivating force in the investment process. It is the reward for undertaking the investment.

Return is crucial to investors. It is the only rational way (after allowing for risk) for investors to compare alternative investments that differ in what they offer. The measurement of actual (historical) returns is necessary for investors to assess how well they have done. And finally, the historical return plays a large part in the estimation of future, unknown returns.

Realized Versus Expected Return

It is important at the outset to distinguish clearly between the two concepts of return described in Chapter 1: realized return and expected return. Both terms are used extensively in investment discussions.

Realized return is what the term implies; it is ex post (after the fact) return, or return that was or could have been earned. Realized return has occurred.

Example. A deposit of \$100 in a bank on January 1 at a stated annual interest rate of $5\frac{1}{4}$ will be worth \$105.25 one year later. The actual or realized return for the year is \$5.25/\$100, or 5.25%. Similarly, the total annual return on the Standard & Poor 500 Composite Index for 1989 was about 31.5%.

This was the actual (realized) return if an investor bought the entire index on January 1, 1989, and sold on December 31, 1989. ▪

Expected return is the return from an asset that investors anticipate (expect) they will earn over some future period. It is a predicted return, subject to uncertainty, and may or may not occur. Investors should be willing to purchase a particular asset if the expected return is adequate, but they must understand that their expectation may not materialize. If not, the realized return will differ from the expected return. In fact, realized returns on securities show considerable variability. Although investors may receive their expected returns on risky securities on a long-run average basis, they generally do not do so on a short-run basis.

The Components of Return

Return on a typical investment consists of two components. The basic component that usually comes to mind is the periodic cash receipts (or income) on the investment, either interest or dividends. The second component is also important, particularly for common stocks but also for longer-term bonds and other fixed-income securities. This is the appreciation (or depreciation) in the price of the asset, commonly called the capital gain or loss. It is the difference between the purchase price and the price at which the asset can be or is sold; therefore, it can be a gain or a loss.

Income The income from an investment opportunity consists of one or more cash payments paid at specified intervals of time. Interest payments on most bonds, for example, are paid semiannually, whereas dividends on common stocks are usually paid quarterly. The distinguishing feature of these payments is that they are paid in cash by the issuer to the holder of the asset.

The term ***yield*** is often used in connection with this component of return. Yield refers to the income component in relation to some price for a security. For our purposes here, the price that is relevant is the purchase price of the security.

Example. The yield on a 10%-coupon bond purchased at a price of $900 is 11.11% ($100/$900). The yield on a common stock paying $5 in dividends per year and purchased for $50 per share is 10%.[1]

It is very important to remember that yield is not, for most purposes, the proper measure of return from a security, as Box 5-1 points out. The capital gain or loss must also be considered. ▪

[1]There are other yield measures, several of which are discussed in the next chapter.

BOX 5-1

YIELD VERSUS TOTAL RETURN

The 1838 Bond-Debenture Trading Fund is a closed-end recently trading at 20. For years it paid out $2 a year unfailingly. But the dividend was cut to $1.86 in 1987, and this year it's likely to come down another 4 cents. Robert Vitale, a soft-spoken 59-year-old who manages the portfolio, is apologetic: "Some people depend on the dividend for their living, the elderly, people like that," he says. "Nobody wants to see it cut."

But, in spite of the pressures on him, Vitale has done pretty well for his shareholders. The portfolio's total return is excellent. Total return is yield, plus or minus capital gains and losses. If a fund has a handsome yield but loses principal, its total return will be lousy. If it has a relatively low yield but makes the capital grow, its total return will be good. The 1838 Fund's total return has averaged 12.5% a year compounded over the past decade, after expenses. That easily beats the 11.2% return for the Merrill Lynch Corporate/Government bond index, which of course does not reflect any expenses.

There's a lesson here for investors: Don't buy a fund, not even a bond fund, on yield alone. The bond market today is almost as volatile as the stock market. Look, then, for a bond fund that has a record of steering the treacherous shoals of the bond market and delivering a good total return. People who buy funds for their yields are fools. You should buy for total return, and, if you need spending money, simply cash in some of your shares.

Source: Excerpted by permission of *Forbes* magazine, September 4, 1989. © Forbes, Inc., 1989.

Price Appreciation (Depreciation) The other component of return is the change in price on the asset (if any). Price appreciation is the amount by which the sale price of a security exceeds the purchase price (this is often referred to as a **capital gain**). A sale price lower than the purchase price results in price depreciation, often referred to as a **capital loss.**[2] Many investors have capital gains as their primary objective. Investors often expect this component to be larger than the income component.

This concept involves only the difference between the proceeds from selling a security and its original cost. An investor can buy an asset and sell it one day, one hour, or one minute later for a capital gain or loss.

Total Return Having examined the two components of a security's return, it remains to add them together (algebraically) to form total return, which for any security is defined as

[2]Capital gains and losses can be either paper gains (losses) or realized gains (losses). The security must be sold before a gain or loss is realized.

$$\text{Total return} = \text{Income} \begin{array}{c} + \text{ Price appreciation} \\ \text{or} \\ - \text{ Price depreciation} \end{array} \tag{5-1}$$

Equation 5-1 is a conceptual statement for total return. To implement this concept, it should be stated differently, as is done following. *The important point is that a security's total return consists of the sum of two components, income and price change.* Note that either component can be zero for a given security over any given time period.

Example. A bond purchased at par and held to maturity provides a stream of income in the form of interest payments. A bond purchased for $800 and held to maturity provides both income and a price change. The purchase of a non-dividend-paying stock that is sold six months later produces either a capital gain or a capital loss, but no income. ■

Measuring Returns

Investors need to measure returns, whether realized or expected. A correct measurement must incorporate the two components of return, income and price change, into a total return as discussed earlier. Returns across time or from different securities can be measured and compared using the total return concept.

Total Return The **total return** for a given holding period is a decimal (or percentage) return concept relating all the cash flows received by an investor during any designated time period to the amount of money invested in the asset. Sometimes called *holding period yield,* it is defined as

$$TR = \frac{\text{Any cash payments received + Price changes over the period}}{\text{Price at which the asset is purchased}} \tag{5-2}$$

All the items in Equation 5-2 are measured in dollars. The dollar price change over the period, defined as the difference between the beginning (or purchase) price and the ending (or sale) price, can be either positive (sales price exceeds purchase price) or negative (purchase price exceeds sales price). Netting the two items in the numerator together and dividing by the purchase price results in a decimal return figure that can easily be converted into percentage form. Note that in using the TR, the two components of return, yield and price change, have been measured.[3]

[3]This can be seen more easily by rewriting Equation 5-2 to show specifically its income and price change components.

$$TR = \frac{\text{Cash payments received}}{\text{Purchase price}} + \frac{\text{Price change over the period}}{\text{Purchase price}}$$

The first term is a yield component, whereas the second term measures the price change.

The general equation for calculating TR is

$$\text{TR} = \frac{\text{CF}_t + (P_\text{E} - P_\text{B})}{P_\text{B}} \tag{5-3}$$

where

CF = cash flows during the measurement period t
P_E = price at the end of period t or sale price
P_B = purchase price of the asset or price at the beginning of the period
PC = change in price during the period or P_E minus P_B

The cash flows for a bond come from the interest payments received; those for a stock come from the dividends received. For some assets, such as a warrant, there are no cash flows, only a price change. Part A of Figure 5-1 illustrates the calculation of TR for a bond, a common stock, and a warrant. Although one year is often used for convenience, this calculation can be applied to periods of any length.

In summary, the total return concept is valuable as a measure of return because it is all-inclusive, measuring the total return per dollar of original investment. It facilitates the comparison of asset returns over a specified period, whether the comparison is of different assets, such as stocks versus bonds, or different securities within the same type, such as several common stocks. Remember that using this concept does not mean that the securities have to be sold and the gains or losses actually realized.

A. Total Return (TR) Calculations

I. Bond TR

$$\text{Bond TR} = \frac{I_t + (P_\text{E} - P_\text{B})}{P_\text{B}} = \frac{I_t + \text{PC}}{P_\text{B}}$$

I_t = the interest payment(s) received during the period,
P_B and P_E = the beginning and ending prices, respectively
PC = the change in price during the period.

Example. Assume the purchase of a 10%-coupon Treasury bond at a price of \$960, held one year, and sold for \$1020. The TR is

$$\text{Bond TR} = \frac{100 + (1020 - 960)}{960} = \frac{100 + 60}{960} = 0.1667, \text{ or } 16.67\% \quad \blacksquare$$

II. Stock TR

$$\text{Stock TR} = \frac{D_t + (P_\text{E} - P_\text{B})}{P_\text{B}} = \frac{D_t + \text{PC}}{P_\text{B}}$$

D_t = the dividend(s) paid during the period

Example. 100 shares of DataShield are purchased at \$30 per share and sold one year later at \$26 per share. A dividend of \$2 per share is paid.

$$\text{Stock TR} = \frac{2 + (26 - 30)}{30} = \frac{2 + (-4)}{30} = -0.0667, \text{ or } -6.67\% \quad ■$$

III. Warrant TR

$$\text{Warrant TR} = \frac{C_t + (P_E - P_B)}{P_B} = \frac{C_t + PC}{P_B} = \frac{PC}{P_B}$$

where C_t = any cash payment received by the warrant holder during the period. Because warrants pay no dividends, the only return to an investor from owning a warrant is the change in price during the period.

Example. Assume the purchase of warrants of DataShield at \$3 per share, a holding period of six months, and the sale at \$3.75 per share.

$$\text{Warrant TR} = \frac{0 + (3.75 - 3.00)}{3.00} = \frac{0.75}{3.00} = 0.25, \text{ or } 25\% \quad ■$$

B. Return Relative Calculations

The return relative for the preceding bond example shown is

$$\text{Bond return relative} = \frac{100 + 1020}{960} = 1.1667$$

The return relative for the stock example is

$$\text{Stock return relative} = \frac{2 + 26}{30} = 0.9333$$

The return relative for the warrant example is

$$\text{Warrant return relative} = \frac{3.75}{3.00} = 1.25$$

To convert from a return relative to a TR, subtract 1.0 from the return relative.

FIGURE 5-1 ***Examples of Total Return and Price Relative Calculations***

Return Relative It is often necessary to measure returns on a slightly different basis. This is particularly true when calculating cumulative wealth or a geometric mean because negative returns cannot be used in the calculation. The **return relative,** sometimes referred to as a *holding period return,* solves this problem by adding 1.0 to the total return. Although return relatives may be less than 1.0, they will always be greater than zero, thereby eliminating negative numbers.

Example. A total return of 0.10 for some holding period is equivalent to a return relative of 1.10, and a total return of -0.15 is equivalent to a return relative of 0.85.

Equation 5-3 can be modified to calculate return relatives directly by using the price at the end of the holding period in the numerator, rather than the change in price, as in Equation 5-4.

$$\textit{Return relative} = \frac{CF_t + P_E}{P_B} \qquad (5\text{-}4)$$

▪

Examples of return relative calculations for the same three assets as the preceding are shown in Part B of Figure 5-1.

Using Measures of Return

As an illustration of the calculation and use of TRs, consider Table 5-1, which shows the Standard & Poor's (S&P) 500 Stock Composite Index for the years 1926 through 1989. Included in the table are end-of-year values for the index, from which capital gains and losses can be computed, and dividends on the index, which constitute the income component. The TRs for each year can be calculated as shown at the bottom of the table, where, as a demonstration of these calculations, the TR for 1981 is calculated.

Example. In 1981 the market, as measured by the S&P 500 Composite Index, had a TR of -4.85%, or return relative of .9515. In 1982, in contrast, the same market index showed a TR of 20.37%, or return relative of 1.2037.

The TR is a useful measure of return for a specified period of time. Also needed in investment analysis are statistics to describe a series of returns. For example, investing in a particular stock for 10 years or a different stock in each of 10 years could result in 10 TRs, which must be described by one or more statistics. ▪

Arithmetic Mean The most familiar statistic to most people is the arithmetic mean. Therefore, the word *mean* will refer to the arithmetic mean unless otherwise specified. The arithmetic mean, customarily designated by the symbol $\bar{X}$ (X-bar), is

$$\bar{X} = \frac{\Sigma X}{n} \qquad (5\text{-}5)$$

or the sum of each of the values being considered divided by the total number of values n.

Example. Using data from Table 5-1 for the 10 years of the 1970s ending in 1979, the arithmetic mean is calculated in Table 5-2 as

$$\begin{aligned}\bar{X} &= [3.51 + 14.12 + 18.72 + (-14.50) \ldots + 18.24]/10 \\ &= 73.84/10 \\ &= 7.38\% \quad \blacksquare\end{aligned}$$

Geometric Mean The arithmetic mean return is appropriate as a measure of the central tendency of a distribution consisting of returns calculated for a particular time, such as a year. However, when percentage changes in value over time are involved, the arithmetic mean of these changes can be misleading. A different mean, the **geometric mean,** is needed to describe accurately the "true" average rate of return over multiple periods. The geometric mean return measures compound, cumulative returns over time. It is often used in investments and finance to reflect the *growth* of invested funds; that is, it measures the realized change in wealth over multiple periods.

The geometric mean is defined as the *n*th root of the product resulting from multiplying a series of returns together, as in Equation 5-6.

$$G = [(1 + R_1)(1 + R_2) \ldots (1 + R_n)]^{1/n} - 1 \tag{5-6}$$

where R is a series of returns in TR form. Note that adding 1.0 to each return, or R, produces a return relative. Return relatives are used in calculating geometric mean returns, because TRs, which can be negative, cannot be used.[4]

Example. Continuing the example from Table 5-1, consisting of the 10 years of data ending in 1979 for the S&P 500, the geometric mean would be as shown in Table 5-2:

$$\begin{aligned}G &= [(1.0351)(1.1412)(1.1872)(.855) \ldots (1.1824)]^{1/10} - 1 \\ &= 1.0578 - 1 \\ &= 0.0578, \text{ or } 5.78\% \quad \blacksquare\end{aligned}$$

The geometric mean reflects compound, cumulative returns over time. Thus, $1.00 invested in the S&P 500 Composite Index would have compounded at an average annual rate of 5.78% over the period 1970–1979. Notice that this geometric average rate of return is considerably lower than the arithmetic average rate of return of 7.38% because it reflects the variability in the returns.

---

[4]An alternative method of calculating the geometric mean is to find the log of each X, sum them, divide by n, and take the antilog.

TABLE 5-1 ***Standard & Poor's 500 Composite Index (1941–1943 = 10), Dividends in Index Form and Total Returns (TRs), 1926–1989***

Year	End-of-Year Index Value	Div.	TR%	Year	End-Of-Year Index Value	Div.	TR%
1926	13.49	0.69	—	1956	46.67	1.74	6.44
1927	17.66	0.77	36.620	1957	39.99	1.79	−10.478
1928	24.35	0.85	42.695	1958	55.21	1.75	42.436
1929	21.45	0.97	−7.926	1959	59.89	1.83	11.791
1930	15.34	0.98	−23.916	1960	58.11	1.95	0.284
1931	8.12	0.82	−41.721	1961	71.55	2.02	26.605
1932	6.89	0.50	−8.990	1962	63.10	2.13	−8.833
1933	10.10	0.44	52.975	1963	75.02	2.28	22.504
1934	9.50	0.45	−1.485	1964	84.75	2.50	16.302
1935	13.43	0.47	46.316	1965	92.43	2.72	12.271
1936	17.18	0.72	33.284	1966	80.33	2.87	−9.986
1937	10.55	0.80	−33.935	1967	96.47	2.92	23.727
1938	13.21	0.51	30.047	1968	103.86	3.07	10.843
1939	12.49	0.62	−0.757	1969	92.06	3.16	−8.319
1940	10.58	0.67	−9.928	1970	92.15	3.14	3.509
1941	8.69	0.71	−11.153	1971	102.09	3.07	14.118
1942	9.77	0.59	19.217	1972	118.05	3.15	18.719
1943	11.67	0.61	25.691	1973	97.55	3.38	−14.502
1944	13.28	0.64	19.280	1974	68.56	3.60	−26.028
1945	17.36	0.66	35.693	1975	90.19	3.68	36.917
1946	15.30	0.71	−7.776	1976	107.46	4.05	23.639
1947	15.30	0.84	5.490	1977	95.10	4.67	−7.165
1948	15.20	0.93	5.425	1978	96.11	5.07	6.393
1949	16.76	1.14	17.763	1979	107.94	5.70	18.240
1950	20.41	1.47	30.549	1980	135.76	6.16	31.480
1951	23.77	1.41	23.371	1981	122.55	6.63	−4.847
1952	26.77	1.41	17.711	1982	140.64	6.87	20.367
1953	24.81	1.45	−1.167	1983	164.93	7.09	22.312
1954	35.98	1.54	51.229	1984	167.24	7.53	5.966
1955	45.48	1.64	30.962	1985	211.28	7.90	31.057
				1986	242.17	8.28	18.539
				1987	247.08	8.81	5.665
				1988	277.72	9.73	16.339
				1989	353.40	11.05	31.229

$$TR\% = \frac{(P_t - P_{t-1}) + D_t}{P_{t-1}} (100)$$

For 1981:

$$TR\% = \frac{(122.55 - 135.76) + 6.63}{135.76} (100)$$

$$= -4.85\%$$

Source: Standard & Poor's Statistical Service, *Security Price Index Record*. New York: Standard & Poor's, 1986, pp. 134–137. Updated from monthly issues of Standard & Poor's *Current Statistics*. Reprinted by permission of Standard & Poor's Corporation.

TABLE 5-2 ***Calculation of the Arithmetic and Geometric Mean for the Years 1970–1979 for the S&P 500 Stock Composite Index***

Year	S&P 500 TRs (%)	S&P 500 Index Return Relatives
1970	3.51	1.0351
1971	14.12	1.1412
1972	18.72	1.1872
1973	−14.50	0.8550
1974	−26.03	0.7397
1975	36.92	1.3692
1976	23.64	1.2364
1977	−7.17	0.9283
1978	6.39	1.0639
1979	18.24	1.1824

$$\text{Arithmetic mean} = \frac{3.51 + 14.12 + 18.72 + \ldots + 18.24}{10}$$

$$= 7.38\%$$

$$\text{Geometric mean} = (1.0351)(1.1412)(1.1872)\ldots(1.1824)]^{1/n} - 1$$

$$= (1.7534)^{1/10} - 1$$

$$= 1.0578 - 1$$

$$= 0.0578 \text{ or } 5.78\%$$

Source: Based on data in Table 5-1.

The geometric mean will always be less than the arithmetic mean unless the values being considered are identical. The spread between the two depends on the dispersion of the distribution: The greater the dispersion, the greater the spread between the two means.

INVESTMENT CALCULATIONS

Obviously, a calculator or computer is needed to calculate the geometric mean in most situations. Calculators with power functions can be used to calculate roots. Alternatively, *The Investment Calculator* available with this text can be used on a personal computer. Go to the "Statistics" section, the first choice in the menu, and hit **ENTER.** Next, using the TR data from Table 5-2, enter the number of periods and designate that yields are to be used. After entering "P" for ex post, enter the 10 TR values, including negative signs. Hit **F1** to show the arithmetic mean, geometric mean, and standard deviation (to be discussed later). Note that the two means are as discussed previously.

Arithmetic Versus Geometric Mean When should we use the arithmetic mean and when should we use the geometric mean? The answer depends on the investor's objective. The arithmetic mean is a useful measure of average (typical) performance over single periods, whereas the geometric mean is a better measure of the change in wealth over time (multiple periods).

Example. As an illustration of how the arithmetic mean can be misleading in describing returns over multiple periods, consider the data in Table 5-3, which show the movements in price for two stocks over two successive holding periods. Both stocks have a beginning price of \$10. Stock A rises to \$20 in period 1 and then declines to \$10 in period 2. Stock B falls to \$8 in period 1 and then rises 50% to \$12 in period 2. For stock A the indicated annual average arithmetic rate of change in price is 25%. This is clearly not sensible, because the price of stock A at the end of period 2 is \$10, the same as the beginning price. The geometric mean calculation gives the correct annual average rate of change in price of 0% per year.

For stock B the arithmetic average of the annual percentage changes in price is 15%. However, if the price actually increased 15% each period, the ending price in period 2 would be \$10 × 1.15 × 1.15 = \$13.23. We know that this is not correct, because the price at the end of period 2 is \$12. The annual geometric rate of return, 9.54%, produces the correct price at the end of period 2: \$10 × 1.0954 × 1.0954 = \$12. ■

As these simple examples demonstrate, over multiple periods the geometric mean shows the true average rate of growth; that is, the rate at which an invested dollar grows. On the other hand, we should use the arithmetic mean to represent the likely or typical performance for a single period. To see this, consider the TR data for the S&P Index for the years 1970–1979 as described earlier. Our best representation of any one year's performance would be the arithmetic mean of 7.38%, because it was necessary to average this rate of return for a particular year, given the wide spread in the yearly numbers, in order to *realize* an actual growth rate of 5.78% after the fact. Thus, the average annual return for the three years 1970–1972 of 12.12% was more than offset by the average annual return for the two years 1973–1974 of −20%.

TABLE 5-3 ***Contrasting the Arithmetic and Geometric Means***

Stock	Period 1	Period 2	Annual Arithmetic Rate of Return	Annual Geometric Rate of Return
A	\$20	\$10	[100% + (−50%)]/2 = 25%	$[2.0(.5)]^{1/2} - 1 = 0\%$
B	\$ 8	\$12	[−20% + (50%)]/2 = 15%	$[.8(1.5)]^{1/2} - 1 = 9.5\%$

Example. Assume that the returns for two consecutive years were 16.76% and −2.0%. The arithmetic mean return for these two years would be exactly 7.38%; however, \$1 invested at these rates of return would have grown to \$1 × 1.1676 × .98 = \$1.1442, a geometric mean rate of return of only 6.97%. Based only on these two observations, our best estimate of the average return for next year would be 7.38%, *not* 6.97%. ■

Arithmetic and Geometric Means for Financial Assets To see how the preceding returns measures are typically used, consider Table 5-4, which shows the average annual geometric and arithmetic returns for major financial assets for the period 1926–1989. These data are from the Ibbotson and Sinquefield studies as published by Ibbotson Associates on a regular basis. They are widely known, used, and quoted.

Table 5-4 indicates that common stocks, as measured by the well-known Standard & Poor's 500 Composite Index, had a geometric mean annual return over this 64-year period of 10.3%. This means that \$1 invested in the market index at the beginning of 1926 would have grown at an average compound rate of 10.3% over this very long period. In contrast, the arithmetic mean annual return for stocks was 12.4%. The best estimate of the "average" return for stocks in any one year would be 12.4%, not the 10.3% geometric mean return. The difference between these two means is related to the variability of the stock return series (variability is discussed later).

Table 5-4 also shows that small company stocks (primarily, the smallest quintile of NYSE stocks according to market value) had a geometric mean return of 12.2% and an arithmetic mean of 17.7%, the highest numbers recorded in this data set. The spread between the two numbers reflects the even greater variability of this series.

These stock return numbers will be discussed in detail in Chapter 8.

Finally, long-term and intermediate-term government and corporate bonds are reported, as well as Treasury bills and the inflation rate. As we would expect, the returns are lower than those for stocks. Notice the small differences between the geometric and arithmetic means, reflecting the much lower levels of variability in these series. These bond return numbers will be discussed in Chapter 6.

Wealth Index Returns such as TRs measure *changes* in the level of wealth. As we have seen, we can express this change as an arithmetic average or as a growth rate (geometric mean). At times, however, it is more desirable to measure *levels* of wealth (or prices) rather than changes. In other words, we measure the *cumulative* effect of returns over time, typically on the basis of \$1 invested. To capture the cumulative effect of returns, we use index values, or indices. The value of the *cumulative wealth index*, V_n, is computed as

$$V_n = V_0\,(1 + R_1)(1 + R_2)\ .\ .\ .\ (1 + R_n) \qquad (5\text{-}7)$$

TABLE 5-4 ***Summary Statistics of Annual Returns for Major Financial Assets, 1926–1989***

Series	Geometric Mean	Arithmetic Mean	Standard Deviation
Common stocks	10.3%	12.4%	20.9%
Small company stocks	12.2	17.7	35.3
Long-term corporate bonds	5.2	5.5	8.5
Long-term government bonds	4.6	4.9	8.6
Intermediate-term government bonds	4.9	5.0	5.5
U.S. Treasury bills	3.6	3.7	3.4
Inflation rates	3.1	3.2	4.8

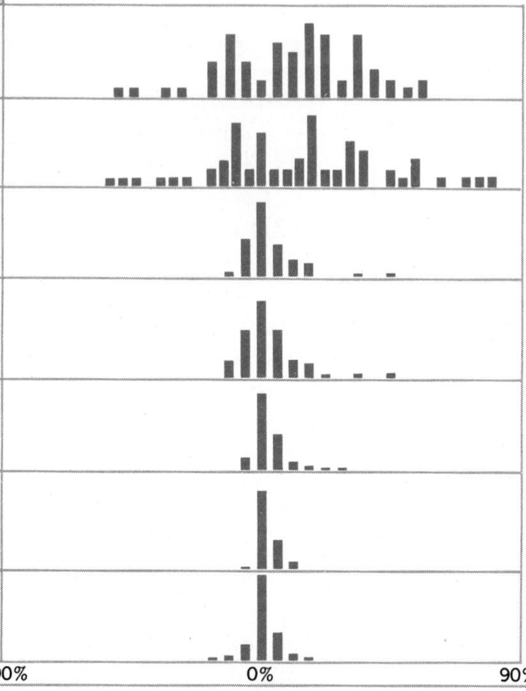

Source: Ibbotson, Roger G., and Rex A. Sinquefield, *Stocks, Bonds, Bills, and Inflation* (SSBI), 1989, updated in *SSBI 1990 Yearbook,*™ Ibbotson Associates, Chicago, p. 31. All rights reserved.

where

V_n = the cumulative wealth index as of the end of period n
V_0 = the beginning index value, typically 1.00
$R_{1,n}$ = the periodic TRs in decimal form

Example. For the S&P total returns in Table 5-1, the cumulative wealth, or ending wealth index, for the period 1926–1931 would be

$$V_{1931} = 1.00\,(1.36620)(1.42695)(0.92074)(0.76084)(0.58279)$$
$$= 0.79591$$

Thus, $1 invested at the end of 1926 (the beginning of 1927) would have been worth only 80 cents by the end of 1931, because of the losses sustained in the last three years. ■

Figure 5-2 shows the wealth indices for the major financial assets and inflation from the Ibbotson Associates data, as discussed earlier. Notice that the series starts at $1 at the end of 1925 and shows the cumulative results of investing in each of these assets by the end of 1989. As Figure 5-2 shows, the returns on stocks have completely dominated the returns on bonds over this period.

Wealth indices demonstrate the use of the geometric mean.

Example. The ending wealth value of 534.45 for the S&P 500 in Figure 5-2 is the result of compounding at 10.3% for 64 years, or

$$\begin{aligned} V_n &= V_0(1.103)^{64} \\ &= \$1.00\ (530.68) \\ &= \$530.68 \text{ (difference caused by rounding error)} \end{aligned}$$ ▪

The tremendous ending wealth for "small" stocks as shown in Figure 5-2 speaks for itself. One dollar invested in these stocks would have grown to $1628.59, which is calculated in exactly the same manner as the preceding. Remember, however, that the variability of this series is considerably larger.

Of course, the single most striking feature of Figure 5-2 is the tremendous difference in ending wealth between stocks and bonds. This reflects the impact of compounding substantially different mean returns over long periods of time, which produces almost unbelievable results. ▪

Compounding and Discounting The use of compounding in the previous section points out the importance of this concept, and its complement, discounting. Both are important in investment analysis and are used often. Compounding involves **future values** resulting from compound interest—earning interest on interest. As we saw, the calculation of wealth indices involves compounding at the geometric mean return over some historical period.

Present value (discounting) is the value today of a dollar to be received in the future. Such dollars are not comparable, because of the time value of money; to be comparable, they must be discounted back to the present. Present value concepts will be used extensively in Chapter 9, and in other chapters as needed, such as Chapter 7.

Tables are readily available for both compounding and discounting, and calculators and computers make these calculations a simple matter. These tables are available at the end of this text.

Risk

Risk and return go together in investments and finance. It is not sensible to talk about returns without talking about risk, because investment decisions

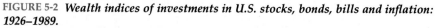

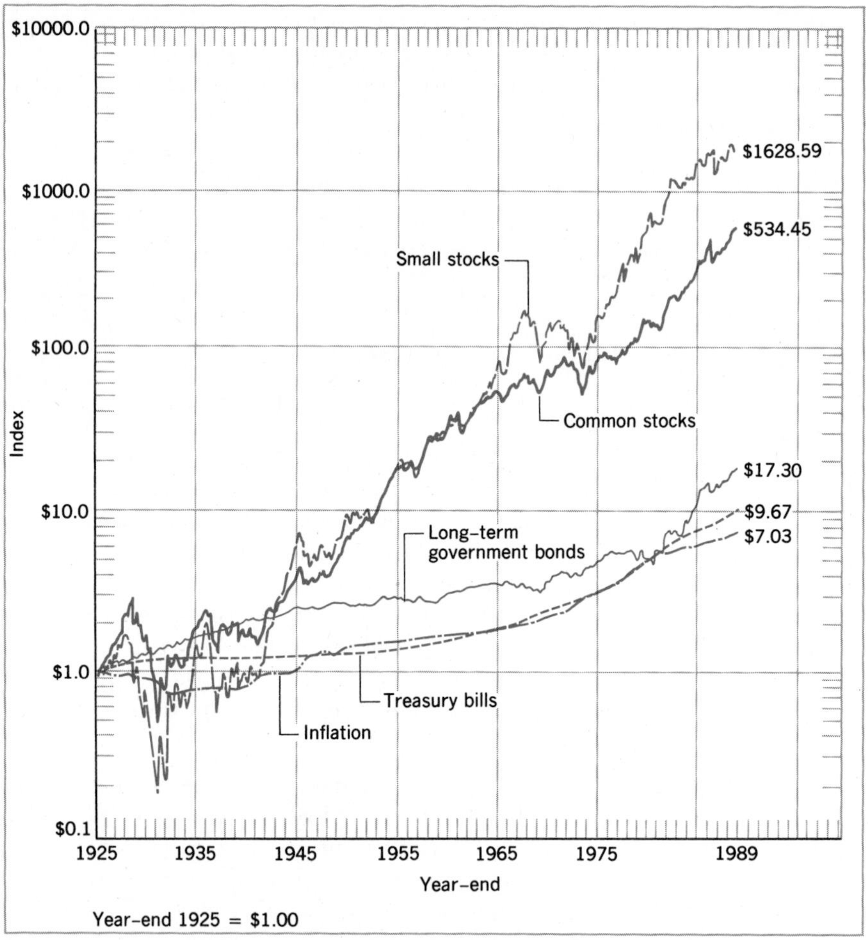

FIGURE 5-2 ***Wealth indices of investments in U.S. stocks, bonds, bills and inflation: 1926–1989.***
Source: Ibbotson, Roger G., and Rex A. Sinquefield, *Stocks, Bonds, Bills, and Inflation* (SBBI), updated in *Stocks, Bonds, Bills and Inflation 1990 Yearbook*™, Ibbotson Associates, Chicago.

involve a risk–return trade-off. Investors must constantly be aware of the risk they are assuming, know what it can do to their investment decisions, and be prepared for the consequences.

Risk was defined in Chapter 1 as the chance that the actual outcome from an investment will differ from the expected outcome. Specifically, what is of concern to most investors is that the actual outcome will be less than the expected outcome. The more variable the possible outcomes that can occur (i.e., the broader the range of possible outcomes) the greater the risk.

INVESTMENTS INTUITION

It is important to remember how expected return and risk go together. An investor cannot reasonably expect larger returns without being willing to assume larger risks. Consider the investor who wishes to avoid any risk (on a practical basis). Such an investor can deposit money in an insured savings account, thereby earning a guaranteed return of a known amount. However, this return will be fixed and the investor cannot earn more than this rate. Although risk is effectively eliminated, the chance of a large return is also. To have the opportunity to earn a larger return, investors must be willing to assume larger risks.

Sources of Risk

What makes a financial asset risky? Traditionally, investors have talked about several sources of risk, such as interest rate risk and market risk. The specific sources of risk applicable to bonds and stocks will be discussed separately in Chapters 6 and 8. Our purpose here is simply to point out that the total risk for any financial asset is a function of one or more general sources of risk.

Interest Rate Risk Interest rate risk is the variability in a security's return resulting from changes in the level of interest rates. Such changes affect all securities inversely; that is, other things being equal, security prices move inversely to interest rates. The reason for this is tied up with the valuation of securities, a subject discussed later. Interest rate risk affects bonds more directly than common stocks and is a major risk faced by all bondholders. As interest rates change, bond prices change in an inverse direction.

Market Risk Market risk is the variability in returns due to fluctuations in the overall market—that is, the aggregate stock market. All securities are exposed to market risk, although it affects primarily common stocks.

Market risk includes a wide range of factors exogenous to securities themselves, including recessions, wars, structural changes in the economy, and changes in consumer preferences.

Inflation Risk A factor affecting all securities is purchasing power risk, or the chance that the purchasing power of invested dollars will decline. With uncertain inflation, the real (inflation-adjusted) return involves risk even if the nominal return is safe (e.g., a Treasury bond). This risk is related to interest rate risk, since interest rates generally rise as inflation increases, because leaders demand additional inflation premiums to compensate for the loss of purchasing power.

Business Risk The risk of doing business in a particular industry or environment is called business risk. For example, U.S. Steel faces unique problems as the nation's largest steel producer. Similarly, General Motors faces unique problems as a result of such developments as the global oil situation and Japanese imports.

Financial Risk Financial risk is associated with the use of debt financing by companies. The larger the proportion of assets financed by debt (as opposed to equity), the larger the variability in the returns, other things being equal. Financial risk involves the concept of financial leverage.

Liquidity Risk Liquidity risk is the risk associated with the particular secondary market in which a security trades. An investment that can be bought or sold quickly and without significant price concession is considered liquid. The more uncertainty about the time element and the price concession, the greater the liquidity risk. A Treasury bill has little or no liquidity risk, whereas a small OTC stock may have substantial liquidity risk.

Total Risk

Investors must do more than simply be aware of the sources of risk. They must be able to quantify, or measure, risk. We therefore discuss the measurement and estimation of the total risk to an investor from one or more financial assets and then do the same for a specific measure of risk—market risk or systematic risk—that is a widely discussed and used cornerstone of modern portfolio theory. Although these are the two best-known and most often used measures of risk, assessing investment risk remains an unresolved issue. Every intelligent investor knows that risk is a key component of investment decisions, but evaluating risk precisely remains an art and not a science. See Box 5-2 for a *Wall Street Journal* assessment of risk.

Measuring Total Risk Risk is often associated with the dispersion in the likely outcomes. Dispersion refers to **variability.** Risk is assumed to arise out of variability, which is consistent with our definition of risk as the chance that the actual outcome of an investment will differ from the expected outcome. If an asset's return has no variability, in effect it has no risk. Thus, a one-year Treasury bill purchased to yield 10% and held to maturity will, in fact, yield (a nominal) 10%. No other outcome is possible, barring default by the U.S. government, a possibility not considered reasonable.

Consider an investor analyzing a series of returns (TRs) on the major

BOX 5-2

MORE ART THAN SCIENCE IN WEIGHING INVESTMENT RISK

Most investors know they are supposed to be weighing risk against return in making investment decisions. But how to put a number on the riskiness of a particular investment or portfolio?

Unfortunately, like many aspects of managing one's money, gauging investment risk is both more complex and less certain than most people would like. So what is this thing called risk that financial professionals can gauge so differently?

Risk has traditionally been equated with the volatility of investment returns. Small-company stocks are deemed riskier than large-company stocks, for instance, because the best years for small stocks have been more stupendous and the worst years more sickening.

Along those lines, financial advisers often measure the "standard deviation," or variance, of an investment's short-term returns from its own average return over a longer period. Standard deviations are calculated for entire portfolios to size up the best and worst performances they are likely to turn in.

Similarly, investors may see references to "beta," a calculation of the volatility of a particular stock or mutual fund relative to a broad market indicator such as the Standard & Poor's 500-stock index. The lower the beta or standard deviation, the lower the risk.

Calculation of future risk, however, is the subject of much debate. For instance, is it appropriate to use the high volatility of bond returns over the past several years, the lower volatility over several decades, or someone's best guess?

Regardless of what kind of analysis is used, advisers say some risks aren't adequately addressed by standard mathematical measures. Where real estate investments are concerned, for example, there is the risk of having to wait months to find a buyer. Even more important, the focus on a one-year horizon can blind investors to the longer-term risk of not generating high enough returns to stay ahead of inflation or provide comfortably fore retirement.

John Markese, director of research for American Association of Individual Investors in Chicago, says: "Some people, in trying to avoid risk, put all their money in Treasury bills. But the likelihood of their achieving their wealth goals may be virtually zero."

Advisers can address that longer-term risk by estimating the portfolio return an investor needs to build enough cash to meet long-term goals. Then, usually using standard deviations, they can also calculate probabilities that a particular portfolio will deliver that target return or, say, beat inflation over an extended period.

Source: Adapted from Karen Slater, "More Art Than Science in Weighing Investment Risk," *The Wall Street Journal*, August 24, 1989, pp. C1 and C10. Reprinted by permission of *The Wall Street Journal*,

types of financial assets over some period of years. Knowing the mean of this series is not enough. The investor needs to know something about the variability in the returns. A *histogram* presents a frequency distribution pictorially, using a vertical bar for each class in a frequency distribution. The vertical axis of such a diagram shows the frequency (or relative frequency), and the horizontal axis represents the value of the class.

Consider the histograms (distributions) of returns for major financial assets for the period 1926–1989 shown in Table 5-4. Common stocks show the largest variability (dispersion) in returns, with "small" common stocks showing even greater variability.[5] Corporate bonds have a much smaller variability and therefore a more compact distribution. Intermediate-term government bonds are less risky, and Treasury bills the least risky.[6] These distributions therefore are even more compact.

The risk of these distributions can be assessed with an absolute measure of dispersion, or variability. The most commonly used measure of dispersion over some period of years is the **standard deviation** which measures the deviation of each observation from the mean of the observations and is a reliable measure of the variability because all the information in a sample is used.[7] The standard deviation is a measure of the total risk of an asset or a portfolio. It captures the total variability in the asset's or portfolio's return, whatever the source(s) of that variability.

The standard deviation can be calculated as

$$s = \left[\frac{\Sigma (X - \overline{X})^2}{n - 1} \right]^{1/2} \tag{5-8}$$

where

s = standard deviation
X = each observation in the sample
$\overline{X}$ = the mean of the observations
n = the number of returns in the sample.

Knowing the returns from the sample, one can calculate the standard deviation fairly easily.

---

[5]In the Ibbotson–Sinquefield analysis, *size* refers to the capitalization (price times number of shares outstanding). The smallest quintile of NYSE stocks, based on capitalization, is chosen to represent the equities of smaller companies.

[6]The reason for the distribution of Treasury bonds, which have no practical risk of default, is that this is a distribution of annual returns, where negative numbers are possible. Thus, a Treasury bond purchased at $1000 on January 1 could decline to, say, $900 by December 31, resulting in a negative TR for that one year period.

[7]The variance is the standard deviation squared. The variance and the standard deviation are similar and can be used for the same purposes; specifically, in investment analysis, both are used as measures of risk. The standard deviation, however, is used more often.

TABLE 5-5 ***Calculating the Historical Standard Deviation***

Year	TR (%), X	$X - \bar{X}$	$(X - \bar{X})^2$	
1970	3.51	−3.87	14.98	
1971	14.12	6.74	45.43	
1972	18.72	11.34	128.6	
1973	−14.50	−21.88	478.73	
1974	−26.03	33.41	1116.23	
1975	36.92	29.54	872.61	
1976	23.64	16.26	264.39	
1977	−7.17	14.55	211.70	
1978	6.39	−.99	.98	
1979	18.19	10.81	116.86	
		$\Sigma(X - \bar{X})^2 =$	3250.51	
			$\frac{3250.51}{9}$	= 361.17
			$(361.17)^{1/2}$	= 19.00%

Example. The standard deviation of the 10 TRs (1970–1979) for the Standard & Poor's 500 Index, as shown in Table 5-2, can be calculated as shown in Table 5-5. ■

Referring back to Table 5-4, notice the standard deviations for each of the listed assets. The standard deviation reflects the dispersion of the returns over the 64-year period covered in the data. The standard deviations clearly show the wide dispersion in the returns from common stocks compared with bonds and Treasury bills. Furthermore, smaller common stocks (i.e., the smallest quintile of stocks on the NYSE, based on market values) can logically be expected to be riskier than all common stocks taken together, and the standard deviation indicates a much wider dispersion. Common stocks had a standard deviation of returns of 20.9%, about two and one-half times that of long-term government and corporate bonds and six times that of Treasury bills. Common stocks are more risky, with more variable returns (greater dispersion), and this is reflected in their standard deviation. The smallest quintile of NYSE stocks is even more risky and has a standard deviation that is considerably higher—35.3%—than the 20.9% for all stocks taken together.

In summary, the standard deviation of return measures the total risk of one security or the total risk of a portfolio of securities. The historical standard deviation can be calculated for individual securities portfolios of securities using TRs for some specified period of time. This ex post value is useful in evaluating the total risk for a particular historical period and in estimating the total risk that is expected to prevail over some future period, a subject to which we now turn.

Components of Total Risk The standard deviation is a statistical measure of variability and, as such, is a proper measure of the variability in the returns from securities. However, standard deviation measures total risk, whereas only part of the total risk may be relevant in portfolios held by investors.

The traditional sources of risk identified previously as causing variability in returns seem to be of two general types: those that are pervasive in nature, such as market risk or interest rate risk, and those that are specific to a particular security issue, such as business or financial risk. Therefore, a logical way to divide total risk into its components is to make a distinction between a general (market) component and a specific (issuer) component. These two components, referred to in investment analysis as systematic risk and unsystematic risk, are additive, so that

$$\text{Total risk} = \text{Systematic risk} + \text{Unsystematic risk} \tag{5-9}$$

The variability in a security's total returns that is not related to overall market variability is called the **unsystematic (nonmarket) risk.** This is the risk that is unique to a particular security.

Unsystematic risk is related to such factors as business and financial risk. Although all securities tend to have some unsystematic risk, it is generally referred to in connection with common stocks.

As will be shown in Part Seven on portfolio management, an investor can construct a diversified portfolio and eliminate part of the total risk, the diversifiable or nonmarket part (unsystematic part). What is left is the nondiversifiable portion, or the market risk (systematic part). This part of the risk is inescapable, because no matter how well an investor diversifies, the risk of the overall market cannot be avoided. If the stock market declines sharply, most stocks will be adversely affected; if it rises strongly, as in the years 1985 and 1989, most stocks will appreciate in value. These movements occur regardless of what any single investor does. Clearly, market risk is critical to all investors. Variability in a security's total returns that is directly associated with overall movements in the general market or economy is called **systematic** or **market risk.** Virtually all securities have some systematic risk, whether bonds or stocks, because systematic risk directly encompasses interest rate risk, market risk, and inflation risk. In the discussion, however, the emphasis will be on the systematic risk of common stocks. In this case, systematic risk is that part of the variability correlated with the variability of the stock market as a whole.

A measure is needed of this unavoidable systematic or nondiversifiable risk. Based on modern portfolio theory, **beta** has emerged as such a measure. Beta's usefulness as a measure of risk is briefly discussed here. The measurement of risk for common stocks will be discussed in Chapter 8.

Beta is a relative measure of risk—the risk of an individual stock rela-

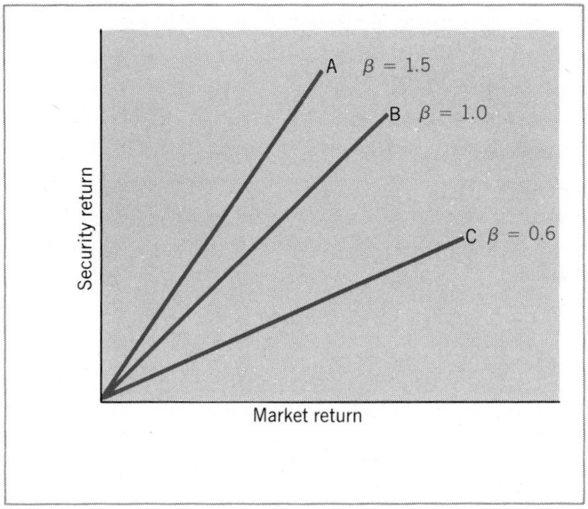

FIGURE 5-3 ***Risk–return trade-offs representing betas of 1.5 (A), 1.0 (B), and 0.6 (C).***

tive to the market portfolio of all stocks.[8] If the security's returns move more (less) than the market's returns as the latter changes, the security's returns have more (less) **volatility** than those of the market. For example, a security whose returns rise or fall on average 15% when the market return rises or falls 10% is said to be an aggressive, or volatile, security.

Beta is the slope of the regression line relating a security's returns to those of the market. If the slope of this relationship for a particular security is a 45-degree angle, as shown for security B in Figure 5-3, the beta is 1.0. This means that for every 1% change in the market's return, *on average* this security's returns change 1%. If the line is steeper, the beta is higher, meaning that the volatility is greater.

Example. In Figure 5-3 Security A's beta of 1.5 indicates that, on average, security returns are 1.5 times as volatile as market returns, both up and down. If the line is less steep than the 45-degree line, beta is less than 1.0; this indicates that, on average, a stock's returns have less volatility than the market as a whole. For example, security C's beta of 0.6 indicates that stock returns move up or down generally only 60% as much as the market as a whole. ■

In summary, the aggregate market has a beta of 1.0. More volatile (risky) stocks have betas larger than 1.0, and less volatile (risky) stocks have betas smaller than 1.0. As a *relative* measure of risk, beta is very convenient.

---

[8]The market as a whole can be thought of in terms of a market index such as the Standard & Poor 500 Composite Index or the Dow-Jones Industrial Index (as discussed in Chapter 10).

INVESTMENTS INTUITION

If an investor is considering a particular stock and is informed that its beta is 1.9, this investor can recognize immediately that the stock is very risky, in relation to the average stock, because the average beta for all stocks is 1.0. Many brokerage houses and investment advisory services report betas as part of the total information given for individual stocks. For example, *The Value Line Investment Survey,* referred to in Chapter 4, reports the beta for each stock covered, as do such brokerage firms as Merrill Lynch.

Estimating Returns and Risk

A frequency distribution is used to describe a group of numbers representing past events, that is, actual occurrences. Frequency distributions of returns summarize some sample data. Analysts often refer to the realized returns for a security, or class of securities, over time.

Realized returns are important, particularly in that they help investors to form expectations about future returns. In the final analysis, however, investors must concern themselves with their best estimate of return over the next year, or six months, or whatever. What about the estimation of returns, which is what investors must actually contend with in managing their portfolios?

The TR is applicable whether measuring realized returns or estimating future (expected) returns. It considers everything the investor can expect to receive over any specified future period; therefore, because it is inclusive, the TR is useful in conceptualizing the estimated returns from securities.

To estimate the returns from various securities, investors must estimate the future stream of payments these securities are likely to provide. The basis for doing this for bonds and stocks will be covered in their respective chapters. For now it is sufficient to remind ourselves of the uncertainty of estimates of the future, a problem emphasized at the outset of our discussion in Chapter 1.

Dealing with Uncertainty

The future is uncertain, which means that the returns expected from securities involve risk. The future return is not known; it must be estimated. To repeat, future return is an expected return and may or may not actually be realized. An investor may expect the TR on a particular security to be 0.10 for the coming year, but in truth this is only a "point estimate." Risk, or the chance of an unexpected return, is involved when investment decisions are made.

Probability Distributions To deal with the uncertainty of returns, investors need to think explicitly about a security's distribution of probable TRs. In other words, investors need to keep in mind that though they may expect a security to return 10%, for example, this is only a one-point estimate of the entire range of possibilities. Given that investors must deal with the uncertain future, a number of possible returns can, and will, occur.

In the case of a Treasury bond paying a fixed rate of interest, only one outcome is possible for the next interest payment. Barring total collapse of the economic system, the interest payment will be made with 100% certainty. The probability of occurrence is 1.0, because no other outcome is possible. With the possibility of two or more outcomes, which is the norm for common stocks, each possible likely outcome must be considered and a probability of its occurrence assessed. The result of considering these outcomes and their probabilities together is a probability distribution consisting of the specification of the likely returns that may occur and the probabilities associated with these likely returns.

Probabilities represent the likelihood of various outcomes and are typically expressed as a decimal (sometimes fractions are used). The sum of the probabilities of all possible outcomes must be 1.0, because they must completely describe all the (perceived) likely occurrences.

How are these probabilities and associated outcomes obtained? In the final analysis, they are subjective estimates. Past occurrences (frequencies) are usually relied on heavily in estimating the probabilities. However, the past must be modified for any changes expected in the future.

Probability distributions can be either discrete or continuous. With a *discrete probability distribution,* a probability is assigned to each possible outcome. In Figure 5-4*a*, five possible TRs are assumed for a stock for next year. Each of these five possible outcomes has an associated probability, with the sum equal to 1.0.

With a *continuous probability distribution,* as shown in Figure 5-4*b*, an infinite number of possible outcomes exist. Because probability is now measured as the area under the curve in Figure 5-4*b*, the emphasis is on the probability that a particular outcome is within some range of values.

The most familiar continuous distribution is the normal distribution depicted in Figure 5-4*b*. This is the well-known "bell-shaped curve" often used in statistics. It is a two-parameter distribution in that the mean and the variance fully describe it.

Calculating Expected Return To describe the single most likely outcome from a particular probability distribution, it is necessary to calculate its **expected value,** or expected return. The expected value is the average of all

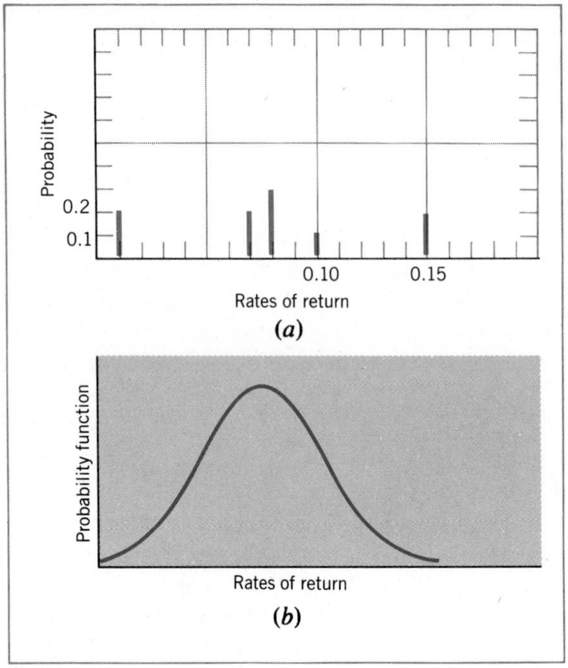

FIGURE 5-4 ***(a) A discrete probability distribution. (b) A Continuous probability distribution.***

possible outcomes, where each outcome is weighted by its respective probability of occurrence. Expected value for any security or portfolio *i* is therefore

$$EV_i = \sum_{i=1}^{n} X_i P(X_i) \tag{5-10}$$

where

EV_i = the expected value of the distribution for security or portfolio i
X_i = the value of the ith possible outcome
$P(X_i)$ = the probability of the ith possible outcome
n = the number of possible outcomes

Example. The expected value of the discrete probability distribution in Figure 5-4*a* is 0.08.[9] ■

Calculating Expected Risk To estimate the total risk expected over some future time period the standard deviation is used once again. In this discus-

---

[9]This is calculated as follows:

$$EV_i = \sum_{i=1}^{n} X_i P(X_i) = 0.01(0.2) + 0.07(0.2) + 0.08(0.3) + 0.10(0.1) + 0.15(0.2) = 0.08.$$

sion we are concerned with the total risk expected to prevail over some future time period, which may differ (sometimes significantly) from that which occurred in the past.

To measure the expected variability in outcomes, probability distributions can be used. The standard deviation is a measure of the spread or dispersion in the probability distribution. The larger this dispersion, the larger the standard deviation.

To calculate the standard deviation from the probability distribution, first calculate the expected value of the distribution using Equation 5-10. Essentially, the same procedure used previously to measure risk is also used to *estimate* risk, but now the probabilities associated with the outcomes must be included, as in Equation 5-11.

$$s = \sqrt{\sum_{i=1}^{n} [(X_i - EV_i)^2 P(X_i)]} \qquad (5\text{-}11)$$

where all terms are as defined previously.

Example. The standard deviation of the hypothetical stock *i*'s returns shown in Figure 5-4*a* is calculated in Table 5-6. *The Investment Calculator* can also be used to make this calculation. ■

The standard deviation, combined with the normal distribution referred to earlier, can provide some useful information about the dispersion. In a normal distribution, the probability that a particular outcome will be above (or below) a specified value can be determined. With one standard deviation on either side of the expected value of the distribution, 68.3% of the outcomes will be encompassed; that is, there is a 68.3% probability that the actual outcome will be within one (plus or minus) standard deviation of the expected value. The probabilities are 95% and 99% that the actual outcome will be within two or three standard deviations, respectively, of the expected value.

TABLE 5-6 ***Calculating the Standard Deviation Using Expected Data***

(1) Possible Return	(2) Probability	(3) (1)×(2)	(4) X_i-EV_i	(5) $(X_i-EV_i)^2$	(6) $(X_i-EV_i)^2P(X_i)$
0.01	0.2	0.002	−0.070	0.0049	0.00098
0.07	0.2	0.014	−0.010	0.0001	0.00002
0.08	0.3	0.024	0.000	0.0000	0.00000
0.10	0.1	0.010	0.020	0.0004	0.00004
0.15	0.2	0.030	0.070	0.0049	0.00098
	1.0	0.080=EV			0.00202

$s = (0.00202)^{1/2} = 0.0449 = 4.49\%$

Calculating a standard deviation ex ante (before the fact) using probability distributions involves subjective estimates of the probabilities and the likely returns. However, this cannot be avoided, because future returns are uncertain. The prices of securities are based on investors' expectations about the future. The relevant standard deviation in this situation is the ex ante standard deviation and not the ex post based on realized returns. Although standard deviations based on realized returns are often used as proxies for ex ante standard deviations, investors should be careful to remember that the past cannot always be extrapolated into the future without modifications. Ex post standard deviations may be convenient, but they are subject to errors.

One important point about the estimation of standard deviation is the distinction between individual securities and portfolios. Standard deviations for well-diversified portfolios are reasonably steady across time, and therefore historical calculations may be fairly reliable in projecting the future. Moving from well-diversified portfolios to individual securities, however, renders historical figures much less reliable.

Arithmetic vs. Geometric Mean Again An important issue arises when we consider expected values from probability distributions. Most investment alternatives have uncertain future returns. The expected cash flows from these opportunities are the means of the probability distributions of the future values.[10]

When returns are derived from probability distributions for multiple periods, the arithmetic mean is the correct measure to use as the discount rate for these multiple periods. This is because we are dealing with the expected ending wealth of the investment as some point in the future, which involves uncertainty. The arithmetic mean, if compounded over the period involved, produces the best estimate of the mean of the probability distribution of ending wealth because it allows for the uncertainty involved. Since the one thing that we can be confident of when investing is that the future is uncertain, we should use the arithmetic mean, not the geometric mean, in estimating the ending wealth of an investment involving a probability distribution.[11]

The Risk–Return Relationship

In Chapter 1 and again in this chapter the emphasis has been on how risk and return go together in investments. The foundation of investment deci-

[10]This discussion is based on Ibbotson Associates, *Stocks, Bonds, Bills and Inflation: 1989 Yearbook* (Chicago: Ibbotson Associates, 1989), pp. 122–123.

[11]The geometric mean would be appropriate as an estimate of the future growth rate under conditions of continuous compounding. The Ibbotson Associates *1989 Yearbook* has a detailed example of why the arithmetic mean is appropriate under these circumstances (see pp. 122–123).

sions, the risk–return trade-off, was shown in Chapter 1 (Figure 1-1). That trade-off shows a positive linear relationship between expected return and risk, with expected return increasing as risk increases. Again, rational risk-averse investors will not willingly assume more risk unless they expect to receive additional (and adequate) return.

Now that both return and risk have been discussed in this chapter, it remains to put the two together, as in Chapter 1. However, this will now be done slightly differently to facilitate the discussion and analysis in subsequent chapters. Although the previous discussion about expected return–risk is entirely appropriate and valid, investors usually think in terms of a required rate of return; therefore, it is necessary to relate risk and required rate of return.

The Required Rate of Return

The **required rate of return** for a security is defined as the minimum expected rate of return needed to induce an investor to purchase it. That is, given its risk, a security must offer some minimum expected return before a particular investor can be persuaded to buy it.

What do investors require (expect) when they invest? First of all, investors can earn a riskless rate of return by investing in riskless assets such as Treasury bills. This risk-free rate of return is designated RF. Investors will expect this risk-free rate as a minimum; furthermore, they will expect a risk premium to compensate them for the additional risk assumed by investing in a risky asset. These two components constitute the required rate of return.

The Risk-free Rate of Return The risk-free rate of return (RF), such as the return on Treasury bills, is a nominal return. It consists of a real rate of return and an inflation premium. The real rate of return (i.e., the pure time value of money) is the basic exchange rate in the economy, or the price necessary to induce someone to forego consumption and save in order to consume more in the next period. This real rate of interest is defined within a context of no uncertainty and no inflation. What matters are the investment opportunities available to investors, which are dependent on the real growth rate of the economy.[12]

Because inflation, in fact, is present in the economy, the nominal RF rate must contain a premium for expected inflation. Investors strive to realize the rate of exchange between present and future consumption, which assumes no price changes. If they anticipate a rise in prices, an additional premium is required to maintain the real rate of interest. For

[12]The economy's real growth rate is a function of the basic determinants of economic growth: (1) changes in the size of the labor force and the number of hours worked and (2) the productivity of the labor force.

example, if the real rate of interest is about 2% and investors anticipate 5% inflation for next year, the risk-free rate should *approximate* 7%. Such a premium should maintain the purchasing power of the real rate of interest to be earned over the next year, 2%. In summary, as an approximation[13]:

Risk-free rate of return = Real rate of return + Inflation premium (5-12)

The Risk Premium In addition to the risk-free rate of return available from riskless assets, rational risk-averse investors purchasing a risky asset expect to be compensated for this risk. There would be no reason for risk-averse investors to purchase a risky asset that promised no return beyond that available from a riskless asset. Therefore, risky assets must offer **risk premiums** above and beyond the riskless rate of return. And the greater the risk of the asset, the greater the promised risk premium must be.

The risk premium must reflect all the uncertainty involved in the asset. Thinking of risk in terms of its traditional sources, such components as the business risk and the financial risk of a corporation would certainly contribute to the risk premium demanded by investors for purchasing the common stock of the corporation. After all, the risk to the investor is that the expected income (return) will not be realized because of unforeseen events. The particular business that a company is in clearly will affect significantly the risk to the investor. One has only to look at the automobile and steel industries in the last few years to see this. And the financial decisions that a firm makes (or fails to make) will also affect the riskiness of the stock. Navistar, for example, faced with adverse business conditions, skirted bankruptcy in part because of large debts that had to be repaid (or negotiated).

Understanding the Required Rate of Return The required rate of return for any investment opportunity can be expressed as in Equation 5-13.

Required rate of return = Risk-free rate + Risk premium (5-13)

It is important to note that there are many financial assets, and therefore many different required rates of return. The average required rate of return on bonds is different from the average required rate of return on preferred stocks, and both are different from that generally required from common stocks, warrants, or puts and calls. Furthermore, within a particular asset category such as common stocks, there are many required rates of return. Common stocks cover a relatively wide range of risk, from conservative utility stocks to small, risky high-technology stocks.

It is also important to be aware that the level of required rates of return changes over time. For example, required rates of return change as infla-

[13]The actual calculation involves adding 1.0 to both the real rate and the inflation premium, multiplying the two together, and subtracting the 1.0 from the product. In the example given, $[(1 + 0.02)(1 + 0.05)] - 1.0 = 0.071$, or 7.1%.

tionary expectations change, because the inflation premium is a component of the risk-free rate of return, which in turn is a component of the required rate of return. Required rates of return were higher at year-end 1980 than at year-end 1982 because of the large difference in inflationary expectations between those two periods.

The overall level of required rates of return also changes as the risk premiums change. Investor pessimism will increase the risk premium and the required rate; investor optimism lowers both.

Risk and Required Rate of Return

Figure 5-5 integrates the required rate of return with risk. Although this figure closely resembles Figure 1-1, there are two important differences:

1. Required rate of return is on the vertical axis, whereas expected return was used in Figure 1-1. Remember, however, that the required return is simply the minimum expected return that will induce investors to purchase a security.
2. Risk is still on the horizontal axis, but now it is measured specifically as beta, the measure of relative market risk.

Figure 5-5 shows that the intercept on the vertical axis remains RF. The relationship between the required rate of return and risk (beta) is linear, as represented by the line RFX. Securities with high (low) betas have high (low) risk, and therefore high (low) required rates of return.

The stock market as a whole (as proxied by an index such as the Standard & Poor 500 Composite Index) has a beta of 1.0. Its required rate of return is MR, as shown by the dotted line in Figure 5-5 extending from the

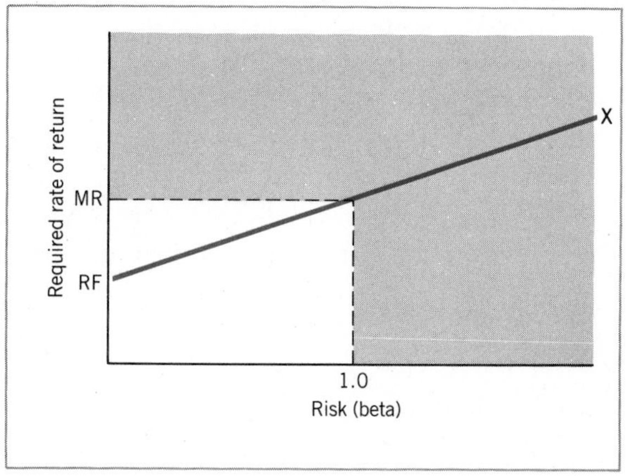

FIGURE 5-5 ***The trade-off between the required rate of return and risk (beta)—the capital asset pricing model or security market line.***

linear trade-off where a beta of 1.0 is represented. This required rate of return on the market index, MR, equals the expected rate of return on the market index when the market is in equilibrium. That is, assuming that the forces of supply and demand in the market have stabilized, the expected return for the market is equal to the required return. Although both rates can and do change over time, in an efficient market it is reasonable to assume equilibrium unless there are indications to the contrary.

The linear trade-off depicted in Figure 5-5 is a very important concept in investments and finance. This relationship is expressed in equation form as

$$k_i = \text{RF} + B_i(\text{MR} - \text{RF}) \tag{5-14}$$

where

k_i = the required (expected) rate of return for asset i
RF = the risk-free rate of return
B_i = the beta for security i
MR = the required (expected) rate of return on the stock market as a whole

Equation 5-14 is called the **capital asset pricing model** (CAPM). It is also referred to (in Figure 5-5) as the **security market line** (SML). Because of its importance, it will be discussed both here and in other parts of the text.

Capital Asset Pricing Model (CAPM)

The CAPM relates the required rate of return for any security i with the relevant risk measure for that security, its beta. Beta is the relevant measure of risk that cannot be diversified away in a portfolio of securities and, as such, is the measure that investors should consider in their portfolio management decision process.

The CAPM is a simple but elegant statement. It says that the required rate of return on an asset is a function of the two components of the required rate of return—the risk-free rate and the risk premium. Thus,

$$\begin{aligned} k_i &= \text{Risk-free rate} + \text{Risk premium} \\ &= \text{RF} + B_i(\text{MR} - \text{RF}) \end{aligned}$$

The CAPM provides an explicit measure of the risk premium. It is the product of the beta for a particular security i and the **market risk premium,** MR − RF:[14]

[14]The slope of the line RFX in Figure 5-4 is the market risk premium, MR − RF. This is the excess return for the market as a whole; that is, the return above the risk-free rate for assuming the risk of the market as a whole. The market risk premium reflects the additional return that investors usually expect for buying risky securities rather than the riskless asset.

$$\text{Risk premium for security } i = B_i(\text{market risk premium}) = B_i(\text{MR} - \text{RF}) \quad (5\text{-}15)$$

INVESTMENTS INTUITION

Equation 5-15 shows that securities with betas greater than the market beta of 1.0 *should have* larger risk premiums than that of the average stock and therefore, when added to RF, larger required rates of return.[15] This is exactly what investors must expect, since beta is a measure of risk, and greater risk should be accompanied by greater return. Conversely, securities with betas less than that of the market are less risky and *should have* required rates of return lower than that for the market as a whole. This will be the indicated result from the CAPM, because the risk premium for the security will be less than the market risk premium and, when added to RF, will produce a lower required rate of return for the security.[16]

Conclusions on Risk and Return

Return and risk go together. Investors expect larger returns to be associated with larger risks. They must anticipate earning their required rate of return before they can be induced to purchase a security. This required rate is related to risk both intuitively—clearly, risk and return go together—and formally through the CAPM.

Summary

- Return and risk go together in investments—indeed, these two parameters are the underlying basis of the subject. Everything an investor does, or is concerned with, is tied directly or indirectly to return and risk.
- The term *return* can be used in different ways. It is important to distinguish between realized (ex post, or historical) return and expected (ex ante, or anticipated) return.

[15]The assumption throughout this discussion is that MR is greater than RF. This is the only reasonable assumption to make, because the CAPM is concerned with expected returns (i.e., ex ante returns). After the fact, this assumption may not hold for particular periods; that is, over historical periods such as a year RF has exceeded MR, which is sometimes negative.

[16]The risk premium on the security will be less than the market risk premium, because we are multiplying by a beta less than 1.0.

- The two components of return are income and price change.
- The total return is a percentage return concept that can be used for any security. The return relative, which adds 1.0 to the total return, is used when calculating the geometric mean of a series of returns.
- The geometric mean measures the compound rate of return over time. The arithmetic mean, on the other hand, is simply the average return for a series and is used to measure the typical performance for a single period.
- Risk is the other side of the coin—risk and expected return should always be considered together. An investor cannot reasonably expect to earn large returns without assuming greater risks.
- The general components of risk have traditionally been categorized into interest rate risk, market risk, inflation risk, business risk, financial risk, and liquidity risk. Each security has its own sources of risk, which we will discuss when we discuss the security itself.
- Historical returns can be described in terms of a frequency distribution and their variability measured by use of the standard deviation.
- When returns are estimated over the future, it is important to remember the uncertainty involved. Probability distributions can be used to express the possible outcomes and the standard deviation can be estimated. It provides useful information about the distribution of returns and aids investors in assessing the possible outcomes of an investment.
- The modern components of risk are systematic risk attributable to exogenous (market) forces, and the unsystematic risk attributable to unique (nonmarket) forces. Unsystematic risk can be diversified away.
- The beta coefficient, measuring the volatility in a security's returns, is a relative measure of risk, relating the movements in the return of a given security to the movements in the market's returns. A high beta (compared to the market beta of 1.0) indicates larger volatility and larger risk.
- The risk–return trade-off diagram relates the required rate of return demanded by investors to the risk actually assumed in a portfolio.
- The required rate of return consists of the risk-free rate of return available to investors without assuming risk plus a risk premium. The risk-free rate of return is composed of a real rate of return plus an inflation premium, whereas the risk premium is composed of the product of the beta for a security and the market's risk premium.
- The formal statement relating the required rate of return for a security to its risk, as represented by beta, is called the capital asset pricing model (CAPM) or security market line (SML).
- The CAPM states that the required rate of return is related to the relevant risk of an asset, given the risk-free rate of return available to all investors. Higher risk requires a higher *expected* return.

Key Words

Beta
Capital asset pricing model (CAPM)
Capital gain
Capital loss
Expected return
Expected value
Future value
Geometric mean
Market risk premium
Present value
Realized return
Required rate of return
Return relatives
Risk
Risk premium
Security market line (SML)
Standard deviation
Systematic (market) Risk
Total return
Unsystematic (nonmarket) Risk
Variability
Volatility
Yield

Questions

5-1 Distinguish between historical return and expected return.

5-2 How long must an asset be held to calculate a TR?

5-3 Define the components of total return. Can any of these components be negative?

5-4 Distinguish between TR and return relative.

5-5 When should the geometric mean return be used to measure returns? Why will it always be less than the arithmetic mean (unless the numbers are identical)?

5-6 When should the arithmetic mean be used in talking about stock returns?

5-7 What is the difference between a frequency distribution and a probability distribution?

5-8 Refer to Table 5-4. How can you explain the standard deviation for riskless government bonds compared to that of corporate bonds?

5-9 According to Table 5-4, common stocks have generally returned more than bonds. How, then, can they be considered more risky?

5-10 Distinguish between market risk and business risk. How is interest rate risk related to inflation risk?

5-11 Classify the six traditional sources of risk as either systematic or unsystematic types of risk.

5-12 Define risk. How does the use of the standard deviation as a measure of risk relate to this definition of risk?

5-13 Explain verbally the relationship between the geometric mean and a wealth index.

5-14 Why is beta a relative measure of risk? Is standard deviation?

5-15 Given a stock with a beta of 0.85, what would investors expect its return to do if the market rose 15%? Would it surprise you if this stock failed to do as expected?

5-16 How can the standard deviation for a particular stock be estimated? How reliable is the estimate for a particular stock compared with a portfolio of stocks?

5-17 What is meant by the required rate of return for a security? How is it related to risk?

5-18 What are the components of the required rate of return? What role does the inflation premium play in this concept?

5-19 What is the equation for required rate of return? Which variable in the equation would appear to be the most difficult to obtain?

5-20 In Figure 5-5, do you think line RFX could slope downward?

5-21 What is the significance of the CAPM? What is the difference between the market's risk premium and an individual security's risk premium?

5-22 What could cause a change in the required rate of return? When the United States experienced an oil embargo in 1974, what effect, if any, do you think this had on investors' required rates of return?

5-23 As Table 5-4 shows, the geometric mean return for stocks over a 64-year period has been around 10%. The returns on corporate bonds in recent years has averaged around this amount, leading some to recommend that investors avoid stocks and purchase bonds because the returns are similar (or even better on bonds) and the risk is far less. Critique this argument.

Demonstration Problems

5-1 Calculate total returns using the following information for XPO, a hypothetical company.

Year	(1) End-of-Year Price (P_t)	(2) Calendar-Year Dividends (D_t)	(3) Capital Gain (Loss) ($P_t - P_{t-1}$)	(4) Total Return in $ (2)+(3) = TR	(5) TR % [100(4) ÷ P_{t-1}]
19X1	$24.70	$1.11	—	—	—
19X2	27.20	1.26	$2.50	$3.76	15.22
19X3	36.30	1.42	9.10	10.52	38.68
19X4	35.75	1.58	−.55	1.03	2.84
19X5	38.25	1.62	—	—	—

A. Capital gain (capital loss) and income. The 19X5 income is the calendar-year dividend of $1.62. The 19X5 capital gain (loss) is the end-of-year price in 19X5 minus the end-of-year 19X4 price—$38.25 − $35.75 = $2.50. The total return for calendar-year 19X5 is equal to income + capital gain = $1.62 + $2.50 = $4.12. Had you bought XPO on January 1, 19X5 for $35.75 per share and held for the calendar year, you would have had a total return of $4.12 per share.

B. What was this return (r) in percentage form (r%)?

$$TR = \frac{\$TR}{P_{t-1}} = \frac{\$4.12}{\$35.75} = 0.1152 = r, \qquad r\% = 100r = 11.52\%$$

C. The same result is obtained as

$$r = \frac{D_t}{P_{t-1}} + \frac{PC}{P_{t-1}} = \frac{\$1.62}{\$35.75} + \frac{\$2.50}{\$35.75} = 0.0453147 + 0.069930 \approx 0.1152$$
$$= r,\ r\% = 11.52$$

D. With the additional information that the price at the end of calendar-year 19X0 was \$25.50, we can calculate the values for 19X1 as capital gain = −\$0.80, and total return = \$0.31. The TR% is equal to 1.216%.

5-2 The following information for IBM is used in Problems 5-2 and 5-3.

Year (t)	(1) End-of-Year Price (P_t)	(2) Calendar-Year Dividends (D_t)	TR%
19X0	\$ 74.60	\$ 2.88	—
19X1	64.30	3.44	−9.2%
19X2	67.70	3.44	10.6
19X3	56.70	3.44	−11.2
19X4	96.25	3.44	75.8
19X5	122.00	3.71	30.6

The *arithmetic* mean of the holding period for IBM, 19X1–19X5:

$$\frac{\Sigma(TR\%)}{n} = \frac{96.6}{5} = 19.32\%$$

5-3 The *geometric* mean of the holding period for IBM, 19X1–19X5: The geometric mean in this example is the fifth root of the product of the $(1 + r)$ version of the TR%. Let us take it by steps. We formed the TR% by multiplying the decimal by 100 to get $r\%$. Now back up to the $(1 + r)$:

Year	TR% = r%	r	$(1 + r)$
19X1	−9.2%	−0.092	0.908
19X2	10.6	0.106	1.106
19X3	−11.2	−0.112	0.888
19X4	75.8	0.758	1.758
19X5	−30.6	0.306	1.306

The geometric mean is $GM = [(1 + r_1)(1 + r_2) \ldots (1 + r_n)]^{1/n} - 1$. So we want the fifth root of the product (0.908)(1.106)(0.888)(1.758)(1.306) = 2.047462654, and

$$(2.047462654)^{1/5} = 1.1541 = (1 + r),\ r = 0.1541,\ r\% = 100r = 15.41\%$$

5-4 The differences in meaning of the arithmetic and geometric mean, holding IBM stock over the period January 1, 19X1, through December 31, 19X5, for two different investment strategies:

Strategy A—keep a fixed amount (say, $1000) invested and do *not* reinvest returns.

Strategy B—reinvest returns and allow compounding.

First, take IBM's TRs and convert them to decimal form (r) for strategy A, and then to $(1 + r)$ form for strategy B.

Strategy A				Strategy B			
Jan 1 Year	Amt. Invested x	r_i	Return	Jan. 1 Year	Amt. Inv. x	$(1 + r_t)$	Terminal Amt.
19X1	$1000	−0.092	−$92.00	19X1	$1000	0.908	$908.00
19X2	1000	0.106	106.00	19X2	908.00	1.106	1004.25
19X3	1000	−0.112	−112.00	19X3	1004.25	0.888	891.77
19X4	1000	0.758	758.00	19X4	891.77	1.758	1567.74
19X5	1000	0.306	306.00	19X5	1567.74	1.306	2047.46
19X6	1000			19X6	2047.46		

Using strategy A, keeping $1000 invested at the beginning of the year, total returns for the years 19X1–19X5 were $966, or $193.20 per year average ($966/5), which on a $1000 investment is $193.20/1000 = 0.1932, or 19.32% per year—the same value as the arithmetic mean in Problem 5-2, earlier.

Using strategy B, compounding gains and losses, total return was $1047.46 (the terminal amount $2047.46 minus the initial $1000). The average annual rate of return in this situation can be found by taking the nth root of the terminal/initial amount:

$$[2047.46/1000]^{1/5} = (2.04746)^{1/5} = 1.1541 = (1 + r),\ r\% = 15.41\%$$

which is exactly the set of values we ended up with in Problem 5-3 previously when calculating the geometric mean.

5-5 The calculation of the standard deviation: Using the TR values for IBM for the five years 19X1–19X5, the deviation of the values from the mean ($\bar{Y}$) can be illustrated graphically.

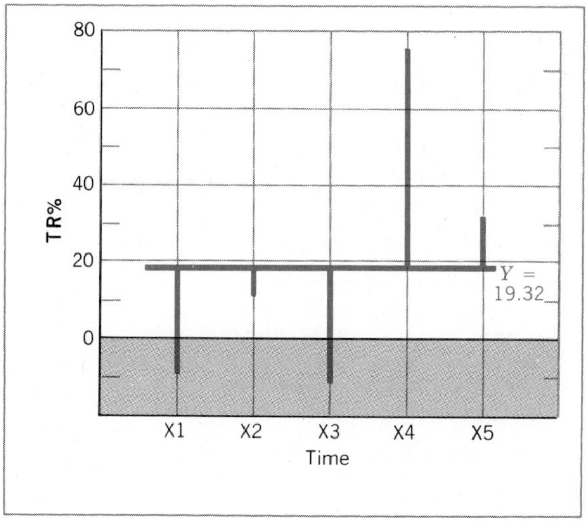

The numerator for the formula for the variance of these Y_t values is $\Sigma(Y_t-\bar{Y})^2$, which we will call SS_y, the sum of the squared deviations of the Y_t around $\bar{Y}$. Algebraically, there is an alternative formula that is simpler:

$$SS_y = \Sigma(Y_t-\bar{Y})^2 = \Sigma Y^2_t - \frac{(\Sigma Y_t)^2}{n}$$

Using IBM's annual total returns, the SS_y will be calculated both ways.

Year	Y_t = TR	$(Y_t - \bar{Y})$	$(Y_t - \bar{Y})^2$	Y_t^2
19X1	−9.2%	28.52	813.3904	84.64
19X2	10.6	−8.72	76.0384	112.36
19X3	−11.2	−30.52	931.4704	125.44
19X4	75.8	56.48	3189.9904	5745.64
19X5	30.6	11.28	127.2384	936.36
Sum	96.6	-0-	5138.1280	7004.44

$$\bar{Y} = 19.32\%$$

$$SS_y = \Sigma (Y_t - \bar{Y})^2 = 5138.128, \text{ and also}$$

$$SS_y = \Sigma Y_t^2 - \frac{(\Sigma Y_t)^2}{n} = 7044.44 - \frac{(96.6)^2}{5} = 5138.128$$

The variance is the "average" squared deviation from the mean:

$$s^2 = \frac{SS_y}{(n-1)} = \frac{5138.128}{4} = 1284.532 \text{ "squared percent"}$$

The standard deviation is the square root of the variance:

$$s = (s^2)^{1/2} = (1284.532)^{1/2} = 35.84\%$$

The standard deviation is the same units of measurement as the original observations, as is the arithmetic mean.

5-6 The calculation of annual total returns for bonds: we will look at bond prices on the basis of $100 par, as bond prices are quoted in *The Wall Street Journal*. The coupon rate on this long-term bond was 10% at the time of purchase—January 1, 19X1. Market interest rates moved upward at that time and the price of the bond fell, recovered somewhat in 19X4, but fell off again in 19X5. The coupon rate of 10%, however, guaranteed a $10 per year interest return (I_t). The data are

	(1) P_B Beginning Year Price	(2) P_e —End-of- Year Price	(3) $ I_t (0.10)($100)	(4) $ $P_E - P_B$ = PC	(5) $ Return (3) + (4)	(6) TR% [(5)/(1)]100
19X1	$100.00	$88.00	$10.00	−12.00	−2.00	−2.00%
19X2	88.00	74.50	10.00	−13.50	−3.50	−3.98
19X3	74.50	66.00	10.00	− 8.50	1.50	2.01
19X4	66.00	76.00	10.00	10.00	20.00	30.30
19X5	76.00	72.00	10.00	______	______	______

First let's fill in the blanks for columns 4, 5, and 6. The change in price, PC, is

$$P_E - P_B = \$72 - \$76 = -\$4$$

and the return is I_t = $10 minus the $4 capital loss, or $6.00. The TR is

$$\text{TR} = \frac{10 + (-4)}{76} = \frac{6}{76} = 0.078947, \text{ or } 100(0.0789) = 7.89\%$$

5-7 Risk-free rate, inflation premium, and required rate of return for IBM. An investor on January 1, 19X7, has the following expectations for the calendar year 19X7: market return, 15%; inflation rate, 5%; real rate of return, 3%; and B_i for IBM = 1.1.

$$\text{RF} = 3\% + 5\% = 8\%$$

The risk premium for IBM would be

$$\text{Risk premium (IBM)} = (1.1)(15\% - 8\%) = (1.1)(7\%) = 7.7\%$$

and the required rate of return for IBM would be

$$\text{RR} = 8\% + 7.7\% = 15.7\%$$

Problems

5-1 Using the data for IBM from Demonstration Problem 5-2, calculate the capital gain (loss) and total dollar return for the years 19X1–19X5 and confirm the 19X3 and 19X4 TRs.

5-2 Assume an investor in a 28% marginal tax bracket buys 100 shares of a stock for \$40, holds it for five months, and sells it at \$50. What tax, in dollars, will be paid on the gain?

5-3 Calculate the TR and the return relative for the following assets:

(a) A preferred stock bought for \$70 per share, held one year during which \$5 per share dividends are collected, and sold for \$63.

(b) A warrant bought for \$11 and sold three months later for \$13.

(c) A 12% bond bought for \$870, held two years during which interest is collected, and sold for \$930.

5-4 Calculate the future value of \$100 at the end of 5, 10, 20, and 30 years, given an interest rate of 12%. Calculate the present value of \$1 to be received at the end of those same periods, given the same interest rate.

5-5 Show that the geometric mean return for XPO (Demonstration Problem 5-1) for the five years 19X1 to 19X5 is 13.15%.

5-6 (a) Calculate, using a calculator, the arithmetic and geometric mean rate of return for the Standard and Poor 500 Composite Index (Table 5-1) for the years 1980–1985.

(b) Calculate, using a calculator, the standard deviation of TRs (from Table 5-1) for the years 1980–1985.

5-7 Calculate the index value for the S&P 500 (Table 5-2) assuming a \$1.00 investment at the beginning of 1980 and extending through the end of 1989. Using only these index values, calculate the geometric mean for these years.

5-8 Replicate Demonstration Problem 5-4 for the XPO data, showing Strategy A (not investing returns) and Strategy B (reinvesting returns and allowing compounding).

5-9 Show that the standard deviation for XPO's five annual TRs is equal to 15.042%.

5-10 Assume that for 1991 an investor expects the following to occur: the real risk-free rate will be 2%, expected inflation will be at a rate of 6%, and the risk premium on the S&P 500 will be 9%. What is the investor's required rate of return on stocks for that year?

5-11 Assume a risk-free rate of 7%, a beta for IBM of 1.1, and an expected return for the market index of 16%. Calculate, using the CAPM, the required rate of return for stock *i*.

5-12 Verify, using *The Investment Calculator,* that the TRs for IBM shown in Demonstration Problem 5-2 are correct.

NOTE: When using *The Investment Calculator* to calculate TRs and return relatives, when asked for "Number of Periods" enter the number of periods for which returns are to be calculated, not the number of periods for which you have data. This allows the program to put the beginning price at time period 0 and calculate a TR for the first year. Thus, in solving this problem for the years 19X1–19X5, enter 5 as the number of periods and place the price for 19X0 at time period 0.

5-13 Using the TRs for the years 1927–1931 from Table 5-1, determine the geometric mean for this period. Show how the same result can be obtained from the ending wealth index value for 1931 of 0.79591.

5-14 Using data for three periods, construct a set of TRs that will produce a geometric mean equal to the arithmetic mean.

5-15 Verify that the standard deviation for IBM for the years 19X1–19X5 (as shown in Demonstration Problem 5-5) is 35.84%.

5-16 According to Table 5-4, the standard deviation for all common stocks for the period 1926–1989 was 20.9%. Using data from Table 5-1, calculate the standard deviation for the years 1980–1989 and compare your results.

5-17 Verify that the standard deviation calculated manually in Table 5-5 is correct. Change the 1975 TR from 36.92 to 26.92 and recalculate the standard deviation. What happened, and why?

5-18 Verify that the estimated standard deviation for the stock in Table 5-6 is correct. If you change the 15% possible return to 12%, what happens to the standard deviation?

Selected References

A basic guide to the CAPM, beta, and related concepts can be found in

Harrington, Diana R. *Modern Portfolio Theory and the Capital Asset Pricing Model: A User's Guide.* Englewood Cliffs, N.J.: Prentice-Hall, 1983.

The best-known source for returns and risks of major financial assets is

Ibbotson Associates, Inc. *Stocks, Bonds, Bills and Inflation: Yearbook.* Annual. Chicago: Ibbotson Associates.

100

PART 2

Fixed-Income Securities: Analysis and Valuation

- CHAPTER 6 The Basics of Bonds
- CHAPTER 7 Bond Valuation and Analysis

CHAPTER 6

The Basics of Bonds

Bonds are an important part of the investment alternatives available to investors. One of the basic types of securities, bonds offer investors the opportunity to earn stable nominal returns with low risk of loss of principal if held to maturity. Bonds also offer investors the chance to earn large returns by speculating on interest rate movements. Given the increase in interest rate volatility that has occurred in recent years, these potential returns—and potential losses—have increased.

Bonds vary widely in individual features, giving investors an opportunity to choose those that closely match their risk preferences, maturity needs, and/or tax situations. For these reasons investors should understand the fundamentals of bonds, which are covered in this chapter. In the following chapter, the discussion centers on how to analyze and manage bonds.

Understanding Bonds

General Characteristics

Bonds can be described simply as long-term debt instruments representing a contractual obligation, or IOU, on the part of the issuer. The buyer of a newly issued coupon bond is lending money to the issuer who, in turn, agrees to pay interest on this loan and repay the principal at a stated maturity date.

Bonds are **fixed-income securities** because the interest payments and the principal repayment for a typical bond are specified at the time the bond is issued and fixed for the life of the bond. At the time of purchase, the bond buyer knows the future stream of payments to be received from buying and holding the bond to maturity. Barring default by the issuer, these payments will be received at specified intervals until maturity, at which time the principal will be repaid. However, if the buyer decides to sell the bond before maturity, the price received will depend upon the level of interest rates at that time. In this case, the bond buyer is exposed to interest rate risk, and the bond return that will be realized for any particular holding period is by no means certain.

The *par value* (principal) of most bonds is $1000, and we shall use this number as the amount to be repaid at maturity.[1] Most bonds are *coupon bonds,* where **coupon** refers to the periodic interest payment paid by the issuer to the holder of the bonds.[2] *Interest on bonds is typically paid semiannually.*

[1]The par value is almost never less than $1000, although it easily can be more.

[2]The terms *interest income* and *coupon income* are interchangeable.

Example. A 10-year, 10%-coupon bond has a dollar coupon of $100 (10% of $1000); therefore, knowing the percentage coupon rate is the same as knowing the coupon payment in dollars.[3] This bond would pay interest of $50 on a specified date every six months. The $1000 principal would be repaid on a specified date 10 years hence. ▪

The typical bond matures (terminates) on a specified date and is technically known as a *term bond*. The phrase **term-to-maturity** is used to denote how much longer the bond will be in existence. In contrast, a *serial bond* has a series of maturity dates. Thus, one issue of serial bonds may mature in specified amounts year after year, and each specified amount could carry a different coupon.

It is important to note the legal ramifications of a bond. Failure to pay either interest or principal on a bond constitutes default for that obligation. Default, unless quickly remedied by payment or a voluntary agreement with the creditor, leads to bankruptcy. A filing of bankruptcy by a corporation initiates litigation and involvement by a court, which works with all parties concerned.[4]

Specific Characteristics

Every bond issue is a contractual obligation between the seller (issuer) and the buyers (investors). Legal conditions that must be met by the issuer are spelled out in an *indenture* or contract. A trustee representing the bondholders is appointed to ensure that the issuer meets its obligations.

Example. A good example of the trustee acting on behalf of bondholders occurred in 1989 when the Washington Public Power Supply System, which as mentioned in Chapter 2 defaulted on $2.25 billion of its municipal bonds in 1983, tried once again to sell new bonds. Chemical Bank, the

---

[3]The coupon rate is calculated as follows:

$$\text{Coupon rate} = \frac{\text{Stated (coupon) interest per year}}{\text{Par (face) value of the bond}}$$

The coupon rate is a fixed rate, given the bond's issuance. It can never vary.

[4]Several options are available in the case of bankruptcy. The firm could be liquidated if its liquidation value is likely to exceed its value if it continued to operate under a reorganization plan. If liquidated, proceeds must be divided among creditors and other claimants according to bankruptcy procedures. Alternatively, a court can seek a reorganization of a firm if its assets appear valuable enough in a going concern. Such a plan requires substantial concurrence by the affected creditors, who receive new claims on the reorganized firm. A third alternative for a firm is voluntarily to seek an "arrangement" under Chapter XI of the Federal Bankruptcy Act. Under Chapter XI, the firm is protected by the court from its creditors while it attempts to work out a plan for paying its debt that creditors will accept.

trustee for the defaulted bonds, threatened to go to court to obtain some $1 billion for holders of the old bonds. The new bond sale was postponed. ▪

Although the typical bond investor never gets involved with most of the provisions of the indenture, he or she should be concerned with certain aspects of any bond being considered. The most important aspect to many investors is the **call provision,** which gives the issuer the right to "call in" the bonds, thereby depriving investors of that particular fixed-income security. Exercising the call provision becomes attractive to the issuer when market interest rates drop enough below the coupon rate on the outstanding bonds for the issuer to save money.[5] Although costs are incurred to call the bonds, such as a "call premium" and administrative expenses, issuers expect to sell new bonds at a lower interest cost, thereby replacing existing higher-interest-cost bonds with new, lower-interest-cost bonds.[6]

INVESTMENTS INTUITION

The call feature is a disadvantage to investors who must give up the higher-yielding bonds. The wise bond investor will note carefully the bond issue's provisions concerning the call, carefully determining the earliest date at which the bond can be called. Some investors have purchased bonds at prices above face value and suffered a loss when the bonds were unexpectedly called in and paid off at face value.[7]

It is important to determine what a bond's yield will be if it is called at the earliest date possible (which is explained later in the chapter). Some bonds are not callable. Some older Treasury bonds can be called within five years of the maturity date.[8]

A second characteristic of many bond issues is the requirement of a **sinking fund,** which provides for the orderly retirement of the bond issue during its life. The provisions of a sinking fund vary widely. It can be stated as a fixed or variable amount and as a percentage of the particular issue outstanding or the total debt of the issuer outstanding.[9]

---

[5]There are different types of call features. Some bonds can be called any time during their life, given a short notice of 30 or 60 days. Many callable bonds have a "deferred call" feature, meaning that a certain time period after issuance must expire before the bonds can be called. Popular time periods in this regard are 5 and 10 years.

[6]The call premium often equals one year's interest if the bond is called within a year; after the first year, it usually declines at a constant rate.

[7]A bond listed as "nonrefundable" for a specified period can still be called in and paid off with cash in hand. It cannot be refunded through the sale of a new issue carrying a lower coupon.

[8]Treasury bonds issued after February 1985 cannot be called.

[9]Payments may be required beginning in the year after issue, or beginning several years later.

Any part or all of the bond issue may be retired through the sinking fund by the maturity date. One procedure for carrying out the sinking fund requirement is simply to buy the required amount of bonds on the open market each year. A second alternative is to call the bonds randomly. Again, investors should be aware of such provisions for their protection.

A third characteristic of bonds that may be important to the bondholder is the *collateral* behind them. Bonds are **senior securities,** meaning they are senior to any preferred stock and to the common stock of a corporation in terms of priority of payment and in case of bankruptcy and liquidation. However, within the bond category itself there are various degrees of security. A **mortgage bond,** for example, represents a secured position whereby the issuing corporation pledges certain real assets as security.

A common type of unsecured bond is the **debenture,** which is a bond backed only by the overall financial soundness of the issuer. Investors who purchase debentures are general creditors, protected only by the overall viability of the issuer. Obviously, financially strong corporations are the most likely sellers of debentures, whereas the financially weak may have to resort to pledging some of their assets as collateral. Debentures can be subordinated, resulting in a claim on income that stands below (subordinate to) the claim of the other debentures.[10]

A fourth characteristic of some bond issues is the **conversion feature,** which means that the holder has the option, under specified terms, to exchange the convertible bonds for shares of common stock. By turning the bonds into the corporation, the convertible owner can receive a stated number of shares of common stock. An owner of convertibles enjoys the income stream of a fixed-income security while holding an option on the underlying common stock.

INVESTMENTS INTUITION

Investors do not receive the conversion option free. The issuer sells convertible bonds at a lower interest rate than would otherwise be paid, resulting in a lower interest return to investors. Convertibles are analyzed in Chapter 16.

New Bond Features

In Chapter 2 we discussed some new bond securities that have been created, pointing out that **zero-coupon bonds** are the most radical innovation

[10]Other types of corporate bonds exist, including *collateral trust bonds,* which are backed by other securities; for example, a parent firm may pledge the securities of one of its subsidiaries as collateral. *Equipment obligations* (or equipment trust certificates) are backed by specific real assets such as railroad engines, airplanes, and so on. A trustee is typically used to hold the assets involved with both collateral trust bonds and equipment obligations.

in the format of a traditional bond. "Zeros" are bought at a discount and redeemed for face value at maturity.

Example. Amax, Inc. issued zeros in 1982. The bonds had an issue price of $225 per $1000 bond, with maturity in 1992. ▪

Zero-coupon bonds appeal to investors for several reasons. First, they can purchase maturities that fit their particular requirements, such as a child's educational needs 15 years from time of purchase. More important, zeros can lock in a fixed rate of return for a long period, thereby eliminating reinvestment risk (to be discussed later in the chapter). This allows investors to know from the outset the exact rate of return they will earn if the zeros are held to maturity.

Zero-coupon bonds are not popular with taxable investors because taxes must be paid each year as though interest were earned.[11] They can be suitable for investors who do not pay taxes, such as pension funds or individual IRA or Keogh accounts. For those investors who wish to speculate on changes in interest rates, zeros offer maximum price volatility, responding sharply to interest rate changes. For example, 30-year zeros can decline in price three times as much as long-term, risky coupon bonds if interest rates rise.

Particularly in the case of zero-coupon bonds, holders must be aware of the call feature. Both corporate and municipal zeros can be, and often are, called. With a coupon-paying bond, investors would realize quickly that the bond had been called because they expect to receive an interest check every six months. But investors could miss a call notice for a zero, particularly if they move often.

Variations of the zero-coupon bond are also the big innovation in federal securities. This started with receipts such as "TIGRs" and "CATs" that were sold at discount and backed by Treasury bonds (see Chapter 2). These securities were created in 1982 by a process known as *coupon stripping*, whereby receipts are sold against each coupon as well as the principal of the underlying Treasury bond issue.[12]

In 1985 the Treasury created its STRIPS, or Separate Trading of Registered Interest and Principal of Securities. Under this program, certain Treasury issues can be "stripped" to create zero-coupon Treasury securities that are direct obligations of the Treasury rather than receipts representing

---

[11]Such bonds are said to be taxed on annual "accretion," or the interest the bonds theoretically accumulate each year.

[12]The 1986 Tax Act authorized the sale of "stripped" municipals, which separate the interest payments on the bonds from principal payments (in effect, each becomes a separate zero-coupon security). The first of these bonds were sold in late 1986, immediately after the tax bill became law.

claims on the Treasuries, as in the case of TIGRs or CATs. STRIPS now dominate the zero-coupon Treasury market.

In the corporate area, bond fads come and go.[13] The traditional corporate "vanilla" bond (i.e., the basic fixed-income security with no special features) is in style when inflation is under control and no other significant external forces distort the marketplace. For example, in July 1982, which approximates the beginning of the great bond market rise that started in 1982, only 46% of the corporate bond offerings were of the conventional variety. In contrast, by November 1982, 81% of new corporate issues were vanilla bonds, because the need for new features had subsided.[14]

Municipal bonds have several new features. The "put" bond can be resold by the investor to the municipality that issued it at a stated price (e.g., 95% of par value). This option, in effect, provides a floor for the bond's price and thereby protects investors from most of the loss possibility arising from interest rate risk.

A new wrinkle for municipal bond issuers is to offer a replacement issue for an outstanding issue of high-coupon bonds and use the proceeds to buy enough Treasury bonds to cover the interest obligations on the old issue until they can be called. The federal backing raises the effective rating of the old bond to the highest category, causing a jump in its market value.[15] The owners can then trade these bonds for a larger number of the new issue and end up owning more bonds at no additional cost.

Still another variation in this area is the municipal bond guarantee, an irrevocable guarantee made by a private party other than the issuer when the bonds are first sold. In effect, the issuer insures the bonds because the guarantor is a source of collateral. Guaranteed bonds should help the issuer, who requests and pays for the insurance, by lowering costs. They may comfort the bondholder—in the industry, this practice is called "sleep insurance"—who ultimately pays the cost in the form of lower yields. It is estimated that the cost of insurance on long-term bonds to investors is about 25 basis points. It should be noted that the companies providing debt-service guarantees vary in their own creditworthiness.[16]

---

[13]This discussion is based on Daniel Hertzberg, "Some Gimmicks Used to Sell Bonds Sour as Rates Fall, Inflation Slows," *The Wall Street Journal,* December 14, 1982, p. 33.

[14]Several, but not all, of the new bond features were intended as inflation hedges and included commodity-backed bonds with face values indexed to certain commodity prices that might be expected to outpace inflation; stock-indexed bonds linking the interest rate paid on the bond to some stock market factor; floating-rate bonds with interest rates that periodically increase with market interest rates in general; and warrants sold with bonds allowing the owners to buy, within a stated period, more bonds at the same yield. Because these warrants are generally detachable from the bonds, they can be sold in the marketplace to speculators.

[15]Since the period to call is generally less than 10 years, the new quality and shorter maturity (less risk) raises the value of the bonds.

[16]See Ben Weberman, "Promises, Promises," *Forbes,* June 16, 1986, p. 179.

Information on Bonds

Bond Ratings

Bonds are rated as to the relative probability of default by several organizations, the best known of which probably are the two financial services companies discussed in Chapter 4, Standard & Poor's (S&P) and Moody's. These organizations provide investors with **bond ratings,** a current opinion on the quality of most large corporate and municipal bonds as well as commercial paper. As independent organizations with no vested interest in the issuers, Standard & Poor's and Moody's can render objective judgments on the relative merits of their securities. This helps the investor judge the quality of an issue. By carefully analyzing the issues in great detail, the rating firms, in effect, perform the *credit analysis* for the investor.

Ratings are made by committees within the rating organizations and are assigned to specific issues of bonds rather than the issuer itself. The ratings reflect the rating companies' judgments of the ability and determination of the issuer to fulfill their contractual obligations. The emphasis is on the likely prosperity of the issuer, not on the resources the investor can expect in the event of financial difficulties. The ratings are tied closely to the financial statements of the issuer. A particular bond issue's rating will change if the financial condition of the issuer changes enough to warrant it.

Standard & Poor's bond ratings consist of letters ranging from AAA, AA, A, BBB, and so on, to D (Moody's corresponding letters are Aaa, Aa, A, Baa, etc., to D). Plus or minus signs can be used to provide more detailed standings within a given category.[17] Figure 6-1 shows Standard & Poor's rating definitions. Included is a brief explanation of the considerations on which the ratings are based.

The first four categories, AAA through BBB, represent "investment-grade" securities. AAA securities are judged to have very strong capacity to meet all obligations, whereas BBB securities are judged to have adequate capacity. Institutional investors typically must confine themselves to bonds in these four categories. Other things being equal, bond ratings and bond yields are inversely related.

Bonds rated BB, B, CCC, and CC are considered as speculative securities in terms of the issuer's ability to meet its contractual obligations. There are significant uncertainties with these securities, although they are not without positive factors. Bonds rated C are currently not paying interest, and bonds rated D are in default.

Of the large number of corporate bonds outstanding, traditionally more than 80% have been rated A or better (based on the value of bonds outstanding). Utilities and finance companies have the fewest low-rated

[17]Moody's uses numbers (i.e., 1, 2, and 3) to designate quality grades further. For example, bonds could be rated Aa1 or Aa2. Major rating categories for Moody's include: Aaa, Aa, A, Baa, Ba, B, Caa, Ca, and C.

S&P'S DEBT RATING DEFINITIONS

A Standard & Poor's corporate or municipal debt rating is a current assessment of the creditworthiness of an obligor with respect to a specific obligation. This assessment may take into consideration obligors such as guarantors, insurers, or lessees.

The debt rating is not a recommendation to purchase, sell, or hold a security, inasmuch as it does not comment as to market price or suitability for a particular investor.

The ratings are based on current information furnished by the issuer or obtained by S&P from other sources it considers reliable. S&P does not perform an audit in connection with any rating and may, on occasion, rely on unaudited financial information. The ratings may be changed, suspended, or withdrawn as a result of changes in, or unavailability of, such information, or for other circumstances.

The ratings are based, in varying degrees, on the following considerations:

1. Likelihood of default—capacity and willingness of the obligor as to the timely payment of interest and repayment of principal in accordance with the terms of the obligation;
2. Nature of and provisions of the obligation;
3. Protection afforded by, and relative position of, the obligation in the event of bankruptcy, reorganization, or other arrangement under the laws of bankruptcy and other laws affecting creditors' rights.

AAA Debt rated 'AAA' has the highest rating assigned by Standard & Poor's. Capacity to pay interest and repay principal is extremely strong.

AA Debt rated 'AA' has a very strong capacity to pay interest and repay principal and differs from the highest rated issues only in small degree.

A Debt rated 'A' has a strong capacity to pay interest and repay principal although it is somewhat more susceptible to the adverse effects of changes in circumstances and economic conditions than debt in higher rated categories.

BBB Debt rated 'BBB' is regarded as having an adequate capacity to pay interest and repay principal. Whereas it normally exhibits adequate protection parameters, adverse economic conditions, or changing circumstances are more likely to lead to a weakened capacity to pay interest and repay principal for debt in this category than in higher rated categories.

Debt rated 'BB', 'B', 'CCC', 'CC', and 'C' is regarded as having predominantly speculative characteristics with respect to capacity to pay interest and repay principal. 'BB' indicates the least degree of speculation and 'C' the highest. While such debt will likely have some quality and protective characteristics, these are outweighed by large uncertainties or major exposures to adverse conditions.

BB Debt rated 'BB' has less near-term vulnerability to default than other speculative issues. However, it faces major ongoing uncertainties or exposure to adverse business, financial, or economic conditions which could lead to inadequate capacity to meet timely interest and principal payments. The 'BB' rating category is also used for debt subordinated to senior debt that is assigned an actual or implied 'BBB–' rating.

B Debt rated 'B' has a greater vulnerability to default but currently has the capacity to meet interest payments and principal payments. Adverse business, financial, or

FIGURE 6-1 ***Standard & Poor's debt rating definitions.***
Source: Standard & Poor's Credit Week, January 19, 1987, p. 8. Reprinted by permission of Standard & Poor's Corporation.

economic conditions will likely impair capacity or willingness to pay interest and repay principal. The 'B' rating category is also used for debt subordinated to senior debt that is assigned an actual or implied 'BB' or 'BB–' rating.

CCC Debt rated 'CCC' has a currently identifiable vulnerability to default, and is dependent upon favorable business, financial, and economic conditions to meet timely payment of interest and repayment of principal. In the event of adverse business, financial, or economic conditions, it is likely to have the capacity to pay interest and repay principal. The 'CCC' rating category is also used for debt subordinated to senior debt that is assigned an actual or implied 'B' or 'B–' rating.

CC The rating 'CC' is typically applied to debt subordinated to senior debt that is assigned an actual or implied 'CCC' rating.

C The rating 'C' is typically applied to debt subordinated to senior debt which is assigned an actual or implied 'CCC–' debt rating.

C1 The rating 'C1' is reserved for income bonds on which no interest is being paid.

D Debt rated 'D' is in default. The 'D' rating category is also used when interest payments or principal repayments are expected to be in default at the payment date, and payment of interest and/or repayment of principal is in arrears.

Plus (+) or minus (−): The ratings from 'AA' to 'CCC' may be modified by the addition of a plus or minus sign to show relative standing within the major rating categories.

Provisional ratings: The letter 'p' indicates that the rating is provisional. A provisional rating assumes the successful completion of the project being financed by the debt being rated and indicates that payment of debt service requirements is largely or entirely dependent upon the successful and timely completion of the project. This rating, however, while addressing credit quality subsequent to completion of the project, makes no comment on the likelihood of, or the risk of default upon failure of, such completion. The investor should exercise his or her own judgment with respect to such likelihood and risk.

L The letter 'L' indicates that the rating pertains to the principal amount of those bonds where the underlying deposit collateral is fully insured by the Federal Savings & Loan Insurance Corp. or the Federal Deposit Insurance Corp.

* Continuance of the rating is contingent upon S&P's receipt of an executed copy of the escrow agreement or closing documentation confirming investments and cash flows.

N.R. Indicates no rating has been requested, that there is insufficient information on which to base a rating, or that S&P does not rate a particular type of obligation as a matter of policy.

Debt Obligations of Issuers outside the United States and its territories are rated on the same basis as domestic corporate and municipal issues. The ratings measure the creditworthiness of the obligor but do not take into account currency exchange and related uncertainties.

Bond Investment Quality Standards: Under present commercial bank regulations issued by the Comptroller of the Currency, bonds rated in the top four categories ('AAA', 'AA', 'A', 'BBB', commonly known as "investment grade" ratings) are generally regarded as eligible for bank investment. In addition, the laws of various states governing legal investments impose certain rating or other standards for obligations eligible for investment by savings banks, trust companies, insurance companies and fiduciaries generally.

FIGURE 6-1 *(Continued)*

bonds, and transportation companies the most (because of problems with bankrupt railroads). Less is known about the ratings of state and local government bonds, but the majority apparently are rated in the top three categories based on value.

Both institutional and individuals investors rely heavily on bond ratings in evaluating the relative quality of an issue, because Standard & Poor's and Moody's have compiled excellent records in making their judgments. Very few defaults have occurred since the 1930s, and this is particularly true of the bonds in the top four investment-grade categories. However, this excellent record does not solve all the bond investor's problems.

Despite their widespread acceptance and use, bond ratings have some limitations. In roughly one-fourth of the cases the two agencies disagree on their evaluations. Furthermore, because most bonds are in the top four categories, it seems safe to argue that not all issues in a single category (such as A) can be equally risky. And it is standard practice to rate unsecured debentures one rating lower than the mortgage bonds of the same corporation, although both are directly tied to the prosperity of the same issuer. Finally, it is extremely important to remember that *bond ratings are a reflection of the relative probability of default,* which says little or nothing about the absolute probability of default.

Other Bond Information

Several sources of information, referred to in Chapter 4, are of particular value to the potential bond investor. These include government sources such as the *Federal Reserve Bulletin* and the *Treasury Bulletin* as well as the publications provided by Standard & Poor's and Moody's.[18] These sources provide bond investors with all the technical information they are likely to require.

For investors wishing to do fundamental analysis on a particular corporate issuer, Moody's and Standard & Poor's sources provide balance sheet and income statement data that permit investors to assess the availability of earnings for servicing debt obligations, the amount of fixed charges the corporation has obligated itself to pay, and so forth. These same sources also provide the bond ratings discussed earlier, and bond investors rely heavily on these ratings because they are so well known and have proved to be very reliable. Thus, investors can easily and quickly obtain an indica-

---

[18]Reviewing from Chapter 4, these include the Standard & Poor's *Bond Guide,* published monthly, which contains various types of financial information on a large number of bonds, and Moody's *Bond Record,* which provides similar information. In addition, Moody's publishes various manuals, including the *Municipal and Government Manual,* the *Industrial Manual,* and the *OTC Industrial Manual,* which provide detailed information on the various bond issues. For a current weekly source of information, Moody's *Bond Survey* discusses conditions in the marketplace and lists both recent and forthcoming bond offerings.

tion of the relative likelihood of default by the issuer. They then must decide for themselves if they are willing to assume the risk of, say, a BBB-rated bond. Although the return will exceed that of a higher-rated bond, the quality is presumably lower.

Bond investors need information other than that pertaining to the details of the bond issue itself. They should pay particular attention to current and prospective economic conditions such as the trend of the economy. Specifically, investors should be concerned with the likely movement of interest rates, which directly affects bond prices. Since no one can consistently make accurate predictions of interest rate movements, the uncertainty is great when investors purchase bonds and subject themselves to interest rate risk.

Some sources of information about interest rate movements, both actual and prospective, are brokerage houses and investment advisory services. Merrill Lynch, for example, publishes the *Bond Market Comment*, which contains useful information on interest rate movements and analysis.

It is possible to find considerable information about bonds in the popular press. Well-known financial papers such as *The Wall Street Journal* and *Barron's* carry bond quotes and feature articles about interest rates, bond issues, current economic projections, strategies being followed by various investors, and other subjects.[19] *Money* magazine often features articles on fixed-income securities, and *Forbes* carries a regular column that discusses all types of fixed-income investments. *The Value Line Investment Survey* now devotes part of every weekly issue to fixed-income securities.

Reading Bond Information

Figure 6-2 is an excerpt from the *corporate bond* page carried daily in *The Wall Street Journal* that reports on corporate and (a few) foreign bonds traded on the New York Stock Exchange. This page also shows Amex bonds. Note that the total volume on the day shown was only $54.5 million and that only 594 domestic bonds traded that day on the exchange. As discussed in Chapter 3, the bond market is primarily an over-the-counter market.

The summary information at the top of the page shows the total volume for the preceding day, the number of issues traded (including advances, declines, and no changes), and some information on the Dow Jones Bond Averages.

---

[19]This source provides information for U.S. government bonds that are publicly traded and for many of the agency bonds that are of interest. It carries only listed issues of corporate bonds, however, just a small part of the total outstanding. If current market quotes are needed for bonds not carried in the *Journal* or *Barron's*, alternative sources are available, although not necessarily easily accessible. The *Bank and Quotation Record* summarizes price information on a monthly basis for many corporate issues, as well as U.S. governments, agencies, and municipals. In addition, *The Blue List* contains extensive price quotes for municipal issues and is widely used by institutions.

Consider the third bond listed in Figure 6-2, one of the several outstanding bond issues of Alabama Power. This 9%-coupon bond maturing in the year 2000 would be referred to by bond investors as the "9s of '00." Alabama Power will pay 9% of $1000 ($90) in interest per year per bond, with the actual payments to be made semiannually ($45 every six months). On a specified maturity date in the year 2000, Alabama Power will repay the holders of the bonds the $1000 principal, and this bond issue will terminate.

The first column after the name and coupon-year description is the "cur yld," or **current yield,** which is the rounded-off ratio of the coupon to the current market price (in this example, it is 9.2%—$9.00/98, which is actually 9.18%). As explained later in this chapter, this is only one measure of return for a bond, and it is not the best.[20] The next column is the volume figure, or the number of bonds traded on a given day.

The next column indicates the closing price for the day, and the last column shows the net change in closing price from the preceding day's closing (or from the last day the issue was traded). This bond lost $6.26 (−5/8) in price from the previous day's closing price.

It is important to note that bond prices are quoted as a percentage of par value. By convention, corporates and Treasuries use 100 as par rather than 1000. Therefore, a price of 90 represents $900, and a price of 55 represents $550 using the normal assumption of a par value of $1000. Each "point," or a change of "1," represents 1% of $1000, or $10. The easiest way to convert quoted bond prices to actual prices is to remember that they are quoted in percentages, with the common assumption of $1000 par value.[20]

Example. A closing price of 101⅜ represents 101.375% of $1000, or $1013.75. ▪

It appears from this example that an investor could purchase the Alabama bond for $98 on that day. Actually, bonds trade on an **accrued interest** basis. This means that the bond buyer must pay the bond seller the price of the bond plus the interest that has been earned (accrued) on the bond since the last semiannual interest payment. This allows an investor to sell a bond anytime without losing the interest that has accrued. It is important that bond buyers remember this additional "cost" when buying a bond because prices are quoted in the paper without the accrued interest.

[20]The current yield captures only the income component of total return, ignoring the price change component.

NEW YORK EXCHANGE BONDS

CORPORATION BONDS
Volume, $54,370,000

Bonds	Cur Yld	Vol	Close	Net Chg.
AL Lb 7¾14	cv	7	111¼	+ 1¼
Advst 9s08	cv	8	84½	+ 1
AlaP 9s2000	9.2	5	98	− ⅝
AlaP 8⅞s03	9.3	15	95½	+ ½
AlaP 10½05	10.2	12	102½	− ½
AlaP 9¼07	9.6	10	96¼	− 1⅞
AlaP 9½08	9.6	5	98½	+ ¾
AlskAr 6⅞14	cv	5	89	...
AlskH 17¾91	16.0	15	111	+ ½
vjAlgl 10¾99f	...	8	28½	+ 1⅛
vjAlgl 9s89mf	...	6	27	...
AlldC zr92	...	233	79⅛	...
AlldC zr96	...	12	61¾	+ ¾
AlldC zr2000	...	102	38	+ ¼
AldC dc6s90	6.2	2	97¼	...
AlldC zr95	...	40	61¼	+ ⅝
AlldC zr07	...	50	20½	− ½
AlldC zr09	...	95	16½	− ¼
AMAX 14¼90	14.2	15	100 13/32	+ ⅜
AmBas 14⅞98	16.8	365	88½	+ 1⅜
Amdur 5½93	cv	10	50⅝	− 1⅞
ABrnd 8⅝90	8.7	246	99¼	− ¼
vjACM 6¾91f	cv	38	30	− ¾
AExC 11¼00	11.0	1	102¼	− ⅝
AmGn 9⅜08	9.6	6	98	...
AmGnFn zr90s	...	9	92 17/32	+ 1/32
ATT 5⅝95	6.5	5	86⅝	− ⅛
ATT 6s00	7.6	16	79	...
ATT 5⅛01	7.0	81	72¾	+ ½
ATT 8¾00	8.9	289	98½	− ¼
ATT 7s01	8.3	52	84⅝	− ¼
ATT 7⅛03	8.5	77	84	− ⅛
ATT 8.80s05	9.1	86	96⅜	− ⅛
ATT 8⅝s07	9.2	131	93¾	− ⅝
ATT 8⅝26	9.5	568	91	− ⅝
Ames 10s95	11.3	5	88½	+ ½
Ames 7½14	cv	99	54½	+ 2
Amoco 6s91	6.2	5	96¼	...
Amoco 9.2s04	9.2	6	100	− 1
Amoco 7⅞07	8.9	12	88¾	− ⅞
AmocoCda 7⅜13	6.1	66	120	...
Ancp 13⅞02f	cv	10	74	− 4
Andarko 5¾12	cv	5	107⅞	+ 1⅞
Anhr 8s96	8.5	20	94½	...
Anhr 8⅝16	9.6	45	90	− 1
ArizP 10⅝00	10.5	29	101	+ ⅞
AshO 11.1s04	10.9	2	102	...
AshO 6¾14	cv	10	94½	+ ¼
Atchsn 4s95	5.2	23	76⅞	+ ⅞
ARch 10⅜95	9.8	130	106	− ⅞
ARch 9½96	9.4	40	101	+ ⅜
ARch 9¼93	9.1	20	101¼	+ ⅛
Avnet 6s12	cv	64	91	...
BRE 9½08	cv	1	97¾	+ ½
Bally 6s98	cv	30	60	+ ¾
Bally 10s06	cv	198	68	− ½
BalGE 8⅜06	9.3	1	89¾	− ⅛
BalGE 8¼07	9.3	10	88½	− ¾
BalGE 9⅛16	9.4	1	96⅝	− 3
Banka 8⅞05	9.6	5	92	− ¼
Banka 8¾01	9.4	10	93¼	...
Bkam zr90	...	13	95 9/32	+ ¼
Bkam zr92	...	188	78½	− ¼
BnkTr 8⅛99	9.0	5	90¼	− ¼
BnkTr 8⅝02	9.4	5	92	− 2
BarcA zr90s	...	33	95⅛	+ 1
BellCn 9s08	9.4	50	96⅛	− 1¾
BellPa 8⅝06	9.1	10	95⅛	...
BellPa 9⅝14	9.6	85	100	− ½
BellPa 9¼19	9.3	5	99⅛	− ¾
BrkHa zr04	...	160	40	+ ¼
BestPr 12⅝96	13.0	9	97	− 1
BethSt 6⅞99	9.0	1	76¾	+ 1⅜
BethSt 9s00	10.1	10	89¼	...
BethSt 8⅜01	10.3	30	81½	− ⅜
Bevrly 7⅝03	cv	60	52½	...
BlkBst zr04	...	15	28	− 1
BoisC 7s16	cv	28	95⅜	− ⅞
BoltBer 6s12	cv	5	49¼	+ 1¼
BrkUn 9⅛95	9.1	20	100⅜	− ⅛
BwnSh 9¼05	cv	2	95½	...
BwnFer 6¼12	cv	69	105¾	+ ¼
BurNo 8.6s99	9.0	5	96	− 1
BurNo 9⅝96	9.6	350	100¾	[illegible]

Bonds	Cur Yld	Vol	Close	Net Chg.
BusInd 5½07	cv	50	61	+ 6
CBI 7s11	...	25	117½	+ 1¾
CBS 10⅞95	10.5	13	103¾	+ ¾
CIGNA 8.2s10	cv	113	97½	− ¼
CIT 8.8s93	8.9	5	99	− 1
CIT 11½05	11.2	50	102¼	− 1½
CUC zr96	cv	26	54	+ 1½
CPc4s perp	9.5	2	42¼	− 1
CPC 4sr	9.2	10	43½	...
CapHd 12¾06	11.8	20	108	+ 1
Carolco 14s93	15.4	10	91	...
CaroFrt 6¼11	cv	1	68	...
CaroT 9⅛00	9.1	10	100	...
CartHaw 12½02	15.1	7	82¾	+ 1⅞
Champ 6½11	cv	52	93	+ ½
ChartC 12s99	13.3	21	90	+ 3
CPoM 8⅞09	9.4	20	94⅛	− ⅞
CPoM 9s18	9.6	12	93½	+ ¼
CPWV 9¼19	9.5	25	97¾	− 3
ChvrnC 10¾95	10.4	15	103⅜	− ½
ChvrnC 7⅞97	8.3	10	94⅝	+ 1⅞
ChvrnC 9¾17	9.8	4	100	+ ⅛
Chvrn 5¾92	6.1	15	93¾	+ ⅝
Chvrn 7s96	7.7	6	91	− ⅛
Chvrn 8¾05	9.1	5	96½	− ⅜
Chvrn 8½95	8.6	25	98⅜	+ ⅛
Chvrn 8¾96	8.9	195	97⅞	− ½
Chvrn 9⅜16	9.6	10	97½	...
ChckFul 7s12	cv	54	64	− ½
Chryslr 8s98	8.8	10	90¾	+ ⅛
Chryslr 12¾92	12.1	12	105	...
Chryslr 12s15	12.0	77	100⅜	− ⅛
Chryslr 9.6s94	9.7	40	98½	...
Chryslr 10.95s17	11.3	10	97	...
Chryslr 10.4s99	10.5	10	98⅝	...
ChryF 8.35s91	8.5	10	98¼	− ¼
ChryF 13¼99	12.3	10	108	+ 1½
ChryF 7⅞91	8.1	1	96¾	− ¾
CirclK 8¼05	cv	2	21	...
CirclK 12¾97	29.0	10	44	+ ⅛
CirclK 7¼06	cv	47	24½	− 1½
CirclK 13s97	44.8	50	29	...
Citicp 8.8s04t	9.3	66	95⅛	− ⅛
Clmt zrD06	...	8	17¼	...
ClevEl 8¾05	9.6	5	91	+ ¼
ClevEl 9¼09	9.9	10	93⅛	− 1⅛
Coastl 11¼96	10.9	10	103¼	...
Coastl 8.48s91	8.7	305	98	+ ⅛
Coastl 11⅛98	10.8	17	103	+ 1
ColuG 9⅛95	9.1	1	100	...
ColuG 8⅜96	8.7	5	96	+ 1⅜
ColuG 7½97J	8.3	10	90	− ⅞
Cmdis 9.65s02	10.3	9	94	+ 1½
CmwE 8s03	9.3	5	86	− 1
CmwE 8¾05	9.6	10	91	− ⅝
CmwE 8⅛07J	9.4	21	86	− 1
CmwE 8⅛07D	9.5	6	85¼	+ ¼
CmwE 8¼07	9.4	12	87⅜	...
CmwE 9⅛08	9.8	10	93¼	− ¾
CmwE 10⅝95	10.3	20	103⅛	+ ⅜
Compq 6½13	cv	21	135	+ 1
Consec 12¾97	15.5	64	82	− 1
ConEd 9⅜00	9.3	16	100½	− ½
ConEd 8.4s03	9.1	25	92	− ½
ConEd 9⅛04	9.2	101	99	+ ½
CnNG M 8⅜96	8.6	5	97	− 1
CnPw 7½01	8.9	50	84	...
CnPw 7½02O	9.1	1	82⅛	− 1
CnPw 9¾06	9.9	5	98	+ ⅛
CnPw 8⅞07	9.4	10	94	+ 1
vjCtlInf 9s06f	cv	49	6⅛	+ ⅛
CtlDat 12¾91	12.6	46	101½	+ ½
CtlDat 8½11	cv	1	86½	+ ½
CoopCo 10⅝05	cv	185	65¼	− ⅛
Copwld 9.92s08	cv	1	104½	+ ½
Crane 7s93	7.5	2	93¼	+ ¼
CrayRs 6⅛11	cv	16	81¼	+ ¼
CritAc 12s13	11.8	3	102	...
CumE zr05	...	25	27	− ½
Dana 8⅞08	9.9	1	90	...
Dana dc5⅞06	cv	40	75	− ½
Datpnt 8⅞06	cv	48	22	− 2
DaytH 10¾13	10.3	9	104	+ ¼
DetEd 6.4s98	7.9	20	81⅛	+ ⅛
DetEd 9.15s00	9.4	8	97	+ ¾
DetEd 9⅞04	9.9	5	100	+ ¼

Quotations as of 4 p.m. Eastern Time
Wednesday, February 28, 1990

Volume $54,550,000

SALES SINCE JANUARY 1
(000 omitted)

1990	1989	1988
$2,090,614	$1,219,481	$1,353,048

	Domestic Wed.	Domestic Tue.	All Issues Wed.	All Issues Tue.
Issues traded	594	598	596	603
Advances	216	271	217	273
Declines	247	187	248	190
Unchanged	131	140	131	140
New highs	9	8	9	8
New lows	20	14	20	14

Dow Jones Bond Averages

−1989− High	−1989− Low	−1990− High	−1990− Low		−1990− Close	−1990− Chg.	−1990− %Yld	−1989− Close	−1989− Chg.
94.15	87.35	93.04	90.68	20 Bonds	91.19	+0.01	9.63	88.14	+ 0.02
95.26	86.95	94.48	91.71	10 Utilities	92.13	+0.15	9.58	87.83	+ 0.03
93.26	87.60	91.60	89.56	10 Industrials	90.26	−0.13	9.68	88.45	....

Bonds	Cur Yld	Vol	Close	Net Chg.
Dow 8⅞2000	9.0	56	98⅜	+ ⅛
Dow 8.92000	9.1	16	98⅛	− 1⅞
Dow 8½s06	9.2	12	92¾	− ¼
Dow 7⅞07	9.1	5	87	− 1
duPnt 8½06	9.1	20	93¼	...
duPnt dc6s01	7.8	30	77¼	− ⅜
duPnt 8½16	9.4	5	90¾	+ ¼
duPnt 7½93	7.7	8	96⅞	+ ⅞
DukeP 7¾03	8.8	1	87¾	+ ¼
DukeP 8⅛03	8.9	18	90⅞	+ ⅝
DukeP 9¾04	9.5	10	102⅝	− ⅛
DukeP 8⅜06	9.4	10	89½	− 2⅝
DukeP 8⅛07	9.2	60	88	...
DuqL 9s06	9.4	8	96	...
DuqL 10⅛09	10.2	89	99	+ ½
ECL 9s89f	...	1	91	+ 1
EKod 8⅝16	9.9	219	87¼	− ¾
Eaton 9s16	10.0	20	90⅜	+ ⅛
EmbSuit 10½94	11.7	13	90	...
EmbSuit 11s99	12.0	60	92	...
Ens 10s01	cv	35	105	...
Equitc 10s04	cv	20	25½	− ½
Exxon 6s97	7.2	149	83⅝	− ⅜
Exxon 6½98	7.6	27	85⅜	− ⅝
Fairfd 13¼92	20.4	3	65	...
FdHL zr92	...	55	81¾	+ ⅜
FedN zr14s	...	100	12	+ ¼
FedN zr19s	...	500	7⅞	...
Fldcst 6s12	cv	10	66	+ ¾
FUnRE 10¼09	cv	1	102	...
FleetFn 8½10	cv	47	118	− 2½
Flemg 6½96	cv	5	92	+ ½
FreptM 8¾13	cv	1	120	+ 3
Fuqua 9½98	10.8	63	88	− 1
GRC 14.30s04	14.3	89	100	...
GTE 12¼94	11.3	20	106	+ ⅛
GnDev 12⅞95	24.8	140	52	+ ¾
GnDev 12⅝05	30.1	82	41⅞	− ⅝
GnDyn 9s16	9.9	2	90⅝	− 1⅜
GnEl 5.3s92	5.5	3	97	...
GnEl 7½96	7.9	11	95¼	+ ¼
GnEl 8½04	9.0	10	94⅝	− 1¾
GnHme 15½95f	...	145	13	+ ½
GnHme 12¾98f	...	237	12	− ½
GnInst 7¼12	cv	14	99½	+ 1½
GMA 7⅛90	7.2	6	99	...
GMA 8s93M	8.2	108	97¼	+ ¼
GMA 7¾94	8.2	40	94⅜	− ¾
GMA 7¼95	7.9	10	92¼	− ⅛
GMA 7.85s98	8.7	140	90¾	− ¼
GMA 8⅞99	9.1	111	97	− ¼
GMA 8¾s00	9.1	56	96⅛	+ ⅛
GMA 8⅛96	8.6	25	94⅝	+ ⅛
GMA 8s02	9.0	5	89⅜	− 1
GMA 8.65s08	9.5	5	91½	− ¾
GMA 11¾00	11.5	50	102	− ⅞
GMA dc6s11	8.9	71	67½	− ¼
GMA zr12	...	81	140¾	− ¼

Bonds	Cur Yld	Vol	Close	Net Chg.
GMA 10⅜95	10.1	179	102⅜	− 1
GMA 9¼93	9.2	128	100⅜	...
GMA 8½91	8.5	50	100	− ⅜
GMA 8⅞96	9.0	161	98⅜	...
GMA 8s90	8.0	26	99½	+ ¼
GMA 8⅛92	8.2	65	98⅝	+ ⅛
GMA 8s93J	8.2	130	97	− ¼
GMA 8s93O	8.3	82	96¾	− ⅛
GMA 8s94	8.3	25	95⅞	+ ¼
GMA 7⅞97	8.6	20	91⅝	− 1¼
GMA 7.45s94	7.9	79	94	+ ¼
GaPw 8⅛01	9.2	5	88¾	+ ⅛
GaPw 7½02D	8.9	21	83⅞	− ½
GaPw 8⅝04	9.4	15	91¾	+ 1½
GaPw 11⅝00	11.3	1	103	+ ½
GaPw 11¾05	11.4	15	103½	...
GaPw 9¾08	9.8	20	99¾	− ⅛
GaPw 10s16J	10.2	16	98⅜	+ ¼
GaPw 10s16A	10.2	5	98½	+ ¼
Getty 14s00	13.6	20	103	...
GdNgF 13¼95	15.8	453	83⅝	− 1⅝
GtNoR 2⅝10	6.8	10	38⅞	− 2⅛
GtNor 2⅝10r	6.8	10	38½	...
GreyF zr94	...	20	63½	+ 1
GrowGp 12½94	13.8	10	90½	+ ½
GrowGp 8½06	cv	7	85	− 1
Grumn 9¼09	cv	47	80	+ 1
GlfRes 12½04	16.2	11	77⅛	− ⅞
HalwdGp 13½09	...	95	73½	+ ½
Harris 7¾01	9.0	10	86	+ 3½
Hercul 8s10	cv	15	90½	...
HmeDep 6¾14	cv	6	131½	+ 2
HomFSD 6½11	cv	55	92	+ 4½
HmGrp 14⅞99	17.9	114	83	− 1
HonyF 8.2s98	9.1	1	90	...
HousF 8⅜03	9.2	5	91	− 1
Huffy 7¼14	cv	8	100	...
Humn 8½09	cv	34	109	− 1
IBM Cr 8s90	8.0	100	99¾	...
ICN 12⅞98	18.3	25	70½	+ ½
IllBel 8¼16	9.0	3	91½	− 1¾
IllPw 9⅜16	10.0	65	93⅝	+ ⅝
IndBel 10s14	9.7	5	103	...
IndBel 8⅛17	9.0	1	90	+ ½
InspRs 8½12	cv	10	90	+ 2
vjItgRs 10¾96f	...	250	3	− ¼
Intlgc 11.99s96	28.2	15	42½	+ ½
IBM 9⅜04	9.3	69	100¾	+ ⅜
IBM 7⅞04	cv	167	97½	− ⅛
IBM 9s98	8.9	522	101	+ ⅛
InMin 9.35s00	9.6	50	97	+ ¾
InMin zr05	...	2	28½	+ ½
IPap dc5⅛12	...	2	58½	+ ½
IntRec 9s10	cv	21	64½	+ ½
IntJh 7¾11	cv	1	58	+ 2
Jamswy 8s05	cv	3	68	− ½
vjJonsLl 6¾94f	...	4	13	+ 2
vjJoneL 6¾94f				

FIGURE 6-2 ***Excerpt from the "New York Exchange Bonds" page from*** *The Wall Street Journal*, March 1, 1990.

Source: The Wall Street Journal, March 1, 1990, p. C 14. Reprinted by permission of *The Wall Street Journal*, © 1990 Dow Jones & Company, Inc. All Rights Reserved Worldwide.

Example. A 10%-coupon bond purchased shortly before the next interest payment date would cost almost $50 more than the stated price of the bond. ▪

The reason that the price of the Alabama Power bond is below 100 (i.e., $1000) is that market yields on bonds of this type rose slightly after this 9%-coupon bond was issued. The lower coupon on this particular Alabama Power bond is less competitive with the going market interest rate for comparable newly issued bonds, and the price declined to reflect this. Some of the bond prices to be seen in Figure 6-2 were selling at **premiums** (prices above par value), reflecting a decline in market rates after that particular bond was sold. Quite a few were selling at **discounts** (prices below par value of $1000) because the state coupons are less than the prevailing interest rate on a comparable new issue.

Other items of interest in Figure 6-2 are the number of different bond issues a single corporation may have outstanding at a given time. Alabama Power, for example, had five different issues reported on this observation date. Many utilities show the same pattern, as do some nonutilities—notice, for example, GMA (General Motors Acceptance Corporation), with numerous different issues outstanding.

Now consider the first bond listed on the page, "AL Lb." The small *cv* under the current yield column indicates that this is a convertible bond, which can be converted at the holder's option into common stock of the same corporation. These bonds require a different type of analysis and will be discussed in Chapter 16.

Finally, note the zero-coupon bonds in the figure, as shown by the designation *zr.* Of course, zeros have no current yield and must always sell at a discount.

The Wall Street Journal also carries quotations on government securities, including Treasury bills, notes and bonds, and agency issues. Figure 6-3 shows quotations excerpted from "Treasury Bonds, Notes, and Bills" (starting with 1990 maturities and going up).

With Treasury notes and bonds, maturities were available on the same date for various periods up to the year 2020 (in Figure 6-3), with coupons ranging from 3% to 15.75%. Note that U.S. government bond prices are quoted in 32nds. Thus, a bond price of 100.4 means 100 and 4/32.

One other difference between government bonds and corporate bonds is that for the former the "yield" column is the yield to maturity, whereas for the latter it is current yield. These can be quite different, as explained later in the chapter.

Notice the "Stripped Treasuries" shown in Figure 6-3. As explained earlier, these are the new zero-coupon offerings of the Treasury.

Treasury bills pay no coupons but are sold at a discount from par value (the minimum denomination is $10,000). For these pure-discount instruments the total return is the difference between the price paid for the bill and its maturity value. The yields on Treasury bills are calculated and quoted on

TREASURY BONDS, NOTES & BILLS

Wednesday, February 28, 1990

Representative Over-the-Counter quotations based on transactions of $1 million or more as of 4 p.m. Eastern time.

Decimals in bid-and-asked and bid changes represent 32nds; 101.01 means 101 1/32. Treasury bill quotes in hundredths. a-Plus 1/64. b-Yield to call date. d-Minus 1/64. k-Nonresident aliens exempt from withholding taxes. n-Treasury notes. p-Treasury note; nonresident aliens exernpt from withholding taxes.

Stripped Treasuries -- a-Stripped interest. b-Treasury bond; stripped principal. c-Treasury note; stripped principal.

Source: Bloomberg Financial Markets

GOVT. BONDS & NOTES

Rate	Maturity	Bid	Asked	Bid Chg.	Yld.
7.12	Feb 90p	99.30	100.01	...	4.70
7.25	Mar 90p	99.27	99.30	...	7.78
7.37	Mar 90p	99.27	99.30	− .01	7.90
10.50	Apr 90n	100.07	100.10	...	7.65
7.62	Apr 90p	99.28	99.31	...	7.62
7.87	May 90p	99.28	99.31	− .01	7.85
8.25	May 90	99.31	100.05	...	7.31
8.12	May 90p	99.30	100.01	−1.01	7.84
11.37	May 90p	100.19	100.22	...	7.75
7.25	Jun 90p	99.21	99.25	+ .01	7.83
8.00	Jun 90p	99.28	100.00	...	7.90
10.75	Jul 90n	100.28	101.00	− .01	7.90
8.37	Jul 90p	100.02	100.06	...	7.86
7.87	Aug 90p	99.27	99.31	− .01	7.92
9.87	Aug 90p	100.22	100.26	− .01	8.02
10.75	Aug 90n	101.05	101.09	...	7.84
8.62	Aug 90p	100.06	100.10	...	7.97
6.75	Sep 90p	99.04	99.08	...	8.08
8.50	Sep 90p	100.02	100.06	− .01	8.14
11.50	Oct 90n	101.27	101.31	− .02	8.16
8.25	Oct 90p	99.31	100.03	− .01	8.07
8.00	Nov 90p	99.26	99.30	− .01	8.06
9.62	Nov 90n	100.29	101.01	...	8.06
13.00	Nov 90n	103.04	103.08	− .01	8.13
8.87	Nov 90p	100.13	100.17	− .01	8.10
6.62	Dec 90p	98.23	98.27	− .01	8.07
9.12	Dec 90p	100.21	100.25	− .01	8.11
11.75	Jan 91n	102.30	103.02	+ .01	8.03
9.00	Jan 91p	100.19	100.23	− .02	8.16
7.37	Feb 91p	99.05	99.09	− .03	8.16
9.12	Feb 91p	100.24	100.28	− .02	8.15
9.37	Feb 91p	101.01	101.05	− .02	8.14
6.75	Mar 91p	98.13	98.17	− .01	8.19
9.75	Mar 91p	101.12	101.16	− .03	8.26
12.37	Apr 91n	104.08	104.11	− .02	8.23
9.25	Apr 91p	100.31	101.03	− .02	8.23
8.12	May 91p	99.23	99.27	− .02	8.25
14.50	May 91n	107.10	107.14	+ .01	7.89
8.75	May 91p	100.14	100.18	− .02	8.25
7.87	Jun 91n	99.12	99.16	− .01	8.26
8.25	Jun 91p	99.26	99.30	− .02	8.29
7.75	Jul 91p	99.05	99.09	− .02	8.29
13.75	Jul 91n	106.25	106.29	− .03	8.31
7.50	Aug 91p	98.25	98.30	− .03	8.28
8.75	Aug 91p	100.14	100.18	− .04	8.33
14.87	Aug 91n	109.08	109.13	+ .09	7.92

Rate	Maturity	Bid	Asked	Bid Chg.	Yld.
12.62	May 95	116.17	116.23	− .12	8.57
8.87	Jul 95p	101.09	101.13	− .14	8.54
10.50	Aug 95p	108.05	108.11	− .14	8.55
8.62	Oct 95p	100.08	100.12	− .14	8.54
9.50	Nov 95p	104.00	104.04	− .14	8.57
11.50	Nov 95	112.26	113.00	− .16	8.57
9.25	Jan 96p	102.31	103.03	− .16	8.56
8.87	Feb 96p	101.10	101.14	− .15	8.56
9.37	Apr 96p	103.19	103.23	− .16	8.58
7.37	May 96p	94.05	94.09	− .16	8.58
7.87	Jul 96p	96.17	96.21	− .16	8.56
8.00	Oct 96p	97.05	97.09	− .17	8.54
7.25	Nov 96p	93.08	93.12	− .15	8.57
8.00	Ja 97p	97.07	97.10	− .17	8.52
8.50	May 97p	99.15	99.19	− .19	8.57
8.62	Aug 97p	100.05	100.09	− .18	8.57
8.87	Nov 97p	101.15	101.19	− .19	8.58
8.12	Feb 98p	97.10	97.14	− .20	8.57
9.00	May 98p	102.11	102.15	− .19	8.57
9.25	Aug 98p	103.27	103.31	− .20	8.58
7.00	May 93-98	90.21	91.07	+ .06	8.51
3.50	Nov 98	89.12	90.14	− .21	4.86
8.87	Nov 98p	101.19	101.23	− .22	8.59
8.87	Feb 99p	101.21	101.25	− .21	8.58
8.50	May 94-99	99.15	99.25	− .10	8.53
9.12	May 99p	103.10	103.14	− .22	8.57
8.00	Aug 99p	96.13	96.17	− .20	8.54
7.87	Nov 99p	95.19	95.23	− .20	8.53
8.50	Feb 00p	99.28	100.00	− .22	8.50
7.87	Feb 95-00	94.28	95.02	− .19	8.62
8.37	Aug 95-00	98.04	98.10	− .19	8.62
11.75	Feb 01	121.11	121.17	− .25	8.67
13.12	May 01	131.14	131.20	− .28	8.66
8.00	Aug 96-01	95.09	95.15	− .21	8.63
13.37	Aug 01	133.20	133.26	− .28	8.66
15.75	Nov 01	151.03	151.09	−1.00	8.68
14.25	Feb 02	140.19	140.25	− .31	8.70
11.62	Nov 02	122.01	122.07	− .28	8.70
10.75	Feb 03	115.18	115.24	− .27	8.70
10.75	May 03	115.23	115.29	− .26	8.70
11.12	Aug 03	118.25	118.31	− .28	8.70
11.87	Nov 03	124.28	125.02	− .29	8.70
12.37	May 04	129.14	129.20	− .31	8.70
13.75	Aug 04	141.03	141.09	−1.01	8.68
11.62	Nov 04k	123.20	123.26	− .31	8.72
8.25	May 00-05	96.17	96.23	− .24	8.64
12.00	May 05k	127.06	127.12	− .31	8.71

Rate	Maturity	Bid	Asked	Bid Chg.	Yld.
.00	May 02a	34.29	35.13	− .14	8.69
.00	Aug 02a	34.05	34.21	− .13	8.69
.00	Nov 02a	33.14	33.30	− .13	8.69
.00	Feb 03a	32.23	33.06	− .13	8.69
.00	May 03a	32.01	32.16	− .13	8.69
.00	Aug 03a	31.11	31.26	− .12	8.69
.00	Nov 03a	30.23	31.06	− .13	8.68
.00	Feb 04a	30.00	30.16	− .13	8.69
.00	May 04a	29.12	29.28	− .13	8.69
.00	Aug 04a	28.24	29.07	− .12	8.69
.00	Nov 04a	28.04	28.20	− .13	8.69
.00	Feb 05a	27.17	28.00	− .12	8.69
.00	May 05a	26.30	27.14	− .13	8.69
.00	Aug 05a	26.12	26.27	− .12	8.69
.00	Nov 05a	25.27	26.10	− .13	8.68
.00	Feb 06a	25.09	25.24	− .13	8.68
.00	May 06a	24.24	25.07	− .13	8.68
.00	Aug 06a	24.07	24.22	− .12	8.68
.00	Nov 06a	23.24	24.07	− .12	8.67
.00	Feb 07a	23.07	23.21	− .12	8.68
.00	May 07a	22.23	23.06	− .12	8.68
.00	Aug 07a	22.09	22.23	− .11	8.67
.00	Nov 07a	21.26	22.08	− .11	8.67
.00	Feb 08a	21.11	21.25	− .11	8.67
.00	May 08a	20.28	21.10	− .12	8.67
.00	Aug 08a	20.14	20.28	− .11	8.67
.00	Nov 08a	20.02	20.16	− .12	8.65
.00	Feb 09a	19.21	20.02	− .11	8.65
.00	May 09a	19.07	19.21	− .12	8.65
.00	Aug 09a	18.28	19.10	− .10	8.63
.00	Nov 09a	18.19	19.01	− .11	8.60
.00	Feb 10a	18.04	18.18	− .11	8.62
.00	May 10a	17.23	18.04	− .11	8.63
.00	Aug 10a	17.11	17.24	− .10	8.63
.00	Nov 10a	17.02	17.16	− .10	8.60
.00	Feb 11a	16.21	17.02	− .09	8.62
.00	May 11a	16.10	16.22	− .10	8.62
.00	Aug 11a	15.30	16.11	− .11	8.62
.00	Nov 11a	15.21	16.01	− .10	8.61
.00	Feb 12a	15.10	15.23	− .10	8.61
.00	May 12a	15.01	15.13	− .10	8.60
.00	Aug 12a	14.22	15.03	− .11	8.60
.00	Nov 12a	14.14	14.26	− .10	8.59
.00	Feb 13a	14.05	14.17	− .10	8.58
.00	May 13a	13.28	14.08	− .10	8.57
.00	Aug 13a	13.20	14.00	− .10	8.56
.00	Nov 13a	13.12	13.24	− .10	8.55
.00	Feb 14a	13.06	13.17	− .09	8.52
.00	May 14a	12.29	13.09	− .10	8.52
.00	Aug 14a	12.21	13.01	− .10	8.51
.00	Nov 14a	12.16	12.27	− .09	8.48
.00	Feb 15a	12.09	12.20	− .09	8.47
.00	May 15a	12.02	12.13	− .09	8.45
.00	Aug 15a	11.26	12.05	− .09	8.45
.00	Nov 15a	11.20	11.31	− .09	8.43
.00	Feb 16a	11.16	11.27	− .09	8.39
.00	May 16a	11.11	11.22	− .09	8.36

STRIPPED TREASURIES

.00	May 90a	98.13	98.14	...	7.66
.00	Aug 90a	96.13	96.15	+ .01	7.93
.00	Nov 90a	94.17	94.20	...	7.97
.00	Feb 92a	92.16	92.19	...	8.17
.00	May 91a	90.18	90.22	− .01	8.26
.00	Aug 91	88.21	88.26	− .02	8.29
.00	Nov 91a	86.28	87.02	− .03	8.28
.00	Feb 92a	84.29	85.04	− .03	8.38
.00	May 92a	83.06	83.13	− .03	8.39
.00	Aug 92a	81.12	81.19	− .05	8.44
.00	Nov 92a	79.23	79.31	− .06	8.43
.00	Feb 93a	77.30	78.07	− .07	8.47
.00	May 93a	76.10	76.19	− .08	8.49
.00	Aug 93a	74.22	75.00	− .08	8.49
.00	Nov 93a	73.06	73.16	− .09	8.48
.00	Feb 94a	71.17	71.27	− .10	8.52
.00	May 94a	70.02	70.13	− .09	8.52
.00	Aug 94a	68.18	68.29	− .10	8.52
.00	Nov 94a	67.07	67.19	− .10	8.50
.00	Feb 95a	65.21	66.01	− .13	8.54
.00	May 95a	64.10	64.22	− .13	8.54
.00	Aug 95a	62.31	63.12	− .11	8.53
.00	Nov 95a	61.21	62.02	− .12	8.54
.00	Feb 96a	60.08	60.22	− .13	8.56
.00	May 96a	59.00	59.14	− .11	8.56
.00	Aug 96a	57.24	58.06	− .10	8.56
.00	Nov 96a	56.18	57.00	− .10	8.56
.00	Feb 97a	55.08	55.22	− .11	8.59
.00	May 97a	54.03	54.17	− .10	8.59
.00	Aug 97a	52.29	53.11	− .11	8.60
.00	Nov 97a	51.26	52.08	− .11	8.60
.00	Feb 98a	50.21	51.04	− .11	8.61
.00	May 98a	49.18	50.01	− .12	8.62
.00	Aug 98a	48.16	48.31	− .12	8.62
.00	Nov 98a	47.17	48.00	− .11	8.61
.00	Feb 99a	46.13	46.29	− .13	8.63
.00	May 99a	45.14	45.30	− .13	8.63
.00	Aug 99a	44.15	44.31	− .13	8.63
.00	Nov 99a	43.19	44.02	− .11	8.62
.00	Feb 00a	42.20	43.03	− .11	8.63
.00	May 00a	41.22	42.06	− .13	8.64
.00	Aug 00a	40.25	41.09	− .13	8.64
.00	Nov 00a	39.30	40.14	− .13	8.64
.00	Feb 01a	39.00	39.15	− .13	8.66
.00	May 01a	38.06	38.21	− .12	8.66
.00	Aug 01a	37.10	37.26	− .14	8.67
.00	Nov 01a	36.17	37.01	− .14	8.67
.00	Feb 02a	35.21	36.05	− .14	8.69

TREASURY BILLS

.00	Mar 01 '90	7.81	7.38	...	7.48
.00	Mar 08 '90	7.91	7.69	+ .35	7.81
.00	Mar 15 '90	7.81	7.69	+ .05	7.82
.00	Mar 22 '90	7.96	7.63	+ .25	7.77
.00	Mar 29 '90	7.19	7.13	− .06	7.26
.00	Apr 05 '90	7.63	7.56	+ .07	7.72
.00	Apr 12 '90	7.79	7.75	+ .06	7.93
.00	Apr 19 '90	7.88	7.84	+ .06	8.04
.00	Apr 26 '90	7.96	7.91	+ .16	8.12
.00	May 03 '90	7.83	7.78	+ .05	8.00
.00	May 10 '90	7.83	7.78	+ .05	8.01
.00	May 17 '90	7.73	7.69	+ .02	7.92
.00	May 24 '90	7.79	7.75	+ .06	8.00
.00	May 31 '90	7.78	7.75	+ .05	8.01
.00	Jun 07 '90	7.80	7.75	+ .08	8.03
.00	Jun 14 '90	7.75	7.72	+ .04	8.01
.00	Jun 21 '90	7.76	7.72	+ .05	8.02
.00	Jun 28 '90	7.72	7.69	+ .07	8.00
.00	Jul 05 '90	7.78	7.75	+ .06	8.08
.00	Jul 12 '90	7.77	7.72	+ .07	8.06
.00	Jul 19 '90	7.76	7.72	+ .06	8.07
.00	Jul 26 '90	7.74	7.69	+ .04	8.05
.00	Aug 02 '90	7.75	7.72	+ .04	3.09
.00	Aug 09 '90	7.74	7.69	+ .07	8.07
.00	Aug 16 '90	7.70	7.66	+ .05	8.05
.00	Aug 23 '90	7.72	7.69	+ .03	8.10
.00	Aug 30 '90	7.73	7.69	+ .04	8.11
.00	Sep 27 '90	7.66	7.59	+ .03	8.01
.00	Oct 25 '90	7.68	7.63	+ .05	8.07
.00	Nov 23 '90	7.68	7.63	+ .04	8.09
.00	Dec 20 '90	7.64	7.59	+ .05	8.08
.00	Jan 17 '91	7.58	7.53	+ .05	8.05
.00	Feb 14 '91	7.57	7.53	+ .05	8.08

FIGURE 6-3 ***Excerpt from "Treasury Bonds, Notes & Bills" from** The Wall Street Journal.* *Source:* Excerpted from *The Wall Street Journal,* March 1, 1990, p. C 15. Reprinted by permission of *The Wall Street Journal,* © 1990 Dow Jones & Company, Inc. All Rights Reserved Worldwide.

an *annualized yield basis* in both primary and secondary markets.[21] Reading the daily "Treasury Issues" section of *The Wall Street Journal* (the Treasury bill section is shown in the last part of Figure 6-3), an investor can see the bid quote, the asked quote, and the discount rate yield for Treasury bills trading in the secondary market. Yields are quoted in hundredths.

---

[21]The yield, or discount rate, on a Treasury bill can be calculated as

$$\text{Discount rate} = \frac{\text{Face value} - \text{Issue price}}{\text{Face value}} \times \frac{360}{\text{Days to maturity}}$$

For example, consider a Treasury bill with a face value of $10,000 issued at a price of $9777, maturing in 91 days. The discount rate is

$$\frac{\$10{,}000 - \$9777}{\$10{,}000} \times \frac{360}{91} = 8.82\%$$

INVESTMENTS INTUITION

Do not be confused because the bid is larger than the asked for Treasury bills. The bid and asked quotes are percentage discounts from face value. The bid quote is the discount rate derived from the price that dealers in these securities will pay to buy them from investors. The larger the discount, the smaller the price.[22] The asked quote is the discount rate derived from the prices at which dealers will sell to investors—the smaller the asked rate, the larger the price. Therefore, as is true for stocks traded in the traditional over-the-counter market, dealers stand ready to sell Treasury bills to investors for a price exceeding what they would pay investors wishing to sell. The difference between the bid and asked quotes represents the dealers' spread, or profit.

Treasury bills trade on the basis of a 360-day year, whereas bonds typically trade on a 365-day-year basis. Treasury bills can be adjusted to a bond equivalent (or investment yield) basis, allowing investors to compare bill yields with the returns from securities with coupons.[23]

The Bond Market

Traditionally, the market for long-term bonds has differed from the stock market in that it is basically a primary market, or market for new issues. Institutional investors have been major purchasers of bonds because regulatory constraints favored such purchases, and on an overall basis they dominate the bond market. Since institutional investors buy in large volume and often hold the bonds until maturity, the volume of trading for existing bonds (the secondary market) historically has been small. Although the secondary market for bonds is increasingly important, the historical nature of the bond market must be recognized.

Investors in the Bond Market

A variety of institutional investors, government agencies, foreign governments, and the Federal Reserve System channel funds into Treasury and

[22]That is, the seller of a one-year-maturity Treasury bill would receive the bid price, or (100% − x.x%) × $10,000, where *x.x%* is the stated "bid" yield.

[23]The bond equivalent basis is

$$\text{Bond equivalent basis} = \frac{\text{Total dollar discount}}{\text{Purchase price}} \times \frac{365}{91} = 9.15\%$$

Note that the bond equivalent yield is always greater than the yield in discount form.

agency securities. Households, which include personal trusts and non-profit organizations, steadily increased their ownership during the 1980s, holding almost $860 billion of Treasuries and agencies by the end of 1988 (including $110 billion in savings bonds).

In 1989 individual investors bought Treasury bills in record amounts because of the high interest returns at the time—about 9%. They bought large amounts of Treasury bonds in 1990. Although investors often buy these securities through their broker or bank, many now buy directly at Treasury auctions through "noncompetitive bidding," agreeing to accept the average price and interest rate among competitive bids.[24]

As for corporate bonds, households directly held only $53 billion in 1980, and a little over twice that amount by the beginning of 1990. This amounted to less than 10% of the corporate bonds outstanding. These figures are consistent with the traditional situation in the bond market—that life insurance companies and pension funds (including state and local funds) are major purchasers of corporate bonds. Private financial institutions hold over $1 trillion of corporate bonds.

The municipal bond market traditionally was an institutional market, with commercial banks and property and casualty insurance companies buying substantial amounts of these bonds in any one year. However, individuals have become a strong force in the municipal bond market because inflation has pushed them into higher tax brackets, where the tax exempt feature of municipals becomes attractive. Individuals became the market in 1982, with over 95% of the net new supply of municipals being bought by individuals either directly or indirectly through investment company funds specializing in tax-exempts.

INVESTMENTS INTUITION

The Tax Reform Act of 1986 enhanced the appeal of municipals to investors, particularly high-bracket investors, because it devastated tax shelters in general and eliminated or limited many other deductions. Municipal bonds emerged as one of the major investment opportunities available to investors.[25]

---

[24]Investors can purchase new Treasury securities directly from the Treasury by participating in the "Treasury Direct" system.

[25]Investors need to remember that tax reform established three categories of municipals: (1) most municipals remain exempt from federal income taxes; (2) some municipals are exempt from federal income taxes but are subject to the alternative minimum tax; (3) some municipals are subject to both federal income taxes and the alternative minimum tax.

Trading Bonds

Chapter 3 outlined trading conditions in the secondary bond markets. Although some corporate bonds are traded on the exchanges, primarily the NYSE, such issues constitute only a small part of total bond trading. For example, the trading volume for bonds traded on the NYSE, the largest centralized bond market operated by an exchange, averages only about $30 million a day. There are approximately 2500 corporate and foreign bonds listed on the NYSE bond exchange, but total trading volume for the year recently has been less than $10 billion (par value). Therefore, the listed market in bonds is small and thin.

As noted in Chapter 3, the secondary bond market is primarily an over-the-counter market, with dealers making a market in the various issues. These may be brokerage firms or commercial banks, which are well-known dealers in governments, agencies, and municipals. *Most corporate bonds are traded over the counter, as are all governments, agencies, and municipals.*

Some sectors of the bond market, such as U.S. government bonds, have been quite active and are becoming more so. In fact, the secondary market for Treasury securities is the most liquid secondary market in the world. The large amounts of government securities outstanding and the continuing large flows into these securities make this the dominant segment of the bond market for most investors.

Unlike the homogeneous government bond market, the corporate bond market is heterogeneous and has experienced declining credit quality despite its overall size—of some 10,000 issues and a market value approximately 60% that of Treasuries. Although some issues may be actively traded (e.g., utility issues), because of the interest in high-yielding securities, other issues may be quite inactive. Individual investors are well advised to consider the relative illiquidity of a small (less than $100,000) position in corporate bonds. Such a position can be liquidated, but it may take longer than a comparable trade in government bonds or common stocks and price concessions often must be made. On the New York Stock Exchange, the spread can range from one to two points (one point = $10) on active issues and up to five points or more on inactive issues. Including commissions, an investor could pay as much as $600 on a $10,000 order. Some experts recommend that the average investor not buy bonds in amounts less that $100,000 unless he or she plans to hold them 5 or 10 years.[26]

The municipal securities market generally is not active. Although there are perhaps 50,000 separate issuers of these securities, the total market value is less than half that of Treasuries. Because of the large number of

---

[26]This information is based on Ben Weberman, "Comparison Shopping," *Forbes,* October 6, 1986, p. 203.

small bond issues in this market, substantial illiquidity exists, and potential bond purchasers should be aware of this before they buy. Prices can vary sharply from dealer to dealer. This is particularly true for individual investors trading small numbers of bonds. And it is even true for institutions at times.

Example. Wells Fargo Bank, seeking to sell $100,000 of bonds for a client in 1989, asked nine dealers for bids and received offers with a spread of $3902.[27] ▪

Although more individual investor funds have flowed into this market in recent years, it remains an over-the-counter dealer market subject to difficulties in trading.

Important Trends in the Bond Market—Junk Bonds

No discussion of the bond market would be complete without considering one of the major events in bonds in the 1980s—the creation and use of "junk bonds." These bonds have had a major impact on financial markets and corporate America and have generated considerable media attention.

Junk bonds are high-risk, high-yield bonds. They carry ratings of BB (S&P) or Ba (Moody's) or lower, with correspondingly higher yields.[28] They can carry coupons of 12%, 13%, 15%, and even 16% (a Resorts International issue carried a coupon of 16.625%). An alternative, and more reassuring, name used to describe this area of the bond market is the *high-yield debt market*.[29] Junk bonds are issued in connection with

1. Mergers.
2. Leveraged buyouts.
3. Companies with heavy debts to repay—such as bank loans.
4. Stock buybacks by corporations.

As with many other investment items, junk bonds illustrate how our dynamic capital markets adjust to new developments. Rising interest rates caused institutional investors to consider the relative attractiveness of lower-rated, and therefore higher-yielding, securities. At the same time, the upsurge in takeovers and mergers created a need for a new approach to financing these transactions. Such well-known figures as T. Boone Pickens used junk bonds to help finance their takeover attempts, and Drexel Burn-

---

[27]See Tom Herman, "Small Investors Can Lose Way in Muni Maze," *The Wall Street Journal*, July 31, 1989, p. C1.

[28]As shown in Figure 6-1, bonds rated BB or below are regarded as "having predominantly speculative characteristics with respect to capacity to pay interest and repay principal."

[29]See Edward I. Altman and Scott A. Nammacher, *Investing in Junk Bonds: Inside the High Yield Debt Market* (New York: John Wiley, 1987) for a good discussion of this market.

ham Lambert helped to develop this market by persuading institutions to buy such bonds. Drexel's Michael Milken is widely credited with changing investors' (in particular, large institutional investors') views of junk bonds. Drexel became both the biggest underwriter and the biggest dealer in the junk bond market.

The junk bond market grew significantly in the 1980s, exceeding $120 billion by 1986 and $200 billion by 1989 before declining in 1990. Institutional investors such as insurance companies, pension funds, and bond mutual funds were significant holders of junk bonds. The high-yield mutual bond funds, representing in effect individual investors, owned about one-fourth of all junk bonds.

Junk bonds mostly trade over the counter on an infrequent basis, and often in secret, known only to the buyer and seller. Price quotations on certain junk bonds can vary widely from firm to firm. Junk bond prices respond sharply to changes in the issuer's financial situation. Investors concentrate more on the issuer's cash flow than on the general movements in interest rates.

Junk bonds have been purchased widely by investors reaching for higher yields. A number of studies suggest that a diversified portfolio of junk bonds shows average returns higher than otherwise available and adequate enough to compensate for the additional risk taken. At times, the yield in excess of Treasury securities is over 4%, and in mid-1989 it was over 5%. And individual results can be spectacular. For example, the return in the second quarter of 1989 alone for Continental Airlines was over 16%, and over 15% for Hospital Corporation of America.

As the amount of these bonds increased in the 1980s, so did the problems involved with them. Defaults averaged about $4 billion a year for the late 1980s, but increased at a more rapid rate in 1989. Three issuers alone accounted for over $2 billion of junk bond problems in 1989—Eastern Airlines, Integrated Resources, and Southmark. The price of the Integrated Resources 12.25% senior subordinated notes dropped $400 in one week in 1989, an incredible loss within such a short time by any standard.

How risky are junk bonds? Investors can incur losses with bonds that stop paying interest or bonds that are "forced restructurings," which usually bail out the company at the expense of the investor. One estimate is that losses on such transactions amount to 60 cents on the dollar.[30] A basic problem here is that the measurement of defaults and troubled exchange offers varies from source to source. Wall Street firms tend to put the figure at about 2% (as a percentage of total junk bonds underwritten since their inception). A well-known study by Edward Altman in 1985 put the annual default rate at 2.4% of dollar volume. In mid-1989 Moody's Investors Ser-

[30]This information is based on Linda Sandler, "Junk Bond Defaults Are Spreading; Investors Debate Next Casualties," *The Wall Street Journal*, July 20, 1989, p. C1.

vice found that an average 3.3% of issuers defaulted each year between 1970 and 1988.

One indication of forthcoming trouble for a particular issue is when the market yield rises to obviously misaligned levels. For example, in mid-1989 some junk bonds were yielding 17%, suggesting strongly that the market viewed such bonds as candidates for restructuring, and a few more were yielding 30%, indicating clearly that the market expected a restructuring soon. A strong fear by junk bond investors is that the economy will slide into recession, endangering even more the issuer's ability to service the debt. Junk bond mutual funds tend to be priced on the basis of *event risk*, a term applied to junk bonds to indicate that their fortunes are tied more to the specific risks of the company than to interest rates.

The impact of junk bonds has been immense. They revolutionized takeover tactics and clearly contributed to the rash of hostile takeover bids in the 1980s, making possible the overthrow of many corporate managers. Examples of hostile-takeover bids include Gulf Oil and Revlon. Since takeovers—both real and rumored—have a significant impact on the stock market as the prices of potential candidates are rapidly driven up, and junk bonds are often used to finance the takeover (or stock buyback by the corporation), junk bond activities have impacted the entire stock market.

Junk bonds suffered sharp declines in 1989, and junk bond returns on a total basis were negative. In 1989 Drexel Burnham Lambert, the primary promotor of junk bonds, pleaded guilty to six counts of securities violations and settled for a fine of $650 million. In February 1990, Drexel filed for bankruptcy. By early 1990 the market for junk bonds was quite illiquid, with investors often not having any bids for their bonds. In such an environment, corporate issuers began to repurchase their junk bonds at severely depressed prices.

Bond Returns and Risks

Why Buy Bonds?

A wide range of investors participate in the fixed-income securities marketplace, ranging from individuals who own a few government or corporate bonds to large institutional investors who own billions of dollars of bonds. Most of these investors are presumably seeking the basic return—risk characteristics that bonds offer; however, quite different overall objectives can be accomplished by purchasing bonds. It is worthwhile to consider these points.

As fixed-income securities, bonds are desirable to many investors because they offer a steady stream of interest income over the life of the obligation and a return of principal at maturity. The promised yield on a bond held to maturity (assuming default does not occur) is known at the time of purchase. Investors who buy bonds and hold them to maturity can effectively lock in a *promised* return and plan accordingly. Barring default by the issuer, the buyers will have the bond principal returned to them at maturity. By holding to maturity investors can escape the risk that interest rates will rise, thereby driving down the price of the bonds. Nevertheless, other risks remain.

Some investors are interested in bonds exactly because bond prices will change as interest rates change. If interest rates rise (fall), bond prices will fall (rise). These investors are interested not in holding the bonds to maturity but rather in earning the capital gains that are possible if they correctly anticipate movements in interest rates. Because bonds can be purchased on margin, large potential gains are possible from speculating on interest rates (of course, large losses are also possible).

Bond speculators encompass a wide range of participants, from financial institutions to individual investors. All are trying to take advantage of an expected movement in interest rates.

Much speculation has occurred recently in the bond markets. In the past, bonds were viewed as very stable instruments whose prices fluctuated very little in the short run. This situation has changed drastically, however, with the bond markets becoming quite volatile. Interest rates in the early 1980s reached record levels, causing large changes in bond prices.

Now that we know why investors purchase and sell bonds, we can analyze some basic information about the returns from, and risks of, investing in bonds. This will allow us to proceed directly to the valuation and analysis of bonds in the next chapter.

Bond Returns

As noted in Chapter 5, the total return on bonds can be separated into two components, which helps to explain why bonds appeal to both conservative investors seeking steady income and aggressive investors seeking capital gains. Conservative investors usually view bonds as fixed-income securities because they expect specified payments from the bonds at specified times. The payments consist of either coupon income on a semiannual basis and the return of principal at maturity or, with zero-coupon bonds, the return of principal at maturity.

The second source of potential returns to bondholders arises from the behavior of bond prices. Capital gains and losses occur because bonds are purchased and sold before maturity. Bond prices are determined by several factors, including time to maturity, coupon, and the general level of interest rates (these factors are discussed in the next chapter).

The most important variable that affects a bond at any time is the behavior of interest rates in the marketplace. *Holding other factors constant, the determining factor in the behavior of bond prices is the behavior of interest rates.* There is an inverse relationship between the two—as market interest rates rise (fall), bond prices decline (rise). Therefore, investors can earn capital gains (or suffer losses) from bonds just as they do with stocks. If they purchase bonds and market interest rates fall, the prices of the bonds will rise. Conversely, if interest rates rise after the purchase, the prices of the bonds will decline.

The behavior of bond prices is more complex than the inverse relationship between bond prices and market interest rates. Different bonds react in different ways to a given change in market rates. Other factors that affect prices include the time to maturity, the coupon, the call feature, and the rating on the bond. Although the result is a complex system of bond price changes, what is important to investors is that they have the opportunity to earn large returns by speculating on the behavior of bond prices.

Measuring Returns

Several measures of the yield, or return, on a bond are available and are sometimes used by investors. (Current yield, defined as the ratio of the coupon interest to the current market price, was discussed earlier in the section entitled "Reading Bond Information.")[31] The most commonly used measure of return for a bond is the yield to maturity. Because yield to maturity is a *promised* yield, the realized compound yield must be considered to measure *realized* performance. Another measure to be considered by bond investors is the yield to the first call date. Finally, the total return concept from Chapter 5 is discussed.

Yield to Maturity The rate of return on bonds most often quoted to investors is the **yield to maturity (YTM),** defined as the *promised* compounded rate of return an investor will receive from a bond purchased at the current market price and held to maturity. Similar to the Internal Rate of Return (IRR) in financial management, the yield to maturity is the interest rate that equates the present value of the cash flows to be received on the bond to the initial investment in the bond, which is its current price. It captures the coupon income to be received on the bond as well as any capital gains and losses realized by purchasing the bond for a price different from face value and holding to maturity.

The calculation of yield to maturity involves equating the current market price (MP) of a bond with its discounted future coupon payments and principal repayment. Note that the market price, the coupon, the number of years to maturity, and the face value of the bond are known, and the discount rate or yield to maturity is the variable to be determined.[32]

[31]The current yield is clearly superior to the coupon rate because it uses the current market price. However, it is not a true measure of the return to a bond purchaser because it does not account for the difference between the bond's purchase price and its eventual redemption at par value.

[32]A traditional method for calculating YTM, used by bond traders and others, is the use of bond tables. These tables provide investors with a YTM, given the coupon rate, the price of

$$P = \sum_{t=1}^{2n} \frac{C_t/2}{(1 + r/2)^t} + \frac{FV}{(1 + r/2)^{2n}} \tag{6-1}$$

where

P = the market price of the bond in question
r = the yield to maturity to be solved for
C = the coupon in dollars
n = the number of years to maturity
FV = the face or par value

To illustrate the trial-and-error (iteration) process involved in a yield-to-maturity calculation, the yield-to-maturity concept is illustrated by referring to the present value tables at the end of the text. The purpose is simply to demonstrate what is happening with the YTM. These problems are easily solved today by calculator or computer, as explained later.

Example. A 10%-coupon bond has 10 years remaining to maturity. Assume that the bond is selling at a discount with a current market price of \$885.30. Because of the inverse relation between bond prices and market yields, it is clear that yields have risen since the bond was originally issued, because the price is less than \$1000. Using Equation 6-1 to solve for yield to maturity,

$$\$885.30 = \sum_{t=1}^{20} \frac{\$50}{(1 + r/2)^t} + \frac{\$1000}{(1 + r/2)^{20}}$$

---

the bond, and the time to maturity. They can also be used to determine the price of a bond when the yield (and the other factors) are known.

To find the YTM on a bond using these tables, do the following steps:

1. Choose the page in the bond table corresponding to the appropriate coupon rate. There is a page for each different coupon.
2. Select the column with the appropriate maturity date.
3. Find the price of the bond in the appropriate maturity column and read across this row to the left column which contains the resulting YTM.

An approximation formula exists for calculating YTM. It relates the net annual effective cash flow to the average amount of money invested in the bond during the ownership period. Effectively, the investor is assumed to have an average investment of this amount in the bond as the price gradually converges to \$1000, as it must by the maturity date.

$$\text{Approximate yield to maturity} = \frac{\text{Coupon Interest} \begin{array}{l} + \text{ Amortized discount} \\ \quad\text{or} \\ - \text{ Amortized premium} \end{array}}{(\text{Current market price} + \text{Par value})/2} \tag{6-2}$$

Example. Consider the preceding bond with a 10% coupon and a term to maturity of 10 years. If it is purchased by an investor as a current market price of \$885.30, the approximate yield to maturity is [\$100 + (\$114.70/10)]/[\$885.30 + 1,000)/2] = 11.83%.

Since both the left-hand side of Equation 6-1 and the numerator values (cash flows) on the right side are known, the equation can be solved for YTM. Because of the semiannual nature of interest payments, the coupon (which in this example was $100) is divided in half and the number of periods (10 in this example) is doubled. What remains is a trial-and-error process to find a discount rate (YTM) that equates the inflows from the bond (coupons plus face value) with its current price (cost). Different rates are tried until the left-hand and right-hand sides are equal. In this example, the solution is 12%.[33]

$$\$885.30 = \$50(\text{present value of an annuity, } 6\% \text{ for 20 periods}) + \$1000\,(\text{present value factor, } 6\% \text{ for 20 periods})$$

$$\$885.30 = \$50(11.4699) + \$1000(0.3118)$$

$$\$885.30 = \$885.30$$ ▪

INVESTMENT CALCULATIONS

It is relatively easy today to find financial calculators or personal computers that already are set up to solve YTM problems. Although it is important to understand the concept of the YTM calculation as explained earlier, to actually calculate a YTM it is always convenient to use some program. *The Investment Calculator* contains a YTM routine as part of the "Duration and Bond Analysis" module. To use it, simply input the current price of the bond, the coupon rate in place of the YTM, the annual coupon in dollars, the number of years to maturity, and the face value, which is always $1000 in this text.

Example. For the problem above involving a 10%, 10-year bond selling at $885.30, inputting these values into the program produces a YTM of 12%. ▪

The YTM calculation for a zero-coupon bond is based on the same process expressed in Equation 6-1—equating the current price to the future cash flows. Because there are no coupons, the process reduces to Equation 6-3, with all terms as previously defined:

$$r = [\text{FV}/P]^{1/2n} - 1 \tag{6-3}$$

[33]The present value of an annuity factor for 6% for 20 periods, 11.4699, is taken from Table A-4 at the end of the text; 0.3118, the present value of a $1 for 6% for 20 periods, is taken from Table A-2.

Example. A zero-coupon bond has 12 years to maturity and is sold for \$300. Given the 24 semiannual periods, the power to be used in raising the ratio of \$1000/\$300, or 3.333, is 0.04167 (calculated as $1/(2 \times 12)$). Using a calculator with power functions shows a value of 1.0514. Subtracting the 1.0 and multiplying by 100 leaves a *semiannual* yield of 5.145%, or an annual yield, or *r*, of 10.29%. Because YTM numbers typically are stated on an annual basis, the yield as calculated from equation 6-3 must be doubled. ▪

It is important to understand that YTM is a promised yield, because investors will earn the indicated yield only if the bond is held to maturity and only if the coupons are reinvested at the YTM. Obviously, no trading can be done for a particular bond if the YTM is to be earned. The investor simply buys and holds. What is not so obvious to many investors, however, is the reinvestment implications of the YTM measure.

Realized Compound Yield The YTM calculation assumes that the investor reinvests all coupons received from a bond at a rate equal to the computed YTM, thereby earning **interest on interest** over the life of the bond.

Example. For a bond with a YTM of 10%, this 10% will be earned *only* if each of the coupons is reinvested at a 10% rate. ▪

If the investor spends the coupons, or reinvests them at a rate different from the assumed reinvestment rate of 10%, the **realized compound yield** actually earned will differ from the promised YTM. Coupons can be reinvested at rates higher or lower than the computed YTM.

This interest-on-interest concept significantly affects the realized return. The exact impact is a function of coupon and time to maturity, with reinvestment becoming more important as either coupon or time to maturity rises, or both.

INVESTMENTS INTUITION

Consider what happens when investors purchase bonds at high YTMs, such as when interest rates reached very high levels in the summer of 1982. Unless they reinvested the coupons at the promised YTMs, investors did not actually realize these high promised yields. For the promised YTM to become a realized YTM, coupons had to be reinvested at the record rates existing at that time, an unlikely situation for a high-YTM bond with a long maturity. The subsequent decline in interest rates during the fall of 1982 illustrates the fallacy of believing that one has "locked up" record yields during a relatively brief period of very high interest rates.

To illustrate the importance of interest on interest in YTM figures, Table 6-1 shows the total realized return under different assumed reinvestment rates for a 10% noncallable 20-year bond purchased at face value. If the reinvestment rate exactly equals the YTM of 10%, the investor realizes a 10% compound yield when the bond is held to maturity, with $4040 of the total dollar return from the bond attributable to interest on interest. At a 12% reinvestment rate, the investor realizes a 11.14% compound return, with almost 75% of the total return coming from interest on interest ($5738/7738). With no reinvestment of coupons (spending them as received), the investor achieves only a 5.57% realized return. Clearly, the reinvestment portion of the YTM concept is critical.

The realized compound yields shown in Table 6-1 can be calculated using the following formula:

$$rcy = \left[\frac{\text{Total future dollars}}{\text{Purchase price of bond}} \right]^{1/2n} - 1.0 \qquad (6\text{-}3)$$

Example. For the bond calculations shown in Table 6-1, consider the realized compound yield at an assumed reinvestment rate of 12%. The future value per dollar invested equals the total return, $7738, plus the cost of the bond, $1000, or $8738. Therefore,

TABLE 6-1 ***Realized Yield, Using Different Reinvestment Rate Assumptions, for a 10% 20-Year Bond Purchased at Face Value***

Coupon Income[a] ($)	Assumed Reinvestment Rate (%)	Amount Attributable to Reinvestment[b] ($)	Total Return[c] ($)	Realized Return[d] (%)
2000	0%	0	2000	5.57
2000	5%	1370	3370	7.51
2000	8%	2751	4751	8.94
2000	9%	3352	5352	9.46
2000	10%	4040	6040	10.00
2000	11%	4830	6830	10.56
2000	12%	5738	7738	11.14

[a]Coupon income = $50 coupon received *semiannually* for 20 years = $50 × 40 periods.
[b]Amount attributable to reinvestment = total return minus coupon income. This is also known as the interest on interest.
[c]Total return = sum of an annuity for 40 periods, $50 semiannual coupons (Example: at 10% reinvestment rate, $50 × [5%, 40 period factor of 120.80] = $6040.)
[d]Realized return = [Future Value per Dollar Invested]$^{1/N}$ − 1, where future value per dollar invested = (total return + the cost of bond)/cost of the bond. The result of this calculation is the realized compound return on a semiannual basis. To put this on an annual basis, this figure must be doubled.

$$\begin{aligned} rcy &= [\$8738/1000]^{1/40} - 1.0 \\ &= [8.738]^{0.025} \\ &= 1.05569 - 1.0 \\ &= 0.05569, \text{ or } 5.569\% \text{ on a semiannual basis} \end{aligned}$$

Once again, to place this on an annual basis, multiply by 2. The annual *rcy* is 5.569% × 2 = 11.14%. ▪

Bond investors today often make specific assumptions about future reinvestment rates in order to cope with the reinvestment rate problem. Given their assumptions, they can calculate the realized yield to be earned if that assumption turns out to be accurate.

One of the advantages of a zero-coupon bond is the elimination of reinvestment rate risk. Investors know at the time of purchase the YTM that will be realized when the bond is held to maturity.

Yield to Call Most corporate bonds, and some government bonds, are callable by the issuers, typically after some deferred call period. For bonds likely to be called, the yield-to-maturity calculation is unrealistic. A better calculation is the promised **yield to call.** The end of the deferred call period, when a bond first can be called, is often used for the yield-to-call calculation. This is particularly appropriate for bonds selling at a premium (i.e., high-coupon bonds with market prices above par value).[34]

To calculate the yield to first call, the YTM formula (Equation 6-1) is used, but with the number of periods until the first call date substituted for the number of periods until maturity and the call price substituted for face value. These changes are shown in Equation 6-4.

$$P = \sum_{t=1}^{2c} \frac{C_t/2}{(1 + \text{YTC}/2)^t} + \frac{\text{CP}}{(1 + \text{YTC}/2)^{2c}} \tag{6-4}$$

where

CP = the call price to be paid if the bond is called
YTC = yield to first call
c = number of periods until the first call date

It is important to remember that bond prices are calculated on the basis of the lowest yield measure. Therefore, for premium bonds selling above a certain level, yield to call replaces yield to maturity, because it produces the lowest measure of yield.[35]

---

[34]That is, bonds with high coupons (and high yields) are prime candidates to be called.

[35]The technical name for the point at which yield to call comes into play is the "crossover point," which is a price and is approximately the sum of par value and one year's interest. For a discussion of this point, see S. Homer and M. Leibowitz, *Inside the Yield Book* (Englewood Cliffs, N.J.: Prentice-Hall, 1972), Chapter 4.

Total Return As explained in Chapter 5, the total return for any security includes both an income component and a price change component. The formula for a bond's total return is repeated as Equation 6-5.[36]

$$\text{Total return} = \frac{C_t + \text{PC}}{P_t} \tag{6-5}$$

Example. Assume an investor buys a 10% coupon bond for $1075, holds it for one year, collects $100 in interest, and sells the bond for $1050. The total return for this one-year period is

$$\text{One-year total return} = \frac{100 + (-25)}{1075}$$
$$= 6.98\%$$

On the other hand, assume the investor had held the bond only six months, collected one $50 coupon, and sold the bond for $1110. The total return for this six-month period would be

$$\text{Six-month total return} = \frac{50 + 35}{1075}$$
$$= 7.91\%$$ ▪

Bond Risk

Bonds have their own sources of risk, just as common stocks and other securities do. Bondholders are promised a stream of interest payments and a repayment of the principal or par value, but they are subject to several sources of risk in actually realizing these returns; specifically: (1) interest rate, (2) default, (3) reinvestment rate, (4) inflation, (5) maturity, (6) call, and (7) liquidity risks.

Interest Rate Risk The major risk facing all bondholders is changes in interest rates. Prices of outstanding bonds must change inversely with changes in current market interest rates. When the market interest rate declines (rises), prices of bonds outstanding rise (fall).

Interest rate risk is the change in the price of a security as a result of changes in market interest rates. This variability in prices is caused by changes in interest rate levels, which are very powerful forces that affect all securities markets. Although investors normally discuss interest rate risk in

---

[36]The subscript t stands for time and refers to a holding period. C is the bond's coupon interest payment in dollars during holding period t. P is the bond's price at the beginning of holding period t, and PC is the change in bond price over the period.

connection with bond analysis, it is important to remember that this risk has significant implications for common stocks. It is discussed again when we consider the sources of risk to an owner of common stocks.

Example. Consider a new issue of AAA-rated 20-year corporate bonds sold by IBM. If existing AAA corporate bonds with comparable features are yielding 10%, the new IBM bonds will yield approximately 10%. An investor buying these bonds today for $1000 each will receive $100 in interest income each year for 20 years and will have $1000 returned for each bond at the end of the 20 years unless IBM defaults, a most unlikely event. Barring default, and recognizing the erosion of all financial assets by inflation, the investor assumes no further risk as to the value of the principal by holding the bonds to maturity. However, if the bonds are sold before maturity, the investor is exposed to interest rate risk.

Assume that the investor sells the bonds five years after purchasing them and that the interest rate on comparable bonds has risen to 12%. Potential buyers of this bond will not pay the original purchaser $1000 for the five-year-old IBM bonds. Why should they, when they can buy new bonds with comparable features yielding 12%? As a result of the upward shift in interest rates, the price of these bonds must decline below $1000, allowing the purchaser to receive approximately 12% on them.

The same forces apply in the opposite direction. If interest rates decline, bond prices rise. Obviously, investors would prefer the higher interest rates on the old bonds, other things being equal. By purchasing old, higher-yielding bonds, they will drive the price up and the yield down until yields again reach an equilibrium. ▪

Default Risk Corporate bonds and municipals, as discussed earlier, are subject to default—the failure to pay the specified interest payments or repay the principal at the time specified in the indenture. Bonds carry strict obligations and the failure to make a specified payment as called for is a serious event.

Default risk does not exist for U.S. Treasury securities, at least on a practical basis. Although some U.S. agency securities are not directly guaranteed by the federal government, the belief is that the Treasury would not permit one of these agencies to default. Corporates and municipals are always subject to some risk, however small, of default by the issuer. The two major rating agencies, Standard & Poor's and Moody's, are good sources of information on default risk.

Reinvestment Rate Risk As we saw in the preceding discussion, YTM calculations make certain assumptions about the reinvestment of the coupons received during the life of a bond. If the stated YTM is actually to be earned, cash flow must be reinvested at the stated YTM. Reinvestment rate risk is the risk that this will not occur, leaving the investor with a lower yield because the cash flows were reinvested at a lower rate.

Inflation Risk Fixed-income securities by definition promise specified payments at specified periods. Since the payment in dollars is fixed, the value of the payment in real terms declines as the price level rises. This risk of the real return being less than the nominal (dollar) return is referred to as inflation risk.

Inflation risk will be accounted for in the next chapter when the level of interest rates is discussed. However, it can be noted that inflation risk is really the risk of unanticipated inflation. If anticipated, inflation is reflected in nominal riskless interest rates that investors use in valuing bonds. Thus, investors are compensated for that part of inflation that is anticipated but may not be compensated for unanticipated inflation.

Maturity Risk Maturity risk refers to the fact that the further into the future an investor goes in purchasing a long-term security, the more risk there is in the investment (other things being equal). The environment 30 years from now, when some long-term bonds mature, can scarcely be envisioned today. Thus, investing for the long term involves substantial risk, and bond investors wish to be compensated for this risk with an additional premium for lending long term rather than short term.

Call Risk As explained earlier in the chapter, many corporate bonds are callable. Issuers have the option of redeeming a bond before the maturity date, typically after the first five years a bond is outstanding. Bonds will not be called unless it is to the issuer's advantage; it is not likely to be to the bondholder's advantage. When interest rates decline, bonds carrying higher coupons are likely to be called. The call risk to a bondholder, therefore, is that higher-coupon bonds will have to be given up.

Liquidity (Marketability) Risk Liquidity risk is concerned with the secondary market where a security is traded. A security is liquid if it can be sold easily and quickly with (at most) small price concessions. Although Treasury securities are very liquid, the corporate bond market is less so. This is particularly true for "small" positions (less than $100,000).

The risk that bondholders face is taking on new dimensions as leveraged buyouts (LBOs) and other corporate refinancings occur at a rapid rate. This situation is discussed in Box 6-1.

Measuring Risk

As noted, there are several sources of risk for bonds. In measuring risk, however, there is no measure comparable to the beta for equity securities (at least in the sense of a measure that is widely recognized and used).

BOX 6-1

THE BONDHOLDERS' COLD NEW WORLD

The talk of the securities world these days is Metropolitan Life Insurance Co.'s lawsuit against RJR Nabisco. Since 1984 the hapless holders of blue-chip corporate bonds have seen their securities devalued as issuers fell prey to leveraged buyouts or other debt-laden deals. Now staid Met Life is fighting mad and banging on the courthouse door.

Screwing the bondholder is the very stuff that LBOs are made of. In that notorious RJR deal, the hit—albeit on paper—was about $1 billion on $5.4 billion of outstanding debt. Less well known is the leveraged recap by Quantum Chemical, formerly National Distillers & Chemical. Quantum, which has revenues of $2.9 billion, borrowed $1.1 billion in order to stave off possible raiders by paying out more than its entire net worth as a cash dividend to shareholders. In that one, bondholders lost about $105 million on securities that were issued less than a year before.

Between 1984 and 1988 there were 254 downgrades of industrial debt by Moody's Investors Service as a result of takeovers, buyouts, or defensive maneuvers by companies borrowing heavily to avoid a raid. The rating agency estimates that $160 billion worth of bonds have been downgraded, clipping bondholders for at least $13 billion. Not surprisingly, these creditors are talking about "theft."

As exercised as bondholders may be about their losses, they haven't attracted much sympathy. That may be because the average bondholder is an institutional investor, a pro, even though the money he is managing in a pension fund, a mutual fund, or the general account at a life insurance company comes from small investors. The losses are mostly on paper and will be negligible if the bonds are paid off in full at maturity. If debt-heavy corporations begin to topple in droves, the damage could be huge.

Source: Excerpted from Gary Hector, "The Bondholders' Cold New World," *Fortune*,

Nevertheless, it is always appropriate to talk about the dispersion in actual or expected returns.

Recall from Chapter 5 that the risk of an investment involves the idea that the actual outcome on any security or portfolio will be different from the expected outcome. Risk is typically assessed by measuring the dispersion in outcomes—the greater the dispersion, the greater the risk. Standard deviation, or variance, is a measure of dispersion or total risk and is the most widely used measure of dispersion. It can be used to measure ex post (historical) risk or ex ante (expected) risk.

Whether they realize it or not, investors are dealing with a probability distribution of possible returns when they consider investing in a bond. Assuming this distribution is normal, a comparison of the returns from bond A with those from bond B will indicate which is riskier. If the standard deviation of A is 5% and that for B it is 3%, A can be said to be riskier.

Useful information can be derived from historical data using the standard deviation (and the assumption that the distribution of returns is normal, or approximately so). One standard deviation on either side of the mean encompasses about 68% of the TRs in the distribution; ± 2 encompasses about 95% of the TRs; and ± 3 encompasses about 99%.

Example. Knowing that all AAA corporate bonds had an average TR of 12% per year for the last 10 years with a standard deviation of 2% and that the distribution was normal, you know that 68% of the returns were within the range of 10% to 14%, or 2% on either side of the mean. In this scenario, investors experienced little risk roughly two-thirds of the time, and even 95% of the time the returns did not go below 8%. Based on this information, investors can decide if they are willing to take the risk of these outcomes if they expect this same situation to prevail in the future.

As another example, consider the situation where someone says that the expected return on a bond rated B for the next year is 18% but that the estimated standard deviation is 10%. The significance of this statement can be understood quickly. Two standard deviations around this expected value encompass *negative* returns. ▪

The Historical Returns and Risks on Bonds

Investments is a forward-looking subject, with participants interested in what will happen over some future holding period. Throughout this text we discuss the valuation and analysis of securities in order to help us make intelligent estimates of the future returns from, and risks of, securities. Nevertheless, it is important to know what has happened in the past. Otherwise, investors have no reasonable basis for judging their future estimates.

INVESTMENTS INTUITION

If during the last 60 years, which encompasses severe depressions as well as periods of very high inflation, bonds in any one year never returned 30% or experienced a 20% loss, it would be unlikely for them to do so in the foreseeable future. However, it would not be impossible. The past therefore cannot simply be extrapolated into the future with no adjustments and no considerations. But knowing what the returns and risk for the major types of securities have been in the past is useful information.

One of the best-known series of returns for the major types of securities, used in Chapter 5, is that of Ibbotson Associates, Inc., produced on an annual, quarterly, and monthly basis in both printed and disk format. This is a statistical examination of the total rates of return on a monthly and annual basis for common stocks, long-term corporate bonds, long-term and intermediate-term U.S. government bonds, and inflation. In addition, for stocks and U.S. government bonds, the total returns are broken down into returns attributable only to income and only to capital appreciation.

Table 6-2 shows the returns and risk (as measured by the standard deviation) on bonds for the period 1926–1989. Notice that both arithmetic mean and geometric mean returns are shown. As discussed in Chapter 5, the geometric mean for each of the series represents the compound annual rate of return and is less than the arithmetic mean. Geometric means measure the change in wealth over time, whereas the arithmetic mean is a better measure of the "typical" performance over individual periods.

Table 6-2 shows that, over this 64-year period, long-term corporates, long-term governments, and intermediate-term governments had annual geometric mean returns of 5.2%, 4.6%, and 4.9% respectively, and similar arithmetic mean annual returns. The standard deviations were low, 8.5%, 8.6%, and 5.5%, respectively.[37] Although in the late 1970s and early 1980s investors became accustomed to high interest rates and the idea that bond returns should be considerably higher than these numbers indicate, for many years bond returns were low because inflation was very low or nonexistent.

Why did intermediate-term government bonds outperform long-term government bonds over this period? The answer lies in the fact that yields in general rose significantly over this period, producing capital losses for some annual holding periods. The longer the maturity of a bond, other things equal, the greater the capital loss. Thus, long-term bonds did not perform as well as intermediate-term bonds.

The fact that the measurement of returns on an annual basis can result in some negative returns on bonds can be clearly demonstrated in connection with an additional point about bond returns and risk. An investor in fixed-income securities always has as one important option choosing between long-term bonds and short-term instruments. Assume the investor has an investment horizon of one year and decides whether to invest in short-term instruments or long-term bonds at the beginning of each year. How would such an investor have fared over a period encompassing the recent major inflationary experience of the United States as well as the strong markets of the mid-1980s?

---

[37]It is important to recognize that the measurement process used to produce these numbers produces, *on an annual basis,* some losses on corporates and governments in certain years. Since the returns are measured annually based on year-end prices, bond price declines during the year can produce negative total returns *for that year.*

TABLE 6-2 ***Rates of Return on Long-Term Bonds and Treasury Bills, 1926–1989***

Series	Geometric Mean (%)	Arithmetic Mean (%)	Standard Deviation (%)
Long-term corporate bonds	5.2	5.5	8.5
Long-term government bonds	4.6	4.9	8.6
Intermediate government bonds	4.9	5.0	5.5
U.S. Treasury bills	3.6	3.7	3.4
Inflation	3.1	3.1	4.8

Source: Ibbotson, Roger G., and Rex A. Sinquefield, *Stocks, Bonds, Bills and Inflation* (SSBI), 1989, updated in *SSBI 1990 Yearbook*, Ibbotson Associates, Chicago.

Consider the annual returns on long-term government bonds and short-term Treasury bills for the 20-year period 1970–1989.[38] Inflation started its upward trend in the late 1960s as a result of President Johnson's financing policies, and interest rates and inflation declined dramatically in the last half of 1982. Therefore, this is an excellent period in which to demonstrate the potential returns on bonds, as well as their riskiness.

The annual total returns on long-term bonds were negative in 6 of the 20 years between 1970 and 1989, with four negative years in a row (1978–1981). Because of their short-term nature, Treasury bills always produce a positive total annual return (unless the data are bad, as happened in one of the early years in the 1930s). Furthermore, shorts outperformed longs in three additional years when bond returns were positive (1973, 1977, and 1983). Thus, investing in long-term government bonds *on an annual basis* is not a riskless strategy because short-term money market instruments outperformed long-term bonds in 9 out of 20 recent years. Nevertheless, on an average annual compound-rate-of-return basis, Treasury bonds outperformed Treasury bills for the period 1970–1989 (9.0% versus 7.6%) primarily because of very large TRs for corporates in 1982, 1985, 1986, and 1989 of 40%, 31%, 24%, and 18%, respectively.

Long-term bond returns can be extraordinary from time to time. On the very first page of this text the following question was posed: Is it possible to have earned 40% or more in one year by investing in default-free Treasury securities? The answer is yes! Two agency issues, one from the Federal Home Loan Mortgage Corporation and one from the Federal Housing Administration, produced incredible annual returns of roughly 49% each in 1982. A 30-year Treasury bond, the safest long-term instrument

[38]These figures are based on *Stocks, Bonds, Bills and Inflation: 1990 Yearbook* (Chicago: Ibbotson Associates, 1990).

BOX 6-2

THE CASE FOR BONDS

Bonds are the Rodney Dangerfield of financial investments. They don't get much respect. They were defined in an early 1980s parody of the *Wall Street Journal* as "fixed-rate instruments designed to fall in price." Even though bonds have produced acceptable—some may dare to say attractive—returns in recent years, most investors still remain skeptical. They remember how badly bonds did in the 1960s and 1970s, when they were actually earning negative returns.

The arguments against bonds are easy to make. Over the long pull their total return (interest payments plus capital gains and losses) has been far inferior to that of common stocks. Over the past 60 years, stocks have returned a compound annual 10%, about 7 percentage points better than the average rate of inflation over the period. On the other hand, high-grade corporate bonds—even with their better performance in the Eighties—have eked out a rate of return of only about 5%. In inflation-adjusted terms, bonds yielded 2%, versus 7% for stocks; thus stocks did $3\frac{1}{2}$ times as well as bonds.

Nevertheless, I believe the case today for bonds is extraordinarily persuasive. Why? Because bonds are priced more attractively than they were in the past. Let me explain.

If investors had known 30 years ago that inflation would become a major problem—if they had correctly forecast that the general economy, inflation rates, exchange rates and therefore interest rates, would become increasingly volatile—bonds would not have been priced to give such inadequate total returns. But remember that our smartest economists were claiming in the early 1960s that inflation (then at 1%) was dead and that even minor fluctuations in economic activity could be "fine-tuned" away. Economists and investors were egregiously wrong. But they are not likely to be wrong forever.

The point is that you shouldn't invest with a rearview mirror. What was a poor investment over the past 60 years will not necessarily be one over the next 60.

Investors learn, and new information about inflation and volatility does get incorporated into market prices. Bonds today reflect the poorer inflation outlook and the greater instability of bond prices. The issue is not how poorly bond investors fared in the 1950, 1960s and 1970s. The issue is, Will bonds produce a generous return in the future?

The case for bonds is a simple one. Bond yields are unusually generous in historical context, in comparison with inflation, and in relation to the returns available today from common stocks.

In the old days—before serious inflation—corporate bond buyers could expect nominal yields of 5% or less. Today, investors in high-quality corporates can receive almost double digit yields. Very safe utility bonds (such as those of the regional Bell operating companies, the baby Bells) yield nearly 10%. They are reasonably free of "event risk"—the risk of a leveraged takeover of the company, which could impair the quality of presently outstanding bonds. That is 10%, total return being the sum of dividends and capital appreciation. Today, the best Wall Street estimates of future dividend and earnings growth, the raw materials needed to produce a growth in capital values, are in the vicinity of 6% to 7%. Adding the growth component to the current dividend yield of the market, now less than 4%, produces a forward-looking return from stocks in the 10% to $10\frac{1}{2}$ range.

Thus, at today's market values, very high quality bonds are priced to yield almost as much as common stocks. Remember that historically stocks have delivered five percentage points more total return than bonds. So bonds now provide some of the best relative values ever. To be sure, bonds are now rationally considered more volatile and riskier than they once were, and they should give returns that are appropriately higher. But stocks are still far more risky than bonds, and it is possible that panic-depressive bond investors have overdiscounted the risks.

In summary, bonds deserve a place in everyone's portfolio. They are particularly appropriate for IRAs, thrift plans and other tax-protected retirement plans, where interest can compound free of tax.

Source: Adapted from Burton G. Malkiel, "The case for bonds," *Forbes*, June 26, 1989, pp. 180–185. Reprinted by permission of Burton Malkiel.

known to humankind, produced an annual return of 41%. High-grade corporate bonds did even better![39]

The Future for Bond Returns and Risk

It seems fitting to close this discussion by considering future bond returns, since investors invest for the future, not the past. As we know well by now, the future is uncertain and unpredictable. Nevertheless, financial market observers can and do make predictions about the future. One well-known observer, Professor Burton Malkiel, has presented a case for bonds for the 1990s. Given that he made a case for stocks for the 1980s, and stocks performed exceptionally well in that decade, Professor Malkiel's arguments are well worth considering.

Summary

- Bonds are creditor instruments and, by definition, fixed-income securities.
- A typical (i.e., coupon) bond offers a stream of fixed interest payments and the return of a specified principal (typically, $1000), all at designated dates.
- Since bonds involve specific contractual obligations on the part of the issuer, failure to meet such obligations results in default and possibly bankruptcy.
- Important characteristics of a bond include the call feature, giving the issuer the right to call in a bond issue by paying it off; the sinking fund, representing periodic payments by the issuer to pay off the bond; the

[39]See Martin L. Leibowitz, "Future Directions of Bond Portfolio Management," reprinted in *The Revolution in Techniques for Managing Bond Portfolios* (Charlottesville: The Institute of Chartered Financial Analysts, 1983).

collateral behind the bond, which may range from none (for a debenture) to the pledge of real property (for a mortgage bond); and the convertibility feature, allowing the bondholder to turn in the bond to the issuer for a specified number of shares of common stock.

- Zero-coupon bonds pay no interest during the bond's life but are instead sold at a discount and held to maturity.
- New municipal bond features include federal backing, guarantees, "stripped" format, and put bonds.
- Bonds are rated, primarily by Standard & Poor's Corporation and by Moody's, as to their relative probability of default. Ratings range from AAA (the highest) to D (those bonds in default), with the first four grades (AAA through BBB) considered investment grade. Municipal bonds and commercial paper are also rated.
- Information sources available for bonds include specific information on the issuer and information on the economy and interest rates, the major factor affecting bond price changes.
- The bond market is basically a primary market. It is a market for new issues traditionally dominated by institutional investors.
- Although corporate bonds are traded on exchanges, primarily the NYSE, most bond trading is done over the counter.
- Although the U.S. government and agency markets are very active, the corporate and municipal markets are not active markets for the average investor.
- Junk bonds became an important component of the bond market in the 1980s, significantly impacting both corporate managements and bond investors.
- The yield to maturity is the promised fully compounded rate of return to be earned on a bond by purchasing and holding to maturity.
- The YTM calculation assumes reinvestment of all coupons at the computed YTM rate. The interest-on-interest concept is an important part of the YTM calculation.
- The major source of bond risk is interest rate risk, whereby a change in interest rates causes an inverse change in bond prices. Inflation risk, default risk, reinvestment rate risk, maturity risk, call risk, and liquidity risk are other sources of bond risk.
- According to the Ibbotson-Sinquefield data for 1926–1989, the average annual geometric rate of return on bonds has been 5.2% for corporates and 4.6% for long-term governments. Bonds have been much safer than common stocks, as shown by standard deviations of roughly 40% those for stocks.

Key Words

Accrued interest
Bonds
Bond ratings
Call provision
Conversion feature
Coupon

Current yield
Debenture
Discount
Event risk
Fixed-income securities
Interest on interest
Interest rate risk
Junk bond
Mortgage bond
Par value
Premium
Realized compound yield
Senior securities
Sinking fund
Term-to-maturity
Yield to call
Yield to maturity (YTM)
Zero-coupon bonds

Questions

6-1 Are all bonds fixed-income securities?

6-2 What is the difference between a debenture and a mortgage bond?

6-3 Is the call feature an advantage or a disadvantage to an investor? In what interest rate environment would you expect issuers to call in bonds, other things being equal?

6-4 Distinguish between a vanilla bond, a zero-coupon bond, and a floating-rate bond. How can a bond be guaranteed?

6-5 What is the probability of default for an A-rated bond? Why might an investor purchase a BB-rated bond, which is below investment grade?

6-6 What "macro" information should be of primary concern to bond investors? What are some sources of such information?

6-7 Using Figure 6-2, consider the fourth bond listed. What is the annual coupon in dollars for this bond, and when does it mature? What is the current yield? What other yield measure should investors consider?

6-8 Referring to question 6-7, find the first convertible bond on the page and decide whether it is selling as a "bond" or because it is valuable currently to convert it into common stock. Find the first premium bond and explain why this bond is selling at a premium.

6-9 Referring again to question 6-7, translate the closing price of the first bond listed into its "true" price (based on $1000 par).

6-10 Assume a normal distribution for the corporate bond information in Table 6-2. Roughly two-thirds of the time, what range would be expected for annual returns? 95% of the time?

6-11 What is the relative size of the government securities market versus the corporate and municipal sectors? List, in order of descending importance, the role of individual investors in these three markets.

6-12 How are bonds traded? where? What limitations, if any, do individual investors face in trading the various types of bonds?

6-13 How can bonds appeal to the most conservative investor as well as the speculator?

6-14 Name the sources of risk for a bond. Which sources are most applicable to corporate bonds? to Treasury bonds?

6-15 How can bond risk be measured?

6-16 What directly accounts for the dramatic bond returns in 1982 and 1985? What are the implications to bond investors?

6-17 What is the relationship between the level of, and changes in, interest rates, and bond speculation?

6-18 Why is the current yield not a true measure of a bond's return?

6-19 What are the disadvantages to an investor of purchasing 10 or 15 corporate bonds?

6-20 How do junk bonds originate? What is meant by event risk?

6-21 If YTM is a promised yield, why do investors not use only the realized compound yield?

6-22 What does it mean to say that YTM is a promised yield?

6-23 What is meant by *interest on interest?*

6-24 Which bond is more affected by interest-on-interest considerations?
(a) Bond A—12% coupon, 20 years to maturity.
(b) Bond B—6% coupon, 25 years to maturity.

Problems

6-1 Calculate the total return for a 9% bond purchased at 86, held one year, and sold for 92. Given this information, what statements can be made about interest rates?

6-2 Given the following information, calculate the current yield, the yield to maturity, and the total return for each bond:
(a) A bond purchased at $940, maturing in three years, with an 8% coupon.
(b) A bond purchased at $1150, maturing in 10 years, with a 15% coupon.
(c) A bond bought at par, with a coupon of 12%, which matures in one year.

6-3 Calculate the two components of total return for a 13% coupon bond bought at $73 and sold three years later for $83.

6-4 Calculate the YTM for a 10-year zero-coupon bond sold at $400. Recalculate the YTM if the bond had been priced at $300.

6-5 Calculate the realized compound yield for a 10% bond with 20 years to maturity and an expected reinvestment rate of 8%, purchased at $1000.

6-6 Consider a 12% 10-year bond purchased at face value. Based on Table 6-1, and assuming a reinvestment rate of 10%, calculate
(a) The total return.
(b) The interest-on-interest.
(c) The realized return.

6-7 Calculate the yield to first call for a 10%, 10-year bond that is callable five years from now. The current market price is $970 and the call price is $1050. Explain why the YTC is greater than the YTM.

6-8 Calculate the YTM for the following bonds.
(a) A 12%, 20-year bond with a current price of $975.
(b) A 6%, 10-year bond with a current price of $836.
(c) A 9%, 8-year bond with a current price of $714.

6-9 Akron Rubber's bonds, the 10s of 2005, are selling at 109 3/8. Exactly 14 years remain to maturity. Determine the
(a) Current yield.
(b) Yield to maturity.

6-10 Using Problem 6-8, assume that 28 years remain to maturity. How would the yield to maturity change? Does the current yield change?

6-11 Archer Products' bonds, the 11s of 2006, sell to yield 12.5%. Exactly 15 years remain to maturity. Determine the current market price of the bonds. If the YTM had been 11.5%, what would the price of the bonds be? Explain why this difference occurs.

6-12 A 12% coupon bond has 20 years to maturity. It is currently selling for 20% less than face value. Determine its YTM.

Selected References

Detailed information on fixed-income securities can be found in

Fabozzi, Frank J., and Pollack, Irving M. editors. *The Handbook of Fixed Income Securities*, 2nd ed. Homewood, Ill.: Dow-Jones-Irwin, 1986.

A complete discussion of junk bonds can be found in

Altman, Edward I., and Nammacher, Scott A. *Investing in Junk Bonds: Inside The High Yield Debt Market*. New York: John Wiley, 1987.

Measuring fixed-income performance is discussed in

Anthony, Robert N. "How to Measure Fixed-Income Performance Correctly." *The Journal of Portfolio Management*, Winter 1985, pp. 61–65.

CHAPTER 7

Bond Valuation and Analysis

What determines the price of a security? The answer is value! A security's estimated value determines the price that investors place on it in the open market.

A security's *intrinsic value,* or economic value, is the present value of the expected cash flows from that asset. Any security purchased is expected to provide one or more cash flows some time in the future. These cash flows could be periodic, such as interest or dividends, or simply a terminal price or redemption value, or a combination of these. Since these cash flows occur in the future, they must be discounted at an appropriate rate to determine their present value. The sum of these discounted cash flows is the economic (intrinsic) value of the asset. Calculating intrinsic value, therefore, requires the use of present value techniques. Equation 7-1 expresses the concept:

$$Value_{t=0} = \sum_{t=1}^{n} \frac{Cash\ flows}{(1 + k)^t} \tag{7-1}$$

where

$Value_{t=0}$ = the value of the asset now (time period 0)
$Cash\ flows$ = the future receipts and repayment (or sales price)
k = the appropriate discount rate
n = number of periods over which the cash flows are expected

To solve Equation 7-1 and derive the intrinsic value of a security, it is necessary to determine the following:

1. The expected *cash flows* from the security. This includes the size and type of cash flows, such as dividends, interest, face value to be received at maturity, or expected price of the security at some point in the future.
2. The *timing* of the expected cash flows. Since the returns to be generated from a security occur at various times in the future, they must be properly documented for discounting back to time period 0 (today). Money has a time value, and the timing of future cash flows significantly affects the value of the asset today.
3. The *discount rate,* or required rate of return demanded by investors. The discount rate used will reflect the time value of the money and the risk of the security. It is an opportunity cost, representing the rate forgone by an investor in the next best alternative with comparable risk.

Bond Valuation

Using the intrinsic value model for valuing any security, the price of a bond should equal the present value of its expected cash flows.[1] The coupons and the principal repayment are known, and the present value is determined by discounting these future payments from the issuer at an appropriate discount rate, or market yield, for the issue. The same equation that was used in the last chapter to solve for yield to maturity, Equation 6-1, is used here, except now we solve for price, because we know the appropriate discount rate, *r*.

Equation 6-1, which is used to solve for both yield to maturity and the intrinsic value of a coupon bond, is restated here as Equation 7-2:

$$\text{IV} = \sum_{t=1}^{2n} \frac{C_t/2}{(1 + r/2)^t} + \frac{\text{FV}}{(1 + r/2)^{2n}} \tag{7-2}$$

where

IV = the intrinsic or present value of the bond today (time period 0)
C = the annual coupons or interest payments
FV = the maturity value (or par value) of the bond
n = the number of years to maturity of the bond
r = the appropriate discount rate or market yield for the bond

Previous discussion did not elaborate on the fact that in order to conform with existing payment practices on bonds of paying interest semiannually rather than annually, the discount rate being used (r), and the coupon (C_t) on the bond must be divided by 2, and the number of periods must be doubled. Equation 7-2 is the equation that underlies published bond quotes and standard bond practices.

For purposes of discussion, we will illustrate the calculation of bond prices by referring to the present value tables at the end of the text, which can always be used to solve these problems if necessary. The present value process for a typical coupon-bearing bond involves three steps, given the dollar coupon on the bond, the face value, and the current market yield applicable to a particular bond:

1. Using the *present value of an annuity* table (Table A-4 in the appendix), determine the present value of the coupons (interest payments).
2. Using the *present value* table (Table A-2 in the appendix), determine the present value of the maturity (par) value of the bond. For our purposes, the maturity value will always be $1000.
3. Add the present values determined in steps 1 and 2 together.

---

[1]As discussed in Chapter 6, an investor purchasing a bond must also pay to the seller the accrued interest on that bond.

Example. Consider newly issued bond A with a three-year maturity, sold at par to yield 10%. Assuming semiannual interest payments of $50 per year for each of the next three years, the value of bond A, based on Equation 7-2, is

$$PV(A) = \sum_{t=1}^{6} \frac{\$50}{(1 + 0.05)^t} + \frac{\$1000}{(1 + 0.06)^6} = \$50(5.0757) + \$1000(0.7462)$$

$$= \$999.99, \text{ or } \$1000$$

which, of course, agrees with our immediate recognition that the bond's value would have to be $1000 since it has just been sold at par. ▪

Now consider bond B, with characteristics identical to A's, issued five years ago when the interest rate demanded for such a bond was 7%. Assume that the current discount rate (or market yield) on bonds of this type is 10% and that the bond has three years left to maturity. Investors certainly will not pay $1000 for bond B and receive the dollar coupon of $70 per year, or $35 semiannually, when they can purchase bond A and receive $100 per year. However, they should be willing to pay a price determined by the use of Equation 7-2.

$$PV(B) = \sum_{t=1}^{6} \frac{\$35}{(1 + 0.05)^t} + \frac{\$1000}{(1 + 0.05)^6} = \$35(5.0757) + \$1000(0.7462)$$

$$= \$923.85$$

Thus, bond B is valued, as is any other asset, on the basis of its future stream of benefits (cash flows), using a discount rate that properly reflects the risk involved. Since the numerator is always specified for coupon-bearing bonds at time of issuance, the only problem in valuing a typical bond is to determine the denominator or discount rate.

The discount rate (or required yield), r, in Equation 7-2 can be observed in the marketplace. It is the current market rate being earned by investors on comparable noncallable bonds with the same maturity and the same credit quality (in other words, it is an opportunity cost). Thus, the effect of interest rates is incorporated into the discount rate used to solve the present value model.

Solving for the price of a bond is an easy procedure in today's financial world using either a personal computer or a financial calculator.

INVESTMENT CALCULATIONS

The Investment Calculator that accompanies this text can be used to calculate the price of a bond given the required market yield or YTM, the life of the bond, the dollar coupon, and the face value (always $1000). Simply go to that part of the software from the main screen and input the values.

Example. For a 10% bond with 10 years to maturity, when the required market yield or YTM is 12%, skip the first data request (for the price of the bond), enter 12 as the yield to maturity (or r), enter $100 as the *annual coupon*, enter 10 as the number of years, and enter $1000 as the face value. You need not enter the next two items concerning callable bonds. Press **F1,** and the program will quickly produce the correct price, using semiannual discounting, of $885.30. ▪

Explaining Bond Prices and Yields

Borrowers supply securities to the financial markets, whereas lenders seek securities as an investment. Equilibrium security prices and interest rates (yields) are determined simultaneously as part of the same process. The price of a security and its rate of return or yield are determined at the same time as different aspects of the borrowing and lending of loanable funds.

An important part of the interest rate–security price determination process is the effect of an increase or decrease on the demand for loanable funds. An increase in the demand for loanable funds leads to an increase in the supply of securities, a new lower equilibrium price for securities, and a higher equilibrium interest rate on loanable funds. An increase in the supply of loanable funds leads to an increase in the demand for securities, a new higher equilibrium price for securities, and a lower equilibrium interest rate on loanable funds.

This analysis summarizes a fundamental fact about the relationship between bond prices and bond yields: *Bond prices move inversely to interest rates.* When the level of interest rates demanded by investors on new issues changes, the yields that they require on all bonds already outstanding will change also. For these yields to change, the prices of these bonds must change. This fundamental fact about the relationship between bond prices and market interest rates is illustrated in Table 7-1 for a 10%-coupon bond. Prices for the bond are shown for market yields from 6% to 14% and for maturity dates from 1 to 30 years.

Table 7-1 shows that for any given maturity, the price of a bond will decline as the market yield increases and increase as the market yield declines from the 10% level. This inverse relationship is the basis for understanding, valuing, and managing bonds. Figure 7-1 shows this relationship using data from Table 7-1.

TABLE 7-1 ***Bond Prices and Market Yields (10% Coupon Bond)***

	Bond Prices at Different Market Yields and Maturities				
Time to Maturity	6%	8%	10%	12%	14%
1	$1038.27	$1018.86	$1000	$981.67	$963.84
5	1170.60	1081.11	1000	926.40	859.53
10	1297.55	1135.90	1000	885.30	788.12
15	1392.01	1172.92	1000	862.35	751.82
20	1462.30	1197.93	1000	849.54	733.37
25	1514.60	1214.82	1000	842.38	723.99
30	1553.51	1226.23	1000	838.39	719.22

INVESTMENT CALCULATIONS

The bond prices in Table 7-1 were calculated using *The Investment Calculator,* as explained earlier. For each column of Table 7-1, corresponding to a particular market yield, it is necessary to change only the number of years on the "Duration and Bond Analysis" screen. Figure 7-1 was produced with a spreadsheet program using the prices in Table 7-1 for the 10-year maturity and adding to them the prices at 2%, 4%, 16%, 18%, and 20%, also calculated from *The Investment Calculator.*

INVESTMENTS INTUITION

We now know that the market yields and prices of all bonds—both new and outstanding—are directly related to interest rate behavior. It is obvious, therefore, that current market interest rates, and any expected change in market interest rates, are the key variables to analyze and monitor in understanding the behavior of bond prices and yields.

In the following discussion, the basic components of market interest rates will be analyzed because of their critical importance in the bond decision process. In addition to analyzing the components of nominal interest rates (i.e., the level of rates), we shall also consider two important dimensions of interest rate behavior:

1. The differences in yields for a given category of bonds, which is known as the term structure of interest rates.

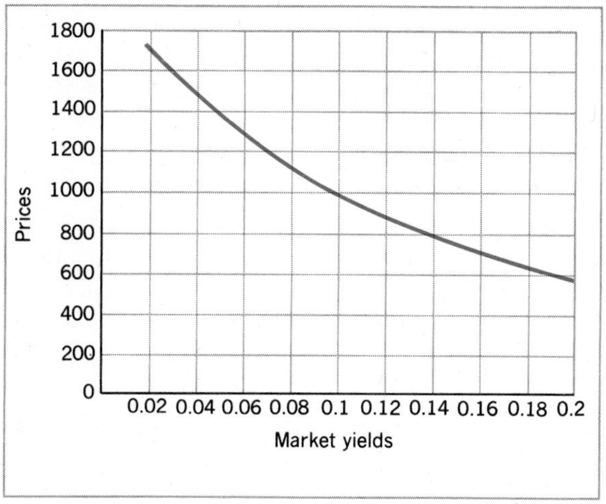

FIGURE 7-1

2. The differences in yields that exist between different sectors or types of bonds, typically referred to as yield spreads.

The Level of Market Interest Rates: A Simple Explanation

Explaining interest rates is a complex task that involves substantial economics reasoning and study. Such a task is not feasible in this text.[2] What is feasible is to assess the basic determinants of actual interest rates with an eye toward recognizing the factors that affect market interest rates and cause them to fluctuate. The bond investor who understands the foundations of market rates can then rely on expert help for more details and be in a better position to interpret and evaluate such help.

The basic foundation of market interest rates is the marginal physical productivity of capital (i.e., the rate at which capital physically reproduces itself). It is the opportunity cost of foregoing consumption, representing the rate that must be offered to individuals to persuade them to save rather than consume. This rate is sometimes referred to as the **real rate of interest,** because it is not affected by price changes or risk factors.[3] It is assumed by

[2]Most money and banking texts contain a good, concise discussion of interest rates. A detailed analysis can be found in James C. Van Horne, *Financial Market Rates and Flows,* 3rd ed. (Englewood Cliffs, N.J.: Prentice-Hall, 1990).

[3]The real rate of interest cannot be measured directly. It is often estimated by dividing (1.0 + MIR) by (1.0 + EI), where MIR is the market interest rate and EI is expected inflation. This result can be approximated by subtracting estimates of inflation from nominal (market) interest rates (on either a realized or expected basis). Some economists believe estimates of the real rate are subject to large errors. See G. Santoni and C. Stone, "The Fed and the Real Rate of Interest," *Review, FRB of St. Louis,* Vol. 69, No. 10 (December 1982), pp. 8–18.

some economists to be about 2% to 3% a year.[4] Designated RR in this discussion, it was discussed in Chapter 5 under required rate of return.

Nominal interest rates on top-quality securities are composed of the RR plus an adjustment for inflation. A lender who lends $100 for a year at 10% will be repaid $110. But if inflation is 12% a year, the $110 that the lender receives upon repayment of the loan is worth only (1/1.12) ($110), or $98.21. Lenders therefore expect to be compensated for the expected rate of price change in order to leave the real purchasing power of wealth unchanged. This inflation adjustment can, *as an approximation for discussion purposes,* be added to the real rate of interest.[5] Unlike RR, which is often assumed to be reasonably stable with time, adjustments for expected inflation vary widely with time.

It is important to note that we are talking here about *expected inflation,* not realized inflation. Financial markets are forward-looking, and interest rates incorporate what investors expect to happen rather than what has happened. One of the best sources of expected inflation data is the survey of consumers conducted by the University of Michigan in its *Survey of Consumers.* Participants are asked to predict how much prices will change in the next year. Figure 7-2 shows the survey results for 1970–1989. It is clear that inflation expectations rose sharply during two periods in the 1970s, reaching a peak in 1980. Inflation expectations declined substantially through the first half of the 1980s, reaching a low point in early 1986 and then rising in 1987 and 1988. Notice that for several years in the 1980s inflation expectations remained above the actual rate of inflation. At year-end 1989 households were expecting CPI increases of about 5% for 1990.

Thus, *for short-term risk-free securities,* such as three-month Treasury bills, the nominal interest rate is a function of the real rate of interest and inflationary premiums. This is expressed as Equation 7-3, in which EI = the expected inflation and MIR_{RF} = market interest rates for short-term, risk-free securities. *As an approximation:*

$$MIR_{RF} = RR + EI \tag{7-3}$$

The short-term risk-free rate of interest changes as these two variables change. They could move in the same direction or opposite directions. The change in inflationary expectations is the key variable affecting the change in the risk-free rate of interest. The wide fluctuations in the Treasury bill rate that occur over time are primarily attributable to changes in inflation.

All market interest rates, whether for risk-free (Treasury) securities or for risky securities, are affected by a *time factor.* That is, although long-

---

[4]There is a common perception that real interest rates have been high in the 1980s. See Stephen G. Cecchetti, "High Real Interest Rates: Can They Be Explained?" *Economic Review: Federal Reserve Bank of Kansas City,* September/October 1986, pp. 31–41.

[5]The correct procedure is to multiply (1 + the real rate) by (1 + the expected rate of inflation), and subtract 1.0. For purposes of our discussion the additive relationship is satisfactory.

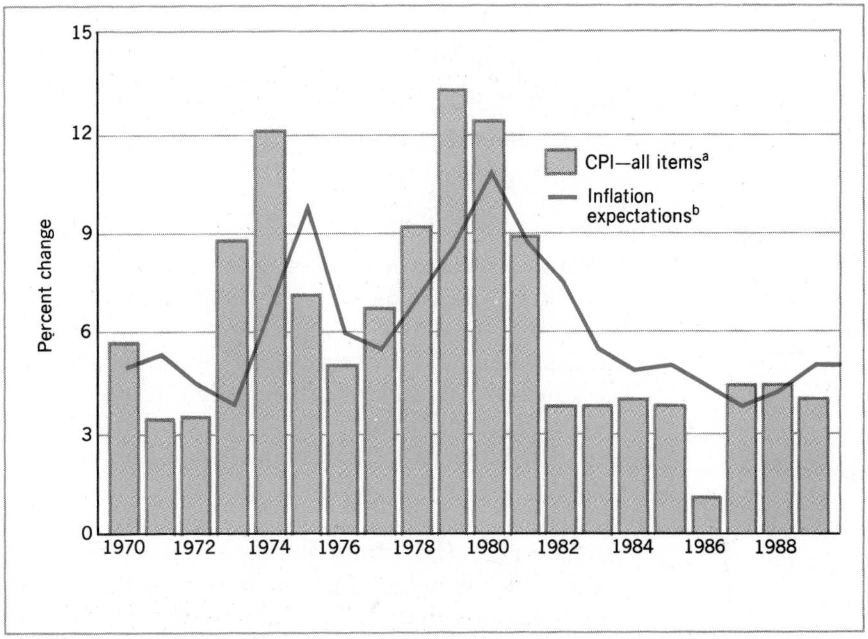

FIGURE 7-2 ***Consumer price index and inflation expectations.***
Source: Economic Trends, Federal Reserve Bank of Cleveland, January 1990, p. 6.

term Treasury bonds are free from default risk in the same manner as Treasury bills, Treasury bonds typically yield more than bills. The maturity factor generally increases the bond investor's risk. Normally, the longer the term of maturity, the higher the yield on a bond, everything else held constant. This is true for all types of bonds, whether Treasuries, corporates, or municipals. The term structure of interest rates, which accounts for the relationship between time and yield for a given type of bond, is discussed later.

Market interest rates other than those for riskless Treasury securities are also affected by a third factor, a *risk factor,* which lenders require as compensation for the risk involved. This risk premium is associated with the issuer's own particular situation or with a particular market factor. In contrast, both RR and EI are economic factors that originate from forces external to the bond issuer or market factor.

These issue characteristics unique to a given issuer that constitute the risk premium include whether the bonds are callable or not, whether they are secured or unsecured, the degree of marketability, and the tax treatment accorded certain securities. Another important characteristic discussed in Chapter 6 is the risk of default. Both corporate and municipal bonds carry some risk of default for which investors expect to be compensated. Market interest rates for corporate bonds exceed those for U.S. Treasury securities, with everything else held constant, because there is some risk of default on the corporates.

The risk premium is often referred to as the yield spread or yield differential. We shall consider it following the discussion of the term structure of interest rates.

Term Structure of Interest Rates

The **term structure of interest rates** refers to the relationship between time to maturity and yields for a particular category of bonds. This relationship holds for a given time. Ideally, other factors are held constant, particularly the risk of default. The easiest way to do this is to examine U.S. Treasury securities, which have no risk of default, have no sinking fund, and are taxable. By eliminating those that are callable and those that have some special features, a quite homogeneous sample of bonds is obtained for analysis.

Yield Curves The term structure is usually plotted in the form of a **yield curve,** which is a graphical depiction of the relationship between yields and time for bonds that are identical except for maturity. The horizontal axis represents time to maturity, whereas the vertical axis represents yield to maturity. Figure 7-3 shows the yield curves most often observed, each of which indicates that interest rates vary with the time to maturity.

Figure 7-3*a* shows yield curves for certain periods in 1988 and 1989 for Treasury securities. The upward-sloping curve in October 1988 is considered typical because interest rates that rise with maturity are considered the "normal" pattern. Notice that by spring of 1989 the yield curves were "humped," peaking in this case at the two-year note. Also note that for the March 1989 yield curve the three-month Treasury bill rate was actually above the 30-year bond rate, but in April it was back below it.

Figure 7-3*b* shows additional yield curves for Treasuries in 1989. Note the downward-sloping curves for June and July, with short rates above long rates. These "inverted" yield curves are unusual and are thought by some market participants to indicate that short-term rates will fall.

Figure 7-3*c* shows the different shapes that yield curves can take during extraordinary interest rate movements. Shown here are the yield curves for U.S. Treasuries at the start of the big interest rate movement in the summer of 1982 and roughly six months later. The curve at July 7, 1982, was downward sloping, as might be expected when interest rates are peaking. Six months later, the yield curve had returned to "normal"—upward sloping.

Term Structure Theories A theory of the term structure of interest rates is needed to explain the shape and slope of the yield curve and why it shifts over time. Three theories traditionally advanced are the expectations

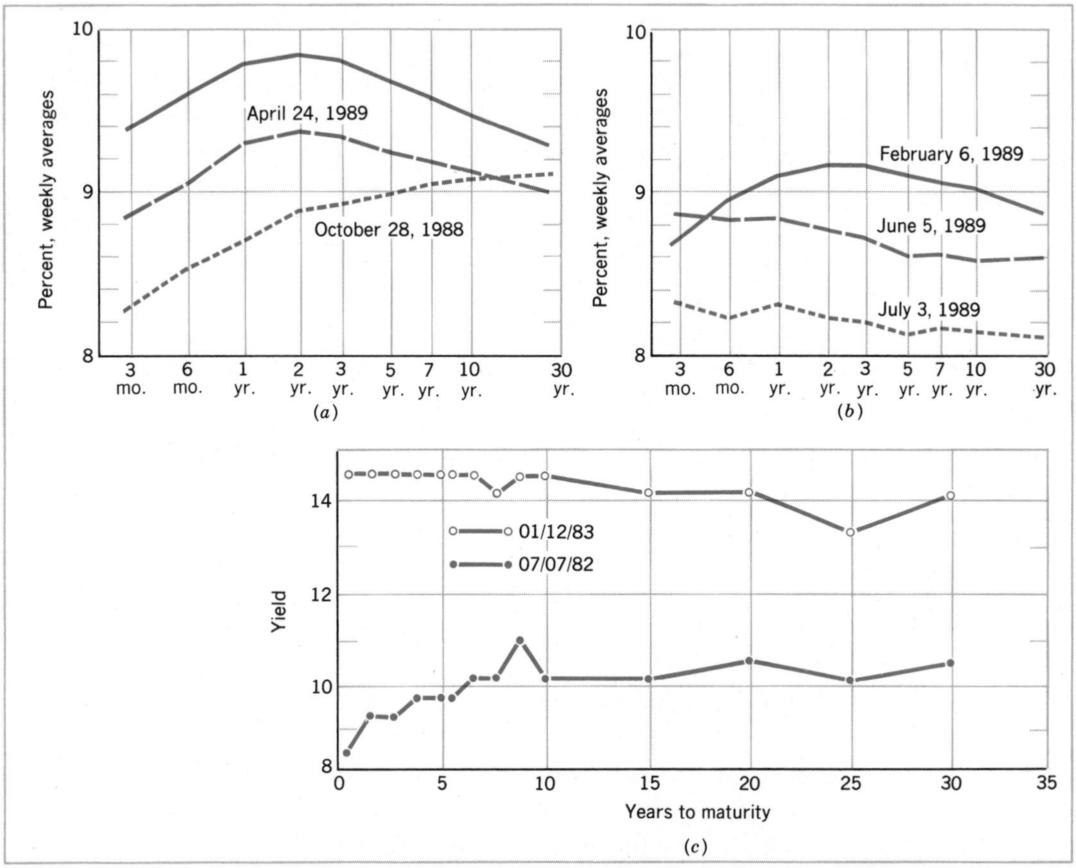

FIGURE 7-3 ***Yield curves for Treasury Securities.***
Source: (*a*) *Economic Trends,* Federal Reserve Bank of Cleveland, May, 1989, p. 15. (*b*) *Economic Trends,* Federal Reserve Bank of Cleveland, July, 1989, p. 19. (*c*) Merrill Lynch, Pierce, Fenner & Smith., *Fixed Income Selector,* First Quarter 1983, p. 9. This graph is reprinted by permission of Merrill Lynch, Pierce, Fenner & Smith Incorporated. © 1983 Merrill Lynch, Pierce, Fenner & Smith Incorporated.

theory, the liquidity premium theory, and the market segmentation theory. These theories are explained in Appendix 7-A.

Regardless of which of the three theories of the term structure of interest rate is correct, it seems reasonable to assert that investors demand a premium from long-term bonds, because of their additional risk. After all, uncertainty increases with time, and long-term bonds are more sensitive to interest rate fluctuations than are short-term bonds. Given that this is a logical argument, what does the historical evidence indicate?

The Ibbotson Associates data, referred to earlier in connection with the returns on financial assets, contain bond "horizon premiums" for the years

1926–1989. A bond *horizon premium* is defined as the return on long-term Treasury bonds minus the return on Treasury bills. The data indicate that the annual arithmetic mean horizon premium for that period was 1.2 (the geometric mean was 0.9). Unanticipated and rising inflation resulted in large unanticipated capital losses for bondholders over the historical period. Adding back the annual rate of capital losses of 0.26% to the historical horizon premium of 1.2%, Ibbotson Associates estimates that investors will expect a maturity premium of about 1.5% in the future despite the lower figure experienced in the past![6]

Yield Curve Implications All three of the theories of the term structure of interest rates have implications for the slope of the yield curve. In brief, under the market segmentation theory, the yield curve will change as the demand for or supply of securities in various parts of the maturity range changes. Such changes may have little or no effect on other parts of the yield curve. Under the liquidity preference theory, upward-sloping curves should predominate because of the uncertainty premiums on longer-term securities. The yield curve will shift as expectations about future rates change. Finally, under the expectations theory, the shape of the yield curve at any point in time has implications about the expectations of market participants:

1. If the yield curve slopes upward, the implication is that future short rates are expected to rise.
2. If the yield curve slopes downward, the implication is that future short rates are expected to fall.
3. If the yield curve is horizontal (flat), the implication is that future short rates are expected to equal the current short rate. Such a curve reflects a state of transition.

Risk Premiums—Yield Spreads

Assume that market interest rates on risk-free securities are determined as just explained. If the expected rate of inflation rises, the level of rates also rises. Similarly, if the real rate of interest were to decline, market interest rates would decline; that is, the level of rates would decrease. Furthermore, as seen in the term structure analysis, yields vary over time for issues that are otherwise homogeneous. The question that remains is, "Why do rates differ between different bond issues or segments of the bond market?"

The answer to this question lies in what is referred to in bond analysis as yield spreads (or yield differentials or risk differentials). **Yield spreads** refer to the relationships between bond yields and the particular issuer and

---

[6]See Ibbotson Associates, *Stocks, Bonds, Bills and Inflation: 1990 Yearbook,* p. 141.

issue characteristics and constitute the risk premiums referred to earlier. Yield spreads are often calculated among different bonds holding maturity constant. They are a result of the following factors:

1. Differences in quality, or risk of default. Clearly, other things being equal, a bond rated BAA will offer a higher yield than a similar bond rated AAA because of the difference in default risk.
2. Differences in call features. Bonds that are callable have higher YTMs than othewise identical noncallable bonds. If the bond is called, bondholders must give it up, and they could replace it only with a bond carrying a lower YTM. Therefore, investors expect to be compensated for this risk.
3. Differences in coupon rates. Bonds with low coupons have a larger part of their YTM in the form of capital gains.
4. Differences in marketability. Some bonds are more marketable than others, meaning that their liquidity is better. They can be sold either quicker or with less of a price concession, or both. The less marketable a bond, the higher the YTM.
5. Differences in tax treatments.

Clearly, yield spreads are a function of the variables connected with a particular issue or issuer. Investors expect to be compensated for the risk of a particular issue, and this compensation is reflected in the risk premium. However, investors are not the only determining factor in yield spreads. The actions of borrowers also affect them. Heavy Treasury financing, for example, may cause a narrowing of the yield spreads between governments and corporates as the large increase in the supply of Treasury securities pushes up the yields on Treasuries.

Yield spreads among alternative bonds may be positive or negative at any time. Furthermore, the size of the yield spread changes over time. Whenever the differences in yield become smaller, the yield spread is said to "narrow"; as the differences increase, it "widens." It seems reasonable to assume that yield spreads widen during recessions, because investors become more risk averse. Since the probability of default is greater during a recession, investors demand more of a premium. On the other hand, yield spreads narrow during boom periods. There is some historical evidence to support that this does, in fact, occur.

As one example of yield spreads, consider Table 7-2, which shows selected spreads between municipal bonds, on the one hand, and corporate Aaa bonds and Treasuries, on the other.[7] As noted, one of the factors causing risk premiums or yield spreads is different tax treatments. During 1986, investors contemplated the significant tax law changes that were

[7]Moody's top bond rating of Aaa is comparable to Standard & Poor's top rating of AAA.

TABLE 7-2 ***Yield Spreads—Municipal Bonds vs. Corporates and Treasuries***

Month	Corporate Aaa Bonds	Long-term Treasury Securities
January 1986	197	151
February 1986	223	168
March 1986	192	108
April 1986	159	43
May 1986	155	53
June 1986	126	41
July 1986	137	38
August 1986	151	54
September 1986	178	100
October 1986	178	98
November 1986	183	98

Source: U.S. Financial Data, The Federal Reserve Bank of St. Louis, December 18, 1986.

ultimately signed by President Reagan in late 1986. Through the first eight months of 1986, expectations of tax liabilities caused the spreads between municipal bonds and other long-term securities to fluctuate substantially, with the basis point spread (100 basis points = 1%) between corporates and municipals ranging from 126 to 223), and that for Treasuries ranging from 38 to 168. The reason was the great uncertainty about the prospects of tax reform and what would happen to both the overall tax rate and the treatment of municipal bonds (which, of course, were always exempt from federal taxes). However, once the general shape of the tax package became relatively clear in September, the spreads between municipals and these other two securities stabilized.[8]

As Table 7-2 shows, the spreads between municipals and both corporates and Treasuries fluctuated substantially from January through August 1986. Notice the very small differences for September, October, and November.

Although the structure of yield spreads and their changes over time are complex, some general relationships account for most of the yield spreads that do exist.

1. Different types of bonds (e.g., U.S. Treasuries versus corporates and municipals.[9]
2. Different qualities within the same type of bond (e.g., AAA corporates versus A corporates).

[8]The changes in the tax treatment of certain types of municipals were made retroactive to August 15, 1986.

[9]These yield spreads were shown in Figure 2-3 in Chapter 2.

3. Different coupons within the same type or quality (e.g., a current-coupon Treasury bond versus a low-coupon Treasury bond).

Relationships Between Bond Yields And Prices

The previous section examined the nature of market interest rates and the periodic changes in them. It was shown that investors need to be concerned with three types of changes in interest rates: changes in the level of rates, the term structure, and the yield spread. When the level of rates for new securities changes, investors also change their required returns on outstanding bonds. To obtain this change in required return or yield, the bond price must change.

What is the exact relationship between changes in yields (interest rates) and price? The response of a bond's price to a change in yield is a function of several variables, which will be described in the next section as a set of bond theorems. Furthermore, understanding the concept of duration provides important insights about the sensitivity of bond price changes to changes in interest rates. Therefore, duration will be explained following the discussion of bond theorems.

Malkiel's Bond Price Theorems

Burton Malkiel derived five theorems about the relationship between bond prices and yields.[10] Using the bond valuation model, he showed that the changes in the price of a bond (i.e., its volatility), given a change in yields, are a function of the following (given par value, always assumed to be $1000):

1. Time to maturity.
2. Coupon.
3. Prevailing interest rate.

Malkiel's five bond price theorems are explained, with examples, in Figure 7-4. The practical implication of Malkiel's derivations for bond investors is the conclusion that the two bond variables of major importance in assessing the change in the price of a bond, given a change in interest rates, are its coupon and its maturity. It can be summarized as follows:

> A decline (rise) in interest rates will cause a rise (decline) in bond prices, with the most volatility in bond prices occurring in longer-maturity bonds and bonds with low coupons.

---

[10]Ibid., pp. 83–84. Burton G. Malkiel, "Expectations, Bond Prices, and the Term Structure of Interest Rates," *Quarterly Journal of Economics,* May 1962, pp. 197–218.

1. *Bond prices move inversely to bond yields (given a fixed coupon).* This principle is clearly shown in the present value analysis of Table 7-1.
2. *Bond price volatility and time to maturity are directly related.*

Example: Given two 10% coupon bonds and a drop in market rates from 10% to 8%, we can see from Table 7-1 that the price of the 15-year bond will be $1172.92 and the 25-year bond, $1214.82.

3. *The percentage price change described in Theorem 2 increases at a diminishing rate as the term to maturity increases.*

Example. The price of the 15-year 10%-coupon bond in Theorem 2 increased $172.90, or 17.29%, when market rates declined by 2%, whereas the price of the same bond with a maturity of 25 years increased only 21.48%. Thus, the marginal percentage change in price decreases as maturity increases.

4. *Holding maturity constant, a decrease in yields raises bond prices more than a corresponding increase in yields lowers prices.*

Example. For the 15-year 10%-coupon bond, the price would be $1172.90 if market rates were to decline from 10% to 8% and $862.35 if they rose from 10% to 12%. In absolute terms, the capital gains (losses) from a decline (increase) in market yields will exceed (be less than) the capital losses (gains) resulting from a comparable increase (decrease) in market yields.

5. *Bond price fluctuations (volatility) and bond coupons are inversely related.*

Example. The price of the 10% coupon bond rises to $1172.92, an increase of 17.3%, if yields drop to 8% whereas the price of a 15% coupon bond will rise from $1383.98 to $1604.90, a *percentage increase* of only 16%.

FIGURE 7-4 ***Malkiel's bond price theorems.***

Therefore, (1) a bond buyer, in order to receive the maximum price impact of an expected change in interest rates, should purchase low-coupon, long-maturity bonds, and (2) an investor holding bonds or contemplating their purchase should, if an increase in interest rates is expected (or feared), concentrate on those bonds with large coupons or short maturities, or both.

These five relationships provide useful information for bond investors by demonstrating how the price of a bond changes as interest rates change. Although investors have no control over the change and direction in market rates, they can exercise control over the coupon and maturity, both of which have significant effects on bond price changes. Nevertheless, it is cumbersome to calculate various possible price changes on the basis of these theorems. What is needed is a measure that relates the price sensitivity of a bond to all these factors. Such a measure, called duration, is available.

Duration

Although maturity is the traditional measure of a bond's lifetime, it is inadequate, because it focuses on only the return of principal at the maturity date. Two 20-year bonds, one with an 8% coupon and the other with a 15% coupon, do not have identical *economic* lifetimes. The investor will recover the original purchase price much sooner with the 15%-coupon bond. Therefore, a measure is needed that accounts for the entire pattern (both size and timing) of the cash flows over the life of the bond—the effective maturity of the bond. Such a concept, called **duration,** was conceived over 50 years ago by Frederick Macaulay.[11]

$$\text{Duration} = \text{Number of years needed to fully recover purchase price of bond, given present values of its cash flows}$$

$$= \text{Weighted average time to recovery of all interest payments plus principal}$$

$$= \sum_{t=1}^{N} t \frac{\dfrac{C_t}{(1+r)^t}}{\displaystyle\sum_{t=1}^{N} \frac{C_t}{(1+r)^t}} \qquad (7\text{-}4)$$

where

C_t = the cash receipt in period t (interest or principal)
r = the yield to maturity on the bond
t = time period when any cash receipt occurs

The denominator of Equation 7-4 is simply the present value of a bond, as given previously in Equation 7-2. The numerator of Equation 7-4 is the present value of any year's cash receipt. Therefore, the cash receipt in each year is weighted in relation to the present value of the bond. Duration is obtained by multiplying each year's weighted cash receipt by the number of years when each is to be received, and summing. *Note that duration is measured in years.*

Table 7-3 provides an example of calculating the duration for a bond. This is a 10%-coupon bond with six years remaining to maturity. *For ease of exposition,* coupons are assumed to be paid annually. The bond is priced at $950.73, and the YTM is 11.17%.

The cash flows consist of the six $100 coupons plus the return of

---

[11]Frederick R. Macaulay, *Some Theoretical Problems Suggested by the Movement of Interest Rates, Bond Yields and Stock Prices in the United States Since 1856* (New York: National Bureau of Economic Research, 1938).

TABLE 7-3 ***An Example of Calculating the Duration of Bond Using a 10%-Coupon, Six-Year-Maturity Bond Priced at $950.73***

(1) Year	(2) Cash Flow	(3) Present Value Factor[a]	(4) Present Value of (2)	(5) Present Value ÷ Price	(6) (1) × (5)
1	100	.8995	89.95	.0946	.0946
2	100	.8091	80.91	.0851	.1702
3	100	.7278	72.78	.0766	.2297
4	100	.6547	65.47	.0689	.2755
5	100	.5889	58.89	.0619	.3097
6	1100	.5298	582.73	.6129	3.6775
			950.73	1.0000	4.7572 = 4.76 years

[a]Using 11.17% as the YTM.

principal at the end of the sixth year. Notice that the sixth-year cash flow of $1100 ($100 coupon plus $1000 return of principal) accounts for 61% of the value of the bond and contributes 3.68 years to the duration of 4.76 years. In this example the other five cash flows combined contributed roughly one year to the duration. The duration of 4.76 years is almost 1.25 years less than the term to maturity of six years. As we explain, duration will always be less than time to maturity for bonds that pay coupons.

INVESTMENT CALCULATIONS

Duration may be calculated easily, using *The Investment Calculator.* Required inputs are the price of the bond, the number of years to maturity, the market yield, the annual dollar coupon, and the face value of $1000.

Why is duration important in bond analysis and management? First, it tells us the difference between the effective lives of alternative bonds. For example, with an 8% yield to maturity and an 8% coupon, a 10-year bond has an effective life (duration) of 7.25 years, whereas a 20-year bond has an effective life of 10.60 years—quite a different perspective, given that the second has a term to maturity of twice the first. Furthermore, under these conditions, a 50-year bond has an effective life of only 13.21 years.[12] The reason for the sharp differences between the term to maturity and the duration is that cash receipts received in the distant future have very small present values and therefore add little to a bond's value.

[12]These numbers, and the basis for this discussion, are taken from Richard W. McEnally, "Duration as a Practical Tool for Bond Management," *The Journal of Portfolio Management*, Summer 1977, pp. 53–56.

Second, the duration concept is used in certain bond management strategies, particularly immunization, as explained later.

Third, duration is a measure of price volatility, a very important part of any bond analysis. Malkiel's bond price theorems are inadequate to examine all aspects of bond price volatility. This issue is considered in some detail in the next section.

How is duration related to the key bond variables previously analyzed?

1. The coupon is inversely related to duration. This is logical because higher coupons result in quicker recovery of the bond's value, resulting in a shorter duration.
2. Duration and yield to maturity are inversely related. Higher yields produce lower present values of cash receipts received far out in time, thereby diminishing their relative value.
3. As illustrated earlier, duration expands with time to maturity but at a decreasing rate, particularly beyond 15 years time to maturity. Even between 5 and 10 years time to maturity, duration is expanding at a significantly lower rate than in the case of a time to maturity of up to 5 years, where it expands rapidly.

Figure 7-5 illustrates some relationships between time to maturity and duration.[13] The following observations can be made from Figure 7-5:

1. In general, duration increases with maturity.
2. For all bonds paying coupons, duration is always less than maturity.
3. For a zero-coupon bond, duration is equal to time to maturity.
4. For a deep-discount bond (the 3%-coupon bond selling to yield 15%), a point is reached at which duration actually decreases as maturity increases.
5. During periods of high interest rates, long-term bonds resemble intermediate-term bonds much more than when interest rates are low, based on duration. The 15%-coupon bond selling to yield 15% in Figure 7-5, illustrating a period of high interest rates, has a duration that does not increase much as time to maturity increases.
6. In a period of low interest rates, as illustrated by the 15%-coupon bond selling to yield 6%, duration increases rapidly with time to maturity.

Using the Duration Concept The real value of the duration measure to bond investors is that it combines coupon and maturity, the two key variables to be manipulated in response to expected changes in interest rates.

---

[13]This discussion is based on William L. Nemerever, "Managing Bond Portfolios Through Immunization Strategies," reprinted in *The Revolution in Techniques for Managing Bond Portfolios* (Charlottesville: The Institute of Chartered Financial Analysts, 1983).

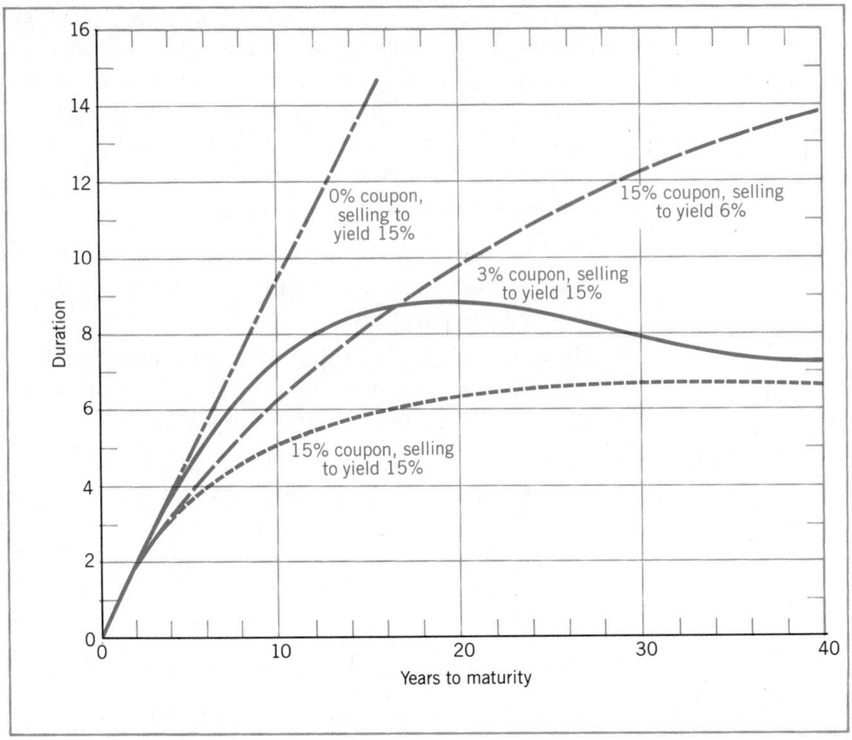

FIGURE 7-5 ***An illustration of Duration versus time to maturity for some hypothetical bonds.***
Source: William L. Nemerever, "Managing Bond Portfolios Through Immunization Strategies," Reprinted in *The Revolution in Techniques for Managing Bond Portfolios,* The Institute of Chartered Financial Analysts, Charlottesville, Va., 1983, p. 104. Reproduced from *The Revolution in Techniques for Managing Bond Portfolios,* The Institute of Chartered Financial Analysts, 1983. By permission.

As noted earlier, duration is positively related to maturity and negatively related to coupon. However, bond price changes are directly related to duration.

The term **modified duration** refers to Macaulay's duration in Equation 7-4 divided by $(1 + r)$, or

$$\text{Modified duration} = \text{Duration}/(1 + r) \tag{7-5}$$

The modified duration can be used to calculate the percentage price change in a bond for a given change in the r. This is shown by Equation 7-6, which is an *approximation:*

$$\begin{array}{l}\text{Approximate}\\ \text{percentage change}\\ \text{in bond price}\end{array} \approx \frac{-D}{(1 + r)} \times \begin{array}{l}\textit{Percentage point}\\ \textit{change in the r}\end{array} \tag{7-6}$$

Example. The bond in Table 7-3 with a duration of 4.76 years would decline in price approximately 0.86% if the r changed by 0.20% (or 20 basis points) from 11.17% to 11.37%.[14] That is,

$$-4.28\,(+0.0020) = -0.00856 = -0.86\% \quad ▪$$

It is important to note that Equation 7-6 is only an approximation for large changes in the bond yield. For very small changes in the required yield there is no problem, but as the changes become larger the approximation becomes poorer. The problem is that modified duration produces symmetric percentage price change estimates using Equation 7-6 (if r had decreased 0.20%, the price change would have been +0.86%) when, in actuality, the price–yield relationship, as shown in Figure 7-1, is not linear. This relationship is actually *convex*, and calculations of price changes should properly account for this convexity. Such discussions are beyond the scope of this text but can be found in advanced discussions.[15]

What does this analysis of price volatility mean to bond investors? It means that to obtain the maximum (minimum) price volatility from a bond, investors should choose bonds with the longest (shortest) duration. If an investor already owns a portfolio of bonds, he or she can act to increase the duration of the portfolio if a decline in interest rates is expected and the investor is attempting to achieve the largest price appreciation possible. Fortunately, duration is additive, which means that a bond portfolio's duration is a weighted average of each individual bond's duration.

Although duration is one measure of bond risk, and an important one, it is not necessarily always the appropriate one. Duration measures volatility, which is important but is only one aspect of the risk in bonds. If an investor considers volatility an acceptable proxy for risk, duration is the measure of risk to use. Duration may not be a complete measure of bond risk, but it does reflect some of the impact of changes in interest rates.

Bond Strategies and Management

It is appropriate to end this chapter with a discussion of the approaches that bond investors can use in managing their bond portfolios, or the bond portion of their overall portfolio. This requires more than an understanding of the basic factors affecting the valuation and analysis of bonds, which were discussed earlier in this chapter.

---

[14]The modified duration would be −4.76/1.117 = 4.28; multiplying by the 0.2-percentage-point rise in YTM produces an expected change in price for the bond of about −0.86%, or a new price of about $941.65.

[15]See Frank J. Fabozzi and T. Dessa Fabozzi, *Bond Markets: Analysis and Strategies* (Englewood Cliffs, N.J.: Prentice-Hall, 1989), Chapter 4.

Bond investing has become increasingly popular, no doubt as a result of record interest rates in recent years. Unfortunately, the theoretical framework for bond portfolio management has not been developed to the same extent as that for common stocks. In some ways common stocks have been more "glamorous," and more attention has been devoted to them. Furthermore, more data exist for common stocks, undoubtedly because the most prominent stocks trade on the New York Stock Exchange where daily prices can be collected and analyzed. The same is not true for bonds. Even today an investor cannot call most brokers and obtain instantaneous, current quotes on many bonds.

Despite the lack of a complete theory of bond portfolio management, investors must manage their bond portfolios and make investment decisions. Different bond investors have derived different strategies to follow, depending on their risk preferences, knowledge of the bond market, and investment objectives.

For organizational purposes, and because this scheme corresponds to the two broad strategies an investor can follow, we will first discuss passive management of bond portfolios and then active management.

Passive Management Strategies

A number of investors accept the idea that securities are fairly priced in the sense that the expected return is commensurate with the risk taken. This belief can justify a **passive management strategy,** meaning that the investor does not actively seek out trading possibilities in an attempt to outperform the market. Such a position is supported by evidence of the type presented in Figure 7-6, which shows the performance of bond managers during the years 1981–1985. During this period more managers fell below the bond index than exceeded it. Has the situation changed? According to information compiled by Trust Universe Comparison Service and reported in mid-1989 by *Forbes,* over the preceding five years the managers of fixed-income portfolios had an annualized total return of 14.4% compared to 14.5% for a bond index—and this was before fees! According to *Forbes,* "the average pension fund" would have been better off by investing bond monies in a passive manner rather than in an active manner.[16]

A passive investment strategy does not mean that investors do nothing. They still must monitor the status of their portfolios in order to match their holdings with their risk preferences and objectives. Conditions in the financial markets change quickly, and investors must do likewise when necessary. Passive management does not mean that investors accept changes in market conditions, securities, and so on, if these changes cause undesirable changes in the securities they hold.

[16]Taken from Steve Kichen, "The *Forbes*/TUCS Institutional Portfolio Report," *Forbes,* August 21, 1989, p. 112.

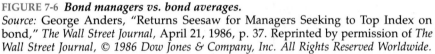

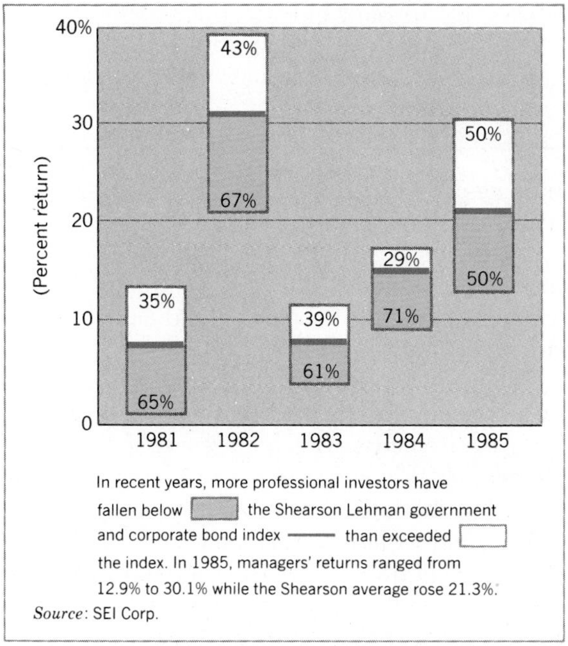

FIGURE 7-6 ***Bond managers vs. bond averages.***
Source: George Anders, "Returns Seesaw for Managers Seeking to Top Index on bond," *The Wall Street Journal,* April 21, 1986, p. 37. Reprinted by permission of *The Wall Street Journal, © 1986 Dow Jones & Company, Inc. All Rights Reserved Worldwide.*

In following a passive management approach, bond investors must first assess the factors that were discussed earlier to determine whether the bonds to be held are suitable investment opportunities. Thus, investors must assess default risk and diversify their holdings to protect themselves against changes in the probability of default. Similarly, call risk must be examined at the outset. Ideally, investors may be able to find bonds that are not callable over the period that they will be held. The higher the coupon on a bond, the more likely it is to be called. A third factor affecting investors is the marketability of a bond. Some bonds cannot be readily sold without a price concession, a lag in the time required to sell the bond, or both.

INVESTMENTS INTUITION

Other factors for the passive bond investor to consider at the outset of the program and to monitor during the life of the investment include a current income requirement and taxes. Some bond investors need large current yields. This suggests large coupons, other things being equal. Taxes are also a factor, because what matters to investors is the after-tax return. Municipal securities may be a good choice for investors in high marginal tax brackets because of their exemption from federal taxes. Treasury securities, on the other hand, are exempt from state (and most city) taxes.

Strategies for investors following a passive bond management approach include the following.

Buy and Hold An obvious strategy for any investor interested in nonactive trading policies is simply to buy and hold. Having considered the factors just mentioned, this investor chooses a portfolio of bonds and does not attempt to trade them in a search for higher returns. An important part of this strategy is to separate from that set the most promising bonds that meet the investor's requirements. This requires some knowledge of bonds and markets. Simply because an investor is following a basic buy-and-hold strategy does not mean that selection is unimportant. It is important to know such facts as the yield advantage of agency securities over U.S. Treasuries, the yield advantage of utilities over industrials, and other factors.

A buy-and-hold strategy can accommodate various degrees of investor passivity. At one extreme, investors could try to duplicate the overall bond market by purchasing a broad cross section of bonds. This strategy has now become easy to accomplish as the result of bond index funds, a relatively new creation that is gaining in popularity. An example is the Vanguard bond market fund, a highly diversified fund that seeks to match the performance of the Salomon Brothers Broad Investment-Grade Bond Index. There are no investment advisory fees to pay with this fund, and total annual operating expenses are expected to be 25 cents per $100 of fund assets. Given the performance of bond managers shown in Figure 7-6, bond index funds may become a popular alternative for investors.

Other buy-and-hold investors may search out alternatives that are better than current holdings and trade accordingly. Finally, some investors may use timing considerations, switching from short maturities to long and back again as conditions warrant.

Immunization The strategy of immunizing (protecting) a portfolio against interest rate risk (i.e., changes in the general level of interest rates) is called **immunization.** To see how such a strategy works, think of interest rate risk as being composed of two parts:

1. The **price risk,** resulting from the inverse relationship between bond prices and required rates of return.
2. The **reinvestment rate risk,** resulting from the uncertainty about the rate at which future coupon income can be reinvested. The YTM calculation assumes that future coupons from a given bond investment will be

reinvested at the calculated yield to maturity. If interest rates change so that this assumption is no longer operable, the bond's realized YTM will differ from the calculated (expected) YTM.

Notice that these two components of interest rate risk move in opposite directions. If interest rates rise, reinvestment rates (and therefore income) rise, whereas the price of the bond declines. The converse of this statement also holds. In effect, the favorable results on one side can be used to offset the unfavorable results on the other. This is what immunization is all about, protecting the portfolio against interest rate risk by canceling out its two components.

The duration concept discussed earlier is the basis for immunization theory. Specifically, a portfolio is said to be immunized (the effects of interest rate risk neutralized) if the duration of the portfolio is made equal to a preselected investment horizon for the portfolio. Note carefully what this statement says. An investor with, say, a 10-year horizon does not choose bonds with 10 years to maturity but bonds with a duration of 10 years—quite a different statement. This will usually require holding bonds with maturities in excess of the investment horizon.[17]

Immunization is included in this discussion of passive strategies for reasons of simplicity. However, this simple discussion of *classical immunization* does not convey the real-world problems involved in implementing such a strategy. In truth, *this strategy is not easy to implement, and it is not a passive strategy in application.* To achieve immunization as discussed here requires frequent rebalancing because duration should always be equal to the investment horizon. An investor simply cannot set duration equal to investment horizon at the beginning of the process and ignore the bond, or portfolio, thereafter.

Active Management Strategies

Although bonds can be and many times are purchased to be held to maturity, often they are not. Henry Kaufman, a well-known forecaster of interest rates, has formulated some new precepts concerning interest rates, one of which is that "bonds are bought for their price appreciation potential and not for income protection."[18] Many bond investors feel this way and use **active management strategies.** Such strategies typically seek to profit from active management of bonds by either:

---

[17]For additional information on reinvestment rate risk, see R. W. McEnally, "How to Neutralize Reinvestment Rate Risk," *The Journal of Portfolio Management*, Spring 1980. Also, see Nemerever, "Managing Bond Portfolios."

[18]Henry Kaufman, "New Precepts of Interest Rates" (Salomon Brothers Inc.), reprinted in *1982 CFA Study Guide III* (Charlottesville, Va.: The Institute of Chartered Financial Analysts, 1981).

1. Playing an anticipated change in interest rates, because we know that bond prices will change as well.

or

2. Identifying *relative* mispricing between the various instruments in the fixed-income market.

We will consider each of these in turn.

Forecasting Interest Rates Changes in interest rates are the key factor affecting bond prices because of the inverse relationship between changes in bond prices and changes in interest rates. When interest rate declines are projected by the investor, action should be taken to invest in bonds, and the right bonds, for price appreciation opportunities. When interest rates are expected to rise, the objective is to minimize losses by not holding bonds or holding bonds with short maturities.

How does an investor forecast interest rates? Not very well, on a consistent and accurate basis, because interest rate forecasting is a notoriously difficult proposition. Nevertheless, reasonable forecasts can be made about the likely growth rate of the economy and the prospects for inflation, both of which affect interest rates and, therefore, bond investors. For an example of making a case for bonds at the beginning of a year, based on expectations about the economy, see Box 7-1.

Assuming that an investor has a forecast of interest rates, what strategy can be used? The basic strategy is to change the maturity of the portfolio; specifically, an investor should lengthen (shorten) the maturity of a bond portfolio when interest rates are expected to decline (rise).

It is important to be aware of the trade-offs in strategies involving maturity.

1. Short maturities sacrifice price appreciation opportunities and usually offer lower coupons (income), but serve to protect the investor when rates are expected to rise.
2. Longer maturities have greater price fluctuations; therefore, the chance for bigger gains (and bigger losses) is magnified. However, longer maturities may be less liquid than Treasury bills.

One form of interest rate forecasting, **horizon analysis,** involves the projection of bond performance over a planned investment horizon. The investor evaluates bonds being considered for purchase over a selected holding period in order to determine which will perform the best. To do this, the investor must make assumptions about reinvestment rates and future market rates and calculate the *realized compound yields* for the bonds being considered. Note that this is different from using the yield-to-maturity concept, which does not require expectations to be integrated into the analysis. Horizon analysis requires the user to make assumptions about reinvestment

BOX 7-1

MAKING A CASE FOR BONDS

For those who can ignore daily fluctuations and stick with convictions, this is the time to take long positions in bonds. The 30-year Treasury, currently priced to yield 8% to maturity, will do well in 1990, as yields decline slightly and prices rise. Inflation will moderate with the weakening economy. Although the Consumer Price Index has climbed 4.7% in the past year (November 1989 over November 1988), up from the 4.2% year-earlier rate, it will probably come through this year with a gain of only 3%.

Don't expect this bullish trend to take hold without interruptions. The bond market is volatile. Take advantage of the short-term swings in market sentiment. Buy long bonds or extend your maturities whenever the majority of market commentators is taking a pessimistic stand and Treasury bond prices have dropped to the lower end of a trading range.

Most forecasters expect little change after a slight dip in short-term rates and slight change in intermediate and long-term yields during 1990. The yield curve, they add, will remain flat. Short-term money market instruments will pay just a fraction of a percent less than long-term bonds. There will be no bonus for going long.

Nonsense. This status-quo prognostication is typical of those who look back a short period and project the same trends out for an extended period. As an example, from early 1989 through about August, the bond markets were quite volatile. In a period of recession-free economics, T bond yields climbed to a peak 9.3% in March, before tumbling to less than 8% in July. At that time, most of the analyses predicted wide bond market movements.

Since then, rates have remained in a narrow 7.7%-to-8.25% trading range. Economists, with typical short memories, see only that latter-year stability as they look ahead.

One explanation of the market's narrow trading range to date is that Federal Reserve credit policy adjustments have been muted by Board Chairman Alan Greenspan. He is responsible for the central bank's tendency to adjust to economic changes gradually and with a considerable lag.

However, as the economy continues to get sluggish—perhaps slowing to no growth at all—it will become evident to Greenspan that he must accede to those wishing to stimulate more aggressively. Short-term yields will plunge 1% to 2%, and long-term bond yields will fall by 1%. Sometime in 1990, probably this summer, the federal funds rate target, a proxy for credit policy, will have been reduced to 7% or less, against 8.5% now. Three-month T bills will drop from the current 7.9% yield (on a bond-equivalent basis) to 6% or so by year-end. Long-term T bonds, paying 8% as the year began, will be yielding only 7% next December. The yield curve will steepen, restoring the historically more common pattern in which investors taking longer maturities get slightly better yields.

Source: Excerpted by permission of *Forbes* magazine, January 22, 1990, © *Forbes*, Inc., 1990.

rates and future yields but allows him or her to consider how different scenarios will affect the performance of the bonds being considered.

Bond Swaps Managers of bond portfolios attempt to adjust to the constantly changing environment for bonds (and all securities) by engaging in what are called **bond swaps.** The term usually refers to the purchase and sale of bonds in an attempt to improve the rate of return on the bond portfolio by identifying temporary mispricings in the market. There are several different types of bond swaps, the best known of which are discussed briefly in Figure 7-7.[19]

Use of Newer Techniques The bond markets have changed rapidly in recent years because of numerous structural changes and the record level of interest rates that have occurred. Along with these changes have come new techniques for the active management of fixed-income portfolios.

The distinction between the bond market and the mortgage market is now blurred, with mortgage instruments competing in the capital markets in the same manner as bonds. The mortgage has been transformed into a security, and the mortgage market has become more uniform and standardized. These securities are alternatives to bonds, especially corporate bonds, and can be used in the portfolio as substitutes.

Financial futures are now a well-known part of the investor's alternatives. The use of futures has grown tremendously. They are used to hedge positions and to speculate on the future course of interest rates. Futures will be discussed in more detail in Chapter 17.

Building a Bond Portfolio

Having reviewed some active and passive strategies for managing a bond portfolio, it is appropriate to consider how to go about building a bond portfolio. The first consideration, which is true throughout the range of investment decisions, is to decide on the risk–return trade-off that all investors face. If an investor seeks higher expected returns, he or she must be prepared to accept a greater risk. Figure 1-1 is applicable to bonds alone. To see this, think of the two broad objectives that investors can have with a bond portfolio, as discussed in Chapter 6.

1. Conservative investors view bonds as fixed-income securities that will pay them a steady stream of income. In most cases the risk is small, and federal government issues have practically no risk of default. These investors tend to use a buy-and-hold approach.

Investors following this strategy seek to maximize their current income subject to the risk (quality of issue) they are willing to assume—corporates should return more than Treasury issues, BAA should return more than A

[19]For a complete discussion of these swaps, see Homer and Leibowitz, *Inside the Yield Book.*

1. The substitution swap involves bonds that are perfect (or very close) substitutes for each other with regard to characteristics such as maturity, quality rating, call provisions, marketability, and coupon payments. The only difference is that at a particular time, the two bonds sell at slightly different prices (and, therefore, a different yield to maturity). The swap is made into the higher-yielding bond, which, if its yield declines to that of the other bond, will provide capital gains as well as a higher current yield.
2. A pure yield pickup swap involves no expectations about market changes, as does the substitution swap (where the buyer expects the yield on the higher-yielding bond to drop). This swap simply involves selling a lower-yielding bond and purchasing a higher-yielding bond of the same quality and maturity. The motivation is strictly to obtain higher yield.
3. The rate anticipation swap is based on a forecast of interest rates. When rates are expected to rise (fall), swaps are made into short (long) maturity bonds (or cash). Because of greater interest rate fluctuations in recent years, interest rate anticipation swaps will probably become increasingly popular relative to other types of swaps.
4. The intermarket spread (sector) swap is designed to take advantage of expected changes in the yield spread relationships between various sectors of the bond market. For example, a bond investor may perceive a misalignment between Treasury bonds and utility bonds. If the yield spread between the two sectors is too wide and is expected to narrow, a switch may be made into the higher-yielding security.

FIGURE 7-7 ***Major types of bond swaps.***

or AA or AAA, longer maturities should return more than short maturities, and so on.

INVESTMENTS INTUITION

Even conservative investors in bonds must consider a number of factors. Assume that an investor wishes to purchase only Treasury issues, thereby avoiding the possible risk of default. Careful consideration should be given to the maturity of the issue, since the range is from Treasury bills of a few months duration to bonds maturing in the twenty-first century. Obviously, the investor's choice will depend to a large extent on interest rate forecasts. Even conservative buy-and-hold investors probably should avoid long-term issues if interest rates are expected to rise over an extended period of time. Finally, these investors may wish to consider the differences in coupons between issues. Previous discussion has shown that the lower the coupon on a bond, the higher the price volatility. Although many investors in this group may plan to hold to maturity, conditions can change.

2. Aggressive investors are interested in capital gains arising from a change in interest rates. There is a substantial range of aggressiveness, from the really short-term speculator to the somewhat less aggressive investor willing to realize capital gains over a longer period while possibly earning high yields.

The short-term speculator studies interest rates carefully and moves into and out of securities on the basis of interest rate expectations. If rates are expected to fall, this investor can buy long-term, low-coupon issues and achieve maximum capital gains if the interest rate forecast is correct. Treasury bonds can be bought on margin to further magnify gains (or losses). Treasury securities, for example, can be purchased on 10% margin. The speculator often uses Treasury issues (the highest-quality bond available) or high-grade corporates in doing this kind of bond trading. It is not necessary to resort to low-quality bonds.

Another form of aggressive behavior involves seeking the highest total return, whether from interest income or capital gains. Investors who follow this strategy plan on a long horizon in terms of holding a portfolio of bonds but engage in active trading during certain periods when such actions seem particularly appropriate. One such period was 1982, when bonds were offering record yields to maturity and interest rates were widely expected to decline. Even mildly aggressive investors could purchase Treasury bonds yielding high-coupon income and have a reasonable expectation of capital gains. The downside risk in this strategy at this time was small. These investors still needed to consider maturity and coupon questions, however, because no interest rate decline can be assumed with certainty.

Summary

- Any security's intrinsic value is the sum of its discounted cash flows. To find this value, it is necessary to identify the amount and timing of the cash flows and the appropriate discount rate to be used in the present value process.
- Using an appropriate market yield as the discount rate, the present value (price) of a bond can easily be found using present value tables or a calculator. If the price of the bond is known, the yield to maturity (discount rate) can be determined.
- The key to bond yields and prices is interest rates. Three important aspects of interest rates are the level of rates over time, the term structure of interest rates, and yield spreads.
- The level of market interest rates for short-term, risk-free securities is a function of the real rate of interest and inflationary expectations. Inflationary expectations are the key variable in understanding changes in market rates for short-term, default-free securities.
- The term structure of interest rates denotes the relationship between

market yields and time to maturity. A yield curve graphically depicts this relationship with upward-sloping curves being the norm.

- None of the three prevalent theories to explain term structure—the expectations theory, the liquidity preference theory, and the market segmentation theory—is dominant.
- Yield spreads are the relationship between bond yields and particular bond features such as quality and callability. Differences in type, quality, and coupon account for most of the yield spreads.
- Malkiel's bond theorems show that bond price volatility is a function of the time to maturity, coupon, par value of the bond, and prevailing interest rate. The two variables of major importance are coupon and maturity.
- Maximum price volatility is achieved with low-coupon, long-maturity bonds.
- Duration, the weighted average time (years) to recovery of all interest payments plus principal, shows the effective life of a bond.
- Bond price changes are directly related to duration, which combines coupon and maturity, the two key variables affecting a bond's price.
- Passive bond strategies include buy and hold and immunization.
- Active management strategies include forecasting interest rates, bond swaps, and other new techniques such as the use of futures.

Key Words

Active management strategy
Bond swaps
Duration
Expectations theory
Horizon analysis
Immunization
Intrinsic value
Liquidity preference theory
Market segmentation theory
Modified duration
Passive management strategy
Price risk
Real rate of interest
Reinvestment rate risk
Term structure of interest rates
Yield curve
Yield spread

Questions

7-1 How is the intrinsic value of any asset determined? How are intrinsic value and present value related?

7-2 How is the price of a bond determined? Why is this process relatively straightforward for a bond?

7-3 What effect does the use of semiannual discounting have on the value of a bond in relation to annual discounting?

7-4 Define YTM. How is YTM determined?

7-5 Why is YTM important?

7-6 Distinguish between promised yield and realized yield. How does interest on interest affect realized return?

7-7 How can bond investors eliminate the reinvestment rate risk inherent in bonds?

7-8 Describe three aspects of market interest rates, carefully distinguishing between the three.

7-9 How can one describe, verbally and graphically, the relationship between time to maturity and yields for a particular category of bonds?

7-10 Briefly discuss the three existing theories of the term structure of interest rates.

7-11 What factors explain yield spreads?

7-12 What are the implications of Malkiel's bond price theorems to bond investors? Which two bond variables are shown to be of major importance in assessing bond price changes?

7-13 How does duration differ from time to maturity? What does duration tell you?

7-14 How is duration related to time to maturity? to coupon? Do the same relationships hold for a zero-coupon bond?

7-15 Assume that a bond investor wishes to maximize the potential price volatility from a portfolio of bonds about to be constructed. What should this investor seek in the way of coupon, maturity, and duration?

7-16 Is duration a complete measure of bond risk? Is it the best measure?

7-17 Identify and explain two passive bond management strategies.

7-18 Explain the concept of immunization. What role, if any, does duration play in this concept?

7-19 Identify and explain two specific active bond management strategies. Are the two related?

7-20 What does an upward-sloping yield curve imply about the expectations of investors? a downward-sloping curve?

7-21 It is August 1, 1982, and you have correctly forecast that interest rates will soon decline sharply. Assuming that you will invest only in fixed-income securities and that your time horizon is one year, how would you construct a portfolio?

7-22 When would investors find bonds with long maturities, selling at large discounts, particularly unattractive as investment opportunities?

7-23 Describe the four bond swaps. Indicate the assumption(s) being made by an investor in undertaking these swaps.

7-24 How can horizon analysis be used to manage a bond portfolio?

Demonstration Problems

Calculating the price of a bond, illustrating Equation 7-2. Consider a bond with the following characteristics:

C = an \$80 coupon = (0.08)(\$1000)
par = \$1000 face value

r = 0.10, the discount rate, the going market interest rate on similar securities

n = exactly three years, the time to maturity

under two different conditions:
(a) Annual coupon payments, \$80 is received at the end of each year.
(b) Semiannual coupon payments, \$40 is received every six months.

Under either condition the price of the bond is the present value of the discounted future returns. The returns, and their discounted values, are as follows:

Future Date	Assumption a		Assumption b	
6 months			\$40 ÷ (1.05) =	\$ 38.095
1 year	\$80 ÷ (1.10) =	\$ 72.726	\$40 ÷ $(1.05)^2$ =	36.281
1.5 years			\$40 ÷ $(1.05)^3$ =	34.554
2 years	\$80 ÷ $(1.10)^2$ =	66.116	\$40 ÷ $(1.05)^4$ =	32.908
2.5 years			\$40 ÷ $(1.05)^5$ =	31.341
3 years	\$80 ÷ $(1.10)^3$ =	60.105	\$40 ÷ $(1.05)^6$ =	29.849
3 years	\$1000 ÷ $(1.10)^3$ =	751.315	\$1000 ÷ $(1.05)^6$ =	746.215
Price		\$950.26		\$949.243

Since the discount rate (10%) exceeds the coupon rate (8%), the bond is selling at a discount. The prices differ because of the timing of the coupon payments.

7-2 Here is an equivalent formula, used in bond tables, that appears more complex but is easier to calculate. For the bond described in 7-1, the value of the sum of the coupon payments can be calculated together with the discounted value of par. For the annual coupons (condition a):

$$P = \frac{C}{r}\left[1 - \frac{1}{(1+r)^t}\right] + \frac{\text{Par}}{(1+r)^t} = \frac{80}{0.10}\left[1 - \frac{1}{(1.10)^3}\right] + \frac{1000}{(1.10)^3}$$

$$= 198.948 + 751.315 = \$950.26$$

With semiannual compounding:

$$P = \frac{C/2}{r/2}\left[1 - \frac{1}{(1+r/2)^{2t}}\right] + \frac{\text{Par}}{(1+r/2^{2t}} = \frac{40}{0.05}\left[1 - \frac{1}{(1.05^{6}}\right] + \frac{1000}{(1.05)^6}$$

$$= 203.028 + 746.215 = \$949.24$$

7-3 Calculating duration, using the information from 7-1, with semiannual coupon payments for the bond. This is an abbreviated form of Table 7-3.

Future Date	pv of cash flows	(2) ÷ 949.243	years	(3) × (4)
6months	38.095	0.04013	0.5	0.02007
1 year	36.281	0.03822	1.0	0.03822

1.5 years	34.554	0.03640	1.5	0.05460
2 years	32.908	0.03467	2.0	0.06934
2.5 years	31.341	0.03302	2.5	0.08255
3 years	29.849	0.03145	3.0	0.09435
3 years	746.215	0.78612	3.0	2.35836
Sum	949.246	1.00120		2.71749

Notice that Equation 7-4 will have to be revised to use (YTM/2) and $2t$ as the power in order to calculate the exact duration shown here.

Problems

7-1 Using the information in Demonstration Problem 7-1, if the coupon rate for the bond is 10% and the discount rate is 8%, with the same three years to maturity, show that the price of the bond is $1051.54 with annual discounting and $1052.24 with semiannual discounting. Use a calculator to determine the discount factors.

What would be the price of this bond if both the coupon rate and the discount rate were 10%?

7-2 Using the information in Demonstration Problem 7-2, solve for the price of the bond in Problem 7-1 using both annual and semiannual discounting. Use a calculator to solve these problems.

7-3 With reference to Problem 7-2, what would be the price of the bond if the coupon were paid quarterly?

7-4 Calculate the price of a 10% coupon bond with eight years to maturity, given an appropriate discount rate of 12%, using both annual and semiannual discounting. Use the tables contained in the appendix at the end of the text.

7-5 Calculate the price of the bond in Problem 7-4 if the maturity is 20 years rather than 8 years. Use semiannual discounting and the tables in the appendix.

Which of Malkiel's principles are illustrated when comparing the price of this bond to the price determined in Problem 7-1?

7-6 Using the bond from Problem 7-1, which is a 10%, 3-year bond with a price of $1052.24, where the market yield is 8%, calculate its duration using the format illustrated in Table 7-3.

7-7 Using the duration and other information calculated in Problem 7-6, determine

(a) The modified duration.

(b) The percentage change in the price of the bond if r changes .50%.

7-8 The YTM on a 10%, 15-year bond is 12%. Calculate the price of the bond.

7-9 Calculate the duration of a 12%-coupon bond with 10 years remaining to maturity and selling at par.

7-10 Given the duration calculated in Problem 7-9, calculate the percentage change in bond price if the market discount rate for this bond rises by .75%.

7-11 Consider a junk bond with a 12% coupon and 20 years to maturity. The current required rate of return for this bond is 15%. What is its price? What would its price be if the required rate of return rose to 17%? 20%?

7-12 A 12%-coupon bond with 10 years to maturity is currently selling for $913.41. Determine the modified duration for this bond. YTM = 13.61%.

7-13 Consider a 4%-coupon bond with 15 years to maturity. Determine the YTM that would be necessary to drive the price of this bond to $300.

7-14 Determine the point at which duration decreases with maturity for a 4% bond with an original maturity of 15 years. Use increments in maturity of five years. The market yield on this bond is 15%.

Selected References

A discussion of real interest rates is contained in

Cecchetti, Stephen G. "High Real Interest Rates: Can They Be Explained?" *Economic Review: Federal Reserve Bank of Kansas City,* September/October 1986, pp. 31–41.

Bond return strategies for investors are discussed in

Fong, H. Gifford, and Fabozzi, Frank J. "How to Enhance Bond Returns with Naive Strategies." *The Journal of Portfolio Management,* Summer 1985, pp. 57–60.

A classic discussion of bond yields and analysis is

Homer, S., and Leibowitz, Martin L. *Inside the Yield Book.* Englewood Cliffs, N.J.: Prentice-Hall, 1972.

A good discussion of duration and reinvestment rate risk can be found in

McEnally, Richard W. "How to Neutralize Reinvestment Rate Risk." *The Journal of Portfolio Management,* Spring 1980, pp. 59–63.

Interest rate risk and related concepts are discussed in

Maloney, Kevin J., and Yawitz, Jess B. "Interest Rate Risk, Immunization, and Duration." *The Journal of Portfolio Management,* Spring 1986, pp. 41–48.

APPENDIX 7-A

Theories of the Term Structure of Interest Rates

1. The **expectations theory** of the term structure of interest rates asserts that financial market participants determine security yields such that the return from holding an n-period security equals the average return expected from holding a series of one-year securities over the same n periods. In other words, the long-term rate of interest is equal to an average of the short-term rates that are expected to prevail over the long-term period.

In effect, the term structure consists of a set of forward rates and a current known rate. *Forward rates* are rates that are expected to prevail in the future; that is, they are unobservable but anticipated future rates.

Under the expectations theory, long rates must be an average of the present and future short-term rates. For example, a three-year bond would carry an interest rate that is an average of the current rate for one year and the expected forward rates for the next two years. The same principle holds for any number of periods; therefore, the market rate for any period to maturity can be expressed as an average of the current rate and the applicable forward rates. Technically, the average involved is a geometric rather than an arithmetic average.

For expositional purposes:[20]

${}_tR_n$ = the current known yield (i.e., at time t) on a security with n periods to maturity

${}_{t+1}r_n$ = the yield expected to prevail one year from today (at time $t + 1$) for n periods—these are forward rates

[20] This discussion is based on J. C. Poindexter and C. P. Jones, *Money, Financial Markets and the Economy* (St. Paul, Minn.: West Publishing, 1980), Chapter 9.

The rate for the three-year bond referred to above must be a geometric average of the current one-year rate ($_tR_1$) and the expected foreward rates for the subsequent two years.

Therefore, in equation form,

$$(1 + {}_tR_3) = [(1 + {}_tR_1)(1 + {}_{t+1}r_1)(1 + {}_{t+2}r_1)]^{1/3} - 1.0 \qquad \text{(7-A1)}$$

where

$(1 + {}_tR_3)$ = the rate on a three-year bond.
$(1 + {}_tR_1)$ = the current known rate on a one-year bond.
$(1 + {}_{t+1}r_1)$ = the expected rate on a bond with one year to maturity beginning one year from now.
$(1 + {}_{t+2}r_1)$ = the expected rate on a bond with one year to maturity beginning two years from now.

Example. Assume the current one-year bond rate ($_rR_1$) is 0.07, the two forward rates are 0.075 ($_{t+1}r_1$) and 0.082($_{t+2}r_1$). The rate for a three-year bond, $(1 + {}_tR_3)$, would be

$$\begin{aligned}(1 + {}_tR_3) &= [(1.07)(1.075)(1.082)]^{1/3} - 1.0 \\ &= 1.07566 - 1.0 \\ &= 0.07566, \text{ or } 7.566\%\end{aligned}$$

The same principle applies for any number of periods. Any long-term rate is a geometric average of consecutive one-period rates. ▪

Forward rates cannot be easily measured, but they can be inferred for any one-year future period. The expectations theory, however, does not say that these future expected rates will be correct; it simply says that there is a relationship between rates today and rates *expected* in the future.

Under this hypothesis, investors can expect the same return regardless of the choice of investment. Any combination of securities for a specified period will have the same expected return. For example, a five-year bond will have the same expected return as a two-year bond held to maturity plus a three-year bond bought at the beginning of the third year. The assumption under this hypothesis is that expected future rates are equal to computed forward rates. Profit-seeking individuals will exploit any differences between forward rates and expected rates, ensuring that they equilibrate.

2. The **liquidity preference theory** states that interest rates reflect the sum of current and expected short rates, as in the expectations theory, plus liquidity (risk) premiums. Because uncertainty increases with time, investors prefer to lend for the short run. Borrowers, however, prefer to borrow for the long run in order to be assured of funds. Investors receive a liquidity premium to induce them to lend long term, while paying a price premium (in the form of lower yields) for investing short term.

The difference between the liquidity preference theory and the expectations theory is the recognition that interest rate expectations are uncertain. Risk-averse investors seek to be compensated for this uncertainty. Forward rates and estimated future rates are not the same. They differ by the amount of the liquidity premiums.

3. The third hypothesis for explaining the term structure of interest rates is the **market segmentation theory.** Under this hypothesis, rates on securities with different maturities are effectively determined by the conditions that prevail in the different maturity segments of the market. Thus, securities with different maturities are imperfect substitutes for one another. Changes in the interest rates of various maturities affect the rates on other maturities little or not at all.

In the segmented markets approach, market participants may operate only within certain maturity ranges, or may at least concentrate their activities in such ranges. Banks, for example, emphasize short-term assets because of their emphasis on liquidity, whereas life insurance companies have traditionally taken a long-run view. They can predict their future liabilities quite well because of the accuracy of mortality estimates, and thus can afford to invest in longer-term securities. Under this hypothesis, the shape of the yield curve is influenced by the various market participants and the amount of funds they have for investment.

Which of these theories is correct? The issue of the term structure has not been resolved; although many empirical studies have been done, the results are at least partially conflicting. Therefore, definitive statements cannot be made. In actual bond practice, market observers and participants tend not to be strict adherents to a particular theory. Rather, they accept the reasonable implications of all three and try to use any information in assessing the shape of the yield curve. Thus, many focus on expectations but allow for liquidity premiums.

Since the 1930s upward-sloping yield curves have been the norm, as would be predicted by the liquidity preference theory. And this theory is more compatible than the other two with the study of investments, which emphasizes the risk–return trade-off that exists. The liquidity preference theory stresses the idea that because of larger risks, longer maturity securities require larger returns or compensation.[21]

---

[21]The expectations theory categorizes investors as return maximizers, whereas the market segmentation theory categorizes investors as risk minimizers.

APPENDIX 7-B

A Transition from Bonds to Common Stocks: The Analysis and Valuation of Preferred Stock

In Chapter 2 preferred stock was classified for investment analysis purposes as a fixed-income security, although technically it is an equity security. It is best described as a hybrid security, having some characteristics similar to fixed-income securities (i.e., bonds) and some similar to common stocks. It seems appropriate, therefore, to discuss the analysis and valuation of preferred stock between the valuation of bonds (this chapter) and the valuation of common stocks (Chapter 9). Preferred stock serves as a transition between these two basic types of securities.

Analysis

Preferred stock can be described as a perpetuity, or perpetual security, since it has no maturity date and will pay the indicated dividend forever. Although perpetual, many preferred stock issues carry a sinking fund, which provides for the retirement of the issue, usually over a period of many years. Furthermore, many preferred stocks are callable by the issuer, which also potentially limits the life of preferreds. Finally, roughly half of all preferred stocks issued in recent years are convertible into common stock.

Therefore, although preferred stock is perpetual by definition, in reality many of the issues will not remain in existence in perpetuity.

Preferred stock dividends, unlike common stock dividends, are fixed when the stock is issued and do not change. These dividends are specified as an annual dollar amount (although paid quarterly) or as a percentage of par value, which is often either $25 or $100. The issuer can forgo paying the preferred dividend if earnings are insufficient. Although this dividend is specified, failure to pay it does not result in default of the obligation, as with bonds. Most preferred issues have a cumulative feature, which requires that all unpaid preferred dividends must be paid before common stock dividends can be paid.

Investors regard preferred stock as less risky than common stock because the dividend is specified and must be paid before a common stock dividend can be paid. They regard preferreds as more risky than bonds, however, because bondholders have priority in being paid and in case of liquidation. Investors should, therefore, require higher rates of return on preferred stock than on bonds of the same issuer, but a smaller required return than on common stocks. A complicating factor in this scenario, however, is that 70% of dividends received by one corporation from another are excludable from corporate income taxes, making preferred stock attractive as an investment for corporations. As a result of this tax feature, preferred stocks often carry slightly lower yields than bonds of comparable quality.

Valuation

The value of any perpetuity can be calculated as follows:

$$V_p = \frac{C}{(1 + k_p)} + \frac{C}{(1 + k_p)^2} + + \ldots = \frac{C}{k_p} \tag{7B-1}$$

where

V_p = the value of a perpetuity today
C = the constant annual payment to be received
k_p = the required rate of return appropriate for this perpetuity

Because preferred stock is a perpetuity, Equation 7B-1 is applicable in its valuation. We simply substitute the preferred dividend (D) for C and the appropriate required return (k_{ps}) for k_p, resulting in Equation 7B-2.

$$V_{ps} = \frac{D}{k_{ps}} \tag{7B-2}$$

A preferred stock, or any perpetuity, is easy to value because the numerator of Equation 7B-2 is known, and fixed, forever. No present value calculations are needed for a perpetuity, which simplifies the valuation process considerably. If any two of the values in 7B-2 are known, the third can easily be found.

Example. As an example of the valuation analysis, consider the \$2.675 cumulative preferred stock of Carolina Power and Light Company (CP&L), with a par value of \$25. This \$2.675 annual dividend is fixed. To value this preferred, investors need to estimate the required rate of return appropriate for a preferred stock with the degree of riskiness of CP&L. Suppose the *k*, or required rate of return, is 10%. The value of this preferred would be

$$V_{\text{CP\&L}} = \frac{\$2.675}{0.10}$$

$$= \$26.75$$

On the other hand, a required rate of return of 11% would result in a value of \$24.32.

If the current price for this preferred, as observed in the marketplace, is used in Equation 7B-2, the yield can be solved by using Equation 7B-3.

$$k_{ps} = \frac{D}{P_{ps}} \qquad \text{(7B-3)}$$

▪

Example. A price of \$30 indicates a yield, or required rate of return, of about 8.92%. ▪

INVESTMENTS INTUITION

Notice from Equation 7B-2 that as the required rate of return rises, the price of the preferred stock declines; obviously, the converse is also true. Because the numerator is fixed, the value (price) of a preferred stock changes as the required rate of return changes. At the time of the price observation for CP&L, the range for the preceding 52 weeks was $\$26\frac{5}{8}$ to $\$30\frac{7}{8}$. The $\$30\frac{7}{8}$ price indicates that interest rates (and required returns) declined during this 52-week period to such a level as to make the value of the preferred rise to this price.

Over a period of years the price for the CP&L preferred ranged from $\$17\frac{7}{8}$ to \$31. A price of \$31 implies a required return of 8.63% at some point during this time span, and the price of $\$17\frac{7}{8}$ implies a required rate of return of 14.97%. Clearly, investors' required rates of return fluctuate across time as interest rates and other factors change. As rates fluctuate, so do preferred stock prices.

100

PART 3

COMMON STOCKS: ANALYSIS AND VALUATION

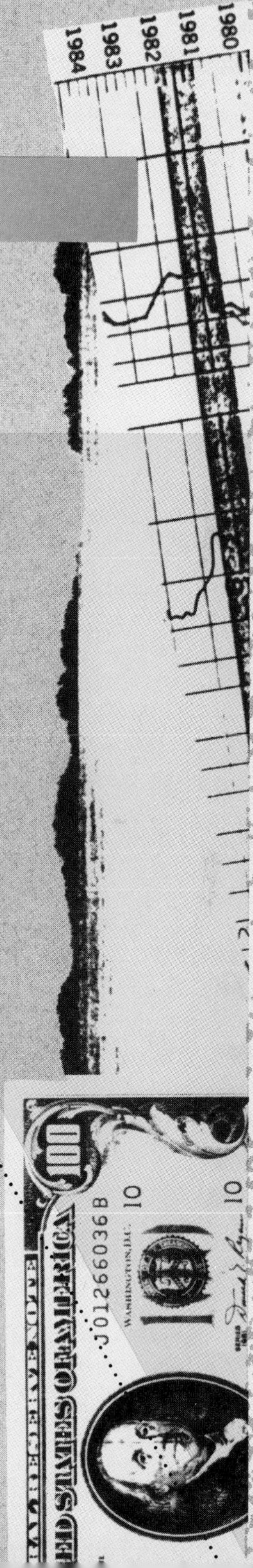

CHAPTER 8

Common Stocks

After discussing fixed-income securities in the preceding two chapters, the next logical step is to consider common stocks (equity securities). In many respects common stocks are easier to describe because they do not have the many technical features of fixed-income securities, such as sinking funds, call features, and maturity risks. On the other hand, they are much more difficult to analyze and value. Several chapters are needed to consider the basic approaches to valuing and selecting common stocks.

Understanding Common Stocks

General Characteristics

The *charter* is the document issued by a state to permit the formation of a corporation. Because each state has its own laws of incorporation, some states (such as Delaware) with relatively favorable laws issue more charters than others. Charters are generally uniform on many details, including the collective rights of the stockholders and their specific rights as individual owners.[1] In effect, stockholder rights are governed by the laws of the state granting the charter. Charters can be amended with approval of a specified percentage of the voting stock and with approval from the appropriate officials of the chartering state.

Quite simply, common stocks denote an equity (ownership) interest in a corporation. The stockholders are the owners of the corporation, entitled to all remaining income after the fixed-income claimants (including preferred stockholders) have been paid; also, in case of liquidation of the corporation, they are entitled to the remaining assets after all other claims (including preferred stock) are satisfied. Because they are entitled to any income and assets remaining after payments to all other claimants, common stockholders are referred to as the *residual claimants* of a corporation.[2]

Common stockholders, as the owners, have control of a corporation—at least in principle.[3] Stockholders are entitled to attend the annual meeting

[1]Collective rights include amending the charter, electing directors, issuing securities, and entering into mergers. Specific rights include the right to vote, the right to sell shares, and the right to share in the residual assets of the corporation if it is dissolved.

[2]The *preemptive right* in a corporation's charter grants existing stockholders the first right to purchase any new common stock sold by the corporation. The "right" is a piece of paper giving each stockholder the option to buy a specified number of new shares, usually at a discount, during a specified short period of time. Because of this, rights are valuable and can be sold in the market.

[3]The *voting rights* of the stockholders give them legal control of the corporation. In theory, the board of directors controls the management of the corporation, but in many cases the effective result is the opposite. Stockholders can regain control if they are sufficiently dissatisfied.

and to vote on major corporate issues, such as electing directors and issuing new shares of stocks. Most vote by *proxy*, meaning that the stockholder authorizes someone else (typically management) to vote his or her shares. Sometimes proxy battles occur, whereby one or more groups unhappy with corporate policies seek to bring about changes.

Stockholders also have limited liability, meaning that the stockholders cannot lose more than their investment in the corporation. In the event of financial difficulties, creditors have recourse only to the assets of the corporation, leaving the stockholders protected. This is perhaps the greatest advantage of the corporation and the reason it has been so successful.

Specific Characteristics

Par value for a common stock, unlike a bond or preferred stock, is not a significant economic variable. Corporations can make the par value any number they choose, and $1 often is used today. Some corporations issue no-par stock. New stock is usually sold for more than par value, with the difference recorded on the balance sheet as "capital in excess of par value."

The **book value** of a corporation is the accounting value of the equity as shown on the books (i.e., balance sheet). It is the sum of common stock outstanding, capital in excess of par value, and retained earnings. Dividing this sum, or total book value, by the number of common shares outstanding produces the *book value per share.* In effect, book value is the accounting value of the stockholders' equity. Although book value per share is not irrelevant in making investment decisions, market value per share remains the critical item of interest to investors.

Example. Merck and Company, a major health products company, reported $2855.8 million as total stockholders' equity for year-end 1988. This is the book value of the equity. Based on the weighted average shares outstanding of 395.6 million for that year, the 1988 book value per share was $7.22. ▪

The **market value** (i.e., price) of the equity is the variable of concern to investors. The *aggregate market value* for a corporation, calculated by multiplying the market price per share of the stock by the number of shares outstanding, represents the total value of the firm as determined in the marketplace. The market value of one share of stock, of course, is simply the observed current market price.

Dividends are the only cash payments regularly made by corporations to their stockholders. They are decided upon and declared by the board of directors and can range from zero to virtually any amount the corporation can afford to pay (typically, up to 100% of present and past net earnings). Although roughly three-fourths of the companies listed on the NYSE pay dividends, stockholders are not guaranteed dividends. At best, they can reasonably "expect" the dividend to be a certain amount in the future or to grow by a certain amount. The ratio of dividends to earnings is known as the **payout ratio.** It indicates the percentage of a firm's earnings paid out in cash to its stockholders. The complement of the payout ratio, or (1.0 − payout ratio), is the *retention ratio.*

Example. Merck's 1988 earnings were $3.05, and it paid an annual dividend of $1.28. Merck's payout ratio was $1.28/$3.05, or 42%. ▪

Dividends are declared and paid quarterly. To receive a declared dividend, an investor must be a *holder of record* on the specified date that a company closes its stock transfer books and compiles the list of stockholders to be paid. However, to avoid problems the brokerage industry has established a procedure of declaring that the right to the dividend remains with the stock until four days before the holder-of-record date. On this fourth day, the right to the dividend leaves the stock; for that reason this date is called the *ex-dividend* date.

Example. Assume that the board of directors of Merck meets on May 24 and declares a quarterly dividend, payable on July 2. May 24 is called the *declaration date.* The board will declare a *holder-of-record date*—say, June 7. The books close on this date, but Merck goes *ex-dividend* on June 3. To receive this dividend, an investor must purchase Merck by June 2. The dividend will be mailed to the stockholders of record on the *payment date,* July 2. ▪

Stock dividends and stock splits attract considerable investor attention. A **stock dividend** is a payment by the corporation in shares of stock instead of cash. A **stock split** involves the issuance of a larger number of shares in proportion to the existing shares outstanding. With a stock split, the book value and par value of the equity are changed; for example, each would be cut in half with a two-for-one split. However, on a practical basis, there is little difference between a stock dividend and a stock split.

Example. A 5% stock dividend would entitle an owner of 100 shares of a particular stock to an additional five shares. A two-for-one stock split would double the number of shares of the stock outstanding, double an individual owner's number of shares (e.g., from 100 shares to 200 shares), and cut the price in half at the time of the split. ▪

The New York Stock Exchange reported 142 stock distributions in 1989, consisting of 71 stock dividends and 71 stock splits (most of which were two-for-one). Stock data, as reported to investors in sources such as *The Value Line Investment Survey* and in the company's reports to stockholders, typically are adjusted for all stock dividends and stock splits.

Example. Merck declared a three-for-one stock split on April 26, 1988, effective May 4, 1988. According to its annual report, "All share and per share amounts for the current and prior periods presented in these financial statements reflect this stock split." ▪

INVESTMENTS INTUITION

The important question to investors is the value of the distribution, whether a dividend or a split. It is clear that the recipient has more shares (i.e., more pieces of paper), but has anything of real value been received? The answer is that, other things being equal, these additional shares do not represent additional value. Quite simply, the pieces of paper, stock certificates, have been repackaged. For example, if you own 1000 shares of a corporation that has 100,000 shares of stock outstanding, your proportional ownership is 1%; with a two-for-one stock split, your proportional ownership is still 1%, because you now own 2000 shares out of a total of 200,000 shares outstanding. If you were to sell your newly distributed shares, however, your proportional ownership would drop to 0.5%.

Of course, if a stock dividend is accompanied by a higher cash dividend resulting from higher earnings, the price of the stock may be bid up. But the increase in value is due to the fundamental determinants of stock prices—in this case, expectations about future earnings and dividends—and not to the stock dividend itself.

New Developments

Common stocks, unlike bonds, basically have not changed in format. For example, there is no equity equivalent to the zero-coupon bond. There is, however, a new equity equivalent of the junk bond.

This new development is *stub stocks*, which represent the smali equity that remains in a company that has issued large amounts of debt. Most of the companies with stub stocks have negative net worth, and all have stockholders' equity that is less than the debt outstanding.

Some stubs are created by buyouts, as in the case of RJR Nabisco, and others by self-imposed recapitalizations.[4]

Example. USG and Harcourt Brace Jovanovich repelled corporate raiders by borrowing and paying a large dividend. The remaining value of their

[4]This information is based on Roger Lowenstein, "Stub Stocks Soar, and Investors Latch Onto the Trend," *The Wall Street Journal*, August 18, 1989, p. C1.

equity was small relative to the debt claims, which have priority both in distribution of the firm's income and in case of bankruptcy. Harcourt counted on selling assets to pay off debt, while USG faced a yearly interest expense of roughly $300 million. ▪

From an investor's standpoint, stub stocks offer a chance for a very large gain. In contrast, although junk bonds may offer a high yield, junk bond investors at best will have only their principal returned. As an example, Holiday, the hotel operator, paid a $65-a-share dividend in 1987 to fend off a takeover. After paying down debt by some $1 billion, its shares were up 158% in less than a year.

Given their large potential returns, investors should expect a large risk to accompany these securities, and they would be correct in that assessment. Stubs are very volatile, outperforming the general market on the upside and underperforming it on the downside. Indexes of stubs have been created so that they can more easily be followed.

Stock Information

Using Stock Information

As discussed in Chapter 4, a common stock investor has numerous sources of information. These sources can be "free," such as brokerage or financial press recommendations, or costly, involving a subscription fee to an investment advisory or information service. The information can be in the form of recommended stocks (and portfolios) or basic (raw) data and/or data calculated for specific purposes (e.g., financial ratios or time series trends of changes in the money supply). Finally, information is available in both published and computerized formats.

To understand the valuation process for stocks, common stock investors should organize and think about information as it is used in security analysis. At the end of the next chapter, as a lead-in to Chapters 10–12 on fundamental security analysis, a suggested framework for common stock analysis will be presented. This framework calls for first analyzing the economy and overall state of the stock market, next analyzing industries, and finally, analyzing individual companies. Each of these chapters will review information pertaining to their respective stages of analysis.

Reading Common Stock Information

Figure 8-1 is an excerpt from the New York Stock Exchange (NYSE) page carried daily in *The Wall Street Journal*. A similar page appears in virtually every daily newspaper.

We shall use as an example the first company listed on the page, AAR Corporation. The first two figures reported are the high and low prices

NEW YORK COMPOSITE

Quotations as of 4:30 p.m. Eastern Time
Friday, March 2, 1990

-A-A-A-

	52 Weeks Hi	52 Weeks Lo	Stock	Sym	Div	Yld %	PE	Vol 100s	Hi	Lo	Close	Net Chg
	37½	24¾	AAR	AIR	.48	1.5	19	155	31⅝	31⅜	31⅜	...
n	9¾	8½	ACM OppFd	AOF	1.26	13.8	...	73	9¼	9⅛	9⅛	– ⅛
	11⅝	10½	ACM Gvt Fd	ACG	1.26	11.2	...	556	11¼	11⅛	11¼	...
n	9⅞	7⅞	ACM MgdIncFd	AMF	1.01	12.4	...	336	8¼	8⅛	8⅛	...
	12⅛	11½	ACM MgdMultFd	MMF		...	...	318	11⅞	11¾	11¾	– ⅛
	11½	10	ACM SecFd	GSF	1.26	11.5	...	1022	11⅛	11	11	– ⅛
	9⅜	8⅛	ACM SpctmFd	SI	1.01	11.1	...	409	9⅛	9	9⅛	...
▲	21⅜	11½	AL Labs A	BMD	.16	.7	22	453	22¼	21½	21½	+ ⅛
	4⅛	3⅛	AMCA	AIL	.12e	3.7	41	94	3¼	3¼	3¼	...
	6⅛	3⅜	AM Int	AM		...	7	591	3¾	3½	3½	– ⅛
	23½	16⅜	AM Int pf		2.00	12.1	...	23	16⅞	16½	16½	– ⅜
	107¼	52½	AMR	AMR		...	9	5098	61¾	60¾	61⅜	+ ⅞
	5½	3⅛	ARX	ARX		...	...	113	3½	3¼	3½	+ ⅛
	72¾	39	ASA	ASA	3.00a	5.7	...	902	52¾	52	52⅜	– ⅝
	70⅜	50⅜	AbbotLab	ABT	1.40	2.2	17	3574	65⅝	64⅝	65	+ ½
	17¼	11¼	Abitibi g	ABY	.50	...	...	83	13	12⅞	12⅞	...
	13	8⅞	AcmeCleve	AMT	.40	4.1	11	35	10	9¾	9⅞	– ⅛
	9¾	6	AcmeElec	ACE	.32	3.6	12	11	9	8⅞	9	+ ⅛
	38½	27	Acuson	ACN		...	21	506	33⅜	32⅞	33⅜	+ ½
	16½	12⅞	AdamsExp	ADX	2.06e	13.1	...	118	15¾	15½	15¾	+ ¼
	15⅜	7¼	AdobeRes	ADB		...	...	105	13	12⅞	12⅞	...
	20¼	16⅞	AdobeRes pf		1.84	9.8	...	6	18¾	18¾	18¾	...
	21⅝	19⅞	AdobeRes pf		2.40	11.4	...	33	21¼	21⅛	21⅛	– ⅛
	10½	6⅞	AdvMicro	AMD		...	6	8855	9⅛	8¾	9	+ ¼
	35	28¼	AdvMicro pf		3.00	10.0	...	144	30	29¾	29⅞	+ ¼
	10⅛	5	Advest	ADV	.16	2.4	9	12	6¾	6⅝	6¾	+ ⅛
	62½	48½	AetnaLife	AET	2.76	5.4	9	1973	51⅛	50⅝	51	...
	14	9⅞	AffilPub	AFP	.24	2.2	...	116	10¾	10½	10¾	+ ⅛

	52 Weeks Hi	52 Weeks Lo	Stock	Sym	Div	Yld %	PE	Vol 100s	Hi	Lo	Close	Net Chg
	25	16⅛	Ahmanson	AHM	.88	4.5	10	2849	19⅜	18⅞	19⅜	+ ¼
	3⅞	**2**	**Aileen**	**AEE**		...	...	**30**	**2¼**	**2¼**	**2¼**	**+ ⅛**
	50¼	40	AirProduct	APD	1.32	2.8	12	1395	46⅝	45⅞	46½	+ ⅞
	43	22⅛	AirbornFrght	ABF	.60	1.4	16	306	43	42½	43	+ ½
	25⅛	15½	Airgas	ARG		...	16	80	17¼	17	17¼	+ ⅛
	20¾	18⅜	Airlease	FLY	2.40	12.5	10	13	19⅜	19¼	19¼	...
	10¼	8½	AlaPwr pf		.87	9.2	...	8	9½	9½	9½	...
	98⅝	88¼	AlaPwr pf		9.00	9.6	...	z100	93½	93½	93½	+1¾
	103½	93	AlaPwr pf		9.44	9.3	...	z900	101	99½	101	+3
	91	80⅞	AlaPwr pf		8.28	9.5	...	z40	87½	87½	87½	+ ½
	30½	19¼	AlaskaAir	ALK	.20	.9	8	714	22¾	22¼	22¾	+ ½
	23½	15¾	AlbanyInt	AIN	.35	1.9	10	65	18¼	18⅛	18⅛	– ⅛
s	26⅝	16⅜	AlbertoCl	ACV	.20	.9	19	205	22	21⅜	21¾	+ ½
s	**20¾**	**13⅞**	**AlbertoCl A**	**ACVA**	**.20**	**1.2**	**15**	**324**	**17¼**	**16⅜**	**17¼**	**+ ⅞**
	60¼	38⅝	Albertsons	ABS	.80	1.5	17	951	53¾	52	52⅞	– ⅝
s	25⅛	18⅞	Alcan	AL	1.12	5.4	6	4410	21	20¾	20⅞	...
	36⅝	25⅜	AlcoStd	ASN	.84	2.7	11	339	30⅞	30	30¾	+ ¾
	34	23⅜	Alex&Alex	AAL	1.00	3.7	19	248	27	26⅝	27	+ ⅜
	71¾	45½	Alexanders	ALX		...	25	19	48¼	47⅝	47⅞	– ¾
	103½	80¾	AlleghanyCp	Y	1.63t	1.9	10	17	84½	84½	84½	...
	1¾	⅛	vjAllegInt	AG		...	...	267	7/16	⅜	13/32	...
	13¾	**7/16**	**vjAllegInt pfC**			...	...	**66**	**⅝**	**⅝**	**⅝**	**– 1/16**
	41⅝	32⅜	AllegLud	ALS	1.20	3.0	7	1089	39¾	38¼	39¾	+1⅝
	42½	35⅝	AllegPwr	AYP	3.16	7.7	11	964	41	40½	40⅞	+ ⅝
	16⅞	9	AllenGp	ALN		...	16	54	11¾	11¾	11¾	+ ⅛
n	25½	12¼	Allergan	AGN	.12e	.8	...	1318	15	14⅞	15	+ ¼
	16¼	11½	AllncCapMgt	AC	1.60e	10.2	18	150	15⅞	15⅝	15¾	+ ⅛
	25⅜	22½	AlldIrishBk pf		1.08e	4.6	...	78	23½	23⅜	23½	...
	27⅝	6⅛	AlliedPdts	ADP		...	9	215	6¾	6⅝	6⅝	+ ⅛
	40⅜	31¾	AlliedSgnl	ALD	1.80	5.0	10	1792	36	35¼	35¾	+ ¼
	10⅞	10	AllstMunIn	ALM	.78a	7.6	...	259	10¼	10⅛	10¼	...
	10⅛	9¼	AllstMunInII	ALT	.73a	7.3	...	313	10	9¾	10	+ ⅛

FIGURE 8-1 ***An excerpt from the New York Stock Exchange composite transactions page from* The Wall Street Journal.**
Source: The Wall Street Journal, March 5, 1990, p. C3. Reprinted by permission of *The Wall Street Journal,* © 1990 Dow Jones & Company, Inc. All Rights Reserved Worldwide.

during the preceding 52 weeks. This information aids investors in assessing the range over which the stock has traded during the previous year. Following the abbreviation for the name of the company and the stock symbol, the current annual dividend per share is shown. Based on *The Wall Street Journal* practice of annualizing the most recent quarterly declaration, AAR paid an annual dividend equal to \$0.48 per share. Since dividends are paid quarterly, the actual payment would have been \$0.12 per share per quarter based on the information shown here. Also shown is the **dividend yield** in percentage form, 1.5% for AAR. This is found by dividing the annual dividend by the current market price, \$31.375 (and rounding off).

The next figure, 19, is the **P/E ratio,** or **multiplier,** for AAR. It is calculated as

$$\text{P/E ratio} = \frac{\text{Current price}}{\text{Actual earnings this year}} \tag{8-1}$$

Equation 8-1 simply states that the P/E ratio is the ratio of the current market price to the firm's earnings. It is an indication of how much the market as a whole is willing to pay for AAR per dollar of reported earnings.

It is standard investing practice to refer to stocks as selling at, say, 10 times earnings, or 15 times earnings. Such a classification has traditionally been used by investors to categorize stocks. Growth stocks, for example, having typically sold at high multiples compared to the average stock, because of their expected high earnings growth. In the 1960s, stocks such as McDonald's, Avon, and Disney sold at P/E ratios of 40–60, or 40–60 times earnings. The average stock during that time might have been selling for 10–18 times earnings, reflecting their average growth-in-earnings prospects and average risk. Conservative blue chip stocks usually sell at relatively low P/E ratios.

Obviously, the reported P/E ratio discussed earlier is an *identity,* because it is calculated simply by dividing the current price by the latest 12-month earnings. However, variations of this ratio are often used in the valuation of common stocks, as explained in the next chapter. In fact, the P/E ratio in its various forms is one of the best-known and most often cited variables for most investors.[5]

Following the P/E ratio is yesterday's sales in hundreds of shares. For the day being reported, 15,500 shares of AAR stock were traded.

The last three entries are the high, low, and close, respectively, for AAR during its trading on the previous day. This stock reached a high of $31.625 per share on one of the markets included in the composite quotations for the NYSE, and it also declined to a low of $31.375 per share on one of these markets. It actually closed, or last traded, at $31.375 per share. The net change in the last column refers to the difference between yesterday's closing price and the previous day's closing price. In the case of AAR, there was no net change from the previous day.[6]

Consider next the tenth and eleventh entries for "AM Int." The entry

[5]In calculating P/E ratios, on the basis of either the latest reported earnings or the expected earnings, problems can arise when comparing P/E ratios among companies if some of them are experiencing, or are expected to experience, abnormally high or low earnings. To avoid this problem, some market participants calculate a *normalized* earnings estimate. Normalized earnings are intended to reflect the "normal" level of a company's earnings; that is, transitory effects are presumably excluded, thus providing the user with a more accurate estimate of "true" earnings.

[6]The letters *wt* following a name abbreviation on the stock exchange page refer to a warrant for that particular corporation. Information identical to stocks is reported for warrants, except that warrants pay no dividends. However, an investor desiring additional information about this or any other warrant—such as the terms of conversion into common stock—must consult some source of information such as an investment advisory service that carries information on warrants—for example, the *Value Line Options and Convertibles Service* or the *R.H.M. Survey of Warrants, Options, and Low-Priced Stock.*

"AM Int pf" represents a preferred stock issue for that corporation. All information is identical to that of a common stock except the P/E ratio is not reported because it has no relevance, since a preferred stock pays a fixed dividend and, other things being equal, increased earnings will not result in a higher valuation for the preferred. These securities generally move like bonds, responding to interest rates. Notice that a corporation may have several issues of preferred stock outstanding. (See Alabama Power, "AlaP," as an example.[7])

Information about the American Stock Exchange (Amex) is identical to that for the New York Stock Exchange, though there are fewer companies, and the companies are typically smaller. Warrants and some preferreds also are listed on the American. Investors should also know how to read information about stocks in the over-the-counter market. As explained in Chapter 3, an increasing number of OTC stocks are being traded in the NASDAQ National Market System. The information for these issues is identical to that carried for the NYSE, and therefore the discussion of NYSE information applies here.

In the case of the "traditional" over-the-counter stocks, for NASDAQ-traded stocks only a bid price and an asked price are reported, as opposed to high, low, and close prices on the exchanges. Consider the following hypothetical example for Arcus:

Stock & Div	Sales 100s	Bid	Ask	Net Chg.
Arcus	11	$5\frac{1}{2}$	$5\frac{3}{4}$	$\frac{1}{8}$

The bid price is what a dealer is willing to pay for the stock, and therefore what an investor should be able to sell shares for. The asked price is what the dealer will sell the shares for, and therefore what an investor will have to pay (of course, brokerage commissions will also be due in most cases). In the case of Arcus, there is a one-fourth point ($0.25) spread between the bid and asked price. The net change figure shown for over-the-counter stocks is the difference between *bid* prices on successive days.

The other information carried for these stocks includes the dividend, although the overwhelming majority of these companies pay no dividend, and the sales in hundreds of shares for the previous day. Arcus paid no dividend, and 1100 shares were traded on this hypothetical day.[8]

---

[7]One last point to note is the letters that appear beside certain stocks, such as the *g* beside Abitibi. These letters refer to footnotes, carried on a nearby page, that provide additional information, particularly dividend information.

[8]Additional OTC quotes are carried in papers such as *The Wall Street Journal*. Only weekly bid and asked quotes are shown for these stocks.

The Stock Market

In contrast to the bond market, the stock market is primarily a secondary market. The aggregate amount of new common stock issued by corporations every year is small compared to the trading on the organized exchanges—the New York Stock Exchange, the American Stock Exchange, the regional exchanges—and the over-the-counter market. In the first half of the 1980s new common stock offerings averaged roughly $17 billion per year. However, when this activity is compared to the secondary markets for common stocks, the relative importance is clear. For example, by the beginning of the 1990s the reported dollar volume on the New York Stock Exchange alone was over $1.5 trillion. Clearly, it is the secondary market for common stocks that is of major importance.

One important trend that should be noted is the continuing shrinkage in the supply of stocks because of company repurchases, mergers, and leveraged buy-outs. Total retirements for only the first half of 1989 were estimated at $125 billion, whereas only $9 billion of new stocks was sold.[9] Figure 8-2 shows the shrinkage of stock for the last half of the 1980s by netting new stock sales against shares retired.

One interesting aspect of this shrinkage in the supply of stocks is its effect on stock prices. Some analysts view it as bullish (positive) on a straight demand–supply basis. This trend was said to create confidence among money managers because of the reduced supply and availability of cash to buy the remaining stocks. One estimate is that 20% of the total market gain since 1984 could be attributed to the reduced supply.

Investors in the Stock Market

In discussing investors in the stock market, it is desirable to separate ownership from trading activity. In Chapter 3 we learned that over 50% of the reported volume on the NYSE was large-block transactions (an indication of institutional activity) compared to 43% for NASDAQ/NMS. Institutional participation on the OTC market has been rising gradually, but did not increase significantly in the last half of the 1980s.

Hosueholds, a proxy for individual investors, traditionally have been the major *owners* of common stocks. A 1985 survey by the NYSE indicated that some 47 million individual U.S. investors owned stock, either directly or in a stock mutual fund. One out of every four adults owned stock. Seven out of 10 of these stockowners owned NYSE-listed issues.

Individuals are important in other markets as well. Figure 8-3 shows the distribution of holdings of NASDAQ/NMS common stocks in 1989 by market value of holdings and by shares held. Three groups are repre-

---

[9]The information in these paragraphs is based on Craig Torres, "Rapid Stock-Supply Shrinkage Continues," *The Wall Street Journal,* July 14, 1989, p. C1.

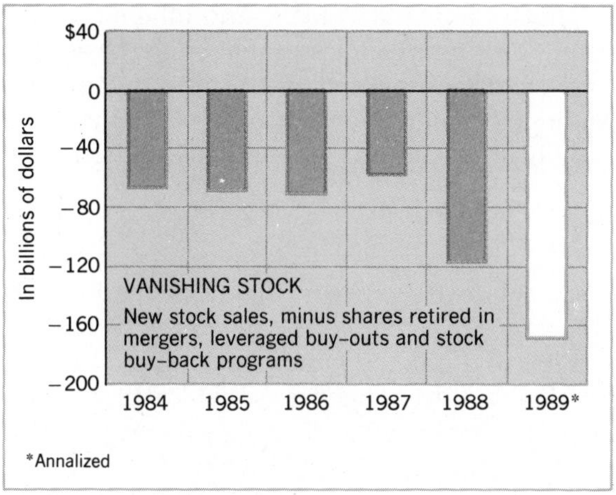

FIGURE 8-2 ***New stock sales minus shares retired, 1984–1989.***
Source: Craig Torres, "Rapid Stock-Supply Shrinkage Continues," *The Wall Street Journal*, July 14, 1989, p. C1.
Source: The Wall Street Journal. Reprinted by permission of *The Wall Street Journal*, © 1989 Dow Jones & Company, Inc. All Rights Reserved Worldwide.

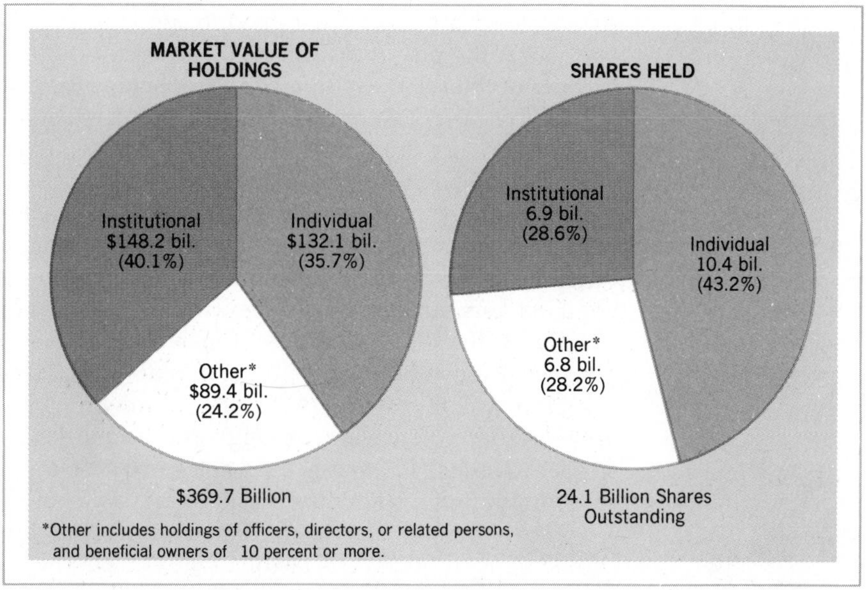

FIGURE 8-3 ***Distribution of holdings of NASDAQ/NMS common stocks: 1989.***
Source: National Association of Securities Dealers, *Fact Book 1990*, p. 42. Reprinted by permission.

sented: institutions, individuals, and others (insiders, large stockholders, and so on). This figure indicates that on the basis of shares held individuals were the single most important group, owning 43% of the total shares outstanding. Individuals account for 36% of the market value of NASDAQ/NMS holdings, which was second to institutional holdings of 40%.

Trading Stocks

Some parallels exist between the stock market and the bond market in terms of trading. As noted in Chapter 6, although the markets for U.S. government and agency bonds are active and liquid, the corporate and municipal sectors are much less so, at least for the average investor. In the case of stocks, the New York Stock Exchange is a very active, liquid market, with trades occurring smoothly within a carefully monitored framework. Prices may fluctuate sharply as a result of changes in investor expectations, but such changes are orderly, and investors can buy or sell with reasonable confidence that the prices are "fair" (i.e., represent orderly transactions within a monitored environment).

The American Stock Exchange is designed to imitate the NYSE, and thus has similar trading procedures. The role of the specialist is essentially the same as that on the NYSE, although capital requirements are smaller. Active stocks are usually assigned to specialist firms that may have several partners at the post to handle orders. Certain trading policies are different because of the relatively thin supply of shares for many Amex stocks.[10]

In the over-the-counter market, the corporations being traded may range from very large (e.g., Food Lion Supermarkets and Coors Beer) to very small firms unknown to most investors; therefore, the market for particular shares may be very active or very inactive. Bid–asked spreads may range from one-eighth point to two points or more. The small investor can trade in the OTC market more easily than in the corporate or municipal bond markets, investing only a few hundred dollars or less. As discussed in Chapter 3, the OTC market is of increasing importance and continues to enhance its position relative to the organized exchanges.

How well does NASDAQ work for individual investors? This is not an easy question to answer. Although auction markets such as the NYSE use specialists, the OTC market uses dealers, a system that can produce differences in trading results. Box 8-1 illustrates some of these differences.

The extent of active stock market trading by individual investors should depend on several factors. One is their knowledge. Do they understand how stocks are valued, traded, and managed? A second factor is their belief about the relationship between a security's value and its price. Are the two usually identical, and if not, can a typical investor expect to spot the difference? A third factor is the trade-offs to be made between direct

---

[10]For example, specialists cannot accept stop orders for round lots.

BOX 8-1

OVER-THE-COUNTER AND UP-THE-CREEK?

The party line at the NASD is that Nasdaq is even more efficient than the exchanges. Nasdaq is big and successful, no question about that. It has captured a lot of business from the American exchange in the past decade. But whether this trend is to the good of the investing public is another matter. Fact is, NASD's decentralized market-making system maintains sometimes enormous spreads between bid and asked prices, with the result that investors are nicked badly when they want to trade. They are nicked in ways that would be illegal on an exchange floor.

Case in point: On Mar. 21, a smart investor we know—call him Harry—placed a limit order at one of the nation's largest brokerage firms to sell 200 shares of Mine Safety Appliances, at 48 or better. Harry thought a sale was guaranteed when Nasdaq reported prices above 48. He watched in amazement as the stock traded as high as 48 on at least five days in early April, at $48\frac{1}{2}$ on Apr. 3, and at 49 on Apr. 12, and still there was no sale. His order wasn't executed until April 14 when the high for the day was $48\frac{3}{4}$, but all he got was 48—minus a fat commission.

Harry wasn't the only person shortchanged in this affair. How about the customer who paid 49 when, unbeknownst to him, Harry's $48 stock was lying on the table?

Here's what would have happened on either the New York or the American. Let's suppose that on the day the seller puts in his order Mine Safety is quoted at 47 to 49. That means a specialist in the stock stands ready to buy at 47 and to sell at 49. If Harry were desperate to sell, he would accept the 47 offered by the specialist, and the specialist would then take the 200 shares into inventory.

Harry, however, is in no hurry to sell. He gives his broker a limit order to sell at 48, an order the broker transmits to the specialist's post. Now let's say Jane phones her broker, wishing to buy 200 shares. It's quoted at 47 to 49, she is told. If she has any brains, she puts in a limit order: Buy at 48 or better. Her order also goes to the specialist, who is required to cross it with Harry's (assuming no one is offering a better price or got in line ahead of Harry).

Both Harry's and Jane's brokers make commissions on this trade. The specialist gets a fee for executing the limit orders—and he can also make a good living from trades that buyers or sellers are desperate to make.

Why wasn't Harry sold out on those days when Nasdaq showed Mine Safety transactions at 48 or higher? Because buyers and sellers didn't have a chance to meet. The over-the-counter market has no specialist post. Instead, dealers in the stock—in Mine Safety's case, there are 11—post their own bid and ask prices. If the best price among the dealers is a bid of 47 and an ask of 49, orders to buy or sell at 48 simply sit idle.

Here are some ways to minimize transaction costs:

- Don't place market orders if you can help it.
- Don't trade over-the-counter stocks for small gains.
- Don't place stop-loss orders in o-t-c stocks.
- Let your broker know when you are unhappy.

Source: Adapted from Richard L. Stern, "The widespread phenomenon," *Forbes*, June 26, 1989, pp. 232–235. Excerpted by permission of *Forbes* magazine, June 26, 1989. © Forbes, Inc., 1989.

investing and indirect investing through the purchase of investment company shares.

Each of these issues will be addressed in subsequent chapters. Readers then can decide for themselves the extent to which active stock market trading is desirable.

Common Stock Returns and Risks

As with bonds, we need to analyze basic information about the returns from, and risks of, investing in common stocks. This information will form a basis for the discussion of the valuation and analysis of stocks in the next chapter.

Common Stock Returns

As we learned in Chapter 5, the returns on common stocks can be separated into two parts: dividends and capital gains or losses. The total return from common stocks is

$$\text{TR} = \text{Dividend yield} + \text{CG(L)} \tag{8-2}$$

where TR is the total return on a stock during any specified period, dividend yield is the ratio of dividend to market price, and CG(L) is the capital gain or loss resulting from the purchase of a stock at one price and its subsequent sale at a different price.[11]

Many investors think of common stocks as vehicles for large (hopefully!) capital gains, although quite a few end up with capital losses. It is this part of the total return that really excites most investors in common stocks. Nevertheless, dividends are a substantial part of the total return from a common stock. Some common stocks, such as utilities, are bought primarily for their dividend yield. Historically, dividends have been about half of the total return from common stocks.

Figure 8-4 indirectly illustrates the impact of the income component, or dividends, on the total returns from common stocks. Recall from Chapter 5 that indices of cumulative wealth can be constructed that show the cumulative level at any point of an initial investment, typically $1.00. Figure 8-4 shows that $1.00 invested in common stocks at the end of 1925 would have been worth $534.45 at the end of 1989. The capital appreciation component of this total return series would have stood at $27.70 per dollar invested at the end of 1925. Although not shown, the income component would have amounted to $18.91 per dollar invested at the end of 1925.

According to the Ibbotson–Sinquefield data referred to in Chapter 5

[11]Note that in the case of a short sale, the capital gain or loss would be the difference between the sale price and the subsequent purchase price.

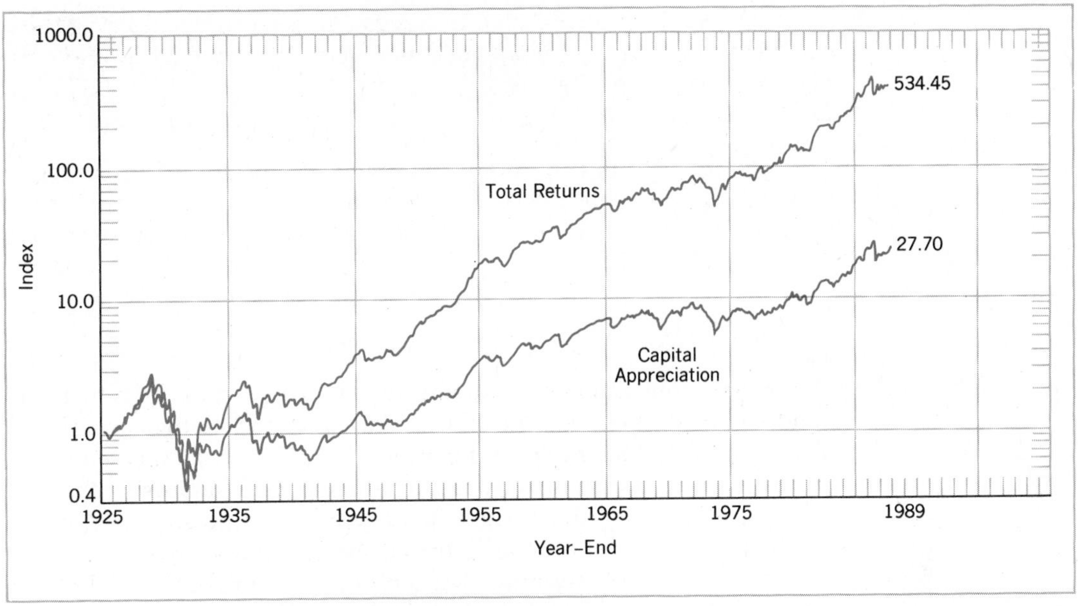

FIGURE 8-4 ***Total returns and capital appreciation indexes for the S&P 500, 1926–1989.***
Source: Roger G. Ibbotson and Rex A. Sinquefield, *Stocks, Bonds, Bills, and Inflation* (SSBI), 1989, updated in *SSBI 1990 Yearbook,* Ibbotson Associates, Chicago, 1990, p. 34. All rights reserved.

and discussed later, the geometric mean annual return for the capital appreciation component of the total return on common stocks has been 5.3%. The geometric mean annual return for the income component has been 4.7%. The two together, plus a small reinvestment rate return, combine to form the 10.3% total return for common stocks that on a wealth index basis for the period 1926–1989, results in the ending value of 534.45 shown in Figure 8-4.[12]

INVESTMENTS INTUITION

The implications of these data are important for stock investors. The income component of a stock's return can have a major effect on its total return. For stocks in general, the income component has been, on average, almost as important as the capital appreciation compo-

[12]Differences occur because of rounding errors. Nevertheless, the process is as follows: Raise 1.047, the income component, to the 64 power, obtaining a value of 18.905. The product of this value and the 27.70 noted earlier is approximately equal to the $534 final wealth number for common stocks.

nent. The Tax Reform Act of 1986 resulted in capital gains being taxed at the same rate as dividends, thereby eliminating the preferential treatment of capital gains.

Investors are paying increasing attention to the income component, and publications concerned with investing are emphasizing the income component more. See Box 8-2 for an analysis by *Forbes* of the dividend component.

Measuring Returns

The income component of common stock returns is measured by the dividend yield. For example, the *current yield* on a stock is the current annual dividend divided by the current market price. The *estimated yield* on a stock is the estimated dividend to be paid for some period, such as for the next 12 months, divided by the current market price. As noted, dividend yield measures only part of the total return from a common stock.

As a conceptual measure, TR is a proper measure of the total return on a common stock. It captures both components of the possible return from a stock, and therefore accounts for everything that an investor receives (or will receive).

Reviewing once again (from Chapter 5), the formula for TR on a common (or preferred) stock is

$$TR_{CS} = \frac{D_t + PC}{P_B} \tag{8-3}$$

where D_t represents the dividend received during a given period t, such as a year, a month, or a quarter; PC measures the change in price during the period; the P_B represents the beginning or purchase price.

The total return is a useful measure of return. It is easy to use as a measure of the return that has occurred, say, over the past year, for one stock, a portfolio, or the market as a whole. It is also useful in trying to estimate the future returns from securities. To do so, however, an investor must estimate the future price in order to calculate the PC term, and estimating price at any point in the future is difficult, at best. Such an estimation process requires the use of probability distributions and expected values, as explained in Chapter 5.

Common Stock Risks

Sources of Risk We discussed the sources of risk applying to all securities in Chapter 5 and those applying to bonds in particular in Chapter 6. We shall do the same here for common stocks, first using traditional terminology and then using modern terminology.

BOX 8-2

SOME INSIGHTS ON THE INCOME COMPONENT OF STOCK RETURNS

No longer are high-yielding stocks only for widows and orphans. Beginning last year, dividends have been taxed no higher than capital gains. That makes high-yielding stocks attractive to a class of investors who used to shun them.

It won't do, however, to go for the stocks with the fattest yields. Some of those dividends are imperiled by inadequate or slow-growing earnings, factors that come back to haunt the dividend seeker as much as the capital gains investor. Occidental Petroleum, for example, has a \$2.50 annual dividend, but that dividend has not been increased in seven years, during which time inflation has cut the dividend's purchasing power by 20%. The prospect for future increases is not good, either, since the company has been paying out more than it earns.

A solid dividend payer, by contrast, pays out less than half its net income and maintains the real value of the dividend in a period of inflation. A stock now yielding a modest 4% but enjoying a 10% annual increase in the dividend will, in ten years, be yielding over 10% on its original price.

Pfizer is one company that has recently kept its dividend whole in purchasing power. This pharmaceutical company, moreover, has paid a dividend every year since 1901 and has increased it in each of the last 21 years. The stock has roughly tripled since early 1974, and the dividend is up fivefold. At the indicated \$2.20 rate for 1989, the yield is almost 12% on original investment for someone who bought 15 years ago.

Source: Adapted from Evan Sturza, "Growth Yields," *Forbes*, April 17, 1989, p. 222. Excerpted by permission of *Forbes* magazine, April 17, 1989. © Forbes, Inc., 1989.

Market risk is that part of a security's total risk that is dependent on fluctuations in the stock market as a whole; that is, a part of the movement in the price of an individual security (or a portfolio) is attributable to movement in the overall market. This risk is caused by broad forces independent of an individual security. For example, the Dow Jones Average dropped significantly when news of President Kennedy's assassination reached the floor of the New York Stock Exchange (it was closed early as a result).

Virtually all securities' prices are affected by the movements of the overall stock market. However, the degree of effect varies among securities, with some being more affected than others. Overall, market risk is the single most important risk affecting the price movements of common stocks.

The significance of market risk can be appreciated by considering the stock market crash that occurred on October 19, 1987. The Dow Jones Industrial Average peaked on August 25, 1987 at 2722. It dropped the week prior to October 19 approximately 10%, declining some 130 points the preceding Friday alone. On that infamous Monday in October, the stock market, as measured by the Dow Jones Average, dropped 508 points—a decline of some 22%. Thus, from the market high on August 27 to the close of business on October 19, the market declined some 36%—a staggering loss by any historical comparison. The loss for the month of October alone was roughly 29%.

The impact of such a market decline is obvious. Virtually every investor who held common stocks in long positions suffered losses because virtually every stock declined in price. Most portfolios suffered losses comparable to that of the Dow. For example, Fidelity Magellan mutual fund, the most successful equity mutual fund of the 1980s, suffered a loss of roughly 33% in the month of October. Therefore, an investor in Magellan experienced a paper loss of one-third of the value of his or her holdings in Magellan in one month. This is market risk at its most dramatic in modern investing history.

Of course, as in other aspects of investments, there are two sides that should be considered. From August 1982 through the high on August 25, 1987, the market advanced at a 29% *annual* compound rate—a phenomenal rate of increase. Most investors who were long did very well during this period. Furthermore, despite a "mini-crash" drop of 190 points in one day in October 1989, by mid-1990 the market had advanced over 70% from the level that was reached on October 19, 1987.

One can argue that many sharp movements in the market (either up or down) are unjustified from an economic standpoint. Nevertheless, the possibility of such movements always exists, and they do occur. What matters is that most stocks tend to move together. If the market declines drastically, most stocks are adversely affected, and if the market rises strongly, most stocks are positively affected. The Standard & Poor 500 Index showed a gain of 31.5% in 1989. Virtually all investors holding a diversified portfolio of S&P 500 stocks enjoyed outstanding performance in 1989.

Various writers on the subject sometimes refer to specific, or company-unique, risks in connection with common stocks, including business risk, financial risk, industry risk, political risk, and management risk. The last two are self-explanatory, and somewhat abstract.

Business risk involves the probability of a company suffering losses or profits less than expected for a given period because of adverse circumstances in that company's particular line of activity. This risk could occur because of external forces such as trade restrictions, a worldwide recession, or hostilities with a foreign country that constitutes much of the market for a company's products. Internally, business risk comes about because of such factors as efficiency considerations, poor planning, or illegal activities by employees.

Financial risk involves the use of debt in financing the assets of a firm. The use of fixed-cost financing affects the earnings per share available to the stockholders, magnifying both gains and losses. This process is called **leverage.** Because of the risk of default, and therefore possible bankruptcy, arising from the use of debt, variability in a company's returns should increase with the use of financial leverage. The same is true of operating leverage, defined as the change in operating profit resulting from a change in sales volume. The higher the operating leverage, other things being equal, the higher the variability in returns accruing to the common stockholders.

Industry risk refers to the possibility of virtually all firms in a given industry being adversely affected by some common factor that does not affect, or affects to a much lesser degree, firms outside that industry. The troubled auto industry of the early 1980s is one example.

Summarizing the preceding discussion, the risk applicable to common stocks can be divided into two types: (1) a general component, representing that portion in the variability of a stock's total returns that is directly associated with overall movements in general economic (or stock market) activity; (2) a specific (issuer) component, representing that portion in the variability of a stock's total return that is not related to the variability in general economic (market) activity. In Chapter 5 we labeled these two components systematic and unsystematic risk, and the following summarizes our earlier discussion:

1. Systematic risk is that part of the total variability directly associated with the variability in the overall market. That is, the variability in the returns of all stocks together explains a significant part of the variability in the returns of any one individual stock. Thus, systematic risk is related to and is often referred to as market risk.

2. Unsystematic risk is that part of the total risk not related to the overall market variability—the portion of total variability remaining after the systematic part has been controlled. Because it is unrelated to overall market risk, it is sometimes called nonmarket risk. It is attributable to the unique factors affecting a particular company.

Partitioning of common stock total risk into these two components has become commonplace in investment analysis. The usefulness of this separation will be more evident when we discuss portfolio management.

Measuring Risk

As discussed in Chapter 5, risk is often associated with dispersion in the likely outcomes, and dispersion refers to variability. The standard deviation captures the dispersion or variability and is used as a measure of the total risk for a common stock.[13]

[13]The standard deviation can easily be squared to form the variance, which is an alternative measure of dispersion or risk. Sometimes it is convenient to use standard deviation, and at other times it is convenient to use variance.

The statistical measure of total risk for a common stock, standard deviation, can be quantitatively separated into its two components, systematic risk and unsystematic risk (which was also discussed in Chapter 5). When this is done, the significance of systematic risk can be seen.

$$\begin{aligned}\text{Total risk} &= \text{Systematic risk} + \text{Unsystematic risk} \\ &= \text{Market risk} + \text{Nonmarket risk} \\ &= \text{Nondiversifiable risk} + \text{Diversifiable risk}\end{aligned} \tag{8-4}$$

The unsystematic risk measures that part of the total risk of a common stock that is not related to the aggregate market for all stocks. As shown in the chapters on portfolio management later in the text, when an investor builds a portfolio of stocks, the unsystematic risk is diversified away, or nearly so. This means that the unsystematic risk term in Equation 8-4 will disappear or be reduced to a very small amount. What remains is the first term, which measures systematic risk.

Systematic risk refers to that part of the total risk that is attributable to the aggregate market for all stocks. A key component of the systematic risk is a stock's beta, which was previously explained in Chapter 5. **Beta** is a relative measure of systematic risk—the risk of an individual stock in relation to the overall market, as measured by the volatility of its returns.

To summarize, the average beta for all stocks is 1.0, because the beta for the overall market is 1.0. Thus, a stock with a beta of 1.5 would be considered an aggressive (risky) security, whereas a stock with a beta of 0.5 would be considered defensive (conservative). *On average,* if the beta of a stock is 2, its returns are twice as volatile as the overall market, moving up or down twice as much.

Example. If the overall market declines 5%, a stock with a beta of 2.0 would be expected to decline, on the average, about 10%; if the market rose 10%, it would be expected to rise about 20%. On the other hand, with a beta of 0.8, if the market declined (rose) 5%, this stock should decline (rise) only 0.8 as much, or 4%.[14] ▪

Beta is an index measure of the systematic risk for a common stock. It is measured on a ratio scale; that is, a beta of 2.0 is twice as large as a beta of 1.0, and a beta of 0.5 is half as large. Beta is useful for comparing the relative systematic risk of different stocks and, in practice, is used by investors to judge a stock's riskiness. Stocks can be ranked by their betas. Because the variance of the market is a constant across all securities for a particular period, ranking stocks by beta is the same as ranking them by their absolute systematic risk.[15] Stocks with high (low) betas are said to be high- (low-) risk securities.

---

[14]Betas can also be negative, which would indicate expected changes in return in the opposite direction to the market.

[15]The absolute systematic risk for a stock is the product of the stock's beta squared and the variance of the return for the overall market.

Betas typically are estimated from historical data, regressing TRs for the individual security against the TRs for some market index. As a result, the usefulness of beta will depend on, among other things, the validity of the regression equation. Regardless of how good the fit is, however, beta is an estimate subject to errors. (The software that accompanies this text can be used to calculate a security's data using historical data).

It is important to note that most calculated betas are *ex post* betas. What is actually needed in investment decisions is an *ex ante* beta measuring expected volatility. The common practice of many investors is simply to calculate the beta for a security and assume it will remain constant in the future, a risky assumption in the case of individual securities. Similar to standard deviations, portfolio betas quite often are stable across time, whereas individual security betas often are notoriously unstable. However, this is not an unfavorable outcome for investors, because the basic premise of portfolio theory is the necessity of holding a portfolio of securities rather than only one or a few securities.

One method of estimating beta is to employ the historical regression estimate but subjectively modify it for expected or known changes. In fact, it is logical to begin the estimation of beta using the best estimate of the historical beta.

Substantial evidence has been presented that betas tend to move toward 1.0 over time.[16] Betas substantially larger (smaller) than 1.0 should tend to be followed by betas that are lower (higher), and closer to 1.0. Thus, forecasted betas should be closer to 1.0 than the estimates based solely on historical data would suggest. Several models have been advocated for adjusting betas for this tendency to "regress toward the mean."[17] As a result, it is not unusual to find "adjusted" betas rather than historical betas. Merrill Lynch, for example, adjusts betas for this tendency. Investors who obtain beta information from such sources are actually using estimated betas.

The Historical Return and Risk on Common Stocks

As with the discussion of bonds, this chapter concludes with an analysis of the historical returns on common stocks. Knowledge of the past 60-plus years of returns on risky assets, both on an absolute basis and in relation to other financial assets, is very useful. Perhaps more important, this information should be useful in helping investors to estimate the future returns

---

[16]See M. Blume, "Betas and Their Regression Tendencies," *Journal of Finance,* Vol. X, No. 3 (June 1975), pp. 785–795; and R. Levy, "On the Short-Term Stationarity of Beta Coefficients," *Financial Analysts Journal,* Vol. 27, No. 5 (December 1977), pp. 55–62.

[17]See M. Blume, "On the Assessment of Risk," *Journal of Finance,* Vol. V, No. 1 (March 1971), pp. 1–10; and O. Vasichek, "A Note on Using Cross-Sectional Information in Bayesian Estimation of Security Betas," *Journal of Finance,* Vol. 8, No. 5 (December 1973), pp. 1233–1239.

from stocks. In the absence of extraordinary inflation or major structural changes in our economy, it is simply unrealistic to expect future annual returns on common stocks over many years to average, say, 30%. On the other hand, investors need not be overly worried that annual returns will average as little as, say, 5% a year over a period of many years.

The Ibbotson–Sinquefield (IS) data, discussed in Chapter 5 (Table 5-4), provide detailed figures for the returns and risk of common stocks. This source reports monthly and annual returns for Standard & Poor's 500 Composite Index from 1926 to date. These returns include both dividends and capital gains or losses (i.e., they are monthly or yearly TRs.)

Table 8-1 repeats (from Table 5-4) the arithmetic mean, geometric mean, and standard deviation of annual returns for common stocks for the years 1926–1989. The geometric annual rate of return has averaged 10.3% for this 64-year period, an impressive figure in comparison with alternatives such as bonds. However, this return, or the 12.4% average annual arithmetic mean, was not achieved without significant risk, as shown by the standard deviation of 20.9%. This standard deviation is roughly two and one-half times that of government and corporate bonds, and almost five times that of Treasury bills (refer to Table 5-4).

Table 8-1 also shows the returns and risk of "small" common stocks. *Small,* in this case, refers to the bottom quintile of New York Stock Exchange stocks ranked by market value. It is reasonable to expect these smaller stocks to be more risky than the largest stocks on the NYSE, such as IBM or AT&T, and their returns generally to be larger. The average annual compound returns for this long period was almost 2% higher, and the annual arithmetic return was over 5% higher. The trade-off, however, was the large jump in risk from 20.9% to 35.3%, as measured by the standard deviation. This is another good demonstration of the risk–return trade-off.

Finally, Table 8-1 shows the so-called **equity risk premium** for common stocks, defined as the difference between the return on common stocks and the return on riskless assets (Treasury bills). In other words, this is the *additional* annual average compensation that investors received for assum-

TABLE 8-1 ***Annual Rates of Return and the Equity Risk Premium for Common Stocks, 1926–1989***

	Geometric Mean (%)	Arithmetic Mean (%)	Standard Deviation (%)
Common stocks	10.3	12.4	20.9
Small stocks	12.2	17.7	35.3
Common stock risk premium (stocks − Treasury bills)	6.5	8.6	20.8

Source: Roger G. Ibbotson and Rex A. Sinquefield, *Stocks, Bonds, Bills, and Inflation* (SSBI), 1989, updated in *SSBI 1990 Yearbook,* Ibbotson Associates, Chicago, pp. 21 and 46.

ing the additional risk of common stock ownership as opposed to risk-free assets. Each investor has to decide if this average risk premium is adequate compensation for the additional risk. Furthermore, the investor must decide if it will be adequate in the future.

As shown in Table 8-1, the arithmetic mean equity risk premium averaged 8.6% over this long period of time, but with considerable variability. This is a useful benchmark figure to keep in mind when attempting to forecast aggregate stock market returns. Since the equity risk premium is the additional compensation beyond the risk-free rate, adding the premium to the current yield on Treasury bills provides one estimate of the expected return on aggregate market returns.

The message from Table 8-1, in conjunction with Table 5-4, is very clear. Common stocks have provided more than twice the annualized return of corporate bonds and government bonds over a 64-year period, but at a cost of roughly two and one-half times the risk; for "small" stocks, the comparable figures are three times as much return, but at over four times the risk. Most investors in common stocks should continue to enjoy higher returns than investors in fixed-income securities, but they will have to assume higher risk to do so. In any year or over a period of years, their returns may be less than those available in alternative assets, and sometimes they will be negative.

We can better appreciate the risk, as well as the return potential, of common stocks by considering a shorter segment of time, such as periods of years. Table 5-1 showed the annual returns on the Standard & Poor's 500 Composite Index for the years 1926–1989. These data clearly demonstrate both the potential returns and the riskiness of common stocks over various time periods. The average return over a longer period can be high in comparison with other securities, such as bonds, but over shorter periods the variability, both up and down, can be great.

We can calculate the annual compound rate of return for any period of years in Table 5-1 by calculating the geometric mean. Doing so allows us to make comparisons of the actual realized rate of return over various periods of time.

Example. The compound annual rate of return on the S&P 500 Composite Index for the years 1980 and 1981 was 11.8%, consisting of a gain of 31.5% in 1980 and a loss of 4.9% in 1981, calculated as

$$\begin{aligned} 1.315(0.951) &= (1.251) \\ 1.251^{1/2} &= 1.118 \\ 1.118 - 1.0 &= 0.118, \text{ or } 11.8\% \end{aligned}$$

▪

It is clear from even a cursory examination of Table 5-1 that the compound annual rate of return can vary widely depending upon the particular years being considered. For example, the years 1973–1977 included three with negative total returns, whereas the 10 years of the 1980s showed outstanding performance.

As the number of years increases, the compound average return is likely to approach the long-run compound average return on common stocks of approximately 10%. However, investors run the risk of investing at the beginning of 1973, for example, and finding that at the end of 1974 their *compound annual* total rate of return was −20%. They are motivated, though, with the hope of being one of those who invested at the beginning of 1988 and finding that at the end of 1989 their *compound annual* total rate of return was 23.5%.

Notice in Table 5-1 that over the 10-year period 1980–1989, only one year showed a loss. Historically, however, for the period 1926–1989, 30% of the time the annual total returns have been negative (Table 5-1 shows that 19 out of 64 years had a negative TR).

Why Investors Buy Stocks

At the end of Chapter 6 we presented Malkiel's case for bonds as an investment for the 1990s. It seems appropriate, therefore, to show why investors invest in common stocks, and the results of doing so over long periods of time.

Wilson and Jones have constructed returns for common stocks, corporate bonds, and commercial paper for the period December 1870 through December 1989, roughly doubling the period covered by the Ibbotson data discussed earlier.[18] They arrived at these returns by reconstructing the Cowles stock index data that begin at the end of 1870. Data for the two fixed-income series were constructed from historical series, and the monthly returns were calculated in a manner comparable to the return series for stocks. Taken together, this is the longest time period yet observed for the returns on these major assets.

Figure 8-5 shows the wealth indices for these three assets, assuming an investment of $1.00 at the end of 1870. As we can see, the result for stocks for this very long time period is staggering relative to bonds, paper, and inflation. The wealth index for stocks increased over 20,000 times, compared with 588 times for bonds and 486 times for commercial paper.

Based on Figure 8-5, and assuming the future will be similar to the past, ask yourself the following question: "If I plan to invest for a *long time period,* and recognizing the risk involved, what should I invest in—stocks, bonds, or paper?" If you have trouble answering this question, return to Chapter 1 and start over.

[18]Jack W. Wilson and Charles P. Jones, "Returns on Stocks, Bonds and Commercial Paper: Long-Term Construction, Analysis, and Comparisons," Faculty Working Paper No. 117, North Carolina State University, April 1988. Updated regularly.

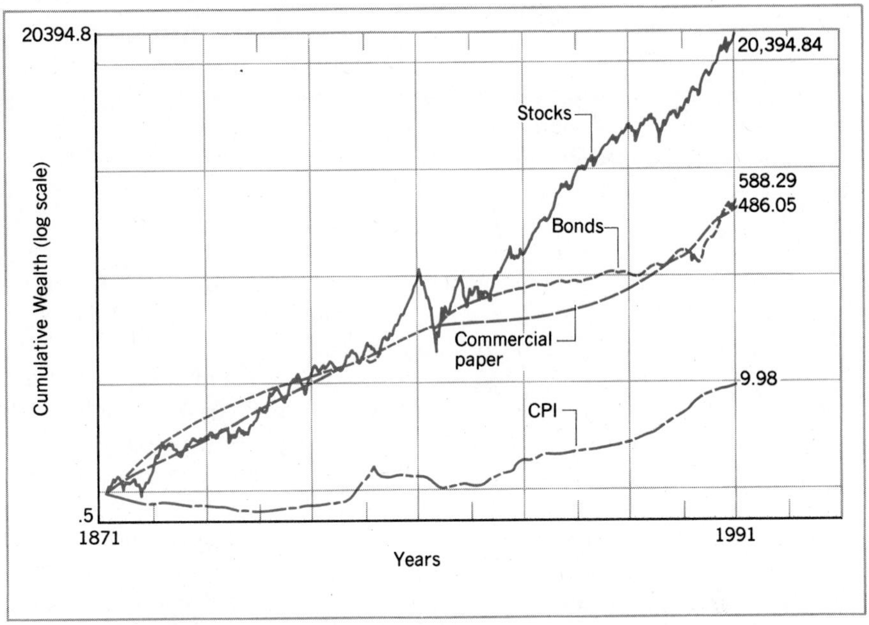

FIGURE 8-5 ***Cumulative wealth indices for stocks, bonds, and commercial paper, and the cumulative CPI—1871–1989.***
Source: Jack W. Wilson and Charles P. Jones, unpublished manuscript.

Summary

- Common stocks (equity securities) represent an ownership position in corporations. The stockholders are the owners, exercise control, and have limited liability.
- The par value of a common stock is relatively insignificant. The book value is the accounting value of the equity. Market value is the variable of interest to stockholders, because on a per-share basis it is the price of the stock, and stock prices are of major interest to investors.
- Quarterly dividends, the only cash payments made by a corporation, depend upon the board of directors.
- Stock dividends and stock splits represent a repackaging of the pieces of paper (stock shares) evidencing ownership. Other things being equal, they do not represent direct economic value.
- Much information is available on stocks and should be organized along market–industry–company lines. Daily price and volume information is readily available in major newspapers.
- The stock market is primarily a secondary market in which existing shares are traded among investors. Institutional investors have dominated the NYSE for many years, accounting for a substantial portion of its total activity. Individual investors dominate the other exchanges.

- Trading on the New York Stock Exchange is very smooth and orderly. Overall, Amex trading is similar, but supplies of many of these stocks are thin. Over-the-counter trading ranges from very active to very inactive, depending on the particular issue.
- Returns on common stocks consist of the dividend yield plus the capital gain (or loss). Dividend yield measures only the income component of the total return, whereas the TR captures both components of total return.
- Common stock risk sources include market risk, interest rate risk, inflation risk, and others. These sources of risk can be separated into systematic and unsystematic components.
- The total risk for a common stock is measured by the standard deviation.
- A relative measure of systematic risk is the beta coefficient, which measures the volatility of a stock's returns. Unsystematic risk can be diversified away in a portfolio, leaving the systematic risk, which cannot be diversified away.
- Historically, common stocks have averaged about 10% compound annual return, but with a standard deviation two to three times that of government and corporate bonds. "Small" common stocks have had even larger average returns and risk.

Key Words

Beta
Book value
Business risk
Dividends
Dividend yield
Equity risk premium
Financial risk
Leverage
Market risk
Market value
Payout ratio
P/E ratio (multiplier)
Stock dividend
Stock split
Systematic risk
Unsystematic risk

Questions

8-1 What are the advantages and disadvantages of being a holder of common stock of IBM as opposed to being a bondholder?

8-2 Distinguish between par value, book value, and market value for a corporation.

8-3 Assume that a company in whose stock you are interested will pay their regular quarterly dividend soon. Looking in *The Wall Street Journal*, you see a dividend figure of $3.20 listed for this stock. The board of directors has declared the dividend payable on September 1, with a holder-of-record date of August 15. When must you buy the stock to receive this dividend, and how much will you receive if you buy 150 shares?

8-4 Of what value to investors are stock dividends and splits?

8-5 How does the reporting in *The Wall Street Journal* for a "standard" over-the-counter stock differ from those over-the-counter stocks traded on the NASDAQ National Market?

8-6 Why is the stock market considered a "secondary" market?

8-7 How important are institutional investors in NYSE total trading?

8-8 How does trading in the over-the-counter market compare to trading in the corporate and municipal bond markets from the standpoint of the average individual investor?

8-9 What is the relative importance, historically, of the two components of common stock returns?

8-10 How can you measure the income component of stocks?

8-11 What are the sources of risk for common stocks?

8-12 Distinguish between systematic and unsystematic risk.

8-13 What is meant by the risk premium for common stocks? Looking at the historical record, would you expect to find much variation in annual risk premiums?

8-14 How is the systematic risk, in relative terms, calculated for a stock?

8-15 What were some factors that affected the unsystematic return for Chrysler Corporation during the 1980s?

8-16 Why is beta a relative measure of risk?

8-17 How can the total risk of a common stock by measured? How is beta related to this measure?

8-18 What is meant by the term *equity risk premium?* Of what significance is it to an investor trying to forecast the return for the overall market next year?

Problems

8-1 Calculate the total return (TR) for a stock purchased at $45 and sold one year later for $57. During the year $3 in dividends were received.

8-2 Calculate the TR for a stock purchased for $32 and sold 11 months later for $27.50.

8-3 Refer to Allegheny Power common stock shown in Figure 8-1 (designated "AllegPwr"). Assume that this stock was purchased exactly one year earlier at its 52-week low. Using the closing price for the stock as shown in Figure 8-1, calculate the TR for this one-year holding period.

8-4 Using the geometric mean for common stocks in Table 8-1, show that the ending wealth for the period 1926–1989 is approximately 530. Using the geometric mean for small common stocks as shown in Table 8-1, what is the ending wealth for this same period?

8-5 Using the information in Table 8-1 and an expected return for Treasury bills for next year of 8%, estimate the required rate of return for the market as a whole for next year.

8-6 Based on the data in Problem 8-5, estimate the required rate of return for Syntex next year if its beta is 1.1.

8-7 Refer to the information in Table 5-1. Show how the compound annual average rate of return for the years 1985–1989 can be calculated from the data for each of the individual years 1985–1989.

8-8 The following information is available for Zebos Computer Software:

	TR Zebos	TR Market Index
19X0	4.71	6.39
19X1	16.83	18.24
19X2	31.52	31.48
19X3	−2.36	−4.85
19X4	11.33	20.37
19X5	17.72	22.31
19X6	3.52	5.97
19X7	15.81	31.06
19X8	10.78	18.54
19X9	−9.33	−12.67

(a) Based only on your observations of the returns for Zebos and the market index as presented, do you think this stock is more risky or less risky than the market, using volatility as the measure of risk?
(b) Using *The Investment Calculator,* calculate the beta for Zebos. Does this beta conform with your intuitive analysis from (a)?
(c) What percentage of the total risk is systematic risk? Why do you think this percentage is so high?
(d) Change the 19X7 TR for Zebos to 25.81. What effect would you expect this to have on the beta for Zebos? Confirm your response by recalculating the beta with this one change.

Selected References

The best-known sources of information on stock returns is

Ibbotson Associates, Inc. *Stocks, Bonds, Bills and Inflation: Yearbook.* Annual. Chicago: Ibbotson Associates.

Factual source of information on common stocks are

NASDAQ Fact Book. Annual. Washington, D.C.: National Association of Securities Dealers, Inc.

New York Stock Exchange Fact Book. Annual. New York: New York Stock Exchange, Inc.

CHAPTER 9

Common Stock Valuation and Analysis

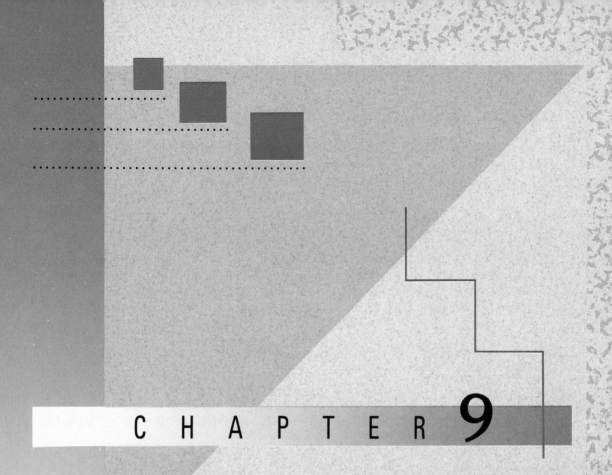

What determines the value of a common stock? What approaches are commonly used by investors interested in valuing and/or selecting stocks? How well can these approaches be expected to work? These questions will be answered in the next few chapters. Because of the complexity of common stocks and the related questions that are raised in their analysis, several chapters are needed to describe adequately the most frequently used analysis and selection processes.

There are two traditional and well-known approaches to analyzing and/or selecting common stocks: fundamental analysis and technical analysis. However, the significant amount of research in recent years on the concept of efficient markets has widespread implications for the analysis and valuation of common stock. Therefore, our discussion of common stocks will be built around these approaches and any implications from the efficient markets literature.

Traditionally, fundamental analysis has occupied the majority of resources devoted to the analysis of common stocks. All investors should understand the logic of, and rationale for, fundamental analysis. It deserves, and will receive, careful consideration. The other approach, technical analysis, is analyzed in Chapter 13, while the efficient market concept, which has implications for both approaches, is discussed in Chapter 14.

Approaches for Analyzing and Selecting Stocks

The two basic approaches, technical and fundamental analysis, are described briefly here, followed by a consideration of efficient market concepts and implications. The fundamental approach is then developed in some detail in the remainder of this chapter, thereby setting the stage for the next three chapters, which analyze the fundamental approach in a specific, recommended order.

Technical Analysis

One of the two traditional strategies long available to investors is technical analysis, which will be examined in detail in Chapter 13. In fact, technical analysis is the oldest strategy and is traceable back to at least the late nineteenth century.

The term ***technical analysis*** refers to the methodology of forecasting fluctuations in securities prices. This methodology can be applied either to individual securities or to the market as a whole (i.e., forecasting a market index such as the Dow Jones Industrial Average).

The rationale behind technical analysis is that the value of a stock is primarily a function of supply and demand conditions. These conditions, in turn, are determined by a range of factors, from scientific to opinions and guesses. The market uses all these factors in determining the changes in prices. These prices will move in trends that may persist, with changes in trends resulting from changes in supply and demand conditions. The idea that these changes can be detected by analyzing the action of the market itself characterizes technical analysis.

In its purest sense, technical analysis is not concerned with the underlying economic variables that affect a company or the market; therefore, the causes of demand and supply shifts are not important. The basic question to be asked can be stated as follows: Does excess demand exist for a stock, and can it be detected by studying either the patterns of past price fluctuations or the movements of certain technical indicators or rules? Technicians study the market using graphical charting of price changes and volume of trading over time. Also, a number of technical indicators are used.

Fundamental Analysis

Fundamental analysis is based on the premise that any security (and the market as a whole) has an **intrinsic value,** or the "true" value as estimated by an investor. This value is a function of the firm's underlying variables, which combine to produce an expected return and an accompanying risk. By assessing these fundamental determinants of the value of a security, an estimate of its intrinsic value can be determined. This estimated intrinsic value can then be compared to the current market price of the security. Similar to the decision rules used for bonds in Chapter 7, there are decision rules for common stocks when fundamental analysis is used to calculate intrinsic value. These rules will be stated later in the chapter.

In equilibrium, the current market price of a security reflects the average of the intrinsic value estimates made by investors. An investor whose intrinsic value estimate differs from the market price is, in effect, differing with the market consensus as to the estimate of either expected return or risk, or both. Investors who can perform good fundamental analysis and spot discrepancies should be able to profit by acting before the market consensus reflects the correct information.

Efficient Markets Implications

One of the most significant developments in recent years is the proposition that securities markets are efficient. This idea has generated considerable controversy concerning the analysis and valuation of securities because of its significant implications for investors. Regardless of how much (or how little) an investor learns about investments, and regardless of whether an investor ends up being convinced by the efficient markets literature, it is prudent to learn something about this idea early in one's study of investments. Much evidence exists to support the basic concepts from this hypothesis, and it cannot be ignored simply because one is uncomfortable with the idea or because it sounds too improbable. It is appropriate to consider this concept at the outset of any discussion about the valuation of common stocks.

The **efficient market hypothesis (EMH)** is concerned with the assessment of information by investors. Security prices are determined by expectations about the future. Investors use the information available to them in forming their expectations. If security prices fully reflect all the relevant information that is available and usable, a securities market is said to be efficient.

If the stock market is efficient, prices reflect their fair economic value as estimated by investors. Even if this is not strictly true, prices may reflect their approximate fair value after transaction costs are taken into account, a condition known as "economic efficiency." In such a market, where prices of stocks depart only slightly from their fair economic value, investors should not employ trading strategies designed to "beat the market" by identifying undervalued stocks.

The implications of an efficient market are extremely important for investors. They include one's beliefs about how to value securities in terms of the other two approaches—the fundamental and the technical approach. This, in turn, encompasses questions about the time and effort to be devoted to these two approaches. Other implications include the management of a portfolio of securities. For example, should management be active or passive? Efficient market proponents often argue that less time should be devoted to the analysis of securities for possible inclusion in a portfolio and more to such considerations as reducing taxes and transaction costs and maintaining the chosen risk level of a portfolio over time.

The rise, and increasing acceptance, of the efficient-markets concept has had an impact on traditional investing practices. Hardest hit has been technical analysis. If prices fluctuate in accordance with the efficient markets model, there is little chance that pure technical analysis is valid.

The EMH concept also has implications for fundamental analysis. If the market is efficient, prices will react quickly to new information. With many active investors buying and selling, prices should be close to their fair economic values. However, fundamental analysis is still needed in an efficient market, because if it was not being done, the market would be less efficient. In fact, one can argue that it is the very fact that investors do fundamental analysis, in the belief that the market is not efficient, that makes the market efficient.

Common Stock Valuation Using Fundamental Analysis

Two basic fundamental approaches to the valuation of common stocks are typically used in the securities world: the present value approach and the P/E ratio (multiple of earnings) approach. The present value analysis is similar to the process considered for bonds in Chapter 7. The future stream of benefits to be received from a common stock is discounted back to the present at the investor's required rate of return. The P/E ratio approach is probably more widely used by practicing security analysts. A stock is said to be worth some multiple of its future earnings. In effect, investors determine the value or price of a stock by deciding how many dollars (the multiple) they are willing to pay for every dollar of estimated earnings.

The Present Value Approach

The classic method of calculating intrinsic value involves the use of present value analysis, often referred to as the *capitalization of income method.* As explained in Chapter 7, the value of any security can be estimated by a present value process involving the capitalization (discounting) of income. That is, the current value of a security is equal to the discounted (present) value of the future stream of cash flows that the investor expects to receive from the asset. Repeating from Chapter 7,

$$\text{Value} = \sum_{t=1}^{n} \frac{\text{Cash flows}}{(1 + k)^t} \tag{9-1}$$

where

k = the required rate of return[1]

To use such a model, the investor must

1. Estimate a discount rate, or appropriate required rate of return (which can be thought of as the sum of the risk-free rate and risk premium as explained in Chapter 5).
2. Estimate the amount and timing of the future stream of cash flows.
3. Use these two components in a present value model to estimate the intrinsic value, which is then compared to the current market price of the security.

Figure 9-1 summarizes the present value process used in fundamental analysis. It emphasizes the factors that go into valuing common stocks. The exact nature of the present value process used by investors in the market-

[1]This concept is explained in Chapter 5.

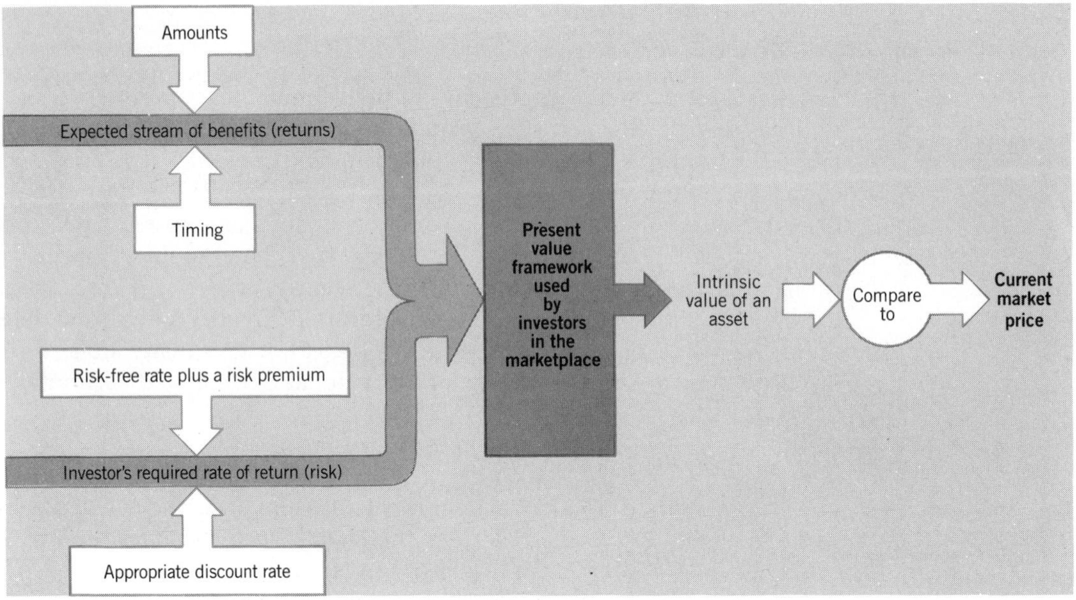

FIGURE 9-1 ***The present value approach to valuation.***

place depends upon assumptions made about the growth in the expected stream of benefits, as explained later.

The Required Rate of Return for a Common Stock The general concept of a required rate of return was discussed in Chapter 5 and was used specifically in Chapter 7 to value bonds. It is appropriate to review this concept for common stocks.

An investor who is considering the purchase of a common stock must assess its risk and, given its risk, the *minimum expected rate of return* that will be required to induce the investor to make the purchase. This minimum expected return, or required rate of return, is an opportunity cost.

What is the relationship between the required rate of return and risk for a common stock? Chapter 1 described the underlying premise of investments—a trade-off between risk and expected return in which the larger the risk assumed, the larger the expected return should be to compensate for the risk. Remember, however, that the return referred to is *expected* return. Expectations may not materialize because of unforeseen events, or simply because expected return is a probability distribution with less than 100% probability of a particular return occurring.

The trade-off between the required rate of return and risk is considered to be linear, as shown in Figure 9-2, which reviews and enhances the discussion in Chapter 5. The required rate of return (usually represented in

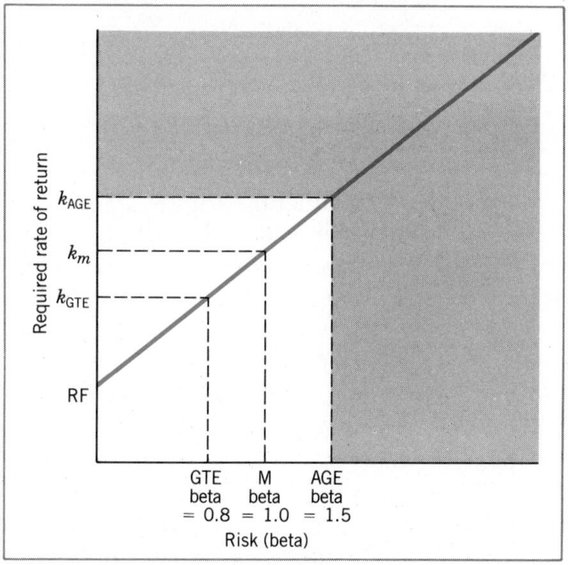

FIGURE 9-2 ***The trade-off between required rate of return and risk for common stocks.***

finance by the letter *k*) is on the vertical axis, risk is on the horizontal axis, and the vertical intercept is the risk-free rate of return that can be earned on a riskless asset. It is important to remember that the horizontal axis in Figure 9-2 uses beta to measure risk. As explained in the previous chapter, beta is a measure of nondiversifiable or systematic risk for a stock. It is the relevant measure of risk when investors hold portfolios of common stocks.

Figure 9-2 indicates that the required rate of return increases as the risk, measured by beta, increases. The stock market taken as a whole has a beta of 1.0, indicated by point M in the diagram. The required rate of return for all stocks is therefore k_M. Now conisder a stock with a beta lower than 1.0; for example, assume that General Telephone and Electronics has a beta of 0.8. Its required rate of return, k_{GTE}, will be below k_M, because its risk (beta) is less than that of the market. On the other hand, if a stock such as A. G. Edwards, a large, publicly traded brokerage firm, has a beta of 1.50, this indicates substantially greater risk than the market as a whole, and investors require a higher rate of return, k_{AGE}.

Recall from Chapter 5 that the trade-off between required rate of return and risk illustrated in Figure 9-2 can be expressed in equation form. The required rate of return for any common stock (e.g., stock *i*) is[2]

$$k_i = RF + B_i(RM - RF) \tag{9-2}$$

[2]This equation was explained in detail in Chapter 5.

where

k_i = the required rate of return for stock i (the RR_i in Chapter 5)
RF = the risk-free rate or rate of return on a riskless asset
RM = the required rate of return on the market
B_i = the risk (beta) of stock i

This equation, known as the capital asset pricing model (CAPM), is one of the key developments in finance and, rightly or wrongly, underlies much of modern investment analysis. The CAPM provides us with a statement for the required rate of return for a common stock.

The Expected Cash Flows for a Common Stock The other component that goes into the present value framework is the expected stream of benefits. Just as the value of a bond is the present value of any interest payments plus the present value of the bond's face value that will be received at maturity, the value of a common stock is the present value of all the cash flows to be received from the issuer (corporation). The question is, "What are the cash flows for a stock, how much can be expected, and when will they be received?"

INVESTMENTS INTUITION

To find which cash flows are appropriate in the valuation of a common stock, ask yourself the following question: If I buy a particular common stock and place it in a special trust fund for the perpetual benefit of myself and my heirs, what cash flow will be received? The answer is dividends, because this is the only cash distribution that a corporation actually makes to its stockholders. Although a firm's earnings per share in any year belong to the stockholders, corporations generally do not pay out all their earnings to their stockholders.

Stockholders may plan to sell their shares sometime in the future, resulting in a cash flow from the sales price. As shown later, however, even if investors think of the cash flow from common stocks as a combination of dividends and a future price at which the stock can be sold, this is equivalent to the stream of all dividends to be received on the stock.

What about earnings? Are they important? Can they be used as the expected cash flow? The answer is yes to both questions. Dividends are paid out of earnings, so earnings are clearly important. And the second approach to fundamental analysis, to be considered later, uses the earnings and a P/E ratio to determine intrinsic value. Therefore, earnings are an important part of fundamental analysis; in fact, earnings receive more attention from investors than any other single variable.

If all earnings are paid out as dividends, they will be accounted for as dividends. If earnings are retained by the corporation, they presumably will be reinvested, thereby enhancing future earnings and, ultimately, dividends. The present value analysis should not count the earnings reinvested currently and also paid later as dividends. If properly defined and separated, these two variables would produce the same results. This means that more than one present value model is possible.[3] However, it is always correct to use dividends in the present value analysis.

Because dividends are the cash flow stream to be received directly by investors, it is appropriate to have a valuation model based on dividends. We will now consider such a model, the dividend discount model, which is the foundation of valuation for common stocks.

The Dividend Discount Model

In adapting Equation 9-1 specifically to value common stocks, the cash flow comes from dividends expected to be paid in each future period. Since dividends are the only cash payment a stockholder receives directly from a firm, *dividends are the foundation of valuation for common stocks.* An investor or analyst using this approach would carefully study the future prospects for a company and estimate the likely dividends to be paid. Also, the analyst would estimate an appropriate required rate of return or discount rate based on the risk foreseen in the dividends, and given the alternatives available. Finally, he or she would discount to the present and add together the estimated future dividends, properly identified as to amount and timing.

The present value approach to calculating the value of a common stock is conceptually no different from the approach used in Chapter 7 to value bonds, or in Appendix 7-B to value preferred stock. Specifically, Equation 9-1 adapted for common stocks, where dividends are the cash flow, results in Equation 9-3. This equation, known as the **dividend discount model (DDM),** states that the value of a stock today is the discounted value of all future dividends:

$$V_{CS} = \frac{D_1}{(1 + k_{CS})} + \frac{D_2}{(1 + k_{CS})^2} + \frac{D_3}{(1 + k_{CS})^3} + \ldots + \frac{D_\infty}{(1 + k_{CS})^\infty} \quad (9\text{-}3)$$

$$= \text{Dividend discount model}$$

where

$D_1, D_2, \ldots$ = the dividends expected to be received in each future period

k_{CS} = the discount rate applicable for an investment with this degree of riskiness (again, the opportunity cost of a comparable risk alternative)

[3]Besides dividends and earnings, cash flow (earnings after tax plus depreciation) has been suggested for these models.

Two immediate problems with Equation 9-3 are

1. The last term in Equation 9-3 indicates that investors are dealing with infinity. They must value a stream of dividends that may be paid forever, since common stock has no maturity date.
2. The dividend stream is uncertain; there are no specified number of dividends, if in fact any are paid at all. Dividends must be declared periodically by the firm's board of directors (technically, they are declared quarterly as explained in Chapter 8). Furthermore, the dividends for most firms are expected to grow over time; therefore, investors usually cannot simplify Equation 9-3 as in the case of a preferred stock.[4] Only if dividends are not expected to grow could such a simplification be made. Although such a possibility exists, it is unusual.

How are these problems resolved? The first problem, that Equation 9-3 involves an infinite number of periods and dividends, will be resolved when we deal with the second problem, specifying the expected stream of dividends. However, from a practical standpoint this problem is not as troublesome as it first appears. At reasonably high discount rates, such as 12%, 14%, or 16%, dividends received 30 or 40 years in the future are worth very little today, so that investors need not worry about them.

The conventional solution to the second problem is to make some assumptions about the *expected growth* of dividends over time. The investor or analyst estimates or models the future stream of dividends or a price that is expected to exist at some point in the future, or both. To do this, he or she classifies each stock into one of three cases, depending on the expected growth rate of the dividends. In summary,

> The dividend discount model is operationalized by estimating the expected future dividends to be paid by a company. This is accomplished by modeling the expected growth rate(s) in the dividend stream.

A time line will be used to represent the three alternative growth rate versions of the dividend discount model. All stocks that pay a dividend, or that are expected to pay dividends sometime in the future, can be modeled using this approach. It is important to keep in mind during this discussion that the dividend currently being paid on a stock (or the most recent dividend paid) is designated as D_0 and is, of course, known. Investors must estimate the future dividends to be paid, starting with D_1, the dividend expected to be paid in the next period. The three growth rate models for dividends are

1. A fixed dollar dividend equal to the current dividend being paid, D_0, to be paid every year from now to infinity. This is typically referred to as *the no-growth model*:

[4]Refer to Appendix 7-B for the valuation of preferred stock.

D_0	D_0	D_0	D_0	...	D_0	Dividend stream
0	1	2	3	...	∞	Time period

2. A dividend that is growing at a constant rate g, starting with D_0. This is typically referred to as *the constant or normal growth version of the dividend discount model*:

D_0	$D_0(1 + g)^1$	$D_0(1 + g)^2$	$D_0(1 + g)^3$	...	$D_0(1 + g)^\infty$	Dividend stream
0	1	2	3	...	∞	Time period

3. A dividend that is growing at variable rates, for example, g_1 for the first four years and g_2 thereafter. This can be referred to as *the multiple-growth version of the dividend discount model*:

D_0	$D_1 = D_0(1 + g_1)$	$D_2 = D_1(1 + g_1)$	$D_3 = D_2(1 + g_1)$	$D_4 = D_3(1 + g_1)$
0	1	2	3	4

$D_5 = D_4(1 + g_2)$	...	$D_\infty = D_{\infty-1}(1 + g_2)$	Dividend stream
5	...	∞	Time period

The Zero-Growth Model. The fixed dollar dividend model reduces to a perpetuity. Assuming a constant *dollar* dividend, Equation 9-3 would simplify to the *no-growth model* shown as Equation 9-4.

$$V_{CS} = \frac{D_0}{k_{CS}} = \text{Zero-growth version of the dividend discount model} \qquad (9\text{-}4)$$

where D_0 is the constant dollar dividend expected for all future time periods and k_{CS} is the opportunity cost or required rate of return.

The no-growth case is equivalent to the valuation process for a preferred stock because, exactly like a preferred stock, the dividend (numerator of Equation 9-4) is fixed forever.[5] Therefore, a no-growth common stock is a perpetuity and is easily valued once k_{CS} is determined.

The Constant-Growth Model. The other two versions of the DDM indicate that to establish the benefits stream, which is to be subsequently discounted, it is first necessary to compound some beginning dividend into the future. Obviously, the higher the growth rate used, the greater the future amount; furthermore, the longer the time period, the greater the future amount.

A well-known scenario in valuation is the case in which dividends are expected to grow at a constant rate over time. This *constant growth model* is shown as Equation 9-5.[6]

---

[5]The valuation of preferred stock is explained in Appendix 7-B.

[6]The constant growth model is often referred to as the Gordon model (named after Myron J. Gordon, who played a large part in its development and use).

$$V_{CS} = \frac{D_0(1+g)}{(1+k_{CS})} + \frac{D_0(1+g)^2}{(1+k_{CS})^2} + \frac{D_0(1+g)^3}{(1+k_{CS})^3} + \ldots + \frac{D_0(1+g)^\infty}{(1+k_{CS})^\infty} \quad (9\text{-}5)$$

where D_0 is the current dividend being paid and growing at the constant rate g, and k_{CS} is the appropriate discount rate.

Equation 9-5 can be simplified to the following equation[7]:

$$V_{CS} = \frac{D_1}{k - g} = \text{Constant growth version of the dividend discount model} \quad (9\text{-}6)$$

where D_1 is the dividend expected to be received at the end of year 1.

Equation 9-6 is used whenever it is reasonable to assume a constant growth rate for dividends. In actual practice it is used quite often because of its simplicity and because it is the best description of the actual behavior of a large number of companies and, in many instances, the market as a whole.

Example. Assume Summa Corporation is currently paying \$1.00 per share in dividends and investors expect dividends to grow at the rate of 5% a year for the foreseeable future. For investments at this risk level, investors require a return of 15% a year. The value of Summa will be

$$V = \frac{D_1}{k - g}$$

$$V = \frac{\$1(1.05)}{0.15 - 0.05} = \$10.50$$

Note that the current dividend of \$1.00 (D_0) must be compounded one period because *Equation 9-6 requires the dividend expected to be received one period from now* (D_1). ▪

In valuation terminology, D_0 represents the dividend currently being paid, and D_1 represents the dividend expected to be paid in the next period. If D_0 is known, D_1 can always be determined[8]:

$$D_0 = \text{Current dividend}$$

$$D_1 = D_0(1 + g)$$

where g is the expected growth rate of dividends.

An examination of Equation 9-6 quickly demonstrates the factors affecting the price of a common stock, assuming the constant growth version of the dividend discount model to be the applicable valuation approach. If the

---

[7]Note that k must be greater than g or nonsensical results are produced. Equation 9-5 collapses to Equation 9-6 as the number of periods involved approaches infinity.

[8]D_2 can be determined as $D_0(1 + g)^2$ or $D_1(1 + g)$.

market lowers the required rate of return for a stock, price will rise (other things being equal). If investors decide that the expected growth in dividends will be higher as the result of some favorable development for the firm, price will also rise (other things being equal). Of course, the converse for these two situations also holds—a rise in the discount rate or a reduction in the expected growth rate of dividends will lower price.

The present value or intrinsic value calculated from Equation 9-6 is quite sensitive to the estimates used by the investor in the equation. Relatively small variations in the inputs can change the estimated price by large percentage amounts.

Example. For Summa, assume the following:

1. The discount rate used, (k), is 16% instead of 15%, with other variables held constant:

$$P = \frac{\$1(1.05)}{0.16 - 0.05} = \$9.55$$

In this example, a one-percentage-point rise in k results in a 9% decrease in price, from \$10.50 to \$9.55.

2. The growth rate (g) is 6% instead of 5%, with other variables held constant:

$$\mathrm{P} = \frac{\$1(1.06)}{0.15 - 0.06} = \$11.77$$

In this example, a one-percentage-point rise in g results in a 12% increase in price, from \$10.50 to \$11.77.

3. The discount rate rises to 16%, and the growth rate declines to 4%:

$$\mathrm{P} = \frac{\$1(1.04)}{0.16 - 0.04} = \$8.67$$

In this example, the price declines from \$10.50 to \$8.67, a 17% change. ▪

These differences suggest why stock prices constantly fluctuate as investors make their buy and sell decisions. Even if all investors use the constant growth version of the dividend discount model to value a particular common stock, many different estimates of value will be obtained because of the following:

1. Each investor has his or her own required rate of return, resulting in a relatively wide range of values of k.
2. Each investor has his or her own estimate of the expected growth rate in dividends. Although this range may be reasonably narrow in most valua-

tion situations, small differences in g can produce significant differences in price, everything else held constant.

Thus, at any point in time for a particular stock, some investors are willing to buy, whereas others wish to sell, depending on their evaluation of the stock's prospects. This helps to make markets active and liquid.

The Multiple Growth Model. Many firms grow at a rapid rate (or rates) for some number of years and then slow down to an "average" growth rate. Other companies pay no dividends for a period of years, often during their early growth period. The constant growth model discused earlier is unable to deal with these situations; therefore, a model is needed that can. Such a variation of the DDM is the *multiple growth model.*

Multiple growth is defined as a situation in which the expected future growth in dividends must be described using two or more growth rates. Although any number of growth rates is possible, most stocks can be described using two or possibly three. It is important to remember that at least two different growth rates are involved—*this is the distinguishing characteristic of multiple growth situations.*

A number of companies have experienced rapid growth that could not be sustained forever. During part of their lives their growth exceeded that of the average company in the economy, but later the growth rate slowed. Examples from the past include McDonald's, Disney, Polaroid, Xerox, and IBM.

To capture the expected growth in dividends under this scenario, it is necessary to model the dividend stream during each period of different growth. It is reasonable to assume that at some point the company's growth will slow down to that of the economy as a whole. At this time the company's growth can be described by the constant growth model (Equation 9-6). What remains, therefore, is to model the exact dividend stream up to the point at which dividends change to a normal growth rate and to find the present value of all the components.

A well-known multiple growth model is the two-period model. This model assumes near-term growth at an unusual rate for some period (typically, 2–10 years) followed by a steady long-term growth rate that is sustainable (i.e., a constant growth rate as discussed earlier). This can be described in equation form as

$$V_0 = \sum_{t=1}^{n} \frac{D_0(1+g_1)^t}{(1+k)^t} + \frac{D_n(1+g_c)}{k-g} \frac{1}{(1+k)^n} \qquad (9\text{-}7)$$

where

V_0 = the intrinsic value of the stock today
D_0 = the current dividend
g_1 = the supernormal (or subnormal) growth rate for dividends

g_c = the constant growth rate for dividends
k = required rate of return
n = the number of periods of supernormal (or subnormal) growth
D_n = the dividend at the end of the abnormal growth period

Notice in Equation 9-7 that the first term on the right side defines a dividend stream covering n periods, growing at a high (or low) growth rate of g_1, and discounted at the required rate of return k. This term covers the period of supernormal (or subnormal) growth, at which time the dividend is expected to grow at a constant rate forever. The second term on the right-hand side is the constant growth version discussed earlier, which takes the dividend expected for the next period, $n + 1$, and divides by the difference between k and g.[9] Notice, however, that the value obtained from this calculation is the value of the stock at the beginning of period $n + 1$ (or the end of period n), and it must be discounted back to time period zero by multiplying by the appropriate discount (present value) factor. Conceptually, the valuation process being illustrated here is

P = Discounted value of all dividends through the unusual growth period n + discounted value of the constant-growth model, which covers the period $n + 1$ to ∞

Think about the second term in Equation 9-7 as representing a P_n, or the expected price of the stock derived from the constant growth model as of the end of period n. The constant growth version of the dividend discount model is used to solve for expected price at the end of period n, which is the beginning of period $n + 1$. Therefore,

$$P_n = \frac{D_{n+1}}{k - g_c}$$

Because P_n is the expected price of the stock at the end of period n, it must be discounted back to the present. When added to the value of the discounted dividends from the first term, the intrinsic value of the stock today (V_0) is produced.

Example. Figure 9-3 illustrates the concept of valuing a multiple growth rate company. In this example, the current dividend is \$1.00 and is expected to grow at the higher rate (g_1) of 12% a year for five years, at the end of which time the new growth rate (g_c) is expected to be a constant 6% a year. The required rate of return is 10%.

The first step in the valuation process illustrated in Figure 9-3 is to determine the dollar dividends in each year of supernormal growth. This is

---

[9]The dividend at period $n + 1$ is equal to the dividend paid in period n compounded up by the new growth rate, g_c. The designation $n + 1$ refers to the first period after the years of abnormal growth.

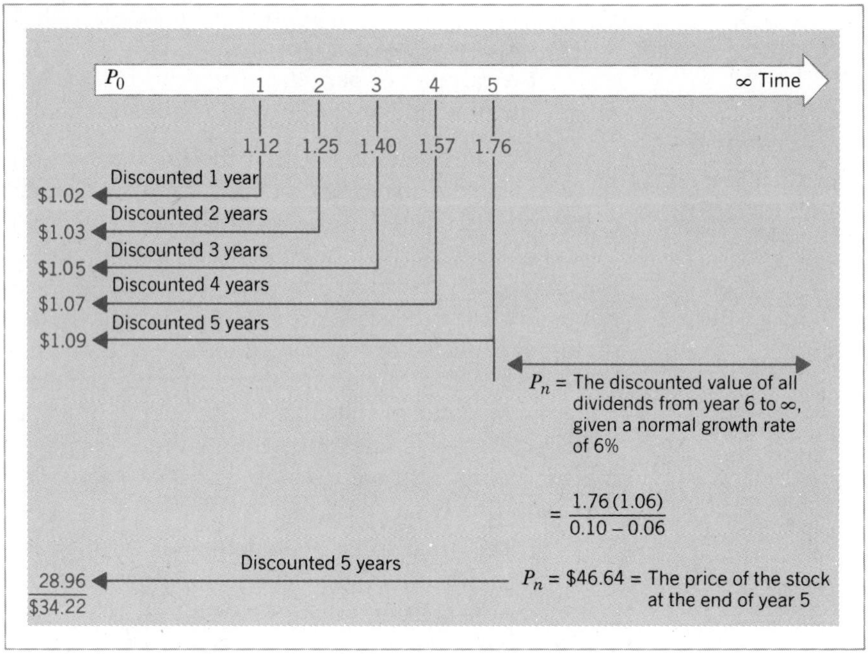

FIGURE 9-3 ***Illustration of a hypothetical supernormal growth company.***

done by compounding the beginning dividend, $1.00, at 12% for each of five years, producing the following[2]:

$$
\begin{aligned}
D_0 &= \$1.00 \\
D_1 &= \$1.00(1.12) = \$1.12 \\
D_2 &= \$1.00(1.12)^2 = \$1.25 \\
D_3 &= \$1.00(1.12)^3 = \$1.46 \\
D_4 &= \$1.00(1.12)^4 = \$1.57 \\
D_5 &= \$1.00(1.12)^5 = \$1.76
\end{aligned}
$$

Once the stream of dividends over the supergrowth period has been determined, they must be discounted to the present using the required rate of return of 10%. Thus,

$$
\begin{aligned}
\$1.12(0.909) &= \$1.02 \\
\$1.25(0.826) &= \$1.03 \\
\$1.46(0.751) &= \$1.05 \\
\$1.57(0.683) &= \$1.07 \\
\$1.76(0.621) &= \underline{\$1.09} \\
& \$5.26
\end{aligned}
$$

Summing the five discounted dividends produces the value of the stock for its first five years only, which is $5.26. To evaluate years 6 on, when constant growth is expected, the constant growth model is used.

$$
\begin{aligned}
P_n &= \frac{D_{n+1}}{(k - g_c)} \\
&= \frac{D_6}{(k - g_c)} \\
&= \frac{D_5(1.06)}{(k - g_c)} \\
&= \frac{\$1.76(1.06)}{0.10 - 0.06} \\
&= \$46.64
\end{aligned}
$$

Thus, \$46.64 is the expected price of the stock at the beginning of year 6 (end of year 5). It must be discounted back to the present, using the present value factor for five years and 10%, 0.621. Therefore,

$$
\begin{aligned}
P_n \text{ discounted to today} &= P_n \text{ (PV factor for five years, 10\%)} \\
&= \$46.64(0.621) \\
&= \$28.96
\end{aligned}
$$

The last step is to add the two present values together:

\$ 5.26	=	Present value of the first five years of dividends
28.96	=	Present value of the price at the end of year 5, representing the discounted value of dividends from year 6 to ∞
\$34.22	=	V_0, the present value of this multiple growth rate stock

▪

Dividends, Dividends—What About Capital Gains? In their initial study of valuation concepts, investors often are bothered by the fact that the dividend discount model contains only dividends, and an infinite stream of dividends at that. Although this is true, many investors are sure that (1) they will not be here forever and (2) they really want capital gains. Dividends may be nice, but buying low and selling high is wonderful! Since so many investors are interested in capital gains, which by definition involves the difference between the price paid for a security and the price at which this security is later sold, a valuation model should seemingly contain a stock price somewhere. Thus, in computing present value for a stock, investors are interested in the present value of the expected price two years from now, or six months from now, or whatever the expected, and finite, holding period is. How can price be incorporated into the valuation—or should it be?

In truth, the only cash flows that an investor needs to be concerned with are dividends. Expected price in the future is built into the dividend discount model given by Equation 9-3—it is simply not visible. To see this, ask yourself at what price you can expect to sell a common stock that you have bought. Assume, for example, that you purchase today and plan to hold for three years. The price you receive three years from now will reflect the buyer's expectations of dividends from that point forward (at the end of years 4, 5, etc.). The price today of the stock is equal to

$$P_0 = \frac{D_1}{(1 + k_{CS})} + \frac{D_2}{(1 + k_{CS})^2} + \frac{D_3}{(1 + k_{CS})^3} + \frac{P_3}{(1 + k_{CS})^3} \tag{9-8}$$

But P_3 (the price of the stock at the end of year 3), is, in turn, equal to the discounted value of all future dividends from year 4 to infinity. That is,

$$P_3 = \frac{D_4}{(1 + k_{CS})^4} + \frac{D_5}{(1 + k_{CS})^5} + \ldots + \frac{D_\infty}{(1 + k_{CS})^\infty} \tag{9-9}$$

Substituting Equation 9-9 into 9-8 produces Equation 9-3, the basic dividend discount model. Thus, the result is the same whether investors discount only a stream of dividends or a combination of dividends and price. Since price at any point in the future is a function of the dividends to be received after that time, the price today for a common stock is best thought of as the discounted value of all future dividends.

Intrinsic Value

After making careful estimates of the expected stream of benefits and the required rate of return for a common stock, the intrinsic value of the stock is obtained through the present value analysis—that is, the dividend discount model. This is the objective of fundamental analysis. What does intrinsic value imply? Traditionally, investors and analysts specify a relationship between the intrinsic value (IV) of an asset and its current market price (CMP). Specifically:

If IV > CMP, the asset is undervalued and should be purchased or held if already owned.

If IV < CMP, the asset is overvalued and should be avoided, sold if held, or possibly sold short.

If IV = CMP, this implies an equilibrium in that the asset is correctly valued.

An important question to ask at this point is, "What do you really have when you valued an asset by determining its intrinsic value?" The intrinsic value of an asset is that value that exists when the asset is correctly valued—its "true" value based on the capitalization of income process. Intrinsic value is simply the present value concept used in a financial context.

INVESTMENTS INTUITION

A problem with intrinsic value is that it is derived from a present value process involving estimates of uncertain (future) benefits and use of (varying) discount rates by different investors. Therefore, the same asset may have many intrinsic values—it depends on who, and how many, are doing the valuing. This is why, for a particular asset on a particular day, some investors are willing to buy and some to sell. Because future benefits are uncertain and investors have differing required rates of return, the use of fundamental valuation models will result in varying estimates of the intrinsic value of an asset. The market price of an asset at any point in time is, in this sense, the consensus intrinsic value of that asset for the market.

Does the problem of varying estimates of value render valuation models useless? No, because individual investors cannot make intelligent investment decisions without having an intelligent estimate of the value of an asset. If General Motors is currently priced at $55 a share, is it a good buy for you? It may or may not be, depending on your own required rate of return (discount rate), your estimate of the future benefit stream to be derived from owning GM, and certain other factors.[10]

Example. Assume that you require 18% to invest in GM; that is, your opportunity cost for alternative investment opportunities of similar risk is 18%. Also, assume that the current dividend is $6.25 and is expected to grow at the rate of 6% a year for the indefinite future. Based on these figures and using the constant growth dividend discount model, the intrinsic value (justified price) of GM to you would be estimated at approximately $52 per share. Based on the intrinsic value principle, GM is overvalued and should not be purchased if the current market price of GM is more than $52 per share, which it is in our example. ▪

Notice that this valuation process tells you that if you could pay $52 per share of GM, you will earn your required rate of return of 18%, *if* the assumed dividend growth rate is correct. You can, therefore, pay $50 per share, or $45, or $48, and earn more than the required rate of return.

Other investors with different opinions about k and g may be on the margin valuing this security, only slightly higher or slightly lower than $55. They are potential traders if the price moves slightly, or if news causes even slight variations in their k or their g.

[10] As shown in Part VII, securities should be chosen on the basis of a portfolio concept—that is, how they fit together to form a unified whole.

INVESTMENTS INTUITION

The valuation process can establish justified prices for assets or indicate whether or not you can *expect* to earn your required rate of return on a prospective asset. Remember, however, that you are not assured of earning your required rate of return. Investment decisions always involve a forward-looking process. Estimates are made under uncertainty, based on the best information available. But even the best estimates may not be realized. As discussed in Chapter 1, uncertainty will always be the dominant feature of the environment in which investment decisions are made.

The P/E Ratio Approach

An alternative fundamental analysis method of valuation often used by practicing security analysts is the P/E ratio or **earnings multiplier** approach. In fact, this method is used more often than dividend discount models by practicing security analysts, although DDMs command more and more attention and are now quite commonly discussed by investors, the popular press, and investment publications.[11] Although the P/E ratio model appears easier to use than DDMs, its very simplicity can cause investors to forget that estimation of the uncertain future is involved here also. This is an important point to remember. *Every valuation model and approach, properly done, requries estimates of the uncertain future.*

The conceptual framework for the P/E model is not as solidly based on economic theory as the DDM. However, a P/E ratio model is consistent with the present value analysis, because it concerns the intrinsic value of a stock or the aggregate market, exactly as before.

Recall from Chapter 8 that the P/E ratio as reported daily in such sources as *The Wall Street Journal* is simply an identity calculated by dividing the current market price of the stock by the latest 12-month earnings. As such, it tells investors the price being paid for each $1 of earnings.

Example. In early 1990, investors were willing to pay 29 times (the most recent 12-month) earnings for Newmont Mining but only 16 times earnings for IBM. Ford was selling at only six times earnings. ▪

[11]For example, the November/December 1985 *Financial Analysts Journal* was devoted to dividend discount models.

These reported P/E ratios provide no basis for valuation other than showing the underlying identity on which the P/E valuation model is based: This identity is[12]

$$P_0 = E_0 \times P_0/E_0 \tag{9-10}$$

To implement the earnings multiplier model and estimate the value of the stock today, we must estimate the values on the right-hand side of Equation 9-10, producing an estimated value, V_E. The basic equation then becomes

$$V_E = \text{estimated earnings} \times \text{justified P/E ratio} \tag{9-11}$$

Example. A stock with estimated earnings of \$3 per share should be worth \$45 if investors are willing to pay 15 times expected earnings. This value will change as estimates of earnings or the justified P/E changes. ▪

Determinants of the P/E Ratio What determines a P/E ratio? To answer this question, the P/E ratio can be derived from the dividend discount model, which, as we have seen, is the foundation of valuation for common stocks. We shall illustrate this process only for the case of constant growth. If a multiple-period growth model is applicable to the stock being considered, a different formulation from the one presented here would be needed.

Start with Equation 9-6, the value of a stock using the constant growth version of the model. To keep the terminology in terms of price, we use P_E to represent estimated price from the model.

$$P_E = \frac{D_1}{k - g} \tag{9-12}$$

Divide both sides of Equation 9-5 by expected earnings, E_1, to obtain

$$P_E/E_1 = \frac{D_1/E_1}{k - g} \tag{9-13}$$

Equation 9-13 indicates those factors that affect the estimated or theoretical P/E ratio, which are the factors on the right side of Equation 9-13:

1. The dividend payout ratio, D/E.
2. The required rate of return.
3. The expected growth rate of dividends.

---

[12]E_0 here refers to the earnings used to calculate the P/E ratio as reported; for example, in the case of *The Wall Street Journal* it is the most recent 12-month earnings.

The following relationships should hold, other things being equal:

1. The higher the payout ratio, the higher the P/E.
2. The higher the expected growth rate, g, the higher the P/E.
3. The higher the required rate of return, k, the lower the P/E.

It is important to remember the phrase "other things being equal" because usually other things are not equal and the preceding relationships do not hold by themselves. It is obvious, upon reflection, that if a firm could increase its estimated P/E ratio, and therefore its market price, by simply raising its payout ratio, it would be very tempted to do so. However, such an action would in all likelihood reduce future growth prospects, lowering g, and thereby defeating the increase in the payout. Similarly, trying to increase g by taking on particularly risky investment projects will cause investors to demand a higher required rate of return, thereby raising k. Again, this will work to offset the positive effects of the increase in g.

Variables 2 and 3 are typically the most important factors in the preceding determination of the P/E ratio because a small change in either can have a large effect on the P/E ratio.

Example. Assume that the payout ratio is 60%. By varying k and g, and therefore changing the difference between the two (the denominator in Equation 9-13), investors can assess the effect on the P/E ratio as follows:

Assume $k = 0.15$ and $g = 0.07$

$$P/E = \frac{D_1/E_1}{k - g}$$

$$P/E = \frac{0.60}{0.15 - 0.07}$$

$$= \frac{0.60}{0.08} = 7.5$$

Now assume $k = 0.16$ and $g = 0.06$

$$P/E = \frac{0.60}{0.10} = 6$$

or that $k = 0.14$ and $g = 0.08$

$$P/E = \frac{0.60}{0.06} = 10$$

Think about each of these P/E ratios being used as a multiplier with an expected earnings for stock i for next year of $3.00. The possible prices for stock i would be $22.50, $18, and $30, respectively, which is quite a range, given the small changes in k and g that were made.

Most investors intuitively realize that the P/E ratio should be higher for companies whose earnings are expected to grow rapidly. However, how much higher is not an easy question to answer. The market will assess the degree of risk involved in the expected future growth of earnings—if the higher growth rate carries with it a high level of risk, the P/E ratio will be affected accordingly. Furthermore, the high growth rate may be attributable to several different factors, some of which are more desirable than others. For example, rapid growth in unit sales due to strong demand for a firm's products is preferable to favorable tax situations, which may change, or liberal accounting procedures, which one day cause a reversal in the firm's situation.

P/E Ratios and Interest Rates The P/E ratio reflects investor optimism and pessimism. It is related to the required rate of return. As the required rate of return increases, other things being equal, the P/E ratio decreases, as can be seen from Equation 9-13.

The required rate of return, in turn, is related to interest rates, which are the required returns on bonds. As interest rates increase, required rates of return on all securities, including stocks, also generally increase. As interest rates increase, bonds become more attractive compared to stocks on a current return basis.

Based on these relationships, an inverse relationship between P/E ratios and interest rates is to be expected. As interest rates rise (decline), other things equal, P/E ratios should decline (rise). Table 9-1 shows interest rates (yields) on corporate, federal, and municipal bonds, yields on pre-

TABLE 9-1 ***The Relationship Between Yields and P/E Ratios, 1976–1989***

	Yields				
Year	AAA Industrial	Long-Term Treasuries	Municipals	Preferred Stock	P/E Ratio
1989	9.26	8.45	7.00	8.75	14.69
1988	9.71	8.94	7.36	9.23	11.68
1987	9.38	8.64	7.14	8.37	14.12
1986	9.02	8.14	6.95	8.76	16.52
1985	11.37	10.75	8.60	10.49	14.15
1984	12.71	11.99	9.61	11.59	9.95
1983	12.04	10.84	8.80	11.02	11.67
1982	13.79	12.23	10.86	12.53	11.13
1981	14.17	12.87	10.43	12.36	7.98
1980	11.94	10.81	7.85	10.57	9.16
1979	9.63	8.74	5.92	9.07	7.31
1978	8.73	7.89	5.52	8.25	7.79
1977	8.02	7.06	5.20	7.60	8.73
1976	8.43	6.78	5.66	7.97	10.84

Source: Federal Reserve *Bulletins*. The P/E ratios for the Standard & Poor's 500 Stock Index are based on calendar year earnings and end-of-year prices from Standard & Poor's Statistical Service, *Security Price Index Record*. Reprinted by permission.

ferred stocks, and P/E ratios for the Standard & Poor's 500 Composite Index for the years 1976–1989. Although the interest rate data are based on averages of monthly data during the year, whereas the P/E ratio data are based on year-end figures, the inverse relationship between the two can be seen clearly. As interest rates rose from 1976 through 1981, the P/E ratio on the S&P 500 Composite Index declined. Conversely, as interest rates declined from 1982 through 1986, the P/E ratio on the stock composite rose. Interest rates rose in 1987 and 1988, and the P/E ratio declined in each year relative to 1986. Finally, interest rates declined in 1989, and the P/E ratio rose.

INVESTMENTS INTUITION

Notice in Table 9-1 how the yields on preferred stocks tend to track the yields on bonds. Preferred stock, although technically an equity security, should behave like a fixed-income security because of the fixed dividend payment. Preferred stocks are substitutes for bonds in the eyes of many investors interested in obtaining a fixed, steady stream of payments.

Which Approach to Use?

We have described the two most often used approaches in fundamental analysis—the dividend discount model and the P/E ratio (multiplier) model. Which should be used?

In theory, the dividend discount model is a correct, logical, and sound position. The best estimate of the current value of a company's common stock is probably the present value of the (estimated) dividends to be paid by that company to its stockholders. However, some analysts and investors feel that this model is unrealistic. After all, they argue, no one can forecast dividends into the distant future with very much accuracy. Technically, the model calls for an estimate of all dividends from now to infinity, which is an impossible task. Finally, many investors want capital gains and not dividends, so for some investors it is not desirable to focus only on dividends.

The previous discussion dealt with these objections that some raise about the dividend discount model. Can you respond to these objections based on this discussion?

Possibly because of the objections to the dividend discount model cited here, or possibly because it is easier to use, the earnings multiplier or P/E model remains a popular approach to valuation. It is a less sophisticated and more intuitive model. In fact, understanding the P/E model can help investors to understand the dividend discount model. Because dividends are paid out of earnings, investors must estimate the growth in earnings before they can estimate the growth in dividends or dividends themselves.

Rather than view these approaches as competing alternatives, it is better to view them as complements. Each is useful, and together they provide analysts with a better chance of valuing common stocks. There are several reasons for viewing them as complementary:

1. The P/E model can be derived from the constant growth version of the dividend discount model. They are, in fact, alternative methods of looking at value. In the dividend discount model, the future stream of benefits is discounted. In the P/E model, an estimate of expected earnings is multiplied by a P/E ratio or multiplier.
2. Dividends are paid out of earnings. To use the dividend discount model, it is necessary to estimate the future growth of earnings. The dividends used in the dividend discount model are a function of the earnings for the firm, an estimate of which is used in the earnings multiplier model.
3. Finally, investors must always keep in mind that valuation is no less an art than a science, and estimates of the future earnings and dividends are subject to error. In some cases it may be desirable to use one or the other method, and in other cases both methods can be used as a check on each other. The more procedures investors have to value common stocks, the more likely they are to obtain reasonable results.

Regardless of which approach is used, it is important to remember that valuation using fundamental analysis, or any other approach, is always subject to error. This is because we are dealing with the uncertain future. *No matter who does the analysis, or how it is done, mistakes will be made.*

In the three chapters that follow, we will utilize extensively the overall logic of the fundamental valuation approach—namely, that the intrinsic value of a common stock, or the aggregate market, is a function of its expected returns and accompanying risk, as proxied by the required rate of return. The dividend discount model and the P/E ratio model will be used interchangeably to illustrate the fundamental valuation process.

Other Valuation Techniques

Other valuation techniques, based on fundamental analysis concepts, are used by investors. We shall discuss two that are often mentioned.

Price to book value is calculated as the ratio of price to stockholders' equity as measured on the balance sheet (and explained in Chapter 12). It is sometimes used to value companies, particularly financial companies. Banks have often been evaluated using this ratio because the assets of banks have book values and market values that are similar. It is also used in merger and acquisition analysis.

A valuation technique that has received attention recently is the **price/sales ratio (PSR).** This ratio is calculated as a company's total market value (price times number of shares) divided by its sales. In effect, it indicates what the market is willing to pay for a firm's revenues.

Example. In 1988 General Mills had sales of $5179 million. Based on an average of the high and low price for the year of $51 and 87 million shares outstanding, the total market value was $443.7 million. The PSR ratio, therefore, was 0.86. Thus, General Mills was selling at 86% of its annual sales. ▪

Some stocks, such as defense stocks, sold at very low PSRs in early 1989, around 25 cents on the sales dollar. At the same time, other stocks, such as the drug stocks, sold anywhere from 1.60 to 4.56 per sales dollar. The ratios for the drug companies would be considered "high," leaving little room for disappointment.

A Framework for Fundamental Analysis

It is obvious that under either of these fundamental approaches an investor will have to work with individual company data. Does this mean that the investor should plunge into a study of company data first and then consider other factors such as the industry within which a particular company operates or the state of the economy? The answer is *No!* The proper order in which to proceed in fundamental analysis is, first, to analyze the overall economy and securities markets; second, to analyze the industry within which a particular company operates; and finally, to analyze the company, which involves the factors affecting the valuation models described earlier.

Thus, the preferred order for fundamental security analysis is (1) the economy and market, (2) the industry, and (3) the company. This approach will be used for the next three chapters. Following is the justification for this approach.

Economy/Market

It is very important to assess the state of the economy and the outlook for primary variables such as corporate profits and interest rates. Investors are heavily influenced by these variables in making their everyday investment decisions. If a recession is likely, or under way, stock prices will be heavily affected at certain times during the contraction. Conversely, if a strong economic expansion is under way, stock prices will be heavily affected, again at particular times during the expansion. Thus, the status of economic activity has a major impact on overall stock prices. It is, therefore, very important for investors to assess the state of the economy and its implications for the stock market.

In turn, the stock market impacts on each individual investor. Investors cannot very well go against market trends. If the market goes up (or down) strongly, most stocks are carried along. Company analysis is likely to be of limited benefit in a year such as 1974, when the stock market was down 25%. Conversely, many investors did well in the years 1975 and 1976 regardless of their specific company analysis, because the market was up 20% and 24% respectively.

In a well-known study several years ago, King analyzed the relationship between market returns and individual stock returns.[13] (He also assessed industry effects, which we will consider later.) King found that for an earlier period of time (1927–1960), roughly half of the variance for an average stock was explained by the overall market. Although the impact of the overall market on a stock's returns seems to have declined in the years following those studied, it remains very substantial.

Another indication of the overall market impact is that on earnings for a particular company. Available evidence suggests that from one-fourth to one-half of the variability in a company's annual earnings is attributable to the overall economy (plus some industry effect).[14]

The economy also significantly affects what happens to various industries. One has only to think of the effects of import quotas, record high interest rates, and so forth, to see why this is so. Therefore, economy analysis must precede industry analysis.

Industry Analysis

After completing an analysis of the economy and the overall market, an investor can decide if it is a favorable time to invest in common stocks. If so, the next step should be industry analysis. King identified an industry factor as the second component (after overall market movements) affecting the variability in stock returns.

Individual companies and industries tend to respond to general market movements, but the degree of response can vary significantly. Industries undergo significant movements over both relatively short and relatively long periods. Industries will be affected to various degrees by recessions and expansions. For example, the heavy goods industries will be severely affected in a recession (examples include the auto and steel industries in the 1981–1982 recession). Consumer goods will probably be much less affected during such a contractionary period. During a severe inflationary period such as the late 1970s and very early 1980s, regulated industries such as utilities were severely hurt by their inability to pass along all price increases. Finally, new "hot" industries emerge from time

---

[13]See B. King, "Market and Industry Factors in Stock Price Movement," *Journal of Business*, Vol. 39 (1966), pp. 139–190.

[14]See Edwin J. Elton and Martin J. Gruber, *Modern Portfolio Theory and Investment Analysis*, 3rd ed. (New York: John Wiley, 1987).

to time and enjoy spectacular (if short-lived) growth. Examples include synthetic fuels and genetic engineering.

Company Analysis

Although the first two steps are important and should be done in the indicated order, great attention and emphasis should be placed on company analysis. Security analysts are typically organized along industry lines, but the reports that they issue usually deal with one (or more) specific companies.

The bottom line for companies, as far as most investors are concerned, is earnings per share. There is a very close relationship between earnings and stock prices, and for this reason most attention is paid to earnings. Dividends, after all, are paid out of earnings. The dividends paid by companies are closely tied to earnings, but not necessarily the current quarterly (or even annual) earnings.

A number of factors are important in analyzing a company. However, because investors tend to focus on earnings and dividends, we need to understand the relationship between these two variables, and between them and other variables. We also need to consider the possibilities of forecasting earnings and dividends.

Because dividends are paid out of earnings, we will concentrate on earnings in our discussion of company analysis in Chapter 12. Earnings are the real key to the fundamental analysis of a common stock. A good understanding of earnings is vital if an investor is to understand, and carry out, fundamental analysis.

The Framework in Perspective

It is useful to summarize the framework for fundamental analysis we are using because the following three chapters will be based on this framework.

Figure 9-4 depicts the fundamental valuation process. We shall examine the economy and market first, then industries, and finally individual companies. Fundamental valuation is usually done within the context of a present value model, primarily the dividend discount model, or a multiplier (P/E ratio) model. In either case, the two components of the value of any security being examined are (1) the expected stream of benefits, either earnings or dividends, and (2) the required rate of return or discount rate—alternatively, the multiplier or P/E ratio.

We need to concentrate on these two factors as we systematically proceed through the three levels of analysis: economy/market, industry, and company.

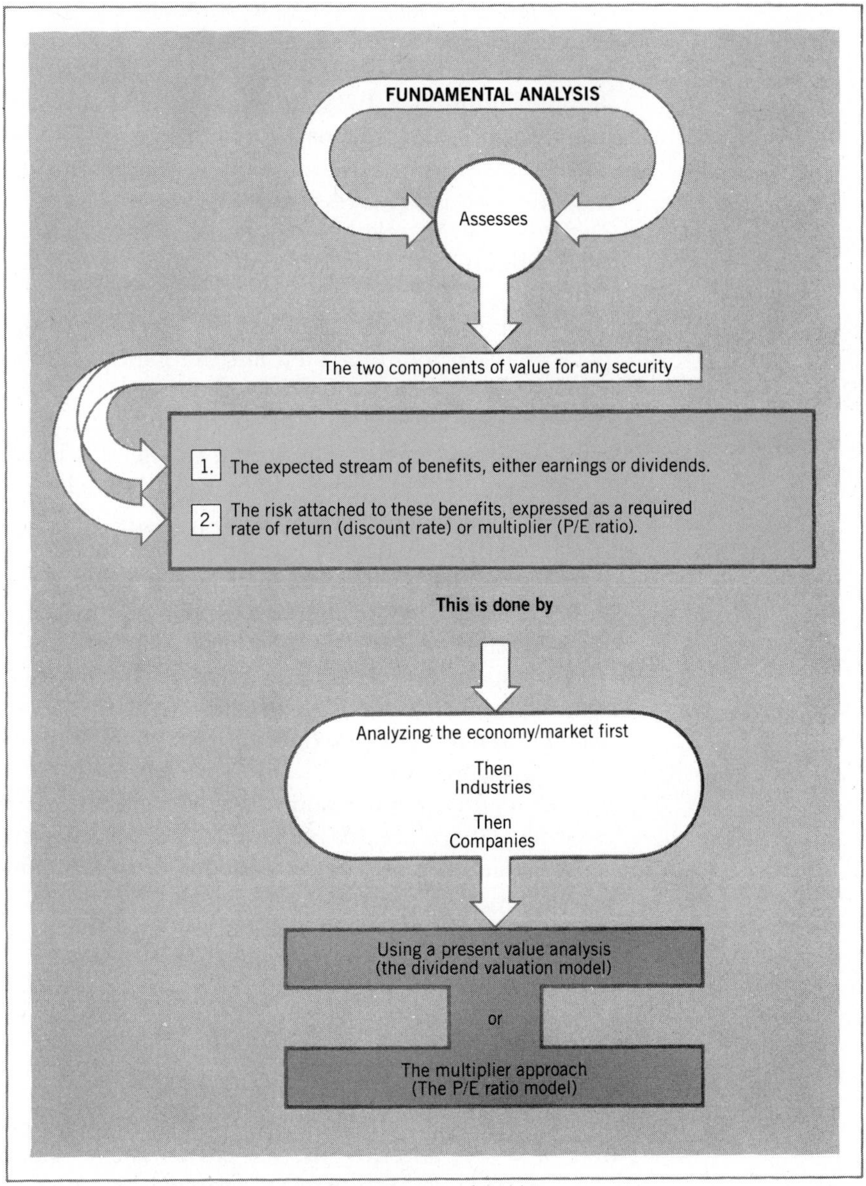

FIGURE 9-4 ***A framework for fundamental analysis.***

Summary

- Two primary approaches for analyzing and selecting common stock are fundamental analysis and technical analysis. Efficient market considerations should be taken into account.

- Fundamental analysis seeks to estimate the intrinsic value of a stock, which is a function of its expected returns and risk. Two fundamental approaches to determining value are the present value approach and the earnings multiplier (P/E ratio) approach.
- The present value approach for common stocks is similar to that used with bonds. A required (minimum) expected rate of return must be determined, based on the risk-free rate and a risk premium.
- There is a direct relationship between beta and required return, represented by the CAPM, which provides an equation for the estimation of required return.
- As for expected returns, since dividends are the only cash flows directly paid by a corporation, they are the logical choice for a present value model.
- According to the dividend discount model, the value of a stock today is the discounted value of all future dividends. To account for an infinite stream of dividends, stocks to be valued are classified by their expected growth rate in dividends.
- If no growth is expected, the dividend discount model reduces to a perpetuity. If two or more growth rates are expected, a multiple growth model must be used in which the future stream of dividends is identified before being discounted.
- The constant growth version of the dividend discount model is most often used; it reduces to the ratio of the dividend expected next period to the difference between the required rate of return and the expected growth rate in dividends.
- The dividend discount model is sensitive to the estimates of the variables used in it; therefore, investors will calculate different prices for the same stock while using an identical model. This model implicitly accounts for the terminal price of a stock.
- The multiplier or P/E ratio approach is based on the identity that a stock's current price is the product of its actual earnings per share and the P/E ratio. It follows that the P/E ratio can be calculated by dividing the current price by the actual earnings per share.
- To implement the P/E ratio approach to estimate the value of a stock, we must estimate the earnings and the P/E ratio for the next period.
- The P/E ratio itself is a function of the dividend payout ratio, the required rate of return, and the expected growth rate of dividends.
- Also, P/E ratios are inversely related to interest rates because interest rates are directly related to required rates of return.
- To perform fundamental analysis correctly, investors need a framework. The proper order for fundamental analysis is to analyze the market and economy first, then industries, and then companies.
- The aggregate market is the most pervasive influence on any single stock, carrying most stocks with it as it moves up or down; therefore, assessing the overall situation should be the first step in analyzing stocks.

- Because stocks grouped as industries tend to move together, industries should be analyzed second.
- Finally, individual companies must be analyzed.
- The basic techniques of fundamental analysis, the present value approach and the P/E ratio approach, can be used at each of the three levels—market, industry, and company.

Key Words

Dividend discount model
Earnings multiplier
Efficient market hypothesis (EMH)
Fundamental analysis
Intrinsic value
Price to book value
Price–sales ratio
Technical analysis

Questions

9-1 What is meant by "intrinsic value"? How is it determined?

9-2 How can the required rate of return for a stock be estimated? What difficulties are likely to be encountered?

9-3 Why can earnings not be used as readily as dividends in the present value approach?

9-4 What is the dividend discount model? Write this model in equation form.

9-5 What problems are encountered in using the dividend discount model?

9-6 Describe the three possibilities for dividend growth. Which is the most likely to apply to the typical company?

9-7 Since dividends are paid to infinity, how is this problem handled in the present value analysis?

9-8 Demonstrate how the dividend discount model is the same as a method that includes a specified number of dividends and a terminal price.

9-9 Assume that two investors are valuing General Foods Company and have agreed to use the constant growth version of the dividend valuation model. Both use $3.00 a share as the expected dividend for the coming year. Are these two investors likely to derive different prices? Why or why not?

9-10 Once an investor calculates intrinsic value for a particular stock, how does he or she decide whether or not to buy it?

9-11 How valuable are the P/E ratios shown daily in *The Wall Street Journal?*

9-12 What factors affect the P/E ratio? How sensitive is it to these factors?

9-13 What is the recommended order for doing fundamental analysis? Why is this sequence deemed proper?

9-14 Some investors prefer the P/E ratio model to the present value analysis on the grounds that the latter is more difficult to use. State these alleged difficulties and respond to them.

9-15 Indicate the likely direction of change in a stock's P/E ratio if
(a) The dividend payout decreases.
(b) The required rate of return rises.
(c) The expected growth rate of dividends rises.
(d) The riskless rate of return decreases.

Demonstration Problems

9-1 Hilton Coffee Company is currently paying a dividend of $2.00 per share, which is not expected to change. Investors require a rate of return of 20% to invest in a stock with the riskiness of Hilton. Calculate the intrinsic value of the stock.

The first step in solving a common stock valuation problem is to identify the type of growth involved in the dividend stream. The second step is to determine if the dividend given in the problem is D_0 or D_1.

In this problem it is clear that the growth rate is zero and that we must solve a zero-growth valuation problem (Equation 9-4). The second step is not relevant here because all of the dividends are the same.

$$V_0 = \frac{D_0}{k}$$

$$= \frac{\$2.00}{.20}$$

$$= \$10.00$$

9-2 Wilshire Publishing is currently paying a dividend of $2.00 per share, which is expected to grow at a constant rate of 7% per year. Investors require a rate of return of 16% to invest in stocks with this degree of riskiness. Calculate the implied price of Wilshire.

Since dividends are expected to grow at a constant rate, we use the constant growth version of the dividend discount model (Equation 9-6). Note carefully that this equation calls for D_1 in the numerator and that the dividend given in this problem is the current dividend being paid, D_0. Therefore, we must compound this dividend up one period to obtain D_1 before solving the problem.

$$D_1 = D_0(1 + g)$$

$$= \$2.00\ (1.07)$$

$$= \$2.14$$

and

$$V_0 = \frac{D_1}{k - g}$$

$$= \frac{\$2.14}{.16 - .07}$$

$$= \$23.78$$

9-3 Wella Chemicals is currently selling for $60 per share and is expected to pay a dividend of $3.00. The expected growth rate in dividends is 8% for the foreseeable future. Calculate the required rate of return for this stock.

To solve this problem, note first of all that this is a constant growth model problem. Second, note that the dividend given in the problem is D_1 because it is stated as the dividend to be paid in the next period. To solve this problem for k, the required rate of return, we simply rearrange Equation 9-6:

$$k = \frac{D_1}{P_0} + g$$

$$= \frac{\$3.00}{\$60} + .08$$

$$= .13$$

Note that we could also solve for g by rearranging Equation 9-6 to do so.

9-4 Wiley Bookcases has been undergoing rapid growth for the last few years. The current dividend of $2.00 per share is expected to continue to grow at the rapid rate of 20% a year for the next three years. After that time Wiley is expected to slow down, with the dividend growing at a more normal rate of 7% a year for the indefinite future. Because of the risk involved in such rapid growth, the required rate of return on this stock is 22%. Calculate the implied price for Wiley.

We can recognize at once that this is a multiple growth case of valuation because more than one growth rate is given. To solve for the value of this stock, it is necessary to identify the entire stream of future dividends from year one to infinity and discount the entire stream back to time period zero. After the third year, a constant growth model can be used which accounts for all dividends from the beginning of year four to infinity.

We first calculate the dividends for each individual year of the abnormal growth period and discount each of these dividends at the required rate of return.

$$D_1 = \$2.00\,(1 + .20) = \$2.40$$

$$D_2 = \$2.00\,(1 + .20)^2 = \$2.88$$

$$D_3 = \$2.00\,(1 + .20)^3 = \$3.46$$

Present value of the first 3 years of dividends

$$\$2.40\,(.820) = \$1.97$$
$$2.88\,(.672) = 1.94$$
$$3.46\,(.551) = 1.91$$
$$= \$5.82$$

Present value of the stock at the end of year 3

$$P_3 = \frac{\$3.46\,(1.07)}{.22 - .07} = \$24.68$$

Present value of P_3 at time period zero

$$P_0 = \$24.68\,(.551) = \$13.60$$

Present value of the stock at time period zero

$$V_0 = \$5.82 + \$13.60 = \$19.42$$

Note that the price derived from the constant model is the price of the stock at the end of year three, which is equivalent to the price of the stock at the beginning of year four. Therefore, we discount it back three periods to time period zero. Adding this value to the present value of all dividends to be received during the abnormal growth period produces the intrinsic value of this multiple-growth-period stock.

Problems

9-1 Johnson Products is currently selling for $45 a share with an expected dividend in the coming year of $2.00 per share. If the growth rate in dividends expected by investors is 9%, what is the required rate of return for this stock?

9-2 Assume that Wilson Industries is expected by investors to have a dividend growth rate of 8% a year over the foreseeable future and that the required rate of return for this stock is 13%. The current dividend being paid (D_0) is $2.25. What is the price of the stock?

9-3 Wolfe Wigs is currently selling for $50 per share and pays $3.00 in dividends ($D_0$). Investors require 15% return on this stock. What is the expected growth rate of dividends?

9-4 Frankish Poultry pays $1.50 a year in dividends, which is expected to remain unchanged. Investors require a 15% rate of return on this stock. What is its price?

9-5 (a) Given a preferred stock with an annual dividend of $3.00 per share and a price of $40, what is the required rate of return?

(b) Assume now that interest rates rise, leading investors to demand a required rate of return of 9%. What will the new price of this preferred stock be?

9-6 An investor purchases the common stock of a well-known home builder, Drac's Shacks, for $25 per share. The expected dividend for the next year is $3.00 per share and the investor is confident that the stock can be sold one year from now for $30. What is the implied required rate of return?

9-7 (a) The current risk-free rate (RF) is 10% and the expected return on the market for the coming year is 15%. Calculate the required rate of return for: (1) stock A, with a beta of 1.0, (2) stock B, with a beta of 1.7, and (3) stock C, with a beta of 0.8.

(b) How would your answers change if RF in part (a) were to increase to 12%, with the other variables unchanged?

(c) How would your answers change if the expected return on the market changes to 17%, with the other variables unchanged?

9-8 Woods Wisconsin Cheese, Inc., is currently selling for $60 and paying a $3.00 dividend.

(a) If investors expect dividends to double in 12 years, what is the required rate of return for this stock?

(b) If investors had expected dividends to approximately triple in six years, what would the required rate of return be?

9-9 Bright Brass, Inc. is currently selling for $36, paying $1.80 in dividends, and investors expect dividends to grow at a constant rate of 8% a year.

(a) If an investor requires a rate of return of 14% for a stock with the riskiness of Bright Brass, is it a good buy for this investor?

(b) What is the maximum an investor with a 14% required return should pay for Bright Brass? What is the maximum if the required return is 15%?

9-10 Joy Juice, Inc. sells at $32 per share, and the latest 12-month earnings are $4 per share with a dividend payout of 50%.

(a) What is Joy's current P/E ratio?

(b) If an investor expects earnings to grow by 10% a year, what is the projected price for next year if the P/E ratio remains unchanged?

(c) Assuming that the payout ratio will remain the same, the expected growth rate of dividends is 10%, and an investor has a required rate of return of 16%, would this stock be a good buy? Why or why not?

(d) If interest rates are expected to decline, what is the likely effect on Joy's P/E ratio?

9-11 The required rate of return for Trieste industries is 15.75%. The stock pays a current dividend of $1.30, and the expected growth rate is 11%. Calculate the formula price.

9-12 In Problem 9-11, assume that the growth rate is 16%. Calculate the formula price for this stock.

9-13 Baumer Legal Services is a rapidly growing firm. Dividends are expected to grow at the rate of 18% annually for the next 10 years. The growth rate after the first 10 years is expected to be 7% annually. The current dividend is $1.82. Investors require a rate of return of 19% on this stock. Calculate the intrinsic value of this stock.

9-14 Turner Software Products is currently paying a dividend of $1.20. This dividend is expected to grow at the rate of 30% a year for the next 5 years, followed by a growth rate of 20% a year for the following 5 years. After 10 years, the dividend is expected to grow at the rate of 6% a year. The required rate of return for this stock is 21%. What is its intrinsic value?

9-15 In Problem 9-14, assume that the growth rate for the first five years is 25% rather than 30%. How would you expect the value calculated in Problem 9-14 to change? Confirm your answer by calculating the new intrinsic value.

Selected References

A discussion of the price—earnings ratio can be found in

Beaver, William, and Dale Morse. "What Determines Price-Earnings Ratios?" *Financial Analysts Journal,* July–August 1978, pp. 65–76.

The dividend discount model is discussed in

Farrell, James L. "The Dividend Discount Model: A Primer." *Financial Analysts Journal,* November–December 1985, pp. 16–25.

Nagorniak, John J. "Thoughts on Using Dividend Discount Models." *Financial Analysts Journal,* November–December 1985, pp. 13–15.

Rie, Daniel. "How Trustworthy Is Your Valuation Model?" *Financial Analysts Journal,* November–December 1985, pp. 42–48.

100

PART 4

Common Stocks: The Fundamental Approach

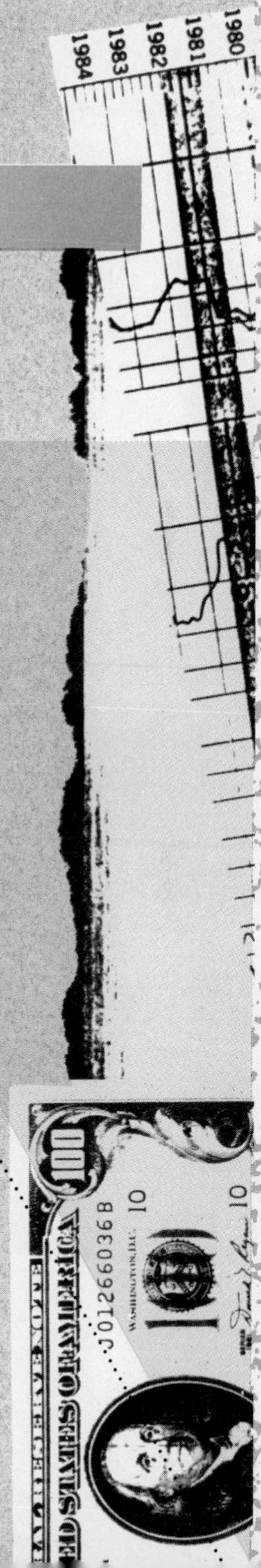

CHAPTER 10

Market Analysis

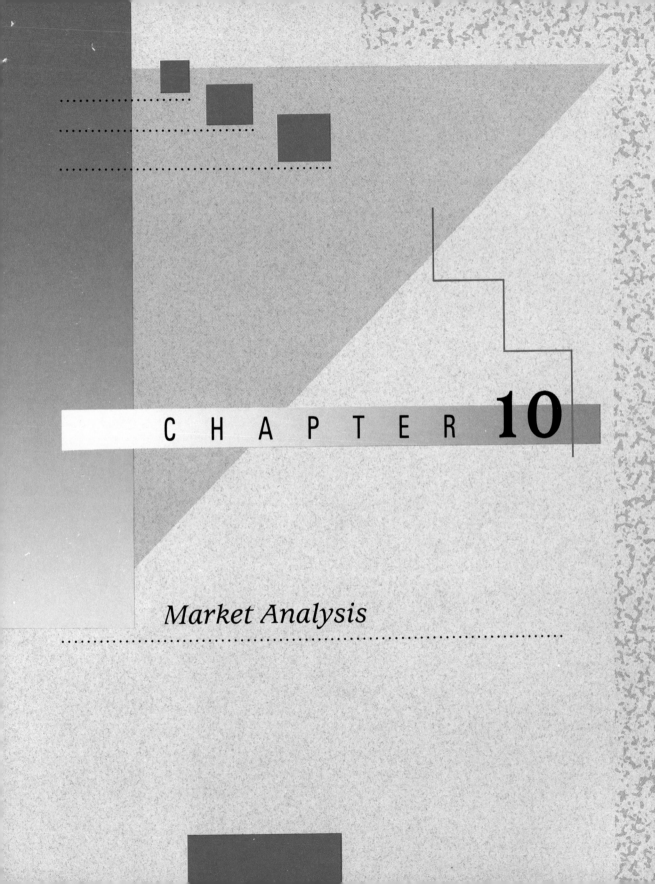

As discussed in the last chapter, the recommended procedure in fundamental security analysis is to analyze the aggregate stock market first, then industries, and finally individual companies. This chapter considers the first step, market analysis.

We shall examine several aspects of market analysis. First, what is meant by the "market." Although it is a popular expression among investors, what exactly are investors talking about when they discuss the "market"? Second, the importance of market analysis needs to be considered. Why is market analysis the first step in fundamental analysis?

Ultimately, investors must make intelligent judgments about the current state of the market and possible changes in the future. Is it at unusually high or low levels, and what is it likely to do in the next three months or year or five years? A logical starting point in assessing the market is to understand the economic factors that determine stock prices. Understanding the current and future state of the economy is the first step in understanding what is happening and what is likely to happen to the market.

Based on a knowledge of the economy–market relationship, the market can be valued using the procedures discussed in Chapter 9. In effect, valuation concepts can be applied to the market as well as to individual securities. The final issue we consider in this chapter is the process involved in forecasting the market. Although investors cannot expect to be consistently correct in doing this, they can expect to make some intelligent inferences about major trends in the market. Because of the market's impact on investor success, investors should at least attempt some basic forecast of the market's likely direction over some future period.

What Is the "Market"?

How often have you heard someone ask, "How did the market do today?" or, "How did the market react to that announcement?" Virtually everyone investing in stocks wants a general idea of how the overall market for equity securities is performing, both to guide their actions and to act as a benchmark against which to judge the performance of their securities. Furthermore, several specific uses of market indicators can be identified, as discussed in the next section.

Uses of Market Indicators

Market indicators are needed to tell investors how all stocks in general are doing at any time or to give them a "feel" for the market. Many investors are encouraged to invest if stocks are moving upward, whereas downward trends may encourage some to liquidate their holdings and invest in money market assets or funds.

Historical records of market averages are useful for gauging where the market is in a particular cycle and possibly for shedding light on what will happen. Assume, for example, that the market has never fallen more than $x\%$, as measured by some index, in a six-month period. Although this is no guarantee that such a decline will not occur, this type of knowledge aids investors in evaluating their potential downside risk over some period of time.

Market averages and indices are useful to investors in quickly judging their overall portfolio performance. Because stocks tend to move up or down together, the rising or falling of the market will indicate to the investor in a general way how he or she is likely to do. Of course, to determine the exact performance, each investor's portfolio must be measured individually, a topic to be discussed in Chapter 22.

Technical analysts need to know the historical record of the market in seeking out patterns from the past that may repeat in the future. Detection of such patterns is the basis for forecasting the future direction of the market using technical analysis, considered in Chapter 13.

Market averages and indices are also used to calculate betas, an important measure of risk discussed in Chapters 5 and 8. An individual security's returns are regressed on the market's returns in order to estimate the security's beta, or relative measure of systematic risk.

Because the "market" is simply the aggregate of all security prices, it is most conveniently measured by some index or average of stock prices. Investors, therefore, need to know about the various market indicators.

Stock Market Indicators

Several issues must be dealt with in the construction of a stock market index or indicator. The most important involve the composition of the index, the weighting procedure used, and the method of calculation.

What is the composition of the index? Is a subsample of one exchange to be used, or a subsample from the major exchanges? Furthermore, should a subsample from the over-the-counter (OTC) market be included? Alternatively, should every stock on an exchange, or exchanges, be used, and if so, how should OTC stocks be handled (e.g., every active OTC stock or every OTC stock for which daily quotes are available)?

If investors need a broad measure of stock performance, several markets (NYSE, Amex, and OTC) need to be included. If investors want to know the performance of the "largest" stocks, a measure of NYSE performance may be sufficient. Some market indicators use subsamples of one or more markets, whereas others use every stock on one or more markets. It is important to be aware of compositional differences among the various market indicators.

A second issue involves the weighting procedure used in constructing the index. Does each stock receive equal weight, or is each weighted by its market value (i.e., market price multiplied by shares outstanding). Alternatively, the indicator could be price weighted, resulting in higher-priced stocks carrying more weight than lower-priced stocks.

The third issue is the calculation procedures used. The primary question here is whether an index or an average is being used.

A **market average** is an arithmetic average of the prices for the sample of securities being used. It shows the arithmetic mean behavior of the prices at a given time. A **market index,** on the other hand, measures the current price behavior of the sample in relation to a base period established for a previous time. Indices, therefore, are expressed in relative numbers, whereas averages are simply arithmetic means (weighted or unweighted). The use of an index allows for more meaningful comparisons over long periods of time because current values can be related to established base period values.

The Dow-Jones Averages are arithmetic averages, but virtually all the other market measures are indices.

The Dow Jones Averages

The best-known average in the United States is the **Dow Jones Industrial Average (DJIA),** probably because it is carried by *The Wall Street Journal.*[1] It is the oldest market indicator, originating in 1896 and modified over the years.[2] The DJIA is computed from 30 leading industrial stocks whose composition changes slowly over time to reflect changes in the economy. This average is said to be composed of **blue chip stocks,** meaning large, well-established, and well-known companies.

In principle, calculation of the DJIA involves adding up the prices of the 30 stocks in the index and dividing by 30 to obtain the average. This is not done because of stock splits and dividends. Instead, the divisor is adjusted to reflect the stock splits and dividends that have occurred. The divisor has decreased over time and today is less than 1.0. As a result, a one-point change in the DJIA does not represent a change of $1.00 in the value of an average share; rather, the change amounts to only a few cents.

---

[1]There are three other Dow Jones averages: the transportation, the public utility, and the composite. The first two encompass 20 and 15 stocks, respectively, and the composite consists of these two groups plus the DJIA (i.e., 65 stocks). Each average is calculated similarly to the DJIA, with changes made in the divisor to adjust for splits and other factors. Daily information on these averages can be found in *The Wall Street Journal* and other newspapers.

[2]The first average of U.S. stocks appeared in 1884 and consisted of 11 stocks, mostly railroads. See H. L. Butler and R. F. DeMong, "The Changing Dow Jones Industrial Average," *Financial Analysts Journal*, July–August 1986, pp. 59–62.

You should keep this in mind the next time someone gets excited about a 10- or 20-point rise in one day in the DJIA.

The DJIA is calculated as:

$$DJIA_t = \Sigma P_{it}/n^* \tag{10-1}$$

where P is the price of a stock i at time t and n^* indicates an adjusted divisor.

It is important to note that the DJIA is a price-weighted series. Although it gives equal weight to equal *dollar* changes, high-priced stocks carry more weight than low-priced stocks. A 1% change in the price of stock A at $200 will have a much different impact on the DJIA from that of a 1% change in stock B at $20. This also means that as high-priced stocks split and their prices decline, they lose relative importance in the calculation of the average, whereas nonsplit stocks increase in relative importance. This bias against growth stocks, which are the most likely stocks to split, can result in a downward bias in the DJIA.

The DJIA has been criticized because of its use of only 30 stocks, because it is priced weighted (rather than value weighted), and because the divisor is not adjusted for stock dividends of less than 10%. Nevertheless, it is the oldest continuous indicator of the stock market, and it remains *the* prominent index for many investors. The DJIA does fulfill its role as a "blue chip" indicator and, as we shall see, fluctuations in the Dow are similar to fluctuations in other market indicators based primarily on NYSE stocks. Proposals have been made to make it more representative.[3]

Standard & Poor's Stock Price Indexes

Standard & Poor's Corporation, which publishes financial data for investors, also publishes five market indices, including a 400-stock Industrial Average, a 40-stock Utility Average, a 20-stock Transportation Average, a 40-stock Financial Average, and finally, all of these combined into a 500-stock Composite Index.[4] The latter is carried in the popular press and is often referred to by investors as a "good" indicator of what the market is doing.

Unlike the Dow Jones Industrial Average, the **S&P 500 Composite Index (S&P 500)** is a market value index. It is expressed in relative numbers with a base period set to 10 (1941–1943). To calculate the index, the market value of all firms is calculated (current market price times number of shares) and this total value is divided by the market value of the 500

[3]For an article on improving the Dow Jones Industrial Average, see Butler and DeMong, "The Changing Dow Jones Average."

[4]Standard & Poor's also publishes indices for various groupings of stocks, covering specific industries, low-priced stocks, high-grade stocks, and so on.

securities for the base period. This relative value is multiplied by 10, representing the base period.[5] In equation form, the S&P 500 is calculated as

$$\text{S\&P}_{500} = \frac{\Sigma P_{it}Q_{it}}{\Sigma P_{ib}Q_{ib}}\,(k) \tag{10-2}$$

where

P = the price of a stock i at time t
Q = number of shares of stock i at time t
b = the base period
k = is the base number

Example. A current value of 200 for the S&P 500 would indicate that the average price of the 500 stocks in the index has increased by a factor of 20 in relation to the base period. ▪

The S&P 500 is obviously a much broader measure than the Dow, and should be more representative of the general market. However, it consists primarily of NYSE stocks, and it is clearly dominated by the largest corporations.[6] All stock splits and dividends are automatically accounted for in calculating the value of the index because the number of shares currently outstanding (i.e., after the split or dividend) and the new price are used in the calculation. Unlike the Dow Jones averages, each stock's importance is based on relative total market value instead of relative per-share price.

Example. IBM has a market value that is more than 10 times as great as that of Apple Computer; therefore, a 1% change in IBM's price has more than 10 times the impact of a 1% change in Apple's price. ▪

Despite the well-known methodology for calculating the S&P 500 Index, different values are reported for this index, as shown in Table 10-1. As these figures indicate, the S&P's performance in 1988 varied by more than half a percentage point, depending on the firm doing the calculations. The reasons for the variations lie in such factors as when the dividends included in the total return calculation are considered to be received—on the declaration date or the payment date.[7]

Does such a difference matter? Yes! in the world of professional money management, managers often are compensated on the basis of how well they perform relative to the S&P 500. Since success is often measured in hundredths of a percentage point, differences such as those in Table 10-1

[5]Before multiplying by 10, the S&P 500 at any point in time can be thought of as the price, in relation to the beginning price of $1, of all stocks in the index weighted by their proportionate total market values.

[6]The S&P 500 contains some bank and insurance company stocks traded in the OTC market.

[7]The information in this discussion is based on James A. White, "Will the Real S&P 500 Please Stand Up?" *The Wall Street Journal*, January 26, 1989, p. C1.

TABLE 10-1 ***S&P 500 returns as calculated by different sources (from company reports)***

Firm	S&P 500 Estimates 1988	1987	1986
Indata	16.30	5.10	18.50
Salomon Brothers	16.34	5.60	18.50
Frank Russell	16.50	5.16	18.23
CDA Investment	16.50	5.20	18.60
Lipper Analytical	16.55	5.25	18.71
SEI Corp.	16.60	5.25	18.67
Standard & Poor's Corp.	**16.61**	**5.10**	**18.50**
Mellon Bank	16.64	5.11	18.28
American National Bank	16.81	5.23	18.47
Wilshire Associates	16.83	5.23	18.55
Bankers Trust	16.84	5.13	18.66

Source: James A. White, "Will the Real S&P 500 Please Stand Up?" *The Wall Street Journal*, January 26, 1989, p. C1. Reprinted by permission of *The Wall Street Journal*, © 1990 Dow Jones & Company, Inc. All Rights Reserved Worldwide.

are significant. Which is the correct figure? No one knows for certain, because Standard & Poor's has been unable to establish its figure as the official one after not paying attention to the issue for many years.

New York Stock Exchange Index

The *NYSE Composite Index* is broader still, covering all stocks listed on the NYSE. It is similar to the S&P indexes in that it is a total-market-value-weighted index. The base index value is 50 (as of year-end 1965).[8]

The NYSE Composite Index, although comparable to the S&P indexes, is a true reflection of what is happening on the NYSE, because it covers all stocks listed.[9] Thus, an investor who purchases a variety of NYSE stocks may find this index to be a better reflection of average performance against which to measure the performance of his or her securities.

American Stock Exchange Index

The American Stock Exchange introduced a new index in 1973, replacing the previous index based on price changes. The base period, August 31, 1973, was assigned an index number of 100. This index is similar to the S&P

[8]Subindexes are available and include Industrial, Utility, Transportation, and Financial.

[9]This is the only available index limited only to the NYSE but covering all the stocks on it.

and NYSE indices in that it is based on market values. All common stocks, warrants, and American Depository Receipts (ADRs) listed on the Amex are covered in this index. ADRs (discussed in Chapter 20) are tradable receipts for the shares of foreign corporations, with the actual shares remaining in the country of origin.

NASDAQ Indexes

The National Association of Security Dealers produces 11 indexes in total. Seven basic NASDAQ indexes cover industrials, banks, insurance, other finance, transportation, utilities, and all companies together in a Composite Index. These indices are similar to the S&P and NYSE indexes. The base period January 1971 is assigned a value of 100 for the Composite Index and the Industrial Index.

In addition to these, the NASDAQ/NMS Industrial Index and the NASDAQ/NMS Composite Index were begun on July 10, 1984, with an initial value for each of 100. The NASDAQ-100 and NASDAQ–Financial were begun in February 1, 1985, with an initial value of 250. Each consists of the 100 largest market-capitalized firms in their respective categories.

The Media General Composite Market Value Index

The Media General Financial Weekly publishes the Media General (M/G) Composite Index, which covers all NYSE and Amex stocks as well as over 800 OTC stocks. It is a market-value-based index that uses January 2, 1970, as its base. This index is very broad, second only to the Wilshire Index (discussed next), and is available weekly in *The Media General Financial Weekly,* which provides detailed information on market measures and market activity.[10]

The Wilshire Index

The broadest of all indicators is the *Wilshire Index,* representing the dollar market value of all NYSE and Amex stocks plus all actively traded OTC stocks. In effect, it is the total price for stocks for which daily quotations can be obtained.[11] It is quoted in billions of dollars, with a base of $1.404 billion set to December 31, 1980.

The Wilshire Index is reported daily in *The Wall Street Journal* and is graphed in each *Forbes* issue.

---

[10]*The Media General Financial Weekly* also carries the DJIA (monthly high and low) on an inflation-adjusted basis.

[11]This index typically is referred to as the Wilshire 5000. Since it currently contains some 6000 stocks, *Forbes* is now referring to it as the Wilshire Index. More than 80% of the stocks covered are NYSE stocks, with about 15% OTC.

Value Line Index

The Value Line Investment Survey, discussed in Chapter 4, publishes several indices, including the *Value Line Composite Index.* Value Line is unique in that it publishes an equally weighted geometric average of stock prices. This average is based on the roughly 1700 companies in the 90+ industries that Value Line chooses to cover in its reports.[12] June 1961 is assigned the base index of 100.

Since the Value Line company is a well-known investment advisory service, its indices receive attention. Investors, however, should be aware of how these unique indices differ from the others. All stocks are equally weighted. Since a daily net percentage change in price is computed for the stocks, each stock in the index has the same percentage weight.[13] Therefore, a 20% movement in a stock's price has the same impact on the index, whether 10 million or 100 million shares are outstanding. Neither a stock's market value nor its price level will impact the index. The small, low-priced stocks covered by Value Line will have the same impact as the larger stocks. In effect, the Value Line Composite is an unweighted index covering a broad cross section of stocks. Some market observers feel that because it is unweighted, it is more reflective of general market trends.

In March 1988, Value Line introduced a new index, the *Value Line Arithmetic Index (VLA).* The *change* in this arithmetically averaged index is the sum of the price *changes* for all stocks in the index divided by the number of stocks. Value Line sees this index as a good estimate of the price performance of an equal dollar portfolio of stocks, whereas changes in the geometric index provide a good estimate of the *median* price changes of the stocks covered.

Relationships Between Market Averages

As the previous discussion indicates, there are numerous measures of the "market," ranging from the DJIA to the Wilshire Index. It is obvious that the overall market can be, and is, measured in several different ways.

The following observations about the various market indexes can be made:

1. Although the DJIA contains only 30 stocks and has often been criticized because of this and the manner in which the average is computed, it

---

[12]Specifically, Value Line publishes an Industrial, Rail, Utility, and Composite Index. More than 80% of these stocks are listed on the NYSE.

[13]To compute the VL Index, the closing price of each stock for a given day is divided by the preceding day's close (which is set at an index of 100). The geometric average of these indexes of change is calculated by finding the nth root of the product of the n changes (where n is approximately 1700). Finally, the geometric average of change for the day is multiplied by the preceeding value of the average to obtain the new value.

parallels the movements of the broader market-value-weighted index *involving NYSE stocks*—specifically, the NYSE and S&P 500 indexes. The correlation between the price changes for the three indexes (S&P, NYSE, and DJIA) has been very high, on the order of .90; however, this does not mean that the DJIA will show similar percentage changes over all intervals of time, particularly smaller intervals.

2. The S&P 500 and the NYSE Composite Index are virtually identical in their patterns. The S&P 500 stocks are contained within the NYSE Composite Index and account for most of its total market value.[14]
3. The greatest divergence in market indexes occurs when comparisons are made between those indexes that involve only NYSE stocks and those that cover other exchanges or NYSE stocks plus stocks from other exchanges. The Amex Index and/or the NASDAQ Composite can perform quite differently in certain years relative to indexes such as the S&P 500.

In addition to the long-term movements in market measures, investors may wish to consider short-term movements. In this case, dramatic differences can, and do, occur between the various market measures. Table 10-2 shows the percentage change for five of the market measures previously discussed for four- and 52-week periods as of August 16, 1982, and August 15, 1983—one year apart.

Table 10-2 indicates that for the four weeks preceding August 16, 1982, all five market measures were up, with the DJIA doubling the broader market measures. On the other hand, for the preceding four weeks one year later, four market indicators were down and the Amex was up; furthermore, the DJIA declined less than the other three.

Table 10-2 also indicates the substantial differences that can occur in market indicators over a period of one year. For the year preceding August 1982, the Amex was down twice as much as the other market measures, with the DJIA showing the smallest (but still substantial) decline. For the year preceding August 1983, all market indicators reflect the great bull market for that period, but the Amex gain was almost twice that of the DJIA. Notice how well Amex and NASDAQ stocks performed, with the Wilshire Index performance in between that of the NYSE-based measures and the measures covering non-NYSE stocks.

Why Is Market Analysis Important?

Now that we know what the "market" is, we can consider again the importance of market analysis. The aggregate market remains the largest single

[14]The importance of this can be realized by noting that the 50 biggest companies in the S&P 500 Index account for more than 50% of its weighting.

TABLE 10-2 ***Four- and 52-Week Percentage Changes in Five Measures of the Stock Market as of Mid-August 1982 and 1983***

	Wilshire 5000	DJIA	NYSE Composite	Amex	NASDAQ Composite
August 16, 1982					
Last 4 weeks	1.6	3.4	1.7	1.7	1.0
Last 52 weeks	−16.3	−11.3	−14.5	−30.0	−17.3
August 15, 1983					
Last 4 weeks	−1.2	−0.8	−1.1	0.5	−2.5
Last 52 weeks	57.9	48.2	53.2	92.8	86.3

Source: Forbes, August 16, 1982, p. 83, and August 15, 1983, p. 107. Reprinted by permission.

factor explaining fluctuations in both individual stock prices and portfolios of stocks.

To appreciate the importance of the market's impact on individual stock prices, Table 10-3 shows "stock performance relative to market" for the Dow Jones Industrial 30 stocks. This information is from a *Forbes* analysis of 778 stocks and is based on the latest 12 months of performance as of March 23, 1989. The first column shows the percentage price change over the period; the second column shows the percentage price change relative to the market (a score of 100 means a stock tied the market for this period).[15]

Table 10-3 indicates that for the 12-month period analyzed, most of the 30 Dow Jones Industrials performed very close to the market. Boeing was a clear exception on the high side, and Goodyear was a clear exception on the low side. Although a few other stocks performed differently from the market, the market's impact on many of the stocks is obvious, as shown by Allied Signal, Alcoa, American Telephone, Bethlehem Steel, Chevron, Eastman Kodak, Exxon, General Electric, McDonalds, Minnesota Mining, Proctor & Gamble, Sears, Texaco, United Technologies, Westinghouse, and Woolworth (all within the range of 94–106). It is clear from Table 10-3 that the market has a major impact on the price performance of individual stocks.

Of even greater importance is the market's effect on a diversified portfolio. As shown in Chapter 19, the basic tenet of portfolio theory is to diversify into a number of securities (properly chosen). For adequately diversified portfolios, market effects account for 90% and more of the variability in the portfolio's return. In other words, for a well-diversified portfolio, which each investor should hold, the market is the dominant factor affecting the variability of its return.

[15] *Forbes* measured the market using the *Investor's Daily* index supplied by William O'Neil & Company.

TABLE 10-3 ***Percentage Price Change and Performance Relative to the Market for a 12-Month Period for the 30 Stocks in the DJIA***

	% Price Change	Relative Price Performance
Allied Slg	1	94
Alcoa	0	93
Amer Exp	19	111
Amer T & T	14	105
Beth Steel	10	102
Boeing	40	130
Chevron	14	106
Coca Cola	29	120
DuPont	21	112
East Kod	9	101
Exxon	4	97
Gen Elec	5	97
Gen Motors	17	108
Goodyear	−28	67
IBM	0	92
Int Paper	6	98
McDonalds	10	102
Merck	17	108
Minn M & M	12	104
Navistar	−13	81
Phil Morr	26	116
Primerica	−22	72
Proct & Gm	15	106
Sears	14	106
Texaco	15	106
USX	0	92
Union Carb	29	115
United Tch	6	98
Westnghs	5	98
Woolworth	4	96

Source: "The Forbes 500 on Wall Street," *Forbes,* May 1, 1989, pp. 294–341. Excerpted by permission of *Forbes* magazine, May 1, 1989, © Forbes, Inc., 1989.

INVESTMENTS INTUITION

In the final analysis, most investors are heavily influenced and affected by the market. If it goes up strongly, as it did in the latter part of 1982 and again in 1985 and 1986, most investors make money. If it goes down sharply, as in 1974 and October 1987, most investors lose money. It is quite difficult to go against the market successfully.

Table 10-2 dramatically shows the importance of market analysis for one-year periods, which can be generalized to other time periods. Over the period from mid-August 1981 through mid-August 1982, most investors lost money, because all the markets were down substantially. On the other hand, the corresponding period one year later was one of the record high periods in modern stock history. Virtually all investors gained during this period, whether they held NYSE stocks or other stocks, whether they were conservative or aggressive, and whether they knew anything at all about valuing stocks or were simply astute enough to invest in August 1982 because they correctly discerned the future trend of the market.

Judging the Level of the Market

Judgments by investors about the overall market, based on the level of one of the market indicators discussed earlier, should be put into perspective. For example, is the market "too high" if the Dow is at 2500 at a particular point in time? Or at 3000? An investor cannot answer this question by looking only at the level of the market!

Understanding the Stock Market

Now that we know what the "market" is and why market analysis is important, we can begin to understand, value, and forecast the market. This section is concerned with understanding the market.

What determines stock prices? In Chapter 9, we established the two determinants of stock prices—the expected benefits stream (earnings or dividends) and the required rate of return (or its counterpart, the P/E ratio). Although these are the ultimate determinants of stock prices, a more complete model is desirable when attempting to understand the stock market. Such a model is shown in Figure 10-1, which is a flow diagram of stock price determination described by Keran several years ago. It shows clearly the variables that interact together to determine stock prices.[16]

Figure 10-1 shows four exogenous (independent) variables that ultimately affect stock prices: the potential output of the economy (Y^*), which is a nonpolicy variable, and three policy variables (i.e., variables subject to government policy decisions)—the corporate tax rate (t_x), changes in government spending or fiscal policy (G), and changes in nominal money (M). All variables to the right of the gray area are determined within the economy (and are called endogenous variables).

The two primary exogenous policy variables, G and M, affect stock prices through two channels.

---

[16]See Michael W. Keran, "Expectations, Money, and the Stock Market," *Review*, Federal Reserve Bank of St. Louis, Vol. 53, No. 1 (January 1971), pp. 16–31.

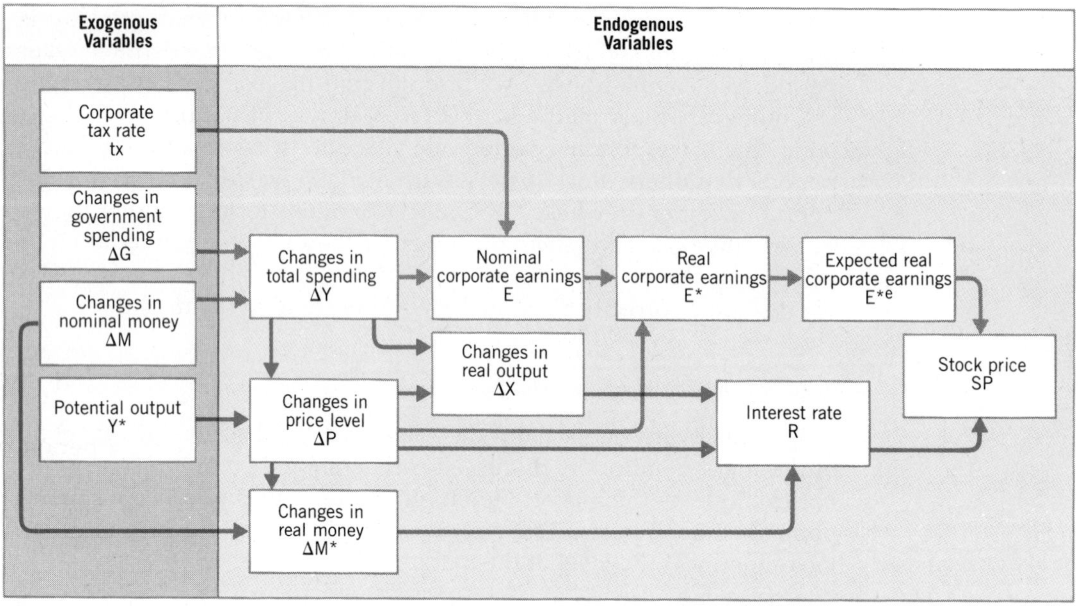

FIGURE 10-1 ***A flow diagram of stock price determination.***
Source: Michael W. Keran, "Expectations, Money, and the Stock Market," *Review,* Federal Reserve Bank of St. Louis, January 1971, p. 27.

1. They affect total spending (Y), which, together with the tax rate (t_x), affects corporate earnings.[17] Expected changes in (real) corporate earnings (E^*) are *positively* related to changes in stock prices (SP).
2. They affect total spending, which together with the economy's potential output (Y^*) and past changes in prices, determine current changes in prices (P). Y and P determine current changes in real output (X). Changes in X and P generate expectations about inflation and real growth, which in turn influence the current interest rate (R). Interest rates have a *negative* influence on stock prices (SP).

Although alternative flow diagrams of the type shown in Figure 10-1 could be constructed, this model is entirely reasonable and logical as a description of stock price determination. It indicates the following major factors that determine stock prices. Three active policy variables—fiscal policy (government spending), monetary policy (money supply), and the corporate tax rate—plus potential output affect three changes. These changes—total spending, price level, and real money—ultimately affect corporate earnings and interest rates, which, in turn, determine stock prices.

[17]Technically, both the current level and lagged changes in Y affect corporate earnings.

Corporate Earnings, Interest Rates, and Stock Prices

As shown in the Keran model in Figure 10-1, the ultimate determinants of stock prices are expected corporate earnings and interest rates (which serves as a proxy for investors' required rate of return). Therefore, it is important to consider in more detail the relationships among these variables over time.

It is logical to expect a close relationship between corporate profits and stock prices. The discussion of fundamental analysis in Chapter 9 showed that price, or value, for one stock or the market as a whole should be a function of the expected stream of benefits to be received (cash flows) and the required rate of return demanded by investors. Therefore, if the economy is prospering, investors would expect corporate earnings and dividends to rise and, other things equal, stock prices to rise.

Figure 10-2 shows corporate profits after taxes over a long period of time on both a current and inflation-adjusted basis. Notice how corporate profits declined in 1970, 1974, 1980, and 1982. The years 1969, 1973, and 1981 had negative total returns for the S&P 500 index (see Table 10-4). The stock market presumably was looking ahead in these three cases and discounting the expected decline in corporate earnings. On a broader basis,

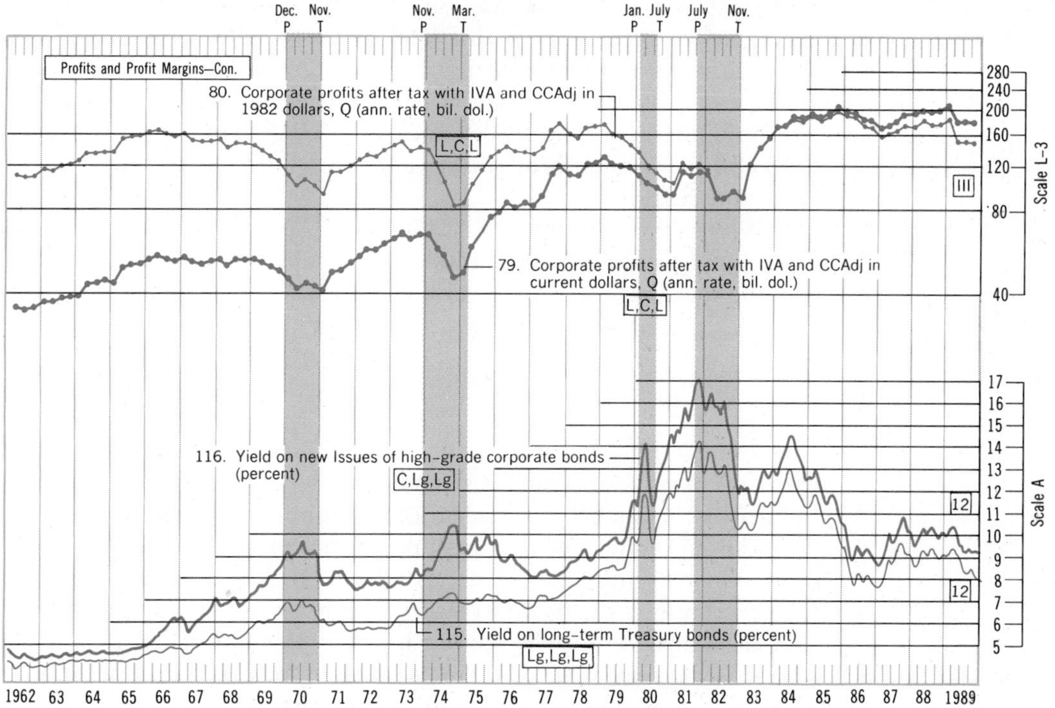

FIGURE 10-2 ***Stock prices, corporate earnings, and yields on long-term bonds.*** *Source: Business Conditions Digest*, December 1989, pp. 29 and 34.

the general trend for the 1980s for corporate profits was clearly upward, and the 1980s represents one of the great decades in the performance of stocks.

In analyzing data such as Figure 10-2, remember that two factors determine the price or value of the market (or a single stock)—earnings (or dividends) and a risk factor (discount rate). Other things often are not equal—earnings may rise, but the discount rate may also rise, and if strong enough can cause a decline in stock prices. Or, as in late 1982, stock prices may rise sharply while corporate profits decline significantly.

Interest rates, the other final component in the determination of stock prices as shown in Figure 10-1, are a basic component of discount rates, with the two usually moving together. It is necessary, therefore, to consider the relationship between interest rates and stock prices.

Figure 10-2 also shows interest rates for long-term corporates and Treasuries. There is clearly a relationship between interest rate movements and stock prices, just as there is with GNP and corporate profits, but in this case the relationship is inverse—as interest rates rise (fall), stock prices fall (rise), other things being equal.

To understand the relationship between stock prices and interest rates, consider the following relationship. Notice in Figure 10-2 that interest rates rose in 1974, whereas the opposite occurred in 1980. The year 1974 was a bad one for stock prices, with a total return of −26%, whereas 1980 was a good year, with a total return of 31%. Also notice the dramatic decline in interest rates in the latter half of 1982, which marked the beginning of the great bull market of the 1980s. Note the decline in interest rates starting in 1984 and continuing through 1985 and 1986. Stocks performed well during this same period.

Why is there an inverse relationship? Recall from Chapter 9 that the basic fundamental valuation model is given by the following equation (assuming the constant growth version of the dividend discount model):

$$V_0 = \frac{D_1}{k - g} \tag{10-3}$$

The k in Equation 10-3 is the required rate of return (discount rate) to be used by investors in discounting future cash flows. It is the rate of return that investors demand in order to invest in common stocks. This rate can be thought of as the sum of a riskless rate of return plus a risk premium determined by the riskiness of the stock being valued. Most observers use the rate on Treasury securities as a proxy for the riskless rate of return, because Treasuries have no practical risk of default. Therefore, the discount rate k is intimately tied to interest rates, and that is why the Keran model (or any other model) can use interest rates in discussing stock price determination.

INVESTMENTS INTUITION

If interest rates rise, the riskless rate rises because it is tied to interest rates, and, other things equal, the required rate of return (discount rate) rises because the riskless rate is one of its two components.

Valuing the Market

To value the market using the fundamental analysis approach explained in Chapter 9, determinants of the market, as previously explained, are used—specifically, the expected stream of benefits and the rate of return required by investors (or, alternatively, a multiplier or P/E ratio). The following estimates are needed:

1. The stream of benefits—earnings or dividends.
2. The required rate of return or the earnings multiplier.

These estimates are used in Equations 10-3 and 10-5, which were explained in Chapter 9:

$$V_0 = \frac{D_1}{k - g} \tag{10-3}$$

$$P_0/E_1 = \frac{D_1/E_1}{k - g} \tag{10-4}$$

$$P_0 = P_0/E_1 \times E_1 \tag{10-5}$$

where

D_1 = expected dividends
E_1 = expected earnings
k = discount rate or required rate of return
g = expected rate in dividends or earnings

These equations apply equally to the aggregate market or an individual stock. Here we are concerned with an aggregate market index such as the S&P 500 Composite Index. Conceptually, the value of this index is the discounted value of all future cash flows to be paid (i.e., the index value of dividends). Alternatively, it is the estimated earnings on the S&P 500 Index multiplied by the estimated P/E ratio, or multiplier. In summary,

$$\text{Value of S\&P 500 today} = \frac{\text{Dividends to be paid on index next period}}{\text{Required rate of return} - \text{Expected growth rate in dividends}}$$

or

Value of S&P 500 = estimated earnings on the index × estimated P/E ratio

We shall focus our discussion on the multiplier approach.

The Earnings Stream

Estimating earnings for a market index for a future period is not easy. Several steps are involved.

The item of interest is the earnings per share for a market index or, in general, corporate profits after taxes. The latter variable is related to GNP, the broadest measure of economic activity. Corporate earnings after taxes are derived from corporate sales, which in turn are related to GNP.

A detailed, complete fundamental analysis would involve estimating each of these variables, starting with GNP, then corporate sales, working down to corporate earnings before taxes, and finally to corporate earnings after taxes. Each of these steps can involve various levels of difficulty, as the following points suggest.

1. To move from GNP to corporate sales, it may be possible to use a regression equation with percentage change in GNP as the independent variable and percentage change in corporate sales as the dependent variable. Based on this regression equation, a prediction could be made of sales given a forecast of change in GNP.
2. To obtain corporate earnings after tax, it is necessary to estimate a net profit margin, which is a volatile series. An alternative is to estimate a gross profit margin by considering those factors that affect the gross margin, including unit labor costs, the utilization rate of plant and equipment, and the inflation rate. After obtaining an estimate of the gross profit margin, multiplying by the sales (per share) estimate would provide an estimate of earnings before depreciation and taxes. Both of these factors would have to be estimated and deducted to obtain an estimate of expected earnings (per share) for the coming year.

Figure 10-2 showed corporate earnings over a long period of time. The volatility and trends in corporate earnings are obvious from the figure.

For a per-share perspective of earnings for the market, consider Table 10-4, which shows prices, earnings, and other selected variables for the S&P 500 Index for almost a 30-year period. Note that the earnings for the S&P 500 have trended up over this long period, but with definite dips and setbacks. The percentage changes from year to year can be quite sharp.

The Multiplier

The multiplier to be applied to the earnings estimate is as important as the earnings estimate. Investors sometimes mistakenly ignore the multiplier and concentrate only on the earnings estimate. The multiplier is more volatile than the earnings component and, therefore, even more difficult to predict. Consider Table 10-4 again, which also shows the P/E ratio for the Standard & Poor's 500 Index over the same period as that for the earnings discussed earlier.

The P/E ratio for the market was low in the postwar period, perhaps

TABLE 10-4 ***Prices, Earnings, Dividends, and Several Calculated Variables for the Standard & Poor's 500 Index, 1960–1989***[a]

				Based on Year-End Prices			
	End-of-Year Prices	Earnings	Dividends	TR (%)[b]	P/E[c]	Dividend Yield (D/P)100(%)	Dividend Payout
1960	58.11	3.27	1.95	0.28	17.77	3.36	59.63
1961	71.55	3.19	2.02	26.60	22.43	2.82	63.32
1962	63.10	3.67	2.13	−8.83	17.19	3.38	58.04
1963	75.02	4.02	2.28	22.50	18.66	3.04	56.72
1964	84.75	4.55	2.50	16.30	18.63	2.95	54.95
1965	92.43	5.19	2.72	12.27	17.81	2.94	52.41
1966	80.33	5.55	2.87	−9.99	14.47	3.57	51.71
1967	96.47	5.33	2.92	23.73	18.10	3.03	54.78
1968	103.86	5.76	3.07	10.84	18.03	2.96	53.30
1969	92.06	5.78	3.16	−8.32	15.93	3.43	54.67
1970	92.15	5.13	3.14	3.51	17.96	3.41	61.21
1971	102.09	5.70	3.07	14.12	17.91	3.01	53.86
1972	118.05	6.42	3.15	18.72	18.39	2.67	49.07
1973	97.55	8.16	3.38	−14.50	11.95	3.46	41.42
1974	68.56	8.89	3.60	−26.03	7.71	5.25	40.49
1975	90.19	7.96	3.68	36.92	11.33	4.08	46.23
1976	107.46	9.91	4.05	23.64	10.84	3.77	40.87
1977	95.10	10.89	4.67	−7.16	8.73	4.91	42.88
1978	96.11	12.33	5.07	6.39	7.79	5.28	41.12
1979	107.94	14.76	5.70	18.24	7.31	5.28	38.62
1980	135.76	14.82	6.16	31.48	9.16	4.54	41.57
1981	122.55	15.36	6.63	−4.85	7.98	5.48	43.75
1982	140.64	12.64	6.87	20.37	11.13	4.88	54.35
1983	164.93	14.03	7.09	22.31	11.67	4.30	50.53
1984	167.24	16.64	8.81	5.97	10.05	4.50	45.25
1985	211.28	14.61	7.90	31.06	14.46	3.74	54.07
1986	242.17	14.48	8.28	18.54	16.72	3.13	57.18
1987	247.08	17.50	8.81	5.67	14.12	3.57	50.34
1988	277.72	23.76	9.73	16.34	11.68	3.50	40.95
1989	353.40	24.06	11.05	31.23	14.69	3.13	45.93p

Source: From Standard & Poor's Statistical Service; Security Price Index Record, 1980 ed., p. 134–137: Plus update issues of *Current Statistics* through 1989. Reprinted by permission.

[a]Values for recent years are subject to revision.

[b]TR = $100[P_t - P_{t-1} + D_t)/P_{t-1}]$.

[c]P/E is earnings during the calendar year divided by the end-of-year price; the dividend yield is calculated similarly. The dividend yield is defined differently from that reported in Standard & Poor's sources.

because investors were expecting record inflation resulting from stifled demand. As the economy progressed and the dire predictions did not materialize, the P/E ratio began to rise in the early 1950s, reaching 19 by 1958 and remaining around that level through 1972. Table 10-4 shows that as inflation heated up in 1973, the multiplier started to decline, and by 1974 it was less than half its previous level—a drastic cut for such a short time. Therefore, what was considered normal (about 17) in the 1960s and early 1970s was not the norm in the late 1970s and early 1980s. The lesson from this analysis is obvious: Investors cannot simply extrapolate P/E ratios, because dramatic changes occur over time. Perhaps the most that can be said is that in the postwar period, P/E ratios of broadly based indices have ranged from an average of about 7 to an average of about 17.

Putting the Two Together

It should be obvious by now that valuing the aggregate market is not easy. Nor will it ever be, because it involves estimates of the uncertain future. And if valuing the aggregate market were relatively easy, many investors would become wealthy by knowing when to buy and sell stocks.

As noted, it is difficult to analyze all the complicated details required to do fundamental market analysis. It involves studying utilization rates, tax rates, depreciation, GNP, and other factors, plus applying some sophisticated statistical techniques. It is instructive, however, to analyze some general results of our basic valuation techniques. Regardless of the difficulty in doing market analysis, and the extent to which an analyst or investor goes, the methodology just outlined is the basis on which to proceed.

As an example of *conceptually* valuing the market, consider the information in Table 10-4, keeping in mind that these are end-of-year values for the Standard & Poor's 500 Composite Index. *Be very careful to understand what will be done here.* We shall "value" the market in *hindsight,* based on ex post (and year-end) values. We shall interpret what did happen. To value the market in actuality, an investor must forecast the two components of value, earnings and P/E ratios. The reasoning process we shall use is applicable whenever and however one values the market.

Consider what happened to the market in 1974. Earnings on the S&P 500 Composite Index increased from year-end 1973 to 1974 ($8.16 to $8.89), but investors became pessimistic because of the energy crisis. The required rate of return demanded by investors rose, which had a negative impact on the P/E ratio (notice in Figure 10-2 that interest rates rose in 1974). Stock prices declined sharply, from 97.55 to 68.56, because the steep decline in the multiplier more than offset the increase in earnings for the year. The important point of this analysis is that an investor trying to value the market for the year ahead, at the beginning of 1974, had to estimate what was likely to happen to the earnings stream for the market and to the P/E ratio (or discount rate). Estimating the earnings is only half the story, and the less important half in many cases.

The years 1981 and 1982 offer a good contrast. Stock prices declined in 1981 and rose in 1982, whereas earnings rose in 1981 and declined in 1982. The multipliers must have been moving in the opposite direction (interest rates moved in opposite directions in those years—see Figure 10-2).

The year 1982 offers a good example for market valuation. A very strong bull market began in August of 1982, which was widely attributed to a decline in interest rates and to investor belief that this decline would continue. Interest rates are closely related to discount rates (required rates of return). With a decline in the discount rate, other things being equal, the multiplier rose and stock prices rose. Although earnings on the S&P declined for the year 1982, they rose sharply in 1983, and the stock market presumably was looking ahead.

The conclusion of this analysis is that to value the market, an investor must analyze both factors that determine value: earnings (or dividends) and multipliers (or required rates of return). More important, the investor must make some type of forecast of these variables in order to forecast the market.

Forecasting Changes in the Market

Most investors want to forecast changes in the market. They want not only to be aware of what the market is doing currently, and why, but also to know where it is likely to go in the future.

It is important to note that it is not reasonable to expect to forecast exact future market levels or precise changes in the market. This is impossible for anyone to do consistently. As will be shown in Chapter 14, there is strong evidence that the market is efficient, one implication of which is that changes in the market cannot be predicted on the basis of information about previous changes. Another implication is that even the professionals cannot *consistently* forecast the market using available information.

What we are seeking here are general clues as to the market's direction and the duration of a likely change. For example, to say that we are confident the market will go to 3000 or 1000 (as measured by the Dow Jones Industrial Average) one year from now is foolish.

This discussion is organized around two approaches. First, some of the techniques related to the economic variables that affect the business cycle and stock prices are used. The second approach involves the fundamental valuation model used in the discussion of market valuation.

Using Economic Variables to Forecast the Market

The Business Cycle The **business cycle** reflects movements in economic activity as a whole, which is comprised of many diverse parts. The diversity of the parts ensures that business cycles are virtually unique, with no two parts identical. However, cycles do have a common framework, with a beginning (a trough), a peak, and an ending (a trough). Thus, economic activity starts in depressed conditions, builds up in the expansionary phase, and ends in a downturn, only to start again (perhaps because of government stimulus).

The typical business cycle in the United States seems to consist of an expansion averaging about three and a half years and a contraction averaging about one year. Obviously, however, these are only averages and cannot be relied on exclusively to interpret current or future situations. The longest expansion on record, for example, covered 106 months from February 1961 through December 1969, and the March 1975 to January 1980 expansion lasted 58 months. Business cycles cannot be neatly categorized as to length and turning points at the time they are occurring. Only in hindsight can such nice distinctions be made.

To make use of business cycle data, an investor needs to monitor indicators of the economy. A good source of help in this regard is the National Bureau of Economic Research (NBER), a private nonprofit organization.

The NBER dates the business cycle when possible. The duration of the contraction and expansion is measured in addition to other pertinent data. In their examination process, the NBER attempts to identify those components of economic activity that move at different times from each other. Such variables can serve as indicators of the economy in general.

Current practice is to identify leading, coincident, and lagging **composite indexes of general economic activity.** This information can be found in *Business Conditions Digest*, including the median lead or lag for each series in relation to the business cycle and several characteristics of each series.

The NBER has focused on 12 leading indicators as representing the best combination of desirable characteristics, including stock prices and money supply. The 12 indicators taken as a composite have generally turned up three to four months before a recovery, and they have usually turned down eight to nine months before a recession begins.

The coincident and lagging indicators serve to confirm (or not) the indications of the leading series. If the leading index signal is not confirmed first by the coincident index and then by the lagging index, investors should reconsider the signal.[18]

Figure 10-3 shows these three composite indexes. The index of leading indicators moves roughly in line with stock prices.

We have now established that certain composite indices can be helpful in forecasting or ascertaining the position of the business cycle. However, stock prices are one of the leading indicators, tending to lead the economy's turning points, both peaks and troughs. What is the investor who is trying to forecast the market to do?

---

[18]The Bureau of Economic Analysis now publishes a "composite index of four roughly coincident indicators" to condense the information from the most important monthly indicators into a summary measure. See Keith M. Carlson, "Monthly Economic Indicators: A Closer Look at the Coincident Index," *Review*, Federal Reserve Bank of St. Louis, November 1985, pp. 20–30.

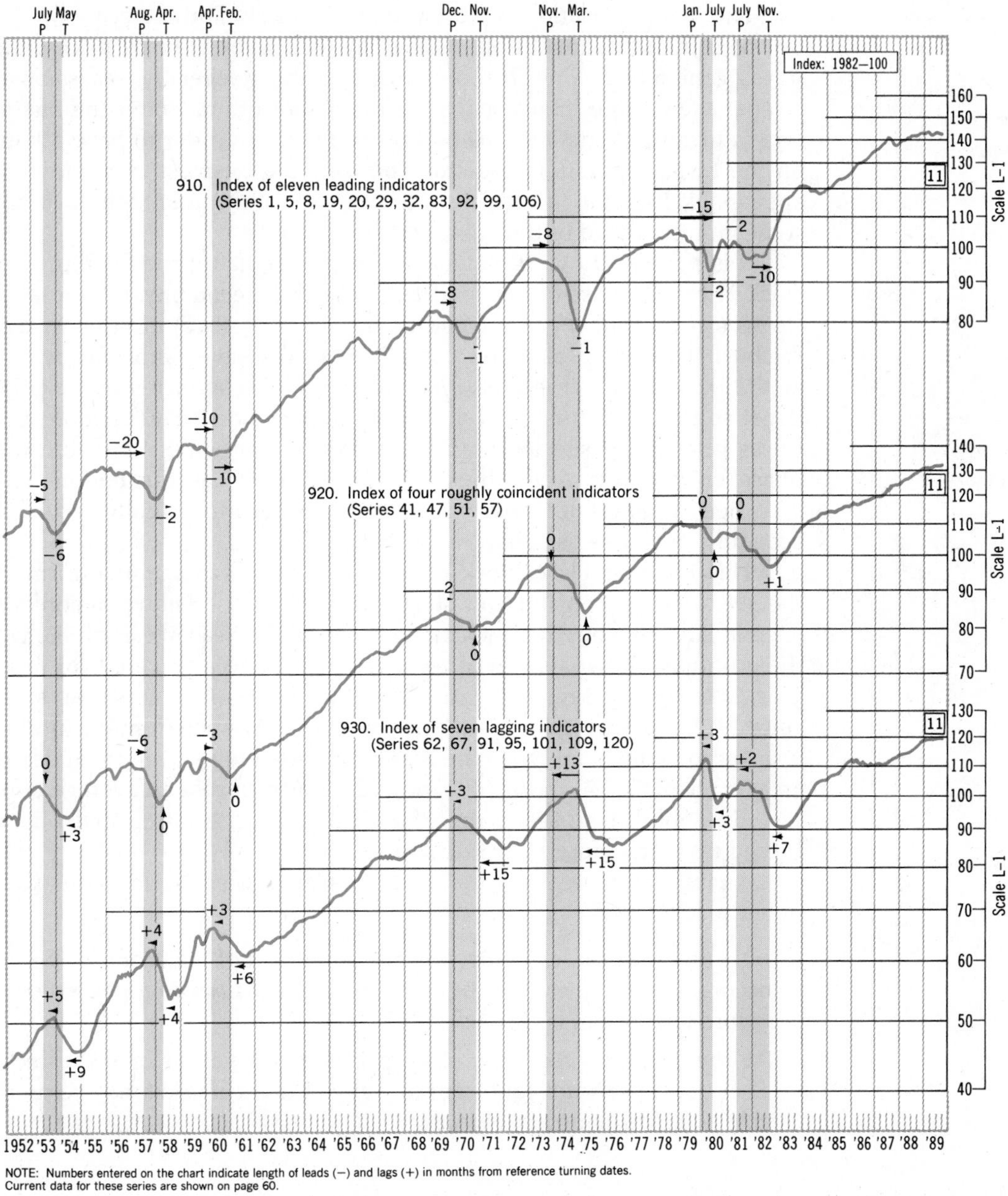

FIGURE 10-3 ***Composite indexes of leading, coincident, and lagging indicators.***
Source: Business Conditions Digest, December 1989, p. 10.

This leading relationship between stock prices and the economy must be taken into account in forecasting likely changes in stock prices. Stock prices generally decline in recessions, and the steeper the recession, the steeper the decline. However, investors need to think about the business cycle's turning points months before they occur in order to have a handle on the turning points in the stock market. If a business cycle downturn appears likely in the future, it is also likely that the market will turn down some months ahead of the economic downturn.

It is possible to be somewhat more precise about the leading role of stock prices. Because of this tendency to lead the economy, total return on stocks (on an annual basis) could be negative (positive) in years in which the business cycle peaks (bottoms). Stock prices have almost always risen as the business cycle is *approaching* a trough. These increases have been large, so that investors do well during these periods. Furthermore, stock prices often drop suddenly as the business cycle enters into the initial phase of recovery. After the previous sharp rise as the bottom is approached, a period of steady prices or even a decline typically occurs. The economy, of course, is still moving ahead.

This business cycle–stock price relationship was again confirmed in the 1982–1983 expansion and stock market boom.[19] The recession worsened in late 1982, but the stock market soared, whereas in early 1983, when the economy showed signs of recovery, stock prices wavered for a time. This action was consistent with the previous 10 major business slumps since 1929. Measuring the Dow Jones Industrial Average from the low point in a slump to the point when the economy started to recover, the index rose an average of 27.8%. In the following 12 months, it rose an average of only 17%. In only three cases of the 10 did the index rise faster after business turned up than before.

An investor forecasting the market using business cycle factors should note the following:

1. If the investor can recognize the bottoming out of the economy before it occurs, a market rise can be predicted, at least *based on past experience,* before the bottom is hit.
2. As the economy recovers, stock prices may level off or even decline. Therefore, a second significant movement in the market may be predictable, again *based on past experience.*

[19]This discussion is based on Alfred L. Malabre, Jr., "Perverse Stocks," *The Wall Street Journal,* February 2, 1983, p. 1.

INVESTMENTS INTUITION

Why is the market a forecaster of the economy? Basically, investors are discounting future earnings, because, as the valuation analysis in Chapter 9 showed, stocks are worth today the discounted value of all future cash flows. Current stock prices reflect investor expectations of the future. Stock prices adjust quickly if investor expectations of corporate profits change. Of course, the market can misjudge corporate profits, resulting in a false signal about future movements in the economy.

An alternative explanation for stock prices leading the economy involves an investor change in the required rate of return, which again would result in an immediate change in stock prices. Note that the valuation model allows for a change in confidence (psychological elements) because a change in investor confidence changes the required rate of return (in the opposite direction). Thus, our valuation model encompasses psychological elements, which are sometimes used in explaining market movements.

There is an interesting piece of information about P/E ratios and recessions.[20] Based on the last 10 economic slumps, the P/E ratio is higher at the end of the slump than at its low point in the slump. In other words, the market P/E usually rises just before the end of the slump. It then remains roughly unchanged over the next year.

Monetary Variables Because of its importance in the economy, monetary policy is assumed to have an important effect on stock prices. Thus, to understand stock prices, investors must understand monetary variables, and to forecast the market, investors must take into account likely changes in the money supply.

The supposed relationship between changes in the money supply and changes in stock prices is direct, with the former leading the latter.[21] Several studies have examined this relationship. Most of the earlier studies found that a relationship does exist and that money leads stock prices.[22] However, later evidence suggests that the market anticipates the changes

[20]See Malabre, "Perverse Stocks."

[21]This relationship was first hypothesized by Beryl Sprinkel, *Money and Stock Prices* (Homewood, Ill.: Irwin Publishing, 1964).

[22]See, for example, Kenneth Homa and Dwight Jaffe, "The Supply of Money and Common Stock Prices," *The Journal of Finance,* December 1971; and Michael Hamburger and Lewis Kochin, "Money and Stock Prices: The Channels of Influence," *The Journal of Finance,* May 1972.

in monetary growth, so that investors cannot use past changes in money supply as a means of outperforming the market. For example, Rozeff found that stock market movements were related to money supply movements, both current and future, indicating that the market has the lead role.[23] This is another indication of market efficiency, an issue considered in Chapter 14. One study found that excess money growth causes a negative reaction in stock prices at the time of announcement only. This effect was the result of the "unexpected" portion of the money growth rate. Causality tests supported "causality" only from stock returns to money growth.[24]

Interest Rates Stock prices are clearly related to changes in interest rates, as established earlier. The implications of this relationship are clear. If interest rates are expected to decline, stock prices will be expected to rise. An excellent example of this can be found in 1982, when interest rates were at record highs and finally began to decline in the late summer (see Figure 10-2). Stock prices rose sharply over the next 12 months. A second example of this relationship is the period from mid-1984 to mid-1986.

Using Valuation Models to Forecast the Market

Based on the valuation models developed earlier, it is necessary to use one of two approaches.

1. Use D_1, k, and g, based on Equation 10-1, $V_0 = D_1/(k - g)$.
2. Use E and P/E, based on Equation 10-3, $P_0 = (E_1)P_0/E_1$.

If we wish to try to forecast the market, we must form some judgments about likely changes in these variables. As an example of trying to forecast the market, consider Figure 10-4, which shows Value Line's "Industrial Composite" (IC) of over 900 industrial, retail, and transportation companies, accounting for about 80% of all income earned by nonfinancial corporations in the United States. Per-share figures are based on the total number of shares outstanding for all the companies in the composite.[25] The data shown in Figure 10-4 include actual and forecasted earnings per share (EPS), dividends per share (DPS), growth rates for these and other variables, and several balance sheet and income statement items.

Note that the performance of the IC during the recession periods con-

---

[23]See Michael Rozeff, "The Money Supply and the Stock Market—The Demise of a Leading Indicator," *Financial Analysts Journal*, September–October 1975.

[24]John Sims, "Money Supply and Stock Returns—Does a Relationship Exist," Unpublished manuscript, University of North Carolina, 1982.

[25]The Industrial Composite is weighted by company size. The price action of the Industrial Composite is influenced by company size, with larger corporations having a greater influence than smaller corporations. In contrast, the Value Line geometric averages are unweighted; that is, they are influenced equally by the price movements of each stock.

INDUSTRIAL COMPOSITE

RECENT PRICE	37	P/E RATIO	13.5 (Trailing: 12.5 / Median: 10.5)	RELATIVE P/E RATIO	1.07	DIV'D YLD	3.2%	VALUE LINE	868

High:	11.4	12.5	12.2	12.9	14.0	18.9	18.1	18.3	22.4	22.0	26.2	30.9	42.8	34.3	41.5	
Low:	7.3	10.2	10.0	9.6	11.1	11.6	13.0	12.0	16.3	17.4	19.3	23.3	24.1	27.8	31.5	

Target Price Range: 1992 1993 1994

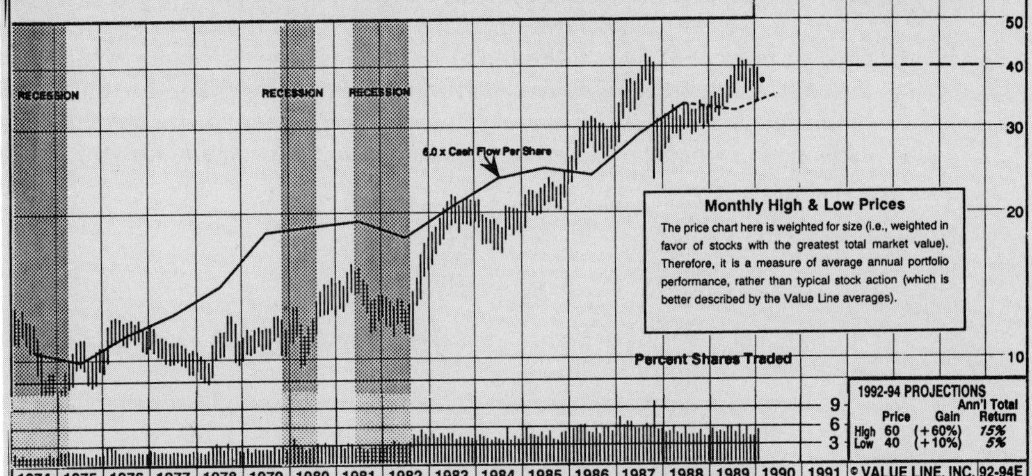

Monthly High & Low Prices

The price chart here is weighted for size (i.e., weighted in favor of stocks with the greatest total market value). Therefore, it is a measure of average annual portfolio performance, rather than typical stock action (which is better described by the Value Line averages).

1992-94 PROJECTIONS

	Price	Gain	Ann'l Total Return
High	60	(+60%)	15%
Low	40	(+10%)	5%

1974	1975	1976	1977	1978	1979	1980	1981	1982	1983	1984	1985	1986	1987	1988	1989	1990	1991	© VALUE LINE, INC.	92-94E
19.82	20.64	22.69	25.76	28.98	34.12	38.73	40.98	39.80	41.09	44.17	47.04	45.72	51.97	56.39	*60.00*	*62.85*		Sales per sh A	*76.15*
1.73	1.65	1.88	2.07	2.36	3.05	3.13	3.21	2.97	3.43	3.93	4.12	3.99	4.83	5.59	*5.60*	*5.90*		"Cash Flow" per sh	*7.40*
1.08	.95	1.15	1.27	1.43	1.97	1.89	1.83	1.42	1.70	2.07	1.99	1.81	2.46	3.00	*2.80*	*3.00*		Earnings per sh B	*3.90*
.36	.37	.42	.49	.54	.63	.69	.71	.71	.74	.81	.88	.92	1.11	1.10	1.20p	*1.28*		Div'ds Decl'd per sh	*1.65*
1.47	1.48	1.46	1.69	1.97	2.63	3.05	3.43	3.21	2.73	3.06	3.52	3.12	3.29	3.89	*3.90*	*4.05*		Cap'l Spending per sh	*4.75*
7.11	7.50	8.02	8.86	9.77	11.10	12.42	13.23	13.58	14.64	15.38	16.12	16.66	18.53	19.18	*20.80*	*22.65*		Book Value per sh C	*29.35*
45.48	45.81	47.23	47.70	48.29	49.18	50.12	51.32	52.11	52.17	52.24	52.40	53.03	52.21	52.37	*52.50*	*53.00*		Common Shs Outst'g D	*54.50*
8.9	10.5	10.0	8.8	7.8	6.3	7.8	8.7	10.1	11.9	9.8	11.4	15.6	14.1	10.6	*13.0*	*Bold figures are*		Avg Ann'l P/E Ratio	*12.5*
1.25	1.40	1.28	1.15	1.06	.91	1.04	1.06	1.11	1.01	.91	.93	1.06	.94	.88	*1.00*	*Value Line*		Relative P/E Ratio	*1.05*
3.8%	3.7%	3.6%	4.4%	4.9%	5.1%	4.6%	4.5%	5.0%	3.7%	4.0%	3.9%	3.3%	3.2%	3.4%	3.3%p	*estimates*		Avg Ann'l Div'd Yield	*3.4%*

CAPITAL STRUCTURE as of Fiscal Year 1988 A

Total Debt $851.0 bill. **Due in 5 Yrs** $517.1 bill.
LT Debt $578.5 bill. **LT Interest** $59.7 bill.

Incl. $29.3 bill. capitalized leases;
$19.4 bill. convertible debt.
(LT interest earned: 5.3x; total interest coverage: 3.9x) (36% of Cap'l)

Leases, Uncapitalized Annual rentals $31.5 bill.
Pension Liability $7.4 bill. in '88 vs. $9.1 bill. in '87

Pfd Stock $27.7 bill. **Pfd Div'd** $1.9 bill.

Incl. $12.2 bill. convertible preferred. (2% of Cap'l)

Common Stock 52.37 bill. shs.

(52.91 bill. fully diluted shs.) (62% of Cap'l)

1980	1981	1982	1983	1984	1985	1986	1987	1988	1989	1990	1991		92-94E
1940.8	2103.3	2073.7	2143.6	2307.5	2464.6	2424.4	2713.0	2952.8	*3150*	*3330*		Sales ($bill) A	*4150*
12.9%	12.1%	11.6%	12.8%	13.7%	13.5%	12.8%	13.5%	14.7%	*14.0%*	*14.0%*		Operating Margin	*14.5%*
62.1	70.9	79.4	87.7	95.0	108.0	114.7	125.0	136.2	*145*	*155*		Depreciation ($bill)	*190*
96.0	95.4	76.8	93.4	112.7	109.9	98.9	129.0	158.6	*150*	*160*		Net Profit ($bill)	*215*
48.6%	46.3%	47.9%	47.1%	46.2%	47.6%	43.5%	41.8%	37.6%	*37.5%*	*37.5%*		Income Tax Rate	*37.5%*
4.9%	4.5%	3.7%	4.4%	4.9%	4.5%	4.1%	4.8%	5.4%	*4.8%*	*4.8%*		Net Profit Margin	*5.2%*
246.6	250.8	243.0	268.6	262.9	263.6	276.8	310.3	391.8	*400*	*425*		Working Cap'l ($bill)	*475*
242.1	281.4	306.4	306.3	340.0	383.8	438.8	469.3	578.5	*725*	*700*		Long-Term Debt ($bill)	*700*
639.9	697.8	730.9	788.3	829.9	871.0	912.0	994.6	1032.0	*1120*	*1230*		Net Worth ($bill)	*1630*
12.1%	11.1%	9.0%	10.0%	11.2%	10.4%	8.9%	10.3%	11.7%	*10.0%*	*10.0%*		% Earned Total Cap'l E	*11.0%*
15.0%	13.7%	10.5%	11.8%	13.6%	12.6%	10.8%	13.0%	15.4%	*13.5%*	*13.0%*		% Earned Net Worth	*13.0%*
9.7%	8.6%	5.4%	6.9%	8.5%	7.3%	5.4%	7.1%	9.5%	*8.0%*	*7.5%*		% Retained to Comm Eq F	*7.5%*
37%	40%	50%	43%	40%	44%	51%	46%	40%	*43%*	*44%*		% All Div'ds to Net Prof	*43%*

CURRENT POSITION ($BILL.)	FY '86	FY '87	FY '88 A
Cash Assets	185.9	201.9	204.2
Receivables	348.0	409.1	640.0
Inventory G	292.5	322.7	340.0
Other	107.8	116.1	128.3
Current Assets	934.2	1049.8	1312.5
Accts Payable	234.7	263.8	289.7
Debt Due	129.0	141.9	272.5
Other	293.7	333.8	358.5
Current Liab.	657.4	739.5	920.7

ANNUAL RATES of change (per sh)	Past 10 Yrs.	Past 5 Yrs.	Est'd '86-'88 to '92-'94
Sales	7.0%	5.0%	*7.0%*
"Cash Flow"	8.5%	8.5%	*7.5%*
Earnings	6.5%	8.0%	*8.0%*
Dividends	8.0%	8.0%	*8.0%*
Book Value	7.0%	5.0%	*8.5%*

Fiscal Year Begins	QUARTERLY SALES ($bill.) A Qtr. I	Qtr. II	Qtr. III	Qtr. IV	Full Fiscal Year
1986	591.7	604.0	582.9	645.8	2424.4
1987	623.8	674.5	672.5	742.2	2713.0
1988	692.1	740.2	723.7	796.8	2952.8
1989	770p	785p	795p	*800*	*3150*
1990	*810*	*825*	*840*	*855*	*3330*

Fiscal Year Begins	EARNINGS PER SHARE A B Qtr. I	Qtr. II	Qtr. III	Qtr. IV	Full Fiscal Year
1986	.40	.52	.50	.39	1.81
1987	.52	.67	.64	.63	2.46
1988	.65	.81	.76	.78	3.00
1989	.78p	.73p	.67p	*.62*	*2.80*
1990	*.70*	*.75*	*.75*	*.80*	*3.00*

Cal-endar	QUARTERLY DIVIDENDS PAID Mar.31	Jun.30	Sep.30	Dec.31	Full Year
1986	.23	.24	.22	.23	.92
1987	.28	.29	.27	.27	1.11
1988	.27	.28	.27	.28	1.10
1989	.30p	.30p	.30p	.30p	1.20p
1990					

EXPLANATION: The Industrial Composite consists of approximately 900 industrial, retail, and transportation companies. These companies account for about 80% of the income earned by all U.S. non-financial corporations. The figures shown in the statistical array differ from those reported by the U.S. Commerce Department in the national income accounts because they (a) are based on stockholder accounting techniques rather than Internal Revenue Service bookkeeping methods and (b) include the reported results of just the larger companies. Financial data and stock market values for these about 900 companies have been pooled as if they belong to one giant conglomerate. Per-share figures are computed on the basis of the total number of common shares outstanding for all the companies at yearend. Forecasts for the Industrial Composite have been published in *Selection & Opinion* since July 11, 1975.

(A) Co. fiscal yrs. end between 5/1 of yr. shown and 4/30 of next yr. Fiscal yrs. for about 80% of co.'s end 12/31. (B) Based on yr.-end shs. outstand'g. Excl. disc. ops.: '74–'79, '81, –1¢; '82, –2¢; '83, –5¢; '84, –5¢; '85, –7¢; '86, –2¢; '87, 3¢; '88, 1¢. Excl. spec. items: '76, '78–'80, 1¢; '81, 4¢; '82, –3¢, '84, –1¢; '85, –23¢; '86, –24¢; '87, –3¢; '88, 2¢. (C) Incl. intan. In '88: $149.1 bill., $2.85/sh. (D) In bill. (E) (Net prof. + ½ l.-t. int.) ÷ (l.-t. debt + net worth, incl. intan.) (F) (Net prof. – all div'ds) ÷ com. eq. (G) About ⅔ LIFO. p: preliminary.

February 23, 1990

FIGURE 10-4 ***Value Lines's Industrial Composite of over 900 industrial, retail, and transportation companies.***
Source: The Value Line Investment Survey, "Selection and Opinion," February 23, 1990, p. 868. Copyright © 1990 by Value Line Publishing Inc. Used by permission.

forms with our previous discussion. Also notice the sharp market drop in October 1987 and the subsequent strong recovery.

First, we can analyze two of the figures given at the top of Figure 10-4: a recent price of 37 and a P/E ratio of 13.5. Value Line's estimate of the EPS for 1989 at this time (February 1990) was \$2.80, as shown on the third row of the data ("Earnings Per Share").[26] Using the P/E ratio model of valuation explained in Chapter 9 based on the assumption of constant growth,

$$P_0 = P_0/E_1 \times E_1$$
$$P_0 = 13.5 \times \$2.80$$
$$\approx \$37$$

The value of the IC was (approximately) a combination of a P/E of 13.5 and expected earnings of \$2.80.

Assuming a constant growth dividend discount model for the market, an estimate of the required rate of return for 1989 was as follows[27]:

$$k = D_1/P + g$$
$$= 1.20/37 + 0.08$$
$$= 0.112$$

Solving Equation 10-2,

$$P_0/E_1 = \frac{D_1/E_1}{k - g}$$
$$= \frac{1.20/2.80}{0.112 - 0.08}$$
$$= 13.4$$

Thus, the models and variables discussed in Chapter 9 are internally consistent with these data.

Now what about forecasts, or at least likely possibilities? First, assume that the spread between k and g, 0.032, holds. Using Value Line's 1990 estimates of D and E,

$$\text{Estimated P/E} = \frac{1.28/3.00}{0.032}$$
$$= \frac{0.427}{0.032}$$
$$= 13.3$$

[26]As of the publication date for this information, fourth quarter 1989 earnings for the Composite was not known, and therefore the 1989 earnings were still an estimate.

[27]The g value of 0.08 is taken from the estimates of growth in the bottom left panel. The dividend figure is taken from the fourth line of the data and is a preliminary estimate for 1989.

In this scenario, if the spread between k and g remains constant, the P/E would be expected to decrease slightly because of the small decrease in the payout ratio. If the earnings estimate for 1990 is high enough to offset this slight decline, the estimated price or value for the market would be higher.

Example. Assume the estimated earnings by Value Line for 1990 is applicable. The estimated price, P_E, would be

$$\begin{aligned} P_E &= \text{estimated P/E} \times \text{estimated earnings} \\ &= 13.3 \times 3.00 \\ &= \$39.90 \end{aligned}$$

Thus, one estimated price for the IC, \$39.90, is 7.8% higher than the recent price given in Figure 10-4 of \$37. ▪

Example. Assumptions could be made about a change in the spread between k and g, which would change the P/E ratio. What if the spread narrowed to 0.022, as a result of k declining from 0.112 to 0.102? Assume estimated earnings of \$3.00.

$$\text{Previous} \qquad k - g = 0.112 - 0.08 = 0.032$$

$$\text{New} \qquad k - g = 0.102 - 0.08 = 0.022$$

$$\begin{aligned} \text{Estimated P/E} &= \frac{0.427}{0.022} \\ &= 19.40 \\ P_E &= \text{estimated P/E} \times \text{estimated } E \\ &= 19.40 \times 3.00 \\ &= \$58.20 \end{aligned}$$

A 1% decline in k, leading to a 1% drop in the spread between k and g, results in a substantially higher estimated price for the IC, from \$37 to \$58.20, or a 57% change. ▪

On the other hand, assume that k rises 1% because of an increase in either the riskless rate of return or the risk premium demanded by investors.

Example. Estimated earnings continue to be \$3.00.

$$\begin{aligned} \text{Estimated P/E} &= \frac{0.427}{0.122 - 0.08} \\ &= 10.2 \end{aligned}$$

and

$$\begin{aligned} P_E &= \text{Estimated P/E} \times \text{Estimated E} \\ &= 10.2 \times \$3.00 \\ &= \$30.60 \end{aligned}$$

Assuming no change in the estimated earnings, these calculations suggest a lower estimated price for the IC of $30.60. ▪

The foregoing examples illustrate the fundamental analysis approach to forecasting the market using some data that are readily available to investors. Such forecasts are not easy, at best, and are clearly subject to errors, some often substantial. Investors can count on the unexpected occurring. Nevertheless, it is possible for the average investor to make some intelligent and useful forecasts of the market at certain times, at least as to direction. In 1974, for example, it was not too difficult to believe that the market could rise in the future, given the low point it had reached. If the economy could be expected to improve after the shock of the energy crunch, earnings could be expected to hold steady or improve. More important, if investor pessimism could be expected to decrease to any extent, the P/E ratio should increase, and therefore stock prices would increase. And this is exactly what happened!

Another example is 1981–1982, when interest rates had reached record levels in the United States and the economy was in a recession. Investors had only to convince themselves that some recovery would occur, thereby increasing earnings, or more important, that interest rates would decline, thereby lowering the required rate of return (i.e., raising the P/E ratio). This is exactly what happened, of course, launching the great bull market of mid-1982 to mid-1983.

Investors should attempt to apply the foregoing type of analysis when estimating the future. Although it is not a perfect process by any means, useful forecasts of likely market trends can be made. Also keep in mind that a number of "market indicators" exist and are touted by various individuals and/or organizations. Box 10-1 contains an example of one such indicator.

Summary

- The "market" is the aggregate of all security prices and is conveniently measured by some average or, most commonly, by some index of stock prices.
- Market measures range from the narrowest New York Stock Exchange measure, the Dow Jones arithmetic mean averages, to the broadest, the Wilshire index. In between are two broader measures of the NYSE, the Standard & Poor's indexes and the New York Stock Exchange indexes.
- Other market measures include the American Stock Exchange Index, the

BOX 10-1

THE DOW YIELD AS A MARKET INDICATOR

You've heard of price-to-sales, price-to-book, the price/earnings ratio and more. Now consider the Dow yield as a worthwhile market indicator. This is defined as the total dividends paid by the 30 Dow Jones industrial stocks, divided by the stocks' aggregate price.

Richard C. Young, president of Young Research & Publishing, an economic and monetary research firm based in Newport, R.I., has compiled some fascinating time series using the Dow yield. For instance, only once since the 1920s has the yield on the Dow finished the year below 3%. That was in 1965. The next year the market shed a quarter of its value. More recently, a dropping yield on the Dow (caused by strong stock price rises) tipped Young that a crash might be coming when it dipped below 3% during the summer of 1987. Young has found that the Dow's normal yield is 4.5%, and that anything over that is a strong buy signal.

Source: Adapted from Thomas Jaffe, "More today, more tomorrow," *Forbes*, May 15, 1989, p. 164. Excerpted by permission of *Forbes* magazine, May 15, 1989, © Forbes, Inc., 1989.

NASDAQ indexes, the Media General Composite Market Value Index, and the Value Line indexes.

- The three indexes based on NYSE stocks (Dow Jones, S&P, and NYSE Composite Index) show high correlations between daily percentages of price changes. There are major divergences between these three indexes and those covering other exchanges, such as the Amex and the OTC market.
- Over short-run periods, significant differences do occur among the various market measures.
- Aggregate market analysis is important because a substantial part of the average stock's return is attributable to the market. Movements in the overall market are the dominant factor affecting the return of a diversified portfolio.
- To understand the market (i.e., what determines stock prices) it is necessary to think in terms of a valuation model. The two determinants of aggregate stock prices are the expected benefits stream (earnings or dividends) and the required rate of return (alternatively, the P/E ratio).
- Keran's model is useful for visualizing the economic factors that combine to determine stock prices. In trying to understand the market in conceptual terms, it is appropriate to think of corporate earnings and interest rates as the determinants of stock prices.
- Corporate earnings are directly related to stock prices, whereas interest rates are inversely related.

- To value the market, investors should think in terms of corporate earnings and the P/E ratio (alternatively, the dividend valuation model could be used).
- Although valuing the market can never be easy, it is possible to make some intelligent estimates by considering what is likely to happen to corporate profits and P/E ratios (or interest rates) over some future period, such as a year.
- In forecasting likely market changes, investors can examine economic variables such as money supply, output, price levels, and government spending that affect the business cycle and stock prices.
- Leading, lagging, and coincident indicators may be helpful in predicting changes in the market. It is important to remember that stock prices typically lead the economy.
- An alternative approach to forecasting likely changes in the market is to apply the valuation model based on dividends or earnings.

Key Words

Blue chip stocks
Business cycle
Composite indexes of general economic activity
Dow-Jones Industiral Average
Market average
Market index
S&P 500 Composite Index (S&P 500)

Market Indexes and Averages:
Averages:
- **The Dow Jones Industrial Average (also, Transportation, Public Utility, and Composite averages)**

Indexes: (arranged from smallest number of companies in index to largest)

New York Stock Exchange:
- **Standard & Poor's 400 Industrial Index**
- **Standard & Poor's 500 Composite Index**
- **New York Stock Exchange Index**

American Stock Exchange:
- **American Stock Exchange Index**

Over-the-Counter:
- **NASDAQ Indexes**

Composite Indices:
- **The Value Line Industrial Average**
- **The Value Line Composite Average**
- **The Media General Composite Index**
- **The Wilshire Index**

Questions

10-1 Name at least four distinct uses for market indicators.

10-2 What are the advantages and disadvantages of using the Dow Jones Industrial Average?

10-3 Express in equation form the method for calculating the S&P 500 Composite Index.

10-4 What is the difference between the S&P 500 Composite Index and the NYSE Composite Index? How closely can they be expected to parallel each other?

10-5 Why is the Value Line index unique among market indicators?

10-6 Why is market analysis so important?

10-7 What are the two determinants of stock prices? How are these two determinants related to a valuation model?

10-8 How can the Keran model use interest rates as one of the two determinants of stock prices when the interest rate does not appear in either the dividend valuation model or the earnings multiplier model?

10-9 In terms of the Keran model, how can the Federal Reserve affect stock prices?

10-10 What is the historical relationship between stock prices, corporate profits, and interest rates?

10-11 How can investors value the market?

10-12 What was the primary cause of the rise in stock prices in 1982?

10-13 What is the "typical" business cycle–stock price relationship?

10-14 If an investor can determine when the bottoming out of the economy will occur, when should stocks be purchased—before, during, or after such a bottom? Would stock prices be expected to continue to rise as the economy recovers (based on historical experience)?

10-15 Can money supply changes forecast stock price changes?

10-16 What is the historical relationship between the market's P/E ratio and recessions?

10-17 Based on Table 10-4, what is the likely explanation for the stock market's lackluster performance in the last half of the 1970s?

10-18 Suppose that you know *with certainty* that corporate earnings next year will rise 15% above this year's level of corporate earnings. Based on this information, should you buy stocks?

Problems

10-1 In the text the Value Line Industrial Composite is used in an example of market valuation. For this problem, the Standard & Poor's 400 Industrial Index and Equations 10-3, 10-4, and 10-5 are used. The annual data for the years 19X1–19X6 are provided:

Year	End-of-Year Price (P)	Earnings (E)	Dividends (D)	P/E	(D/E)100 (%)	(D/P)100 (%)
19X1	107.21	13.12	5.35	8.17	40.78	4.99
19X2	121.02	16.08	6.04	7.53	37.56	4.99

19X3	154.45	16.13	6.55	9.58	40.61	4.24
19X4	137.12	16.70	7.00	8.21	41.92	5.11
19X5	157.62	13.21	7.18	11.93	54.35	4.56
19X6	186.24	15.24	6.97			

The 19X6 values in italics are projected, like those of the Value Line Industrial Composite:

a. Calculate the 19X6 values for those columns left blank.
b. Why would you expect this index to differ from the Value Line Index?
c. On the assumption that $g = 0.095$, calculate k for 19X6 using the formula $k = D/P + g$ and show that $k = 0.132425$.
d. Using the 19X6 values in Equation 10-4, show that P/E = 12.22.
e. Assuming a projection that 19X7 earnings will be 25% greater than the 19X6 value, show that projected earnings for the S&P 400 are expected to be 19.05.
f. Assuming further that the dividend-payout ratio will be 0.40, show that projected dividends for 19X7 will be 7.62.
g. Using the projected earnings and dividends for 19X7, and the same k and g used in problem c, show that Equation 10-4 yields an expected P/E for 19X7 of 10.69.
h. Using these expected values for 19X7, evaluate Equation 10-5, and show that the expected price is 203.61.
i. Recalculate the values for 19X7 P/E and P, using the same $g = 0.095$, but with (1) $k = 0.14$, (2) $k = 0.13$, and (3) $k = 0.12$.

Selected References

The relationship between stock prices and the economy is discussed in

Pearce, Douglas K. "Stock Prices and the Economy." *Economic Review*. Federal Reserve Bank of Kansas City, November 1983, pp. 7–22.

Stock market cycles are discussed in

Renshaw, Edward F. "The Anatomy of Stock Market Cycles." *The Journal of Portfolio Management*, Fall 1983, pp. 53–57.

A discussion of the theory of stock price movements can be found in

Schiller, Robert J. "Theories of Aggregate Stock Price Movements." *The Journal of Portfolio Management*, Winter 1984, pp. 28–37.

A more in-depth analysis of forecasting stock prices is

Umstead, David. "Forecasting Stock Market Prices." *Journal of Finance*, May 1977, pp. 427–441.

A good overall view of the economy can be found in

United States Government Printing Office, *Economic Report of the President*, yearly.

CHAPTER 11

Industry Analysis

The second step in the fundamental analysis of common stocks is industry analysis. An investor who is convinced that the economy and the market are attractive for investing should proceed to consider those industries that promise the most opportunities in the coming years. In the 1990s, for example, investors probably will not view basic U.S. industries such as autos and steel with the same enthusiasm they would have 15 or 20 years earlier. On the other hand, it is obvious that the telecommunications and computer-related industries are going to change the way in which most Americans live.

In this chapter we shall consider the *conceptual issues* involved in industry analysis. The basic concepts of industry analysis are closely related to our previous discussion of valuation principles. Although the actual security analysis of industries as done by professional security analysts is tedious, these concepts can be applied by investors in several ways, depending on the degree of rigor sought, the amount of information available, and the specific models used. What we seek to accomplish here is to learn to think analytically about industries.

The significance of industry analysis can be established by considering the performance of various industries over multiple-year periods. This analysis will indicate the value to investors of selecting certain industries while avoiding others. We will also establish the needs for investors to continue analyzing industries by showing the inconsistency of industry performance over consecutive yearly periods. Such a demonstration justifies an analysis of industries, which will be done following this discussion.

Performance of Industries over Time

The Value of Industry Analysis

Before embarking on industry analysis, it is worthwhile to consider its value. To establish the value of industry analysis, we can assess the performance of industry groups over long periods of time.[1] Standard & Poor's calculates weekly stock price indices for a variety of industries, with data available for a 40-year period. Since the data are reported as index numbers, long-term comparisons of price performance can be made for any industry covered.

Table 11-1 shows the price performance of selected industries for the

[1]This discussion is taken from H. A. Latané, D. L. Tuttle, and C. P. Jones, *Security Analysis and Portfolio Management* (New York: Ronald Press, 1975), pp. 427–431.

TABLE 11-1 ***Standard & Poor's Weekly Stock Price Indexes for Selected Industries Using 1973 Data and Three Different Base Periods, and Selected Price Indexes Using 1982, 1986, and 1989 Data and a Base of 1941–43 = 10***

	1941–1943 = 10		1950 = 10	1960 = 10
	1973	1950	1960	1973
Computer and business equipment	1450	20	113	46
(without IBM)	433	17	59	42
Electronics (major companies)	685	23	96	31
Drugs	245	14	43	41
Oil (composite)	145	22	30	23
Capital goods	119	18	33	20
S&P 400 Industrial Average	121	18	32	20
Gold mining	64	10	16	39
Aerospace	46	12	38	10
Sugar	30	16	13	15
Textile apparel	31	13	21	11
Lead and zinc	17	12	8	18

	1941 – 1943 = 10		
	1982	1986	1989
Oil well equipment and service	1312	999	1702
Computer and business equipment	1412	2032	—
Drugs	248	540	967
S&P 400 Industrial Average	156	270	—
Textile apparel	63	174	198
Aerospace	179	322	359
Chemicals (diversified)	57	32	41
Copper	55	52	—
Broadcast media	889	2255	5137
Steel	32	28	51
Shoes	108	149	323

Sources: H. A. Latané, D. L. Tuttle, and C. P. Jones, *Security Analysis and Portfolio Management* (New York: Ronald Press, 1975), pp. 427–429; Standard & Poor's *Statistical Service: Security Price Index Record.* Price data are as of December 1982 and 1989 (monthly averages of weekly indexes). Reprinted by permission of John Wiley & Sons, Inc. and Standard & Poor's.

years 1973 and 1950 (using 1941–1943 as the base), for 1960 (using 1950 as a base), for 1973 (using 1960 as a base), and 1982, 1986, and 1989 (using 1941–1943 as a base). The S&P 400 Industrial Index in 1973 was 12 times (121/10) its 1941–1943 level, a continuously compounded average in excess of 8% annually over this 31-year period. However, this average growth rate consisted of widely varying performance over the industries covered by Standard & Poor's.

Over the 31-year period 1943–1973, office and business equipment did extremely well (145 times what it was in 1941–1943), thanks primarily to IBM; without IBM this industry was still 43 times larger than its base. The electronics industry also did well, rising to almost 69 times its beginning level (685/10). At the other extreme, the lead and zinc industry was less than two times its beginning level, and the sugar and textile apparel industries were only three times their beginning levels. Notice how the capital goods industry paralleled the Industrial Average.

Over shorter periods of time, as the last two columns at the top of Table 11-1 show, industries perform quite differently. During the 1950s, for example, the price index for the electronics industry increased almost tenfold (i.e., the index was 96), whereas that for the textile apparel industry increased only twofold, with the sugar and lead–zinc industries doing much worse.

Standard & Poor's has changed industry classifications over time because of changes in the economy. The lower half of Table 11-1, therefore, shows selected and matched Standard & Poor's Industry Stock Price indexes for the end of 1982 and the end of 1986, based on 1941–1943, and those comparable indexes that were reported at the end of 1989. This provides both a 40-year-plus picture of industry performance, which approximates the maximum investing lifetime of many individuals, and a look at how much change can occur in shorter periods of three (1986–1989), four (1982–1986) and seven (1982–1989) years.

Tremendous differences existed for industries in the 1980s. Notice how Chemicals declined and then rallied but remained below the 1982 value. On the other hand, Oil-well equipment and service had declined by 1986 but made a significant recovery by 1989. Broadcast media did very well over the period ending in 1986 and had more than doubled again by 1989. Shoes more than doubled from 1986 through 1989. The performance of Drugs remained strong in the 1980s, with prices up over 40% in 1989 alone.

Even over very short periods, such as one month, industries can perform very differently. A dramatic example is the performance of industry groups around the great market crash of October 1987, when the S&P 500 Index declined some 22 percent in one month. All industries were clobbered during this unprecedented decline in stock prices; however, some industries suffered only small declines, whereas others suffered large ones. Table 11-2 shows the smallest and biggest losers, based on percentage change in stock prices, from September 30 to October 30.

According to Table 11-2, the electric utility industry and the telephone industry experienced a small loss relative to the average. As would be expected by most market observers, on a relative basis industries such as beverages, food, household products and drug companies declined less than the manufacturing and industrial sectors. For example, the machine tool industry lost 41% and miscellaneous metals lost 39%. Nevertheless, toy companies suffered a loss of almost 42 percent, and the leisure time industry lost 40%. Clearly, the losses suffered by virtually all investors in October, 1987 varied widely depending upon the particular industries held.

TABLE 11-2 ***Standard & Poor's Industry Groups with the Best and Worst Performances Based on Percentage Change in Stock Price from 9/30/87 to 10/30/87***

Best Performers		Worst Performers	
Electric companies	−3.5%	Toys	−41.8%
Telephone	−8.1	Machine tools	−41.3
Property/casualty insurers	−14.0	Leisure time	−40.3
Beverages-Brewers	−14.6	Miscellaneous metals	−39.4
International oils	−14.7	Gold	−38.3
Houshold products	−15.2	Offshore drilling	−38.0
Multi-line insurance	−15.3	Auto trucks and parts	−36.8
Diversified health care	−15.9	Paper containers	−35.0
Beverages-Soft drinks	−16.3	Electronics-Semiconductors	−33.9
Food companies	−17.2	Tires and rubber goods	−33.8
Drug companies	−17.4	Manufactured housing	−33.2
Medical products, supplies	−18.4	Miscellaneous financial	−32.7
Restaurants	−18.8	Aluminum	−32.6
Computer software, services	−18.9	Retail department stores	−32.1
		Homebuilding	−31.8
Standard & Poor's 500	−21.8%		
Dow Jones Industrials	−23.2		

Source: Karen Slater, "Not All Industries Suffered Alike in Stock Market's Cruelest Month," *The Wall Street Journal*, November 2, 1987, p. 33. Reprinted by permission of *The Wall Street Journal*, © 1987 Dow Jones & Company, Inc. All Rights Reserved Worldwide.

Consistency of Industry Performance

The previous section established the value of industry analysis from a long-term perspective. Those investors who select the growth industries and maintain their positions will generally receive far better returns than those who have the misfortune to concentrate in industries that perform poorly over long periods of time.

Can relative industry performance be predicted reliably on the basis of past success, as measured by previous price performance? To answer this question, consider Table 11-1 again. Assume that an investor calculated the top part of the table sometime in 1974, when the 1973 data were available. Should this investor count on past performance to carry him or her through the next several years—for example, through 1982? The answer is *no!*

As the bottom of the table shows, the computer business and equipment industry, a spectacular performer through 1973, was lower by 1982—in other words, the great growth was over. Although this was still a phenomenal industry over the 40 years 1943–1982, with a 141-fold increase, it was an even better 31-year performer (through 1973), with a 145-fold increase. The drug industry, a strong performer over the 1943–1973 period, was virtually unchanged in 1982. On the other hand, textile apparel had an index of 63 by 1982, compared to 31 in 1973, and that of aerospace was 179 versus 46. Furthermore, both of these industries showed dramatic increases over the three-year period 1982–1985.

What about industry performance over shorter periods of time? Should investors screen industries to find those that are currently performing well and are, therefore, likely to be the source of the most promising opportunities, from which company analysis will be done? To answer this question, consider Table 11-3, which shows price performance by industries for 52-week periods ending in mid-November for the years 1980, 1981, and 1982; that for 52-week periods ending in late September for the years 1984, 1985, and 1986; and that for 52-week periods ending in mid-September for the years 1987, 1988, and 1989.[2]

In 1980 the rare metals industry ranked first (out of 60 covered) for the 52-week period ending in mid-November of that year. This industry as a whole had experienced a 121% increase in price over the previous year. However, an investor choosing this industry on the basis of this performance would have been disappointed over the subsequent two years, as the rank and performance dropped to 60 (last) in 1981 with a one-year decline of 39% and was in fifty-fourth place in 1982 with a one-year decline of 11%. Similarly, the oil and natural gas services industry went from third place in 1980, with a previous year gain of 104%, to fifty-third place in 1981 (−26%), and to sixtieth place (last) in 1982 (−41%).

On the other hand, consider the retail department store industry, which was in fifty-seventh place in 1980 (−1%). By 1981 it was in the fourteenth position (9%), and by 1982, in the first position, with a previous yearly gain of 80%. The automotive industry also showed a dramatic turnaround, rising from last place in 1980 to tenth place in 1982.

Finally, note the leather shoes industry. It was a steady performer during this three-year period, rising from the top third of the 60 industries in 1980 to almost the top decile in 1982.

The middle part of Table 11-3 tells the same basic story for the years 1984–1986. Aerospace went from eighth place to fifty-third, whereas savings and loans went from sixtieth to fifth. Textiles and leather shoes improved dramatically from 1984 to 1986.

The bottom part of Table 11-3 contains similar examples for the years 1987–1989.

Table 11-3 is compiled from *The Media General Financial Weekly*, which provides a front-page ranking of 60 industries, including industry performance (rank and percentage change) for the current week, as well as the last 4, 13, and 52 weeks. This analysis also shows the company in each industry with the highest and lowest performance for each of the four

[2]The author wishes to thank *The Media General Financial Weekly* for providing these data.

TABLE 11-3 ***Media General Industry Ranks and Percentage Price Performance over 52-Week Periods for Three-Year Intervals for Selected Industries***

	Previous 52-Week Price Performance as of Mid-November					
	1980		1981		1982	
	Rank	Percent Change	Rank	Percent Change	Rank	Percent Change
Oil, natural gas services	(3)	104	(53)	−26	(60)	−41
Metals, rare	(1)	121	(60)	−39	(54)	−11
Savings and loans	(52)	9	(56)	−30	(5)	55
Shoes	(19)	39	(9)	16	(7)	50
Automotive	(60)	−8	(44)	−16	(10)	44
Retail—department stores	(57)	−1	(14)	9	(1)	80
Electronics	(6)	70	(29)	−1	(42)	15

	Previous 52-Week Price Performance as of Late September					
	1984		1985		1986	
	Rank	Percent Change	Rank	Percent Change	Rank	Percent Change
Aerospace	(8)	7	(24)	15	(53)	10.5
Textile manufacturing	(53)	−19	(10)	22	(8)	56
Shoes—leather	(58)	−28	(18)	19	(12)	43
Savings and loans	(60)	−30	(4)	35	(5)	52
Airlines	(24)	−7	(3)	40	(52)	12
Drug manufacturers	(36)	−11	(8)	27	(7)	48
Food–meats–dairy	(20)	10	(7)	28	(3)	57

	Previous 52-Week Price Performance as of Mid-September					
	1987		1988		1989	
	Rank	Percent Change	Rank	Percent Change	Rank	Percent Change
Airlines	(48)	21	(39)	−17	(1)	66
Textiles—apparel	(44)	27	(59)	−33	(10)	37
Electronics	(18)	48	(10)	−8	(60)	−2
Retail—apparel	(42)	30	(58)	−31	(5)	50
Precision instruments	(16)	49	(54)	−24	(58)	5.6
Utilities—electric	(60)	−8.3	(4)	−1.3	(51)	15.4

Source: The Media General Financial Weekly, issues of November 17, 1980, November 16, 1981, and November 15, 1982, September 24, 1984, September 23, 1985, September 22, 1986, September 21, 1987, September 19, 1988, and September 18, 1989, p. 1. Courtesy of Media General Financial Services, Inc. Richmond, Virginia.

periods. These weekly data are unique and provide a valuable source of information to investors.

In summary, although industry analysis is clearly valuable over time, with some industries far outperforming others, industry rankings on some periodic basis (e.g., yearly or quarterly) are not consistent. Investors cannot simply choose those industries that have performed well recently and expect them to continue to do so for the next several periods. Perhaps just as important, investors should not ignore industries simply because their recent performance has been poor. Their subsequent performance over relatively short periods of time may be, and often is, at the opposite extreme! It is necessary, therefore, to learn the basic concepts about industry analysis. First, however, let us consider what an industry is.

What Is an Industry?

At first glance, the term *industry* may seem self-explanatory. After all, everyone is familiar with the auto industry, the drug industry, and the electric utility industry. But are these classifications as clear-cut as they seem? For example, a consumer can drink beer out of glass containers or aluminum cans or steel cans. Does this involve one industry, containers, or three—the glass, steel, and aluminum industries (or perhaps two: glass and metals)?

The problem becomes even more messy when companies in diversified lines of business are considered.

Example. Harvey Group is an American Stock Exchange company that showed the following breakdown by sales for one year: retailing of professional and home audio and video equipment, 56%; food brokerage, 44%; however, by percentage of total profits the breakdowns are 32% and 68%, respectively. In what industry is Harvey Group? It is not easy to classify such a company, particularly in relation to Cascade Natural Gas, a New York Stock Exchange company whose only activity is the distribution of natural gas in 84 communities in Washington and Oregon. ▪

There are complications in classifying even a seemingly "clear" example such as General Motors, the world's largest automobile manufacturer. In 1984 GM acquired EDS, a computer services firm, and in 1985 it acquired Hughes Aircraft.

The message is clear. Industries cannot casually be identified and classified, at least in many cases. It seems safe to assert that industries have been, and will continue to become, more mixed in their activities and less identifiable with one product or service.

Classifying Industries

Regardless of the problems, analysts and investors need methods with which to classify industries. One well-known and widely used system is the

Standard Industrial Classification (SIC) system based on Census data and developed to classify firms on the basis of what they produce.[3] SIC codes have 11 divisions, designated A through K. For example, agriculture–forestry–fishing is Industry Division A; mining is B; retail trade is G; and K, the last group, is nonclassifiable establishments. Within each of these divisions are several major industry groups, designated by a two-digit code. The primary metal industries, for example, are a part of Division D, manufacturing, and are assigned the two-digit code 33.

The major industry groups within each division are further subdivided into three-, four-, and five-digit SIC codes to provide more detailed classifications. A specific industry is assigned a three-digit code, as are entire companies.[4] Plants carrying out specific functions (such as producing steel) are assigned four-digit SIC codes. A five-digit code indicates a specific product. Thus, the larger the number of digits in the SIC system, the more specific the breakdown.

SIC codes have aided significantly in bringing order to the industry classification problem by providing a consistent basis for describing industries and companies. Analysts using SIC codes can focus on economic activity in as broad, or as specific, a manner as desired.

Other Industry Classifications

The SIC system of industry classification is probably the most consistent system available, and possibly the easiest to use. However, it is not the only industry designation in actual use. Standard & Poor's Corporation, at the end of 1982, provided weekly stock indices on approximately 100 industry groupings (or parts of industries). Many of these series go back 30 or 40 years.

The Value Line Investment Survey covers roughly 1700 companies, divided into approximately 90 industries, with a discussion of industry prospects preceding the company analysis. As discussed later, these industry classifications could be important, because *Value Line* ranks their expected performance (relatively) for the year ahead.

Still another very useful industry classification system is that of *The Media General Financial Weekly,* discussed earlier, which divides stocks into 60 industries. Since Media General is one of the few consistent (weekly) sources of past price performance by industries, these classification systems can also be quite useful to investors.

Other sources of information use different numbers of industries in presenting data. The important point to remember is that no one industry classification system is widely used in the standard investment publications.

---

[3]See *Census of Manufacturers* (Washington, D.C.: U.S. Government Printing Office).

[4]Companies involved in several lines of activity are assigned multiple SIC codes.

Analyzing Industries

Industries, as well as the market and companies, are analyzed through the study of a wide range of data, including sales, earnings, dividends, capital structure, product lines, regulations, innovations, and so on. Such analysis requires considerable expertise and is usually performed by industry analysts employed by brokerage firms and other institutional investors.

A useful first step is to analyze industries in terms of their stage in the life cycle. The idea is to assess the general health and current position of the industry. A second step is to assess the position of the industry in relation to the business cycle and macroeconomic conditions. A third step involves a qualitative analysis of industry characteristics designed to assist investors in assessing the future prospects for an industry. Each of these steps will be examined in turn.

The Industry Life Cycle

Many observers believe that industries evolve through at least three stages: the pioneering stage, the expansion stage, and the stabilization stage. There is an obvious parallel in this idea to human development. The concept of an **industry life cycle** could apply to industries or product lines within industries. The industry life cycle concept is depicted in Figure 11-1, and each stage is discussed in the following section.

Pioneering Stage In the pioneering stage, rapid growth in demand occurs. Although a number of companies within a growing industry will fail at this stage because they will not survive the competitive pressures, most experience rapid growth in sales and earnings, possibly at an increasing rate. The

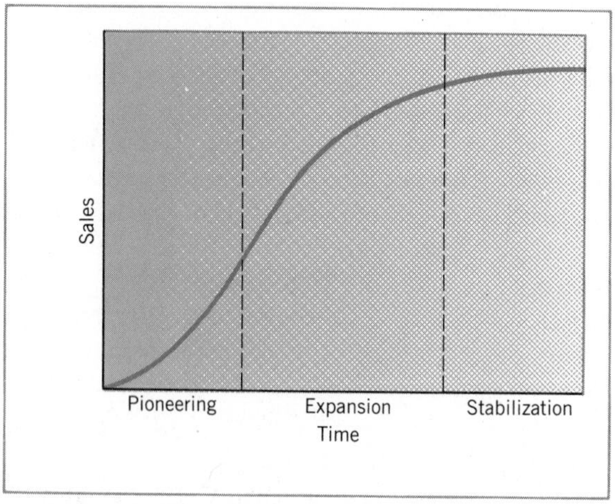

FIGURE 11-1 ***The industry life cycle.***

opportunities available may attract a number of companies, as well as venture capital. Considerable jockeying for position occurs as the companies battle each other for survival, with the weaker firms failing and dropping out. Investor risk in an unproved company is high, but so are expected returns if the company succeeds. At the pioneering stage of an industry it can be difficult for security analysts to identify the likely survivors, just when the ability to identify the future strong performers is most valuable. By the time it becomes apparent who the real winners are, their prices may have been bid up considerably beyond what they were in the earlier stages of development.

In the early 1980s, the microcomputer business—both hardware and software—offered a good example of companies in the pioneering stage. Given the explosion in expected demand for these products, many new firms entered the business hoping to capture some share of the total market. By 1983, there were an estimated 150 manufacturers of home computers, a clearly unsustainable number over the longer run.

Expansion Stage In the second stage of an industry's life cycle, the expansion stage, the survivors from the pioneering stage are identifiable. They continue to grow and prosper, but the rate of growth is more moderate than before.

At the expansion stage of the cycle, industries are improving their products and perhaps lowering their prices. They are more stable and solid, and at this stage they often attract considerable investment funds. Investors are more willing to invest in these industries now that their potential has been demonstrated and the risk of failure has decreased.

Financial policies become firmly established at this stage. The capital base is widened and strengthened. Dividends often become payable, further enhancing the attractiveness of these companies to a number of investors.

Stabilization Stage Finally, industries evolve into the stabilization stage (sometimes referred to as the maturity stage), at which point the growth begins to moderate. Sales may still be increasing, but at a much slower rate than before. Products become more stadardized and less innovative, the marketplace is full of competitors, and costs are stable, rather than decreasing through efficiency moves, for example. Industries at this stage continue to move along, but without significant growth. Stagnation may occur for considerable periods of time, or intermittently.

Assessing the Industry Life Cycle This three-part classification of industry evolution is helpful to investors in assessing the growth potential of different companies in an industry. Based on the stage of the industry, they can better assess the potential of companies within that industry. However, there are limitations to this type of analysis. First, it is only a generalization, and investors must be careful not to attempt to categorize every industry, or all companies within a particular industry, into neat categories that may not apply. Second, even the general framework may not apply to some industries that are not categorized by many small companies struggling for survival. Finally, the bottom line in security analysis is stock prices, a function of the expected stream of benefits and the risk involved.

The industrial life cycle tends to focus on sales and share of the market and investment in the industry. Although all these factors are important to investors, they are not the final items of interest. Given these qualifications to industry life cycle analysis, what are the implications for investors?

The pioneering stage may offer the highest potential returns, but it also offers the greatest risk. Several companies in a particular industry will fail, or do poorly. Such risk may be appropriate for some investors, but many will wish to avoid the risk inherent in this stage.

The maturity stage is to be avoided by investors interested primarily in capital gains. Companies at this stage may have relatively high dividend payouts because their growth prospects are fewer. These companies often offer stability in earnings and dividend growth.

Perhaps a fourth stage could be added to the analysis of the industrial life cycle—decline, on either a relative or absolute basis. Clearly, investors should seek to spot industries in this stage and avoid them. In the 1990s, as the United States continues in the era of information processing, certain industrial sectors will decline (in some cases this decline has already started).

It is the second stage, expansion, that is probably of most interest to investors. Industries that have survived the pioneering stage often offer good opportunities, as the demand for their products and services is growing more rapidly than the economy as a whole. Growth is rapid but orderly, an appealing characteristic to investors.

Business Cycle Analysis

A second way to analyze industries is by their operating ability in relation to the economy as a whole. That is, some industries perform poorly during a recession, whereas others are able to weather it reasonably well. Some industries move closely with the business cycle, outperforming the average industry in good times and underperforming it in bad times. Investors, in analyzing industries, should be aware of these relationships.

Most investors have heard of, and are usually seeking, growth companies. In *growth industries* earnings are expected to be significantly above the average of all industries, and such growth may occur regardless of setbacks in the economy. Drugs have been a growth industry in the past, as have color television, office equipment, and computers. Growth industries in the 1980s included genetic engineering, microcomputers, and new medical devices. Current and future growth industries include robotics and cellular telephones. Clearly, one of the primary goals of fundamental security analysis is to identify the growth industries of the near and far future.

At the opposite end of the scale are the *defensive industries,* which are least affected by recessions and economic adversity. Food has long been considered such an industry. People must eat, and they continue to drink beer, eat frozen yogurt, and so on, regardless of the economy. Public utilities might also be considered a defensive industry.

Cyclical industries are most volatile—they do unusually well when the economy prospers and are likely to be hurt more when the economy falters. Durable goods are a good example of the products involved in cyclical industries. Autos, refrigerators, and stereos, for example, may be avidly sought when times are good, but such purchases may be postponed during a recession, because consumers can often make do with the old units. Countercyclical industries also exist, actually moving opposite to the prevailing economic trend. The gold mining industry is known to follow this pattern.

These three classifications of industries according to economic conditions do not constitute an exhaustive set. Additional classifications are possible and logical. For example, some industries are **interest sensitive,** that is, particularly sensitive to expectations about changes in interest rates. The financial services industry, the banking industry, and the real estate industry are obvious examples of interest-sensitive industries. Another is the building industry.

What are the implications of these classifications for investors? To predict performance of an industry over shorter periods of time, investors should carefully analyze the stage of the business cycle and the likely movements in interest rates. If the economy is heading into a recession, cyclical industries are likely to be affected more than other industries, whereas defensive industries are the least likely to be affected. With such guidelines investors may make better buy or sell decisions. Similarly, an expected rise in interest rates will have negative implications for the savings and loan industry and the home building industry, whereas an expected drop in interest rates will have the opposite effect.

These statements reinforce the importance of market analysis. Not only do investors need to know the state of the economy and market before deciding to invest, but such knowledge is valuable in selecting, or avoiding, particular industries.

As an example of applying business cycle considerations to industry analysis, consider the situation in 1982–1983. The great bull market of 1982–1983 officially began on August 13, 1982. One year later, the market, as measured by the Dow Jones Industrial Average, was up approximately 50%. Every industry appreciated during this span, ranging from more than 250% for the brokerage industry to less than 1% for the entertainment industry.

Investors who understood the economy–industry relationship realized that the cyclical industries were likely to do well as the economy improved. And, in fact, some of the largest gains were made by cyclical industries:

metals, up 135%; autos, up 98%; airlines, up 80%; and aluminum, up 76%. Some of these industries were still showing depressed earnings well into the bull market, but as several popular press articles noted in 1983, investors recognized that cyclical movements should occur in certain industries and acted accordingly.[5]

The interest-sensitive industries soared before and during this period, as investors anticipated a drop in interest rates. By mid-1982, many investors were, or already had been, looking for an improvement in the business cycle, with a corresponding drop in interest rates. Realizing that this situation would be favorable for industries substantially affected by interest rates, investors bought accordingly. And finally, lower interest rates, other things being equal, mean higher stock prices. Higher stock prices, in turn, suggest the possibility of increasing trading by investors, resulting in more brokerage commissions for the brokerage industry, which, as noted, was the best performer over this one-year period.

In 1980–1981, on the other hand, the economy experienced recession and sharply rising interest rates. Cyclical industries did poorly—autos were in last place in 1980 and forty-fourth in 1981. The November 1981 performance record for the previous 12 months showed metals in last place, with heavy building fifty-ninth, aerospace fifty-fourth, heavy machinery forty-eighth, chemicals forty-seventh, and so on.

On a short-run basis, consider again Table 11-2. According to some analysts at the time, the industries hit hardest by the crash of 1987 were those thought to be most affected in the case of a slowdown in economic growth. The strongest performers in October 1987 were the "classical defensive types of stocks."[6] As Table 11-2 shows, the electric utilities showed the smallest loss during that month. Table 11-3 shows that the electric utility industry was ranked fourth in 1988 as investors presumably sought safety; however, for the same period in 1989 this industry ranked only fifty-first out of 60 as investors switched to the stronger-performing industries in the face of a strong move upward in the S&P 500 Index.

INVESTMENTS INTUITION

Clearly, business cycle analysis for industries is a logical and worthwhile part of fundamental security analysis. Industries are sensitive to the business conditions and interest rate expectations at any given time, and the smart investor will think carefully about these factors.

[5]See Gary Putka, "Some See Activity of Certain Groups as Sign of Possible Leadership Shift," *The Wall Street Journal*, June 13, 1983, p. 47.

[6]See Karen Slater, "Not All Industries Suffered Alike in Stock Market's Cruelest Month," *The Wall Street Journal*, November 2, 1987, p. 33.

Qualitative Aspects of Industry Analysis

The analyst or investor should consider several important qualitative factors that can characterize an industry. Knowing about these factors will help investors to analyze a particular industry and will aid in assessing its future prospects.

The Historical Performance As we have learned, some industries perform well and others perform poorly over long periods of time. Although performance is not always consistent and predictable on the basis of the past, an industry's track record should not be ignored. In Table 11-1 we saw that the lead and zinc industry performed poorly in both 1950 and 1960 (in relation to the base of 1941–1943). It continued to do badly in 1973. The office and business equipment industry and the electronics industry, on the other hand, showed strength at the 1950 and 1960 checkpoints and continued to do well in 1973.

Investors should consider the historical record of sales and earnings growth and price performance. Although the past cannot simply be extrapolated into the future, it does provide some useful information.

Competition The nature of the competitive conditions in an industry can provide useful information in assessing its future. Is the industry protected from the entrance of new competitors as a result of control of raw materials, prohibitive cost of building plants, the level of production needed to operate profitably, and so forth?

According to one analysis, the intensity of competition in an industry determines that industry's ability to sustain above average returns.[7] This intensity is not a matter of luck, but a reflection of underlying factors that determine the strength of five basic competitive factors:

1. Threat of new entrants.
2. Bargaining power of buyers.
3. Rivalry between existing competitors.
4. Threat of substitute products.
5. Bargaining power of suppliers.

These factors are seen as ranging from intense in some industries (e.g., tires and paper) where spectacular profits do not occur to mild in other industries (e.g., cosmetics and toiletries) where high returns are not unusual.

Investors need to consider carefully the future ability of particular

---

[7]See Michael E. Porter, "Industry Structure and Competitive Strategy: Keys to Profitability," *Financial Analysts Journal*, July–August 1980, pp. 30–41.

industries to compete both at home and abroad. Assessing these five factors is a good way to start.

Government Effects Government regulations and actions can have significant effects on industries. The investor must attempt to assess the results of these effects or, at the very least, be well aware that they exist and may continue.

Consider the breakup of AT&T as of January 1, 1984. This one action changed the telecommunications industry permanently, and perhaps others as well. As a second example, the deregulating of the financial services industries resulted in banks and savings and loans competing more directly with each other, offering consumers many of the same services. Such an action has to affect the relative performance of these two industries as well as some of their other competitors, such as the brokerage industry (which can now also offer similar services in many respects).

Structural Changes A fourth factor to consider is the structural changes that occur in the economy. As the United States continues to move from an industrial society to an information–communications society, major industries will be affected. New industries with tremendous potential are, and will be, emerging, whereas some traditional industries, such as steel, may never recover their former positions.

Structural shifts can occur even within relatively new industries. For example, in the early 1980s the microcomputer industry was a young, dynamic industry with numerous competitors, some of whom enjoyed phenomenal success in a short time. The introduction of microcomputers by IBM in 1982, however, forever changed that industry. Other hardware manufacturers sought to be compatible with IBM's personal computer and suppliers rushed to supply items such as software, printers, and additional memory boards. Virtually every part of the industry was significantly affected by IBM's decision to enter this market.

Evaluating Future Industry Prospects

Ultimately, investors are interested in expected performance in the future. They realize that such estimates are difficult and are likely to be somewhat in error, but they know that equity prices are a function of expected parameters, not past, known values. How, then, is an investor to proceed?

Ideally, investors would like to value industries along the lines discussed in Chapter 9 for the market. They would like to be able to estimate the expected earnings for an industry and the expected multiplier and combine them to produce an estimate of value. However, this is not easy to do. It requires an understanding of several relationships and estimates of several variables. Fortunately, considerable information is readily available to help investors in their analysis of industries. Investors should be aware of the primary sources of information about industries and the nature of the information available. These issues are discussed later.

The next best alternative to detailed industry analysis is to apply the concepts discussed here in a general way. To determine industry performance for shorter periods (e.g., one year), investors should ask themselves the following types of questions:

1. Given the current and prospective economic situation, which industries are likely to show improving earnings?
2. Which industries are likely to show improving P/E ratios; or, what is the likely direction of interest rates and which industries would be most affected by a significant change in interest rates? A change in interest rates, other things being equal, leads to a change in the discount rate (and a change in the multiplier).
3. Which industries are likely to be most affected by possible future political events, such as a new administration, renewed inflation, new trade restrictions an increase in defense spending, and so on?
4. Are investors valuing future (and uncertain) payoffs too highly?

To forecast industry performance in the long run, investors should ask the following questions:

1. Which industries are obvious candidates for growth and prosperity over, say, the next decade? (In the 1980s, such industries as microcomputers, the software industry, telecommunications, and cellular telephones could have been identified.)
2. Which industries appear likely to have difficulties as the United States changes from an industrial to an information-collecting and processing economy? (Possible candidates are automobiles and steel.)

As with all security analysis, there are several ways to proceed in analyzing industries. Much of this process is common sense. For example, if you can reasonably forecast a declining number of competitors in an industry, it stands to reason that, other things being equal, the remaining firms will be more profitable. For an example of this type of industry analysis, see Box 11-1.

Sources of Industry Information

General Information Several sources provide basic data on industries, including the following:

1. Standard & Poor's: (a) *The Annual Analysis Handbook* with monthly supplements provides per-share statistics for the industries covered. The data include sales, profit margin, income taxes, depreciation, earnings, dividends, capital expenditures, and so on. (b) The *Industry Survey* cov-

BOX 11-1

FEW IS MORE

When does less equal more? Acquisition binges that shrink the number of players in an industry, and thereby the competition, allow for vastly more profits for the survivors. It's almost surefire.

You can apply the same principle to investing in stocks: Invest in industries where the number of competitors has fallen to a handful.

Look at the airline industry as a 1980s example. Deregulation led to price wars, which led to red ink, which led to a myriad of takeovers, causing much increased concentration. And that has led to tremendous rate hikes recently. You can feel it when you fly. The price you pay for a ticket will reflect the reduction in competition.

Where can you see hot-off-the-press mass consolidations to tip us off on fat future profits? The clearest sign I see is in the auto parts market, with particular emphasis on replacement parts. About 19% of the industry has consolidated in the last 18 months. According to various other estimates, in the last five years the auto parts industry has lost between one-third and one-half of its participants. It has been very much an acquire-or-be-acquired world.

One reason is that, at the original equipment level, the big three automakers have signaled they want fewer and higher-quality suppliers, à la Japanese-style management. But perhaps the main cause is simply that there has been too much competitive price bashing—too many bashers. Retail prices for replacement parts are too low.

But remember, the darkest hour is just before the price goes up. Here's the telling aspect: After recent mergers, the three biggest players make up over 75% of the muffler market—original equipment and replacement. There may be a little more consolidation, but not much, and soon thereafter you can expect higher prices for mufflers, especially for the big kids on the block.

The whole trend to concentration in auto and replacement parts verges on, and is likely to become, what introductory economics texts call "oligopoly"—the nearest thing to monopoly power the law allows. Higher prices on Main Street should translate directly to higher prices on Wall Street.

Source: Adapted from Kenneth L. Fisher, "Few Is More," *Forbes*, May 1, 1989, p. 406. Excerpted by permission of *Forbes* magazine, May 1, 1989, © Forbes, Inc., 1989.

ers major industries with basic analysis revised annually and current analysis revised quarterly. (c) Standard & Poor's *Register* provides Standard Industrial Classification codes for all companies.[8]

2. *Robert Morris Associates Annual Studies* and *Dun & Bradstreet Key Business Ratios* provide ratios for a number of industries.

---

[8]Each four-digit code, starting with industry 0111 and going through industry 9661, includes companies under it in alphabetical order.

The *Quarterly Financial Report for Manufacturing, Mining and Trade Corporations*, published jointly by the Federal Trade Commission and the Securities and Exchange Commission, provides timely information on individual industries. Included are data on sales, net profit, and so forth. Individual industries can be compared to groups of industries (e.g., all mining corporations) and to all manufacturing corporations.

Forbes magazine has an annual rating of industry performance in its early January issue. Five-year figures on profitability and growth of sales and earnings are shown for a large number of industries and for individual companies within these industries.[9] An excerpt is shown in Figure 11-2.[10] Thus, this source provides investors with calculated information they can use to assess industries (and companies within those industries).

The Value Line Investment Survey covers both individual companies and the industries that the covered companies comprise. Companies are organized by industry, with each weekly issue giving information on several industries at a time. A write-up of industry developments, financial data, and trends introduces each group of companies (industry) covered by Value Line. Investors can obtain data on such variables as industry sales, operating margin, profit margin, tax rate, and capital structure.

Value Line estimates industry statistics for both the current year and the coming year. It also *ranks* all industries in terms of timeliness (probable performance over the next 12 months); therefore, investors have a unique and readily available short-term forecast. Figure 11-3 shows a weekly ranking of all industries covered by Value Line.

As discussed earlier in the chapter, *The Media General Financial Weekly* publishes up-to-date weekly information on 60 industries, showing price performance over four recent periods. This is a convenient source of recent industry performance.

Specific Information Many publications that contain specific industry information are available. Industry magazines are a good example, including such publications as *Chemical Week* and *Automotive News*. Another source of specific industry information is trade associations, which compile statistics for their particular industries. Examples include the American Banker's Association and the Iron and Steel Institute.

Obviously, brokerage firms prepare many reports on both companies and industries. Because their research analysts are typically organized along industry lines, reports are often issued on specific industries.

---

[9]Additional information includes the debt/equity ratio, return on total capital, and the net profit margin.

[10]Figure 11-2 is excerpted from the "Computers and Electronics" grouping used by *Forbes*.

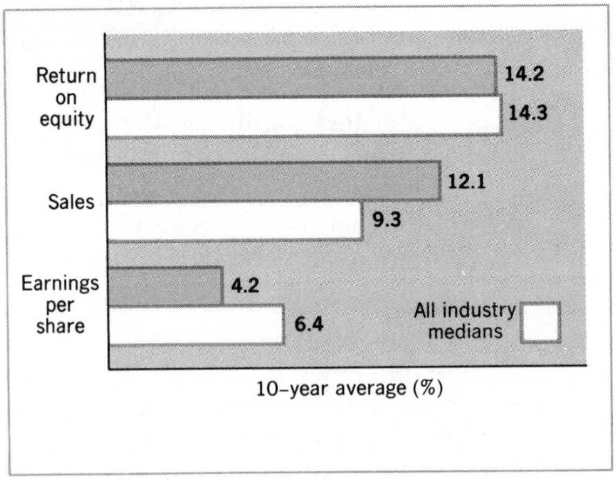

Computers & communications	Profitability					Growth						Sales	Net income
	Return on equity					Sales			Earnings per share				
Company	10-year average %	5-year average %	latest 12 mos %	Return on capital latest 12 mos %	Debt/capital %	10-year average %	5-year average %	latest 12 mos %	10-year average %	5-year average %	latest 12 mos %	latest 12 mos $mil	latest 12 mos $mil
Hardware													
Apple Computer	36.6	31.6	43.2	36.2	0.0	38.4	28.5	29.8	37.3	41.6	14.6	5,284	454
Mark IV Industries	29.0	32.7	21.8	7.1	85.7	40.6	96.2	113.4	35.1	50.9	14.9	945	24
Cray Research	28.9	30.8	17.5	16.4	13.0	39.5	37.8	33.3	39.4	42.7	23.5	785	125
EG&G	26.7	25.1	21.2	19.6	2.4	11.9	7.8	20.8	12.9	5.6	6.8	1,614	69
Intergraph	25.2[a]	18.6	12.5	12.1	1.0	39.4[a]	23.2	6.5	38.4[a]	15.2	−5.2	831	81
Molex	25.1	23.4	14.8	14.2	1.3	19.3	21.0	9.1	17.6	16.1	−8.5	577	57
Premier Industrial	21.7	21.8	29.2	26.1	2.8	8.1	9.4	10.7	13.5	14.9	16.3	607	71
AMP	20.7	20.3	19.6	18.0	4.7	11.3	11.3	7.9	9.2	13.3	−1.8	2,812	297
IBM	20.1	17.1	14.0	11.3	17.9	11.7	7.6	9.3	6.8	−2.3	7.2	63,185	5,514
Thomas & Betts	18.1	18.5	17.6	15.7	9.6	8.6	12.3	7.5	5.8	12.0	−3.0	535	55
Hewlett-Packard	17.0	15.6	18.2	17.7	7.7	17.4	14.2	21.0	15.2	10.2	4.8	11,899	829
SCI Systems	16.5	15.1	4.3	4.7	61.5	45.0	24.9	23.8	29.6	15.6	−65.3	1,050	7
NCR	16.4	17.7	18.6	16.0	9.0	8.0	10.4	−0.6	7.8	13.8	−0.4	5,972	414
Prime Computer	16.1[a]	11.0	def	def	19.5	24.6[a]	22.0	8.9	NM	−12.5	P-D	1,558	−145
Marshall Industries	15.7	17.5	16.1	13.2	20.2	21.5	19.5	14.4	21.8[a]	22.3	−4.8	529	20
Northern Telecom	15.4	14.5	7.0	6.1	20.8	13.3	14.1	14.1	NM	NM	−47.8	5,852	191
Tandem Computers	15.0	13.8	13.1	12.7	4.8	38.0	25.4	24.2	30.3	23.5	21.9	1,633	118
Carlisle Cos	15.0	11.0	11.0	10.6	8.4	7.1	4.8	0.2	NM	−6.0	−9.1	562	21
Digital Equipment	14.9	16.3	12.6	12.7	1.6	22.5	20.8	8.8	15.8	34.7	−17.1	12,931	1,000
Analog Devices	14.8	12.1	11.4	10.5	3.6	19.3	12.5	7.9	17.3	NM	17.4	458	39
Amdahl	14.3	19.1	16.8	14.5	6.4	19.5	19.7	16.2	14.9	37.6	−14.2	2,021	175
Western Digital	14.2	22.1	6.5	6.8	33.0	62.2[a]	69.7	10.8	NM	NM	−58.4	970	19
Intel	13.0	14.5	16.4	14.7	14.9	16.7	15.7	8.8	19.3	NM	−34.1	2,959	354
Motorola	12.2	11.2	14.5	15.0	16.2	13.0	11.7	16.4	NM	NM	15.3	9,179	490
Wang Laboratories	11.4	3.2	def	def	35.4	31.1	13.2	−11.5	NM	−17.5	P-D	2,743	−500
Perkin-Elmer	10.6	7.9	def	def	5.1	6.9	3.0	−32.7	3.8	5.6	P-D	784	−24
Harris Corp	10.3	8.1	2.8	3.5	23.8	9.3	5.7	26.2	−4.4	NM	−59.5	2,506	26

D-D: Deficit to deficit. D-P: Deficit to profit. P-D: Profit to deficit. def: Deficit. NA: Not available. NE: Negative equity. NM: Not meaningful a: Nine-year average. b: Eight-year average. c: Four-year average. d: Three-year average. For further explanation, see page 120.

Sources: FORBES; Value Line Data Base Service via Lotus CD Investment.

FIGURE 11-2 **Forbes** ***annual industry analysis for the computers and communication industry, 1990.***
Source: Forbes, "Annual Report on American Industry," January 8, 1990, p. 134. Reprinted by permission of *Forbes* magazine, January 8, 1990. © Forbes Inc., 1990.

INDUSTRIES, IN ORDER OF TIMELINESS*

Arrow (▲▼) before name indicates that a **significant change in Rank** has occurred since the preceding week.

1 Drug	25 Food Processing	49 Electric Utility (East)	73▲Maritime
2 Investment Co.(Foreign)	26 Investment Co.(Domestic)	50 Metal Fabricating	74 Diversified Co.
3 Shoe	27 Gold/Silver Mining	51 Retail (Special Lines)	75 Homebuilding
4 Beverage	28 Insurance (Diversified)	52 Semiconductor	76 Computer & Peripherals
5 Medical Supplies	29 Packaging & Container	53 Broadcasting/Cable TV	77 Chemical (Diversified)
6 Oilfield Services/Equip.	30 Chemical (Specialty)	54 Office Equip & Supplies	78 Newspaper
7 Computer Software & Svcs	31 Foreign Electronics	55 Natural Gas (Distrib.)	79 Manuf. Housing/Rec Veh
8 Advertising	32 Metals & Mining (Ind'l)	56 Canadian Energy	80 Air Transport
9 Household Products	33▲Home Appliance	57▼Tobacco	81 Recreation
10 European Diversified	34 Toiletries/Cosmetics	58 Retail Store	82 Bank
11 Toys & School Supplies	35 Investment Co. (Income)	59 Bank (Midwest)	83 Real Estate
12 Machinery (Const&Mining)	36 Machine Tool	60 Electric Util. (Central)	84 R.E.I.T.
13 Industrial Services	37 Electronics	61 Railroad	85 Textile
14 Restaurant	38 Aluminum	62 Furn./Home Furnishings	86 Auto & Truck (Foreign)
15 Coal/Alternate Energy	39 Chemical (Basic)	63 Precision Instrument	87 Publishing
16 Insurance(Prop/Casualty)	40 Drugstore	64 Steel (Integrated)	88 Aerospace/Defense
17 Petroleum (Producing)	41 Metals & Mining (Div.)	65 Steel (General)	89 Thrift
18 Natural Gas(Diversified)	42 Steel (Specialty)	66▼Auto Parts (Replacement)	90 Cement
19 Financial Services	43 Tire & Rubber	67 Food Wholesalers	91 Trucking/Transp. Leasing
20 Medical Services	44 Retail Building Supply	68 Securities Brokerage	92 Bank (Canadian)
21 Electrical Equipment	45 Machinery	69 Apparel	93 Auto & Truck
22 Insurance (Life)	46 Paper & Forest Products	70 Building Materials	94 Hotel/Gaming
23 Telecom. Equipment	47 Telecom. Services	71 Copper	95 Auto Parts (OEM)
24 Grocery	48 Petroleum (Integrated)	72 Electric Utility (West)	

***Based on the Timeliness ranks of the stocks in the industry**

FIGURE 11-3 ***Weekly Industry Rankings in order of timeliness by* The Value Line Investment Survey**

Source: The Value Line Investment Survey, "Summary of Advices and Index, March 2, 1990, p. 24. Copyright © 1990 by Value Line Publishing Inc. Used by permission.

Summary

- Industry analysis is the second of three steps in fundamental security analysis, following aggregate market analysis but preceding individual company analysis. The objective is to identify those industries that will perform best in the future in terms of returns to stockholders.
- Is industry analysis valuable? Yes, because over the long term some industries perform much better than others.
- Industry performance is not consistent; past price performance does not always predict future price performance. Particularly over shorter periods such as one or two years, industry performance rankings may completely reverse themselves.
- Although the term *industry* at first seems self-explanatory, industry definitions and classifications are not straightforward, and the trend toward diversification of activities over the years has blurred the lines even more.
- The Standard Industrial Classification system, a comprehensive scheme for classifying major industry groups, specific industries, specific functions, and specific products, brings some order to the problem.
- A number of investment information services, such as Standard & Poor's, Value Line, and Media General, use their own industry classifications.
- To analyze industries, a useful first step is to examine their stage in the life cycle, which in its simplest form consists of the pioneering, expan-

sion, and maturity stages. Most investors will usually be interested in the expansion stage, in which growth is rapid and risk is tolerable.

- A second industry analysis approach is business cycle analysis. Industries perform differently at various stages in the business cycle.
- A third phase involves a qualitative analysis of important factors affecting industries.
- Investors interested in evaluating future industry prospects have a wide range of data available for their use. These data can be used for a detailed, in-depth analysis of industries using standard security analysis techniques for examining recent ratings of industry performance (e.g., the *Forbes* data in Figure 11-2) or for ranking likely industry performance (e.g., the Value Line industry rankings in Figure 11-3).

Key Words

Cyclical industries
Industry life cycle
Interest-sensitive industries
Standard Industrial Classification (SIC) system

Questions

11-1 Why is it difficult to classify industries?

11-2 Why is industry analysis valuable?

11-3 Name some industries that you would expect to perform well in the next five years and in the next 10–15 years.

11-4 How consistent is year-to-year industry performance?

11-5 What are the stages in the life cycle for an industry? Can you think of other stages to add?

11-6 Name an industry that is currently in each of the three life cycle stages.

11-7 In which stage of the life cycle do investors face the highest risk of losing a substantial part of the investment?

11-8 Which industries are the most sensitive to the business cycle? the least sensitive?

11-9 Explain how aggregate market analysis can be important in analyzing industries in relation to the business cycle.

11-10 Explain the concept used in valuing industries.

11-11 What sources of information would be useful to an investor doing a detailed industry analysis?

11-12 Explain how Figure 11-2 might be useful to an investor doing industry analysis.

Selected References

Livingstone, Miles. "Industry Movements of Common Stocks." *Journal of Finance*, June 1977, pp. 861–874.

One of the most detailed and well-known analyses of industries can be found in Michael Porter's work. See, as an example:

Porter, Michael E. "Industry Structure and Competitive Strategy: Keys to Profitability." *Financial Analysts Journal*, July–August 1980, pp. 30–41.

Porter, Michael E. *Competitive Advantage: Creating and Sustaining Superior Performance.* New York: Free Press, 1985.

CHAPTER 12

Company Analysis

Given that market analysis indicates a favorable time to invest in common stocks and that an investor has analyzed industries to find those with the most promising future, it remains to choose promising companies within those industries. The last step in fundamental analysis, therefore, is to analyze individual companies. An investor should think in terms of, and analyze to the extent practical, the two components of fundamental value: earnings or dividend streams, and a required rate of return or P/E ratio.

Fundamental Analysis

Fundamental analysis at the company level involves analyzing basic financial variables in order to estimate intrinsic value. These variables include sales, profit margins, depreciation, the tax rate, sources of financing, asset utilization, and other factors. Additional analysis could involve the firm's competitive position in its industry, labor relations, technological changes, management, foreign competition, and so on. The end result of fundamental analysis is an estimate of the two factors that determine a security's (or industry's or the market's) value: a cash flow stream and a required rate of return (alternatively, a P/E ratio).

As discussed in Chapter 9, the dividend discount model is one of two basic frameworks most often used for explaining common stock valuation. Assuming that the dividend growth rate for a particular company can be expected to be constant over the future, the dividend discount model reduces to the normal constant growth version shown as Equation 12-1 (Equation 9-5 from Chapter 9):

$$\text{Intrinsic value} = V_{cs} = \frac{D_1}{k-g} \qquad (12\text{-}1)$$

where

V_{cs} = the estimated value of the common stock today
D_1 = the expected dollar dividend to be paid next period
k = the required rate of return
g = the estimated future growth rate of dividends

In fundamental analysis the **intrinsic value** of a stock is its justified price, the price justified by a company's fundamental financial variables.

Alternatively, for a short-run estimate of intrinsic value the earnings multiplier model could be used. Intrinsic value is the product of the estimated earnings for a company and the estimated multiplier or P/E ratio, as shown in Equation 12-2.[1]

$$\text{Intrinsic value} = \text{Estimated EPS} \times \text{Justified P/E ratio} \qquad (12\text{-}2)$$

Using either Equation 12-1 or Equation 12-2, a stock's calculated intrinsic value is compared to its current market price. If the intrinsic value is larger than the current market price, the stock would be considered undervalued—a buy. If intrinsic value is less than the market price, the stock would be considered overvalued and should be avoided or possibly sold if owned; further, an overvalued security could be sold short.

INVESTMENTS INTUITION

Based on the preceding, we can state that the intrinsic value of a share of stock is a function of

Using the dividend discount model:

$$\text{Intrinsic value} = f(D_1, k, \text{and } g)$$

Using the multiplier model:

$$\text{Intrinsic value} = f(E_1, \text{P/E})$$

For purposes of discussion, we concentrate on earnings and P/E ratios for several reasons. First, dividends are paid from earnings. Although the two series are not perfectly correlated, future dividend growth typically must come from the future earnings growth. Second, the close correlations between earnings changes and stock price changes is well documented and can be demonstrated graphically. To see why investors and security analysts focus so much attention on earnings, consider Figure 12-1, which shows the 50 best and worst stocks for a five-year period. The top 50 stocks from the sample of 650 companies studied showed a five-year price appreciation of 182%, with a change in EPS of 199%; for the bottom 50 performers, with a price depreciation of −62%, the change in EPS was −61%. This figure dramatically illustrates the importance of EPS in common stock analysis. Although most comparisons of earnings and stock prices are not as striking as those in Figure 12-1, EPS changes and price changes typically are very closely related for the best-performing and worst-performing stocks and are clearly related for stocks in general.

[1]Technically, to calculate the intrinsic value of a stock using the multiplier method, analysts often determine what is called the normalized EPS, defined as the normal earnings for a company under typical operating conditions. Thus, unusual impacts on earnings are adjusted for, such as nonrecurring earnings or extraordinary earnings.

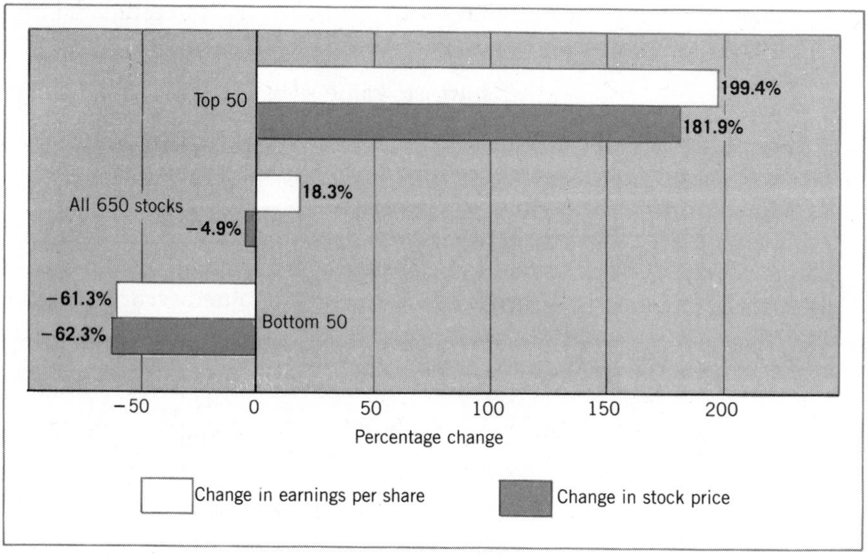

FIGURE 12-1 ***Median changes in earnings and stock price: five-year horizon, 1966–1970.***
Source: V. Niederhoffer and P. J. Regan, "Earnings Changes, Analysts' Forecasts and Stock Prices," *Financial Analysts Journal*, Vol. 28 (May–June 1972), p. 71. Reprinted by permission.

Understanding Earnings

If investors are to focus on **earnings per share (EPS)** for a company, the key component in security analysis, they should understand how EPS is derived and what it represents. For investors an EPS figure is the bottom line—the item of major interest—in a company's financial statements. Furthermore, they must understand EPS before they can attempt to estimate it.

The Financial Statements

Investors rely heavily on the **financial statements** of a corporation, which provide the major financial data about companies. To illustrate certain points in this general discussion, we shall examine the 1989 financial statements for EG&G, Inc., a producer of technical and scientific products and services for customers worldwide.

The Balance Sheet The balance sheet shows the portfolio of assets for a corporation, as well as its liabilities and owner's equity, at one point in time. The amounts at which items are carried on the balance sheet are dictated by accounting conventions. Cash is the actual dollar amount, whereas marketable securities could be at cost or market value (EG&G's is at cost). Stockholders' equity and the fixed assets are on a book value basis.

The balance sheet for EG&G, shown in Table 12-1, is for the year 1989, which also includes data for 1988.[2] The asset side is divided into current assets and long-term assets (labeled as property, plant, and equipment) plus investments and other assets. In the case of EG&G, the net property, plant, and equipment is small compared to the current assets, whereas in the case of General Motors, for example, the fixed assets exceed the current assets.

The liabilities on a balance sheet are divided between current liabilities (payable within one year) and permanent liabilities (which include stockholders' equity). For 1989, EG&G had $256 million in current liabilities, $8.8 million in long-term debt, and $349 million in stockholders' equity, plus miscellaneous items. Note that the stockholders' investment includes 30.051 million shares of stock outstanding as of 1989 with a par value of $1, some capital in excess of par value, and a substantial amount of retained earnings ($345 million). It is important to recognize that the retained earnings item does not represent "spendable" funds for a company; rather, it designates that part of previous earnings not paid out as dividends. Although 1 million shares of preferred stock have been authorized by the board of directors, no shares were outstanding at the end of 1989.[3]

A number of financial ratios can be calculated from balance sheet data that help assess the company's financial strength (e.g., the current ratio, a measure of liquidity, or the debt-to-total-assets ratio, a measure of leverage). Some of these ratios will be demonstrated later in the analysis.

The Income Statement This statement is used more frequently by investors, not only to assess current management performance but also to estimate the future profitability of the company. The income statement represents flows for a particular period, usually one year. Table 12-2 shows the income statement for EG&G covering the years 1989, 1988, and 1987 (many income statements show only the current and previous years).

The key item for investors on the income statement is the after-tax net income, which, divided by the number of common shares outstanding, produces earnings per share. Earnings from continuing operations are used to judge the success of the company and are almost always what is reported by the financial press. Nonrecurring earnings, such as net extraordinary items that arise from unusual and infrequently occurring transactions, are separated from income from continuing operations.

Table 12-2 clearly illustrates the "flow" in an income statement. Start-

[2]Standard practice in financial statements is to show at least two years of results, allowing comparisons to be made.

[3]As explained in Chapter 2, preferred stock, though often treated by investors as a fixed-income security, is in fact an equity security and is shown as part of the stockholders' equity.

TABLE 12-1 ***Consolidated Balance Sheet, EG&G, Inc., 1989***

(Dollars in thousands)	1989	1988
Current Assets:		
Cash and cash equivalents	$ 28,581	$ 41,949
Accounts receivable (Note 3)	237,489	201,803
Inventories (Note 4)	116,976	100,861
Other (Note 15)	24,303	19,767
Total Current Assets	407,349	364,380
Property, Plant and Equipment:		
At cost (Note 5)	208,458	186,419
Less—Accumulated depreciation and amortization	135,408	117,982
Net Property, Plant and Equipment	73,050	68,437
Investments (Note 6)	38,968	62,833
Intangible and Other Assets (Note 7)	124,036	43,613
Total Assets	$643,403	$539,263
Current Liabilities:		
Short-term debt (Note 8)	$104,531	$ 34,182
Accounts payable	51,985	50,960
Accrued expenses (Note 9)	99,646	88,085
Total Current Liabilities	256,162	173,227
Long-Term Debt (Note 8)	8,859	14,843
Deferred Income Taxes (Note 15)	3,573	8,780
Other Long-Term Liabilities (Note 12)	25,822	10,066
Stockholders' Equity (Note 10):		
Preferred stock—$1 par value, authorized 1,000,000 shares; none outstanding	—	—
Common stock—$1 par value, authorized 100,000,000 shares; issued 30,051,000 shares in 1989 and 30,052,000 shares in 1988	30,051	30,052
Capital in excess of par value	5,728	5,994
Retained earnings	345,429	298,166
Cumulative translation adjustments (Note 1)	2,095	(571)
	383,303	333,641
Less—Cost of shares held in treasury; 1,054,000 shares in 1989 and 41,000 shares in 1988	34,316	1,294
Total Stockholders' Equity	348,987	332,347
Total Liabilities and Stockholders' Equity	$643,403	$539,263

Source: Annual Report to Stockholders, 1989, EG&G, Inc., p. 44. Courtesy of EG&G, Inc.,

ing with revenues (net sales plus other income), costs and expenses are deducted, the largest of which are cost of sales. The difference (adjusted for certain items as necessary) is "income before income taxes," which for EG&G in 1989 was $99.8 million.[4] Subtracting a provision for taxes leaves a

[4]Interest expense and interest, and gains and losses on investments and dispositions are included in "other expenses."

TABLE 12-2 ***Consolidated Statement of Income, EG&G, Inc., 1989***

(Dollars in thousands except per share data)	1989	1988	1987
Sales (Note 1):			
Products	$1,091,321	$ 909,777	$ 823,721
Services	558,837	496,503	441,122
Total sales	1,650,158	1,406,280	1,264,843
Costs and Expenses (Notes 4, 11, 12, and 13):			
Cost of Sales:			
Products	894,544	718,356	649,140
Services	477,371	420,580	374,625
	1,371,915	1,138,936	1,023,765
Selling, general and administrative expenses	179,850	169,334	159,344
Total costs and expenses	1,551,765	1,308,270	1,183,109
Income From Operations	98,393	98,010	81,734
Other income (expense), net (Note 14)	1,393	(624)	3,023
Income Before Income Taxes	99,786	97,386	84,757
Provision for Federal and foreign income taxes (Note 15)	29,936	28,729	27,216
Net Income	$ 69,850	$ 68,657	$ 57,541
Earnings Per Share (Note 16)	$ 2.40	$ 2.30	$ 1.92

Source: Annual Report to Stockholders, 1989, EG&G, Inc., p. 45. Courtesy of EG&G, Inc.

net income (total dollars) of $69.9 million, which, divided by the weighted number of shares outstanding, produces EPS of $2.40.[5]

Certifying the Statements The earnings on an income statement are derived on the basis of **generally accepted accounting principles (GAAPs).** The company adheres to a standard set of rules developed by the accounting profession on the basis of historical costs, which can be measured objectively. An auditor from an independent accounting firm certifies that the earnings have been derived according to accounting standards in a statement labeled the "auditor's report." Note that the auditor's report does not guarantee the accuracy or the quality of the earnings in an absolute sense, but only that the statements present fairly the financial position of the company for a particular period. The auditors are certifying, in effect, that generally accepted accounting principles were applied on a consistent basis. The Financial Accounting Standards Board (FASB), which succeeded the Accounting Principles Board of the American Institute of Certified Public Accountants in 1972, currently formulates accounting standards.

[5]In 1989, the weighted average shares for EG&G, which is used to calculate EPS, was 29.131 million.

The Problem with Reported Earnings

Although earnings in particular, and financial statements in general, are derived on the basis of GAAPs and are certified in an auditor's report, a problem exists with earnings. The problem, simply stated, is that reported EPS for a company (i.e., accounting EPS) is not a precise figure that is readily comparable over time, and the EPS for different companies often are not comparable to each other.

The problem with earnings is that alternative accounting principles can be, and are, used to prepare the financial statements. Many of the items in the balance sheet and income statement can be accounted for in at least two ways, resulting in what one might call the "conservative" treatment and the "liberal" treatment of EPS. Given the number of items that constitute the financial statements, the possible number of acceptable (i.e., that conform to GAAPs) combinations that could be used is enormous. Holding everything else constant, such as sales, products, and operating ability, a company could produce several legal and permissible EPS figures, depending solely on the accounting principles used.

Example. *Forbes* magazine once illustrated how a single company, using only two sets of principles (liberal and conservative), could produce in one year an EPS of $1.99 per share or an EPS of $3.14, a number more than 50% higher.[6] ▪

The question that investors must try to answer is, "Which EPS best represents the true position of a company?" A good example of the problem with earnings, and how reported income can be made to vary, is shown in Box 12-1. This illustration ties this whole issue together nicely—the problem, the role of the SEC and the accounting profession, and the plight of the investor.

Reported EPS is a function of the many alternative GAAPs in use. In truth, it is extremely difficult, if not impossible, for the "true" performance of a company to be reflected consistently in one figure. And each company is different, so is it reasonable to expect one accounting system to capture the true performance of all companies? The business world is complex, and one can make a case for the necessity of alternative treatments of the same item or process, such as inventories or depreciation.

Accountants are caught in the middle, between investors, who want a clean, clear-cut EPS figure, and company management, which wishes to present the financial statements in the most favorable light. After all, management hires the accounting firm, and, subject to certain guidelines, management can change accounting firms. As long as the company follows GAAPs, it may be difficult for the accountant to resist management pres-

[6]See "What Are Earnings? The Growing Credibility Gap," *Forbes*, May 15, 1967, pp. 28–29.

BOX 12-1

EARNINGS HELPER

No one ever said accounting was an exact science. How inexact it can be has been illustrated in two recent cases: Cineplex Odeon and Blockbuster Entertainment. Both companies minimized the amortization of assets to the benefit of reported earnings.

What's going on here? When it comes to amortization and depreciation, Generally Accepted Accounting Principles provide only the vaguest of guidelines. Management is supposed to write off assets over their estimated useful lives. But asset life expectancy is highly subjective, and is influenced by a myriad of factors. If something happens that will reduce (or lengthen) an asset's useful life, should management be required to change the depreciation schedule, to better reflect economic reality?

For their part, the accountants retort that they're doing the best they can—that when reviewing depreciation, they look at engineering reports, industry practices and the company's historical use of its assets. Even so, they say, it is difficult to pass judgment on how much value can be squeezed from the assets.

As a result, the corporation's auditors will probably go along with management's judgment as long as the writeoff period doesn't diverge too much from general industry practice. *Yet the permissible variations are so great as to make it difficult to compare two companies' earnings without intimate knowledge of their accounting practices* [emphasis added].

What can an investor do? Under Generally Accepted Accounting Principles, whenever a company stretches out the lives of its assets, management must note (but not justify) any material change in the reported earnings in the footnotes to the annual report. And an accounting shift from accelerated to straight-line depreciation must be both footnoted and justified—although the justification can be vague.

In December 1987 the SEC asked the American Institute of Certified Public Accountants to consider having any change in the length of depreciation highlighted in the auditor's report accompanying financial statements. Presumably this would draw attention to the change and put investors on the alert.

But the accountants retort that disclosure in the footnotes is enough. Says Daniel Guy, vice president for auditing for the American Institute of Certified Public Accountants: "Footnotes are very important. Why is it necessary to highlight them? I can't imagine anyone being hoodwinked by changes in depreciation anyway." Maybe so, but some pretty smart investors were taken in by the Cineplex Odeon and Blockbuster Entertainment amortization schedules.

Source: Adapted from Dana Wechsler, "Earnings helper," *Forbes,* June 12, 1989, pp. 150, 153. Excerpted by permission. *Forbes* magazine, June 12, 1989, © Forbes, Inc., 1989.

sure to use particular principles, as Box 12-1 points out. At some point, an accounting firm may resign as a company's auditor as a result of the problems and pressures that can arise.

It is also true that the FASB faces conflicting demands when it formulates or changes accounting principles. Various interest groups want items accounted for in specific ways. The end result is that the "standards" issued by the FASB are often compromises that do not fully resolve the particular issue, and in some cases, they may create additional complications. Since its formation, the FASB has issued numerous standards and exposure drafts and has tackled some very difficult issues, such as inflation accounting and foreign currency translations. Much remains to be done, however, and this will probably remain true for a long time.

Should the FASB falter in its job, or investors actively demand more action in the way of "tighter" accounting rules, the government could intervene and issue its own rulings. The Securities and Exchange Commission has the authority to do this because corporations must file detailed financial data with it. In fact, the SEC has issued some definitions of acceptable accounting practices over the years, thereby acting as a prod to the accounting groups to continue their progress. On the other hand, as Box 12-1 demonstrates, the SEC may feel it is unable to insist upon more conformity, preferring instead to have the accounting profession take the responsibility.

INVESTMENTS INTUITION

It is important for all investors to remember that reported EPS is not the precise figure that it first appears to be. Unless adjustments are made, EPS may not be comparable on either a time series or a cross-sectional basis. This is true of the market as a whole and of individual companies.

Some EPS figures are better than others in the sense that they have been derived using more conservative principles. In other words, they are of higher quality. In an article on the quality of earnings, Bernstein and Seigel stated[7]:

> a company's reported earnings figure is often taken by the unsophisticated user of financial statements as the quantitative measure of the firm's well-being. Of course, any professional knows that earnings numbers are in *large part* the product of conscious and often subjective choices between various accounting treatments and business options, as well as of various external economic factors. . . . If he wants to assess the true earning power of each

[7]See Leopold Bernstein and Joel Seigel, "The Concept of Earnings Quality," *Financial Analysts Journal*, July–August 1979.

company, the financial statement user must make some determination of the "quality of its earnings" [emphasis added].

Example. In mid-1989, some analysts were warning that the quality of corporate earnings had deteriorated steadily for several years and that the market had not yet reflected this decline. According to one estimate, "true" operating profits declined some 16% in three years (first quarter 1986 through first quarter 1989), whereas reported profits for the S&P 500 Index were some 72% higher.[8] One investment strategist estimated that the elimination of deferred tax credits on balance sheets added a one-time gain of $1.25 to average S&P 500 earnings of $27.50 for the year. ▪

Quality assessments are typically difficult to make and require considerable expertise in accounting and financial analysis. The best advice for the investor is to go ahead and use the reported EPS because it is all that is normally available, and the majority of investors will also have to rely on this figure. Investors should, however, be aware of the potential problems involved in EPS and constantly keep in mind its nature and derivation. References can be found periodically in sources such as *Forbes* and *The Wall Street Journal* on the quality of earnings[9].

The Determinants of Earnings

On a company level, EPS is the culmination of several factors working in succession. We shall examine these determining factors in steps by analyzing, through financial ratios, the variables that interact to determine a company's EPS. This financial ratio analysis is a part of the fundamental analysis done by security analysts, and it can help investors to understand earnings, both currently and prospectively. The ratios involved in each step are shown on the left side; their application to EG&G's data for 1989 is on the right side.

STEP 1 *What determines EPS?*

$$\text{EPS} = \text{ROE} \times \text{Book value per share} \tag{12-3}$$

where ROE is the return on equity and book value per share is the stockholders' equity.

	For EG&G	$	Return
$\text{EPS} = \dfrac{\text{net income after taxes}}{\text{Shares outstanding}}$	$= \dfrac{\$69{,}850{,}000}{29{,}131{,}000}$	$= \$2.40$	—

[8]This information is based on Barbara Donnelly, "Quality of Corporate Profit Fades, but Market's Bulls Fail to Notice," *The Wall Street Journal,* June 29, 1989, p. C1.
[9]See Donnelly, "Quality of Corporate Profit Fades," p. C1.

				Return	Leverage factor
ROE =	$\frac{\text{Net income after taxes}}{\text{Stockholders' equity}}$	= $\frac{\$69{,}850{,}000}{\$348{,}987{,}000}$	=	—	0.200
Book value =	$\frac{\text{Stockholders' equity}}{\text{Shares outstanding}}$	= $\frac{\$348{,}987{,}000}{29{,}131{,}000}$	=	\$11.98	—

Note that two factors, ROE and book value, determine the EPS. The ROE is the rate at which stockholders earn on their portion of the capital used to finance the company. Book value measures the accounting value of the stockholders' equity. In EG&G's case in 1989 the ROE was 20% and the book value was $11.98 per share.[10] Therefore, EPS equaled

$$\$11.98 \times 0.200 = \$2.40$$

STEP 2 *What determines ROE?*

The **return on equity (ROE)** is the product of the company's profitability on its assets and its financing decisions, as expressed in Equation 12-4.

$$\text{ROE} = \text{ROA} \times \text{Leverage} \qquad (12\text{-}4)$$

where ROE is the return on assets and leverage reflects how the assets are financed (i.e., owners' money or creditors' money).

				Return	Leverage factor
ROE	= $\frac{\text{Net income}}{\text{Equity}}$	= $\frac{\$69{,}850{,}000}{\$348{,}987{,}000}$	=	0.200	—
ROA	= $\frac{\text{Net income}}{\text{Total assets}}$	= $\frac{\$69{,}850{,}000}{\$643{,}403{,}000}$	=	0.109	—
Leverage	= $\frac{\text{Total assets}}{\text{Equity}}$	= $\frac{\$643{,}403{,}000}{\$348{,}987{,}000}$	=	—	1.84

Return on assets (ROA) is a fundamental measure of firm profitability, reflecting how effectively and efficiently the firm's assets are used. Obviously, the higher the net income for a given amount of assets, the better the return. For EG&G, the return on assets is 0.109. The ROA can be improved by increasing the net income more than the assets (in percentage terms) or by using the existing assets even more efficiently.

The **leverage** ratio measures how the firm finances its assets.[11] Basically, it can finance with either debt or equity. Debt is a cheaper source of financing, but a more risky method, because of the fixed interest payments

---

[10]This book value calculation uses weighted shares outstanding in 1989.

[11]Leverage can be measured in several ways, such as the ratio of total debt to total assets or the ratio of debt to equity.

that must be systematically repaid on time to avoid bankruptcy. Leverage can magnify the returns to the stockholders (favorable leverage) or diminish them (unfavorable leverage). Thus, any given ROA can be magnified into a higher ROE by the judicious use of debt financing. The converse, however, applies—injudicious use of debt can lower the ROE below the ROA.

In 1989, EG&G's ratio of total debt to total assets was about 45%.[12] Thus, the creditors were financing slightly less than one-half of the assets, and the stockholders were underwriting the remainder. To capture the effects of leverage we shall use a multiplier. Dividing total assets by equity produces an *equity multiplier* of 1.62, which can be used as the measure of leverage.

Combining these two factors, ROA and leverage, for EG&G to obtain ROE results in (allowing for rounding error) the following:

$$\text{ROE} = 1.84 \times 0.109 = 0.20$$

In sum, both the investment decision (the ROA) and the financing decision (leverage) affect the returns to the stockholders. A firm can use its assets effectively, resulting in a high ROA, and can decrease this ratio by poor financing decisions. Conversely, it can experience mediocre returns from its assets but boost the ROA figure by clever financing. Finally, a firm could do a very good or very bad job on both determinants of ROE. To understand the EPS fully for a given company, investors should examine both how the assets are used and how they are financed.

Example. Assume the ROA for EG&G remains at 0.109 but that any asset increase is financed by additional debt. Let us assume that the equity multiplier goes to 2.00, which is the same as assuming that the debt ratio goes to 0.50 of total assets.

$$\begin{aligned}\text{ROE} &= 0.109 \times 2.00 \\ &= 0.218\end{aligned}$$

In this example, the ROE is boosted almost 2 percentage points which, in turn, increases the EPS, other things equal. ▪

As long as the marginal debt cost is less than the marginal return on assets, the additional debt financing will increase the ROE and therefore the EPS (although this is not evident in the analysis). What does not show here, however, is the impact of leverage on the risk of the firm. Remember that in this analysis we are examining only the determinants of EPS but that two factors, EPS and a multiplier, are required to determine value. An increase in leverage may raise the riskiness of the company more than

[12]This does not count deferred federal income taxes.

enough to offset the increased EPS, thereby lowering the value of the company.

STEP 3 *What determines return on assets?*

ROA is an important measure of a firm's profitability. It is determined by two factors, as shown in Equation 12-5:

$$\text{ROA} = \text{Net income margin} \times \text{Turnover}$$

$$\text{ROA} = \frac{\text{Net income}}{\text{Total assets}} = \frac{\$69{,}850{,}000}{\$643{,}403{,}000} = 0.127$$

$$\text{Net income margin} = \frac{\text{Net Income}}{\text{Sales}} = \frac{\$69{,}850{,}000}{\$1{,}650{,}158{,}000} = 0.042 \qquad (12\text{-}5)$$

$$\text{Turnover} = \frac{\text{Sales}}{\text{Total assets}} = \frac{\$1{,}650{,}158{,}000}{\$643{,}403{,}000} = 2.565$$

The first item affecting ROA, the net income margin, measures the firm's earning power on its sales (revenue). How much net return is realized from sales, given all costs? Obviously, the more the firm earns per dollar of sales, the better. EG&G's net income margin is 4.2%.

Turnover is a measure of efficiency. Given some amount of total assets, how much in sales can be generated? The more sales per dollar of assets, where each dollar of assets has to be financed with a source of funds bearing a cost, the better it is for a firm. The firm may have some assets that are unproductive, thereby adversely affecting its efficiency. EG&G's turnover rate is 2.565; combining the two ratios,[13]

$$\text{ROA} = 0.042 \times 2.565 = 0.108$$

Again, one of the determinants of ROA may be able to offset poor performance in the other. The net income margin may be low, but the firm may generate more sales per dollar of assets than comparable firms. Conversely, poor turnover may be partially offset by high net profitability.

STEP 4 *What determines the net income margin?*

The net income margin is a function of two ratios:

$$\text{Net income Margin} = \frac{\text{Net income}}{\text{EBIT}^{14}} \times \frac{\text{EBIT}}{\text{Sales}} \qquad (12\text{-}6)$$

---

[13]Rounding errors account for any differences.

[14]EBIT is computed as income before income taxes (from Table 12-2) plus 1989 interest expense of $9,125,000 (obtained from the footnotes accompanying the statements).

where

EBIT = Earnings before interest and taxes

$$\textit{Net income margin} = \frac{\text{Net income}}{\text{Sales}} = \frac{\$69{,}850{,}000}{\$1{,}650{,}158{,}000} = 0.042$$

$$\textit{Income ratio} = \frac{\text{Net income}}{\text{EBIT}} = \frac{\$69{,}850{,}000}{\$108{,}911{,}000} = 0.641$$

$$\textit{Operating efficiency} = \frac{\text{EBIT}}{\text{Sales}} = \frac{\$108{,}911{,}000}{\$1{,}650{,}158{,}000} = 0.066$$

The income ratio relates the net income after tax to the EBIT. It reflects the impact of interest and taxes on net income. If these variables decline, the income ratio rises, as does the net income margin (if other things are equal). Firms can lower taxes through the use of credits, such as the investment tax credit and a credit for net operating losses suffered in earlier years. Interest expense, for a given amount of debt, will decline as market interest rates decline. Of course, the firm could also change the amount of debt it uses to finance its assets.

The EBIT/sales ratio is a measure of the firm's ability to operate efficiently. EBIT reflects the earnings before the financing decision is accounted for by subtracting the interest expense, and before the provision for income taxes. The larger the EBIT per dollar of sales, the better. In effect, the EBIT reflects the gross margin on sales.

For EG&G, the net income margin is

$$0.641 \times 0.066 = 0.042, \text{ or } 4.2\%$$

The advantage of analyzing these earnings determinants is to be able to determine the strengths and weaknesses of a particular company. Various factors interrelate to determine EPS. Some of these factors (e.g., the financing decision) are under the control of the company's management, but others are not (e.g., the *marginal* tax rate paid by corporations and the level of market interest rates).

INVESTMENTS INTUITION

On a conceptual basis, it is easy to see how these factors affect EPS. Consider the manufacturers of home computers in the early 1980s. Early entrants in the business were able to expand volume as the total sales grew, thereby gaining operating efficiency. This increasing efficiency had an impact on EBIT/sales and led to an increase in EPS (during this time, profit margins held). With increasing competition, however, the net income margin declined as prices were cut to meet the competition. The ROA was negatively affected and this led to a decline for most companies in ROE and EPS, in some cases by disastrous dimensions.

Which Earnings Are Important?

Figure 12-1 showed the importance of reported earnings. A logical question to ask next is, "Should stocks that experience the largest growth in EPS have the largest risk-adjusted returns?" A study by Elton, Gruber, and Gultekin examined the risk-adjusted excess returns available from buying stocks on the basis of next year's growth in earnings.[15] They found that those stocks with the highest future growth in EPS showed the highest risk-adjusted returns. For the 30% of the companies with the highest growth in EPS, the risk-adjusted excess return was 7.48%; for the 30% with the lowest growth, the risk-adjusted excess return was −4.93%. Clearly, therefore, growth in reported earnings affects stock prices in a highly significant manner.

Thus, the EPS that investors use to value stocks is the future (expected) EPS. Current stock price is a function of the future stream of earnings and the P/E ratio, not the past earnings. If investors knew what the EPS for a particular company would be next year, they could achieve good results in the market.

One method of assessing the future EPS for a company is to estimate the company's EPS growth rate. Knowing the current EPS and the growth rate in EPS, future EPS can be calculated easily. That is,

$$E_1 = E_0(1 + g)$$

where

E_1 = next period's EPS
E_0 = current EPS
g = the expected growth rate in EPS

$$E_2 = E_0(1 + g)^2$$

and so on.

Therefore, the logical questions to answer are, "What determines earnings growth, g?" and "How well can such growth be predicted?"

[15] E. Elton, M. Gruber, and M. Gultekin, "The Usefulness of Analyst Estimates of Earnings," unpublished manuscript, 1978. This article is discussed in E. Elton and M. Gruber, *Modern Portfolio Theory and Investment Analysis*, 3rd ed. (New York: John Wiley, 1987), pp. 435–436.

Analyzing and Forecasting Earnings Growth

As noted, investors should be concerned with future growth in the EPS for a company. What determines the earnings growth rate?

The growth rate of earnings or dividends, g, is a function of the ROE (r) and the **retention rate** (b), as in Equation 12-7[16]:

$$g = rb \qquad (12\text{-}7)$$

where the retention rate is 1 − dividend payout ratio.

To estimate g, therefore, it is necessary to estimate r and b. Payout ratios for most companies vary over time, but reasonable estimates can often be obtained for a particular company. We have previously examined ROE and found that it is a function of three forces: asset efficiency, net income margin, and leverage.

Using the ratios developed from the previous section:

$$\text{ROE} = \frac{\text{Sales}}{\text{Assets}} \times \frac{\text{Net income}}{\text{Sales}} \times \frac{\text{Assets}}{\text{Equity}} \qquad (12\text{-}8)$$

Example. EG&G's 1989 ROE, as discussed, was 0.20. Using Equation 12-8,

$$\begin{aligned}\text{ROE} &= \frac{\$1{,}650{,}158{,}000}{\$643{,}403{,}000} \times \frac{\$69{,}850{,}000}{\$1{,}650{,}158{,}000} \times \frac{\$643{,}403{,}000}{\$348{,}987{,}000} \\ &= 2.576 \times 0.042 \times 1.84 \\ &= 0.199, \text{ or } 19.9\%\end{aligned}$$

Rounding error accounts for the difference. ▪

To estimate the future growth rate for EG&G, it is necessary to estimate those factors that will affect the ROE and the retention rate.

Example. In the case of EG&G, the payout ratio for a recent number of years averaged about 27%. The retention rate was therefore about 73%. The ROE for these same years averaged about 21.9%. For EG&G, investors might assume that the average of these years is the best estimate of the future and therefore g would be estimated as

$$g = 0.73\ (0.219) = 0.16, \text{ or } 16\% \quad ▪$$

[16]Technically, g is defined as the expected growth rate in dividends. However, the dividend growth rate is clearly influenced by the earnings growth rate. Although dividend and earnings growth rates can diverge in the short run, such differences would not be expected to continue for long periods of time. The standard assumption in security analysis is that g represents the growth rate for both dividends and earnings.

Although the payout ratio variable has been quite stable for EG&G, it is usually difficult to estimate the three factors that determine ROE—efficiency, net income margin, and leverage. EG&G's financial ratios are reasonably stable, but they do change from year to year.

Equation 12-7 is one of the principal calculations in fundamental security analysis and is often used by analysts. An alternative to estimating the components of the growth rate is to use the past g values to predict future growth. Again, *the important variable in company analysis is the change in earnings over some future period.* How well does the past growth rate of earnings for a particular company predict the future growth rate?

Predicting Earnings Growth

As we have seen, the intrinsic value and actual market price of a common stock are directly (positively) related to the level and growth of its EPS. Therefore, one of the most important parts of company analysis, and of fundamental security analysis in general, is the projection of earnings growth. Other things being equal, those companies with strong earnings growth in the future are the most probable candidates for further strong price appreciation. Earnings changes (i.e., growth) are the key to fundamental stock analysis.

Given the importance of earnings growth, the logical question becomes, "Is past growth an indicator of future growth?" An investor might naturally assume that stocks with previous high growth rates of EPS would have high growth rates in the future. Unfortunately, empirical studies do not support this assumption; according to available evidence, both British and American companies exhibited a lack of persistence in earnings trends.[17]

Example. Ford Motor Company showed an annual rate of change in EPS for a particular 10-year period and five-year period ending in the same year of 17% and 42%, respectively.[18] Was it reasonable to assume that such growth rates would persist in an industry as competitive as automobiles? In the case of EG&G, a relatively stable company that normally has demonstrated steady growth in EPS since 1969 (i.e., EPS increased in each successive year until 1986), the EPS growth rate for the years 1989 and 1988 was 4% and 20%, respectively, but for 1986 it was negative. Which of these growth rates, if any, is most likely to continue in the future?

---

[17]See, for example, I. M. D. Little, "Higgledy Piggledy Growth," *Bulletin of the Oxford University Institute of Economics and Statistics,* Vol. 24 (November 1962), pp. 389–412; R. Trent, "Corporate Growth Rates: An Analysis of Their Intertemporal Association," *Southern Journal of Business,* Vol. 4 (October 1969), pp. 196–210; and J. Lintner and R. Glauber, "Higgledy-Piggledy Growth in America," unpublished manuscript, 1969 (this article is discussed in Elton and Gruber, *Modern Portfolio Theory,* pp. 431–432).

[18]*The Value Line Investment Survey,* December 26, 1986, p. 105.

Because of the lack of consistency in earnings trends, investors, who need estimates of future EPS, cannot simply assume that trends will continue. They can estimate the expected growth in dividends or earnings or they can use EPS forecasts, provided either mechanically (i.e., by equation) or by security analysts. Since earnings forecasts are widely available from brokerage houses and other organizations, or can be computed by calculator or computer, investors need to consider the use, and value, of earnings forecasts.

Working with Earnings Forecasts

The preceding discussion has established two important points in the fundamental security analysis process for individual companies.

1. EPS is the key to future price changes in a common stock. Stocks with large earnings changes are the most likely candidates to show large price changes, either positive or negative.
2. The earnings growth rate, or persistence in the earnings trend, is not easily predicted. Investors cannot simply use the past rate of growth in EPS to predict the future rate of growth.

The investors' problem therefore is to determine (1) how to obtain an earnings forecast, (2) which forecast provides the more useful information (mechanical estimates or analysts' estimates), and (3) how expectations of future earnings can best be used in selecting stocks. We shall consider each of these topics in turn.

Obtaining a Forecast of EPS

Security Analysts' Estimates of Earnings Among the most obvious sources of earnings forecasts are security analysts, who make such forecasts as a part of their job. Because of the widespread availability of this type of earnings information, it is worthwhile to examine how valuable the earnings projections of security analysts are.[19]

Malkiel and Cragg, in a well-known study of the earnings forecasts of security analysts, found that these estimates were not very accurate.[20] The correlations between the rate forecast and the realized growth rate were low. The analysts apparently relied heavily on past growth rates, which, as noted previously, is not a reliable method of forecasting earnings growth.

---

[19] *The Value Line Investment Survey,* for example, forecasts quarterly earnings for several quarters ahead for each company covered.

[20] B. Malkiel and J. Cragg, "Expectations and the Structure of Share Prices," *American Economic Review,* Vol. 60 (September 1970), pp. 601–617.

The average correlation coefficient between actual earnings growth and forecast growth for the five institutional investors studied was only 0.35.

Niederhoffer and Regan, in the study that showed the association between earnings and stock prices (Figure 12-1), also examined analysts' ability to forecast earnings for one year (1970). Figure 12-2 shows the top and bottom 50 companies (and a random 50 companies) from the sample in terms of actual price changes for one year, the actual earnings change, and the forecast earnings change. For the top 50 companies, analysts underestimated the earnings changes in 89% of the cases for which estimates were available. For the bottom 50 companies, the analysts overestimated the earnings for every single company for which data were available; that is, the actual earnings for these companies were less than the forecast earnings.

Elton, Gruber, and Gultekin, in the study cited earlier, found that investors could not earn excess returns by buying and selling stocks on the basis of the consensus estimate of earnings growth (the consensus estimate was defined as the average estimate of security analysts at major brokerage houses).

Mechanical Estimates of Earnings An alternative method of obtaining earnings forecasts is the use of various mechanical procedures such as time series models. In deciding what type of model to use, it is necessary to consider some of the evidence on the behavior of earnings over time.

Studies of the behavior of the time path of earnings have produced mixed results. Most of the early studies indicated randomness in the growth rates of annual earnings, as discussed earlier. Other studies found some evidence of nonrandomness. And more recent studies, particularly of quarterly earnings, have indicated that the time series behavior of earnings is not random.

Time series analysis involves the use of historical data to make earnings forecasts. The model used assumes that the future will be similar to the past. The series being forecast, EPS, is assumed to have trend elements, an average value, seasonal factors, and error. The moving average technique is a simple example of the time series model for forecasting EPS. Exponential smoothing, which assigns differing weights to past values, is an example of a more sophisticated technique. A regression equation would represent another sophisticated technique for making forecasts; the regression equation could handle several variables, such as trend and seasonal factors.

Which Forecasts Are Best? Evidence for the superiority of mechanical forecasts or of estimates by security analysts is mixed. Earlier studies found that analysts' forecasts were not more accurate than sophisticated time series forecasts.[21] A later study by Brown and Rozeff (BR) that re-

[21]See J. Cragg and B. Malkiel, "The Consensus and Accuracy of Some Predictions of the Growth of Corporate Earnings," *Journal of Finance*, March 1968, pp. 67–84, and E. Elton and M. Gruber, "Earnings Estimates and the Accuracy of Expectational Data," *Management Science*, April 1972, pp. 409–424.

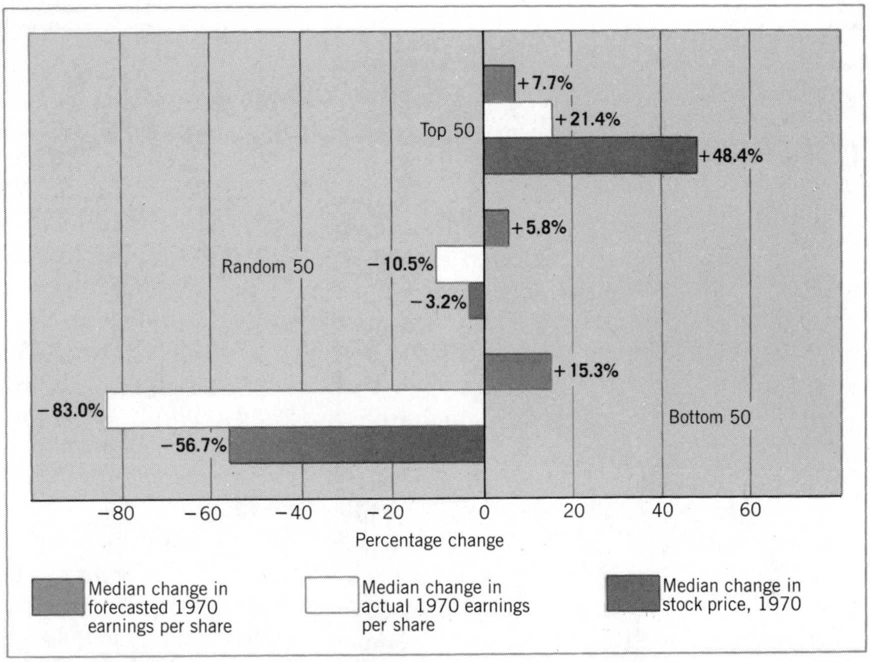

FIGURE 12-2 ***Median changes in forecasted earnings, actual earnings, and stock price: one-year horizon.***
Source: V. Niederhoffer and P. J. Regan, "Earnings Changes, Analysts' Forecasts and Stock Prices," *Financial Analysts Journal,* Vol. 28 (May–June 1972), p. 71. Reprinted by permission.

ceived considerable attention found the opposite—the results "overwhelmingly" favored the analysts.[22] BR found that earnings forecasts made by *The Value Line Investment Survey* were consistently significantly better than those produced by well-known time series models, including the sophisticated Box–Jenkins method. Such a finding is reassuring from an economic theory standpoint because analysts' forecasts cost more than time series forecasts.

Even if investors accept the results of this study as to the *relative* superiority of analysts' forecasts, the message in Figure 12-2 remains true today. Analysts often over- or underestimate the earnings that are actually realized. However, uncertain earnings forecasts provide opportunities for investors. Analysts often are wrong, and if investors can make better forecasts of earnings, they can expect to profit from their astuteness. See Box 12-2 for a good description of how analysts' estimates sometimes vary widely and the opportunities this presents.

[22] L. Brown and M. Rozeff, "The Superiority of Analyst Forecasts as Measures of Expectations: Evidence from Earnings," *The Journal of Finance,* Vol. 33 (March 1978), pp. 1–16.

BOX 12-2

EARNINGS GUESSTIMATES

A popular academic theory says that you can't beat the market because any company's expected future earnings are fully reflected in today's stock price. It's a compelling theory when applied to the likes of IBM. Dozens of experts follow this stock, they are in pretty close agreement, and they tend to adjust their earnings forecasts up and down in unison. It would be pretty hard to outguess them.

But what about Magma Copper? Security analysts are all over the lot. Three months ago the average 1989 forecast was $1.13 a share. Now the mean estimate is up to $1.60. Not only that, behind this consensus forecast of $1.60 lie estimates ranging from 75 cents to $2.

With so much variation in the figures, there is opportunity for an investor who can make an informed guess about future earnings. That's because, as New York University finance professors Edwin Elton and Martin Gruber have shown, stock prices reflect the consensus, or average estimates, of analysts. If you have reason to believe the analysts are too bearish on earnings, you stand a good chance of making money on the stock by buying it.

The Institutional Brokers Estimate System, a service of New York brokerage firm Lynch, Jones & Ryan, tracks consensus estimates on 3,500 firms. That's a starting point. Where you have reason to think that the consensus is wrong, you can profit.

Consider Bethlehem Steel, about which there is much disagreement: Forecasts for 1989 earnings range from $3.80 a share to a high of $9. Richard Henderson, an analyst at Donaldson, Lufkin & Jenrette's Pershing Securities, comes in at the high end of the range and argues that Bethlehem Steel will double in price this year. The steelmaker presently trades at 25, or five times earnings. If Henderson's $9 estimate is on the mark and the stock were to trade at the same multiple as at present, Henderson's target of $50 would be approached. Is Henderson right? Or the consensus? You decide.

"A 1-cent-per-pound difference in the price of copper translates into 21 cents in Phelps Dodge's aftertax earnings," notes Smith Barney metals analyst William Siedenberg. And the price of copper can be extremely volatile: Between January and February it dropped 30 cents. Siedenberg expects that the average price of copper will be a little lower this year than in 1988. That's why he is estimating that Phelps Dodge will earn $10 a share in 1989, near the low end of the range. But Nicholas Toufexis of Prudential-Bache, whose forecast is $18, argues that the AIDS crisis in Zaire and the lack of capital spending in Peru will hurt the supply of copper, put the price up and make current purchases highly profitable.

Afraid to try outguessing the analysts? Don't be. The record shows that their forecasts are often wide of the mark.

Source: Adapted from Christopher Palmeri, "Earnings guesstimates," *Forbes*, April 17, 1989, pp. 216, 218, and 220. Excerpted by permission. *Forbes* magazine, April, 17 1989, © Forbes, Inc., 1989.

Actual EPS Versus Expectations About EPS

We have established that earnings changes and stock price changes are highly correlated. We have also discussed the necessity of forecasting EPS and how these forecasts can be obtained. What remains is to examine the role of expectations about earnings in selecting common stocks.

The association between earnings and stock prices is more complicated than simply demonstrating a correlation (association) between earnings changes and stock price changes. Investor expectations are also important in an environment dominated by uncertainty. Investors must form expectations about EPS, and these expectations should be incorporated into stock prices if markets are efficient. Although these expectations are often inaccurate, they play a key role in affecting stock prices. Malkiel and Cragg, in the study cited earlier, concluded that in making accurate one-year predictions, "It is far more important to know what the market will think the growth rate of earnings will be next year rather than to know the (actual) realized long-term growth rate."[23]

Similarly, Niederhoffer and Regan found in their study that the actual change in earnings of most of the best-performing companies was higher than that predicted by the analysts. For the worst-performing companies, the actual change in earnings was less than predicted. Therefore, the difference, or *earnings surprise factor,* is associated with significant adjustments in the price of the stock.

As Latané and Jones have pointed out, new information about a stock is unexpected information.[24] What is important about EPS in terms of stock prices is the difference between what the market (i.e., investors in general) was expecting the EPS to be and what was actually reported by the company. Unexpected information about earnings calls for a revision in investor probability beliefs about the future and therefore an adjustment in the price of the stock.

To assess the impact of the surprise factor in EPS, Latané and Jones developed a model to express and use the earnings surprise factor in the quarterly EPS of companies. The resulting criterion represents the difference between the actual EPS for a company and the EPS expected by the market. The latter variable is obtained from one of the mechanical models referred to earlier—a simple time series regression involving the quarterly EPS of a particular company. By subtracting the expected EPS from the actual EPS, the unexpected earnings component is obtained. This is then standardized for size differences among companies, and the result is called **standardized unexpected earnings (SUE).** SUE is calculated as follows[25]:

[23]Malkiel and Cragg, "Expectations and the Structure of Share Prices," p. 616.

[24]H. Latané and C. Jones, "Standardized Unexpected Earnings—A Progress Report," *The Journal of Finance*, Vol. 32 (December 1977), pp. 1457–1465.

[25]This is explained in ibid., p. 1457. The standardization variable is the standard error of estimate for the estimating regression equation.

$$\text{SUE} = \frac{\text{Actual quarterly EPS} - \text{Forecast quarterly EPS}}{\text{Standardization variable}} \qquad (12\text{-}9)$$

The SUE concept is designed to capture the surprise element in the earnings just referred to; in other words, the difference between what the market expects the company to earn and what it actually does earn. A favorable earnings surprise, where the actual earnings exceed the market's expectation, should bring about an adjustment to the price of the stock as investors revise their probability beliefs about the earnings of the company; conversely, an unfavorable earnings surprise should lead to a downward adjustment in price—in effect, the market has been disappointed in its expectations.

Latané and Jones have shown that the absolute size of the SUE calculated for a large sample of stocks is nicely distributed around 0.0, with fewer observations in the tails of the distribution and more observations toward the center (i.e., SUEs around 0.0).[26] In doing this, stocks can be categorized by SUEs that are divided into increments of 1.0. Thus, SUE classifications can range from all stocks with a SUE ≤ -4.0 (category 1), all between -4.0 and -3.0 (category 2), and so on, up to the most positive category, all stocks with SUEs > 4.0 (category 10). The larger the SUE (either positive or negative), the greater the unexpected earnings and therefore, other things being equal, the larger the adjustment in the stock's return should be. Stocks with small SUEs (between $+1.0$ and -1.0) have little or no unexpected earnings and therefore should show little or no subsequent adjustment in stock return.

In conclusion, stock prices are affected not only by the level of and growth in earnings, but also by the market's expectations of earnings. Investors should be concerned with both the forecast for earnings and the difference between the actual earnings and the forecast. Therefore, fundamental analysis of earnings should involve more than a forecast, which is difficult enough—it should involve the role of the market's expectations about earnings.

Fundamental Security Analysis in Practice

We have analyzed several important aspects of fundamental analysis as it is applies to individual companies. Obviously, such a process can be quite detailed, involving an analysis of a company's sales potential, competition, tax situation, cost projections, accounting practices, and so on. Nevertheless, regardless of detail and complexity, the underlying process is as described. Analysts and investors are seeking to estimate a company's earn-

[26] Henry A. Latané and Charles P. Jones, "Standardized Unexpected Earnings—1971–77," *The Journal of Finance*, Vol. 34 (June 1979), pp. 717–724.

ings and P/E ratio and determine if the stock is undervalued (a buy) or overvalued (a sell).

Figure 12-3 shows an excerpt from a brokerage recommendation issued in August 1989 for Upjohn Company, a pharmaceutical company. The information in this report is concise, but it illustrates nicely the points discussed earlier. Notice in particular the earnings information, based on

---

Richard R. Stover
(212) 237-2441
Adele M. Haley
(212) 237-2340

August 11, 1989

THE UPJOHN COMPANY
(NYSE: UPJ)

Reiterating our recommendation—Strong buy

Price 8/11/89	Analyst Stock Rating	1989 Price Range	EPS (FY: Dec.) 1988A	1989E	1990E	Cal. Yr. P/E 1989E	1990E	Indicated Dividend	Yield
37 ⅞	1	38 · 28	$1.90	$2.16	$2.60	17.5×	14.6×	$0.88	2.3%

Shares Outstanding: 185.2 million
Market Value of Common: $6.9 million
Average Daily Volume: 801,700
Estimated Float: 172.3million

DJIA: 2683.99
S&P 500: 344.74
Est. 3–5 Year Growth Rate: 16–22%
HQ: Kalamazoo, MI

We are adjusting modestly our 1990 EPS estimate and reaffirm our strong buy recommendation on Upjohn shares. The stock has outperformed the market in the 2Q and is exceptionally well positioned for continued follow-through. Selling at a P/E multiple of 14.6 times our 1990 estimate, Upjohn is at the low end of its valuation channel. While some of Upjohn's recent strength reflects investor speculation of takeover/merger (in light of recent activities in the Drug Group), the fundamentals of the Company are steadily improving. There is potential for considerable upside surprise as the consensus estimate—now in the $2.30–2.40 range for 1990—is adjusted upward. We urge investors to establish/build positions for outstanding visible above-average growth. Our confidence reflects the following observations:

Fundamental security analysis in a brokerage report.
Source: Adapted from The Upjohn Company, Alex. Brown & Sons, Inc., Baltimore, Maryland, August 11, 1989. Reprinted by permission.

the date of the report (August 11, 1989). Actual 1988 earnings of $1.90 are reported, and 1989 and 1990 earnings are estimated. P/E ratios, to be discussed later, are also calculated.

Notice the statements in the report: "Upjohn is at the low end of its valuation channel" and "the fundamentals of the Company are steadily improving." Also notice the statement about "surprises," which was discussed earlier and which is an important factor in security analysis:

"There is potential for considerable upside surprise as the consensus estimate—now in the $2.30–2.40 range for 1990—is adjusted upward." This consensus estimate refers to the average estimate of EPS as provided by security analysts. As discussed, this is one of two ways for investors to obtain earnings forecasts.

The P/E Ratio

The other half of the valuation framework in fundamental analysis is the price/earnings (P/E) ratio, or multiplier. The P/E ratio (reported in *The Wall Street Journal* and other newspapers) indicates how much per dollar of earnings investors currently are willing to pay for a stock—that is, the price for each dollar of earnings. In a sense, it represents the market's summary evaluation of a company's prospects.

Example. In September 1989, EG&G was selling for about 14 times latest 12-month earnings of $2.27, and about 13 times Value Line's estimate for 1989 earnings of $2.50. The average annual P/E ratios for EG&G for the years 1984–1988 were 17, 18.2, 20.6, 17.6, and 14.2, respectively. ▪

In effect, the P/E ratio is a measure of the relative price of a stock. In September 1989, for example, investors were willing to pay about 50 times earnings for Centel, but only six times earnings for Asarco.[27] What are the reasons for such a large difference? To answer this question, it is necessary to consider the determinants of the P/E ratio.

Determinants of the P/E Ratio

Reviewing earlier discussion, the expected P/E ratio is conceptually a function of three factors[28]:

$$\text{P/E} = \frac{D_1/E_1}{k - g} \tag{12-10}$$

[27]These P/E ratios were based on the most recent four quarters of earnings.

[28]Equation 12-3 is based on the constant growth version of the dividend valuation model.

where

D_1/E_1 = the expected dividend payout ratio
k = the required rate of return for the stock
g = expected growth rate in dividends

Investors attempting to determine the P/E ratio that will prevail for a particular stock should think in terms of these three factors, and their likely changes. Each of these will be considered in turn.

The Dividend Payout Ratio Dividends are clearly a function of earnings (although accounting earnings and cash, out of which dividends are paid, are not necessarily closely related). The relationship between these two variables, however, is more complex than simply current dividends being a function of current earnings. Dividends paid by corporations reflect established practices (i.e., previous earnings level) as well as prospects for the future (i.e., expected future earnings).

The majority of corporations listed on the NYSE and Amex pay dividends, and many of the actively traded over-the-counter stocks act as if dividends matter significantly to investors. Consequently, dividends, once established at a certain level, are maintained at that level if at all possible. Dividends are not reduced until and unless there is no alternative. Also, dividends are not increased until it is clear that the new, higher level of dividends can be supported. The result of these policies is that dividends adjust with a lag to earnings.

The P/E ratio can be expected to change as the expected dividend payout ratio changes. The higher the expected payout ratio, other things being equal, the higher the P/E ratio. However, "other things" are seldom equal. If the payout rises, the expected growth rate in earnings and dividends, g, will probably decline, thereby adversely affecting the P/E ratio. This decline occurs because less funds will be available for reinvestment in the business, thereby leading to a decline in the expected growth rate, g.

The Required Rate of Return As explained in Chapter 5 (Equation 5-19), the required rate of return, k, is a function of the riskless rate of return and a risk premium. Thus, k is equal to

$$k = \text{RF} + \text{RP} \tag{12-11}$$

The riskless rate of return can be proxied by the Treasury bill rate. The risk premium is the additional compensation demanded by risk-averse investors before purchasing a risky asset such as a common stock.

Discounted cash flow models, discussed in Chapter 9, can be used to estimate the required rate of return for a company. Rearranging Equation 9-5 indicates that k is equal to the current dividend yield plus the expected growth rate in earnings. A study by Harris suggests that a consensus forecast of earnings growth by analysts can be used successfully as a proxy for the dividend growth rate in solving for k.[29] Since analysts' growth forecasts are readily available on a large number of stocks, this approach may offer a straightforward method of estimating required rates of return.

At the company level, the risk premium for a stock can be thought of as a composite of business risk, financial risk, and other risks, which were explained in Chapter 8. Other risks could include the liquidity, or marketability, of a particular stock. As a general rule, large NYSE companies are more liquid than small OTC stocks.

Based on Equation 12-11, the following statements can be made about a company's required rate of return:

1. Other things being equal, if the risk-free rate, RF, rises, k will rise. Thus, in periods of high interest rates such as 1980–1981, k typically will be higher than in periods such as 1982–1983, when interest rates had declined from the high levels of 1980–1981.
2. Other things being equal, if the risk premium rises (falls), as a result of an increase (decrease) in business risk, financial risk, or other risks, k will rise (fall).

The relationship between k and the P/E ratio is inverse: *Other things equal,* as k rises, the P/E ratio declines; as k declines, the P/E ratio rises. The required rate of return is a discount rate, and discount rates and P/E ratios move inversely to each other. To understand this, consider the simplest case in valuation—no growth (in other words, EPS will remain at a fixed dollar amount forever). Rather than using an earnings multiplier, think of capitalizing the earnings. To do this, analysts use the **E/P ratio,** which is the reciprocal of the P/E ratio (i.e., E/P = [1/(P/E)]).

$$V_0 = \text{Intrinsic value} = \frac{E_0}{\text{E/P}} \tag{12-15}$$

Rather than use a multiplier of, say, 10, an E/P ratio or capitalization rate of 0.10 can be used. It is obvious that if this capitalization rate increased, V_0 would decline.

The Expected Growth Rate The third variable affecting the P/E ratio is the expected growth rate of dividends, g.[30] We know that $g = br$, making the expected growth rate a function of the return on equity (r) and the retention rate (b). The higher either of these variables are, the higher g will be. What

[29]See Robert S. Harris, "Using Analysts' Growth Forecasts to Estimate Shareholder Required Rates of Return," *Financial Management*, Spring 1986, pp. 58–67.

[30]Remember that in the constant-growth version of the dividend valuation model, the growth rate in dividends is equivalent to the growth rate in earnings and to the growth rate in the price of the stock for all future time periods.

about the relationship between g and P/E? P/E and g are directly related—the higher the g, other things being equal, the higher the P/E ratio.

Investors should be willing to pay more for a company with expected rapid growth in earnings in relation to a company with expected slower growth in earnings. A basic problem in fundamental analysis, however, is determining how *much* more investors should be willing to pay for growth. In other words, how high should the P/E ratio be? There is no precise answer to this question. It depends upon such factors as the following:

1. The confidence that investors have in the expected growth. In the case of EG&G, for example, investors may be well justified in expecting a rapid rate of growth for the next few years because of previous performance, management's ability, and the high estimates of growth described in investment advisory services. This may not be the case for another company, where, because of competitive inroads and other factors, the high growth prospects are at great risk—consider Apple Computer, for example, which constantly faces the IBM challenge in home computers, as well as the challenge of other manufacturers.
2. The reasons for the earnings growth can be important. Is it a result of great demand in the marketplace, or a result of astute financing policies that could backfire if interest rates rise sharply or the economy enters a severe recession? Is growth the result of sales expansion or cost cutting (which will be exhausted at some point)?

EG&G's P/E Ratio

In analyzing the P/E ratio for EG&G, we first ask what model describes the expected growth for EG&G. Given this company's recent rapid growth, its stated objective of a long-term growth in earnings of 15%, and Value Line's estimate of its expected future growth, we probably would not choose the constant growth version of the dividend valuation model. Instead, we should evaluate EG&G by using a multiple growth model. At the end of the 1980s, EG&G was expected (by Value Line, for example) to enjoy rapid growth for at least a few more years. At some point, however, this growth can be expected to slow down to a more normal rate.

Given the growth prospects for EG&G, a constant growth model is not strictly applicable for estimating a P/E ratio because it assumes constant growth in dividends and earnings over all future time periods. However, the same variables will affect the P/E ratio. Furthermore, at some time in the future, the expected rate will slow down to a more normal rate of growth, and at that point the P/E ratio for the *next* year will be

$$\frac{P}{E_{n+1}} = \frac{D_{n+1}/E_{n+1}}{k - g}$$

where n is the year that the abnormal growth ends.

Why P/E Ratios Vary Among Companies

Stock prices reflect market expectations about earnings. Companies that the market believes will achieve higher earnings growth rates will tend to be priced higher than companies that are expected to show low earnings growth rates. Thus, a primary factor in explaining P/E ratio differences among companies is investor expectations about the future growth of earnings. Variations in the rate of earnings growth will also influence the P/E.

Table 12-3 shows one of *The Value Line Investment Survey*'s weekly rankings of the lowest- and highest-P/E stocks out of the more than 1700 companies covered. The lowest estimated current P/E ratios ranged from 0.6 to 7.3, whereas the highest ranged from 90.0 to 30.4.

The low-P/E ratio stocks in Table 12-3 were dominated by the banks and savings and loans and other industries and companies with special problems. Note that both Ford and Chrysler showed up in this list, compiled at the beginning of March 1990. The high-P/E stocks include a wide variety of businesses, many of which appear to be good growth prospects in the the 1990s (e.g., computers and medical services and supplies), and some that appear to be highly speculative (e.g., gold and silver mining). Other activities represented in the high-P/E set include real estate, drugs, and petroleum. Each of these areas represented expected growth opportunities in the early 1990s, as assessed by investors in early 1990.

Additional Company Analysis

In modern investment analysis, the risk for a stock is based on its beta coefficient, as explained in Chapters 5 and 8. Beta reflects the relative systematic risk for a stock, or the risk that cannot be diversified away. The higher the beta coefficient, the higher the risk for an individual stock, and the higher the required rate of return.

Beta measures the volatility of a stock's returns—its fluctuations in relation to the market. According to *The Value Line Investment Survey,* the beta for EG&G was around 1.00 at the beginning of 1990. Therefore, we know that EG&G had the same relative systematic risk as the market as a whole; that is, its price fluctuates, *on average,* in line with the market. If, for example, the market is expected to rise 20% over the next year, investors could expect, *on average,* for EG&G to rise 20% based on its beta of 1.00. Investors who are seeking a stock of average riskiness could be interested in EG&G in this hypothetical situation. In a market decline, EG&G would be expected to decline no more, *on average,* than the market. If the market declines 20%, for example, EG&G would be expected, on average, to decline in price by 20%.

TABLE 12-3 *VL Ratings by P/E Ratio*

LOWEST P/Es

Stocks whose estimated current P/E ratios are lowest

Page No.	Stock Name	Recent Price	Current P/E Ratio	Timeliness	Safety Rank	Industry Group	Industry Rank
1419	Wheeling-Pitts. Steel	10	0.6	–	5	Steel (Integrated)	64
1416	LTV Corp.	1⅝	0.8	–	5	Steel (Integrated)	64
671	Gen'l Development	5¾	2.8	3	4	Real Estate	86
1369	Eagle-Picher Ind.	6	2.9	4	5	Diversified Co.	74
2032	Midlantic Corp.	20	3.0	5	2	Bank	85
660	Michigan Nat'l Corp.	44	3.6	3	3	Bank (Midwest)	57
887	Standard Pacific, L.P.	14	3.7	3	4	Homebuilding	77
1161	GLENFED Inc.	15	3.8	3	3	Thrift	82
2062	Hallwood Group	4⅜	4.0	–	5	Financial Services	23
1177	Lomas & Nettleton Mtg.	4⅜	4.0	5	3	R.E.I.T.	87
885	PHM Corp.	8½	4.2	4	4	Homebuilding	77
1327	Portec, Inc.	4⅜	4.4	4	5	Machinery	45
1551	Galoob (Lewis) Toys	9⅛	4.6	2	4	Toys & School Supplies	11
104	Ford Motor	46	4.7	4	2	Auto & Truck	93
626	AmBase Corp.	9	4.7	3	3	Insurance(Prop/Casualty)	18
1155	CalFed Inc.	17	4.8	3	3	Thrift	82
649	Cont'l Bank Corp.	17	4.8	4	3	Bank (Midwest)	57
103	Chrysler	17	4.8	5	3	Auto & Truck	93
881	Kaufman & Broad Home	12	4.9	–	4	Homebuilding	77
2018	Equimark Corp.	11	4.9	3	4	Bank	85
1570	Bank of Montreal	29	4.9	2	3	Bank (Canadian)	81
258	British Airways (ADR)	33	5.0	3	3	Air Transport	78
869	Owens-Corning	22	5.1	3	3	Building Materials	69
838	Telefonica Espana ADR	23	5.1	3	3	European Diversified	3
929	Federal Paper Board	23	5.2	3	3	Paper & Forest Products	46
1181	Property Capital Trust	12	5.3	4	2	R.E.I.T.	87
943	Stone Container	21	5.4	3	4	Paper & Forest Products	46
1192	Morgan Stanley	61	5.4	3	3	Securities Brokerage	62
624	Inco Limited	24	5.5	–	3	Metals & Mining (Ind'l)	31
1014	Honeywell, Inc.	83	5.5	2	3	Electrical Equipment	17
1035	Cubic Corp.	18	5.5	2	3	Electronics	37
922	Bohemia, Inc.	22	5.5	2	3	Paper & Forest Products	46
1245	Phelps Dodge	56	5.5	3	3	Copper	70
560	Gen'l Dynamics	37	5.5	4	2	Aerospace/Defense	90
1154	Boston Bancorp	16	5.6	3	3	Thrift	82
2060	Green Tree	12	5.6	2	4	Financial Services	23
1010	Franklin Electric	8½	5.7	–	4	Electrical Equipment	17
1784	Prime Motor Inns	12	5.7	5	3	Hotel/Gaming	95
886	Ryland Group	19	5.7	3	3	Homebuilding	77
2020	First Fidelity Bancorp	21	5.8	4	2	Bank	85
2028	MNC Financial	21	5.8	3	2	Bank	85
1164	HomeFed Corp.	32	5.9	4	3	Thrift	82
1257	Vista Chemical	35	5.9	–	4	Chemical (Basic)	32
1251	Georgia Gulf	39	5.9	–	3	Chemical (Basic)	32
1880	Akzo N.V. (ADR)	31	5.9	3	3	Chemical (Diversified)	75
1655	Service Merchandise	5½	6.0	–	5	Retail Store	56
1216	De Beers Consol.	18	6.0	–	3	Gold/Diamond (S.A.)	—
580	Thiokol Corp.	12	6.0	–	3	Aerospace/Defense	90
2109	Cyclops Inds.	29	6.0	–	4	Steel (Specialty)	41
641	Selective Ins. Group	18	6.0	3	3	Insurance(Prop/Casualty)	18

Page No.	Stock Name	Recent Price	Current P/E Ratio	Timeliness	Safety Rank	Industry Group	Industry Rank
1586	Pioneer Fin'l Serv.	15	6.0	1	3	Unassigned	—
1871	Cyprus Minerals	26	6.0	3	3	Coal/Alternate Energy	10
1899	Gaylord Container 'A'	7⅛	6.1	–	5	Unassigned	—
261	KLM Royal Dutch	18	6.2	3	3	Air Transport	78
583	United Industrial Corp.	9	6.2	4	3	Aerospace/Defense	90
884	NVR L.P.	4½	6.2	4	4	Homebuilding	77
2036	Security Pacific	40	6.2	3	3	Bank	85
1252	Lyondell Petrochemical	21	6.3	–	4	Chemical (Basic)	32
644	Ameritrust Corp.	21	6.3	3	2	Bank (Midwest)	57
1237	Asarco Inc.	27	6.3	3	3	Copper	70
636	Orion Capital	20	6.3	3	3	Insurance(Prop/Casualty)	18
2037	Shawmut National	15	6.3	4	2	Bank	85
621	Cleveland-Cliffs	30	6.4	2	3	Metals & Mining (Ind'l)	31
665	Society Corp.	31	6.4	3	1	Bank (Midwest)	57
229	MEDIQ Inc.	3	6.4	4	4	Medical Supplies	6
2048	Wells Fargo & Co.	75	6.4	2	2	Bank	85
930	Georgia-Pacific	43	6.5	2	3	Paper & Forest Products	46
569	Martin Marietta	39	6.5	2	3	Aerospace/Defense	90
1246	Reynolds Metals	54	6.5	3	3	Aluminum	38
822	British Steel (ADR)	23	6.6	–	2	European Diversified	3
2038	Signet Banking Corp.	29	6.6	3	3	Bank	85
2026	Fleet/Norstar Fin'l	23	6.7	3	2	Bank	85
924	Bowater Inc.	24	6.7	3	3	Paper & Forest Products	46
1207	NWNL Cos.	31	6.8	3	2	Insurance (Life)	20
619	AMAX Inc.	24	6.8	3	3	Metals & Mining (Ind'l)	31
591	Copperweld Corp.	16	6.8	–	5	Metal Fabricating	49
2004	BankAmerica Corp.	29	6.8	3	3	Bank	85
2110	Laclede Steel	15	6.9	3	3	Steel (Specialty)	41
2044	UJB Financial Corp.	17	6.9	4	3	Bank	85
949	Willamette Ind.	50	6.9	2	3	Paper & Forest Products	46
562	Grumman	14	6.9	4	3	Aerospace/Defense	90
1433	Sun Distributors L.P.	13	6.9	–	4	Unassigned	—
658	Manufacturers Nat'l	50	6.9	3	2	Bank (Midwest)	57
708	Cincinnati Gas & Elec.	31	7.0	3	3	Electric Util. (Central)	59
201	United Illuminating	31	7.0	3	4	Electric Utility (East)	52
1195	Salomon Inc.	23	7.0	3	3	Securities Brokerage	62
2106	Allegheny Ludlum	39	7.0	3	3	Steel (Specialty)	41
933	Int'l Paper	51	7.0	3	3	Paper & Forest Products	46
2014	Citizens & Southern	28	7.1	3	3	Bank	85
652	First Chicago	35	7.1	4	3	Bank (Midwest)	57
888	Toll Brothers	3½	7.1	3	5	Homebuilding	77
1179	Mortgage & Rlty Trust	13	7.1	4	3	R.E.I.T.	87
2009	Barnett Banks Inc.	30	7.1	3	2	Bank	85
1355	JLG Industries	17	7.2	3	4	Machinery (Const&Mining)	12
686	SouthTrust Corp.	21	7.2	3	2	Unassigned	—
2017	Dominion Bankshs.	19	7.2	3	2	Bank	85
882	Lennar Corp.	19	7.2	3	4	Homebuilding	77
925	Champion Int'l	28	7.2	3	3	Paper & Forest Products	46
1208	Provident Life 'B'	23	7.2	3	2	Insurance (Life)	20
1501	Arden Group 'A'	54	7.3	3	4	Grocery	25

HIGHEST P/Es

Stocks whose estimated current P/E ratios are biggest

Page No.	Stock Name	Recent Price	Current P/E Ratio	Timeliness	Safety Rank	Industry Group	Industry Rank
669	Deltona Corp.	4½	90.0	–	5	Real Estate	86
222	Diasonics Inc.	3⅜	85.0	3	4	Medical Supplies	6
1648	Neiman-Marcus	16	80.0	–	4	Retail Store	56
1173	Federal Rlty. Inv. Trust	20	80.0	4	2	R.E.I.T.	87
1381	Kysor Ind'l	11	78.6	5	3	Diversified Co.	74
585	Wyman-Gordon	14	77.8	4	3	Aerospace/Defense	90
1486	Rymer Foods Inc.	8½	77.3	3	5	Food Processing	26
668	AMREP Corp.	7¼	73.0	4	4	Real Estate	86
1227	Homestake Mining	20	71.4	3	3	Gold/Silver Mining	28
1068	Int'l Rectifier	7⅛	71.0	2	5	Semiconductor	40
431	Bow Valley Inds.	12	70.6	3	3	Canadian Energy	48
1839	Noble Affiliates	16	66.7	2	3	Petroleum (Producing)	21
1840	Oryx Energy Co.	46	66.7	–	3	Petroleum (Producing)	21
1106	SCI Systems	9¾	65.3	4	3	Computer & Peripherals	79
160	Tektronix, Inc.	13	65.0	4	3	Precision Instrument	66
1376	Interlake Corp.	7⅝	63.3	–	4	Diversified Co.	74
507	Ecolab Inc.	25	62.5	5	3	Chemical (Specialty)	30
2118	DST Systems	10	62.5	4	3	Computer Software & Svcs	8
921	Abitibi-Price	13	61.9	4	3	Paper & Forest Products	46
1866	Varco Int'l	8⅜	60.0	2	5	Oilfield Services/Equip.	4
1384	Masco Inds.	6	60.0	4	4	Diversified Co.	74
1095	Gen'l DataComm	4⅛	58.6	3	4	Computer & Peripherals	79
467	Transco Energy	41	55.4	3	3	Natural Gas(Diversified)	15
268	Builders Transport	13	54.2	–	3	Trucking/Transp. Leasing	92
766	LIN Broadcasting	112	54.1	–	3	Telecom. Services	53
412	Hamilton Oil	30	53.6	3	3	Petroleum (Integrated)	47
1280	Beverly Enterprises	4¾	53.3	3	5	Medical Services	16
564	Hi-Shear Inds.	13	52.0	4	3	Aerospace/Defense	90
1259	ALZA Corp. 'A'	38	51.4	2	3	Drug	1
1847	Wainoco Oil	9⅛	50.6	3	4	Petroleum (Producing)	21
1843	Sun Energy Partners	13	50.0	–	4	Petroleum (Producing)	21
1176	L & N Housing	11	50.0	4	3	R.E.I.T.	87
113	Subaru of America	6½	50.0	–	3	Auto & Truck (Foreign)	73
1773	Aztar Corp.	5¾	48.3	5	4	Hotel/Gaming	95
442	Shell Canada	40	47.1	4	3	Canadian Energy	48
2069	PS Group Inc.	32	45.7	4	3	Financial Services	23
279	Yellow Freight Sys.	25	45.5	4	3	Trucking/Transp. Leasing	92
676	Texas Pacific Land Trust	34	44.2	3	1	Real Estate	86
1617	Tultex Corp.	7⅜	43.5	5	3	Apparel	76
422	Quaker State Corp.	13	43.3	4	3	Petroleum (Integrated)	47
1222	Amer. Barrick Res.	19	43.2	2	3	Gold/Silver Mining	28
1402	Tyler Corp.	8⅝	43.0	–	3	Diversified Co.	74
1774	Bally Mfg.	12	42.9	5	4	Hotel/Gaming	95
1266	Genentech	27	42.9	–	3	Drug	1
1358	Stone & Webster	36	42.9	5	1	Machinery (Const&Mining)	12
1534	Coca-Cola Enterprises	14	42.4	4	3	Beverage	7
1371	Fuqua Ind.	22	42.3	5	3	Diversified Co.	74
1846	Union Texas Petr.	19	42.2	3	3	Petroleum (Producing)	21
563	Hexcel Corp.	16	42.1	5	3	Aerospace/Defense	90
1831	Anadarko Petroleum	32	42.1	3	3	Petroleum (Producing)	21

Page No.	Stock Name	Recent Price	Current P/E Ratio	Timeliness	Safety Rank	Industry Group	Industry Rank
1833	DEKALB Energy Co.	32	41.6	–	3	Petroleum (Producing)	21
758	C-TEC Corp.	19	41.3	4	3	Telecom. Services	53
2042	Sterling Bancorp	9⅜	40.9	3	3	Bank	85
832	Racal Telecom (ADR)	63	40.6	–	3	European Diversified	3
1564	NEC Corp. (ADR)	64	40.0	2	3	Foreign Electronics	24
303	Frisch's Restaurants	22	40.0	4	3	Restaurant	19
1766	Outboard Marine	24	40.0	5	3	Recreation	84
454	Enron Corp.	54	39.7	3	3	Natural Gas(Diversified)	15
2008	Bank of New York	38	38.8	3	2	Bank	85
1261	Amgen	58	38.7	1	4	Drug	1
1074	Teradyne Inc.	8⅞	38.7	3	3	Semiconductor	40
1708	Petrie Stores	22	38.6	3	3	Retail (Special Lines)	50
1223	Battle Mtn. Gold Co.	16	38.1	3	3	Gold/Silver Mining	28
2013	Citicorp	25	37.3	4	3	Bank	85
1229	Newmont Mining	52	37.1	2	4	Gold/Silver Mining	28
1566	Pioneer Elec. (ADR)	89	36.8	1	3	Foreign Electronics	24
352	Primark Corp.	8¾	36.7	–	3	Industrial Services	13
1377	Itel Corp.	19	36.5	3	4	Diversified Co.	74
1562	Kyocera Corp. (ADR)	92	36.1	3	3	Foreign Electronics	24
1215	Blyvoor Gold ADR	3⅝	36.0	–	4	Gold/Diamond (S.A.)	—
441	Renaissance Energy	27	36.0	1	4	Canadian Energy	48
145	Finnigan Corp.	15	35.7	4	4	Precision Instrument	66
438	Numac Oil & Gas	7¾	35.5	3	3	Canadian Energy	48
1339	Cincinnati Milacron	18	35.3	3	3	Machine Tool	36
1228	LAC Minerals	12	35.3	3	3	Gold/Silver Mining	28
806	Walbro Corp.	15	34.9	3	3	Auto Parts (Oem)	94
629	Cont'l Corp.	29	34.9	3	2	Insurance(Prop/Casualty)	18
1286	Omnicare Inc.	7¼	34.8	3	3	Medical Services	16
2055	CUC Int'l	16	34.8	–	4	Financial Services	23
416	Murphy Oil Corp.	44	34.6	3	3	Petroleum (Integrated)	47
620	Brush Wellman	21	34.4	4	3	Metals & Mining (Ind'l)	31
218	Collagen Corp.	17	34.0	1	4	Medical Supplies	6
449	Burlington Resources	43	33.9	–	3	Natural Gas(Diversified)	15
581	TransTechnology	11	33.3	4	3	Aerospace/Defense	90
1573	Nat'l Bank of Canada	11	33.3	4	3	Bank (Canadian)	81
1815	N.Y. Times	24	33.3	4	2	Newspaper	80
1765	Orion Pictures	20	33.3	3	5	Recreation	84
276	Ryder System	19	33.3	5	3	Trucking/Transp. Leasing	92
1813	Media General	30	33.3	5	3	Newspaper	80
760	Century Tel. Enterprises	26	32.9	3	3	Telecom. Services	53
874	Republic Gypsum	4⅞	32.7	4	3	Building Materials	69
718	Illinois Power	18	32.7	3	4	Electric Util. (Central)	59
527	Raychem Corp.	26	32.5	4	3	Chemical (Specialty)	30
1070	Micron Technology	12	32.4	4	4	Semiconductor	40
1225	Echo Bay Mines	16	32.0	3	3	Gold/Silver Mining	28
1231	Placer Dome	19	31.7	3	3	Gold/Silver Mining	28
1303	AMCA Int'l Ltd.	3¾	31.7	3	4	Machinery	45
417	Occidental Petroleum	28	31.5	3	3	Petroleum (Integrated)	47
1568	TDK Corp. (ADR)	42	31.3	4	3	Foreign Electronics	24
448	Arkla Inc.	24	30.4	3	2	Natural Gas(Diversified)	15

Factual material is obtained from sources believed to be reliable, but the publisher is not responsible for any errors or omissions contained herein.

Source: The Value Line Investment Survey, "Summary of Advices and Index," March 9, 1990, p. 35.

INVESTMENTS INTUITION

It is extremely important in analyses such as these to remember that beta is a measure of volatility, indicating what can be expected to happen, *on average*, to a stock when the overall market rises or falls. In fact, EG&G, or any other stock, will not perform in the predicted way every time. If it did, the risk would disappear. Investors can always find examples of stocks that, over some specific period of time, did not move as their beta indicated they would. This is not an indictment of the usefulness of beta as a measure of volatility; rather, it suggests that the beta relationship can only be expected to hold *on the average*.

In trying to understand and predict a company's return and risk, we need to keep in mind that the return is a function of two components. The systematic component is related to the return on the overall market and is the product of the beta coefficient and the return on the market, as explained. The other component is the unique part attributable to the company itself and not to the overall market. It is a function of the specific positive or negative factors that affect a company independent of the market.

Summary

- The analysis of individual companies, the last of three steps in fundamental security analysis, encompasses all the basic financial variables of the company, such as sales, management, competition, and so on. On a specific level, it involves applying the valuation procedures explained in earlier chapters.
- Intrinsic value (a company's justified price) can be estimated using either a dividend valuation model or an earnings multiplier model. It is then compared to the current market price in order to determine if the stock is undervalued or overvalued.
- An important first step in fundamental analysis is to understand the earnings per share (EPS) of companies. To do this, the financial statements are used.
- The balance sheet shows the assets and liabilities at a specific date, whereas the income statement shows the flows during a period for the items that determine net income.
- Although these statements are certified by the accounting profession, alternative accounting principles result in EPS figures that are not precise, readily comparable figures.
- EPS is the result of the interaction of several variables.
- Changes in earnings are directly related to changes in stock prices. To

assess expected earnings, investors can consider the earnings growth rate, which is the product of ROE and the earnings retention rate.

- The lack of persistence in these growth rates may lead investors to consider EPS forecasts, available mechanically or from analysts. Both are subject to error. The evidence is mixed on which method is better, although a recent study favors analysts' forecasts.
- The difference between actual and forecast EPS is important because of the role of the market's expectations about earnings. Standardized unexpected earnings (SUE) attempts to evaluate the unexpected portion of quarterly earnings.
- The price/earnings (P/E) ratio is the other half of the earnings multiplier model, indicating the amount per dollar of earnings investors are willing to pay for a stock. It represents the relative price of a stock, with some companies carrying high P/E ratios and others having low ones.
- The P/E ratio is influenced directly by investors' expectations of the future growth of earnings and the payout ratio, and inversely by the required rate of return.
- P/E ratios vary among companies primarily because of investors' expectations about the future growth of earnings. If investors lower their expectations, the price of the stock may drop while earnings remain constant or even rise.
- The beta coefficient, the measure of volatility for a stock, indicates the *average* responsiveness of the stock's price to the overall market, with high- (low-) beta stocks exhibiting larger (smaller) changes than the overall market, on average.

Key Words

E/P ratio
Earnings per share (EPS)
Financial statements
Generally accepted accounting principles (GAAPs)
Intrinsic value
Leverage
Retention rate
Return on assets (ROA)
Return on equity (ROE)
Standardized unexpected earnings (SUE)

Questions

12-1 What is the intrinsic value of a stock?

12-2 How can a stock's intrinsic value be determined?

12-3 What are the limitations of using Equation 12-1 to determine intrinsic value?

12-4 What is meant by *GAAP?*

12-5 What are the problems with estimating accounting earnings?

12-6 What does the auditor's report signify about the financial statements?

12-7 Using *The Wall Street Journal, Barron's, Forbes,* and other business publications, find an example of a company whose recent accounting practices affected EPS in a way that illustrates the problem with earnings.

12-8 What is the concept of earnings quality?

12-9 Outline, in words, the determination process for EPS.

12-10 Explain the role that financing plays in a company's EPS.

12-11 Assuming that a firm's return on assets exceeds its interest costs, why would it not boost ROE to the maximum through the use of debt financing, since higher ROE leads to higher EPS?

12-12 How can the earnings growth rate be determined?

12-13 How well do earnings growth rates for individual companies persist across time?

12-14 How can investors obtain EPS forecasts? Which source is better?

12-15 What role do earnings expectations play in selecting stocks?

12-16 How can the unexpected component of EPS be used to select stocks?

12-17 Explain the relationship between SUE and fundamental security analysis.

12-18 Describe at least two variations in calculating a P/E ratio.

12-19 Using the *Value Line Investment Survey,* list the average annual P/E ratio for the following companies for the last five years: Apple Computer, EG&G, Coca Cola, and Philadelphia Electric. What conclusions can you draw from this analysis?

12-20 What are the variables that affect the P/E ratio? Is the effect direct or inverse for each component?

12-21 Holding everything else constant, what effect would the following have on the P/E ratio of a company?

(a) An increase in the expected growth rate of earnings.
(b) A decrease in the expected dividend payout.
(c) An increase in the risk-free rate of return.
(d) An increase in the risk premium.
(e) A decrease in the required rate of return.

12-22 Why would an investor want to know the beta coefficient for a particular company? How could this information be used?

12-23 Is beta the only determinant of a company's return?

12-24 Using Table 12-3, update from *Value Line* the P/E ratios for the first 10 companies in both the lowest and highest set. What does this tell you about the stability of the P/E ratio over time?

Problems

12-1 GF is a large producer of food products. In 19X5, the percentage breakdown of revenues and profits was as follows:

	Revenues(%)	Profits(%)
Packaged foods	41	62
Coffee	28	19
Processed meat	19	13
Food service—other	12	6
	100	100

International operations account for about 22% of sales and 17% of operating profit.

For the 19X1–19X5 fiscal years, ending March 21, the number of shares outstanding (in millions) and selected income statement data were (in millions of dollars) as follows:

Shares Outst.	Year	Revenues	Oper. Inc.	Cap. Exp.	Deprec.	Int. Exp.	Net Income Bef Tax	Net Income After Tax
49.93	19X1	$5472	$524	$121	$77	$31	$452	$232
49.97	19X2	5960	534	262	78	39	470	256
49.43	19X3	6601	565	187	89	50	473	255
49.45	19X4	8351	694	283	131	152	418	221
51.92	19X5	8256	721	266	133	139	535	289

(a) For each year calculate operating income as a percentage of revenues.
(b) Net profits after tax as a percentage of revenues.
(c) After-tax profits per share outstanding (EPS).

The balance sheet data for the same fiscal years (in millions of dollars) were as follows:

Year	Cash	Current Assets	Current Liabilities	Total Assets	Long-Term Debt	Common Equity
19X1	$291	$1736	$845	$2565	$251	$1321
19X2	178	1951	1047	2978	255	1480
19X3	309	2019	929	3103	391	1610
19X4	163	2254	1215	3861	731	1626
19X5	285	2315	1342	4310	736	1872

(d) Calculate the ratio of current assets to current liabilties for each year.
(e) Calculate the long-term debt as a percentage of common equity.
(f) For each year calculate the book value per share as the common equity divided by the number of shares outstanding.
(g) Calculate ROE.
(h) Calculate ROA.
(i) Calculate leverage.

(j) Calculate the net income margin.
(k) Calculate turnover.
(l) Calculate the EBIT.
(m) Calculate the income ratio.
(n) Calculate operating efficiency.
(o) On the basis of Parts (d) through (n), evaluate the current status of the health of GF, and the changes over the period.

12-2 Combining information from the S&P reports and some estimated data for 19X7, the following calendar-year data, on a per-share basis, are provided:

Year	Price Range Low High	Earnings	Dividends	Book Value	(D/E) 100(%)	Annual Avg. P/E	ROE = E/Book
19X1	\$26.5–\$35.3	\$4.56	\$1.72	\$25.98	37.7	7.0	17.6%
19X2	28.3– 37.0	5.02	1.95	29.15	38.8	6.2	17.3
19X3	23.5– 34.3	5.14	2.20	32.11	42.8	5.8	16.0
19X4	27.8– 35.0	4.47	2.20	30.86		7.7	
19X5	29.0– 47.8	5.73	2.30	30.30		6.8	
19X6	36.6– 53.5	6.75	2.40	39.85			
19X7		6.75	2.60	44.00			

(a) Calculate the D/E, ROE, and TR for 19X4, 19X5, and 19X6 (use the average of the low and high prices to calculate TRs).
(b) Show that from 19X2 through 19X6 the per annum growth rate in dividends was 6.9% and for earnings was 8.2%.
(c) Using the current price of \$47, with estimated earnings for 19X7 of \$6.75, show that the P/E would be evaluated as 6.96.
(d) On the basis of the annual average P/E ratios shown above and your estimate in Problem c, assume an expected P/E of 7. If an investor expected the earnings of GF for 19X7 to be \$7.50, show that the intrinsic value would be \$52.50.
(e) What factors are important in explaining the difference in the P/E ratios of EG&G and GF?
(f) From your calculation of the growth rate of dividends in Problem b, assume that the annual rate is 7%. If the required rate of return for the stock is 12% and the expected dividend payout ratio is 0.4, show that P/E = 8.
(g) If the dividend payout ratio is 0.4 and the return on equity is 15%, evaluate Equation 12-7 and show that $g = 0.09$.
(h) Using $k = 0.14$ and $g = 0.09$, with expected 19X7 dividends of \$2.60, show that the intrinsic value is \$52.
(i) Assume the "beta" for GF is 0.8 relative to EG&G's beta of 1.0. Is this information of any help in explaining the different P/E ratios of these two companies?

Selected References

The practitioner's side of stock valuation is discussed in

Chugh, Lal C., and Meador, Joseph W. "The Stock Valuation Process: The Analysts' View." *Financial Analysts Journal*, November/December 1984, pp. 41–44.

A more complete analysis of the SUE concept can be found in

Jones, Charles P., Rendleman, Richard J., and Latané, Henry A. "Stock Return and SUEs During the 1970s." *The Journal of Portfolio Management*, Winter 1984, pp. 18–22.

Dividend discount models are discussed in

Nagorniak, John J. "Thoughts on Using Dividend Discount Models." *Financial Analysts Journal*, November/December 1985, pp. 13–15.

100

PART 5

Common Stocks: Other Approaches

- CHAPTER 13 Technical Analysis
- CHAPTER 14 Efficient Markets

CHAPTER 13

Technical Analysis

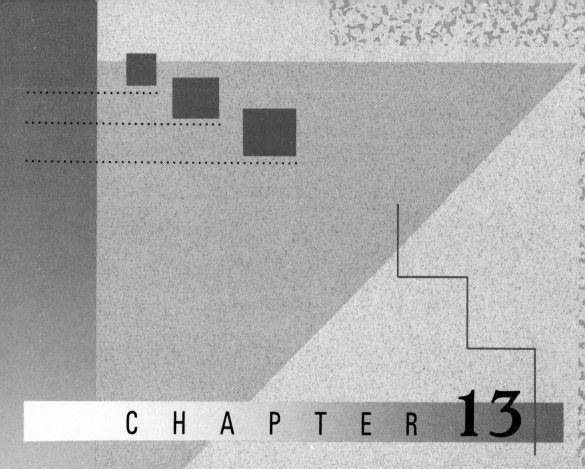

As discussed in Chapter 9, technical analysis is the other traditional approach for selecting stocks. This approach is entirely different from the fundamental approach discussed in the last four chapters.

Although it is the oldest approach (dating back to the late 1800s), the technical approach to common stock selection is extremely controversial. The techniques discussed in this chapter appear at first glance to have considerable merit, because they seem intuitive and plausible, but they have been severely challenged in the last two decades:

Someone learning about investments should (and, in all likelihood, will) be exposed to technical analysis, because many investors, investment advisory firms, and the popular press talk about it and use it. As noted, it has been around for a long time and is widely known. Furthermore, it may produce some insights into the psychological dimension of the market. Even if this approach is incorrect, many investors act as if it is correct. However, today's investors should be aware of the best current evidence about an approach or concept. As we shall see in this chapter and in Chapter 14, extensive evidence challenges the validity, and likelihood of success, of technical analysis. Therefore, the prudent course of action is to study this topic and try to make an objective evaluation of its validity and usefulness.

The discussion in this chapter seeks to strike a reasonable balance. Although it is desirable to know about technical analysis, the persuasive documentation questioning its usefulness argues for a streamlined approach to its study. Accordingly, we shall not discuss all the published techniques, or consider any of them in great detail. The interpretation of virtually all these techniques typically is a matter of judgment. This is particularly true for charting, which is quite subjective in interpretation. A reader interested in the fine points of charting should consult one of the references devoted to that subject.[1]

Although technical analysis can be applied to securities other than common stocks, conventional technical analysis emphasizes either the aggregate stock market or individual common stocks. Therefore, we restrict our discussion in this chapter to common stocks.

What Is Technical Analysis?

Technical analysis can be defined as the use of specific market data for the analysis of both the aggregate stock market and individual stocks. It is

[1]See, for example, R. Edwards and J. Magee, *Technical Analysis of Stock Trends,* 5th ed. (Springfield, Mass.: John Magee, 1966).

sometimes called *market or internal analysis*, because it utilizes the record of the market itself to attempt to assess the demand for, and supply of, shares of a stock or the entire market.

Technical analysis is based on published market data as opposed to fundamental data, such as earnings, sales, growth rates, or government regulations. **Market data** include the price of a stock or the level of a market index, volume (number of shares traded), and technical indicators (explained later), such as the short interest ratio. Many technical analysts feel that only such market data, as opposed to fundamental data, are relevant.

The objective of technical analysis is timing—predicting short-term price movements in either individual stocks or a market indicator. This is accomplished by studying the action of the market or stock through an analysis of price and volume data, or certain technical indicators. Note that technicians are interested not in price levels but in price changes. They attempt to forecast trends in price changes.

Recall that in fundamental analysis the dividend discount model produces an estimate of a stock's intrinsic value, which is then compared to the market price. Fundamentalists believe that their data, properly evaluated, indicate the worth or intrinsic value of a stock. Technicians, on the other hand, believe that it is extremely difficult to estimate intrinsic value or to derive much benefit from such a number if it is estimated. Technicians believe that it is virtually impossible to obtain and analyze *good* information consistently; in particular, they are dubious about the value to be derived from an analysis of published financial statements. Instead they focus on market data as an indication of the forces of supply and demand for a stock or the market.

The following points summarize technical analysis:

1. Technical analysis is based on published market data.
2. The focus of technical analysis is timing. The emphasis is on likely price changes.
3. Technical analysis focuses on internal factors by analyzing movements in the market and/or a stock. Fundamental analysis, in contrast, focuses on economic and political factors, which are external to the market itself.
4. Technicians tend to concentrate more on the short run. The techniques of technical analysis are designed to detect likely price movements over a relatively short time. Fundamentalists, on the other hand, have a substantial interest in the intermediate and longer run.

The Rationale of Technical Analysis

Technical analysis is based on the proposition that prices are determined by the interaction of demand and supply and reflect the net optimism (pessimism) of market participants. Since all investors are not in agreement on price, the determining factor at any point in time is the net demand (or lack thereof) for a stock based on how many investors are optimistic or pessimistic. Furthermore, once the balance of investors becomes optimistic (pessimistic), this mood is likely to continue for the near term and can be detected by various technical indicators.

INVESTMENTS INTUITION

Clearly, prices are determined in the marketplace by the forces of supply and demand. Many market participants would agree that investors have differing amounts of information on which to base their decisions. A key question in assessing technical analysis concerns the information that investors use to make their decisions. Technicians believe that investors use a wide variety of factors, including those not related to the fundamental value of a company (e.g., rumors and irrelevant information). If this is the case, one cannot rely solely on a sound fundamental model to determine the intrinsic value of a stock. However, according to technicians, market data can be used to assess trends in market psychology. In effect, prior price movements can be used to assess future price movements.

A second key question concerns trends in prices and the detection of these trends. A major assumption in technical analysis is that trends in stock prices occur and continue for considerable periods of time. The rationale for this is that investors do not receive and interpret information equally; some receive it earlier or assess it better than others. For example, market professionals who follow the market daily may learn of important developments before the average investor. The same is true of the large institutional investors who constantly seek out new information about stocks.

The effect of the process by which prices adjust to new information, as far as technicians are concerned, is one of a *gradual adjustment* toward a new (equilibrium) price. As the stock adjusts from its old equilibrium level to its new level, the price tends to move in a trend. Stock prices require time to adjust to the change in supply and demand.

Technicians assume that the process of change from the old equilibrium to the new can be detected by the action of the stock (or the market) itself. What is important is to be able to recognize a change in the supply–demand relationship quickly and take the appropriate action. The reason the change is taking place is not important, only the fact that it is taking place.

The rationale of technical analysis can be summarized as follows:

1. Prices are determined by the forces of demand and supply.
2. Many factors affect demand and supply, including fundamental factors and "market psychology" factors.
3. Stock prices tend to move in trends as the stock price adjusts to a new equilibrium level.
4. Trends can be analyzed, and changes in trends detected, by studying the action of price movements and trading volume across time.

A Framework for Technical Analysis

Technical analysis is primarily considered with improving timing decisions. What matters is the change in prices (as opposed to the level of prices). Technicians are attempting to discern trends in demand and supply in order to forecast short-term movements in price.

Technical analysis can be applied to both the aggregate market and individual stocks. Either can be analyzed by graphs (charts) and, in some cases, by technical indicators that are applicable to both.

Price and volume are the primary tools of the technical analyst. Technicians believe that the forces of supply and demand show up in patterns of price and volume. Volume data are used to gauge the general condition in the market and to help assess its trend. The evidence seems to suggest that rising (falling) stock prices are usually associated with rising (falling) volume. If stock prices rise but volume activity does not keep pace, technicians would be skeptical about the upward trend. An upward surge on contracting volume would be particularly suspect. A downside movement from some pattern or holding point, accompanied by heavy volume, would be taken as a bearish sign.

It should be noted that technical analysis has evolved over time. It is much more than the charting of individual stocks or the market. Technicians today often seek to understand investor sentiment by examining what is happening in the overall market environment. They also engage in "contrary analysis," which is more of an intellectual process than a technique. The idea here is to go against the crowd when the crowd starts thinking alike.

Figure 13-1 depicts the basics of the technical analysis approach to selecting common stocks. We discuss technical indicators first, which often are concerned primarily with the aggregate market, although several are also applied to individual stocks. We then consider charting, which is primarily associated with individual stocks.[2]

[2]A good source of current information on technical indicators is *Barron's*, a weekly newspaper.

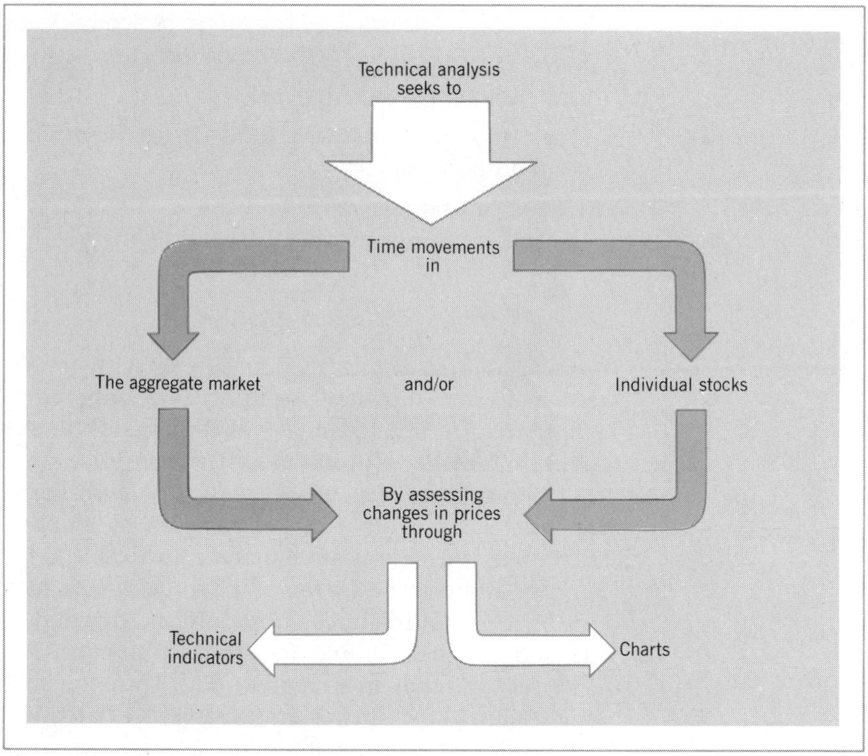

FIGURE 13-1 ***The technical analysis approach to common stock selection.***

Aggregate Market Analysis

Technical analysis is often applied to the aggregate market, as represented by an index such as the Dow Jones Industrial Average or the Standard & Poor's 500 Composite Index. The purpose is to predict changes in the overall market. Most of the techniques used have been available for many years. References to technical analysis of the market can be seen regularly in the popular press and in several investment advisory letters. For example, references may be made about the market penetrating a resistance level, or finding support at a particular level.[3]

The Dow Theory

The oldest and best-known theory of technical analysis is the **Dow theory,** originally developed in the late 1800s by the editor of *The Wall Street Jour-*

---

[3]See, for example, Standard & Poor's *Investor's Monthly,* March 1990, p. 1.

nal.[4] Although Charles H. Dow developed it to describe past price movements, William Hamilton followed up by using it to predict movements in the market (it is not concerned with individual securities). The Dow theory was very popular in the 1920s and 1930s, and articles offering support for it appear periodically in the literature.[5]

The basis of the Dow theory is the existence of three types of price movements:

1. Primary moves, a broad market movement that lasts several years.
2. Secondary (intermediate) moves, occurring within the primary moves, which represent interruptions lasting several weeks or months.
3. Day-to-day moves, occurring randomly around the primary and secondary moves.

The term ***bull market*** refers to an upward primary move, whereas ***bear market*** refers to a downward primary move. A major upward move is said to occur when successive rallies penetrate previous highs, whereas declines remain above previous lows. A major downward move is expected when successive rallies fail to penetrate previous highs, whereas declines penetrate previous lows.

The secondary or intermediate moves give rise to the so-called technical corrections, which are often referred to in the popular press. These corrections supposedly adjust for excesses that have occurred. These movements are of considerable importance in applying the Dow theory.

Finally, the day-to-day "ripples" occur often and are of minor importance. Even ardent technical analysts usually do not try to predict day-to-day movements in the market.

Figure 13-2 illustrates the basic concept of the Dow theory, although numerous variations exist. The primary trend, represented by the dotted line, is up through time period 1. Although several downward (secondary) reactions occur, these "corrections" do not reach the previous low. Each of these reactions is followed by an upward movement that exceeds the previously obtained high. Trading volume continues to build over this period. Although prices again decline after time period 1 as another correction occurs, the price recovery fails to surpass the last peak reached (this is referred to as an abortive recovery). When the next downward reaction occurs, it penetrates the previous low. This could suggest that a primary downturn or new bear market has begun, although this is subject to confirmation, as mentioned later.

---

[4]For a good discussion of the Dow theory, see R. Teweles and E. Bradley. *The Stock Market*, 4th ed. (New York: John Wiley, 1982), pp. 307–322.

[5]See, for example, D. Glickstein and R. Wublels, "Dow Theory Is Alive and Well!" *The Journal of Portfolio Management*, Vol. 9 (Spring 1983), pp. 28–32.

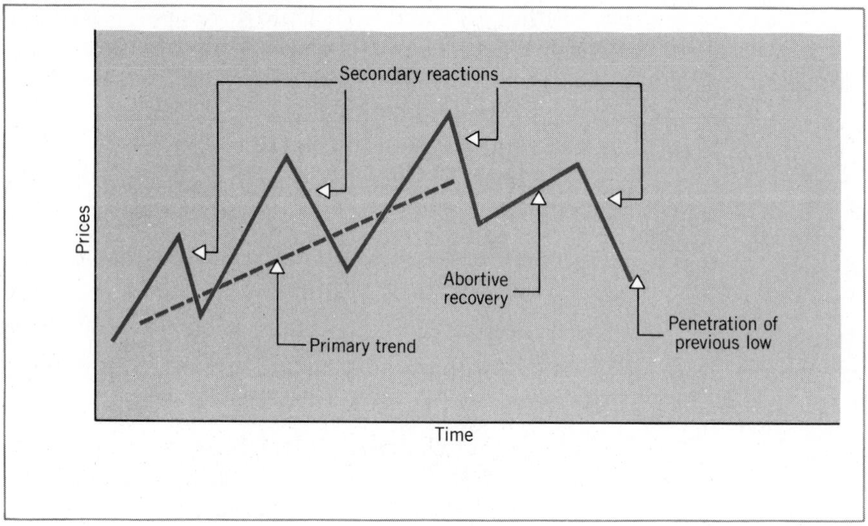

FIGURE 13-2 ***The basic concept of the Dow theory.***

The Dow theory is intended to forecast the start of a primary movement. It will not forecast how long the movement will last. It is important to note that, as originally conceived, the Dow Jones Industrial and Rail averages (which was later replaced by the Transportation Average) must *confirm* each other for the movement to be validated. It is also important to note that confirmation is up to each user of the Dow theory. The trend will continue as long as the averages confirm each other. Only these averages matter—extensive records are not required, chart patterns are not studied, and so on.

The Dow theory is subject to a number of criticisms.[6] Studies of its success rate have been disappointing (e.g., over periods of as much as 25 years, investors would have been more successful with a buy-and-hold policy in the same stocks). It is obvious that today's economy is vastly different from that existing when the theory was developed. Confirmations are slow to arrive and are often unclear when they do. The amount of price movement needed for a confirmation is ambiguous.

One problem with the Dow theory is the many versions available. The theory is interpreted in various ways by its users and may therefore be predicting different (and conflicting) movements at the same time. See Box 13-1 for an interesting discussion of differing interpretations of the Dow theory.

[6]This discussion is based on Teweles and Bradley, *The Stock Market*, pp. 320–321.

BOX 13-1

BULL? OR BEAR?

When is a buy signal not a buy signal? When it's issued by the venerable Dow Theory.

According to *Market Logic*, edited by Norman Fosback and Glen Parker, the Dow Theory flashed a buy signal on Feb. 16, 1988. But according to Richard Russell's *Dow Theory Letters*, the Dow Theory has been bearish since Oct. 15, 1987!

Dow left lots of room for argument. Such as: How large must a secondary reaction be? And how much time do the averages have after a secondary reaction to reconfirm the original primary trend? After all, countertrend movements occur every day. So not just any secondary reaction will do.

Richard Russell thought that the preconditions for a Dow Theory sell signal were met prior to the 1987 crash. Following the Aug. 25 high, a secondary correction lasted until Sept. 21. In their subsequent rally up to Oct. 2, both the DJI and DJT failed to surpass their Aug. 25 highs. And on Oct. 15, both averages closed below their Sept. 21 lows—triggering a sell signal.

But some Dow Theorists disagreed with Russell. According to them, Russell hadn't given stocks enough time following their Sept. 21 low to see if they could surpass their old highs. The rally that did occur lasted just nine trading sessions, short of the three-week minimum that they claimed was the traditional definition. So, while Russell got credit for getting out prior to the crash, not everyone agreed that the bull market was over.

Subsequent events seem to have supported these bullish Dow Theorists, as the DJI has since recovered all but a couple hundred of its 1,000-point drop. But Russell is sticking to his guns. He believes it is very bearish that the DJI has not joined the DJT in making a new alltime high. A buy signal wouldn't occur, he says, until and unless it does so.

Fosback and Parker, however, argue that a Dow Theory buy signal does not require the averages to make alltime highs. A buy signal requires only that both averages surpass their previous reaction highs, which has happened already.

Source: Adapted from Mark Hulbert, "Bull? Or Bear?" *Forbes*, July 24, 1989, p. 340. Excerpted by permission of *Forbes* magazine, July 24, 1989, © Forbes, Inc., 1989.

The *advance–decline line* measures, on a cumulative basis, the net difference between the number of stocks advancing in price and the number of stocks declining in price. Subtracting the number of declines from the number of advances produces the net advance for a given day (which, of course, can be negative). The advance–decline line, often referred to as the breadth of the market, results from accumulating these numbers across time.

The advance–decline line is compared to a stock average, in particular the Dow Jones Industrial Average, in order to determine if movements in this market indicator have also occurred in the market as a whole. The two normally move together. If both are rising (declining), the overall market is said to be technically strong (weak). If the advance–decline line is rising while the average is declining, the decline in the latter should reverse itself. Particular attention is paid to a divergence between the two during a bull market. If the average rises while the line weakens or declines, this indicates a weakening in the market and the average would be expected to reverse itself and start declining.

Moving Averages

A popular technical technique for analyzing both the overall market and individual stocks is that of a *moving average of prices*, which is used to detect both the direction and the rate of change. Some number of days of closing prices is chosen for the calculation of a moving average. A well-known average for identifying major trends is the 200-day moving average (alternatively, a 30-week moving average).[7] After initially calculating the average price, the new value for the moving average is calculated by dropping the earliest observation and adding the latest one. This process is repeated daily (or weekly). The resulting moving average line supposedly represents the basic trend of stock prices.

A comparison of the current market price to the moving average produces a buy or sell signal. The general buy signal is when actual prices rise through the moving average on high volume, with the opposite applying to a sell signal. Specific signals of an upper turning point (a sell signal) are the following:

1. Actual price is below the moving average, advances toward it, does not penetrate the average, and starts to turn down again.
2. Following a rise, the moving average flattens out or declines, and the price of the stock or index penetrates it from the top.
3. The stock price rises above the moving average line while the line is still falling.

Buy signals would be generated if these situations were turned upside down.

Figure 13-3 shows a 200-day moving average for the Wilshire Index plotted against the index itself. This graph is shown in *Forbes* on a regular basis and is therefore available to investors, although obviously with some lag. The graph may take on real significance in view of an article that states that since the beginning of 1981, each of the six times the Wilshire Index crossed its 200-day moving average and remained there, a new bull or bear phase was confirmed. See Box 13-2.

---

[7]For identifying intermediate trends, a 10-week moving average is often used.

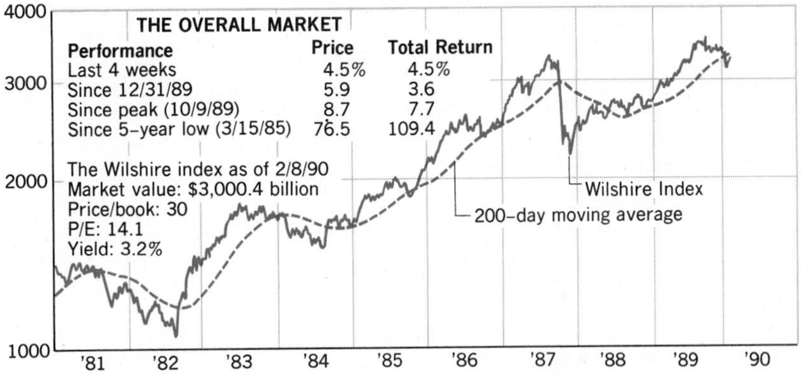

FIGURE 13-3 ***A 200-day moving average plotted with the Wilshire Index.***
Source: The *Forbes* Wall Street Review, *Forbes,* March 5, 1990, p. 157. Reprinted by permission of *Forbes* magazine, March 5, 1990, © Forbes, Inc., 1990.

The Confidence Index

The Confidence Index, published weekly by *Barron's*, attempts to measure investor optimism and pessimism by examining investor actions in the bond market. It is calculated as follows:

$$\text{Confidence Index} = \frac{\text{Yield on 10 high-grade corporate bonds}}{\text{Average yield on 40 Dow Jones bonds}} \qquad (13\text{-}1)$$

Since high-grade bonds should always yield less than lower-quality bonds, the Confidence Index should always be less than 1.0. As investors become more optimistic about the future, the difference between the two yields in the index decreases (i.e., the default risk premium narrows and the ratio increases). As investors become more pessimistic about the future, the difference between the two yields increases (i.e., the default risk premium rises) and the ratio decreases. Because the bond market tends to be dominated by institutional investors, the Confidence Index is viewed by some as a barometer of sophisticated investors' expectations (and behavior).

Advocates of the Confidence Index believe that it should move in the same direction as the stock market because increased confidence in the bond market should lead to increased confidence in the stock market. Therefore, an increase (decrease) in the index is a buy (sell) signal. If the Confidence Index leads the market, it can be useful as an indicator.[8] Because it is available weekly in *Barron's*, it is a convenient and accessible indicator.

Although the bond and stock markets generally move together, there is no theoretical reason that confidence in the bond market should precede confidence in the stock market. The latter is considered by most observers

---

[8]Lead time is believed by advocates to be between two months and one year.

BOX 13-2

HOW YOU CAN MOVE WITH THE AVERAGES

To most individuals, "technical indicators" are either for the pros or for the birds. The use of charts and statistical measures to divine the direction of the stock market tends to baffle many investors. Others argue that such techniques are great at explaining what has happened but don't help much in forecasting what lies ahead. In truth, the "technical analysts" have been getting more respect from Wall Street lately for their predictive abilities.

One technical indicator these analysts are watching closely right now as a pointer to the market's overall direction is the relationship of key market indexes like the Dow to the indexes' longer-term "moving averages." These averages smooth out the market's day-to-day oscillations into a longer-term trend covering anywhere from a few days to a year or more.

To technicians, bells go off any time the daily price of a major index like the Wilshire or Dow moves decisively across its 200-day moving average, because that event historically has augured a fundamental change in direction for the market. A fall below the trend line is bearish, while a rise above it is very bullish. Each of the six times the Wilshire crossed its 200-day moving average since the beginning of 1981 and stayed there, the development has confirmed a new bull or bear phase. Investors who used this technique with the Wilshire were warned of the cataclysmic Oct. 19, 1987, crash, although not by much. The Wilshire exactly hit its 200-day moving average on the Thursday before Black Monday and smashed through it on the following day, giving quick-witted investors a little time to heed the warning. The last time such a cross occurred, in April 1988, it signaled investors to get back into the market.

Such decisive traversals are fairly infrequent. That is why using moving averages is generally considered a good timing technique for investors who want to avoid being caught in major bear markets but don't want to get whipsawed by intermediate shifts. It can be tough, though, to distinguish a significant fall below or surge above the average from a temporary dip or rise. The most recent close call occurred in early November when the Wilshire dropped close to its moving average, then bounced back.

Source: Adapted from 1/8/90 issue of *U.S. News & World Report*. Reprinted by permission.

to be the preeminent discounter of future events. In fact, the Confidence Index does not always lead the market and has given a number of false signals. Thus, its record as a predictor is mixed at best.

Mutual Fund Liquidity

Mutual funds (a form of investment company, to be discussed in Chapter 18) are institutional investors who own and manage a portfolio of securities on behalf of their shareholders. Mutual fund managers will vary their cash (liquidity) positions across time, depending on their expectations for the market. Because of the availability of data on these funds, the ratio of cash and cash equivalents (e.g., Treasury bills) to the total assets of the fund can be obtained on a timely basis.

One technical position with regard to mutual fund liquidity is that the larger the liquidity percentage, the more bullish it is for the market. The rationale involves the potential buying power represented by this liquidity—as it is committed to the market, prices will be driven up. Similarly, a low level of liquidity indicates little available money for purchases by the mutual funds, a bearish sign.

What is a high or low level of liquidity? Probably 5% to 12% cash and cash equivalents is considered normal. A bearish signal was given when the liquidity level reached 5% to 6% until the mid-1970s, whereas 7% to 8% is the current range often used to signal a bear market. A level above 10% is typically considered bullish, with recent emphasis on the 11% to 12% range.[9] (For one piece of factual evidence, consider the liquidity position of common stock mutual funds in August 1982, the start of a very strong bull market. At that time, 12% of their assets was in cash.)

Short Interest Ratio

The **short interest ratio** is defined as

$$\text{Short interest ratio} = \frac{\text{Total shares sold short}}{\text{Average daily trading volume}} \qquad (13\text{-}2)$$

The short interest (number of shares sold short) is calculated on the twentieth day of the month and appears subsequently in *The Wall Street Journal*, listed by stock name for both the New York and American exchanges. Although the ratio can be calculated for an individual stock, this information typically is used in aggregate market analysis. In effect, the ratio indicates the number of days necessary to "work off" the current short ratio.[10] It is considered to be a measure of investor sentiment.

Investors sell short when they expect prices to decline; therefore, it would appear, the higher the short interest, the more investors are expecting a decline. A large short interest position for an individual stock should indicate heavy speculation by investors that the price will drop. However, many technical analysts interpret this ratio in the opposite manner. With this reverse interpretation, a *high* short interest ratio is taken as a *bullish* sign, because the large number of shares sold short represents a large number of shares that must be repurchased in order to close out the short

[9]The liquidity level can be found in *Barron's* "Monthly Mutual Fund Indicators." It is listed as "Liquid Asset Ratio (Equity and Balanced)."

[10]For example, a ratio of 1.0 means that the outstanding short interest approximates a day's trading volume.

sales (if the ratio is low, the required purchases are not present). In effect, the short seller must repurchase, whether his or her expectations were correct or not. The larger the short sale ratio, the larger the potential demand that is indicated. Therefore, an increase in the ratio indicates more "pent up" demand for the shares that have been shorted.

The short interest ratio for a given month should be interpreted in relation to historical boundaries, which historically were in the range of 1.0–2.0 for the NYSE. A short interest ratio above 2.0 would have been considered extremely bullish, whereas a ratio below 1.0 would indicate weakness; therefore, if the ratio rises above the range considered normal, a buy signal would be generated, and if it falls below 1.0, a sell signal would be generated. However, increased trading in stock options and futures (discussed in Chapters 15 and 17, respectively), which provide investors with new ways to hedge short positions, has distorted the historical boundaries.

The short interest ratio increased in the mid-1980s to a typical range of 2.0–3.0. Therefore, a bullish signal would be given by a rise to (or above) 3.0, and a bearish signal would be given by a ratio approaching 2.0. In 1988 and 1989 it was typically between 3.0 and 4.0, approaching 4.0 for NYSE stocks at the end of 1988 and reaching this level in April 1989, a high in modern investing history.[11] And the market performed well in 1989. On the other hand, short selling activity was vigorous before the market crash of 1987, suggesting the opposite interpretation—high short interest related to a market decline.

For investors interested in the short interest, *The Wall Street Journal* reports each month NYSE and Amex issues for which a short interest position of at least 100,000 shares existed or for which a short position change of 50,000 shares occurred from the previous month. On an individual stock basis, comments in *The Wall Street Journal* suggest that a significant increase in the short position is a bearish sign, whereas a significant decrease is a bullish sign.

Contrary Opinion

Several indicators are based on the theory of **contrary opinion.** The idea is to trade contrary to most investors, who supposedly almost always lose—in other words, to go against the crowd. This is an old idea on Wall Street, and over the years technicians have developed several measures designed to capitalize on this concept. We shall consider some of the best-known traditional contrary opinion indicators as well as one of the newer indicators.

Odd-Lot Theory According to the **odd-lot theory** small investors who often buy or sell odd lots (less than 100 shares of stock) are usually wrong

[11]The short interest ratio for OTC stocks as measured by those on the National Market System must be interpreted differently. For example, in early 1989 it was 2.6 for these stocks.

in their actions at market peaks and troughs. Supposedly, such investors typically buy (sell) when the market is at or close to a peak (bottom).

To take advantage of the (wrong) actions of these investors, an indicator must be calculated. Several are available, but a commonly used one is the odd-lot index, defined as

$$\text{Odd-lot index} = \frac{\text{Odd-lot sales}}{\text{Odd-lot purchases}} \tag{13-3}$$

A decline in this index would indicate more purchases in relation to sales by small investors, suggesting they are optimistic. According to contrary opinion, it is time to sell—to go against the "man in the street." Conversely, a rise in this index would indicate more sales relative to purchases, a sign of pessimism by small investors but an opportune time for a contrarian to buy.

A variation of the odd-lot index is the odd-lot short sales ratio, defined as follows[12]:

$$\text{Odd-lot short sales ratio} = \frac{\text{Odd-lot short sales}}{\text{Total odd-lot sales}} \tag{13-4}$$

As short sales by odd-lotters increase (decrease), these investors are becoming more pessimistic (optimistic). For a contrarian, it is time to buy (sell). The rationale for this ratio is the same as before. Odd-lotters are expected to sell short at precisely the wrong time; that is, prior to a rise in prices.

Regardless of which odd-lot indicator is used, odd-lot theories have not been particularly successful. Small investors have often been correct in their judgments, particularly since the 1970s. This analysis seems to have proved incorrect at least as often as it has proved accurate. Many market professionals today do not believe in odd-lot theories.

The Opinions of Investment Advisory Services *Investors Intelligence*, an investment advisory service, samples weekly the opinions of about 135 investment advisory services and calculates an index of investment service opinions. It has found that, on average, these services are most bearish at the market bottom and least bearish at the market top. This index, published since 1963, is now available weekly and is widely quoted in the investing community.

The "bearish sentiment index" is calculated as the ratio of advisory services that are bearish to the total number with an opinion. When this index approaches 60%, the Dow Jones Industrial Average supposedly tends to go from bearish to bullish; as it approaches 15%, the opposite

[12]This ratio is often used by technicians to confirm the general odd-lot indicator.

occurs. Thus, a contrarian should react in the opposite direction of the sentiment these services are exhibiting.

The reason for this seeming contradiction to logic—that investment advisory services are wrong at the extremes—is attributed to the fact that these services tend to follow trends rather than forecast them. Thus, they are reporting and reacting to what has happened rather than concentrating on anticipating what is likely to happen.

How well does this sentiment index work? According to the editor of *Investors Intelligence,* it caused the newsletter to be completely bullish in July 1982, immediately preceding the start of the great bull market of August 1982–August 1987. It also caused the newsletter to go bearish two months before the crash of October 1987. On the other hand, a recent study of the index by two finance professors found that the index was wrong about 50% of the time—in other words, it was of no value. They attributed the strong belief in the index partly to people seeing patterns in random data.[13]

Mutual Fund Liquidity It is interesting to note that mutual fund liquidity can be used as a contrary opinion technique. Under this scenario, mutual funds are viewed in a manner similar to odd-lotters—they are presumed to act incorrectly before a market turning point. Therefore, when mutual fund liquidity is low because the funds are fully invested, contrarians believe that the market is at, or near, a peak. The funds should be building up cash (liquidity); instead they are extremely bullish and are fully invested. Conversely, when funds hold large liquid reserves, it suggests that they are bearish; contrarians would consider this a good time to buy because the market may be at, or near, its low point.

Put/Call Ratio Some technical analysts believe that people who play the options market are, as a group, almost consistent losers. Speculators buy calls when they expect stock prices to rise, and they buy puts when they expect prices to fall. Because they are generally more optimistic than pessimistic, the **put/call ratio** is typically 0.50–0.60.[14] Such a ratio indicates that only five or six puts are purchased for every 10 calls purchased. When this ratio rises to 0.70, it indicates pessimism on the part of speculators in options, but to some technical analysts this is a buy signal. A ratio below 0.40 would be a sell signal because of the rampant optimism such a ratio indicates. A ratio of 0.60 would be neutral.

According to some research on the put/call ratio for 1983–1986, it generally gave useful signals using the 0.70 and 0.40 guidelines. However, so

---

[13]This information is based on John R. Dorfman, "This Stock Market Sign Often Points the Wrong Way," *The Wall Street Journal,* January 26, 1989, p. C1.

[14]The discussion in these two paragraphs is based on Earl C. Gottschalk, Jr., "Using 'Dumb Money' as a Market Guide," *The Wall Street Journal,* January 17, 1989, p. C1.

many trades were generated that it would be difficult to make money because of commissions.

Individual Stock Analysis

We turn our attention now from an analysis of the aggregate market to an analysis of individual common stocks. Technicians are interested in both.

Technical Indicators

Some of the technical indicators discussed earlier can be applied to individual stocks as well as the aggregate market. Moving averages, for example, are used for individual stocks as well as for the market. Moving average series are available from financial advisory services such as *Daily Graphs,* which offers weekly charts on over 2600 companies. Each chart includes both a 200-day and a 10-week moving average. As noted, the short interest ratio can also be calculated for individual stocks, and the short interest on many NYSE and Amex stocks is reported monthly in *The Wall Street Journal* along with the short interest position for the market.

To assess individual stock price movements, technicians generally rely on charts or graphs of price movements. A second popular technique is that of relative strength analysis.

Charts of Price Patterns

The **charting** of price patterns is one of the classic technical analysis techniques. Technicians believe that stock prices move in trends, with price changes forming patterns that can be recognized and categorized. By visually assessing the forces of supply and demand, technicians hope to be able to predict the likely direction of future movements.

Technical analysts rely primarily on bar charts and point-and-figure charts. We shall discuss each of these in turn. During this discussion, keep in mind two terms often used by technicians—*support level* and *resistance level.* A **support level** is the level of price (or, more correctly, a price range) at which a technician expects a significant increase in the demand for a stock; a **resistance level,** on the other hand, is the level of price (range) at which a technician expects a significant increase in the supply of a stock. Support levels tend to develop when profit taking causes a reversal in a stock's price following an increase. Investors who did not purchase earlier are now willing to buy at this price, which becomes a support level. Resistance levels tend to develop after a stock declines from a higher level. Investors are waiting to sell the stocks at a certain recovery point. At certain price levels, therefore, a significant increase in supply occurs and the price will encounter resistance moving beyond this level.

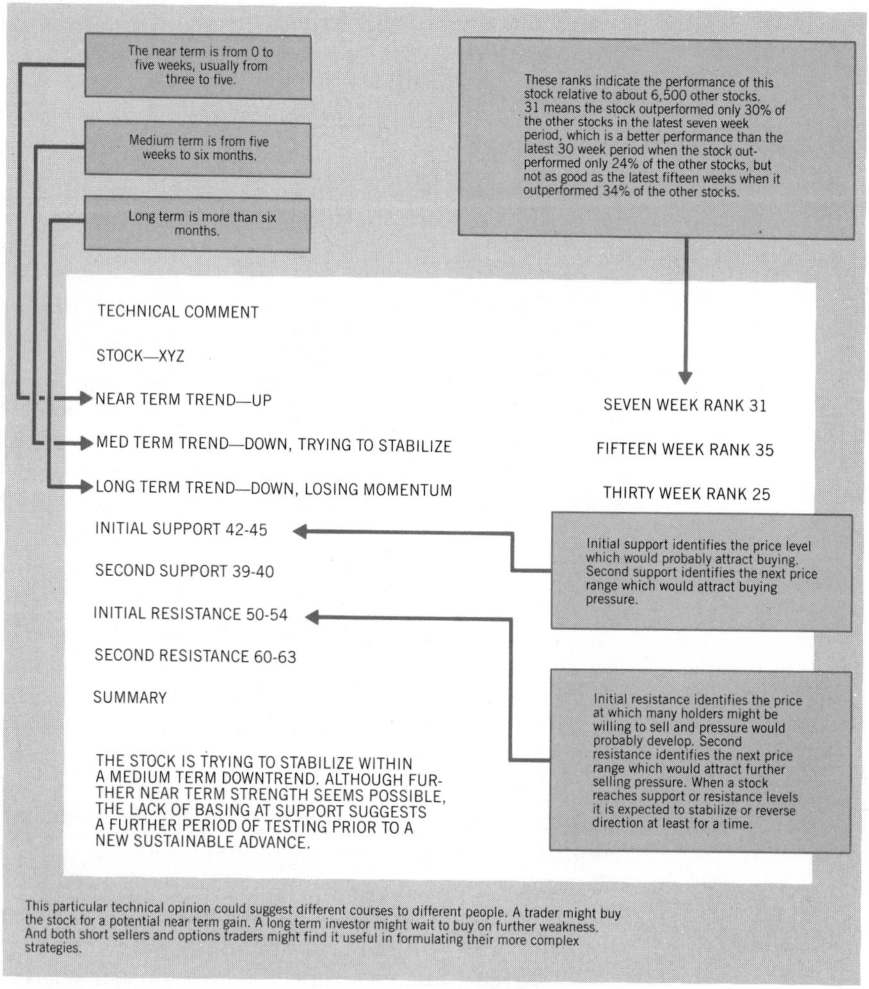

The near term is from 0 to five weeks, usually from three to five.
Medium term is from five weeks to six months.
Long term is more than six months.
These ranks indicate the performance of this stock relative to about 6,500 other stocks. 31 means the stock outperformed only 30% of the other stocks in the latest seven week period, which is a better performance than the latest 30 week period when the stock out-performed only 24% of the other stocks, but not as good as the latest fifteen weeks when it outperformed 34% of the other stocks.
TECHNICAL COMMENT
STOCK—XYZ
NEAR TERM TREND—UP
MED TERM TREND—DOWN, TRYING TO STABILIZE
LONG TERM TREND—DOWN, LOSING MOMENTUM
SEVEN WEEK RANK 31
FIFTEEN WEEK RANK 35
THIRTY WEEK RANK 25
INITIAL SUPPORT 42-45
SECOND SUPPORT 39-40
INITIAL RESISTANCE 50-54
SECOND RESISTANCE 60-63
SUMMARY
THE STOCK IS TRYING TO STABILIZE WITHIN A MEDIUM TERM DOWNTREND. ALTHOUGH FURTHER NEAR TERM STRENGTH SEEMS POSSIBLE, THE LACK OF BASING AT SUPPORT SUGGESTS A FURTHER PERIOD OF TESTING PRIOR TO A NEW SUSTAINABLE ADVANCE.
Initial support identifies the price level which would probably attract buying. Second support identifies the next price range which would attract buying pressure.
Initial resistance identifies the price at which many holders might be willing to sell and pressure would probably develop. Second resistance identifies the next price range which would attract further selling pressure. When a stock reaches support or resistance levels it is expected to stabilize or reverse direction at least for a time.
This particular technical opinion could suggest different courses to different people. A trader might buy the stock for a potential near term gain. A long term investor might wait to buy on further weakness. And both short sellers and options traders might find it useful in formulating their more complex strategies.

FIGURE 13-4 ***A technical opinion from a brokerage firm.***
Source: "A Technical Explanation," *Investments for a Changing Economy,* Merrill Lynch, February/March 1983, p. 9. © Copyright Merrill Lynch 1983. All rights reserved. Reprinted by permission.

Figure 13-4 shows a technical opinion from a brokerage firm report. Several of the terms just discussed, such as resistance and support levels, are mentioned; furthermore, trends covering different periods of time are assessed.

Bar Charts Probably the most popular chart in technical analysis, and clearly the simplest, **bar charts** are plotted with price on the vertical axis while time is shown on the horizontal axis. Each day's price movement is represented by a vertical bar whose top (bottom) represents the high (low) price for the day. (A small, horizontal tick may be used to designate the closing price for the day.) The bottom of a bar chart usually shows the trading volume for each day, permitting the simultaneous observation of both price and volume activity. The time intervals do not have to be days, but could be weeks, months, or anything else a particular preparer may choose. *The Wall Street Journal* carries a bar chart of the Dow Jones averages each day on the page with NYSE quotations.

Figure 13-5 shows a daily bar chart for Unfloppy Disks, Inc. The technician using charts will search for patterns in the chart that can be used to predict future price moves. Note in Figure 13-5 the strong uptrend occurring over a period of months. This trend ended with a rally on high volume (at point 1 in the figure) that forms part of the left shoulder of a famous chart pattern called a head-and-shoulders pattern. In the left shoulder there is initial strong demand followed by a reaction on lower volume (2), and then a second rally with strong volume, carrying prices still higher (3). Profit taking again causes prices to fall to the so-called neckline (4), thus completing the left shoulder (the neckline is formed by connecting previous low points. A rally occurs, but this time on low volume, and again prices sink back to the neckline. This is the head (5). The last step is the formation of the right shoulder, which in this case occurs with light volume (6). Growing weakness can be identified as the price approaches the neckline. As can be seen in Figure 13-5, a downside breakout occurs on heavy volume, which is considered by technicians to be a sell signal.

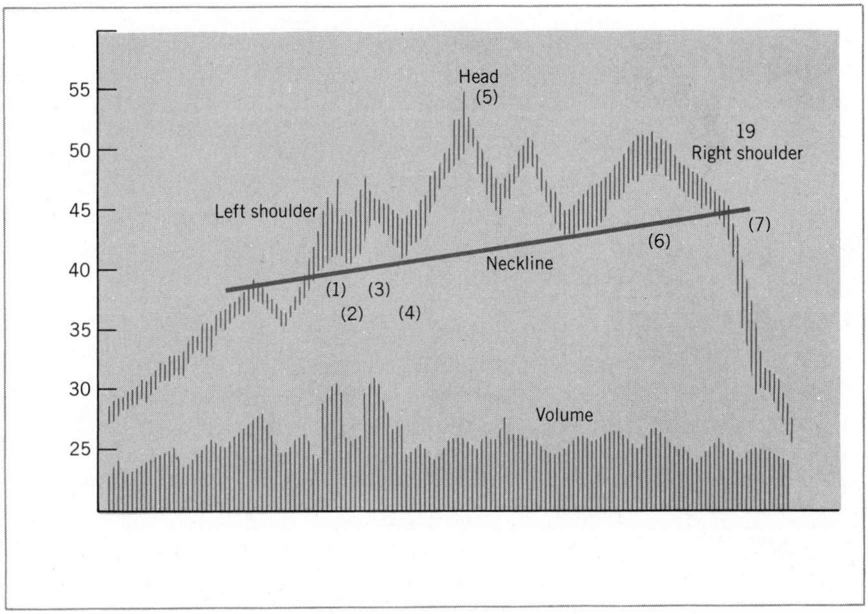

FIGURE 13-5 ***A bar chart for Unfloppy Disks, Inc.***

What about other patterns? The number of such patterns considered by technicians is very large. Some of the possible patterns include flags, pennants, gaps (of more than one type), triangles of various types (e.g., symmetrical, ascending, descending, and inverted), the inverted saucer or dome, the triple top, the compound fulcrum, the rising (and falling) wedge, the broadening bottom, the duplex horizontal, rectangles, and the inverted V.

It is obvious that numerous patterns are possible and can usually be found on a chart of stock prices. It is also obvious that most, if not all, of these patterns are much easier to identify in hindsight than at the time they are actually occurring.

Point-and-Figure-Charts A **point-and-figure** chart is somewhat more complex in that it shows only significant price changes, and volume is not shown at all. It also attempts to predict the amount of the future price movements. Although the horizontal axis still depicts time, specific calendar time is not particularly important (some chartists do show the month in which changes occur).

An X is typically used to show upward movements; an O is used for downward movements. Each X or O in a particular chart may represent $1 movements, $2 movements, $5 movements, and so on, depending upon how much movement is considered significant for that stock. An X or O is recorded only when the price moves by the specified amount.

Figure 13-6 shows a point-and-figure chart for several days for a hypothetical company called Gigantic Computers. Note the lack of a time dimension in this chart. Instead, only significant price changes, in this case $1, are

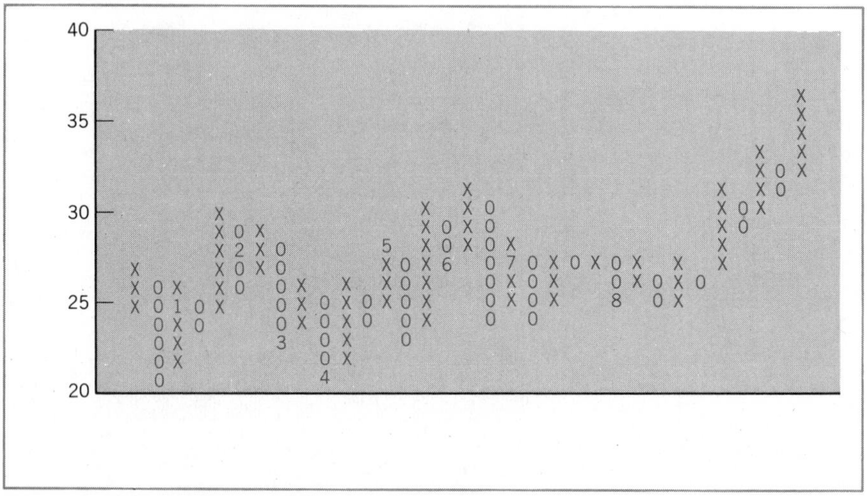

FIGURE 13-6 ***A point-and-figure chart for Gigantic Computers. X = $1 upward price change, O = $1 downward price change (numbers indicate months).***

recorded. An X is recorded for each $1 uptick and an O for each $1 downtick. A new column is started each time the direction of price change is reversed.

A point-and-figure chart is designed to compress many price changes into a small space. By doing this, areas of "congestion" can be identified. A congestion area is a compacted area of price fluctuations (i.e., a closely compacted horizontal band of Xs and Os). The technician studies a congestion area in search of a "breakout," which will indicate an expected upward or downward movement in stock price. In Figure 13-6 the congestion at month 8 leads to an upward breakout.

Some Evidence on Price Charts There are many chart patterns, some of which were mentioned earlier, and numerous technicians analyzing and interpreting these patterns. It is impossible to demonstrate conclusively the lack of predictive significance in charting. Very few *scientific* studies of the ability of chart patterns to predict the future direction of price movements have been conducted. One such study is relevant in considering the likelihood of success of this activity.

Levy studied the predictive significance of "five-point" chart patterns. A five-point chart pattern is one with two highs and three lows, or two lows and three highs. As Figure 13-7 shows, there are 32 possible forms that this chart can assume. As Levy noted,[15]

> The avid chartist will recognize, among the thirty-two patterns, several variations of channels, wedges, diamonds, symmetrical triangles, head and shoulders, reverse head and shoulders, triple tops, and triple bottoms. Each of these formations allegedly reflects underlying supply/demand and support/resistance conditions which have implications as to future price behavior. A common belief among chartists is that the appearance of certain patterns followed by a "breakout" gives a profitable buy or sell signal [p. 316, courtesy of The University of Chicago Press].

Using daily prices for 548 NYSE stocks over a five-year period (1964–1969), Levy found 19,077 five-point patterns. Of these, 9383 were followed by a breakout and were therefore studied. The results indicated that although some patterns did produce better results than others, none performed very differently from the market. Deducting brokerage commissions, *none* of the 32 patterns was found to have any "profitable forecasting ability in either [bullish or bearish] direction." The really surprising conclusion of this study, however, concerned the charts themselves. Again, to quote Levy:

> Even more important, an evaluation of the six distinct best and worst patterns for the four holding periods uncovers an extraordinary contradiction between the lessons of the chartist's textbook and the empirical evidence generated by

---

[15]See R. Levy, "The Predictive Significance of Five-Point Chart Patterns," *The Journal of Business,* Vol. 44 (July 1971), pp. 316–323. © 1971 by the University of Chicago. All rights reserved.

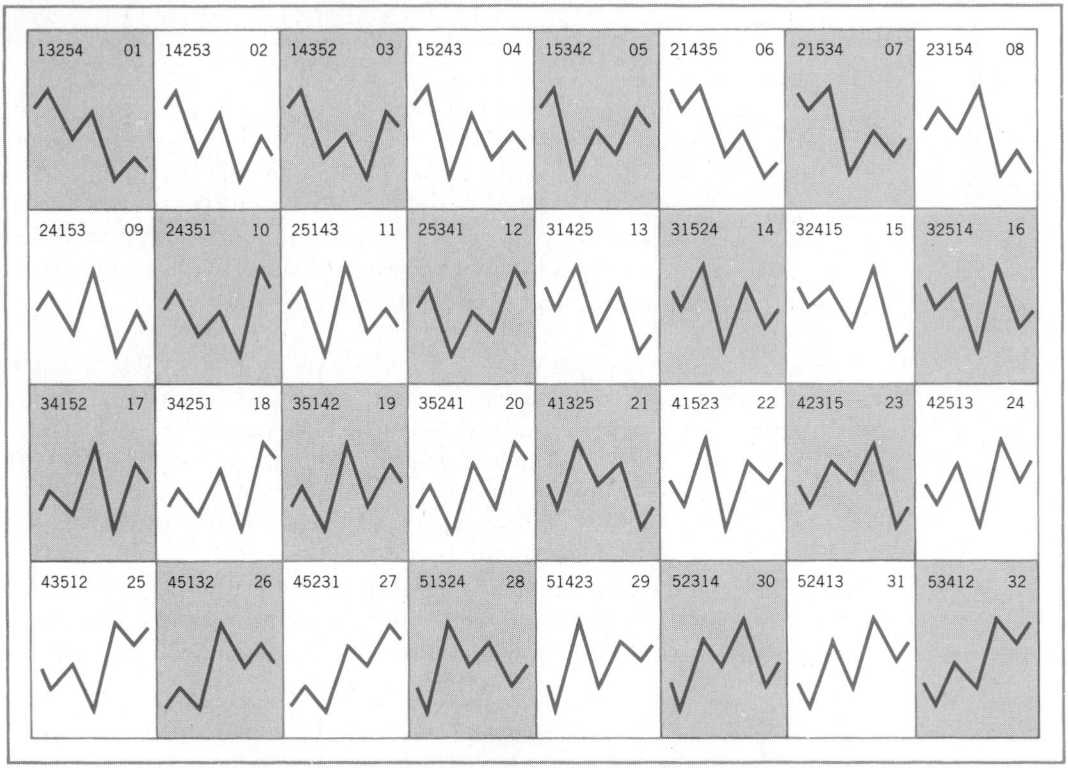

FIGURE 13-7 ***Possible forms of a five-point chart pattern.***
Source: Robert A. Levy, "The Predictive Significance of Five-Point Chart Patterns," *The Journal of Business,* The University of Chicago Press, July 1971, p. 317. By permission of the University of Chicago Press. © 1971 by the University of Chicago.

> these tests. For example, the best performing patterns would probably be characterized as bearish by most technicians, and conversely, the worst performing patterns would, in two of the three cases, be characterized as bullish [p. 322, courtesy of the University of Chicago Press].

Opinions about charting vary widely. The evidence is not conclusive—at least to everyone's satisfaction. The controversy will continue.

Relative Strength

A well-known technique used to forecast individual stocks (or industries) is relative strength analysis. The *relative strength* for a given stock is calculated as the ratio of the stock's price to a market index, or an industry index, or the average price of the stock itself over some previous period. These ratios can be plotted to form a graph of relative price across time. In effect, the graph shows the strength of the stock relative to its industry, the market, or whatever.

Numerous investment information services provide information on relative strength. For example, *The Value Line Investment Survey* divides a stock's price by the Value Line Composite Average and plots this relative strength ratio for each company it covers. In the example page from *Value Line* (see Figure 4-4 in Chapter 4) covering EG&G, the relative price strength is shown in the plot at the top of the page.

The relative strength of a stock over time may be of use in forecasting. Because trends are assumed to continue for some time, a rising ratio indicates relative strength, that is, it indicates a stock that is outperforming the market and that may continue to do so. As they do with most technical indicators, technicians interpret some of these signals in different ways.

Relative strength analysis lends itself well to computerized stock analysis. This probably accounts for its popularity among institutional investors who own highly automated and sophisticated data analysis systems. In fact, the extent to which a number of institutional investors use relative strength techniques and have the means to observe changes at about the same time can affect the volatility of a stock.

The relative strength concept gained considerable attention in 1967 with the publication of an article by Levy that claimed very strong investment results through the use of relative strength.[16] Subsequent investigations pointed out several deficiencies in Levy's study.[17] Nevertheless, the concept remains an important part of technical analysis today. New work periodically appears supporting relative strength.[18]

Testing Technical Analysis Strategies

It is important to consider what constitutes a fair test of a technical trading rule. The adjustments that should be made include at least the following:

1. *Risk.* If the risk involved in two strategies is not comparable, a fair comparison cannot be made. As we know, other things being equal, a more risky strategy would be *expected* to outperform a less risky strategy.
2. *Transaction and other costs (e.g., taxes).* Several technical trading rules appeared to produce excess returns before transaction costs were de-

---

[16]R. Levy, "Random Walks: Reality or Myth," *Financial Analysts Journal*, Vol. 23 (November–December 1967), pp. 69–77.

[17]M. Jensen, "Random Walks: Reality or Myth," *Financial Analysts Journal*, Vol. 23 (November–December 1967), pp. 77–85; and M. Jensen and G. Bennington, "Random Walks and Technical Theories: Some Additional Evidence," *Journal of Finance*, Vol. 25 (May 1970), pp. 469–482.

[18]For example, a 1981 paper by Bohan indicated support for relative strength analysis over the years 1969–1980. J. Bohan, "Relative Strength: Further Positive Evidence," *The Journal of Portfolio Management*, Vol. 8 (Fall 1981), pp. 36–39.

ducted. After such costs were deducted, however, the rules were inferior to a buy-and-hold strategy, which generates little costs.

3. *Consistency* Can the rule outperform the alternative over a reasonable period of time, such as five or 10 years? Any rule may outperform an alternative for a short period, but it will not be too useful unless it holds up over some longer term.
4. *Out-of-sample validity.* Has the rule been tried on data other than that used to produce the rule? It is always possible to find a rule that works on a particular sample if enough rules are tried; that is, it is possible to torture the data until it confesses.

A well-known technical trading rule is the so-called **filter rule.** A filter rule specifies a breakpoint for an individual stock or a market average, and trades are made when the stock price change is greater than this filter.

Example. Buy a stock if the price moves up 10% from some established base, such as a previous low, hold it until it declines 10% from its new high, and then sell it and possibly go short. ▪

Several studies of filters have been conducted. Fama and Blume tested 24 filters (ranging from 0.5% to 50%) on each of the 30 Dow Jones stocks.[19] Before commissions, several of the filters were profitable, in particular the smallest (0.5%). After commissions, however, average returns were typically negative or very small. Brokerage commissions more than offset any gains that could be exploited. The low correlations found in the statistical tests were insufficient to provide profitable filter trading rules.

A popular technical trading rule that often appears in investment advisory publications is relative strength, defined as the ratio of a stock's current price to that of an industry or market index (or the stock's average price over some previous period). Robert Levy developed and claimed success for a relative strength technique based on the previous 26 weeks of price data for the stock and the market.[20] Stocks with the highest relative strength were selected and replaced as necessary when a new ranking showed a decline in one of the top group. Levy presented results for some cutoff points that were superior to a buy-and-hold strategy, after brokerage costs.

Subsequent work by others indicated several problems with Levy's work, including a failure to adjust for risk and taxes.[21] Specifically, Levy's portfolios were more risky than a buy-and-hold strategy and involved short-term gains, which were taxed at higher rates than long-term gains at that time. Perhaps most important, Levy fitted his model to the same

---

[19]E. Fama and M. Blume, "Filter Rules and Stock-Market Trading," *Journal of Business: A Supplement*, Vol. 39 (January 1969), pp. 2–21.

[20]See note 16.

[21]See note 17.

database for which he subsequently presented his results. He tried 68 variations of the basic idea. Independent analysis of his work, involving other time periods and risk adjustments, produced results that were inferior to a buy-and-hold strategy.

Obviously, many different variations of the relative strength technique can be tested by varying the time period over which the average price is calculated and the percentage of the top stocks selected. If we conduct enough tests, we can find a rule that produces favorable results on a particular sample. Therefore, before we conclude that a trading rule of this type is successful, we should conduct a fair test as outlined earlier. Risks must be comparable and appropriate costs must be deducted. Finally, the rule should be tried on a different sample of stocks.

Some Conclusions About Technical Analysis

Technical analysis often appeals to those beginning a study of investments because it is easy to believe that stock prices form repeatable patterns over time or that certain indicators should be related to future market (or individual stock) price movements. Most people who look at a chart of a particular stock will immediately see what they believe to be patterns in the price changes and clear evidence of trends that should have been obvious to anyone studying it. How should we view this situation?

On the one hand, academicians (and numerous practitioners) are highly skeptical of technical analysis, to say the least. Most academic discussions at the college level dismiss, or seriously disparage, this concept. A primary reason is that thorough tests of technical analysis techniques have failed to confirm their value, given all costs and considering an alternative, such as a buy-and-hold strategy.

In addition to these reasons, other troubling features of technical analysis remain. First of all, several interpretations of each technical tool and chart pattern are not only possible, but usual. One or more of the interpreters will be correct (more or less), but it is virtually impossible to know ex ante (beforehand) who these will be. Ex post (after the fact), we will know which indicator or chart, or whose interpretation, was correct, but only those investors who used that particular information will benefit. Tools such as the Dow theory are well known for their multiple interpretations by various observers who disagree over how the theory is to be interpreted.

Furthermore, consider a technical trading rule (or chart pattern) that is, in fact, successful. When it gives its signal on the basis of reaching some specified value (or forms a clear picture on a chart), it correctly predicts movements in the market or some particular stock. Such a rule or pattern, if observed by several market participants, will be self-destructive as more and more investors use it. Price will reach its equilibrium value quickly, taking away profit opportunities from all but the quickest. Some observers will start trying to act before the rest on the basis of what they expect to happen (e.g., they may act before a complete head and shoulders forms). Price will then reach an equilibrium even quicker, so that only those who act earliest will benefit. Eventually, the value of any such rule will be negated entirely.

INVESTMENTS INTUITION

No inherent reason exists for stock price movements to repeat themselves. For example, flipping a fair coin 100 times should, on average, result in about 50 heads and 50 tails. There is some probability that the first 10 tosses could produce 10 heads. However, the chance of such a pattern repeating itself is very small.

As we shall see in the next chapter, strong evidence suggests that stock price *changes* over time follow a "random walk"—in effect, any patterns formed are accidental, but not surprising. See Box 13-3 for a good discussion of random occurrences.

On the other hand, it is impossible to test all the techniques of technical analysis and their variations and interpretations. In fact, technical analysis has not been tested thoroughly. The techniques of technical analysis are simply too numerous, and technical analysis is broader than the use of only price information. Therefore, absolutely definitive statements cannot be made about this subject. A good example of the omissions in this area is the use of volume in technical strategies. Although volume is a recognized part of technical analysis, few tests have been conducted on its use in conjunction with the rest of technical analysis.[22]

Second, in fairness, many technical analysts recognize that technical analysis is not the key to riches and that it will not solve the investing problem of what stocks to buy, and when. These analysts view technical analysis as a supplement or complement to a broader analysis. They do not ignore fundamental analysis, but perhaps use technical analysis to screen for companies that will then be analyzed by fundamental analysis.

What can we conclude about technical analysis? On the basis of all available evidence, it is difficult to justify technical analysis. The studies that have been done in support of this concept have produced, at best, weak support. Studies done in support of the efficient market hypothesis, on the other hand, are much stronger and are nearly unanimous in their conclusions that technical analysis does not work. It is time, therefore, to turn to a consideration of the efficient market hypothesis.

---

[22]For additional discussion of these points, see O. Maurice Joy and Charles P. Jones, "Should We Believe the Tests of Market Efficiency?" *Journal of Portfolio Management*, Summer 1986, pp. 49–54.

BOX 13-3

GAMBLER'S PARADOX

Many economists and those who use fundamental economic data in their work argue that commodity and stock prices are randomly generated, and, therefore, no matter what historically based method one might employ, it is impossible to predict tomorrow's or next month's prices. Technicians who employ such things as moving averages, chart and price patterns, computer programs and the like, of course, don't agree with such a position.

One reason that it is difficult to find common ground between the two schools of thought is that there is no general agreement about how commodity and stock prices are produced. If the underlying process is random and/or independent, it is probably impossible to predict future price movements. But if prices are either nonrandom and/or dependent, then there is some pattern to prices, and, with the appropriate tools, one should be able to detect that pattern.

The mathematical definitions of randomness and independence are not obvious, but the concepts can be made clear by an example. Suppose you have a small jar filled with 50 white and 50 black balls. Take out 1 ball at a time, note its color and replace it in the jar, then withdraw another ball. If you do this repeatedly, you will generate a random and independent sequence of colors. It is random because each and every ball had an equal chance of being selected. It is independent because the choice of the first ball had no effect on the selection of the second and succeeding balls.

If the process is truly independent and you have a "run" of six white balls, will that affect the probability of getting a white ball on the seventh selection? Of course not. But so many people believe the opposite that the phenomenon has been given a name—"the gambler's paradox" or "maturity of chance." Unfortunately, for gamblers and everyone else, if the process is truly independent—that is, if you have not inadvertently biased it in some way—then the probability of drawing a white ball is still 0.5. The previous six selections have no effect on the outcome of the seventh.

If you like challenges, try to convince someone who is holding a pair of so-called hot dice and has just rolled six consecutive sevens at a crap table that the seventh roll is completely independent of the previous six. According to John Scarne, a well-known writer on gambling, the longest color win recorded at roulette in an American casino occurred in Saratoga, N.Y. in 1943, when the color red came up 32 times. The odds against this happening are in the billions. Some might call this a miracle, but it is well to keep in mind that the odds are exactly the same against a series of alternate occurrences of red and black, odd, even or any other arbitrary series of 32 events.

The only thing that makes this run remarkable is that one color turned up in the string. Scarne reports in his book *Complete Guide to Gambling* that he witnessed a woman make 39 consecutive passes at the crap table. The odds against such an event make the roulette example seem like an everyday occurrence. Such events would normally break any gambling house, but table limits prevent the winnings from becoming astronomical. (I would still want to check the dice in the latter example.)

But back to commodity price behavior. If you believe that you can predict the behavior of commodity prices, then it is necessary to assume, at least implicitly, that prices are nonrandom, dependent or both. Otherwise, you are involved in a gambler's paradox, and, in the long run, whatever system you use will not work.

Source: Adapted from Stanley W. Angrist's column, *Forbes* magazine, December 2, 1985. Excerpted by permission of *Forbes* magazine, December 2, 1985. © Forbes, Inc., 1985.

Summary

- Technical analysis, the other approach to selecting securities, is the oldest approach available to investors and in many respects the most controversial.
- Technical analysis relies on published market data, primarily price and volume data, to predict the short-term direction of individual stocks or the market as a whole. The emphasis is on internal factors that help to detect demand–supply conditions in the market.
- The rationale for technical analysis is that the net demand (or lack thereof) for stocks can be detected by various technical indicators and that trends in stock prices occur and continue for considerable periods of time. Stock prices require time to adjust to the change in supply and demand.
- Price and volume are primary tools of the technical analyst, as are various technical indicators. Technical analysis can be applied to both the aggregate market and individual stocks.
- Aggregate market analysis originated with the Dow theory, the best-known technical theory. It is designed to detect the start of major movements.
- Other technical indicators of the aggregate market include, but are not limited to, the following:
  1. Moving averages, used to detect both the direction and the rate of change in prices.
  2. The advance–decline line (breadth of market), used to assess the condition of the overall market.
  3. The Confidence Index, which attempts to measure investor optimism and pessimism.
  4. Mutual fund liquidity, which uses the potential buying power (liquidity) of mutual funds as a bullish or bearish indicator.
  5. Short interest ratio, which assesses potential demand from investors who have sold short.
  6. Contrary opinion, which is designed to go against the crowd. Included here are the odd-lot theory, the odd-lot short sales theory, the put-call ratio, and the opinions of investment advisory services.
- When applied to individual stocks, technical analysis can involve some of the same indicators just described. It also involves the use of charts of price patterns to detect trends that are believed to persist over time.
- The most often used charts are bar charts, which show each day's price

movement as well as volume, and point-and-figure charts, which show only significant price changes as they occur.

- Numerous chart "patterns" are recognizable to a technician. However, all patterns are subject to multiple interpretations because different technicians will read the same chart differently.
- Some scientific evidence suggests that patterns based on "five-point chart patterns" have no validity.
- A second well-known technique used for individual stocks is determination of relative strength, which shows the strength of a particular stock in relation to its average price, its industry, or the market.

Key Words

Bar chart	**Filter rule**	**Resistance level**
Bear market	**Market data**	**Short interest ratio**
Bull market	**Odd-lot theory**	**Support level**
Charting	**Point-and-figure chart**	**Technical analysis**
Contrary opinion	**Put/call ratio**	
Dow theory	**Relative strength**	

Questions

13-1 Describe the rationale for technical analysis.

13-2 Differentiate between fundamental analysis and technical analysis.

13-3 What do technicians assume about the adjustment of stock prices from one equilibrium position to another?

13-4 What role does volume play in technical analysis?

13-5 What is the purpose of the Dow theory? What is the significance of the "confirmation" signal in this theory?

13-6 How does the Dow theory forecast how long a market movement will last?

13-7 Using a moving average, how is a sell signal generated?

13-8 Why is the advance–decline line referred to as an indicator of the breadth of the market?

13-9 Why would an increase in the Confidence Index be a buy signal?

13-10 What is the rationale for the theory of contrary opinion?

13-11 How is the odd-lot index calculated? How is it used as a buy or sell signal?

13-12 Why is a rising short interest ratio considered to be a bullish indicator?

13-13 Distinguish between a bar chart and a point-and-figure chart.

13-14 What is relative strength analysis?

13-15 On a rational economic basis, why is the study of chart patterns likely to be an unrewarding activity?

13-16 Is it possible to prove or disprove categorically the validity of technical analysis?

13-17 Assume that you know a technical analyst who claims success on the basis of his or her chart patterns. How might you go about scientifically testing this claim?

13-18 How do the new contrarians differ from the more traditional contrarians?

13-19 Why do stock price movements repeat themselves?

13-20 Look at the bar chart of the Dow Jones averages on the next-to-last page of *The Wall Street Journal*. Does this chart cover a sufficient time period to apply the Dow theory?

13-21 With reference to question 20, why would this chart, or possibly several of these charts covering a number of months, be useful in trying to apply the Dow theory?

13-22 What new financial instruments have caused the short interest ratio to be less reliable? Why?

13-23 Describe a bullish sign when using a moving average. A bearish sign. Do the same for the advance–decline line.

13-24 Consider the plot of stock X in the following diagram. The plot shows weekly prices for one year, based on a beginning price of $30.

(a) Using Figure 13-5, do you see any five-point chart patterns in this figure?

(b) Do you see any other patterns in this chart that might help you to predict the future price of this stock?

(c) What is your forecast of this stock's price over the next three months?

(d) If this price series were to be generated using random numbers, do you think it could resemble this plot?

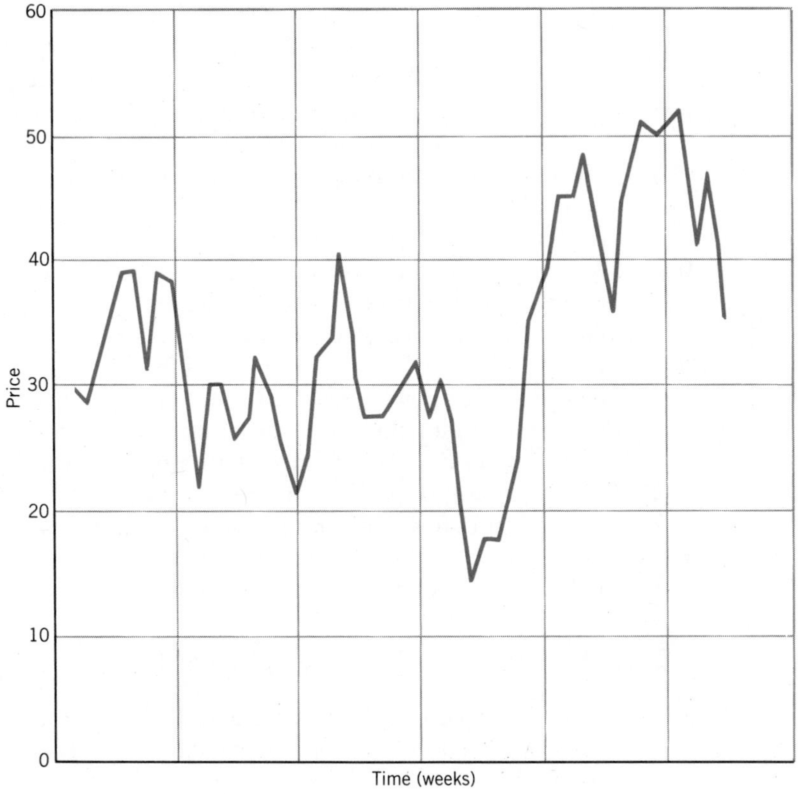

Selected References

Support for the Dow theory can be found in

Glickstein, D., and Wublels, R. "Dow Theory Is Alive and Well!" *The Journal of Portfolio Management*, Spring 1983, pp. 28–32.

A rigorous examination of stock price dependence can be found in

Greene, M., and Fielitz, B. "Long-Term Dependence in Common Stock Returns." *Journal of Financial Economics*, May 1977, pp. 339–349.

A different view of tests of technical analysis can be found in

Joy, O. M., and Jones, Charles P. "Should We Believe the Tests of Market Efficiency?" *Journal of Portfolio Management*, Summer 1986, pp. 49–54.

One of the classic commentaries on this and other subjects is

Malkiel, Burton G. *A Random Walk Down Wall Street*, 5th college ed. New York: W. W. Norton, 1990.

The forecasting of stock prices is discussed in

Umstead, David. "Forecasting Stock Market Prices." *Journal of Finance*, May 1977, pp. 427–441.

CHAPTER 14

Efficient Markets

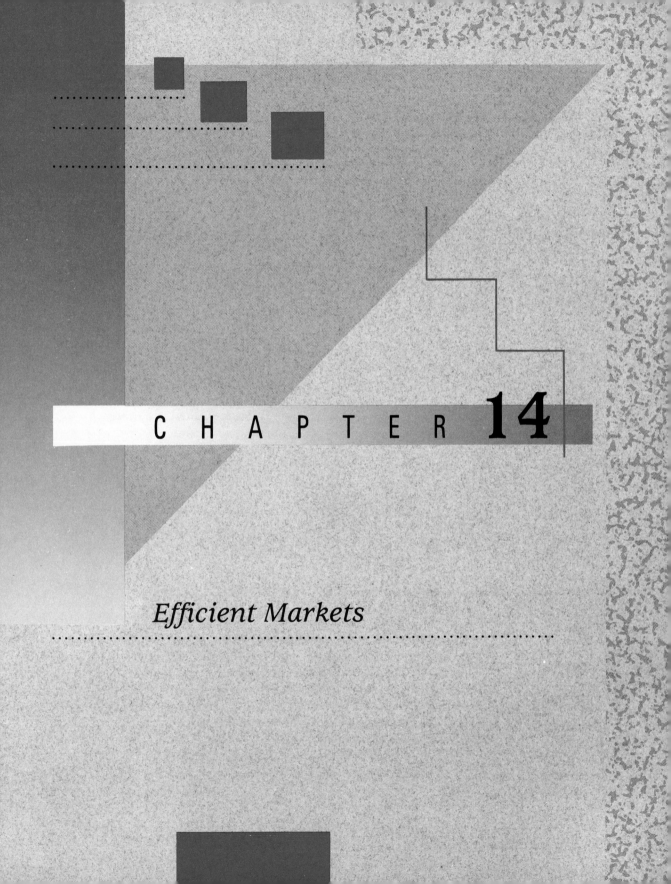

We now have considered fundamental and technical approaches for selecting stocks. Investors using either (or both) of these approaches must take into account the possibility that securities markets, in particular the market for common stocks, are efficient. As explained later, *efficient* refers to quick and accurate reflection of information in prices.

In an efficient market many traditional investing activities, such as technical analysis and even "typical" fundamental analysis, are suspect at best and useless at worst. Needless to say, such a proposition has generated tremendous controversy, which continues today. The idea of an efficient market remains controversial, and a number of participants refuse to accept it. This is not surprising in view of the enormous implications that an efficient market has for everyone concerned with securities. Some market participants' jobs and reputations are at stake, and they are not going to accept this concept readily.

Because of its significant impact and implications, the idea that markets are efficient deserves careful thought and study. Beginners should approach it with an open mind. The fact that some well-known market observers and participants reject this idea does not reduce its validity. Nor is it going to disappear, because too much evidence exists to support it. The intelligent approach for investors, therefore, is to learn about it and from it.

First, we consider what an efficient market is and what it means. Although the concept of market efficiency applies to all financial markets, we concentrate on the equities market. The evidence that has accumulated in support of the concept will be sampled, as well as some evidence of possible market anomalies (i.e., inefficiencies). Finally, the implications of efficient markets to investors will be considered.

The Concept of an Efficient Market

What Is an Efficient Market?

As we know from our study of valuation models in previous chapters, stock prices are determined by investors on the basis of the expected cash flows to be received from a stock and the risk involved. Investors use all the information they have available or can reasonably obtain. This information set consists of both known information and beliefs about the future (i.e., information that can reasonably be inferred). Regardless of its form, information is the key to the determination of stock prices and therefore is the central issue of the efficient markets concept.

An **efficient market (EM)** is defined as one in which the prices of securities fully reflect all known information quickly and accurately. Let us consider the meaning of this definition.

> *Fully reflect.* The EM concept postulates that investors will assimilate all information into prices in making their buy and sell decisions. Therefore, the current price of a stock incorporates all information.
>
> *All known information.* The EM concept assumes that all known information is reflected in the price, including not only past information (e.g., last year's or last quarter's earnings), but also current information as well as events that have been announced but have not yet transpired (such as a forthcoming stock split). Furthermore, information that can reasonably be inferred is also assumed to be reflected in price. For example, if many investors believe that interest rates will soon decline, prices will reflect this belief before the actual decline occurs.
>
> *Quickly and accurately.* This part of the definition often causes beginners some problems. The EM concept does not require that the adjustment be literally instantaneous, only that it occur very quickly as information becomes known. Given the extremely rapid dissemination of information in the United States through electronic communications equipment, which virtually all brokerage houses and institutional investors have, information is spread very quickly, almost instantaneously, to market participants with access to these sources. For individual investors without this access, important information can be received, at the latest, the following day in such sources as *The Wall Street Journal.*

As for "accurately," again the EM concept does not claim, or require, a perfect adjustment. Rather, the EMH says that the adjustment in prices resulting from information is "unbiased." This means that the expected value of the adjustment error is zero—sometimes too large and at other times too small, but on average balancing out and correct. The new price does not have to be the new equilibrium price, but only an unbiased estimate of the final equilibrium price that will be established after investors have fully assessed the input of the information.

Figure 14-1 illustrates the concept of market efficiency for one company for which a significant event occurs that has an effect on its expected profitability. It is assumed here that the stock's excess return—that part not explained by overall market movements—is zero on a typical day. Date 0 in Figure 14-1 is the announcement date for the event. Before the announcement date, the stock's excess returns are zero. On the day of announcement the excess return is positive, and the adjustment is complete by day 1. At day 2, and thereafter, the previous pattern resumes.

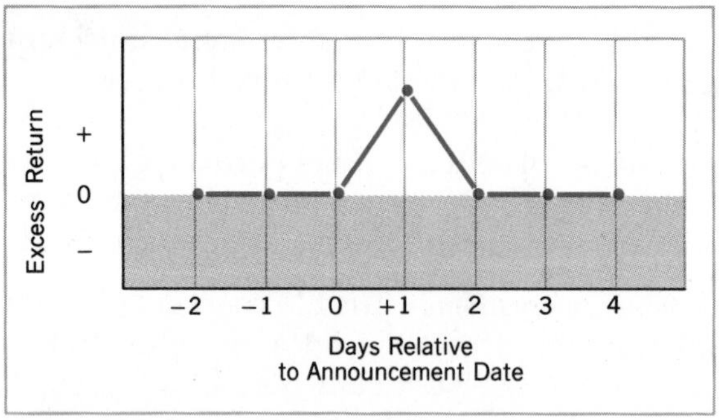

FIGURE 14-1 ***The adjustment of security prices in an efficient market.***

Why the Market Can Be Expected to Be Efficient

If all this seems too much to expect, consider the situation from the following standpoint. It can be shown that an efficient market can exist if the following events occur:

1. A large number of rational, profit-maximizing investors exist who actively participate in the market by analyzing, valuing, and trading stocks. These investors are price takers; that is, one participant alone cannot affect the price of a security.
2. Information is costless and widely available to market participants at approximately the same time.
3. Information is generated in a random fashion such that announcements are basically independent of one another.
4. Investors react quickly and accurately to the new information, causing stock prices to adjust accordingly.

These conditions may seem strict, and in some sense they are. Nevertheless, consider how closely they parallel the actual investments environment. There is no question that a large number of investors are constantly "playing the game." Both individuals and institutions follow the market closely on a daily basis, standing ready to buy or sell when they think it is appropriate. The total amount of money at their disposal at any one time is significant.

Although the production of information is not costless, for institutions in the investments business, generating various types of information is a necessary cost of business, and many participants receive it "free."[1] It is widely available to many participants at approximately the same time, as information is announced on radio, television, and teletype around the country.

---

[1]Obviously, investors pay for such items in their brokerage costs and other fees.

Information is, for the most part, generated in a random fashion in the sense that most investors cannot predict when companies will announce significant new developments, when wars will break out, when strikes will occur, when currencies will be devalued, when important leaders will suddenly suffer a heart attack, and so forth. Although there is some dependence in information events over time, by and large announcements are independent and occur more or less randomly.

INVESTMENTS INTUITION

Ask yourself why investors would not react quickly to information as it is announced. Many monitor the market daily, have funds with which to act, and are seeking to make money. They are going to act, and act quickly. You have only to observe some stocks with the largest changes in prices on the NYSE on a given day and then check the news stories for that day to see that this is true.

If, as we have shown, the preceding conditions for an EM are generally met in practice, the result is a market in which investors adjust security prices rapidly and accurately to reflect random information coming into the market. Prices reflect fully all available information. Furthermore, price changes are independent of one another and move in a random fashion. The price change occurring today is independent of the one yesterday, because it is based on investors' reactions to new, independent information coming into the market today.

The implications of an efficient market for security analysts, money managers, and investors are enormous. See Box 14-1 for a discussion of some of these implications as well as a professional investment consultant's views on why the market is efficient and where most of those concerned with managing money have gone wrong.

Forms of Market Efficiency

If, as discussed, the conditions for market efficiency are actually met, exactly how efficient is the market and what does this imply for investors? We first consider the question of efficiency, including the major evidence in support of this concept. We then consider the implications to investors of an efficient market.

We have defined an efficient market as one in which all information is reflected in stock prices quickly and, on balance, accurately. Thus, the key to assessing market efficiency is information, in all of its various forms. When we speak of information, we mean not only the type of information, but its quality and the speed with which it is disseminated among investors.

Standard practice since 1970 is to discuss the EM concept in the form of

BOX 14-1

THE MARKET IS BEATING THE INVESTMENT MANAGERS

In the 23 years he has spent scouting the higher reaches of Wall Street, business strategy consultant Charles Ellis figures he has logged "maybe 5000 days" assessing the capabilities of many of the nation's top money managers. What has he concluded about the profession from all these labors?

That by and large money managers are "tough, clever, tenacious," but he is underwhelmed by their performance. Ellis reckons that nearly two out of every three professionally managed funds, measured cumulatively over the last 15 years, have failed to do as well in equities as Standard & Poor's 500 stock average. "The fact is," says Ellis, "the investment managers are not beating the market. The market is beating them."

How to explain that mediocrity on the part of people who are "tough, clever, tenacious"? Ellis, who brings a nice blend of the theoretical and workaday experience to the topic, thinks the great mass of money managers have failed to recognize a dramatic change in the market.

Ellis is not in the business of managing money, but of advising a long list of blue-chip institutional clients on business strategy. Managing partner of the Connecticut-based Greenwich Associates, Ellis, now 48, first came to The Street in the early Sixties. In those days, he says, beating the game was no great shakes. Institutional investors accounted for only 30% of the market. Now, however, borne on a flood of rising cash flow, institutional investors account for what Ellis says is 80% of the market. The institutions have virtually become the stock market.

So? The market has been institutional for a long time. What's new? What's new, Ellis says, is that the thousands of analysts and money managers prowling the market sweep up most of the bargains before they become real bargains. The market, in short, has become highly efficient.

Since money managers spend a lot of time taking in one another's analytical wash, only a truly perceptive minority can consistently get the edge of superior knowledge over the rest of the mob. Look at *Forbes'* mutual fund ratings. Only a handful of managers—Lindner Fund, Sequoia Fund and Mutual Shares—keep popping up in the winner's circle.

Further, given the drag of management fees and other costs, it takes about 1.6% of assets for the average institutional investor to keep the joint running. Since investors demand an equity premium—a premium over the risk-free rate of return for choosing to invest in stocks—a money manager has to wring an extra 25% above the historical 6% equity premium to enable his client to keep up with the market. Ellis thinks that the majority of money men find grinding out even that bare minimum "surprisingly difficult."

That comes as no great epiphany to devotees of the efficient market theory, who argue that the anthill army of analysts at work have made the market so efficient that it is unbeatable over the long haul. You can beat the market only by joining it; in effect, by replicating it with a portfolio of "index" stocks.

Ellis brings something different to the party. He thinks there are rewards to be had in taking carefully measured above-market risks, and his consulting work has given him an unusual insight into where the money men have gone wrong.

Ellis thinks many money men would do better if clients understood long-term investing. Corporate pension funds, for example, are often administered by in-house bureaucrats whose long-range career paths lead to other jobs. The fund is just one more rung up the ladder. The result, says Ellis in his book (*Investment Policy, How to Win the Loser's Game,* Dow Jones-Irwin), is that the people who hire and fire the money managers prefer noncontroversial investment policies to the less stereotyped kind of investing that alone yields superior results. In Ellis' words, they seek "the most acceptable near-term balance between desires for superior returns and avoidance of unusual or unorthodox positions. . . . They above all . . . avoid distressing risk to their own careers."

And what's happening on the money managers' side of the portfolio? "The very same thing," says Ellis. "They are understandably cautious, compromising with a defensive tilt, seeking 'not to lose' over a three-to-five-year time horizon." Says Ellis of the corporate types who choose investment managers: "Most of these people are good corporate managers, but they act as any ordinary person with a minimum of investment experience would."

In short, they are we—fated to buy high and sell low because of a constitutional inability to make a long-range plan and stick to it. The psychological and tactical hazards of the game are such, Elis argues, that the number of investors able to outdo the market over long periods is very small indeed.

Yes, there are people who can beat the market fairly consistently. Ellis bows in the direction of such standouts as T. Rowe Price; Warren Buffett, chairman of Berkshire Hathaway; and the Vanguard Group's John Neff. Ellis even has some of his own cash running with Buffett and Neff, whom he puts in the star-quality Pantheon of "maybe 20" individuals. Twenty, mind you, out of thousands.

Ellis advocates what he calls a "coffee-can portfolio," a term he borrowed from Bob Kirby of the Capital Group in Los Angeles to describe a cross section of the U.S.' best-managed companies held for the long pull. You can increase the reward potential by adding as much risk in the shape of more volatile stocks as you feel comfortable with. He also puts in a good word for a mix of well-managed mutual funds for individuals.

"It's not exciting," chuckles Ellis. "It takes the fun out of watching the averages and quarterly reports, talking to friends and worrying about the market." Maybe you prefer the fun of doing your own trading. That's okay, Ellis says, "but it's a loser's game. Don't try to win, try not to lose."

Source: Richard Phalon, "Winning a Loser's Game," *Forbes,* March 10, 1986, pp. 136–137 and 139. Excerpted by permission of *Forbes* magazine, March 10, 1986. © Forbes, Inc., 1986.

the **efficient market hypothesis (EMH),** which is simply the formal statement of market efficiency previously discussed.[2] The EMH is concerned with the extent to which security prices fully reflect all available information and, for expositional purposes, is divided into the following *cumulative* levels.

[2]See E. Fama, "Efficient Capital Markets: A Review of Theory and Empirical Work," *Journal of Finance,* Vol. 25, No. 2 (May 1970), pp. 383–417.

1. Weak Form One of the most traditional types of information used in assessing security values is the market data discussed in Chapter 13. If security prices are determined in an efficient market, historical price data should already be reflected in current prices and should be of no value in predicting future price changes. Since price data are the basis of technical analysis, technical analysis that relies on the past history of price information is of little or no value.

Tests of the usefulness of price data are called **weak-form** tests of the EMH. If the weak form of the EMH is true, past price changes should be unrelated to future price changes. Another way to say this is that stock changes over time should be independent, or nearly so.

The correct implication of a weak-form efficient market is that the past history of price information is of no value in assessing future changes in price. It is not correct to state, as is sometimes done, that the best estimate of price $t + 1$ is the current (time t) price, because this implies an expected return of zero. The efficient market in no way implies that the expected return on any security is zero.

2. Semistrong Form A more comprehensive level of market efficiency involves not only known and publicly available price data, but all publicly known and available data, such as earnings, dividends, stock split announcements, new product developments, financing difficulties, and accounting changes. A market that quickly incorporates all such information into prices is said to show **semistrong-form** efficiency. Note that a semistrong efficient market encompasses the weak form of the hypothesis because market data are part of the larger set of all publicly available information.

Tests of the semistrong EMH are tests of the *lag* in the adjustment of stock prices to announcements of information. A semistrong efficient market implies that investors cannot act on new public information after its announcement and expect to earn above-average risk-adjusted returns. If lags exist in the adjustment of stock prices to certain announcements, the market is not fully efficient in the semistrong sense.

3. Strong Form The most stringent form of market efficiency is the **strong form,** which asserts that stock prices fully reflect *all* information, public and nonpublic. If the market is strong-form efficient, no group of investors should be able to earn, over a reasonable period of time, excess rates of return by using publicly available information in a superior manner. Professionally managed portfolios are most often tested in this regard.

An extreme version of the strong form holds that all nonpublic information, including information that may be restricted to certain groups such as corporate insiders and specialists on the exchanges, is immediately re-

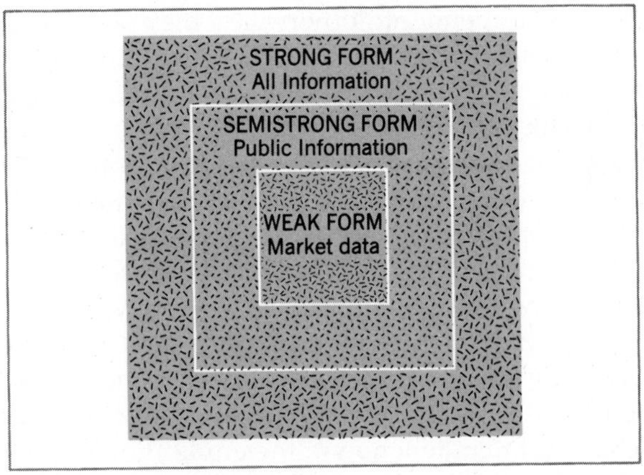

FIGURE 14-2 ***Cumulative levels of market efficiency and the information associated with each level.***

flected in prices. In effect, this version refers to monopolistic access to information by certain market participants.

Strong-form efficiency encompasses the weak and semistrong forms and represents the highest level of market efficiency. Figure 14-2 depicts graphically these three levels of market efficiency.

Evidence on Market Efficiency

Because of the significance of the efficient markets hypothesis to all investors, and because of the controversy that surrounds the EMH, we shall examine the empirical evidence on market efficiency. Many studies have been done over the years, and continue to be done. Obviously, we cannot begin to discuss them all, nor is it necessarily desirable to discuss several in detail. Our purpose here is to present an idea of how these tests are done, the scope of what has been done, and the results. The empirical evidence will be separated into tests of the three forms of market efficiency previously discussed.

It is important to note that the key to testing the validity of any of the three forms of market efficiency is the *consistency* with which investors can earn returns in excess of those commensurate with the risk involved. Short-lived inefficiencies appearing on a random basis do not constitute evidence of market inefficiencies, at least in an economic (as opposed to a statistical) sense.

Weak-Form Evidence

As noted, weak-form efficiency means that price data are incorporated into current stock prices. If prices follow nonrandom trends, stock price changes are dependent; otherwise, they are independent. Therefore, weak-form tests involve the question of whether all information contained in the sequence of past prices is fully reflected in the current price.

The weak-form EMH is related to, but not identical with, an idea from the 1960s called the *random walk hypothesis.* If prices follow a random walk, *price changes* over time are random (independent).[3] The price change for today is unrelated to the price change yesterday, or the day before, or any other day. This is a result of the scenario described at the outset of the chapter. If new information arrives randomly in the market and investors react immediately to it, changes in prices will also be random.

One way to test for weak-form efficiency is to test statistically the independence of stock price changes. If the statistical tests suggest that price changes are independent, the implication is that knowing, and using, the past sequence of price information is of no value to an investor. In other words, trends in price changes do not exist.

INVESTMENTS INTUITION

It should be apparent upon reflection that we are talking about price changes and not about the level of price itself. Obviously, a $60 stock has a price on any given day that will be related closely to its price tomorrow, since it is unlikely in one day to go much above $62 or much below $58. Also, we are not concerned with whether the change in today's price, say $+\frac{1}{2}$, is related to the change in tomorrow's price, say $-\frac{1}{4}$. Dollar price changes such as these are also related. The issue centers on percentage price changes over time—are they related or not?

A second way to test for weak-form efficiency, after testing the purely statistical nature of price changes, is to test specific trading rules that attempt to use past price data. If such tests legitimately produce risk-adjusted returns beyond that available from simply buying a portfolio of stocks and holding it until a common liquidation date, after deducting all costs, it would suggest that the market is not weak-form efficient.

Statistical Tests of Price Changes Stock price changes in an efficient market should be independent. Two simple statistical tests of independence are the serial correlation test and the signs test. The first, *the serial correlation test,* involves measuring the correlation between price changes for various lags, such as one day, two days, and so on. The second, *the signs test,* involves classifying each price change by its sign, which means whether it

[3]Technically, the random walk hypothesis is more restrictive than the weak-form EMH. Stock prices can conform to weak-form efficiency without meeting the conditions of a random walk.

was +, 0, or − (regardless of amount). Then the "runs" in the series of signs can be counted and compared to known information about a random series. If there are persistent price changes, the length of the runs will indicate this.

A test of randomness in stock prices can be traced back to the turn of this century, but modern tests began in the 1950s. A well-known test was conducted by Eugene Fama, who studied the daily returns on the 30 Dow Jones Industrial stocks.[4] Using serial correlation analysis to test for statistically significant correlation coefficients, Fama tested lags ranging from one to 10 days. Of the 30 stocks and 10 possible lags, a few correlation coefficients were found to differ statistically from zero, but the level was small. Only a very small percentage of any successive price change could be explained by a prior change. Serial correlation tests by other researchers invariably reached the same conclusion.

The signs test also supports independence. Although some "runs" do occur, they fall within the limits of randomness, since a truly random series exhibits some runs (several + or − observations in succession). Fama found, using the same data, a very small tendency for one-day runs to persist. Longer runs of four, nine, and 16 days did not persist. Overall, the results are what would be expected from a random series.

Technical Trading Rules The statistical tests described here demonstrate that trends, other than those consistent with a random series, do not exist in stock prices. However, those who believe that such trends not only exist but can be used successfully argue that the statistical tests do not detect more sophisticated or realistic strategies. In general, we are talking about technicians who, as noted in the previous chapter, believe that stock prices exhibit trends that can be detected through technical analysis. Therefore, although statistical tests are important and support the idea that such technical trading will prove useless, it remains necessary to investigate such rules, using actual trading strategies.

An almost unlimited number of possible technical trading rules could be tested. Obviously, all of them cannot be examined, but if a sufficient number are examined and found to be ineffective, the burden of proof shifts to those who argue that such techniques have value. And this is exactly the situation that prevails. There is very little evidence that a technical trading rule based solely on past price and volume data can, after all proper adjustments have been made, outperform a simple buy-and-hold strategy.

This is perhaps a good place in the discussion to note the difference between *statistical dependence* and *economic dependence* in stock price changes.

---

[4]E. Fama, "The Behavior of Stock Market Prices," *Journal of Finance*, Vol. 38, No. 1 (January 1965), pp. 34–105.

The statistical tests discussed earlier detected some small amount of dependence in price changes.[5] All of the series could not be said to be completely statistically independent. However, they were economically independent in that one could not exploit the small statistical dependence that existed. After brokerage costs, excess returns disappear, and, after all, this is the bottom line for investors—can excess returns be earned with a technical trading rule after all costs are deducted?

Weak-Form Contraevidence DeBondt and Thaler have tested an "overreaction hypothesis," which states that people "overreact" to unexpected and dramatic news events.[6] Applied to stock prices, the hypothesis is that, as a result of overreactions, "loser" portfolios outperform the market after their formation.

DeBondt and Thaler found that over a half-century period, loser portfolios of 35 stocks outperformed the market by an average of almost 20% for a 36-month period after portfolio formation. Winner portfolios earned about 5% less than the market. Interestingly, the overreaction seems to occur mostly during the second and third year of the test period.

This tendency for stocks that experience extreme returns to go through subsequent price reversals after portfolios are formed, and for the effect to be observed years after portfolio formation, has clear implications for market efficiency. Specifically, it indicates substantial weak-form inefficiencies, because DeBondt and Thaler are testing whether the overreaction hypothesis is *predictive*. In other words, according to their research, knowing past price changes appear to help significantly in predicting future price changes.

Semistrong-Form Evidence

Weak-form tests, of both the statistical and the trading rule types, are numerous and almost unanimous in their findings (after necessary corrections and adjustments have been made). Semistrong tests, on the other hand, are less numerous and somewhat more diverse in their findings, although they clearly support the proposition that the market adjusts to new public information rapidly.

Semistrong-form tests are tests of the speed of price adjustments to public information. The question is whether investors can use publicly available information to earn excess returns, after proper adjustments. As a benchmark, we can use a buy-and-hold strategy with equivalent risk, or perhaps the market as a whole.

We shall consider a sampling of often-cited studies of semistrong effi-

[5]Stock returns tend to exhibit a slight positive correlation.

[6]Werner F. M. DeBondt and Richard Thaler, "Does the Stock Market Overreact?" *The Journal of Finance*, July 1985, pp. 793–805.

ciency without developing them in detail. What is important is to obtain a feel for the wide variety of information tested and the logic behind these tests. The methodology and a detailed discussion of the results are not essential for our purposes. We shall consider five issues as examples of semistrong efficiency tests, recognizing that other examples exist and could have been chosen.

Following the discussion of strong-form efficiency evidence, we consider some contraevidence to semistrong efficiency. This evidence suggests that lags do occur in the adjustment of stock prices to certain information. Although these examples are also not an exhaustive list, fewer documented examples of lags in the adjustment of stock prices to information have been presented.

1. *Stock splits.* An often cited study of the long-run effects of stock splits on returns was done by Fama, Fisher, Jensen, and Roll (FFJR).[7] This paper was the first **event study,** which means that a company's stock returns are examined to determine the impact of a particular event on the stock price. The methodology involves using a cumulative abnormal returns (CAR) methodology based on an **index model** of stock returns. An index model states that security returns are determined by a market factor (index) and a unique company factor. A beta coefficient captures the sensitivity of the firm's return to the market's return.

Company-unique returns are the residual error terms representing the difference between the security's actual return and that given by the index model. In other words, after adjusting for what the company's return should have been, given the index model, any remaining portion of the actual return is an **abnormal return** representing the impact of a particular event. The **cumulative abnormal return** is the sum of the individual abnormal returns over the period of time under examination.

In and of itself, as we know from Chapter 8, a stock split adds nothing of value to a company and, therefore, should have no effect on the company's total market value. Clearly, a security's return should be unaffected after a stock split if the market is efficient because this information should have been reflected in the stock's price at or before the announcement of the split.

FFJR found that although the stocks they studied exhibited sharp increases in price prior to the split, abnormal (i.e., risk-adjusted) returns after the split were very stable. Thus, the split itself did not affect prices. The results indicate that any price adjustments occurred prior to a split, not afterward, which supports the semistrong form of market efficiency. Furthermore, investors could not gain by purchasing stocks after the announcement of the split; they would have to purchase before the split itself. In

[7]E. Fama, L. Fisher, M. Jensen, and R. Roll, "The Adjustment of Stock Prices to New Information," *International Economics Review,* Vol. 10, No. 1 (February 1969), pp. 2–21.

other words, for a typical individual stock, by the time a stock split is announced the market has discounted any favorable effects implied, so that investors cannot gain by acquiring stocks after the announcement.

2. *Money supply changes.* As noted in Chapter 10, a relationship exists between money supply and economic activity, and between money supply and stock prices. Several studies, in assessing the relationship between money supply growth and stock prices, find that changes in anticipated money supply growth rates are reflected in stock prices before the changes occur.[8] If the changes are unexpected, they are reflected in price almost immediately on the disclosure of the information necessary to assess the situation. Therefore, the market appears to be semistrong efficient with respect to changes in the money supply.

3. *Accounting changes.* Several studies have examined the effects on stock prices of announcements of accounting changes. The accounting changes include depreciation, the investment tax credit, inventory reporting (LIFO versus FIFO), and other items.

The issue of accounting announcements requires some explanation. Essentially, two different types of changes are involved:

1. The change may affect only the manner in which earnings are reported to stockholders, and therefore should not affect stock prices. The reason for this is that such changes do not affect the firm's cash flows, and thus its real economic value.
2. The change may affect the economic value of the firm by affecting its cash flows. This is a true change and should therefore generate a change in market prices. In an efficient market, stock prices should adjust quickly to the announcement of this type of change.

In general, the studies indicate that the market is able to distinguish the superficial changes described in type 1 from the real changes described in type 2. For example, switching depreciation methods from accelerated to straight-line for *shareholder reporting purposes* will affect shareholder earnings but not cash flows, and the evidence indicates no long-lasting effect on stock prices.[9] This is the result that would be expected in an efficient market. On the other hand, a change from FIFO to LIFO decreases taxes for the firm making the switch, thereby affecting the real value of the firm positively by increasing the cash flows. In an efficient market, price changes associated with such a change should be positive. What is interesting is that studies have found an increase in stock prices for some period preceding the switch from FIFO to LIFO.[10]

---

[8]See Chapter 10.

[9]R. Kaplan and R. Roll, "Investor Evaluation of Accounting Information: Some Empirical Evidence," *The Journal of Business,* Vol. 45, No. 2 (April 1972), pp. 225–257.

[10]R. Abdel-Khalik and J. McKeown, "Understanding Accounting Changes in an Efficient Market: Evidence of Differential Reaction," *Accounting Review* (October 1978), pp. 851–868.

4. *Dividend announcements.* Does the market anticipate changes in dividends? To answer this question, it is necessary to build a model of dividend policy in order to be able to make predictions of dividends. This allows a surprising dividend change to be separated from what is anticipated by the market. By concentrating only on unanticipated dividend changes, some assessment of market efficiency can be made. Two early studies of this question both found that, in general, the market seems to adjust to the new information quickly. In fact, much of the adjustment is in anticipation of the announcement itself.[11]

5. *Reactions to other announcements.* Investors are constantly given a wide range of information concerning both large-scale events and items about particular companies. Each of these types of announcements has been examined for the effects on stock prices.

One study examined the impact of major world events on stock prices.[12] In an efficient market the adjustment of stock prices to such announcements should be rapid, preventing investors from earning excess returns as the information becomes publicly available. Stock prices were examined prior to the announcement and at the market opening following the announcement as well as on the following two days. Although there were some variations in the results, investors would have been unable to profit by purchasing stocks when the market opened following the announcement. In general, a semistrong efficient market was indicated.

Another example of this type of announcement or story concerns the usefulness of the "Heard in the Street" column in *The Wall Street Journal.* This daily feature highlights particular companies and analysts' opinions on stocks. Although this is often the first disclosure of such information to the general public, it is reasonable to assume that analysts' estimates have already been made available to their respective firms' customers.

A study of the impact of the publication of this information on stock returns showed a positive effect on the order of 1% to 2%.[13] Unless transaction costs are smaller than this, however, market efficiency would seem to prevail. This is an example of economic efficiency—the abnormal returns indicated are not large enough to justify exploiting the small discrepancies that appear to exist.

Strong-Form Evidence

The strong form of the EMH states that stock prices immediately adjust to and reflect all information, public or otherwise. In general, this means that

---

[11]R. Pettit, "Dividend Announcements, Security Performance, and Capital Market Efficiency," *Journal of Finance,* Vol. 27, No. 5 (December 1972), pp. 993–1007; and R. Watts, "The Informational Content of Dividends," *The Journal of Business,* Vol. 45, No. 2 (April 1973), pp. 191–211.
[12]F. Reilly and E. Drzycimski, "Tests of Stock Market Efficiency Following Major World Events," *The Journal of Business Research,* Vol. 1 (Summer 1973), pp. 57–72.
[13]P. Davies and M. Canes, "Stock Prices and the Publication of Second-Hand Information," *The Journal of Business,* Vol. 51 (January 1978), pp. 43–56.

no group of investors can earn excess returns through a superior ability to analyze publicly available information. Investors who transform public information into private information do not gain by doing so. At the extreme, the strong form holds that even those investors with monopolistic access to information cannot gain by using this information.

One way to test for strong-form efficiency is to examine the performance of groups presumed to have access to "true" nonpublic information. If such groups can consistently earn above-average risk-adjusted returns, the extreme version of the strong form would not be supported. We shall consider corporate insiders, a group that presumably falls into the category of having monopolistic access to information.

We shall also consider the performance of professionally managed portfolios as a test of whether any group of investors can earn excess returns. The availability of data makes this group a logical one to analyze in assessing the strong-form assertion that all information is fully reflected in prices and that no type of investor can earn excess returns through superior ability.

Corporate Insiders A corporate insider is an officer, director, or major stockholder of a corporation. Such individuals might be expected to have valuable inside information. Insiders are required by the Securities and Exchange Commission (SEC) to report their purchase or sale transactions each month. This information is made public several weeks later.

Most studies of corporate insiders find that they consistently earn above-average profits.[14] Insiders have access to privileged information and are able to act on it and profit before the information is made public. This is logical and not really surprising. It is a violation of strong-form efficiency, however, which requires a market in which no investor can consistently earn abnormal profits.

Investors without access to this private information can observe what the insiders are doing by studying the publicly available reports they must make to the SEC. Several investment information services compile this information and sell it to the public in the form of regularly issued reports, and it is available weekly in *Barron's* and *The Wall Street Journal*. Furthermore, such services as *The Value Line Investment Survey* report insider transactions for each company they cover. Some studies of the performance of stocks after publication of these SEC reports indicate that above-average returns could have been earned on the basis of this publicly available information.[15] Which form of market efficiency do these findings point to, and why?

---

[14]See, for example, J. Jaffe, "Special Information and Insider Trading," *The Journal of Business*, Vol. 47 (July 1974), pp. 410–428.

[15]S. Pratt and C. DeVere, "Relationship Between Insider Trading and Rates of Return for NYSE Common Stocks, 1960–1966," included in J. Lorie and R. Brealey, eds., *Modern Developments in Investment Management* (New York: Praeger Publishers, 1972), pp. 268–279.

Portfolio Managers An interesting test of market efficiency is the performance of professional portfolio managers, particularly mutual fund managers, for whom a considerable amount of data is available. This can be considered a test of strong-form efficiency if it is assumed that these managers are free to use any type of information and stock selection techniques they choose. These professionals manage their portfolios on a continual basis with staffs of experts to assist them. Presumably, if valuable information is available to be discovered, these investors should be among the first to discover and use it.

Most of the evidence available on the historical performance of mutual funds suggest that the managers of these portfolios have been unable to achieve consistently superior performance. A well-known study by Michael Jensen analyzed 115 mutual funds during the period 1945–1964.[16] On a net basis (i.e., less fund expenses), the average fund earned 1.1% *less* per year than an unmanaged portfolio of similar risk. Jensen was unable to detect a management contribution sufficient to offset fund expenses, which supports strong-form efficiency as presented here.

In an article appearing several years after Jensen's, Norman Mains corrected what he felt to be biases in Jensen's article against the managed funds.[17] His results suggest a neutral performance, on average, on a net basis. On a gross basis the majority of funds performed positively. Thus, managers would seem to be able to earn enough to pay fund expenses (unlike Jensen's findings), but not enough to benefit the fund's shareholders.

An early study of mutual funds by William Sharpe supports the Jensen findings.[18] Sharpe found that of 34 funds examined, only 11 performed equal to or better than the Dow Jones Industrial Average (on a net basis). A later study by John McDonald also supports Jensen, finding no benefit to shareholders from active management.[19] And, as noted, most other studies have found similar results. On the other hand, Friend, Blume, and Crockett found good performance for mutual funds compared to certain random selection techniques.[20]

---

[16]M. Jensen, "The Performance of Mutual Funds in the Period 1945–1964," *Journal of Finance,* Vol. 23 (May 1968), pp. 389–416.

[17]N. Mains, "Risk, the Pricing of Capital Assets, and the Evaluation of Investment Portfolios: Comment," *The Journal of Business,* Vol. 50 (July 1977), pp. 317–384.

[18]W. Sharpe, "Mutual Fund Performance," *The Journal of Business,* Vol. 39 (January 1966), pp. 119–138.

[19]J. McDonald, "Objectives and Performance of Mutual Funds, 1960–1969," *Journal of Financia and Quantitative Analysis,* Vol. 9 (June 1974), pp. 311–333.

[20]I. Friend, M. Blume, and J. Crockett, *Mutual Funds and Other Institutional Investors* (New York: McGraw-Hill, 1970).

Implications of the Efficient Market Hypothesis

The nonexhaustive evidence on market efficiency presented here is impressive in its support of market efficiency. What are the implications to investors? How should investors analyze and select securities and manage their portfolios if the market is efficient?

As mentioned earlier, technical analysis and the EMH directly conflict with each other. Technicians believe stock prices exhibit trends that persist across time, whereas the weak-form EMH states that price (and volume) data are already reflected in stock prices. EMH proponents believe that information is disseminated rapidly and that prices adjust rapidly to this new information. If prices fully reflect the available information, technical trading systems that rely on a knowledge and use of past trading date cannot be of value.

Although technical analysis cannot be categorically refuted because of its many variations and interpretations, the evidence accumulated to date overwhelmingly favors the weak-form EMH and casts doubt on technical analysis. The evidence is such that the burden of proof has shifted to the proponents of technical analysis to demonstrate, in a correctly conducted test (e.g., adjusting for transaction costs and risk), that technical analysis outperforms a buy-and-hold strategy.

The EMH also has implications for fundamental analysis, which seeks to estimate the intrinsic value of a security and provide buy or sell decisions depending on whether the current market price is less than or greater than the intrinsic value. The evidence that has been accumulated to date suggests that discrepancies do, in fact, exist from time to time and from security to security. There is no theoretical reason that an investor could not do a superior job of analysis and profit thereby. However, the EMH suggests that investors who use the same data and make the same interpretations as other investors will experience only average results.

What is necessary in fundamental analysis, given the evidence on market efficiency, is to perform clearly *superior* fundamental analysis. For example, an investor must estimate future variables such as earnings better than other investors, or at least more consistently. This investor must derive more and better insights from information that is publicly available to all investors. The evidence on the EMH suggests that it is quite difficult, although by no means impossible, for investors to do this.

What about money management activities? Assume for a moment that the market is efficient. What would this mean to the money management process, that is, to professional money managers? The most important effect would be a reduction in the resources devoted to assessing individual securities. For the manager to act in this respect, he or she would have to believe that an analyst had come up with some superior insights. Passive strategies would become the norm; nevertheless, the portfolio manager would still have tasks to perform in this efficient market. These tasks would consist of at least the following[21]:

1. *The degree of diversification.* As will be seen in Chapter 19, the basic tenet of good portfolio management is to diversify the portfolio. The manager would have to be certain that the correct amount of diversification had been achieved.
2. *The riskiness of the portfolio.* Depending on the type of portfolio being managed and its objectives, the manager must achieve a level of risk appropriate for that portfolio. This would involve assessing the risk and establishing the appropriate position.
3. *The maintenance of the desired risk level.* It may be necessary to make changes in the portfolio that would keep the risk level at the intended level.
4. *The tax status of the investor.* Investors are interested in the amount of return they are allowed to keep after taxes. Accordingly, their tax situation should be kept in mind as investment alternatives are considered. Tax-exempt portfolios have their own needs and interests.
5. *Transaction costs.* Trading costs can have a significant impact on the final performance of the portfolio. Managers should seek to reduce these costs to the extent possible and practical.

Before deciding that these tasks may be all that is left to do in the portfolio management process in the face of an efficient market, we should examine some evidence that suggests possibilities for investors interested in selecting stocks. This evidence is in contrast with that discussed thus far and constitutes a good conclusion for this chapter by indicating that regardless of how persuasive the case for market efficiency is, the final answer is not in and may never be.

Evidence of Market Anomalies

Having considered the type of evidence supporting market efficiency, we can appropriately consider some other work that raises questions. These examples are sometimes referred to as **market anomalies,** meaning that the results are in contrast to what would be expected in a totally efficient market. They cannot easily be explained away. We shall examine several anomalies that have generated much attention and have yet to be satisfactorily explained. However, investors must be cautious in viewing any of these anomalies as a stock selection device guaranteed to outperform the market. There is no such guarantee because empirical tests of these anoma-

---

[21]See J. Lorie and M. Hamilton, *The Stock Market: Theories and Evidence* (Homewood, Ill.: Richard D. Irwin, 1973), pp. 106–108.

lies may not approximate actual trading strategies that would be followed by investors. Furthermore, if anomalies exist and can be identified, investors should still hold a portfolio of stocks rather than concentrating on a few stocks identified by one of these methods. As we shall see in Chapter 19, diversification is crucial for all investors.

Earnings Announcements

The adjustment of stock prices to earnings announcements has been studied in several papers, opening up some interesting questions and possibilities. It is obvious that earnings announcements, because of the importance of earnings in the valuation process, are important to investors. Such announcements contain information that should, and does, affect stock prices. The questions that need to be answered are as follows:

1. How much of the earnings announcement is new information and how much has been anticipated by the market—in other words, how much of the announcement is a "surprise"?
2. How quickly is the "surprise" portion of the announcement reflected in the price of the stock? Is it immediate, as would be expected in an efficient market, or is there a lag in the adjustment process? If a lag occurs, investors have a chance to realize excess returns by quickly acting on the publicly available earnings announcements.

To assess the earnings announcement issue properly, it is necessary to separate a particular earnings announcement into an expected part and an unexpected part, a dichotomy discussed in Chapter 12. The expected part is that portion anticipated by investors by the time of announcement and requiring no adjustment in stock prices, whereas the unexpected part is unanticipated by investors and requires an adjustment in price.

Latané, Tuttle, and Jones studied quarterly earnings reports in 1968 and found them to be positively correlated with subsequent short-term price movements, thereby indicating a lag in the adjustment of stock prices to the information in these reports.[22] Following several papers that examined the value of quarterly earnings in stock selection, Latané, Jones, and Rieke in 1974 developed the concept of standardized unexpected earnings (SUE) as a means of investigating the earnings surprises in quarterly data.[23] As explained in Chapter 12, SUE is defined as

---

[22]See H. A. Latané, Donald L. Tuttle, and Charles P. Jones, "E/P Ratios vs. Changes in Earnings in Forecasting Future Price Changes," *Financial Analysts Journal*, January–February 1969, pp. 117–120, 123.

[23]For a discussion of much of this literature, see O. Joy and C. Jones, "Earnings Reports and Market Efficiencies: An Analysis of Contrary Evidence," *Journal of Financial Research*, Vol. 2 (Spring 1979), pp. 51–64.

$$\text{SUE} = \frac{\text{Actual earnings} - \text{Predicted earnings}}{\text{Standardization factor to adjust for size differences}}$$

$$= \frac{\text{Unexpected earnings}}{\text{Standard error of the estimate}}$$

The actual quarterly earnings are the earnings reported by the company and available on brokerage house wire services the same day as reported, or in *The Wall Street Journal* the following day. Predicted earnings for a particular company are estimated from historical earnings data before the earnings are reported. As each company's earnings are announced, the SUE can be calculated and acted on. Companies with high (low) unexpected earnings are expected to have a positive (negative) price response.

Latané and Jones have documented the performance of SUE in a series of papers. SUE was shown to have a definite relationship with subsequent excess holding period returns. In one paper the authors documented the precise response of stock prices to earnings announcements using a large sample of stocks (over 1400) for the 36 quarters covering mid-1971 to mid-1980.[24] Daily returns were used, allowing the exact response of stock prices to quarterly earnings announcements to be analyzed before, on, and after the day the earnings were announced.

Figure 14-3 shows a similar analysis for an updated period through mid-1984 involving a sample size ranging from about 1700 companies per quarter to almost 2000 companies. SUEs are separated into 10 categories based on the size and sign of the unexpected earnings. Category 10 contains all SUEs larger than 4.0 and category 1 contains all SUEs smaller than −4.0; categories 5 and 6 contain the smallest unexpected earnings. **Excess returns** are calculated for each security as the difference between a security's return for each day and the market's return for that day. These excess returns are cumulated for the period beginning 63 days before the announcement date of earnings through 63 days following the announcement date (there are approximately 63 trading days in a quarter). As Figure 14-3 shows, the SUE categories follow a monotonic discrimination, with category 10 performing the best and category 1 performing the worst. Categories 5 and 6 show virtually no excess returns after the announcement date of earnings, as would be expected.

Figure 14-3 indicates that although a substantial adjustment to the forthcoming earnings announcements occurs before the actual announcement, a substantial adjustment also occurs after the day of announcement. This is the unexplained part of the SUE puzzle. In an efficient market, prices should adjust quickly to earnings, rather than with a lag.

---

[24]See Charles P. Jones, Richard J. Rendleman, and Henry A. Latané, "Stock Returns and SUEs during the 1970s," *The Journal of Portfolio Management*, Winter 1984, pp. 18–22.

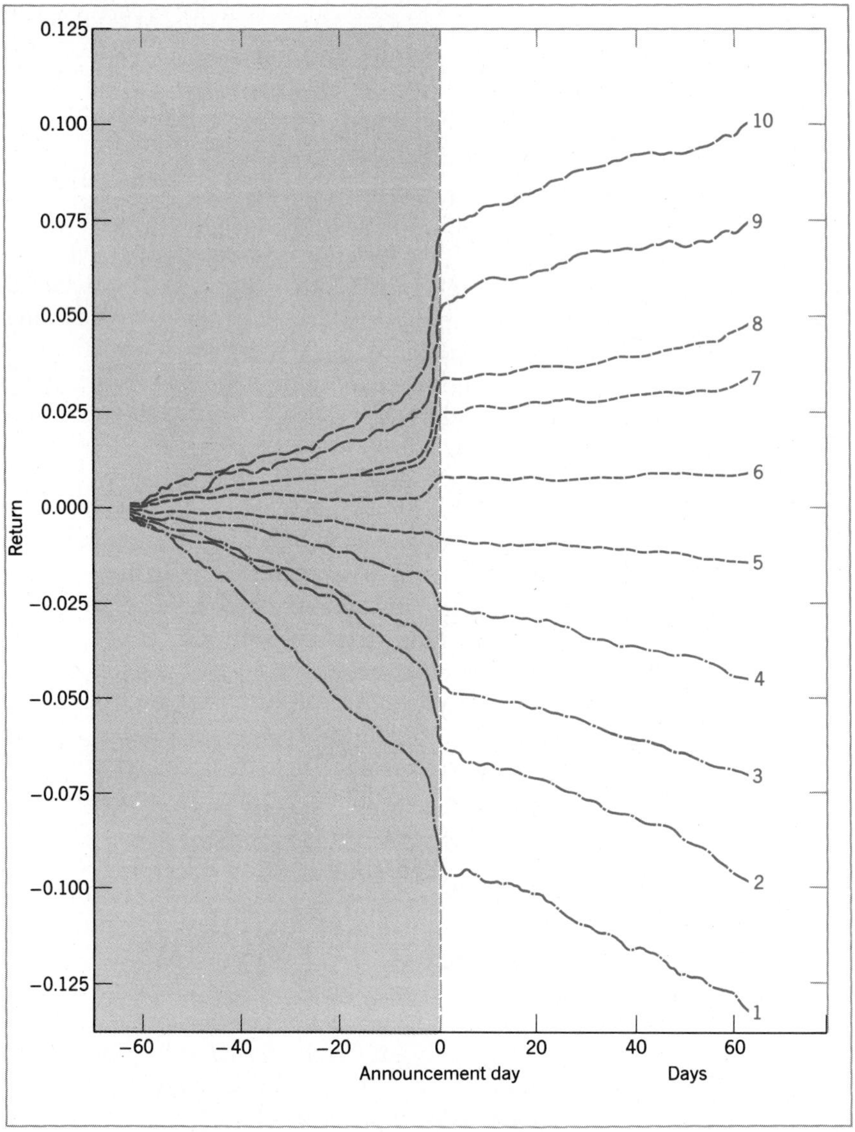

FIGURE 14-3 ***Cumulative excess returns surrounding the announcement date of earnings for 10 SUE categories, mid-1975 to mid-1984.***

By the mid-1980s, considerable evidence had been presented about the relationship between unexpected earnings and subsequent stock returns. Although such evidence is not in any way conclusive, it cannot be easily dismissed. Different researchers, using different samples and different techniques, have examined the unexpected earnings issue and have found similar results.[25] It must be emphasized, however, that techniques such as SUE are not a guarantee of major success for investors. The relationships discussed are averages and do not necessarily reflect what any single investor would experience.

Low P/E Ratios

One of the more enduring concepts in investments concerns the price/earnings (P/E) ratio discussed earlier in the valuation chapters. A number of investors believe that low-P/E stocks, on average, outperform high-P/E stocks. The rationale for this is not explicit, but the belief persists.

Basu studied this issue by ranking stocks by their P/E ratios and comparing the results of the high P/E ratio group with those of the low P/E ratio group 12 months following purchase.[26] Since the P/E ratio is known information and presumably reflected in price, a relationship between the P/E ratio and subsequent returns should not exist if the market is efficient. The results of Basu's study indicated that the low-P/E ratio stocks outperformed the high P/E ratio stocks. Furthermore, risk was not a factor. After various adjustments for risk, the low-P/E stocks were still superior performers.

These results attracted considerable attention because of their implications for the concept of market efficiency and because the P/E ratio is an easy, well-known strategy to use in selecting stocks. Subsequently, questions about the validity of the P/E were raised by other academic researchers in studies of the firm size effect, which is discussed later as another anomaly.

In response to the questions raised, Basu conducted a study to reexamine the relationship between the P/E ratio, the size effect, and returns on NYSE stocks for the period 1963–1980.[27] He found that the stocks of low-P/E firms generally had higher *risk-adjusted* returns than firms with high P/E ratios. This P/E ratio effect, furthermore, was significant even after differences in firm size were adjusted for. Controlling for differences in both risk and P/E ratios, Basu found that the size effect virtually disappeared.

In view of some research suggesting that the P/E effect is confined to low-beta-risk securities, a recent study examined the P/E anomaly with

---

[25]See, for example, C. M. Bidwell III, "A Test of Market Efficiency: SUE/PE," *The Journal of Portfolio Management* (Summer 1979), pp. 53–58; and O. M. Joy, R. H. Litzenberger, and R. W. McEnally, "The Adjustment of Stock Prices to Announcements of Unanticipated Changes in Quarterly Earnings," *Journal of Accounting Research,* Autumn 1977, pp. 207–225.

[26]S. Basu, "Investment Performance of Common Stocks in Relation to Their Price–Earnings Ratios: A Test of the Efficient Market Hypothesis," *Journal of Finance,* Vol. 32, No. 2 (June 1977), pp. 663–682.

[27]S. Basu, "The Relationship Between Earnings' Yield, Market Value and Return for NYSE Common Stocks: Further Evidence," *Journal of Financial Economics,* Vol. 12 (June 1983), pp. 129–156.

respect to both total risk and systematic risk.[28] The results indicate that the P/E effect is not confined to low-beta-risk securities. Regardless of the risk measure used, low-P/E securities provided significant positive excess returns across all risk levels.

The P/E ratio anomaly remains unexplained. Until it is refuted, however, it appears to offer investors a potential strategy for investing that could produce returns superior to many alternatives they may be using. And investing in low-P/E stocks continues to be advocated by some well-known commentators. For example, David Dreman recommends that investors ignore professional investment advice and select stocks with low-P/E ratios. His hypothesis in that low-P/E stocks may be unwanted currently, but if they have strong finances, high yields, and good earnings records, they almost always do well eventually.

In his articles in *Forbes*, Dreman periodically discusses studies showing the results of selecting low-P/E stocks. For example, he has reported on a study of almost 1500 stocks (on average) over the 22-year period 1963–1985. This time span included three major bull and bear markets and a wide range in the Dow Jones Industrial Average. As Table 14-1 shows, the lowest quintile of P/E ratio stocks far outperformed the other four quintiles, virtually doubling the highest P/E quintile. Results are measured annually based only on the P/E ratios. According to Dreman, $10,000 invested in the lowest quintile would have resulted in $630,042 compared to $88,169 for the highest P/E group (assuming annual switching).[29]

Investors need to be careful when following the low-P/E strategy. Although a diversified portfolio, as always, is critical, rigid adherence to a low-P/E strategy could result in an inadequately diversified portfolio. Dreman has indicated that he takes a minimum of 25 stocks in 15–18 industries and that "most [low-P/E stocks] have significant problems or very good reasons why you don't want to own them."[30] Only about one in 10 candidates on the basis of the low P/E pass his additional screens, such as dividend yields higher than average and accelerating earnings growth over the past. Dreman also suggests an emphasis on large stocks as opposed to small-company stocks.

According to some evidence, the low-P/E strategy does not do well in turbulent markets, nor in periods of slow economic growth. However, these stocks may perform well in a "full-blown" bear market because of their higher dividend yields.[31] Overall, the low-P/E strategy should be

---

[28]See David Goodman and John Peavy, "The Risk Universal Nature of the P/E Effect," *Journal of Portfolio Management* (Summer 1985), pp. 14–17.
[29]See David Dreman, "A Strategy for All Seasons," *Forbes*, July 14, 1986, p. 118.
[30]This quote, as well as the general discussion surrounding it, is taken from Barbara Donnelly, "That Low-P/E Gold Might Really Be Lead," *The Wall Street Journal*, April 25, 1989, p. C1.
[31]Ibid.

TABLE 14-1 ***Annual Returns from P/E Quintiles, Mid-1963 to Mid-1985***

P/E Group	Total Return	Appreciation	Dividend
Lowest	20.7%	15.4%	5.3
Second lowest	15.7	10.2	5.5
Middle	10.7	6.0	4.7
Second Highest	10.4	6.7	3.7
Highest	10.4	8.2	2.2

Source: David Dreman, "A Strategy for All Seasons," *Forbes,* July 14, 1986, p. 118. Excerpted by permission of *Forbes* magazine, July 14, 1986. © Forbes Inc., 1986.

viewed as a long-run strategy, to be pursued through both good and bad markets.

The Size Effect

A third anomaly is the firm **size effect,** referred to earlier. In a well-publicized study, Rolf Banz found that the stocks of small NYSE firms earned higher *risk-adjusted* returns than the stocks of large NYSE firms (on average).[32] This "size effect" appears to have persisted for over 40 years. Mark Reinganum, using a sample of both NYSE and Amex firms, also found abnormally large risk-adjusted returns for small firms.[33] Both of these researchers attributed the results to a misspecification of the CAPM rather than to a market inefficiency. That is, both Banz and Reinganum, in the face of persistent abnormal returns attributed to the size effect, were unwilling to reject the idea that the market could have inefficiencies of this type.

Additional research on the size effect indicates that "small" firms with the largest abnormal returns tend to be those that have recently become small (or have recently declined in price), that either pay no dividend or have a high dividend yield, that have low prices, and that have low P/E ratios.[34] Keim found that roughly 50% of the return difference reported by Reinganum is concentrated in January.[35]

[32]R. Banz, "The Relationship Between Returns and Market Value of Common Stocks," *Journal of Financial Economics,* Vol. 9 (March 1981), pp. 3–18.

[33]M. Reinganum, "Misspecification of Capital Asset Pricing: Empirical Anomalies Based on Earnings Yield and Market Values," *Journal of Financial Economics,* Vol. 9 (March 1981), pp. 19–46.

[34]See, for example, Donald B. Keim, "Dividend Yields and the January Effect," *Journal of Portfolio Management,* Winter 1986, pp. 54–60. Keim finds that the largest abnormal returns accrue to smaller firms either paying no dividends or having high dividend yields.

[35]These results, as well as a discussion of most of the anomalies, can be found in Donald B. Keim, "The CAPM and Equity Return Regularities," *Financial Analysts Journal,* May–June 1986, pp. 19–34.

The January Effect

Several studies in the past have suggested that seasonality exists in the stock market. Recent evidence of stock return seasonality has grown out of studies of the size anomaly explained in the previous section. Keim studied the month-to-month stability of the size effect for all NYSE and Amex firms with data for 1963–1979.[36] His findings again supported the existence of a significant size effect (a 30.5% small-size premium). However, roughly half of this size effect occurred in January, and more than half of the excess January returns occurred during the first five trading days of that month. The first trading day of the year showed a high small-firm premium for every year of the period studied. The strong performance in January by small-company stocks has become known as the **January effect.**[37]

Another paper by Keim documented once again the abnormal returns for small firms in January. Keim also found a yield effect—the largest abnormal returns tended to accrue to firms either paying no dividends or having high dividend yields.[38]

According to the Ibbotson data discussed in earlier chapters, in almost 90% of the years since 1926, small stocks outperformed large stocks. The data indicate that some 40% of the average total return per year for small-company stocks occurs in the month of January alone. This information is available and has been widely discussed in the press.[39]

> **INVESTMENTS INTUITION**
>
> The interesting question from a market efficiency standpoint is why this should continue as more and more people learn about the January effect. After all, no calculations as such are needed to implement a "January strategy." All that is needed is to buy, sometime in December, several small-company stocks or a mutual fund that holds such stocks.

Recent evidence on the January effect, as measured by the performance of the NASDAQ Composite Index for the month of January, is:[40]

---

[36]See Donald B. Keim, "Size-Related Anomalies and Stock Return Seasonality," *Journal of Financial Economics*, Vol. 12 (1983), pp. 13–32.

[37]See Richard Roll, "Vas ist das? The Turn of the Year Effect and the Return Premium of Small Firms," *Journal of Portfolio Management*, (1983), pp. 18–28. Roll also found a turn-of-the-year effect with abnormal returns for small firms on the last trading day in December.

[38]See Donald B. Keim, "Dividend Yields and the January Effect," *The Journal of Portfolio Management*, Winter 1986, pp. 54–60.

[39]See, for example, Earl C. Gottschalk Jr., "It's the 'January Effect,' but Will It Occur Next Month?" *The Wall Street Journal*, December 14, 1988, p. C1.

[40]These percentage price changes are available from data in NASD's *NASDAQ Fact Book* and current periodicals that report stock market indices.

1986	+3.3%
1987	+12.4%
1988	+4.3%
1989	+5.2%
1990	−8.6%

Thus, the interesting question now about the January effect is, "Does 1990 represent the end of the January effect, or was it a temporary departure from the documented behavior of the price performance of small firms in January?"

The Value Line Phenomenon

As discussed in Chapter 4, *The Value Line Investment Survey* is the largest, and perhaps best-known, investment advisory service in the country. *Value Line* ranks each of the roughly 1700 stocks it covers from 1 (best) to 5 (worst) as to its "Timeliness"—probable relative price performance within the next 12 months. These timeliness ranks, which are updated each week, have been available since 1965.

The performance of the five rankings categories has been spectacular, based on *Value Line's* calculations. For example, the complete record of *Value Line* rankings for timeliness from 1965 through 1986 showed that the ranking system clearly discriminates in a monotonic order. Without allowing for changes in ranks (equal amounts are invested in each stock in each grouping at the beginning of the year and held for 12 months without allowing for subsequent changes in ranking), Group 3 stocks performed in an average manner (using the average of the stocks covered by *Value Line*), whereas Groups 1 and 2 performed much better than either the average or the two market measures reported. On the other hand, shortselling Groups 4 and 5 would have been unsuccessful. Allowing for changes in ranks produced spectacular results, with Group 1 up over 13,000% and Group 5 down almost 100%. However, such a procedure would have resulted in a prohibitive portfolio turnover rate.[41]

The Value Line Investment Survey now reports regularly a comparison of the performance of its Group 1 stocks with four other strategies: low P/E low cap (small size), low price book value, and low price/sales. Figure 14-4 shows this performance as of late 1989. Each of the five strategies is plotted relative to the Value Line Composite Index. This figure provides some information on two of the strategies discussed earlier, low P/E and the size effect, as well as two valuation techniques discussed in Chapter 9, P/book value and price/sales. Figure 14-4 appears to make a good case for the *Value Line* ranking system based on the performance of its Group 1 stocks.

[41]These results were reported in "Selection and Opinion," *The Value Line Investment Survey*, January 23, 1987, p. 719.

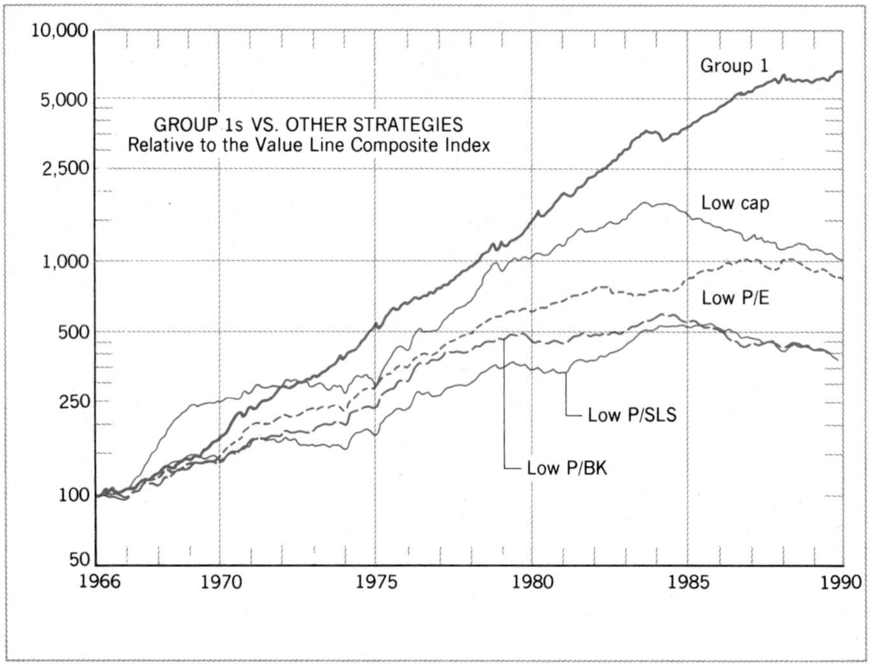

FIGURE 14-4 **Value Line's *Group 1 stocks and four other strategies relative to the Value Line Composite Index, 1966 to late 1989.***
Source: "Selection and Opinion," *The Value Line Investment Survey,* October 27, 1989, p. 138. Copyright © 1989 by Value Line Publishing Inc. Used by permission.

Some Conclusions About Market Efficiency

Given all of the evidence about market efficiency discussed previously—the studies supporting it as well as the anomalies evidence—what conclusions can be drawn? In truth, no definitive conclusion about market efficiency can be stated. The evidence in support of market efficiency is persuasive because of the large amount of research done over many years by numerous investigators. Nevertheless, the evidence of anomalies has yet to be explained satisfactorily. And many technicians and fundamentalists are convinced that they can outperform the market, or at least provide more benefits than cost. Paradoxically, this belief helps to make the market efficient.

INVESTMENTS INTUITION

The paradox of efficient markets and active investors is that investors, in an attempt to uncover and use important information about security prices, help to make the market efficient. In other words, in the course of searching out undervalued and overvalued stocks, investors discover information and act on it as quickly as possible. If the information is favorable, the discoverers will buy immediately, and if unfavorable, they will sell immediately. As investors scramble for information and attempt to be the first to act, they make the market more efficient. If enough of this activity occurs, all information will be reflected in prices. Thus, the fact that a number of investors do not believe in the EMH results in actions that help to make the market efficient.

In the final analysis it is probably best to accept the idea that the market is quite efficient, but not totally. Most of the research done to date suggests that information is received and acted on quickly, and generally the correct adjustments are made. To outperform the market, fundamental analysis beyond the norm must be done. The fundamental analysis that is routinely done every day is already reflected in stock prices. The marginal value of one more investor performing the same calculations that have been done by other investors is zero. And until more evidence to the contrary is forthcoming, technical analysis remains questionable at best.

Simon Keane has argued that investors must choose between a belief in operational efficiency and operational inefficiency.[42] In an operationally efficient market some investors with the skill to detect a divergence between price and semistrong value earn economic rents. For the majority of investors, however, such opportunities are not available. An operationally inefficient market, on the other hand, contains inefficiencies that can be spotted by the average investor. The evidence to date suggests that investors face an operationally efficient market.[43]

Some anomalies do seem to exist, and since the late 1970s the flow of research reporting on anomalies has accelerated.[44] These anomalies require considerable work to document scientifically and do not represent a guarantee of investment riches; however, these anomalies appear to offer opportunities to astute investors. The reasons for the existence of these anomalies remain unsettled. The quantity and quality of the research in this area has undermined the extreme view that the market is so perfectly efficient that no opportunities for excess returns could possibly exist.

One difficult problem for those who believe in efficient markets is the crash of October 1987. The S&P 500 Index lost over 20% in one day. Is it really reasonable to argue that investors, efficiently discounting informa-

[42]See Simon Keane, "The Efficient Market Hypothesis on Trial," *Financial Analysts Journal*, March–April 1986, pp. 58–63. This paper presents an excellent discussion of the current efficient market debate.

[43]For evidence that the market is not perfectly efficient and therefore offers investors investment opportunities, see Robert F. Vandell and Robert Panino, "A Purposeful Stride Down Wall Street," *The Journal of Portfolio Management*, Winter 1986, pp. 31–39.

[44]A special edition of the *Journal of Financial Economics* in 1978 was devoted to this contrary evidence.

BOX 14-2

DANGEROUSLY INEFFICIENT

Strange that so many academics still cling to the illusion that the stock market is an efficient pricing mechanism. If the stock market were truly efficient, it would never have reached 2700 on the Dow in the summer of 1987, nor would it have crashed to 1750 little more than a month later. To argue that this was efficient pricing would be to argue that the corporate world lost one-third of its real value in a single month. Clearly this is an unsustainable view.

Despite piles of research from academics and government regulatory agencies, there is still no clear consensus on what triggered Black Monday. But it happened and could happen again, without reasonable cause, says Avner Arbel, 52, professor of finance at Cornell University. Arbel isn't lulled by the market's subsequent recovery. He is convinced that the crash is but a symptom of dangerous inefficiency in the stock market.

The theory certainly does not hold true today, says Arbel. No single kernel of information can account for the market's precipitous crash. To Arbel, this indicates that the stock market was riding a wave of speculative buying. In academic terms, the stock market had become inefficient. What's more, Arbel warns that unless the causes of this inefficiency are corrected, another crash is likely.

Arbel thinks he knows what lies behind the inefficient and volatile pricing: insider trading. He argues that today's stock market gyrations are largely fueled by information not available to the general public—especially takeover rumors. The big moves in stocks have mostly been in takeover situations and the like, and here, Arbel says, the mass of investors are at an enormous disadvantage vis-a-vis the dealmakers, big traders and institutions.

With investing increasingly dominated by institutions, Arbel has reached the radical conclusion that there are really two stocks markets in the U.S., each running on a different pool of information. The first market we all know about. It consists of the traditional stock exchanges, where prices are based on information provided by news accounts, brokerage analysts and disclosure documents filed with the Securities & Exchange Commission.

More sinister is a second market, or what Arbel calls the "shadow market." Here the stock prices of companies involved in mergers and restructurings are determined away from the market, be it in a company's boardroom or in the offices of its investment banker. Generally, this information isn't available to the public on a timely basis. Instead, it remains the preserve of a few big institutions and professional traders. In time, prices on the traditional stock markets rise or fall to meet the shadow market, leaving savvy shadow players clutching fat profits.

"How can pricing be efficient if stocks double overnight because of discussions that go on in boardrooms?" Arbel gripes.

Soured on the game, he says, individual investors have turned away from the market. "In an odd way the small investor knows the market is inefficient, and he doesn't trust it."

To make the stock market more efficient, Arbel would eliminate the specialist system, which failed to hold up stock prices in the face of massive selling. He would also create one centralized market and one government agency to oversee it. During heavy downward market moves, Arbel supports a halt in trading to give the market a chance to catch its breath. To help alleviate small investors' fears, Arbel recommends more effective policing of institutional activity and more timely public disclosure of merger negotiations.

In short, Arbel wants to see more federal policing. But is that really the answer? A market that prices stocks so cheaply that they are susceptible to substantial premiums in takeover situations may not be efficient in the first place. Could it be that a takeover game, far from being a cause of inefficiency, is itself a product of pricing inefficiency?

Source: Adapted from Matthew Schifrin, "Dangerously Inefficient," *Forbes*, July 10, 1989, pp. 60–61. Excerpted by permission of *Forbes* magazine, July 10, 1989, © Forbes, Inc., 1989.

tion, decided in one day that the market should be valued some 20% less? Not many people, including efficient market proponents, are comfortable making this argument. For a discussion of how the market crash can be interpreted relative to market efficiency, see Box 14-2.

The controversy about market efficiency remains. Every investor is still faced with the choice between an active and passive investment strategy.

Summary

- Investors must consider the implications of efficient markets for investment decisions.
- An efficient market is defined as one in which the prices of securities fully reflect all known information quickly and accurately.
- The conditions that guarantee an efficient market can be shown to hold to a large extent: many investors are competing, information is widely available and generated more or less randomly, and investors react quickly to this information.
- To assess market efficiency, three cumulative forms (or degrees) of efficiency are discussed: the weak form, the semistrong form, and the strong form. The weak form involves market data, whereas the semistrong and strong form involve the assimilation of all public and private information, respectively. The weak-form evidence, whether statistical tests or trading rules, strongly supports the hypothesis.
- Many tests of semistrong efficiency have been conducted, including, among others, stock splits, money supply changes, accounting changes, dividend announcements, and reactions to other announcements. Although all the studies do not agree, the majority support semistrong efficiency.
- Strong-form evidence takes the form of tests of the performance of groups presumed to have "private" information and of the ability of professional managers to outperform the market. Insiders apparently are

able to do well, although the decisions of the managers of mutual funds have not been found to add value.

- Most knowledgeable observers accept weak-form efficiency, reject strong-form efficiency, and feel that the market is, to a large degree, semistrong efficient. This casts doubt on the value of technical analysis as well as conventional fundamental analysis.
- Although the EMH does not preclude investors from outperforming the market, it does suggest that this is quite difficult to accomplish and that the investor must do more than the norm.
- Even if the market is efficient, money managers still have activities to perform, including diversifying the portfolio, choosing and maintaining some degree of risk, and assessing taxes and transaction costs.
- Several major "anomalies" that have appeared over the last several years have yet to be satisfactorily explained. These anomalies, which would not be expected in a totally efficient market, are as follows:
  1. *Unexpected earnings, as represented by SUE.* The market appears to adjust with a lag to the earnings surprises contained in quarterly earnings. SUE has been shown to be a monotonic discriminator of subsequent short-term (e.g., three-month) stock returns.
  2. *P/E ratios.* Low-P/E stocks appear to outperform high-P/E stocks over annual periods, even after adjustment for risk and size.
  3. *The size effect.* Small firms have been shown to outperform large firms, on a risk-adjusted basis, over a period of many years.
  4. *The January effect.* Much of the abnormal return for small firms occurs in the month of January, possibly because tax-induced sales in December temporarily depress prices, which then recover in January.
  5. *Value Line's performance.* The *Value Line* rankings for timeliness have performed extremely well over the period 1965–1986 and appear to offer the average investor a chance to outperform the averages.

Key Words

Abnormal return
Cumulative abnormal return
Efficient market (EM)
Efficient market hypothesis (EMH)
Event study
Excess returns
Index model
January effect
Market anomalies
Semistrong form
Size effect
Strong form
Weak form

Questions

14-1 What is meant by an efficient market?

14-2 Describe the three forms of market efficiency.

14-3 What are the conditions for an efficient market? How closely are they met in reality?

14-4 Why is a market that is weak-form efficient in direct opposition to technical analysis?

14-5 What do semistrong market efficiency tests attempt to test for?

14-6 Describe two different ways to test for weak-form efficiency.

14-7 Distinguish between economic significance and statistical significance.

14-8 If the EMH is true, what are the implications for investors?

14-9 Could the performance of mutual fund managers also be a test of semistrong efficiency?

14-10 Describe the money management activities of a portfolio manager who believes that the market is efficient.

14-11 What are market anomalies? Describe four.

14-12 If all investors believe that the market is efficient, could that eventually lead to less efficiency in the market?

14-13 What is the relationship between SUE and fundamental analysis?

14-14 What other types of events or information could be used in semistrong-form tests?

14-15 What are the benefits to society of an efficient market?

14-16 If the market moves in an upward trend over a period of years, would this be inconsistent with weak-form efficiency?

14-17 Do security analysts have a role in an efficient market?

14-18 Evaluate the following statement: "My mutual fund has outperformed the market for the last four years. How can the market be efficient?"

14-19 What are the necessary conditions for a scientific test of a technical analysis trading rule?

14-20 Are filter rules related to timing strategies or stock selection strategies? What alternative should a filter rule be compared with?

14-21 Assume that you analyze the activities of specialists on the NYSE and find that they are able to realize consistently above-average rates of return? What form of the EMH are you testing?

14-22 What are some possible explanations for the size anomaly?

14-23 Can technical analysis ever be completely invalidated?

14-24 How can data on corporate insiders be used to test both the semistrong and the strong forms of the EMH?

14-25 How can data on the performance of mutual funds be used to test both the semistrong and the strong forms of the EMH?

14-26 Assume that the price of a stock remains constant from time period 0 to time period 1, at which time a significant piece of information about the stock becomes available. Draw a diagram that depicts the situation if (a) the market is semistrong efficient and (b) there is a lag in the adjustment of the price to this information.

14-27 How is the SUE concept related to technical analysis?

14-28 What is meant by an operationally efficient market?

Problems

14-1 Calculate the SUE for a stock with actual quarterly earnings of $0.50 per share and expected quarterly earnings of $0.30 per share. The standard error of estimate is 0.05. Is this a good buy?

Selected References

An alternative explanation of market anomalies can be found in

Arbel, Avner. "Generic Stocks: The Key to Market Anomalies," *The Journal of Portfolio Management*, Summer 1985, pp. 4–13.

One of the best articles available on efficient markets is:

Keane, Simon. "The Efficient Market Hypothesis on Trial" *Financial Analysts Journal*, March–April 1986, pp. 58–63.

100

PART 6

Additional Investment Opportunities

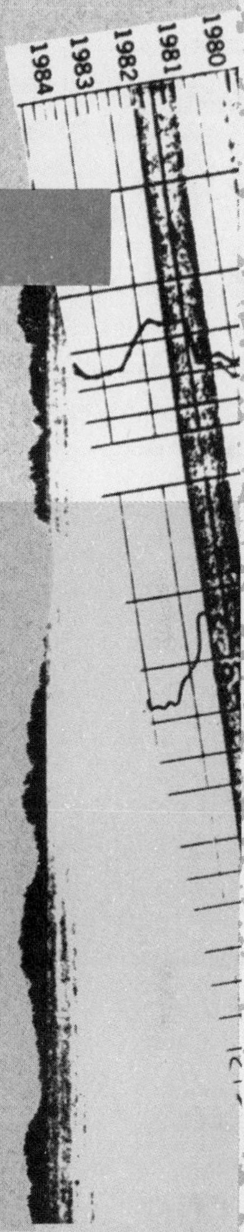

- CHAPTER 15 Options
- CHAPTER 16 Warrants and Convertible Securities
- CHAPTER 17 Futures Markets
- CHAPTER 18 Investment Companies

CHAPTER 15

Options

Rather than trade directly in common stocks, investors can purchase securities representing a claim—an option—on a particular stock or group of stocks. This option gives the holder the right to receive or deliver shares of stock under specified conditions. The option need not be exercised (and often will not be worth exercising). Instead, an investor can simply buy and sell these **equity-derivative securities,** which are securities that derive all, or part, of their value from the equity of the same corporation. Gains or losses will depend on the difference between the purchase price and the sales price.

This chapter will discuss put and call options. Chapter 16 will discuss warrants and convertibles. All three are equity-derivative securities.[1]

Background

Options, which represent claims on an underlying common stock, are created by investors and sold to other investors. The corporation whose common stock underlies these claims has no direct interest in the transaction, being in no way responsible for the creation, termination, or execution of puts and calls.

A **call** option gives the holder the right to buy (or "call away") 100 shares of a particular common stock at a specified price any time before a specified expiration date.[2]

Example. An IBM six-month call option at $100 per share gives the buyer the right (an option) to purchase 100 shares of IBM at $100 per share from a writer (seller) of the option any time during the six months before the specified expiration date.[3] Investors purchase calls if they expect the stock price to rise because the price of the call and the common stock will move together. Therefore, calls permit investors to speculate on a rise in the price of the underlying common stock without buying the stock itself.

A **put** option gives the buyer the right to sell (or "put away") 100 shares of a particular common stock at a specified price before a specified

[1]Rights, another equity-derivative security, were briefly discussed in Chapter 2. They are not discussed further because of their minor importance to most investors.

[2]It is important to remember throughout this discussion that the standard option contract on the organized exchanges is for 100 shares of the underlying common stock; therefore, when we speak of buying or selling *a* call or *a* put, we mean one contract representing an option on 100 shares of stock.

[3]Options that can be exercised any time before expiration are known technically as American options. A European option, in contrast, can only be exercised at maturity.

expiration date. If exercised, the shares are sold by the owner (buyer) of the put contract to a writer (seller) of this contract who has been designated to take delivery of the shares and pay the specified price.

Example. A writer (seller) of an IBM six-month put at $100 per share is obligated, under certain circumstances, to receive from the holder of this put 100 shares of IBM for which the writer will pay $100 per share. Investors will purchase a put if they expect the stock price to fall, because the value of the put will rise as the stock price declines. Therefore, puts allow investors to speculate on a decline in the stock price without selling the common stock short. ▪

Why Options Markets?

An investor can always purchase shares of common stock if he or she is bullish about the company's prospects, or if the investor is bearish, he or she can sell short. Why, then, should we create these indirect claims on a stock as an alternative way to invest? Several reasons have been advanced, including the following:

1. In the case of calls, an investor can control (for a short period) a claim on the underlying common stock for a much smaller investment than required to buy the stock itself. In the case of puts, an investor can duplicate a short sale without a margin account and at a modest cost in relation to the value of the stock.
2. The buyer's maximum loss is known in advance. If an option expires worthless, the most the buyer can lose is the cost (price) of the option.
3. Options provide leverage—magnified gains (in percentage terms) in relation to buying the stock; furthermore, options can provide greater leverage than fully margined stock transactions.
4. Puts and calls expand the opportunity set available to investors, making available risk–return combinations that would otherwise be impossible or that improve the risk–return characteristics of a portfolio. For example, an investor can sell the stock short and buy a call, thereby decreasing the risk on the short sale for the life of the call.[4]
5. Options can reduce total portfolio transaction costs. Although transaction costs at the single trade level may be higher for options, this need not be true for the total trades made for a portfolio.
6. Using options on a market index such as the S&P 500, an investor can participate in the overall movement of the market, or protect a portfolio against adverse market movements, with a single trading decision.

[4]Most stocks do not have puts and calls available. Several hundred stocks constitute the active options market.

Understanding Options

Options Terminology

To understand puts and calls, one must understand the terms used in connection with them. Since 1973, when options trading on organized exchanges began, the following terms of put and call contracts have been standardized: the price at which the put or call can be exercised, the expiration date, and the number of shares (100) involved in each contract. Our discussion applies specifically to options on the organized exchanges.[5] Important options terms include the following:

1. *Exercise (strike) price.* The **exercise (strike) price** is the per-share price at which the common stock may be purchased (in the case of a call) or sold to a writer (in the case of a put). Most stocks in the options market have options available at several different exercise prices, thereby providing investors with a choice. For stocks with prices greater than $25, the strike price changes in increments of $5; for those under $25, the increment is $2.50. As the stock price changes, options with new exercise prices are added.

Example. If IBM's market price is around $100, options may be available with the following strike prices: $90, $95, $100, $105, $110, $115, $120, and $125. The holder of an IBM $95-exercise-price call option has the right, if he or she chooses, to exercise the option by paying $95 per share, or $9500 (plus commission) for 100 shares, and take delivery of 100 shares of IBM common stock. The holder of an IBM $95-exercise-price put could, if he or she chooses, deliver 100 shares of IBM stock and receive $9500 (less commission), or $95 per share. If IBM were to rise in price to $125, new options would be created with strike prices of $130, $135, and so on. In effect, the strike prices adjust to the changing price of the stock.

2. *Expiration date.* The **expiration date** is the last date at which an option can be exercised.[6] All puts and calls are designated by the month of expiration. Originally, calendar cycles included January–April–July–October, February–May–August–November, or March–June–September–December. As one month in the cycle expired, another was added to take its place. The farthest expiration date possible was the end of the farthest three-month interval—a maximum of nine months.[7]

---

[5]Puts and calls existed for many years before these organized exchanges. They could be bought or sold in the over-the-counter market through brokers who were part of the Put and Call Dealers and Brokers Association. Members of this association endeavored to satisfy investor demands for particular options on a case-by-case basis. The terms of each individual contract (price, exercise date, etc.) had to be negotiated between buyer and seller. This was clearly a cumbersome, inefficient process.

[6]American-style options can be exercised any time prior to expiration; European-style options can be exercised only at expiration.

[7]The exact expiration day is the Saturday following the third Friday of the exercise month.

The options exchanges currently offer sequential options and other shorter-term patterns. Examples include November–December–January, November–December–February, and November–December–March in one cycle, and January–February–March, January–February–April, and January–February–May in another.

3. *Option premium.* The **option premium** is the price paid by the option buyer to the writer (seller) of the option, whether put or call. The premium is stated on a per-share basis for options on organized exchanges, and since the standard contract is on 100 shares, the premium represents hundreds of dollars.

Example. An option premium stated as $3 represents $300, $15 represents $1500, and so on.

Figure 15-1 is an excerpt from *The Wall Street Journal's* "Listed Options Quotation" page.[8] The most active options for the day for each of the five markets are indicated on the right side of the page. Notice that for the Chicago Board the most active options included an option on a market index, the S&P 100 (which will be discussed later).

Example. Consider the options for Paramount Communications shown in the third column as taken from *The Wall Street Journal* for November 2, 1989. Calls are shown first, followed by puts, and there are three expiration dates for each (in this example, November, December, and March). Six exercise prices are available for Paramount: $50, $55, $60, $65, $70, and $75. Thus, an investor had a potential choice of 6 (exercise prices) × 3 (expiration dates) = 18 call options on this stock, and 18 put options.[9] ▪

Options sold on these exchanges are protected against stock dividends and stock splits; therefore, if either is paid during the life of an option, both the exercise price and the number of shares in the contract are adjusted as necessary. Options traded on organized exchanges are not protected against cash dividends, however, and this can have significant effects on option values. When a cash dividend is paid, the stock price should decline to reflect this payment. Any event that reduces the stock price reduces the value of a call and increases the value of a put.

---

[8]This excerpt shows only a few of the options traded, but all five markets that trade options—the Chicago Board Option Exchange, the American Stock Exchange, the Pacific Stock Exchange, the Philadelphia Stock Exchange, and the New York Stock Exchange—are carried on this page and would be read in the same manner.

[9]Stock letter *s* indicates that options are unavailable for certain exercise prices and exercise dates; the *r* indicates that a particular option was not traded that day.

LISTED OPTIONS QUOTATIONS

Thursday, November 2, 1989

Options closing prices. Sales unit usually is 100 shares.
Stock close is New York or American exchange final price.

Option & NY Close	Strike Price	Calls–Last			Puts–Last		
		Nov	Dec	Mar	Nov	Dec	Mar
MayDS	50	r	1/2	r	r	r	r
Mc Don	27 1/2	s	4	s	s	r	s
30 5/8	30	1 1/4	1 7/8	2 7/8	3/8	3/4	1 5/8
30 5/8	32 1/2	s	3/4	s	s	r	s
30 5/8	35	r	1/4	13/16	r	r	r
N C R	55	r	r	r	r	r	1 1/4
59 7/8	60	1 1/8	2 5/8	r	1 1/16	2	r
59 7/8	65	r	7/8	2 3/8	r	r	6
59 7/8	70	r	r	1 1/4	9 3/8	r	r
NorSo	40	r	1/2	1 1/8	r	r	r
Oracle	20	2 3/4	3 1/4	4 5/8	r	7/8	1 1/8
22 3/4	22 1/2	1 1/4	2 1/8	2 3/4	1 1/16	1 3/8	r
22 3/4	25	1/2	1 1/4	2 1/8	r	2 7/8	3 1/2
22 3/4	30	1/8	r	1 1/8	r	r	r
OutbdM	25	2	2 1/2	3 1/2	r	1/2	1 1/4
26 7/8	30	r	7/16	1	3 1/8	r	4 1/8
26 7/8	35	r	1/4	1/2	r	8 1/4	r
Pall	30	r	r	r	r	r	3/4
31 7/8	35	r	r	1 1/4	r	r	r
ParaCm	50	8	9	11 3/4	r	r	r
58	55	4	5 3/4	8	3/4	2	r
58	60	1 5/8	3	6	3 1/2	5	6 1/4
58	65	5/8	1 11/16	3 1/2	r	8 3/4	r
58	70	5/16	1 1/4	2 5/8	r	r	r
58	75	s	5/8	1 9/16	s	r	r
RalPur	80	2	3	5 3/8	1	2	3 5/8
80 3/4	85	1/4	1 3/8	3 1/2	5	5	6 3/4
80 3/4	90	r	1/2	1 7/8	r	10 1/8	r
80 3/4	105	s	r	3/8	s	r	r
SherW	30	r	r	r	r	r	5/8
33 7/8	35	1/4	1/2	r	r	r	r
SwAir	20	r	r	r	r	r	1
22 3/4	22 1/2	7/8	1 3/8	r	r	5/8	r
22 3/4	25	r	1/2	1 1/2	r	r	r
22 3/4	30	r	1/4	r	r	r	r
Syntex	40	5 5/8	6	6 3/4	1/16	1/2	r
45 3/8	45	1 3/8	2 3/8	4	1 1/8	2	2 3/4
45 3/8	50	3/8	1	2	r	5 3/4	6 1/2
45 3/8	55	3/16	1/2	1 1/8	r	r	r
45 3/8	60	s	3/16	s	s	r	s
Tektrn	17 1/2	r	r	1 3/4	r	r	r
17 5/8	20	r	1/2	1 1/16	r	2 3/4	r
17 5/8	22 1/2	1/8	r	r	r	r	r
Telcrd	40	r	5/8	r	r	r	r
Telxon	5	2 3/4	r	r	r	r	r
7 5/8	7 1/2	r	r	1 3/4	r	r	r
7 5/8	12 1/2	s	1/8	r	s	r	r
Toys	35	2 5/8	3 3/4	r	r	5/8	1 1/2
38	40	3/8	1	2	r	r	3 3/4
UCamp	35	r	r	r	r	5/8	r
36 3/4	40	1/8	5/8	1 9/16	3	r	4
36 3/4	45	s	3/16	r	s	r	r
Walmrt	35	r	r	7 1/4	r	3/8	7/8
41	40	1 13/16	2 1/2	4	7/8	1 1/4	2
41	45	3/16	1/2	1 3/4	3 1/2	r	r
Whirlp	35	r	3/8	r	r	r	r
Whitmn	25	3 1/8	r	4 5/8	r	r	3/4
28	30	5/16	11/16	1 5/8	r	2 3/4	3 1/8
28	35	r	1/4	11/16	r	r	r
28	40	r	1/16	r	r	r	r

Total call vol 253,140 **Call open int** 3,084,714
Total put vol 192,264 **Put open int** 1,471,153

r-Not Traded. s-No Option.

MOST ACTIVE OPTIONS

CHICAGO BOARD

		Sales	Last	Chg.	N.Y. Close
CALLS					
SP100	Nov320	20608	2 3/4	– 1 1/4	315.52
SP100	Nov315	17992	5 1/4	– 1 3/4	315.52
SP100	Nov325	16163	1 5-16	–11-16	315.52
I B M	Nov100	9814	1	– 7-16	98
SP100	Nov330	6610	9-16	– 1/4	315.52
PUTS					
SP100	Nov315	22071	5 1/8	+ 1	315.52
SP100	Nov310	16224	3 5/8	+ 7/8	315.52
SP100	Nov320	13551	7 3/4	+ 1 5/8	315.52
SP100	Nov305	9993	2 1/2	+ 9-16	315.52
SP100	Nov300	8463	1 3/4	+ 3/8	315.52

AMERICAN

		Sales	Last	Chg.	N.Y. Close
CALLS					
AFamly	Nov20	3852	1 1/2	– 5/8	20 1/2
Apple	Nov45	2701	15-16	– 1 1/8	44
A M R	Nov75	2567	2 1/8	– 1	72
AFamly	Nov22 1/2	2409	13-16	– 3/8	20 1/2
A M R	Nov70	2252	4 1/2	– 7/8	72
PUTS					
MMIdx	Nov520	1584	7 1/4	+ 1 3/4	523.85
A M R	Nov65	1375	7/8	+ 1/8	72
MMIdx	Nov500	1136	2 3/4	+ 5/8	523.85
Merril	Jan30	1073	3 1/4	+11-16	27 1/4
Chase	Dec35	1035	3/4	– 3-16	36 1/2

PHILADELPHIA

		Sales	Last	Chg.	N.Y. Close
CALLS					
GaGulf	Nov55	2586	1 3/8	+13-16	54
GnInst	Nov40	1624	1 3-16	+ 7-16	39 5/8
GaGulf	Nov50	1138	4 3/4	+ 2 1/4	54
GnInst	Dec40	1121	2 1/8	+ 5/8	39 5/8
F N M	Nov45	1118	3/8	– 1-16	40

		Sales	Last	Chg.	N.Y. Close
PUTS					
LinB	Nov100	2017	5-16	– 3-16	112
LinB	Dec100	2012	2 5/8	+ 1/8	112
Time	Dec120	1580	1 1/2	– 1/4	130 3/4
LinB	Nov105	1326	5/8	– 1/8	112
LinB	Nov110	1112	1 9-16	– 1-16	112

PACIFIC

		Sales	Last	Chg.	N.Y. Close
CALLS					
Compaq	Nov90	5190	3 3/8	– 13 5/8	89
Compaq	Nov95	4657	1 1/2	– 10 1/4	89
Compaq	Nov105	3043	7-16	–3 9-16	89
Compaq	Nov100	2857	3/4	– 7	89
Compaq	Dec100	1764	2 1/2	– 7 1/4	89
PUTS					
Compaq	Nov85	2680	1 3/4	+ 1 5/8	89
Compaq	Nov90	2630	3 3/4	+ 3 1/2	89
Compaq	Nov95	2352	6 7/8	+6 5-16	89
Compaq	Nov100	1855	11	+ 9 3/4	89
Hilton	Nov85	1361	3/4	....	95 7/8

NEW YORK

		Sales	Last	Chg.	N.Y. Close
CALLS					
DigCom	Nov22 1/2	950	1/8	– 3-16	18 1/2
CSoup	Nov50	682	3/4	+ 1-16	47 5/8
DigCom	Nov20	615	7-16	– 1/8	18 1/2
QntmCp	Nov11 1/4	605	5-16	– 5-16	10 5/8
DigCom	Dec20	453	7/8	– 1/8	18 1/2
PUTS					
CSoup	Nov45	415	11-16	– 5-16	47 5/8
CSoup	Dec40	300	5/8	+ 1/8	47 5/8
CSoup	Dec45	262	1 3/8	– 1/4	47 5/8
CSoup	Nov50	223	2 3/4	– 5/8	47 5/8
FruitL	Feb10	220	5/8	+ 1/8	11 3/4

FIGURE 15-1 ***An Excerpt from "Listed Options Quotations" section of* The Wall Street Journal.**
Source: The Wall Street Journal, November 3, 1989, p. C1. Reprinted by permission of *The Wall Street Journal.*

How Options Work

As noted, a standard call (put) contract gives the buyer the right to purchase (sell) 100 shares of a particular stock at a specified exercise price any time before the expiration date. Both puts and calls are created by sellers who write a particular contract. Sellers (writers) are investors, either individuals or institutions, who seek to profit from their beliefs about the underlying stock's likely price performance, just as the buyer does. *Note that the buyer and the seller have opposite expectations about the likely performance of the underlying stock, and therefore the option itself.* Specifically, the call writer expects the price of the stock to remain roughly steady or perhaps move down, whereas the call buyer expects the price of the stock to move upward, and relatively soon. The put writer expects the price of the stock to remain roughly steady or perhaps move up, whereas the put buyer expects the price of the stock to move down, and relatively soon.

Example. Consider an individual named Carl who owns 100 shares of Paramount common and is optimistic about Paramount's long-run prospects. However, Carl feels that the price of Paramount will be flat, or possibly decline somewhat, over the next three months. Carl wishes to earn a short-run return on his Paramount position while holding the stock, which can be accomplished by selling a (covered) call option on the shares.

Carl instructs his broker to write (sell) a March call option on Paramount at a strike price of $55. For writing this option, Carl will receive a premium from the buyer. The premium amount is a function of supply and demand conditions and is determined by several factors that we shall examine later. The buyer pays the premium plus brokerage commissions, and the seller receives this premium less brokerage commissions. As we can see from Figure 15-1, the premium is $4 (i.e., $400, since 100 shares are involved). What happens now? Three courses of action are possible.

1. *The option may expire worthless* three months from now because the stock did not appreciate. Assume that the price of Paramount subsequently declines to $48 by the expiration date. The call gives the buyer (owner) the right to purchase Paramount from Carl for $55, but this would make no sense when Paramount can be purchased on the open market at $48. Therefore, the option will expire worthless. The buyer will lose the $400 investment, and Carl will gain the premium while continuing to own the Paramount shares.

2. If Paramount appreciates, a call buyer has *the right to exercise* the option and Carl could be called upon to meet this exercise. This means that the buyer pays Carl $5500 (the $55 exercise price multiplied by 100 shares) and receives 100 shares of Paramount. Assume the price has appreciated to $65 before expiration and the buyer exercises the option. The call buyer now owns 100 shares of Paramount worth $65 per share, for which the buyer paid $55 per share (plus the $4 per share for the call option itself). An immediate sale of Paramount in the market would result in a $600 gross profit for the call owner, or $6500 − ($5500 + $400). Brokerage costs would have to be included to obtain a net profit figure.

3. If Paramount appreciates, the value (price) of the call will also appreciate. The owner can simply *sell the call in the secondary market* to another investor who wishes to speculate on Paramount. Listed options are traded continuously on the five exchanges mentioned; therefore, buyers call their broker and instruct him or her to sell. Most investors trading puts and calls do not exercise those that are valuable; instead, they simply sell them on the open market, just as they would the common stock if they owned it.[10] ▪

Puts work the same way as calls, except in reverse. Again, a writer creates a particular put contract and sells it for the premium that the buyer pays. The writer believes that the underlying common stock is likely to remain flat or appreciate, and the buyer believes it is likely to decline.

Note the obligation of a put writer (seller). Assume a writer sells a March Paramount put at an exercise price of $60 when the stock price is $58, as in Figure 15-1. The premium is $3\frac{1}{2}$, or $350, which the buyer of the put pays and the writer receives (brokerage costs would be involved in both cases). Suppose the price of Paramount declines to $50 just before the expiration date. The put owner (buyer), who did not own Paramount previously, could instruct the broker to purchase 100 shares of Paramount in the market for $50. The buyer could then exercise the put, which means that a chosen writer must accept the 100 shares of Paramount and pay the put owner $60 per share, or $6000 total (although the current market price is only $50). The put buyer grosses $650 ($6000 received less $5000 cost of 100 shares less the $350 for the put). The put writer suffers an immediate paper loss. (Brokerage costs have once again been omitted in the example.)

As in the case of a call, two other courses of action are possible in addition to the exercise of the put as just described. First, the put may expire worthless, because the price of the common did not decline or did not decline enough to justify exercising the put. Second, and far more likely, the put owner can sell the put in the secondary market for a profit (or a loss). As in the case of calls, most put buyers plan to resell their options in the options market, rather than exercise them.

The Mechanics of Trading

Secondary Markets Five option exchanges constitute the secondary market: the Chicago Board, the American, the Philadelphia, the Pacific, and the

[10]One of the implications of the option pricing model to be considered later is that calls on stocks that do not pay a cash dividend should never be exercised before the expiration date. Calls on stocks paying a cash dividend might be exercised before the expiration date.

New York. All five exchanges are continuous markets, similar to stock exchanges. These markets provide liquidity to investors, a very important requirement for successful trading. Investors know that they can instruct their broker to buy or sell whenever they desire at a price set by the forces of supply and demand.

These exchanges have made puts and calls a success by standardizing the exercise date and exercise price of contracts. One Paramount March 60 call option is identical to every other Paramount March 60 call option.

The same types of orders discussed in Chapter 3—in particular, market, limit, and stop orders—are used in trading puts and calls.[11] Certificates representing ownership are not used for puts and calls; instead transactions are handled as bookkeeping entries. Option trades settle on the next business day after the trade.

The secondary markets for puts and calls have worked well in the years since the Chicago Board Options Exchange (CBOE) started operations in 1973. Trading volume has been large, and the number of puts and calls available has expanded. Starting in early 1990, the market for options expanded with the approval by the SEC for any of the five options exchanges to trade options on any exchange-traded stock if no other exchange is doing so and the stock meets certain requirements.[12] All exclusive trading privileges are scheduled to be eliminated on January 21, 1991, ending completely the monopoly that individual exchanges have had on options for a particular stock.[13]

The chairman of the SEC was on record in early 1990 as wanting to see the five exchanges move toward an electronic linkage. This would permit customers' orders to flow quickly to the market with the best price. Such a linkage and multiple listing of options should benefit investors by narrowing the spreads between bid and asked prices.

The Clearing Corporation The **options clearing corporation (OCC)** performs a number of important functions that contribute to the success of the secondary market for options. It functions as an intermediary between the brokers representing the buyers and the writers. That is, once the brokers representing the buyer and the seller negotiate the price on the floor of the exchange, they no longer deal with each other, but with the OCC.

Through their brokers, call writers contract with the OCC itself to deliver shares of the particular stock, and buyers of calls actually receive

---

[11] Although available, the manner in which some types of orders are executed on some of the options exchanges varies from that used on the stock exchanges.

[12] It was already possible for more than one options exchange to trade options on OTC stocks meeting regulatory rules.

[13] This information, and the paragraph following, is based on Stanley W. Angrist, "Trading in Stock Options to Expand Starting Today," *The Wall Street Journal*, January 22, 1990, pp. C1 and C10.

the right to purchase the shares from the OCC. Thus, the OCC becomes the buyer for every seller and the seller for every buyer, guaranteeing that all obligations will be met. This prevents the risk and problems that could occur as buyers attempted to force writers to honor their obligations. Instead, both buyers and sellers count on the OCC to enforce their contracts. The net position of the OCC is zero, because the number of contracts purchased must equal the number sold.

Investors wishing to exercise their options inform their brokers, who in turn inform the OCC of the exercise. The OCC randomly selects a broker on whom it holds the same written contract, and the broker selects a customer who has written these options to honor the contract. Writers chosen in this manner are said to be assigned an obligation or to have received an assignment notice.[14] Once assigned, the writer cannot execute an offsetting transaction to eliminate the obligation. Thus, a call writer who receives an assignment must sell the underlying securities, and a put writer must purchase them.

One of the great advantages of a clearinghouse is that transactors in this market can easily cancel their positions. Since the OCC maintains all the positions for both buyers and sellers, it can cancel out the obligations of writers wishing to terminate their position. For example, a call writer can terminate the obligation to deliver the stock anytime before the expiration date (or assignment) by making a "closing purchase transaction" at the current market-determined price of the option. The OCC offsets the outstanding call written with the call purchased in the closing transaction. A put writer can also close out a position at any time by making an offsetting transaction.

To protect itself, the OCC requires that its member firms whose customers have written options provide collateral to it in order to protect the OCC against defaults by writers. The member firms, in turn, require its customers who have written options to provide collateral for their written positions. With regard to puts and calls, **margin** refers to the collateral that option writers provide their brokers to ensure fulfillment of the contract in case of exercise.

Options cannot be purchased on margin. Buyers must pay 100% of the purchase price.

Brokerage Commissions All brokerage commissions are negotiable, as explained in Chapter 3. The major brokerage houses typically charge more than discount brokers, who advertise that they may save an investor 50% or more on option commissions.

Example. The following data provide an idea of brokerage commissions on puts and calls using a major discount brokerage service. The commis-

---

[14]Assignment is virtually certain when an option expires in the money.

sion rate is calculated as a percentage of the dollar value of the transaction. For example, on transactions up to $2500, the commission rate is $29 plus 1.6% of the principal amount. The minimum option commission is $37.25 plus $1.75 per contract, whereas the maximum charge is $40 per contract on the first two contracts, plus $4 per contract thereafter. This is only one example. Commissions vary between brokerage houses. ▪

When an option is exercised, both the buyer of the stock (the exerciser) and the seller of the stock (who is assigned the obligation) must pay brokerage commissions.

Analyzing Basic Options Strategies

In this section we analyze some basic options strategies used by investors. We first consider the buyer's standpoint and then the writer's (seller of the option). Following these basic strategies, we consider more sophisticated approaches.

Buying Options

Many individual investors purchase calls and puts at some point in their investment program. Calls are more popular than puts, just as buying long is more popular than selling short.

Buying Calls Investors buy calls because they are bullish (optimistic) about the price of the underlying stock. They wish to have a claim on the stock that will allow them to profit if their expectations are correct. The use of calls minimizes the initial investment, specifies the maximum loss that can be suffered, and provides the potential for maximum leverage (the ratio of profit to dollars invested).[15]

Investors always have the alternative of purchasing the stock itself. In doing so, their profit or loss is a direct (linear) function of the price of the stock at any point in time. To see this, examine Figure 15-2, which shows the profit–loss relationship for a stock that can currently be purchased for $48. If the price drops to $40, the investor loses $8; if the price rises to $60, the investor gains $12. The profit or loss from buying a stock is directly tied to movements in its price, both up and down.

Alternatively, investors can purchase calls, changing their profit and loss possibilities.

Example. Assume that at the current stock price of $48, a six-month call with an exercise price of $50 could be purchased for a premium of $4 (i.e., $400). If this call expires worthless, the maximum loss is the $400 premium

[15]Of course, the leverage can be harmful, maximizing the losses.

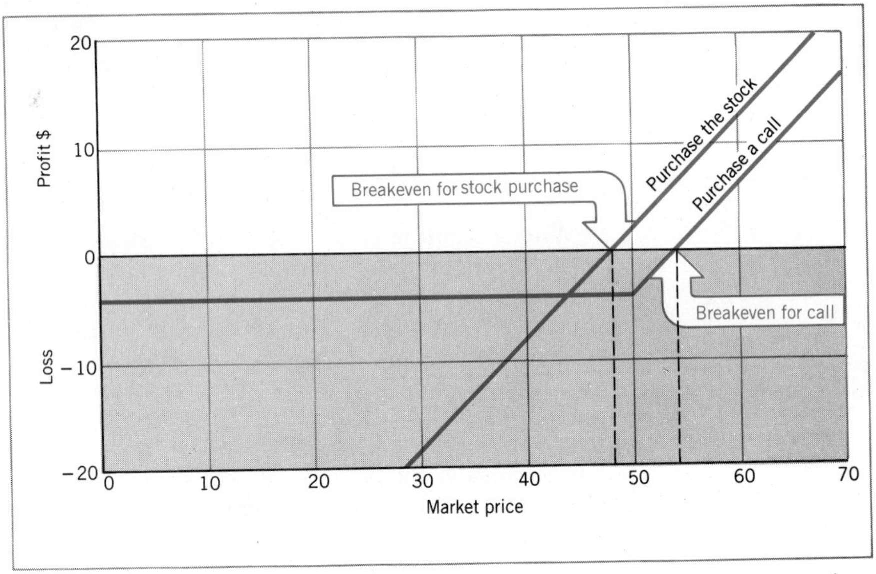

FIGURE 15-2 ***The profit and loss possibilities from purchasing a call versus purchasing the underlying common stock.***

(we shall ignore brokerage costs in these examples). This is shown in Figure 15-2 by the profit–loss line for the call. Notice that up to the exercise price of $50, the loss to the investor is $4 (i.e., $400). The break-even point for the investor is the sum of the exercise price and the premium, or $50 + $4 = $54; therefore, the profit–loss line for the purchase of a call crosses the break-even line at $54. If the price of the stock rises above $54, the value of the call will increase with it at least point for point, as shown by the two parallel lines above the profit–loss line. ▪

Figure 15-2 demonstrates why many investors purchase calls. Their loss is limited to the premium, no matter how much the price of the stock declines. For those investors interested in "taking a flyer," a call option may be a good alternative. As the stock price rises, the price of the call will keep pace, no matter how high the stock price rises.

Now consider what calls can do for an investor through leverage. Calls provide maximum leverage for speculative purposes.

Example. Assume an investor believes Syntex common, priced at $48, will appreciate in the next six months. A six-month call with an exercise price of $50 is available on Syntex for $4. The investor can either (ignoring commissions) buy 100 shares of Syntex common for $4800 or buy 12 call contracts, representing 1200 shares of Syntex, for $4800.

Should Syntex advance to $57 before expiration, the gross profit would be $900 on the 100 shares of common and at least 12 × $300 = $3600 on the

12 call contracts.[16] An investor in the calls could realize about four times the profit available on the stock itself for the same initial investment. ▪

Investors must *always* remember that the losses with calls could be large, or total. The high return potential is accompanied by large risk. Ask yourself what happens in the previous example if the stock is at $49 six months from now. Ignoring commissions, purchasing the stock would produce $100 in profit, whereas the option strategy could result in a total loss, because the calls are not worth exercising.[17]

Another potential reason for buying calls is to protect a short sale. An investor who has sold a stock short because of an expected drop in price can protect against an unexpected rise in price by purchasing a call on the shorted stock. If the stock price declines, the cost of the call option can be viewed as insurance. If the stock price rises, the call can be exercised and the stock acquired and delivered to cover the short sale.

Buying Puts Investors buy puts when they are bearish (pessimistic) about the price of the underlying common stock. Since a put gives the owner the right to sell the underlying stock at the specified exercise price, a decline in price will allow the put owner to purchase the stock at a lower price and deliver it to the writer of the put at the higher exercise price.

When bearish about a particular stock, investors can sell a stock short. If they do this, their profit or loss will be a direct (linear) function of the price of the stock at any point in time, as shown in Figure 15-3. For expositional purposes, we shall again use the example of a stock currently selling for $48. A short sale produces a downward-sloping line that intersects the break-even line at $48. Below this price, the investor profits from a short sale at $48; above this line, the investor would lose—as the stock price rises, the potential loss increases.

Alternatively, investors can purchase puts, changing their profit and loss possibilities.

Example. Assume that a four-month put with an exercise price of $50 could be purchased for a premium of $4. This put is currently worth exercising and as the price of the stock declines it becomes more valuable. The break-even point is $50 − $4 = $46, and as the stock price declines below this level, the value of the put keeps pace. If the price of the stock rises above $50, the loss from the put position can never exceed $4; the loss from selling short, however, continues to increase as the stock price rises. Just as with calls, put buyers are protected against potential losses. The most that

[16]The break-even point is assumed to be the sum of the $50 exercise price and the $4 premium, or $54, and the intrinsic value of the call to be at least $7.

[17]As this became obvious, the calls could be sold before maturity to recover a small part of the investment.

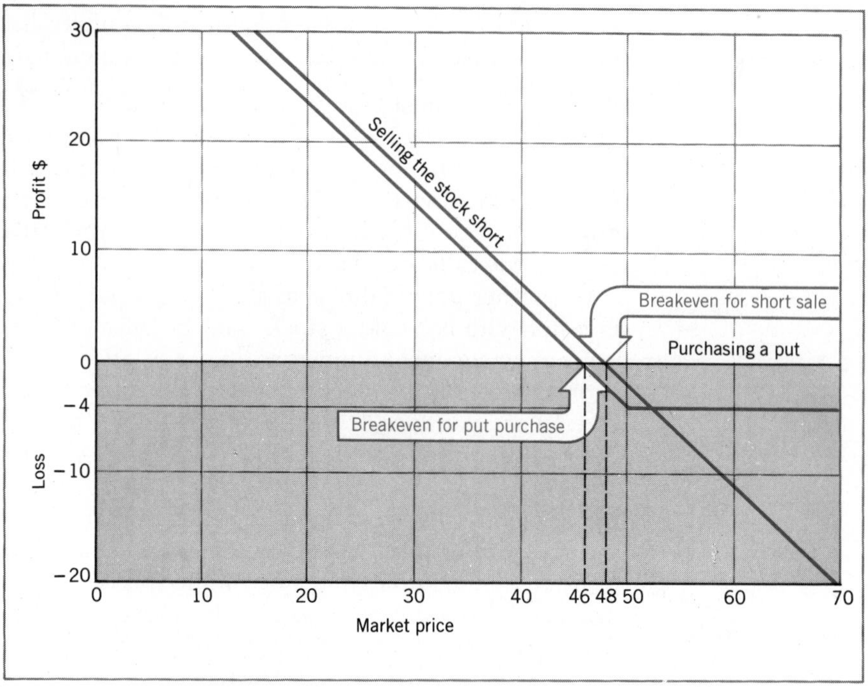

FIGURE 15-3 ***The profit and loss possibilities from buying a put versus selling short the underlying common stock.***

can be lost with a put is its premium, or price. With short selling, the losses theoretically are unlimited because the stock price could rise to any level. ▪

Put buyers, like call buyers, can maximize the leverage potential involved in a transaction. In other words, put buying is a chance to earn big profits on a relatively small investment.

Example. An investor believes the price of Dow Chemical will decline within the next four months from its current price of \$91. Based on actual prices, a four-month put with an exercise price of \$95 was available for \$6 $\frac{1}{2}$. The investor, wishing to speculate on a belief that the price will decline, could, for \$4550, either (1) sell short 100 shares of Dow—a margin deposit (at 50%) would be required—or (2) buy seven put contracts at \$6 $\frac{1}{2}$ each. Assume that the investor's judgment is correct and that Dow's price declines to \$80 three months later. The profit, as a percentage of the money invested, would be (1) for selling short = \$91 − \$80 = \$1100/\$4550 = 24% or (2) for buying puts = \$850 × 7 = \$5950/\$4550 = 131%.[18] ▪

[18]The intrinsic value of the put would be \$15 (\$95 − \$80). Subtracting the premium of \$6$\frac{1}{2}$ leaves a profit of \$8$\frac{1}{2}$ (\$850) per contract. The put could be worth more than \$15, because of any remaining time value.

Again, the purchase of puts provides leverage, which magnifies gains, but also magnifies losses. If Dow's price remained around $95 or rose, the puts would expire worthless and the total investment would be lost. The short seller would also lose in this case, but the position would not have to be closed out.

INVESTMENTS INTUITION

These examples illustrate *the great risk with options—because of their short maturity, the investor's expectations must be realized in a relatively short time*. It is not enough to be correct in one's assessments—you must be right in a relatively short period of time.

Puts also can be used to protect an investor's profit.

Example. Assume a stock owned by an investor has appreciated from $50 to $70. Perhaps the investor feels the stock price could appreciate even more, but there is concern over a market decline that may include this stock. In these circumstances, the investor could purchase a put with an exercise price of $70 and offset the lost profits should the stock price decline. This occurs when the investor exercises the put and delivers the stock already owned, receiving the exercise price of $70 ▪

Writing Options

Both individuals and institutional investors write options. A call option written against stock owned by the writer is said to be *covered*. If a writer does not own the stock, a *naked* call option is involved, since the writer may be required to deliver stock not owned if the call is exercised. A put writer who is short the stock is "covered," otherwise the put writer is "naked."

Writing Calls To write a call is to sell a call; that is, the call writer enters into a contract to sell a claim on a particular stock. If the writer owns the stock, he or she has sold a covered call; if the stock is not owned, he or she has sold a naked call.

The writer is obligated to deliver the stock at the stated exercise price if called on to do so when the holder of the call exercises it. The writer will receive the exercise price per share for the stock delivered, which could exceed the price originally paid by the writer for the stock.

Example. Assume that an investor purchased 100 shares of Syntex last year for $40 per share and this year, with the stock price at $48, writes a (covered) six-month call with an exercise price of $50. The writer receives a premium of $4. This situation is illustrated in Figure 15-4.

If called on to deliver his or her 100 shares, the investor will receive $50

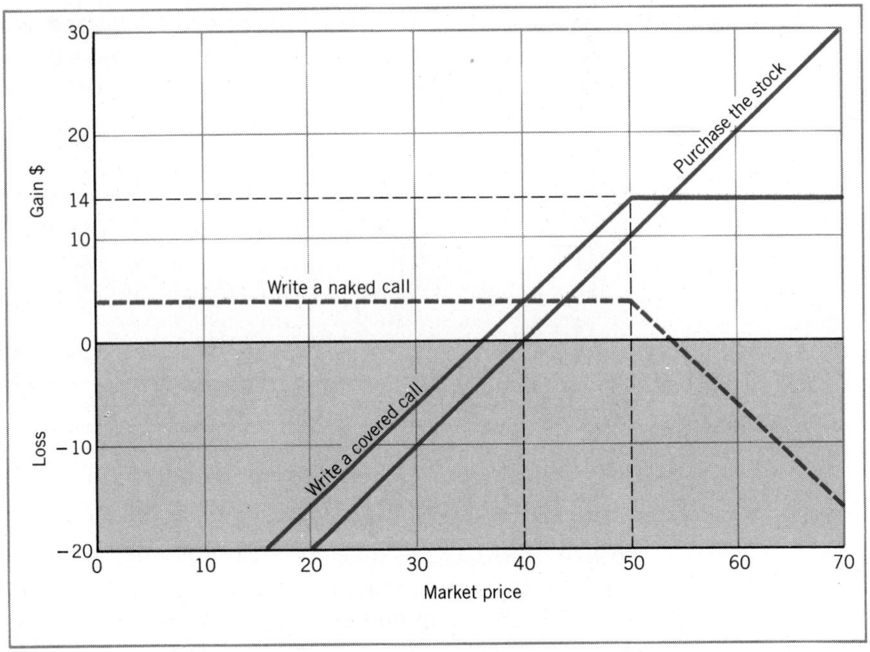

FIGURE 15-4 ***The profit and loss possibilities from writing naked calls, covered calls, and purchasing the underlying common stock.***

per share, plus the $4 premium, for a gross profit of $14 per share (since the stock was purchased at $40 per share). However, the investor gives up the additional potential gain if the price of this stock rises above $50—shown by the flat line to the right of $50 for the covered call position in Figure 15-4. If the price rises to $60 after the call is sold, for example, the investor will gross $14 per share but could have grossed $20 per share if no call had been written. ▪

Writing a naked call is also illustrated (by the broken line) in Figure 15-4. If the call is not exercised, the writer profits by the amount of the premium, $4. The naked writer's break-even point is $54. This position will be profitable if the price of the stock does not rise above this break-even point. Notice that the potential gain for the naked writer is limited to $4. The potential loss, however, is large. If the price of the stock were to rise sharply, the writer could easily lose an amount in excess of what was received in premium income.

Why write a call? The call writer may be seeking the income from the premium. Writing calls against stocks owned is often considered to be a conservative strategy that supplements the dividend income on stocks held. If the calls expire unexercised, the call writer retains the premium and the stock. The premium also provides the covered writer with some downside protection in case the price of the stock declines. The annualized premium from writing six-month calls is approximately 15% of the stock price.

Writing covered calls is one form of a *hedged position*, which with simple strategies such as those discussed here involves puts or calls and the underlying stock. In a hedged position, options are used to protect the stock against unfavorable outcomes. The writing of covered calls is the most common hedge.

Remember that the writer of a call can terminate the contract at any time before its expiration by purchasing a comparable call option. The clearing corporation cancels the position when this "closing purchase transaction" is made.

Writing Puts Writers (sellers) of puts are seeking the premium income just as call writers are. The writer obligates him or herself to purchase a stock at the specified exercise price during the life of the put contract. If stock prices decline, the put buyer may purchase the stock and exercise the put by delivering the stock to the writer, who must pay the specified price.

Note that the put writer may be obligated to purchase a stock for, say, \$50 a share when it is selling in the market for \$40 a share. This represents an immediate paper loss (less the premium received for selling the put). Also note that the put writer can cancel the obligation by purchasing an identical contract in the market. Of course, if the price of the stock has declined since the put was written, the price of the put will have increased and the writer will have to repurchase at a price higher than the premium received when the put was written.

Example: Figure 15-5 illustrates the position for the seller of a put. Using the previous figures, a six-month put is sold at an exercise price of \$50 for a

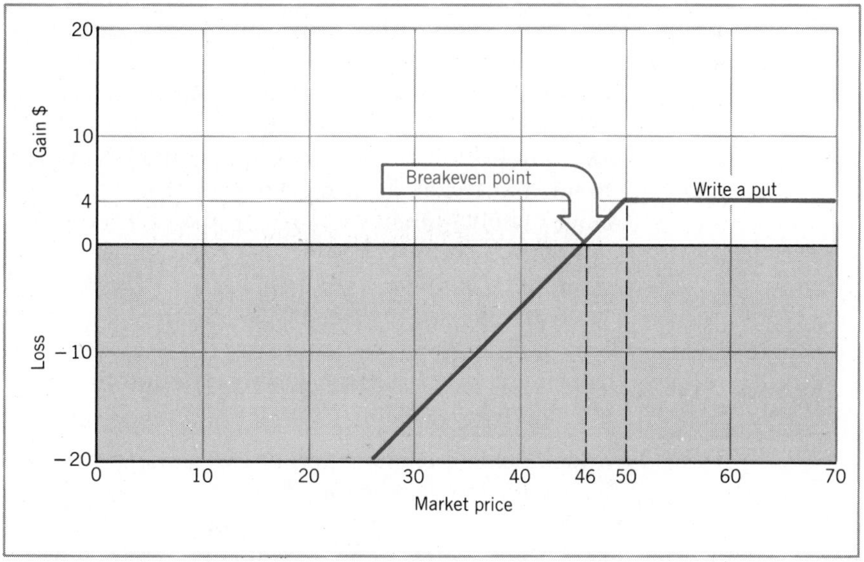

FIGURE 15-5 ***The profit and loss possibilities from writing a put.***

premium of $4. The seller of a naked put receives the premium and hopes that the stock price remains at or above the exercise price. As the price of the stock falls, the seller's position declines. The seller begins to lose money below the break-even point, which in this case is $50 − $4 = $46. Losses could be substantial if the price of the stock declines sharply. The price of the put will increase point for point as the stock price declines. Therefore, to close out this position, the put seller may have to repurchase the contract at a substantially higher price. ▪

More Sophisticated Options Strategies

Puts and calls offer investors a number of opportunities beyond the simple strategies discussed in the previous section. We shall briefly examine some combinations of options that can be written or purchased, and we shall consider the use of spreads.

Combinations of Options

Options can be mixed together in numerous ways. The typical combinations are a straddle, a strip, and a strap. A **straddle** is a combination of a put and a call on the same stock with the same exercise date and exercise price. A purchaser of a straddle believes that the underlying stock price is highly volatile and may go either up or down. Buying the straddle eliminates the need to call the market correctly. The buyer of the straddle can exercise each part separately, and therefore can profit from a large enough move either way. However, the price of the stock must rise or fall enough to equal the premium on both a put and a call; therefore, the straddle buyer must be confident that the underlying stock has a good chance of moving sharply in at least one direction.

Straddles can also be sold (written). As is always true about the two sides in an option contract, the seller believes that the underlying stock price will exhibit small volatility but could go up or down. Like the purchaser, the writer does not forecast a likely movement in one direction rather than the other.

Example. Consider a stock selling at $75 with a six-month straddle available with an exercise price of $75 and, for simplicity, call and put prices of $5 each. The seller of such a straddle is protected in the range of $65–85 (ignoring commissions). The buyers hope that the price exceeds one of these boundaries before expiration. ▪

A *strip* is a combination of two puts and a call on the same security, again with the same expiration date and exercise price. In this case, the purchaser believes the probability of a price decline exceeds the probability of a price rise and therefore wants two puts (but also wants some protection in the opposite direction). The seller obviously believes the opposite.

A *strap* is similar to a strip but combines two calls with a put. Here, of course, the purchaser believes the probability of a price increase exceeds that for a price decrease, and again, the writer expects the opposite.

Spreads

Rather than being only the buyer or the seller of various combinations of puts and calls, an investor can be both simultaneously by means of a spread. A **spread** is defined as the purchase and sale of an equivalent option varying in only one respect. Its purpose is to reduce risk in an option position, and it is a popular practice.

The two basic spreads are the *money spread* and the *time spread.* A money spread involves the purchase of a call option at one exercise price and the sale of the same-maturity option, but with a different exercise price. For example, an investor could buy an IBM January 80 call and sell an IBM January 90 call.

A time spread involves the purchase and sale of options that are identical except for expiration dates. For example, an investor could buy an IBM January 90 call and sell an IBM April 90 call.

Investors use particular spread strategies, depending on whether they are bullish or bearish.

Example. Assume you are bullish about IBM but wish to reduce the risk involved in options. IBM is selling for $84, with four-month call options available at exercise prices of $90 and $80 for $3 and $8, respectively. A bullish money spread would consist of buying the $80 call and selling the $90 call. Your net cost is now $5, which is the maximum you could lose if the calls expire worthless because the price of IBM dropped sharply. If IBM rises, you purchase the $90 call to offset the $90 call sold, resulting in a loss. However, your $80 call will be worth at least the price of the stock minus the exercise price of $80, and when this is netted against your loss on the $90 transaction, you will have a net gain. In effect, you give up some potential profit (what could have been earned on the $80 call alone) to reduce your risk (by reducing your net cost) if the stock price declines.

Option Pricing

A General Framework

In this section we shall examine the determinants of the price of a put or call. Recall that the current market price is referred to as the premium.

Special terminology is used to describe the relationship between the exercise price of the option and the current stock price. If the price of the common stock, S, exceeds the exercise price of a call, E, that call is said to be *in the money.* This means that the call has an immediate exercisable value. On the other hand, if the price of the common is less than the exercise price of a call, it is said to be *out of the money.* Finally, calls that are *near the money* are those with exercise prices slightly greater than current market price, whereas calls that are *at the money* are those with exercise prices equal to the stock price.

These same definitions also apply to puts, but in reverse. In summary,

If $S > E$, a call is in the money and a put is out of the money.

If $S < E$, a call is out of the money and a put is in the money.

If $S = E$, an option is at the money.

The price of a call option can be dichotomized in the following manner. If a call is in the money (the market price of the stock exceeds the exercise price for the call option) it has an *immediate* value equal to the difference in the two prices. This value will be designated as the **intrinsic value** of the call; it could also be referred to as the option's minimum value, which in this case is positive. If the call is out of the money (the stock price is less than the exercise price), the intrinsic value is zero; in this case, the price of the option is based on its speculative appeal. Summarizing,

$$\text{Intrinsic value of a call} = \text{Maximum (stock price} - \text{exercise price) or 0} \quad (15\text{-}1)$$

Example. Paramount common stock closed at \$58 on the day shown in Figure 15-1. This means that the 50 and 55 call options were in the money because the stock price was greater than the exercise price, whereas the other four were out of the money (and had intrinsic values of zero). The intrinsic value of the December 50 call was

$$\text{Intrinsic value of Dec. 50 call} = \$58 - \$50 = \$8$$ ▪

Puts work in reverse. If the market price of the stock is less than the exercise price of the put, the put is in the money and has an intrinsic value. Otherwise, it is out of the money and has a zero intrinsic value. Thus:

$$\text{Intrinsic value of a put} = \text{Maximum (exercise price} - \text{stock price) or 0} \quad (15\text{-}2)$$

Example. For Paramount puts, the 60, 65, 70, and 75 puts are in the money, because they are worth exercising on this particular date (ignoring transaction costs); that is, a put holder could buy the stock at the current market price and sell it to the writer at the specified exercise price. The intrinsic value of the Dec. 60 put was

$$\text{Intrinsic value of Dec. 60 put} = \$60 - \$58 = \$2$$ ▪

An option's premium almost never declines below its intrinsic value. The reason is that market arbitragers, who constantly monitor option prices for discrepancies, would purchase the options and exercise them, thus earning riskless returns. **Arbitragers** are speculators who seek to earn a return without assuming risk by constructing riskless hedges.

Option prices almost always exceed intrinsic values; the amount of excess reflects the option's potential appreciation, or **speculative premium.** Such excesses exist because buyers are willing to pay a price for potential future stock price movements. This part of the option's price reflects its time value.[19] Clearly, time has a positive value—the longer the time to expiration for the option, the more chance it has to appreciate in value. However, holding the stock price constant, options are a *wasting asset* whose value approaches intrinsic value as expiration approaches. In other words, as expiration approaches, the time value of the option declines to zero.

Example. Notice that the premiums for Paramount calls and puts in Figure 15-1 increase as maturity increases; that is, premiums increase from the November contracts to the March contracts. ▪

The speculative premium can be calculated as the difference between the option price and the intrinsic value:

$$\text{Speculative premium} = \text{Option price} - \text{Intrinsic value} \qquad (15\text{-}3)$$

Example. For the Paramount options shown in Figure 15-1:

$$\text{Speculative premium of Dec. 50 call} = \$9 - \$8 = \$1$$

$$\text{Speculative premium of Dec. 60 put} = \$5 - \$2 = \$3 \quad ▪$$

We can now understand the premium for an option as the sum of its intrinsic value and its speculative premium, or

$$\text{Premium or Option price} = \text{Intrinsic value} + \text{Speculative premium} \qquad (15\text{-}4)$$

Example. For the Paramount options:

$$\text{Premium for Dec. 50 call} = \$8 + \$1 = \$9$$

$$\text{Premium for Dec. 60 put} = \$2 + \$3 = \$5 \quad ▪$$

Notice an important point about options based on the preceeding discussion. An investor who owns a call option and wishes to acquire the underlying common stock will always find it preferable to sell the option and purchase the stock in the open market rather than exercise the option (at least if the stock pays no dividends). Why? Because otherwise, he or she will lose the speculative premium on the option.

Example. Consider the Paramount December 50 call option, with the market price of the common at $58. An investor who owned the call and

[19]The time value of a call can be calculated as the sum of the call price and the striking price less the stock price. If a call has no intrinsic value—that is, it is out of the money—its price and its time value are equal.

wanted to own Paramount common would be better off to sell the option at $9 and purchase the common for $58, for a net investment of $49. Exercising the call option, the investor would have to pay $50 per share for shares of stock worth $58 in the market, a gain of $8 per share (brokerage commissions are ignored in this example). ▪

Boundaries on Option Prices

In the previous section we learned what the premium, or price, of a put or call consists of, but we do not know why options trade at the prices they do and the range of values they can assume. In this section we shall learn about the boundaries for option prices, and in the next section we shall discuss the exact determinants of options prices.

The value of an option must be related to the value of the underlying security. The basic relationship is most easy to understand by considering an option just prior to expiration, when there is no speculative premium. If the option is not exercised, it will expire immediately, leaving the option with no value. Obviously, investors will exercise it only if it is worth exercising (if it is in the money).

Figure 15-6 (*a*) shows the values of call and put options at expiration, assuming a strike price of $50. At expiration, a call must have a value that is the maximum of 0 or its intrinsic value. Therefore, the line representing the value of a call option must be horizontal at $0 up to the exercise price and then rise as the stock price exceeds the exercise price. Above $50 the call price must equal the difference between the stock price and the exercise price.

For puts the situation is reversed. At expiration, a put must have a value that is the maximum of 0 or its intrinsic value. Therefore, the line in Figure 15-6(*a*) representing the value of a put option must be horizontal

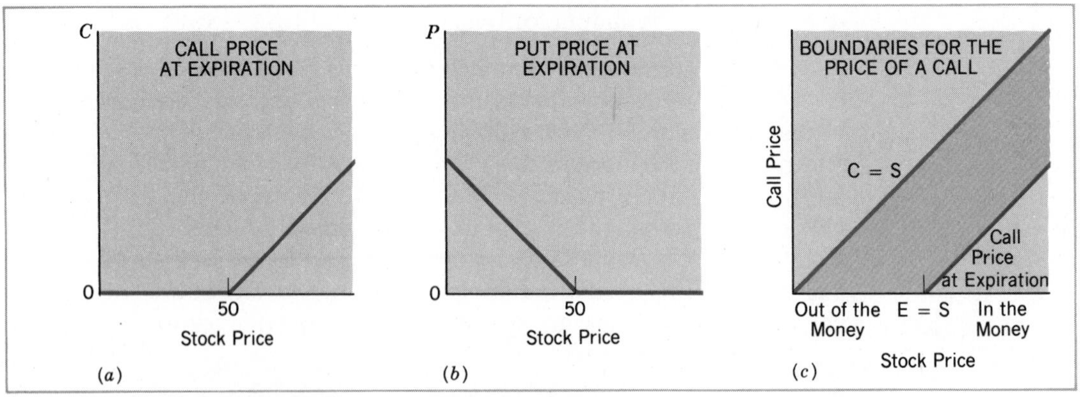

FIGURE 15-6 ***Determining option prices.***

beyond the exercise price. Below $50 the put price must equal the difference between the exercise price and the stock price.

What is the maximum price an option can assume? To see this think of a call. Since the call's value is derived from its ability to be converted into the underlying stock, it can never sell for more than the stock itself. It would not make sense to pay more for a call on one share of stock than the price of the stock itself. Therefore, the maximum price for a call is the price of the underlying stock.

Based on the preceding, we can establish the upper and lower boundaries for the price of a call option as shown in Figure 15-6(*b*). The upper boundary is a 45° line from the origin representing a call price equal to the stock price.[20] The lower boundary is the price of the option at expiration, which must be either zero or its in-the-money value. This is represented by the 45° line starting at the exercise price. The lower boundary also can be interpreted as the value of the call at the moment the call is exercised, or its intrinsic value.

The analysis in Figure 15-6(*b*) establishes boundaries for the price of a call. We can make some additional general statements, such as that a call with a lower exercise price must sell at a higher price than an identical call with a higher exercise price and that, other things equal, the greater the maturity, the greater the value of the call. However, to understand fully the price of a call option, we must use a formal model of call prices, which is done next.

The Black–Scholes Model

Fischer Black and Myron Scholes have developed a model for the valuation of call options that is widely accepted and used in the investments community.[21] The formula itself is mathematical and appears to be very complex; however, it is widely available on calculators and computers. Numerous investors estimate the value of calls using the **Black–Scholes model.**

The Black–Scholes model uses five variables to value the call option of a *non–dividend-paying stock.* These five variables, all but the last of which are directly observable in the market, are as follows:

1. The price of the underlying stock.
2. The exercise price of the option.
3. The time remaining to the expiration of the option.
4. The interest rate.
5. The variability of the underlying stock price.

---

[20]Think of this as a call with a zero exercise price and an infinite maturity.

[21]F. Black and M. Scholes, "The Pricing of Options and Corporate Liabilities," *Journal of Political Economy,* Vol. 81 (May–June 1973), pp. 637–654.

The first two variables are of obvious importance in valuing an option, because, as noted before, they determine the option's intrinsic value—whether it is in the money or not. If it is out of the money, it has only a time value based on the speculative interest in the stock.

Time to expiration is also an important factor in the value of an option, because, as noted, value increases with maturity, other things being equal. The relationship between time and value is not proportional, however. The time value of an option is greatest when the market price and the exercise price are equal. If the option is already in the money, a rise in the stock price will not result in the same percentage gain in the option price that would occur in the previous situation. And finally, for out-of-the-money options, part of the time remaining will be used for the price of the stock to reach the exercise price.

The interest rate affects option values because of the opportunity cost involved. Buying an option is a substitute to some degree for buying on margin, on which interest must be paid. The higher interest rates are, therefore, the more interest cost is saved by the use of options. This adds to the value of the option and results in a direct relationship between the value of a call option and interest rates in the market.

The last factor, and the only one not directly observable in the marketplace, is the variability in the price of the underlying stock. Volatility is associated with risk, as discussed in Chapter 5. The greater the risk, the *higher* the price of a call option because of the increased potential for the stock to move up. Therefore, a positive relation exists between the variability of the stock and the value of the call option.

The Black–Scholes option pricing formula can be expressed as[22]

$$\text{CP} = \text{CMP}[N(d_1)] - \frac{\text{EP}}{e^{rt}}[N(d_2)] \qquad (15\text{-}5)$$

where

CP = the price of the call option
CMP = current market price of the underlying common stock
$N(d)_1$ = the cumulative density function of d_1
EP = the exercise price of the option
e = the base of natural logarithms = approximately 2.71828
r = the continuously compounded riskless rate of interest on an annual basis
t = the time remaining before the expiration date of the option, expressed as a fraction of a year
$N(d_2)$ = the cumulative density function of d_2

[22]This model applies to non–dividend-paying stocks.

To find d_1 and d_2, it is necessary to solve these equations:

$$d_1 = \frac{\ln(\text{CMP/EP}) + (r + 0.5\sigma^2)t}{(\sigma[(t)^{1/2}])} \tag{15-6}$$

$$d_2 = d_1 - (\sigma[(t)^{1/2}]) \tag{15-7}$$

where

ln(CMP/EP) = the natural log of (CMP/EP)
σ = the standard deviation of the annual rate of return on the underlying common stock

The five variables previously listed are needed as inputs. Variables 1–4 are immediately available. Variable 5 is not, however, because what is needed is the variability *expected* to occur in the stock's rate of return. Although historical data on stock returns are typically used to estimate this standard deviation, variability does change over time. A formula user should try to incorporate expected changes in the variability when using historical data. To do this, the user should examine any likely changes in either the market's or the individual stock's variability.

Variables 1–3 should be identical for a given stock for everyone using the Black–Scholes model. Variable 4 should be identical or very close among formula users, depending on the exact proxy used for the riskless rate of interest. Variable 5 will vary among users, providing different option values. Empirical studies have shown that estimates of the variance obtained from other than historical data are more valuable than the estimates based on historical data. Since the price of an option can be observed at any time, it is possible to solve the Black–Scholes formula for the implied standard deviation of the stock's return. Henry Latané and Richard Rendleman found that better forecasts of the actual standard deviation could be obtained by preparing forecasts from the model itself.[23]

Example. The following is an example of the use of the Black–Scholes option pricing formula:

Assume

CMP = \$40
EP = \$45
r = 0.10
t = 0.5 (6 months)
σ = 0.45

[23]H. Latané and R. Rendleman, Jr., "Standard Deviations of Stock Price Ratios Implied in Option Prices," *The Journal of Finance*, May 1976, pp. 369–382.

Step 1: *Solve for d_1.*

$$d_1 = \frac{\ln(40/45) + [(0.10 + 0.5(0.45)^2]\,0.5}{0.45\,[(0.5)^{1/2}]}$$

$$= \frac{-0.1178 + 0.1006}{0.3182}$$

$$= -0.054$$

Step 2: *Use a cumulative probability distribution table to find the value of $N(d_1)$.*

$$N(d_1) = 0.4801$$

where $d_1 = -0.054$

Step 3: *Find d_2.*

$$d_2 = -0.054 - [0.45((0.5)^{1/2})]$$
$$= -0.372$$

Step 4: *Find $N(d_2)$.*

$$N(d_2) \approx 0.3557$$

Step 5: *Solve for CP.*

$$\text{CP} = \text{CMP}[0.4801] - \text{EP}[\text{antilog} - (0.1)(0.5)][0.3557]$$

$$= 19.20 - 45(0.9512)(0.3557)$$

$$= 19.20 - 15.23$$

$$= \$3.97$$

The theoretical (fair) value of the option, according to the Black–Scholes formula, is $3.97. If the current market price of the option is greater than the theoretical value, it is overpriced; if less, it is underpriced. ▪

INVESTMENT CALCULATIONS

Using *The Investment Calculator,* choose "Option Pricing—Black–Scholes" from the main menu. Enter, in order, the current market price of the stock, $40; the exercise price, $45, the interest rate, 0.10; the time to expiration, 183 days (which is 0.5 years); and the standard deviation, 0.45. The program calculates the price of this call as $3.96.

Hedge Ratios. A key concept with options is their use as a hedging device. Although risky assets themselves, options can be used to control risk. In particular, options can be used to control the riskiness inherent in common stocks.

To hedge a long stock position with options, an investor would write one call option while simultaneously buying a certain number of shares of common. This number is given by the **hedge ratio,** which is $N(d_1)$ from the Black–Scholes model.[24] The hedge ratio for an option, commonly referred to as the option's *delta,* indicates the change in the price of the option for a $1 change in the price of the common. Since the hedge ratio with a call option is $N(d_1)$, for a put option it is $N(d_1) - 1$.

Example. In the preceding example, $N(d_1)$ was 0.48; therefore, for every call option written, 0.48 shares of the common would be required to hedge the position. For a standard 100-share option contract, 48 shares of stock would be required. A $1 increase in the price of the stock should produce a $0.48 change in the price of the option. The loss on the call options written is 100 × $0.48, or $48, which is offset by the gain on the 48 shares of stock of $48. A perfectly hedged position leaves total wealth unchanged. ▪

The fact that hedge ratios are less than 1.0 indicates that option values change with stock prices on less than a one-for-one basis. That is, *dollar movements* in options prices are smaller than dollar movements in the underlying stock; however, *percentage* price changes on the option generally will be greater than percentage price changes on the stock.

Put Prices

To establish put prices, we can take advantage of the principle of put–call parity.

The **put–call parity** principle expresses the relationship between the prices of puts and calls on the same stock that must hold if arbitrage is to be ruled out. In other words, unless the price of the put and the call bear a certain relationship to each other, there will be opportunities for earning riskless profits (arbitrage). The put–call parity can be expressed as

$$\text{Price of put} = \text{EP}/(e^{rt}) - \text{CMP} + \text{CP} \qquad (15\text{-}8)$$

where all terms are as defined before.

Example. Use the information for the call given earlier. Since the Black–Scholes model uses continuous interest, the discount factor is expressed in

---

[24]Technically, the hedge ratio is the slope of the functional relationship between the value of the option (vertical axis) and the value of the stock (horizontal axis), evaluated at the current stock price.

continuous form.[25] It is equal to e^{rt}, or $e^{.10(.5)}$. Using a calculator, this value is 1.051. Therefore,

$$\text{Price of put} = 45/1.051 - 40 + 3.96 = \$6.78 \quad ▪$$

INVESTMENT CALCULATIONS

Using *The Investment Calculator,* the price of the put is calculated as $6.76.

The Status of Option Pricing Models

Development of the Black–Scholes (BS) model was a very significant event and has had a major impact on all options investors, both directly and indirectly. This model has been the basis of extensive empirical investigations into how options are priced. Other models have subsequently been developed. Since the BS model can be used to value options, providing investors with an estimate of the option's intrinsic value, the state of option pricing theory is important.

Although the numerous studies that have been conducted offer general support for the BS model, deficiencies have been noted. Furthermore, the results of these studies have not always been consistent. For example, Fischer Black found that the BS model underpriced deep out-of-the-money call options (and overpriced deep-in-the-money calls), whereas James MacBeth and Larry Merville reported biases that were exactly the opposite.[26] Gultekin et al. tested the BS model and found results in agreement with Black and exactly the opposite of MacBeth and Merville.[27]

A reasonable consensus of the options studies that have been conducted is desirable. Dan Galai, in a summary of the empirical tests of option-pricing models, concludes the following[28]:

1. The BS model works well for at-the-money options, although unexplained deviations still occur.

---

[25]The value e^k is the equivalent of $(1 + r)$ in continuous compounding. If r is 5%, the value of e^k is $e^{.05}$, or 1.051.

[26]See Fischer Black, "Fact and Fantasy in the Use of Options," *Financial Analysts Journal,* July–August 1975, pp. 36–72; J. MacBeth and L. J. Merville, "An Empirical Examination of the Black–Scholes Call Option Pricing Model," *The Journal of Finance,* December 1979, pp. 1173–1186 and MacBeth and Merville, "Tests of the Black–Scholes and Cox Call Option Valuation Models," *The Journal of Finance,* May 1980, pp. 285–301.

[27]See N. Gultekin, R. Rogalski, and S. Tinic, "Option Pricing Model Estimates: Some Empirical Results," *Financial Management,* Spring 1982, pp. 58–69.

[28]See Dan Galai, "A Survey of Empirical Tests of Option-Pricing Models," in Menachem Brenner, ed., *Option Pricing: Theory and Applications* (Lexington, Mass.: Lexington Books, 1983), pp. 45–80.

2. The biases noted earlier for deep-in-the-money and deep-out-of-the-money options do exist.
3. No other model consistently does better than the BS model in explaining actual option prices.

The deviations and biases that appear to remain in option pricing models may derive from several sources. Deviations of model prices from market prices appear to be significantly related to the extent to which options are in or out of the money. William Sterk has presented evidence suggesting that this in- and out-of-the-money bias depends on the magnitude of the dividend on the underlying stocks studied.[29] Another problem is that the true stock price volatility is unobservable.

In summary, the best evidence to date, taken together, indicates that although some statistically significant biases may exist in the prices generated by the option pricing models, the validity of these models remains intact. What are the implications of this for market efficiency?

Market Efficiency and Investor Returns The option pricing models can be used to test for the possibility of trading rules to exploit any economically viable biases in option prices. Continuing with his summary of the empirical tests of option-pricing models, Galai concludes that, although actual prices do deviate from model predictions, the options market appears to be quite efficient; that is, traders do not appear able consistently to earn above-normal profits after commissions and taxes.[30] Galai believes that the studies indicate that non–exchange members are unable as well to earn above-normal profits consistently.

An Investor's Perspective on Puts and Calls

What Puts and Calls Mean to Investors

We examined earlier some simple strategies using puts and calls and briefly considered some more sophisticated strategies. It is important for investors to have an overall perspective on puts and calls and consider what they really add to the investment process.

Options contracts are important to investors in terms of the two dimensions of every investment decision that we have emphasized throughout this book—the return and risk from an asset or portfolio. Furthermore, the return–risk modification properties of puts and calls vary significantly from other derivative instruments such as futures contracts, which we shall consider in Chapter 17.

---

[29]See William E. Sterk, "Option Pricing: Dividends and the In- and Out-of-the-Money Bias," *Financial Management*, Winter 1983, pp. 47–53.
[30]Galai, "A Survey of Empirical Tests," p. 69.

The important point about options and portfolio return and risk is that the impact of options is not symmetrical. As we saw when we discussed basic strategies (Figures 15-2–15-5), the use of options changes the potential distribution of returns. For example, Figure 15-2 shows that unlike the purchase of a stock, the purchase of a call results in a horizontal segment for the line representing profit and loss possibilities. Another way to say this is that the distribution is *truncated,* because in the case of buying a call the most the investor can lose is the premium, regardless of what happens to the stock price. The same is true when purchasing a put—relative to the profit–loss line (Figure 15-3) when selling short, the distribution of possible profits and losses from purchasing a put is truncated—if the stock price continues to rise, adversely affecting the investor, the most that can be lost from the put purchase is the premium.

Purchasing call options is like purchasing insurance. A call represents insurance on the underlying stock. If the price of the stock goes up, the value of the call does also, but if the price declines, the call owner is insured against losses beyond the premium paid for the call. The premium, or price paid for the call, is the cost of the insurance.

A put also represents insurance. To see this, consider the strategy known as a *protective put.* In this situation, an investor buys a stock and simultaneously buys a put on that stock. This protects the investor against a sudden sharp drop in the price of the stock. The cost of this insurance is the cost of the put. Obviously, if the price of the stock rises, which is what the investor is betting, the profits will be less than they otherwise would be by the amount of the put price.

Portfolio Insurance. The potential return/risk modification properties of options, and particularly the insurance aspects discussed previously, are well illustrated by the technique known as **portfolio insurance.** This term refers to investment strategies designed to hedge portfolio positions by providing a minimum return on the portfolio while simultaneously providing an opportunity for the portfolio to participate in rising security prices. This asset management technique became very popular in the 1980s, with many billions of dollars of assets insured.

There are several methods of insuring a portfolio, including options, futures, and the creation of "synthetic options." In practice, it is common to use futures contracts on market indexes (as discussed in Chapter 17). However, in principle, options can be used in portfolio insurance strategies, and their use illustrates the basic nature of a hedge.

The idea behind portfolio insurance with regard to options is simple. A protective put can be purchased that allows the portfolio to be sold for an amount sufficient to provide the minimum return. The remaining portfolio funds are invested in the usual manner. The protective put provides insurance for the portfolio by limiting losses in the event stock prices decline.

The portfolio's value at the end of the period must equal or exceed the exercise price of the put.

Example. An investor wishes to ensure a minimum return of 5 percent. For simplicity, we assume the investor starts with \$1.00.[31] One unit of a stock market index sells for \$0.9097 whereas a European put (exercisable only at expiration) on this index can be bought for \$0.0903. This put has a strike price of \$1.05. The investor has used portfolio insurance to ensure a 5 percent minimum return. If the value of the stock index exceeds \$1.05 by the end of the investing period, the investor is ahead that much and allows the put to expire worthless. If the value of the index is less than \$1.05 by the end of the period, the investor can exercise the option and sell the stock index for \$1.05, thereby earning the required 5-percent minimum return on the initial investment of \$1.00. Portfolio insurance has provided protection against the downside while allowing the investor to participate in stock price advances. ▪

This example illustrates the conceptual use of puts in portfolio insurance strategies. The same outcome could be achieved by a strategy combining puts and fixed-income investment. In practice, however, puts and calls are not used to insure portfolios because those typically available to investors are American and not European. Being exercisable at any time makes American options not only more valuable than corresponding European options but also much more costly for portfolio insurance purposes. Furthermore, it generally is not possible to find puts and calls with the exact time to expiration, exercise price, and so on that matches a particular portfolio.

It should also be noted that portfolio insurance is not costless. The first cost is the cost of the option itself. In our example, the put cost \$0.0903. Obviously, if stocks advance and the put expires worthless, the cost of the put has been lost relative to an uninsured strategy. This can be thought of as the *insurance premium*. The other cost is an *opportunity cost*. An investor who places 100 percent of investment funds in the stock index would participate fully in any market rise. In our example, the insured investor would participate in only 90.97 percent of any market rise.

The Evolutionary Use of Options

Puts and calls on organized options exchanges have been available to investors since 1973. The creation of organized options exchanges has made puts and calls a viable investment alternative for many investors. The clearinghouse guarantees the performance of every option contract, all of whose

[31]This example is based on Richard J. Rendleman and Richard W. McEnally, "Assessing the Costs of Portfolio Insurance," *Financial Analysts Journal* (May–June 1987), pp. 27–37.

key parameters are standardized. Most important, an active secondary market, which did not exist prior to 1973, is provided. Thus, investors are assured of being able to trade puts and calls on a continuous basis during the life of the option.

Puts and calls traded on organized exchanges have been a major success. By the beginning of 1990 there were more than 650 stocks on which options could be bought and sold. Trading volume has expanded tremendously. The CBOE has seen its market share decline somewhat as the new exchanges began trading. However, it still handles a significant percentage of total trades.

Puts and calls have been popular with individual investors since the beginning of CBOE trading, although the manner in which they are viewed has changed somewhat. At first, options were viewed more or less as speculative instruments. They often were brought for their leverage possibilities. Covered option writing was used to enhance portfolio yields. Although these uses continue today, by the 1980s options had proved themselves as a respectable investment alternative and had begun to attract institutional attention. Changes in regulations occurred that, in effect, encouraged institutional interest in options. Pension funds, insurance companies, and banks began to receive clearance for the trading of options, provided that such trading met the guidelines under which they normally operate.

Institutions have begun to hire "portfolio options strategists" to assist them in trading options. One use of options for institutions is to hedge their portfolios by writing calls against stocks in the portfolio that have appreciated significantly. The institutions doing this insure themselves against a decline in prices equal to the income earned from writing the calls; meanwhile, the holdings continue to pay dividends and represent long-term investments in the companies.

Thus, in the 1990s options are increasingly valued for their use in strategic portfolio management. Options allow investors to create strategies that expand the set of outcomes beyond what could be achieved in the absence of options. In other words, investors and investment managers sometimes need the nonsymmetric distributions of returns that options can provide. Options strategies increase the set of contingencies that can be provided for, as the following example illustrates.[32]

Example. A portfolio manager wishes to ensure some guaranteed minimum return while having some chance at the upward return potential. One illustration of this is a pension fund that faces a minimum actuarial payoff but still wishes to participate in the upside potential of a portfolio.

---

[32]This discussion is based on Richard Bookstaber, "The Use of Options in Performance Structuring," *Journal of Portfolio Management*, Summer 1985, pp. 36–37.

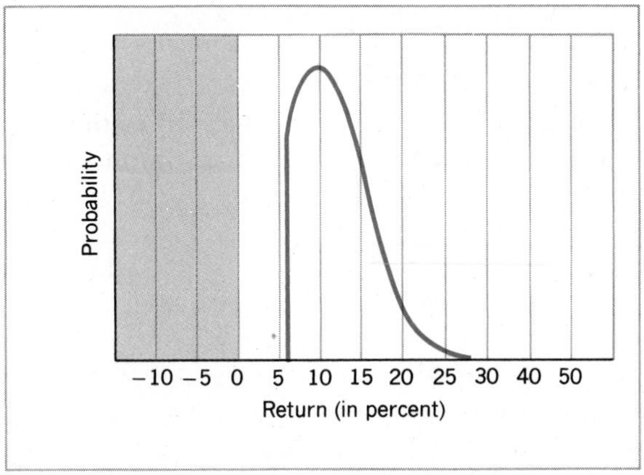

FIGURE 15-7 ***The return distribution that might be preferred by the portfolio manager. (The probability of a large loss is eliminated.)***
Source: Richard Bookstaber, "The Use of Options in Performance Structuring," *The Journal of Portfolio Management*, Summer 1985, p. 37. Reprinted by permission.

This situation, illustrated by Figure 15-7, cannot be handled by conventional portfolio management techniques. ▪

Stock Index Options and Interest Rate Options

The newest innovation in the options market are **stock index options** and **interest rate options.** Because most investor interest is in stock index options, we shall confine our discussion to them after listing the interest rate options that are available.

Primary interest rate options include options traded on the Chicago Board Options Exchange on Treasury notes and on Treasury bonds, on short-term interest rates, and on long-term interest rates. Other interest rate options are available on Treasury bills and on mortgage-backed securities.

The Basics of Stock Index Options

In mid-1990, stock index options were available on the following broad market indexes: the S&P 100 Index, the S&P 500 Index, the New York Stock Exchange Index, the Major Market Index, the Value Line Index, the Financial News Composite Index, the International Market Index, the Institutional Index, and the National OTC Index. Index options were also available on various industry subindexes, including the Computer Technology Index, the Oil Index, the Utilities Index and the Gold/Silver Index. In additional, index options were available for an Institutional Index and a NYSE Beta Index.[33]

In 1986 the S&P 500 Index option was converted to a European-style contract, meaning it cannot be exercised until the contract expires. The predictable exercise date appeals to institutional investors when they attempt to hedge their portfolios against losses in volatile markets. Hedgers using standard index options may find their hedges exercised before the contracts expire, thereby giving an edge to the European-style contracts. The Institutional Index is also European-style.

Stock index options enable investors to trade on general stock market movements or industries in the same way that they can trade on individual stocks. Thus, an investor who is bullish on the market can buy a call on a market index, and an investor who is bearish on the overall market can buy a put. The investor need only make a market decision, not an industry or an individual stock decision.

Overall, stock index options are similar to the options listed on the options exchanges. As usual, the exercise price and the expiration date are uniformly established. Investors buy and sell them through their broker in the normal manner. The major difference in the two is that, unlike stock options, which require the actual delivery of the stock upon exercise, buyers of index options receive cash from the seller upon exercise of the contract. The amount of cash settlement is equal to the difference between the closing price of the index and the strike price of the option multiplied by a specified dollar amount.

Index option information is read in the same manner as that for stock options. Figure 15-8 shows an example of the information carried in *The Wall Street Journal* for the S&P 500 Index option.

Example. To illustrate the cash settlement procedure used for index options, assume that an investor holds a NYSE Index option with a strike price of 135. This investor decides to exercise the option on a day that the NYSE Composite Index closes at 139.5. The investor will receive a cash payment from the assigned writer equal to $100 multiplied by the difference between the option's strike price and the closing value of the index, or

$$\begin{array}{lcl} \text{NYSE Composite Index close} & = & 139.5 \\ \text{NYSE Index option strike price} & = & \underline{135.0} \\ & & 4.5 \times \$100 = \$450 \end{array}$$

Note the use of the $100 multiplier for the NYSE Index option. The multiplier performs a function similar to the unit of trading (100 shares) for

[33]The Institutional Index is based on an index of 75 stocks most widely held by institutional investors. The Beta Index is a price-weighted index designed to track the performance of 100 of the most volatile stocks traded on the NYSE.

Following is an example of S&P 500 index option prices as they appear in the financial tables of the *Wall Street Journal.*

S&P 500 INDEX

Strike	Calls—Last			Puts—Last		
Price	Jun	Jul	Sep	Jun	Jul	Sep
220	...	$\frac{1}{4}$	...	...	...	...
225	...	...	$17\frac{7}{8}$	$\frac{1}{16}$	...	$2\frac{13}{16}$
230	$8\frac{7}{8}$	$10\frac{3}{8}$	...	$\frac{5}{16}$	$1\frac{11}{16}$	$4\frac{1}{4}$
235	$4\frac{1}{2}$	$7\frac{3}{8}$	...	$1\frac{1}{16}$	$2\frac{1}{2}$	$5\frac{7}{8}$
240	$2\frac{1}{8}$	$4\frac{3}{8}$	$8\frac{3}{8}$	$3\frac{3}{8}$	5	8
245	$\frac{7}{8}$	$2\frac{15}{16}$	$4\frac{7}{8}$	$7\frac{5}{8}$	$8\frac{1}{8}$	...
250	$\frac{1}{4}$	$1\frac{11}{16}$	...	$12\frac{1}{8}$	...	...
255	$\frac{1}{16}$	$\frac{3}{4}$	$3\frac{3}{4}$	...	...	...

Total call volume 3,338 — Total call open int. 51,270

Total put volume 3,741 — Total put open int. 52,239

The index: High 240.08; Low 238.23. Close 239.58, −0.38

(Callouts: 1 — Sep; 2 — Last; 3 — Strike Price; 4 — Total call/put volume; 5 — Total call/put open int.; 6 — The index.)

1. *Expiration months.* SPX options trade in the two nearby months plus three months from the March–June–September–December cycle.
2. *Last.* The option's last sale price (premium per share). Option premiums are expressed in terms of dollars and fractions per unit of the index. Each point represents \$100. The minimum fraction is $\frac{1}{16}$ (\$6.25) for series trading below 3, and $\frac{1}{8}$ (\$12.50) for all other series.
3. *Strike price.* The price at which the index may be bought or sold.
4. *Volume.* Number of call and put options traded. Total volume is the sum of calls and puts.
5. *Open interest.* The number of option contracts that were open at the end of the previous trading season. Each unit represents a buyer and a seller who still hold exercisable contracts. Total open interest is the sum of calls and puts.
6. *Index values.* The day's high, low and closing index values, with the daily price change.

S&P 500 options are European-style options; they are exercised only at expiration. At expiration the value of an S&P 500 call is the amount by which the index exceeds the strike price. The value of a put is the amount the index is below the put's strike price. If the index closes below the strike price of an expiring call, or above the strike price of an expiring put, the option expires worthless.

Suppose, for example, that the index closes at 224.50 on the last trading day for

FIGURE 15-8 ***Understanding index option information.***
Source: Reprinted from *A Basic Guide to SPX,* © 1986. Chicago Board Options Exchange Inc., by permission.

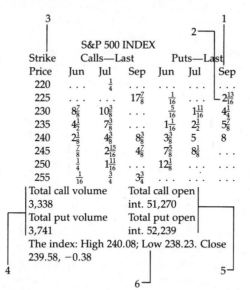

September SPX options. A September 220 call would have an in-the-money value of 4.50—the closing index price of 224.50 minus the call strike price of 220, or \$450 (4.50 × \$100). A September 220 put under these same circumstances would expire worthless.

The principal difference between equity and index options is *cash settlement* upon exercise. The exercise of an equity option requires delivery of the underlying security. With S&P 500 index options, only cash changes hands. Exercise of an index option gives the holder the in-the-money cash difference between the exercise price multiplied by \$100 and the closing index value multiplied by \$100.

FIGURE 15-8 ***(Continued)***

a stock option in that it determines the total dollar value of the cash settlement. Since options on different indexes may have different multipliers, it is important to know the multiplier for the stock index being used.

Strategies with Stock Index Options

The strategies with index options are similar to those for individual stock options. Investors expecting a market rise buy calls, and investors expecting a market decline buy puts. The maximum losses from these two strategies—the premiums—are known at the outset of the transaction. The potential gains can be large because of the leverage involved with options.

Example. In September, an investor expects the stock market to rise strongly over the next two or three months. This investor decides to purchase a NYSE Index November 130 call, currently selling for $3\frac{1}{2}$, on a day when the NYSE Index closed at 129.5. Assume that the market rises as expected by the investor to a mid-November level of 139.86 (an 8% increase). The investor could exercise the option and receive a cash settlement equal to the difference between the index close (139.86) and the exercise price of 130, multiplied by \$100, or[34]

139.86 NYSE Index close
130.00 Call exercise price
9.86 × \$100 = \$986

▪

The leverage offered by index options is illustrated in this example by the fact that an 8% rise in the index leads to a 182% profit on the option position [(\$986 − \$350)/\$350] = 181.7%]. Obviously, leverage can, and often does, work against an investor. If the market declined or remained flat, the

[34]Before exercising, the investor should determine if a better price could be obtained by selling the option.

entire option premium of $350 could be lost. As with any option, however, the investor has a limited loss of known amount—the premium paid.

Investors can use stock index options to hedge their positions. For example, an investor who owns a diversified portfolio of stocks may be unwilling to liquidate his or her portfolio but is concerned about a near-term market decline. Buying a put on a market index will provide some protection to the investor in the event of a market decline; in effect, the investor is purchasing a form of market insurance. The losses on the portfolio holdings will be partially offset by the gains on the put. If the market rises, the investor loses the premium paid but gains with the portfolio holdings. A problem arises, however, in that the portfolio holdings and the market index are unlikely to be a perfect match. The effectiveness of this hedge will depend upon the similarity between the two.

Example. Assume an investor has a portfolio of NYSE common stocks currently worth $39,000. It is October and this investor is concerned about a market decline over the next couple of months. The NYSE Index is currently at 130, and a NYSE Index December 130 put is available for 3. In an attempt to protect the portfolio's profits against a market decline, the investor purchases three of these puts, which represent an aggregate exercise price of $39,000 (130 × 100 × 3 = $39,000).[35]

Assume that the market declines 10% by mid-December. If the NYSE Index is 117 at that point,

$$\begin{aligned} \text{Put exercise price} &= 130 \\ \text{NYSE Index price} &= \underline{117} \\ & \quad 13 \times \$100 \times 3\text{ (puts)} = \$3900 \end{aligned}$$

If the value of the investor's portfolio declines exactly 10%, the loss on the portfolio of $3900 would be exactly offset by the total gain on the three put contracts of $3900. It is important to note, however, that a particular portfolio's value may decline more or less than the overall market as represented by one of the market indexes such as the NYSE Composite Index. The value of a particular portfolio may decline less or more than the change in the index.

As before, if the option is held to expiration and a market decline (of a significant amount) does not occur, the investor will lose the entire premium paid for the put(s). In our example, the investor could lose the entire $900 paid for the three puts. This could be viewed as the cost of obtaining "market insurance." ▪

Stock index options can be useful to institutional investors (or individuals) who do not have funds available immediately for investment but antici-

[35]The exercise value of an index option, like any stock option, is equal to 100 (shares) multiplied by the exercise price.

pate a market rise. Buying calls will allow such investors to take advantage of the rise in prices if it does occur. Of course, the premium could be lost if the anticipations are incorrect.

Investors can sell (write) index options, either to speculate or to hedge their positions. As we saw in the case of individual options, however, the risk can be large. If the seller is correct in his or her beliefs, the profit is limited to the amount of the premium; if incorrect, the seller faces potential losses far in excess of the premiums received from selling the options. It is impractical (or impossible) to write a completely covered stock index option because of the difficulty of owning a portfolio that exactly matches the index at all points in time. Although the writer of an individual stock call option can deliver the stock if the option is exercised, the writer of a stock index call option that is exercised must settle in cash and cannot be certain that gains in the stock portfolio will *fully* offset losses on the index option.[36]

The Popularity of Stock Index Options

Stock index options appeal to speculators because of the leverage they offer. A change in the underlying index of less than 1% can result in a change in the value of the contract of 15% or more. Given the increased volatility in the financial markets in recent years, investors can experience rapid changes in the value of their positions.

Introduced in 1983, stock index options quickly became the fastest-growing investment in the United States. Much of the initial value was accounted for by professional speculators and trading firms. As familiarity with index options increased, individual investors assumed a larger role in this market.

Summary

- Equity-derivative securities consist of puts and calls, created by investors, and warrants and convertible securities, created by corporations.
- A call (put) is an option to buy (sell) 100 shares of a particular stock at a stated price any time before a specified expiration date. The seller receives a premium for selling either of these options, and the buyer pays the premium.
- Advantages of options include a smaller investment than transacting in the stock itself, knowing the maximum loss in advance, leverage, and an expansion of the opportunity set available to investors.
- Buyers of calls expect the underlying stock to perform in the opposite

[36]Writers of index options are notified of their obligation to make a cash settlement on the business day following the day of exercise.

direction from the expectations of put buyers. Writers of each instrument have opposite expectations from the buyers.

- The basic strategies for options involve a call writer and a put buyer expecting the underlying stock price to decline, whereas the call buyer and the put writer expect it to rise. Options may also be used to hedge against a portfolio position by establishing an opposite position in options on that stock.
- More sophisticated options strategies include combinations of options, such as strips, straps, and straddles and spreads which include money spreads and time spreads.
- Options have an intrinsic value ranging from $0 to the "in the money" value. Most sell for more than this, representing a speculative premium.
- According to the Black–Scholes option valuation model, value is a function of the price of the stock, the exercise price of the option, time to maturity, the interest rate, and the volatility of the underlying stock.
- The available empirical evidence seems to suggest that the options market is efficient, with trading rules unable to exploit any biases that exist in the Black–Scholes or other options pricing models.
- Interest rate options and stock index options are available to investors.
- Stock index options are a popular innovation in the options area that allows investors to buy puts and calls on broad stock market indexes and industry subindexes.
- The major distinction with these option contracts is that settlement is in cash.
- In effect, stock index options allow investors to make only a market decision and/or to purchase a form of market insurance.
- The strategies with index options are similar to those for individual stock options. Investors can both hedge and speculate.

Key Words

Arbitragers
Black–Scholes model
Call
Equity–derivative securities
Expiration date
Exercise (strike) price
Hedge ratio
Interest rate options
Intrinsic value
Margin option premium
Options
Options clearing corporation (OCC)
Put
Put–call parity
Speculative premium
Spread
Stock index options
Straddle

Questions

15-1 Distinguish between a put and a call and a warrant.

15-2 What are the potential advantages of puts and calls?

15-3 Explain the following terms used with puts and calls:
   a. Strike price
   b. Naked option
   c. Premium
   d. Out-of-the-money option

15-4 Who writes puts and calls? Why?

15-5 What role does the options clearing corporation play in the options market?

15-6 What is the relationship between option prices and their intrinsic values? Why?

15-7 What is meant by the time premium of an option?

15-8 Explain the factors used in the Black–Scholes option valuation model. What is the relationship between each factor and the value of the option?

15-9 Give three reasons an investor might purchase a call?

15-10 Why do investors write calls? What are their obligations?

15-11 What is a straddle? When would an investor buy one?

15-12 What is a spread? What is its purpose?

15-13 Explain two types of spreads.

15-14 Why is the call or put writer's position considerably different from the buyer's position?

15-15 What is an index option? What index options are available?

15-16 What are the major differences between a stock option and an index option?

15-17 How can a put be used to protect a particular position? a call?

15-18 How does writing a covered call differ from writing a naked call?

15-19 Summarize Galai's conclusions about the available empirical evidence on options.

15-20 What is the significance of the industry subindex stock index options?

15-21 Assume that you own a diversified portfolio of 50 stocks and fear a market decline over the next six months.
   a. How could you protect your portfolio during this period using stock index options?
   b. How effective would this hedge be?
   c. Other things being equal, if your portfolio consisted of 150 stocks, would the protection be more effective?

15-22 Assume that you expect interest rates to rise and that you wish to speculate on this expectation. How could interest rate options be used to do this?

15-23 What does it mean to say that an option is worth more alive than dead?

15-24 Which is greater for an option relative to the underlying common, dollar movements or return volatility? Why?

Problems

15-1 The common stock of Teledyne trades on the NYSE. Teledyne has never paid a cash dividend. The stock is relatively risky. Assume that the beta for

Teledyne is 1.3 and that Teledyne closed at a price of \$162. Hypothetical option quotes on Teledyne are as follows:

Strike	Call			Put		
Price	Apr	Jul	Oct	Apr	Jul	Oct
140	$23\frac{1}{2}$	s	s	$\frac{3}{8}$	s	s
150	16	21	25	1	$3\frac{3}{4}$	r
160	$8\frac{7}{8}$	14	20	3	7	9
170	3	9	$13\frac{1}{4}$	9	10	11
180	$1\frac{1}{4}$	$5\frac{1}{4}$	9	r	20	r

r = not traded; s = no option offered.

Based on the Teledyne data, answer the following questions:

a. Which calls are in the money?

b. Which puts are in the money?

c. Why are investors willing to pay $1\frac{1}{4}$ for the 180 call but only 1 for the 150 put, which is closer to the current market price?

15-2 Based on the Teledyne data answer the following:

a. Calculate the intrinsic value of the April 140 and the October 170 calls.

b. Calculate the intrinsic value of the April 140 and the October 170 puts.

c. Explain the reasons for differences in intrinsic values between a and b.

15-3 Using the Teledyne data, answer the following:

a. What is the cost of 10 October 150 call contracts in total dollars? From the text, what is the commission? Total cost?

b. What is the cost of 20 October 160 put contracts in total dollars? What is the commission? Total cost?

c. On the following day, Teledyne closed at \$164. Which of the options would you have expected to increase? Decrease?

d. The new quote on the October 150 call was 26. What would have been your one-day profit on the 10 contracts? What is the net profit (after commissions)?

e. The new quote on the October 160 put was $7\frac{1}{2}$. What would have been your one-day profit on the 20 contracts? Net profit?

f. What is the most you could lose on these 20 contracts?

15-4 Assume that the value of a call option using the Black–Scholes model is \$8.94. The interest rate is 8% and the time to maturity is 90 days. The price of the underlying stock is \$47.375, and the exercise price is \$45. Calculate the price of a put using the put-call parity relationship.

15-5 Using the Black–Scholes formula, calculate the value of a call option given the following information:

Stock price = \$50

Exercise price = \$45

Interest rate = 7%

Time to expiration = 90 days

Standard deviation = 0.4

What is the price of the put using the same information?

15-6 Using the information in Problem 15-5, determine the sensitivity of the call value to a change in inputs by recalculating the call value if

a. The interest rate doubles to 14% but all other values remain the same.
b. The standard deviation doubles to 0.8 but all other values remain the same.

Which change causes the greatest change in the value of the call? What can you infer from this?

15-7 Given the following information, determine the number of shares of stock that must be purchased to form a hedged position if one option contract (covering 100 shares of stock) is to be written.

Stock price = $100

Exercise price = $95

Interest rate = 8%

Time to expiration = 180 days

Standard deviation = 0.6

15-8 Given the information in Problem 15-7, determine how the value of the call would change if

a. The exercise price is $100.
b. The time to expiration is 80 days (use the original exercise price of $95).
c. The time to expiration is 8 days.

15-9 Determine the value of Ribex call options if the exercise price is $40, the stock is currently selling for $2 out of the money, the time to expiration is 90 days, the interest rate is .10, and the variance of return on the stock for the past few months has been .81.

15-10 Using the information in Problem 15-9, decide intuitively whether the put or the call will sell at a higher price and verify your answer.

Selected References

Some empirical results from the option pricing model can be found in

Gultekin, N. Bulent, Rogalski, Richard J., and Tinic, Seha M. "Option Pricing Model Estimates: Some Empirical Results." *Financial Management*, Spring 1982, pp. 58–69.

A complete discussion of options can be found in

Ritchken, Peter. *Options: Theory, Strategy, and Applications.* Glenview, Ill.: Scott, Foresman, 1987.

CHAPTER 16

Warrants and Convertible Securities

Chapter 15 discussed one of the equity-derivative securities—options. This chapter continues that discussion by analyzing two other equity-derivative securities, warrants and convertible securities. As with options, these securities derive part or all of their value from the underlying common stock. Unlike options, however, which are created by investors, warrants and convertible securities are created by corporations. Although not as popular as options with many investors, these securities are viable investment alternatives.

Warrants

The definition of a warrant is very similar to that of the call option discussed in Chapter 15. A **warrant** is an option to purchase, within a specified time period, a stated number of shares of common stock at a specified price. The following are important differences between calls and warrants:

1. Warrants are issued by corporations, whereas puts and calls are created by investors (whether individuals or institutions).
2. Warrants typically have maturities of at least several years, whereas listed calls expire within several months.
3. Warrant terms are not standardized—each warrant is unique.

Warrants are most often issued attached to bonds as a "sweetener," allowing the corporate issuer to obtain a lower interest rate (i.e., financing cost).[1] The warrants can be detached and sold separately. In effect, a purchaser of bonds with detachable warrants is buying a package of securities.

Warrants are sometimes issued in conjunction with an acquisition or reorganization. They may also be issued during a new stock sale as partial compensation to the underwriters or as part of a common stock offering to investors.

The attractiveness of warrants to investors declined in recent years. The principal reason for this was the proliferation of alternative equity-derivative securities, including not only puts and calls but also financial futures and futures options (both of which are explained in Chapter 17). By the early 1990s, however, the popularity of warrants was once again increasing, primarily in connection with bond issues. Larger and better-capitalized companies, such as American Express and MCI Communications, were issuing warrants.

[1]This is particularly true of companies with small capitalizations.

Characteristics of Warrants

A warrant provides the owner with an exercisable option on the underlying common stock of the issuer—that is, a claim on the equity. However, the warrant holder receives no dividends and has no voting rights.

All conditions of a warrant are specified at issuance. Although the issuer may set any expiration date, typically it is 3–10 years.[2] In a number of cases, the expiration date can be extended. Warrants often provide for a one-to-one ratio in conversion, allowing the holder to purchase a number of common shares equal to the number of warrants converted. However, any conversion rate can be specified by the company, and fractional shares may be involved.[3] The *exercise price,* defined as the per-share amount to be paid by the warrant holder on exercise, is also specified at issuance. It always exceeds the market price of the stock at the time the warrant is issued.

Example Pier 1 Imports, Inc., a specialty retailer of imported home furnishings and related items, issued a warrant as part of a 20-year debenture offering (a good example of a sweetner).[4] Each $1000 11.5% debenture carried 42 warrants with it, exercisable at $22 cash per share on a one-to-one basis. ▪

Some warrants contain provisions under which the corporate issuer can call the warrant or alter the expiration date if certain conditions transpire.

Example The Pier 1 warrants were callable anytime for $18. The expiration date could be accelerated by up to two years if the common closed at or above $40 for 10 consecutive trading days. ▪

Why Buy Warrants?

Warrants offer investors a cheaper way to speculate on a particular common stock because the purchase of a given number of warrants is always cheaper than the purchase of a corresponding number of common stock shares. Therefore, investors can establish a given equity position for a considerably smaller capital investment through the use of warrants.

Investors trade warrants on the exchanges and over the counter exactly as they would common stock. They call their broker, usually trade in

---

[2]A few warrants are perpetual (i.e., they never expire).

[3]Warrant conversions are usually adjusted automatically for any stock dividends or splits.

[4]The original information for Pier 1 is taken from *The Value Line Convertible Survey, Part I: The Convertible Strategist,* Vol. 14, No. 35 (September 12, 1983), p. 118. This Value Line service, which is separate from the *Investment Survey* discussed in Chapter 4, is an excellent source of information on warrants, convertibles, and puts and calls.

round lots, and pay normal brokerage commissions.[5] Most investors never exercise warrants but simply buy and sell them in pursuit of capital gains.

Investors are interested in warrants primarily because of their speculative appeal. Warrants provide *leverage* opportunities. Leverage produces larger percentage gains (and also losses) than the underlying common stock for given fluctuations in the price of the common.

Example. On one observation date, the Pier 1 common stock traded at $18.25 and the warrant traded at $5.75. Since an investor would have to pay $22 to exercise this warrant and receive a share of stock, no one would be willing to do so at that time. Nevertheless, investors were willing to pay $5.75 per warrant to speculate on future price movements. Assume, for example, the stock doubled in price to $36.50 per share (100% appreciation). The warrant at that point would be worth a minimum of $14.50 minus the $22 exercise price). This would represent a gain of $8.75 per warrant, or 152% appreciation. In fact, this warrant would probably sell for more than $14.50, because of increased investor interest, resulting in an even larger appreciation percentage relative to the common.

This example demonstrates the leverage potential possible from a warrant. Other things being equal, the warrant price will appreciate more *percentage-wise* than the common stock price for a given increase in the common. (Accordingly, if the stock price declines, the percentage decline of the warrant price will often be greater.)

The primary disadvantage of warrants is that they are *wasting assets.* Unless the price of the stock rises enough to make exercise worthwhile, the price of the warrant will decline over time and the warrant eventually will expire worthless.

Valuing Warrants

As is true for every financial asset, a warrant has value because of an expected future return of some type. In the case of warrants, since no dividends are paid, the expected return must be realized in the form of capital appreciation, or price change. Warrant valuation, therefore, involves an understanding of the price range in which a warrant may trade.

INVESTMENTS INTUITION

Because warrants, like options, are equity-derivative securities, warrant prices must fluctuate within certain boundaries because the warrant price must bear a relationship with the price of the underlying

---

[5]Prior to 1970, the NYSE had not permitted the trading of warrants for many years.

stock. Otherwise, arbitragers would buy one security while simultaneously selling the other and earn a profit. For example, if a warrant could be exercised for one share of stock at $10 per share and the stock was selling for $20 per share, the warrant could not sell for less than $10. If it did, it would pay arbitragers to purchase the warrant and exercise it, in effect buying the stock for less than $20 per share.

Warrants fluctuate in price between a minimum and maximum value, just as options do, as explained in Chapter 15.[6] The *maximum value of a warrant* is the price of the underlying common stock. The price of a warrant, which is a claim on the common stock, can never exceed the price of the stock itself because no return beyond the value of the stock is possible. In fact, most warrant prices never reach their maximum value because warrants are an expiring asset—their time value decreases as they approach maturity.

The *minimum value of a warrant* is the difference between the market price of the common and the warrant's exercise price, *if this spread is positive.* This difference must hold, at least approximately, or arbitragers could purchase the warrant, exercise it immediately, and sell the common stock received, thereby earning a profit. If the spread is negative (the exercise price exceeds the market price), the minimum price (MP) of the warrant is zero. Thus,

$$\begin{aligned} MP &= \$0, \text{ if } CMP < EP \\ MP &= (CMP - EP) \times N, \text{ if } CMP > EP \end{aligned} \tag{16-1}$$

where

MP = minimum price of a warrant
CMP = current market price of the stock
EP = the exercise price of the warrant
N = number of common shares received per warrant exercised

Equation 16-1 is often referred to as the **theoretical (calculated) value of a warrant,** because it produces the *intrinsic value* of a warrant. In actuality, warrants typically sell above this calculated value. The amount in excess of the formula value is referred to as the *premium*. The premium can be calculated by rearranging Equation 16-1 into 16-2.

$$\text{Premium} = \begin{matrix}\text{Market price}\\ \text{of the warrant}\end{matrix} - \begin{matrix}\text{Minimum price}\\ \text{of the warrant}\end{matrix} \tag{16-2}$$

Example Returning to the Pier 1 Imports warrants, the following calculations can be made, using the prices previously cited as an example.

[6]For simplicity, this discussion assumes a one-to-one purchase ratio between the warrant and the common.

Minimum price for Pier 1 warrants = \$0 because CMP < EP

The minimum price would have to be considered zero because the current market price was less than the exercise price (obviously, the price cannot be negative).

The premium would be calculated as

Premium for Pier 1 warrants = \$5.75 − \$0 = \$5.75

On the observation date, the Pier 1 Imports warrant was selling for a premium of \$5.75 above its minimum price. Investors were willing to pay this because the warrant was selling at slightly less than one-third the price of the common and the maximum loss was relatively small (i.e., \$5.75 per warrant). As shown earlier, the potential return could be large because of the leverage involved. ▪

Some warrants, of course, are in the money—the stock price exceeds the exercise price.

Example. Tyco Toys issued a warrant with an exercise price of \$16.50. On one observation date, the price of the common was \$20.25 and the price of the warrant was \$7.88. Therefore, the minimum price of the warrant was \$3.75, and it was selling for a premium of \$7.88 − \$3.50, or \$4.38. ▪

Figure 16-1 shows the relationships that exist among the market price of the warrant, the warrant, the minimum (theoretical) price as given by Equation 16-1, the maximum price of the warrant, and the premium. The minimum price line starts at EP, the exercise price of the warrant. The minimum price of the warrant rises (becomes positive) as the price of the stock exceeds the exercise price. Notice that as the price of the common

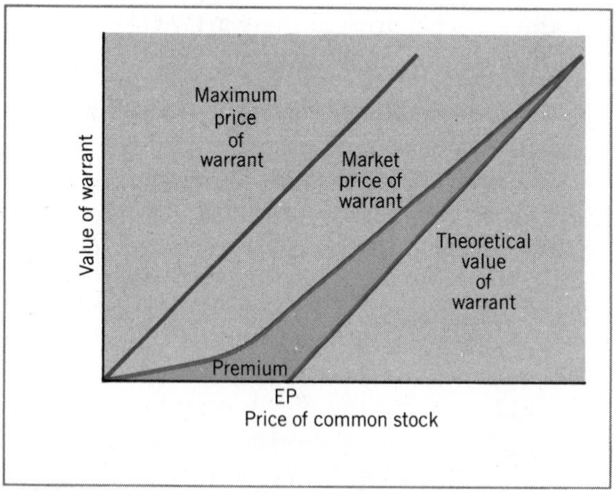

FIGURE 16-1 ***Relationships between the value of a warrant and the price of the underlying common stock (EP = exercise price of the warrant).***

stock continues to increase, the size of the premium decreases, a phenomenon that will be discussed later. Finally, note the line representing the maximum price for the warrant. Why is this drawn at a 45° angle?

The Speculative Value of a Warrant

What determines the premium investors will pay for a warrant, that is, its speculative value? Since investors typically purchase warrants to speculate on the underlying common stock, some obvious factors will affect the premium, or speculative potential, of the warrant. These include the following:

1. *Remaining warrant life.* Clearly, other things being equal, the larger the remaining life of a warrant, the more valuable it is. A warrant that currently is unattractive to exercise may become attractive six months, two years, or eight years from now as a result of appreciation in the common. Most investors are well advised not to purchase a warrant with less than three years remaining to maturity.
2. *Price volatility of the common.* Other things being equal, the more volatile the price of the underlying common, the more likely the warrant is to appreciate during a given time period. Investors are willing to pay larger premiums for such a warrant.
3. *The dividend on the underlying common.* Since warrant holders receive no dividends, an inverse relationship exists between the warrant premium and the expected dividend on the common.
4. *The potential leverage of the warrant.* As previously explained, warrant prices rise (and decline) faster, in percentage terms, than the price of the stock. Some warrants have greater leverage possibilities than others and therefore command larger premiums.

In connection with the leverage potential of the warrant, notice in Figure 16-1 that the premium becomes smaller as the price of the stock rises. Why? As the stock price increases, the leverage potential decreases. In other words, the ability of the warrant to magnify percentage gains on the amount invested decreases as the price of the stock rises.

Example. Consider the following examples for the Pier 1 Imports warrant, assuming the same stock price of $18.25 and the same warrant price of $5.75 as previously used.

Stock price doubles from $18.25 to $36.50	100% gain
Theoretical value of warrant rises $5.75 to $14.50	152% gain
Stock price rises an additional 50% from $36.50 to $54.75	50% gain
Theoretical value of warrant rises from $14.50 to $32.75[7]	126% gain

[7]$54.75 − 22 = $32.75 theoretical value; $32.75 − 14.50/14.50 = 126% gain.

Stock price rises an additional 25% from \$54.75 to \$68.44	25% gain
Theoretical value of warrant rises from \$32.75 to \$46.44	42% gain

▪

Convertible Securities

A third form of equity-derivative securities is the convertible bond or convertible preferred stock, both of which permit the owner to convert the security into common stock under specified conditions. These **convertible securities** ("convertibles") carry a claim on the common stock of the same issuer, which is *exercisable at the owner's initiative.*[8] If the option is never exercised, the convertible bond remains in existence until its maturity date, whereas a convertible preferred could remain in existence forever, since preferred stock has no maturity date.

Unlike puts and calls and warrants, convertible securities derive only part of their value from the option feature (i.e., the claim on the underlying common stock). These securities are valuable in their own right, as either bonds or preferred stock. Puts and calls and warrants, on the other hand, are only as valuable as the underlying common stock. They have no value beyond their claim on the common stock.

Convertibles have increased in popularity in recent years because they offer a unique combination of equity and bond characteristics.

Terminology for Convertible Securities

Convertible securities, whether bonds or preferred stock, have a certain terminology.

1. The **conversion ratio** is the number of shares of common stock that a convertible holder receives on conversion, which is the process of tendering the convertible security to the corporation in exchange for common stock.[9]

2. The **conversion price** is the par value of the bond or preferred divided by the conversion ratio.[10]

$$\text{Conversion price} = \frac{\text{Par value}}{\text{Conversion ratio}} \qquad (16\text{-}3)$$

3. The **conversion value** is the convertible's value based on the current price of the common stock. It is defined as

$$\text{Conversion value} = \text{Conversion ratio} \times \text{Current price of common} \qquad (16\text{-}4)$$

---

[8] Many convertible bonds cannot be converted for an initial period of 6–24 months.

[9] Forced conversion results when the issuer initiates conversion by calling the bonds.

[10] It is obvious that the conversion privilege attached to a convertible can be expressed in either conversion ratio or conversion price terms. Both the conversion price and the conversion ratio are almost always protected against stock splits and dividends.

4. The **conversion premium** is the dollar difference between the market price of the security and its conversion value.

$$\text{Conversion premium} = \text{Market price of convertible} - \text{Conversion value} \qquad (16\text{-}5)$$

Convertible securities are, by construction, hybrid securities. They have some characteristics of debt or preferred stock and some characteristics of the common stock on which they represent an option. Therefore, to value them one must consider them in both contexts. This will be done first for convertible bonds and than for convertible preferred stock.

Convertible Bonds

Convertible bonds are issued by corporations as part of their capital-raising activities. Similar to a warrant, a convertible feature can be attached to a bond as a sweetener, thereby allowing the issuer to obtain a lower interest cost by offering investors a chance for future gains from the common stock. Convertibles are sometimes sold as temporary financing instruments with the expectation that over a period of months (or years) the bonds will be converted into common stock. The bonds are a cheaper source of financing to the issuer than the common stock, and their gradual conversion places less price pressure on the common stock. Finally, convertibles offer a corporation the opportunity to sell common stock at a higher price than the current market price. If the issuer feels that the stock price is temporarily depressed, convertible bonds can be sold at a 15% to 20% premium. The result of this premium is that the price of the stock must rise by that amount before conversion is warranted.

Most bonds, whether convertible or not, are callable by the issuer. This results in additional concerns for the convertible bondholder.

Convertible bonds are typically issued as debentures. They are often subordinated to straight (nonconvertible) debentures, increasing their risk. Using S&P and Moody's bond ratings, most convertible bonds are one class below a straight debenture issue. Nevertheless, convertible bonds enjoy good marketability. Large issues on the New York Stock Exchange are often actively traded, in contrast to many nonconvertible issues of the same quality.

Analyzing Convertible Bonds

A convertible bond offers the purchaser a stream of interest payments and a return of principal at maturity. It also offers a promise of capital gains if the price of the stock rises sufficiently. To value a convertible bond, it is necessary to account for all of these elements. The convertible bond model is illustrated graphically to provide a framework for analysis. We shall then illustrate the components of value individually.

Graphic Analysis of Convertible Bonds Figure 16-2 shows the components of the convertible bond model. This diagram depicts the expected relationships for a typical convertible bond. The horizontal line from PV (par value) on the left to the maturity value (MV) on the right provides a reference point; any bond sold at par value would start out at PV, and all bonds will mature at their maturity value. If such a bond is callable, the call price will be above the par value in the early years because of the call premium; by maturity this price would converge to the maturity value.

Each convertible bond has an **investment value (IV)** or straight-debt value, which is the price at which a convertible would sell to equal the yield on a comparable nonconvertible. In other words, the investment value is the convertible's estimated value as a straight bond. By evaluating the coupons and the maturity value of the convertible at the going required rate of return for a comparable straight bond, the beginning investment value can be determined. Remember that the straight (i.e., nonconvertible) bond has a higher market yield because it does not offer a speculative play on the common stock. The investment value is represented in Figure 16-2 by the line from IV to MV.

Each convertible has a conversion value at any point in time. The original conversion value (point CV) is established by multiplying together the conversion ratio and the price of the common stock at the time the convertible is issued. The conversion value curve in Figure 16-2 is then drawn on the assumption that the price of the stock will grow at a constant rate, g; that is,

$$P_1 = P_0(1 + g)$$
$$P_2 = P_1(1 + g)$$

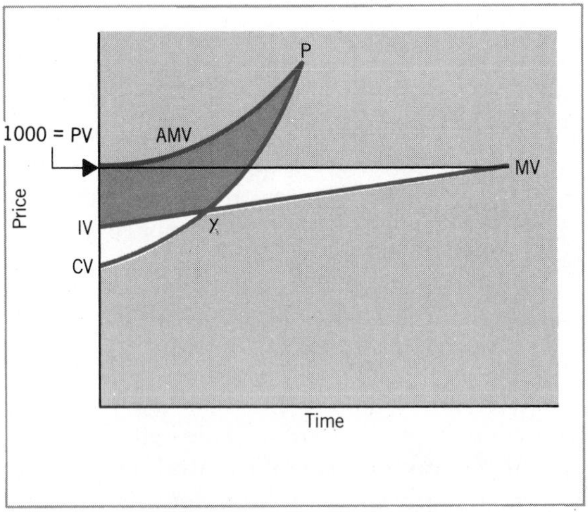

FIGURE 16-2 ***Conceptual model for understanding convertible bonds.***

and so forth. Obviously, this is an expected relationship and may not occur in this manner. Using this assumption, the conversion value rises above the par value as the price of the stock rises, tracing out the curve CV–*P* in Figure 16-2.

Finally, because the convertible often sells at a premium, it is necessary to draw an actual market value (AMV) curve, which is shown in Figure 16-2 as AMV–*P*. This curve eventually approaches the conversion value curve as the conversion value increases. This is attributable primarily to the fact that the convertible may be called, forcing conversion. If this occurs, the convertible holder can receive only the conversion value. Therefore, investors are not likely to pay more than this for the convertible.

The shaded area in Figure 16-2 is the premium over conversion value, which declines as the market price of the convertible rises. This reflects the fact that the bond is callable.

Bond Value Every convertible bond has an investment value or regular bond value, which is the price at which the bond would sell with no conversion option. This price is given by the present value calculations for a bond, as explained in Chapter 7.

$$BV = \sum_{t=1}^{2n} \frac{C_t/2}{(1 + r/2)^t} + \frac{FV}{(1 + r/2)^{2n}} \tag{16-6}$$

where

BV = intrinsic value or present value of the bond
C = the interest payments (coupons)
FV = par value of the bond
n = number of years to maturity
r = appropriate required rate of return

Example As an example of convertible bond valuation, consider the 8.5s of 2008 convertible debenture of Hartmarx Corporation (formerly, Hart, Schaffner & Marx), a NYSE-listed manufacturer of men's clothing. According to *The Value Line Convertible Survey,* this bond, issued in late 1982, was convertible into 34.095 common shares, which is its conversion ratio.[11] The conversion price at that time was \$29.33, or \$1000/34.095.[12] At one observation point after its issuance, the common stock of Hartmarx was selling at 35 $\frac{1}{8}$ while this debenture was selling at \$1210. The conversion value of Hartmarx at that observation point was therefore 34.095 × \$35.125 = \$1197.59. ▪

[11]*The Value Line Convertible Survey, Part I: The Convertible Strategist,* Vol. 14, No. 30 (August 8, 1983), p. 150.

[12]Many convertible bonds have a conversion price that increases over time.

In the case of the Hartmarx bond, the expiration date was set at January 15, 2008.[13] Valuing this bond at the observation point just used (after the July 15 interest payment) meant that 24.5 years remained to maturity, or 49 semiannual interest payments. Based on *The Value Line Convertible Survey's* assigned investment grade value of 0 for this issue and the market rates in effect at that time, 12.2% was chosen as the applicable discount rate for a bond of this risk category.[14] Therefore, the bond or investment value for this Hartmarx convertible debenture was[15]

$$\begin{aligned} BV &= \sum_{t=1}^{49} \frac{\$42.75}{(1 + 0.061)^t} + \frac{\$1000}{(1 + 0.061)^{49}} \\ &= \$717.23 \end{aligned}$$

Of course, the bond value fluctuates over time as market interest rates change.

Conversion Value Every convertible bond has a conversion value, or the value of the common stock received upon conversion. At the time of issuance, a convertible bond has a conversion value equal to the market price of the common stock multiplied by the number of shares of stock that can be received by converting. As noted, the conversion price is usually set 15% to 20% above the current market price of the common, so that conversion would not be worthwhile. Over time, if the price of the common stock grows, the conversion value should also grow at the same rate. This happened for the Hartmarx bond, which, as noted, had a conversion value of $1197.59.

Minimum (Floor) Value Every convertible bond has a **floor value,** or minimum value. A convertible will always sell *for no less than* the larger of (1) its bond (investment) value or (2) its conversion value.

Even if the value of the conversion feature is zero, with virtually no prospect of a change in this value, a convertible bond would have a minimum price of its investment or straight bond value (i.e., its value as a nonconvertible debt instrument). If the price were to decline below this value, bond investors would buy it because its yield would be greater than alternative comparable bonds. The bond value for the Hartmarx debenture as of the valuation date was $717.23, the absolute minimum price for this bond as of that time.

---

[13]The Hartmarx debenture was not callable before January 15, 1985 (unless the common stock closed at $44 or more for 30 consecutive trading days).
[14]This information is available in each weekly issue.
[15]To solve this equation the present value of the annuity must be found using the formula $1/[(1 - (1 + r)^n)/r]$. The present value factor for 49 periods can be found as $1/(1.061)^{49}$.

INVESTMENTS INTUITION

In a similar manner, a convertible bond cannot sell below its conversion value. If it did, arbitragers would buy the bond, convert it into common stock, and sell the shares, or simply establish an equity position at a cost lower than would otherwise be possible. Since the Hartmarx conversion value of $1197.59 was higher than its bond value, this was its minimum, of floor, value at the time of these calculations.

In Figure 16-2, the line IV-*Y*-P represents the minimum market value for the convertible bond. This minimum market value is made up of part of the investment value line (IV to *Y*) and part of the conversion value curve (*Y* to *P*). We can call this the effective market value floor.

Actual Bond Value (Price) Convertible bonds usually sell at prices above their minimum value, which, as we have seen, is the higher of the bond value or the conversion value. This difference between the actual bond value and the effective market value floor is the premium.

Example. The Hartmarx bond was selling at $1210 at the observation point with a conversion value of $1197.59. The dollar premium, therefore, was the difference, or $12.41. ▪

The reasons convertibles sell at premiums include the following:

1. The conversion option has a positive value because the right to convert any time during the life of the bond is valuable and investors are willing to pay for it. In effect, this is equivalent to owning a call on the stock, and calls command positive premiums.
2. A convertible bond offers investors downside protection, thereby decreasing their risk. If the price of the common declines sharply, resulting in a sharp decline in the conversion value, the convertible will still sell as a bond and will have a bond value determined by the present value of interest payments and principal. This dual minimum-price feature of convertibles reduces investors' risk and commands a premium in doing so.

The Option Pricing Model The key to valuing a convertible is to value its premium. To value convertible premiums it is possible to use, at least in principle, the option pricing model explained in the previous section. Why? Because, in effect, a convertible security is a call option on the underlying common stock (a complex call, to be sure). As such, the premium should be amenable to interpretation using the option pricing model.

Although the model is difficult, at best, to apply directly, it can be used to indicate how certain factors will impact the premium. This will help investors to gauge their relative size.

Using the five variables in the Black–Scholes call option model from Chapter 15, the following relationships can be noted:

1. *The price of the underlying stock.* Clearly, a higher stock price is associated with a higher premium.
2. *The exercise price of the option.* The lower the effective exercise price (i.e., the higher the conversion ratio), the larger the premium should be, other things being equal.
3. *The time remaining to the expiration of the option.* In the case of convertibles, the option feature is available throughout the life of the security. Because most bonds are callable, however, the expected call date would be the effective expiration date. The longer the time to maturity, the higher the premium.
4. *The interest rate.* This acts as an opportunity cost in affecting the value of a call. The higher the interest rate, other things being equal, the higher the value of a call, and therefore the higher the convertible premium.
5. *The volatility of the underlying stock price.* The more volatility in stock price, the more likely the price is to rise, thereby involving the speculative appeal of convertibles and raising the premium.

Other Factors to Consider In evaluating convertible bonds, certain details should be kept in mind in addition to the preceding factors.

1. When a convertible bond is converted, the holder loses the accrued interest from the last interest payment date. Furthermore, if a holder converts after the ex dividend date, the common stock dividend on the newly received common shares could be lost. Since the issuer can call the bonds and force conversion, these factors can be important. It is not unusual for issuers to choose a time favorable to themselves.
2. A bond is subject to call if the market price exceeds the call price. Investors who pay a premium over the conversion value in these circumstances run a risk of having the bond called as the company forces conversion.

Buying Convertible Bonds

Why should investors consider convertible bonds? Are there disadvantages?

Advantages: Convertible bonds offer investors a unique combination of an income stream from a fixed-income security and a chance to participate in the price appreciation of the common stock. Convertibles offer downside protection in relation to owning the common stock, because regardless of what happens to the price of the common, the convertible bond will not decline below its value as a straight bond. They offer upside potential, because a convertible bond must always be worth at least its conversion as the price of the common stock rises. Furthermore, the yield on a convertible bond usually exceeds that of the common stock, and interest payments have first order of priority.[16] Compared to common stock owners, convertible bond holders enjoy a yield advantage while awaiting appreciation in the stock price.

Disadvantages: Convertible bonds yield less than do straight bonds of similar risk and maturity. Investors must give up some yield to receive the conversion feature. Convertibles are callable, and in many cases the issuer can and will force conversion. When a convertible bond is called, the holder will choose the better alternative—accept the call price or convert into common stock. If a corporation calls a bond at, say, $1100 (face value of $1000 plus one year's interest of $100 for a call premium), and the conversion value is, say, $1200, the bondholders in effect are forced to convert. They give up their fixed-income security and the chance for future capital gains from the common stock.

Risk and Return on Convertible Bonds

Few studies have been done on convertible bonds. One recent study that does shed light is by Edward Altman. He analyzed convertible bond behavior during the 1980s and drew the following conclusions[17]:

1. Convertible issues, which typically are unsecured and subordinated, tend to be small, with a median issue size in 1987 of about $35 million.
2. Both investment grade and non–investment grade convertibles had a lower average yield to maturity than comparable straight debt.
3. For the period 1983–1987, the average total returns on convertibles was less than that for high-yield straight debt, government bonds, the NYSE Index, and the S&P 500 Index using as a sample all convertible bonds covered by *Value Line*.
4. High-yield straight debt was significantly less volatile than either the convertible bond sample or the stock market indexes.
5. There was a high correlation between convertible bonds and stock market returns, which suggests that convertible performance is heavily dependent on stock market activity.

---

[16] In the case of Hartmarx, the yields at the observation point were 7% and 2.7%, respectively, a 4.3% yield advantage for the convertible.

[17] These findings are taken from Edward I. Altman, "The Convertible Debt Market: Are Returns Worth the Risk?" *Financial Analysts Journal*, July–August 1989, pp. 23–31.

6. On the basis of mutual fund data for convertible bond funds, government bond funds, and high-yield straight debt funds, convertible security funds did not do particularly well over a three-year period and a five-year period. However, the convertible funds had almost twice the total return over a 10-year period, apparently reflecting the strong performance of the stock market during that time.
7. The default loss on convertibles exceeded that of straight debt for every year examined.

Convertible Preferred Stock

A convertible preferred stock offers investors fixed quarterly dividends forever plus an option on the underlying common stock. This security is often issued in connection with mergers.

Convertible preferreds differ from convertible bonds in the following ways:

1. The conversion privilege does not expire.
2. The conversion rate does not change, as it often does with bonds.
3. Conversion can take place immediately upon issuance.

Example As an example of a convertible preferred stock, consider the \$3.75 B convertible preferred of Potlatch Corporation, which produces wood and paper products. It is convertible into 0.943 common shares and can be exchanged for the 7.5s 2011 convertible bonds at the company's option. At one observation point, the common was selling for 55 (providing a dividend yield of 2.8%) while the preferred was selling for \$60.25.[18] ▪

Analyzing Convertible Preferreds

A convertible preferred offers investors an infinite stream of quarterly dividends and a chance to participate in any appreciation in the common stock. Each of these elements for convertible preferreds must be accounted for and valued, exactly as they were in the case of convertible bonds.

Preferred Stock Value As Appendix 7-B pointed out, a preferred stock is valued using a simple perpetuity formula:

$$P_{ps} = \frac{D}{K_{ps}} \tag{16-7}$$

[18]All the data for the Potlatch convertible preferred are available in *The Value Line Convertible Survey, Part I: The Convertible Strategist*, August 18, 1986, p. 142.

where

P_{ps} = the value of the preferred stock
D = the fixed annual dividends
K_{ps} = the appropriate required rate of return

If K_{ps} rises, the value of the preferred will decline because D is permanently fixed and does not change. Thus, the value of a preferred stock changes as the required rate of return demanded by investors changes.

Reversing Equation 16-7, the required rate of return (yield) on the preferred is

$$K_{ps} = \frac{D}{P_{ps}} \tag{16-8}$$

Example For Potlatch, the calculation is

$$K_{PO} = \$3.75/\$60.25 = 6.2\%$$

Investors could purchase this convertible preferred stock, receive a 6.2% yield, and have an option on the common stock of Potlatch. What is this option worth? ▪

Conversion Value The conversion value of the Potlatch convertible preferred is

$$CV_{PO} = .943 \times \$55 = \$51.87$$

This convertible is selling at a typical premium over conversion value, which can be calculated as

$$\text{Premium over conversion value} = \frac{\text{Market price of preferred} - \text{Conversion value}}{\text{Conversion value}}$$

$$= \frac{\$60.25 - \$51.87}{\$51.87}$$

$$= 16.1\%$$

The percentage premium indicates the extent to which the common stock must appreciate before the preferred stockholder would enjoy capital gains. Thus, the common stock would have to appreciate 16% before the conversion value would be equal to the price of the preferred stock. Thereafter, if the common appreciated, the preferred would also, regardless of whether investors were willing to pay a premium for the preferred.

Buying Convertible Preferreds

Convertible preferreds, like any other security, have advantages and disadvantages. As always, there are return and risk issues to consider. As for advantages, the preferred has priority over the common in payment of dividends and in case of liquidation while offering a claim on the underlying common stock, the value of which may appreciate over time. The dividend yield on a convertible preferred is almost always higher than that on the common stock, since preferreds are viewed by investors as fixed-income securities.

Example. In the case of Potlatch, the dividend yield on the preferred was more than twice that of the common. This return offered some downside protection on the price of the preferred stock, in relation to the common stock, because as stock prices decline the convertible preferred can trade on its merits as a preferred stock, offering a competitive return. *Value Line* estimated that the Potlatch preferred would share in only 50% of any decline in the common. ▪

Disadvantages include a lower yield than a comparable straight (nonconvertible) preferred stock. Convertible preferreds, like any other preferreds, are affected by a rise in interest rates (required rate of return). Because the yield on a convertible preferred is lower than that on a comparable nonconvertible preferred, the impact on the price as a result of a rise in interest rates will be greater for the convertible. Finally, if the common stock price rises, the preferred will not rise as much. *Value Line* estimated that the Potlatch preferred would share 70% of any rise in the common.

Summary

- Warrants are options to purchase common stock from corporations for a specified price and time, which is usually a period of years.
- Warrants offer leverage opportunities and require a smaller outlay than purchase of the stock. Percentage-wise, warrants usually appreciate (or depreciate) more than the stock price.
- Warrants have a minimum value, as calculated by the theoretical value formula, and a maximum value, which is the price of the stock.
- The amount above the minimum price at which a warrant sells is its premium. The premium is affected by the remaining warrant life, the price volatility of the common, any dividends, and the potential leverage of the warrant. The leverage decreases as the stock price increases.
- Convertible securities consist of bonds and preferred stock, which are valuable in their own right.
- Convertible bonds are issued as debentures and are always worth at least their straight debt value.

- A convertible bond may be priced on the basis of its investment value or its conversion value, the higher of which is its floor value. Convertibles usually sell above either of these values.
- The amount above the floor value at which convertibles sell is referred to as the premium. Investors are willing to pay a premium for the conversion option and the downside protection resulting from the straight debt value.
- Convertible preferred stock is similar to bonds, but the conversion privilege never expires. This security has a minimum value—the value of a preferred stock paying a fixed dividend forever. In addition, it has a conversion value and often sells at a premium over that value.
- Convertible preferreds offer investors downside protection, but a lower yield than a comparable nonconvertible preferred.

Key Words

Conversion premium
Conversion price
Conversion ratio
Conversion value
Convertible securities
Floor value
Investment value (IV)
Theoretical (calculated) value of warrant
Warrant

Questions

16-1 Why are warrants issued?
16-2 Why buy warrants?
16-3 What is the range of a warrant's price? Under what conditions will it approach either end of this range?
16-4 What is meant by the premium on a warrant? What factors affect this premium?
16-5 Explain the relationship between the leverage potential of a warrant and the price of the underlying stock.
16-6 Distinguish between the conversion ratio, the conversion price, and the conversion value.
16-7 Why do corporations issue convertible bonds?
16-8 What is meant by the floor value of a convertible bond?
16-9 Why do convertible bonds sell at premiums?
16-10 Explain the relationship between the factors in the Black–Scholes option model and the premium on convertible bonds.
16-11 What are the advantages of buying convertible bonds? What are the disadvantages?
16-12 How do convertible preferred stocks differ from convertible bonds?
16-13 What are the advantages of convertible preferreds? What are the disadvantages?

16-14 What does the percentage conversion premium on a convertible preferred stock indicate?

16-15 What risks are all convertible securities exposed to?

16-16 Explain what is meant by the theoretical value of a warrant?

16-17 Why might a corporation extend a warrant's expiration date?

16-18 Why does the market value of a convertible bond approach the conversion value as the conversion value increases?

16-19 What are the basic differences between purchasing a warrant and purchasing the underlying common stock? between a call and a warrant?

Problems

16-1 The price of the Hartmarx common was about $26.50 when the convertible bond described in the chapter was issued. Determine the percentage conversion premium at that time if the bond was issued at par.

16-2 At a subsequent observation point to the one used in the chapter, Pier 1 Imports common stock was trading at $15.875, with the warrant of $5.25.

a. Determine the theoretical value of the warrant at this time.

b. Determine its premium. .

c. How would you justify the warrant's price at this point?

16-3 Golden Nugget had a warrant attached to its bond issue, the 8.38s of 1993. Assume a price quote on the bond of $745.00. The warrant expires on July 1, 1993. The price of the warrant is currently quoted at $4.13. The market price of the common stock is $11.25. The per-share exercise price is $18.00 and the conversion ratio is 1.0.

a. On the basis of this bond quote, is the current market interest rate greater or less than 8.38?

b. Using Equation 16-1, calculate the minimum price on this warrant.

c. Using Equation 16-2, calculate the premium.

d. The relationship between the value of the warrant and the price of common stock is shown in Figure 16-1. On that figure, the minimum price line starts at a common stock price of EP. For Golden Nugget, what is the value of EP?

e. For the market prices of Golden Nugget and for the market prices of the warrants shown here, calculate the minimum prices (Equation 16-1) and the premium values (Equation 16-2).

Stock Price	Minimum Value	Actual Warrant Price	Premium
$ 5.00		$ 1.50	
11.25		4.13	
12.50		5.00	
18.00		8.00	
20.00		9.00	

25.00	13.00
35:00	22.00
50.00	36.00
70.00	54.00

f. Use these values to construct the graph for Golden Nugget based on Figure 16-1.

g. What should be expected regarding the value of the premiums:
   (1) As we approach July 1, 1993?
   (2) If the price of Golden Nugget should become quite stable around $15 per share?
   (3) If earnings of Golden Nugget become stable at $2.00 per share, with a steady dividend payout ratio of 0.50?

16-4 Pan American World Airways has several convertible bond issues outstanding. One issue is the 15s of 1998. Upon issue of this bond it was specified that each $1000 par bond is convertible to stock at a conversion price of $5.50 per share. Assume that the quoted price on the bond is $1350. The closing price on Pan Am's common stock is $7.25.

a. Using Equation 16-3, calculate the conversion ratio. Explain what this means.
b. Using Equation 16-4, calculate the conversion value.
c. Using Equation 16-5, calculate the conversion premium.
d. Using Equation 16-6, assuming 14 years to the maturity date of the bond (t) and a required rate of return (r) of 12%, show that the bond value is $1199, using our computational formula (C = $150) of

$$BV = \frac{C}{r}\left[1 - \frac{1}{(1+r)^t}\right] + \frac{Par}{(1+r)^t}$$

e. What is the actual bond value?
f. What is the minimum price on the bond?

16-5 For the Pan Am convertible bond, the 15s of 98, assume that market interest rates rose, requiring the rate of return (r) to be 13%, but the price of Pan Am common stock fell to $6.50.

a. What would happen to the market price of the bond?
b. Calculate (1) the conversion value and (2) the minimum (floor) value.
c. What do you expect to happen to the value of the premium.

16-6 Pan Am also has outstanding the convertible bond of 5.25s of 89. Assume this bond has five years to maturity at $1000 par value. The current market price of this bond is $700.00.

a. Using a required rate of 14%, calculate the bond value (t = 5).
b. The market price of Pan Am common stock is $7.00. The conversion ratio is 60.753. Calculate (1) the conversion price and (2) the conversion value.
c. Explain why the bond is selling at such a deep discount, whereas the 15s of 98 are selling at a premium.

Selected References

A basic discussion of convertible bonds as an investment can be found in

Bierman, Harold, Jr. "Convertible Bonds as Investments." *Financial Analysts Journal*, March–April 1980, pp. 59–61.

Basic discussions of warrants and convertibles can be found in

Ritchie, John C., Jr. "Convertible Bonds and Warrants." In Frank J. Fabozzi and Irving M. Pollack, eds. *The Handbook of Fixed Income Securities*. Homewood, Ill.: Dow Jones-Irwin, 1983.

CHAPTER 17

Futures Markets

Futures markets are one of the fastest-growing areas in all of investments. New instruments in this area have proliferated, and techniques involving the use of futures, such as program trading, have captured wide media attention. Of particular importance to many investors is the array of financial futures now available. Anyone studying investments should understand what futures contracts are, how they can be used, and the wide variety of choices now available.

Understanding Futures Markets

Why Futures Markets?

Physical commodities and financial instruments typically are traded in cash markets. A *cash contract* calls for immediate delivery and is used by those who need a commodity now (e.g., food processors). Cash contracts are not cancellable unless both parties agree. The current cash prices of commodities and financial instruments can be found daily in such sources as *The Wall Street Journal*.

There are two types of cash markets, spot markets and forward markets. Spot markets are markets for immediate delivery.[1] The *spot price* refers to the current market price of an item available for immediate delivery.

The **forward markets** are markets for deferred delivery. The *forward price* is the price of an item for deferred delivery.

Example. Suppose that a manufacturer of high school and college class rings is gathering orders to fill for this school year and wishes to ensure an established price today for gold to be delivered six months from now, when the rings will actually be manufactured. The spot price of gold is not the manufacturer's primary concern, because the gold will not be purchased until it is needed for the manufacturing process. However, to reduce its risk the manufacturer is interested in contracting for gold to be delivered in six months at a price established today. This will allow the manufacturer to price its rings more accurately.

Our manufacturer could find a gold supplier who was willing to enter into a **forward contract,** which is simply a commitment today to transact in the future. The other party to the contract, such as a mining company, agrees to deliver the gold six months from now at a price negotiated today. Both parties have agreed to a deferred delivery at a sales price that is

[1]"Immediate" means in the normal course of business. For example, it may normally take two days for an item to be delivered after being ordered.

currently determined. No funds have been exchanged. Both parties have reduced their risk in the sense that the mining company knows what it will receive for the gold when it is sold six months from now and the ring manufacturer knows what it will pay for the gold when it actually needs to take delivery six months from now. ▪

INVESTMENTS INTUITION

Obviously, one of the parties may be disappointed six months later when the price of gold has changed, but that is the advantage of hindsight—if investors could foresee the future, they would know what to do to start with and would not have to worry about risk.

Forward contracts are centuries old, traceable back to at least the ancient Romans and Greeks. Organized **futures markets,** on the other hand, go back to the mid–nineteenth century in Chicago. Futures markets are, in effect, organized and standardized forward markets. An organized exchange standardizes the nonstandard forward contracts, establishing such features as the contract size, the delivery dates, the condition of the items that can be delivered, and so forth. Only the price and number of contracts are left for futures traders to negotiate. Individuals can trade without personal contact with each other because of the centralized marketplace. Performance is guaranteed by a third party, relieving one party to the transaction from worrying that the other party will fail to honor its commitment.

Current U.S. Futures Markets

To most people, futures trading traditionally has meant trading in futures contracts for commodities such as wheat, soybeans, and gold. However, money can be thought of simply as another commodity, and financial futures have become a particularly viable investment alternative for numerous investors. Therefore, futures contracts currently traded on U.S. futures exchanges can be divided into two broad categories: commodities and financials. Each of these two broad categories can be further subdivided as shown in Table 17-1. As we can see, the futures markets involve trading in a variety of both commodities and financials.

For each type of contract, such as corn or silver, different delivery dates are available. Each contract will specify the trading unit involved, and where applicable, the deliverable grade necessary to satisfy the contract.

The Structure of Futures Markets

As noted, futures contracts are traded on designated *futures exchanges,* which are voluntary, nonprofit associations. There are several major U.S.

TABLE 17-1 ***Futures Contracts Traded in the United States, by Categories***

The major commodities traded in the United States can be classified into the following categories (as shown in *The Wall Street Journal*):

	I. Commodities
Grains and oilseeds:	Wheat, corn, oats, soybeans, soybean oils, soybean meal, barley, flaxseed, rapeseed, rye, and canola
Livestock and meats:	Cattle (both live and feeders), pork bellies, and hogs
Foods:	Cocoa, coffee, orange juice, and sugar
Fibers:	Cotton
Metals:	Copper, gold, platinum, silver, and palladium
Oil:	Gasoline, heating oil, crude oil, gas oil
Wood:	Lumber
	II. Financials
Interest rates:	Treasury bills, Treasury notes, Treasury bonds, municipal bond index, 30-day interest rate, mortgage-backed, Eurodollars
Stock indexes:	S&P 500 Index, NYSE Composite Index, Major Market Index, CRB Index, KC Value Line Index, and KC Mini Value Line
Foreign currencies:	Japanese yen, West German mark, Canadian dollar, British pound, Swiss franc, Australian dollar, and U.S. Dollar Index.

exchanges.[2] Futures exchanges typically are nonprofit firms operated on behalf of their members. Memberships are held by individuals and, like stock exchange seats, can be traded at market-determined prices. The exchange provides an organized marketplace where established rules govern the conduct of the members. The exchange is financed both by membership dues and by fees charged for services rendered.

All memberships must be owned by individuals, although they may be controlled by firms. Members can trade for their own accounts or as agents for others. For example, floor traders trade for their own accounts, whereas floor brokers (or commission brokers) often act as agents for others. Futures commission merchants (FCM) act as agents for the general public, for which they receive commissions. Thus, a customer can establish an account with an FCM, who in turn may work through a floor broker at the exchange.

An important role in every futures transaction is played by the *clearing-*

[2]The commodity futures and futures options exchanges include the following: Chicago Board of Trade (CBT), Chicago Mercantile Exchange (CME), Commodity Exchange, New York (CMX), International Petroleum Exchange (IME), Kansas City Board of Trade (KCBT), Mid-America Commodity Exchange (MCE), New York Coffee Sugar & Cocoa Exchange (CSCE), New York Cotton Exchange (CTN), New York Futures Exchange (NYFE), the New York Mercantile Exchange (NYM), and the Philadelphia Board of Trade (PBOT). In early 1990 the New York Mercantile Exchange (Merc) and the Commodity Exchange (Comex) agreed to a tentative merger plan.

house, which ensures the fulfillment of each futures contract by placing itself between the parties to each transaction. Essentially, the clearinghouse for futures markets operates the same as the clearinghouse for options, which was discussed in some detail in Chapter 15. Buyers and sellers settle with the clearinghouse, not each other. Thus, the clearinghouse, and not another investor, is actually on the other side of every transaction.

The clearinghouse ensures that all payments are made as specified, and it stands ready to fulfill a contract if either buyer or seller defaults. It thereby helps to facilitate an orderly market in futures, because any buyer or seller can always close out a position and be assured of payment. A failure by the clearinghouse to perform would ruin the futures market.

Futures contracts are standardized, transferable agreements whose prices fluctuate constantly; they are legal contracts, and such items as quantity and price are spelled out precisely and cannot be changed. However, futures contracts are not securities and are not regulated by the Securities and Exchange Commission. The Commodity Futures Trading Commission (CFTC), a federal regulatory agency, is responsible for regulating trading in all domestic futures markets. In practice, the National Futures Association, a self-regulating body, has assumed some of the duties previously performed by the CFTC. In addition, each exchange has a supervisory body to oversee its members.

The Mechanics of Trading

Basic Procedures

A **futures contract** is a commitment to buy or sell at a specified future settlement date a designated amount of a commodity or financial asset. It is a legally binding contract by two parties to make or take delivery of the item at some time in the future. The seller (sometimes called the short) of the futures contract agrees to make delivery, and the buyer (the long) of the contract agrees to take delivery, at a currently determined market price. Selling short in futures trading means only that a contract not previously purchased is sold.

Note that a contract is not really being sold or bought, as in the case of Treasury bills, stocks, or CDs, because no money is exchanged at the time the contract is entered into. The seller and the buyer are agreeing to make and take delivery, respectively, at some future time for a price agreed upon today.

It is extremely important to remember that, unlike an options contract, *a futures contract involves a specific obligation to take or make delivery.* However, futures contracts can be settled by delivery or by offset. Delivery, or settlement of the contract, occurs in months that are designated by the various exchanges for each of the items traded. Delivery occurs in less than 2% of all transactions.[3] **Offset** is the typical method of settling a contract. Holders liquidate a position by arranging an offsetting transaction. This means that buyers sell their positions and sellers buy their positions sometime prior to delivery. Thus, to eliminate a futures market position, the investor simply does the reverse of what was done originally. It is essential to remember that if a futures contract is not offset, it must be closed out by delivery.

Each exchange establishes price fluctuation limits on the various types of contracts. Typically, a minimum price change is specified. In the case of corn, for example, it is 0.25 cent per bushel, or $12.50 per contract. A *daily price limit* is in effect for all futures contracts except stock index futures. For corn it is 10 cents per bushel ($500 per contract) above and below the previous day's settlement price.

With stocks, short selling can be done only on an uptick, but futures have no such restriction. Stock positions, short or long, can literally be held forever. However, futures positions must be closed out within a specified time, either by offsetting the position or by making or taking delivery.

Unlike stocks, there are no specialists on futures exchanges. Each futures contract is traded in a specific "pit," in an auction market process where every bid and offer compete without priority as to time or size. A system of "open outcry" is used, where any offer to buy or sell must be made to all traders in the pit.

Brokerage commissions on commodities contracts are paid on the basis of a completed contract (purchase and sale), rather than on each purchase and sale, as in the csae of stocks. As with options, no certificates exist for futures contracts.

The **open interest** indicates contracts not offset by opposite transactions or delivery; that is, it measures the number of contracts outstanding.

Margin

Recall that in the case of stock transactions the term *margin* refers to the down payment in a transaction in which money is borrowed from the broker to finance the total cost. **Futures margin,** on the other hand, refers to the "good faith" (or earnest money) deposit made by the transactor to ensure the completion of the contract. It is not a downpayment because ownership of the underlying item is not being transferred. In effect, margin is a performance bond. Because no credit is being extended, there is no interest expense on that part of the contract not covered by the margin as there is when stocks are purchased on margin.[4] In futures trading, unlike stock trading, margin is the norm.

---

[3] Instruments that can be used in a delivery are explicitly identified in delivery manuals issued by the appropriate exchange.

[4] With futures, customers often receive interest on margin money deposited. A customer with a large enough requirement (roughly, $15,000 and over) can use Treasury bills as part of the margin.

Each exchange sets its own minimum *initial margin* requirements (in dollars). Furthermore, brokerage houses can require a higher margin and typically do so. The margin required for futures contracts, which is small in relation to the value of the contract itself, represents the equity of the transactor (either buyer or seller).

In addition to the initial margin requirement, each contract requires a *maintenance margin* or *variation margin*, below which the investor's equity cannot drop. If the market price of a futures contract moves adversely to the owner's position, the equity declines. If the decline is substantial, bringing the equity below the maintenance or variation margin, a **margin call** occurs, requiring the transactor to deposit additional cash or close out the account. To understand precisely how this works, we must first understand how profits and losses from futures contracts are debited and credited daily to an investor's account.

All futures contracts are **marked to the market** daily, which means that all profits and losses on a contract are credited and debited to each investor's account every trading day.[5] Those contract holders with a profit can withdraw the gains, whereas those with a loss will receive a margin call when the equity falls below the specified variation margin.

Example. Table 17-2 illustrates how accounts are marked to the market daily and how a margin call can occur. Consider an investor who buys a stock index futures contract for 75 (the pricing of these is explained later) and a second investor who sells (shorts) the same contract at the same price. Assume these contracts are on the NYSE Composite Index, where each point in the price is divided into 20 "ticks" worth $25 each.[6] For example, a price advance from 75 to 76, or one point, represents an advance of 20 ticks worth $25 each, or $500. Each investor puts up an initial margin of $3500. Table 17-2 traces each investor's account as it is marked to the market daily.[7]

At the end of day 1, the price of the contract has dropped to a settlement price of 74.5, a decrease of 10 ticks with a total value of $250. This amount is credited to the seller's account because the seller is short, and the price has dropped; conversely, $250 is debited to the buyer's account because the buyer is long, and the price moved adversely to this position. Table 17-1 shows that the current equity at the end of day 1 is $3250 for the buyer and $3750 for the seller.

Now assume that two weeks have passed, during which time each

[5]This is not true of forward contracts, where no funds are transferred until the maturity date.

[6]The NYSE Composite Index Futures Contract is quoted in the same manner as the index itself; for trading purposes, however, the contract is quoted in units called "ticks," each worth 0.05 of one point.

[7]This example is similar to an illustration in *Introducing New York Stock Exchange Index Futures* (New York Futures Exchange), p. 8. The level of the index used here is for illustrative purposes only. I wish to thank the N.Y. Futures Exchange for their help with this example.

TABLE 17-2 *Investor Accounts, Using Stock Index Futures, Marked to the Market*

	Buyer (Long)	Seller (Short)
Account after one day		
Original equity (Initial margin)	$3500	$3500
Day 1 mark to the market	(250)	250
Current equity	$3250	$3750
Account after two weeks		
Original equity (initial margin)	$3500	$3500
Cumulative mark to the market	2125	(2125)
Current equity	$5625	$1375
Withdrawable excess equity	$2125	
Margin call		$2125

Source: Based on *Introducing New York Stock Exchange Index Futures,* New York Futures Exchange, p. 8. Reprinted by permission of the New York Futures Exchange, Inc. Copyright, 1984.

account has been marked to the market daily. The settlement price on this contract has reached 79.25. The aggregate change in market value for each investor is the difference between the current price and the initial price multiplied by $500, the value of one point in price, which in this example is

$$79.25 - 75 = 4.25 \times \$500 = \$2125$$

As shown in Table 17-2, this amount is currently credited to the buyer because the price moved in the direction the buyer expected; conversely, this same amount is currently debited to the seller, who now is on the wrong side of the price movement. Therefore, starting with an initial equity of $3500, after two weeks the cumulative mark to the market is $2125. This results in a current equity of $5625 for the buyer and $1375 for the seller. The buyer has a withdrawable excess equity of $2125, because of the favorable price movement, whereas the seller has a margin call of $2125.[8] ▪

INVESTMENTS INTUITION

This example illustrates what is meant by the expression that futures trading is a zero-sum game. The aggregate gains and losses net to zero. The aggregate profits enjoyed by the winners must be equal to the aggregate losses suffered by the losers.

[8]If the investor's current equity drops below the maintenance level required (which in this case is $1500), he or she receives a margin call and must add enough money to bring the account back to the initial margin level.

Using Futures Contracts

Who uses futures, and for what? Traditionally, participants in the futures market have been classified as either hedgers or speculators. **Hedgers** buy or sell futures contracts in order to offset the risk in a cash position.[9] By taking a position opposite to that of one already held, at a price set today, hedgers plan to reduce the risk of adverse price fluctuations—that is, to hedge the risk of unexpected price changes.

In a sense, the real motivation for all futures trading is to reduce price risk. With futures, risk is reduced by having the gain (loss) in the futures position offset the loss (gain) on the cash position. A hedger is willing to forego some profit potential in exchange for having someone else assume part of the risk. It is important to note the trade-off involved here: *Hedging reduces the risk of loss, but it also reduces the return possibilities relative to the unhedged position.* Thus, hedging is used by people who are uncertain of future price movements and want to protect themselves against adverse price movements.

Figure 17-1 illustrates the hedging process as it affects the return–risk distribution. Notice that the unhedged position has a greater chance of a larger loss, but also a greater chance of a larger gain. The hedged position has a smaller chance of a low return but also a smaller chance of a high return.

Hedging is not an automatic process. It requires more than simply taking a position. Hedgers must make timing decisions as to when to initiate and end the process. As conditions change, hedgers must adjust their hedge strategy.

One aspect of hedging that must be considered is "basis" risk. The **basis** is defined as the difference between the spot price of the commodity being hedged and the price of the futures contract used as a hedge. The basis is positive (negative) if cash prices are higher (lower) than prices in the futures market.

Basis = Current cash price − Futures price[10]

Example. If the S&P 500 Index settles at 200.75 while the S&P 500 Futures Stock Index closes at 200.30, the basis is 0.45. ▪

The basis fluctuates in an unpredictable manner and is not constant during a hedge period. **Basis risk,** therefore, is the risk hedgers face as a result of unexpected changes in basis. Changes in the basis will affect the hedge position during its life. However, a hedge will reduce risk as long as

---

[9]The cash position may currently exist (a cash hedge) or may be expected to exist in the future (an anticipatory hedge).

[10]Technically, a basis exists for each outstanding futures contract and can differ, depending on the maturity of the contracts. Most references to basis refer to the nearby futures contract.

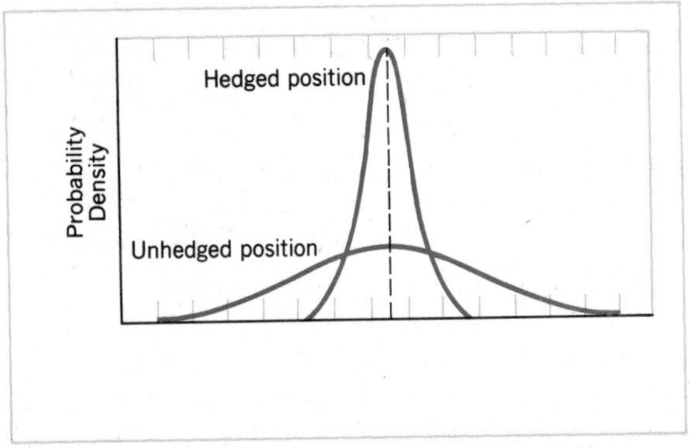

FIGURE 17-1 ***Return distributions for hedged and unhedged positions.***

the variability in the basis is less than the variability in the price of the asset being hedged. At maturity, the futures price and the cash price must be equal, resulting in a zero basis (transaction costs can cause discrepancies).

The significance of basis risk to investors is that risk cannot be entirely eliminated. Hedging a cash position will involve basis risk. Ultimately, the usefulness of financial futures is dependent on how well the cash price follows the futures price.

In contrast to hedgers, **speculators** buy or sell futures contracts in an attempt to earn a return. Speculators are willing to assume the risk of price fluctuations, hoping to profit from them. Some speculators are professionals who do this for a living; others are amateurs, ranging from the very sophisticated to the novice.

Speculators are very valuable to the proper functioning of the futures market, absorbing the excess demand or supply generated by hedgers. Speculators contribute to the liquidity of the market and reduce the variability in prices over time.

The futures markets serve a valuable economic purpose by allowing hedgers to shift risks to speculators. The risk of price fluctuations is shifted from participants unwilling to assume such risk to those who are. Another economic function performed by futures markets is price discovery. Because the price of a futures contract reflects current expectations about values at some future date, transactors can establish current prices against later transactions.

Financial Futures

Financial futures provide investors more of an opportunity to "fine-tune" the risk–return characteristics of their portfolios. In recent years, this has become more important as interest rates have become much more volatile and as investors have sought new techniques to reduce the risk of equity positions. In fact, one can argue that the drastic changes that have occurred in the financial markets in the last 15–20 years have generated a genuine need for new financial instruments that allow market participants to deal with these changes.

The procedures for trading financial futures are the same as those for any other commodity, with few exceptions. At maturity, stock index futures settle in cash because it would be impossible or impractical to deliver all the stocks in a particular index.[11] Unlike traditional futures contracts, stock index futures typically have no daily price limits (although they can be imposed).

We shall divide the subsequent discussion of financial futures into the two major categories of contracts, interest rate futures and stock index futures. Hedging and speculative activities within each category will be discussed separately.

Interest Rate Futures

Bond prices are highly volatile, and investors are exposed to adverse price movements. Financial futures, in effect, allow bondholders and others who are affected by volatile interest rates to transfer the risk. In fact, one of the primary reasons for the growth in financial futures is that portfolio managers and investors are trying to protect themselves against adverse movements in interest rates. An investor concerned with protecting the value of fixed-income securities must consider the impact of interest rates on the value of these securities.

Today's investors have the opportunity to consider several different **interest rate futures** contracts that are traded on two exchanges.[12] The International Monetary Market specializes in short-maturity instruments, including Treasury bills and Eurodollars. The Chicago Board of Trade (CBT) specializes in long-maturity instruments, including Treasury notes, Treasury bonds, and GNMAs.

Table 17-3 describes some futures contracts on fixed-income securities. Contracts are available on GNMA mortgages and U.S. Treasury bonds and notes in trading units of $100,000 and on Treasury bills in trading units of $1 million. The contracts for U.S. government securities are by far the most important.

---

[11]Gains and losses on the last day of trading are credited and debited to the long and short positions in the same way—marked to the market—as was done for every other trading day of the contract. Therefore, not only is there no physical delivery of securities, but the buyer does not pay the full value of the contract at settlement.

[12]The Chicago Board of Trade launched financial futures trading in 1975 by opening trading in Government National Mortgage Association (GNMA or Ginnie Mae) bonds. The concept accelerated in 1976, when the International Monetary Market started trading in Treasury bills. Treasury bond futures appeared in 1977.

TABLE 17-3 ***Characteristics of Interest Rate Futures Contracts***

Contract	Where Traded[a]	Contract Size or Trading Unit	Minimum Fluctuations
Treasury bonds	CBT	$100,000 par value 8% coupon[b]	$\frac{1}{32}$ or $31.25
10-Year Treasury notes	CBT	$100,000 par value	$\frac{1}{32}$ or $31.25
Treasury bills	IMM	$1 million face value	1 basis point
GNMA	CBT	$100,000 principal balance with 8% coupon[c]	$\frac{1}{32}$ or $31.25

[a]CBT = Chicago Board of Trade; IMM = International Monetary Market.
[b]Bonds with other coupons are usable with price adjustments.
[c]Other coupons and principal amounts that are equivalent to $100,000, 8% can be used.

Reading Quotes

As an illustration of the quotation (reporting) system for interest rate futures, Table 17-4 shows some hypothetical quotes for the Treasury Bond contract on the CBT. These hypothetical quotes are intended only to illustrate relationships that typically exist. The value of the contract is $100,000, and the price quotations are percentages of par, with 32nds shown. Since one point is $1000, $\frac{1}{32}$ is worth $31.25. Thus, a price of $75\frac{16}{32}$ is equal to $75,500. Table 17-4 indicates that there were eight different contract months for the Treasury bond contract, covering a period of slightly more than two years—since the first contract, December, could have been purchased prior to that month.

In this illustration, the December futures contract opened at $74\frac{20}{32}$ of par, traded in a range of $74\frac{30}{32}$ to $74\frac{20}{32}$, and settled at $74\frac{25}{32}$, which translates into a yield of 11.816.[13] Notice that the change in price, $+\frac{8}{32}$, is opposite the change in yields, −0.042. In both cases, changes are measured from the previous day's respective variables.

Hedging with Interest Rate Futures

We now consider an example of using interest rate futures to hedge positions. Obviously, other examples could be constructed involving various transactors, such as a corporation or financial institution; various financial instruments, such as a portfolio of GNMAs or Treasury bills; and various scenarios under which the particular hedger is operating. Our objective is simply to illustrate the basic concepts. Since a short hedge is by far the more common, we shall concentrate on it.

[13]Futures prices on Treasury bonds are quoted with reference to an 8%, 20-year bond. Settlement prices are translated into a settlement yield to provide a reference point for interest rates.

TABLE 17-4 ***Hypothetical Quotes for One Day for the Various Maturities of the Treasury Bond Futures Contract***

	Open	High	Low	Settle	Change	Yield Settle Change	Open Interest
Dec. 19X0	74-20	74-30	74-20	74-25	+8	11.816–0.042	100,845
March 19X1	74-06	74-13	74-03	74-07	+8	11.911–0.041	24,566
June	73-28	73-31	73-21	73-25	+8	11.985–0.042	16,548
Sept.	73-13	73-16	73-09	73-13	+8	12.049–0.042	12,563
Dec.	72-32	73-06	72-30	73-03	+8	12.103–0.043	8,576
March 19X2	72-22	72-30	72-23	72-27	+8	12.146–0.042	7,283
June	72-15	72-23	72-16	72-20	+8	12.184–0.042	4,801
Sept.	72-12	72-17	72-10	72-14	+8	12.217–0.042	702
Dec.	—	—	—	72-09	+8	12.245–0.042	141
March 19X3	—	—	—	72-05	+8	12.267–0.042	58

Short Hedge. Suppose an investor has a bond portfolio and wishes to protect the value of his or her position.[14] For example, a pension fund manager holds $1 million of 11.75% Treasury bonds due 2005–10. The manager plans to sell the bonds three months from now (June 1) but wishes to protect the value of the bonds against a rise in interest rates.

To protect the position, the manager hedges by going short (selling) in the futures market. As illustrated in Table 17-5, the manager sells 10 September contracts (since each contract is worth $100,000) at a current price of 83–06. In this example, interest rates rise, producing a loss on the cash side (i.e., in the prices of the bonds held in the cash market) and a gain on the futures side (i.e., the manager can cover the short position at a lower price, which produces a profit). The futures position thus offsets 67% of the cash market loss.[15]

The primary reason that the manager in this example offset only 67% of the cash market loss is that the T-bond contract is based on 8%-coupon bonds, whereas the manager was holding 11.75% bonds. The dollar value of higher-coupon bonds changes by a larger dollar amount than the dollar value of lower-coupon bonds for any change in yields. One way to overcome this difference is to execute a "weighted" short hedge, adjusting the number of futures contracts used to hedge the cash position. With the

[14]This example is taken from *U.S. Treasury Bond Futures* (Chicago: Chicago Board of Trade), p. 10.

[15]The $89,062.50 gain is calculated as follows: The gain per contract is $83\frac{6}{32} - 74\frac{9}{32} = 8\frac{29}{32}$, or 8.90625% of par value. Multiplying the gain of 8.90625% by par value = $8,906.25 per contract, and for 10 contracts the total gain is $89,062.50.

TABLE 17-5 ***Illustration of Hedges Using Interest Rate Futures: A Short Hedge***

Cash Market	Futures Market
Short Hedge	
June 1	June 1
Holds $1 million 11¾% Treasury bonds due 2005–10. Current market price: 117-23 (yield 9.89%)	Sells 10 T-bond futures contracts at a price of 83–06
September 1	September 1
Sells $1 million of 11¾% bonds at 104–12 (yield 11.24%)	Buys 10 T-bond futures contracts at 74–09
Loss: $133,437.50	Gain: $89,062.50

example data in Table 17-5, selling 14 September contracts would offset 93.4% of the cash market loss.[16]

The Importance of Basis Note that risk cannot be eliminated completely from a hedge transaction such as the short hedge just illustrated because basis risk cannot be completely eliminated. Recall that basis is the difference between the price of the item being hedged and the price of the futures contract used to hedge it. The basis fluctuates over time and cannot be predicted precisely. Changes in the basis can affect the final results while the hedge is in effect. Nevertheless, basis fluctuations are usually less volatile than price fluctuations.

A short hedge benefits from a strengthening basis (futures prices decline faster than cash prices or cash prices rise faster than futures prices). If the basis weakens, as in the short hedge example, the hedge loses some of its effectiveness.

Speculating with Interest Rate Futures

Investors may wish to speculate with interest rate futures as well as to hedge with them. To do this, investors make assessments of likely movements in interest rates and assume a futures position that corresponds with this assessment. If the investor anticipates a rise in interest rates, he or she will sell one (or more) interest rate futures, because a rise in interest rates will drive down the prices of bonds and therefore the price of the futures contract. The investor sells a contract with the expectation of buying it back later at a lower price. Of course, a decline in interest rates will result in a loss for this investor, since the price will rise.

Assume that in November a speculator thinks that interest rates will

[16]The market value of the 14 futures contracts changes from $1,164,625 to $1,039,937.50. The cash market values change from $1,177,187.50 to $1,043,750. Different Treasury bonds are related to the nominal 8%-coupon, 20-year-maturity bond used in the contract by means of a set of conversion factors that represent the relative values of the various deliverable bonds. The conversion factor for the 11.75%-coupon bond used in this example, rounded off, is 1.40.

rise over the next two weeks and wishes to profit from this speculation. The investor can sell one December Treasury bond futures contract at a price of, say, $90\frac{20}{32}$. Two weeks later the price of this contract has declined to $88\frac{24}{32}$ because of rising interest rates. This investor would have a gain of $1\frac{28}{32}$, or $1875 (each $\frac{1}{32}$ is worth $31.25) and could close out this position by buying an additional contract.

The usefulness of interest rate futures for pursuing such a strategy is significant. A speculator who wishes to assume a short position in bonds cannot do so readily in the cash market (either financially or mechanically). Interest rate futures provide the means to short bonds easily.

In a similar manner, investors can speculate on a decline in interest rates by purchasing interest rate futures. If the decline materializes, bond prices and the value of the futures contract will rise. Because of the leverage involved, the gains can be large; however, the losses can also be large if interest rates move in the wrong direction.

Stock Index Futures

Stock index futures trading was initiated in 1982 with several contracts quickly being created. Investors can trade futures contracts on the NYSE Composite, the S&P 500, and the Value Line Index. The contract size for each of these indexes is $500 times the index level. Contracts are also available on the Major Market Index, with a multiplier of $250, and the Mini Value Line Index, with a multiplier of $100.[17] The S&P 500 contract is the most popular stock index futures contract.

Delivery is not permitted in stock index futures because of its impracticality. Each contract is settled by cash on the settlement day, when any unsettled contracts are settled by taking an offsetting position using the price of the underlying index.[18]

Stock index futures offer investors the opportunity to act on their investment opinions concerning the future direction of the market. They need not select individual stocks, and it is easy to short the market. Furthermore, investors who are concerned about unfavorable short-term market prospects but remain bullish for the longer run can protect themselves in the interim by selling stock index futures.

Hedging with Stock Index Futures

Common stock investors hedge with financial futures for the same reasons that fixed-income investors use them. Investors, whether individuals or institutions, may hold a substantial stock portfolio that is subject to the risk

[17]This is most, but not all, of the contracts available as they change over time.

[18]The final settlement price is set equal to the closing index on the maturity date.

of the overall market, that is, systematic risk. A futures contract enables the investor to transfer a part or all of the risk to those willing to assume it. Stock index futures have opened up new, and relatively inexpensive, opportunities for investors to manage market risk through hedging.

Chapter 8 pointed out the two types of risk inherent in common stocks: systematic risk and unsystematic risk. Diversification will eliminate most or all of the unsystematic risk in a portfolio, but not the systematic risk. Although an investor could adjust the beta of the portfolio in anticipation of a market rise or fall, this is not an ideal solution, because of the changes in portfolio composition that might be required.

Investors can use financial futures on stock market indexes to hedge against an overall market decline; that is, investors can hedge against systematic or market risk. By selling the appropriate number of contracts against a stock purchase, the investor protects against systematic risk while attempting to earn the unique part of a stock's return. In effect, stock index futures contracts give an investor the opportunity to protect his or her portfolio against market fluctuations.

To hedge market risk, investors must be able to take a position in the hedging asset (in this case, stock index futures) such that profits or losses on the hedging asset offset changes in the value of the stock portfolio. Stock index futures permit this because changes in the futures prices themselves generally are highly correlated with changes in value of the stock portfolios that are caused by marketwide events. The more diversified the portfolio, and therefore the lower the unsystematic risk, the greater the correlation between the futures contract and the stock positions.

Figure 17-2 shows the price of the S&P 500 Index futures plotted against the value of a portfolio that is 99% diversified; that is, market risk accounts for 99% of its total risk.[19] The two track each other very closely, which demonstrates that stock index futures can be very effective in hedging the market risk of a portfolio.

Short Hedges Since so much common stock is held by investors, the short hedge is the natural type of contract for most investors. *Investors who hold stock portfolios hedge market risk by selling stock index futures, which means they assume a short position.*

A short position can be implemented by selling a forward maturity of the contract. The purpose of this hedge is to offset (in total or in part) any losses on the stock portfolio with gains on the futures position. To implement this defensive strategy, an investor would sell one or more futures contracts. Ideally, the value of these contracts would equal the value of the stock portfolio. If the market falls, leading to a loss on the cash (the stock

[19]This example is taken from Charles S. Morris, "Managing Stock Market Risk with Stock Index Futures," *Economic Review*, June 1989, pp. 3–16.

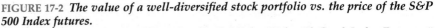

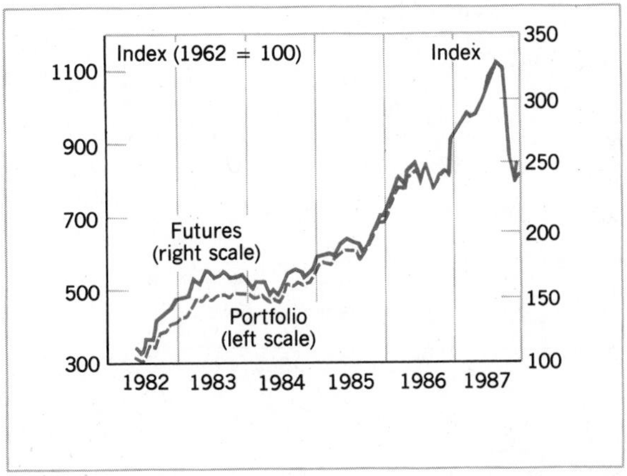

FIGURE 17-2 ***The value of a well-diversified stock portfolio vs. the price of the S&P 500 Index futures.***
Source: Charles S. Morris, "Managing Stock Market Risk with Stock Index Futures," *Economic Review,* June 1989, p. 9.

portfolio) position, stock index futures prices will also fall, leading to a profit for the sellers of the stock index futures.

The potential reduction in price volatility that can be accomplished by hedging is shown in Figure 17-3, which compares the performance of a well-diversified portfolio (the unhedged portfolio) with the same portfolio hedged by sales of the S&P 500 Index futures. Clearly, there is much less variability in the value of the hedged portfolio as compared to the value of the unhedged portfolio—in fact, the volatility of the returns is some 91% lower.[20] Notice in particular what happened in the great market crash of October 1987. The value of the unhedged portfolio fell some 19% whereas the value of the hedged portfolio fell only 6%. Thus, although the unhedged portfolio was well diversified, it was severly impacted by the market crash. On the other hand, even the hedged portfolio did not escape without a loss.

Example. Table 17-6 (top) illustrates the concept of a short hedge using the Standard & Poor's Index when it was at 173. Assume that an investor had a portfolio of stocks valued at $90,000 that he or she would like to protect against an anticipated market decline. By selling one S&P stock index future at 173, the investor has a short position of $86,500, because the value of the contract is $500 times the index quote. As the table illustrates, a decline in the stock market of 10% results in a loss on the stock portfolio of $9000 and a gain on the futures position of $8650 (ignoring commissions).

[20]See ibid.

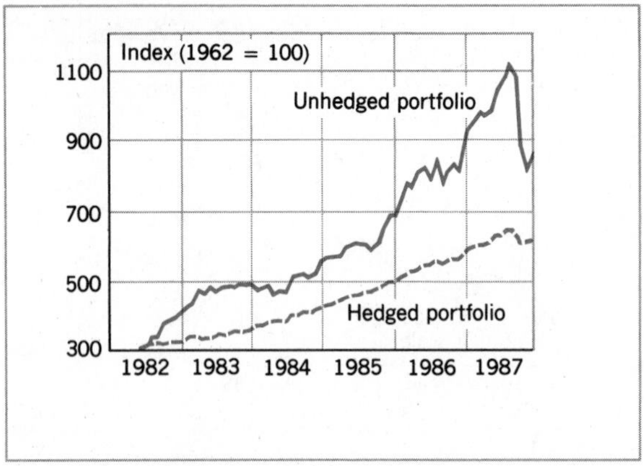

FIGURE 17-3 ***The value of a well-diversified portfolio vs. the value of the same portfolio hedged by sales of S&P 500 Index futures.***
Source: Charles S. Morris, "Managing Stock Market Risk with Stock Index Futures," *Economic Review,* June 1989, p. 10.

Examples of Short and Long Hedges Using Stock Index Futures

	Current Position	Pos. Following a 10% Market Drop	Change in Pos.
Short Hedge			
(Long position) dollar value of portfolio	$90,000	$81,000	$(9000)
(Short position) sell one S&P 500 futures[a] contract at 173	86,500	77,850	8650
Gain or loss from hedging			(350)

	Current Position	Position or Cost Following a 10% Market Rise	Change in Position or Cost of Position
Long Hedge			
Buy one S&P 500 futures contract at 173	$86,500	$95,150	$8650
Amount of money to be invested in stocks (cost of stock position)	75,000	82,500	(7500)
Gain or loss from hedging			1150

[a]Value of the futures contracts is $500 × index.

Thus, the investor almost makes up on the short side what is lost on the long side. ▪

Long Hedges The long hedger generally wishes to reduce the risk, while awaiting funds to invest, of having to pay more for an equity position when prices rise. Potential users of a long hedge include the following:

1. Institutions with a regular cash flow who use long hedges to improve the timing of their positions.
2. Institutions switching large positions who wish to hedge during the time it takes to complete the process. (This could also be a short hedge.)

Example. Assume an investor with $75,000 to invest believes that the stock market will advance but has been unable to select the stocks he or she wishes to hold. By purchasing one S&P 500 Index future, the investor will gain if the market advances. As shown in Table 17-6, a 10% market advance will increase the value of the futures contract $8650. Even if the investor has to pay 10% more (on average) for stocks purchased after the advance, he or she still gains, because the net hedge result is positive.

Limitations of Hedging with Stock Index Futures Although hedging with stock index futures can reduce an investor's risk, typically risk cannot be eliminated completely. As with interest rate futures, basis risk is present with stock index futures. It represents the difference between the price of the stock index futures contract and the value of the underlying stock index. A daily examination of the "Futures Prices" page of *The Wall Street Journal* will show that each of the indexes quoted under the respective futures contracts differs from the closing price of the contracts.[21]

Basis risk as it applies to common stock portfolios can be defined as the risk that remains after a stock portfolio has been hedged.[22] What is important to note here is that stock index futures hedge only systematic (market) risk. This means that when we consider a stock portfolio hedged with stock index futures, the basis risk is attributable to unsystematic (nonmarket or firm-specific) risk.

Figure 17-4(*a*) illustrates the effects of basis risk by comparing the value of a relatively undiversified portfolio with the price of the S&P 500 futures contract. In contrast to Figure 17-2, where the portfolio was 99% diversified, this portfolio is only 66% diversified. Although the two series are related, the relationship is in no way as close as that illustrated in Figure 17-2. Therefore, stock index futures will be less effective at hedging the total risk of the portfolio, as shown in Figure 17-4(*b*). In this situation, the variance of returns on the hedged portfolio is only 27% lower than the unhedged position. Note that in the crash of October 1987 both portfolios fell sharply, demonstrating that the hedge was relatively ineffective (the hedged position did better than the unhedged position, but not by much).

---

[21]Futures prices are generally more volatile than the underlying indexes and therefore diverge from them. The index futures tend to lead the actual market indexes. If investors are bullish, the futures are priced at a premium, with greater maturities usually associated with greater premiums. If investors are bearish, the futures are normally priced at a discount, which may widen as maturity increases.

[22]This discussion is based heavily on Morris, "Managing Stock Market Risk with Stock Index Futures," pp. 11–13.

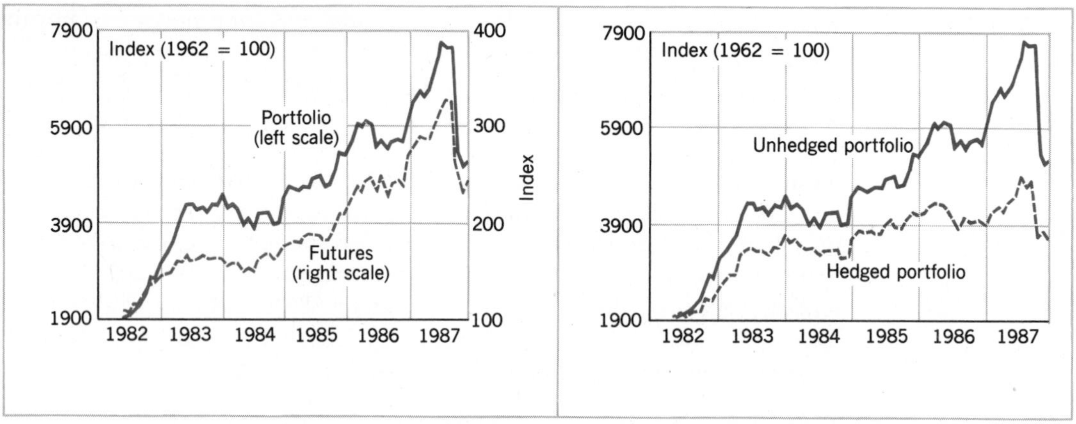

FIGURE 17-4 ***(a)*** ***The value of a relatively undiversified stock portfolio and the price of the S&P 500 index futures contract. (b) The value of the unhedged portfolio and the same portfolio hedged by sales of S&P 500 futures contracts.***
Source: Charles S. Morris, "Managing Stock Market Risk with Stock Index Futures," *Economic Review,* June 1989, pp. 12, 13.

From this analysis we can conclude that stock index futures generally do not provide a good hedge for relatively undiversified portfolios.

Speculating with Stock Index Futures

In addition to the previous hedging strategies (and others not described), investors can speculate with stock index futures if they wish to profit from stock market volatility by judging and acting on the likely market trends. Stock index futures are effective instruments for speculating on movements in the stock market because

1. Minimal costs are involved in establishing a futures position.
2. Stock index futures mirror the market, offering just as much risk.

We can refer to one group of speculators as "active traders." These individuals are willing to risk their capital on price changes they expect to occur in the futures contracts. Such individuals are often sophisticated investors who are seeking the opportunity for large gains and who understand the risk they are assuming.

Strategies of active traders basically include long and short positions. Traders who expect the market to rise buy index futures. Because of the high leverage, the profit opportunities are great; however, the loss opportunities are equally great. The same is true for traders expecting a market decline who assume a short position by selling a stock index futures contract. Selling a contract is a convenient way to go short the entire market. It can be done anytime (no wait for an uptick, as with stock short sales).

Another form of speculation involves *spreaders,* who establish both long and short positions at the same time. Their objective is to profit from changes in price relationships between two futures contracts. These include the following:

1. The *intramarket spread,* also known as a calendar or time spread. This spread involves contracts for two different settlement months, such as buying a March contract and selling a June contract.
2. The *intermarket spread,* also known as a quality spread. This spread involves two different markets, such as buying a NYSE contract and selling a Value Line contract (both for the same month).

Spreaders are interested in relative price as opposed to absolute price changes. If two different contracts appear to be out of line, the spreader hopes to profit by buying one contract and selling the other and waiting for the price difference to adjust. This adjustment may require the spread between the two contracts to widen in some cases and narrow in others.

Program Trading

A force of considerable magnitude has hit Wall Street. It is called **program trading,** and it has captured much attention and generated considerable controversy. It leads to headlines attributing market plunges at least in part to program trading, as happened on October 19, 1987, when the Dow Jones Industrial Average fell over 500 points.

Program trading involves the use of computer-generated orders to buy and sell securities based on arbitrage opportunities. The arbitrage occurs between common stocks, on the one hand, and index futures and options, on the other. Large institutional investors seek to exploit differences between the two sides. Specifically, when stock index futures prices rise substantially above the current value of the stock index itself (e.g., the S&P 500), these investors sell the futures and buy the underlying stocks, typically in "baskets" of several million dollars. Because the futures price and the stock index value must be equal when the futures contract expires, these investors are seeking to "capture the premium" between the two, thereby earning an arbitrage profit. That is, they seek high risk-free returns by arbitraging the difference between the cash value of the underlying securities and the prices of the futures contracts on these securities. In effect, they have a hedged position and should profit regardless of what happens to stock prices.

Normally, program traders and other speculators "unwind" their positions during the last trading hour of the day the futures expire. At this time, the futures premium goes to zero, because, as noted, the futures price at expiration must equal the stock index value.

The headlines about program trading often reflect the results of rapid selling by the program traders. For whatever reason, traders decide to sell the futures. As the price falls, stock prices fall also. When the futures price drops below the price of the stock index, tremendous selling orders can be unleashed. These volume sell orders in stocks drive the futures prices even lower.

Summary

- A futures contract designates a specific amount of a particular item to be delivered at a specified date in the future and a currently determined market price.
- Buyers assume long positions and sellers assume short positions. A short position indicates only that a contract not previously purchased is sold.
- Most contracts are settled by offset, whereby a position is liquidated by an offsetting transaction.
- Margin, the norm in futures trading, is the "good faith" deposit made to ensure completion of the contract.
- All futures contracts are marked to the market daily, meaning that all profits and losses are credited and debited to each investor's account daily.
- Contracts are traded on designated futures exchanges, which set minimum price changes and may establish daily price limits.
- Futures positions must be closed out within a specified time. There are no certificates and no specialists to handle the trading.
- Hedgers buy or sell futures contracts to offset the risk in some other position.
- Speculators buy or sell futures contracts in an attempt to earn a return and are valuable to the proper functioning of the market.
- Interest rate futures, one of the two principal types of financial futures, allow investors to hedge against, and speculate on, interest rate movements.
- Investors can, among other transactions, execute short hedges to protect their long positions in bonds.
- Stock index futures are available on the NYSE Composite Index, the S&P 500 Index, and the Value Line Index.
- Investors can use stock index futures to hedge the systematic risk of common stocks, that is, broad market movements.
- Short hedges protect a stock position against a market decline, and long hedges protect against having to pay more for an equity position because prices rise before the investment can be made.

Key Words

Basis
Basis risk
Forward contract
Forward markets
Financial futures
Futures contract
Futures margin
Futures markets
Hedgers
Interest rate futures
Margin call
Marked to the market
Offset
Open interest
Program trading
Speculators
Stock index futures

Questions

17-1 Carefully describe a futures contract.

17-2 Explain how futures contracts are valued daily and how most contracts are settled.

17-3 Describe the role of the clearinghouses in futures trading.

17-4 What determines if an investor receives a margin call?

17-5 Describe the differences between trading in stocks and trading in futures contracts.

17-6 How do financial futures differ from other futures contracts?

17-7 Explain the differences between a hedger and a speculator.

17-8 What is meant by basis? When is the basis positive?

17-9 Given a futures contract on Treasury bonds, determine the dollar price of a contract quoted at 80-5, 90-24, and 69-2.

17-10 When might a portfolio manager with a bond position use a short hedge involving interest rate futures?

17-11 Is it possible to construct a perfect hedge? Why or why not?

17-12 What is the difference between a short hedge and a weighted short hedge using interest rate futures?

17-13 Why would an investor have preferences among the different stock index futures?

17-14 What type of risk does stock index futures allow investors to hedge? Why would this be desirable?

17-15 Explain how a pension fund might use a long hedge with stock index futures.

17-16 When would an investor likely do the following?
a. Buy a call on a stock index.
b. Buy a put on interest rate futures.

17-17 What is program trading? How does it work?

Problems

17-1 Assume that an investor buys one March NYSE Composite Index futures contract on February 1 at 67.5. The position is closed out after five days.

The prices on the four days after purchase were 67.8, 68.1, 68, and 68.5. The initial margin is $3500.

a. Calculate the current equity on each of the next four days.
b. Calculate the excess equity for these four days.
c. Calculate the final gain or loss for the week.
d. Recalculate a, b, and c assuming that the investor had been short over this same period.

17-2 Given the information in Problem 17-1, assume that the investor holds until the contract expires. Ignore the four days after purchase and assume that on the next to last day of trading in March that the investor was long and the final settlement price on that date was 70.5. Calculate the cumulative profit.

17-3 Calculate the dollar gain or loss on Treasury bond futures contracts ($100,000) per contract for the following transactions. In each case the position is held six months before closing it out.

a. Sell 10 T-bond contracts at a price of 82-80 and buy 10 at 76-12.
b. Sell 10 T-bond contracts at a price of 80-14 and buy 10 at 77.
c. Buy 15 T-bond contracts at 62-10 and sell 15 at 64-24.
d. Sell one T-bond contract at 70-14 and buy one at 78-08.

17-4 Assume a portfolio manager holds $1 million of 8.5% Treasury bonds due 1994–99. The current market price is 76-2, for a yield of 11.95%. The manager fears a rise in interest rates in the next three months and wishes to protect this position against such a rise by hedging in futures.

a. Ignoring weighted hedges, what should the manager do?
b. Assume T-bond futures contracts are available at 68, and the price three months later is 59-12. If the manager constructs the correct hedge, what is the gain or loss on this position?
c. The price of the Treasury bonds three months later is 67-8. What is the gain or loss on this cash position?
d. What is the net effect of this hedge?

Selected References

A good discussion of institutional hedging via futures can be found in

Figlewski, Stephen. *Hedging with Financial Futures for Institutional Investors: From Theory to Practice.* Cambridge, Mass.: Ballinger, 1986.

A basic guide to financial futures is

Schwartz, Edward W., Hill, Joanne M., and Schneeweis, Thomas. *Financial Futures: Fundamentals, Strategies, and Applications.* Homewood, Ill.: Richard D. Irwin, 1986.

A discussion of using interest rate futures in investment management can be found in

Trainer, Francis H., Jr. "The Uses of Treasury Bond Futures in Fixed-Income Portfolio Management." *Financial Analysts Journal,* January–February 1983, pp. 27–34.

A complete discussion of futures and options can be found in

Marshall, John F. *Futures and Option Contracting: Theory and Practice.* Cincinnati: South-Western Publishing Company, 1989.

APPENDIX 17-A

Futures Options

In Chapter 15 we discussed options (puts and calls) on common stocks. In this chapter we discussed two types of futures contracts, interest rate futures and stock index futures. The latest innovation in financial instruments is a combination of the two, **futures options.** The development of this new instrument is a good example of the ever-changing financial markets in the United States, where new instruments are developed to provide investors with opportunities that did not previously exist.

Options, both puts and calls, are offered on both interest rate futures and stock index futures. Specifically, the following financial futures options were available in early 1990 as reported in the popular press[23]:

Options on foreign exchange: Pound, mark, Swiss franc, yen, Canadian dollar, Australian dollar, and sterling.

Options on interest rate futures: U.S. Treasury bills, notes, and bonds.

Options on stock index futures: The S&P 500 Index (traded on the Chicago Mercantile Exchange) and the NYSE Composite Index (traded on the New York Futures Exchange).

Options on commodities: agricultural, oil, livestock, metals, and lumber

Recall from Chapter 15 that an option provides the purchaser with the right, but not the *obligation,* to exercise the claim provided by the contract. An option on a futures contract gives its owner the right to assume a long or short position in the respective futures contract. If this right is exercised, the holder's position will be at the exercise (strike) price of the option that

[23]Futures options are also available for several agricultural commodities as well as copper, gold, and silver.

was purchased. For example, the exerciser of a call option buys the futures contract at the exercise price stated in the call option.

The key elements of an option contract on a particular futures contract are the exercise price and the premium. As in the case of stock options, premiums are determined in competitive markets. Each put and call option is either in the money or out of the money. With an in-the-money call option, the exercise price is less than the current price of the underlying futures contract (if the exercise price is greater than the current price, it is out of the money). For put options, the reverse is true.

Figure 17-A1 shows the relationships between premiums on put and call futures options. The exercise (strike) price is on the horizontal axis. As the strike price rises above the current futures price, the premiums on calls decline, whereas the premiums on puts rise. If the strike price was below the current futures price, the reverse would be true.

Options on futures contracts can serve some of the same purposes as the futures contracts themselves. Specifically, both futures contracts and options can be used to transfer the risk of adverse price movements from hedgers to speculators. For example, the portfolio manager with bond holdings (a long position) who expects a rise in interest rates can hedge against the risk of the capital losses resulting from such a rise by selling futures contracts on Treasury bonds. Alternatively, futures options on Treasury bonds could be used to hedge against this risk because the option's

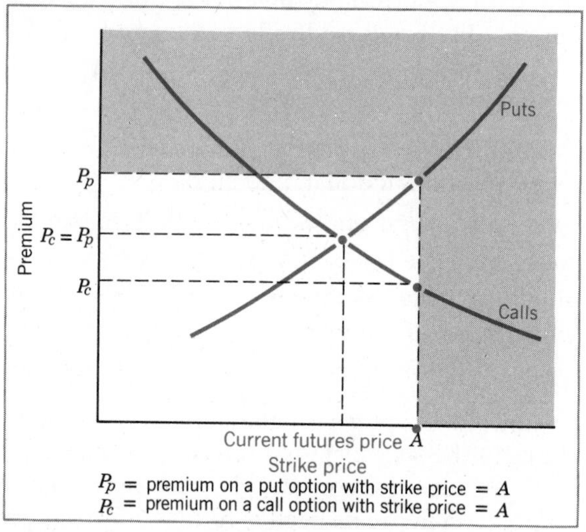

FIGURE 17-A1 ***Relationship between premiums on put and call options on futures contracts.***
Source: Michael T. Belongia and Thomas H. Gregory, "Are Options on Treasury Bond Futures Priced Efficiently?" *Review,* Federal Reserve Bank of St. Louis, January 1984, p. 8.

price will change in response to a change in the price of the underlying commodity.

A rise in interest rates is bearish (bond prices will fall); therefore, the portfolio manager would either buy a put or sell a call. The value of these options would rise as the price of the futures contract declined. On the other hand, an investor bullish on bond prices (i.e., one who expects interest rates to decline) would either buy a call or sell a put. In addition to these simple strategies, a number of spreading techniques can be used with options on Treasury bond futures.

The general appeal of options on futures contracts is the limited liability assumed by the purchaser. Unlike a futures contract, which has to be settled by some means (typically, by offset), the purchaser, once the contract is bought, has no additional obligation. Moreover, unlike futures, the purchaser is not subject to margin calls. Even if a speculator in futures is ultimately correct in his or her expectations, margin calls in the interim can wipe out all the equity. A writer (seller) of an option on a futures contract, however, does have an obligation to assume a position (long or short) in the futures market at the strike price if the option is exercised. Sellers must deposit margin when opening a position.

Questions

17A-1 With regard to futures options, fill in the following blanks with either "less than" or "greater than." The current futures price is 75.

a. Put options with strike prices ______ 75 are in the money.
b. Call options with strike prices ______ 75 are out of the money.
c. Put options with strike prices ______ 75 are out of the money.
d. Call options with strike prices ______ 75 are in the money.

CHAPTER 18

Investment Companies

In Chapter 2 we pointed out that an important alternative to investing directly in securities, indirect investing, is accomplished by the purchase of shares in investment companies, which offer investors a wide range of return–risk opportunities. Investors may be able to accomplish their objectives as well through indirect investing as through direct investing (i.e., doing it themselves). A thorough understanding of investment companies is essential for making intelligent decisions about investment programs.

Investment companies had become an extremely popular investment alternative by the dawn of the 1990s. By the beginning of 1990, 25% of households owned at least one fund, up from only 6% of households in 1980. The explosion in the number of funds available and the growth of their total assets are unprecedented. At the beginning of the 1990s, mutual funds held slightly less than $1 trillion in assets, an increase of 1000% since 1980. Consider the following figures, which describe only the mutual fund portion of the total investment companies available to investors[1]:

1. The total assets of all mutual funds (including money market funds) amounted to $51 billion in 1976. In 1990 the total assets of one mutual fund company, Fidelity Investments, exceeded this number by a considerable amount. One of Fidelity's funds, the Magellan Fund, had assets on January 1, 1990, of over $12 billion.
2. Mutual fund sales (excluding money market funds) totaled $4 billion in 1976, $10 billion in 1980, and $40 billion in 1983. Following sales of $46 billion in 1984, sales more than doubled to $114 billion in 1985 and almost doubled again in 1986, reaching $216 billion. Sales in 1987, 1988, and 1989 were $191, $95 billion, and $126 billion, respectively.
3. There were 452 mutual funds of all types in existence at the end of 1976. By the beginning of 1990 the number approximated 3000.

Mutual funds may well be *the* investment of the 1990s for many individual investors, particularly small investors. Regardless of whether this prediction turns out to be true or not, investment companies are a very important alternative for investors, and therefore deserve their careful attention.

Understanding Investment Companies

In this section we shall discuss the basic definition and nature of investment companies and outline the types of investment companies.

[1]Detailed figures on investment companies can be found in the *Mutual Fund Fact Book*, Investment Company Institute, 1775 K Street, Washington, D.C.

What Is an Investment Company?

An **investment company** can be defined as a financial service organization that sells shares in itself to the public and uses the funds it raises to invest in a portfolio of securities such as money market instruments, stocks, and bonds. By pooling the funds of thousands of investors, a widely diversified set of financial assets can be purchased and the company can offer its owners a variety of services.

Example. Suppose an investment company called the Health Fund is formed to invest in the common stocks of health-related firms that are expected to benefit from the tremendous amount of money spent by Americans on health care. Health Fund might sell 20 million shares to the public for $10 a share, raising $200 million. Once the fund is started, it invests in the common stocks of various companies in the health field industry, such as Pfizer Drugs, Abbott Labs, and Syntex. Health Fund now owns a portfolio of stocks, and, in turn, is owned by investors who purchased shares of it. These investors, if so disposed and financially able, could have constructed a similar portfolio directly by purchasing the same stocks bought by the Health Fund. By purchasing Health Fund, they own a percentage of its portfolio, and, in effect, they are stockholders in the companies owned by Health Fund. An investment company, therefore, is a *pure intermediary:* it performs a basic service—buying and selling securities—for its shareholders that they could perform for themselves.[2] ▪

An important factor affecting investment company organization is the Internal Revenue Service classification of a *regulated investment company.* If a company meets the prescribed conditions and is so classified, it can elect to pay no federal taxes on any distributions of dividends, interest, and realized capital gains to its shareholders. The investment company acts as a *conduit,* "flowing through" these distributions to stockholders, who pay their own marginal tax rates on them; in effect, fund shareholders are treated as if they held the securities in the fund's portfolio. After all, investment companies are pure intermediaries, and thus shareholders should pay the same taxes they would pay if they owned the shares directly. Meeting these conditions results in the following[3]:

1. Dividends and interest are taxable to a fund only if retained; therefore, after operating costs are deducted, all such income is usually paid out.

[2]Note, however, that investment companies provide a variety of services for their shareholders, at least some of which cannot be performed as easily or conveniently by many investors.
[3]To qualify as a regulated investment company, a fund must earn at least 90% of all income from security transactions and distribute at least 90% of all interest and dividend income. Furthermore, the fund must diversify its assets. For at least 50% of the portfolio, no more than 5% of the fund's assets can be invested in the securities of any one issuer, and a position in any one security cannot exceed 25% of the fund's assets.

2. Realized capital gains are taxable to a fund only if retained; if distributed to shareholders, they are taxable to them.

Investment companies are required by the Investment Company Act of 1940 to register with the SEC.[4] This detailed regulatory statute contains numerous provisions designed to protect shareholders.[5] Most states also regulate investment companies.

Types of Investment Companies

All investment companies begin by selling shares in themselves to the public. Most investment companies are managed companies, offering professional management of the portfolio as one of the benefits. One less-well-known type of investment company is unmanaged. We shall begin with the unmanaged type and then discuss the two types of managed investment companies. After we consider each of the three, we shall concentrate our discussion on mutual funds, the most popular type of investment company for the typical individual investor.

Unit Investment Trusts An alternative form of investment company from the normal managed type is the Unit Investment Trust, traditionally an *unmanaged,* fixed-income security portfolio put together by a sponsor and handled by an independent trustee. Redeemable trust certificates representing claims against the assets of the trust are sold to investors at net asset value plus a small commission. All interest (or dividends) and principal repayments are distributed to the holders of the certificates. Most unit investment trusts hold tax-exempt securities.

The assets underlying a unit investment trust are almost always kept unchanged, although certain portfolio changes may be dictated by changing events. In the case of fixed-income securities, the trust ceases to exist when the bonds mature.

It is possible to redeem units of the trust. The sponsor makes a market in these certificates for those who wish to sell. Generally, the units are sold back at the net asset value. It is also possible to find secondary markets for unit trusts among brokers and dealers.

A new innovation in the 1990s is the *stock trust* designed for small investors. Typical initial investment is $1000, and a typical projected holding period is one to five years.[6] The primary benefit touted is diversifica-

---

[4]The 1940 act was amended in 1970. These amendments, among other things, prohibited the charging of excessive commissions to share purchasers and the payment of excessive fees to investment company advisors.

[5]Investment companies are also regulated under the Securities Acts of 1933, the Securities Exchange Act of 1934, and the Investment Advisers Act of 1940.

[6]This information is based on Karen Slater, "Asking $1,000 a Pop, Stock Trusts Aim to Lure Small Investors," *The Wall Street Journal,* January 30, 1990, p. C1.

tion, with the trusts holding between 10 and 40 stocks. Like a bond trust, these trusts intend to keep their positions basically unchanged, selling an individual stock only in the event of major problems with the company.

In addition to achieving diversification with a relatively small initial investment, investors in stock trusts know exactly what they are buying. Furthermore, they reduce significantly the portfolio management fees normally associated with mutual funds and ranging from 0.75% to 1.25% of assets. On the negative side, trust sales commissions can be as much as 4% for a one-year trust, and some investors worry about the lack of portfolio management implicit in a trust.

In general, *unit investment trusts are passive investments*. They are designed to be bought and held, with capital preservation as a major objective. Investors gain diversification, professional management that takes care of all the details, the purchase of securities by the trust at a cheaper price than if purchased individually, and minimum operating costs. They lose the ability to make rapid, inexpensive or costless changes in their positions if conditions change.

Closed-End Investment Companies One of the two types of managed investment companies, **closed-end investment companies** usually sell no additional shares of their own stock after the initial public offering. Therefore, their capitalizations are fixed unless a new public offering is made. The shares of a closed-end fund trade in the secondary markets (e.g., on the exchanges) exactly like any other stock. To buy and sell, investors use their brokers, paying (receiving) the current price at which the shares are selling plus (less) brokerage commissions.[7]

Because shares of closed-end funds trade on exchanges, their prices are determined by the forces of supply and demand. Interestingly, however, the market price is seldom equal to the actual per share value of the closed-end shares, which is referred to as the **net asset value (NAV)**. The NAV of an investment company share is computed by calculating the total market value of the securities in the portfolio, subtracting any trade payables, and dividing by the number of mutual fund shares currently outstanding.[8]

[7]A special type of closed-end fund is the dual-purpose fund. It differs from other investment companies in that it has a limited life and sells two classes of shares to investors. At its inception, equal dollar amounts of income and capital shares are sold, with the proceeds used to purchase a portfolio of assets as usual. However, the *income shareholders* receive all interest and dividends yielded by the assets, and at the termination date of the fund they receive a special redemption value. *Capital shareholders*, on the other hand, are entitled to all assets not received by the income shares; therefore, they receive everything remaining at the termination date. The life of dual-purpose funds ranges from 10 to 20 years. A new fund can be formed at that time or the capital shares can be paid off by liquidating all remaining assets.

[8]Total market value of the portfolio is equal to the product of each security's current market price multiplied by the number of shares of that security owned by the fund.

Example. If the total market value of the securities held by the previously mentioned Health Fund is $300 million on a day when 25 million shares of Health Fund are owned by shareholders, the NAV is $300/25 = $12 per share. ▪

Historically, the market prices of closed-ends have ranged from roughly 5% to 20% below their NAVs. In this situation, the closed-end is said to be selling at a **discount:** if the market price exceeds the NAV, as it sometimes does for some closed-end funds, the fund is said to be selling at a **premium.** Although several studies have addressed the question of why these funds sell at discounts and premiums, no totally satisfactory explanation has been widely accepted by all market observers.[9]

Example. As an illustration of the discount phenomenon, consider the following data for Super Fund, a hypothetical closed-end investment company.

	19X1	19X2	19X3	19X4	19X5
NAV	$16.24	11.33	12.85	13.76	12.00
Closing price	$12.38	9.50	9.88	11.25	10.62
Dividends	$ 0.23	0.15	0.15	0.15	0.14
Capital gains distributions	$ 1.04	1.38	1.17	0.92	1.21
% Discount (rounded)	24	16	23	18	12

The percentage discounts from NAV for the five-year period range from 12 to 24%, with an average of 19%.[10] ▪

By purchasing a fund at a discount, an investor is actually buying shares in a portfolio of securities at a price below their market value. Therefore, even if the value of the portfolio remains unchanged, an investor can gain or lose if the discount narrows or widens over time; that is, a difference exists between the portfolio's return and the shareholder's return.

Example. Assume that an investor purchased shares in the Super Fund at year-end 19X2 and sold at year-end 19X3. Based on NAV, the portfolio return was

$$\text{Portfolio return} = \frac{\text{Ending NAV} - \text{Beginning NAV} + \text{Dividends} + \text{Capital gains distributions}}{\text{Beginning NAV}}$$

[9]See, for example, B. Malkiel, "The Valuation of Closed-End Investment Companies," *Journal of Finance*, June 1977, pp. 847–856.

[10]The percentage discount can be calculated as

$$\text{Percentage discount from NAV} = [(\text{NAV} - \text{Closing price})/\text{NAV}]\ 100$$

$$= \frac{\$12.85 - 11.33 + 0.15 + 1.17}{\$11.33}$$

$$= 0.251, \text{ or } 25.1\%$$

The shareholder's return, however, is the total return, calculated using closing prices.

$$\text{Shareholder's return} = \frac{\$9.88 - 9.50 + 0.15 + 1.17}{\$9.50}$$

$$= 0.179, \text{ or } 17.9\%$$

A shareholder would have realized 17.9% during 19X3 on a total return basis, whereas the portfolio's performance was 25.1%. The percentage discount widened in 19X3. ▪

Funds trade at premiums as well as discounts. At the beginning of 1990, while such well-known closed-end funds as Adams Express and Tri-Continental were trading at discounts of approximately 11% and 16%, respectively, the Korea Fund was trading at an astounding premium of approximately 87%, an increase from the previous year's premium of 63%. In other words, investors buying the shares of Korea Fund were willing to pay about 87% more than the net asset value of the fund to obtain the shares.

Mutual Funds **Open-end investment companies,** which are popularly referred to as **mutual funds,** continue to sell shares to investors after the initial sale of shares that starts the fund. Mutual funds are the most popular form of investment company for the typical investor.

Owners of fund shares can sell them back to the company (redeem them) any time they choose; the mutual fund is legally obligated to redeem them. Investors purchase new shares, and redeem their existing shares, at the net asset value (NAV), which, as explained earlier, is the value of a single share in the fund. The NAV is calculated daily, and new purchases and sales are made at the most recently calculated NAV. Thus, the capitalization of an open-end investment company is continually changing as new investors buy additional shares and some existing shareholders cash in by selling their shares back to the company.

Mutual funds are corporations, typically formed by an investment advisory firm that selects the board of trustees (directors) for the company. The trustees, in turn, hire a separate management company, normally the investment advisory firm, to manage the fund. The management company is contracted by the investment company to perform necessary research and to manage the portfolio, as well as handle the administrative chores, for which it receives a fee.

Example. Fidelity Investments is a mutual fund company offering dozens of different funds to the public. FMR is a corporation that acts as investment adviser to the "Fidelity family of funds" as well as certain other funds that are generally offered to limited groups of investors. The stock of FMR is wholly owned by a holding company, FMR Corporation, which, in effect, is the Fidelity Company. ▪

Some funds use a sales force to reach investors, with shares available from brokers, insurance agents, and financial planners. In an alternative form of distribution called direct marketing, the company uses advertising and direct mailing to appeal to investors. About 70% of all stock, bond, and income fund sales are made by funds using a sales force.[11]

There are economies of scale in managing portfolios. Expenses rise as assets under management increase, but not at the same rate as revenues. Because investment managers can oversee various amounts of money with few additional costs, management companies seek to increase the size of the fund(s) being managed. Many operate several different funds simultaneously.

Mutual funds can be subdivided into those that charge a sales fee (load funds) and those that do not (no-load funds). A **load fund** charges investors for the costs involved in selling the fund. This sales fee, added to the fund's NAV, has traditionally been a maximum of 8.5%.

Example. On a $1000 purchase, with an 8.5% load fee, an investor would pay $85 "commission," acquiring only $915 in shares.[12] ▪

The load fee percentage usually declines with the size of the purchase. Typically, there is no redemption fee when shares are redeemed, although in the early 1980s some funds began charging redemption fees in the 1% to 3% range. All of these fees must be stated in the **prospectus,** which is designed to describe a particular fund's objectives, policies, operations, and fees. Investors should carefully read a fund's prospectus before investing.

The load or sales charge goes to the marketing organization selling the shares, which could be the investment company itself or brokers. The fee is split between the sales person and the company employing that person. The old adage in the investment company business is that "mutual fund shares are sold, not bought," meaning that the sales force aggressively sells the shares to investors. However, the percentage of stock and bond funds with the full 8.5% sales fee declined from almost one-third of such funds in 1980 to only about 5% of all such funds at the beginning of 1990.

In contrast to the load funds, **no-load** mutual funds are bought at net asset value directly from the fund itself. No sales fee is charged because

[11]Equity funds have equal sales from direct marketing and sales forces. The majority of bond and income fund sales are made by sales forces.

[12]Note that this is an effective charge of 9.3% ($85/$915).

there is no sales force to compensate. Investors must seek out these funds by responding to advertisements in the financial press, and purchase and redeem shares by mail, wire, or telephone.[13] Quite a few funds are said to be "low-load" funds, with sales charges of 2% to 3%. A single investment company—for example, Fidelity Investments—may simultaneously offer both no-load funds and low-load funds.

A question that is often asked is, "If the no-load funds charge no sales fee, how is the investment company compensated?" The answer is that all funds, open-end and closed-end, load funds and no-load funds, charge the shareholders an *expense fee*. This fee is paid out of the fund's income, derived from the dividends, interest, and capital gains earned during the year.

The annual expense fee consists of *management fees*, overhead, and 12b-1 fees, if any.[14] Typical annual management fees begin at 0.5% of the fund's total market value (in other words, 50 cents per year per $100 of assets under management).[15] Some funds reduce the fee as the fund's assets under management increase.

Funds show the total expenses as an "annual expense ratio" (percentage of assets). The average operating expenses for all mutual funds is around 1.25% of assets. The average for stock funds is 1.6% of assets.

Mutual Funds

There are two major types of mutual funds:

1. Money market funds (including short-term municipal bond funds)
2. Equity, bond, and income funds

In effect, money market funds concentrate on short-term investing by holding portfolios of money market assets, and equity, bond, and income funds concentrate on longer-term investing by holding mostly capital market assets.

Money Market Funds One of the major innovations in the investment company industry has been the creation, and subsequent phenomenal growth, of the money market funds. These funds were created in 1974, when interest rates were at record high levels. They grew tremendously in 1981–1982 when short-term interest rates were again at record levels and

[13]On any given day, the last few pages of *The Wall Street Journal* contain several ads for mutual funds.

[14]The Securities and Exchange Commission allows funds to charge a "distribution fee," often called a 12b-1 fee. This fee is a fraction of a percent of the fund's average assets.

[15]The management fee for money market funds is less.

investors seeking to earn these high short-term rates found that they generally could not do so directly.[16]

This situation has changed with the deregulation of the thrift institutions, and competition has increased dramatically for investors' short-term savings. Banks can now offer money market deposit accounts (MMDAs) (discussed in Chapter 2) that pay money market rates and are insured. Although their average current yield was less than that of the money market funds in 1984 and 1985, MMDAs have attracted record amounts of funds. As a result, money market assets grew from $2 billion in 1974 to $207 billion by 1982, and totaled $359 billion by the beginning of 1990—an increase of about $85 billion from the beginning of 1989.

Money market funds are open-end investment companies that operate like a traditional mutual fund except that their portfolios consist of money market instruments such as Treasury bills, negotiable CDs, and prime commercial paper.[17] Some funds hold only bills, whereas others hold various mixtures. In 1989, as Table 18-1 shows, commercial paper accounted for almost 50% of the total assets held by these funds, with repurchase agreements and commercial bank CDs a distant second and third respectively. The average maturity of these portfolios was around 30 days.

Alternative forms of money market funds are the *short-term municipal bond fund,* also called a *tax-exempt money market fund,* and the *short-term state municipal bond funds,* which invest only in the issues of a single state. These funds, available since 1979, invest in municipal securities with short maturities.

Investors in money market funds pay neither a sales charge nor a redemption charge, but they do pay a management fee. Interest is earned and credited daily. The shares can be redeemed at any time by phone or wire. Many funds offer check-writing privileges for checks of $500 or more, with the investor earning interest until the check clears.[18]

Money market funds provide investors with a chance to earn the going rates in the money market while enjoying broad diversification and high liquidity. Although investors may assume little risk because of the diversification and quality of these instruments, money market funds are not insured. Banks and thrift institutions have emphasized this point in competing with money market funds for the savings of investors.

---

[16]Recall that the money market instruments discussed in Chapter 2 have large minimum investments, ranging from $10,000 for Treasury bills to a more typical $100,000 in the case of negotiable certificates of deposit and banker's acceptances.

[17]Currently, three types of money market funds exist. General-purpose fund are those with a varying mix of clients, both individuals and institutions. Broker–dealer funds, the largest of the three in terms of assets, are managed by brokerage firms, and their clients are primarily individuals. Finally, institutional funds are designed exclusively for institutions such as banks and businesses.

[18]Shareholders have made only limited use of the check-writing privilege, however, indicating that they regard money market funds primarily as a way to save.

TABLE 18-1 *Money Market Fund Asset Composition, 1989 (billions of dollars)*

Money Market Fund Asset Composition Yearend 1989 (billions of dollars)	
U.S. Treasury Bills	$7.4
Other Treasury Securities	7.4
Other U.S. Securities	21.0
Repurchase Agreements	54.9
Commercial Bank CDs	33.6
Other Domestic CDs	7.6
Eurodollar CDs	26.4
Commercial Paper	179.1
Bankers Acceptances	7.5
Cash Reserves	0.1
Other	13.7
Total Net Assets	$358.7
Average Maturity (Days)	38
Number of Funds	463

Source: Reprinted by permission of the Investment Company Institute, *1990 Mutual Fund Fact Book,* p. 32.

Equity, Bond, and Income Funds[19] The board of directors (trustees) of an investment company *must* specify the objective that the company will pursue in its investment policy. The companies try to follow a consistent investment policy, according to their specified objective. Investors purchase funds on the basis of their objectives.

The Investment Company Institute, a well-known organization that represents the investment company industry, uses 19 major categories of investment objectives for equity, bond, and income funds. These are identified and explained in Figure 18-1.

As Figure 18-1 shows, investors using these funds have a wide range of investment objectives. Traditionally, investors often opted for growth funds, which seek capital appreciation, or balanced funds, which seek both income and capital appreciation. Now investors can choose from global funds, either bonds or stocks, precious metal funds, municipal bond funds, and so forth. Growth funds remain the largest single category of funds, followed by municipal bond funds and aggressive growth funds, respectively.

Table 18-2 shows the portfolio composition of the equity, bond, and income funds as of year-end 1989. As we would expect, equities (both common and preferred) represent a substantial portion of total assets. In the 1950s and 1960s, the mutual fund industry concentrated on equity funds. However, as we can see from Table 18-2, bonds have become a much

[19]The Investment Company Institute uses this terminology.

Aggressive Growth Funds seek maximum capital gains as their investment objective. Current income is not a significant factor. Some may invest in stocks of businesses that are somewhat out of the mainstream, such as fledgling companies, new industries, companies fallen on hard times, or industries temporarily out of favor. Some may also use specialized investment techniques such as option writing or short-term trading.

Balanced Funds generally have a three-part investment objective: 1) to conserve the investors' initial principal, 2) to pay current income, and 3) to promote long-term growth of both this principal and income. Balanced funds have a portfolio mix of bonds, preferred stocks, and common stocks.

Corporate Bond Funds, like income funds, seek a high level of income. They do so by buying bonds of corporations for the majority of the fund's portfolio. The rest of the portfolio may be in U.S. Treasury bonds or bonds issued by a federal agency.

Flexible Portfolio Funds may be 100 percent invested in stocks OR bonds OR money market instruments, depending on market conditions. These funds give the money managers the greatest flexibility in anticipating or responding to economic changes.

GNMA or Ginnie Mae Funds invest in mortgage securities backed by the Government National Mortgage Association (GNMA). To qualify for this category, the majority of the portfolio must always be invested in mortgage-backed securities.

Global Bond Funds invest in the debt securities of companies and countries worldwide, including the U.S.

Global Equity Funds invest in securities traded worldwide, including the U.S. Compared to direct investments, global funds offer investors an easier avenue to investing abroad. The funds' professional money managers handle the trading and recordkeeping details and deal with differences in currencies, languages, time zones, laws and regulations, and business customs and practices. In addition to another layer of diversification, global funds add another layer of risk—exchange-rate risk.

Growth Funds invest in the common stock of well-established companies. Their primary aim is to produce an increase in the value of their investments (capital gains) rather than a flow of dividends. Investors who buy a growth fund are more interested in seeing the fund's share price rise than in receiving income from dividends.

Growth and Income Funds invest money in the common stock of companies that have had increasing share value but also a solid record of paying dividends. This type of fund attempts to combine long-term capital growth with a steady stream of income.

High-yield Bond Funds maintain at least two-thirds of their portfolio in lower-rated orporate bonds (Baa or lower by Moody's rating service and BBB or lower by Standard and Poor's rating service). In return for a generally higher yield, investors must bear a greater degree of risk than for higher-rated bonds.

FIGURE 18-1 ***The number of mutual funds for selected years.***
Source: Reprinted by permission of the Investment Company Institute, *1990 Mutual Fund Fact Book,* p. 22.

Income (Bond) Funds seek a high level of current income for their shareholders by investing at all times in a mix of corporate and government bonds.

Income (Equity) Funds seek a high level of current income for their shareholders by investing primarily in equity securities of companies with good dividend-paying records.

Income (Mixed) Funds seek a high level of current income for their shareholders by investing in income-producing securities, including both equities and debt instruments.

International Funds invest in equity securities of companies located outside the U.S. Two thirds of their portfolios must be so invested at all times to be categorized here.

Long-term Municipal Bond Funds invest in bonds issued by states and municipalities to finance schools, highways, hospitals, airports, bridges, water and sewer works, and other public projects. In most cases, income earned on these securities is not taxed by the federal government, but may be taxed under state and local laws. For some taxpayers, portions of income earned on these securities may be subject to the federal alternative minimum tax.

Option/Income Funds seek a higher current return by investing primarily in dividend-paying common stocks on which call options are traded on national securities exchanges. Current return generally consists of dividends, premiums from writing options, net short-term gains from sales of portfolio securities on exercises of options or otherwise, and any profits from closing purchase transactions.

Precious Metals/Gold Funds maintain two thirds of their portfolios invested in securities associated with gold, silver, and other precious metals.

State Municipal Bond Funds—Long-term work just like other long-term municipal bond funds (see above) except their portfolios contain the issues of only one state. A resident of that state has the advantage of receiving income free of both federal and state tax. For some taxpayers, portions of income from these securities may be subject to the federal alternative minimum tax.

U.S. Government Income Funds invest in a variety of government securities. These include U.S. Treasury bonds, federally guaranteed mortgage-backed securities, and other government notes.

FIGURE 18-1 ***(Continued)***

more important component of the aggregate portfolio for these funds. Notice in particular the importance of long-term Treasury bonds.

Mutual Fund Data

Figure 18-2 shows the number of mutual funds for selected years since 1940. There were no money market funds until 1974, and by the end of 1989 there were 664. There were over 2000 stock, bond, and income funds.

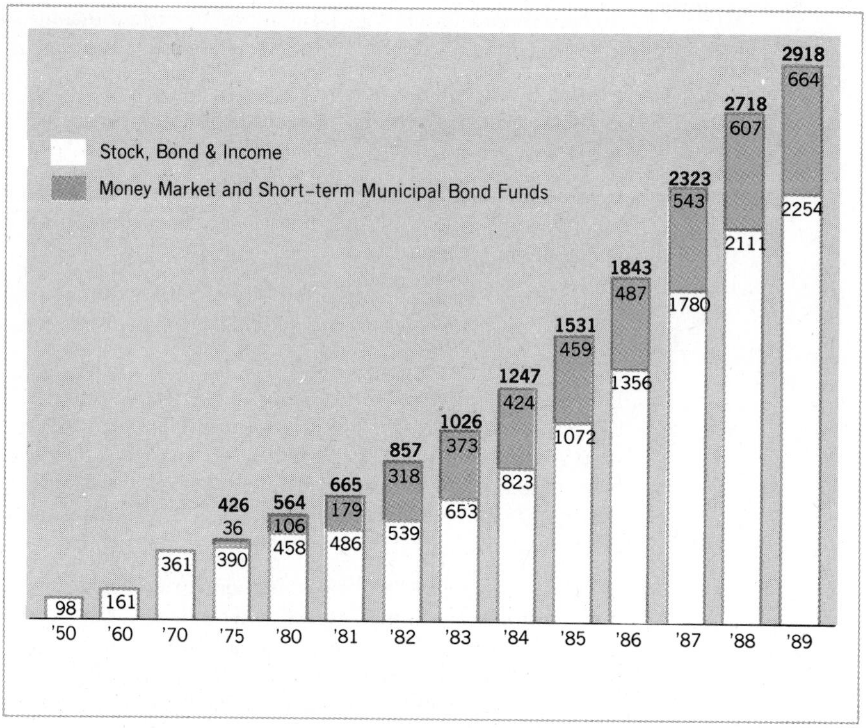

FIGURE 18-2 ***Types of equity, bond, and income funds.***
Source: Reprinted by permission of the Investment Company Institute, *1990 Mutual Fund Fact Book,* p. 17–18.

TABLE 18-2 ***Portfolio Composition of Equity, Bond, and Income Funds, 1989 (billions of dollars)***

Portfolio Composition of Equity, Bond, and Income Funds Yearend 1989 (billions of dollars)	
Common Stock	$241.3
Preferred Stock	4.6
Municipal Bonds (long-term)	85.0
Corporate Bonds	53.0
U.S. Gov't. Sec. (long-term)	118.1
U.S. Gov't. Sec. (short-term)	11.0
Liquid Assets	33.8
Other	7.1
Total Net Assets	$553.8

Source: Reprinted by permission of the Investment Company Institute, *1990 Mutual Fund Fact Book,* p. 31.

The percentage distribution of total net assets by type of fund has changed dramatically since the mid-1970s, as shown in Figure 18-3. Whereas equity funds constituted about 34% of total mutual fund net assets in 1979, by 1989 this percentage had declined to only 25%, and bond–income funds grew from 18% to 31%. Thus, bond and income funds now constitute a bigger share of total mutual fund assets than do equity funds. Money market funds declined from 48% of assets in 1979 to 37% in 1989. The new category of short-term municipal bond funds did not exist in 1979, but constituted 7% of all assets by 1989.

Analyzing Mutual Funds

As noted, investors have a basic choice. They can design a portfolio of securities by doing their own analysis, with or without the aid of other parties such as brokers. Alternatively, they can simply invest in shares of an investment company, which will invest the funds on their behalf in an existing portfolio. This decision is an important one that confronts all investors and should be considered carefully.

Advantages and Disadvantages of Owning Mutual Fund Shares

Because of its importance, we shall discuss in detail the benefits and costs of indirect investing through investment companies. By analyzing the costs and benefits, investors can decide whether to purchase securities directly or indirectly.

Choosing between direct and indirect investing is not always difficult. For example, an investor wishing to invest in money market instruments such as negotiable CDs or commercial paper may have no alternative because of the large minimum denominations that these securities carry. Also, an investor with less than $10,000 to invest cannot purchase even one Treasury bill. As another example, the alternatives are poor for many investors interested in corporate or municipal bonds if they wish to obtain the benefits of diversification and good liquidity (in case they need to sell before maturity). Unless they have considerable funds (at least $100,000) to invest and some knowledge about the bond markets, the unit investment trusts or a regular bond fund specializing in municipals or corporates are often the most sensible way to invest.

When the choice between direct and indirect investing is not clear, it is important to weigh the potential benefits and costs of owning investment company shares. In general, the following discussion applies to any of the three types of investment company shares, but we shall concentrate specifically on mutual funds.

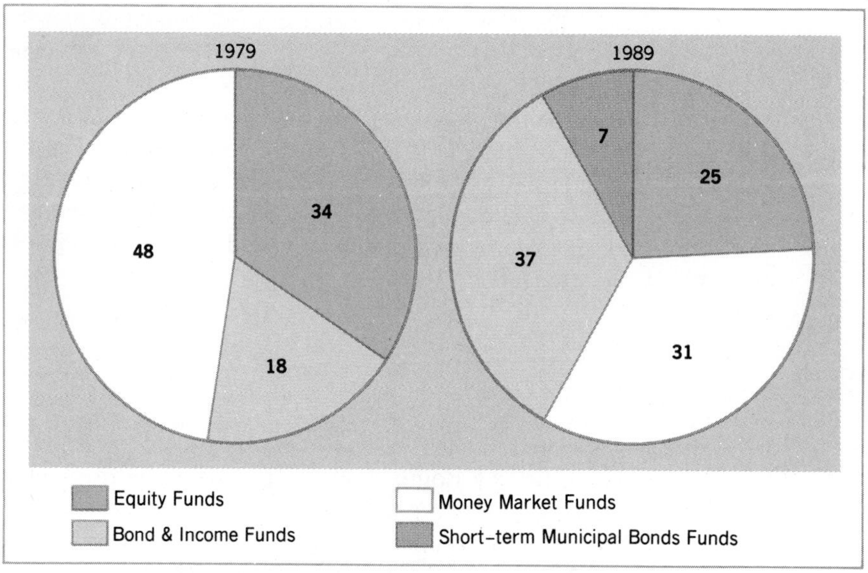

FIGURE 18-3 ***Percent distribution of total net assets by type of fund.***
Source: Reprinted by permission of the Investment Company Institute, *1990 Mutual Fund Fact Book,* p. 21.

Benefits The benefits include the following:

Diversification Perhaps the single greatest benefit of owning shares in a mutual fund is the instantaneous diversification conferred on the investor. As we shall see in Part Seven, one of the most important tenets of modern portfolio theory is the necessity of diversifying one's holdings among several assets in order to reduce risk. Investors may find this impossible to do if they have limited funds to invest, or expensive in terms of brokerage costs even with adequate funds. Mutual funds, on the other hand, are required by both the Internal Revenue Code and the Investment Company Act of 1940 to meet certain diversification standards.

Overall, mutual funds offer very substantial diversification. Some funds hold over 100 different securities, and sometimes as many as 200. On the other hand, other funds are not as well diversified. In particular, *speciality funds* or *sector funds* specializing in certain industries, commodities, or geographic areas may be quite poorly diversified.

Variety of Objectives A large number of mutual funds are available with a wide variety of objectives. Investors can probably find one or more funds to meet their objectives. Funds specialize in stocks, bonds, and combinations thereof. With stocks, some funds are broadly diversified and others specialize in a particular industry, commodity, concept, or geographical area. With bonds, some funds are broadly diversified in Treasury securities, corporates, or municipals.

Thus, investors can typically find funds to suit their investment outlook, tax situation, income needs, and risk preferences. There is virtually a fund for everyone.

Services Mutual funds offer a wide variety of services to their shareholders:

1. *Record keeping.* The funds maintain and compile complete records of the shareholder's activity for a given year, including the dividends, interest, and capital gains received by the shareholder. This is a great convenience for income tax purposes.
2. *Handling of securities.* Mutual funds typically arrange for the physical custody of all securities in the portfolio. This includes the collection of all dividends and interest.
3. *Fund swaps.* Increasingly, investors are taking advantage of the exchange privilege—the ability to switch their holdings among the *family of funds* being managed by a given investment advisor. The fees charged for purchase of shares are reduced, or even eliminated, for existing shareholders.[20] Thus, shareholders may decide to switch from one fund emphasizing capital gains to another emphasizing maximum current income, either taxable or tax-exempt.

   Figure 18-4 shows the dollar value of sales exchanges among all types of mutual funds. Exchanges have increased at an incredible rate, nearly quadrupling from 1983 to 1989.
4. *Accumulation and withdrawal plans.* Many funds permit the *automatic reinvestment* of all dividends into shares of the fund at net asset value.[21] Thus, investment income dividends and capital gains distributions can be reinvested automatically in additional shares. In 1988, about 62% of the investment income dividends paid out by mutual funds was reinvested. Some funds also permit specified monthly withdrawals by the shareholder, based either on a fixed dollar amount or a fixed percentage of the shareholder's assets. A minimum investment amount is usually required to start a withdrawal plan.
5. *IRA and Keogh plans.* Many funds provide investors with a tax shelter through the use of Individual Retirement Accounts (IRAs) and Keogh plans for the self-employed.

---

[20]Fees are usually at a level approximating the cost of the bookkeeping process of converting the account.

[21]Some load funds reinvest investment income at the fund's offering price; however, no fund charges a load to reinvest capital gain distributions. The National Association of Securities Dealers has limited the maximum load chargeable on reinvested dividends to 7.5%.

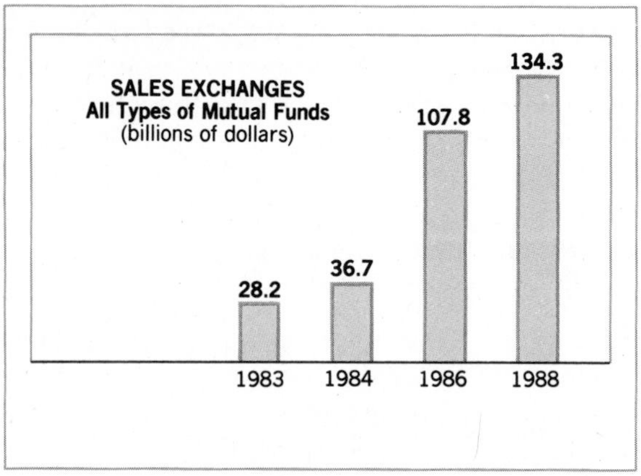

FIGURE 18-4 ***Sales exchanges, all types of mutual funds (billions of dollars).*** *Source:* Reprinted by permission of the Investment Company Institute, *1990 Mutual Fund Fact Book,* p. 26.

Costs The costs of mutual funds include the following:

Load Fee The most obvious cost of mutual fund ownership is the sales charge paid by owners of load fund shares. As noted before, this sales charge is substantial, averaging about 8.5% (an effective cost of 9.3%). Of course, these fees can be avoided if a comparable no-load fund can be found, which is often the case.[22]

Although load fees are "front-end" charges, paid by investors to buy into a load fund, a major area of contention in recent years is the so-called *12b-1 fees*. These fees are named after an SEC regulation that allows fund sponsors to deduct from fund assets compensation for brokers who sell the funds. The rationale for such fees is that by increasing the sales of a fund as a result of the compensation, the fund will become larger and economies of scale will lower the cost to investors of operating the fund. Some bond funds have charged 12b-1 fees of 1% or more, which clearly takes away from the investor's results. Often the funds that charge these fees are very large in terms of assets—in effect, they already have economies of scale. Investors should carefully examine the 12b-1 fees charged by funds.

Annual Expenses Every fund charges an annual management fee, roughly 0.5% of asset market value, to compensate for the research and management costs incurred by the fund.[23] Operating expenses of the fund, including custodian, accounting, legal, and postage costs, must also be paid by the

[22]Closed-end shares can also be purchased on the exchanges by paying regular brokerage fees.
[23]The management fee is usually the largest component of a fund's expenses. It covers salaries, office space and accessories, and the cost of portfolio management.

shareholders. Annual expenses are deducted from the assets of the fund. As noted previously, the annual expense ratio for the average stock fund is 1.6%, although the variation is large.

Transaction Costs Like any investor, investment companies must pay transaction costs to buy and sell securities.[24] They have an advantage over individual investors, however, because of the large blocks they trade and their power to negotiate favorable commissions—available evidence suggests brokerage commissions of about 6 cents a share. Obviously, brokerage commissions can be reduced by holding down portfolio turnover.[25] Some funds have relatively low turnover, whereas others turn over almost their entire portfolio regularly. By 1989 the average equity fund turnover was over 90%, up from 25% in the mid-1970s.

A possible "hidden" transaction cost for investment companies is the price pressure caused by the trading of a large block. Buying or selling a large block may drive the price up or down beyond what would have occurred with a smaller number of shares. An additional transaction cost is the market maker's bid–ask spread (which applies to both listed and OTC stocks). These "hidden" transaction costs have been estimated at about 0.6%.[26]

Superfluous Diversification Adequate diversification is absolutely essential to the sound management of portfolios; however, some mutual funds may hold as many as 200 securities in their portfolios. This is more than is needed to reduce risk and will tend to negate the positive effects of a few good performers in the portfolio. The fund's performance will tend to parallel the market average, as does an index fund, although it is attempting to outperform such funds.

The Active Management Cost If securities markets are basically efficient, as suggested by the efficient market hypothesis, investment companies can generate too much expense by unsuccessfully trying to time market moves or buy (sell) under- (over-) valued securities. And the evidence on mutual fund performance considered in Chapter 14 suggests that this is probably the case. Given the importance of this topic, we shall consider it again.

Assessing Mutual Fund Performance

Measuring Performance Returns on mutual funds (or closed-end funds) can be calculated in the same manner as the total return measure explained

[24]Brokerage costs are treated as capital items rather than expenses.

[25]The SEC defines turnover for investment companies as the lesser of sales or purchases divided by average assets.

[26]See David Henry, "High Churnover," *Forbes*, March 10, 1986, p. 146.

in Chapter 5. The total return during a particular period (both income and price appreciation) is related to the price at the beginning of the period.

Example. Consider the hypothetical Wonder Fund, a diversified common stock fund that at year-end 19X7 has 97% of its assets in common stocks. Net asset values per share at year-end 19X6 and 19X7 are $7.75 and $8.59, respectively. During 19X7, $0.56 in income (dividends and interest) and $0.33 in capital gains are distributed to shareholders. Thus, total shareholder return on Wonder Fund in 19X7 is 22.3%, calculated as

$$\text{Shareholder total returns} = \frac{\$8.59 - \$7.75 + \$0.89}{\$7.75}$$

$$= 22.3\%$$

▪

What can be said about the performance of Wonder Fund based on this information? The first comparison that is usually made is to the "market" during the same period. Assume that the S&P 500 Composite Index for 19X7 shows a total return (TR) of 20.4%. Therefore, Wonder outperforms the market for that year. But is this enough information to conclude anything about this one company's performance? The answer is *no!* Investors should ask several questions about a particular fund they own or are considering purchasing.

The first and most important question concerns the risk involved: Did Wonder assume more risk than is represented in a market index such as the S&P 500? As we established in Chapter 1, the basis of investment decisions is that a risk–return trade-off is involved. Risk and expected return go together; therefore, if a particular fund assumes more risk than the market average, its return is expected to be larger.

Example Consider total return data for Wonder Fund and the S&P 500 for the years 19X0 through 19X9. Assume that the respective standard deviations of the annual returns for Wonder Fund and the market index are 19.69% and 20.94% and that the beta for the fund is 0.90. Therefore, Wonder shows less total risk (standard deviation) and less market risk (beta) than did the market index over this time period. ▪

The second question that should be raised concerns performance over time. The fact that a fund performs well in one particular year is not reassuring for the longer run. Luck or short-term insights can play a role in performance. It is important to assess the consistency of performance over time. Assume that the mean return over this 10-year period for Wonder is 12.46%, whereas that for the S&P 500 was 8.45%. Furthermore, assume that except for 19X7, Wonder performed better than the market on an absolute basis for each year during 19X0 through 19X9. This analysis appears to suggest that Wonder has performed well.

Relative consistency of performance is also important. Assume that the *Forbes* ratings (explained later) of performance in both up and down markets show that Wonder has a relative rating of C in both up and down markets. This indicates that the fund did not do as well as 50% of all the funds rated during up markets (it was in the third quartile); on the other hand, it did better than 50% of all funds in down markets (it was in the second quartile).[27] Thus, on a relative ranking basis, Wonder is not a standout. To make the list of consistent performers over the period studied by *Forbes,* a fund had to achieve a ranking of B or higher in both up and down markets—a feat usually accomplished by only a few funds.

A third area to question is expenses. A fund that performs well may have large expenses as it searches for undervalued securities or tries to time market movements. Assume that Wonder has annual expenses of $0.36 per $100 of average net assets. This figure, which includes both operating expenses and management fees, compares to an average of about $0.75 to $0.90. However, Wonder has a sales charge of 7.25% (with reduced charges beginning at $5000). This will clearly reduce the performance for an investor in the year of purchase. Of course, calculating shareholder returns over a longer period will diminish the relative impact of the sales charge. Nevertheless, the load fee remains a significant item to consider, and investors always have the option of no-load funds.

The Performance Record Chapter 14 discussed the performance of portfolio managers as one indication of market efficiency. Several studies of mutual fund performance were mentioned, most of which found that mutual funds do not outperform market averages on a risk-adjusted basis. A summary of these findings, together with those of other studies, suggests the following[28]:

1. Active portfolio management by mutual fund managers seems to produce positive results *gross* of fund expenses, but not *net* of fund expenses.
2. The risk of mutual funds is reasonably stable over time, and past risk levels can be used to predict future risk (obviously, by no means perfectly).
3. Consistency in individual fund performance typically has not been found. Although a few funds seem to perform well over a period of time, such results can be accounted for by the laws of probability. This issue, however, remains unsettled.

Thus, empirical studies of mutual fund performance suggest that active portfolio management does not increase shareholder welfare. For the typical

[27]In the *Forbes* ratings, a C in an up market represents the third quartile of Performance (A+ and A cover the first quartile, and B covers the second quartile); on the down side, A and B cover the first quartile; C, the second; D, the third; and F, the last.

[28]Other studies include J. McDonald, "Objectives and Performance of Mutual Funds, 1960–1969," *Journal of Financial and Quantitative Analysis,* June 1974, pp. 311–333.

mutual fund investor, this evidence suggests that mutual funds should not be purchased primarily to obtain exceptional management performance.

One perspective on the performance of professional portfolio managers can be obtained by considering the following:

1. For the period 1981–1985, the Salomon Broad Bond Index outperformed 81% of professionally managed bond portfolios.[29]
2. For all equity mutual funds considered together, for the 10 years through December 31, 1988, the annual average performance for the funds was 15.4% vs. 16.3% for the S&P 500 (not adjusted for sales charges).[30]
3. For one five-year period ending in 1989, less than 40% of all U.S. stock mutual funds outperformed the S&P 500 Index.

An interesting point to consider when discussing the performance records of investment companies is the relative performance of closed-end funds versus that of mutual funds. For a discussion of some difficulties in performance, see Box 18-1.

Investor Alternatives to Actively Managed Funds

As noted in the previous discussion, the performance of mutual funds relative to a market index such as the S&P 500 Index has not been impressive. For example, the average stock fund in the 1980s showed an average annualized return of 15.2%, impressive performance relative to the long-run annual average return on stocks from the Ibbotson data or to other investment alternatives such as bonds or CDs. However, the comparable figure for the S&P 500 for the same time period was 17.6%, some 2.4 percentage points more.[31]

One result of the overall poor performance of mutual funds has been the creation and growth of index funds. A special type of mutual fund, the **index fund** is designed to parallel the movements of a stock market average or a bond index.

A stock index fund may consist of all the stocks in a well-known market average such as the Standard & Poor 500 Composite Stock Index. No attempt is made to forecast market movements and act accordingly, or to select under- or overvalued securities. A bond index fund is designed to match the performance of some well-known bond index, such as the Salomon Index. In either case, expenses are kept to a minimum, including

[29]This information is collected by SEI Funds Evaluation survey and reported in materials issued by The Vanguard Group as part of their material on the Vanguard Bond Market Fund.
[30]See Investment Company Institute, *Mutual Fund Fact Book 1989*, p. 24.
[31]See, "Oh, What a Decade!", *Money*, February 1990, p. 129.

BOX 18-1

TWINS BUT NOT IDENTICAL TWINS

Which is a better buy, the $352 million American Capital Harbor Fund or the closed-end $77 million American Capital Convertible Securities? At first glance, it's hard to choose. They're both balanced funds. James Behrmann, 45, runs both.

Yet Behrmann has done much better with the closed-end fund. Measured by the performance of its portfolio (that is, on net asset value, rather than the trading price of the fund's shares), American Capital Convertible has returned 11.5% a year over the past five years. Harbor has returned only 8.7% a year.

Why the substantial difference in results? As an open-end fund, American Capital Harbor stands ready to cash out any shareholder at the value of his share of the portfolio. American Capital Convertible, in contrast, has a fixed number of shares outstanding, and holders can't turn them in for redemption at asset value, as with a mutual fund. This difference forces Behrmann to run the two funds somewhat differently from each other.

Because of Harbor's potential need to meet redemptions, Behrmann stacks the open-end fund's portfolio with larger, more liquid issues, and maintains more cash in it. His closed-end fund, by contrast, is almost always fully invested in convertibles. At year-end 1988, for instance, Harbor had 5.8% of its assets in short-term investments, versus 3.7% for the closed-end.

In some ways it is hard to compare performance between closed-ends and mutual funds, because closed-ends frequently sell at discounts from asset value and occasionally at a premium; thus the value of the shares can move independently of the underlying investment results. Strip out this difference, however, and closed-end funds are the clear winner. Here's the score:

The average closed-end equity fund outperformed the S&P 500 over one, three and ten years (though it lost ground to the market over the last five years). The average mutual (or open-end) fund failed to beat the market during any of these periods.

What about overhead costs? They tend to run slightly higher on closed-ends, but a lower average portfolio turnover for closed-ends probably more than makes up for this in the form of lower transaction costs.

Other things being equal, it would seem that the closed-end is better for the investor. There's one thing, however, that is often very unequal between an open-end and a closed-end, and that is the cost of getting into it. So, before choosing, it's smart to check this out.

In American Capital's case, the entry cost is a strong reason to prefer the closed end. The closed-end vehicle for James Behrmann's expertise is currently available at an 8% discount from asset value, which means that you can get a dollar of assets for 92 cents (or about 93 cents, including a broker's commission). The open-end fund, however, has an 8.5% load, which means that each dollar of assets will cost you more than $1.00.

Today, with most closed-ends selling at big discounts from asset value, the closed-end is the clear choice for the smart investor. One caveat: Though discounts are currently at a high level, they have gone even higher in the past; if the discounts were to widen further, the closed-ends would underperform mutual funds. An investor's results depend not only on what happens to the portfolio but on what happens to the discount or premium. If he gets in at a premium and sells at a discount, he can fare poorly even if the portfolio manager is doing a good job. That's why brand-new closed-ends are a bad buy. They come out at a 7.5% premium and then usually slump to a discount.

Suppose the discount does nothing, simply remains the same. In that case, buyers of steeply discounted closed-ends earn a higher yield than holders of the open-end clone.

Source: Adapted from Jonathan Clements, "Twins But Not Identical Twins," *Forbes*, May 1, 1989, pp. 402–403. Excerpted by permission of *Forbes* magazine, May 1, 1989. © Forbes, Inc., 1989.

research costs (security analysis), portfolio managers' fees, and brokerage commissions. Index funds can be run efficiently by a small staff.

Example The Vanguard Group of Investment Companies offers its "Vanguard Index Trust" portfolios to allow investors to duplicate the broad market of all common stocks at a low cost. *The 500 Portfolio* consists of stocks selected to duplicate the S&P 500, which represents 70% of the overall market. *The Extended Market Portfolio,* consisting of a statistically selected sample of the Wilshire 4500 (stocks not included in the S&P 500), represents the other 30% of the market. By using both of these funds an investor can duplicate the overall market at very low expense. The Vanguard 500 portfolio had a 1989 expense ratio of 0.21%, said to be the lowest of any equity mutual fund. There are no sales charges or exit charges of any kind. ▪

INVESTMENTS INTUITION

Index funds have arisen in response to the growing body of evidence concerning the efficiency of the market, and they have grown as evidence of the inability of mutual funds to consistently, or even very often, outperform the market continues to accumulate. If the market is efficient, many of the activities normally engaged in by funds are suspect; that is, the benefits are not likely to exceed the costs. And as previously indicated, the available evidence indicates that many investment companies have failed to match the performance of broad market indexes.

Obtaining Information on Investment Companies

Because of their popularity and prominence in the investments world, and the fact that they are heavily regulated under the Investment Company Act of 1940, considerable information is available on investment companies.

This information originates with the companies themselves, the popular press, and specialized services devoted to funds and/or carrying specialized information on investment companies as part of their overall coverage. We shall discuss each of these information sources in turn.

Investment companies must file a registration statement with the SEC disclosing their investment policies, practices, and so on. In addition, they must make available to stockholders a prospectus that outlines in detail the fund's operations.[32]

For daily results, investors usually consult *The Wall Street Journal*, which carries daily quotations on many open-end funds as well as a weekly listing on Monday. *Barron's*, a weekly financial newspaper, carries a comprehensive list of quotations, including yields and capital gains for the previous 12 months. *Barron's* also carries a list of closed-end funds with both the NAV and the current market price (and therefore the discount or premium), including quotes on the dual-purpose funds.

To show the types of information available in the financial press as well as to illustrate some of the concepts we have discussed earlier in this chapter, consider the information shown in Table 18-3. Although the data are hypothetical, they simulate the actual data that can be observed in the financial press.

Consider first the kind of data to be seen daily in papers such as *The Wall Street Journal*. The top of Table 18-3 shows a small portion of the page on mutual funds, using as an example the family of funds run by an investment advisor operating under the corporate name National Funds Group. This company operates six funds, offering investors a wide choice of objectives. The net asset value of each of the funds is known, along with the offer price, or the price at which National will sell investors shares of each fund. The difference in these two prices is the load fee, or sales charge. Notice that the high-yield fund is a no-load fund and carries the "N.L." designation under the offer price. The NAV change shows the change in the closing NAV from the previous day. There was no change in the NAV of the High Yield fund from the previous day.

In the second half of the table, we see how our hypothetical funds performed for the week, as reported in *Barron's*. The 52-week high and low NAVs are shown, as well as the week's closing NAV. Dividend payments, including both income and capital gains, are for the latest 12 months.

Based on Table 18-3, the following observations can be made as a "typical" case. As we would expect, the Aggressive Frontiers fund, seeking maximum capital gains, has shown the widest fluctuation in NAV in the last 52 weeks. This fund holds volatile securities that rise and fall more than

[32]Complete information about operations is supplied to shareholders at least twice a year; most companies supply it four times a year.

TABLE 18-3 *Data for One Hypothetical Family of Mutual Funds, the National Funds Group*

The National Funds Group	NAV	Offer Price	NAV Change
	Daily Data		
National Income	6.12	6.55	+0.04
National Growth	14.62	15.90	+0.06
National High Yield	5.00	N.L.	—
National Aggressive Frontiers	8.16	8.90	+0.03
National Tax-free	9.14	9.60	−0.02
National Balanced	8.45	9.14	+0.01

	52 Weeks					
	High NAV	Low NAV	Close NAV	Week's Change	Income Dividends	Capital Gains
		Weekly Data				
National Income	7.02	5.98	6.10	+0.12	1.12	
National Growth	18.36	11.82	14.70	+0.18	0.60	0.95
National High Yield	6.12	4.62	5.02	+0.02	1.50	
National Aggressive Frontiers	22.14	4.82	8.03	+0.25	0.38	1.78
National Tax-free	9.38	9.00	9.12	−0.09	0.89	
National Balanced	8.80	7.12	8.40	+0.06	0.90	0.50

corresponding market movements. This fund and the other common stock fund (Growth), along with the Balanced fund, have paid shareholders both income and capital gains in the last 52 weeks. The Growth fund has paid more in capital gains, whereas the Balanced fund has paid more in income. The High Yield fund (a junk bond fund), with the highest income payout, has paid only interest income, whereas the Income fund, with the next highest payout, has paid both interest and dividends. The tax-free fund has paid a smaller amount of income, which is exempt from federal taxation.

Several organizations provide detailed data about investment companies. One of the best known is an annual publication by Wiesenberger Investment Companies Service entitled *Investment Companies,* which contains numerous statistics for over 500 mutual funds, including a history, investment objectives, sales charges, statistical history, and, for many funds, a 10-year performance analysis.[33] An example of this coverage is shown in Figure 18-5 for Affiliated Fund, Inc.

Forbes, a biweekly investment magazine, provides an annual rating of investment company performance in its early September issue. Several hundred funds are rated using the format shown in Figure 18-6. Both risk and return aspects are considered, and performance is related to up and

[33]The Wiesenberger firm also publishes a quarterly update on the long-run performance of many funds, entitled *Management Results,* and a monthly report on short-run performance (plus dividends), entitled *Current Performance and Dividend Record.*

AFFILIATED FUND, INC.

Affiliated Fund was formed in 1934 as a diversified common stock open-end investment company. Its investments are supervised by Lord, Abbett & Co., which performs similar services for twelve other funds bearing the Lord Abbett name. Affiliated Fund's investment objective is long-term growth of capital and income, without excessive fluctuations in market value.

The portfolio usually consists principally of common stocks believed to be selling at the most reasonable prices in relation to value. Investments are in "large, seasoned companies that are expected to show above-average growth and that are in sound financial condition."

At the close of 1988, the fund was 86% invested in common stocks, of which a substantial portion was in five industries: electric utilities (10.6% of net assets); office equipment and communication (9% each); oil & gas (7.9%), and financial (7.1%). The five largest individual common stock holdings were IBM (5.4%); Mobil (4.5%); Citicorp (3.2%); USX (3.1%), and American Telephone (2.8%). The rate of portfolio turnover during the latest fiscal year was 27% of average assets. Unrealized appreciation in the portfolio at the calendar year-end was 7.3% of net assets.

Special Services: An open account arrangement serves for accumulation and for automatic dividend reinvestment. Income dividends are invested at the offering price. Regular investments of $50 or more may be made automatically through pre-authorized checks drawn against the investor's checking account. The withdrawal plan is available to accounts worth $10,000 or more at the current offering price. Monthly or quarterly payments may be either a specified amount or at an annual rate. Prototype corporate profit-sharing plans, Keogh Plans, 403(b) and 401(k) tax-sheltered plans, Individual Retirement Accounts (including payroll-deduction IRAs), and Simplified Employee Pension programs are available.

Statistical History

	AT YEAR-ENDS								ANNUAL DATA				
						% of Assets in							
Year	Total Net Assets ($)	Number of Share-holders	Net Asset Value Per Share ($)	Offer-ing Price ($)	Yield (%)	Cash & Gov't	Bonds & Pre-ferreds	Com-mon Stocks	Income Div-idends ($)	Capital Gains Distribu-tion ($)	Expense Ratio (%)	Offering Price ($) High	Low
1988	3,267,040,273	207,390	9.20	9.92	4.7	11	3*	86	0.48	0.35	0.43	10.64	9.46
1987	3,235,758,463	212,769	8.93	9.63	5.3	4	5*	91	0.58	1.34	0.37	14.99	8.84
1986	3,170,898,409	187,477	10.50	11.32	4.4	5	7	88	0.55	1.14**	0.32	12.84	10.45
1985	2,529,281,086	165,107	9.91	10.68	4.9	7	6	87	0.56	0.81	0.32	11.06	9.50
1984	2,095,833,599	155,799	8.98	9.68	5.2	3	5*	92	0.53	0.48	0.32	10.42	8.83
1983	2,061,615,155	152,121	9.41	10.15	4.7	4	5	91	0.52	0.82	0.33	11.26	9.13
1982	1,784,211,202	149,619	8.59	9.26	5.8	3	—	97	0.56	0.33**	0.36	9.48	7.28
1981	1,580,559,665	148,596	7.75	8.36	6.3	4	—	96	0.56	0.49	0.34	9.98	8.17
1980	1,719,544,589	150,677	8.78	9.47	5.0	8	—	92	0.51	0.71	0.38	10.37	7.77
1979	1,539,977,140	157,466	8.05	8.68	5.0	3	1*	96	0.45	0.44	0.41	9.37	7.57
1978	1,361,289,473	168,599	6.97	7.52	4.5	5	3*	92	0.39	0.31	0.42	8.86	7.22

* Includes a substantial proportion in convertible securities.

** Includes $0.03 short-term capital gains in 1982; $0.08 in 1986.

Directors: John M. McCarthy, Chmn.; Ronald P. Lynch, Pres.; Thomas F. Creamer; Stewart S. Dixon; John C. Jansing; Hansel B. Millican, Jr.; Thomas J. Neff.

Investment Adviser: Lord, Abbett & Co. Compensation to the Adviser is .4 of 1% annually on the first $200 million of net assets of the fund, 2/5 of 1% annually on the next $300 million, .375 of 1% on the next $200 million, .35 of 1% on the next $200 million, and .3 of 1% on assets in excess of $900 million.

Custodian: Morgan Guaranty Trust Company, New York, NY.

Transfer Agent: United Missouri Bank of Kansas City, N.A.

Shareholder Servicing Agent: DST, Inc., P.O. Box 419100, Kansas City, MO 64141.

Distributor: Lord, Abbett & Co., 767 Fifth Ave., New York, NY 10153.

Sales Charge: Maximum is 7¼% of offering price; minimum is ½ of 1% at $4 million. Reduced charges begin at $5,000 and are applicable to initial and subsequent combined purchases of this fund and other funds in the Lord Abbett group on a permanent basis. Minimum is $25,000 for Statement of Intention. Minimum initial purchase is $250.

Distribution Plan: (12b-1) None.

Dividends: Income dividends are paid quarterly in the months of March, June, September and December. Capital gains, if any, are paid optionally in shares or cash in December.

Shareholder Reports: Issued semi-annually. Fiscal year ends October 31. The current prospectus was effective in March.

Qualified for Sale: In all states, DC and PR.

Address: 767 Fifth Ave., New York, NY 10153.

Telephone: (212) 848-1800.

FIGURE 18-5 *A page from* **Investment Companies** *showing the coverage of Affiliated Fund.*

Source: Reprinted by permission from the Wiesenberger Investment Companies Service 1989 Edition, p. 217.

An assumed investment of $10,000 in this fund, with capital gains accepted in shares and income dividends reinvested, is illustrated below. The explanation in the introduction to this section must be read in conjunction with this illustration.

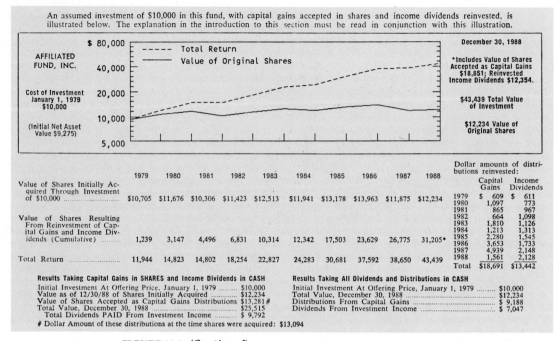

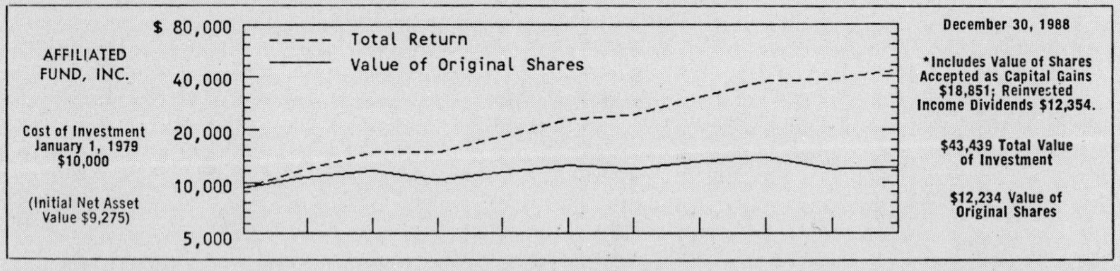

	1979	1980	1981	1982	1983	1984	1985	1986	1987	1988
Value of Shares Initially Acquired Through Investment of $10,000	$10,705	$11,676	$10,306	$11,423	$12,513	$11,941	$13,178	$13,963	$11,875	$12,234
Value of Shares Resulting From Reinvestment of Capital Gains and Income Dividends (Cumulative)	1,239	3,147	4,496	6,831	10,314	12,342	17,503	23,629	26,775	31,205*
Total Return	11,944	14,823	14,802	18,254	22,827	24,283	30,681	37,592	38,650	43,439

Dollar amounts of distributions reinvested:

	Capital Gains	Income Dividends
1979	$ 609	$ 611
1980	1,097	773
1981	865	967
1982	664	1,098
1983	1,810	1,126
1984	1,213	1,313
1985	2,280	1,545
1986	3,653	1,733
1987	4,939	2,148
1988	1,561	2,128
Total	$18,691	$13,442

Results Taking Capital Gains in SHARES and Income Dividends in CASH

Initial Investment At Offering Price, January 1, 1979	$10,000
Value as of 12/30/88 of Shares Initially Acquired	$12,234
Value of Shares Accepted as Capital Gains Distributions	$13,281#
Total Value, December 30, 1988	$25,515
Total Dividends PAID From Investment Income	$ 9,792

Results Taking All Dividends and Distributions in CASH

Initial Investment At Offering Price, January 1, 1979	$10,000
Total Value, December 30, 1988	$12,234
Distributions From Capital Gains	$ 9,188
Dividends From Investment Income	$ 7,047

Dollar Amount of these distributions at the time shares were acquired: $13,094

FIGURE 18-5 ***(Continued)***

down periods for the overall market. Letter ratings are assigned for both market conditions, ranging from A to D in an up market and A to F in a down market.[34] This gives investors some guidance in choosing a fund. If a market rise is expected, for example, the investor might select a fund that has done extremely well during such periods, regardless of its performance in a declining market. On the other hand, a risk-averse investor might prefer a fund that has performed reasonably well in both good and bad markets.

Money magazine devotes articles to mutual funds as well as providing its own rankings of funds. For example, the February 1990 issue carried a 31-page report on mutual funds, ranking some 960 funds on their five-year returns. *Money* provided a "risk-adjusted grade," which compares funds within broad categories on a return–risk basis. This is important because it allows investors to assess the risk of the funds. *Business Week* also rates mutual funds and categorizes each fund as to its level of risk (very high, high, average, low, and very low). Ratings are based on five-year risk-adjusted performance, relative to the S&P 500.

[34]In up markets, 5% of the funds rated by *Forbes* receive a rating of A+; the next 15% receive an A; the next 25%, a B; the next 25%, a C; the next 25%, a D; the bottom 5%, an F. In down markets a similar distribution is used, with ratings ranging from A to F.

Performance in UP —markets—	Performance in DOWN —markets—	Fund/ distributor	Total return: Annual average 1980 to 1980	Total return: Last 12 months	Yield	Assets: 6/30/89 (millions)	Assets: % change '89 vs '88	Maximum sales charge	Annual expenses per $100	
		Standard & Poor's 500 stock average	14.8%	20.4%	3.2%					
		FORBES stock fund composite	12.1%	15.0%	2.3%				$1.58	
		AARP Growth-Capital Growth/ Scudder	—*	32.4%	0.3%	$146	55%	none	$1.15	
		AARP Growth-Growth & Income/ Scudder	—*	20.7	4.2	218	−12	none	1.05	
B	D	ABT Growth & Income Trust/ Palm Beach	10.6%	10.0	3.0	104	−9	4.75%	*1.21*	
•A	•D	ABT Invest-Emerging Growth/Palm Beach	—*	9.8	none	20	−23	4.75	*1.84*	
•D	•A	ABT Invest-Security Income/Palm Beach	—*	23.7	2.1	8	−21	4.75	*2.21*	
D	A	ABT Utility Income Fund/ Palm Beach	11.5	19.4	6.9	116	−2	4.75	*1.19*	
B	C	Acorn Fund/ Acorn	14.8	19.9	2.0	738	39	none	0.80	
		Adam Investors/ Conway, Luongo	—*	16.7	2.5	3	−53	none	1.99	
D	B	Adams Express/closed end	12.2	13.7	2.9	512	8	NA	0.52	
		Advantage Growth Fund/ Advest	—*	19.0	1.4	28	1	4.00r	2.39	
C	B	Affiliated Fund/Lord Abbett	14.8	11.9	4.8	3,469	1	7.25	0.43	
F	C	Afuture Fund	Afuture	3.2	9.7	2.5	9	−9	none	1.60
D	B	Aim Equity-Charter Fund/ [1]AIM	11.8	21.8	2.9	66	−6	5.50	*1.65*	

•Fund rated for two periods only; maximum allowable grade A. *Fund not in operation for full period. *Expense ratio is in italics if the fund has a shareholder-paid 12b-1 plan exceeding 0.1% (hidden load)pending or in force.* r:Includes back-end load that reverts to distributor. NA:Not applicable or not available. [1]Formerly Charter Fund.

FIGURE 18-6 ***An excerpt from the annual* Forbes *ratings of mutual funds, 1989 "Annual Fund Ratings," September 4, 1989, p. 200.***
Source: Reprinted by permission. *Forbes* magazine, September 4, 1989, © Forbes, Inc., 1989.

A rapidly expanding source of information and investment advice is provided by the mutual fund newsletters sold by individuals and companies to mutual fund shareholders. Some newsletters specialize in the funds for one company; for example, at least four cover only the funds of Fidelity. At the beginning of 1990 some 40 newsletters were being sold.

Summary

- An investment company is a financial service organization that invests in a portfolio of securities on behalf of its own shareholders. It offers investors a way to invest indirectly by purchasing shares in the investment company, which, in turn, invests in a portfolio of securities.
- Investment companies consist of open-end companies (popularly called mutual funds), closed-end companies, and unit investment trusts.
- An open-end fund continuously sells shares in itself to the public and redeems them when its investors wish to sell.
- Closed-end funds have a fixed number of shares of stock outstanding and trade on exchanges like any other security.
- Mutual funds can be divided into load funds, which charge a sales fee to investors who purchase shares, and no-load funds, which do not. The average sales fee historically has been 8.50%.
- All funds charge their shareholders for the expenses involved, including a management fee.
- Two major categories of investment companies are the money market funds and the equity, bond, and income funds.
- Money market funds offer investors a chance to own money market instruments, which typically have large face values, that will earn current money market rates.
- Equity, bond, and income funds invest primarily in stocks and bonds. They can be organized into common stock funds (which can be broken down into funds with different growth and income objectives as well as international funds and precious metals funds), balanced funds, income funds, option/income funds, and various types of bond funds.
- The potential benefits of owning investment company shares include diversification, an opportunity to choose from a variety of objectives, and a range of services such as record keeping, fund swaps, accumulation and withdrawal plans, and IRA and Keogh plans.
- The actual and potential costs include any load fee, the management fee, administrative fees, transaction costs, superfluous diversification, and active management cost. These benefits and costs must be evaluated by investors within a framework that considers their own situation and alternatives.
- The question of fund performance remains unsettled. Considerable evidence suggests that the funds do not outperform the market when all

relevant factors are considered. In assessing performance, shareholder returns should be measured using the TR concept.

- Investors should also assess the risk, the consistency in performance over time, and the expenses involved. Index funds are increasing in popularity.
- Because they are closely regulated, investment companies must provide information to investors on a timely basis. On a daily and weekly basis, sources such as *The Wall Street Journal* and *Barron's* are useful. Several services cover funds in detail, such as the Wiesenberger Service and *Forbes*.

Key Words

Closed-end investment company	Load funds	Open-end investment company
Discount	Management fee	Premium
Index funds	Mutual funds	Prospectus
Investment company	Net asset value (NAV)	
	No-load funds	

Questions

18-1 Explain what is meant by the term *pure intermediary.*

18-2 What is the difference between an open-end investment company and a closed-end investment company? a load fund and a no-load fund?

18-3 It has been said that many closed-end funds are "worth more dead than alive." What is meant by this expression?

18-4 Which investment companies charge a management fee, and what is its size, on average?

18-5 What does it mean for an investment company to be regulated?

18-6 List the benefits of a money market fund for investors? List the disadvantages. What alternative investment is a close substitute?

18-7 What is meant by an investment company's "objective"? List the various objectives pursued by equity, bond, and income funds.

18-8 How does a unit investment trust differ from an investment company?

18-9 What is meant by the statement that the portfolio manager's results differ from the shareholder's results for the closed-end investment company?

18-10 List the advantages offered by investment companies. What are the costs, both actual and potential?

18-11 Based on a consensus of the studies of mutual fund performance, what can be said about their returns and risk?

18-12 Examine the latest *Forbes* rating of mutual funds (August of each year). How many funds achieved a high rating in both up and down markets (B or better)?

18-13 List some reasons that an investor might prefer a closed-end fund to an open-end fund.

18-14 What do you think is the explanation for the fact that load funds dominate no-load funds in sales?

18-15 How is net asset value calculated for an investment company? How closely correlated could you expect changes in NAVs to be with changes in market indexes?

18-16 What is meant by a "fund swap"?

18-17 How can risk measures be calculated for investment companies?

Problems

18-1 Using the following data for GoGrowth Fund, Inc., calculate the shareholder total returns (TR) for the years 19X2, 19X3, 19X4, and 19X5 (ignore the sales charge).

Year	Income Dividends ($)	Capital Gains Distributions ($)	NAV per share ($)
19X5	$0.56	$0.49	$7.75
19X4	0.51	0.71	8.78
19X3	0.45	0.44	8.05
19X2	0.39	0.31	6.97
19X1	0.37	0.15	7.41

18-2 a. GoGrowth began calendar year 19X7 with a NAV of $8.59 and ended the year with a NAV of $9.51. During the year it paid $0.51 in dividends and distributed $0.82 in capital gains. Calculate Affiliated's TR for 19X7.

b. GoGrowth has a front-end load. Assume you purchased 100 shares at $8.59 on January 1, 19X7, and the load was 7.25%. For what amount did you write your check? How much do you have invested?

c. Calculate your 19X7 calendar-year TR, net of your transaction cost.

d. The TR on the S&P 500 for 19X7 was 22.4%. Compare your TR on GoGrowth, both before and after transaction cost, with the market. Is this a fair comparison?

e. Assume that you had bought 100 shares of a no-load fund, and it had a TR of 25%. Compare GoGrowth's TR, both before and after transaction cost, with this fund. Is this a fair comparison?

18-3 Value Line has a family of no-load mutual funds. For each of their five funds, the relevant shareholder values are shown in the following table.

Fund	NAV 12-31-X2($)	Dividends($)	Capital Distribution($)	NAV 12-30-X3
Value Line Fund	$14.28	$0.55	$0.75	$12.87
Bond Fund	12.76	1.34	0.28	11.85
Income	7.01	0.56	0.14	6.77
Leveraged Growth	18.82	0.64	0.02	19.66
Special Situations	13.83	0.45	—	16.11

a. Calculate the calendar-year TR for each fund. The TR on the S&P 500 was 22.4%. Evaluate 19X3's performance for each fund.
b. Compare each fund's TR with the (net of transaction cost) TR of Affiliated.
c. In the text, different kinds of function are described. From the names of these Value Line funds, can you identify the type of fund?
d. Based on c, try ranking these funds from highest risk to lowest risk.

18-4 A better comparison of fund performance is possible by looking at several years of TRs. For the five Value Line funds, the annual TRs are provided along with the TR for the S&P 500. The mean, standard deviation, and beta are also provided. (All Value Line data courtesy of Wiesenberger Financial Services.)

a. On the basis of the standard deviation of the TRs, and the betas, do the risks match with your rankings in Problem 18-3(d)?
b. Compare the 10-year results on average annual yield with the average for Affiliated in the text. How does Affiliated compare?
c. Compare the average TR and the risk of each fund with the market. Do the results of the Income Fund surprise you?
d. For each fund, in how many years was the performance better than the market?

	Fund TR%					
Year	Value Line	Bond Fund	Income	Leveraged Growth	Special Situations	S&P 500 TR%
1973	10.5%	—	−15.9%	−48.2%	−45.7%	−14.5%
1974	−22.4	—	−16.1	−30.6	−29.2	−26.0
1975	39.2	—	41.7	59.1	47.0	36.9
1976	42.5	—	34.5	46.7	52.7	23.6
1977	9.5	—	1.8	51.1	12.3	−7.2
1978	19.3	—	11.1	27.6	21.2	6.4
1979	44.0	—	27.6	26.2	43.5	18.2
1980	41.6	—	26.8	29.5	54.4	31.5
1981	2.4	—	16.2	15.9	−2.3	−4.8
1982	28.9	33.2	29.9	28.6	23.1	20.4
Mean	17.5	—	15.8	20.6	17.7	8.4
Standard deviation	27.1	—	20.3	34.5	34.6	20.9
Beta	1.2	—	0.9	1.2	1.5	1.0

e. Which funds seem to have better performance than the market? Generally, does it appear that mean returns above the market are associated with undertaking greater risk?

18-5 The following hypothetical values and prices are for publicly traded closed-end mutual funds.

Fund	Net Asset Value($)	Stock Price($)
Adams Express	$16.90	$15.85
Salomon Bros.	14.23	15.50
Tri-Continental	23.70	23.40

a. Calculate the discount or the premium.
b. Express these differences as a percentage of the NAV.
c. What reasons can you think of for these differences?

18-6 For the Super Fund data given in the text:
a. Verify that the percentage discounts are as given.
b. Calculate the portfolio performance for each of the other four years. The closing NAV in 19X0 was $11.55.
c. Calculate stockholder's TRs for each of the other four years. The closing price as of 19X0 was $8.25.
d. Compare the portfolio results with the shareholder's results. Compare both with the TRs for the S&P 500 as given in Chapter 5. What can you conclude?

18-7 Dual-purpose funds are typically initiated with an equal amount of income shares and capital shares. Assume a fund is initiated with $40 million, divided equally between the income shareholders and the capital shareholders.
a. Show that the leverage ratio for income shareholders, and for capital shareholders, is 2.
b. What would be your leverage ratio if you bought 10 shares of the income and 10 shares of the capital?

Selected References

A good source of annual information on mutual funds is
Mutual Fund Fact Book. Washington, D.C.: Investment Company Institute.

A detailed source of information on investment companies is
Wiesenberger Investment Company Service. Annual Editions. Boston: Warren, Gorham, & Lamont.

100

PART 7

Portfolio Management

- CHAPTER 19 Portfolio Theory
- CHAPTER 20 International Investing and Extended Diversification
- CHAPTER 21 Capital Market Theory
- CHAPTER 22 Measuring Portfolio Performance

CHAPTER 19

Portfolio Theory

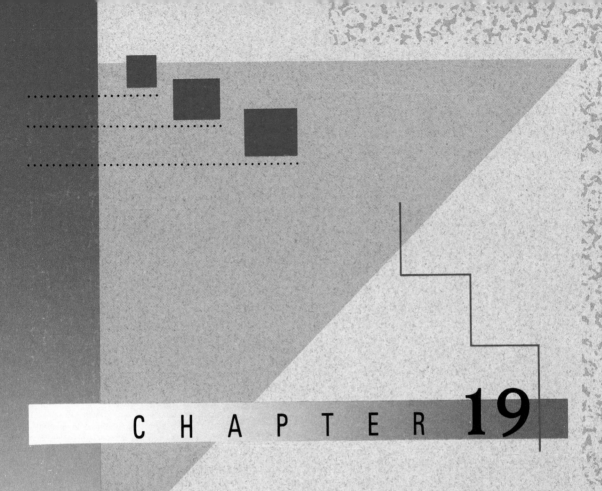

In earlier chapters we discussed the valuation and selection of common stocks using the fundamental approach. We also discussed technical analysis and the implications of efficient markets. Various securities that investors can choose in a direct investing program have been analyzed, ranging from bonds to financial futures. Finally, the alternative of investing directly through investment companies was analyzed in the previous chapter.

For the remainder of this text our emphasis will shift to a consideration of portfolios rather than of individual securities. The word *portfolio* simply means the combination of assets invested in and held by an investor, whether an individual or an institution. Technically, a portfolio encompasses the investor's entire set of assets, real and financial. In this text, however, we are concentrating on financial assets. Most people hold portfolios of assets (both real and financial), whether because of planning and knowledge or as a result of unrelated decisions.

The study of all aspects of portfolios can be designated **portfolio management.** This broad term encompasses the concepts of portfolio theory, a very important part of investments and the specific focus of this chapter. We shall analyze the classic portfolio theory model developed by Markowitz and learn how to simplify the process of obtaining inputs for this model by using the single index model. Appendix 19-A illustrates a procedure for determining optimal portfolios, which vastly simplifies the calculations and provides a simple stock-screening device that portfolio managers and investors can use to make operational investment decisions.

The Markowitz Model

In the early 1950s, Harry Markowitz originated the basic portfolio model that underlies modern portfolio theory.[1] Before Markowitz, investors dealt loosely with the concepts of return and risk. Although they were familiar with the concept of risk, they usually did not quantify it. Investors have known intuitively for many years that it is smart to diversify, that is, not to "put all of your eggs in one basket." Markowitz, however, was the first to develop formally the concept of portfolio diversification. He showed quantitatively why, and how, portfolio diversification works to reduce the risk of a portfolio to an investor.

Markowitz sought to organize the existing thoughts and practices into

[1]See H. Markowitz, "Portfolio Selection," *Journal of Finance*, Vol. 7 (March 1952), pp. 77–91; and *Portfolio Selection: Efficient Diversification of Investments* (New York: John Wiley, 1959).

a more formal framework and answer a basic question: Is the risk of a portfolio equal to the sum of the risks of the individual securities comprising it? Markowitz was the first to develop a specific measure of portfolio risk and to derive the expected return and risk for a portfolio. His model is based on the expected return and risk characteristics of securities and is, in essence, a theoretical framework for analyzing risk–return choices.

Markowitz was also the first to derive the concept of an **efficient portfolio,** defined as one that has the smallest portfolio risk for a given level of expected return, or the largest expected return for a given level of risk. Investors can identify efficient portfolios by specifying an expected portfolio return and minimizing the portfolio risk at this level of return. Alternatively, they can specify a portfolio risk level they are willing to assume and maximize the expected return on the portfolio for this level of risk.

Rational investors will seek efficient portfolios because these portfolios promise maximum expected return for a specified level of risk, or minimum risk for a specified expected return. Given their importance, we should know how they are determined. To determine an efficient set of portfolios, it is necessary to determine the expected return and standard deviation of return for each portfolio. To do this we need to understand the Markowitz model.

Markowitz made some basic assumptions in developing his model: investors (1) like return and dislike risk, (2) act rationally in making decisions, and (3) make decisions on the basis of maximizing their expected utility. Thus, investor utility is a function of expected return and risk, the two major parameters of investment decisions.[2] The model itself is based on equations for the expected return and risk of a portfolio. To solve these equations, some values are needed for the relevant variables. Before analyzing these inputs, however, we should clearly understand the types of data that are used to provide the inputs for the portfolio model.

Ex Post Versus Ex Ante Calculations

Portfolios are built to be held over some future time period. Portfolio theory is concerned with **ex ante** events, meaning expected future events. If we wish to make portfolio decisions for the future, we must use ex ante values.[3] On the other hand, if we wish to evaluate portfolio performance for some previous period, we calculate the actual return and risk values for that period—**ex post** values.

---

[2]This assumption does not exclude other objectives, which do exist. Markowitz noted that there are "certain conceivable circumstances under which an investor would prefer a nonefficient portfolio" (*Portfolio Selection,* p. 281).

[3]*Ex ante* means "before the fact"; *ex post* means "after the fact."

INVESTMENTS INTUITION

Because we know the historical data, it is often convenient to use ex post values as proxies for the ex ante values needed in the portfolio model. In fact, historical data should be examined and used as a basis for estimating ex ante values; however, it is important to remember that portfolio models call for ex ante values that may, and often do, differ from the historical data. Investor expectations are crucial in determining security prices. When ex post data are used as a proxy for the required ex ante values, the assumption being made (either implicitly or explicitly) is that such realizations will be repeated in the future, which may or may not be true.

Inputs Needed

The Markowitz analysis generates efficient portfolios based on a set of inputs supplied by an investor (or security analyst).

1. The expected return, E(R), for every security being considered.
2. The standard deviation of returns, SD(R), as a measure of the risk of each security.
3. The covariance—a measure of relationships—between securities' rates of return.

We shall discuss the first two of these now and the third after an initial consideration of portfolios. For purposes of illustrating portfolio concepts, we shall use two companies, one real and one hypothetical: EG&G and General Fudge (GF). EG&G, as discussed in Chapter 12, is a technology-oriented company that grew rapidly in the 1970s and early 1980s. In recent years investors in EG&G stock earned high total returns (TRs), as can be seen in the following data (in percentage form)[4]:

	19X0	19X1	19X2	19X3	19X4	19X5	19X6	19X7	19X8	19X9
EG&G	−2.7	−28.9	14.8	21.7	5.6	67.2	70.0	80.3	−8.3	44.7
GF	−12.0	−19.1	63.4	15.4	9.4	7.7	10.4	−3.2	11.9	32.3
Market	−14.5	−26.0	36.9	23.6	−7.2	6.4	18.2	31.5	−4.8	20.4

Investors in EG&G also assumed substantial risk. The standard deviation of the 10 TRs is 37.3%, with three negative TRs; the calculated beta is 1.21, indicating greater volatility than the market as a whole.[5] Given this perfor-

[4]These data are taken from a recent 10-year period.

[5]These betas are calculated later in the chapter from the 10 annual TRs.

mance record, EG&G could appeal to investors as a growth company with above-average expected return–risk possibilities.

GF, on the other hand, is a stable company with a much lower average TR over the same period, 11.6%, and a standard deviation of TRs of 23%, roughly two-thirds that of EG&G. The calculated beta is 0.78. As a general rule, stockholders gained less and lost less in any one year with GF than with EG&G. Thus, GF would seem to be a good contrast to the more volatile EG&G, which, as discussed later, is a key point when building portfolios.

The first two inputs needed for the Markowitz model are discussed in the following two sections. Note that we shall be discussing individual securities in these two sections.

Expected Return on a Security Investors buy stocks for their future returns; therefore, portfolio models must be formulated ex ante. Because the world is uncertain, security returns are really probability judgments. To calculate the expected returns on security *i*, an investor needs an estimate of the realistically obtainable returns from the security plus the likelihood of occurrence (i.e., probabilities) for each possible return.[6]

Example. Assume that an investor is estimating the expected return for EG&G for a forthcoming time period. The investor must estimate the possible returns and their associated probabilities. As a basis for doing this, it would be logical to examine prior stockholder returns; however, it is also necessary to incorporate expected conditions for the coming period. Examining the TRs shown earlier and modifying these figures for expected events, the investor might decide that there is a

40% chance of a very large TR, say 60%

20% chance of a better-than-market-average TR, say 15%

20% chance of a small TR, say 5%

20% chance of a negative TR, say −15% ▪

These probabilities sum to 1.0, as they must in a complete probability distribution, because they are exhaustive (we are assuming that all possible events are expressed). The potential returns must ultimately reflect expectations of the future rather than be merely averages from the past. Because the future is uncertain, all investors will not agree on the potential returns and the associated probabilities.

[6]As explained in Chapter 5, these are the two components of a probability distribution.

Given the probability distribution of potential returns for a security, its expected return, $E(R_i)$, can be calcuated as the expected value of the probability distribution[7]:

$$E(R_i) = \sum_{k=1}^{m} (P_k)\, PR_k \qquad (19\text{-}1)$$

where

$E(R_i)$ = the expected return on any security i
P_k = the probability of occurrence of each potential rate of return
PR_k = The potential returns for a security
m = the number of potential returns for each security

Example. The expected return for EG&G is calculated in Table 19-1 as

$$E(R_{EG\&G}) = 0.4(60\%) + 0.2(15\%) + 0.2(5\%) + 0.2(-15\%) = 25\%$$ ▪

Risk of a Security To measure the risk of any security we use the variance (or its square root, the standard deviation) of the expected returns. For discussion purposes these two variables are assumed to be interchangeable. Statistically, the variance measures the dispersion of returns around its expected value. The greater the dispersion in returns, the greater the risk and the greater the variance or standard deviation. Therefore, variance is a logical and consistent measure of the risk of a security to an investor.

To calculate the expected variance or standard deviation for an individual security, the following equations can be used:

$$VAR(R_i) = \sigma_i^2 = \sum_{k=1}^{m} (PR_k - E(R_i))^2\, P_k \qquad (19\text{-}2)$$

$$SD(R_i) = \sigma_i = \Big[\sum_{k=1}^{m} (PR_k - E(R_i))^2\, P_k\Big]^{1/2} \qquad (19\text{-}3)$$

where $VAR(R_i)$ is the variance of the return on any security and $SD(R_i)$ is the standard deviation of the return, and all other terms are as previously defined.

Example. As an illustration of these calculations, the lower portion of Table 19-1 shows the calculation of the variance and standard deviation for EG&G, based on the data in the top. The variance of the EG&G return is 0.091; taking the square root of this number, the standard deviation of the return is 30.2%. ▪

---

7 It is always assumed that $\sum_{k=1}^{m} P_k = 1$.

TABLE 19-1 ***Hypothetical Probability Distribution of Potential Returns for EG&G***

(1) Potential Return (PR)	(2) Probability (P)	(3) (1) × (2)
	Calculating the Expected Return for EG&G	
0.60	0.4	0.24
0.15	0.2	0.03
0.05	0.2	0.01
−0.15	0.2	−0.03
	1.0	$E(R_{EG\&G})$ = 0.25 = 25%

(1) PR	(2) $E(R_{EG\&G})$	(3) $PR - E(R_{EG\&G})$	(4) $[PR - E(R_{EG\&G})]^2$	(5) Probability	(6) (4) × (5)
		Calculating the Variance and Standard Deviation of Expected Return for EG&G			
0.60	0.25	0.35	0.1225	0.4	0.049
0.15	0.25	−0.10	0.01	0.2	0.002
0.05	0.25	−0.20	0.04	0.2	0.008
−0.15	0.25	−0.40	0.16	0.2	0.032
				Variance =	0.091
				Standard deviation =	$\sqrt{0.091}$
				=	30.2%

Using the previous calculations, the expected return and the expected variance of return would be calculated for each individual security being considered for inclusion in a portfolio. For example, the same calculations would be made for General Fudge based on an estimated probability distribution for the next period. Assuming these inputs are now calculated, we can consider the portfolio's expected return and risk.

Portfolio Return

The expected return on any portfolio is easily calculated as a weighted average of the individual securities' expected returns. The weights used are the proportions of total investable funds invested in each security. The combined portfolio weights are assumed to sum to 100% of total investable funds.

Example. With equal dollar amounts in three securities, the portfolio weights are 0.333, 0.333, and 0.333. Under the same conditions with a portfolio of five securities, each security would have a portfolio weight of 0.20. ▪

The expected return of a portfolio can be calculated as

$$E(R_p) = \sum_{i=1}^{n} W_i \, E(R_i) \tag{19-4}$$

where

$E(R_p)$ = the expected return on the portfolio[8]
W_i = the proportion of investable funds placed in security i
$E(R_i)$ = the expected return on security i
n = number of securities

Example. Consider a three-stock portfolio consisting of stocks G, H, and I with expected returns of 12%, 20%, and 17%, respectively. Assume that 50% of investable funds is invested in security G, 30% in H, and 20% in I. The expected return on this portfolio is

$$E(R_p) = 0.5(12\%) + 0.3(20\%) + 0.2(17\%) = 15.4\% \quad ▪$$

Regardless of the number of assets held in a portfolio, or the proportion of total investable funds placed in each asset, the expected return on the portfolio is *always* a weighted average of the expected returns for individual assets in the portfolio.

INVESTMENTS INTUITION

The expected return for a portfolio must fall between the highest and lowest expected returns for the individual securities making up the portfolio—exactly where is determined by the percentages of investable funds placed in each of the individual securities in the portfolio.

Portfolio Risk

The remaining computation in the basic portfolio model is that of the risk of the portfolio. In the Markowitz model, risk is measured by the variance (or standard deviation) of the portfolio's return, just as in the case of each individual security. It is at this point that the basis of modern portfolio theory emerges, which can be stated as follows:

> Although the expected return of a portfolio is a weighted average of the expected returns of the individual securities in the portfolio, the risk (as measured by the variance or standard deviation) is *not* a weighted average of the risk of the individual securities in the portfolio. Symbolically,

$$E(R_p) = \sum_{i=1}^{n} W_i\, E(R_i) \tag{19-4}$$

[8]The subscript i is used to denote an individual security whereas p is used to denote a portfolio.

But

$$VAR(R_p) \neq \sum_{i=1}^{n} W_i \, VAR(R_i) \tag{19-5}$$

It is precisely because Equation 19-5 is an inequality that investors can reduce the risk of a portfolio beyond what it would be if risk were, in fact, simply a weighted average of the individual securities' risk. Portfolio risk depends not only on the weighted average of the risks of the individual securities in the portfolio, but also on the relationships, or covariances, among the returns on securities in the portfolio. Thus,

> Portfolio risk is a function of each individual security's risk and the covariances between the returns on the individual securities. Stated in terms of variance, portfolio risk is

$$VAR(R_p) = \sum_{i=1}^{n} W_i^2 \, VAR(R_i) + \sum_{i=1}^{n} \sum_{\substack{j=1 \\ i \neq j}}^{n} W_i W_j \, COV(R_i, R_j) \tag{19-6}$$

where

$VAR(R_p)$ = the variance of the return on the portfolio
$VAR(R_i)$ = the variance of return for security i
$COV(R_i, R_j)$ = the covariance between the returns for securities i and j
W_i = the percentage of investable funds invested in security i
$\sum_{i=1}^{n} \sum_{j=1}^{n}$ = a double summation sign indicating that n^2 numbers are to be added together (i.e., all possible pairs of values for i and j)

INVESTMENTS INTUITION

The intuitive nature of portfolio risk can be seen by considering Equation 19-6. The first term on the right side of Equation 19-6 is the weighted individual security risks. The second term of the equation, the weighted relationships between securities' returns, can assume a positive value, a negative value, or a zero value, depending upon the exact relationships among the securities. This term can

1. Add to the weighted individual security risks if the term is positive.
2. Add nothing to the weighted individual security risks if the term has a value of zero.
3. Reduce the weighted individual security risks if the term has a negative value.

Clearly, the relationships among the returns on securities are a central part of portfolio theory. In our earlier discussion of the inputs needed for the Markowitz model, the third input listed was the covariances for each pair of securities' rates of return. We shall now consider this input involving the relationships between securities in detail.

Covariance The covariance is an absolute (as opposed to relative) measure of the degree of association between the returns for a pair of securities. ***Covariance*** is defined as the extent to which two variables covary (move together) over time. As is true throughout our discussion, the variables in question are the returns (TRs) on two securities. The covariance can be

1. Positive, indicating that the returns on the two securities tend to move in the same direction at the same time; when one increases (decreases), the other tends to do the same.
2. Negative, indicating that the returns on the two securities tend to move inversely; when one increases (decreases), the other tends to decrease (increase).
3. Zero, indicating that the returns on two securities are independent and have no tendency to move in the same or opposite directions together.

The formula for calculating covariance is

$$COV(R_i, R_j) = E([PR_i - E(R_i)][PR_j - E(R_j)]) \tag{19-7}$$

$$= \sum_{k=1}^{m} P_k([PR_{ik} - E(R_i)]\,[PR_{jk} - E(R_j)])$$

If all returns are equally likely to occur, the covariance is equal to

$$= \frac{1}{m} \sum_{k=1}^{m} [PR_{ik} - E(R_i)]\,[PR_{jk} - E(R_j)]$$

where

$COV(R_i, R_j)$ = the covariance between securities i and j
PR_i = the potential return on security i
$E(R_i)$ = the expected value of the return on security i
m = number of likely outcomes for a security for the period

Example. To illustrate the calculation of a covariance, Table 19-2 repeats the annual TRs for EG&G and GF and uses this *ex post* data to calculate a covariance between EG&G and GF. In effect, we assume here that each of the returns is equally likely to occur. However, it must be remembered that the model user should determine if the likely future covariations will be different from those of the past; if they will be different, the future expected covariances should be used. ▪

TABLE 19-2 ***Annual TRs for EG&G and General Fudge, and Calculation of the Covariance Between Them***

	TR% $EG\&G_i$	TR% GF_j	$R_i - E(R_i)$	$R_j - E(R_j)$	$[R_i - E(R_i)][R_j - E(R_j)]$
1973	−2.7	−12.0	−29.2	−23.6	689.12
1974	−28.9	−19.1	−55.4	−30.7	1700.78
1975	14.8	63.4	−11.7	51.8	−606.06
1976	21.7	15.4	−4.8	03.8	−18.24
1977	05.6	09.4	−20.9	−02.2	45.98
1978	67.2	07.7	40.7	−03.9	−158.73
1979	70.0	10.4	43.5	−01.2	−52.2
1980	80.3	−03.3	53.8	−14.9	−801.62
1981	−08.3	11.9	−34.8	0.3	−10.44
1982	44.8	32.3	18.3	20.7	378.81
					Σ = 1167.4
Mean	26.5	11.6			Covariance = 116.74
σ	37.3	23.3			

An examination of the TRs for these two companies indicates that their movements are quite different. General Fudge sometimes has a large TR, whereas EG&G has a much lower one, with the reverse being also true. In two of the years one stock's TR was negative and the other's was positive; furthermore, in the other eight years the TRs had the same sign but did not necessarily move in the same direction from the previous year.

The calculated covariance between these two stocks is 116.74, a low covariance; this is not surprising, given the differences in their TR movements over this period. However, an investor cannot judge the size of this covariance in the abstract. The question is, "How low is low—what is a low (or high) covariance?" To answer the question of the relative association between two securities' returns, we must refer to the correlation coefficient, because it is bounded.

The Correlation Coefficient To account for the effect of the covariations between securities, which is done in the second term of equation 19-6, it is necessary to estimate the correlation coefficient between each pair of securities, i and j. As used in portfolio theory, the ***correlation coefficient*** (r_{ij}) is a statistical measure of the extent to which the returns on any two securities are related; however, it denotes only association, not causation. It is a relative measure of association that is bounded by +1.0 and −1.0, with

$$r_{ij} = +1.0 = \text{perfect positive correlation}$$

$$r_{ij} = 0.0 = \text{no correlation}$$

$$r_{ij} = -1.0 = \text{perfect negative (inverse) correlation}$$

Figure 19-1 illustrates these three cases for two securities. With perfect positive correlation, the returns have a perfect direct linear relationship.

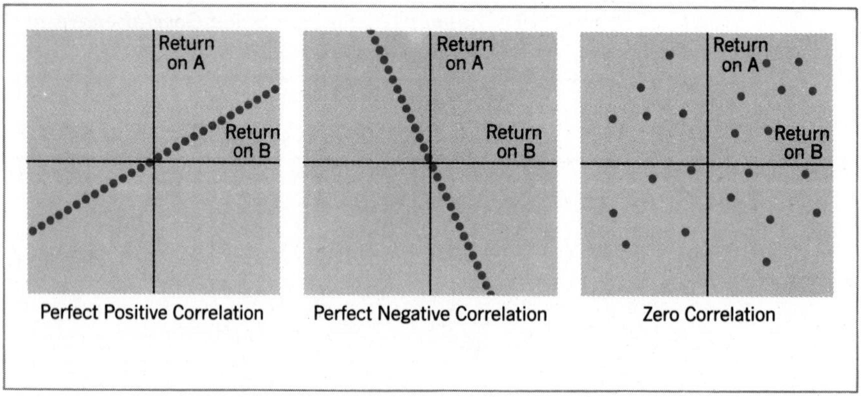

FIGURE 19-1 ***Returns on two securities. (a) perfect positive correlation; (b) perfect negative correlation; (c) no correlation.***

Knowing what the return on one security will do allows an investor to forecast perfectly what the other will do.

With perfect negative correlation, the securities' returns have a perfect inverse linear relationship to each other; therefore, knowing the return on one security provides full knowledge about the return on the second security. When one security's return is high, the other is low.

With zero correlation, there is no relationship between the returns on the two securities. A knowledge of the return on one security is of no value in predicting the return of the second security.

Combining securities with perfect positive correlation provides no reduction in portfolio risk. The risk of the resulting portfolio is simply a weighted average of the individual risks of the securities. As more securities are added under the condition of perfect positive correlation, portfolio risk remains a weighted average. There is no risk reduction.

Combining two securities with zero correlation (statistical independence) reduces the risk of the portfolio. If more securities with uncorrelated returns are added to the portfolio, significant risk reduction can be achieved. However, portfolio risk cannot be eliminated.

Finally, combining two securities with perfect negative correlation could eliminate risk altogether. This is the principle behind hedging strategies, some of which were discussed in Chapter 17.

In the real world, these extreme correlations are rare. Rather, securities typically have some positive correlation with each other. Thus, although risk can be reduced, it usually cannot be eliminated. Other things being equal, investors wish to find securities with the least positive correlation possible. Ideally, they would like securities with negative correlation or low positive correlation, but they generally will be faced with positively correlated security returns.

Relating the Correlation Coefficient and the Covariance

The covariance and the correlation coefficient are linked in the following manner:

$$\text{COV}(R_i, R_j) = r_{ij}\ \text{SD}(R_i)\ \text{SD}(R_j) \tag{19-8}$$

Equation 19-6 can therefore be restated to an equivalent expression, Equation 19-9, by substituting the right side of 19-8 for $\text{COV}(R_i, R_j)$ in 19-6.

$$\text{VAR}(R_p) = \sum_{i=1}^{n} W_i^2\ \text{VAR}(R_i) + \sum_{\substack{i=1 \\ i \neq j}}^{n} \sum_{j=1}^{n} (W_i)(W_j)(r_{ij})\ \text{SD}(R_i)\ \text{SD}(R_j) \tag{19-9}$$

Knowing the covariance, we can easily calculate the correlation coefficient by rearranging Equation 19-8 to 19-10:

$$r_{ij} = \frac{\text{COV}_{ij}}{\text{SD}_i\ \text{SD}_j} \tag{19-10}$$

Example. The correlation coefficient for EG&G and General Fudge is

$$r_{\text{EG\&G,GF}} = \frac{116.74}{(37.3)(23.3)} = 0.149 = 0.13$$

Thus, based on the historical data there is low positive correlation between EG&G and General Fudge. This is a good example of the types of securities that investors would like to combine in their portfolios, *given a world of mostly positive correlation coefficients between the returns on securities.* ▪

Understanding Portfolio Risk

Having considered the correlation coefficient and the covariance as measures of the association between securities' returns, we are now in a position to understand portfolio risk better. We have said that to calculate portfolio risk, we must account for two factors (from Equation 19-6):

1. Weighted individual security risks (i.e., the variance of *each* individual security, weighted by the percentage of investable funds placed in each individual security).
2. Weighted relationships between securities (i.e., the covariation between the securities' returns, again weighted by the percentage of investable funds placed in each security).

We can now better understand Equation 19-6, or its equivalent, Equation 19-9. One of Markowitz's real contributions to portfolio theory is his insight about the relative importance of these two factors. As the number of securities held in a portfolio increases, the importance of each individual security's risk (variance) decreases, while the importance of the covariance relationships increases. In a portfolio of 500 securities, for example, the contribution of each security's own risk to the total portfolio risk will be extremely small; portfolio risk will consist almost entirely of the covariance risk between securities.

To see this, consider the first term in Equation 19-6 or 19-9:

$$\sum_{i=1}^{n} W_i^2 \, VAR(R_i)$$

Assume equal amounts are invested in each security. The proportions, or weights, will be in $1/n$. Rewriting this term produces

$$\sum_{i=1}^{n} ((1/n)^2) \, VAR(R_i) = \frac{1}{n} \sum_{i=1}^{n} [VAR(R_i)/n]$$

The term in brackets represents an average variance for the stocks in the portfolio. As n becomes larger, this average variance becomes smaller, approaching zero for large values of n. Therefore, the risk of a well-diversified portfolio will be largely attributable to the impact of the second term in Equation 19-6 or 19-9.

We can rewrite Equation 19-6 into a shorter format:

$$VAR(R_p) = \sum_{i=1}^{n} \sum_{j=1}^{n} W_i W_j \, COV(R_i, R_j) \tag{19-11}$$

$$VAR(R_p) = \sum_{i=1}^{n} \sum_{j=1}^{n} W_i W_j \, r_{ij} \, SD(R_i) \, SD(R_j) \tag{19-12}$$

These equations account for both the variance and the covariances because when $i=j$, the variance is calculated; when $i \neq j$, the covariance is calculated.

To calculate portfolio risk using either Equation 19-11 or Equation 19-12, we need estimates of the variance for each security and estimates of the correlation coefficients or covariances. Both variances and correlation coefficients can be (and are) calculated using either ex post or ex ante data. If an analyst uses ex post data to calculate the correlation coefficient or the covariance and then uses these estimates in the Markowitz model, the implicit assumption is that the relationship that existed in the past will continue into the future. The same is true of the variances. If the historical variance is thought to be the best estimate of the expected variance, it should be used; however, it must be remembered that the variance and the correlation coefficient can change over time (and does).

After calculating (or estimating) the variances for each security and the covariances for every pair of securities, the portfolio risk can be calculated.

The importance of the covariance (or correlation coefficient) can be seen in the following simple example for a portfolio of two securities. By focusing on only two securities, the impact of different covariances (or correlation coefficients) on the total risk of the portfolio can be easily seen.

The Two-Security Case The risk of a portfolio, as measured by the standard deviation of returns, for the case of two securities, X and Y, is

$$SD(R_p) = [W_X^2 \, VAR(R_X) + W_Y^2 \, VAR(R_Y) + 2(W_X)(W_Y)(r_{X,Y}) \, SD(R_X) \, SD(R_Y)]^{1/2} \tag{19-13}$$

Example. Using the *historical data* for EG&G and GF, the mean annual TRs for this period were 26.3% and 11.6%, respectively, with standard deviations of 37.3% and 23.3%. Let us assume that the correlation coefficient between their returns is +0.15. To see the effects of changing the correlation coefficient, assume that the weights are 0.5 each—50% of investable funds is to be placed in each security. With these data, the standard deviation, or risk, for this portfolio would be

$$\begin{aligned} SD(R_p) &= [(0.5)^2(0.373)^2 + (0.5)^2(0.233)^2 + 2(0.5)(0.5)(0.373)(0.233)\, r_{EG\&G,GF}]^{1/2} \\ &= [0.0348 + 0.0136 + 0.0435\, r_{EG\&G,GF}]^{1/2} \end{aligned}$$

since $2(0.5)(0.5)(0.373)(0.233) = 0.0435$. The risk of the portfolio clearly depends heavily on the value of the third term, which in turn depends on the correlation coefficient between the returns for EG&G and GF. To assess the potential impact of this, consider the following cases: an r of +1, +0.5, +0.15, 0, −0.5, and −1.0. Calculating portfolio risk under each of these scenarios produces the following portfolio risks:

$$\begin{aligned} r &= +1.0: & SD(R_p) &= [0.0348 + 0.0136 + 0.0435(1.0)]^{1/2} &= 30.3\% \\ r &= +0.5: & SD(R_p) &= [0.0348 + 0.0136 + 0.0435(0.5)]^{1/2} &= 26.5\% \\ r &= +0.15: & SD(R_p) &= [0.0348 + 0.0136 + 0.0435(0.15)]^{1/2} &= 23.4\% \\ r &= 0.0: & SD(R_p) &= [0.0348 + 0.0136]^{1/2} &= 22.0\% \\ r &= -0.5: & SD(R_p) &= [0.0348 + 0.0136 + 0.0435(-0.5)]^{1/2} &= 16.0\% \\ r &= -1.0: & SD(R_p) &= [0.0348 + 0.0136 + 0.0435(-1.0)]^{1/2} &= 7.0\% \end{aligned}$$

▪

These calculations clearly show the impact on portfolio risk of combining securities with less than perfect positive correlation. The risk of the portfolio steadily decreases from 30.3% to 7% as the correlation coefficient declines from +1.0 to −1.0.

Conclusions About Portfolio Risk Our discussion of portfolio risk can be summarized in the following points:

1. The risk for a portfolio encompasses not only the individual security risks but also the covariances between all pairs of securities.

2. As shown in the two-security cases above, the importance of the covariance term can equal the combined importance of the individual securities' risks. Therefore, when adding a security to a portfolio, the average covariance between it and the other securities in the portfolio is more important than the security's own risk.
3. Three factors, not two, determine portfolio risk: individual variances, the covariances between securities, and the weights (percentage of investable funds) given to each security.[9]

Calculating Portfolio Return and Risk: An Example

Having considered both of the key parameters of the portfolio model, we now examine an example of building a portfolio using our two securities, EG&G and GF. Assume an investor is considering investing \$20,000 in stocks. The investor has decided to buy either EG&G, GF, or a combination of the two. If a portfolio is to be held, the investor has decided to invest half of the funds in EG&G and the other half in GF. The investor believes that the expected return and risk estimates for EG&G in Table 19-1 are reasonable and makes the following estimates for GF for the coming year based on a judgment that GF will enjoy an exceptionally good year: $E(R_{GF}) = 23\%$ and $SD(R_{GF}) = 25\%$. Note that $W_{EG\&G} = \$10{,}000/\$20{,}000 = 0.5$, and therefore $W_{GF} = 1.0 - W_{EG\&G} = 0.5$

$$E(R_p) = 0.5(25\%) + 0.5(23\%) = 24\%$$

$$SD(R_p) = [(0.5)^2(0.30)^2 + (0.5)^2(0.25)^2 + 2(0.5)(0.5)(0.15)(0.30)(0.25)]^{1/2}$$

$$= [0.0225 + 0.0156 + 0.0056]^{1/2} = 20.9\%$$

By combining GF with EG&G, the investor builds a portfolio with a greater expected return and less risk than if GF were held alone. These beneficial portfolio effects are attributable to the low positive correlation between the returns on these two securities.

Notice that *having established the portfolio weights*, W_1 and W_2, the calculation of the expected return on the portfolio is independent of the calculation of portfolio risk. The expected return will not change if some other variable in the risk calculation changes. For example, assume that the correlation coefficient between EG&G and GF is −0.15 instead of +0.15. The expected return on the portfolio remains 24%. The risk would now be

$$SD(R_p) = [(0.5)^2(0.3)^2 + (0.5)^2(0.25)^2 + 2(0.5)(0.5)(-0.15)(0.30)(0.25)]^{1/2}$$

$$= 18\%$$

[9]Both expected return and risk change as the weights change, whereas only the risk changes as the correlation coefficient changes.

The risk of this portfolio declines because of the beneficial effects of combining negatively correlated stocks. Therefore, holding everything else constant, risk can be reduced without affecting expected return, if the correlation between securities can be reduced.

The two-security case can be generalized to the n-security case. Portfolio risk can be reduced by combining assets with less than perfect positive correlation; furthermore, the smaller the positive correlation, the better.

Determining Efficient Portfolios

Having discussed the expected return and risk of portfolios in detail, we can now consider how the efficient portfolios of the Markowitz model are actually derived. Figure 19-2 illustrates the basic idea of an efficient set of

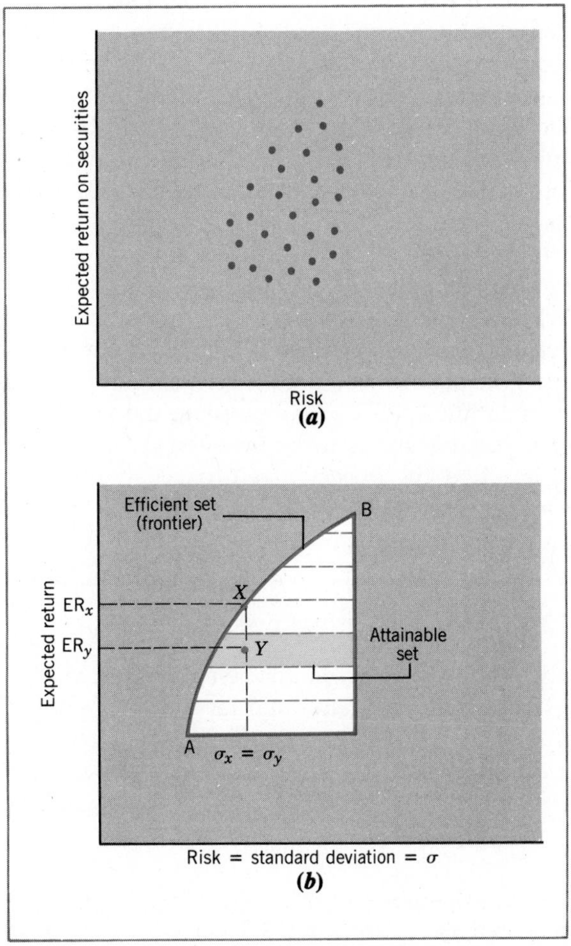

FIGURE 19-2 **(a)** ***Expected returns and risk for a group of securities;*** **(b)** ***the efficient set of portfolios.***

portfolios. First, note that the vertical axis is expected return and the horizontal axis is risk (as measured by the standard deviation). These are the standard axes in portfolio theory, and this diagram will be applied throughout this discussion. It is very important always to keep in mind that portfolio theory is concerned with the returns anticipated for the future (i.e., the expected returns).

In Figure 19-2*a* the expected returns and risks of a hypothetical group of securities have been plotted for the year 19X8. By combining these securities into various combinations, an infinite number of portfolio alternatives is possible. These possibilities are illustrated in Figure 19-2*b* and include the entire shaded area, which represents the many combinations of expected return and risk obtainable by forming portfolios. In portfolio theory, this area is referred to as the "attainable set" of portfolios—these portfolios are possible, but not necessarily preferable.

The curve AB represents the **efficient set (frontier)** of portfolios. This set dominates all interior portfolios (the remaining attainable set of portfolios) because it offers the largest expected return for a given amount of risk, or the smallest risk for a given expected return.[10] To see this consider portfolio *X* on the efficient frontier and portfolio *Y* in the attainable set. Although both have the same level of risk, *X* has a larger expected return; therefore, portfolio *X* dominates portfolio *Y* and would be preferred by investors. The same type of comparisons could be made with other portfolios with the same result. The efficient set of portfolios is the optimal set of portfolios for investors.

Technically, the basic Markowitz model is solved by a complex technique called quadratic programming. Since the model is easily solved by computer, the details need not concern us. It is important to note, however, that the solution involves manipulating the portfolio weights, or percentages of investable funds to be invested in each security. In other words, having inputted the expected returns, standard deviations, and correlations for the securities being considered, this is the only variable that can be manipulated to solve the portfolio problem.

INVESTMENTS INTUITION

Think of efficient portfolios as being derived in the following manner. The inputs are obtained and a level of desired expected return for a portfolio is specified—for example, 10%. Then all combinations of securities that can be combined to form a portfolio with an expected return of 10% are determined, and the one with the smallest variance

[10]The dominance principle in portfolio theory states that at a given level of risk investors prefer the portfolio with the highest expected return, or that for a given level of expected return investors prefer the portfolio with the least risk. All other portfolios are then dominated.

of return is selected as the efficient portfolio. Next, a level of portfolio expected return of 11%, for example, is specified, and the process is repeated. This continues until the feasible range of expected returns is processed. Of course, the problem could be solved by specifying levels of portfolio risk and choosing that portfolio with the largest expected return for the specified level of risk.

Selecting an Optimal Portfolio

Once the efficient set of portfolios is determined using the Markowitz model, investors must select the portfolio most appropriate for them from the full set. The Markowitz model does not specify one optimum portfolio. It generates the efficient frontier of portfolios, all of which, by definition, are optimal portfolios (for a given level of expected return or risk).

To select the expected return—risk combination that will satisfy an individual investor's personal preferences, indifference curves (which are assumed to be known for an investor) are used. These curves, shown in Figure 19-3 as a family of four curves, describe investor preferences; curve 1 is preferable to 2, which is preferable to 3, which is preferable to 4.[11]

The optimal portfolio for any investor occurs at the point of tangency between the investor's highest indifference curve and the efficient frontier. In Figure 19-3 this occurs at point 0. This portfolio maximizes investor utility because the indifference curves reflect investor utility preferences. Notice that curves U_2 and U_1 are unattainable and that U_3 is the highest indifference curve for this investor that is tangent to the efficient frontier. On the other hand, U_4, though attainable, is inferior to U_3, which offers a higher expected return for the same risk (and therefore more utility).

Note that on a practical basis, conservative investors would select portfolios on the left end of the efficient frontier AB because these portfolios have less risk (and, of course, less expected return). Conversely, aggressive investors would choose portfolios toward point B because these portfolios offer higher expected returns (along with higher levels of risk).

The Single Index Model

The Markowitz model generates the correct solution to the portfolio problem; that is, given a set of inputs, the Markowitz efficient-set procedures produce *the* optimal set of portfolios. It does so, however, at considerable

[11]Indifference curves are derived from utility analysis and represent the loci of equal utility in return–risk space. Although positively sloped in this analysis (because of the assumption that investors like larger returns and dislike risk), their exact shape depends upon investor preferences for taking risk.

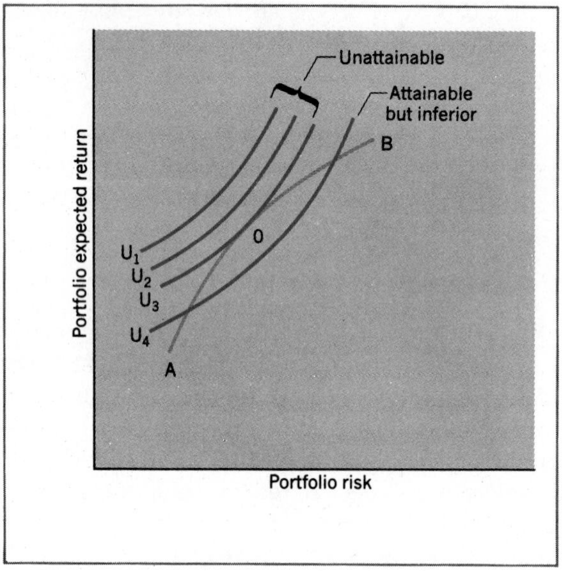

FIGURE 19-3 ***Selecting the optimal portfolio on the efficient frontier.***

cost. The major problem with the Markowitz model is that it requires a full set of covariances between the TRs of all securities being considered. There are $[n(n - 1)]/2$ unique covariances for a set of n securities.[12]

Example. If an analyst is considering 100 securities, it will be necessary to estimate [100(99)]/2 = 4950 unique covariances. For 250 securities, the number is [250(249)]/2 = 31,125 covariances. ▪

Obviously, estimating large numbers of covariances quickly becomes a major problem for model users. Since many institutional investors follow as many as 250 or 300 securities, the number of inputs required may become an impossibility. In fact, until the basic Markowitz model was simplified in terms of the covariance inputs, it remained primarily of academic interest.

In his original work, Markowitz suggested using an index to which securities are related as a means of generating covariances. William Sharpe, following Markowitz, developed the **single index model,** which relates returns on each security to the returns on a common index.[13] A broad market index of common stock returns is generally used for this purpose.[14]

[12]Although for n securities there are $n(n - 1)$ total covariances, $COV_{ij} = COV_{ji}$; therefore, there are only one-half as many unique covariances.
[13]W. Sharpe, "A Simplified Model for Portfolio Analysis," *Management Science* 9 (January 1963), pp. 277–293.
[14]There is no requirement that the index be a stock index. It could be any variable thought to be the dominant influence on stock returns.

The single index model can be stated as

$$R_{it} = a_i + b_i R_{Mt} + e_{it} \tag{19-14}$$

where

R_{it} = the random return (TR) on security i in period t
R_{Mt} = the random return (TR) on the market index in period t
a_i = the constant return unique to security i
b_i = measure of the sensitivity of the stock's return to the return on the market index
e_{it} = the random residual error in period t, or the difference between the actual return for some period and the return expected given the market return

To estimate the single index model, the TRs for stock i can be regressed on the corresponding TRs for the market index. Estimates will be obtained of a_i (the constant return on security i that is earned regardless of the level of market returns) and b_i (the beta coefficient that indicates the expected increase in a security's return for a 1% increase in market return).

The return on stock i in period t, conditional on a given market return in period t, is simply $a_i + b_i R_{Mt}$. The residual error, e_{it}, is the difference between the actual return for stock i in period t and its expected return. For any one period these error terms can be positive or negative. Over multiple periods the error term should average out to be zero.

Example. To illustrate the calculation of the single index model, we shall use the TR data for EG&G and GF presented earlier in the chapter along with the TRs for the S&P 500. Fitting a regression equation to each of these companies with the S&P 500 as the market index, the fitted equations are:

$$R_{EG\&G} = 16.3 + 1.21 R_{S\&P\ 500}$$

$$R_{GF} = 5.1 + 0.78 R_{S\&P\ 500}$$

▪

When the TRs for each stock are plotted against the market index TRs, and a regression line is fitted to these points, the *characteristic lines* shown in Figure 19-4 result. As can be seen, EG&G has a higher intercept (a_1) then GF (16.3 versus 5.1). This is the unique part of the return, that is, the return on each company when the market return is zero. EG&G's unique return is quite high.

The beta for EG&G is greater than 1.0 because this company's returns are more volatile than the market. On the other hand, GF's beta is considerably less than the market's beta of 1.0, indicating less volatility. This is shown in Figure 19-4 by the slopes of the characteristic lines, with EG&G having the steeper slope.

The single index model assumes that the market index is unrelated to

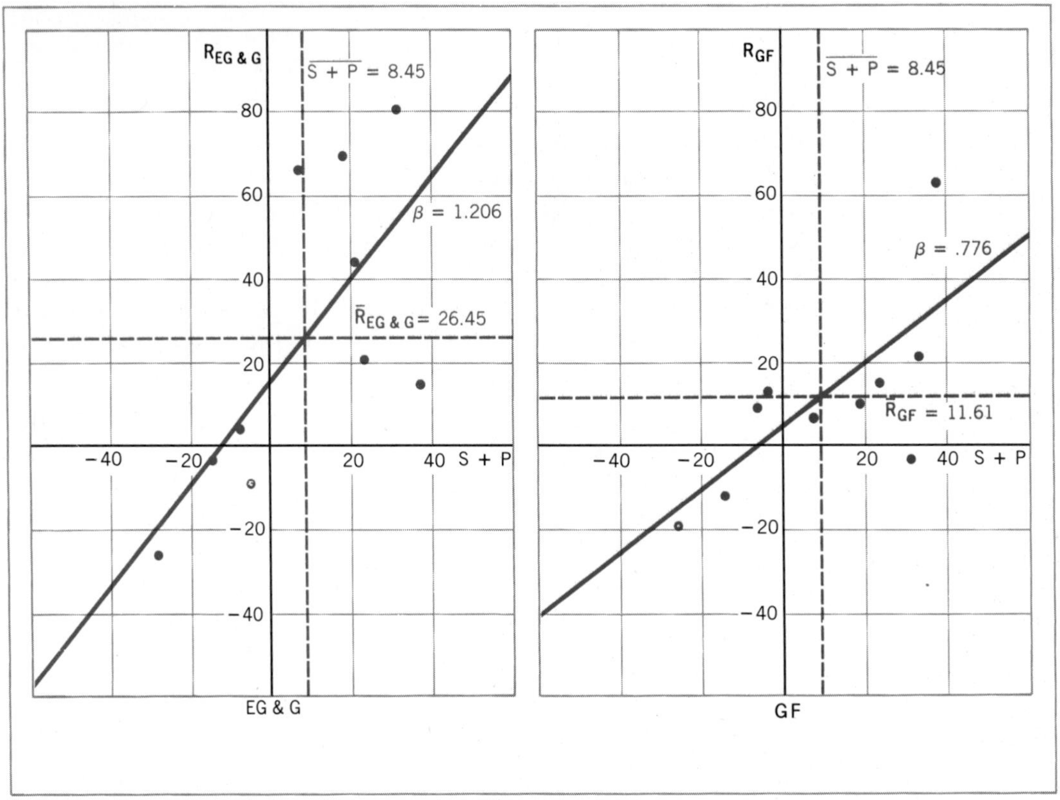

FIGURE 19-4 ***Characteristic lines for EG&G and GF using annual TRs.***

the residual error.[15] It is also assumed that securities are related only in their common response to the return on the market; that is, the residual errors for security i are uncorrelated with those of security j. This is the key assumption of the single index model because it implies that stocks covary together only because of their common relationship to the market index. In other words, there are no influences on stocks beyond the market, such as industry effects.[16]

The single index model can be used in at least two ways:

1. To simplify the estimations for the inputs to the Markowitz variance–covariance model.

---

[15]The use of regression analysis in estimating the single index model guarantees that these two variables will be uncorrelated.

[16]The use of regression analysis does not guarantee that this will be true. Instead, it is a specific simplifying assumption that, in fact, may or may not be true.

2. To solve the portfolio analysis problem directly; that is, to obtain the expected return and risk for portfolios.

Each of these will be considered in turn.

Using the Model to Estimate the Inputs

The single index model can be used to simplify greatly the estimations of the inputs needed for the basic Markowitz model. From the previous analysis, we know that, to generate the efficient set of portfolios, we need the expected return on each security, the variance of return on each security, and the covariances between each pair of securities.

Based on the single index model, the following equations can be used to obtain the inputs:

$$E(R_i) = a_i + b_i E(R_M) \tag{19-15}$$

$$VAR(R_i) = b_i^2[VAR\ (R_M)] + VAR\ (e_i) \tag{19-16}$$

$$COV(R_i, R_j) = b_i\, b_j\ VAR(R_M) \tag{19-17}$$

To implement these equations, the user needs a_i, b_i, and VAR(e_i). An expected return for the market index is also needed, as well as an estimate of its future variance. All of these variables may be estimated on the basis of historical data, by probability judgments about the future, or by a combination of the two.

Example. To illustrate implementation of these equations, consider the two stocks previously used, EG&G and GF. The calculated a_i and b_i are 16.3 and 1.21 for EG&G, 5.1 and 0.78 for GF. Assume that the market has an expected return of 10%, with an expected standard deviation of 20% (variance of 400). The expected return for each security would be

$$\text{EG\&G} = 16.3 + 1.21\ (10) = 28.4\%$$

$$\text{GF} = 5.1 + 0.78\ (10) = 12.9\%$$

▪

The variances and covariances could be calculated in a similar manner, using the VAR(e_i) from an estimation of Equation 19-14. Notice that in the case of the covariance, the calculation reduces to the product of the two betas and the variance of the market. For these two companies, this would be

$$COV = (1.21)(0.78)(400) = 377.5$$

Here we see the critical assumption of the single index model—securities are related only in their common response to the market index. The residual error terms for stock *i* are uncorrelated with the residual error terms for stock j. All correlation between security returns is reflected in the b term. If in fact this is not true, Equation 19-17 is incorrect.

Using the single index model for a sample of 250 securities, only 250 estimates of the b_i and the variance of the market index must be estimated to obtain the covariances needed. In contrast, the Markowitz model requires [250(249)]/2 unique covariance estimates. Clearly, the single index model greatly simplifies the problem of obtaining covariances.

The single index model requires $3n + 2$ total pieces of data to implement, where n is the number of securities being considered.

Example. The 250 securities mentioned earlier would require $3n + 2 = 3(250) + 2 = 752$ estimates, consisting of 250 estimates of a_i, 250 estimates of b_i, 250 variances of the residual errors [VAR(e_i)], one estimate of the expected return on the market index, and one estimate of the expected variance on the market index. ▪

In contrast, the full variance–covariance model of Markowitz requires $[n(n + 3)]/2$ estimates for n securities.

Example. In the case of the 250 securities, [250(253)]/2 = 31,625 total pieces of data, or

250 expected returns
+ 250 variances
+ [250(249)]/2 covariances
= 31,625 total pieces of data

▪

Using the Model for Portfolio Analysis

The single index model can be used to solve the portfolio problem directly; that is, the portfolio analysis problem can be reformulated in terms of expected return and variance on the market index. Rather than estimate the inputs for the Markowitz model, we can directly estimate the expected return and risk for a portfolio based on relationships involved with the single index model.

Since expected return on a portfolio is always a weighted average of the expected returns on individual securities, we can calculate $E(R_p)$ as a weighted average of the single index model's equation for the expected return on individual securities (Equation 19-15).

$$E(R_p) = \sum_{i=1}^{n} W_i[E(R_i)] = \sum_{i=1}^{n} W_iE[a_i + b_iE(R_M)] \quad (19\text{-}18)$$

$$= \sum_{i=1}^{n} W_ia_i + \sum_{i=1}^{n} W_ib_iE(R_M)$$

The characteristics of the single index model are such that

$$a_p = \sum_{i=1}^{n} W_i a_i \tag{19-19}$$

$$b_p = \sum_{i=1}^{n} W_i b_i \tag{19-20}$$

In other words, the portfolio a, a_p, is a weighted average of the individual security a_i's, and the portfolio b, b_p, is a weighted average of the individual security b_i's. Therefore, the expected return for a portfolio can be rewritten as

$$E(R_p) = a_p + b_p E(R_M) \tag{19-21}$$

As illustrated in Equation 19-16, the single index model partitions the risk on an individual security into two parts:

$$VAR(R_i) = b_i^2\, VAR(R_M) + VAR(e_i)$$

To estimate directly the variance of a portfolio, we need a weighted average of these two parts. Taking advantage of Equation 19-20 for the beta of a portfolio, $VAR(R_p)$ becomes

$$VAR(R_p) = [b_p]^2\, VAR(R_M) + \sum_{i=1}^{n} W_i^2\, VAR(e_i) \tag{19-22}$$

As a portfolio is diversified, the second term of Equation 19-22, the weighted unsystematic risk of the portfolio, declines drastically (this will be considered in more detail in the next chapter). The first term, the systematic risk of a portfolio, cannot be eliminated through diversification. Therefore, as the residual risk is reduced through diversification, for well-diversified portfolios the portfolio risk approaches

$$VAR(R_p) = [b_p]^2\, VAR(R_M) \tag{19-23}$$

and

$$SD(R_p) = b_p[SD(R_M)] \tag{19-24}$$

Estimating Portfolio Return and Risk: An Example

As we did with the Markowitz model, we can estimate the portfolio expected return and risk for a two-stock portfolio consisting of EG&G and GF. Assume again that an investor has $20,000 to invest and plans to invest $10,000 in each stock; therefore, the weights in each will be 0.5. The expected return for the market is 10% with a standard deviation of 20%. Assume the following values for each stock:

	a	b	VAR(e_i)
EG&G	16	1.2	850
GF	5	0.8	310

Using Equation 19-18:

$$E(R_p) = [0.5][16 + 1.2(10)] + [0.5][5 + 0.8(10)] = 20.5$$

Using Equations 19-19 and 19-20 to calculate the a and b for the portfolio and Equation 19-21 to calculate $E(R_p)$,

$$\begin{aligned} E(R_p) &= a_p + b_p E(R_M) \\ &= 10.5+1.0(10) = 20.5 \end{aligned}$$

In calculating the risk of this portfolio, note that the weighted systematic risk is

$$[b_p]^2 \text{ VAR}(R_M) = 1.0(400) = 400$$

whereas the weighted unsystematic risk is

$$[0.5]^2(850) + [0.5]^2(310) = 290$$

Therefore, total risk for the portfolio equals the sum of the two parts, or

$$\text{VAR}(R_p) = 400 + 290 = 690$$

and

$$\text{SD}(R_p) = [690]^{1/2} = 26.3\%$$

Multi-index Models

As noted in the previous section, the single index model assumes that stock prices covary only because of common movement with one index, specifically that of the market. Some researchers have attempted to capture some nonmarket influences by constructing multi-index models. Probably the most obvious example of these potential nonmarket influences is the industry factor.[17] A multi-index model is of the form

$$E(R_i) = a_i + b_i R_M + c_i \text{NF} + e_i \tag{19-25}$$

where NF is the nonmarket factor and all other variables are as previously defined. Equation 19-25 could be expanded to include three, four, or more indexes.

[17]In a well-known study, Benjamin King found a common movement between securities, beyond the market effect, associated with industries. See B. King, "Market and Industry Factors in Stock Price Behavior," *Journal of Business*, Vol. 39 (January 1966), pp. 139–190.

It seems logical that a multi-index model should perform better than a single index model because it uses more information about the interrelationships between stock returns. In effect, the multi-index model falls between the full variance–covariance method of Markowitz and Sharpe's single index model.

How well do these models perform? Given the large number of possible multi-index models, no conclusive statement is possible. However, one well-known study, by Kalman Cohen and Jerry Pogue, found that the single index model outperformed a multi-index model in that it produced more efficient portfolios.[18] This study, using industry classifications, found the single index model not only was simpler but led to lower expected risks.

It is worth noting that the multi-index model tested by Cohen and Pogue (and by Elton and Gruber) actually reproduced the *historical* correlations better than the single index model.[19] However, *it did not perform better ex ante,* which is the more important consideration, because portfolios are built to be held for a future period of time.

Evaluation of the Single Index Model

The single index model is a valuable simplification of the full variance–covariance matrix needed for the Markowitz model. An obvious question to ask is how it performs in relation to the Markowitz model.

In his original paper developing the single index model, Sharpe found that two sets of efficient portfolios—one using the full Markowitz model and one using his simplification—generated from a sample of stocks were very much alike.[20] A later study also found that the Sharpe model did no worse than the Markowitz model in all tests conducted, and in tests using shorter time periods it performed better.[21]

In summary, the single index model performs very well and is a major step forward in the evolution of portfolio theory. It simplifies the calculations of the inputs needed in the Markowitz model. In addition, the model leads to the derivation of useful measures of risk that will be used in Chapter 20 to derive a theory of capital markets. Furthermore, the use of the single index model makes possible an even more significant simplification in the determination of optimal portfolios, as explained in the appendix.

---

[18]K. Cohen and J. Pogue, "An Empirical Evaluation of Alternative Portfolio Selection Models," *Journal of Business*, Vol. 46 (April 1967), pp. 166–193.
[19]E. Elton and M. Gruber, "Estimating the Dependence Structure of Share Prices—Implications for Portfolio Selection," *Journal of Finance*, Vol. 5 (December 1973), pp. 1203–1232.
[20]Sharpe, "A Simplified Model."
[21]G. Frankfurter, H. Phillips, and J. Seagle, "Performance of the Sharpe Portfolio Selection Model: A Comparison," *Journal of Financial and Quantitative Analysis*, June 1976, pp. 195–204.

Summary

- Portfolio theory/management is concerned with an investor's portfolio—the combination of assets invested in and held by an investor.
- Basic portfolio theory originated with Harry Markowitz, based on the expected return and risk characteristics of securities.
- Investors seek efficient portfolios, defined as those with maximum return for a specified risk of minimum risk for a specified return. The efficient set (frontier) of portfolios can be calculated from equations for the expected return and risk for a portfolio.
- The expected return for a portfolio is a weighted average of the individual securities' expected returns.
- Portfolio risk is not a weighted average of individual security risks because it is necessary to account for the covariations between the returns on securities. Once determined, the weighted covariance term can be added to the weighted variance of the securities to determine portfolio risk.
- To determine the covariations between securities' returns, it is necessary to calculate the covariance or the correlation coefficient, either of which can be positive, negative, or zero. Investors seek to reduce positive correlation, which is typical, as much as possible.
- Portfolio risk depends not only on the variances and covariances, but also on the weights for each security (as does the portfolio expected return). The weights are the variables to be manipulated in solving the Markowitz portfolio model.
- After generating the efficient set of portfolios, an investor chooses one based on the point of tangency between the efficient frontier and the investor's highest indifference curve.
- The single index model greatly simplifies the calculations for the covariances in the Markowitz model by relating the return on each security to that of a market index. This model assumes that the only reason that stocks move together is because of a common relationship to the market.
- Using this model, the investor can determine the expected return, variance, and covariance for every security with only $3n + 2$ estimates.
- The single index model appears to perform as well as multi-index models on an ex ante basis and to compare very favorably with the full variance–covariance model of Markowitz.
- The single index model makes it possible to simplify greatly the calculations involved in determining optimum portfolios by using the Elton–Gruber–Padberg techniques explained in the appendix.

Key Words

Correlation coefficient
Covariance
Ex ante
Ex post
Efficient portfolio
Efficient set (frontier)
Portfolio management
Single index model

Questions

19-1 Evaluate this statement: With regard to portfolio risk, the whole is not equal to the sum of the parts.

19-2 What is meant by an efficient portfolio?

19-3 How is expected return for one security determined? For a portfolio?

19-4 Calculate the number of covariances needed for an evaluation of 500 securities using the Markowitz model. Also, calculate the total number of pieces of information needed.

19-5 Using the Sharpe model, how many covariances would be needed to evaluate 500 securities? How many total pieces of information?

19-6 How many, and which, factors determine portfolio risk?

19-7 The Markowitz approach is often referred to as a mean-variance approach. Why?

19-8 What is the key assumption underlying the single index model?

19-9 When, if ever, would a stock with a large risk (standard deviation) be desirable in building a portfolio?

19-10 What is the relationship between the market model, the single index model, and the characteristic line?

19-11 What is the relationship between the correlation coefficient and the covariance, both qualitatively and quantitatively?

19-12 Using the Markowitz analysis, how does an investor select an optimal portfolio?

19-13 What is the excess return to beta ratio? What are its advantages in relation to the Markowitz model?

19-14 Explain two different uses for the single index model.

19-15 Many investors have known for years that they should not "put all of their eggs in one basket." How does the Markowitz analysis shed light on this old principle?

19-16 What is a multi-index model? Give an example of one. If multi-index models are able to reproduce historical correlations better than the single index model, are they preferable?

19-17 Why do rational investors seek efficient portfolios?

19-18 How would the expected return for a portfolio of 500 securities be calculated?

19-19 Given a set of inputs, explain conceptually how efficient portfolios are determined.

Demonstration Problems

19-1 Calculate portfolio return and risk for the two-security case discussed in the chapter, assuming ex ante returns and standard deviations as follows:

	EG&G		GF
Return (%)	25		23
Standard deviation (%)	30		25
Covariance		112.5	

The correlation coefficient, r, is +0.15. We can calculate expected portfolio returns and risk for different weights (W). We shall use intervals of 0.20, and we will illustrate the calculations using $W_i = 0.8$.

$$\text{Expected return} = (0.8)(25) + (0.2)(23) = 24.6\%$$

$$\text{Variance} = (0.8)^2(30)^2 + (0.2)^2(25)^2 + (2)(.8)(.2)(112.5) = 637$$

$$\text{Standard deviation} = (637)^{1/2} = 25.2\%$$

The complete results are as follows:

Proportion In		(1)	(2)	(3)
EG&G W_i	GF $W_j = (1 - W_i)$	Portfolio Expected Returns (%)	Variance	Standard Deviation (%)
1.0	0.0	25.0	900	30.0
0.8	0.2	24.6	637	25.2
0.6	0.4	24.2	478	21.9
0.4	0.6	23.8	423	20.6
0.2	0.8	23.4	472	21.7
0.0	1.0	23.0	625	25.0

Notice that the expected return on the portfolio declines as the proportion invested in EG&G, which has the higher expected return, receives less weight. The portfolio standard deviation, on the other hand, first declines and then rises.

19-2 Use the single index model to calculate expected portfolio returns and risk for the two-security case. We make slightly different assumptions from those in Problem 19-1, with the alphas, betas, and the mean square unsystematic errors for EG&G and General Fudge as follows:

	Alpha	Beta	Unsystematic Errors	Expected S&P 500 Values
EG&G	16	1.2	850	Return = 10%
General Fudge	5	0.8	310	Standard deviation = 20%

We use the following values for different portfolio weights to obtain the numbers in columns 1–7.

$$\text{Alpha} = 16W_i + 5W_j = a_p$$

$$\text{Beta} = 1.2W_i + 0.8W_j = b_p$$

Expected return = $a_p + b_p(10) = E(R_p)$
Systematic risk = $400b_p^2 = S$
Unsystematic risk = $850\ W_i^2 + 310\ W_j^2 = N$
Variance = columns 4 + 5
Standard deviation = square root of column 6.

For example, with $W_i = 0.8$:

$a_p = 0.8(16) + 0.2(5) = 13.8$
$b_p = 0.8(1.20) + 0.2(.80) = 1.12$
$E(R_p) = 13.8 + 1.12(10) = 25\%$
$S = 400(1.12)^2 = 502$
$N = 850(0.8) + 350(0.2) = 556$
Variance = 502 + 556 = 1058
Standard deviation = $(1058)^{1/2} = 32.5$

Weights		(1)	(2)	(3)	(4)	(5)	(6)	(7) Standard
W_i	W_j	a_p	b_p	R_p(%)	S	N	Variance	Deviation (%)
1.0	0.0	16.0	1.20	28.0	576	850.0	1426	37.8
0.8	0.2	13.8	1.12	25.0	502	556.4	1058	32.5
0.6	0.4	11.6	1.04	22.0	433	355.6	788	28.1
0.4	0.6	9.4	0.96	19.0	369	247.6	616	24.8
0.2	0.8	7.2	0.88	16.0	310	232.4	542	23.3
0.0	1.0	5.0	0.80	13.0	256	310.0	566	23.8

19-3 Calculate the characteristic line for EG&G. Let Y be the annual TRs for EG&G and X be the TRs for the S&P 500 Index (the values are shown in the text). The summary statistics are as follows:

$$n = 10$$

$$\Sigma Y = 264.5 \quad \Sigma Y^2 = 19{,}503.65$$

$$\Sigma X = 84.5 \quad \Sigma X^2 = 4{,}660.31$$

$$\Sigma XY = 6995.76$$

$$SS_y = \Sigma(Y - \bar{Y})^2 = \Sigma Y^2 - \frac{(\Sigma Y)^2}{n} = 12{,}507.625$$

$$SS_x = \Sigma(X - \bar{X})^2 = \Sigma X^2 - \frac{(\Sigma X)^2}{n} = 3946.285$$

$$SS_{xy} = \Sigma(X - \bar{X})(Y - \bar{Y})^2 = \Sigma XY - \frac{(\Sigma X)(\Sigma Y)}{n} = 4760.735$$

$$\hat{\beta} = \frac{SS_{xy}}{SS_x} = 1.206384$$

$$\hat{a} = \bar{Y} - \hat{\beta}\bar{X} = 16.256$$

$$\hat{Y} = 16.256 + 1.206X$$

Analysis of Variance Source (Risk)	Sum of Squares	No. of Observations	Variance	
Total SS_y	= 12,507.625	$n - 1 = 9$	1389.736	= Total variance
Systematic $\beta^2 SS_x$	= 5,743.275	$n - 1 = 9$	638.142	= Systematic variance
Unsystematic	= 6,764.350	$n - 1 = 9$	751.594	= Unsystematic variance

Problems

19-1 Calculate the expected return and risk (standard deviation) for General Fudge for 198X, given the following information:

Probabilities	0.15	0.20	0.40	0.10	0.15
Expected returns:	0.20	0.16	0.12	0.05	−0.05

19-2 Four securities have the following expected returns: A = 15%, B = 12%, C = 30%, and D = 22%. Calculate the expected returns for a portfolio consisting of all four securities under the following conditions:

(a) The portfolio weights are 25% each.

(b) The portfolio weights are 10% in A, with the remainder equally divided among the other three stocks.

(c) The portfolio weights are 10% each in A and B, and 40% each in C and D.

19-3 Assume the additional information provided below for the four stocks in Problem 19-2.

		Correlations with			
	SD(%)	A	B	C	D
A	10	1.0			
B	8	0.6	1.0		
C	20	0.2	−1.0	1.0	
D	16	0.5	0.3	0.8	1.0

(a) Assuming equal weights for each stock, what are the standard deviations for the following portfolios?

(1) A, B, and C

(2) B and C

(3) B and D
(4) C and D

(b) Calculate the standard deviation for a portfolio consisting of stocks B and C, assuming the following weights: (1) 40% in B and 60% in C; (2) 60% in C and 40% in B.

(c) In part a, which portfolio(s) would an investor prefer?

19-4 Given the following information for a set of portfolios, determine which of these portfolio(s) would constitute the efficient set.

Portfolio	Expected Return (%)	Standard Deviation (%)
1	10	20
2	12	24
3	8	16
4	6	12
5	9	21
6	20	40
7	18	36
8	8	15
9	11	19
10	12	22
11	14	26

19-5 Assume that the expected return on the market is 10% with a standard deviation of 20%. The following information is available for stocks A, B, and C.

	a	*b*	Residual Error or VAR(e_i)
A	3	1.4	300
B	1	0.7	500
C	20	1.0	200

Using the single index model, answer the following:

(a) Calculate the expected return for each stock.

(b) Calculate the variance, and standard deviation, for each stock.

(c) Which of the three securities is the riskiest if 100% of an investor's wealth can be invested in only one security?

(d) Under the same conditions as c, which security is more risky—b or c?

(e) Which security is least risky when added to a well-diversified portfolio?

19-6 Using the format of Demonstration Problem 19-2 (weights in increments of 0.2), calculate the data as calculated in that problem (alpha, beta, etc.) for the following two companies.

	X	Y
Alpha	1.0	−10.0
Beta	1.0	1.6
Unsystematic risk	650	1500

19-7 Given the following information, and using the example of Demonstration Problem 19-3, show that the characteristic line for this company is

$$\hat{Y} = 5.055 + 0.776X$$

$\Sigma X = 264.5$; $\Sigma X^2 = 4660.31$; $\Sigma Y = 116.1$; $\Sigma Y^2 = 6217.13$; $\Sigma XY = 4042.23$
$SS_x = 3946.285$; $SS_y = 4869.209$; $SS_{xy} = 3061.185$

19-8 Given the following information for four securities

Security	1	2	3	4
E(R)%	10	12	14	18
VAR(R)	300	350	400	450

$r(1,2) = 0.2$; $r(1,3) = 0.4$; $r(1,4) = 0.6$; $r(2,3) = 0.1$; $r(3,4) = 0.9$; $r(2,4) = 0.5$.

Calculate five efficient portfolios using the Markowitz analysis, an upper boundary of 25%, and a lower boundary of 10%. Use the "with" short sale procedure.

(a) What is the highest expected return from these five portfolios?
(b) What is the lowest standard deviation from these five portfolios?
(c) Which portfolios involve short sales?
(d) What portfolio should be preferred by an investor?

19-9 Using the information in 19-8, determine the effects of changing the correlation coefficient between securities 1 and 2 from 0.20 to −0.20.

(a) What is the effect on the expected return of the portfolio?
(b) What is the effect on the variance of the portfolios?

Selected References

A good discussion of the intricacies of portfolio theory can be found in

Elton, Edwin J., and Gruber, Martin J. *Modern Portfolio Theory and Investment Analysis*, 3rd ed. New York: John Wiley, 1987.

An interesting discussion by Markowitz can be found in

Markowitz, Harry. "Markowitz Revisited." *Financial Analysts Journal*, September–October 1976, pp. 47–52.

APPENDIX 19-A

Simple Techniques for Determining Optimum Portfolios

Based on the single index model, Edwin Elton, Martin Gruber, and Manfred Padberg (EGP) have developed procedures for determining optimal portfolios that are easy to implement compared to the techniques discussed earlier—the computations can even be made without the aid of a computer. Furthermore, the procedures indicate why a stock does or does not enter into an optimal portfolio.[22]

We shall refer to this technique for determining the efficient frontier as the EGP technique. To implement it, the single index model must be accepted as the description of the comovement between securities. If this assumption is made, a single number can be used to measure the desirability of adding a stock to an optimal portfolio. This measure is the stock's **excess return to beta ratio,** defined as

$$\text{Excess return to beta} = \frac{E(R_i) - RF}{b_i} \tag{19-A1}$$

with all terms as previously defined.

In words, Equation 19-A1 is the ratio of the extra return, beyond what is offered on a risk-free asset, to the stock's nondiversifiable (i.e., systematic) risk. The higher the ratio, the more desirable the stock for inclusion in a portfolio.

[22]E. Elton, M. Gruber, and M. Padberg, "Optimal Portfolios From Simple Ranking Devices," *Journal of Portfolio Management*, Vol. 3 (Spring 1978), pp. 15–19; E. Elton, M. Gruber, and M. Padberg, "Simple Criteria for Optimal Portfolio Selection: Tracing Out the Efficient Frontier," *Journal of Finance*, Vol. 13 (March 1978), pp. 296–302.

Example. Using the expected returns for EG&G and GF estimated earlier from the single index model, the excess return to beta ratios would be (assuming a risk-free rate of 5%)

$$\text{EG\&G} = \frac{28.4 - 5}{1.21} = 19.3$$

$$\text{GF} = \frac{12.9 - 5}{0.78} = 10.1$$

▪

To use the EGP technique, the following steps are performed. (This discussion will omit the formulas necessary to calculate certain variables, but the example below illustrates the calculations necessary to use this technique.)

1. Calculate the excess return to beta ratio for each stock being considered.
2. Rank all stocks on this ratio from highest to lowest.
3. Using a specified formula, calculate a cut-off point C^*, which is based on the characteristics of all stocks that belong in the optimum portfolio.
4. Knowing C^*, select all stocks with an excess return-to-beta ratio above C^*.
5. Using another formula, calculate the percentage of investable funds to invest in each security. The residual variance of each security plays a major part in this calculation.

EGP note that their technique produces results equivalent to those produced by the quadratic programming technique of the Markowitz model. Obviously, the calculations are much less complex and involved. Furthermore, additional stocks can be evaluated immediately by calculating this ratio. In fact, the attractiveness of stocks can be evaluated before the calculations for an optimal portfolio are initiated.

The Elton–Gruber–Padberg procedures greatly simplify the entire process of obtaining optimum portfolios. The calculations required are reduced enormously, although the final results are the same as would be produced using the more involved procedures. Perhaps more important, this procedure produces a very simple screening device (the excess return to beta ratio) that many portfolio managers and investors can readily use to evaluate securities to determine immediately if they warrant inclusion in the optimal portfolio, which was not previously possible.

Example. This example is highly simplified and designed to illustrate the principles of portfolio composition. Using six corporations, and slightly different assumed ex ante values, first rank in descending order on the basis of excess returns to beta (shown in column 1 below). Continuing the assumption that the expected market yield is 10% and the risk-free yield is 5%, the values in the first five columns are assumed.

Ranked Corporation	(1) $\frac{(R_i - RF)}{\beta_i}$	(2) α_i	(3) B_i	(4) $(R_i - RF)$	(5) $N = \sigma^2$	(6) C_i	
1. EG&G	14.0%	9.8	1.2	16.8%	800	4.884	
2. GF	10.0	5.0	.8	8.0	400	6.949	
3. PepsiCo	8.0	3.0	1.0	8.0	640	7.172	
4. IBM	8.0	3.0	1.0	8.0	500	7.347	C* = 7.0
5. NCNB	4.0	−2.2	1.2	4.8	800	6.705	
6. EAL	1.0	−9.4	1.6	1.6	1,600	5.949	

Using a tedious computational process, the cumulative C_i for the portfolio is calculated in column 6. For an investor with a cut-off point, C* = 7, the optimum portfolio would include EG&G, GF, PepsiCo, and IBM, and NCNB and EAL would be excluded. This model further allows the computation of the appropriate portfolio weights using the formula

$$Z_i = \left[\frac{\beta_i}{\sigma^2} \right] \left[\frac{(R_i - RF)}{\beta_i} - C^* \right] = \left[\frac{\text{Column 3}}{\text{Column 5}} \right] [\text{Column 1} - 7.0]$$

For the four securities to be included in the portfolio, the Z_i are as follows:

Security		Z_i	$W_i = Z_i/\Sigma Z_i$	
EG&G		0.0105	0.52	
GF		0.0060	0.30	
PepsiCo		0.0015625	0.08	
IBM		0.0020	0.10	
	$\Sigma Z_i =$	0.0200625	1.00	$= \Sigma W_i$

and the $W_i = Z_i/\Sigma Z_i$.

Problems

For EG&G and GF the expected returns calculated from the single index model, on the assumption of an expected market return of 10%, are 28.4% for EG&G and 12.9% for GF. Assume an RF of 5%. The excess return to beta ratio for each stock is

$$\text{EG\&G: } \frac{(28.4 - 5)}{1.21} = 19.34$$

$$\text{GF: } \frac{(12.9 - 5)}{0.78} = 10.13$$

Using the alpha and betas for the following four corporations, and the same expected market return (10%) and risk-free yield (5%), calculate the excess return to beta for each of four corporations, and in combination with EG&G and GF, show the six corporations rank, from high to low, in the following order:

Corporation	Excess Return to Beta	Beta	Alpha
1. EG&G	19.34	1.21	16.30
2. GF	10.13	0.78	0.10
3. PepsiCo		1.01	0.96
4. IBM		1.06	0.55
5. NCNB		1.13	−1.50
6. EAL		1.62	−10.70

CHAPTER 20

Capital Market Theory

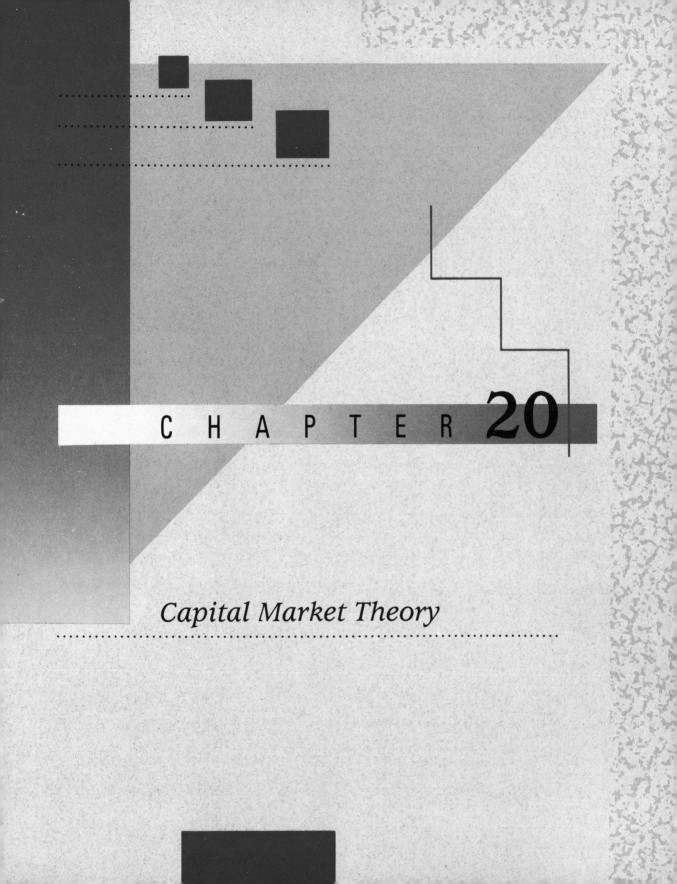

This chapter is a natural sequel to the last one because capital market theory starts where Markowitz portfolio theory ends. **Capital market theory** describes the pricing of capital assets in the marketplace. The objective is to provide a model that can be used to price risky assets.[1]

Portfolio theory is normative, describing how investors should act in selecting an optimal portfolio of securities. Capital market theory is positive, describing how assets are priced in a market of investors using the Markowitz portfolio model. Capital market theory is based on the concept of efficient diversification discussed in the previous chapter.

Assumptions of Capital Market Theory

Capital market theory builds on Markowitz portfolio theory. Each investor is assumed to diversify his or her portfolio according to the Markowitz model, choosing a location on the efficient frontier that matches his or her return–risk preferences. Because of the complexity of the real world, additional assumptions must be made:

1. All investors have identical probability distributions for future rates of return. They have indentical (or homogeneous) expectations with respect to the three inputs of the portfolio model explained in the previous chapter: expected returns, the variance of returns, and the correlation matrix.
2. All investors have the same one-period time horizon.
3. All investors can borrow or lend money at the risk-free rate of return (designated RF in this text).
4. There are no transaction costs.
5. There are no personal income taxes—investors are indifferent between capital gains and dividends.
6. There is no inflation.
7. No single investor can affect the price of a stock through his or her buying and selling decisions.
8. Capital markets are in equilibrium.

Most, or all, of these assumptions appear unrealistic and disturb many individuals encountering capital market theory for the first time. However,

---

[1]Much of this analysis is attributable to the work of Sharpe. See W. Sharpe, "Capital Asset Prices: A Theory of Market Equilibrium Under Conditions of Risk," *The Journal of Finance*, Vol. 19 (September 1964), pp. 425–442. Lintner and Mossin developed a similar analysis.

the important issue is how well the theory predicts or describes reality, and not how realistic its assumptions are. If capital market theory does a good job of explaining the returns on risky assets, it will be very useful and the assumptions made in deriving the theory will be of less importance.

It should be noted that most of these assumptions can be relaxed without significant effects on the capital pricing asset model (CAPM) or its implications. Another way to say this is that the CAPM is robust.[2] Although the results from such a relaxation of the assumptions may be less clear-cut and precise, no significant damage is done. Many of the conclusions of the basic model still hold.

Finally, it is worth noting that all of the assumptions are not necessarily unrealistic. For example, some institutional investors are tax-exempt, and their brokerage costs, as a percentage of the transaction, are quite small. Nor is it too unreasonable to assume that for the one-period horizon of the model, inflation may be fully anticipated and, therefore, not a major factor.

Introducing a Risk-free Asset

The key to the development of capital market theory is the introduction of a risk-free asset into the analysis. Investors, in addition to the option of risky assets such as common stocks, always have the option of buying a riskless asset, which for our purposes can be proxied by short-term Treasury securities. A **risk-free asset** is defined as one with a certain expected return and a variance of return of zero. Since variance = 0, the risk-free rate in each period will be equal to its expected value. Furthermore, the covariance between the risk-free asset and any risky asset i will be zero, because

$$\begin{aligned} \text{COV}_{\text{RF},i} &= r_{\text{RF},i}\,\text{SD}_i\,\text{SD}_{\text{RF}} \\ &= r_{\text{RF},i}\,\text{SD}_i\,(0) \\ &= 0 \end{aligned}$$

where r denotes the correlation coefficient and SD denotes the respective standard deviation of asset i or the risk-free asset. Therefore, the risk-free asset will have no correlation with risky assets.

Although the introduction of a risk-free asset appears to be a simple step to take in the evolution of portfolio and capital market theory, it is a very significant step. It allows Markowitz portfolio theory to be extended in such a way that the efficient frontier is completely changed, which in turn leads to a general theory for pricing assets under uncertainty.

---

[2]For a discussion of changing these assumptions, see E. Elton and M. Gruber, *Modern Portfolio Theory and Investment Analysis*, 3rd ed. (New York: John Wiley, 1987), Chapter 11.

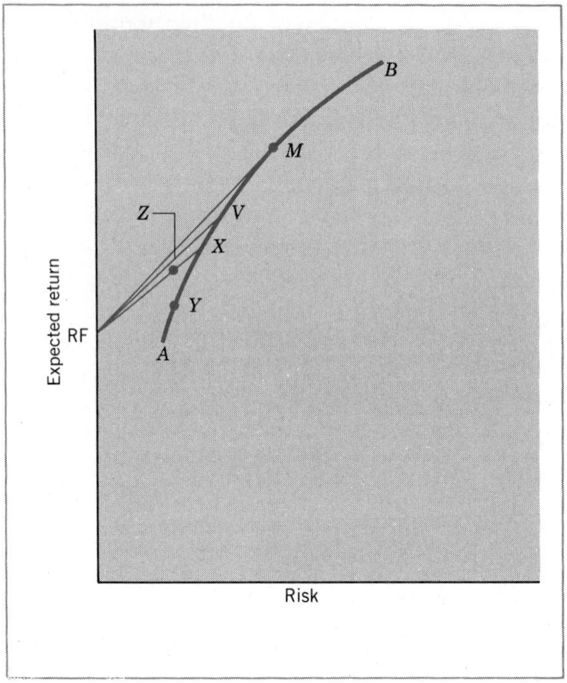

FIGURE 20-1 ***The Markowitz efficient frontier and the lending possibilities resulting from introducing a risk-free asset.***

Combining Risk-free and Risky Assets

Assume that the efficient frontier developed in the last chapter, as shown in Figure 20-1, has been derived by an investor. The arc AB delineates the efficient set of portfolios of risky assets (for simplicity, assume these are portfolios of common stocks). We now introduce a risk-free asset with return RF and SD = 0.

As shown in Figure 20-1, the return on the risk-free asset (RF) will plot on the vertical axis because the risk is zero. Investors can combine this riskless asset with the efficient set of portfolios on the efficient frontier. By drawing a line between RF and various risky portfolios on the efficient frontier, we can examine combinations of risk–return possibilities that did not exist previously.

Consider an arbitrary point on the efficient frontier, risky portfolio *X*. An investor who combines the risk-free asset with portfolio *X* of risky assets would have a portfolio somewhere on the line RF–X (e.g., point Z). Assume this investor places W_{RF} of investable funds in the risk-free asset, and the remainder $(1 - W_{RF})$ in portfolio *X*. The expected return on this combined portfolio *p* would be

$$E(R_p) = W_{RF}RF + (1 - W_{RF})\,E(R_X) \qquad (20\text{-}1)$$

As always, the expected return of a portfolio is a weighted average of the expected returns of the individual assets. Since portfolio X, consisting of risky assets, would always be assumed to have a larger *expected* return than the return on the risk-free asset (RF), the greater the percentage of an investor's funds committed to X, $(1 - W_{RF})$, the larger the expected return on the portfolio.

The standard deviation of this portfolio is

$$SD(R_p) = (1 - W_{RF})\ SD(R_X) \tag{20-2}$$

because $SD_{RF} = 0$ and the correlation between RF and any risky portfolio is zero, eliminating the covariation term. Thus, the standard deviation of a portfolio combining the risk-free asset with a risky asset (portfolio) is simply the weighted standard deviation of the risky portfolio.

Example. Assume that portfolio X has an expected return of 15%, with a standard deviation of 10%, and that the risk-free security has an expected return of 7%. If half of investable funds is placed in each (i.e., $W_{RF} = 0.5$ and $1 - W_{RF} = 0.5$), then

$$E(R_p) = 0.5(7\%) + 0.5(15\%) = 11\%$$

and

$$SD(R_p) = (1.0 - 0.5)10\% = 5\%$$

An investor could change positions on the line RF-X by varying W_{RF}, and hence $1 - W_{RF}$. As more of the investable funds are placed in the risk-free asset, both the expected return and the risk of the portfolio decline. ▪

INVESTMENTS INTUITION

It should be apparent that the segment of the efficient frontier below X (i.e., A to X) in Figure 20-1 is now dominated by the line RF-X. For example, at point Z on the straight line the investor has the same risk as portfolio *Y* on the Markowitz efficient frontier, but Z has a larger expected return.

Lending Possibilities

In Figure 20-1 a new line could be drawn between RF and the Markowitz efficient frontier above point X, for example, connecting RF to point V. Each successively higher line will dominate the preceding set of portfolios. This process ends when a line is drawn tangent to the efficient frontier, given a vertical intercept of RF. In Figure 20-1 this occurs at point M. The set of portfolio opportunities on this line (RF to M) dominates all portfolios below it. Point M, called the market portfolio, is very important in capital market theory and is discussed in the following paragraphs.

The straight line from RF to the efficient frontier at point M, RF–M, dominates all straight lines below it and contains the superior lending portfolios.[3] Lending refers to the purchase of a riskless asset such as Treasury bills, because by making such a purchase, the investor is lending money to the issuer of the securities, the U.S. government. Through a combination of lending (investing funds at a rate of RF) and investing in a risky portfolio of securities, an investor has changed the opportunity set available from the Markowitz efficient frontier.

With the introduction of the possibility of lending (i.e., purchasing a risk-free asset) investors have several alternatives:

1. Invest 100% of investable funds in the riskless asset, providing an expected return of RF and zero risk.
2. Invest 100% of investable funds in risky-asset portfolio *M*, offering, $E(R_M)$, with its risk $SD(R_M)$.
3. Invest in any combination of return and risk between these two points, obtained by varying the proportion W_{RF} invested in the riskless asset.

Each investor would choose a point on this line that corresponds to his or her risk preferences. Formally, this would be where the investor's highest indifference curve is tangent to the straight line. In practical terms this means that the more conservative investors would be closer to the risk-free asset designated by the vertical intercept RF. More aggressive investors would be closer to, or on, point M, representing full investment in a portfolio of risky assets. This latter group, however, can go beyond point M, and it is to this possibility that we now turn.

Borrowing Possibilities

Recall from the assumptions of capital market theory that investors are able to borrow and lend at the risk-free rate RF. Borrowing additional investable funds and investing them together with the investor's own wealth allows investors to seek higher expected returns while assuming greater risk. These borrowed funds can be used to lever the portfolio position beyond point M, the point of tangency between the straight line emanating from RF and the efficient frontier AB. As in the lending discussion, point M represents 100% of an investor's wealth in the risky asset portfolio *M*. The straight line RF–M is now extended upward, as shown in Figure 20-2, and can be designated RF–M–L.

What effect does borrowing have on the expected return and risk for a portfolio? These parameters can be calculated in the usual manner. How-

[3]The concept of dominance is explained in Chapter 19, footnote 10.

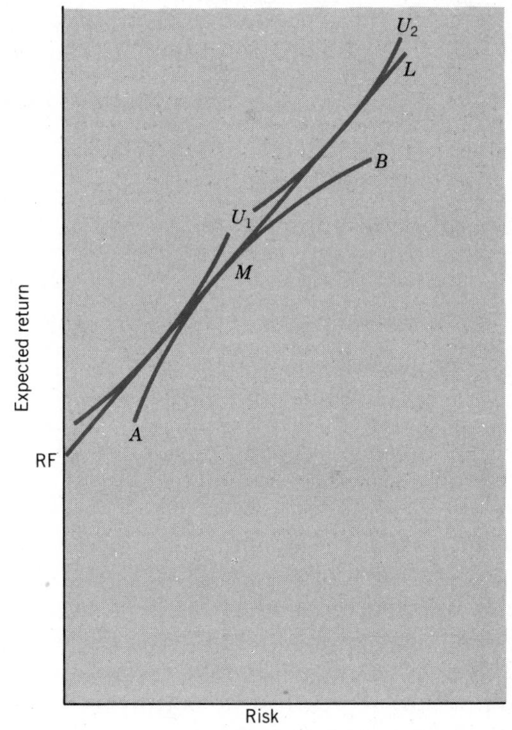

FIGURE 20-2 ***The efficient frontier when lending and borrowing possibilities are allowed.***

ever, the proportions to be invested are now stated differently. Since the proportions to be invested in the alternatives are stated as percentages of an investor's total investable funds, various combinations must add up to 1.0 (i.e., 100%, representing an investor's total wealth). Therefore, the proportion to be borrowed at RF is stated as a negative figure,[4] so that

$$W_{RF} + (1 - W_{RF}) = 1.0 = 100\% \text{ of investor wealth} \qquad (20\text{-}3)$$

Assume an investor can borrow 100% of his or her investable wealth, which, together with the investable wealth itself, will be invested in risky-asset portfolio *M* (i.e., 200% of investable wealth is invested in portfolio *M*). The $1 - W_{RF}$ weight must now equal 2.0 to represent the sum of original wealth plus borrowed funds. To obtain this result, the proportion of in-

[4]Keep in mind that with lending the investor earns a rate RF, whereas with borrowing the investor pays the rate RF on the borrowed funds.

vestable funds to be placed in the risk-free asset is negative—specifically, −1.0. Therefore, the proportion to be invested in portfolio *M* is [1 − (−1)] = 2. Overall, the combined weights are still equal to 1.0, since

$$W_{RF} + (1 - W_{RF}) = 1.0$$

$$-1 + [1 - (-1)] = 1.0$$

The expected return on the investor's portfolio *p*, consisting of investable wealth plus borrowed funds invested in portfolio *M*, is now

$$E(R_p) = W_{RF}\,RF + (1 - W_{RF})E(R_M)$$

$$= -1(RF) + 2E(R_M)$$

The expected return increases linearly as the borrowing increases. The standard deviation of this portfolio is

$$SD(R_p) = (1 - W_{RF})SD(R_M)$$

$$= 2SD(R_M)$$

Risk will increase as the amount of borrowing increases.

Example. Borrowing possibilities (i.e., leverage) are illustrated by the following example. Assume that the expected return on portfolio M is 21%, with $SD(R_M) = 13\%$. The expected risk-free rate, RF, is still 7%, as earlier. However, it now represents the borrowing rate, or the rate at which the investor must pay interest on funds borrowed and invested in the risk asset *M*.

The expected return on this portfolio would be

$$E(R_p) = -1(7\%) + 2(21\%)$$

$$= -7\% + 40\%$$

$$= 33\%$$

The standard deviation of this leveraged portfolio would be

$$SD(R_p) = (1.0 - W_{RF})SD(R_M)$$

$$= [1.0 - (-1.0)]SD(R_M)$$

$$= 2SD(R_M)$$

$$= 26\%$$

The Market Portfolio

Portfolio *M* in Figure 20-2 is called the **market portfolio** of risky securities. It is the highest point of tangency between RF and the efficient frontier. All investors would want to be on the optimal line RF–M–L, and unless they invested 100% of their wealth in RF, would want to own portfolio *M* with some portion of their investable wealth or to invest their own wealth plus borrowed funds in portfolio *M*.

In equilibrium, all risky assets must be in portfolio *M* because all investors are assumed to hold the same risky portfolio. If they do, in equilibrium this portfolio must be the market portfolio consisting of all risky assets. All assets are included in portfolio *M* in proportion to their market value.

Example. If the market value of IBM constitutes 2% of the market value of all risky assets, IBM will constitute 2% of the market value of portfolio M and, therefore, 2% of the market value of each investor's portfolio of risky assets. ▪

In theory, the market portfolio should include all risky assets, both financial (bonds, options, futures, etc.) and real (gold, real estate, etc.), in their proper proportions.[5] Such a portfolio would be completely diversified. The market portfolio is a risky portfolio, and its risk will be designated $SD(R_M)$.

Of course, the market portfolio is unobservable.[6] In practice, the market portfolio is often proxied by the portfolio of all common stocks, which, in turn, is proxied by a market index such as Standard & Poor's 500 Composite Index (which has been used throughout the text). Therefore, to facilitate this discussion, think of portfolio *M* as a broad market index such as the S&P 500 Index.

The Separation Theorem

We have established that all investors will hold combinations of the risk-free asset (either lending or borrowing) and the market portfolio (*M*). By combining these two assets into various portfolios, investors can form efficient portfolios along line RF–M–L in Figure 20-2. Unlike the Markowitz analysis, it is not necessary to match an investor's utility curves with a particular efficient portfolio, because only one efficient portfolio, portfolio *M*, is held by all investors. Rather, the investor uses utility curves to determine where along the new efficient frontier RF–M–L he or she should be. This is the same as deciding how much of investable funds should be lent

[5]The market portfolio contains all marketable assets in the proportions W_i, where

$$W_i = \frac{\text{Total value of the } i\text{th asset}}{\text{Total value of all assets in the market}}$$

[6]Market values and returns have been computed for a "world market wealth portfolio" consisting of stocks, bonds, cash, real estate, and metals. See Roger G. Ibbotson, Laurence B. Siegel, and Kathryn S. Love, "World Wealth: Market Values and Returns," *The Journal of Portfolio Management*, Fall 1985, pp. 4–23.

or borrowed at RF and how much should be invested in portfolio *M*. This decision process is known as the separation theorem.

The **separation theorem** states that the investment decision (which portfolio of risky assets to hold) is separate from the financing decision (how to allocate investable funds between the risk-free asset and the risky asset).[7] The risky portfolio *M* is optimal for every investor regardless of that investor's utility function. This means that *M*'s optimality is determined separately from knowledge of any investor's risk–return preferences. All investors, by investing in the same portfolio of risky assets (*M*) and by either borrowing or lending at the rate RF, can achieve any point on the straight line RF–M–L in Figure 20-2. Each point on the line represents a different expected return–risk trade-off. An investor with utility curve U_1 will be at the lower end of the line, representing a combination of lending and investment in *M*. On the other hand, utility curve U_2 represents an investor borrowing at the rate RF to invest in risky assets—specifically, portfolio *M*.

The concept of the riskless-asset–risky-asset (portfolio) dichotomy is an important one in investments, with several different applications. As we have seen, using the two in combination allows investors to achieve any point on the expected return–risk trade-off that all investors face. Furthermore, some of the new techniques utilize the same two assets. For example, portfolio insurance can be thought of as an *asset allocation strategy* that seeks to rebalance a portfolio between a risky component and a riskless component in order to keep the portfolio return from declining below some specified minimum return.

The New Efficient Frontier

The end result of introducing a riskless asset into the analysis is to create lending and borrowing possibilities and a set of expected return–risk possibilities that did not exist previously. As shown in Figure 20-2, the new frontier is a straight line tangent to the efficient frontier at point M and with a vertical intercept RF. Investors can be anywhere they choose on this line, depending on their risk–return preferences.

The introduction of the risk-free asset significantly changes the efficient frontier. Specifically, the following points emerge:

1. The new efficient frontier is no longer a curve, or arc, as in the Markowitz analysis. It is now linear.
2. Only one portfolio of risky assets is efficient. In the Markowitz analysis, many portfolios of risky assets are efficient.

---

[7]See J. Tobin, "Liquidity Preference as Behavior Towards Risk," *Review of Economic Studies*, February 1958, pp. 65–87.

3. Borrowing and lending possibilities, combined with the one efficient portfolio of risky assets, *M*, offer an investor whatever risk-expected return combination he or she seeks.

The straight line shown in Figure 20-2, which shows the optimal expected returns for any level of portfolio risk, has a special name in capital market theory, as discussed in the next section.

The Capital Market Line

The straight line shown in Figure 20-2 traces out the risk–return trade-off for efficient portfolios, which, as we have seen, is tangent to the Markowitz efficient frontier at point M and has a vertical intercept RF.

This straight line, usually referred to as the **capital market line (CML),** shows the conditions prevailing in the capital markets in terms of expected return and risk. It depicts the *equilibrium conditions* that prevail in the market for efficient portfolios consisting of the portfolio of risky assets or the risk-free asset, or both. All combinations of risky and risk-free portfolios are bounded by the CML, and all investors will end up with portfolios somewhere on the CML.

Consider the equation for the CML, which is shown as a straight line in Figure 20-3 without the now-dominated Markowitz frontier. We know that this line has an intercept of RF. If investors are to invest in risky assets, they must be compensated for this additional risk with a risk premium. The vertical distance between the risk-free rate and the CML at point M in Figure 20-3 is the amount of return expected for bearing the risk of the

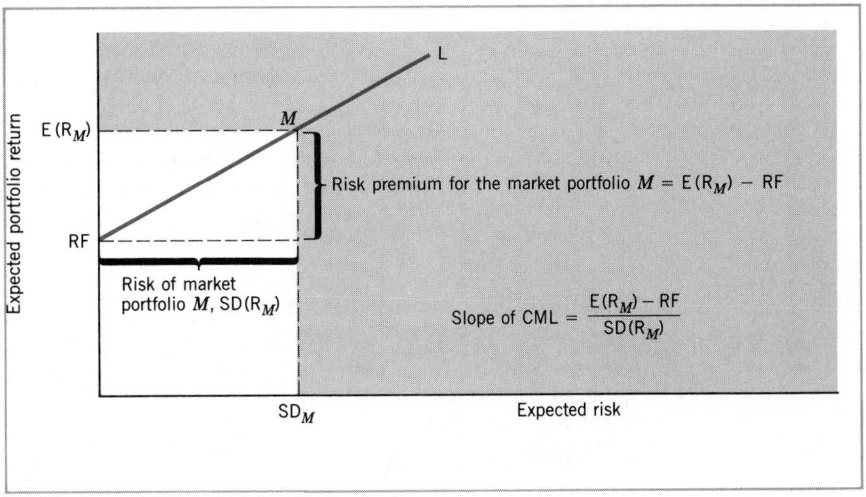

FIGURE 20-3 ***The capital market line and the components of its slope.***

market portfolio, that is, the excess return above the risk-free rate. At that point, the amount of risk for the market portfolio is given by the horizontal dotted line between RF and $SD(R_M)$. Therefore,

$$\frac{E(R_M) - RF}{SD(R_M)} = \text{Slope of the CML} \tag{20-4}$$

$$= \text{Expected return–risk trade-off for efficient portfolios}$$

The slope of the CML is the market price for risk for efficient portfolios. It indicates the additional return that the market demands for each percentage increase in a portfolio's risk, that is, in its standard deviation of return.

Example. Assume, for example, that the expected return on portfolio *M* is 13%, with a standard deviation of 25%, and the RF is 7%. The slope of the CML would be

$$\frac{0.13 - 0.07}{0.25} = 0.24$$

The slope of the CML indicates the equilibrium price of risk in the market. In our example a risk premium of 0.24 indicates that the market demands this amount of return for each percentage increase in a portfolio's risk. ▪

We now know the intercept and slope of the CML. Since the CML is the trade-off between expected return and risk for efficient portfolios, and risk is being measured by the standard deviation, the equation for the CML is

$$E(R_p) = RF + \frac{E(R_M) - RF}{SD(R_M)} SD(R_p) \tag{20-5}$$

where

$E(R_p)$ = the expected return on any efficient portfolio on the CML
RF = rate of return on the risk-free asset
$E(R_M)$ = the expected return on the market portfolio *M*
$SD(R_M)$ = the standard deviation of the returns on the market portfolio
$SD(R_p)$ = the standard deviation of the efficient portfolio being considered

In effect, the expected return for any portfolio on the CML = (price necessary to induce investors to forgo consumption) + (market price of risk) times (amount of risk on the portfolio being considered). Note that:

RF is the price of forgone consumption

$[E(R_M) - RF]/SD(R_M)$ is the market price of risk

$SD(R_p)$ is the amount of risk being assumed on a particular portfolio.

The following points should be noted about the CML:

1. Only efficient portfolios consisting of RF and *M* lie on the CML. Portfolio *M*, the market portfolio of risky securities, contains all securities weighted by their respective market values—it is the optimum combination of risky securities. The risk-free asset has no risk. Therefore, all asset combinations on the CML are efficient portfolios consisting of *M* and RF.
2. The CML must always be upward sloping *ex ante* because the price of risk must always be positive. Remember that the CML is formulated in a world of expected return, and risk-averse investors will not invest unless they expect to be compensated for the risk. The greater the risk, the greater the expected return.
3. On a historical basis, for some particular period of time such as a year or two, or four consecutive quarters, the CML can be downward sloping. This means that the return on RF exceeds the return on the market portfolio. This does not negate the validity of the CML; it merely indicates that returns actually realized differ from those that were expected. Obviously, investor expectations are not always realized (if they were, there would be no risk). Thus, although the CML must be upward sloping ex ante (before the fact), it can be, and sometimes is, downward sloping ex post (after the fact).
4. The CML can be used to determine the optimal expected returns associated with different portfolio risk levels. Therefore, the CML indicates the required return for each portfolio risk level.

The Security Market Line

The capital market line applies only to efficient portfolios. These portfolios contain only systematic risk and no residual (unsystematic) risk. What about individual securities or inefficient portfolios? Can this type of analysis be applied to them?

INVESTMENTS INTUITION

Conceptually, the same type of framework should be applicable for individual securities as for efficient portfolios. After all, the essence of investments is that expected return and risk go together, as explained in Chapter 5. An upward-sloping trade-off should exist between these two variables. The key question, however, is how to measure the risk of an individual security.

Two Sources of Risk

In Chapter 19 the single index model was used to simplify the Markowitz model by greatly reducing the number of covariances that must be calculated. This model was stated in Chapter 19 as

$$R_{it} = a_i + b_i R_{Mt} + e_{it} \tag{20-6}$$

where

R_{it} = the random return on stock i during some period t
R_{Mt} = the random return on the overall market during period t
a_i = the unique part of stock i's return
b_i = the measure of the expected increase in return for security i given a 1% increase in market return
e_{it} = the random residual error in period t (i.e., the difference between the actual return in period t and the predicted return in period t)

Using this model, a security's return can be divided into a unique part and a market-related part. Similarly, a security's total risk, as measured by the standard deviation, can be attributed to two sources.

Taking the variance of Equation 20-6 results in

$$\begin{aligned} \text{VAR } R_i &= \text{VAR } (a_i + b_i R_M + e_i) \\ &= b_i^2(\text{VAR } R_M) + \text{VAR } e_i \qquad (20\text{-}7) \\ &= \text{Systematic risk} + \text{unsystematic risk} \end{aligned}$$

As Equation 20-7 shows, the total risk of a security, as measured by the variance in the rate of return, can be broken down into (1) systematic risk (that part of total risk associated with the variability in the overall market) and (2) unsystematic risk (that part of total risk not related to the variability in the overall market).

$$\text{Systematic risk} + \text{unsystematic risk} = \text{Total risk}$$

The unsystematic risk portion of a security's variance in Equation 20-7 can be diversified away by holding a portfolio of securities. In effect, the unique part of the risk of each security is canceled out, leaving the portion that is attributable to the systematic variance arising from the market.

Figure 20-4 illustrates this concept of declining unsystematic risk in a portfolio of securities. As more securities are added, the unsystematic risk becomes smaller and smaller, and the total risk for the portfolio approaches its systematic risk. Since diversification cannot reduce systematic risk, total portfolio risk can be reduced no lower than the total risk of the market portfolio.

How many securities does it take to eliminate most or all of the unsystematic risk? In a well-known study, Evans and Archer found that the total risk of a 15-stock portfolio was approximately the same as that for the

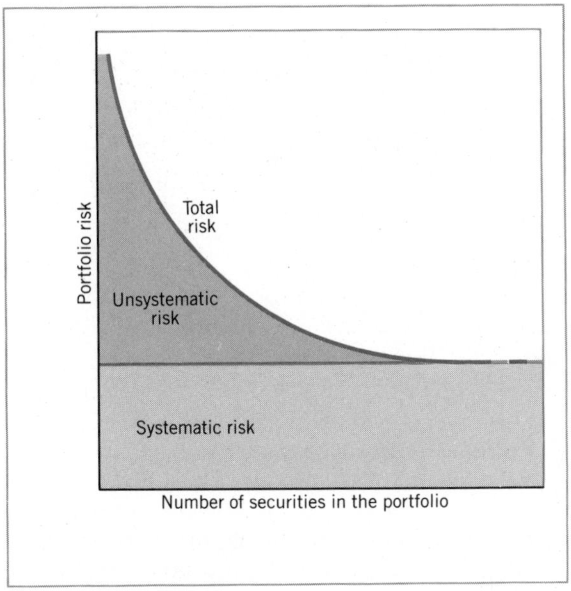

FIGURE 20-4 ***The effect of diversification on portfolio risk.***

market portfolio.[8] The added benefit of additional diversification declined sharply after 15 or 16 securities.

The Expected Return–Risk Relationship

What is important is each security's contribution to the total risk of the portfolio. If a portfolio is completely diversified, the only risk it has is systematic risk. Therefore, the contribution of any one security to the riskiness of a portfolio is its systematic risk.

We can relate each individual security to the risk of the portfolio through its covariance with the market portfolio, $COV_{i,M}$. However, it is more convenient to use a standardized measure of systematic risk, the beta coefficient, by taking advantage of the following relationship:

$$b_i = \frac{COV_{i,M}}{VAR(R_M)} = \frac{SD_i}{SD_M} r_{iM} \tag{20-8}$$

To derive the expected return–risk relationship for one security, recognizing that the contribution of a security to the total risk of a diversified portfolio is its systematic risk, we simply reformulate the expected return–

[8]See J. Evans and S. Archer, "Diversification and the Reduction of Dispersion: An Empirical Analysis," *The Journal of Finance*, Vol. 23 (December 1968), pp. 761–767.

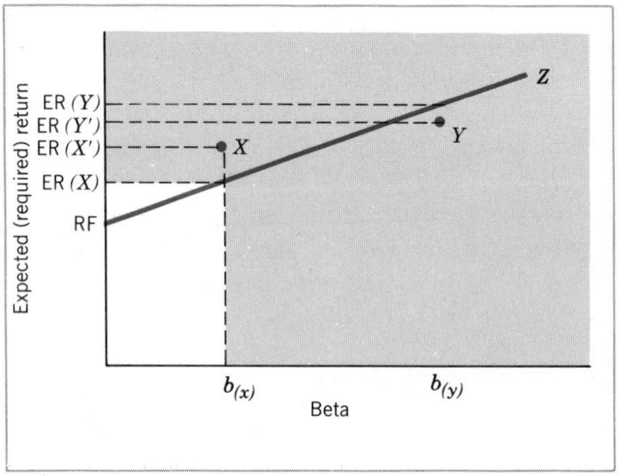

FIGURE 20-5 ***The security market line (SML).***

risk trade-off with beta (the measure of relative systematic risk) on the horizontal axis, as shown in Figure 20-5. The vertical axis remains the expected return, and the intercept of the trade-off on this vertical axis remains the risk-free rate of return, RF.

In Figure 20-5 the vertical axis is the expected, or required, return for an asset. In equilibrium, investors *require* a particular expected return before they will undertake the investment. In Chapter 5 we defined the required rate of return for a security as the minimum expected rate of return needed to induce an investor to purchase it. Given its risk, a security must offer some minimum expected return before a particular investor can be persuaded to purchase it. Thus, in discussing the SML concept, we are simultaneously talking about the required and expected rate of return.

INVESTMENTS INTUITION

As we could (and should) expect, Figure 20-5 again demonstrates that if investors are to seek higher expected returns, they must assume a larger risk. The trade-off between *expected* return and risk must always be positive.[9]

The line RF–Z in Figure 20-5 is called the **security market line (SML).** It depicts the trade-off between risk and required (expected) return for *all assets*, whether individual securities, inefficient portfolios, or efficient portfolios. The SML is the graph of the CAPM explained in Chapter 5. The equation for this relationship is

[9]Again, this relationship may turn out to be negative ex post.

$$E(R_i) = RF + b_i\,(E(R_M) - RF) = SML = CAPM \tag{20-9}$$

where

$E(R_i)$ = the expected required rate of return for security *i*
b_i = the beta or systematic risk for security *i*
$E(R_M)$ = the expected return on the aggregate market

In Equation 20-9, the term (ER_M − RF) is referred to as the market risk premium. It compensates for assuming risk because it is the expected return in excess of that available from buying the risk-free asset. The b_i for a security is calculated from Equation 20-8. Having calculated beta and estimated the market risk premium, the expected return for any security can be calculated from Equation 20-9.

Example. Assume that the beta for EG&G is 1.21, as calculated from Equation 20-8. Also assume that RF is 0.10 and that the expected return on the market is 0.18. The expected return for EG&G can be calculated as

$$\begin{aligned} ER_{EG\&G} &= 0.10 + 1.21(0.18 - 0.10) \\ &= 19.6\% \end{aligned}$$

EG&G's expected return would be 19.6%. Since its beta is larger than that of the market, its expected return should also be larger because the greater the risk assumed, the larger the *expected* return. ▪

INVESTMENTS INTUITION

The CAPM is a simple but elegant statement about expected return and risk for any security or portfolio. If formalizes the basis of investments, which is that the greater the risk assumed, the greater the *expected* return should be. The CAPM states that an investor requires (expects) a return on a risky asset equal to the return on a risk-free asset plus a risk premium, and the greater the risk assumed, the greater the risk premium.

Over- and Undervalued Securities

The SML has important implications for security prices. In equilibrium, each security should lie on the SML because the expected return on the security should be that needed to compensate investors for the systematic risk.

What happens if investors determine that a security does not lie on the SML? To make this determination, they must employ a separate methodology to estimate the expected returns for securities. In other words, a SML can be fitted to a sample of securities to determine the expected (required) return–risk trade-off that exists. Knowing the beta for any stock, one can determine the required return from the SML. Then, estimating the expected return from, say, fundamental analysis, an investor can assess a security in relation to the SML and determine whether it is under- or overvalued.

In Figure 20-5, two securities are plotted around the SML. Security *X* has a high expected return derived from fundamental analysis and plots above the SML. Security *Y* has a low expected return and plots below the SML. Which is undervalued?

Security *X*, plotting above the SML, is undervalued because it offers more expected return than investors require, given its level of systematic risk. Investors require a minimum expected return of ER_X, but security *X*, according to fundamental analysis, is offering ER_X'. If investors recognize this, they will do the following:

Purchase security *X*, because it offers more return than required.
This demand will drive up the price of *X*, as more of it is purchased.
The return will be driven down, until it is at the level indicated by the SML.

Now consider security *Y*. This security, according to investors' fundamental analysis, does not offer enough expected return given its level of systematic risk. Investors require $E(R_Y)$ for security *Y*, based on the SML, but *Y* offers only $E(R_Y')$. As investors recognize this, they will do the following:

Sell security *Y* (or perhaps sell *Y* short), because it offers less than the required return.
This increase in the supply of *Y* will drive down its price.
The return will be driven up for *new* buyers because any dividends paid are now relative to a lower price, as is any expected price appreciation.
The price will fall until the expected return rises enough to reach the SML and the security is once again in equilibrium.

Estimating the SML

To implement the SML approach described here, an investor needs estimates of the return on the risk-free asset, the expected return on the market index, and the beta for an individual security. How difficult are these to obtain?

The return on a risk-free asset, RF, should be the easiest of the three variables to obtain. In estimating RF, the investor can use the return on Treasury bills for the coming period (e.g., a year).

Estimating the market return is more difficult because the expected return for the market index is not observable. And, as noted in Chapter 10, several market indexes could be used. Estimates of the market return could be derived from a study of previous market returns (such as the Standard & Poor's data in Table 5-1 and the Ibbotson–Sinquefield data referred to in

Chapter 8). Alternatively, probability estimates of market returns could be made, and the expected value calculated. This would provide an estimate of both the expected return and the standard deviation for the market.

Finally, it is necessary to estimate the betas for individual securities. This is a crucial part of the CAPM estimation process. The estimates of RF and the expected return on the market are the same for each security being evaluated. Only beta is unique, bringing together the investor's expectations of returns for the stock with those for the market. Beta is the only company-specific factor in the CAPM; therefore, risk is the only asset-specific forecast that must be made in the CAPM.

As noted, beta is usually estimated by fitting a characteristic line to the data (Equation 20-6). However, this is an estimate of the beta called for in the CAPM. The market proxy used in equations such as 20-6 may not fully reflect the market portfolio specified in the CAPM. Furthermore, several points should be kept in mind:

1. We are trying to estimate the future beta for a security, which may differ from the historical beta.
2. In theory, the independent variable R_M represents the total of all marketable assets in the economy. This is typically approximated with a stock market index, which, in turn, is an approximation of the return on all common stocks.
3. The characteristic line can be fitted over varying numbers of observations and time periods. There is no one correct period or number of observations for calculating beta. As a result, estimates of beta will vary. For example, *The Value Line Investment Survey* calculates betas from weekly rates of return for five years, whereas other analysts often use monthly rates of return over a comparable period.
4. The regression estimates of a and b are only estimates of the true a and b, and are subject to error. These estimates may not be equal to the true a and b.
5. As the fundamental variables (e.g., earnings, cash flow) of a company change, b should change. The beta is not perfectly stationary over time. This issue is important enough to be considered separately.

The Accuracy of Beta Estimates

How much association is there between betas in different periods? Stated differently, are betas estimated by Equation 20-6 good estimates of future betas? This question has been closely examined in studies by Blume and Levy.[10] Blume found that in comparing nonoverlapping seven-year periods

[10]See M. Blume, "Betas and Their Regression Tendencies," *The Journal of Finance*, Vol. 10 (June 1975), pp. 785–795; and R. Levy, "On the Short-Term Stationarity of Beta Coefficients," *Financial Analysts Journal*, Vol. 27 (December 1971), pp. 55–62.

for 1, 2, 4, 7, 10, 21, and so on, stocks in a portfolio, the following observations could be made:

1. Betas estimated for individual securities are unstable. They contain relatively little information about future betas.
2. Betas estimated for large portfolios are stable. They contain much information about future betas.

In effect, a large portfolio (e.g., 50 stocks) provides stability because of the averaging effect. Although the betas of some stocks in the portfolio go up from period to period, others go down, and these two movements tend to cancel each other. Furthermore, the errors involved in estimating betas tend to cancel out in a portfolio. Therefore, estimates of portfolio betas show less change from period to period and are much more reliable than are the estimates for individual securities.

Tests of the CAPM

The conclusions of the CAPM are entirely sensible:

1. Return and risk are positively related—greater risk should carry greater return.
2. The relevant risk for a security is a measure of its effect on portfolio risk.

The question, therefore, is how well the theory works. After all, the assumptions on which capital market theory rest are, for the most part, unrealistic. To assess the validity of this or any other theory, empirical tests must be performed. If the CAPM is valid, and the market tends to balance out so that realized security returns average out to equal expected returns, empirical tests should find (over the long run)

$$\bar{R}_i = a_1 + a_2 b_i \qquad (20\text{-}10)$$

where

$\bar{R}_i$ = the average return on security i over some number of periods
b_i = the estimated beta for security i

When Equation 20-10 is estimated, a_1 should approximate the average risk-free rate during the periods studied, and a_2 should approximate the *average market* risk premium during the periods studied.

An extensive literature exists involving tests of capital market theory, in particular, the CAPM. Although it is not possible to summarize the scope of this literature entirely, and to reconcile findings from different studies that seem to be in disagreement, the following points represent a reasonable consensus of the empirical results[11]:

---

[11]For a discussion of empirical tests of the CAPM, see Elton and Gruber, *Modern Portfolio Theory*.

1. The SML appears to be linear. The trade-off between expected (required) return and risk is an upward-sloping straight line.
2. The intercept term, a_1, is generally found to be higher than RF.
3. The slope of the CAPM, a_2, is generally found to be less steep than posited by the theory.
4. Although the evidence is mixed, no persuasive case has been made that unsystematic risk commands a risk premium; in other words, investors are rewarded only for assuming systematic risk.

The major problem in testing capital market theory is that it is formulated on an ex ante basis but can be tested only on an ex post basis. We can never know investor expectations with certainty. Therefore, it should come as no surprise that tests of the model have produced conflicting results in some cases and that the empirical results diverge from the predictions of the model. In fact, it is amazing that the empirical results support the basic CAPM as well as they do. Based on studies of many years of data, it appears that the stock market prices securities on the basis of a linear relationship between systematic risk and return, with diversifiable (unsystematic) risk playing little or no part in the pricing mechanism.

The CAPM has not been proved empirically, nor will it be. In fact, Roll has argued that the CAPM is untestable because the market portfolio, which consists of all risky assets, is unobservable.[12] Roll argues that tests of the CAPM are actually tests of the mean-variance efficiency of the market portfolio. Nevertheless, the CAPM remains a logical way to view the expected return–risk trade-off.

Arbitrage Pricing Theory

The CAPM is not the only model of security pricing. An alternative model that has received attention is the **arbitrage pricing model (APM)** developed by Ross.[13] We can put these N factors together into a model for security returns in the following way:

$$R_i = a_i + b_{i1}F_1 + b_{i2}F_2 + \ldots b_{iN}F_N + e_i \quad (20\text{-}11)$$

where

R_i = the actual return on security i
a_i = the expected return for stock i if all factors have a value of zero
b_i = the return sensitivity of the stock to factor i
F_i = factors common to securities that affect their returns
e_i = unique effect on stock i's return or that part of the return unrelated to the specified factors

[12]See R. Roll, "A Critique of the Asset Pricing Theory's Tests; Part I: On Past and Potential Testability of the Theory," *Journal of Financial Economics*, Vol. 4 (March 1977), pp. 129–176.
[13]This discussion is indebted to Elton and Gruber, *Modern Portfolio Theory*.

Equation 20-11 indicates that the actual return on a security is composed of its expected return and one or more factors (which can have a positive or a negative influence). Therefore, deviations of actual returns from expected returns are attributable to these factors affecting securities.

Equation 20-11 is called a **factor model,** the purpose of which is to express the behavior of security returns. Factor models describe the return-generating process for securities. The relevant factors should be identified by economic analysis of what affects security returns.

A factor model makes no statement about equilibrium. If we make it into an equilibrium model, we are saying something about *expected* returns across securities. APT is an equilibrium theory of expected returns that requires a factor model such as Equation 20-11. As an equilibrium model, the e_i term in Equation 20-11 drops out, the Fs are the expected return per unit of sensitivity, and a_i is approximately equal to the risk-free rate (R_i becomes E_i, the expected return on security).

What about the equilibrium returns that would be provided by securities under this more complex (relative to the CAPM) formulation. Arbitrage pricing theory (APT) demonstrates that portfolios can be formed to eliminate arbitrage profits.[14] The a_i will be the same for all securities (and will approximate RF). The APT makes no statements about the size or the sign of the F_i's. Both the factor model and these values must be identified empirically.

APT is more general than the CAPM. If only one factor exists, the two models can be shown to be identical. The problem with APT is that the factors are not well specified, at least ex ante. To implement the APT model, we need to know the factors that account for the differences among security returns. In contrast, with the CAPM the factor that matters is the market portfolio, a concept that is well understood conceptually. However, as noted earlier, Roll has argued that the market portfolio is unobservable.

Most empirical work suggests that three to five factors influence security returns and are priced in the market. For example, one study identified three explanatory factors priced in the stock market: a general market index, price volatility of energy, and interest rate sensitivity.[15] Because of the newness of APT, however, such results must be regarded as tentative. The question of how security prices and equilibrium returns are established—whether as described by the CAPM or APT or some other model—remains open.

Roll and Ross have argued that APT offers an approach to strategic portfolio planning. The idea is to recognize that a few systematic factors affect long-term average returns. Investigators should seek to identify the few factors affecting most assets in order to appreciate their influence on

---

[14]Arbitrage transactions occur when the prices of two perfect substitutes are not identical. Such transactions produce a risk-free profit with no commitment of capital.

[15]See Robert A. Pari and Son-Nan Chen, "An Empirical Test of the Arbitrage Pricing Theory," *The Journal of Financial Research*, Summer 1984, pp. 121–130.

portfolio returns. Based on this knowledge, they should seek to structure the portfolio in such a way as to improve its design and performance.

Summary

- Capital market theory, based on the concept of efficient diversification, describes the pricing of capital assets in the marketplace.
- Although capital market theory is derived from several assumptions that appear unrealistic, the important issue is the ability of the theory to predict. Relaxation of most of the assumptions does not change the major implications of capital market theory.
- The key to the development of capital market theory is the introduction of a risk-free asset, which, when combined with risky assets through borrowing and lending, changes the efficient frontier from the arc of the Markowitz analysis to a straight line.
- The new efficient frontier has a vertical intercept of RF and is tangent to the old efficient frontier at point M, the market portfolio. In theory, this market-value-weighted portfolio should include all risky assets, although in practice it is typically proxied by a stock market index such as the Standard & Poor's 500.
- The separation theorem states that the decision about which portfolio of risky assets to hold is separate from the decision about how much of an investor's funds should be allocated to the risk-free asset and how much to risky assets.
- All investors can achieve an optimal point on the new efficient frontier by investing in portfolio *M* and either borrowing or lending at the risk-free rate, RF.
- The new efficient frontier is called the capital market line, and its slope indicates the equilibrium price of risk in the market. It is the expected return–risk trade-off for efficient portfolios.
- Ex ante, the CML must always be positive, although ex post it may be negative for certain periods.
- Based on the separation of risk into its systematic and unsystematic components, the security market line (CAPM) can be constructed for individual securities (and portfolios). What is important is each security's contribution to the total risk of the portfolio, as measured by beta.
- Using beta as the measure of risk, the SML depicts the trade-off between required return and risk for securities.
- If the expected returns for securities can be estimated from security analysis, and plotted against the SML, undervalued and overvalued securities can be identified.
- Problems exist in estimating the SML, in particular estimating the betas for securities. The stability of beta is a concern, particularly for individual securities; however, portfolio betas tend to be more stable across time.

- Tests of the CAPM are inconclusive. An ex ante model is being tested with ex post data. It has not been proved empirically, nor is it likely to be, but its basic implications seem to be supported.
- Alternative theories of asset pricing, such as the arbitrage pricing theory, also exist but are unproved.

Key Words

Arbitrage pricing model (APM)
Capital market line (CML)
Capital market theory
Factor model
Market portfolio
Risk-free asset
Security market line (SML)
Separation theorem

Questions

20-1 How do lending possibilities change the Markowitz model? borrowing possibilities?

20-2 What are the implications of the separation theorem for the approach typically followed by most brokers in constructing portfolios for their clients?

20-3 In terms of their appearance as a graph, what is the difference between the CML and the SML?

20-4 What is the "market portfolio"?

20-5 What is the slope of the CML? What does it measure?

20-6 Why does the CML contain only efficient portfolios?

20-7 Based on your knowledge of b_i, write three equivalent expressions for the SML.

20-8 How can the SML be used to identify over- and undervalued securities?

20-9 What happens to the price and return of a security when investors recognize it as undervalued?

20-10 What are the difficulties involved in estimating a security's beta?

20-11 If individual security betas are unstable, can betas be a useful concept?

20-12 How can the CAPM be tested empirically? What are the expected results of regressing average returns on betas?

20-13 How many securities are required to diversify a portfolio adequately?

20-14 With regard to mutual funds, what do you think is meant by the term *superfluous diversification?*

20-15 The CAPM provides required returns for individual securities or portfolios. What uses can you see for such a model?

20-16 What is the relationship betewen the CML and the Markowitz efficient frontier?

20-17 In Figure 20-2, how does an investor decide where to be on the new efficient frontier?

20-18 The CML can be described as representing a trade-off. What is this trade-off? Be specific.

20-19 Draw a diagram of the SML. Label the axes and the intercept.
(a) Assume the risk-free rate shifts upward. Draw the new SML.
(b) Assume that the risk-free rate remains the same as before the change in (a) but that investors become more pessimistic about the stock market. Draw the new SML.

Problems

20-1 The expected return for the market is 12%, with a standard deviation of 21%. The expected risk-free rate is 8%. Information is available for five mutual funds, all assumed to be efficient, as follows:

Mutual Funds	SD (%)
Affiliated	14
Omega	16
Ivy	21
Value Line Fund	25
New Horizons	30

(a) Calculate the slope of the CML.
(b) Calculate the expected return on each of these portfolios.
(c) Rank the portfolios in increasing order of expected return.
(d) Do any of the portfolios have the same expected return as the market? Why?

20-2 Given the market data in Problem 20-1 and the following information for each of five stocks do the following.

Stock	Beta	R_i
1	0.9	12
2	1.3	13
3	0.5	11
4	1.1	12.5
5	1.0	12

(a) Calculate the expected return for each stock.
(b) With these expected returns and betas think of a line connecting them—what is this line?
(c) Assume that an investor, using fundamental analysis, develops the estimates labeled R_i for these stocks. Determine which are undervalued and which are overvalued.
(d) What is the market's risk premium?

20-3 Given the following information:

Expected return for the market, 12%

Standard deviation of market return, 21%

Risk-free rate, 8%

Correlation coefficient between
 Stock A and the market, .8
 Stock B and the market, .6

Standard deviation for stock A, 25%

Standard deviation for stock B, 30%

(a) Calculate the beta for stock A and stock B.
(b) Calculate the required return for each stock.

20-4 Assume that RF is 7%, the estimated return on the market is 12%, and the standard deviation of the market's expected return is 21%. Calculate the expected return and risk (standard deviation) for the following portfolios:
(a) 60% of investable wealth in riskless assets, 40% in the market portfolio
(b) 150% of investable wealth in the market portfolio
(c) 100% of investable wealth in the market portfolio

20-5 Assume that the risk-free rate is 7% and the expected market return is 13%. Show that the security market line, from Equation (20-9) is

$$E(R_i) = 7.0 + 6.0b$$

Assume that an investor has estimated the following values for six different corporations:

Corporation	b_i	R_i (%)
GF	0.8	12
PepsiCo	0.9	13
IBM	1.0	14
NCNB	1.2	11
EG&G	1.2	21
EAL	1.5	10

Calculate the ER_i for each corporation using the SML, and evaluate which securities are over- and which are undervalued.

20-6 On the assumption that RF is expected to be 5% and the expected market return is 13% with an expected standard deviation of 21%, what is the formula for the capital market line?

20-7 On the assumption that RF is expected to be 5% and the expected market return is 15% with an expected standard deviation of 14%, what is the formula for the security market line?

20-8 Using annual data for 10 years, the following ex post values are available for several mutual funds. (S&P 500 Index was used as the market)

R_p = average annual total return
SD_p = the standard deviation of the total returns
a_p and b_p = the constant and slope of the characteristic line.

Mutual Fund	R_p (%)	SD_p(%)	a_p	b_p
A	15.5	19	4.4	0.9
B	14.5	22	1.8	1.0
C	21.0	18	12.4	0.7
D	17.0	27	3.0	1.2
E	13.2	24	3.1	0.8
F	22.0	24	9.4	1.0
G	21.5	23	9.0	.9
H	24.5	27	9.3	1.2
I	9.3	18	−1.6	0.9
J	21.0	21	9.5	0.9
Overall market	12.0	21	0.0	1.0

(a) On the basis of your CML in Problem 20-6, what are the values of the $E(R_p)$ for the funds, assuming that the standard deviations will continue?

(b) (1) On the basis of your SML in Problem 20-1, what are the values of the $E(R_p)$ for the funds?
   (2) Assume that a particular investor was certain that the ex post R_p in the first column were her expected yields. Which funds would that investor consider undervalued and which overvalued?

(c) (1) For the ex post data, how many of the mutual fund portfolios had average annual total returns greater than the market?
   (2) Using standard deviation as the risk measure, rank the funds from low risk to high risk. How many funds had greater risk than the market; how many had lesser risk?
   (3) Using b_i as the risk measure, rank the funds from low risk to high risk. How many funds had greater risk? how many lower?
   (4) Does the rank order of risk using ex post standard deviation agree with rank order using ex post b_i? Discuss ex post measurement of risk relative to ex ante risk.

(d) Using the ex post values for return and risk, does it appear (on the average) that the higher-risk funds achieved higher returns? Discuss.

Selected References

A good discussion of capital market theory can be found in

Elton, Edwin, and Gruber, Martin. *Modern Portfolio Theory and Portfolio Analysis*, 3rd ed. New York: John Wiley, 1987.

CHAPTER 21

International Investing and Extended Diversification

We learned in Chapter 19 the primary implication of portfolio theory—diversify. If markets are even reasonably efficient, prudent investors must diversify to reduce the risk from uncertain future returns. We saw that combining stocks with less than perfect positive correlations results in beneficial risk reduction.

The diversification principle can be applied to assets other than domestic common stocks in order to reduce the risk of the investor's portfolio. In this chapter we pursue this idea further by considering **extended diversification,** defined here to mean investment in foreign securities and tangible (real) assets. Because of its importance and appeal to investors, we separate international investing and consider it in detail.

The Case for Extended Diversification

Logically, investment opportunities should not be limited to one particular asset category, such as bonds or stocks, or to one country, such as the United States. To do so is to ignore a substantial part of what might be called the "World Wealth Portfolio," which represents worldwide opportunities in both financial and tangible assets to either enhance returns or reduce risks, or both.

Figure 21-1 shows a 1980s estimate of the World Wealth Portfolio and variations thereof. Such an estimate is valuable for the *relative* perspective it provides of both the role that equities plays in the overall portfolio as well as that part of total wealth that is constituted by the United States.

Figure 21-1*a* indicates that foreign real estate made up more than 35% of total world wealth, with U.S. real estate constituting an additional 18%. U.S. equities are less than 7% of the total, and foreign equities are less than 5%. Fixed-income securities constitute another 13% of world wealth, split roughly equally between U.S. and foreign sources. Metals are a small percentage, and art is such as small percentage that it does not even register as a significant percentage of the world total, because of rounding.

Figure 21-1*b* shows the distribution of asset classes in the World Wealth Market Portfolio for which returns can be measured, which is referred to as "World Investable Wealth." This more closely represents the opportunity set available to most investors. Excluded are durables, foreign real estate, art, convertible bonds, and venture capital. U.S. real estate becomes the most important item, at over one-third of the total, with residential real estate alone accounting for more than one-fourth of the total wealth. As important as U.S. equities are, they still constitute only 13% of World Investable Wealth. Foreign equities become twice as important, at about 10% of the total, and foreign bonds assume a larger

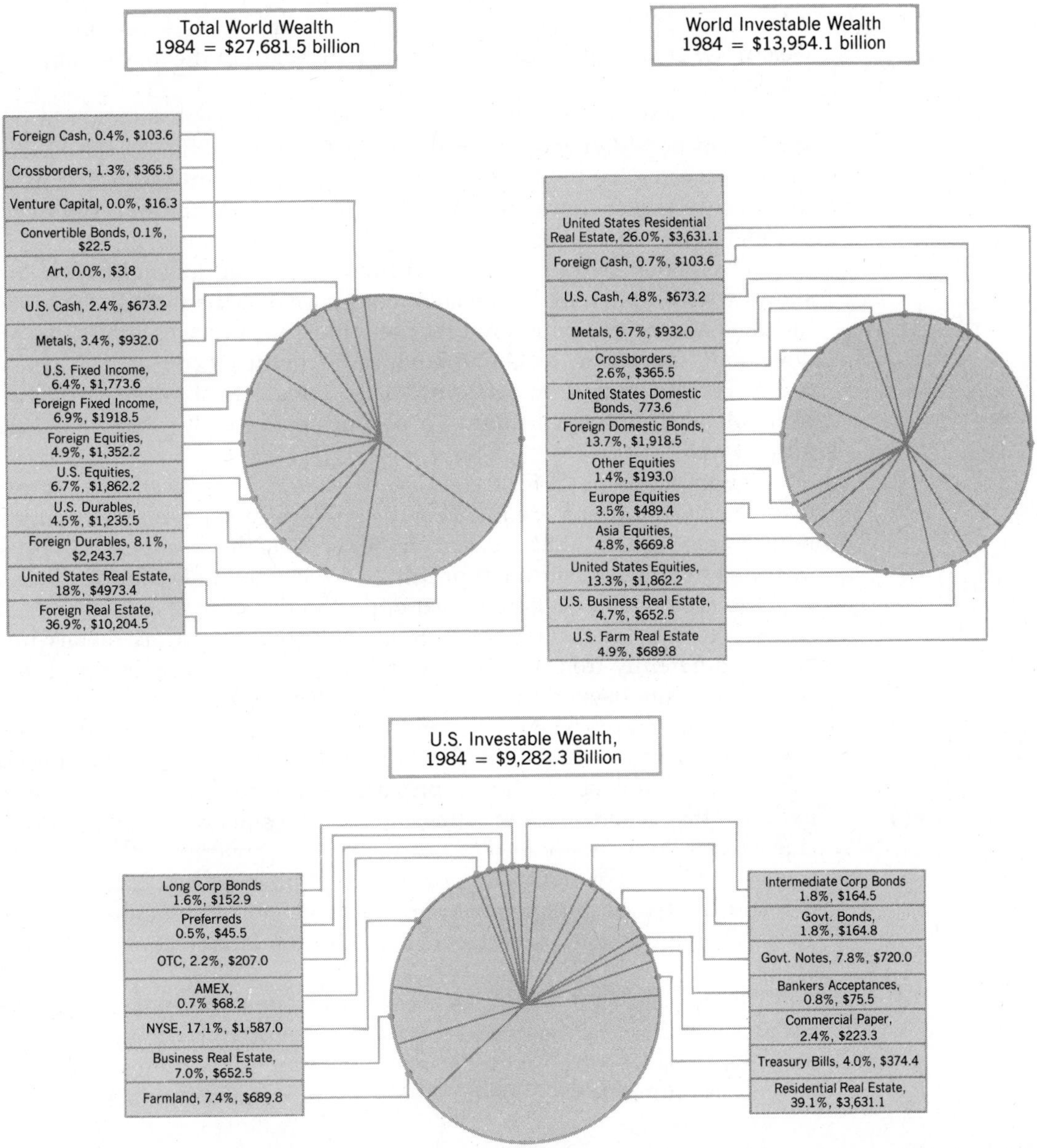

FIGURE 21-1 ***Total investable wealth, world investable wealth, and U.S. investable wealth.***
Source: Roger G. Ibbotson, Laurence B. Siegel, and Kathryn S. Love, "World Wealth: Market Values and Returns," *The Journal of Portfolio Management*, Fall 1985, p. 6. Reprinted by permission.

role, about 14%. U.S. bonds account for about 6% of world investable wealth, whereas metals become a larger percentage of the total, at approximately 7%.

Finally, part (c) of Figure 21-1 puts the United States situation in perspective by considering only U.S. Investable Wealth. Although real estate is the largest category, the importance of the NYSE is clearly seen. It is easily the second largest component of U.S. investable wealth. Also notice the prominent role that Treasury securities plays in this analysis.

What about the return potential from this world portfolio? Table 21-1 shows world capital market total annual returns for the period 1960–1984. Included are the compound return, the arithmetic mean, and the standard deviation. The return on Asian equities far outdistanced other asset returns. Foreign bonds outperformed U.S. bonds. Real estate performed well. Metals, although suffering a decline in the early 1980s, also performed well.

The implications of Figure 21-1 and Table 21-1 are clear. The alternatives for diversification are many, and significant opportunities for higher returns are available, at least based on the record of the recent past. Furthermore, using the diversification principles we learned in the last chapter, it would be reasonable to assume that opportunities for risk reduction exist, because foreign markets as well as tangible assets such as metals may behave differently from U.S. financial markets. Prudent investors should plan to diversify beyond the typical U.S. stocks and bonds.

To begin to appreciate the benefits possible from diversifying beyond domestic common stocks, consider Figure 21-2, which shows the "joys of diversification" on a basis that is applicable directly to investors. The figure indicates that a portfolio consisting of only five equally weighted parts—U.S. stocks, foreign stocks, U.S. corporate and government bonds, real estate, and Treasury bills—outperformed both the S&P 500 Composite Index and the typical professional portfolio manager over the period 1965–1985. Most of the excess gains were derived from foreign equities and real estate.

The message from Figure 21-2 is clear. Extended diversification, from both foreign financial assets and real assets, can produce significant benefits. Investors who confine themselves only to U.S. equities and fixed-income securities are forgoing potentially lucrative opportunities.

International Investing

A very important part of the diversification possibilities available to investors involves the securities of foreign countries. Expanding the opportunity set to include foreign securities should have a positive effect on portfolio performance. However, it also introduces new risk elements, particularly currency risk.

TABLE 21-1 ***World Capital Market Total Annual Returns, 1960–1984***

	Compound Return	Arithmetic Mean	Standard Deviation
Equities			
United States			
NYSE	8.71%	9.99%	16.30%
Amex	7.28	9.95	23.49
OTC	11.47	13.88	22.42
United States total	8.81	10.20	16.89
Foreign			
Europe	7.83	8.94	15.58
Asia	15.14	18.42	30.74
Other	8.14	10.21	20.88
Foreign total	9.84	11.02	16.07
Equities total	9.08	10.21	15.28
Bonds			
United States			
Corporate			
Intermediate-term	6.37	6.80	7.15
Long-term	5.03	5.58	11.26
Corporate total[a]	5.35	5.75	9.63
Government			
Treasury notes	6.32	6.44	5.27
Treasury bonds	4.70	5.11	9.70
U.S. agencies	6.88	7.04	6.15
Government total	5.91	6.10	6.43
United States total	5.70	5.93	7.16
Foreign			
Corporate domestic	8.35	8.58	7.26
Government domestic	5.79	6.04	7.41
Crossborder	7.51	7.66	5.76
Foreign total	6.80	7.01	6.88
Bonds total	6.36	6.50	5.56

	Compound Return	Arithmetic Mean	Standard Deviation
Cash equivalents			
United States			
U.S. Treasury bills	6.25%	6.29%	3.10%
Commercial paper	7.03	7.08	3.20
U.S. cash total	6.49	6.54	3.22
Foreign	6.00	6.23	7.10
Cash total	6.38	6.42	2.92
Real Estate[b]			
Business	8.49	8.57	4.16
Residential	8.86	8.93	3.77
Farms	11.86	12.13	7.88
Real estate total	9.44	9.49	3.45
Metals			
Gold	9.08	12.62	29.87
Silver	9.14	20.51	75.34
Metals total	9.11	12.63	29.69
U.S. Market Wealth Portfolio	8.63	8.74	5.06
Foreign Market Wealth Portfolio	7.76	8.09	8.48
World Market Wealth Portfolio			
Excluding metals	8.34	8.47	5.24
Including metals	8.39	8.54	5.80
U.S. inflation rate	5.24	5.30	3.60

Source: Roger G. Ibbotson, Laurence B. Siegel, and Kathryn S. Love, "World Wealth: Market Values and Returns," *The Journal of Portfolio Management*, Fall 1985, p. 6. Reprinted by permission.

[a]Including preferred stock.

[b]United States only.

The International Securities Markets

Foreign firms issue common stock, just as U.S. firms do. Most issue bonds with characteristics similar to U.S. bonds, as discussed in Chapter 6. Foreign firms and foreign banks also issue money market instruments that are quite comparable to those issued in the United States.

Joys of Diversification: A Broad Portfolio Pays Off

Over the past two decades, a diversified investment index has outpaced the U.S. stock market and the typical portfolio manager. The index consists of five equally weighted parts: U.S. stocks, foreign stocks, U.S. corporate and government bonds, real estate and Treasury bills. This index has grown at a 10.2% compound rate since 1965, compared with 9.4% for the S&P 500-stock index and 7.9% for the median U.S. money manager invested in both stocks and bonds.

Most of the extra gains came from foreign equities and real estate, which raced ahead of U.S. stock for much of the 1970s and early 1980s. Analysts differ on whether this performance will continue. But they say diversified portfolios can be less volatile than all-equity accounts, because swings in different parts of broad portfolio often offset one another somewhat.

Individual investors could approximately duplicate the diversification index with a combination of Treasury bills, stocks of real estate investment trusts or limited partnerships in income-producing real estate, and mutual funds specializing in blue chip and overseas stocks and in fixed-income securities.

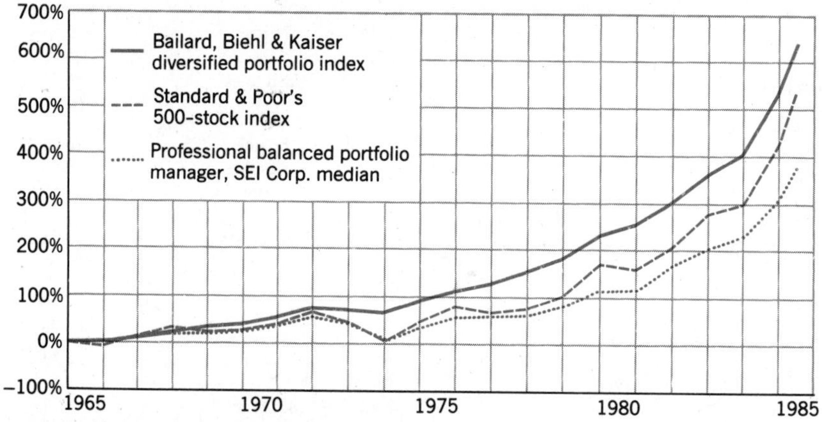

FIGURE 21-2 ***The joys of diversification.***
Source: The Wall Street Journal, September 29, 1986, p. 21. Reprinted by permission of *The Wall Street Journal*, © 1986 Dow Jones & Company, Inc. All Rights Reserved Worldwide.

As we saw in Figure 21-1, foreign equities make up about 10% of *world investable wealth*, whereas U.S. equities account for about 13%. On the other hand, the amount of foreign domestic bonds is double that of U.S. domestic bonds.

All industrialized countries have organized stock exchanges. The volume in most of these markets is large. The Tokyo Stock Exchange is the largest equity market in the world on the basis of dollar value of trading, followed by the NYSE, NASDAQ, and London, respectively. Figure 21-3 shows the dollar volume of equity trading in major world markets.

Some foreign stock markets have grown rapidly in recent years. The Tokyo stock market, for example, grew fourfold in less than seven years in the 1980s. A highly publicized feature of Japanese stocks in the 1980s was their high P/E ratio relative to those in other countries, typically around 60, compared to a range of 12–20 for U.S. stocks.

Each equity market has its own index measure comparable to the Dow Jones Industrial Average and the S&P 500 Index for U.S. stocks. In addi-

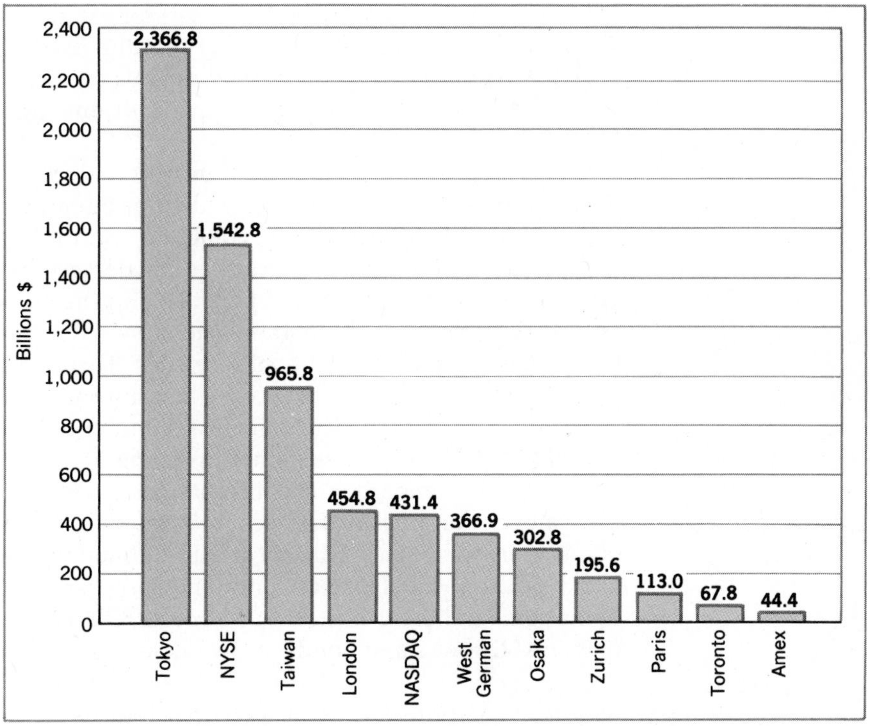

FIGURE 21-3 ***Dollar volume of equity trading in major world markets, 1989.*** *Source:* National Association of Securities Dealers, *Fact Book 1990,* p. 15. Reprinted by permission.

tion, certain international indexes are regularly computed. One of these is the **EAFE Index,** or the Europe, Australia, and Far East Index. This index, compiled by Morgan Stanley Capital International, is, in effect, the non-American world index.

The Benefits of International Investing

Diversification The basic principle of diversification that we learned in Chapter 19 is that by adding to a portfolio assets that are not perfectly correlated with the existing portfolio assets, risk can be reduced. An obvious application of this principle is to add foreign securities to a portfolio of domestic securities. The increased opportunity set made available by foreign markets may provide lower correlations than are possible with domestic securities only.

The typical stock in the United States is correlated with the overall market on the order of .5. Although less than 1.0, and therefore offering diversification benefits, this is still a significant positive correlation. Now consider the correlations of returns between various stock markets and the

U.S. markets. Germany's stock market, for example, is correlated only .32 with the U.S. market, which means that the percentage of common variance between the two is only 10%.[1] Spain's correlation is only .15. On the other hand, as we would expect, Canada is quite highly correlated with the United States.

This information clearly indicates the potential benefits for portfolio diversification that could be derived from international investing. Figure 21-4 indicates the possibilities of combining portfolios with less than perfect correlations to reduce risk. The upper line depicts the relationship between the number of securities in the portfolio and the risk of the portfolio using only U.S. securities. The bottom line shows the same relationship using both domestic and international securities. Throughout the entire range of portfolio sizes the risk is reduced when international investing is considered. And the difference is dramatic—about one-third less.

The benefits of international investing also can be demonstrated by analyzing the standard efficient frontiers we studied in Chapter 19. Figure 21-5 shows the efficient frontier for total stocks and for total stocks and bonds. The total stock efficient frontier dominates the point representing U.S. stocks only, EAFE stocks only, or "world" stocks only. The same is true of the combination of all stocks and bonds relative to U.S. stocks and bonds only, EAFE stocks and bonds, or world stocks and bonds only.

Returns To appreciate some potential returns from international investing, consider Table 21-2, which shows both the annual return and risks from the stocks and bonds of several countries, including the United States. The average annual total return for U.S. investors from investing in each of these markets is shown in the first column. This total return is composed of three components, which are presented in the second, third, and fourth columns as the capital gain, the income component, and the exchange or currency risk, respectively.

Table 21-2 shows that over this 15-year period the returns from both common stocks and bonds from several foreign countries exceeded those for the United States. For example, with stocks the average annual return from West Germany was 16.69%; from Belgium, 19.41%; from Japan, 24.58%; and from Hong Kong, 25.01%. The corresponding figure for the United States was 9.95%. Notice that the EAFE Index showed a return of 17.09% (in U.S. dollars), whereas the world index, which includes the United States, showed a return of 13%. The same is true for bonds, with Japan showing an average annual return of 15.68% and West Germany showing 13.14% compared to the return for the United States of 8.77%.

It is clear from Table 21-2 that the returns on foreign securities for U.S. dollar investors are often superior to what they could earn in domestic

---

[1]These figures, and the corresponding discussion, is taken from Bruno Solnik, *International Investments* (Reading, Mass.: Addison-Wesley, 1988), pp. 38–41.

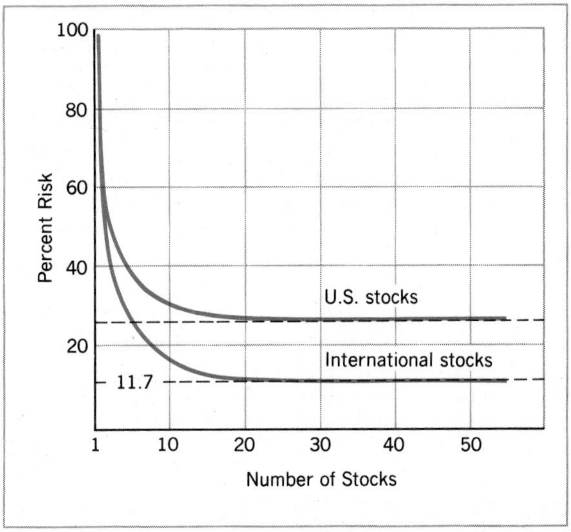

FIGURE 21-4 ***The benefits of international diversification in reducing portfolio risk.***
Source: Bruno Solnik, "Why Not Diversify Internationally Rather Than Domestically," *Financial Analysts Journal,* July 1974. Reprinted by permission.

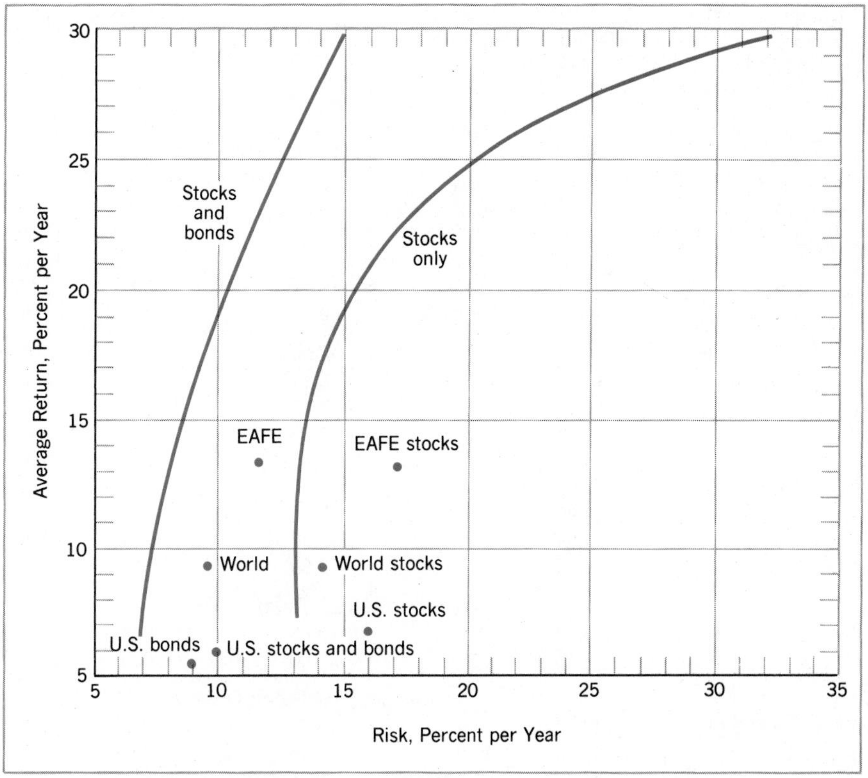

FIGURE 21-5 ***Efficient portfolios, stocks only and stocks and bonds, for both U.S. and international securities.***
Source: Bruno Solnik and B. Noetzlin, "Optimal International Asset Allocation," *The Journal of Portfolio Management,* Fall 1982. Reprinted by permission.

TABLE 21-2 ***Risk and Return Percentages for U.S. Dollar Investors, 1971–1985***

	(1) Annual Return	(2) Capital Gain	(3) Dividend Interest Income	(4) Exchange Gain	(5) Total Risk	(6) Domestic Risk	(7) Exchange Risk
			Stocks				
West Germany	16.69	7.38	4.80	4.51	20.09	15.78	12.17
Belgium	19.41	6.67	11.30	1.44	20.53	15.80	12.14
Denmark	14.51	9.32	5.05	0.14	18.50	16.67	11.14
France	14.62	9.54	6.19	−1.11	25.45	21.60	11.30
Italy	10.65	13.01	3.16	−5.51	27.80	26.27	9.75
Norway	11.51	7.60	4.15	−0.24	28.68	27.11	9.73
Netherlands	17.06	6.73	6.74	3.59	19.30	17.35	11.59
United Kingdom	13.73	11.33	6.01	−3.61	28.28	24.95	10.32
Sweden	18.32	15.43	4.94	−2.05	20.84	18.80	9.75
Switzerland	14.75	5.01	2.96	6.78	20.58	15.75	14.36
Spain	8.24	4.27	8.40	−4.43	22.76	19.39	9.98
Australia	9.28	8.05	4.94	−3.71	26.81	23.26	10.10
Japan	24.58	16.03	2.42	6.14	20.75	16.35	11.16
Hong Kong	25.01	17.05	4.95	3.01	40.86	43.07	6.43
Singapore	11.30	10.90	2.87	−2.48	32.46	32.39	6.01
Canada	10.28	8.16	4.32	−2.20	20.14	18.47	4.29
United States	9.95	5.17	4.78	0.00	15.41	15.41	0.00
			Bonds				
West Germany	13.14	0.40	8.37	4.37	15.19	6.91	12.17
France	10.81	−0.21	12.09	−1.07	13.96	6.69	11.30
Netherlands	13.11	0.67	8.96	3.47	14.10	6.89	11.59
United Kingdom	8.37	−0.47	12.27	−3.44	16.88	11.38	10.32
Switzerland	12.34	0.65	5.05	6.64	15.22	4.24	14.36
Japan	15.68	1.40	8.59	5.70	15.22	6.75	11.16
Canada	7.20	−1.29	10.64	−2.14	10.83	8.67	4.29
United States	8.77	−0.92	9.68	0.00	9.20	9.20	0.00
			Cash				
West Germany	10.46		6.19	4.27	12.10	0.77	12.17
France	11.18		12.25	−1.07	11.38	1.34	11.30
Netherlands	10.59		7.20	3.39	11.67	0.83	11.59
United Kingdom	8.98		12.44	−3.46	10.47	0.95	10.32
Switzerland	10.97		4.42	6.56	14.41	0.77	14.36
Japan	12.90		7.33	5.56	11.19	0.70	11.16
Canada	7.96		10.12	−2.16	4.42	1.00	4.29
United States	9.93		9.93	0.00	1.03	1.03	0.00
			Gold and Gold-Related Vehicles				
	18.97	8.88	10.09	0.00	49.04	49.04	
	15.76	15.76	0.00	0.00	27.58	27.58	
			International Stock Indexes				
World (in U.S.$)	13.00	8.45	4.55	0.00	13.85	13.18	
EAFE (in U.S.$)	17.09	12.91	4.18	0.00	17.21	14.40	

Source: Bruno Solnik, *International Investments*, © 1988, Addison-Wesley Publising Co., Inc., Reading, Massachusetts. From page 45. Reprinted with permission of the publisher.

These calculations are based on monthly index values and coupons obtained from Morgan Stanley Capital International (stocks) and Lombard Odier (bonds, cash).

securities. However, the risks are also often larger, and we know that we must consider both aspects of investing.

The Risks of International Investing

There are several risks from international investing. One of the best known is *political risk,* which is the risk that the country whose financial assets are purchased may invoke changes detrimental to investors. These changes range from the relatively mild, such as a change in the tax law or a tightening of restrictions on the exchange of foreign currency for domestic currency, to the extreme, such as the expropriation of assets.

INVESTMENTS INTUITION

In truth, investors face political risk with all international investments. Obvious examples abound in the emerging nations, and in well-known markets, such as Hong Kong, where major political changes may occur in 1998. But political risk is also present in the most stable of countries. Canada, for example, imposed new taxes on energy firms (as did the United States), and France imposed exchange controls.

International investing is also well known for currency risk. This means that an investor's return from a foreign asset depends not only on the returns on the foreign asset itself, but also on the exchange rate between the currency of that country and the dollar. We shall consider currency risk in some detail after analyzing the overall risks of foreign investing.

Total Risk As we learned in Chapter 19, the total risk of investing is measured by the standard deviation of returns. Table 21-2 shows the total risk of the particular market as measured by the standard deviation of U.S. dollar monthly rates of return.

As the risk column of Table 21-2 indicates, the total risk of all the stock markets shown is larger than that of the United States. For example, Hong Kong and Singapore have more than twice the risk, whereas most other countries have at least one-third more risk. The same was true in the bond markets, with the United States showing the lowest total risk.

Currency Risk We can define **currency risk** as the risk that the rate of return earned by an investor in a foreign market will be adversely affected by conversion of the foreign currency into the domestic currency. For example, an investor interested in the large returns of recent years in the Japanese market faces the risk that a decline in the value of the Yen against the dollar would decrease the return earned from the Japanese investment. The following situation prevails for a U.S. investor:

If the currency of the country in which an investment is made decreases while the return is being earned, the dollar gain on the investment will be decreased. If the currency of the foreign country increases, the dollar gain on the investment will be increased.

Example. Assume an investor in Japanese stocks enjoys a 30% gain in one year. During this period the Yen declines in value, relative to the dollar, by 10%. The return on the Japanese investment is now worth less in dollars as shown by the following calculations:

130%	=	the Japanese investment increased by the 30% return
0.9	=	value of the Yen relative to the dollar
117%	=	percentage of original investment after currency risk

▪

In this example, the investor's return is 17%, not 30%. The reason is that the decline in the value of the Yen affects both the original investment and the return earned on this investment. That is, after the adjustment for the decline in the Yen, the investor lost 10% on the original investment plus another 10% on the 30% return, or a total of 13%. Subtracting this 13% from the total before-currency-adjustment wealth of 130% (100% investment plus return of 30%) produces an after-currency adjustment wealth of 117%, or a return of 17%.

Returning to Table 21-2, the annual returns have been decomposed into capital gains, income, and exchange gain or loss.

Example. For West Germany the total gain of 16.69% for a U.S. investor consisted of an investment return of 12.18% (capital gains plus income) plus an exchange gain of 4.51%, a favorable currency risk situation. In contrast, investors in the United Kingdom suffered a −3.61% exchange loss, which decreased the total investment return of 17.34% to a final return to U.S. investors of 13.73%. ▪

This is currency risk in action, and illustrates how investors both gain and lose from currency risk—at times investment returns are enhanced, and at other times they are diminished.

Most investors hold foreign stocks without hedging away the currency risk. This implicitly is a decision not only to invest in foreign stocks but also to accept the gains or losses accruing from currency risk. In other words, investors face two decisions: (1) what foreign stocks to buy and (2) whether the currency risks should be hedged.

Just how important is currency risk? It is very important for today's investors. Although currency risk may have accounted for only a relatively small part of the variability in dollar-denominated returns from foreign equities in the past, this is no longer true. In the late 1970s and during the 1980s currency risk increased significantly.

According to one study, currency risk accounted for about 23% of the risk (standard deviation) of foreign stock market returns for the period 1975–1987.[2] Exchange rate changes appeared to amplify the variability in foreign stock markets.

According to another study, U.S. investors gain as much in risk reduction by hedging their currency exposure as they do by investing in foreign securities, on an unhedged basis, in the first place.[3] In other words, the *incremental* risk reduction in hedging the foreign component of a portfolio is roughly equal to the risk reduction achieved by investing in foreign securities to begin with.

This evidence suggests that investors should hedge their foreign stock positions against currency risk. Unless an investor is confident that the foreign currency will appreciate during the life of the investment, which is indeed a risky proposition, he or she should attempt to hedge the currency risk implicit in these investments.

What kind of market is the foreign exchange market? It is worthwhile to appreciate the immense size and liquidity of the foreign exchange market—in effect, the world's largest financial market. This market doubled in size in only three years in the late 1980s, reaching average daily trading of over $500 billion by the beginning of the 1990s. In the United States alone, this figure doubled to more than $100 billion in average daily trading. London remains the world's largest currency market, with the United States second and Japan third. Thus, the foreign exchange market is a massive market involving investing, hedging, and speculative activities that flow easily across international borders.

How does an investor hedge against currency risk? The easiest way is to use forward and futures contracts for currency. Near-term contracts (e.g., up to six months) are extremely liquid, the bid–asked quotes have a very narrow spread, and the transaction cost averages perhaps .06% on a six-month contract, or .12% for a year's coverage.[4] Thus, the costs of hedging against currency risk are very small, particularly when compared to the other costs of investing in foreign securities, such as brokerage costs, custodial fees, and so on.

How to Invest Internationally

Exactly as in the case of investing in U.S. stocks, there are two ways to invest internationally: direct and indirect. We consider each of these in turn.

---

[2]See Lee R. Thompson III, "Currency Risks in International Equity Portfolios," *Financial Analysts Journal*, March–April 1988, pp. 68–71.

[3]See André F. Perold and Evan C. Schulman, "The Free Lunch in Currency Hedging: Implications for Investment Policy and Performance Standards," *Financial Analysts Journal*, May–June 1988, pp. 45–50.

[4]See ibid., p. 48.

Direct Investing Obviously, the stocks of foreign firms trade on their own stock exchanges. A stockbroker in the United States can easily buy or sell a security on the Tokyo or London exchanges. As we have seen, however, this entails currency risk as well as several other problems. For example, to collect dividends in Japan an investor must present certificates of ownership to the company (or its agent).

Foreign firms can also arrange to have their shares traded on an exchange or market in another country. In the United States, two methods are available for trading internationally–listed foreign securities.

One alternative is for the shares to be traded directly on an exchange or in the OTC market, exactly like any other company. As of the end of 1988, 31 foreign issues were traded directly on the NYSE, 22 of which were Canadian. NASDAQ, on the other hand, carried 196 issues in 1988 with share volume of 1.5 billion shares.

The second alternative for internationally listed foreign securities to be traded in the United States is via **American Depository Receipts (ADRs)**, which have existed since 1927. ADRs represent indirect ownership of a specified number of shares of a foreign company.[5] These shares are held on deposit in a bank in the issuing company's home country, and the ADRs are issued by U.S. banks called depositories. In effect, ADRs are tradable receipts issued by depositories that have physical possession of the foreign securities through their foreign correspondent banks or custodian.[6] The prices of ADRs are quoted in dollars, and dividends are paid in dollars.

The securities are to be held on deposit as long as the ADRs are outstanding. The bank (or its correspondent) holding the securities collects the dividends, pays any applicable foreign withholding taxes, converts the remaining funds into dollars, and pays this amount to the ADR holders. Holders can choose to convert their ADRs into the specified number of foreign shares represented by paying a fee.

At the beginning of 1990, over 800 companies from over 30 foreign countries were traded on U.S. exchanges as ADRs.[7] Australia constituted some 22% of this total, followed closely by the United Kingdom. Japan was third, at 18%. Over 3 billion ADRs changed hands on major U.S. exchanges in 1989. Examples of well-known companies that trade as ADRs include De Beers Consolidated, Toyota, Volvo, Sony, and Glaxo.

ADRs are an effective way for an American investor to invest in specific foreign stocks without having to worry about currency problems. The only realistic alternative for many Americans is to purchase investment companies specializing in foreign securities.

---

[5]It is not unusual for an ADR issue to represent several of the foreign issuer's underlying shares. Therefore, it is important to know the terms attached.

[6]ADRs are initiated by the depository bank, assuming the corporation does not object.

[7]See Tom Herman and Michael R. Sesit, "ADRs: Foreign Issues With U.S. Accents," *The Wall Street Journal*, February 8, 1990, p. C1.

Indirect Investing As we saw in Chapter 18, investors can invest indirectly rather than do the investing themselves. This means buying and selling the shares of investment companies, either mutual funds (open-end companies) or closed-end funds whose shares are traded on exchanges. This is clearly the easiest and probably the best way for most investors to own foreign stocks, because the funds do everything for them while providing a diversified portfolio of foreign securities.

Funds that specialize in international securities have become both numerous and well known in recent years. Such funds as Fidelity Overseas, Kemper International, T. Rowe Price International Stock, Templeton World Fund, Scudder International, and Dean Witter World Wide are examples of international and global mutual funds of significant size and investor interest.

So-called *international funds* tend to concentrate primarily on international stocks. For example, in 1989 Fidelity Overseas was roughly one-third invested in Europe and one-third invested in the Pacific Basin. Kemper International, on the other hand, had roughly one-sixth of its assets in each of three areas, the United Kingdom, Germany, and Japan. On the other hand, *global funds* tend to keep a minimum of 25% of their assets in the United States. For example, in 1989 Templeton World had over 60% of its assets in the United States, and small positions in Australia and Canada.

Another alternative in indirect investing is the *single-country funds,* which, as their name implies, concentrate on the securities of a single country. These funds are closed-end funds, with a fixed number of shares outstanding. These funds reached new levels of popularity at the end of the 1980s, with three times as many created in 1989 as in 1988. At the beginning of 1990 there were approximately 50 single-country funds listed in New York or London.

As pointed out in Chapter 18, closed-end funds often sell at either a discount or a premium to their net asset value. For example, during 1989 the Brazil Fund sold at a discount of more than 40%, whereas the Spain Fund sold as a premium of more than 120%. The prices of these funds' shares have been more volatile than the market as a whole. For example, following the market crash of 1987, the prices of these funds dropped more than the prices of most individual stocks.

Some developing countries, such as Taiwan and Korea, restrict access to foreign equity ownership, with the result that a single-country fund may be an investor's only readily available alternative for investing in that particular country. Although this may help to explain the premiums on some of these funds, it obviously does not explain the premium on the Spain Fund.

Tangible Assets

In the remainder of this chapter we consider investment in real, or tangible, assets. Such assets are a part of the total set of assets available to investors.

In other words, in addition to the array of financial assets discussed so far, investors can add to their portfolio one or more real assets, such as gold and other precious metals, art, and so forth, as well as real estate. Investors can hold real estate itself or they can invest in a financial asset representing an ownership interest in the underlying real estate.

If tangible assets such as gold and real estate are to be desirable as investment alternatives, they should have favorable return and/or risk characteristics, at least when held as part of a diversified portfolio. To illustrate these possibilities, Table 21-3 presents correlation coefficients for bonds, stocks, real estate, gold, and futures (in two different forms) for the period 1975–1985. As we know from Chapter 19, favorable portfolio effects are possible when assets are less than perfectly correlated with each other, and the less the better, with negative correlations being preferable.

Table 21-3 indicates that gold was negatively correlated with Treasury bills, bonds, stocks, and real estate over this period, suggesting beneficial portfolio effects.[8] Real estate was negatively correlated with Treasury bills, and was moderately positively correlated with bond and stock returns. Futures also show some negative correlations.

Figure 21-6 shows the estimated efficient return–risk frontiers for these assets. The frontiers were estimated using the returns, standard deviations, and correlation coefficients of these assets over this period. Frontier A represents the "standard" strategy of holding bills, bonds, and stocks—that is, the traditional financial assets. Frontier B, on the other hand, represents a strategy of holding bills, bonds, stocks, real estate, and futures. At every level of expected return the risk is reduced with Frontier B relative to Frontier A, with an average risk reduction of 41% along Frontier B. This clearly suggests that investors can improve their positions by considering assets other than the traditional financial assets.

Interestingly, Frontier B in Figure 21-6 does not include gold, despite its favorable negative correlations with the financial assets. The explanation given for these results is that gold's extreme volatility relative to the volatility of the other assets used in the analysis prevented it from showing up on the frontier. For example, for the period analyzed, gold had a standard deviation of almost 39% compared to 16% for stocks and 3% for real estate. This suggests that certain real assets may not always be desirable in investors' portfolios even if they appear to offer certain favorable characteristics such as negative correlations with other assets.

Real Estate

Like international investments, real estate can be very useful in constructing diversified portfolios. Recall that real estate is one of the five parts of

[8]This discussion is based on Scott H. Irwin and Diego Landa, "Real Estate, Futures, and Gold as Portfolio Assets," *Journal of Portfolio Management*, Fall 1987, pp. 29–34.

TABLE 21-3 ***Correlations Among Financial and Real Assets***

	Correlation Coefficients						
	Bonds	Stocks	Real Estate	Buy-and-Hold Futures	Futures Funds	Gold	Inflation Rate
Bills	0.63	0.07	−0.46	−0.42	−0.54	−0.53	−0.66
Bonds		0.46	0.25	−0.33	−0.47	−0.23	−0.77
Stocks			0.51	0.22	−0.56	−0.15	−0.29
Real estate				0.49	0.07	0.41	−0.18
Futures					−0.03	0.52	0.18
Futures funds						0.58	0.55
Gold							0.55

Source: Scott H. Irwin and Diego Landa, "Real Estate, Futures, and Gold as Portfolio Assets," *The Journal of Portfolio Management,* Fall 1987, p. 32. Reprinted by permission.

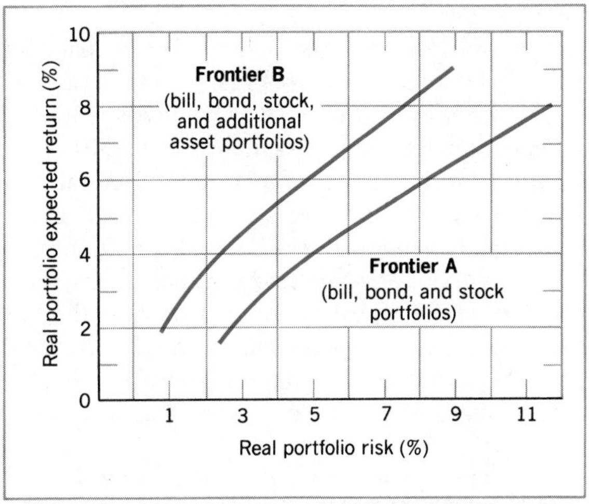

FIGURE 21-6 ***Efficient portfolios for financial assets and financial and real assets***
Source: Irwin and Landa, op. cit., p. 32. Reprinted by permission.

the diversified portfolio illustrated in Figure 21-2. Also recall that real estate constitutes a large percentage of total world assets.

Everyone has a general notion of what "real estate" is. After all, roughly half of all U.S. households own real estate either as their home or as an investment. But the term encompasses a variety of properties, including multifamily dwellings, office buildings, shopping centers, industrial buildings, hotels and motels, and raw land. Unlike the auction markets in which stocks trade, real estate properties must be evaluated as individual "deals," and individual investment judgments can be extremely important.

There are several ways investors can participate in real estate other than direct ownership. These include regular partnerships, limited partnerships (which means that the investor's liability is limited to the amount of the investment), and **real estate investment trusts (REITs)**. REITs are similar to the investment companies discussed in Chapter 18 and offer investors a chance to participate in a large portfolio of real estate holdings with a relatively small investment. Shares of REITs trade on exchanges or over the counter, and, like closed-end investment companies in general, they may sell at discounts or premiums relative to the value of their underlying properties. The highest-quality REITs historically have sold at premiums.

Some REITs hold mortgages whereas "equity" REITs hold primarily properties. Some are "finite-life REITs," which liquidate at a given time in the future, typically 8–10 years. In effect, these REITs are more like limited partnerships.

REITs specialize in a variety of real estate, with some owning regional shopping centers while others own hospitals or nursing homes. Since they are required by law to pay out 95% of their earnings to shareholders, they typically offer high yields.

The bottom line on rates of return from real estate is not clear. Some studies indicate that the nominal rate of return on real estate has compared favorably to other investments over the years, although common stocks did better over certain long periods, such as the 1950s and the 1960s. However, it is important to remember that real estate generally is accepted as a hedge against inflation, and therefore it is worthwhile to consider the real rate of return on real estate. During the inflationary 1970s, for example, real estate performed well as an inflationary hedge and outperformed common stocks on a real (inflation-adjusted) basis. On the other hand, in the relatively low inflation of the 1980s, real estate has not performed as well, as Table 21-4 shows.

Table 21-4 shows the annual total returns (TRs) for the years 1982–1988 for one real estate index, a stock market index, Treasury bills, and a bond

TABLE 21-4 ***Annual Returns on Real Estate, Stocks, Bonds, and Bills***

	FRANK RUSSELL CO. PROPERTY INDEX	S&P 500	3-MONTH T BILLS	SALOMON BOND INDEX[a]
1982	9.5%	21.5%	11.2%	31.8%
1983	13.2	22.5	8.9	8.2
1984	13.1	6.2	10.0	15.0
1985	9.9	31.6	7.8	22.3
1986	6.4	18.6	6.2	15.4
1987	5.4	5.2	5.9	2.6
1988	7.1	16.5	6.8	8.0

[a]Investment-grade issues

Source: James A. White, "Land Ho! Pensions Race for Real Estate," *The Wall Street Journal,* September 19, 1989, p. C1. Reprinted by permission of *The Wall Street Journal,*

index of investment-grade issues.[9] During this time period real estate did not perform very well relative to conventional financial asset alternatives. After subtracting management fees of about 1.2%, the average annual return on real estate barely exceeded that for three-month Treasury bills. Clearly, the returns on real estate for this period do not compare well with those of stock and bond returns.

A major problem with real estate as an investment in the 1980s is the tremendous amount of money that flowed into it. The result was overbuilding, soaring prices for premium properties, and lower rates of return. U.S. pension funds alone increased their stake in commercial real estate from about $17 billion in 1981 to over $70 billion in 1989 and an estimated $120 billion by 1992. This reflected a desire on the part of pension funds to diversify their stock and bond holdings as well as a belief in the real estate market.

In addition to overbuilding, real estate in the 1980s was hurt by the lower inflation that existed during that period. Also, tax reform lessened some of the advantages of real estate.

Investors must be concerned with the effects of an investment alternative on their portfolio of assets. As we saw earlier, real estate offers the potential of negative correlations with other assets. One problem with establishing these correlations, however, is that real estate returns and risks are measured using different indexes of properties. Some of these properties are based on appraisals, and properties trade infrequently. Indexes using such appraisals may behave differently from an index based on true market values (if such an index existed). It is quite possible that appraisal-based indexes understate the actual risk involved.

Table 21-5 shows some efficient portfolio mixes consisting of real estate, stocks, and bonds.[10] The risk of the real estate index has been adjusted upward to match that of the S&P 500 Index, 15.4%, for the period studied. This is done to try to offset the tendency for the risk in real estate returns to be understated because of the appraisal problem. The beneficial effects are achieved because of the negative correlations of the real estate index with the stock index and the bond index. This table suggests that real estate belongs in efficient portfolios in a major way. For example, for a portfolio with an 11% return, real estate constitutes almost 50% of the portfolio. Contrast this with the less than 3% of total assets that real estate constitutes in pension fund portfolios.

---

[9]This discussion is based on James A. White, "Land Ho! Pensions Race for Real Estate," *The Wall Street Journal*, September 19, 1989, p. C1.

[10]This discussion is based on Paul M. Firstenberg, Stephen A. Ross, and Randall C. Zisler, "Real Estate: The Whole Story," *Journal of Portfolio Management*, Spring 1988, pp. 22–34. This is one of the most complete discussions of real estate investing in article-length format.

TABLE 21-5 ***Efficient Portfolio Mixes of Real Estate, Stocks, and Bonds***

Real Estate (Index)	Stocks (S&P 500)	Government Bonds	Mean (%)	Portfolio Standard Deviation (%)
38	13	49	10.40	7.05
41	15	44	10.60	7.09
44	17	39	10.80	7.19
47	18	35	11.00	7.37
50	20	30	11.20	7.61
53	21	26	11.40	7.91
56	23	21	11.60	8.26
58	25	17	11.80	8.66
61	26	12	12.00	9.10
64	28	8	12.20	9.57
67	30	3	12.40	10.80
71	29		12.60	10.61
76	24		12.80	11.22
80	20		13.00	11.92
85	15		13.20	12.70
90	10		13.40	13.54
95	5		13.60	14.42
100	0		13.80	15.35

Source: Paul M. Firstenberg, Stephen A. Ross, and Randall C. Zisler, "Real Estate: The Whole Story," *The Journal of Portfolio Management*, Spring 1988, p. 31. Reprinted by permission.

Precious Metals

Precious metals are of interest to a number of investors and potentially offer attractive returns. However, the returns on precious metals also have been more volatile, at times spectacularly so, such as when silver soared to $50 per ounce but subsequently collapsed.

Table 21-1 shows that the annual compound return for gold over the period 1960–1984 was 9.08% and that for silver was 9.14%. Standard deviations were high—30% and 75%, respectively. Metals outperformed both the U.S. and Foreign Market Wealth Portfolio, but with a much higher standard deviation.

The key characteristic of precious metals has been their potential as an inflation hedge. Investors concerned about inflation and the dimunition in the value of financial assets often turn to precious metals as a hedge against inflation. Several studies report negative correlations between gold returns and stock returns.[11] One researcher has stated that failure to "hold some

[11]See, for example, A. F. Herbst, "Gold Versus U.S. Common Stocks: Some Evidence on Inflation Hedge Performance and Cyclical Behavior," *Financial Analysts Journal*, January–February 1983, pp. 66–74.

significant fraction of gold mining stocks results in suboptimal and economically inefficient allocation of resources and, therefore, is unequivocally imprudent."[12]

Gold-mining stocks also are regarded as havens when investors are frightened. During such times, investors may turn to such defensive stocks as utilities and food issues and to gold-mining stocks, because they often move counter to the market. Thus, if investors are worried about the economy and the general market, they may invest in gold-mining stocks as a "countergroup." Gold also acts as a currency, moving counter to the dollar. Thus, when worldwide events occur to make investors nervous, they may turn to gold.

Table 21-3 indicated that gold is negatively correlated with bills, bonds, and stocks. Note also that futures were negatively correlated with financial assets and that gold can be traded as a futures contract.

One question for investors interested in precious metals is how to invest in them. Alternatives include bullion, coins, mining companies, futures, and mutual fund shares. Buying the metals themselves can involve storage and insurance costs, assay costs, and so forth. Futures contracts offer a low-cost method of betting on the price of metals, but they require a relatively large margin deposit and the risk of margin calls. Purchases of shares of mining companies, such as Asarco and Phelps Dodge, may involve fundamental security analysis of the type discussed in Chapters 10–12. Purchase of investment company shares represents a fairly "pure" play on the precious metals, relieving the investor of having to do the analysis involved to construct a relevant portfolio. However, such a move does not eliminate an investor's risk. If the prices of precious metals do poorly for a period of time, the shares of these funds will reflect that. Investors should view such investments as only one small part of their total portfolio.

Summary

- Extended diversification is defined here as investment in foreign securities and tangible (real) assets.
- The case for extended diversification is the large opportunity set available to investors as illustrated by World Investable Wealth.
- The international securities markets are large and diverse, with securities similar to those traded in the United States.
- Diversification is a major benefit of international investing because of lower correlations among U.S. and foreign securities. When foreign secu-

[12]See E. J. Sherman, "Gold: A Conservative Prudent Diversifier," *Journal of Portfolio Management*, Spring 1982, pp. 21–27.

rities are considered, efficient frontiers dominate those available only with U.S. securities.

- In general, both the return and the risk available from foreign securities have exceeded those available from U.S. securities.
- Currency risk is the risk that the rate of return earned by an investor in a foreign market will be adversely affected by conversion of the foreign currency into the domestic currency. It is a significant part of the total risk of foreign investing.
- Investors should hedge their foreign investments against currency risk unless they are confident that the foreign currency will appreciate during the life of the investment.
- International investing can be accomplished through direct investing, which includes American Depository Receipts, and indirect investing, which involves investment companies.
- One of the benefits of investing in real (tangible) assets is the lower correlations that exist between these assets and financial assets, which in some cases are negative. This results in more optimal efficient frontiers.
- Real estate offers the potential for negative correlations with stocks and bonds and generally is accepted as an inflationary hedge.
- In the mid-1980s the total returns on real estate barely exceeded those for Treasury bills because of the significant lessening of inflationary pressures.
- Precious metals have exhibited both higher returns and higher risks over the last 20–30 years. Gold is typically taken to be negatively correlated with financial assets.
- The key characteristic of precious metals has been their potential as an inflation hedge.

Key Terms

American Depository Receipts (ADRs)
Currency risk
EAFE Index
Extended diversification
Real estate investment trusts (REITs)

Questions

21-1 What is the "intuitive" case for extended diversification?

21-2 What is the largest category of assets in World Investable Wealth? What is the relative importance of U.S. equities?

21-3 Which is the largest equity market in the world on the basis of dollar volume of trading?

21-4 What are the benefits of international investing?

21-5 What kinds of risk can be identified for international investing?

21-6 What is meant by currency risk? When does a U.S. investor lose from currency risk?

21-7 How important is currency risk? Should it be hedged?

21-8 How can Americans invest directly in foreign securities?

21-9 What is an ADR? What advantages do they offer investors?

21-10 How can Americans invest indirectly in foreign securities?

21-11 Distinguish between an international fund and a global fund.

21-12 What is a single-country fund? How are such funds organized?

21-13 What is the correlation between gold, real estate, and financial assets?

21-14 Does the state of the economy tend to affect real estate returns?

21-15 How has real estate performed recently in terms of total returns?

21-16 Do you think the measurement of total returns for real estate is comparable to that of stocks or bonds? Why or why not?

21-17 What is the key characteristic of precious metals that is of most interest to investors?

21-18 What are the alternative ways of investing in precious metals?

21-19 What are the disadvantages of holding precious metals as investments relative to financial assets?

21-20 What other real assets might investors purchase as part of a diversified portfolio?

Problems

21-1 The covariance between U.S. and Canadian stock returns is 225. Calculate the expected return for a portfolio of 30% U.S. securities and 70% Canadian securities if the expected return for U.S. securities is 9.7% and for Canadian securities 7.9%, the standard deviation for U.S. securities is 20.3%, and the standard deviation for Canadian securities is 14.6%.

(a) How would your answer change if the standard deviation for Canadian securities had been higher?

(b) How would your answer change if the weights had been reversed?

21-2 Using the information in Problem 21-1, calculate the standard deviation for the portfolio.

21-3 The covariance between European securities and U.S. securities is 289. The expected return and standard deviation for European securities is 10.6% and 22.1%. Using the information for U.S. securities in Problem 21-1, calculate the expected return and standard deviation for a 30%/70% portfolio.

21-4 Given the following information for U.S. stock returns and Japanese stock returns, and the knowledge that the covariance between them is 265, calculate the portfolio return and risk from combining the two using weighting increments of 0.10 (calculate 11 combinations, ranging from $W_{U.S.} = 1.0$ and $W_J = 0.0$ to $W_{U.S.} = 0.0$ and $W_J = 1.0$.

19X0	−14.5	−19.8
19X1	−26.0	−5.1
19X2	36.9	41.9
19X3	23.6	27.6
19X4	−7.2	−2.3
19X5	6.4	60.2
19X6	18.2	−19.8
19X7	31.5	32.2
19X8	−4.8	19.4
19X9	20.4	1.4
19Y0	22.3	28.7

(a) Which combination produces the highest portfolio return?
(b) Which combination produces the lowest portfolio standard deviation?
(c) What does this example illustrate about the beneficial effects of diversifying with foreign securities?
(d) Based on the results calculated, which portfolio would a smart U.S. investor prefer?

Selected References

A well-known book on international investing is

Solnik, Bruno. *International Investments.* Reading, Mass.: Addison-Wesley, 1988.

CHAPTER 22

Measuring Portfolio Performance

We have now discussed, in an organized and systematic manner, the major components of the investing process. After considering background material, we analyzed bonds and stocks and studied approaches to common stock analysis, with particular emphasis on the fundamental approach. We then considered other assets, such as options and futures, and the alternative of indirect investing. Finally, we studied portfolio management and capital market theory.

One important issue remains—the "bottom line" of the investing process, evaluating the performance of a portfolio. In other words, we need to consider how well various portfolios have performed. Every investor should be concerned with this issue because, after all, the objective of investing is to increase or at least protect financial wealth. If results are unsatisfactory, it must be determined so that changes can be made.

Evaluating portfolio performance is important regardless of whether an individual manages his or her own funds or invests indirectly through investment companies. Direct investing can be time-consuming and have high opportunity costs. If the results are inadequate, why do it (unless the investor simply enjoys it)? On the other hand, if professional portfolio managers are employed, it is necessary to know how well they perform. If manager A consistently outperforms manager B, other things being equal, investors will want to be with A. Alternatively, if neither A nor B outperforms an index fund, other things being equal, investors may prefer neither. The important point is that performance has to be measured before intelligent decisions can be made.

In this chapter we shall discuss what is involved in measuring portfolio performance. It is important to understand the issues of performance evaluation and the overall framework within which evaluation should be conducted. We shall review the well-known measures of portfolio performance and their problems. Box 22-1 describes the investor's plight.

A Framework for Evaluating Portfolio Performance

Assume that in 1990 the GoGrowth mutual fund earned a total return of 20% for its shareholders. As a shareholder, you are trying to assess GoGrowth's performance. What can you say?

Based on the preceding information and our discussion in Chapter 18 on investment company performance, you can legitimately say little or nothing. The primary reason for this is that investing is a two-dimensional process based on return and risk. These two factors are opposite sides of the same coin, and both must be evaluated if intelligent decisions are to be

BOX 22-1

PORTFOLIO RETURN IS A TOUGH FIGURE TO FIND

Most investors have a pretty good idea how major market benchmarks like Standard & Poor's 500-stock index did in 1989. Even if the exact figures aren't on the tips of their tongues, they can easily look them up.

But when it comes to the return on their own portfolios, most people have only the roughest notion. And there aren't any easy answers in the year-end brokerage and mutual-fund statements that outnumber the bills in some investors' mailboxes these days.

Securities firms have added more information to their statements in recent years. But they still don't show an overall performance figure that can be compared with, say, last year's 31.7% total return on the S&P 500. Unless investors do the frequently daunting calculations for themselves, they generally have no way of knowing how their investments stack up.

Mutual-fund investors don't have it much better. Fund companies do report total return figures for each fund, but that's often only part of the answer. People who moved their money around—say, shifting some dollars between a money-market fund and a stock fund—are still left groping in the dark.

Why don't brokerage firms and mutual-fund companies calculate their customers' returns?

Some people suspect that the firms, particularly the brokerages, just don't want to shine a spotlight on performance.

Investors are typically optimistic, adds John Markese, director of research for the American Association of Individual Investors in Chicago. Their guesses at portfolio returns are "invariably higher than what they did make." Securities firms "would be extremely reluctant, I think, to tell you the actual rate of return—particularly after all commissions," he says.

Investors should also take care in selecting appropriate benchmarks to measure their portfolios against. [One adviser] suggests constructing a customized index that represents a hypothetical portfolio with an investment mix similar to that of the investor.

Source: Adapted from Karen Slater, "Portfolio Return Is Tough Figure to Find," *The Wall Street Journal,* January 22, 1990, pp. C1, C21. Reprinted by permission of *The Wall Street Journal,*

made. Therefore, knowing nothing about the risk of this fund, little can be said about its performance. After all, its managers may have taken twice the risk of comparable portfolios to achieve this 20% return.

Given the risk faced by all investors, it is totally inadequate to consider only the returns from various investment alternatives. Although all investors prefer higher returns, they are also risk averse. To evaluate portfolio performance properly, we must determine whether the returns are large enough, given the risk involved. If we are to assess performance carefully, we must evaluate performance on a risk-adjusted basis.

The second reason that little can be said about the performance of GoGrowth is that its 20% return, given its risk, is meaningful only when compared to some benchmark. Obviously, if the average fund or the market returned 25% in 1990, and GoGrowth is average, its performance appears unfavorable. Therefore, it is necessary to make comparisons in performance measurement, and an important related issue is the benchmark to be used in evaluating the performance of a portfolio.

There are, of course, other important issues in evaluating the portfolio's performance. One of these involves evaluating the manager as opposed to the portfolio itself. It is essential to determine how well diversified the portfolio was during the evaluation period, because, as we have seen in the previous two chapters, diversification can reduce portfolio risk. If a manager assumes unsystematic risk, we want to know if he or she earned an adequate return for doing so.

In evaluating the portfolio manager rather than the portfolio itself, an investor should consider the objectives set by the manager and any constraints under which he or she must operate. For example, if a fund's objective is to invest in small, speculative stocks, investors must expect the risk to be larger than that of the typical fund, with substantial swings in the annual realized returns. It is important to determine whether the manager followed the stated objective. Similarly, if a portfolio manager is obligated to operate under certain constraints, these must be taken into account. For example, if a portfolio manager of an equity fund is prohibited from selling short, it is unreasonable to expect the manager to protect the portfolio in this manner in a bear market. If the manager is further prohibited from trading in options and futures, about the only protection left in a bear market is to reduce the equity exposure.

Measures of Portfolio Performance

It is now clear that in measuring portfolio performance, investors must consider both the realized return and the risk that was assumed. Therefore, whatever measures or techniques are used, these parameters must be incorporated into the analysis.

When portfolio performance is evaluated, the total return to the investor is relevant. As discussed throughout this text, a proper measure of this return is the total return (TR), which captures both the income component and the capital gains (or losses) component of return. Furthermore, as discussed, we know that two measures of risk are widely used in investments: standard deviation and beta.

Based on the concepts of capital market theory and the CAPM, and recognizing the necessity to incorporate both return and risk into the analysis, these researchers developed measures of portfolio performance in the 1960s. These measures are often referred to as the **composite (risk-**

adjusted) measures of portfolio performance, meaning that they incorporate both return and risk into the evaluation. These measures, which are often used today, are analyzed in the following section.

The Reward-to-Variability Measure

William Sharpe, whose contributions to portfolio theory have been previously encountered, introduced a composite measure of portfolio performance called the **reward-to-variability ratio (RVAR)** based on his work in capital market theory discussed in the last chapter.[1] Sharpe used it to rank the performance of 34 mutual funds over the period 1954–1963. This measure can be defined as

$$RVAR = \frac{\overline{TR_p} - \overline{RF}}{SD_p}$$

$$= \frac{\text{Excess return}}{\text{Risk}}$$

where

$\overline{TR_p}$ = the average TR for portfolio p during some period of time (we will use annual data)

$\overline{RF}$ = the average risk-free rate of return during the period

SD_p = the standard deviation of return for portfolio p during the period

$\overline{TR_p} - \overline{RF}$ = excess return (risk premium) on portfolio p

The numerator of Equation 22-1 measures the portfolio's **excess return,** or the return above the risk-free rate (RF could have been earned without assuming risk). This is also referred to as the risk premium. The denominator uses the standard deviation, which is a measure of the total risk or variability in the return of the portfolio. Note the following about RVAR:

1. It measures the *excess return* per unit of *total risk.*
2. The higher the RVAR, the better the portfolio performance.

INVESTMENTS INTUITION

Since this is an ordinal (relative) measure of portfolio performance, different portfolios can easily be ranked on this variable. Using only the Sharpe measure of portfolio performance, the portfolio with the highest RVAR would be judged best in terms of ex post performance.

[1]W. Sharpe, "Mutual Fund Performance," *The Journal of Business,* January 1966, pp. 119–138.

TABLE 22-1 ***Annual Shareholder Returns for Three Mutual Funds and TRs for the S&P 500 and Treasury Bills, 1974–1982 (in percentages)***

	New Horizons	Affiliated	Ivy	S&P 500	RF
1974	−38.7	−16	−33	−26	7.9
1975	39.6	39.4	30	36.9	5.8
1976	11.1	34.3	18.2	23.6	5.0
1977	12.7	−6.9	−7.3	−7.2	5.3
1978	20.9	3.2	4.9	6.4	7.2
1979	35.5	28.9	30.9	18.2	10
1980	57.6	24.1	34.7	31.5	11.5
1981	−7.8	0.0	6.0	−4.8	14.1
1982	22.8	23.4	33.0	20.4	10.7
Mean	17.1	14.5	13.0	11	8.6
SD	28.1	19.7	22.8	20.5	—
Beta	1.20	0.92	1.04	1.00	—
R^2	0.77	0.90	0.87		

Source: Reprinted by permission from the *Wiesenberger Investment Companies Service*, 1983 Edition, Copyright © 1983. Warren, Gorham & Lamont, Inc., 210 South Street, Boston, Mass. All Rights Reserved.

As an example of calculating the Sharpe ratio, consider the data for three mutual funds for the years 1974 through 1982, as shown in Table 22-1. These funds were chosen randomly for illustrative purposes only.[2] Annual shareholder returns are shown, based on Wiesenberger data.[3] Table 22-1 also shows the return on the S&P 500 Index for those years, as well as the annual yields on Treasury bills as a proxy for RF.[4]

On the basis of these data, Sharpe's RVAR can be calculated as

$$\text{New Horizons RVAR} = \frac{17.1 - 8.6}{28.1} = 0.302$$

$$\text{Affiliated RVAR} = \frac{14.5 - 8.6}{19.7} = 0.299$$

$$\text{Ivy Fund RVAR} = \frac{13.0 - 8.6}{22.8} = 0.193$$

$$\text{S\&P 500 RVAR} = \frac{11.0 - 8.6}{20.5} = 0.117$$

[2]The use of these funds as examples in no way implies anything about their performance or operations.

[3]The calculation of total shareholder returns for a mutual fund, as well as the use of Wiesenberger data, was explained in Chapter 18.

[4]The annualized Treasury bill rate is taken from the *Economic Report of the President*.

Based on these calculations, we see that all three funds outperformed the S&P 500 Index on an excess return–risk basis during this nine-year period (when interest rates, and therefore RF, were unusually high by historical standards). New Horizons and Affiliated performed almost the same (rounded to two decimal places their performance would be equal) during this period on the basis of RVAR.

Sharpe's measure for these funds is illustrated graphically in Figure 22-1. The vertical axis is the return on the portfolio, and the horizontal axis is standard deviation of returns. The vertical intercept is RF. As Figure 22-1 shows, RVAR measures the slope of the line from RF to the portfolio being evaluated. The steeper the line, the higher the slope (RVAR) and the better the performance. Because of their better performance, Affiliated and New Horizons, with almost identical RVARs, have the highest slope, whereas Ivy's slope is lower. (Affiliated is shown on the same ray with New Horizons in Figure 22-1 because of the closeness of the numbers).

INVESTMENTS INTUITION

In Figure 22-1 we are drawing the capital market line (CML) when we plot the market's return against its standard deviation and have RF as the vertical intercept. Based on the discussion in Chapter 20, all efficient portfolios should plot on this line, and an investor with the ability to borrow and lend at the rate RF should be able to attain any point on this line. Of course, this is the ex post and not the ex ante CML.

The Reward-to-Volatility Measure

At approximately the same time as Sharpe's measure was developed (the mid-1960s), Jack Treynor presented a similar measure called the **reward-to-volatility rate.**[5] Like Sharpe, Treynor sought to relate the return on a portfolio to its risk. Treynor, however, distinguished between total risk and systematic risk, implicitly assuming that portfolios are well diversified.

In measuring portfolio performance, Treynor introduced the concept of the characteristic line, used in earlier chapters to partition a security's return into its systematic and unsystematic components. It is used in a similar manner with portfolios, depicting the relationship between the returns on a portfolio and those of the market. The slope of the characteristic line measures the relative volatility of the fund's returns. As we know, the slope of this line is the beta coefficient, which is a measure of the volatility

[5]J. Treynor, "How to Rate Management of Investment Funds" *Harvard Business Review*, January–February 1965, pp. 63–75.

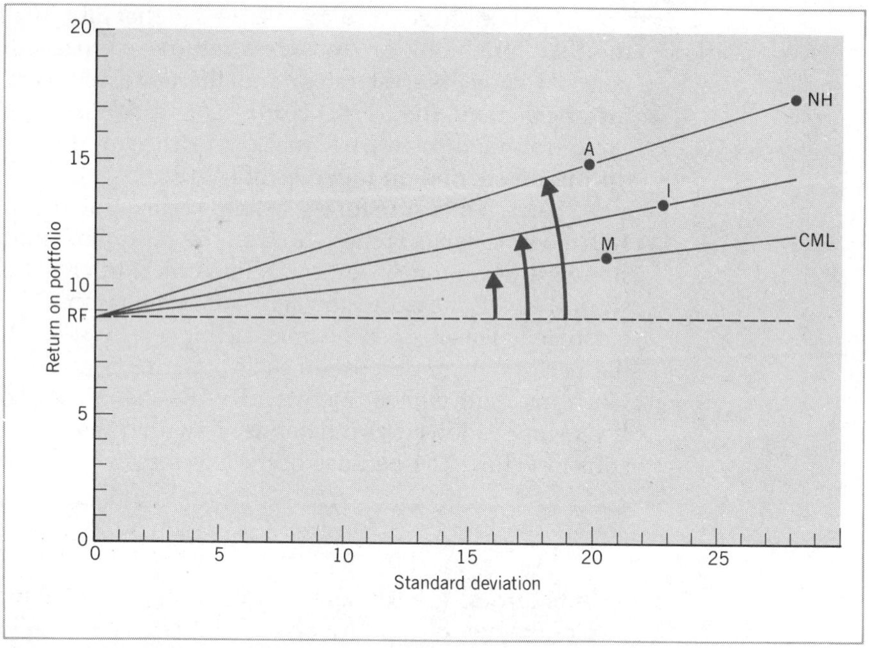

FIGURE 22-1 ***Sharpe's measure of performance (RVAR) for three mutual fund portfolios (A = Affiliated Fund; NH = New Horizons Fund; I = Ivy Fund).***

(or responsiveness) of the portfolio's returns in relation to those of the market index.

Figure 22-2 shows the characteristic lines for New Horizons and Affiliated, corresponding to the data in Table 22-1. As can be seen, New Horizons has the steeper characteristic line, reflecting a higher beta. These characteristic lines are estimated by regressing each fund's returns on the S&P 500 returns for the nine-year period, producing the following equations:

$$\text{New Horizons: } R_p = 3.84 + 1.20\, R_{\text{S\&P 500}}$$

$$\text{Affiliated: } R_p = 4.42 + 0.92\, R_{\text{S\&P 500}}$$

Treynor's measure relates the average excess return on the portfolio during some period (exactly the same variable as in the Sharpe measure) to its systematic risk as measured by the portfolio's beta. The reward-to-volatility (RVOL) ratio is

$$\text{RVOL} = \frac{\overline{TR_p} - \overline{RF}}{b_p} \tag{22-2}$$

$$= \frac{\text{excess return on portfolio } p}{\text{Systematic risk for portfolio } p}$$

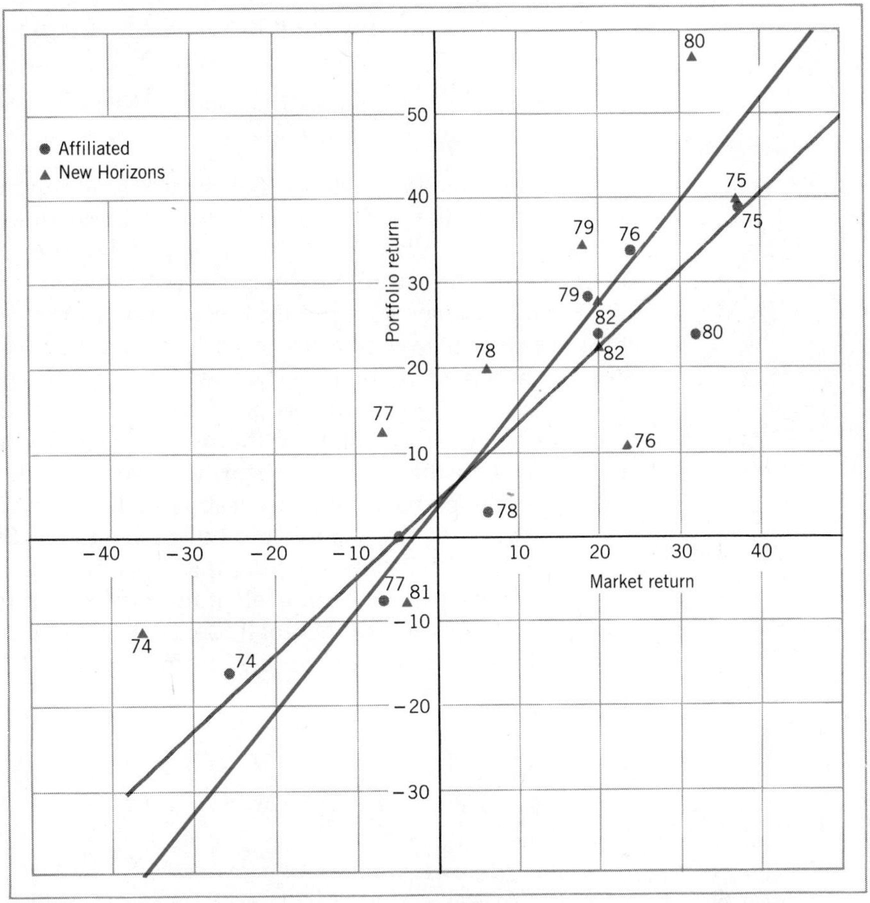

FIGURE 22-2 ***Characteristic lines for Affiliated and New Horizon, 1974–1982.***

where all terms are as previously defined and b_p is the beta for portfolio p.

In this case we are calculating the excess return per unit of systematic risk. As with RVAR, higher values of RVOL indicate better portfolio performance. Portfolios can be ranked on their RVOL, and assuming that the Treynor measure is a correct measure of portfolio performance, the best performing portfolio can be determined.

Using the data in Table 22-1, we can calculate RVOL for the same three portfolios illustrated. Using Equation 22-2

$$\text{New Horizons RVOL} = \frac{17.1 - 8.6}{1.20} = 7.1$$

$$\text{Affiliated RVOL} = \frac{14.5 - 8.6}{0.92} = 6.4$$

$$\text{Ivy Fund RVOL} = \frac{13.0 - 8.6}{1.04} = 4.2$$

$$\text{S\&P 500 RVOL} = \frac{11.0 - 8.6}{1.00} = 2.4$$

These calculations indicate that all three funds outperformed the market on the basis of their excess return–systematic risk ratio. New Horizons, for example, had a higher beta than the other funds, but its higher return was sufficient to compensate for the larger risk (at least in these comparisons).

Figure 22-3 shows a plot of these funds in return-beta space. Again, lines are drawn from the RF to each fund's return–risk point with the steepest line representing the largest slope and the best performance; in other words, the steeper the slope, the better the performance.

As in Figure 22-1, plotting the market data produces the appropriate market line—in this case, the security market line (SML). All three funds plot above the ex post SML, suggesting better performance for the stated level of systematic risk than would be implied by the SML.

The use of RVOL, of course, implies that systematic risk is the proper measure of risk to use when evaluating portfolio performance. (Similarly, the use of RVAR implies that total risk is the proper measure to use when evaluating portfolios.) As we learned in Chapter 21, systematic risk is a

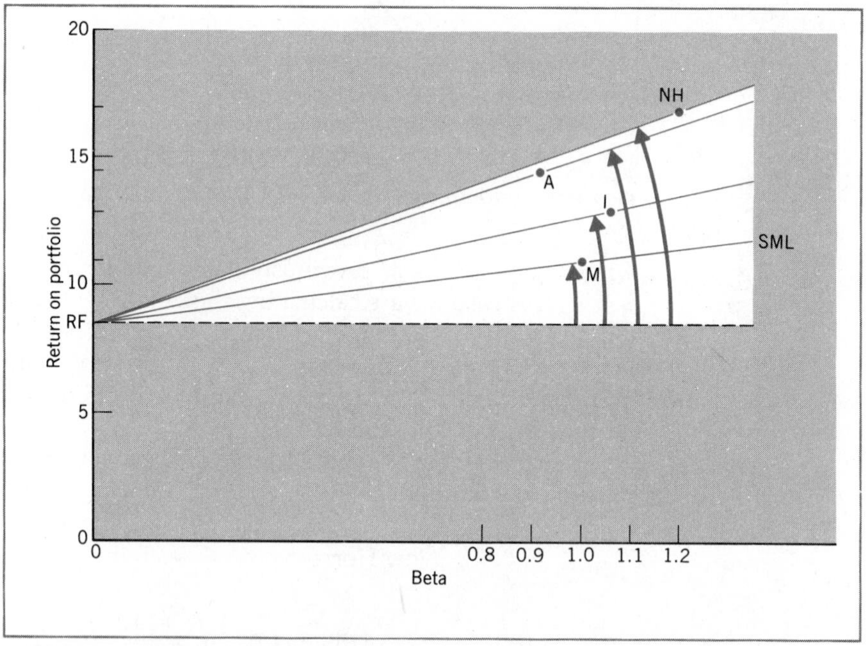

FIGURE 22-3 ***Treynor's measure of performance for three mutual fund portfolios (A = Affiliated Fund; NH = New Horizons Fund; I = Ivy Fund).***

proper measure of risk to use when portfolios are perfectly diversified so that no unsystematic risk remains. (The procedure for measuring the degree of diversification is given in the following discussion.)

Comparing the Sharpe and Treynor Measures

Given their similarity, when should RVAR or RVOL be used, and why? Actually, given the assumptions underlying each measure, both can be said to be correct. Therefore, it is usually desirable to calculate both measures for a set of portfolios that is being evaluated.

The choice of which to use could depend upon the definition of risk. If an investor thinks it correct to use total risk, RVAR is appropriate; however, if the investor thinks that it is correct to use systematic risk, RVOL is appropriate.

What about the rankings of a set of portfolios using the two measures? Our earlier calculations provide the following rankings, where 1 represents the best performance:

	Sharpe	Treynor
New Horizons	1	1
Affiliated	2	2
Ivy	3	3

If the portfolios are fully diversified, the rankings will be identical. As the portfolios become less well diversified, the possibility of differences in rankings increases. This leads to the following conclusion about these two measures: RVAR takes into account how well diversified a portfolio was during the measurement period. Differences in rankings between the two measures can result from substantial differences in diversification in the portfolio. If a portfolio is inadequately diversified, its RVOL ranking can be higher than its RVAR ranking. Such a difference in ranking results from the substantial difference in the amount of diversification in the portfolio. For typical large, professionally managed portfolios, such as broad-based equity mutual funds, the two measures often provide identical, or almost identical, rankings.

This analysis leads to an important observation about Sharpe and Treynor measures. Investors who have all (or substantially all) of their assets in a portfolio of securities should rely more on the Sharpe measure because it assesses the portfolio's total return in relation to total risk, which includes any unsystematic risk assumed by the investor. However, for those investors whose portfolio constitutes only one (relatively) small part of their total assets, systematic risk may well be the relevant risk. In these circumstances, RVOL is appropriate because it considers only systematic risk.

Measuring Diversification

Portfolio diversification is typically measured by correlating the returns on the portfolio with the returns on the market index. This is accomplished as a part of the process of fitting a characteristic line whereby the portfolio's returns are regressed against the market's returns. The square of the correlation coefficient produced as a part of the analysis, called the coefficient of determination, or R^2, is used to denote the degree of diversification. The **coefficient of determination** indicates the percentage of the variance in the portfolio's returns that is explained by the market's returns. If the fund is totally diversified, the R^2 will approach 1.0, indicating that the fund's returns are completely explained by the market's returns. The lower the coefficient of determination, the less the portfolio's returns are attributable to the market's returns. This indicates that other factors, which could have been diversified away, are being allowed to influence the portfolio's returns.

The R^2 figures in Table 22-1 indicate that New Horizons was less diversified than was Affiliated, with an R^2 value of 0.77 compared to Affiliated's 0.90. This lower degree of diversification for New Horizons can be seen in Figure 22-2, which shows that the points around its characteristic line are more dispersed (spread out) than those of Affiliated. Therefore, New Horizons was exposed to more unsystematic risk than the other two funds, presumably because the portfolio managers expected to earn adequate returns to compensate for this risk.

Jensen's Differential Return Measure

A measure related to Treynor's RVOL is Jensen's **differential return measure,** or **alpha** (we shall refer to it simply as alpha); in fact, these two measures can produce, with proper adjustments, identical relative rankings of portfolio performance.[6] Jensen's measure of performance is based on the CAPM discussed in Chapter 20.[7] The expected return for any security (*i*) or portfolio (*p*) was given in Equation 20-9 of Chapter 20 as

$$E(R_p) = RF + b_p[E(R_M) - RF] \tag{20-9}$$

with all terms as previously defined.

Notice that Equation 20-9, which covers any ex ante period *t*, can be applied to ex post periods if investor's expectations are, on the average, fulfilled. Empirically, Equation 20-9 can be approximated as Equation 22-3.

$$R_{pt} = RF_t + b_p[R_{Mt} - RF_t] + E_{pt} \tag{22-3}$$

[6]Jensen's alpha divided by beta is equivalent to Treynor's measure minus the average risk premium for the market portfolio for the period.

[7]M. Jensen, "The Performance of Mutual Funds in the Period 1945–1964," *The Journal of Finance*, May 1968, pp. 389–416.

where

R_{pt} = the return on portfolio p in period t
RF_t = the risk-free rate in period t
R_{Mt} = the return on the market in period t
E_{pt} = a random error term for portfolio p in period t
$[R_{Mt} - RF_t]$ = the market risk premium during period t

Equation 22-3 relates the realized return on portfolio p during any period t to the sum of the risk-free rate and the portfolio's risk premium plus an error term. Given the market risk premium, the risk premium on portfolio p is a function of portfolio p's systematic risk—the larger its systematic risk, the larger the risk premium.

Equation 22-3 can be written in what is called the risk premium (or, alternatively, the excess return) form by moving RF to the left side and subtracting it from R_{pt}, as in 22-4:

$$R_{pt} - RF_t = b_p[R_{Mt} - RF_t] + E_{pt} \qquad (22\text{-}4)$$

where

$R_{pt} - RF_t$ = the risk premium on portfolio p

Equation 22-4 indicates that the risk premium on portfolio p is equal to the product of its beta and the market risk premium plus an error term. In other words, the risk premium on portfolio p should be proportional to the risk premium on the market portfolio if the CAPM model is correct and investor expectations were generally realized (in effect, if all assets and portfolios were in equilibrium).

A return proportional to the risk assumed is illustrated by Fund Y in Figure 22-4. This diagram illustrates an alternative form of the characteristic line discussed earlier, where portfolio returns are related to market returns. In this case the risk-free rate each period, RF_t, is subtracted from both the portfolio's return and the market's return.[8]

Equation 22-4 can be empirically tested by fitting a regression for some number of periods. Portfolio excess returns (risk premiums) are regressed against the excess returns (risk premiums) for the market. If managers earn a return proportional to the risk assumed, this relationship should hold; that is, there should be no intercept term (alpha) in the regression, which should go through the origin, as in the case of Fund Y in Figure 22-4.

Given these expected findings, Jensen argued that an intercept term, alpha, could be added to Equation 22-4 as a means of identifying superior or inferior portfolio performance. Therefore, Equation 22-4 becomes Equation 22-5:

[8]This version is usually referred to as a characteristic line in risk premium or excess return form.

$$R_{pt} - RF_t = a_p + b_p[R_{Mt} - RF_t] + E_{pt} \tag{22-5}$$

The CAPM asserts that equilibrium conditions should result in a zero intercept term. Therefore, the alpha should measure the contribution of the portfolio manager since it represents the average incremental rate of return beyond the return attributable to the level of risk assumed. Specifically: (1) alpha, when significantly positive, is evidence of superior performance (illustrated in Figure 22-4 with portfolio *X*, which has a positive intercept); (2) if alpha is significantly negative, this is evidence of inferior performance (illustrated in Figure 22-4 with portfolio *Z*, which has a negative intercept); (3) if alpha is insignificantly different from zero, this is evidence that the portfolio manager matched the market on a risk-adjusted basis (as in the case of portfolio *Y*).

Note that Equation 22-5 can be rearranged to better demonstrate what a_p really is. Rearranging terms, Equation 22-5 becomes

$$\bar{a}_p = (\overline{R}_p - \overline{RF}) - [b_p(\overline{R}_M - \overline{RF})] \tag{22-6}$$

where the bars above the variables indicate averages for the period measured.

Equation 22-6 states that a_p is the difference between the actual excess return on portfolio *p* during some period and the risk premium on that portfolio that should have been earned, given its level of systematic risk and the use of the CAPM.

As noted, this difference can be positive, negative, or zero. It is important to recognize the role of *statistical significance* in the interpretation of Jensen's measure. Although the estimated alpha may be positive or negative, it may not be significantly different (statistically) from zero. If it is not, we would conclude that the manager of the portfolio being

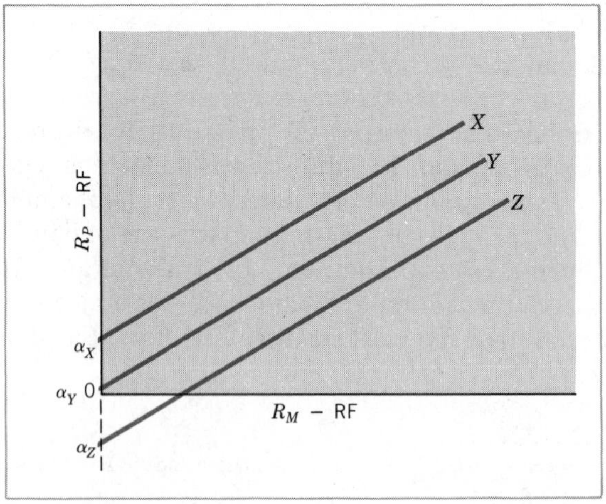

FIGURE 22-4 ***Jensen's measure of portfolio performance for three hypothetical funds.***

evaluated performed as expected; that is, the manager earned an average risk-adjusted return, neither more nor less than would be expected given the risk assumed.

Jensen's performance measure can be estimated by regressing excess returns for the portfolio being evaluated against excess returns for the market (in effect, producing a characteristic line in excess return form). When this was done for the three mutual funds evaluated earlier, the following alphas were found:

Portfolio	Alpha	Standard Error	Significant?
New Horizons	5.64	4.88	No
Affiliated	3.67	2.21	No
Ivy	2.07	2.94	No

All three funds showed positive alphas, and reasonably high ones given the alphas typically observed for mutual funds. If significant, the 5.64 for New Horizons would indicate that this fund, *on the average*, earned an annual risk-adjusted rate of return that was more than 5% above the market average; in other words, New Horizon earned a positive return attributable to factors other than the market, presumably due to the ability of its managers. However, the standard errors for each fund indicate that the alphas are not significantly different from zero.[9] Therefore, we cannot conclude that these three funds exhibited superior performance. As in any regression equation, the coefficients must be statistically significant for any conclusions to be drawn.

Superior and inferior portfolio performance can result from at least two sources. First, the portfolio manager may be able to select undervalued securities consistently enough to affect portfolio performance. Second, the manager may be able to time market turns, varying the portfolio's composition in accordance with the rise and fall of the market. Obviously, a manager with enough ability may be able to do more.

A computational advantage of the Jensen measure is that it permits the performance measure to be estimated simultaneously with the beta for a portfolio. That is, by estimating a characteristic line in risk premium form, estimates of both alpha and beta are obtained at the same time. However, unlike the Sharpe and Treynor measures, each period's returns must be in the estimating process, rather than an average return for the entire period. Thus, if performance is being measured on an annual basis, the annual returns on RF, R_M, and R_p must be obtained.

[9]A general rule of thumb is that a coefficient should be twice its standard error in order to be significant at the 5% level. Alternatively, *t* values can be examined in order to test the significance of the coefficients. For a reasonably large number of observations, and therefore degrees of freedom, *t* values of approximately 2.0 would indicate significance at the 5% level.

Problems with Portfolio Measurement

Using the three composite performance measures just discussed to evaluate portfolios is not without problems. Investors should understand their limitations and be guided accordingly.

First, these measures are derived from capital market theory and the CAPM and are therefore dependent on the assumptions involved with this theory, as discussed in Chapter 20. For example, if the Treasury bill rate is not a satisfactory proxy for the risk-free rate, or if investors cannot borrow and lend at the risk-free rate, this will have an impact upon these measures of performance.

An important assumption of capital market theory that directly affects the use of these performance measures is the assumption of a market portfolio that can be proxied by a market index. We have used the S&P 500 Index as a market proxy, as is often done. However, there are potential problems.

Richard Roll has argued that beta is not a clear-cut measure of risk.[10] If the definition of the market portfolio is changed, for example, by using the New York Stock Exchange Index instead of the S&P 500, the beta can change. This could, in turn, change the rankings of portfolios. Although a high correlation exists among most of the commonly used market proxies, this does not eliminate the problem—that some may be efficient but others are not. This relates to Roll's major point, mentioned in Chapter 20, that using a market portfolio other than the "true" market portfolio does not constitute a test of the CAPM. Rather, it is a test only of whether or not the chosen market proxy is efficient.

According to Roll, no unambiguous test of the CAPM has yet been conducted. This should be kept in mind when considering performance measures based on the CAPM, such as the Treynor and Jensen measures.

Theoretically, each of the three performance measures discussed should be independent of its respective risk measure. However, a number of researchers over the years have found a relationship between them. In some cases the relationship was negative and in others it was positive. In fact, it can be shown that a fundamental relationship does exist between the composite performance measures and their associated risk measure.[11] Given an empirical CML, the relationship between Sharpe's measure and the standard deviation can be instantly derived; similarly, given an empirical SML, the relationship between Jensen's and Treynor's perfor-

---

[10]See R. Roll, "Ambiguity When Performance Is Measured by the Securities Market Line," *The Journal of Finance,* Vol. 33 (September 1978), pp. 1051–1069; "Performance Evaluation and Benchmark Error, Part I," *Journal of Portfolio Management,* Vol. 6 (Summer 1980), pp. 5–12, and Part II (Winter 1981), pp. 17–22.

[11]See J. Wilson and C. Jones, "The Relationship Between Performance and Risk: Whence the Bias?" *The Journal of Financial Research,* Vol. 4 (Summer 1981), pp. 109–117.

mance measures and beta can be derived instantly. The only other variable needed to do these calculations is the mean market return for the period.

Summary

- Portfolio performance, the bottom line in the investing process, is an important aspect of interest to all investors and money managers.
- The framework for evaluating portfolio performance consists of measuring both the realized return and the risk of the portfolio being evaluated, determining an appropriate benchmark to use to compare a portfolio's performance, and recognizing that an evaluation of the portfolio itself is not necessarily equivalent to an evaluation of the portfolio manager.
- The most often used measures of portfolio performance are the composite measures of Sharpe, Treynor, and Jensen, which bring return and risk together.
- The Sharpe and Treynor measures can be used to rank portfolio performance and indicate the relative positions of the portfolios being evaluated. Jensen's measure is an absolute measure of performance.
- The Sharpe and Treynor measures both relate the excess return on a portfolio to a measure of its risk. Sharpe's RVAR uses standard deviation, whereas Treynor's RVOL uses beta.
- Since RVAR implicitly measures the lack of complete diversification in a portfolio and RVOL assumes complete diversification, portfolio rankings from the two measures can differ if portfolios are not well diversified.
- The Sharpe measure is more appropriate when the portfolio constitutes a significant portion of the investor's wealth, whereas the Treynor measure is more appropriate when the portfolio constitutes only a small part of that wealth.
- Jensen's differential return measures the difference between what the portfolio was expected to earn, given its systematic risk, and what it actually did earn. By regressing the portfolio's excess return against that of the market index, alpha can be used to capture the superior or inferior performance of the portfolio manager.
- Based on capital market theory, alphas are expected to be zero. Significantly positive or negative alphas are used to indicate corresponding performance.
- The composite measures are not without their limitations and problems. If there are problems with capital market theory and the CAPM, such problems carry over to performance measurement.
- One problem in particular concerns the market portfolio, which can be measured only imprecisely. Failure to use the true ex ante market portfolio may result in different betas and different rankings for portfolios.

Key Words

Coefficient of determination
Composite (risk-adjusted) measures of portfolio performance
Differential return measure (alpha)
Excess return
Reward-to-variability ratio (RVAR)
Reward-to-volatility ratio (RVOL)

Questions

22-1 Outline the framework for evaluating portfolio performance.

22-2 Why can the evaluation of a portfolio be different from the evaluation of a portfolio manager?

22-3 Explain how the three composite measures of performance are related to capital market theory and the CAPM.

22-4 What role does diversification play in the Sharpe and Treynor measures?

22-5 How can one construct a characteristic line for a portfolio? What does it show?

22-6 How can portfolio diversification be measured? On the average, what degree of diversification would you expect to find for a typical mutual fund?

22-7 For what type of mutual fund discussed in Chapter 18 could you expect to find complete diversification?

22-8 In general, when may an investor prefer to rely on the Sharpe measure? The Treynor measure?

22-9 Explain how Jensen's differential return measure is derived from the CAPM.

22-10 Why is the Jensen measure computationally efficient?

22-11 What role does statistical significance play in the Jensen measure?

22-12 How does Roll's questioning of the testing of the CAPM relate to the issue of performance measurement?

22-13 Illustrate how the choice of the wrong market index could affect the rankings of portfolios.

22-14 In theory, what would be the proper market index to use?

22-15 Explain why the steeper the angle, the better the performance in Figures 22-1 and 22-3.

22-16 If portfolios were evaluated using the Sharpe and Jensen measures, would the same rankings of performance be obtained?

Problems

22-1 The following data are available for five portfolios and the market for a recent 10-year period:

	Average Annual Return (%)	Standard Deviation (%)	b_i	R^2
1	14	21	1.15	0.70
2	16	24	1.1	0.98
3	26	30	1.3	0.96
4	17	25	0.9	0.92
5	10	18	0.45	0.60
S&P 500	12	20		
RF	6			

(a) Rank these portfolios using the Sharpe measure.
(b) Rank these portfolios using the Treynor measure.
(c) Compare the rankings of portfolio 1 and 2. Are there any differences? How can you explain these differences?
(d) Which of these portfolios outperformed the market?

22-2 Consider the five funds shown below:

	a	b	R^2
1	2.0	1.0	0.98
2	1.6[a]	1.1	0.95
3	3.5	0.9	0.90
4	1.2	0.8	0.80
5	0.9[a]	1.20	0.60

[a]Significant at 5% level.

(a) Which fund's returns are best explained by the market's returns?
(b) Which fund had the largest total risk?
(c) Which fund had the lowest market risk? The highest?
(d) Which fund(s), according to Jensen's alpha, outperformed the market?

22-3 The following diagram shows characteristic lines in risk premium form for two portfolios. Assume that the alphas for each portfolio are statistically significant.
(a) Label each axis.
(b) Which fund has the larger beta?
(c) Based on a visual inspection, which fund has the larger absolute alpha?
(d) Which fund outperformed the market?

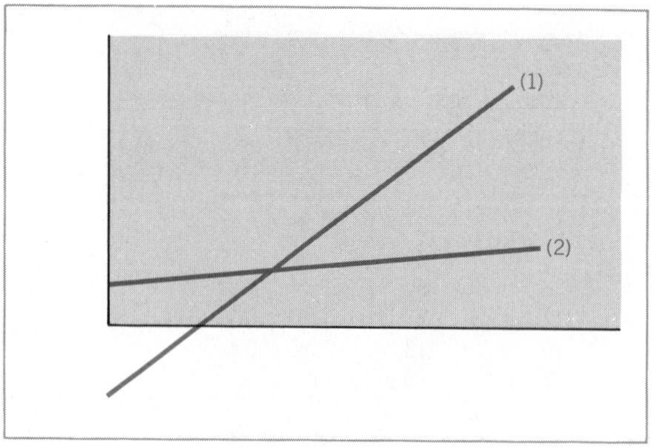

22-4 Annual total returns for the same nine years used in the chapter (1974–1982) are shown below for eight hypothetical mutual funds. The values are like those shown in Table 22-1, and the characteristic lines are calculated using annual market yields. The ex post values shown in the following table are as follows:

Fund	(1) $\bar{R}_i$ (%)	(2) SD_i(%)	(3) a_i	(4) b_i	(5) R^2
A	17.0	20.0	7.53	0.88	0.82
B	19.0	17.8	11.70	0.65	0.57
C	12.3	25.0	3.12	0.83	0.47
D	20.0	24.5	9.00	1.00	0.72
E	15.0	17.4	6.15	0.79	0.88
F	19.0	18.0	10.11	0.83	0.89
G	8.6	19.0	−1.37	0.91	0.95
H	20.0	21.5	9.52	0.93	0.78

where

$\bar{R}_i$ = mean annual total returns for each fund
SD_i = standard deviation of the annual yields
a_i = the constant of the characteristic line
b_i = the slope

Using 8.6% as the risk-free yield, answer the following problems:

a. Calculate Sharpe's RVAR for each of these eight funds, and using the three additional funds given in the text, rank the 11 funds from high to low performance.
b. Calculate Treynor's RVOL for each fund and perform the same ranking as in part a.
c. Using the R^2 in column 5, comment on the degree of diversification of the eight mutual funds. Which fund appears to be the most highly diversified? Which fund appears to be the least diversified?

d. The returns, standard deviations, and characteristic lines were recalculated using the annual Treasury bill rate, as in the text for formula 22-4. The results are shown in the following table in excess yield form:

Fund	$\bar{R}_i$	SD_i	a_i	SE(a)	b_i	t values
A	8.60	20.00	6.57	(3.53)	0.87	2.15
B	10.30	16.90	8.81	(4.78)	0.61	2.23
C	3.70	25.50	1.58	(7.37)	0.86	0.24
D	11.50	25.00	8.98	(5.23)	1.03	1.96
E	6.30	18.09	4.34	(2.51)	0.81	1.91
F	10.80	18.20	8.69	(2.40)	0.83	4.21
G	−0.02	19.80	−2.22	(1.65)	0.92	−1.49
H	11.30	23.40	8.88	(4.20)	0.95	2.40

In the column to the right of the a_i is the calculated standard error of alpha [SE(a)]. The critical value of t for 7 degrees of freedom (number of observations minus 2) for a two-tailed test at the 5% level is 2.365. With a large number of degrees of freedom (more observations), the critical value of t is close to 2.00. The calculated t values are shown in the last column of the table (t for a_i). If the absolute value in that column exceeds 2.365, that fund's alpha is significantly different from zero. On the basis of this test, which funds exhibit above, or below, average performance?

e. Compare the values of a and b calculated in excess yield form with those calculated initially. Can you suggest any generalizations about the relative magnitudes of the a or the b values?

22-5 Given the following information

Period	Market Return	RF	Portfolio 1	Portfolio 2
1	0.12	.07	0.14	0.16
2	0.10	.07	0.18	0.20
3	0.02	.08	0.06	0.04
4	0.20	.08	0.30	0.26
5	0.16	.07	0.21	0.21
6	−0.03	.08	−0.04	−0.06
7	−0.05	.07	−0.04	−0.01
8	0.13	.07	0.14	0.12
9	0.30	.08	0.28	0.32
10	−0.15	.09	−0.20	−0.25

(a) Rank the portfolios on RVAR.
(b) Rank the portfolios on RVOL.
(c) Rank the portfolios on alpha.
(d) Which portfolio had the smaller unsystematic risk?
(e) Which portfolio had the larger beta?

(f) Which portfolio had the larger standard deviation?
(g) Which portfolio had the larger average return?
(h) How are the answers to (f) and (g) related to the results for the composite performance measures?

22-6 Given the following information for three portfolios for a six-year period

Period	Market Return	RF	Portfolio 1	Portfolio 2	Portfolio 3
1	0.10	.05	0.15	0.16	0.17
2	0.02	.06	0.09	0.11	0.13
3	0.20	.08	0.26	0.28	0.18
4	0.30	.09	0.34	0.36	0.42
5	−0.04	.08	−0.02	−0.03	−0.16
6	0.16	.07	0.16	0.17	0.17

Answer (a) through (d) without doing the calculations.
(a) Which portfolio would you expect to have the largest beta?
(b) Which portfolio would you expect to have the largest standard deviation?
(c) Which portfolio would you expect to have the largest R^2?
(d) Which portfolio would you expect to rank first on the basis of RVAR?
(e) Using *The Investment Calculator,* determine the rankings of the three portfolios on RVAR and RVOL.
(f) Which portfolio had the largest alpha?
(g) Which portfolio exhibited the best performance based on the composite measures of performance?

22-7 The following information is available for two portfolios, a market index, and the risk-free rate:

Period	Market Return	RF	Portfolio 1	Portfolio 2
1	0.10	.06	0.10	0.20
2	0.12	.08	0.12	0.24
3	0.20	.08	0.20	0.40
4	0.04	.08	0.04	0.08
5	0.12	.08	0.12	0.24

(a) Without doing calculations, determine the portfolio with a beta of 1.0.
(b) Without doing calculations, determine the beta of portfolio 2.
(c) Without doing calculations, determine the R^2 for each portfolio.
(d) Without doing calculations, what would you expect the alpha of portfolio 1 to be?
(e) What would you expect the RVAR and RVOL to be for portfolio 1 relative to the market?
(f) Verify your answers using *The Investment Calculator.*

Selected References

Some of the problems in performance measurement are discussed in

Ferguson, Robert. "The Trouble with Performance Measurement," *Journal of Portfolio Management*, Spring 1986, pp. 4–9.

A short discussion of performance measurement can be found in

Good, Walter. "Measuring Performance," *Financial Analysts Journal*, May–June 1983, pp. 19–23.

The relationships among the composite measures are explained in

Wilson, Jack, and Jones, Charles. "The Relationship Between Performance and Risk: Whence the Bias?" *The Journal of Financial Research*, Summer 1981, pp. 109–117.

GLOSSARY

A

Abnormal Return Return on a security beyond what would be expected on the basis of its risk.

Accrued Interest Interest that has accrued on a bond since the payment of the last coupon. The purchaser of a bond pays the accrued interest plus the market price.

Active Management Strategy A strategy designed to provide additional returns by active trading.

Allocationally Efficient A market that allocates resources to the most productive uses.

American Depository Receipts (ADRs) Securities representing an ownership interest in the equities of foreign companies. A bank holds the shares in trust and issues depository receipts to American shareholders of the foreign companies. ADRs trade much like other securities.

Arbitrage Pricing Model (APM) An equilibrium theory of expected returns for securities involving few assumptions about investor preferences. It requires a factor model.

Arbitragers Investors who seek discrepancies in security prices in an attempt to earn riskless returns.

Asked Price The price at which the specialist or dealer offers to sell shares.

Association for Investment Management and Research (AIMR) A new organization combining the Institute of Chartered Financial Analysts and the Financial Analysts Federation.

Auction Market A securities market such as the New York Stock Exchange where the prices of securities are determined by the actions of buyers and sellers transacting at a specified location.

B

Bar Chart A chart that is plotted with price on the vertical axis and time on the horizontal axis and that shows each day's price movements. It is probably the most popular chart in technical analysis.

Basis With futures contracts, the difference between the price of the item being hedged (the cash contract) and the price of the futures contract used to hedge it.

Bear market A period of time (usually months) during which measures of the stock market decline.

Beta A measure of volatility, or relative systematic risk, for stock or portfolio returns. Typically found by regressing stock (or portfolio) returns on a market proxy such as the S&P 500.

Bid Price The price at which the specialist or dealer offers to buy shares.

Black–Scholes Model A widely used model for the valuation of call options.

Blocks Transactions involving at least 10,000 shares.

Blue Chip Stocks Stocks of the highest quality, with long records of earnings and dividends—well-known, stable, mature companies.

Bond Long-term debt instrument representing a contractual obligation on the part of the issuer to pay interest and repay principal.

Bond Ratings Letters (e.g., AAA, AA, etc.) assigned to bonds to express their relative probability of default. Widely recognized ratings are done by Standard & Poor's and Moody's.

Bond Swaps An active bond management strategy involving the purchase and sale of bonds in an attempt to improve the rate of return on the bond portfolio. There are several different types of bond swaps.

Book Value The value of a corporation's equity as shown on the books (i.e., balance sheet).

Broker An intermediary who represents either a buyer or a seller in securities transactions and receives a commission. Commission brokers do not take a position in the security.

Bull Market A period of time (usually months) during which measures of the stock market rises.

Business Cycle A period of time during which the aggregate economic activity changes.

Business Risk The risk of a company suffering losses, or profits less than those expected, for some time period because of adverse circumstances in that company's line of activity.

C

Call An option to buy stock at a stated price within a specified period of time.

Call Provision Gives the issuer the right to call in a security and retire it by paying off the obligation.

Capital Asset Pricing Model (CAPM) A model that relates the required rate of return for any security to the risk for that security as measured by beta.

Capital Gain The amount by which the sale price of a security exceeds the purchase price.

Capital Loss The amount by which the sale price of a capital asset is less than its purchase price.

Capital Market The market for long-term securities such as bonds and stocks.

Capital Market Line (CML) The trade-off between expected return and risk for efficient portfolios.

Capital Market Theory A theory that describes the pricing of capital assets in the marketplace.

Cash Account An account in which a customer can make only cash transactions. This is the most common type of brokerage account.

Certificates of Deposit (1) If negotiable, a marketable short-term deposit liability of the issuer that pays a principal (a minimum of $100,000) plus interest at maturity; (2) if nonnegotiable, savings certificates with varying maturities and interest rates.

Chartered Financial Analyst (CFA) A designation for investment professionals signifying the successful completion of three levels of examinations.

Charting The classical technical analysis technique of charting security price trends in order to detect patterns in price movements.

Closed-End Investment Company An investment company with a fixed capitalization whose shares trade on exchanges and over the counter.

Coefficient of Determination The square of the correlation coefficient, measuring the percentage of the variance in the dependent variable that is accounted for by the independent variable.

Collateralized Mortgage Obligations (CMOs) Bonds backed by a trust created to hold Ginnie Mae and other government-guaranteed mortgages. CMOs are issued by brokerage firms.

Composite Indexes of General Economic Activity A series of leading, coincident, and lagging indicators of economic activity that help to assess the status of the business cycle.

Composite (Risk-Adjusted) Measure of Portfolio Performance Portfolio performance measures combining return and risk into one calculation.

Compustat A major computerized source of balance sheet and income statement data about firms.

Constant Growth Model A version of the dividend discount model that assumes that dividends are expected to grow at a constant rate over time. It can be used to solve for the current price of a stock.

Contrary Opinion The idea of trading opposite the majority of investors, who supposedly always lose; to go against the crowd.

Conversion Feature The characteristic of a bond or preferred stock that allows it to be converted into common stock at the option of the convertible security holder.

Conversion Premium With convertible securities, the dollar difference between the market price of the security and its conversion value.

Conversion Price The par value of a bond or preferred stock divided by the conversion ratio.

Conversion Ratio The number of shares of common stock that the owner of a convertible security receives upon conversion.

Conversion Value A convertible security's value based on the current price of the common stock.

Convertible Securities Bonds or preferred stock that are convertible, at the holder's option, into shares of common stock of the same corporation.

Corporate Bonds Long-term debt securities of various types sold by corporations.

Correlation Coefficient A statistical measure of the extent to which two variables are associated. This coefficient ranges from +1.0 (perfect positive correlation) to -1.0 (perfect negative or inverse correlation), with 0.0 being no correlation.

Coupon The dollar interest payment on a bond, equal to the coupon rate multiplied by the face value of $1000.

Coupon Bond Coupon refers to the periodic interest payments paid by the issuer to the bondholders. Most bonds are coupon bonds.

Covariance An absolute measure of the extent to which two variables tend to covary, or move together.

Currency Risk The risk of adverse fluctuations in the relative value of one currency to another.

Current Yield The yield on a security resulting from dividing the interest payment or dividend by the current market price.

Cyclical Industries Industries that usually do well when the economy prospers and that are likely to be hurt when it falters.

D

Dealer An individual (or firm) who buys and sells securities for his or her own account. Dealers in OTC securities profit by the spread between the bid and asked prices.

Debenture An unsecured bond, backed by the general credit of a company.

Differential Return Measure (Alpha) Jensen's measure of portfolio performance. It is the difference between what the portfolio actually earned and what it was expected to earn given its level of systematic risk.

Discount The amount by which a bond or preferred stock sells below its par or face value. For closed-end investment companies, the amount by which the net asset value exceeds the current market price.

Discount Broker Brokerage firms offering execution services at prices typically less than those of full-line brokerage firms.

Dividends The only cash payments regularly made by corporations to their stockholders.

Dividend Discount Model (DDM) A widely used model to value common stocks. This model states that the current price of a stock is equal to the discounted value of all future dividends.

Dividend Yield The dollar dividend on an equity security divided by the market price.

Dow Jones Industrial Average (DJIA) A price-weighted series of 30 leading industrial stocks, used as a measure of stock market activity.

Dow Theory The oldest theory of technical analysis, based on three types of price movements—primary, secondary, and daily.

Duration A measure of a bond's lifetime, stated in years, that accounts for the entire pattern (both size and timing) of the cash flows over the life of the bond.

E

EAFE Index The Europe, Australia, and Far East Index, a value-weighted index of the equity performance of major foreign markets.

E/P Ratio A capitalization rate used to capitalize earnings—the reciprocal of the P/E ratio.

Earnings Multiplier The P/E ratio approach, which states that the price of a stock is equal to the product of its earnings and a multiplier.

Earnings Per Share (EPS) The net income of a corporation divided by the common shares outstanding.

Efficient Market A market in which the prices of securities fully reflect all known information quickly and, on average, accurately.

Efficient Market Hypothesis (EMH) The idea that securities markets are efficient, with the prices of securities reflecting their economic value. This hypothesis is typically broken into the weak, semistrong, and strong forms.

Efficient Portfolio A portfolio that has the largest expected return for a given level of risk or the smallest risk for a given level of expected return.

Efficient Set (Frontier) The set of portfolios generated by the Markowitz portfolio model. These portfolios have the maximum expected return for a given level of risk, or the minimum risk for a given level of expected return.

Equity-Derivative Securities Securities that derive their value in whole or in part by having a claim on the underlying common stock. Examples include options, warrants, and convertibles.

Equity Risk Premium The difference between the return on common stocks and the return on riskless assets (e.g., Treasury bills). It is the additional compensation, over and above the riskless rate of return, for assuming the risk of common stocks.

Equity Securities The nondebt securities of a corporation representing the ownership interest. Includes both preferred and common stock.

Event Study An empirical analysis of stock price behavior surrounding a particular event.

Ex Ante Before the fact—what is expected to occur.

Ex Post After the fact—what has occurred.

Excess Return Return on a security above that of the overall market for the same time period.

Exercise (Strike) Price The per-share price at which the common stock may be purchased (in the case of a call) or sold to a writer (in the case of a put).

Expectations Theory One theory of the term structure of interest rates. It states that the long-term rate of interest is equal to an average of the short-term rates that are expected to prevail over the long-term period.

Expected Return The ex ante return expected by investors over some future holding period. The expected return often differs from the realized return.

Expected Value The weighted average return of a probability distribution, given the likely outcomes and their associated probabilities.

Expiration Date With options, the last date at which an option can be exercised.

Extended Diversification Diversification of a portfolio into real assets, such as real estate and metals.

F

Factor Model Used to depict the behavior of security prices by identifying major factors in the economy that affect large numbers of securities.

Federal Agency Securities Securities issued by federal credit agencies. Federal agency securities are fully guaranteed whereas government-sponsored-agency securities are not.

Filter Rule A well-known technical trading rule specifying a breakpoint for an individual stock or market average. Trades are made when the price change is greater than this filter.

Financial Assets Pieces of paper evidencing a claim on some issuer.

Financial Futures Futures contracts on financial assets such as Treasury bonds, CDs, and stock indexes.

Financial Risk Risk arising from the use of debt in financing the assets of a firm.

Financial Statements The major financial data provided by a corporation, primarily the balance sheet and the income statement.

Fixed-Income Securities Securities with specified payment dates and amounts, primarily bonds and preferred stock.

Floor Value The minimum value for a convertible security.

Forward Contract A contract negotiated currently providing for the exchange, at a future delivery date, of a specified amount of goods for a specified price.

Fourth Market A communications network linking large institutional investors.

Fundamental Analysis The idea that a security has an intrinsic value at any time that is a function of underlying economic variables. Intrinsic value can be estimated by analyzing these variables.

Futures Contracts Agreements providing for the future exchange of a particular asset at a currently determined market price.

Futures Margin The good-faith deposit made by a transactor to ensure the completion of a futures contract.

Futures Markets The organized markets for the trading of futures contracts.

Futures Options Option contracts (both puts and calls) on both interest futures and stock index futures.

Future Value Also referred to as compound value. The terminal value of a beginning amount of money compounded at some interest rate for some period of time.

G

Generally Accepted Accounting Principles (GAAPs) A standard set of rules developed by the accounting profession for the preparation of financial statements.

Geometric Mean The *n*th root of the product of *n* numbers. It is used as a measure of the compound rate of return over time.

GNMA Pass-Through Certificates A federal agency security that monthly passes through the principal and interest payments on the underlying mortgages to the bondholder as the mortgages are repaid.

H

Hedge Ratio The ratio of options written to shares of stock held long in a riskless portfolio.

Hedgers Investors who attempt to minimize the risk of financial loss from adverse price changes by assuming futures positions opposite to cash positions.

Horizon Analysis A form of interest rate forecasting involving the projection of bond performance over a planned investment horizon.

I

Immunization The strategy of immunizing (protecting) a portfolio against interest rate risk by canceling out its two components, price risk and reinvestment rate risk.

Index Funds Mutual funds holding portfolios that attempt to duplicate a market average such as the S&P 500.

Indirect Investing The buying and selling of the shares of investment companies that, in turn, hold portfolios of securities. This is an investor alternative to direct investing.

Individual Retirement Accounts (IRAs) Tax-sheltered accounts available to all income earners. IRA funds can be invested in a wide range of assets.

Industry Life Cycle The evolvement of industries through stages, including the pioneering, expansion, and stabilization stages.

In the Money Denoting an option currently worth exercising.

Instinet An electronic trading network, part of the fourth market.

Institutional Investors Pension funds, investment companies, bank trust departments, life insurance companies, and so forth, all of whom manage large portfolios of securities.

Interest Rate Futures Futures contracts on fixed-income securities such as Treasury bills and bonds, CDs, and GNMA mortgages.

Interest on Interest The process by which bond coupons are reinvested to earn interest, thereby generating interest on interest.

Interest Rate Options Option contracts on fixed-income securities such as Treasury bonds.

Interest Rate Risk The change in the price of a security resulting from a change in market interest rates.

Interest Sensitive Particularly sensitive to expectations about changes in interest rates.

Intermarket Trading System (ITS) A form of a central routing system, consisting of a network of terminals linking together several stock exchanges.

Intrinsic Value The economic value of an asset.

Investment The commitment of funds to one or more assets that will be held over some future time period.

Investment Banking Firm Firms specializing in the sale of new securities to the public, typically by underwriting the issue.

Investment Company A financial service organization that sells shares in itself to the public and uses these funds to invest in a portfolio of securities.

Investments The study of the investment process.

Investment Value (IV) The straight-debt value of a convertible bond.

J

January Effect The observed tendency for stock returns to be higher in January than would be expected.

Junk Bond Bonds that carry ratings of BB or lower, with correspondingly higher yields. The junk bond market is perhaps better referred to as the "high-yield debt market."

L

Leverage The magnification of gains and losses in earnings resulting from the use of fixed-cost financing.

Limit Order An order to buy or sell at a specified (or better) price.

Liquidity The ease with which an asset can be bought or sold quickly with relatively small price changes.

Liquidity Preference Theory One of the theories of the term structure of interest rates. It states that interest rates reflect the sum of current and expected short rates, as in the expectations theory, plus liquidity (risk) premiums.

Load Funds Mutual funds with a sales charge, ranging up to 8.5%.

M

Margin The part of a transaction's value that a customer must pay to initiate the transaction, with the other part being borrowed from the broker. The initial margin is set by the Federal Reserve System. The maintenance margin is the amount, established by brokers and exchanges, below which the actual margin cannot go.

Margin Account An account that permits margin trading, requiring $2000 to open.

Margin Call A demand from the broker for additional cash or securities as a result of the actual margin declining below the maintenance margin.

Marked to the Market The daily process of debiting and crediting gains and losses resulting from changes in future prices.

Market Anomalies Techniques or strategies that appear to be contrary to an efficient market. These anomalies include SUE, the low-P/E strategy, the size effect, and the seasonal effect.

Market Average An arithmetic average of the prices for the sample of securities being used.

Market Data Primarily, stock price and volume data.

Market Index Measures the current price behavior of a sample of stocks in relation to a base period established for a previous time.

Market Model Relates the return on each stock to the return on the market, using a linear relationship with intercept and slope.

Market Order An order to buy or sell at the best price when the order reaches the trading floor.

Market Portfolio The portfolio of all risky assets, with each asset weighted by the ratio of its market value to the market value of all risky assets.

Market Risk The risk to common stocks resulting from a decline in the overall stock market (as measured, for example, by the S&P 500).

Market Risk Premium The difference between the expected return for the market and the risk-free rate of return.

Market Segmentation Theory One of three hypotheses for explaining the term structure of interest rates. It states that rates on securities with different maturities are effectively determined by the conditions that prevail in the different maturity segments of the market.

Market Value The market value of one share of stock is the current market price; for the corporation, it equals market price per share multiplied by the number of shares outstanding.

Marketable Securities Financial assets that are easily and inexpensively traded between investors.

Modified Duration Duration divided by 1 + yield to maturity.

Money Market The market for short-term, highly liquid, low-risk assets such as Treasury bills and negotiable CDs.

Money Market Deposit Accounts (MMDAs) Accounts at banks and thrift institutions with no interest rate ceilings.

Money Market Fund A mutual fund that invests in money market instruments.

Money Market Securities Securities sold in the money market, including Treasury bills, CDs, commercial paper, bankers' acceptances, and so forth.

Mortgage-Backed Securities Securities representing an investment in an underlying pool of mortgages.

Mortgage Bond A bond secured by a claim on real assets.

Municipal Securities Securities issued by political entities other than the federal government and its agencies, such as states and cities and airport authorities.

Mutual Funds The popular name for open-end-investment companies. A mutual fund continually sells and redeems its own shares.

N

NASDAQ The automated quotation system for the OTC market, showing current bid and asked prices for thousands of stocks.

NASDAQ National Market System (NASDAQ/NMS) A combination of the competing market markers in OTC stocks and the up-to-the-minute reporting of trades using data almost identical to that shown for the NYSE and AMEX.

National Association of Securities Dealers (NASD) A self-regulating body of brokers and dealers overseeing OTC practices.

National Market System (NMS) The market system for U.S. securities called for, but left undefined, by the Securities Acts Amendments of 1975.

Negotiated Market A market involving dealers, such as the OTC.

Net Asset Value (NAV) The per share value of an investment company, based on its portfolio. It is equal to the market value of the portfolio held by the company divided by the number of its shares outstanding.

New York Stock Exchange (NYSE) The major secondary market for the trading of equity securities.

No Load Funds Mutual funds that do not have a sales charge (load fee).

NOW (Negotiable Order of Withdrawal) Accounts Checking accounts that pay interest at a specified interest rate.

NYSE Rule 390 This rule states that members must obtain NYSE permission before transacting off the exchange in a listed stock (unless exempted specifically by the exchange).

O

Odd-Lot Theory The idea that small investors who often transact in odd lots (i.e., less than 100 shares) are unsophisticated and usually wrong in their actions.

Offset The typical method of closing out a futures contract by taking a position opposite to that initially taken.

Open-End Investment Company An investment company whose capitalization constantly changes as new shares are sold and outstanding shares are redeemed.

Operationally Efficient Referring to a market with the lowest possible prices for transaction services.

Open Interest In the futures market, the number of contracts currently outstanding on a commodity or financial future.

Options Calls (puts) give the holder the right to buy (sell) 100 shares of stock within a specified period at a specified price.

Options Clearing Corporation (OCC) An organization that stands between buyers and sellers of options to ensure fulfillment of obligations.

Out of the Money Denoting options currently not worth exercising.

Over-the-Counter (OTC) Market A network of securities dealers for the trading of unlisted securities.

P

P/E Ratio (Multiplier) The ratio of stock price to earnings, using historical, current, or estimated data. This ratio is also referred to as the multiplier.

Par Value The value assigned to a security when it is issued. For bonds and preferred stock, par value is equivalent to face value. For common stocks, par value is arbitrary and of little importance.

Passive Management Strategy A strategy whereby investors do not actively seek out trading possibilities in an attempt to outperform the market.

Payout Ratio The ratio of dividends to earnings.

Point-and-Figure Chart A technical analysis chart that shows only significant price changes and does not show volume.

Portfolio The securities held by an investor taken as a group.

Portfolio Insurance An asset management technique designed to provide a portfolio with a lower limit on value while permitting it to benefit from rising security prices. The basic concept involves the purchase of a "protective put" on the portfolio, with the balance of the funds invested in the underlying assets.

Portfolio Management The second step in the investment decision process, involving the management of a group of assets (i.e., a portfolio) as a unit.

Preferred Stock An equity security with an intermediate claim (between the bondholders and the stockholders) on a firm's assets and earnings. Dividends are specified, but can be omitted.

Premium The amount by which a bond or preferred stock exceeds its par or face value. For closed-end investment companies, the amount by which the current market price exceeds the net asset value. In the case of options, the price paid by the option buyer to the seller of the option.

Present Value The discounted value of a future cash flow.

Price to Book Value The ratio of price to stockholders' equity as measured on the balance sheet.

Price Risk That part of interest rate risk involving the inverse relationship between bond prices and required rates of return.

Price/Sales Ratio (PSR) The ratio of a company's total market value to its sales. It indicates what the market is willing to pay for a company's revenues.

Primary Market The market for new issues of securities, typically involving investment bankers.

Private Placement The sale of an issue of securities to an institutional investor.

Program Trading Trading that uses computer-generated orders to buy and sell securities based on arbitrage opportunities between common stocks and index futures and options.

Prospectus A document that provides information about an initial public offering of securities to potential buyers.

Pure Intermediary An organization providing services for its clientele that they could provide for themselves (e.g., investment companies).

Put An option to sell a specified number of shares of stock at a specified price within a specified period of time.

Put–Call Parity The formal relationship between a call and a put on the same item that must hold if no arbitrage is to occur.

Put/Call Ratio The ratio of puts purchased to calls purchased, used as a technical indicator.

R

Real Assets Physical assets, such as gold or real estate.

Real Estate Investment Trusts (REITs) An organization similar to a mutual fund designed to hold a portfolio of real estate–related investments.

Real Rate of Interest The marginal physical productivity of capital, or the opportunity cost of foregoing consumption. It is the basic component of market interest rates.

Realized Compound Yield The rate of return actually earned on a bond, given the reinvestment of the coupons at varying rates.

Reinvestment Rate Risk That part of interest rate risk resulting from uncertainty about the rate at which future interest coupons can be reinvested.

Relative Strength A technical analysis technique involving the ratio of a stock's price to a market index or other index. These ratios are plotted across time to form a graph of relative prices.

Required Rate of Return The minimum expected return on an asset that an investor requires before investing.

Resistance Level The level of price at which a technician expects a significant increase in the supply of a stock.

Restricted Account A margin account where the actual margin is between the initial margin and the maintenance margin. Additional margin purchases are prohibited.

Retention Rate 1.0 minus the payout ratio.

Return on Assets (ROA) A fundamental measure of a firm's profitability, equal to net income divided by total assets.

Return on Equity (ROE) The rate of return on stockholders' equity, equal to net income divided by equity.

Return Relative The total return from an investment for a given period of time, including both yield and capital gain or loss. RRs are stated on the basis of 1.0, which represents no gain or loss.

Reward-to-Variability Ratio Sharpe's measure of portfolio performance. This is the ratio of excess portfolio return (i.e., return minus the risk-free rate) to risk as measured by the standard deviation.

Reward-to-Volatility Ratio Treynor's measure of portfolio performance. It is the ratio of excess portfolio return (i.e., return minus the risk-free rate) to risk as measured by beta.

Rights A short-term (weeks) option permitting the holder to purchase from the corporation a specified number of shares of a new issue of common stock at a specified subscription price.

Risk The chance that the actual return on an investment will be different from the expected return.

Risk-Averse Investor An investor who will not assume a given level of risk unless there is an expectation of adequate compensation for having done so.

Risk-Free Asset An asset with a certain expected return and a variance of return of zero.

Risk-Free Rate of Return The return on a riskless asset, often proxied by the rate of return on Treasury securities.

Risk Premium The additional compensation demanded by investors, above the risk-free rate of return, for assuming risk. The larger the risk, the larger the risk premium.

S

Secondary Market The market where previously issued securities are traded, including both the organized exchanges and the OTC.

Securities and Exchange Commission (SEC) A federal government agency established by the Securities Exchange Act of 1934 to protect investors.

Security Analysis The first part of the investment decision process, involving the valuation and analysis of individual securities.

Security Market Line (SML) An alternative name for the CAPM (see Capital Asset Pricing Model).

Semistrong Form The part of the Efficient Market Hypothesis that states that prices reflect all publicly available information.

Senior Securities Securities ahead of common stock in terms of payment or in case of liquidation; typically, debt securities.

Separation Theorem The idea that the investment decision (which portfolio of risky assets to hold) is separate from the financing decision (how to allocate investable funds between the risk-free asset and the risky asset).

Serial Bonds Bonds that mature at specified stated intervals.

Shelf Rule A rule that permits qualified companies to file a short-form registration and to "place on the shelf" securities to be sold over time under favorable conditions.

Short Interest Ratio A technical analysis indicator used primarily in aggregate market analysis. It is calculated as the ratio of total shares sold short to average daily trading volume.

Short Sale The sale of a stock not owned in order to take advantage of an expected decline in the price of the stock. If the decline occurs, a profit will result when the stock is purchased and the short position is closed.

Single Index Model A model that relates returns on each security to the returns on a market index.

Sinking Fund A fund that provides for the orderly retirement of a bond issue during its life.

Size Effect The observed tendency for smaller firms to have higher stock returns than large firms.

Specialist A member of an organized exchange who is charged with maintaining an orderly market in one or more stocks by buying or selling for his or her own account. The specialist also acts as a broker's broker, executing limit orders for brokers.

Speculative Premium The difference between an option's price and its intrinsic value, reflecting what investors are willing to pay to speculate on future price changes.

Spread The purchase and sale of an equivalent option varying in only one respect, such as time or price.

Standard Deviation A measure of the dispersion of outcomes around the mean (or expected value), used to measure total risk. It is the square root of the variance.

Standard Industrial Classification (SIC) System A system based on Census data used to classify industries on the basis of what the firms produce.

S&P 500 Composite Index (S&P 500) Market value index of stock market activity, with a base of 10 (1941–1943). The S&P Composite Index is a broad and well-known measure of market activity, often used by institutional investors to measure portfolio performance.

Standardized Unexpected Earnings (SUE) A variable used in the selection of common stocks. It is calculated by subtracting expected earnings from actual earnings and dividing the result by the standard error of the regression equation used to estimate the expected earnings.

Stock Dividend A payment by the corporation in shares of stock rather than cash.

Stock Index Futures Futures contracts on stock indexes, including the S&P 500, the NYSE Index, and the Value Line Index.

Stock Index Options Option contracts on a stock market index such as the S&P 500.

Stock Split The issuance by a corporation of a large number of shares of stock in proportion to the existing shares outstanding. A split changes the book value and the par value.

Stop Order An order specifying a certain price at which a market order takes effect.

Straddle A combination of a put and a call on the same stock with the same exercise date and exercise price.

Street Name A designation for an account in which customers' securities are held by a brokerage firm in its name. Customers often leave securities with their brokers for safekeeping.

Strong Form That part of the Efficient Market Hypothesis that states that prices reflect all information, public and private.

Super NOW Account An unrestricted checking account paying money-market rates.

Support Level The level of price at which a technician expects a significant decrease in the supply of a stock.

Syndicate Several investment bankers involved in an underwriting.

Syndicated Offering The sale of a new issue of securities through investment bankers.

Systematic Risk Risk attributable to factors affecting all investments. Also called market risk or nondiversifiable risk.

Systematic (Market) Risk That part of total risk attributable to the market itself.

T

Technical Analysis The methodology of forecasting fluctuations in the prices of securities, whether individual securities or the market as a whole.

Term Structure of Interest Rates Refers to the relationship between time to maturity and yields for a particular category of bonds.

Term to Maturity The remaining life of a bond.

Theoretical (Calculated) Value of a Warrant A formula value for a warrant that produces its intrinsic value. Warrants typically sell above this value.

TIGRs (Tigers) Fixed-income receipts sold at discount (by Merrill Lynch) and backed by U.S. Treasury bonds.

Third Market An OTC market for exchange-listed securities.

Total Return The total return from an investment for a given period of time, including both yield and capital gain or loss. It is stated in percent form.

Treasury Bill A short-term money market instrument sold at discount by the U. S. government.

Treasury Bond Long-term bonds sold by the U.S. government.

U

Unbundle To separate brokerage charges so that customers pay only for those services desired, such as execution services.

Underwriting The process by which investment bankers purchase an issue of securities from an issuer and resell it to the public.

Unlisted Security A security not listed on one of the exchanges.

Unsystematic Risk Also called nonmarket risk or diversifiable risk. It is risk attributable to factors unique to the security.

Unsystematic (Nonmarket) Risk Risk attributable to a security independent of the overall market.

V

Variability Dispersion in the likely outcomes.

Volatility Fluctuations in a security's or portfolio's return.

W

Warrant A corporate-created option to purchase a stated number of common shares at a specified price within a specified time (typically several years).

Weak Form That part of the Efficient Market Hypothesis that states that prices reflect all price and volume data.

Wealth The sum of current income and the present value of all future income.

"Wrap" Account A new type of brokerage account where all costs are wrapped in one fee—the cost of the broker-consultant, the money manager, and transactions costs.

Y

Yield The income return on a security.

Yield Curve A graphical depiction of the relationship between yields and time for bonds that are identical except for maturity.

Yield Spreads The relationship between bond yields and the particular features on various bonds such as quality, callability, and taxes.

Yield to Call A better measure than yield to maturity for bonds likely to be called, using as the time element the end of the deferred call period rather than term to maturity.

Yield to Maturity (YTM) The indicated (promised) compounded rate of return an investor will receive from a bond purchased at the current market price and held to maturity.

Z

Zero-Coupon Bond A bond sold with no coupons. It is purchased at a discount and redeemed for face value at maturity.

INTEREST TABLES

TABLE A–1 Compound (Future) Value Factors for $1 Compounded at R Percent for N Periods

	R =												
N	1%	2%	3%	4%	5%	6%	7%	8%	9%	10%	11%	12%	13%
1	1.01	1.02	1.03	1.04	1.05	1.06	1.07	1.08	1.09	1.1	1.11	1.12	1.13
2	1.02	1.04	1.061	1.082	1.103	1.124	1.145	1.166	1.188	1.21	1.232	1.254	1.277
3	1.03	1.061	1.093	1.125	1.158	1.191	1.225	1.26	1.295	1.331	1.368	1.405	1.443
4	1.041	1.082	1.126	1.17	1.216	1.262	1.311	1.36	1.412	1.464	1.518	1.574	1.63
5	1.051	1.104	1.159	1.217	1.276	1.338	1.403	1.469	1.539	1.611	1.685	1.762	1.842
6	1.062	1.126	1.194	1.265	1.34	1.419	1.501	1.587	1.677	1.772	1.87	1.974	2.082
7	1.072	1.149	1.23	1.316	1.407	1.504	1.606	1.714	1.828	1.949	2.076	2.211	2.353
8	1.083	1.172	1.267	1.369	1.477	1.594	1.718	1.851	1.993	2.144	2.305	2.476	2.658
9	1.094	1.195	1.305	1.423	1.551	1.689	1.838	1.999	2.172	2.358	2.558	2.773	3.004
10	1.105	1.219	1.344	1.48	1.629	1.791	1.967	2.159	2.367	2.594	2.839	3.106	3.395
11	1.116	1.243	1.384	1.539	1.71	1.898	2.105	2.332	2.58	2.853	3.152	3.479	3.836
12	1.127	1.268	1.426	1.601	1.796	2.012	2.252	2.518	2.813	3.138	3.498	3.896	4.335
13	1.138	1.294	1.469	1.665	1.886	2.133	2.41	2.72	3.066	3.452	3.883	4.363	4.898
14	1.149	1.319	1.513	1.732	1.98	2.261	2.579	2.937	3.342	3.797	4.31	4.887	5.535
15	1.161	1.346	1.558	1.801	2.079	2.397	2.759	3.172	3.642	4.177	4.785	5.474	6.254
16	1.173	1.373	1.605	1.873	2.183	2.54	2.952	3.426	3.97	4.595	5.311	6.13	7.067
17	1.184	1.4	1.653	1.948	2.292	2.693	3.159	3.7	4.328	5.054	5.895	6.866	7.986
18	1.196	1.428	1.702	2.026	2.407	2.854	3.38	3.996	4.717	5.56	6.544	7.69	9.024
19	1.208	1.457	1.754	2.107	2.527	3.026	3.617	4.316	5.142	6.116	7.263	8.613	10.197
20	1.22	1.486	1.806	2.191	2.653	3.207	3.87	4.661	5.604	6.727	8.062	9.646	11.523
21	1.232	1.516	1.86	2.279	2.786	3.4	4.141	5.034	6.109	7.4	8.949	10.804	13.021
22	1.245	1.546	1.916	2.37	2.925	3.604	4.43	5.437	6.659	8.14	9.934	12.1	14.714
23	1.257	1.577	1.974	2.465	3.072	3.82	4.741	5.871	7.258	8.954	11.026	13.552	16.627
24	1.27	1.608	2.033	2.563	3.225	4.049	5.072	6.341	7.911	9.85	12.239	15.179	18.788
25	1.282	1.641	2.094	2.666	3.386	4.292	5.427	6.848	8.623	10.835	13.585	17	21.231
30	1.348	1.811	2.427	3.243	4.322	5.743	7.612	10.063	13.268	17.449	22.892	29.96	39.116
35	1.417	2	2.814	3.946	5.516	7.686	10.677	14.785	20.414	28.102	38.575	52.8	72.069
40	1.489	2.208	3.262	4.801	7.04	10.286	14.974	21.725	31.409	45.259	65.001	93.051	132.782
45	1.565	2.438	3.782	5.841	8.985	13.765	21.002	31.92	48.327	72.89	109.53	163.98	244.641
50	1.645	2.692	4.384	7.107	11.467	18.42	29.457	46.902	74.358	117.39	184.56	289.00	450.736

TABLE A–1 Compound (Future) Value Factors for $1 Compounded at R Percent for N Periods

	R =												
N	14%	15%	16%	18%	20%	22%	24%	25%	30%	35%	40%	45%	50%
1	1.14	1.15	1.16	1.18	1.2	1.22	1.24	1.25	1.3	1.35	1.4	1.45	1.5
2	1.3	1.323	1.346	1.392	1.44	1.488	1.538	1.563	1.69	1.823	1.96	2.103	2.25
3	1.482	1.521	1.561	1.643	1.728	1.816	1.907	1.953	2.197	2.46	2.744	3.049	3.375
4	1.689	1.749	1.811	1.939	2.074	2.215	2.364	2.441	2.856	3.322	3.842	4.421	5.063
5	1.925	2.011	2.1	2.288	2.488	2.703	2.932	3.052	3.713	4.484	5.378	6.41	7.594
6	2.195	2.313	2.436	2.7	2.986	3.297	3.635	3.815	4.827	6.053	7.53	9.294	11.391
7	2.502	2.66	2.826	3.185	3.583	4.023	4.508	4.768	6.275	8.172	10.541	13.476	17.086
8	2.853	3.059	3.278	3.759	4.3	4.908	5.59	5.96	8.157	11.032	14.758	19.541	25.629
9	3.252	3.518	3.803	4.435	5.16	5.987	6.931	7.451	10.604	14.894	20.661	28.334	38.443
10	3.707	4.046	4.411	5.234	6.192	7.305	8.594	9.313	13.786	20.107	28.925	41.085	57.665
11	4.226	4.652	5.117	6.176	7.43	8.912	10.657	11.642	17.922	27.144	40.496	59.573	86.498
12	4.818	5.35	5.936	7.288	8.916	10.872	13.215	14.552	23.298	36.644	56.694	86.381	129.746
13	5.492	6.153	6.886	8.599	10.699	13.264	16.386	18.19	30.288	49.47	79.371	125.25	194.62
14	6.261	7.076	7.988	10.147	12.839	16.182	20.319	22.737	39.374	66.784	111.12	181.61	291.929
15	7.138	8.137	9.266	11.974	15.407	19.742	25.196	28.422	51.186	90.158	155.56	263.34	437.894
16	8.137	9.358	10.748	14.129	18.488	24.086	31.243	35.527	66.542	121.71	217.79	381.84	656.841
17	9.276	10.761	12.468	16.672	22.186	29.384	38.741	44.409	86.504	164.31	304.91	553.67	985.261
18	10.575	12.375	14.463	19.673	26.623	35.849	48.039	55.511	112.45	221.82	426.87	802.83	1477.892
19	12.056	14.232	16.777	23.214	31.948	43.736	59.568	69.389	146.19	299.46	597.63	1164.1	2216.838
20	13.743	16.367	19.461	27.393	38.338	53.358	73.864	86.736	190.05	404.27	836.68	1687.9	3325.257
21	15.668	18.822	22.574	32.324	46.005	65.096	91.592	108.42	247.06	545.76	1171.3	2447.5	4987.885
22	17.861	21.645	26.186	38.142	55.206	79.418	113.57	135.52	321.18	736.78	1639.8	3548.9	7481.828
23	20.362	24.891	30.376	45.008	66.247	96.889	140.83	169.40	417.53	994.66	2295.8	5145.9	11222.74
24	23.212	28.625	35.236	53.109	79.497	118.20	174.63	211.75	542.80	1342.7	3214.2	7461.6	16834.11
25	26.462	32.919	40.874	62.669	95.396	144.21	216.54	264.69	705.64	1812.7	4499.8	10819.	25251.17
30	50.95	66.212	85.85	143.37	237.37	389.75	634.82	807.79	2619.9	8128.5	24201.	69348.	191751.1
35	98.1	133.17	180.31	327.99	590.66	1053.4	1861.0	2465.1	9727.8	36448.	130161	444508	.
40	188.88	267.86	378.72	750.37	1469.7	2847.0	5455.9	7523.1	36118.	163437	700037	.	.
45	363.67	538.76	795.44	1716.6	3657.2	7694.7	15994.	22958.	134106	732857	.	.	.
50	700.23	1083.6	1670.7	3927.3	9100.4	20796.	46890.	70064.	497929	.	.	.	.

TABLE A–2 Present Value Factors (at R Percent) for $1 Received at the End of N Periods

	R =												
N	1%	2%	3%	4%	5%	6%	7%	8%	9%	10%	11%	12%	13%
1	.990	.980	.971	.962	.952	.943	.935	.926	.917	.909	.901	.893	.885
2	.980	.961	.943	.925	.907	.890	.873	.857	.842	.826	.812	.797	.783
3	.971	.942	.915	.889	.864	.840	.816	.794	.772	.751	.731	.712	.693
4	.961	.924	.888	.855	.823	.792	.763	.735	.708	.683	.659	.636	.613
5	.951	.906	.863	.822	.784	.747	.713	.681	.650	.621	.593	.567	.543
6	.942	.888	.837	.790	.746	.705	.666	.630	.596	.564	.535	.507	.480
7	.933	.871	.813	.760	.711	.665	.623	.583	.547	.513	.482	.452	.425
8	.923	.853	.789	.731	.677	.627	.582	.540	.502	.467	.434	.404	.376
9	.914	.837	.766	.703	.645	.592	.544	.500	.460	.424	.391	.361	.333
10	.905	.820	.744	.676	.614	.558	.508	.463	.422	.386	.352	.322	.295
11	.896	.804	.722	.650	.585	.527	.475	.429	.388	.350	.317	.287	.261
12	.887	.788	.701	.625	.557	.497	.444	.397	.356	.319	.286	.257	.231
13	.879	.773	.681	.601	.530	.469	.415	.368	.326	.290	.258	.229	.204
14	.870	.758	.661	.577	.505	.442	.388	.340	.299	.263	.232	.205	.181
15	.861	.743	.642	.555	.481	.417	.362	.315	.275	.239	.209	.183	.160
16	.853	.728	.623	.534	.458	.394	.339	.292	.252	.218	.188	.163	.141
17	.844	.714	.605	.513	.436	.371	.317	.270	.231	.198	.170	.146	.125
18	.836	.700	.587	.494	.416	.350	.296	.250	.212	.180	.153	.130	.111
19	.828	.686	.570	.475	.396	.331	.277	.232	.194	.164	.138	.116	.098
20	.820	.673	.554	.456	.377	.312	.258	.215	.178	.149	.124	.104	.087
21	.811	.660	.538	.439	.359	.294	.242	.199	.164	.135	.112	.093	.077
22	.803	.647	.522	.422	.342	.278	.226	.184	.150	.123	.101	.083	.068
23	.795	.634	.507	.406	.326	.262	.211	.170	.138	.112	.091	.074	.060
24	.788	.622	.492	.390	.310	.247	.197	.158	.126	.102	.082	.066	.053
25	.780	.610	.478	.375	.295	.233	.184	.146	.116	.092	.074	.059	.047
30	.742	.552	.412	.308	.231	.174	.131	.099	.075	.057	.044	.033	.026
35	.706	.500	.355	.253	.181	.130	.094	.068	.049	.036	.026	.019	.014
40	.672	.453	.307	.208	.142	.097	.067	.046	.032	.022	.015	.011	.008
45	.639	.410	.264	.171	.111	.073	.048	.031	.021	.014	.009	.006	.004
50	.608	.372	.228	.141	.087	.054	.034	.021	.013	.009	.005	.003	.002

TABLE A–2 Present Value Factors (at R Percent) for $1 Received at the End of N Periods

	R =												
N	14%	15%	16%	18%	20%	22%	24%	25%	30%	35%	40%	45%	50%
1	.877	.870	.862	.847	.833	.820	.806	.800	.769	.741	.714	.690	.667
2	.769	.756	.743	.718	.694	.672	.650	.640	.592	.549	.510	.476	.444
3	.675	.658	.641	.609	.579	.551	.524	.512	.455	.406	.364	.328	.296
4	.592	.572	.552	.516	.482	.451	.423	.410	.350	.301	.260	.226	.198
5	.519	.497	.476	.437	.402	.370	.341	.328	.269	.223	.186	.156	.132
6	.456	.432	.410	.370	.335	.303	.275	.262	.207	.165	.133	.108	.088
7	.400	.376	.354	.314	.279	.249	.222	.210	.159	.122	.095	.074	.059
8	.351	.327	.305	.266	.233	.204	.179	.168	.123	.091	.068	.051	.039
9	.308	.284	.263	.225	.194	.167	.144	.134	.094	.067	.048	.035	.026
10	.270	.247	.227	.191	.162	.137	.116	.107	.073	.050	.035	.024	.017
11	.237	.215	.195	.162	.135	.112	.094	.086	.056	.037	.025	.017	.012
12	.208	.187	.168	.137	.112	.092	.076	.069	.043	.027	.018	.012	.008
13	.182	.163	.145	.116	.093	.075	.061	.055	.033	.020	.013	.008	.005
14	.160	.141	.125	.099	.078	.062	.049	.044	.025	.015	.009	.006	.003
15	.140	.123	.108	.084	.065	.051	.040	.035	.020	.011	.006	.004	.002
16	.123	.107	.093	.071	.054	.042	.032	.028	.015	.008	.005	.003	.002
17	.108	.093	.080	.060	.045	.034	.026	.023	.012	.006	.003	.002	.001
18	.095	.081	.069	.051	.038	.028	.021	.018	.009	.005	.002	.001	.001
19	.083	.070	.060	.043	.031	.023	.017	.014	.007	.003	.002	.001	.
20	.073	.061	.051	.037	.026	.019	.014	.012	.005	.002	.001	.001	.
21	.064	.053	.044	.031	.022	.015	.011	.009	.004	.002	.001	.	.
22	.056	.046	.038	.026	.018	.013	.009	.007	.003	.001	.001	.	.
23	.049	.040	.033	.022	.015	.010	.007	.006	.002	.001	.	.	.
24	.043	.035	.028	.019	.013	.008	.006	.005	.002	.001	.	.	.
25	.038	.030	.024	.016	.010	.007	.005	.004	.001	.001	.	.	.
30	.020	.015	.012	.007	.004	.003	.002	.001	.	.	.	.	.
35	.010	.008	.006	.003	.002	.001	.001	.	.	.	.	.	.
40	.005	.004	.003	.001	.001	.	.	.	.	.	.	.	.
45	.003	.002	.001	.001	.	.	.	.	.	.	.	.	.
50	.001	.001	.001	.	.	.	.	.	.	.	.	.	.

TABLE A–3 Compound Sum Annuity Factors for $1 Compounded at R Percent for N Periods

	R =												
N	1%	2%	3%	4%	5%	6%	7%	8%	9%	10%	11%	12%	13%
1	1	1	1	1	1	1	1	1	1	1	1	1	1
2	2.01	2.02	2.03	2.04	2.05	2.06	2.07	2.08	2.09	2.1	2.11	2.12	2.13
3	3.03	3.06	3.091	3.122	3.152	3.184	3.215	3.246	3.278	3.31	3.342	3.374	3.407
4	4.06	4.122	4.184	4.246	4.31	4.375	4.44	4.506	4.573	4.641	4.71	4.779	4.85
5	5.101	5.204	5.309	5.416	5.526	5.637	5.751	5.867	5.985	6.105	6.228	6.353	6.48
6	6.152	6.308	6.468	6.633	6.802	6.975	7.153	7.336	7.523	7.716	7.913	8.115	8.323
7	7.214	7.434	7.662	7.898	8.142	8.394	8.654	8.923	9.2	9.487	9.783	10.089	10.405
8	8.286	8.583	8.892	9.214	9.549	9.897	10.26	10.637	11.028	11.436	11.859	12.3	12.757
9	9.369	9.755	10.159	10.583	11.027	11.491	11.978	12.488	13.021	13.579	14.164	14.776	15.416
10	10.462	10.95	11.464	12.006	12.578	13.181	13.816	14.487	15.193	15.937	16.722	17.549	18.42
11	11.567	12.169	12.808	13.486	14.207	14.972	15.784	16.645	17.56	18.531	19.561	20.655	21.814
12	12.683	13.412	14.192	15.026	15.917	16.87	17.888	18.977	20.141	21.384	22.713	24.133	25.65
13	13.809	14.68	15.618	16.627	17.713	18.882	20.141	21.495	22.953	24.523	26.212	28.029	29.985
14	14.947	15.974	17.086	18.292	19.599	21.015	22.55	24.215	26.019	27.975	30.095	32.393	34.883
15	16.097	17.293	18.599	20.024	21.579	23.276	25.129	27.152	29.361	31.772	34.405	37.28	40.417
16	17.258	18.639	20.157	21.825	23.657	25.673	27.888	30.324	33.003	35.95	39.19	42.753	46.672
17	18.43	20.012	21.762	23.698	25.84	28.213	30.84	33.75	36.974	40.545	44.501	48.884	53.739
18	19.615	21.412	23.414	25.645	28.132	30.906	33.999	37.45	41.301	45.599	50.396	55.75	61.725
19	20.811	22.841	25.117	27.671	30.539	33.76	37.379	41.446	46.018	51.159	56.939	63.44	70.749
20	22.019	24.297	26.87	29.778	33.066	36.786	40.995	45.762	51.16	57.275	64.203	72.052	80.947
21	23.239	25.783	28.676	31.969	35.719	39.993	44.865	50.423	56.765	64.002	72.265	81.699	92.47
22	24.472	27.299	30.537	34.248	38.505	43.392	49.006	55.457	62.873	71.403	81.214	92.503	105.491
23	25.716	28.845	32.453	36.618	41.43	46.996	53.436	60.893	69.532	79.543	91.148	104.60	120.205
24	26.973	30.422	34.426	39.083	44.502	50.816	58.177	66.765	76.79	88.497	102.17	118.15	136.831
25	28.243	32.03	36.459	41.646	47.727	54.865	63.249	73.106	84.701	98.347	114.41	133.33	155.62
30	34.785	40.568	47.575	56.085	66.439	79.058	94.461	113.28	136.30	164.49	199.02	241.33	293.199
35	41.66	49.994	60.462	73.652	90.32	111.43	138.23	172.31	215.71	271.02	341.59	431.66	546.681
40	48.886	60.402	75.401	95.026	120.8	154.76	199.63	259.05	337.88	442.59	581.82	767.09	1013.704
45	56.481	71.893	92.72	121.02	159.7	212.74	285.74	386.50	525.85	718.90	986.63	1358.2	1874.165
50	64.463	84.579	112.79	152.66	209.34	290.33	406.52	573.77	815.08	1163.9	1668.7	2400.0	3459.507

TABLE A–3 Compound Sum Annuity Factors for $1 Compounded at R Percent for N Periods

	R =												
N	14%	15%	16%	18%	20%	22%	24%	25%	30%	35%	40%	45%	50%
1	1	1	1	1	1	1	1	1	1	1	1	1	1
2	2.14	2.15	2.16	2.18	2.2	2.22	2.24	2.25	2.3	2.35	2.4	2.45	2.5
3	3.44	3.472	3.506	3.572	3.64	3.708	3.778	3.813	3.99	4.172	4.36	4.552	4.75
4	4.921	4.993	5.066	5.215	5.368	5.524	5.684	5.766	6.187	6.633	7.104	7.601	8.125
5	6.61	6.742	6.877	7.154	7.442	7.74	8.048	8.207	9.043	9.954	10.946	12.022	13.188
6	8.536	8.754	8.977	9.442	9.93	10.442	10.98	11.259	12.756	14.438	16.324	18.431	20.781
7	10.73	11.067	11.414	12.142	12.916	13.74	14.615	15.073	17.583	20.492	23.853	27.725	32.172
8	13.233	13.727	14.24	15.327	16.499	17.762	19.123	19.842	23.858	28.664	34.395	41.202	49.258
9	16.085	16.786	17.519	19.086	20.799	22.67	24.712	25.802	32.015	39.696	49.153	60.743	74.887
10	19.337	20.304	21.321	23.521	25.959	28.657	31.643	33.253	42.619	54.59	69.814	89.077	113.33
11	23.045	24.349	25.733	28.755	32.15	35.962	40.238	42.566	56.405	74.697	98.739	130.16	170.995
12	27.271	29.002	30.85	34.931	39.581	44.874	50.895	54.208	74.327	101.84	139.23	189.73	257.493
13	32.089	34.352	36.786	42.219	48.497	55.746	64.11	68.76	97.625	138.48	195.92	276.11	387.239
14	37.581	40.505	43.672	50.818	59.196	69.01	80.496	86.949	127.91	187.95	275.3	401.36	581.859
15	43.842	47.58	51.66	60.965	72.035	85.192	100.81	109.68	167.28	254.73	386.42	582.98	873.788
16	50.98	55.717	60.925	72.939	87.442	104.93	126.01	138.10	218.47	344.89	541.98	846.32	1311.682
17	59.118	65.075	71.673	87.068	105.93	129.02	157.25	173.63	285.01	466.61	759.78	1228.1	1968.523
18	68.394	75.836	84.141	103.74	128.11	158.40	195.99	218.04	371.51	630.92	1064.6	1781.8	2953.784
19	78.969	88.212	98.603	123.41	154.74	194.25	244.03	273.55	483.97	852.74	1491.5	2584.6	4431.676
20	91.025	102.44	115.38	146.62	186.68	237.98	303.60	342.94	630.16	1152.2	2089.2	3748.7	6648.513
21	104.76	118.81	134.84	174.02	225.02	291.34	377.46	429.68	820.21	1556.4	2925.8	5436.7	9973.77
22	120.43	137.63	157.41	206.34	271.03	356.44	469.05	538.10	1067.2	2102.2	4097.2	7884.2	14961.65
23	138.29	159.27	183.60	244.48	326.23	435.86	582.63	673.62	1388.4	2839.0	5737.1	11433.	22443.48
24	158.65	184.16	213.97	289.49	392.48	532.75	723.46	843.03	1806.0	3833.7	8032.9	16579.	33666.22
25	181.87	212.79	249.21	342.60	471.98	650.95	898.09	1054.7	2348.8	5176.5	11247.	24040.	50500.34
30	356.78	434.74	530.31	790.94	1181.8	1767.0	2640.9	3227.1	8729.9	23221.	60501.	154106	383500.1
35	693.57	881.17	1120.7	1816.6	2948.3	4783.6	7750.2	9856.7	32422.	104136	325400	987794	.
40	1342.0	1779.0	2360.7	4163.2	7343.8	12936.	22728.	30088.	120392	466960	.	.	.
45	2590.5	3585.1	4965.2	9531.5	18281.	34971.	66640.	91831.	447019	.	.	.	.
50	4994.5	7217.7	10435.	21813.	45497.	94525.	195372	280255	.	.	.	.	.

TABLE A–4 Present Value Annuity Factors (at R Percent Per Period) for $1 Received Per Period for Each of N Periods

	R =												
N	1%	2%	3%	4%	5%	6%	7%	8%	9%	10%	11%	12%	13%
1	0.990	0.980	0.971	0.962	0.952	0.943	0.935	0.926	0.917	0.909	0.901	0.893	0.885
2	1.970	1.942	1.913	1.886	1.859	1.833	1.808	1.783	1.759	1.736	1.713	1.690	1.668
3	2.941	2.884	2.829	2.775	2.723	2.673	2.624	2.577	2.531	2.487	2.444	2.402	2.361
4	3.902	3.808	3.717	3.630	3.546	3.465	3.387	3.312	3.240	3.170	3.102	3.037	2.974
5	4.853	4.713	4.580	4.452	4.329	4.212	4.100	3.993	3.890	3.791	3.696	3.605	3.517
6	5.795	5.601	5.417	5.242	5.076	4.917	4.767	4.623	4.486	4.355	4.231	4.111	3.998
7	6.728	6.472	6.230	6.002	5.786	5.582	5.389	5.206	5.033	4.868	4.712	4.564	4.423
8	7.652	7.325	7.020	6.733	6.463	6.210	5.971	5.747	5.535	5.335	5.146	4.968	4.799
9	8.566	8.162	7.786	7.435	7.108	6.802	6.515	6.247	5.995	5.759	5.537	5.328	5.132
10	9.471	8.983	8.530	8.111	7.722	7.360	7.024	6.710	6.418	6.145	5.889	5.650	5.426
11	10.368	9.787	9.253	8.760	8.306	7.887	7.499	7.139	6.805	6.495	6.207	5.938	5.687
12	11.255	10.575	9.954	9.385	8.863	8.384	7.943	7.536	7.161	6.814	6.492	6.194	5.918
13	12.134	11.348	10.635	9.986	9.394	8.853	8.358	7.904	7.487	7.103	6.750	6.424	6.122
14	13.004	12.106	11.296	10.563	9.899	9.295	8.745	8.244	7.786	7.367	6.982	6.628	6.302
15	13.865	12.849	11.938	11.118	10.380	9.712	9.108	8.559	8.061	7.606	7.191	6.811	6.462
16	14.718	13.578	12.561	11.652	10.838	10.106	9.447	8.851	8.313	7.824	7.379	6.974	6.604
17	15.562	14.292	13.166	12.166	11.274	10.477	9.763	9.122	8.544	8.022	7.549	7.120	6.729
18	16.398	14.992	13.754	12.659	11.690	10.828	10.059	9.372	8.756	8.201	7.702	7.250	6.840
19	17.226	15.678	14.324	13.134	12.085	11.158	10.336	9.604	8.950	8.365	7.839	7.366	6.938
20	18.046	16.351	14.877	13.590	12.462	11.470	10.594	9.818	9.129	8.514	7.963	7.469	7.025
21	18.857	17.011	15.415	14.029	12.821	11.764	10.836	10.017	9.292	8.649	8.075	7.562	7.102
22	19.660	17.658	15.937	14.451	13.163	12.042	11.061	10.201	9.442	8.772	8.176	7.645	7.170
23	20.456	18.292	16.444	14.857	13.489	12.303	11.272	10.371	9.580	8.883	8.266	7.718	7.230
24	21.243	18.914	16.936	15.247	13.799	12.550	11.469	10.529	9.707	8.985	8.348	7.784	7.283
25	22.023	19.523	17.413	15.622	14.094	12.783	11.654	10.675	9.823	9.077	8.422	7.843	7.330
30	25.808	22.396	19.600	17.292	15.372	13.765	12.409	11.258	10.274	9.427	8.694	8.055	7.496
35	29.409	24.999	21.487	18.665	16.374	14.498	12.948	11.655	10.567	9.644	8.855	8.176	7.586
40	32.835	27.355	23.115	19.793	17.159	15.046	13.332	11.925	10.757	9.779	8.951	8.244	7.634
45	36.095	29.490	24.519	20.720	17.774	15.456	13.606	12.108	10.881	9.863	9.008	8.283	7.661
50	39.196	31.424	25.730	21.482	18.256	15.762	13.801	12.233	10.962	9.915	9.042	8.304	7.675

TABLE A–4 Present Value Annuity Factors (at R Percent Per Period) for $1 Received Per Period for Each of N Periods

	R =												
N	14%	15%	16%	18%	20%	22%	24%	25%	30%	35%	40%	45%	50%
1	0.877	0.870	0.862	0.847	0.833	0.820	0.806	0.800	0.769	0.741	0.714	0.690	0.667
2	1.647	1.626	1.605	1.566	1.528	1.492	1.457	1.440	1.361	1.289	1.224	1.165	1.111
3	2.322	2.283	2.246	2.174	2.106	2.042	1.981	1.952	1.816	1.696	1.589	1.493	1.407
4	2.914	2.855	2.798	2.690	2.589	2.494	2.404	2.362	2.166	1.997	1.849	1.720	1.605
5	3.433	3.352	3.274	3.127	2.991	2.864	2.745	2.689	2.436	2.220	2.035	1.876	1.737
6	3.889	3.784	3.685	3.498	3.326	3.167	3.020	2.951	2.643	2.385	2.168	1.983	1.824
7	4.288	4.160	4.039	3.812	3.605	3.416	3.242	3.161	2.802	2.508	2.263	2.057	1.883
8	4.639	4.487	4.344	4.078	3.837	3.619	3.421	3.329	2.925	2.598	2.331	2.109	1.922
9	4.946	4.772	4.607	4.303	4.031	3.786	3.566	3.463	3.019	2.665	2.379	2.144	1.948
10	5.216	5.019	4.833	4.494	4.192	3.923	3.682	3.571	3.092	2.715	2.414	2.168	1.965
11	5.453	5.234	5.029	4.656	4.327	4.035	3.776	3.656	3.147	2.752	2.438	2.185	1.977
12	5.660	5.421	5.197	4.793	4.439	4.127	3.851	3.725	3.190	2.779	2.456	2.196	1.985
13	5.842	5.583	5.342	4.910	4.533	4.203	3.912	3.780	3.223	2.799	2.469	2.204	1.990
14	6.002	5.724	5.468	5.008	4.611	4.265	3.962	3.824	3.249	2.814	2.478	2.210	1.993
15	6.142	5.847	5.575	5.092	4.675	4.315	4.001	3.859	3.268	2.825	2.484	2.214	1.995
16	6.265	5.954	5.668	5.162	4.730	4.357	4.033	3.887	3.283	2.834	2.489	2.216	1.997
17	6.373	6.047	5.749	5.222	4.775	4.391	4.059	3.910	3.295	2.840	2.492	2.218	1.998
18	6.467	6.128	5.818	5.273	4.812	4.419	4.080	3.928	3.304	2.844	2.494	2.219	1.999
19	6.550	6.198	5.877	5.316	4.843	4.442	4.097	3.942	3.311	2.848	2.496	2.220	1.999
20	6.623	6.259	5.929	5.353	4.870	4.460	4.110	3.954	3.316	2.850	2.497	2.221	1.999
21	6.687	6.312	5.973	5.384	4.891	4.476	4.121	3.963	3.320	2.852	2.498	2.221	2.000
22	6.743	6.359	6.011	5.410	4.909	4.488	4.130	3.970	3.323	2.853	2.498	2.222	2.000
23	6.792	6.399	6.044	5.432	4.925	4.499	4.137	3.976	3.325	2.854	2.499	2.222	2.000
24	6.835	6.434	6.073	5.451	4.937	4.507	4.143	3.981	3.327	2.855	2.499	2.222	2.000
25	6.873	6.464	6.097	5.467	4.948	4.514	4.147	3.985	3.329	2.856	2.499	2.222	2.000
30	7.003	6.566	6.177	5.517	4.979	4.534	4.160	3.995	3.332	2.857	2.500	2.222	2.000
35	7.070	6.617	6.215	5.539	4.992	4.541	4.164	3.998	3.333	2.857	2.500	2.222	2.000
40	7.105	6.642	6.233	5.548	4.997	4.544	4.166	3.999	3.333	2.857	2.500	2.222	2.000
45	7.123	6.654	6.242	5.552	4.999	4.545	4.166	4.000	3.333	2.857	2.500	2.222	2.000
50	7.133	6.661	6.246	5.554	4.999	4.545	4.167	4.000	3.333	2.857	2.500	2.222	2.000

APPENDIX

Instructions for Using

The Investment Calculator Software

Software prepared by

Robert Brooks, University of Alabama
David Swanger, Auburn University
Chuck Warlick, Auburn University

PART ONE
INTRODUCTION

1-1 Compatibility

All programs on this disk are accessible through the file named INVEST.EXE. These programs have been compiled together to speed their selection. This software requires no other software outside the operating system (usually referred to as DOS). This software will run on any 640 K IBM PC and "true" or "100%" compatible, including the IBM AT and XT; also, it may run on computers that are less than "100%" compatible.

1-2 Software Features

The programs on this disk correspond to the content covered in Charles P. Jones's *Investments: Analysis and Management,* Third Edition.

These programs feature

1. Extensive internal checks for input accuracy.
2. Extensive checks for available memory.
3. Full screen field editing.
4. User-friendly menus.
5. Rapid execution of calculations by pressing F1.
6. Sensitivity analysis in selected places by pressing F2.
7. Graphics available in selected places by pressing F3.
8. Filing and retrieval of data in selected places by pressing F4.
9. Printing with a press of a function key by pressing F5.
10. General discussion screen for each program by pressing F10.

1-3 Making a Back-Up Copy

We encourage you to immediately make a back-up copy of this disk to save yourself the trouble of needing a replacement later. The following steps should guide you through this process:

1. Obtain a blank floppy disk.
2. Put the DOS disk in drive A and shut the door.
3. Switch on the computer.
4. Enter the date and time, pressing the RETURN key each time.
5. Place the blank floppy disk into drive B, type FORMAT B: and press RETURN. (CAUTION: Make sure you format the correct floppy!)

6. When asked "Format another (Y/N)?" type N and press RETURN.
7. Place the original Investments disk (the one containing the programs) into drive A, type A: and press RETURN.
8. Type COPY *.* B: and press RETURN.

NOTE: If your screen reports "Write protect error writing drive B: Abort, Retry, Ignore?", check to see if your new disk is write protected.

1-4 Purpose of Software

The extent to which one can comprehend complex financial calculations and apply financial models is usually limited by his/her ability to actually calculate results based on a given set of inputs. Recently, several financial models have been developed that require enormous and tedious mathematical calculations: for example, using option pricing formulae and solving for the optimal portfolio when given a set of constraints and estimated input. There does not appear to be any trend toward models with less mathematical rigor.

These programs can greatly enhance your learning experience by alleviating the hours spent on learning solution methodologies. Also with this time-saving device, the professor and student are left with more time to focus on the economic implications of various financial models. For example, using the Black Scholes Option Pricing program, you can perform sensitivity analysis of the underlying input (the exercise price, stock price, and so forth) and view the results graphically. From this exercise, you will gain a deeper understanding of this pricing model and its implications in practice. This type of exercise would not be practical without software.

This software can be used in several ways. First, it can be used to check your accuracy in working through numerical calculations. Second, it can be used to solve problems like the efficient frontier, which is difficult if not impossible to do by hand. Third, it can be used to conduct sensitivity analysis to gain a better understanding of the relationship of input variables to output variables. Fourth, it can be used to obtain a sense of the practical applications of various pricing relationships, such as the Black Scholes model.

PART TWO SOFTWARE

2-1 General Comments

These programs will run without any accompanying software (with the exception of DOS). They are fast and very easy to use. Help screens are available to aid you in understanding the topic related to the program. Extensive internal checks are also included to be sure the numbers that are input are within appropriate boundaries. (If they are not, the program will indicate the problem).

To start the program, place the floppy containing a copy of the original disk into drive A. (NOTE: Please see Section 1-3 for instructions on making a back-up copy of the original disk.) Move the prompt to the A drive by typing A:. Next, at the A prompt (A>), type INVEST.

After a few moments, the following screen should appear:

```
            THE INVESTMENT CALCULATOR
              Software to Accompany
     INVESTMENTS: ANALYSIS AND MANAGEMENT 3/E
               By Charles P. Jones

          Statistics
          Duration and Bond Analysis
          Beta
          Risk Analysis
          Valuation Model-Dividend
          Moving Average
          Option Pricing-Black Scholes
          Index Futures Option Pricing
          Efficient Portfolios
          Factor Model of APT
          Portfolio Performance Measurement
          Help
```

A program can be accessed by typing the first letter of your selection. For example, the Black Scholes Option Pricing program can be selected by typing O. This software package was designed for a color monitor. For some monochrome screens, the results are suboptimal. If this is the case with your machine, press the ESCAPE key (ESC) and type INVEST -NOCOLOR.

Once a program has been selected, you need to understand how to manipulate data input values. All programs have default values so you can experiment with how it works before you understand what to input. To change data input values, just type over the existing values.

2-2 Statistics

Press "S" to select the Statistics program. The Statistics program allows you to calculate total return and return relative as well as the arithmetic mean, the standard deviation, and the geometric mean for either ex-post data or ex-ante data. In order to use this program, you need to know the number of periods (ex-post data) or the number of "states of nature" (ex-ante data). For ex-post data, you may choose inputting prices and cash flows or yields. Ex-ante data only allows for yields.

You are prompted first whether to input new data or retrieve old data from a previously saved file. Suppose you wish to input new data.

For example, if you have price data and the number of periods is 3, then input 3 for the number of periods, P for (P)rices, and press F1. Next, input the following prices and cash flows:

Time Period	*Price*	*End of Period Cash flow*
0	$100.00	
1	$110.00	$10.00
2	$105.00	$10.00
3	$95.00	$10.00

Use the UP and DOWN ARROW keys to move the cursor to previous entries. If you make a mistake inputting these values, use the BACKSPACE key to delete the incorrect value and retype the correct value. Then just press F1 to show the results.

Time Period	*Total Return*		*Return Relative*
1	20.00%		1.20
2	4.55%		1.05
3	0.00%		1.00
Arithmetic Mean		8.18%	
Standard Deviation		10.48%	
Geometric Mean		7.85%	

When the calculations are complete, we see the upward bias of the arithmetic mean. The arithmetic mean return is appropriate as a measure of the central tendency of a distribution consisting of returns calculated for a particular time, such as a year. However, when percentage changes in value over time are involved, the arithmetic mean of these changes can be misleading. A different mean, the geometric mean, is needed to accurately describe the "true" average rate of return over multiple periods. The geometric mean return is the most descriptive reflection of compound, cumulative returns over time. The standard deviation is a measure of the total risk of an asset or a portfolio. It captures the total variability in the asset's or portfolio's return, whatever the source(s) of that variability.

A similar analysis to that given previously could be performed by using total return rather than prices. Also, ex-ante returns can be used with total return.

NOTE: When using ex-ante total return the probabilities must add up to 100%. You also have the ability to store and retrieve input data.

2-3 Duration and Bond Analysis

The Duration and Bond Analysis program is accessed by typing D. This program calculates several values related to bonds given the following types of data:

1. Market Price of Bond.
2. Yield to Maturity.
3. Annual Coupon Rate.
4. Number of Years to Maturity.
5. Face or Par Value.
6. Number of Years to First Call.
7. Call Price.

This program's output is based on two assumptions. First, the current yield, yield to maturity, and yield to first call are calculated assuming that the market price entered is correct. These yields are used by investors to measure the potential return. Second, the market price, duration, and change in price are calculated assuming that the yield to maturity is correct. Duration and change in price are used as risk measures.

For example, enter the following:

1. Market Price of Bond	$990.00
2. Yield to Maturity	11.%
3. Annual Coupon Rate	100.0
4. Number of Years to Maturity	10
5. Face or Par Value	$1000.0
6. Number of Years to First Call	5
7. Call Price	$1100.00

Pressing F1 to calculate, we see the following results:

Based Market Price		*Based Yield to Maturity*	
Current Yield	10.10%	Market Price	$940.25
Yield to Maturity	10.16%	Duration	6.65 years
Yield to First Call	11.80%	Change in Price	−6.0%

If we change the market price to $1010.00, we now have the following:

	Based on Market Price
Current Yield	9.9%
Yield to Maturity	9.84%
Yield to First Call	11.28%

From these results, we can see that the current yield is below the yield to maturity for bonds trading below par, but the reverse is true for bonds trading above par.

Sensitivity analysis can be performed on the yield to maturity by pressing F2. If a suitable graphics card is available, a graph can be produced to show the relationship between the bond's market price and yield to maturity by pressing F3.

2-4 Beta

When the Beta program is selected, you have the opportunity to select from previously saved input or inputting new data. When inputting new data, you must enter the number of periods of historical data for the market return and the security return. Once the appropriate returns have been entered, press the F1 key to calculate the beta that will appear on the screen.

For example, if the number of periods is 5, you should type 5 and press F1 and you now have the following returns:

Period	*Security Return*	*Market Return*
1	10.00	12.00
2	13.00	15.00
3	15.00	16.00
4	12.00	14.00
5	13.00	12.00

Pressing F1, we see the beta is 0.75. That is, for a 1%-change in the market, this security moves 0.75%. Beta is a measure of volatility, or relative systematic risk, for stock or portfolio returns. It is typically found by regressing stock (or portfolio) returns on a market proxy such as the S&P 500.

2-5 Risk Analysis

The procedure for using the Risk Analysis program is identical to the one used with the Beta program; however, the Risk Analysis program provides more extensive output.

Specifically, the total risk, systematic risk, and unsystematic risk are calculated for both the absolute level as well as the proportion. The total risk of a security, as measured by the variance in the rate of return, can be decomposed into (1) systematic risk—that part of total risk associated with the variability in the overall market and (2) unsystematic risk—that part of the total risk not related to the variability in the overall market. That is,

$$\text{Systematic Risk} + \text{Unsystematic Risk} = \text{Total Risk}$$

For example, from the data given in Section 2-4, we find

		Proportion of Total Risk
Beta	0.75	**************
Total Risk	1.82	100.00%
Systematic Risk	1.34	73.85%
Unsystematic Risk	0.47	26.15%

Thus, we find in this security's return 74% of the variability is related to the market.

2-6 Valuation Model—Dividend

The Dividend Valuation Model program allows up to three stages of dividend growth. This program operates under the assumption that each stage has a fixed level of growth. The required entries are

1. Required Rate of Return.
2. Current Dividend.
3. Number of Growth Stages.
   (a) growth rate of each stage.
   (b) duration of the stage.

The last growth stage is assumed to be to infinity.

Suppose a security has a required 15% rate of return, a current annual dividend of $2.50, and two growth stages. After inputting these values, press F1 to enter the growth rates and duration. Specifically, consider the case where the first growth rate is 20.00% for five years and a growth rate of 5.00% thereafter. Pressing F1, we see the theoretical price is $46.70. If your expectations change and you feel this firm will only be able to maintain a 20.00% growth rate for four years, then change the number of years from five to four. Pressing F1 again, the value of these shares is $42.26.

Sensitivity analysis can be performed on the required rate of return by pressing F2. If a suitable graphics card is available, a graph can be produced to show the relationship between the stock's market price and the required rate of return.

2-7 Moving Average

The Moving Average program calculates the moving average of a series of numbers. As with other programs, storing and retrieving inputs is available. This program requires that you enter the number of periods and the averaging frequency. The averaging frequency is the number of observations over which an average is taken. If the averaging frequency is 12 (monthly data), the moving average is based on the previous 12 months including the current month. A comparison of the current market price to the moving average produces a buy or sell signal. The general buy signal is when actual prices rise through the moving average on high volume, with the opposite applying to a sell signal. As usual in technical analysis, variations of this general rule exist.

Suppose you have 10 values; the averaging frequency is three, and the values are 5, 6, 7, 8, 9, 10, 9, 8, 7, and 6. Pressing F1, we find the moving average is 0.0, 0.0, 6, 7, 8, 9, 9.33, 9, 8, and 7.

2-8 Option Pricing—Black Scholes

When the Black Scholes Option Pricing program is accessed, the following entries are required:

1. Stock Price.
2. Exercise Price.
3. Annual Interest Rate.
4. Time to Expiration (days).
5. Standard Deviation of Stock Returns (decimal).

Consider the following example:

Stock Price	$40.000
Exercise Price	$45.000
Annual Interest Rate	10.00%
Time to Expiration (days)	183.00
Standard Deviation of Stock Returns	0.4500

We see the call price is $3.96 and the put price is $6.76.

The put price is based on the standard put-call parity model. The call price is equal to the stock price minus the discounted exercise price (discounted at the risk-free rate) plus the put price.

The hedge ratio indicates what fraction of shares of stock to buy or sell for each option written in order to have a hedged portfolio.

This program allows sensitivity analysis to be performed on all the underlying parameters. The program will allow you to store outputs for later use and graphs can be produced.

2-9 Index Futures Option Pricing

The Index Futures Option Pricing program is similar in nature to the Black Scholes Option Pricing program. In this program, however, the index value is entered and both the futures value and the futures options values are calculated using a modified Black Scholes Option Pricing equation. (The difference in the models stems from futures having a zero value on the day the position is entered).

Suppose you have the following information:

Spot Index	\$100.00
Exercise Price	\$100.00
Annual Interest Rate	5.00%
Annual Dividend Yield	3.00%
Time to Expiration	182.00%
Standard Deviation of Stock Returns	0.25

Using this information, we find the following:

Futures Index Value	\$101.00
Futures Call Price	7.39
Call Hedge Ratio	0.54
Futures Put Price	\$6.41
Put Hedge Ratio	−0.46

We now see the futures index value is at a premium over the spot rate. Stock index futures offer investors the opportunity to hedge the risk contained in their portfolios as well as speculate on the future direction of the stock market as a whole (as opposed to individual stocks). The stock index futures option contract provides the same opportunities with the advantage of limited risk.

2-10 Efficient Portfolios

The Efficient Portfolios program is a package of four programs—the Markowitz method, with or without short sales, and the Single Index method, with or without short sales. When running the without short sales version, extensive memory is required, and you are allowed to place constraints on the percentage invested in each asset. The program that runs with short sales is less demanding.

This program package allows the calculation of points on the efficient frontier between specified upper and lower bounds. The Markowitz approach requires the expected return, standard deviation, and correlation coefficients for each security. The Single Index approach requires the expected return, beta, and residual standard deviation for each security and the market standard deviation.

The efficient set (frontier) is the set of portfolios generated by the Markowitz model or the Single Index model. These portfolios have the maximum expected return for a given level of risk, or the minimum risk for a given level of expected return. The major problem with the Markowitz model is that it requires a full set of correlations between the returns for all securities being considered. To alleviate this problem, William Sharpe developed the Single Index model, which relates returns from each security to the returns on a common index. The single index model requires less input, which in practice makes it easier to implement.

Suppose you are considering the appropriate amount to invest in stocks or bonds and you are not allowed to short sell. You can use the Markowitz method to solve this problem. Specifically, enter the following:

Number of Securities	2
(W)ith or With (O)ut	W
Upper Bound	20.00
Lower Bound	10.00
Number to Calculate	4
(M)arkowitz or (S)ingle Index Model	M

Pressing F1 to continue, enter the following:

Expected Return 1	10.00%	Standard Deviation 1	10.00%
Expected Return 2	20.00%	Standard Deviation 2	20.00%

for the bonds' and stocks' expected return and variance. Press F1, enter 0.30 for the correlation, and the following results will appear:

Portfolio	1	2	3	4
Return	10.0	13.333	16.667	20.0
Standard Deviation	10.0	10.75	14.682	20.00
Weight 1	100.0	66.667	33.333	0.000
Weight 2	0.0	33.333	66.667	100.000

If we had a target return of 16.667%, we would invest 33.333% in bonds and 66.667% in stocks.

2-11 Factor Model of APT

The Factor Model of APT program calculates the expected return when given the risk-free rate, return sensitivities, and expected return per unit. For example, suppose the risk-free rate is 5.00%, the number of factors is 4, and the factor entries are as follows:

Factor	*Return Sensitivity*	*Expected Return Per Unit*
1	1.00	5.00%
2	0.75	3.00%
3	0.50	7.00%
4	1.50	9.00%

In this case, we find the expected return is 29.25%. According to the Arbitrage Pricing Theory (APT), a security's value changes over time as a result of certain factors such as interest rates or industrial production. In order to implement this model, we need to know the factors that account for the differences among security returns. Most empirical work suggests that three to five factors influence security returns and these factors are priced in the market.

2-12 Portfolio Performance Measurement

The Portfolio Performance Measurement program allows you to store and retrieve inputs. With this program, you can estimate three performance measures for each portfolio, return to variability (RVAR), return to volatility (RVOL), Jensen's ALPHA and the standard error of ALPHA. This program also calculates the average return, standard deviation (SD), and beta.

The data required includes the number of portfolios, the number of periods, the market return, the risk-free rate, and each portfolio's return for each period.

Consider the case with three portfolios, five periods, and the following parameters:

Period	*Market Return*	*Risk-Free Return*	*Portfolio* 1	2	3
1	10.00	6.00	10.00	10.00	12.00
2	15.00	6.00	5.00	15.00	20.00
3	10.00	6.00	15.00	10.00	10.00
4	15.00	6.00	20.00	15.00	20.00
5	10.00	6.00	5.00	10.00	5.00

From this information, we find the following:

Statistic	*Market Return*	*Risk-Free Rate*	*Portfolios* 1	2	3
Mean	12.00	6.00	11.00	12.00	13.40
SD	2.74	NA	6.52	2.74	6.54
Beta	1.00	NA	0.50	1.00	2.20
R-Square	1.00	NA	0.04	1.00	0.85
RVAR	2.19	NA	0.77	2.19	1.13
RVOL	6.00	NA	10.00	6.00	3.36
ALPHA	0.00	NA	2.00	0.00	−5.80

Thus, we can examine the performance of various portfolios. In this case, we can also see that the performance results of portfolio 2 are exactly the same as the "market." We can attribute this to the fact that portfolio 2 returns are the same as the "market." Portfolio 1 does not perform as well as the "market" by the Reward-to-Variability (RVAR) measure, whereas it outperforms the "market" by the Reward-to-Volatility (RVOL) measure and the ALPHA measure. The reverse is true for portfolio 3.

PROGRAM NOTES

System Requirements 640K IBM PC or "100%" compatible.

To Run Program

1. Boot system with DOS.
2. Insert disk containing software into drive A and type A:.
3. Type INVEST.

Potential Problems

1. Program does not appear—check that the disk contains a program called INVEST.EXE and that the disk is in the appropriate drive.
2. Screen appears but does not look clear and you are using an IBM PC clone. Escape out of the program and try typing

```
INVEST -NOCOLOR
```

Program Selection Type the first letter of the desired program.

Program Termination Press the ESCAPE key (ESC). The ESC key backs you out of the program one step at a time.

Data Input Data is input by typing over previous inputs.

Help Screens When inside a program, if the data is incorrectly entered, the program will pop up a window indicating the problem. Also, an initial help screen is provided when you first enter the package. To access this information, type H.

Standard Function Keys (when available)
F1 — calculate results based on specified inputs
F2 — perform applicable sensitivity analysis
F3 — graph the results
F4 — file inputs or outputs to an ASCII file for later use in a word processor, printing or use elsewhere within the program
F5 — print the contents of a window to the default printer
F10 — accesses a discussion screen related to the program

INDEX